书名题签：韩启德

中华科学技术大词典

— 工程技术卷（上）—

全国科学技术名词审定委员会 编

名誉总主编 路甬祥
总 主 编 白春礼

商务印书馆

2019年·北京

图书在版编目(CIP)数据

中华科学技术大词典.工程技术卷.上/全国科学技术名词审定委员会编.—北京:商务印书馆,2019
ISBN 978-7-100-17102-1

Ⅰ.①中… Ⅱ.①全… Ⅲ.①科学名词—名词术语—中国—词典②工程技术—科学名词—名词术语—中国—词典 Ⅳ.①H03②TB-61

中国版本图书馆 CIP 数据核字(2019)第 033841 号

权利保留,侵权必究。

中华科学技术大词典
工程技术卷(上)
全国科学技术名词审定委员会 编

商 务 印 书 馆 出 版
(北京王府井大街36号 邮政编码100710)
商 务 印 书 馆 发 行
北京中科印刷有限公司印刷
ISBN 978-7-100-17102-1

2019年6月第1版　开本787×1092　1/16
2019年6月北京第1次印刷　印张44¼
定价:142.00元

《中华科学技术大词典》

编辑委员会

名誉总主编：路甬祥

总 主 编：白春礼

副 总 主 编（以姓氏笔画为序）：

孙寿山　李济生　张礼和　张伯礼　张焕乔　陆汝钤
陈运泰　武　寅

常务副总主编：刘　青

编辑委员会委员（以姓氏笔画为序）：

丁一汇　于殿利　才　磊　王　杰　王　璞　王存忠
王英杰　仇伟立　叶大年　代晓明　白春礼　冯　军
曲爱国　朱　星　朱建平　乔格侠　任图生　邬　江
刘　青　刘功臣　刘志荣　刘连安　刘虎威　孙寿山
严加安　严海军　李宇明　李胜利　李济生　余桂林
辛德培　汪朝光　宋　彤　张　晖　张玉森　张礼和
张先恩　张伯礼　张柏春　张晓林　张焕乔　陆汝钤
陈　竺　陈运泰　陈超志　武　寅　周明鑑　周洪波
饶克勤　娄　宇　洪定一　顾红雅　奚大华　高素婷
唐绪军　陶文沂　黄　行　黄群慧　韩布新　程　晓
储成才　温昌斌　谢地坤　路甬祥　裴亚军　潘书祥

《中华科学技术大词典·工程技术卷(上)》

(运载工程、土木与建筑工程卷)

编辑委员会

主　编：刘功臣

副主编：娄　宇　仇伟立

编辑委员会委员(以姓氏笔画为序)：

于　鑫　王凤武　王昌兴　王荣生　王振军　王逢辰

仇伟立　朱炳寅　朱晓宁　刘正江　刘功臣　孙　英

杜荣铭　李　华　李　娜　李玉英　李全望　李贵臣

李济生　李爱民　李瑞林　杨守仁　吴宏斌　何士伟

何正良　张建元　张爱华　张惠江　赵芳敏　施　昌

娄　宇　高振勋　唐　正　唐　燕　唐珵珵　黄星元

《中华科学技术大词典》项目部

主　任：张　晖

副主任：代晓明

成　员：吴　颐　白　杨　王　海

路甬祥序

全国科学技术名词审定委员会(以下简称"全国科技名词委")在其成立30多年来工作的基础上,对科学技术名词审定工作和海峡两岸科技名词对照工作的成果进行系统梳理,编纂出版《中华科学技术大词典》,有利于发挥其规范科学技术名词和加强海峡两岸各领域交流的重要作用。同时,也是全国科技名词委工作成果的重要展示。

科学技术名词作为科学技术概念的语言表达,产生于科技领域,应用于社会各个方面,是科技和经济社会融合发展的结晶。通过科学技术名词的规范表述,促进科技理论、知识和思想的传播交流,这是科学技术名词工作的根本宗旨。科学技术名词也是中华文化宝库的重要组成部分,它凝结着人类智慧和中华民族的创造,映射出科学技术和人类文明进步的轨迹。做好科学技术名词审定、公布、推广等各方面工作,有利于传承弘扬中华优秀科学文化,提高全民族科学文化素养,促进社会文明和谐发展,促进国际经济政治、科技文化的交流与合作。依托全国科技名词委30多年来的工作成果,在会聚数千位科技专家和学术精英的智慧结晶、融合现代科学和中华文化的新理念之基础上,编纂出版《中华科学技术大词典》,必将在普及现代科学技术和传承中华优秀文化中发挥积极作用,也具有宝贵的历史价值。

编纂一部集科技名词规范成果之大成的大型工具书,是当前科技名词规范化工作发展的需要。我国科技名词审定工作从全国科技名词委成立伊始,已经在基础科学、工程技术、农业、医学、人文社会科学等领域审定公布了130多种、40多万条的学科规范名词,出版了近30个学科的海峡两岸科技名词对照本,为我国科技发展和两岸科教文化交流发挥了重要的基础性作用。但是,以往的公布和出版工作都是分学科进行的,其优势是有利于开展审定工作,方便单个学科或行业领域的使用,而不足之处在于次序分散,不利于跨学科,以及综合性、交叉性学科领域的使用,也不利于科技名词的系统认知和社会普及。将这些名词系统分类和编纂集成,有利于学科向综合性、交叉性、系统性方向发展和创新。因而,编纂一部综合性的科学技术名词工具书,既是审定公布工作的深化与延伸,也是响应社会各界规范使用科技名词的基本诉求,必将在促进科技文化交流和实现协同创新方面发挥十分重要的作用。

科学技术名词也是海峡两岸科教文化交流的重要载体。由于历史的原因,海峡两岸分隔近70年,其间正是现代科技大发展时期,新名词术语层出不穷,两岸专家分别定名,形成大量名词术语之间的差异。台湾大学一位气象学教授曾举例说,两岸用同一种语言,但对于同样的气象探测设备,大陆称"无线电探空气球",台湾称"雷保";对于同样的云层气象条件,台湾称"逸入",大陆称"夹卷",造成学术交流的障碍。凡此种种概念相同而称谓不同的情况,约占科技名词术语三分之一以上,严重影响到两岸科技、文化、教育、经贸等各领域的交流和发展。海峡两岸各界对名词术语差异所造成的语言障碍都普遍有相似的经历和深刻的认识。1993年4月,两岸第一次"汪辜会谈"顺乎民意，把探讨"海峡两岸科技名词统一"列入了共同协议之中。随之全国科技名词委制定了《关于开展海峡两岸科学技术名词统一工作的意见》，决定加强与台湾地区学者和有关机构的交流合作，促进两岸科技名词的交流对照与统一工作。此后20多年来，两岸科技名词工作成绩斐然，已先后出版了近30种分学科的"海峡两岸名词对照本"。本次编纂出版《中华科学技术大词典》，广泛收集审选了各学科名词，成为囊括近百个学科、约50万条科技名词的综合性大词典。它的问世，将面向海峡两岸民众，释疑解惑，互动交流，协同科学认知，增进文化认同，为两岸科学文化等各领域的交流合作架起桥梁。它是促进科技创新发展，促进中华文化传承，促进两岸交流与祖国统一的科学文化工程，也是两岸专家学者的共同愿望，意义重大、影响深远。

《中华科学技术大词典》的出版，是两岸专家相互配合、共同努力的结果。双方专家也在这次合作中加深了相互了解，取得了广泛共识。大词典的问世是两岸学术界和专家合作的成果，是海峡所不能阻断的科教文化交流的缩影。我相信在两岸专家共同努力下，两岸科教文化的交流会呈现更加良好的局面。

《中华科学技术大词典》的出版，是我国科学技术名词规范化事业不断发展的重要见证，也是两岸科技文化交流中具有重要意义的盛事。故为序，以示衷心祝贺！

路甬祥

2018年8月28日

白春礼序

历经两岸专家学者多年来的共同努力,《中华科学技术大词典》即将问世了,这是两岸科技名词交流对照工作的一件盛事,也是两岸科教文化、经济社会等各个领域交流合作的一项基础工作,我感到由衷的欣慰。

中华文字是历史渊源的载体、民族精神的血脉,是人类文化的瑰丽成果。它不同于西方拼音文字,构成了中国人独有的思维方式和文化传统,使海峡两岸及中华文化圈内所有人民引为自豪。

科学技术名词是中华文化的重要组成部分,许多科学技术名词的定名都折射出中华文化艰辛的发展历程。特别是近代以来,中华民族历经苦难,举步维艰,大批先辈科学家肩负着沉重的历史责任,化解万难,在引进消化西方先进科技概念的基础上,结合中国的文化传统,创制了一大批具有中华文化品位和特点的名词术语,为我国近代科技跟上世界科技的发展创造了条件。

尽管经过了近 70 年的两岸分隔,但共同的历史传统和语言文化,无时无刻不在提醒着人们,海峡两岸同根同源、同文同宗,都是中华文明的继承者、弘扬者。但是,由于两岸社会长期处于相互隔绝的状态,其间正是全球科学技术飞速发展的历史时期,对于人类社会在相互学习、共同发展中产生的科学技术概念,两岸使用同样的文字却分别定名,其表达科学技术概念的词素词义,悄然发生了不同的演变,给两岸人民带来了交流的障碍,影响了两岸科教文化、经济贸易、人文社会等领域的交流合作。早在 30 年前恢复交流后不久,就有大陆学者关注到两岸科技名词的不同发展路径,意识到两岸科技名词的差异是造成两岸认知差距的原因之一,因而呼吁从促进计算机信息处理的角度出发,积极研究并推进海峡两岸科技名词的统一,消除语言障碍。

科技名词交流是海峡两岸专家学者的共同呼声。1993 年首轮"汪辜会谈"达成的协议中就有探讨两岸科技名词统一的内容。全国科学技术名词审定委员会始终积极、稳妥地推动此项工作,这一举措也逐步得到两岸科技界的广泛认同。多年来两岸合作增加,交往频繁,文化上水乳交融,大陆和台湾地区科技名词交流互鉴,不少过去为一方独有的名词术语,已经逐步从分歧趋于一致。在此形势下,两岸合作编纂一部涵盖科学与技术各领域名词术语的科学技术大词典正逢其时。

2010 年 7 月,两岸科学技术领域专家学者议定,在前期合作的基础上,合编《中华科学技术大词典》等辞书;同时双方协商决定利用信息技术,采用云计算平台开展数据库建设。在两岸专家学者多轮协商并形成共识的基础上,大词典编纂工作得以全面展开。

《中华科学技术大词典》的编纂突出了基础性、通用性、实用性,以广泛收录全球通用的现代科技概念为主,适当收录一些双方各自特有的名词术语,反映两岸科学技术名词差异,以方便两岸科技交流和一般民众使用,并为学习汉语的外国人提供帮助。同时为便于两岸读者使用,对于两岸不同的通用字形采取了分别呈现的形式。这种安排不仅便于双方大众阅读,同时也有助于双方逐步了解对方用字用词的现实情况,以达到化异为同的目的。几年来两岸专家学者实事求是、相互尊重、学风严谨、科学务实,奉献了各自的学识和心智,在两岸文化交流合作中又迈出坚实的一步。我们这次编纂出版《中华科学技术大词典》,既是过去两岸科技名词工作的延续,也为今后在更大的领域开展两岸学术交往,为科技文化、经济社会的进一步交流合作创造了基础条件。多年来的两岸科技名词交流实践充分说明,罔顾历史,无论是对传统文化的否定与切割,还是出于政治私利操控的"去中国化",都经不住历史长河的冲刷,终将因得不到公众的支持而烟消云散。维护两岸和平发展是两岸同胞的民意主流,本次编纂工作一直得到台湾方面有关机构和广大专家学者的协助与支持,编纂成果也将为两岸各界共享,成为促进两岸关系和平发展的一件鲜活的、生动的实例。

《中华科学技术大词典》集科学与技术领域名词术语之大成,汇聚了两岸无数专家学者的智慧,必将发挥传承与弘扬中华文化的历史和现实作用。经过两岸专家学者的不懈努力,《中华科学技术大词典》即将出版,借此机会,我谨向30多年来支持和参与科技名词工作的两岸专家学者致以诚挚的敬意!向参与此次词典编纂工作的所有专家学者,向全国科学技术名词审定委员会事务中心和词典项目部的同仁们,向支持本词典出版的国家出版基金规划管理办公室和投入精干队伍保障出版质量的商务印书馆,表示由衷的感谢!

白春礼

2019年夏

前　言

2009年7月，以"推进和深化两岸文化教育交流合作"为主题的第五届两岸经贸文化论坛在长沙举行，倡议两岸民间合作编纂中华语文工具书。2010年7月，两岸合编中华语文工具书第二轮会谈决定，两岸合编的工具书由语言文字领域拓展到科学技术领域，以全国科学技术名词审定委员会（以下简称"全国科技名词委"）和台湾教育研究院为实施者，组织两岸专家合作编纂《中华科学技术大词典》。2011年3月，两岸专家共同提出编纂出版《中华科学技术大词典》的总体方案。2013年12月，《中华科学技术大词典》正式纳入《2013—2025年国家辞书编纂出版规划》，2016年6月《中华科学技术大词典》获得国家出版基金项目支持。

《中华科学技术大词典》成立编辑委员会，由白春礼院士担任总主编，路甬祥院士为名誉总主编。同时设立词典项目部，负责编纂的日常组织工作。各领域先后共有500多位专家学者参加了本词典的编纂和审定。

《中华科学技术大词典》在全国科技名词委审定公布的130多种学科名词和已出版的近30种海峡两岸科技名词对照本的基础上，参考台湾方面公布的名词数据库资料编纂而成。全书共收录96个学科，约50万条科技名词；并实现大陆名与台湾名，中文名和英文名的对照功能。全书按照学科领域和学科特点，共分为10卷，即数理化卷、地学卷、生物学卷、工程技术卷（上、中、下）、农业卷、医学卷、社会科学卷、人文科学卷。

本词典收录的各学科名词具有以下特点：一是在全国科技名词委公布名词的基础上，参照台湾方面的收词范围扩展而来，基本上反映出海峡两岸科学技术发展现状；二是体现了规范性，充分利用科技名词规范化工作的成果；三是注重科学文化的传承，既收录了当代科学技术领域的科技名词，也适当收录了反映中国近代以来科学和文化发展脉络的科技名词。本词典是两岸专家学者对多年来科技名词领域交流、对照和统一工作成果的一次大规模整理和总结，是两岸合作编写工具书的最新成果，是两岸专家学者的智慧结晶，是两岸共同弘扬中华文化的一次重要实践。

本词典作为两岸专家共同参与编纂的工具书，契合了两岸科学技术发展的现实需求，为两岸在科技、教育、文化、经贸等方面的交流合作提供了必不可少的对照性词汇，可成为两岸各领域交流的参考和依据。同时，可用作全球华语地区科技界人士的参考读物。

本词典编纂期间，编审专家以严肃的科学态度，认真工作，持之以恒，默默奉献。台湾教育研究院及台湾各学科的部分专家学者参与了词目编选，特别是对台湾名、英文名等进行了仔细审读。在此，我们向他们表示衷心的感谢。

《中华科学技术大词典》涉及学科广泛,尤其是进行如此大规模的两岸科技名词梳理、遴选、编纂及全面对照,没有先例,难度巨大,编纂中难免会有疏漏错误之处,欢迎广大专家学者和读者批评指正。

《中华科学技术大词典》编辑委员会

2019 年 3 月 1 日

《中华科学技术大词典·工程技术卷(上)》编纂说明

《中华科学技术大词典·工程技术卷(上)》(以下简称《工程技术卷(上)》)是《中华科学技术大词典》的第 4 卷,主要包括运载工程、土木与建筑工程领域的科技名词,涵盖航空科学技术、航海科学技术、航天科学技术、公路科学技术、铁道科学技术、船舶科学技术、建筑学、土木工程、城乡规划学、风景园林学等 10 个分支,共收录词条约 48 600 条。全部词条按照大陆名音序排序,以便查检。

《工程技术卷(上)》收词以全国科学技术名词审定委员会审定、公布的科技名词和已经出版的海峡两岸对照名词为基础。在初稿的基础上组织专家进行了初审,主要工作包括三方面:一是对存在的格式、书写、拼写、翻译不准确等问题进行校正;二是对大陆和台湾名词概念不对应、词条内涵发生变化以及不适合作为科技名词的词汇,进行了调整、替代和删除;三是对初稿中没有却特别基础、重要、常用的词予以收录。分卷编辑据此加以校核,形成一审稿。之后由《中华科学技术大词典》项目部进行数据处理,重点进行各学科词条合库查重筛选,形成二审稿。针对二审稿,第二次组织专家深入细致地复查,解决初审遗留问题,检查处理编辑加工过程中的疏漏,形成三审稿。分卷主编第三次组织专家审查,形成终审稿。终审稿由分卷主编和副主编再次把关,形成报批稿,报送《中华科学技术大词典》编辑委员会审查批准后,交由商务印书馆出版。

本卷词典所涉及的 10 个学科中,航空科学技术、航海科学技术、航天科学技术、公路科学技术、铁道科学技术、船舶科学技术、建筑学、土木工程已公布过科技名词,航海科学技术、船舶科学技术已出版海峡两岸名词对照本,城乡规划学名词和风景园林学名词也正在审定,具有良好的前期工作基础,词条质量较高,为本卷词典的顺利出版打下了坚实的基础。

我们邀请了 36 位专家学者参加了本卷词典的编纂和审定工作。编审专家学者严谨认真的工作态度和默默奉献的工作精神,保证了本书的高质量出版。台湾同仁对相关学科的两岸名词对照工作给予了很大帮助,体现了两岸专家密切合作的精神风范。

《中华科学技术大词典》项目部和全国科学技术名词审定委员会事务中心各审定室的同志们对词典的编纂给予了大力的支持。从组建分卷编辑委员会开始,他们就积极参与,协助联系专家,承担了提供稿件资料、协助组织召开编委会、开展专项检查、誊录与复核编校意见等多项繁杂工作。

值此词典出版之际,我们向所有为词典编纂出版工作做出贡献的专家、学者和同仁们表示衷心的感谢。

由于时间仓促,编者水平有限,难免有各种不足和差错,诚望读者批评指正。

《中华科学技术大词典·工程技术卷(上)》编辑委员会

2019 年 3 月 29 日

目　录

凡例 ·· 2
词目首字音序索引 ·· 4
词目首字笔画索引 ·· 11
词典正文 ·· 1—670
附录 ·· 671
　　国际单位制 ··· 673
　　希腊字母表 ··· 676
　　地质年代表 ··· 677
　　元素周期表 ··· 678

词目英文索引
（二维码）

凡 例

1. 词条收录

1.1 本词典所收词条涵盖基础科学、工程技术、农业科学、医学、社会科学、人文及其他领域共计 96 个学科,例如数学、物理学、化学、天文学、地质学、测绘学、动物学、植物学、航天科学技术、建筑学、机械工程、电子学、材料科学技术、资源科学技术、农学、土壤学、医学、中医药学、经济学、法学、语言学、教育学等。

1.2 本词典收录的词条包括海峡两岸通用的,以及海峡两岸有差异的科学技术名词共约 50 万条。

1.3 本词典收录的词条按照科学技术相关学科领域归类,共分为 10 卷。依次为数理化卷、地学卷、生物学卷、工程技术卷(上、中、下)、农业卷、医学卷、社会科学卷、人文科学卷。

2. 词条构成

2.1 本词典所收词条由词目(中文)及其对应的英文构成。

2.2 词目采用两岸名称对照的形式,大陆名列前,台湾名列后,中间以" / "分隔。例如:

电灼式印刷机/放電式列印機

拉克斯-密格拉蒙定理/拉克斯-米爾格雷定理

2.3 词目的字形,分别采用两岸各自通用的字形。例如:

自然循环/自然循環

作业控制中心/作業控制中心

2.4 词目中的大陆名有两条(或以上)同义词时,分别以两条(或以上)词目列出。例如:

背景/背景

本底/背景

2.5 词目中的大陆名对应两条(或以上)台湾同义词时,台湾名在词目中并行排列,中间以逗号隔开。例如:

出口融资/出口融資,籌集出口資金

横节理/橫節理,交錯劈理,Q 節理

2.6 词目中的大陆名对应两个(或两个以上)台湾名概念时,对应的台湾名分别以①② ……列出。例如:

质量/ ①質量,②品質

槽轮/ ①間歇工作輪,星形輪,日内瓦輪,②有槽帶輪

2.7 词目中大陆名和台湾名中"[ ]"内的字为可省略部分。例如:

等离[子]体动力学/電漿動力學

2.8 词目中大陆名和台湾名中"( )"内的汉字、西文字母、阿拉伯数字、罗马数字为该词的特殊标注(如天体名的备注、化合物结构标示、数学概念的符号标识等)。例如:

虹神星(小行星7号)/虹神星(7號小行星)

聚(β-氨基丙酸)/聚(β-胺基丙酸)

广义(g,k)特征标/廣義(g,k)特徵[標]

2.9 本词典收录的词条不单独标出所属学科。

3. 词目排序

3.1 词目按大陆名的首字汉语拼音字母次序排列，首字同音的按笔画排列，笔画少的在前，多的在后；笔画相同的按起笔笔形(横、竖、撇、点、折)的次序排列，起笔笔形相同的按第二起笔笔形的次序排列，以此类推。首字相同的按第二字的汉语拼音字母次序排列，以此类推。

3.2 词目中含有西文字母或阿拉伯数字、罗马数字时，按词目中的汉字汉语拼音排序；词首或词中的西文字母或阿拉伯数字、罗马数字一律不参加排序。

4. 词目对应的英文(或其他外文)

4.1 词目对应的外文主要为英文，也有极少量的其他文种词语或字母。例如拉丁文、法文、德文及希腊字母等。遇有其他外文时，遵从其特殊形式。

4.2 词目对应的英文，在词目之后列出。例如：

计算机辅助设计/電腦輔助設計 computer-aided design

4.3 词义相同的英文并行排列，中间以逗号隔开。例如：

粗钢/粗鋼 crude steel, raw steel

4.4 英文名词一般采用单数形式，必须或习惯采用复数形式的英文名词除外。

4.5 以人名、地名等命名的专有名词，其对应的英文，首字母为大写。

4.6 英文如有英美拼法差异时，一般采用美式拼法。

4.7 英文中出现拉丁文词时，一般遵从各学科领域的格式惯例。例如：

肠产毒性大肠杆菌/腸產毒性大腸桿菌 enterotoxigenic *Escherichia coli*（生物学卷）

南方古猿/南[方古]猿 *Australopithecus*（地学卷）

奥斯特线虫属/牛胃絲蟲屬 *Ostertagia*（农业卷）

尺头/尺頭 caput ulnare(拉)（医学卷）

4.8 英文中出现汉语拼音转写词语时，一般遵从汉语拼音分词习惯。例如：

芎菊上清丸 xiongju shangqing pills

5. 附录

本词典后附有国际单位制、希腊字母表、地质年代表、元素周期表。

6. 索引

6.1 本词典列有词目首字音序索引和词目首字笔画索引。

6.2 本词典附有词目英文索引(扫描二维码查取)。

词目首字音序索引

(字右边的号码指词典正文的页码)

A

a
阿 1

ai
埃 1
矮 1
霭 1
艾 1
爱 1
碍 1

an
安 1
鞍 3
岸 3
按 3
案 3
暗 3

ang
昂 3

ao
凹 3
奥 3

B

ba
八 4
巴 4
扒 4
拔 4
靶 4
坝 4
罢 4

bai
白 4
百 4
柏 4
摆 4
拜 5

ban
扳 5

班 5
斑 5
搬 5
板 5
版 6
办 6
半 6
伴 8
拌 8
瓣 8

bang
邦 8
绑 8
棒 8
傍 8

bao
包 8
雹 9
薄 9
饱 9
宝 9
保 9
报 11
刨 11
抱 11
暴 11
曝 11
爆 12

bei
杯 12
背 12
北 12
贝 12
备 12
背 13
倍 13
被 13

ben
奔 13
锛 14
本 14
笨 14

beng
崩 14
泵 14

蹦 14

bi
比 14
舭 15
必 15
毕 15
闭 15
秘 16
辟 16
篦 16
壁 16
避 16
臂 16
璧 16

bian
边 16
编 17
鞭 18
扁 18
匾 18
变 18
便 19
辨 19

biao
标 19
彪 21
表 21

bie
别 22

bin
汾 22
宾 22
滨 22
濒 22
殡 22

bing
冰 22
兵 23
丙 23
并 23
病 23

bo
拨 23
波 24
玻 25

剥 25
菠 25
播 25
伯 26
驳 26
泊 26
博 26
搏 26
箔 26
薄 26

bu
补 26
捕 27
哺 27
不 27
布 28
步 29
部 29

C

ca
擦 30

cai
材 30
财 30
裁 30
采 30
彩 31
踩 31

can
参 31
餐 31
残 31

cang
仓 31
苍 31
舱 32
藏 32

cao
操 32
糙 33
槽 33
草 33

ce
册 34
厕 34
侧 34
测 35

ceng
层 37

cha
叉 38
差 38
插 38
茶 38
查 39
岔 39

chai
拆 39
柴 39

chan
觇 39
掺 39
缠 40
产 40
铲 40
阐 40
颤 40

chang
长 40
常 41
厂 42
场 42
倡 42

chao
抄 42
超 42
潮 44

che
车 45
彻 49
掣 49
撤 49

chen
尘 49
沉 49
陈 50

ce
晨 50
衬 50
称 50

cheng
称 50
撑 50
成 50
诚 50
承 50
城 51
乘 59
盛 59
程 59
橙 59
秤 59

chi
吃 59
螭 59
池 59
弛 59
驰 59
迟 59
持 60
尺 60
齿 60
赤 60

chong
冲 60
充 61
虫 62
重 62

chou
抽 62
稠 63
筹 63
臭 63

chu
出 63
初 64
除 65
厨 65
橱 65
处 65
杵 65

储 65
畜 65
触 65

chuan
穿 65
传 66
船 67
椽 71
喘 71
串 71

chuang
窗 71
床 71
创 71

chui
吹 71
垂 71
捶 72
锤 72

chun
春 72
纯 72
醇 73

ci
祠 73
瓷 73
磁 73
次 74
刺 74
葱 74
从 74
丛 74

cu
粗 74
促 75
猝 75

cuan
攒 75
窜 75
催 75
脆 75
淬 75

cun
村 75

存 75

cuo
搓 76
措 76
错 76

D

da
搭 77
达 77
打 77
大 77

dai
呆 80
代 80
带 80
贷 81
怠 81
袋 81
戴 81

dan
担 81
单 81
淡 86
弹 86
蛋 86
氮 86

dang
当 86
挡 86
档 87

dao
刀 87
导 87
岛 88
捣 89
倒 89
到 89
倒 89
道 89

de
德 92

deng		dong		扼	129	费	148	gai		弓	179	gui		盒	220
灯	92	东	116	轭	129	fen		改	163	公	179	归	196	荷	220
登	92	冬	117	恶	129	分	148	钙	163	功	182	规	196	赫	220
蹬	92	氡	117	颚	129	芬	151	盖	163	攻	183	硅	197	褐	220
等	92	动	117			酚	151	概	163	供	183	轨	197	hei	
凳	94	冻	119	en		焚	151	gan		宫	183	柜	200	黑	220
澄	94	洞	119	恩	129	粉	151	干	163	拱	184	贵	200	hen	
磴	94	dou		er		粪	152	甘	165	栱	184	gun		痕	221
di		斗	119	儿	129	feng		坩	165	共	184	辊	200	heng	
低	94	抖	119	耳	129	丰	152	竿	165	贡	185	滚	200	恒	221
堤	96	陡	119	二	129	风	152	杆	165	gou		guo		珩	221
滴	96	du				枫	154	赶	165	勾	185	郭	200	桁	221
狄	96	都	119	═F═		封	154	感	165	沟	185	锅	200	横	221
迪	96	毒	120			峰	155	橄	165	钩	185	国	201	衡	223
敌	96	独	120	fa		锋	155	干	165	构	185	果	203	hong	
笛	96	读	120	发	132	蜂	155	gang		购	185	过	203	轰	223
抵	96	堵	120	乏	134	缝	155	冈	166	gu				烘	223
底	96	赌	120	伐	135	fo		刚	166	估	185	═H═		红	223
地	97	度	120	阀	135	佛	155	钢	166	孤	185			宏	224
帝	103	渡	120	筏	135	fou		缸	169	箍	186	ha		虹	224
递	103	镀	120	法	135	否	155	港	169	古	186	哈	206	洪	224
第	103	duan		发	135	fu		杠	169	谷	186	hai		hou	
蒂	104	端	120	fan		夫	156	gao		股	186	海	206	喉	224
dian		短	121	帆	135	孵	156	高	169	骨	186	氦	209	猴	224
颠	104	段	121	翻	135	敷	156	膏	174	钴	186	han		后	224
典	104	断	121	凡	135	弗	156	告	174	鼓	186	含	209	厚	225
点	104	锻	122	繁	135	伏	156	ge		毂	187	焓	209	候	225
电	105	dui		反	135	扶	156	戈	174	固	187	涵	209	hu	
店	112	堆	122	返	137	服	156	哥	174	故	189	寒	210	呼	225
垫	112	队	122	饭	137	氟	156	搁	174	顾	189	罕	210	弧	226
殿	112	对	122	泛	137	浮	157	割	174	锢	189	汉	210	胡	226
diao		dun		范	137	符	157	歌	174	gua		旱	210	湖	226
凋	112	吨	123	fang		幅	157	阁	174	瓜	189	焊	210	蝴	226
雕	112	墩	123	方	137	辐	158	格	174	刮	189	hang		糊	226
吊	112	镦	124	坊	138	福	158	蛤	174	寡	189	夯	211	互	226
钓	113	蹲	124	芳	138	斧	158	隔	174	挂	189	行	211	户	226
调	113	趸	124	枋	138	俯	158	槅	175	guai		航	211	护	226
掉	114	钝	124	防	138	辅	159	镉	175	拐	190	巷	217	hua	
die		盾	124	妨	138	腐	159	个	175	guan		hao		花	227
跌	114	duo		房	142	负	160	各	175	关	190	毫	217	划	227
迭	114	多	124	仿	142	附	160	铬	175	观	190	豪	217	华	227
叠	114	掇	127	访	143	复	161	gei		官	191	好	217	滑	227
碟	114	舵	127	纺	143	副	162	给	175	管	191	号	217	化	228
蝶	114	惰	127	舫	143	赋	162	gen		贯	192	好	217	划	229
ding				放	143	傅	162	根	175	冠	192	耗	217	画	229
丁	114	═E═		fei		富	162	跟	175	惯	192	he		话	229
顶	114			飞	143	腹	162	艮	176	盥	192			huan	
订	115	e		非	145	覆	162	geng		灌	192	合	217	还	229
钉	115	阿	129	菲	147			耕	176	罐	193	和	218	环	229
定	115	鹅	129	肥	147	═G═		更	176	guang		河	218	缓	232
diu		额	129	肺	147			gong		光	193	荷	219	幻	232
丢	116			沸	148	ga		工	176	广	196	核	219	换	232
				废	147	伽	163								

huang		疾	255	键	273	紧	287	jue		控	314	朗	320	量	332
荒	233	棘	255	溅	273	锦	287	决	299	kou		浪	320	粮	332
皇	233	集	255	鉴	273	谨	287	绝	299	口	315	lao		两	332
黄	233	瘠	257	键	274	尽	287	掘	300	扣	315	捞	320	亮	332
簧	233	几	257	箭	274	进	288	蕨	300	ku		劳	320	量	333
晃	233	挤	257			jiang		近	289	jun		枯	315	老	320	liao	
		给	258	江	274	浸	290	军	300	骷	315	烙	321	疗	333
hui		脊	258	将	274	禁	290	均	300	库	315	le		燎	333
灰	233	计	258	浆	274			龟	301	kua		乐	321	料	333
挥	234	记	260	缰	274	jing		菌	301	挎	315	勒	321	瞭	333
恢	234	纪	260	疆	274	京	290	峻	301	跨	315	lei		lie	
辉	234	技	260	奖	274	经	290	竣	301	块	316	雷	321	列	333
回	234	忌	261	桨	274	惊	291			快	316	垒	322	劣	335
洄	235	季	261	降	274	晶	291	— K —		kuan		累	322	烈	335
毁	235	剂	261			精	291			宽	316	肋	322	猎	335
汇	236	迹	261	jiao		井	292	ka		kuang		类	322	裂	335
会	236	既	261	交	275	肼	292	咖	302	狂	316				
绘	236	继	261	郊	278	景	292	喀	302	矿	316	leng		lin	
彗	236	祭	261	浇	278	警	292	卡	302	框	317	棱	322	邻	335
惠	236	寄	261	胶	278	劲	292	kai		kui		冷	322	林	335
				焦	279	径	292	开	302	亏	317			临	336
hun		jia		角	279	净	293	铠	303	魁	317	li		淋	337
昏	236	加	261	绞	280	竞	293			馈	317	离	324	磷	337
浑	236	家	263	铰	280	敬	293	kan				梨	325	鳞	337
混	236	夹	263	矫	280	静	293	看	303	kun		犁	325	檩	337
		甲	264	脚	280	境	293	勘	303	昆	317	篱	325		
huo		岬	264	搅	280	镜	295	堪	303	捆	317	礼	325	ling	
锪	239	假	264	叫	280			坎	303			里	325	灵	337
活	239	价	265	轿	280	jiu		看	303	kuo		理	325	铃	337
火	240	驾	265	校	280	纠	295			扩	317	锂	326	凌	337
伙	241	架	265	较	281	鸠	295	kang		括	318	力	326	陵	337
货	241	嫁	265	教	281	久	295	康	304	阔	318	历	326	菱	337
获	244			酵	281	酒	295	抗	304			立	327	零	337
霍	244	jian				旧	295			— L —		励	327	岭	338
豁	244	尖	266	jie		救	295	— L —				利	327	领	338
		歼	266	阶	281	就	296	kao		la		沥	327	另	338
— J —		坚	266	接	281			考	305	垃	319	例	328		
		间	266	街	283	ju		靠	305	拉	319	砾	329	liu	
ji		肩	266	子	283	拘	296			喇	320	粒	329	溜	338
几	245	监	266	节	283	居	296	ke		蜡	320			刘	338
击	245	兼	266	杰	284	局	297	柯	305			lian		留	338
机	245	检	266	拮	284	橘	298	科	305	lai		连	329	流	338
矶	250	减	267	洁	284	矩	298	颗	305	来	320	帘	330	琉	339
鸡	250	剪	268	结	284	举	298	壳	306			莲	330	硫	339
奇	250	简	268	捷	285	巨	298	可	306	lan		联	330	馏	339
积	250	碱	268	截	285	拒	298	克	308	兰	320	廉	330	六	339
基	251	见	269	解	285	剧	298	刻	308	拦	320	练	331		
缉	253	件	269	介	286	距	298	客	308	栏	320	炼	331	long	
畸	253	间	269	界	286	锯	298			阑	320	链	331	龙	339
激	253	建	269	借	286	聚	298	ken		蓝	320			笼	340
级	254	剑	273					啃	309	篮	320	liang		隆	340
极	254	健	273	jin		juan		keng		揽	320	良	332		
即	255	舰	273	金	286	捐	299	坑	309	缆	320	凉	332	lou	
急	255	渐	273	筋	287	涓	299					梁	332	娄	340
				襟	287	卷	299	kong		lang				楼	340
								空	310	廊	320				
								孔	314						
								空	314						

词目首字音序索引

漏	340	man		敏	359	ni		耙	373	pin		器	398	qiu	
	lu	蛮	354	ming		尼	367	帕	373	拼	381	憩	398	丘	408
炉	340	满	354	名	359	泥	368		pai	贫	382		qian	秋	408
栌	340	曼	354	明	359	铌	368	拍	373	频	382	千	398	球	408
卤	340	漫	354	鸣	360	霓	368	排	373	品	382	扦	398		qu
鲁	341	慢	354	冥	360	拟	368	牌	375		ping	迁	398	区	409
陆	341		mang	命	360	逆	368	派	375	乒	382	钎	398	曲	410
录	341	芒	354		mo	腻	368		pan	平	382	牵	398	驱	411
鹿	341	忙	354	摹	360		nian	潘	375	评	386	铅	399	屈	411
路	341	盲	354	模	360	年	368	攀	375	苹	386	签	399	趋	411
辂	343		mao	膜	360	黏	369	盘	375	屏	386	前	399	渠	411
露	343	猫	354	摩	361	捻	369	判	375	瓶	387	钳	400	曲	412
	lü	毛	354	磨	361	辗	369		pang		po	潜	400	取	412
闾	344	茅	355	蘑	361	碾	369	旁	375	坡	387	浅	401	去	412
旅	344	锚	355	抹	361		niao		pao	泊	387	欠	401		quan
铝	345	卯	356	末	361	鸟	370	抛	375	泼	387	堑	401	圈	412
履	346	铆	356	没	361	尿	370	跑	375	迫	387	嵌	401	全	412
律	346	冒	356	莫	361		nie	泡	376	破	387		qiang	泉	414
率	346	贸	356	墨	362	镍	370	炮	376		pou	抢	402		que
绿	346	帽	356		mu		ning		pei	剖	387	强	402	缺	414
氯	347		mei	模	362	凝	370	胚	376		pu	墙	402	雀	414
滤	347	梅	356	母	362		niu	陪	376	扑	387	蔷	402	确	414
	luan	煤	356	木	362	牛	370	培	376	铺	387	抢	402	阙	414
峦	347	霉	356	目	362	扭	370	赔	376	蒲	388	强	402		qun
卵	347	每	356	沐	363	纽	370	佩	376	普	388	戗	402	裙	414
乱	347	美	357	苜	363	钮	370	配	376	谱	388		qiao	群	414
	lun	镁	357	牧	363		nong		pen	瀑	388	跷	403		
伦	347		men	钼	363	农	370	喷	377			锹	403	**R**	
轮	347	门	357	墓	363	浓	371	盆	379	**Q**		敲	403		
	luo	闷	357	幕	363		nu		peng			乔	403		ran
罗	348		meng	穆	363	努	371	砰	379		qi	桥	403	燃	416
逻	349	萌	357			怒	371	棚	379	七	389	翘	406	染	418
螺	349	蒙	357	**N**			nü	硼	379	期	389	撬	406		rang
裸	350	孟	357			女	371	膨	379	欺	389		qie	壤	418
洛	350		mi		na		nuan	碰	380	齐	389	切	406	让	418
落	351	弥	357	纳	364	暖	371		pi	其	389		qin		rao
		迷	357	钠	364		nuo	批	380	奇	389	侵	406	扰	418
M		糜	357		nai	挪	371	坯	380	歧	389	亲	406	绕	418
		米	357	奈	364			劈	380	脐	389	禽	406		re
	ma	泌	358	耐	364	**O**		皮	380	骑	389	勤	406	惹	418
麻	352	密	358		nan		ou	毗	380	棋	389	揿	406	热	418
马	352	蜜	358	南	365	欧	372	铍	380	旗	389		qing		ren
玛	352		mian	难	365	呕	372	疲	380	鳍	389	青	406	人	421
码	352	免	358		nang	偶	372	匹	380	企	389	轻	406	刃	424
	mai	面	358	囊	365	耦	372	辟	380	启	389	氢	407	认	424
埋	353		miao		nao				pian	起	389	倾	407	任	424
霾	353	苗	359	挠	365	**P**		偏	380	气	391	清	408	韧	424
麦	353	瞄	359	闹	365			片	381	弃	394	晴	408		ri
脉	353	庙	359		nei		pa		piao	汽	394	请	408	日	424
			mie	内	365	爬	373	漂	381	砌	398		qiong		rong
		灭	359		neng			票	381			穹	408	容	425
			min	能	367		pa		pie						
		民	359			耙	373	撇	381						

词目首字音序索引

溶	426	shai		时	449	耍	463	suo		体	491	退	511	萎	521
熔	426	筛	433	识	450	shuai		梭	482	剃	492	tun		艉	521
融	426	晒	433	实	450	衰	463	缩	482	替	492	吞	511	鲔	522
冗	426	shan		拾	451	摔	463	索	482	tian		囤	511	卫	522
	rou	山	433	食	451	甩	463	锁	483	天	492	tuo		未	524
柔	426	舢	434	蚀	452	shuan				添	494	托	511	位	525
肉	427	闪	434	炻	452	栓	463	=== T ===		田	494	拖	511		wen
	ru	扇	434	史	452	shuang				填	494	脱	512	温	525
茹	427	shang		矢	452	双	463	ta		tiao		驮	512	文	526
蠕	427	伤	434	使	452	霜	467	他	484	条	495	陀	512	纹	527
乳	427	商	434	始	452	shui		塌	484	调	495	驼	513	吻	527
入	427	熵	435	驶	452	水	467	塔	484	挑	496	椭	513	紊	527
	ruan	上	435	示	452	税	474	榻	484	眺	496	拓	513	稳	527
软	427	shao		世	452	睡	474	踏	484	跳	496			问	528
	rui	烧	436	市	453	shun		tai		tie		=== W ===			weng
锐	428	梢	436	式	453	顺	474	胎	484	贴	496			嗡	528
瑞	428	稍	436	势	453	瞬	475	台	484	铁	496	wa		瓮	528
	run	少	436	事	453	shuo		抬	485	ting		挖	514		wo
闰	428		she	饰	454	朔	475	太	485	厅	498	洼	514	涡	528
润	428	蛇	436	试	454		si	钛	486	汀	498	蛙	514	沃	529
	ruo	设	436	视	454	司	475	泰	486	听	498	瓦	514	卧	529
弱	428	社	437	适	455	丝	476		tan	烃	498		wai	握	529
		射	438	室	456	私	476	坍	486	亭	498	外	514		wu
=== S ===		涉	439	释	456	斯	476	摊	487	庭	498		wan	乌	529
		摄	439		shou	撕	476	滩	487	停	498	弯	515	圬	529
	sa		shen	收	456	死	476	谈	487	艇	499	蜿	516	污	529
洒	429	申	439	手	457	四	476	弹	487	tong		完	516	钨	531
撒	429	伸	439	守	458	寺	476	坦	488	通	499	玩	516	屋	531
萨	429	参	439	首	458	伺	476	炭	488	同	501	晚	516	无	531
	sai	砷	439	艏	458	饲	477	探	488	桐	502	碗	516	五	534
塞	429	深	439	寿	459		song	碳	488	铜	502	万	516	午	535
赛	429	神	440	受	459	松	477		tang	统	502	腕	517	伍	535
	san	审	440	狩	459	送	477	汤	489	桶	503		wang	庑	535
三	429	甚	440	授	459		sou	镗	489		tou	王	517	武	535
伞	431	渗	440	售	459	搜	477	唐	489	偷	503	网	517	舞	535
散	431		sheng	兽	459		su	镋	489	头	503	往	517	坞	535
	sang	升	440		shu	苏	477	糖	489	投	503	旺	517	物	535
桑	431	生	441	书	459	素	477		tao	透	504	望	517	误	535
	sao	声	443	枢	459	速	478	掏	489		tu		wei	雾	536
缫	431	牲	444	梳	459	宿	478	逃	489	凸	504	危	518		
扫	431	绳	444	舒	459	塑	478	陶	489	突	504	威	518	=== X ===	
	se	省	445	疏	460	溯	479	淘	489	图	504	微	518		
色	432	圣	445	输	460		suan	套	489	徒	505	韦	519		xi
	sen	盛	445	蔬	460	酸	479		te	涂	505	违	519	西	537
森	432	剩	445	熟	460		sui	特	490	屠	505	围	520	吸	537
	sha		shi	蜀	460	随	479		teng	土	505	桅	520	汐	538
杀	432	失	445	鼠	460	岁	480	藤	491		tuan	维	520	希	538
沙	432	诗	446	束	460	碎	480		ti	湍	509	伪	521	析	538
纱	433	施	446	树	460	隧	480	梯	491	团	509	尾	521	牺	538
刹	433	湿	447	竖	461		sun	踢	491		tui	纬	521	稀	538
砂	433	十	447	数	461	损	482	提	491	推	509	委	521	舾	538
		石	448	shua		榫	482								
				刷	463										

锡	538	削	549	序	560	延	569	仪	581	永	591	乐	605	zhan	
溪	538	消	549	畜	560	严	570	宜	582	泳	591	阅	605	沾	613
熄	538	硝	550	续	560	岩	570	移	582	涌	591	跃	605	毡	613
嬉	538	销	550	絮	560	沿	570	遗	583	用	591	越	605	斩	613
习	538	小	550	蓄	560	研	571	颐	583	佣	592	yun		展	613
席	538	笑	551	xuan		盐	571	疑	583	you		云	605	占	613
洗	538	效	551	宣	561	颜	571	乙	583	优	592	匀	605	栈	613
铣	539			轩	561	檐	571	已	583	邮	592	允	605	战	613
喜	539	xie		悬	561	衍	571	以	583	油	592	陨	605	站	613
戏	539	楔	551	旋	562	掩	571	椅	583	鱿	593	运	605	zhang	
系	539	歇	551	漩	563	眼	571	艺	583	游	593	晕	607	张	614
细	540	协	551	选	563	偃	571	刈	583	有	594	韵	607	章	614
隙	540	胁	552	眩	563	演	571	议	583	右	596			樟	614
xia		斜	552	旋	563	厌	571	异	583	幼	596	Z		涨	614
瞎	540	谐	553	渲	563	宴	571	抑	584	囿	596			丈	614
峡	540	携	553	xue		验	571	邑	584	诱	597	za		账	614
狭	540	写	553	削	563	燕	572	译	584	釉	597	匝	608	胀	614
下	540	泄	553	靴	563	yang		易	584	yu		杂	608	障	614
夏	541	泻	553	穴	563	扬	572	驿	584	迂	597	zai		zhao	
xian		卸	553	学	564	羊	572	疫	584	淤	597	灾	608	招	614
先	541	屑	553	雪	564	阳	572	逸	584	余	597	栽	608	着	615
纤	542	蟹	553	血	564	杨	572	意	584	鱼	597	再	608	爪	615
鲜	542	xin		xun		洋	572	溢	584	娱	597	在	609	找	615
闲	542	心	553	熏	564	仰	572	翼	584	渔	597	载	609	沼	615
弦	542	芯	553	旬	564	养	572	yin		隅	598	zan		兆	615
咸	542	辛	554	寻	564	氧	573	因	585	逾	598	暂	610	照	615
涎	542	锌	554	巡	564	样	573	阴	585	瑜	598	鏨	610	罩	615
衔	542	新	554	询	564	yao		荫	585	宇	598	zao		zhe	
舷	542	薪	554	循	564	腰	573	音	585	羽	598	遭	610	遮	615
显	542	信	554	训	565	邀	573	银	585	雨	598	凿	610	折	615
险	543	xing		迅	565	窑	574	引	585	语	598	早	610	辙	616
县	543	兴	556	驯	565	摇	574	饮	587	郁	599	藻	611	锗	616
现	543	星	556			遥	574	隐	587	育	599	皂	611	褶	616
限	543	行	556	Y		咬	575	印	587	浴	599	造	611	zhen	
线	544	形	558			药	575	饮	588	预	599	噪	611	针	616
xiang		型	559	ya		要	575	ying		阈	600			侦	616
乡	545	性	559			钥	575	应	588	遇	600	ze		珍	616
相	546			压	566	ye		英	588	御	601	责	611	帧	616
香	547	xiong		押	568	椰	575	膺	588	愈	601			真	616
厢	547	汹	559	垭	568	冶	575	鹰	588			zeng		砧	618
箱	547	胸	559	鸭	568	野	575	迎	588	yuan		增	611	诊	618
镶	547	雄	559	芽	568	业	575	荧	588	渊	601	憎	612	枕	618
详	547	xiu		崖	568	叶	575	盈	588	元	601	zha		阵	618
响	547	休	559	衙	569	页	576	营	588	园	601	扎	612	振	618
向	547	修	559	哑	569	曳	576	影	588	原	602	渣	612	震	619
项	548	锈	560	雅	569	夜	576	应	588	圆	603	轧	612	镇	619
巷	548	嗅	560	亚	569	液	576	硬	590	缘	604	闸	612	zheng	
相	548	溴	560	yan		yi		yo		源	604	栅	612	争	619
象	548	xu		氩	569	一	580	哟	591	远	604	炸	613	征	619
像	548	须	560			伊	581	yong		苑	604	zhai		蒸	619
橡	549	虚	560	咽	569	衣	581	拥	591	约	604	摘	613	整	620
xiao		需	560	烟	569	医	581	雍	591	月	604	宅	613	正	621
肖	549	徐	560	淹	569							窄	613		

证	623	纸	628	终	635	昼	639	柱	644	状	650	资	652	足	663
政	623	指	628	钟	635	皱	639	蛀	644	撞	650	子	652	族	663
zhi		趾	629	舯	635	zhu		铸	644	zhui		紫	652	阻	663
之	623	制	629	种	636	珠	639	筑	645	追	650	自	652	组	664
支	623	质	630	踵	636	株	639			锥	650	字	659	祖	665
芝	623	治	631	中	636	诸	639	zhua		坠	651	zong		zuan	
枝	623	致	631	仲	636	猪	639	抓	645	缀	651	宗	659	钻	665
织	623	秩	631	种	636	竹	639	zhuan		zhun		综	659	zui	
知	623	窒	631	重	636	逐	640	专	645	准	651	棕	660	最	665
执	623	蛭	631	zhou		主	640	砖	646	zhuo		总	660	zuo	
直	624	智	631	舟	637	助	642	转	646	桌	651	纵	662	作	669
值	626	滞	631	周	637	住	643	zhuang		卓	651	zou		左	669
职	626	置	632	洲	638	贮	643	庄	648	浊	651	走	663	作	669
植	626			轴	638	注	643	桩	648	着	651	zu		坐	670
止	627	zhong		肘	639	驻	644	装	648	zi		租	663	座	670
		中	632					壮	650	姿	651				

词目首字笔画索引

(字右边的号码指词典正文的页码)

一画		刃	424	见	269	书	459	田	494	记	260	协	551	迁	398
一	580	飞	143	午	535	幻	232	史	452	永	591	西	537	乔	403
乙	583	习	538	牛	370	五画		叫	280	司	475	压	566	传	66
二画		叉	38	手	457	未	524	另	338	尼	367	厌	571	乒	382
二	129	马	352	气	391	末	361	凹	3	民	359	在	609	休	559
十	447	乡	545	毛	354	示	452	四	476	弗	156	百	4	伍	535
丁	114	四画		升	440	击	245	生	441	出	63	有	594	伏	156
厂	42	丰	152	长	40	打	77	矢	452	加	261	存	75	优	592
七	389	王	517	片	381	正	621	失	445	皮	380	页	576	伐	135
八	4	开	302	化	228	扑	387	丘	408	边	16	灰	233	延	569
人	421	井	292	爪	615	扒	4	代	80	发	132	达	77	仲	636
入	427	天	492	反	135	功	182	仪	581			列	333	件	269
儿	129	夫	156	刈	583	去	412	白	4	圣	445	死	476	任	424
几	245	元	601	介	286	甘	165	他	484	对	122	成	50	伤	434
	257	无	531	从	74	世	452	瓜	189	台	295	夹	263	价	265
刀	87	韦	519	分	148	艾	1	丛	74	纠	362	轨	197	伦	347
力	326	云	605	乏	134	古	186	用	591	母	596	划	227	华	227
三画		专	645	公	179	节	283	甩	463	幼	476		229	仰	572
三	429	扎	612	仓	31	本	14	印	587	丝		毕	15	仿	142
干	163	艺	583	月	604	可	306	乐	321	六画		尘	49	伙	241
	165	木	362	欠	401	匝	608		605	邦	8	尖	266	伪	521
亏	317	五	534	风	152	丙	23	册	34	式	453	劣	335	自	652
工	176	支	623	勾	669	左	356	卯	597	迂	193	伊	581
土	505	厅	498	乌	529	石	448	外	514	动	117	光	86	血	564
下	540	不	27	匀	185	右	596	处	65	坏	529	当	610	向	547
大	77	太	485	六	339	布	28	冬	117	寺	476	早	576	后	224
丈	614	区	409	文	526	夯	211	鸟	370	扣	398	曳	62	行	211
万	516	历	326	方	137	龙	339	包	8	扦	315	虫	410		
上	435	匹	380	火	240	平	382	主	640	考	305	曲		舟	637
小	550	车	45	斗	119	灭	359	市	453	托	511	团	509	全	412
口	315	巨	298	计	258	轧	612	立	327	老	320	同	501	会	236
山	433	戈	174	订	115	东	116	闪	434	执	623	吊	112	杀	432
千	398	比	14	户	226	卡	302	兰	320	扩	317	吃	59	合	217
个	175	互	226	认	424	北	12	半	6	扫	431	因	585	兆	615
久	295	切	406	冗	426	占	613	汀	498	地	97	吸	537	企	389
凡	135	瓦	514	心	553	凸	504	汇	236	场	42	岁	480	伞	431
广	196	止	627	尺	60	业	575	头	503	扬	572	帆	135	创	71
门	357	少	436	引	585	旧	295	汉	210	耳	129	回	234	肋	322
之	623	日	424	巴	4	归	196	穴	563	共	184	刚	166	杂	608
已	583	中	632	孔	314	目	362	写	553	芒	354	网	517	危	518
弓	179	队	122	叶	575	让	418	亚	569	肉	427	旬	564
子	652	贝	12	办	6	甲	264	礼	325	芝	623	年	368	负	159
子	283	冈	166	以	583	申	439	训	565	机	245	先	541	名	359
卫	522	内	365	允	605	电	105	议	583	过	203	丢	116	各	175
女	371	水	467	双	463	号	217	必	15	再	608	竹	639	多	124

争	619	好	217	抖	119	串	71	饭	137	迟	59	拥	591	轭	129
色	432	戏	539	护	226	听	498	饮	587	局	297	抵	96	斩	613
壮	650	羽	598	壳	306	吻	527	系	588	改	163	拘	296	轮	347
冲	60	观	190	块	316	吹	71	冻	539	张	614	势	453	软	427
	62	红	223	扭	370	邑	584	疸	119	忌	261	抱	11	到	89
冰	22	驮	512	声	443	囤	511	状	650	陆	341	垃	319	非	145
庄	648	纤	542	报	11	别	22	庞	535	阿	1	拉	319	歧	389
刘	338	驯	565	拟	368	财	30	床	71		129	拦	320	齿	60
齐	389	约	604	芽	568	针	616	库	315	陈	50	拌	8	卓	651
交	275	级	254	花	227	钉	115	疗	333	阻	663	招	614	旺	517
衣	581	纪	260	芬	151	告	174	应	588	附	160	坡	387	果	203
次	74	驰	59	苍	31	乱	347	冷	322	坠	651	拨	23	昆	317
产	40	巡	564	芳	138	利	327	序	560	陀	512	抬	485	国	201
决	299			严	570	私	476	辛	554	妨	142	其	389	明	359
充	61	**七画**		芯	553	每	356	弃	394	努	371	取	412	易	584
闭	15	寿	459	劳	320	兵	23	冶	575	劲	292	苹	386	昂	3
问	528	麦	353	克	308	估	185	闰	428	鸡	250	苷	363	迪	96
羊	572	玛	352	苏	477	体	491	闲	542	纬	521	苗	359	典	104
并	23	形	558	杆	165	伸	439	间	266	驱	411	英	588	固	187
关	190	进	288	杠	169	作	669	纯	269	纱	72	苑	604	呼	225
米	357	吞	511	材	30	伯	26	闷	357	纳	433	范	137	鸣	360
灯	92	远	604	村	75	佣	592	判	375	驳	364	直	624	咖	302
污	529	违	519	极	254	低	94	沐	363	纵	26	茅	355	岸	3
江	274	韧	424	杨	572	住	643	沥	327	纸	662	林	335	岩	570
汐	538	运	605	更	176	位	525	沙	432	纹	628	枝	623	罗	348
池	59	扶	156	束	460	伴	8	汽	394	纺	527	杯	12	岬	264
汤	489	技	260	两	332	皂	611	沃	529	纽	559	枢	143	帕	373
忙	354	扰	418	医	581	伺	476	汹	143		370	柜	200	岭	338
兴	556	扭	129	励	327	佛	155	泛	137	**八画**		杵	65	账	614
宇	598	拒	298	否	155	伽	163	没	361	玩	516	析	538	购	185
守	458	找	615	还	229	近	289	沟	185	环	229	板	5	贮	643
宅	613	批	380	矶	250	彻	49	沉	49	武	535	松	477	图	504
字	659	走	663	歼	266	返	137	快	316	青	406	枫	154	钎	398
安	1	抄	42	来	320	余	597	完	516	责	611	构	185	钓	113
军	300	贡	185	连	329	希	538	宏	224	现	543	枋	138	制	629
许	560	坝	4	轩	561	坐	670	灾	608	玢	22	杰	284	知	623
农	370	攻	183	步	29	谷	186	良	332	表	21	枕	618	迭	114
设	436	赤	60	卤	340	含	209	证	623	规	196	画	229	垂	71
访	143	折	615	坚	266	邻	335	启	389	抹	361	卧	529	牧	363
寻	564	抓	645	肖	549	岔	39	评	386	拑	165	事	453	物	535
艮	176	扳	5	旱	210	肘	639	补	26	坯	380	刺	74	刮	189
迅	565	抢	402	时	449	龟	301	初	64	拓	513	雨	598	和	218
尽	287	坎	303	助	642	免	358	社	437	拔	4	郁	599	季	261
导	87	圳	486	县	543	狂	316	识	450	坦	488	矿	316	委	521
异	583	均	300	里	325	狄	96	罕	210	担	81	码	352	供	183
弛	59	坞	535	呆	80	角	279	诊	618	押	568	厕	34	使	452
	618	抑	584	呕	372	鸠	295	译	584	抽	62	奈	364	例	328
阵	572	抛	375	园	601	条	495	灵	337	拐	190	奇	250	版	6
阳	456	投	503	围	520	卵	347	即	255	拖	511	侦	389	侧	616
收	281	坑	309	吨	123	岛	88	层	37	拍	373	欧	372	侧	34
阶	585	抗	304	足	663	刨	11	尿	370	顶	114	轰	223	佩	376
阴	138	坊	138	邮	592	迎	588	尾	521	拆	39	转	646	货	241

字	页	字	页	字	页	字	页	字	页	字	页	字	页	字	页	字	页	字	页
迫	387	河	218	限	543	茶	38	毗	380	促	75	首	458	陨	605
质	630	沽	613	始	452	荒	233	贵	200	信	554	逆	368	除	65
征	619	油	592	驾	265	荧	588	界	286	皇	233	总	660	险	543
往	517	泊	26	参	31	故	189	虹	224	泉	414	炻	452	怒	371
爬	373		387		439	胡	226	品	382	侵	406	炼	331	架	265
径	292	沿	570	线	544	荫	585	咽	569	追	650	炸	613	盈	588
金	286	泡	376	练	331	茹	427	囹	596	盾	124	炮	376	急	81
刹	433	注	643	组	664	南	365	响	547	待	81	烃	498	柔	426
命	360	泻	553	细	540	药	575	哈	206	衍	571	剃	492	垒	322
斧	158	泌	358	驶	452	标	19	咬	575	律	346	洼	514	绑	8
采	30	泳	591	织	623	栈	613	哟	591	须	560	洁	284	结	284
受	459	泥	368	终	635	枯	315	炭	488	舢	434	洪	224	绕	418
乳	427	沸	148	驻	644	柯	305	峡	540	剑	273	洒	429	绘	236
贫	382	沼	615	绊	8	栌	340	峻	616	逃	489	浇	278	给	175
瓮	528	波	24	驼	513	相	546	贴	496	食	451	浊	651		258
饯	402	泼	387	驿	584		548	骨	186	盆	379	洞	119	绝	299
胖	292	治	631	经	290	查	39	钙	163	胚	376	洄	235	绞	280
肺	147	性	559	贯	192	柏	4	钛	486	脉	353	测	35	统	502
胀	614	学	564			栅	612	钝	124	胎	484	洗	538		
股	186	宝	9	九画		柱	644	钟	635	狭	540	活	239	十画	
肥	147	宗	659	春	72	栏	616	钢	166	独	120	洰	542	耕	176
服	156	定	115	珍	616	树	460	钠	364	飑	21	派	375	耗	217
胁	552	宜	582	玻	25	要	575	钥	575	狩	459	染	418	耙	373
周	637	审	440	毒	120	咸	542	钨	531	贸	356	洛	350	泰	486
昏	236	官	191	型	559	威	518	钩	185	急	255	洋	572	珠	639
鱼	597	空	310	挂	189	研	571	钮	370	蚀	452	洲	638	珀	221
备	12		314	封	154	砖	646	卸	553	峦	347	浑	236	班	5
饰	454	帘	330	持	60	厚	225	缸	169	弯	515	浓	371	素	477
饱	9	穿	408	拮	284	砌	398	拜	5	将	274	恒	221	捞	320
饲	477	实	450	拱	184	砂	568	看	303	奖	274	恢	234	栽	608
变	18	试	454	垭	548	泵	433	矩	298	亭	498	举	298	捕	27
京	290	诗	446	项	315	面	14	毡	613	亮	332	宣	561	振	618
店	112	肩	266	挎	51	耐	358	氡	117	度	120	室	456	载	609
夜	576	房	142	城	365	耍	463	氟	156	迹	261	宫	183	赶	165
庙	359	诚	50	挠	623	牵	398	氢	407	庭	498	突	504	盐	571
底	96	衬	50	政	86	残	31	牲	444	疫	584	穿	65	埋	353
剂	261	视	454	挡	318	轴	638	选	563	姿	651	客	308	捆	317
郊	278	话	229	括	451	轻	406	适	455	亲	406	冠	192	捐	299
废	147	询	564	拾	496	背	12	香	547	音	585	语	598	损	482
净	293	详	547	挑	628		13	种	636	帝	103	扁	18	都	119
盲	354	建	269	指	112	战	613	秋	408	施	446	祖	665	换	232
放	143	录	341	垫	257	觇	39	科	305	闾	344	神	440	热	418
刻	308	居	296	挤	381	点	104	重	62	阀	135	祠	73	捣	89
育	599	刷	463	拼	514	临	336	复	636	阁	174	误	535	埃	1
闸	612	屈	411	挖	3	竖	461	竿	160	差	38	诱	597	莲	330
闹	365	弧	226	按	234	省	445	段	165	养	572	退	511	莫	361
卷	299	弥	357	挥	371	削	549	便	121	美	357	既	261	荷	219
单	81	弦	542	挪	440	哑	569	贷	19	送	477	屋	531		220
炉	340	承	50	甚	217	显	548	顺	81	类	322	昼	639	获	244
浅	401	孟	357	巷	80	冒	542	修	474	迷	357	屏	386	恶	129
法	135	孤	185	带	33	星	356	保	559	娄	340	费	148	真	616
泄	553	降	274	草			556		9	前	399	陆	119	框	317

栱	184	铁	496	浆	274	涌	591	培	376	啃	309	祭	261	密	358
档	87	铃	337	衰	463	宽	316	接	281	跃	605	减	267	谐	553
桐	502	铅	399	高	169	家	263	控	314	蛀	644	毫	217	屠	505
株	639	铆	356	郭	200	宴	571	探	488	蛇	436	麻	352	弹	86
桥	403	铌	368	席	538	宾	22	掘	300	累	322	痕	221		487
桁	221	铍	380	准	651	窄	613	掺	39	崖	568	廊	320	随	479
栓	463	缺	414	座	670	容	425	掇	127	逻	349	康	304	蛋	86
桄	520	氩	569	病	23	案	3	职	626	崩	14	鹿	341	隅	598
格	174	氪	209	疾	255	请	408	基	251	圈	412	章	614	隆	340
桩	648	氧	573	疲	380	朗	320	勘	303	铝	345	商	434	隐	587
校	280	特	490	脊	258	诸	639	菱	337	铜	502	族	663	续	560
核	219	牺	538	效	551	读	120	勒	321	铠	303	旋	562	骑	389
样	573	造	611	离	324	扇	434	黄	233	铣	539		563	绳	444
根	175	乘	59	紊	527	被	13	菲	147	铬	175	望	517	维	520
索	482	敌	96	唐	489	冥	360	萌	357	铰	280	率	346	综	659
哥	174	秤	59	涡	112	调	113	菌	301	铲	40	阈	600	绿	346
速	478	租	663	瓷	73			萎	521	银	585	阐	40	缀	651
配	376	积	250	资	652	谈	487	菠	25	矫	280	着	615	**十二画**	
夏	541	秩	631	凉	332	剥	25	营	588	梨	325		651	斑	5
砗	379	称	50	站	613	展	613	萨	429	犁	325	盖	163	替	492
砝	618	秘	16	剖	387	剧	298	梢	436	移	582	粗	74	堪	303
砷	439	透	504	竞	293	屑	553	梅	356	笨	14	粒	329	塔	484
砾	329	笑	551	部	29	弱	428	检	266	笼	340	断	121	搭	77
破	387	借	286	旁	375	陵	337	梳	459	笛	96	剪	268	越	605
原	602	值	626	旅	344	陶	489	梯	491	符	157	兽	459	趋	411
套	489	倾	407	畜	65	陪	376	桶	503	第	103	焊	210	超	42
逐	640	倒	89			娱	597	梭	482	敏	359	焙	209	揽	320
烈	335	俱	298	阅	605	通	499	救	295	偃	571	清	408	堤	96
顾	189	倡	42	瓶	387	能	367	副	161	袋	81	添	494	提	491
轿	280	候	225	粉	151	难	365	票	381	偶	372	淋	337	博	26
较	281	俯	158	料	333	预	599	酚	151	偷	503	淹	569	喜	539
逗	124	倍	13	兼	266	桑	431	厢	547	售	459	渠	411	揿	406
致	631	健	273	朔	475	验	571	硅	197	停	498	渐	273	插	38
柴	39	臭	63	烘	223	继	261	盛	59	偏	380	混	236	搜	477
桌	651	射	438	烧	436	**十一画**			445	假	264	渊	601	裁	30
监	266	徒	505	烟	569	彗	236	匾	18	衔	542	渔	597	搁	174
紧	287	徐	560	烙	321	球	408	雪	564	盘	375	淘	489	搓	76
晒	433	舭	15	递	103	理	325	辅	158	船	67	液	576	搅	280
眩	563	舯	635	酒	295	琉	339	堑	401	舷	542	淬	75	握	529
鸭	568	舰	273	涉	439	堵	120	虚	560	舵	127	淤	597	斯	476
晃	233	舱	32	消	549	措	76	雀	414	斜	552	淡	86	期	389
哺	27	航	211	涓	299	掩	571	常	41	盒	220	深	439	欺	389
晕	607	舫	143	涡	528	捷	285	晨	50	彩	31	涵	209	联	330
恩	129	爱	1	海	206	排	373	眺	496	领	338	梁	332	散	431
罢	4	脆	75	涂	505	掉	114	眼	571	脚	280	渗	440	惹	418
峰	155	胸	559	浴	599	捶	72	悬	561	脱	512	情	408	敬	293
圆	603	脐	389	浮	156	堆	122	野	575	象	548	惊	291	葱	74
峻	301	胶	278	流	338	推	509	曼	354	逸	584	惯	192	蒂	104
钳	400	留	338	润	428	授	459	晚	516	猪	639	寄	261	落	351
钴	186	皱	639	浪	320	捻	369	畦	389	猎	335	宿	478	棒	8
钻	665	凌	337	浸	290	教	281	距	298	猫	354	窒	631	棱	322
钼	363	桨	274	涨	614	掏	489	趾	629	猝	75	窑	574	棋	389

词目首字笔画索引

字	页	字	页	字	页	字	页	字	页	字	页	字	页	字	页	字	页	字	页
椰	575	链	331	竣	301	靶	4	锤	72	盞	343	膜	360	碾	369
植	626	销	550	阑	320	蓝	320	锥	650	群	414	鲔	522	震	619
森	432	锁	483	阔	318	墓	363	锦	287	殿	112	鲜	542	霉	356
焚	151	锂	326	普	388	幕	363	锶	239	辟	16	疑	583	暴	11
椅	583	锅	200	粪	152	蓄	560	键	274			380	孵	156	瞎	540
棚	379	锈	560	道	89	蒲	388	锯	298	障	614	敲	403	影	588
棕	660	锋	155	港	169	蒙	357	矮	1	嫁	265	豪	217	踢	491
椭	513	锌	554	滞	631	颐	583	稠	63	叠	114	膏	174	踏	484
惠	236	锐	428	湖	226	蒸	619	筹	63	缝	155	遮	615	踩	31
棘	255	掣	49	渣	612	楔	551	签	399	缠	40	腐	159	蝶	114
厨	65	短	121	湿	447	禁	290	简	268	十四画	端	120	蝴	226
硬	590	智	631	温	525	楼	340	毁	235	静	293	旗	389	颚	129
硝	550	氮	86	湍	509	概	163	鼠	460	墙	402	精	291	墨	362
确	414	键	273	溅	273	橡	71	催	75	赫	220	熄	538	镇	619
硫	339	氯	347	滑	227	感	165	像	548	截	285	熔	426	镉	175
裂	335	鹅	129	渡	120	碍	1	魁	317	境	295	漂	381	镍	370
雄	559	剩	445	游	593	硼	379	衙	569	摘	613	漫	354	靠	305
辊	200	稍	436	渲	563	碎	480	微	518	摔	463	滴	96	箱	547
暂	610	程	59	惰	127	碰	380	艇	521	撇	381	漱	563	箭	274
雅	569	稀	538	割	174	碗	516	愈	601	聚	298	演	571	德	92
翘	406	税	474	寒	210	雷	321	遥	574	蔷	402	漏	340	艚	458
紫	652	等	92	富	162	零	337	腻	368	摹	360	慢	354	熟	460
凿	610	筑	645	窜	75	雾	536	腰	573	模	360	赛	429	摩	361
辉	234	筛	433	窗	71	雹	9	腹	162		362	寡	189	瘠	257
敞	42	筒	503	裙	414	辐	157	触	65	榀	175	蜜	358	颜	571
晴	408	筏	135	强	402	输	460	解	285	榻	484	褐	220	糊	226
最	665	筋	287	疏	459	频	382	馏	339	榫	482	谱	388	熵	435
量	332	傅	162	隔	174	鉴	273	廉	331	歌	174	隧	480	潜	400
	333	牌	375	隙	540	睛	359	新	554	遭	610	凳	94	潮	44
喷	377	集	255	絮	560	睡	474	韵	607	醉	281	缩	482	潘	375
晶	291	焦	279	登	92	暖	371	意	584	酸	479	缫	431	澄	94
喇	320	傍	8	缆	320	歇	551	阙	414	碟	114	十五画	憎	612
遇	600	储	65	绰	253	暗	3	粮	332	碱	268	藕	372	额	129
景	292	奥	3	缓	232	照	615	数	461	碳	488	撕	476	劈	380
跌	114	街	283	编	17	畸	253	塑	478	磁	73	撒	429	履	346
跑	375	御	601	缘	604	跨	315	煤	356	殡	22	撑	50	嬉	538
遗	583	循	564	十三画	跷	403	满	354	需	560	撬	406	十六画
蛙	514	舾	538	瑞	428	跳	496	源	604	辗	369	播	25	操	32
蛭	631	艇	499	瑜	598	路	341	滤	347	颗	305	墩	123	燕	572
蛤	174	舒	459	摄	439	跟	175	溴	560	蜡	320	撞	650	薪	554
喘	71	逾	598	填	494	蜂	155	溪	538	蜿	516	撤	49	薄	9
喉	224	釉	597	搏	26	嗅	560	溜	338	骷	315	增	611		26
喀	302	释	456	塌	484	嗡	528	滚	200	锹	403	鞍	3	颠	104
嵌	401	禽	406	鼓	186	置	632	溢	584	锻	122	蕨	300	橱	65
幅	157	腕	517	摆	4	罩	615	溯	479	镀	120	蔬	460	橡	333
帽	356	鱿	593	携	553	蜀	460	滨	22	镁	357	横	221	橙	59
赋	162	鲁	341	搬	5	锗	616	溶	426	舞	535	槽	33	橘	298
赌	120	猴	224	摇	574	错	76	滩	487	稳	527	橡	549	整	620
赔	376	馈	317	毂	187	锚	355	塞	429	熏	564	樟	614	融	426
黑	220	装	648	摊	487	锛	14	谨	287	箍	186	橄	165	甑	368
铸	644	蛮	354	勤	406	锡	538	裸	350	箔	26	敷	156	霍	244
铺	387	就	296	靴	563	锢	189	福	158	管	191	醇	73	錾	610

词目首字笔画索引

辙	616	篱	325	糖	489	藏	32	簧	233	疆	274	警	292	爆	12
餐	31	盥	192	燃	416	檫	571	繁	135	蹚	489	磨	361	二十画及以上	
踵	636	邀	573	濒	22	檩	337	糜	357	蹦	14	藻	611	壤	418
螭	59	衡	223	激	253	磷	337	膺	588	翻	135	攀	375	蠕	427
器	398	膨	379	褶	616	磴	94	豁	244	鳍	389	霪	1	鳞	337
噪	611	雕	112	壁	16	霜	467	臂	16	鹰	588	曝	11	灌	192
镗	489	磨	361	避	16	瞭	333	翼	584	瀑	388	蹲	124	露	343
镜	295	凝	370	缰	274	瞬	475	**十八画**		襟	287	蹬	92	囊	365
憩	398	辨	19	**十七画**		螺	349	鞭	18	壁	16	蟹	553	霾	353
穆	363	壅	591	戴	81	镦	124	藤	491	**十九画**		颤	40	镶	547
篮	320	糙	33	擦	30	黏	369	覆	162	攒	75	瓣	8	罐	193
笆	16														

A

阿尔班山考古遗址/阿塔皮爾卡考古遺址，阿塔普埃卡考古遺址　Archaeological Site of Monte Albán
阿尔多布兰迪尼庄园/阿爾多布蘭迪尼別墅　Villa Aldobrandini
阿根廷草原/潘帕草原　pampas
阿瓜达斯水库/阿瓜達斯水庫　Aguadas historic water reservoirs
阿瓜达斯住宅区/阿瓜達斯住宅區　Aguadas residential areas
阿克巴墓/阿克巴墓　Akbar tomb
阿克雷特法则/阿克萊特法則　Ackeret rule
阿里安住宅/阿里安住宅　house of Arian
阿隆索地租模型/阿隆索[競租]模式　Bid rent mode
阿伦方差/阿倫方差，Allan 變異數，艾倫方差　Allan variance
阿纳沙公园/阿納沙公園　Park Araxá
埃尔塔津古城/埃爾塔津古城　El Tajin Pre-Hispanic City
埃及式门楼/派龍，塔門　pylon
埃及式柱/埃及式柱　Egyptian column
埃斯特庄园/埃斯特莊園　Villa d'Este
矮侧板/下降側　low side
矮端板/矮端板　low end
矮型信号机/矮型號誌　dwarf signal
霭/靄　mist
艾里应力函数/艾利應力函數　Airy stress function
爱奥尼柱式/愛奧尼亞柱式　Ionic order
爱车点/愛車點　car caring point
爱德考克天线/亞德考克天線　Adcook antenna
爱琴建筑/愛琴文化的建築　Aegean architecture
碍航浮标/危險浮標　danger buoy
碍航物/障礙物　obstruction
安定[性]理论/安定性理論　shake down theory
安防控制中心/安全控制室　security control room
安放龙骨日期/安放龍骨日期　date of keel laid
安静休息区/安靜休息區　tranquil rest area
安全/安全保證　security
安全棒/安全棒　safety rod
安全保卫组/保全組　safeguard team
安全报告/安全信文　safety message
安全报警系统/安全警報系統　safety alarm system

安全标志/安全標誌　safety sign, safety mark, safety symbol
安全玻璃/安全玻璃　safety glass, tempered glass
安全操作系统/安全操作系統　secure operation system
安全产水量/安全出水量　safe yield
安全车/安全車　safety car
安全出舱滑道/應急逃生滑道　emergency egress chute
安全出口/安全出口　safety exit
安全措施/安全措施　safety measure
安全挡台/安全擋臺　safety barricade
安全导火索/安全引線　safety fuse
安全岛/安全島，避車島　refuge island, safety island
安全到达保险/安全到達保險　safety arrival insurance
安全灯/安全燈　safety lamp, safe-light
安全地带/安全島　safety island
安全地点/安全地點，安全區　safety place
安全电灯/安全電燈　electric safety lamp
安全电路/安全電路　vital circuit, safety circuit
安全电压/安全電壓　safety voltage
安全吊货钩/安全吊貨鉤　cargo safety hook
安全发火机构/安全發火機構　safe ignition device, safe and arm device
安全阀/安全閥　safety valve, relief valve
安全阀调定压力/安全閥調定壓力　safety valve setting pressure
安全防范产品/安全保護品　security and protection product
安全防范系统/安全防範系統　security and protection system, SPS
安全防范[系统]工程/安全防範系統工程　engineering of security and protection system
安全防护/安全保護　security protection
安全防护设备/安全保護裝置　safety protection equipment
安全防护水平/安全防護水準　level of security
安全符号/安全符號　safety symbol
安全[工作]负荷/安全工作負荷，安全使用負荷　safe working load, SWL

安全工作压强/安全工作壓力　safe working pressure
安全关键件/安全關鍵零組件　safety critical part
安全管道/安全管道　safety corridor
安全管理/安全管理　safety management
安全管理手册/安全管理手冊　safety management manual
安全管理系统/安全管理系統,保全管理系統　security management system, SMS
安全管理证书/安全管理證書　Safety Management Certificate
安全管理制度/安全管理制度　safety management system, SMS
安全航路/安全主航道　safety fairway
安全航速/安全速度　safety speed
安全和解除保险装置/引信安全備位機構　safe and arming device, S and A device
安全呼叫/安全呼叫　safety call
安全呼叫格式/安全呼叫格式　safety call format
安全技术措施/安全技術措施　safety technical measures
安全监测装置/安全監測裝置　safety monitoring assembly
安全降功率系统/安全降功率系統　safety power cutback system
安全教育/安全教育　safety education
安全接点/安全接頭　safety contact, power off contact
安全距离/安全距離　safety distance
安全开关/安全開關　safety switch, safety
安全控制/安全控制　safety control
安全控制电视监视系统/安全控制電視監控系統　safe-control television monitor system
安全控制系统/安全控制系統　safety control system
安全控制信息/安全控制資訊　safety control information
安全联锁/安全聯鎖,安全互鎖　safety interlock
安全逻辑装置/安全邏輯裝置　safety logic assembly
安全帽/安全帽　safety cap, safety helmet
安全门/太平門　exit door, escape door
安全模式/安全狀態　safety mode
安全判据/安全準則　safety criterion
安全判决/安全決策　safety decision
安全判决准则/安全決策法則　safety decision rule
安全驱动器/安全驅動器　safety actuator
安全燃料/安全油料　safety fuel
安全设备试验/安全設備試驗　test on safety equipment
安全设施用地/安全設施用地　land for security facility
安全绳/安全繩　safety rope, safety strap
安全事故/安全事故　safety misadventure
安全寿命设计/安全壽命設計　safe life design
安全水域标志/安全水域標誌　safety water mark
安全索/救生索,攀手索　life line
安全梯/室内逃生梯　emergency staircase, fire escape
安全停堆系统/安全停機系統　safety shutdown system
安全通信/安全通信　safety communication
安全通信程序/安全通信程式　safety communication procedure
安全[通信]网/安全[通信]網　safety net
安全投弹高度/安全投射高度　safe release altitude
安全系数/安全係數,安全因數　safety factor, SF, safety coefficient
安全系统/安全系統　safety system
安全线/安全[側]線　catch siding
安全信号/安全信號　safety signal
安全性/安全性　safety
安全性可靠性大纲/安全性可靠度方案　safety and reliability program
安全遥控/安全遥控　safety command and control
安全业务/安全業務　safety service
安全溢出阀/安全溢出閥　discharge valve
安全应急预案/安全應急方案,安全緊急應變計劃　safety emergency plan
安全应力/安全應力　safe stress
安全用电/安全用電,電氣安全量測　electrical safety measure, safety power consumption, safety in utilizing electric energy
安全优先等级/安全優先順序　safety priority
安全与环保政策/安全與環保政策　safety and environmental protection policy
[安全与解除]保险装置/安全備炸裝置　safety and arming device
安全与联锁装置/安全與聯鎖設施　safety and interlock device
安全裕度/安全限度,安全餘裕,安全客限　margin of safety, safety margin
安全载流量/安全載流量　safe carrying capacity
安全炸药/安全炸藥　safety explosion, explosive charge, safety explosive
安全照明/安全照明　safety lighting
安全整改/安全整流　security promotion
安全执行机构/安全點火機構　safety and firing mechanism

安全指令/安全指令　safety command
安全重要构筑物/安全重要構築物　structure important to safety
安全注射系统/安全噴射系統　safety injection system
安全抓杆/扶手棍,抓條　safety climbing pole
安全装置/安全裝置,安全設備,安全設施　safety device, safety equipment
安全状态/安全狀態,可靠狀態　safe condition
安全自毁/安全自毀　safety self-destruct
安时效率/安［培小］時效率　ampere-hour efficiency
安息香树胶/安息香膠　gum benzoin
安置/住宅改築　rehousing
安置房/安置房,遷置住宅　resettlement housing
安装/安裝　installation
安装拆卸费/安裝拆卸費　mounting and dismounting cost
安装高度/安裝高　mounting height
安装工程费/安裝費用　installation cost
安装焊/工地焊接　site weld
安装焊缝/安裝焊接　erection weld
安装耗油率/安裝耗油率　installed specific fuel consumption
安装环/安裝環　installation ring
安装角/安裝角,傾角,交錯角　angle of incidence, stagger angle
安装接线图/安裝接線圖,裝配接線圖　installation connection diagram
安装节/機架　mount
安装螺栓/裝配螺栓　assembling bolt
安装锚杆台车/錨桿支護臺車　bolting jumbo
安装损失/安裝損失　installation loss
安装图［样］/安裝圖,架設圖　erection drawing
安装推力/安裝後推力　installation thrust
安装误差/安裝誤差　installation error
鞍形舱/鞍形艙　saddle chamber
岸壁效应/岸壁效應　bank effect
岸边淤积/沿岸淤積　shore deposit
岸冰/岸冰　shore ice
岸船通信系统/岸船通信系統　shore-ship communication system, S-S communication system
岸电/岸電　shore power
岸电电缆/岸電電纜　shore connection cables
岸电联锁保护/岸電聯鎖保護　interlock protection of shore power connection
岸电箱/岸電接線盒　shore connection box
岸墙/岸牆　quay wall
岸上管理/岸上管理　shore-based management
岸上维修/岸上維修　shore-based maintenance, SBM
岸台费/岸臺費　coast station charge
岸吸/岸吸力　bank suction
按比例承包/百分比計酬契約　percentage contract
按键电话机/按鍵電話機　key pad telephone set
按键开关/接紐開關　button switch, key switch
按键式拨号盘/小鍵盤,鍵墊　key pad
按钮/按鈕　push-in button
按钮表示/按鈕表示　button indication
按质赔偿/補償損失　compensation for loss
案/長形桌　long table
暗电流/暗電流　dark current
暗沟排水/暗管排水　pipe drainage
暗管排水/暗管排水　pipe drainage
暗涵/暗涵　buried culvert
暗河/埋没河川　buried stream
暗盒/暗盒　cassette, magazine
暗礁/暗礁,伏礁　sunken rock, submerged rock
暗流/潛流　undercurrent
暗渠/暗渠　covered conduit
暗视觉/暗視力,夜間視覺,微光視覺　scotopic vision
暗适应/暗適應　dark adaptation
暗室/暗室,暗房　darkroom
暗榫/短榫　stub tenon
暗挖法/暗挖法　undermining method, subsurface excavation method
暗挖隧道/鑽挖隧道　bored tunnel
暗线/隱藏配線　concealed wiring
暗轴/暗軸　hidden axis
昂/昂　ang, lever
昂尾挑斡/昂尾挑斡　angwei tiaowo
凹槽/刻凹槽　notching
凹底平车/凹底平車　depressed center flat car
凹式平板挂车/彎板拖車　cranked platform trailer
凹凸断面/凹凸斷面　beaded section
凹纹压路机/齒輪輾路機　indenting roller
凹形竖曲线/凹面豎曲線　concave vertical curve
奥德特·芒太罗住宅花园/奧德特·芒太羅住宅花園　Odette Monteiro Garden
奥林达历史中心/奧林達歷史中心　historic center of the town of Olinda
奥米伽/亞米茄　Omega
奥米伽表/亞米茄表　Omega table
奥米伽传播改正量/亞米茄傳播修正值　Omega propagation correction, OPC
奥米伽船位/亞米茄船位　Omega fix
奥米伽导航仪/亞米茄航儀　Omega navigator
奥米伽海图/亞米茄海圖　Omega chart
奥米伽系统/亞米茄系統　Omega system
奥米伽信号格式/亞米茄信號格式　Omega signal format

B

八角截面风洞/八角形風洞 octagon wind tunnel
八角井/八角井 octagonal well
八字锚泊/[八字]雙錨泊 riding to two anchors
八字形桥台/八字形橋臺,翼[牆]形橋臺 flare wing walled abutment, abutment with flare wing wall, splayed abutment
巴比伦建筑/巴比倫建築 Babylonian architecture
巴布尔回忆录/巴布爾回憶錄 Babur-Name
巴布尔墓/巴布爾墓 Babur tomb
巴格/巴格 bagh
巴劳木/娑羅雙木 Bangkirai
巴黎美术学院建筑教育/巴黎美術學院建築教育 Beaux-Arts architecture education
巴洛克建筑/巴洛克建築 Baroque architecture
巴洛克式园林/巴洛克式園林 Baroque style garden
巴拿马运河导缆孔/巴拿馬運河導索器 Panama chock
巴拿马运河吨位/巴拿馬運河噸位 Panama canal tonnage
巴拿马运河吨位证书/巴拿馬運河噸位證書 Panama Canal Tonnage Certificate
巴氏合金/巴比合金,白合金 Babbitt metal
巴氏货油舱清洗系统/巴氏貨油艙清洗系統 Butterworth tank cleaning system
巴西草原/[巴西的]旱性草原 campo
巴西利卡/巴西利卡建築 Basilica
巴西利亚/巴西利亞 Brasilia
扒碴机/軌枕間道碴機 crib ballast remover
拔出试验/拔出試驗 pull out test
拔出阻力/拔出阻力,抗拔力 pull out resistance
拔桩/拔樁 pile extracting
拔桩机/拔樁機 pile extractor
靶板/目標板 target plate
靶场/靶場 range, shooting range, firing range
靶场测量/靶場量測 target range measurement
靶场间测量小组标准/IRIG 標準 Inter-Range Instrumentation Group standards, IRIG standards
靶船/靶船 target ship, target craft
靶机/目標靶機 target drone
靶室/靶室 range tank
坝/壩 dam
坝顶/壩頂 crest of dam
坝顶长度/壩頂長度 crest length
坝顶加高/壩頂加高 heightening of dam
坝高/壩高 height of dam
坝冠/壩頂 crest of dam
坝身/壩體 dam body
坝体/壩體 dam body
坝址勘探/基址探測 site exploration
坝址滤层/壩址濾層 toe filter
罢工条款/罷工保險條款 strike clause
白炽灯/白熾燈,白熱燈 incandescent lamp
白道/白道 moon path, lunar orbit
白点/白點 flake crack, shatter crack, small nucleus fissure
白垩土/白[堊質]黏土 chalky clay
白合金轴承/白合金軸承 white metal bearing
白色硅酸盐水泥/白[波特蘭]水泥 white Portland cement
白霜/白霜 hoar frost
白水表行车/白水表行車 running without water in gage
白天信号灯/日間信號燈 daylight signaling lamp
白铁皮/鍍鋅鐵皮 tinned sheet-iron
白星火箭/白星火箭 white star rocket
白噪声/白噪音,白雜訊 white noise
白噪声测试器/白雜訊測試儀 white noise test set
白昼信号灯/日間訊號燈 daylight signaling light
白棕绳/白棕繩,馬尼拉繩 Manila rope
百分表/針盤指示儀 dial indicator
百分位/百分位 percentile
百货商店/百貨公司 department store
百米桩/百米樁,百公尺樁 100m stake
百帕/百巴斯噶 hectopascal
百万分之几/百萬分之幾 parts per million, ppm
百叶窗/百葉窗 louver
百叶窗油缸/百葉窗油壓缸 oil cylinder of shutter
百叶型风口/通風調節設備 register
柏油碎石路面/柏油碎石路面 tar macadam pavement
摆动承梁/搖承材 swing bolster
摆动角/旋角 swing angle

摆动绞车/旋轉絞車　swing winch
摆动辗压/迴轉鍛造　rotary forging
摆动喷管/球窩噴嘴　gimbaled nozzle
摆动扫描/擺動式掃描　oscillating scan
摆动扫描地球敏感器/擺動掃描地球感測器　swing scanning earth sensor, swing scanning horizon sensor
摆动式机器人/垂擺式機器人　pendular robot
摆动轴/擺動軸　axis of oscillation
摆墩/擺墩,塢墩布置　blocking arrangement
摆幅/動程　throw
摆滚振动/擺滾振動　rock-roll vibration
摆角/旋角　swing angle
摆块/擺塊　centering block
摆块吊/擺塊吊　centering block hanger
摆式车体/擺式車體　pendulum type car body
摆式积分陀螺加速度计/擺式積分陀螺加速度儀　pendulous integrating gyro accelerometer, PIGA
摆式加速度计/擺式加速度儀　pendulous accelerometer
摆式减振器/擺式配重　pendulum damper
摆式罗经/擺式電盤經　pendulous gyrocompass
摆式仪/可攜式擺錘試驗儀　portable pendulum tester
摆式支座/[橋架]搖軸支座,[桁架]伸縮支座　rocker bearing
摆式阻尼器/擺式配重　pendulum damper
摆性/擺性　pendulosity
摆振铰/摇曳鉸　lead-lag hinge
摆轴支座/搖擺式支座　pendulum bearing
拜占庭建筑/拜占庭式建築物[風格]　Byzantine architecture
扳道电话/搬道員電話　switchman telephone
扳道房/調車助手室　switchman cabin
扳道员/調車工,掛鉤工　shunter
班车客运/班車客運　scheduled bus transport
班车线路/班車線路　regular service route
班次/班次　number of runs
班次密度/班次密度　density of runs
班次时刻表/班次時間表　time table of runs
班夫国家公园/班夫公園　Banff National Park
班轮/定期船　liner
班轮公会/定期船公會　liner conference
班轮公会行动守则公约/定期船同盟行動章程公約　Convention on a Code of Conduct for Liner Conference
班轮提单/定期船載貨證券　liner bill of lading
班轮条款/定期船條款　liner term

班轮运输/定期船業務　liner service
班长台/話務長臺,領班臺　chief operator desk
斑马线/斑馬線,人行道　zebra crossing, zebra marking
斑岩/玢岩　porphyrite
斑叶植物/斑葉植物　variegate-leaved plant
搬移费/搬移費　moving charge
搬运式标准/移動式標準　traveling standard
EPS板/EPS板,模塑聚苯乙烯板　expanded polystyrene board, EPS board
GJ板/GJ板,鋼絲網架聚苯芯板　polystyrene core plate of steel wire rack
XPS板/XPS板　extruded polystyrene board, XPS board
板材/[木]板　plank, board
板材负载试验/平板負載試驗,平板載重試驗　plate load test
板材量尺/板尺　board measure
板材轧机/軋板機　plate mill
板垫圈/板墊圈　plate washer
板端错台/板端錯臺　faulting of slab ends
板缝排列/板縫排列　seam arrangement
板肋拱桥/板筋拱橋　slab rib arch bridge
板梁/板梁　plate girder
板梁式钢结构/板梁式鋼結構　plate girder type steel structure
板料/金屬薄板,板金　sheet metal
板料成形/板材成形　sheet forming
板墙加固法/板牆加固法　masonry strengthening with reinforced concrete panel
板桥/板橋　slab bridge
板石/板石,板岩　flag stone, slate
板石铺砌/板石路面　flag stone pavement
板式车架/板框　plate frame
板式轨道/板式軌道　slab track
板式换热器/板式熱交換器　plate heat exchanger
板式基础/板式基礎　slab foundation
板式家具/板式家具產品　panel-type furniture
板式橡胶支座/板式橡膠支座,板式橡膠支承　laminated rubber bearing
板式蒸发器/板式蒸發器　plate-type evaporator
板式住宅/板式住宅　slab-type housing
板栓梁/加榫梁　keyed girder
板体断裂/面板擠壓破壞　slab rupture
板体翘曲/板翹曲　slab warping
板体温度翘曲应力/板體溫度翹曲應力　slab stress due to thermal warping
板瓦/平瓦[片],甋瓦　flat tile

板岩/板岩，板石　slate
板振捣器/板振動器　slab vibrator
板柱-剪力墙结构/板柱-剪力牆結構　slab-column shear wall structure
板柱结构/板柱結構　slab-column structure
板桩/板樁　sheet pile
板桩岸壁/板樁擋土牆　sheet pile bulkhead
板桩堤/板樁堤　sheet pile levee
板桩防波堤/板樁防波堤　sheet pile breakwater
板桩防护栏/板樁攔水幕　sheet pile screen
板桩基础/板樁基礎　sheet pile foundation
板桩截水墙/板樁截水牆　sheet pile cutoff
板桩码头/板樁岸壁　sheet pile quaywall, sheet pile wharf
板桩锚碇/板樁錨　sheet pile anchorage
板桩墙/板樁牆　sheet pile wall
板桩围堰/板樁圍堰　sheet pile cofferdam
板桩帷幕/板樁攔水幕　sheet pile screen
版门/實心門　solid door
办公建筑/辦公大樓　office building
办公区/辦公區　administrative area
办公室/辦公室　office
办理闭塞/閉塞,阻塞　blocking
半闭式给水系统/半閉式給水系統　semi-closed feed water system
半补偿链形悬挂/半補償鏈形懸掛　semi-auto-tensioned catenary equipment
半长轴/半長軸　semi-major axis
半常绿植物/半常綠植物　semi-evergreen plant
半场篮球/半場籃球,街頭籃球　half-court basketball
半潮/半潮　half tide
半潮礁/半潮礁　half tide rock
半潮闸/半潮閘　half tide lock
半城市化/半都市化　peri-urbanization
半穿式桥/半穿式橋　half through bridge
半弹道式再入/半彈道重返　semi-ballistic re-entry
半导体/半導體　semiconductor
半导体器件厂/半導體器材廠　semiconductor device plant
半导体天平/半導體天平　semiconductor balance
半导体制冷/半導體冷凍　semiconductor refrigeration
半岛/半島　peninsula
半岛园/半島園　peninsula garden
半堤半堑/半填半斷面　part-cut and part-fill section, cut and fill section
半地下沥青贮仓/半地下瀝青儲倉　semi-underground asphalt storage
半地下室/半地下室　semi-basement
半电波暗室/半電波暗室　semi-anechoic enclosure
半电池/半電池　half cell
半叠片机座/半疊片機座　semi-laminated frame
半定向式立交/半定向式立體交流道　semi-directional interchange
半独立式住宅/雙建住宅　semidetached house
半段效应/半剖面效應　half section effect
半断面开挖/半斷面開挖　half section excavation
半盾构/半盾構　semi-shield
半分开式扣件/半分開式扣件　semi-separated rail fastening, mixed holding fastening
半分配制电话会议/半分散式電話會議　telephone conference of semi-distribution system
半封闭式厂房/半封閉式廠房　semi-enclosed industrial building
半封闭式制冷压缩机/半封密冷凍壓縮機裝置　semi-hermetic refrigerating compressor unit
半感应式信号控制/半感應號誌控制　semi-actuated signal control
半刚式船台/半剛式船臺　semi-rigid cradle
半刚性基层/半剛性基層　semi-rigid base, semi-rigid base course
半刚性路面/半剛性路面　semi-rigid pavement
半高箱/半高櫃　half height container
半隔水层/阻水層　aquitard
半公共空间/半公共空間　semi-public space
半固定式泡沫灭火系统/半固定泡沫滅火系統　half fixed foam extinguishing system
半挂车/半[搭]拖車　semi-trailer
半挂汽车列车/半拖車組　semi-trailer train
半挂牵引车/大拖車　tractor truck
半灌木/半灌木　subshrub, suffrutex
半滚倒转/半滾倒轉　half roll and half loop
半横向通风/半橫流式通風　semitransverse ventilation, semitransversal ventilation
半即热式水加热器/半即熱式水加熱器　semi-instantaneous heat exchanger, semi-instantaneous water heater
半集装箱船/半貨櫃船　semi-container ship
半价票/半價票　half price ticket
半间接照明/半間接照明　semi-indirect lighting
半铰接式旋翼/半活節式旋轉翼　semi-articulated rotor
半节接管/半節接管　half socket pipe
半结/半套結　half hitch
半解析法/半分析法　semi-analytical method
半解析式惯性导航系统/半解析慣性導航系統

semi-analytic inertial navigation system
半筋斗翻转/殷麥曼轉彎,上昇反轉　Immelmann turn
半径差/半徑差　semidiameter, SD
半径杆/半徑桿,曲拐臂　radius bar, radius rod
半开放式办公室/半開放式辦公室,半開敞辦公室　semi-open space office
半连续性/半連續性　partial continuity
半梁/半梁　half beam
半龙门起重机/半門架起重機　half-portal crane
半路堑式明洞/半路塹式明洞　part cut-type open tunnel, part cut-type tunnel without cover, part cut-type gallery
半履带牵引车/前輪牽引車　half track tractor
半埋外挂/半潛運載　semi-submerged carriage
半密闭式燃[气用]具/煙道氣裝備　flued gas appliance
半密闭自然排气式燃具/半密閉自然排氣式燃具　semi-sealed gas burning appliance of natural exhaust type
半模型/半模型　half model
半模型试验/半模型試驗　half model test
半模型天平/半模型天平　half model balance
半苜蓿叶形立交/部分苜蓿葉交流道　partial clover leaf interchange
半耐寒植物/半耐寒植物　half hardy plant, semi-hardy plant
半平衡舵/半平衡舵　semi-balanced rudder
半潜船/半潛[式]船　semi-submerged ship
半潜式钻井平台/半潛式鑽探平臺　semi-submersible drilling unit, semi-submersible drilling platform
半清洁区/半清潔區域　semi-clean area
半球谐振陀螺/半球形共振陀螺儀　hemispherical resonance gyroscope
半球形壳体/半球形殼體　hemispherical shell
半球形穹顶/半圓屋頂,半圓形天花板　semi-dome
半日潮/半日[週]潮　semi-diurnal tide
半山洞/半山洞　half tunnel
半升力再入/半昇力再入　semi-lift re-entry
半湿喷混凝土机/半濕噴混凝土機　half wet shotcreting machine
半湿润[的]/半濕潤　semi-humid
半衰期/半生期　half life
半双工/半雙向操作　half-duplex operation
半双工操作/半雙工作業　semi-duplex operation
半双工传输/半雙工傳輸　half-duplex transmission
半双工无线电通信/半雙工無線電通訊　semi-duplex radio communication
半水化热石膏/緩凝灰漿　hemihydrate plaster
半私人空间/半私用空間　semi-private space
半通径/半正焦弦　semi-latus rectum
半透膜/半透膜　semi-permeable membrane
半挖半填断面/半挖半填截面　cut and fill section
半坞式船台/半塢式船臺　semi-dock building berth
半消声室/半消聲室　semi-anechoic room
半蓄热式热交换器/半蓄熱式熱交換器　half storage type heat exchanger
半悬舵/半懸舵,半平衡舵　semi-balanced rudder, partially under hung rudder
半循环交路/半循環交路　semi-loop routing
半压力式涵洞/半壓力[式]涵洞　inlet submerged culvert, partial pressure culvert
半夜灯/半夜燈,黃昏燈　evening lamp
半液浮速率陀螺仪/半浮式速率陀螺儀　half floated rate gyro
半阴性地被植物/半陰性地被植物　semi-negative ground cover plant
半硬壳式结构/半硬殼[式結構]　semi-monocoque structure, semi-monocoque
半永久性建筑/半永久建築　semi-permanent building
半永久性桥/半永久[性]橋梁　semi-permanent bridge
半圆法/半圓法　semicircular method
半圆自差/半圓自差　semicircular deviation
半月/半月　half moon
半月分潮/半月潮　fortnightly tide
半再生式生命保障系统/半再生式維生系統　semi-regenerative life support system
半涨潮/半漲潮　half flood
半正弦冲击脉冲/半正弦衝擊脈波　half-sine shock pulse
半直接照明/半直接照明　semi-direct lighting
半致死剂量/半致死劑量　half lethal dose
半致死浓度/半致死濃度　half lethal concentration
半重力式桥台/半重力式橋臺　semi-gravity type abutment
半主动式引信/半主動式引信　semi-active fuze
半主动姿态稳定/半主動姿態穩定　semi-active attitude stabilization
半自动闭塞/半自動閉鎖系統　semi-automatic block system
半自动闭塞机/半自動閉塞機　semi-automatic block machine
半自动闭塞联系电路/半自動閉塞聯繫電路　liaison

circuit with semi-automatic block
半自动测试/半自動測試 semi-automatic test
半自动测试设备/半自動測試裝備 semi-automatic test equipment
半自动称量/半自動稱量 semi-automatic weigh
半自动跟踪/半自動追蹤 semi-automatic tracking
半自动焊机/半自動焊機 semi-automatic welder
半自动化驼峰/半自動式駝峰 semi-automatic hump
半自动化驼峰系统/半自動化駝峰系統 semi-automatic hump system
半自动机械天平/半自動機械天平 auto-manual mechanobalance
半自然环境/半自然環境 semi-natural environment
半自然群落/半自然群集 semi-natural community
半自然生态系统/半自然生態系統 semi-natural ecosystem
半自然植被/半自然植被 semi-natural vegetation
半组合曲轴/半組合曲柄軸 half built-up crankshaft
伴飞/伴飛 accompanying flight
伴流/伴流,跡流 wake
伴流测量/跡流量測 wake survey, wake measurement
伴流横向力/伴流橫向力 transverse force of wake current
伴流模拟/跡流模擬 wake simulation
伴流系数/跡流因數 wake fraction
伴流因数/跡流因數,跡流係數 wake factor, wake coefficient
伴生树种/伴生樹種 associated tree species
伴生种/伴生種 companions, accompanying species
伴随过程参数/伴隨過程參數 accompanying parameter of operation process
拌和厂/拌和工場 mixing plant
拌和功率测定/拌和功率測定 mixing power measurement
拌和宽度测定/拌和寬度測定 mixing width measurement
拌和楼/混凝土配料廠 batch plant
拌和深度测定/拌和深度測定 mixing depth measurement
拌和时间/拌和時間 mixing time
拌和性能试验/拌和性能試驗 mixer performance test
拌浆机/灌漿拌和機 grout mixer
绊线/絆線 trip thread
瓣/瓣 ban
邦德数/邦德數 Bond number
邦戎曲线/龐琴曲線 Bonjean curves

绑带/繃帶 bandage
绑扎/捆縛,縛固 lashing
绑扎板/拉緊板 lashing plate
绑扎棒/拉緊桿 lashing bar, lashing rod
绑扎材料/綁紮材料 lashing materials
绑扎钩/拉緊鉤 lashing hook
绑扎环/拉緊環,D型環 lashing eye
绑扎链/拉緊鏈 lashing chain
绑扎链扣/拉緊鏈扣 chain lashing device
绑扎索/拉緊索 lashing cable
绑扎套筒/拉緊缸 lashing pot
棒捣法/棒搗法 rodding method
棒钢/條鋼 bar steel
棒料/棒料 bar
棒磨式碎石机/棒磨式碎石機 rod mill crusher
棒球场/棒球場 baseball field
棒球场草坪/棒球場草坪 ballpark lawn
棒球运动/棒球 baseball
棒式车架/骨架 bar frame
棒式绝缘子/棒形絕緣子 strut insulator, rod insulator
傍靠补给法/傍靠傳遞法 alongside method
傍山隧道/山坡隧道 sidehill tunnel
傍拖/傍拖 towing alongside
包/封包 packet
包层直径/包層直徑 cladding diameter
包车客运/包車公路客運 chartered bus transport
包车运价/包車運價 charter rate
包覆/包覆,被覆 cladding, covering, coating
包袱彩画/包袱彩畫 brocade-like pattern, baofu caihua
包干计费里程/包乾計費里程 chartered pay mileage
包裹/包裹 package
包裹运费/包裹運費 parcel freight
包含因子/涵蓋因子 coverage factor
包豪斯建筑教育/包豪斯建築教育 Bauhaus architecture education
包机飞行/包租飛行 chartered flight
包间式卧车/臥車 corridor compartment type sleeping car
包交换/分封交換,分組交換 packet switching
包交换网/分封交換網路 packet switching network
包络[曲]线/包絡線 envelope curve
包络图/包絡圖 envelope diagram
包膜控释肥/包膜控釋肥料 coated controlled release fertilizer
包容性/包容性 containment
包容性规划/包容性規劃 inclusive planning

包式终端/分封模式終端機,分封型終端機　packet mode terminal
包厢/包厢,專席　box
包辛格效应/包辛格效應　Bauschinger effect
包罩试验/覆緣試驗　shroud test
包装/包裝　packing, package
包装标号/包裝號碼　packaging code number
包装不牢货/包裝不固貨　insufficiently packed cargo
包装材料/包裝材料　packing materials
包装舱容/包裝貨容積　bale cargo capacity
包装拆器/封包組合拆卸器,配封機　packet assembler-disassembler
包装储运标志/包裝指示性標誌　package indicative mark
包装储运图示标志/貨運標識,揀選作業　pictorial marking for handling of package
包装货/包裝貨　packed cargo
包装货物/包裝貨物,件貨　packed goods, package freight
包装件/包裝件　package, pack
包装鉴定/包裝檢查　inspection of package
包装库/包裝後儲存　packing storage
包装类/包裝分類　packaging group
包装容积/包裝容積　bale capacity
包装运输试验/包裝運輸試驗　transporting test for package
雹暴/雹暴　hailstorm
薄板/板　board
薄板吸收/薄板吸收　panel absorption
薄壁/薄壁　thin wall
薄壁杆/薄壁桿　thin-walled bar
薄壁结构/薄壁結構　thin-walled structure, thin wall structure
薄壁梁/薄壁梁　thin-walled beam
薄壁筒体结构/薄殼鋼管結構　thin-shelled tubular structure
薄壁型钢/薄型鋼　light gage section steel
薄壁轴承/薄壁軸承　thin wall bearing
薄冰/薄冰　sheet ice
薄层假定/薄層假設　thin layer assumption
薄层水流/薄層流　sheet flow
薄腹梁/薄腹梁　thin web girder
薄管取样器/薄管探樣器　thin-walled sampler
薄激波层理论/薄震波層方程式　thin shock-layer theory
薄壳/薄殼　thin shell
薄壳建筑/薄殼建築　stressed-skin construction
薄壳结构/薄殼結構,殼層結構　thin shell structure, shell structure
薄壳取样器/薄壁管取樣器　thin-walled tube sampler
薄片/切片　thin section
薄翼理论/薄翼理論　thin airfoil theory
饱和曝光量/飽和曝光量　saturation exposure
饱和层/飽和區　saturation zone
饱和带/飽和區　saturation zone
饱和单位重[量]/飽和單位重　saturated unit weight
饱和含水量/飽和含水量　saturated water content
饱和记录/飽和記錄　saturation recording
饱和孔隙比/飽和孔隙比　zero air void ratio
饱和流量/飽和流量　saturation volume
饱和流率/飽和流率　saturation volume rate
饱和面/飽和面　plane of saturation
饱和黏土/飽和黏土　saturated clay
饱和区/飽和區　saturation zone
饱和曲线/飽和曲線　saturation curve
饱和缺氧量/飽和缺氧量　oxygen saturation deficit
饱和热直减率/飽和絕熱傾率　saturation adiabatic lapse rate
饱和容量/飽和容量　saturation capacity
饱和溶解氧/飽和溶氧　saturated dissolved oxygen
饱和湿度/飽和濕度　saturated humidity
饱和水/飽和水　water of saturation
饱和水汽压/平衡蒸汽壓　equilibrium vapor pressure
饱和水蒸气压力/飽和水汽壓　saturation vapor pressure
饱和梯度/飽和坡　saturation gradient
饱和烃/飽和碳氫化合物　saturated hydrocarbon
饱和土液化/飽和土壤液化　liquefaction of saturated soil
饱和压力/飽和壓　saturation pressure
饱和蒸汽/飽和蒸汽　saturated steam
饱和蒸汽室/飽和蒸汽室　saturated chamber
饱和蒸汽压力/飽和蒸汽壓力　saturated vapor pressure, saturation steam pressure
饱水率试验/飽和含水量試驗　saturated water content test
宝塔/寶塔　pagoda
保安器/保安器,保護器　protector
保持/保持　hold
保持力矩/保持扭矩　hold torque
保持模式/保持模式　hold mode
保持位/[自]保持位置,吸持位置　maintaining position, holding position
保持系/保持系　maintainer line
保管期/貯藏期,保存期　preservation period

保函/賠償[責任]保證書　letter of indemnity
保护/保護　conservation
保护标志/保護標誌　protective mark
保护层/保護[層]　protection course
[保护层]水养法/水中養護　water curing
保护导体/保護導體　protective conductor
保护地/保護區, 防護區　protected area
保护[地]线/保護線　protective earth wire
保护地栽培建筑设施/保護地栽培建築設施　building and facility of protected culture land
保护电弧焊/掩弧焊接　shielded arc welding
保护电流密度/保護電流密度　protection current density
保护电路/保護電路　protective circuit
保护电容器/保護電容器　protective capacitor
保护电位/保護電位　protective potential
保护范围/保育區　conservation zone
保护关机/保護性關機　protective cut-off
保护规划/保持規劃　conservation planning
保护海底电缆公约/保護海底電纜公約　Convention for the Protection of Submarine Cables
保护火花间隙/保護火花間隙　protective spark gap
保护建筑/保護建築　building conservation, protected building, listed building for conservation
保护接地/保護接地　protective earthing, protective grounding
保护接地中性导体/保護接地中性導體, PEN 線　protective earthing and neutral conductor
保护模式/保護模式　mode of protection
保护膜/膜片　diaphragm
保护培育/保護培育　foster protection
保护区/保護區, 保存區　conservation area, protection zone, protected zone
保护区段/保護區段　overlap protection block section
保护区划定/保護區指定, 保存區指定　conservation zone designation
保护权/保護權　right of protection
保护设施/防護工具　protective equipment
保护生态学/保護生態學　conservation ecology
保护世界文化和自然遗产公约/世界文化遺產暨自然遺產保護公約　Convention Concerning the Protection of the World Cultural and Natural Heritage
保护套管/保護套管　protection sleeve
保护涂层/保護[性]塗層　protective coating
保护位置/保護位置　protective location
保护物种/受保護種　protected species
保护系统/防護系統　protection system
保护线用连接线/保護線用聯軌線　crossbond of protective wire
保护[性]接地/保護[性]接地　protective grounding, protective earthing
保护野生动物标志/野生動物保護標誌　wild animals protection sign
保护用品/防護工具　protective equipment
保价运输/保價運輸　insured transport
保健生态社区/保健生態社區　health ecological community
保精度跟踪角加速度/保精度追蹤角加速度　tracking angle acceleration without degradation
保精度工作范围/保精度作用距離　operating range without degradation
保龄球馆/保齡球室　bowling room, bowling alley
保留林/保護林　reserve forest
保留权/保留權　right of retention
保密通信/保全通信　security communication
保密通信系统/秘密通訊系統　secret communication system
保赔/防護賠償　protection and indemnity, PI
保赔保险/船舶營運人責任保險　PI insurance
保赔协会/防護及賠償協會　protection and indemnity club, PI club
保赔责任险/防護及賠償責任險, 防護及賠償危險　protection and indemnity risk, PI risk
保墒/保濕, 保水性　keep moisture, soil moisture conservation
保守力/保守力　conservative force
保守系/保守系統　conservative system
保水剂/保水劑　water-retaining agent
保水性/保水能力　water retentivity
保税库/保稅倉庫　bond room, bond store
保税码头/保稅碼頭　sufference wharf
保税区/自由關稅區　tariff-free zone
保土坝/保土壩　soil saving dam
保温/保溫, 絕熱, 隔熱　thermal insulation, thermal protection
保温材料/保溫材料, 絕熱材料, 隔熱材料　thermal insulation materials, thermal insulating materials
保温层/保溫層, 隔熱層, [隔熱]襯套　lagging, insulation layer
保温挂车/保溫拖車　thermal insulated trailer
保温货车/保溫車輛　thermal insulated vehicle
保温集装箱/保溫[貨]櫃　thermal container
保温砂浆/保溫砂漿　thermo-retaining mortar, thermal insulation mortar
保温箱/保溫[貨]櫃　thermal container

保温用具/保溫[用]具　thermal protective aid
保温运输/保溫運輸　insulated transport
保险带/保險帶,安全帶　safety belt
保险费/保險費用　insurance charge
保险公司/保險公司　insurance company
保险价值/保險價值　insured value
保险螺母/並緊螺帽　lock nut
保险螺栓/安全螺栓　safety bolt
保险人/保險人　assurer
保险索赔/保險索賠　insurance claim
保险装置/安全裝置　safety device
保向性/航向保持[性]　course keeping quality
保形外挂/共形運載　conformal carriage
保修工程师/保證工程師,保固技師　guarantee engineer
保压停车/保壓停車　stopping at maintaining position
保养/保養　maintenance
保养期/養護週期　maintenance period
保用期/保固期　warranted period
保障系统/支援系統　support system
保障性/支援性　supportability
保障性住房/保障性住房,補貼住房　government-subsidized housing, subsidized housing
保障性住房规划/保障性住房建設規劃　indemnificatory housing planning
保证金/保證金,保留款　retention money
保质期/截止日期,失效日期　expiration date
报潮球/報潮球　tidal ball
报酬/報酬　reward
报告/報告　report
报告程序/報告程式　reporting procedures
报告点/報告點　reporting point, RP
报告厅/報告廳,大禮堂　auditorium, report hall
报关/報關　declaration
报关行/報關行　custom broker
报警/警報　alarm
报警保护系统/警報防護系統　alarm and protection system
报警报文/警報信文　alert message
报警打印/警報列印　alarm printer
报警复核/警報復核　alarm recheck
报警监视系统/警報監視系統　alarm monitoring system
报警接收中心/警報接收中心,接處警中心　alarm receiving center
报警控制设备/警報控制器　alarm controller
报警联动/警報聯動　action with alarm
报警器/警告裝置　warning device
报警区域/警報區　alarm zone
报警数据/警報數據　alert data
报警数据滤除/篩選之警報數據　filtered alert data
报警图像复核/警報圖像復核　video check to alarm
报警限/警報限度　alarm limit
报警响应时间/警報響應時間　response time to alarm
报警装置/警報裝置,警報設施,警告裝置　alarm unit, warning device
报考人/申請發證者　candidate
报头/報頭,標頭　preamble, header
报头开始信号/報頭開始信號　start-of-heading signal
报文/消息,情報,無線電報　message
报务室/無線電室　radio room
刨边机/鉋緣機,邊緣鉋床　edge planer
刨花板/鉋花板,塑合板,碎屑膠合板　shaving board, particle board, chipboard
刨花车/鉋花車　wood chip car
刨平边/鉋光邊　planed edge
刨削/鉋削　planning, shaping, chipping
抱缸/咬缸,缸膠著　piston seizure
抱鼓石/抱鼓石　drum-shaped stone block
抱角石/抱角石,牆角石　corner stone
抱厦/抱廈　covered porch, baosha
抱轴式牵引电动机/抱軸式牽引電動機　axle hung traction motor, nose suspension traction motor
抱轴瓦/抱軸瓦　axle suspension bush
抱轴悬挂装置/懸掛軸承　suspension bearing
抱轴轴承/抱軸軸承　axle hung bearing
暴动和内乱不保/暴動和內亂不保　free of riot and civil commotion
暴风/暴風　squall
暴风警报/暴風警報　storm warning
暴风强度分配形式/暴雨分布型態　storm distribution pattern
暴风雨/暴風雨　heavy rainstorms
暴雨/暴雨　storm rainfall
暴雨地下流量/地下暴雨水流　subsurface storm flow
暴雨径流/暴雨徑流　storm runoff, rainstorm run off
暴雨巨浪/風暴激浪　storm surge
暴雨强度/暴雨強度,降雨強度　rainfall intensity, rainstorm intensity, intensity of storms
暴雨渗流/暴雨滲流　storm seepage
曝光表/曝光計,露光計　exposure meter

曝光过度/燒毀,燃毀,燒壞　burn out
曝光间隔/曝光間隔　exposure interval
曝光宽容度/曝光寬容度　exposure latitude
曝光[量]/曝光　exposure
曝光时间/曝光時間　exposure time
爆胶/膠炸藥　blasting gelatin
爆孔钻/爆孔鑽　blast-hole drill
爆控机构/備炸機構　arming unit
爆破/爆炸　blasting
爆破大石/巨石炸破　boulder blasting
爆破工/施爆人　shotfirer
爆破激振/爆發式激振　vibration excited by explosive action
爆破巨砾/巨石炸破　boulder blasting
爆破漏斗/爆破漏斗　blasting crater
爆破排淤/爆破排淤　blasting discharging sedimentation, silt arresting by explosion, discharge of sedimentation by blasting
爆破速度/爆炸速度　detonation velocity
爆破振动/爆破振動　blasting vibration
爆破振动效应/爆破振動效應　vibration effect of explosion
爆破作业/爆破作業　blasting operation
爆燃/爆炸,爆震　detonation
爆心投影点/爆心投影點　ground zero
爆炸波理论/爆波理論　blast wave theory
爆炸成形/爆炸成形　explosive forming
爆炸冲击仿真器/火工衝擊模擬機　pyroshock simulator
爆炸冲击环境/火工衝擊環境　pyroshock environment
爆炸冲击试验/火工衝擊試驗　pyroshock test
[爆]炸点/爆炸點　burst point
[爆]炸点分布密度/爆炸點分布密度　burst point distribution density
爆炸高度/爆炸高度　burst height
爆炸焊/爆炸焊接　explosion welding
爆炸夯/爆炸夯　explosion rammer
爆炸极限/爆炸極限,爆炸界限　explosive limit
爆炸挤密/爆炸擠密法　blasting compaction
爆炸螺母/爆炸物螺帽　explosive nut
爆炸螺栓/爆炸螺栓　explosive bolt
爆炸品/爆炸品,炸藥　explosive
爆炸上限/爆炸上限值　upper explosive limit
爆炸式夯实机/爆炸式夯土機　explosion compactor, explosion rammer
爆炸事故/爆炸事故　explosion accident
爆炸危险区域/爆炸危險區　explosive hazardous area
爆炸雾号/爆音霧號　explosive fog signal
爆炸下限/爆炸下限值　lower explosive limit
爆炸线/爆發線　explosion line
爆炸信号/爆炸信號　explosive signal
爆炸性粉尘环境/爆炸性粉塵氣氛　explosive dust atmosphere
爆炸性气体环境/爆炸性氣體環境　explosive gas atmosphere
爆炸性气体环境的点燃温度/氣爆區著火溫度　ignition temperature of explosive gas atmosphere
爆炸作用/爆炸作用　explosion action
爆震/爆震,氣爆,爆炸　knock, detonation, blast
杯罐试验/杯罐試驗,燒杯試驗　jar test
背负运输车/背負運輸車　piggyback car
北半球/北半球　northern hemisphere
北冰洋海流/北極海流　arctic current
北大西洋冬季载重线/冬期北大西洋載重線　winter North Atlantic load line
北斗二(天璇)(大熊β)/北斗二(天璇)(大熊β)　Merak
北斗七星/北斗七星　great dipper
北斗一(天枢)(大熊α)/北斗一(天樞)(大熊α)　Dubhe
北方标/北方標　north mark
北河二(双子α)/北河二(雙子α)　Castor
北极/北極　north pole
北极冰/北極陳冰　arctic pack
北极光/北極光　aurora borealis, northern light
北极气团/北極氣團　arctic air mass
北极圈/北極圈　arctic circle
北极星/北極星　north star, Polaris
北极星高度改正量/北極星修正　Polaris correction
北极星求纬度/極星求緯法　latitude by pole star
北京宪章/北京憲章　Beijing Charter
北京坐标系/北京坐標系統　Beijing coordinate system
北落师门(南鱼α)/北落師門(南魚α)　Fomalhaut
北美草原/[北美]大草原　prairie
北天极/北天極　north celestial pole
北向上/北向上　north up
北向陀螺/北向迴轉儀　north gyro
贝[尔]/貝[爾]　bel
贝雷桥/貝雷式橋,活動便橋　Bailey bridge
贝氏体等温淬火/沃斯回火　austempering
备案/備案　submit for record
备餐间/備餐室,配膳室　pantry
备弹量/彈匣容量　ammunition capacity

备电源/備用能源　stand-by power source
备件/備品　spare
备降场/備用停機坪　alternative landing field
备降机场/備用機場　alternate airport
备锚/備便抛錨　set the anchor ready for letting go
备用/備用　stand-by
备用泵/備用泵　stand-by pump
备用电源/備用光源　stand-by power source
备用发电机/備用發電機　stand-by generator
备用发电机组/備用發電機組　stand-by generating set
备用发信机/備用發射機　reserve transmitter
备用飞行操纵系统/備用飛行操縱系統　stand-by emergency flight control system
备用轨/備用軌　stock rail per kilometer of track, emergency rail stored along the way
备用货车/備用車　reserved car
备用机车/備用機車　locomotive in reserve
备用锚/備用錨　spare anchor
备用热源/備用熱源　stand-by heat source
备用设备/交替設施　alternating device
备用收信机/備用接收機　reserve receiver
备用天线/備用天線　reserve antenna
备用照明/備用照明　stand-by lighting
备淤深度/備淤深度　allowance for sedimentation
备展室/備展室　exhibition preparation room
背场背反射太阳电池/背場背反射太陽電池　back surface field and back surface reflection solar cell
背场太阳电池/背面場太陽電池　back surface field solar cell
背反射太阳电池/背面反射太陽電池　back surface reflection solar cell
背风潮/下風潮,順潮　lee tide
背景/背景　background
背景亮光/背景亮光　background light
背景密度/背景密度值,本底密度　background density
背景限光电探测器/背景限制光電探測器　background limited photodetector
背景音/背景音　background sound
背景音乐/背景音樂　background music
背景噪声/背景噪聲　background noise
背景噪声场强/背景雜訊場強[度]　background noise field strength
背景种植/背景種植　background planting
背空化/[葉]背空蝕　back cavitation
背离规则/背離規則　departure from these rules
背鳍/脊鰭　dorsal fin

背绳走/背著走　walkaway
背台指示器/背臺指示器　from indicator
背投室/背景放映機室　background projector room
背投影屏幕/背投影銀幕　rear screen projection
背向散射碎片/反向散射碎片　backscattered debris
背压/背壓,反壓　back pressure
背压式汽轮机/背壓式汽輪機,背壓[蒸汽]渦輪機　back-pressure turbine, back-pressure steam turbine
背压调节器/背壓調整器　evaporator pressure regulator, back pressure regulator
倍程衰减/倍程衰減　double attenuation
倍率/率　rate
倍频程/倍頻程,倍頻帶　octave
倍频衰减/倍頻衰減　frequency doubling attenuation
倍数[测量]单位/[量测]倍數單位　multiple unit of measurement
倍性育种/倍数性育種　ploidy breeding
被保险人/被保險人　insured
被测量/被測量　measurand
[被测量的]变换值/[待測量]變換值　transformed value of a measurand
被串通路/被串通路　disturbed channel
被盗事故/被盜事故　robbery accident, burglary accident
被动安全性/被動安全　passive safety
被动段/被動段　unpowered-flight phase
被动隔振/被動隔振　passive vibration isolation
被动跟踪/被動追蹤　passive tracking
被动红外探测器/被動式紅外裝置,無源紅外線器件　passive infrared correlation device
被动抗性/被動抗力　passive resistance
被动式热控制/被動熱控制　passive thermal control
被动式引信/被動式引信　passive fuze
被动土压力/被動土壓力　passive earth pressure
被动微波遥感/被動微波遙測　passive microwave remote sensing
被动章动阻尼/被動章動控制　passive nutation damping
被动姿态控制/被動姿態控制　passive attitude control
被动姿态稳定/被動姿態穩定　passive attitude stabilization
被抚养人口/被撫養人口,依賴人口　dependent population
被覆层/包覆[料],塗層,塗料　coating
被叫/被叫　called
被叫控制复原方式/被叫用户拆線　called subscriber release

被叫用户/受話方,被呼用戶　called party
被控点/受控點　controlled point
被拖船/被拖船　towed vessel
被追越船/被超越船,被追趕船　overtaken vessel
被子植物/被子植物　angiosperm
锛制方材/大枋木　hewn square
本初子午线/本初子午線　initial meridian
本地差分 GPS/當地差分全球定位系統　local area differential GPS
本地电池/本機電池,自給電池［組］　local battery
本地电信楼/本地電信大樓　local telecommunication building
本地发令/區域命令　local commanding
本地警告/當地警告　local warning
本地用户终端/地面終端臺　local user terminal, LUT
本地增强系统/當地增強系統　local area augmentation system
本地终端/當地終端機　local terminal
本构方程/本構方程　constitutive equation
本构关系/本構關係　constitutive relation
本机平衡/本機平衡　in-field balancing
本体稳定姿态控制系统/本體穩定姿態控制系統　body-stabilized attitude control system
本务走行公里/本務走行公里　leading locomotive running kilometer
本站作业车/本站作業車　local car
本征值/特徵值,固有值　characteristic value, eigenvalue
本质安全电路/本質安全線路　intrinsically safe circuit
本质安全防爆型设备/本質安全防爆型設備　intrinsic safety explosion-proof device
本子午线/初子午線　prime meridian
笨重货/笨重貨　awkward cargo
崩顶碎波/溢出型碎波　spilling breaker
崩岗/崩塌山丘　collapse mound, collapsing hill
崩解性土/崩解土　disintegrated soil
崩解性岩石/崩解岩　disintegrated rock
崩碎波/溢出型碎波　spilling breaker
崩塌/崩塌,崩陷,塌陷　collapse, toppling
崩塌地段路基/崩塌地段路基　subgrade in rock fall district, subgrade in collapse zone
崩坍/崩陷　collapse, fall
泵/泵　pump
泵比转速/泵比角速率　pump specific angular speed
泵舱/泵室　pump room
泵舱通海阀/泵室海水閥　pump room sea valve

泵的抽送率/抽水量　pumpage
泵电动机/泵電動機,泵馬達　pump motor
泵壳/主泵外殼　pump casing
泵流量/泵能量　pump capacity
泵轮/泵葉輪　pump impeller
泵滤网/抽水機濾篩　pump strainer
泵内滤片/泵內濾片　snore piece
泵气蚀系数/泵孔蝕係數　pump cavitation coefficient
泵腔吹除/泵腔吹洩　pump cavity blow-off
泵失速/泵失速　pump stall
泵送混凝土/泵送混凝土　pumped concrete, pump concrete
泵送剂/泵送劑　pumping aid, pumping admixture
泵特性曲线/泵特性曲線　pump characteristic curve
泵吸/泵取,泵［作用］　pumping
泵效率/泵效率　pump efficiency
泵压式供应系统/泵壓式供應系統　turbopump-feed system
泵压式液体火箭发动机/泵壓式液體火箭發動機　turbopump-feed liquid rocket engine
泵压头/泵壓頭　pump head
泵站/泵站　pumping station
泵站排水/抽出排水　pumping drainage
泵支承箱/泵筒支箱　pump supporting box
泵自动切换装置/泵自動切換設施　pump auto-change over device
蹦床/彈躍騰翻器　trampoline
蹦极/蹦極,高空彈跳　bungee jumping
比表面［积］/比表面積　specific surface
比沉积/比沈積　specific deposit
比冲［量］/比衝［量］　specific impulse
比冲效率/比［衝］效率　specific efficiency, specific impulse efficiency
比导磁率/比滲透率　specific permeability
比导电率/比傳導　specific conductivity
比对/比對,比較　comparison
比幅单脉冲/比幅單脈衝　amplitude-comparison monopulse
比刚度/勁度密度比　stiffness-to-density ratio
比功［率］/比功率,比馬力,功率重量比　specific power
比较测量/比較測量　comparison measurement
比较单元/比較單位　comparing unit
比较器/比測儀　comparator
比较式［测量］仪器/比較［量測］儀器　comparison measuring instrument
比较线/比較［路］線,選取線　alternative line
比较行星学/比較行星學　comparative planetology

比力/比力　specific force
比例/比例　proportion
比例尺/比例尺　scale
比例带/比例帶　proportional band
比例导引法/比例導引法　proportional navigation method
比例法/百分比計酬契約　percentage contract
比例放样/比例放樣　scale lofting
比例规/比例規　proportional compass
比例极限/比例極限,比例限度　proportional limit, limit of proportionality
比例加药器/比例加藥機　chemical proportioner
比例加载/比例加載　proportional loading
比例调节器/比例調整器　proportioner, proportional regulator
比例原则/比例原理　principle of proportionality
比流量/比流量　specific discharge
比面积/比[表]面積　specific floor area
比摩阻/比摩擦水頭損失　specific frictional head loss
比能量/比能[量],能量密度　specific energy
比拟正交异性板法/準正交異性板法　quasi orthotropic plate method
比强度/強度密度比　strength-to-density ratio
比热/比熱　specific heat
比热比/比熱比　specific heat ratio
比热容/比熱容量　specific heat capacity
比热容测定仪/比熱熱量計　specific heat calorimeter
比容[积]/比容　specific volume
比容量/比容量　specific capacity
比赛场地/競技場　arena, field of play
比渗透率/比滲透率　specific permeability
比湿/比濕度　specific humidity
比特/比,位元　bit
比特率/位元率　bit rate
比相/比相　phase comparison
比相单脉冲/比相單脈衝　phase comparison monopulse
比相雷达引信/比相雷達引信　phase comparison radar fuze
比压降/比壓降　specific pressure drop
比重/比重　specific gravity
比重环/比重盤　gravity disc
比重量/比重量　weight-power ratio
比重试验/比重試驗　specific gravity test
比转数/比速　specific speed
比浊法/測濁法　turbidimetry
比阻法/比阻法　specific resistivity method
舭/舭,舯膨出部　bilge, bulge
舭板列/舭列板　bilge strake
舭部半径/舭曲半徑　bilge radius
舭部扶手/舭部扶手　underside handholds
舭部升高/[舯]橫斜高　deadrise
舭墩/舭邊墩　bilge block
舭龙骨/舭龍骨　rolling chock, bilge keel
舭肘板/舭腋板　bilge bracket
必要带宽/必須頻帶寬度　necessary bandwidth
必要生活空间/必要生活空間　necessary living space
毕奥-萨伐尔公式/畢奧-薩伐公式　Biot-Savart formula
毕宿五(金牛α)/畢宿五(金牛α)　Aldebaran
闭杯试验/閉杯法試驗　closed cup test
闭合差比值/閉合比　ratio of closure
闭合度/閉合性,閉合比　closure
闭合索/閉合索　closing rope
闭湖/閉口湖泊　closed lake
闭环控制/閉環控制,回路控制　closed-loop control
闭环系统/閉環系統　closed-loop system
闭孔率/密封孔率　rate of closed hole
闭口端管桩/封底管樁　closed end pipe pile
闭口式风洞/閉口式風洞　closed test section wind tunnel
闭路式风洞/閉路式風洞　closed circuit wind tunnel
闭路式轨道电路/閉式軌道電路　close type track circuit
闭路网络/閉路網路　closed network
闭路循环/閉塞系統　closed system
闭路用户组/閉路用戶組　closed user group
闭塞系统/阻塞系統　block system
闭塞分区/閉塞區間　block section
闭塞机/閉塞器　block instrument
闭式加注/閉式加載　closed loading
闭式空气循环冷却系统/封閉式空氣循環冷卻系統　closed air cycle cooling system
闭式冷却水系统/閉式冷卻水系統　closed cooling water system
闭式冷却系统/閉式冷卻系統　closed cooling system
闭式联合碎石机组/封閉型碎石廠　close type crushing plant
闭式喷油器/閉式噴油閥　closed type fuel valve
闭式热水供应系统/封閉式熱水供應系統　closed hot water system
闭式热水热网/閉式熱水熱網　closed type hot water heat supply network
闭式循环/閉合循環　closed cycle
闭式叶轮/罩筒葉輪　shrouded impeller
闭式液压系统/閉式液壓系統　closed type hydraulic

system
闭式自动喷水灭火系统/封閉型自動灑水系統 close type sprinkler system
闭锁/鎖進 lock-in
闭锁机构/鎖定裝置,止動裝置 locking mechanism
闭锁速率/鎖進速率 lock-in rate
闭锁位置/閉鎖位置,鎖倉位置 locked position of coupler
秘鲁草原/秘魯草原,洛馬群落 loma
辟邪/辟邪 bixie
篦子/鐵篦子,烤柵 grate, gridiron, grill
壁/壁,牆 wall
壁板/嵌板,模板單元 panel
壁板颤振/翼段顫振 panel flutter
壁橱/壁櫥,衣帽間 closet
壁灯/壁燈 wall lamp
壁挂/壁氈,壁布 wall hanging
壁柜/壁櫥,衣帽間 closet
壁画/壁畫 fresco
壁画石窟类/壁畫石窟類 grotto-murals type
壁炉/壁爐 fireplace
壁球馆/壁球場 squash court
壁泉/壁泉 wall fountain
壁式插座/壁式插座 wall plug
壁式框架/牆體框架 wall frame
壁宿二(仙女α)/壁宿二(仙女α) Alpheratz
壁压信息法/壁壓訊息法 wall pressure information method
壁纸/牆紙 wall paper
壁柱/壁柱 pilaster
避车洞/避車洞 refuge hole, refuge recess, refuge niche
避车台/避車臺,行人庇護設施,庇護區 refuge platform, refuge
避车线/避車線,退縮線 refuge track, setback line
避风港/避風港 harbor of refuge, sheltering harbor
避风航路/避風航路 routing for storm avoidance
避风锚地/避風錨地 shelter
避雷器/避雷器 lightning arrester, surge arrester
避雷塔/避雷塔 lightning tower
避雷线/避雷針,避雷導體 lightning conductor
避难层/庇護層 refuge floor
避难港/避難港 port of refuge
避难港费用/避難港費用 port of refuge expenses
避难滑道/避火滑道 fire chute
避难疏散场所/避難疏散場所 disaster shelter for evacuation
避难所/庇護所 refuge

避难线/安全側線 refuge siding
避碰灯/防撞燈 anti-collision light
避碰决策/避碰決策 decision making of collision avoidance
避碰行为/避碰行爲 collision avoidance behavior
避碰专家系统/避碰專家系統 collision avoidance expert system
避碰装置/避碰裝置 equipment for collision avoidance
避碰综合决策/綜合避碰決策 synthetical decision making of collision avoidance
避雨棚/避雨亭,避雨處 rain shelter
避震疏散场所/避震疏散場所 seismic shelter for evacuation
臂/臂 arm
臂板电锁器联锁/臂軸承電鎖器聯鎖 interlocking by electric locks with semaphore
臂板接触器/臂軸承接觸器 contact operated by semaphore
臂板信号机/臂軸承號誌,揚旗號誌 semaphore signal
臂板转极器/臂軸承轉極器 pole changer operated by semaphore
臂斗式挖掘机/整括斜面裝置 skimmer equipment
臂距差/曲柄臂距差 difference crank spread
臂距千分表/曲柄軸撓曲針盤量規 crankshaft deflection dial gage
壁山/壁山 wall hill
璧雍/璧雍 imperial academy
边舱/翼櫃,翼艙 wing tank
边侧导坑/側導坑 side drift
边侧庭院/側院 side yard
边墩/邊墩 side keel block
边防检查区/邊防檢查區 immigration check area
边沟/邊溝 side ditch
边际效应/邊際效果 marginal effect
边界层/邊界層,介面層 boundary layer
边界层动量厚度/邊界層動量厚度 boundary layer momentum thickness
边界层动量损失厚度/邊界層動量損失厚度 momentum loss thickness of boundary layer
边界层分离/邊界層分離 separation of boundary layer
边界层厚度/邊界層厚度 boundary layer thickness
边界层积分关系式/邊界層積分關係式 boundary layer integral relations
边界层空气动力学/邊界層空氣動力學 boundary layer aerodynamics

边界层控制/邊界層控制　boundary layer control
边界层理论/邊界層理論　boundary layer theory
边界层内层/邊界層內層　inner layer of boundary layer
边界层能量损失厚度/邊界層能量損失厚度　energy loss thickness of boundary layer
边界层皮托探针/邊界層皮托探管　Pitot probe of boundary layer
边界层外层/邊界層外層　outer layer of boundary layer
边界层位移厚度/邊界層推移厚度　boundary layer displacement thickness
边界层泄除/邊界層吸除　boundary layer bleed
边界刚度矩阵/邊界勁度矩陣　boundary stiffness matrix
边界节点/固定接頭　boundary node
边界景观/邊界景觀　marginal landscape
边界润滑/邊界潤滑　boundary lubrication
边界条件/邊界條件　boundary condition
边界效应/邊界影響　boundary effect
边界修正/邊界校正　boundary correction
边界元/邊界元素　boundary element
边界种植/邊界種植　boundary planting
边孔/邊孔　side hole, side span
边框/邊界　border
边篱/邊籬　boundary fence
边梁/邊梁　edge beam
边幕/舞臺側幕　wing
边抛/道旁棄土　side casting
边坡/邊坡,側面斜坡　side slope
边坡冲蚀/坡面侵蝕　slope erosion
边坡冲刷防治/坡面侵蝕處理　slope erosion treatment
边坡平台/邊坡平臺　plain stage of slope
边坡清筛机/道床肩部清洗機　ballast shoulder cleaning machine
边坡稳定/邊坡穩定　slope stabilization
边坡修整/邊坡修整　slope trimming
边坡植被防护/邊坡植被防護　vegetation on slope
边墙/邊牆,側壁,側牆　side wall
边墙型扩展覆盖喷头/擴大覆蓋面邊牆式灑水噴頭　extended coverage sidewall sprinkler
边扫描边跟踪/掃描同時追蹤　track-while-scan
边搜索边测距/搜索同時測距　range-while-search, RWS
边条/邊條　strake
边条翼/輔助翼,肩翼　strake wing
边缘/邊緣　edge

边缘波/邊緣波　edge wave
边缘城市/邊緣城市　edge city
边缘钢筋/邊緣鋼筋,邊緣加固料　edge reinforcement
边缘跟踪/邊緣追蹤　edge tracking
边缘加工/邊緣[預]加工　edge preparation
边缘检验/邊際檢驗　marginal check
边缘群落/邊緣群落,林緣群落　marginal community, edge community
边缘生境/邊緣棲所　marginal habitat
边缘土地/邊際土地　marginal land
边缘线/邊線　edge line
边缘效应/邊[緣]效應　border effect, edge effect
边缘增强/邊緣增強　boundary enhance
边缘种/邊緣種　edge species
边缘种群/邊緣族群　fringe population, peripheral population
边缘种植/邊緣種植　edge planting
边走边卸阀/邊走邊卸閥　ballast flow control valve
编程/程式編寫　programming
编程人员/程式設計師　programmer
编队/編隊　formation
编队飞行/編隊飛行　formation flight
编发线/編發線　marshalling-departure track
编绘/編集　compilation
编码/編碼　coding
编码分集/編碼分集　code diversity
编码式太阳敏感器/編碼太陽感測器　encoded sun sensor
编码位置数据/編碼之位置數據　encoded position data
编码信息/編碼數據　coded information
编码延迟/密碼遲延　coding delay
编码遥控/編碼遙控　coded telecommand
编目室/編目室　cataloging room
编栅水坝/盾壩　wicker dam
编织带/編織物　braid
编织[法]/編織　weave
编织物/針織物　knitting
编制图/圖集　compiled map
编组/歸組　grouping
编组场/調車場　sorting yard
编组场综合作业自动化/編組場綜合作業自動化　automation of synthetic operation in marshalling yard
编组调车/編組調車　make-up train
编组能力/編組能力　make-up capacity
编组站/編組站　marshalling station, marshalling

yard
鞭梢效应/鞭梢效應　whipping lash effect, whipping effect
鞭状天线/鞭形天線　whip antenna
扁担桩/扁擔樁　pole pile
扁钢/扁鋼，平鋼　flat steel
扁钢丝绳/扁索　flat rope
扁壳/扁殼　shallow shell
扁壳桥/扁殼橋　shell bridge
扁平化设计/扁平化設計　flat design
扁千斤顶/扁千斤頂，平板千斤頂　flat jack
匾道处理/圜道處理　parkway treatment
匾额/額匾　horizontal inscribed board
变薄拉深/壓薄，拉伸，延伸　ironing
变薄旋压/剪力旋壓　power spinning, shear spinning, flow turning
变差/變差　variation
变电所测试车/變電所試驗車　substation testing car
变动支出/變動費用　variable expense
变分法/變分法　variational method
变分原理/變分原理　variational principle
变风量空气调节系统/可變容積空氣調節系統　air conditioning system of variable volume
变风量末端装置/變風量通風終端裝置　variable air volume terminal device
变幅/變幅　derricking
变幅绞车/跨索絞機　spanwire winch, span winch
变更/變更　variation, change order
变更登记/變更登記　registration of alteration
变更径路/路徑變更　route diversion
变更设计/變更設計　altered design
变更通知书/更改通知　notice of design revision, notice of design complement
变工况/可變工作情況　variable working condition
变轨/軌道變更　orbit changing
变轨发动机/軌道機動發動機　orbit maneuver engine
变后掠翼/變後掠機翼　variable backswept wing
变厚度拱坝/不等厚拱壩　variable thickness arch dam
变[化]率/變率　rate of change
变极调速/變極調速　speed regulation by pole changing, pole changing speed control
变极性等离子弧焊/變極性參數電漿弧焊[接]　plasma arc welding with adjustable polarity parameters
变几何燃气轮机/可變幾何形狀燃氣輪機　variable geometry gas turbine
变几何燃烧室/可變幾何燃燒室　variable geometry combustor
变几何设计/可變幾何設計　variable geometry design
变焦镜头/變焦透鏡，可變焦距透鏡　zoom lens
变焦距/變焦距　zoom
变焦立体镜/縮放立體鏡　zoom stereoscope
变焦系统/變焦系統　zoom system, pancreatic system
变截面梁/變斷面梁　beam with variable cross-section
变距铰/變距鉸，軸向鉸　pitch hinge
变距螺桨/變距螺旋槳　variable pitch propeller
变开闭比通气壁/變多孔性多孔壁　variable porosity porous wall
变量泵/變量泵　variable delivery pump, variable capacity pump
变量油马达/變量油馬達　variable displacement oil motor
变流机/旋轉變流器，換流機　convertor, rotary inverter
变流机组/換流機組　converter set
变流量管流/變流量管流　channel flow with variable mass flow rate
变螺距/可變螺距，可變節距　variable pitch
变密度风洞/變密度風洞　variable density wind tunnel
变摩擦式减震装置/變摩擦式減震裝置　variable friction type snubbing device
变扭比/扭矩比　torque ratio
变扭器轴/變扭器軸　torque converter shaft
变频交流电源系统/變頻交流電源系統　variable frequency AC power system
变频器/變頻器，變頻機　frequency changer, frequency convertor, frequency converter
变频调速/變頻調速　speed regulation by frequency variation, variable frequency speed control
变坡点/變坡點，坡度變點，坡度轉折點　point of gradient change, grade change point, point of change of gradient
变视场导引头/變視場導引頭　FOV variable homing head
变水头渗透试验/變水頭透水試驗　falling head permeability test
变送器/發話器，[信號]發射器　transmitter
变速车道/變速車道　speed change lane
变速恒频电源系统/變速恆頻電源系統　variable speed constant frequency AC power system

变速路段/變速區　speed change area
变速区/變速區　speed change area
变速运动/變速運動　non-uniform motion
变推力液体火箭发动机/變推力液體火箭發動機　variable thrust liquid rocket engine
变弯度机翼/可變弧翼　variable camber wing
变位阀/換向閥　changeover valve
变温率/溫度變化率　temperature change rate
变温吸附/變溫吸附　temperature swing adsorption, TSA
变稳飞机/變穩定性飛機　variable stability airplane
变相机/換相機　phase convertor
变向泵/可逆泵　reversible pump
变形/變形　deformation
变形测量表/變形量規　deformation gage
变形缝/變形縫　deformation joint
变形钢筋/竹節鋼筋　deformed bar
变形高温合金/變形高溫合金　wrought superalloy
变形机制/變形機構　mechanism of deformation
变形加工/變形加工　deformation process
变形抗力/變形抵抗　deformation resistance
变形铝合金/變形用鋁合金　wrought aluminium alloy
变形镁合金/變形鎂合金　wrought magnesium alloy
变形模量/變形模數　modulus of deformation
变Z形试验/修正式蛇航試驗,修正式之字航行試驗　modified zigzag maneuver test
变形钛合金/變形鈦合金　wrought titanium alloy
变形椭圆/變形橢圓　indicatrix ellipse
变性混凝土/變態混凝土　metamorphic concrete
变压变频交流电源系统/變壓變頻交流電源系統　variable voltage variable frequency AC power system
变压器/變壓器　transformer, electric transformer
变压器电动势/變壓器電動勢　transformer EMF
变压器过负荷/變壓器過負荷　overload of transformer
变压器箱/變壓器箱　transformer box
变压调速/變壓調速　variable voltage speed control
变压吸附/變壓式吸附法　pressure swing adsorption, PSA
变异中心/變異中心　variation center
变质/變質　degenerate
变质岩/變質岩　metamorphic rock
变阻调压/變阻控制　rheostatic control
便道/臨時道路　temporary road
便利店/便利商店,简便超市　convenience store
便利国际海上运输公约/便利國際海上運輸公約　Convention on Facilitation of International Maritime Traffic
便桥/便橋　detour bridge, temporary bridge
便携电台/攜帶型無線電臺　portable radio set
便携式生命保障系统/可攜式維生系統　portable life support system
辨识/辨識　identification
标称电压/標稱電壓　nominal voltage
标称范围/標稱範圍　nominal range
标称放电电流/標稱放電電流　nominal discharge current
标称功率/標稱功率　nominal power
标称角动量/標稱角動量　nominal angular momentum
标称直径/標稱直徑,公稱直徑　nominal diameter
标称值/標稱值　nominal value
标称周长/標稱週長　nominal perimeter
标称转速/標稱速率　nominal speed
标尺/尺規　scale
标尺垫/三角座鈑　benching iron
标定断开容量/額定斷電容量　rated breaking capacity
标定工况/額定工作狀況　rated working condition
标定功率/額定功率　rated power, rated output
标定功率修正/額定修正　rating corrections
标定接通容量/額定接續容量　rated making capacity
标定热箱法/額定熱箱法　calibrated hot box method
标定值/校正值　calibration value
标定转舵扭矩/額定舵桿扭矩　rated stock torque
标定转速/額定引擎轉速　rated engine speed
标度因素/標度因數,比例因數　scale factor
标杆/標桿　pole beacon, beacon
标杆仪/標桿儀　pole device, pole instrument
标贯装置/貫入裝置　standard penetration equipment
标绘航线/標繪航線　plot a course
标绘距离/標繪距離　plot a distance
标记/標記,記號　marking
标校经纬仪/經緯儀校正　theodolite for calibration
标距/標記長度　gage length
标模实验/標模試驗　calibration-model test
标模试验精密度/校正模型精密度　precision of calibration model
标模试验准确度/校正模型準確度　accuracy of calibration model
标模统校/標模統校　unified calibration of standard model
标牌/標貼　placard
标签/標籤　label

标圈/標圈　aiming circle
标识/標識　sign, landmark
标示牌/揭示板，布告板　bulletin board
标书表格/標書表格　form of tender
标题/標題，名稱　title, heading
标题栏/標題欄　drawing title column
标位分系统/定位子系統　positioning subsystem
标值/指標數　indicated number
标志/標誌，標記　sign, mark symbol, marker
标志尺寸/標稱尺寸　nominal size
标志船/標誌船　marking vessel
标志灯/標誌燈　marker lamp
标志服/標誌服　safety marked coat
标志附牌/標誌附牌　additional panel
标志牌/告示牌　sign board
标志器/信ës器　marker
标志设施/標誌設施　sign device
标志视认性/標誌視認性　sign legibility
标志线/標誌線　pendent wire
标志用图形符号/標誌用圖形符號　graphical symbol for use on sign
标制服装/制服　uniform
标注用符号/標注用符號　symbol for indicating
标柱测速试验/標柱速率試驗　measured mile trial
标桩/標樁　marking stake
标准/標準　standard
标准报告格式/標準報告格式　standard reporting format
标准比冲/標準比衝　standard specific impulse
标准不确定度/標準不確定度　standard uncertainty
标准长度钢轨/標準長度鋼軌，定尺鋼軌　standard length rail
标准操纵性试验/標準操縱性試驗，蛇航試驗　standard maneuvering test
标准层/標準層　typical floor
标准差/標準偏差　standard deviation
标准场强法/標準場強度法　standard field strength method
标准车辆荷载/標準載重汽車荷載　standard truck loading
标准城市地区/標準都會區　standard metropolitan area
标准城市结构/標準都市結構　standard area of urban structure
标准尺寸/標準尺寸　standard size
标准大城市统计区/標準都會統計區　standard metropolitan statistical area
标准大气[压]/標準大氣　standard atmosphere
标准大气状况/標準大氣狀態　standard atmospheric condition
标准钉道/標準釘道　standard rail-spiking
标准定位业务/標準定位業務　standard positioning service, SPS
标准冻结深度/標準凍深　standard frost penetration
标准短管/標準短管　standard short tube
标准额定热负荷/標準額定熱負荷　normal rated heat load
标准方法/標準法　standard method
标准沸点/標準沸點　standard boiling point
标准分路灵敏度/標準分流靈敏度　standard shunting sensitivity
标准刚度/標準勁度　standard stiffness
标准高度/基準高　standard height
标准格式/標準格式　standard form
标准工作条件/標準運行條件　standard operating condition
标准贯入抵抗/標準貫入抵抗　standard penetration resistance
标准贯入度检验/標準穿入度檢驗　standard penetration inspection
标准贯入试验/標準貫入試驗，標準穿入試驗，N值试验　standard penetration test, SPT
标准轨距/標準軌距，標準量規　standard gage
标准航海用语/標準航海用語　standard marine navigational vocabulary, SMNV
标准横向补给法/標準强力法輸送設備　standard tensioned replenishment alongside method
标准滑阀图/標準滑閥圖　standard slide valve diagram
标准化大纲/標準化方案　standardization program
标准化设计/標準單元設計　standard cell design portfolio
标准化声压级差/標準化聲壓位準差　standardized sound pressure level difference
标准化撞击声压级/標準化衝擊聲壓位準　standardized impact sound pressure level
标准货车/標準貨車　standard truck
标准间/標準客房　standard guest room
标准界面说明/標準介面說明　standard interface description
标准进场航线/標準抵達航線　standard arrival route, STAR
标准救火水流/標準救火水源　standard fire stream
标准绝缘法兰接头/典型絕緣凸緣接頭　typical insulating flange joint
标准空档深度/標準空隙深度　standard void depth

标准雷电冲击电压/標準操作衝擊電壓波　standard lightning voltage impulse
标准罗航向/標準羅經航向　standard compass course
标准罗经/標準羅經　standard compass
标准煤/標準煤　standard coal
标准模型/標準模型　standard model
标准模型试验/標準模型試驗　standard model test
标准排放接头/標準排洩接頭　standard discharge connection
标准排水量/標準排水量　standard displacement
标准排泄接头/標準排洩接頭　standard discharge connection
标准喷头/標準噴頭　standard sprinkler
标准频率和时间信号台/標準頻時信號臺　standard frequency and time signal station
标准频率和时间信号业务/標準頻時信號業務　standard frequency and time signal service
标准频率信号/標準頻率信號　frequency reference signal
标准气压高度/標準氣壓高度　standard barometric altitude, standard pressure altitude
标准溶液/標準溶液　standard solution
标准色液/標準色液　standard color solution
标准筛/標準篩　standard sieve
标准设计/標準設計　standard design
标准时/標準時　standard time
标准试验发动机/標準試驗發動機　standard testing motor
标准太阳电池/標準太陽電池　standard solar cell
标准天线法/標準天線法　standard antenna method
标准条件/參考條件　reference condition
标准物质/參考物質,基準物質　reference material
标准物质标准值/參考物質有證數值　certified value of reference material
[标准物质的]定值/[參考物質的]驗證　certification of a reference material
标准[误]差/標準誤差　standard error
标准箱/20呎貨櫃相當數量　twenty equivalent unit, TEU
标准型城市/標準都市結構　standard area of urban structure
标准循环/標準循環　standard cycle
标准仪表离场/標準儀器離場　standard instrument departure, SID
标准有效温度/標準有效溫度　standard effective temperature, SET
标准再入轨道/標準再入軌跡　standard re-entry trajectory
标准轴载/標準軸載重,標準軸負荷　standard axle load
标准桩/標準樁　standard pile
标准状态/標準狀態　standard condition
飑线/颮線　squall line
表/表　list
表层沉积/表層堆積物　surface deposit
表层地质图/表層地質圖　surface geologic map
表层流/表面流　surface current
表观隔声量/視隔音指標　apparent sound reduction index
表观功率/視[在]功率　apparent power
表观密度/表觀密度,視密度　apparent density
表观弹性模数/視彈性模數　apparent modulus of elasticity
表观温度/表觀溫度,表面[輻射]溫度　apparent temperature
表列高度/表列高度　tabulated altitude
表流/片層洪水　sheet flood
表面/表面,外側面　surface, outside face
表面波/表面波　surface wave
表面充电/表面充電　surface charging
表面处理/表面處理　surface treatment
表面处理剂/表面處理劑　surface treating agent
表面粗糙度/表面粗糙度　surface roughness
表面淬火/表面淬火　surface hardening, surface quenching
表面电阻/表面電阻,表面阻力　surface electrical resistance, surface resistance
表面分析仪/表面分析儀器　surface analysis instrument
表面改性/表面改質　surface modification
表面干燥状态/面乾狀態　surface-dry condition
表面构造/表面組織,表面織構　surface texture
表面构造深度/表面織構深度　surface texture depth
表面过滤/表面過濾　surface filtration
表面宏观构造/表面宏觀構造　surface macro texture
表面换热系数/表面散熱係數　surface coefficient of heat transfer
表面换热阻/表面換熱阻　surface resistance of heat transfer
表面活性/表面活力　surface activity
表面活性化结合/表面活性化結合　surface activated bonding
表面活性剂/表面活性劑　surface-active agent, surfactant
表面巨观构造/表面巨觀構造　surface mega texture

表面理论/表面理論　theory of surface
表面力/表面力　surface force
表面裂纹/表面裂紋　external crack
表面摩擦/表面曳力,表阻力　surface drag
表面摩擦系数/表面摩擦係數,地面摩擦係數　surface friction coefficient
表面平整度/表面平坦度,地面平坦度　surface evenness
表面清理/表面清潔　surface cleaning
表面湿润系数/表面濕潤係數　surface wetness fraction
表面式换热器/表面熱交換器　surface heat exchanger
表面式回热器/複熱器　recuperator
表面式空气冷却器/表面空氣冷卻器　surface air cooler
表面式凝汽器/表面冷凝器　surface condenser
表面碳化/表面炭化法　superficial charring
表面涂覆/表面塗層　surface coating
表面拖曳/表面曳力,表阻力　surface drag
表面微观构造/表面微觀構造　surface micro texture
表面涡流/表面渦流　surface eddy
表面压实/表面夯實　superficial compaction
表面硬化/表面硬化　face hardening
表面预处理/表面預處理　surface pretreatment
表面张力/表面張力　surface tension
表面张力贮箱/表面張力推進劑貯箱　surface tension propellant tank
表面整平/表面整平　templet tamper
表面阻力/表面阻力　surface resistance
表盘式调速器/針盤調速器　dial type governor
表上作业法/表上作業法　table dispatching method
表示/指示　indication
表示灯/指示燈　indication lamp
表示灯电源/指示燈電源　power source for indication lamp
表示电路/指示電路　indication circuit
表示对象/指示對象　indicated object
表示杆/指示桿　indication rod
表示连接杆/指示連接桿　connecting rod for indication
表示盘/儀表板　indicating panel
表示器/指示器　indicator
表示周期/指示週期　indication cycle
表土/表土,耕層土　topsoil
表土保护/表土保護　topsoil protection
表土剥离/表土剝離　topsoil stripping
表土堆放/表土堆放　topsoil pile
表土回填/表土回填　topsoil backfill
表土评价/表土評鑒　topsoil evaluation
表土清表/表土清表　topsoil surface clear
表土再利用/表土再利用　topsoil reuse
表现主义/表現主義　expressionism
表型/表[現]型　phenotype
表压力/表壓力　gage pressure
表演区/表演區　acting area
表演艺术中心/表演藝術中心　performing arts center
别墅/別墅　villa
玢岩/玢岩　porphyrite
宾馆/賓館,小型家庭旅館　guesthouse
滨海湖/海岸湖泊　coastal lake
滨海旅游/海岸旅遊　coastal tourism
滨河路堤/濱河路堤　embankment on river bank
滨水区/臨水區　waterfront area
滨滩补给/海岸培養　beach nourishment
濒危世界遗产名录/瀕危世界遺產清單,世界自然遺產名錄　List of World Heritage in Danger
濒危野生动植物种进出口国际贸易公约/瀕臨絕種野生動植物國際貿易公約　Convention on International Trade in Endangered Species of Wild Fauna and Flora
濒危植物/瀕危植物,瀕臨絕種植物　threatened plant, endangered plant
濒危种/瀕危[物]種　threatened species, endangered species
殡仪馆/殯儀館　funeral parlor
殡葬建筑/殯葬建築,喪葬建築　funeral architecture
冰坝/淩壅　ice gorge
冰崩/冰崩　ice avalanche
冰舱/冰艙　ice hold, ice bunker
冰川崩溃/冰川暴裂　glacier burst
冰川沉积/冰川沈積　glacial deposit
冰川地质学/冰河地質學　glacial geology
冰川风/冰川風,冰河風　glacier wind
冰川[河]学/冰河學　glaciology
冰川仪/冰河計　glaciometer
冰带区/冰帶[板列]　ice belt
冰挡/流冰擋　ice guard
冰点/冰點,凝結點　freezing point, solidifying point
冰冻地区/冰凍地區　frost region
冰冻期/冰凍期　ice period
冰冻条款/冰凍條款　ice clause
冰风洞/結冰風洞　icing tunnel
冰封/冰凍封閉,冰阻　icebound
冰封地带/冰障　ice barrier

冰封区域/冰封區域　ice covered area
冰盖/覆冰[量]　ice cover
冰荷载/冰荷載　ice pressure, ice load
冰厚/冰層厚度　ice thickness
冰壶/冰上推石遊戲　curling
冰壶场/冰壺場　curling field
冰湖沉积/冰河湖積土　glacial-lake deposit
冰架/冰架,連岸冰,冰灘　ice shelf
冰间水道/冰間巷道　lead lane
冰壳/脆冰殼　ice rind
冰库/冰庫　ice storage room
冰况报告/冰況報告　ice report
冰况图集/冰況地圖　ice atlas
冰困/冰封　ice bound
冰凌调查/冰凌調査　ice floe survey, frazil ice survey
冰锚/[繫]冰錨　ice anchor
冰面饱和水汽压/冰面平衡蒸汽壓　equilibrium vapor pressure of ice surface
冰碛土/冰碛　moraine, glacial till, till
冰碛物/冰河積層　glacial till
冰情警报/冰情警報　ice warning
冰情巡逻服务/冰區巡邏服務　ice patrol service
冰丘/冰丘,冰堆　ice hummock, hummock
冰球场/滑冰場　rink
冰球馆/冰球館　indoor ice rink, ice hocky rink
冰球运动/冰球運動　ice hockey sport
冰区航行/冰區航行　ice navigation
冰区界限/冰區界線　ice boundary
冰区水道/冰道,冰河　ice channel
冰区拖航/冰區拖纜航　towing in ice
冰山/冰山　iceberg, berg
冰山探测/冰山探測　detection of iceberg
冰蚀/冰銷蝕　ice erosion
冰水堆积/冰積土　glacial-fluvial deposit
冰条纹/冰花　ice fringe
冰图/冰圖　ice chart
冰丸/冰珠　ice pellet
冰箱冷藏车/冰艙冷藏[火]車　ice-bunker refrigerator car
冰形/冰形　icing shape
冰雪路面驾驶/冰雪路面駕駛　driving on snowy and icy road
冰雪运动/冰雪體育　ice and snow sport
冰压力/冰壓力　ice pressure
冰壅/冰脹,冰推作用　ice push
冰原/冰原,冰野　ice field
冰缘线/冰緣線　ice edge
冰载荷/冰負荷　ice load
冰障/冰凌,冰塞　ice jam
冰中操船/冰中操船　shiphandling in ice
冰中护航/冰中護航　convoy in ice
冰锥/冰錐　ice cone
兵工厂/兵工廠　arsenal
丙烯酸地坪涂料/丙烯酸地面塗料　acrylic floor coating
并车电抗器/并聯運轉反應器　parallel operation reactor
并车屏/并車屏　paralleling panel
并励电动机/并聯激勵電動機　shunt excited motor
并联补偿电容器组/并聯補償電容器組　capacitor bank
并联电容补偿装置/并聯電容比較電橋　compensator with parallel capacitance
并联电阻/并聯電阻,分路電阻　shunt resistance
并联复式汽轮机/并列複式蒸汽渦輪機　cross-compound steam turbine
并联供水/并聯供水　parallel water supply
并联火箭发动机/并聯火箭發動機　multi-rocket engine cluster
并联扫描/并聯掃描　parallel scan
并联式轨道电路/并聯式軌道電路　multiply connected track circuit
并联引爆系统/并聯引爆系統　parallel fuzing system
并联运行/并聯運轉　parallel operation
并联运行试验/并聯運轉試驗　parallel-running test
并列断续角焊缝/并列斷續填角焊接　chain intermittent fillet weld
并列式枢纽/并列式樞紐　parallel arrangement type junction
并行传输/平行傳輸　parallel transmission
并行工程/同步工程　concurrent engineering
并置信号点/并置信號點　double signal location
并装提单/并装載貨證券　combined bill of lading
病虫害防治/病蟲害防治　prevention and control of plant diseases and insect pests
病房/病房,病室　ward
病理科/病理檢驗室,病理研究室　pathology laboratory
[病兽]隔离室/病獸隔離室　isolation barn
病原体/病原體　pathogen
病原细菌/病原菌　pathogenic bacteria
拨叉/撥叉　poking fork
拨道/撥道　track lining
拨道机/撥道機　track lining machine
拨道器/撥道器　track lining tool

拨号/撥號　dialing
拨号脉冲/撥號脈衝　dial impulse
拨号盘/撥號盤,標度板　dial
拨号音/撥號音　dialing tone
拨号终端/撥號終端機　dial-up terminal
波/波　wave
λ波/λ震波　λ shock wave
波长/波長　wave length
波长计/波長計　wave meter
波导缝隙阵天线/槽嵌波導天線,開槽波導天線　slotted waveguide antenna
波导线/波導線路　waveguide line
波导线传输方式/波導線路傳輸波式　transmission mode with waveguide line
波[的]传播/波傳播　wave propagation
波的反射/反射波　reflection of wave
波的折射/波浪折射　refraction of wave
波顶/波頂　wave summit
波动/波[動]　wave motion
波动法测桩/波動法測樁　waving inspection for piles
波动方程/波動方程式　wave equation
波动声学/波動聲學　wave acoustics
波陡/波浪尖度　wave steepness
L-波段紧急无线电示标/L頻帶應急指位無線電示標　L-band EPIRB
L-波段紧急无线电示标系统/L頻帶應急指位無線電示標系統　L-band EPIRB system
S波段统一系统/統一S波段系統　unified S-band system
波尔豪森法/柏哈森法　Pohlhausen method
波分复用/波分複用　wavelength devision multiplexing
波峰/波峰,浪峰　wave ridge, wave crest
波峰宽度/波峰寬度　wave crest length
波峰钎焊/波峰焊　wave soldering, flow soldering
波峰因数/峰值因數,波頂因素　crest factor
波腹/波腹　wave loop, antinode
波高/波高　wave height
波高系数/波高係數　wave height coefficient
波谷/波谷　wave trough, wave hollow
波痕/漣漪　ripple mark
波候/波候　wave climate
波激振动/船體波振　springing
波浪/[波]浪　wave
波浪变化/波浪變化　wave variability
波浪补偿器/波浪補償器　swell compensator
波浪传播/波浪前進　propagation of wave
波浪传播线/波浪進行曲線　wave propagation line
波浪等能量线/波浪等能量線　line of wave constant energy
波浪反射/波反射　wave reflection
波浪观测/波浪觀察　wave observation
波浪轨迹/波浪軌跡　wave orbit
波浪力/波力　wave force
波浪流/波浪流　wave-induced current
波浪破碎/洶湧碎波　surging breaker
波浪谱/波譜　wave spectrum
波浪曲折图/波浪曲折圖　wave refraction diagram
波浪绕射图/波浪繞射圖　wave diffraction diagram
波浪绕射系数/波浪繞射係數　coefficient of wave diffraction
波浪生成/起浪　generation of wave
波浪衰减/波浪衰減　wave decay
波浪衰减距离/波浪衰減距離　wave decay distance
波浪水动压力修正/史密斯修正波效應　Smith correction
波浪水分子速度/波浪水分子速度　wave particle velocity
波浪水深因数/波浪水深因數　wave depth factor
波浪特征值/波動特性　wave characteristics
波浪弯矩/波載彎曲力矩　wave bending moment
波浪席/波浪席　wave seating
波浪要素/波浪要素　wave parameter
波浪越顶/越波,跳波,溢漫波　wave overtopping
波浪载荷/波浪負荷　wave load
波浪折射/波折射　wave refraction
波浪中阻力试验/波浪中阻力試驗　resistance test in waves
波[浪]周期/波[浪]週期　wave period
波浪追测/波浪追測　wave hind casting
波列/波列,浪陣　wave train
波龄/波齡　wave age
波流/波浪流　wave-induced current
波门内插测距/波門內插測距　rang gate interpolation ranging
波能传递/波浪能量傳遞　wave energy transmission
波能量/波能　wave energy
波能系数/波浪能量係數　wave energy coefficient
波谱/波譜　wave spectrum
波前/波前[進面]　wave front
波前法/迎頭法　frontal method
波倾角/波面傾角,波面斜率　slope of wave surface
波群速/波群速度　wave group velocity
波射线/波射線　wave ray
波束控制系统/[波]束控制系統　beam controlling system

波束宽度/波束寬度　beam width
波束区/波束區域　beam zone
波束锐化比/敏銳波束比　beam sharpening ratio
波束跃度/波束跳度　beam saltus
波束制导/波束制導　beam riding guidance
波斯传统/波斯傳統　Persian tradition
波斯建筑/波斯建築　Persian architecture
波斯式柱/波斯柱　Persian column
波速/波速　wave celerity, wave velocity, celerity of wave
波速测定/波速測量　wave velocity measurement
波速勘探法/波速調查　wave velocity survey
波特/波特　baud
波特兰矿渣水泥/卜特蘭高爐水泥　Portland blast-furnace cement
波纹板式推力室/波紋板推力室　corrugated plate thrust chamber
波纹地板/波紋地板　corrugated floor
波纹钢桥面/波紋鋼甲板　corrugated steel deck
波纹管涵/皺紋金屬管涵　corrugated metal pipe culvert
波纹护套/波形管套　corrugated sheath
波向/波向　wave direction
波向线/波向線　wave orthogonal
波形/波形　wave form, waveform, wave profile
波形舱壁/波形艙壁　corrugated bulkhead
波形舱口盖/波形艙蓋　corrugated hatchcover
波形发生器/造波機　wave maker, wave generator
波形辐板/波形輪板　corragated wheel plate
波形梁护栏/波形管護欄　corrugated beam barrier
波形膨胀管/波形膨脹管　corrugated expansion pipe
H波型振动/H型振動　H-mode vibration
波型阻力/波型阻力　wave pattern resistance
波衍射/波繞射　diffraction of wave, wave diffraction
波[振]幅/波幅　wave amplitude
波阻/震波阻力,造波抵抗　shock wave drag, wave drag
玻璃布层压制品/玻璃布積層板　glass cloth laminate
玻璃钢船/玻璃纖維強化塑膠船　fiberglass reinforced plastic boat, fiberglass reinforced plastic ship, FRP ship
玻璃钢管/玻璃鋼管　fiberglass tube
玻璃钢护栏/玻璃纖維強化塑膠護欄　fiberglass reinforced plastic fence
玻璃钢结构/玻璃鋼結構　fiberglass reinforced plastic structure
玻璃钢救生艇/玻璃纖維救生艇　fiberglass lifeboat
玻璃钢门窗/玻璃鋼門窗　fiberglass reinforced plastic door and window
玻璃钢桥/玻璃纖維強化塑膠橋　fiberglass reinforced plastic bridge
玻璃家具/玻璃家具　glass furniture
玻璃量筒/玻璃量筒　glass graduate
玻璃马赛克/馬賽克玻璃　glass mosaic
玻璃棉/玻璃綿,玻璃絨　glass wool
玻璃幕墙/玻璃幕牆　glass curtain wall
玻璃贴膜/玻璃膜　glass film
玻璃微珠/玻璃微珠　micro-glass bead
玻璃微珠反射体/玻璃微珠反射體　glass microball reflector
玻璃温室/玻璃溫室　glass greenhouse
玻璃纤维/玻璃纖維　glass fiber
玻璃纤维壁布/玻璃纖維壁布　fiberglass wall covering fabric
玻璃纤维强化复合材/玻璃纖維強化複合材　fiberglass reinforced concrete
玻璃纤维网格布/玻纖網　fiberglass mesh
玻璃纤维增加塑料/玻璃纖維強化塑膠　fiberglass reinforced plastics, FRP, fiberglass reinforced plastics
玻璃纤维增强石膏制品/玻璃纖維石膏板　fiberglass reinforced gypsum
玻璃纤维增强水泥空心条板/玻璃纖維增強水泥空心條板　fiberglass reinforced cement panel with cavity
玻璃纤维增强水泥制品/玻璃纖維增強水泥　fiberglass reinforced cement
玻璃纤维增强塑料/玻璃纖維強化塑膠　fiberglass reinforced plastic
玻纤胎沥青瓦/瀝青漬玻璃纖維瓦板　asphalt shingle made from glass felt
剥层翻修/剝層翻修　peeled resurfacing
剥离强度/撕裂強度　peel strength
剥落试验/去膜試驗　stripping test
剥皮机/剝皮機　peeler
剥蚀/剝蝕,剝離　chipping
菠萝格/默包　Merbau
播音连接器/播音連接器　public address coupling
播音室/播音室,播影室　broadcasting studio, public address room
播音装置/播講裝置,播講系統　public address system
播种/播種　sow
播种机/播種機　seeder
播种盘/播種盤　seed tray

播种器/播種器　garden seeder
播种草坪/播種草坪　seeding lawn
播种繁殖/播種繁殖　sowing propagation
播种量/播種量　seeding quantity
播种苗/實生苗,苗木　tree seedling
播种期/播種期　sowing time, seeding time
伯奈特公园/柏内特公園　Burnett Park
伯努利方程/柏努利方程式　Bernoulli equation
驳岸/園林駁岸　revetment in garden
驳船/駁船　lighter, barge
驳船编队系数/編隊係數　formation coefficient
驳船队/駁船隊　barge train
驳船队编组/駁船隊編組　barge train formation
驳船队形图/駁船隊形圖　sketch of barge train formation
驳船码头/駁船碼頭　lighter wharf
驳门/駁門　port
驳运泵/轉駁泵　transfer pump
泊船处/泊地,錨泊處　road stead
泊位/泊位,航席,停船位置　berth
泊位利用率/泊位利用率　berth occupancy
泊位条款/碼頭收交貨條件　berth term
泊位通过能力/泊位通過能力　berth throughput capacity
泊位租船合同/泊位傭船契約　berth charter party
博什烟度/爐腹發煙器　Bosh smoke unit
博塔弗戈湾/博塔福戈灣　Botafogo bay
博物馆/博物館　museum
搏风板/搏縫板　gable eave board
箔条/干擾絲　chaff
薄膜电阻温度计/薄膜電阻溫度計　thin film resistance thermometer
薄膜技术/薄膜技術　thin film technology
薄膜加热试验/薄膜加熱試驗　thin film heating test
薄膜理论/薄膜理論　membrane theory
薄膜水层/膜帶　pellicular zone
薄膜太阳电池/薄膜太陽能電池　thin film solar cell
薄膜吸收/膜吸收　membrane absorption
薄膜养护/覆膜養護　membrane curing
薄膜养生/覆膜養護　membrane curing
薄膜养生液/薄膜養護液　membrane curing solution
薄膜应力/薄膜應力　membrane stress
薄膜蒸发/薄膜蒸發　thin film evaporation
薄燃料油/稀燃油　thin fuel oil
薄弱楼层/軟弱層　weak storey
薄雾/薄霧　thin fog
补板/補板　patching
补偿板/調整板　compensating plate

补偿棒/填隙棒　shim rod
补偿点/補償點　compensation point
补偿电容器/補償電容　compensation capacitor
补偿量/補償量　compensation dosage
补偿流/補償流　compensation current
补偿坡度/折減坡度　compensating grade
补偿器/[熱膨脹]補償器　compensator, compensator for thermal expansion
补偿式高速摄影机/補償式高速攝影機　compensating high-speed camera
补偿水/補償水　compensation water
补偿调节指针/補償調節指針　compensation adjusting pointer
补偿线圈/補償線圈　compensating coil
补偿因子/補償因子　compensation factor
补偿针阀/補償針閥　compensation needle valve
补偿装置的电抗比/補償器電抗比　reactance ratio of compensator
补偿作用/補償　compensation
补充报告/補充報告　supplementary report
补充电力/補充電力　supplementary power
补充加注/補充　topping, replenishment
补充客票/補充票　additional ticket
补充码/補充碼　complement code
补充说明/補充說明　supplemental instruction
补充[天气]预报/補充[天氣]預報　supplementary weather forecast
补充型号合格证/補充型別檢定證　supplemental type certificate, STC
补焊/補焊　repair welding
补机/補機　banking locomotive
补给船/補給船　delivery ship
补给航速/整補航速　replenishment speed
补给航向/整補航向　replenishment course
补给横距/整補橫距　replenishment distance abeam
补给舰/補給艦　replenishing ship
补给率/補給率　recharge rate
补给水/補給水,補充水　make-up feed water, make-up water
补给线/補給線　feeder line
补给站/補給站　supplying station
补给阵位/整補站　replenishment station
补给直升机/補給直昇機　supplying helicopter
补给纵距/整補縱距　replenishment distance astern
补间铺作/補間鋪作　intercolumnar bracket set, bujian puzuo
补强层/補強層　strengthening course
补燃火箭发动机/分級燃燒火箭發動機　staged

combustion rocket engine
补燃循环/補燃循環 staged combustion cycle
补砂/補砂 resanding
补水率/補充水率 make up water percentage
补水系统/加水系統 water charging system
补水贮存舱/備用給水櫃 reserve feedwater tank
补正板/補正板 aspheric plate
补植/補植 reinforcement planting
补助解/補助解 complementary solution
捕获/截獲 acquisition
捕获带/捕捉帶 pull-in range
捕获辐射/捕獲輻射 trapped radiation
捕获辐射模式/捕獲輻射模式 trapped radiation model
捕获概率/獲得概率 acquisition probability
捕获轨迹法/繫留軌跡法 captive trajectory method
捕获粒子/俘獲粒子 trapped particle
捕获量/漁獲物 catch
捕获灵敏度/擷取靈敏度 acquisition sensitivity
捕获模式/擷取模式 acquisition mode
捕获区/捕獲區 trapping region
捕获视场/獲得視野 FOV of acquisition
捕鲸船/捕鯨船 whaler
捕鲸母船/捕鯨母船,鯨加工船 whale factory ship, whaling mother ship
捕捞机械/漁撈機械 fishing machinery
捕食食物链/捕食食物鏈 predator food chain
捕食效率/捕食效率 predation efficiency
捕食者/捕食者,掠食者 predator
捕蟹船/捕蟹船 crabber
捕鱼技术/漁撈學 fishing technology
捕鱼权/捕魚權 right of fishery
捕捉网/捕捉網 catching net
哺乳室/哺乳室,育嬰室 nursing room
不安全泊位/不良船席,危險泊位 foul berth
不变钢/恆範鋼 Invar
不沉淀物/不沈澱物 nonsettleable matter
不沉性/不沈性 insubmersibility
不成对运行图/不成對運行圖 train diagram not in pairs
不定常空泡/不穩定空泡 unsteady cavities, non-stationary cavities
不定期船舶/不定期輪船 tramp
不定期船运输/不定期船業務 tramp service
不定期货船/不定期貨船 tramp steamer
不定期列车/不定點列車 irregular train
不定芽/不定芽 adventitious bud, indefinite bud
不冻港/不凍港 ice free port

不对称交流电充电/不對稱交流充電 asymmetric alternating current charge
不对称浸水/不對稱浸水,不對稱泛水 unsymmetrical flooding
不对称脉冲轨道电路/不對稱脈衝軌道電路 asymmetrical impulse track circuit
不对称平衡/不對稱平衡 asymmetrical balance
不对称三开道岔/不對稱三開道岔 unsymmetrical three-way turnout, unsymmetrical three-throw turnout
不发火地面/無火花地板 non-sparkling floor
不发射信标/無示標發送 no beacon emission
不分开式扣件/不分開式扣件 non-separated rail fastening, direct holding fastening
不工作时间/不工作時間 non-operative time
不规则波/不規則波[浪] irregular wave
不规则畸变/不規則畸變,偶發畸變 fortuitous distortion
不规则造园时期/不規則造園時期 irregular gardening period
不合格/不合格性 nonconformity
不滑路面/不滑路面 non-skid pavement
不击舟/不擊舟 immovable pleasure boat
不记名提单/不記名載貨證券 blank bill of lading
不间断电源/不間斷電源 uninterruptible power source, UPS
不洁压舱水/不潔壓艙水 dirty ballast
不均一土壤/不規則土壤 erratic subsoil
不均匀运动/變速運動 non-uniform motion
不可避免的事故/不可避免的事故 inevitable accident
不可拆卸的/不可拆卸者 non-removable
不可倒转柴油机/不可逆轉柴油機 non-reversible diesel engine
不可懂串音/不可解串音 unintelligible crosstalk
不可见伤害/不可見傷害 invisible harm
不可抗力/不可抗力 force majeure
不可逆过程/不可逆過程 irreversible process
不可逆助力机械操纵/不可逆助力機械操縱 irreversible boosted mechanical control
不可修复产品/不可修復產品 non-repairable item
不可压缩流体/不可壓縮流體 incompressible fluid
不可预见费/準備金,預備之應變津貼 contingencies, provision for contingency, allowance for contingency
不可转让提单/不可轉讓載貨證券 non-negotiable bill of lading
不利地段/不利地區 unfavorable area to earthquake

resistance, unfavorable area
不利季节/不利季節 unfavorable season
不连续层/突變層 layer of discontinuity
不连续[性]/不連續性 discontinuity
不良地质/不良地質 unfavorable geology
不良锚地/不良船席,危險泊位 foul berth
不毛之地/裸露地 barren land
不明过失/不明過失 inscrutable fault
不明阶段/不明階段 uncertainty phase
不耐寒植物/不耐寒植物,霜凍敏感植物 non-hardy plant, frost-sensitive plants, tender plant
不能工作时间/停機時間,停工時間 down time
不排水分析/不排水分析 undrained analysis
不排水剪力试验/不排水剪力試驗 undrained shear test
不排水条件/不排水條件 undrained condition
不排水下沉沉井/不排水下沈沈井 sinking open caisson by undrained dredging
不排土桩/非排土樁 non displacement pile
不平衡电阻/不平衡電阻 unbalanced resistance
不平衡舵/不平衡舵 unbalanced rudder
不平衡力/不均衡力 unbalanced force
不平整路面/不平路面 uneven road
不清洁提单/不潔載貨證券 foul bill of lading
[不确定度的]A类评定/[不確定度]A類評估 type A evaluation of uncertainty
[不确定度的]B类评定/[不確定度]B類評估 type B evaluation of uncertainty
不确定性分析/不確定[性]分析 uncertainty analysis
不确定圆柱面/不確定圓柱面 critical cylinder
不燃材料/不燃材料 non-combustible materials
不燃烧体/不可燃組分 non-combustible component
不渗透率/不透水率 ratio of impermeability
不适航性/無適航性 unseaworthiness
不适用地区的标志/不適用地區的標誌 closed area marking
不同期重复性/不同期重複性 different term repeatability
不同时到达间隔时间/不同時到達間隔時間 time interval between two opposing trains arriving at station not at the same time
不透水层/非透水層 aquifuge
不透水丁堤/不透水丁堤 impermeable groyne
不透水覆盖层/不透水鋪層 impervious blanket
不透水率/不透水率 ratio of impermeability
不透水墙/截水牆 impermeable wall
不透水系数/不透水因子 impermeability factor

不透水心墙/不透水心牆 watertight core
不透水性/不透水性,水密性 impermeability, water tightness
不透水性试验/不透水試驗,不滲透試驗 impermeability test
不完全饱和/不完全飽和 partial saturation
不完全膨胀/不完全膨脹 under expansion
不完全燃烧/不完全燃燒 imperfect combustion, incomplete combustion
不完全燃烧热损失/不完全燃燒熱損失 heat loss due to incomplete combustion
不完全水舌/不完全水舌 incomplete nappe
不完全溢流/不完全溢流 incomplete overflow
不稳定河槽/不穩定河槽 unstable channel
不稳定河床/移動河床 shifting bed
不稳定环/遲滯環,磁滯環 hysteresis loop
不稳定交通流量/不穩交通流量 unstable traffic flow
不稳定结构/不穩定結構 unstable structure
不稳定流/非定常流 non-stationary flow
不稳定阵雨/不穩定驟雨 instability shower
不限时人工解锁/不限時人工解鎖 manual non-time release
不锈钢/不銹鋼 stainless steel
不锈钢管/不銹鋼管 stainless steel pipe, stainless steel tube
不育系/不育系 sterile line
不在第一港卸的货/留船未卸貨 residue cargo
不摘车修/不摘車修 in-train repair
不整合/不整合 unconformity
不知条款/不知條款 unknown clause
不准入境/禁止入境 entrance prohibited
布查特花园/布查特花園 Butchart Gardens
布袋除尘器/濾袋除塵器 bag dust collector
布管船/布管船 pipeline layer
布景库/舞臺布景庫 stage scenery room
布拉格谐振/布拉格共振 Bragg resonance
布拉休斯定理/布拉斯定理 Blasius theorem
布拉休斯平板解/布拉斯平板解 Blasius solution for flat plate flow
布缆船/布纜船 cable ship, cable layer
布缆机/布纜機 cable laying machine
布雷航海勤务/布雷航海勤務 mine-laying navigation service
布雷舰艇/布雷艦,布雷艇 minelayer
布伦海姆宫苑/布萊納姆宮,布萊尼姆宮 Blenheim Palace Park
布氏硬度试验/布氏硬度試驗,勃氏硬度試驗

Brinell hardness test
布氏［硬］度数／布氏硬度數，勃式硬度數　Brinell figure
布网船／布網船　net layer
布纹粉刷／布紋粉刷　sack-rubbed finish
布线／布纜　cabling
布线系统／布線系統　wiring system
步道／步道　pedestrian path
步进电机／步進馬達　stepping motor
步进角／步進角　stepping angle
步进式／逐步　step-by-step
步进制电话交换机／步進位電話交換機　step-by-step telephone switching system
步距角／步長　step size, step width
步桥／步橋，窄道　cat walk
步入式衣柜／進入壁櫃　walk-in closet
步石／步石，踏腳石　stepping stone
步行板／步行板　foot plank
步行道／人行道　sidewalk, pedestrian path
步行交通设施／安全行人設施　pedestrian facility
步行街／步行街　pedestrian street
步行区／行人專區　pedestrian area
步行商业街／徒步商店街　pedestrian mall
步行上楼式公寓／低層公寓　walkup apartment
步行系统／步行系統　pedestrian system
步行游览路／徒步旅遊線路　walking tour route
步行者友好环境／行人友好環境　pedestrian-friendly environment
步序／步序列，步順序　step sequence
部分出入限制／部分出入管制　partial control of access
部分重复使用运载器／部分重複使用運載器　partial reusable space vehicle
部分防洪／部分防洪　partial flood control
部分仿真／局部［實體］模擬　partial simulation
部分封闭救生艇／部分圍蔽救生艇　partially enclosed lifeboat
部分负荷／部分負荷　partial load
部分负荷工况／部分負荷工況　partial load mode
部分货载／部分貨載　part cargo
部分减低水压／部分減低水壓　partical relief
部分进汽度／部分進汽度　degree of partial admission
部分控制进入／部分出入管制　partial control of access
部分任务训练器／部分任務訓練機　partial task trainer
部分下沉／部分浸水　partial submergence
部分预混［式］燃烧／部分預混［式］燃燒　partially aerated combustion
部分预应力／部分預力　partial prestressing
部分预应力混凝土／部分預力混凝土　partially prestressed concrete
部分预应力混凝土桥／部分預應力混凝土橋　partially prestressed concrete bridge
部分装载舱室／部分裝載艙間　partly filled compartment
部件／組件　component
部件故障检测／零组件失效檢測，元件失效檢測　inspection of component failure

C

擦地角/擦地角　tail down angle
擦地炸机构/擦地炸機構　grazing impact mechanism
擦痕面/斷層滑面　slickenside
擦伤/擦刻　scratching
材/材　timber module, cai
材料拌和均匀度测定/材料拌和均勻度測定　materials mixing uniformity measurement
材料表/材料單　bill of materials
材料堆放区/材料堆放區　material stacking area
材料放气/材料釋氣　material outgassing
材料非线性分析/材料非線性分析　material nonlinear analysis
材料供应计划/施工材料供應計劃　material supply plan
材料明细表/材料表　material list
材料明细清单/材料表　material list
材料强度标准值/材料強度特徵值　characteristic value for strength of material
材料强度分项系数/材料強度部分安全係數　partial safety factor for strength of material
材料强度设计值/材料強度的設計值　design value for strength of material
材料去气/材料除氣　material degassing
材料申请计划/材料申請計劃　material requisition plan
材料试验法/材料試驗法　materials test method
材料输送机械/材料運送機　materials conveyer
材料污染/材料汙染　material contamination
材料消耗定额/材料定額　material consumption norm, material consumption rating
材料性能/材料性能　characteristic of materials, materials property
材料员/料務士　material staff
材料质量损失/材料質量損失　material mass loss
材质不良/材質不良　bad materials
财产损失/財產損害　property damage
财务管理/財務管理　financial management
财务管理信息系统/財務管理資訊系統　financial management information system
财务计划/財務計劃　financial plan, financial planning
财务净现值/財務淨現值　financial net present value, FNPV
财务决算审查/財務決算審查　financial statements review
财务评价/財務評估　financial evaluation
财务效益/財務效益　financial benefit
财务折现率/財務折現率　financial discount rate
财物/財物　property
财源/財源　financial source
裁判席/裁判席　referee seat
采光的总透射比/採光總穿透率　total transmittance of daylighting
采光均匀度/採光均勻度　uniformity of daylighting
采光塔/穹頂天窗　lantern
采光屋顶/屋頂燈，天棚光　roof light
采光系数/晝光因數　daylight factor
采光系数的室内反射光分量/晝光因數的屋內反射成分　internally reflected component of daylight factor
采光系数的室外反射光分量/晝光因數的屋外反射成分　externally reflected component of daylight factor
采光系数的天空光分量/晝光因數的天空成分　sky component of daylight factor
采光系数平均值/晝光因數標準值　average value of daylight factor
采集种条/採集種條　breeding branches collection
采矿船/採礦船　mining dredger
采矿用地/礦業用地　mining land
采料场/借土場　borrowing area
采暖/採暖　heating
采暖地板/採暖地板　heating floor
采暖度日数/採暖度日　heating degree day
采暖装置/採暖系統　heating system
采石/採石　quarrying
采石场/採石場　quarry yard
采血室/採血室　blood sample collecting room
采雪器/採雪樣設備　snow sampling equipment
采样/取樣　sample
采样保持/取樣與保持　sample and hold
采样编码器/取樣編碼器　sampler and coder

采样点/抽樣點　sampling point
采样定理/採樣定理,取樣定理　sampling theorem
采样频率/採樣頻率,取樣頻率　sampling frequency
采样数据系统/取樣資料系統　sampled data system
采珍渔船/採珠船　lugger, pearl boat
采种/種子收集　seed collection
彩度/純度　purity
彩画作/彩畫　decorative painting
[彩]色/[顏]色　color
彩色反转胶片/彩色逆轉軟片　color reverse film
彩色红外胶片/彩色紅外線軟片　color infrared film
彩色混凝土/彩色混凝土　color cement concrete
彩色胶片/彩色軟片　color film, autochrome
彩色沥青/彩色瀝青　colored asphalt
彩色沥青混凝土路面/彩色瀝青混凝土路面　colorful asphalt concrete pavement
彩色路面/著色路面　colored pavement
彩色人行道/彩色人行道　color footway
彩色体/彩色體　color body
彩色透水混凝土/彩色透水混凝土　color pervious concrete
彩色透水沥青/帶色透水瀝青,著色透水瀝青　color porous asphalt
彩色涂层钢板/彩色鋼板　colored coating steel sheet
彩色纹影仪/顏色紋影法　color schlieren system
彩叶植物/彩葉植物　color-leafed plant
踩/踩　cai
参比电极/參比電極,參考電極　reference electrode
参考尺寸/參考尺寸　reference dimension
参考当量/參考當量　reference equivalent
参考面/參考面,基準面　reference surface, reference plane
参考谱/參考譜　reference spectrum
参考椭球/參考橢球體　reference ellipsoid
参考桩/參考樁　recovery peg
参数辨识/參數識別　parameter identification
参数不均匀率/參數不匀率　parameter non-uniform rate
参数化设计/參數化設計　parametric design
参数监控/參數監測　parameter monitoring
参数设定/參數設定　parameter setting
参数水文学/參數水文學　parametric hydrology
参数诊断/參數診斷　parameter diagnosis
参与性评估/參與性評估　participation assessment
参与性设计/參與式設計　participatory design
参与因数/參與因數　participant factor
参与应力/參與應力　participating stress
参照标准/參考標準　reference standard

参照建筑/參照建築　reference building
餐车/餐車　dining car
餐厨垃圾处理厂/廚餘廢棄物處理廠　food waste treatment plant
餐具/食器　eating utensils
餐室/餐室　dining room
餐厅/餐廳　dining room, dining hall
残差/殘[餘誤]差　residual error, residual
残车率/殘車率　rate of bad order cars
残积土/殘餘土　residual soil
残留黏土/殘餘黏土　residual clay soil
残留响应区/殘留響應區　residual response zone
残水旋塞/排洩旋塞　drain cock
残损鉴定/貨損檢驗　survey on damage to cargo
残碳值/殘留碳　carbon residue
残压/殘餘電壓,剩餘電壓　residual voltage
残油标准排放/殘油標準排洩　residual oil standard discharge connection
残余边带发射/殘邊帶發射　vestigial-sideband emission
残余变形/殘留形變　residual deformation
残余电流/殘餘電流,剩餘電流　residual current
残余废气/殘留氣體,剩餘氣　residual gas
残余废气系数/殘氣係數　coefficient of residual gas
残余孔隙水压力/殘餘孔壓力　residual pore pressure
残余气体分析仪/殘餘氣體分析器　residual gas analyzer
残余强度/殘餘強度,剩餘強度　residual strength
残余危险/殘餘危害　residual hazard
残余氧/餘氧　residual oxygen
残余应变/殘留應變　residual strain
残余应力/殘留應力　internal stress, residual stress
残雨/殘雨　residual rain
残渣油/殘油　residual fuel oil
仓储费/倉儲費　storage charge
仓储建筑/倉儲建築　industrial warehouse building, storage building
仓储区/倉儲區,倉庫區　warehouse district
仓储用地/倉儲用地,倉庫用地　land for warehouse, warehouse land
仓储用地规划/儲存空間土地利用規劃　warehouse land-use planning
仓库/倉庫,儲藏室　warehouse, storage
仓库交货/倉庫交貨　delivery ex-warehouse
仓库面积使用率/倉庫面積使用率　storage area utilization ratio
仓库区/倉庫區　warehouse area, warehouse zone
苍古/蒼古,古代遺物,古代遺跡　antiquity

舱/艙　hold, compartment
舱壁/艙壁　bulkhead
舱壁板/艙壁板　bulkhead plate
舱壁防爆填料函/艙壁防爆填料函　anti-explosion bulkhead stuffing box
舱壁扶强材/艙壁防撓材　bulkhead stiffener
舱壁甲板/艙壁甲板　bulkhead deck
舱壁龛/艙壁凹入部　bulkhead recess
舱壁门/艙壁門　bulkhead door
舱壁图/艙壁圖　bulkhead plan
舱底泵/舭[水]泵　bilge pump
舱底水系统/舭水系統　bilge system
舱底水总管/舭水總管　bilge main, bilge main line
舱底污水/舭水,艙底水　bilge water
舱段/艙段　bay section
舱盖/艙蓋　hatch cover
舱盖布/艙口蓋布　hatch tarpaulin
舱盖曳行装置/艙蓋驅動設施　hatch cover driving device
舱口/艙口　hatch opening, hatchway
舱口吊杆/艙口吊桿　hatch boom
舱口端梁/艙口端梁　hatch end beam
舱口盖绞车/艙口蓋絞車,艙口蓋絞機　hatch cover winch
舱口活动横梁/艙口活動梁　hatch beam, portable hatch beam
舱口检验/艙口檢驗　hatch survey
舱口梁/艙口梁　hatch beam
舱口围板/艙口緣圍　hatch coaming
舱口悬臂梁/艙口側半梁　fork beam, hatch side cantilever beam
舱口压条/艙口壓條　hatch batten
舱口装卸指挥人/艙口裝卸指揮人　hatch man
舱口纵桁/艙口側縱梁　hatch side girder
舱门/艙門　cabin door
舱面货/艙面貨,甲板貨　deck cargo
舱面货提单/艙面載貨證券　on deck bill of lading
舱面属具/甲板裝具　deck fittings, deck equipment and fittings
舱内安装设备/裝於艙内之設備　internal mounted equipment
舱内保健设备/艙内健康照護設備　onboard health care facilities
舱内航天服/載具内太空衣　intravehicular space suit
舱内活动服/載具内活動服　intravehicular activity clothing, IVA clothing
舱内活动机器人/太空載具内活動機器人　intravehicular activity robot
舱内货/艙内貨　under-deck cargo
舱内设备/艙内設備　below deck equipment, BDE
舱内医监设备/艙内醫學監測儀器　onboard medical monitoring instrument
舱容图/容積圖,容量圖　capacity plan
舱容系数/貨艙係數　coefficient of hold
舱室/艙室　space
舱室布置/艙内布置　interior arrangement
舱室鉴定/艙室檢查　inspection of chamber
舱室设备/艙室設備　accommodation equipment
舱室属具/房艙屬具　cabin outfit
舱室通风机/艙室[通]風機,房艙通風機　cabin fan, cabin ventilator
舱外安装设备/裝於艙外之設備　externally mounted equipment
舱外航天服/載具外太空衣　extravehicular space suit
舱外活动/太空船外活動　extravehicular activity, EVA
舱外活动机器人/太空載具外活動機器人　extravehicular activity robot
舱外设备/艙面設備　above deck equipment, ADE
舱位登记簿/艙位簿　space book
舱效应/艙效應　chamber effect
舱压安全阀/座艙壓力減壓閥　cabin pressure relief valve
藏品档案室/採集檔案室　collection file room
藏品库区/藏品庫區　collection storage area
操场/操場,球場　sports field, playground
操舵/操舵　steering
操舵拉杆/操舵桿　steering rod
操舵链/舵鏈　steering chain
操舵轮/舵輪　steering wheel
操舵罗航向/駕駛羅經航向　steering compass course
操舵罗经/駕駛羅經　steering compass
操舵目标灯/拖航燈　steering light
操舵试验/操舵試驗　steering test
操舵室/駕駛室　wheel house
操舵索/操舵鋼索　steering wire
操舵台/操舵臺　steering stand
操舵遥控传动装置/操舵液壓遙控裝置　steering telemotor
操舵轴/操舵軸　steering shaft, steering shafting
操舵装置/操舵裝置,操舵機　steering apparatus, steering gear
操艇/操艇　boating
操纵部位转换/控制位置轉換　transfer of control station

操纵导数/控制導數　control derivative
操纵灯号/操縱號燈　maneuvering light signal
操纵杆/操縱桿,控制桿　control rod, joystick
操纵机构/操縱機構,轉向機構　steering unit
操纵缆/操縱線　steering line
操纵力/操縱[控制]力　control force
操纵力和位移/操縱[控制]力和位移　control force and displacement
操纵链/操縱鏈　maneuvering chain
操纵能力受限船/操縱能力受限船　vessel restricted in her ability to maneuver
操纵期望参数/操縱期望參數　control anticipation parameter, CAP
操纵失灵/操縱失靈　out of command
操纵失灵号灯/操縱失靈號燈　out of command light
操纵台/操作控制臺　operating console
操纵限制灯/操縱限制燈　restricted maneuver light
操纵信号/操縱信號,運轉信號　maneuvering signal
操纵信号灯/操船信號燈　maneuvering light
操纵性/操縱性[能],運轉能力　maneuverability, controllability
操纵性衡准/操縱性準則,操縱性標準　criteria of maneuverability
操纵性识别/操縱性識別　maneuverability identification
操纵性试验/操縱性試驗　maneuverability test
操纵性试验水池/操縱性試驗池　maneuvering tank
操作/操作　handling
操作测试程序/操作試驗程式　operation test program, OTP
操作程序/操作程式　operation sequence
操作飞行程序/任務飛行程式　operational flight program, OFP
操作规程/操作規則　operation rule
操作规则/操作規則　operation rule
操作级/操作級　operational level
操作空间/操作空間　operational space
操作力测定/操作力測定,作用力測定　operating force measurement
操作模式/操作模式　operation mode
操作时间/操作時間　operating time
操作说明/操作說明　operating instruction
操作说明书/操作説明書　operation manual
操作污染/操作汙染　operational pollution
操作行程测定/操作距離測定　operating distance measurement
操作与设备手册/操作與設備手冊　operations and equipment manual

操作员/航空器使用人,航空運送人,航空器營運人　operator
操作指令/操作指令　operational command
操作准备/操作準備　operational readiness
糙率/粗度係數　coefficient of roughness
槽/槽　groove, slot
槽齿连接/階式接頭　step joint
槽钢/槽鋼　channel steel
槽钢顶梁/槽形材　channel bar
槽化交口/槽化交口　channalized intersection
槽化线/槽化線　channelizing-line marking
槽孔模片板/長孔樣板　slotted templet
槽口接头/槽舌接合　rabbet joint
槽内处理法/池槽處理　tank treatment
槽式列车/槽式列車　bunker train
槽式输送链/環鏈輸送機　trough-chain conveyor
槽探/槽探　trench test, trenching
槽线/槽線　trough line
槽形板/槽形板　channel slab, trough plate
槽形玻璃/槽形玻璃,U型玻璃　U shape glass
槽形梁/槽形梁　channel beam
槽型舱壁/波形艙壁　corrugated bulkhead
槽型梁/槽型梁,槽形梁　trough girder
草/草　grass
草本/草本　herb
草本地被植物/草本植物區　herbaceous plant
草本植被/草本植被　herbaceous vegetation
草场退化/草地退化　grassland degradation
草丛/草叢　tussock
草地/草地,草原　grassland, grass land
草地改良/草地改良　grassland improvement
草地开发/草地開發　grassland development
草地沙化/草原土地沙化　grassland sandification
草地生态学/草原生態學　grassland ecology
草甸/草甸,濕草原　meadow
草甸草原/濕貧草原,草甸-乾草原植被區　meadow steppe
草甸土/濕草原土　meadow soil
草垫/草墊　hay layer
草栿/草栿　rough beam, caofu
草花/草花　herb flower
草木灰/草木灰　plant ash
草皮/草皮　turf
草坪/草坪　lawn
草坪打孔/草坪打孔　punched on the lawn
草坪打孔机/草坪打孔機,草坪衝孔機　lawn punching machine
草坪岛/草坪島　lawn island

草坪灯/草坪燈　lawn lamp
草坪混播/草坪混播　lawn mixed sowing
草坪机/草坪機　lawn comber
草坪交播/草坪加播　lawn over seeding
草坪绿色期/草坪綠色期　lawn green period
草坪区/草坪區　lawn space
草坪上肥器/草坪加肥器　lawn feeder
草坪扬声器/草坪揚聲器　lawn loudspeaker
草坪植物/草坪植物　lawn plant
草坪质地/草坪質地　lawn texture
草绳/草繩　straw rope
草图/草圖　sketch
草药花坛/草藥花壇　herbaceous flower bed
草原/草原　steppe
草原景观/草原景觀　prairie landscape
草原生态系统/草原生態系統　prairie ecosystem
草原式住宅/草原式住宅　prairie house
草原土壤/草原土　steppe soil
册页[客]票/優待票　coupon ticket
厕所/廁所　lavatory, toilet
侧摆振动/橫擺振動　swaying vibration
侧板/側板　side sheet
侧壁导洞法/側壁導坑法,雙側導坑法　side heading method
侧壁导坑/側壁斜坑　side wall drift
侧壁导坑法/側壁導坑法,雙側導坑法　side heading method
侧壁气垫船/側壁式氣墊船　side waller, sidewall hovercraft
侧窗/側窗　side window
侧道/側道,臨街道路　frontage roadway
侧灯/側燈　side lamp
侧方交会/側方交會法　lateral intersection
侧风/側風　cross wind, sidewind
侧滚振动/橫滾振動　rolling vibration
侧护栏/側面保護　side protection
侧滑/外側滑　side skidding
侧滑角/內側滑角　angle of sideslip
侧缓冲器/側邊緩衝器　side-buffer
侧架立柱/側框架柱　side frame column
侧架上弦杆/側框架上弦桿　side frame top chord
侧架上斜弦杆/側框架上斜弦桿　side frame top oblique chord
侧架弹簧承台/側框架彈簧座　side frame spring seat
侧架下弦杆/側框架下弦桿　side frame bottom chord
侧架下斜弦杆/側框架下斜弦桿　side frame bottom oblique chord
侧脚/側腳　inclination of the corner column, cejiao
侧净空/兩側清除區　side clearway
侧开门箱/側開貨櫃　open side container
侧开泥驳/側漏斗型駁船　side hopper barge
侧靠式渡船/側靠式渡船　side mooring ferry boat
侧廊/走道,通道　aisle
侧力/側[向]力,橫向力　side force, maglev lateral force
侧梁/側梁　side sill
侧流堰/側流堰　side-flow weir
侧门/側門　side door
侧面标志/側面標誌　lateral mark
侧面采光/側面採光,側窗採光　side daylighting
侧面基地线/側面基地線　side lot line
侧面集装箱叉车/側面貨櫃叉車　side container fork lift
侧面角焊缝/側面填角焊接　fillet weld in parallel shear
侧面摩擦/側面摩擦　side friction
侧面燃烧/側面燃燒　side burning
侧模/側模　side form
侧排油阀/側排油閥　side oil outlet valve
侧偏修正角/側偏修正角　windage jump correction angle
侧墙/側牆,側壁,邊牆　side wall
侧墙包板/外側牆板　side sheathing
侧倾车体/可傾式車體　tilting type car body
侧倾轨条/側傾軌條　canted rail
侧渠/側運渠　side canal
侧扫声呐/水平掃描聲納　side scan sonar
侧设望远镜/側望遠鏡　side telescope
侧蚀/橫向沖蝕　lateral erosion
侧视范围/側視範圍　swath steering range
侧视雷达/側視雷達　side-looking radar, SLR
侧视图/側視圖　lateral view, side view
侧台/側臺　side stage
侧庭/側院　side yard
侧推器/側推器,推力裝置　thruster, side thruster
侧限抗压强度试验/側限抗壓強度試驗　confined compression strength test
侧限压缩模量/側限壓縮模量,體側限壓縮模量　constrained modulus, oedometric modulus
侧限压缩试验/圍限壓縮試驗　confined compression test
侧向暗沟/汙水支管　lateral sewer
侧向传声/側向傳播　flanking transmission
侧向反射声/側向反射　lateral reflection

侧向轨道发散火箭/側向彈道發散火箭　lateral trajectory divergence rocket
侧向加速度/橫向加速度　lateral acceleration
侧向碰撞/側面衝撞　side collision
侧向视野/側向視野　field of lateral vision
侧向水平联结系/側向水平聯結系　lateral bracing
侧向土压力/側向土壓力　lateral earth pressure
侧向推力装置/側推裝置　side thrust device
侧向稳定[性]/橫向穩定性　lateral stability
侧向最小安全间距/橫向最低安全間隙　minimum safe lateral clearance
侧斜/[螺]葉歪斜　skew back
侧斜角/[螺葉]歪斜角度　skew angle
侧压堰/側壓堰　weir with end-contraction
侧堰/側堰　slide weir
侧移式舱盖/側滾式艙蓋　side rolling hatch cover
侧移式舱口盖/側移式艙口蓋　side rolling hatch cover
侧音/側音,旁調　side tone
侧音测距/側音測距　side tone ranging
侧院/側院　side yard
侧院线/側院線　side yard line
侧枝/側枝　lateral branch
侧置驾驶杆/側控制桿　side control stick
侧柱/側柱　side post
侧柱连铁/側柱連鐵　side post connecting rail
侧柱内补强/側柱內補強　inside reinforcement of side post
侧撞/側撞　conering
测爆/測定爆發界限　measuring the explosive limit
测爆仪/測爆儀　explosimeter
测冰仪/冰川儀　glaciometer
测波标杆/波高桿　wave staff
测波仪/測波儀　wave gage
测长/測長　distance-to-coupling measurement
测地分系统/大地子系統　geodetic subsystem
测地卫星/測地衛星　geodetic satellite
测点/[觀]測點　observation point, survey point
测定/測流　gauging
测定值/測定值　measured value
测段/測段　segment of survey
测缝计/裂縫探測儀　crack gage, crack meter
测缝仪/量縫計　joint meter
测功器/測功計　dynamometer
测管水头线/靜壓管頭線　piezometric head line
测轨精度/測軌精度　orbit measuring precision
测厚/測厚　thickness measuring
测厚规/測厚規,厚度規,測隙規　thickness gage
测厚仪/測厚規,厚度規,測隙規　thickness gage
测绘/測繪,測量製圖　surveying and mapping
测绘仪/測量儀器　surveying instrument
测角/測角　angle measurement
测角精度/角精確度　angle accuracy
测角器/測角器,測向器,量角器　goniometer
测角误差/測角誤差　angle error
测距尺/塔尺,箱尺　telemeter rod
测距环/測距光網　ranging reticle
测距精度/全距精確度　range accuracy
测距门/測距閘門　distance measuring gate
测距频闪效应/測距頻閃效應　distance measuring stroboscopic effect
测距误差/誤差概率,距誤　range error
测距系统/測距系統　ranging system
测距仪/測距儀　range finder, distance measuring equipment
测距应答器/地面參考站臺　DME transponder
测控/追蹤,遙測和指令　tracking telemetry and command, TT and C
测控保障系统/TT&C 支援系統　supporting system for TT and C
测控仿真系统/TT&C 模擬系統　TT and C simulation system
测控分系统/TT&C 子系統　tracking telemetry and command subsystem, TT and C subsystem
测控覆盖率/TT&C 有效區　TT and C coverage
测控计划/TT&C 計劃　TT and C plan
测控任务/TT&C 任務　TT and C task
测控任务分析/TT&C 任務分析　TT and C task analysis
测控软件/TT&C 軟體　TT and C software
测控实时软件/TT&C 即時軟體　TT and C real-time software
测控事件/TT&C 事件　TT and C event
测控事件序列/TT&C 程式　sequence of TT and C event, TT and C procedure
测控网仿真/TT&C 網路模擬　TT and C network simulation
测控系统/TT&C 系統　TT and C system
测控系统工程/TT&C 系統工程　TT and C system engineering
测控要求/TT&C 要求　TT and C requirement
测控应用软件/TT&C 應用軟體　TT and C application software
测控站/TT&C 站　TT and C station
测控站计算机/TT&C 站電腦　TT and C station computer

测控总体设计/TT&C系统設計　TT and C system design
测控坐标系/TT&C坐標系　coordinate system used in TT and C
测力计/測功計　dynamometer
测力柱/測力柱　load measurement column
测量/測量,量測,測流　survey, measurement, gauging
测量标志/測量標記　surveying marker
[测量]标准/[量測]標準　measurement standard
[测量]标准的保持/[量測]標準的保存　conservation of measurement standard
测量表/量表　measuring watch
[测量]不确定度/[量測]不準確度　uncertainty of measurement
测量程序/量測程式　measurement procedure
测量重复性/測量重複性　repeatability of measurement
测量船/測量船,測量艦　surveying ship, instrumentation ship
测量船配置/測量船配置　instrumentation ship location
[测量]单位/[量測]單位　unit of measurement
[测量]单位符号/[量測]單位符號　symbol of a unit of measurement
[测量]单位制/[量測]單位制　system of units of measurement
测量单元/測定單位　measuring unit
[测量的]算术平均值/[量測]算術平均值　arithmetic average of measurement
测量对象/量測對象　measuring object
测量范围/量測範圍　measurement range
测量方法/測計方法,量測方法　measuring means, method of measurement
测量放样/測量放樣　staking out in survey
测量飞机/測量飛機　instrumentation airplane
[测量]估计值/[量測]估計值　estimate of measurement
测量过程/量測過程　measurement process
测量过程控制/量測過程式控制　measurement process control
测量技术/量測技術　measurement technique
测量结果/量測結果　result of a measurement
[测量结果的]重复性/[量測結果]重複性　repeatability of results of measurement
[测量结果的]复现性/[量測結果]重現性　reproducibility of results of measurement
测量精度/測量精度　survey precision, precision of survey
测量精密度/量測精密度　precision of measurement
测量雷达/儀表級雷達　instrumentation radar
测量链/量測鏈　measuring chain
[测量器具的]示值/[量測儀器]示值　indication of a measuring instrument
测量设备/量測設備　measuring equipment
测量设备特性/量測設備特性　characteristics of measuring equipment
[测量]统计量/[量測]統計量　statistic quantity of measurement
[测量]误差/[量測]誤差　error of measurement
测量系统/量測系統　measuring system
测量线路/測量線路　running line
测量相机/太空測量攝影機　space-born metric camera
测量信号/量測信號　measurement signal
测量信息加工/測量資訊處理　measurement information processing
测量信息接收/測量資訊接收　measurement information receive
测量样本/量測樣本　measurement sample
测量仪表/測量儀表　measuring instrument
测量元素/測量元件　measurement element
测量原理/量測原理　principle of measurement
测量站配置/測站位置　station location
测量准确度/量測準確度　accuracy of measurement
测量总体/量測全體　measurement population
测量组/測量隊　surveying party
测流断面/觀測斷面　hydrometric section
测扭机构/扭力矩測量機構　torque-measuring mechanism
测坡度尺/側坡水尺　slope gage
测深/測深　sounding, depth sounder
测深潮汐订正/測深訂正潮汐　tidal reduction for soundings
测深尺/測深標尺　sounding rod, sounding scale
测深锤/測深[鉛]錘　sound lead, sounding lead, hand lead
测深导航/測深航法　bathymetric navigation
测深杆/測深桿,涉水桿　wading rod
测深管/測深管　sounding pipe
测深机/測深機　sounding machine
测深绳/測深[鋼]繩,測深索　sounding line, sounding wire
测深线/測深繩,測深索　sounding line
测深仪/測深機　sounding machine
测深仪误差/回聲測深儀誤差　echo sounder error

测绳/測繩　measuring rope
测试/測試,試驗　testing
CAMAC 测试/CAMAC 測試　CAMAC test
测试报告/試驗報告　test report
测试参数/測試參數　test parameter
测试程序/試驗計劃　test program
测试点/試驗點　test point
测试段/測試段　measuring section
测试发射操作规程/測試發射操作規則　test-launch operation rules
测试发射预案/測試發射預先計劃　test-launch preplan
测试范围/測試範圍　test area
测试方法/測試方法,試驗法　test method
测试方式/測試模式　test mode
测试分析技术/試驗分析技術　test and analysis technology
测试工作台/測試工作臺　test table
测试环境/測試環境　test environment
测试环路/測試回路　test loop
测试记录/測試記錄　test record
测试技术/測試技術　test technology
测试检查程序/基準常式　benchmark routine, test and check program
测试逻辑/試驗邏輯　test logic
测试目标/測試目標　test target
测试软件/測試軟體　test software
测试设备/試驗裝備　test equipment, test facility
测试设备转运/測試設施轉移　test facility transfer
测试实验室/試驗實驗室　test laboratory
测试数据/試驗數據　test data
测试顺序/試驗程式　test sequence
测试台/測試臺,校驗臺　test desk
测试图形/測試圖形,試驗圖形,試驗型式　test pattern
测试[协调]组/測試組　test coordination team
测试性/可测试性　testability
测试性设计/可測試性設計　testability design
测试仪/測試器　tester
测试指标/測試規格　test specification
测试中心/測試中心　test center
测速/速率試驗,速率試航,速度量測　speed trial, speed measurement
测速板/測速板　chip log
测速场/測速場　speed trial ground
测速发电机/測速發電機　tachogenerator
测速精度/距離變率精確度　range rate accuracy
测速误差/距離變率誤差　range rate error

测温传感器/高溫計傳感器　pyrometer probe
测向灵敏度/方探靈敏度　direction finder sensitivity
测向仪/測向儀　direction finder
测斜仪/測斜儀,傾角計　inclinometer
测压高度/測壓高度　piezometric height
测压排管/測壓排管　pressure rake
测压水头/測壓管水頭　piezometric head
测压元件/測力器　load cell
测氧仪/氧氣分析器　oxygen analyser
测液深标尺/量液深尺　dipstick
测站/測站,測點,儀器站　instrument station, survey station
测者能见地平距离/視程　visible range
[测者]子午圈/天子午線　celestial meridian
测针/點尺　point gage
测重/測重　weight sensing
测阻/測阻　rollability measurement
层/[地]層,皺度　stratum, rugosity
A 层/A 層位　A Horizon
B 层/B 層位　B Horizon
C 层/C 層位　C Horizon
层板胶合结构/多層膠合木料結構　glued laminated timber structure
层板式喷注器/層板式噴注器　platelet injector
层板叶片/積層葉片　laminated blade
层次分析/層次分析　hierarchical analysis
层叠式结构/層疊式結構　piling mode
层高/層高　story height
层合玻璃/層合玻璃　laminated glass
层积云/層積雲　stratus-cumulus
层间剪切/層間剪切　interlaminar shear
层间剪切强度/層間剪切強度,積層間剪強度　interlaminar shear strength
层间水/中間層水　intermediate water
层间位移/層間變位　storey drift
层间应力/層間應力　interlaminar stress
层理/層理　stratification
层流/層流　laminar flow
层流边界层/層流邊界層　laminar boundary layer
层流分离/層流分離　laminar separation
层流机翼/層流翼　laminar flow wing
层流速度/層流速度　laminar velocity
层流翼/層流翼　laminar flow wing
层流翼型/層流翼[切]形　laminar flow aerofoil profile, laminar flow airfoil profile
层铺法/層鋪法　layer spread method
层砌琢石/層砌工　rangework
层燃锅炉/爐箅鍋爐　grate fired boiler, stoker fired

层石砌体/層砌圬工　coursed masonry
层位/層列　tier
层位分类法/層位分類法　pedological classification
层屋顶/網格殼屋面　lamella roof
层压板/膠合板　laminated board
层压成形/層壓成形　laminating molding
层压塑料[制品]/疊合塑膠板　laminated plastic
层云/層雲　stratus
层状腐蚀/層[狀腐]蝕　layer corrosion
层状土/層狀土壤,分層土壤,成層土　stratified soil, laminated soil
叉槽/叉槽　fork pocket
叉车装载机/堆高機　forklift truck, forklift loader
叉道法/叉道法　passing track method
叉簧/鉤形電鍵,鉤頭轉轍器　hook switch
叉手/叉手　inverted V-shaped brace, chashou
叉丝/十字絲　cross-hairs
叉形环/叉形環　fork ring
叉柱造/叉柱造　chazhuzao
叉桩/叉樁　brace pile, coupled batter pile
差别运价/差別運價　differential rate
差错恢复/錯誤復原　error recovery
差错检测/錯誤檢測　error detection
差错控制/誤差控制,錯誤控制　error control
差错漏检率/殘餘誤差率　residual error-rate
差定温探测器/固定昇溫檢測器　rate-of-rise fixed temperature detector
差动操纵摇臂/差動操縱搖臂　differential control crank arm
差动打桩锤/差動樁錘　differential acting pile-hammer
差动舵/差動舵　Jenckel rudder
差动滑轮/差動滑輪組　differential pulley block
差动平尾/差動尾翼,尾部昇降副翼　differential tailplane, taileron
差动油缸/差動氣缸　differential cylinder
差分 GPS/差分全球定位系統　differential GPS, DGPS
差分奥米伽/差分亞米茄　differential Omega
差分测定/差分測定　differential determination
差分测量/差分測量　differential measurement
差分定位/差分定位　differential positioning
差分格式/差分格式　difference scheme
差分观测/較差觀測　differential observation
差分脉码调制/差動式脈衝碼調變　differential pulse-code modulation
差分全球定位系统/差分[式]全球定位系統　differential global positioning system, differential GPS, DGPS
差分调制/微分調變　differential modulation
GPS 差分相位测量/全球定位系統差分相位測量　GPS differential phase measurement
差分移相键控/微分相移鍵控　differential phase shift keying, DPSK
差积曲线/累積殘餘曲線　residual mass curve
差热分析/[示]差熱分析,差[分]熱分析　differential thermal analysis
差压铸造/反壓鑄造　counter pressure casting
差转电台/無線電中繼設備　radio repeating set
差转罗兰 C/差分羅遠 C　differential Loran-C
插拔桩状态/插拔樁狀態　spud driving and pulling condition
插板/閘板　stop log
插板支护/打插板法　inserting plate support, forepoling
插阀/插閥　insert valve
插花/插花　flower arrangement
插花艺术/插花藝術　flower arrangement art
插接/疊接　splicing
插接不良/插接不良　plug-in trouble
插接钢筋/起動桿　starter bar
插接式母线/保護式絕緣母線,封閉式絕緣母線,密集式絕緣母線　plug-in busbar
插孔/插口,插座　jack
插孔排/撐扳條　jack strip
插泥灯/插泥燈　insert mud lamp, mud spotlight
插入机构/引入系統　injection system
插入式混凝土振捣器/插入式混凝土振搗器　immersion type vibrator for concrete
插入式混凝土振动器/插入式混凝土路面振動整實器　internal concrete vibrator
插入式继电器/插入式繼電器　plug-in type relay
插入式振捣器/内部震動機　poker vibrator
插入损耗/插入損耗,介入損失　insertion loss
插入箱/插入箱　insert section
[插]塞/[插]塞,插頭　plug
插穗/插條　cuttings
插削/插削　slotting
插值/内插　interpolation
插座/電源插座　power socket
茶馆/茶藝館　tea house
茶炉/茶水鍋爐　drinking water boiler
茶室/茶藝館　tea house
茶亭/茶亭　tea booth, tea kiosk
茶桌/茶幾　tea table

查号台/查詢檯,詢問檯　information desk
查核与管制/查核與管制　verification and control
查询/詢訊,輪詢　polling
查兹沃斯园/德比夏園　Chatsworth Park, Derbyshire Park
岔道标志/岔道標誌　cross buck sign
岔线/分歧線,支線　spur track
岔心角/叉心角　frog angle
岔枕/岔枕　switch tie, turnout tie
岔中绝缘/岔中絕緣　insulated joint within a turnout
拆除机/拆除工具　demolisher
拆除模板/脱型,拆模　form removal
拆除模壳/脱型,拆模　form removal
拆船/拆船　shipbreaking
拆建比/拆建比　demolition and construction ratio
拆模/拆模　removal of form
拆迁/拆遷,拆除　remove, demolition
拆迁安置/拆遷安置　demolition and resettlement
拆迁补偿/安遷救濟金　relocation compensation, compensation for removal
拆箱间/開箱室　unpacking room
[拆卸]检修/檢修,大修,翻修　overhaul
拆验/拆檢　examination of opened up parts, open-up examination
拆装家具/拆裝家具　furniture disassembly
拆装式桁架/可拆卸的桁架　demountable truss
柴捆/柴捆束　fagot
柴捆坝/柴捆壩　fagot dam
柴捆护岸/柴排護岸　faggotting
柴笼护岸/柴排護岸　faggotting
柴排/柴排,沈排　mattress, willow fascine, firewood raft
柴-燃联合动力装置/柴油燃氣渦輪組合機　combined diesel and gas turbine power plant
柴油沉淀柜/柴油沈澱櫃　diesel oil settling tank
柴油锤打桩架/柴油捶打椿架　diesel hammer pile driving frame
柴油打桩机/柴油打樁機,柴油椿錘　diesel pile driver
柴油电动挖掘机/柴油電動鏟土機　diesel-electric shovel
柴油发电机/柴油發電機　diesel dynamo, diesel generator, diesel engine generator
柴油发电机室/柴油發電機艙　diesel generator room
柴油发电机组/柴油發電機組　diesel generating set
柴油机/柴油機,柴油引擎,狄塞爾引擎　diesel engine
柴油机爆燃/柴油機爆震　engine detonation

柴油机齿轮传动/柴油機齒輪傳動　diesel geared drive
柴油机船/柴油機船,內燃機船　diesel boat, diesel ship, motor ship
柴油机电力传动/柴油機電力傳動　diesel-electric drive
柴油机电力推进装置/柴油[機]電力推進裝置　diesel-electric propulsion plant
柴油机动力装置/柴油機動力裝置　diesel engine power plant
柴油机负荷图/柴油機負載圖　engine load diagram
柴油机机油/柴油機潤滑油　diesel engine lubricating oil
柴油机净重/柴油機淨重　net weight of diesel engine
柴油机排烟/柴油機排煙　diesel smoke
柴油机喷油泵试验台/柴油機噴油泵試驗臺　diesel fuel injection pump tester
柴油机喷油定时测定器/柴油機噴油定時測定器　diesel injection timing tester
柴油机起动试验/柴油機起動試驗　diesel engine starting test
柴油机特性/柴油機特性　diesel engine characteristic
柴油机通气管工作装置/柴油機通氣管裝置　snort, snorkel
柴油机烟度计/柴油機排煙濃度計　diesel smoke meter
柴油机运转范围图/柴油機運轉範圍圖　engine layout diagram
柴油机支座/柴油機支架　engine support
柴油机转速表/柴油機轉速計　diesel engine tachometer
柴油起重机/柴油起重機　diesel crane
柴油-燃气联合动力装置/柴油機-燃氣渦輪機動力裝置　diesel and gas turbine power plant
柴油日用柜/柴油日用櫃　diesel oil daily tank
柴油推土机/柴油鏟土機　diesel shovel
柴油指数/柴油指數　diesel index
柴油主机气动遥控系统/柴油主機氣力遥控系統　pneumatic remote control system for main diesel engine
柴油桩锤/柴油椿錘,柴油打椿機　diesel pile hammer
觇牌水平尺/覘標式水準尺　target staff
掺混气/混合氣體　mixed gas
掺混区/混合區　dilution zone
掺加料/摻合物　admixture
掺锂太阳电池/滲鋰太陽電池　lithium-doped solar cell

掺炭炼钢/摻炭煉鋼　gas carburising
缠绕结构/纏繞結構　winding structure
缠绕类攀缘植物/攀緣植物　twine of climbing plant
缠绕植物/纏繞植物　twining plant
缠腰/纏腰　auxiliary eave, chanyao
缠扎/紮縛　seizing
缠柱造/纏柱造　chanzhuzao
产房/產房　delivery department
产量潜力/出量勢　potential yield
产卵场/產卵場　spawning ground
产率系数/產率係數　yield coefficient
产品保证/產品保證　product assurance
产品保证大纲/產品保證計劃　product assurance program
产品履历书/產品記錄表　product log
产品模型数据交换标准/產品模型數據交換規範　standard for exchange of product model data, STEP model data
产品水/淡化水　product water
产品责任/產品責任　product liability
产品证明书/產品證書　product certificate
产品组装/產品組裝　article assembly
产沙量/泥沙產量　sediment yield
产水量/出水量　water yield
产业布局/產業分布,工業分布　industrial distribution
产业规划/工業規劃　industrial planning
产业集聚区/產業集聚區　industrial agglomeration area
产业集群/產業群聚　industrial cluster
产业结构/產業結構,工業結構　industrial structure
产业链/工業鏈　industry chain
产业园区/產業園區,工業園區　industrial park
产业转型/工業化轉型　industrial transformation
铲除拥包/鏟除擁包　upheaval leveling
铲斗/杓,鏟頭　dipper
铲斗式清岩机/鏟石機　rock shovel
铲斗挖沟机/環斗挖泥機　bucket ladder
铲斗挖泥船/戽斗挖泥船　bucket dredger, dipper dredger
铲斗转盘/鏟斗轉盤　turntable of dipper machine
铲投/鏟土作業　shovelling
铲土机配件/鏟土機配件　shovel attachment
铲扬机/鏟揚機　dipper machine
铲运机/鏟土機,刮土機　scraper, scoper, carrying scraper
铲运机铲斗/轉式刮土機　bowl of scraper, scraper bucket
阐明/判讀,研判,釋義　interpretation
颤动回声/顫動回聲　flutter echo
颤振/顫振,顫動,飄動　flutter
颤振简化模型/顫振简化模型　simplified model of flutter
颤振临界风速/顫振臨界風速　critical wind speed of flutter
颤振模型/顫振模型　flutter model
颤振模型试验/顫振模型試驗　flutter model test
颤振试验/顫振試驗　flutter test
颤振抑制控制/顫振控制　flutter suppression control
颤振余量/顫振邊限　flutter margin
长壁挖掘机/長壁挖掘機　long wall drill
长臂圆规/梁式圓規　beam compass
长波/長波　long wave
长波辐射/長波輻射　long wave radiation
长[插]接/長接　long splice
长城/長城　the Great Wall
长大笨重货物/長大笨重貨物　heavy and bulky goods
长大货物车/長大貨物車　oversize commodity car
长大坡道/長大下坡道　long steep grade, long heavy grade
长定子/長定子　long stator
长短大圆信号干扰/長短大圓信號干擾　interference between longer and shorter circle path signals
长吨/長噸　long ton
长方圆柱投影/長方圓柱投影　rectangle cylindrical projection
长分段式电弧加热器/長分段式電弧加熱器　long segment type arc heater
长峰波/長峰波　long crested waves
长钢轨运输作业列车/長鋼軌運輸作業列車　long welded rail transporting and working train
长轨条/長軌條　long rail string
长轨线路/長鋼軌運　long welded rail track
长货挂车/電桿拖車　pole trailer
长基线干涉仪/長基線干涉儀　long baseline interferometer
长件货/超長貨　lengthy cargo
长交路/長交路　long routing
长宽比/長寬比　length breadth ratio, length-breadth ratio
长期暴露装置/長期照射裝置　long duration exposure facility
长期重复性/長期重現性　long term repeatability
长期调查/長期調查　long time count
长期发展计划/長期發展計劃　long-range

development plan
长期刚度/長期剛度　long term stiffness
长期航天效应/長期太空飛行效應　long term space flight effect
长期力矩/長期力矩　secular torque
长期强度/長期強度　long term strength
长期摄动/長期擾動　secular perturbation
长期生态研究/長期生態研究　long term ecological research, LTER
长期试车/持久試車　endurance test
长期试验/長期實驗　long term experiment
长期稳定性/長期性穩定　long term stability
长期效应组合/長期效應組合　combination for long term action effects
长期雨量计/積時雨量計　totalizer
长日[照]植物/長日照植物　long day plant
长闪光/長閃光　long flash
长射式风洞/長射式風洞　long shot tunnel
长深比/長深比　length-depth ratio
长声/長聲　prolonged blast
长式提单/長式載貨證券　long form bill of lading
长隧道/長大隧道　long tunnel
长条形基础/長條基腳　long strip footing
长途半自动接续/長途半自動接續　toll semi-automatic dialling
长途半自动接续台/長途半自動接續臺　toll switchboard for semi-automatic operation
长途电话交换机/長途電話交換系統　toll telephone switching system
长途电话所/長途電話局　toll telephone office
长途电信枢纽楼/長途電信樞紐樓　long distance telecommunication center, hub building for long distance telecommunication
长途调度台/長途調度臺　trunk dispatcher switchboard
长途接续台/長途接續臺　manual toll switching board
长途客车/公路客運汽車　intercity bus
长途汽车[客运]站/長途客運汽車站　coach station, long distance bus station
长途通信网/長途通信網　toll communication network
长途业务台/長途[接續]和記錄臺　toll service desk
长途中继线/長途中繼線　toll junction line
长途自动电话/長途自動電話　toll automatic telephone
长途自动电话中继器/長途自動電話中繼器　toll automatic switching repeater
长途自动接续/長途自動接續　toll automatic dialling
长尾喷管/尾管噴嘴　tailpipe nozzle
长细比/細長比　slenderness ratio
长弦/長弦　long chord
长线法/長線法　long line method
长线台座成型/長線臺座成型　long line platform moulding
长线张拉台座/長線張拉臺座　stretching bed for longline production
长行程柴油机/長衝程柴油機　long-stroke diesel engine
长延时/長延時　long time delay
长远规划/長期方案　long-range programme
长枕木/長軌枕　long tie
长周期摄动/長週期攝動　long periodic perturbation
长轴/長軸　major axis
长柱试验机/長柱試驗機　long column testing machine
常陈一(猎犬α)/常陳一(獵犬α)　Cor Carole
常规处理/簡便方法　conventional treatment
常规能源/傳統能源　conventional energy
常规潜艇/傳統潛艇　conventional submarine
常规试验/標準試驗　normal test
常规太阳电池/常規太陽電池　conventional solar cell
常规通信信道/正常通信管道　general communication channels
常规推进剂/常規推進劑　conventional propellant
常规[推进剂]加注系统/常規推進劑加注系統　conventional propellant loading system
常规无线电通信/一般無線電通信　general radio communication
常规无线电业务/一般無線電業務　conventional radio service
常规育种技术/常規育種技術　classical breeding
常绿阔叶林/常綠闊葉林　evergreen broad-leaved forest, laurel forest, laurisilvae
常绿林/常綠林　evergreen forest
常绿绿篱/常綠綠籬　evergreen hedge
常绿乔木/常綠樹　evergreen tree
常绿树/常綠樹　evergreen tree
常绿针叶树/常綠針葉樹　evergreen conifer
常绿植物/常綠植物　evergreen plant
常摩擦式减震装置/常摩擦式減震裝置　constant friction type snubbing device
常年性热负荷/常年性熱負荷　year round heating load
常平座/環架懸浮組件　gimbal mount assembly

常设辅助人工照明/常時輔助人工照明　permanent supplementary artificial lighting
常设展厅/常設展廳,固定陳列展廳　permanent exhibition hall
常时微动/常時微動　usual environmental microvibration
常水头渗透试验/定水頭透水試驗法　constant head permeability test
常水位/常水位,中水位,平均水位　mean water level, normal water level stage, ordinary water level
常速/等速率　constant speed
常温连接器/常溫連接器　normal temperature connector
常压热水锅炉/常壓熱水鍋爐　atmospheric hot water boiler
常压碳化工艺/氣壓碳化法　atmosphere pressure carbonization process
常压蒸馏/常壓蒸餾　atmospheric distillation
常用闭塞制/常用閉塞制　regular block system
常用局减/常用局減　quick service
常用制动/行車制動　service braking, service application
常住人口/常住人口,居住人口　permanent population, resident population
常驻水位/滯留水位　standing water level
厂拌法/廠拌法　plant mixing method
厂拌混凝土/廠拌混凝土　plant-mixed concrete
厂界环境噪声/廠界雜訊標準　industrial enterprise noise
厂矿道路/廠礦道路　factory and mine road
厂内线/工業專線,商業專線　industry track
厂前区/廠前區　plant front area
厂区管道/廠用煤氣管　house service gas pipe
厂修/廠修　yard repair
场到场/貨櫃場到場　container yard to container yard, CY to CY
场地/場,位置,地點　site
场地标高/地面高程　ground elevation, land elevation
场地分析/建設場地分析　site analysis
场地复杂程度/場地複雜性　site complexity
场地覆盖层厚度/場地覆蓋層厚度　thickness of site soil layer, thickness of overburden layer
场地类别/場地類別　site category, site classification
场地平面图/基地計劃　site plan
场地平整/場地平整,現場工程,安裝工程　field engineering, site levelling, levelling of ground
场地土/場土　site soil
场地稳定性/場地穩定性　site stability
场地稳定性评价/廠址穩定性評估　site stability evaluation
场地误差/場地誤差　site error
场地振动衰减/場地振動衰減[量]　vibration attenuation of ground
场间联系电路/場間聯繫電路　liaison circuit between yards
场库/場庫　storage yard and warehouse
场面气压高度/場面氣壓高度　barometric altitude above airfield height
场强/場强[度]　field strength
场强测量/場强度量測　field strength measurement
场强测量仪/場强計　field strength meter
场强覆盖区/場强覆蓋區　field strength coverage
场强中值/場强度中值　median of field strength
场曲/像場彎曲　field curvature
场所/場所,地方　place
场所精神/場所精神　genius loci, place spirit
场所营造/場所營造　place making
场站收据/倉庫收貨單　dock receipt
敞顶集装箱/敞頂貨櫃,開頂貨櫃　open top container
敞开式厂房/敞開式廠房　opened industrial building
敞开式汽车库[存]/敞開式汽車庫　open garage
敞开式弹射/敞開彈射　open ejection
敞口管桩/開口管樁　open end pipe pile
敞口式桥/露天橋,開敞橋　open bridge
敞篷货车/敞車　open wagon
倡导性规划/倡導型規劃,倡導式規劃　advocacy planning
抄关/抄關　searching
抄网/抄網　dip net
超倍采样/超倍採樣　super-commutation
超标雨水行泄通道/超標雨水行洩通道　overland flow conveyance pathway for over-standard storm event
超波速流/超波速流　super-wave flow
超差/時角增量超差　excess of hour angle increment
超长超重列车/超長超重列車　exceptionally long and heavy train
超长货附加费/超長貨附加費　extra-length charge
超长货物/超長貨物　exceptional length freight
超长行程柴油机/超長衝程柴油機　super-long stroke diesel engine
超车/超車　overtaking
超车车道/超車車道,超越車道　overtaking lane,

passing lane
超车视距/超車視距　overtaking sight distance
超纯水/超純水　ultra pure water
超大货物/超大貨物　over-size goods
超大型发动机/超大型引擎　super large engine
超大型油轮/超大型原油輪,超級油輪　very large crude oil carrier, ultra large crude carrier, ULCC
超单元/超單元　hyperelement
超导电力推进装置/超導電力推進裝置　superconductor electric propulsion plant
超导电性/超導電性　superconductivity
超导发电机/超導發電機　superconducting generator
超导体/超導體　superconductor
超导体斥力/超導斥力　superconducting repulsion force
超导[性]金属/超導金屬　superconducting metal
超导悬浮系统/超導懸承系統　superconducting suspension system
超低空飞行/超低空飛行　super low altitude flight
超低碳钢/低碳鋼　dead mild steel
超低温预成形/超低溫預成形,極低溫預成形　super cryogenic preforming, super cryogenic temperature preforming
超短波通信/超短波通信　ultra short wave communication
超范围修理/超範圍修理　repair beyond the scope of repairing course
超负荷/過[量]負荷,過載,超載　overload
超负荷功率限/超載限制　overload limit
超负荷试验/超載試驗,過負荷試驗　overload test
超高层建筑/超高層建築　super high-rise building
超高递减距离/超高遞減距離　gradual-decrease distance
超高横坡度/超高順坡　superelevation slope
超高缓和段/超高緩和段　superelevation run off, attainment of superelevation
超高频/超高頻率　ultra high frequency
超高强度钢/超高強度鋼　ultra high strength steel
超高顺坡/超高坡度　superelevation slope
超高速风洞/超高速風洞　hypervelocity wind tunnel
超高速撞击/超高速衝擊　hypervelocity impact
超高速撞击试验/超高速撞擊試驗　hypervelocity impact test
超高效空气过滤器/超低滲透空氣過濾器　ultra low penetration air filter, ULPA filter
超高压锅炉/超高壓鍋爐　super high pressure boiler
超高真空/超高真空　ultra-high vacuum
超高真空物理气相沉积/超高真空物理氣相沈積　ultra-high vacuum physical vapor deposition
超高作业/超高作業　over height stacking operation
超功率事故/超功率事故　super-power accident
超固结比/過壓密比　overconsolidation ratio
超固结土/過壓密土　overconsolidated soil
超固结[作用]/過壓密　overconsolidation
超混杂复合材料/超混成複合材　super hybrid composite
超级市场/超級市場,超市　supermarket
超筋梁/超筋梁　overreinforced beam
超精加工/超精密加工　ultraprecision machining, UPM
超静定/超静定,静不定　statically indeterminate
超静定次数/静不定度　degree of statical indeterminacy
超静定桁架/静不定桁架　indeterminate truss
超静定结构/超静定結構,静不定結構　statically indeterminate structure
超静定力/超静定力,静不定力　statically indeterminate force
超静定梁/超静定梁,静不定梁　statically indeterminate beam
超静定桥梁结构/静不定橋梁結構　statically indeterminate bridge structure
超空化螺旋桨/超空化螺槳　super-cavitating propeller
超临界低温贮存/超臨界低溫儲存　supercritical cryogenic storage
超临界机翼/超臨界機翼　supercritical wing
超临界流/超臨界速流　supercritical flow
超临界速度/超臨界速度　supercritical velocity
超临界翼型/超臨界翼[切]形　supercritical aerofoil, supercritical airfoil profile
超滤/超過濾　ultra filtration
超扭保护装置/超扭[矩]保護設施　overtorque protection device
超前导坑/導向井,導坑　advance heading, pilot drift
超前锚杆/超前錨桿　advance anchor bolt
超前偏置控制/超前偏置控制　lead-bias control
超前探测/超前探測　forward probe
超前探眼/側部鑽孔　flank hole
超前支护/超前支護　advance support, forepoling, spiling
超轻骨料/超輕質骨材　super lightweight aggregate
超轻型飞机/超輕型飛機　ultralight airplane
超群/超群　super group
超群配线架/超群配線架　supergroup distribution frame

超燃冲压发动机/超音速燃燒衝壓發動機 scramjet engine
超深稳定土搅拌机/超深穩定土拌和機 super deep soil stabilizer
超渗雨/超滲雨量 rainfall excess
超声波/超音波 ultrasonic wave, ultrasound wave
超声波查漏仪/超音波偵漏器 ultrasonic leak detector
超声波车辆检测器/超音波車輛探測器 ultrasonic vehicle detector
超声波穿孔/超音波穿孔 ultrasonic perforating
超声波焊/超音波焊接 ultrasonic welding
超声波加工/超音波加工 ultrasonic machining
超声波加湿器/超音波加濕器 ultrasonic humidifier
超声[波]检测/超音波探測,超音波檢驗 ultrasonic testing, UT
超声波检查/超音波檢視 ultrasonic inspection
超声波清洗/超音波清潔 ultrasonic cleaning
超声波软钎焊/超音波軟焊 ultrasonic soldering
超声波探伤/超音波探傷 ultrasonic examination, ultrasonic flaw detection, ultrasonic testing
超声波探伤法/超音波探傷法 ultrasonic method
超声波探伤器/超音波探傷器 ultrasonic detector
超声波探伤仪/超音波探傷儀 ultrasonic flaw detector
超声-回弹综合检测仪/超音波回彈綜合探傷儀 ultrasonic rebound combined detector
超声脉冲测量仪/超音脈衝測量設備 ultrasonic pulse velocity measurement device
超声气体雾化粉末/超音波氣體霧化粉末 ultrasonic gas atomized powder
超声速风洞/超音速風洞 supersonic wind tunnel
超声速流/超音速流 supersonic flow
超声速平板烧蚀试验/超音速板燒蝕試驗 supersonic plate ablation test
超声速通流级/超音速通流級 supersonic through-flow stage
超声探伤/超音波檢視 ultrasonic inspection
超实时仿真/快速即時模擬 super-real-time simulation
超视距空空导弹/超視距空對空飛彈 beyond visual range air-to-air missile, BVRAAM
B超室/B超室,B型超聲[檢查]室 B-mode ultrasound room
超速/超速 overspeed
超速保护装置/超速保護設施 overspeed protection device
超速警告/超速警告 overspeed warning
超速调节器/超速調速器 overspeed governor
超速跳闸机构/超速跳掣機構 overspeed trip mechanism
超速停车装置/超速跳脱 overspeed trip
超塑成形/超塑性成形 superplastic forming
超塑化混凝土/超塑化混凝土 flowing concrete, superplastic concrete
超塑性/超塑性 superplasticity
超塑性成形-扩散连接/超塑性成形及擴散結合 superplastic forming and diffusion bond, SFDB
超塑性锻造/超塑性鍛造 superplastic forging
超挖/超挖 overbreak
超微粒子/超細顆粒 ultrafine particle
超温试车/超溫試驗 overtemperature test
超限货物/超限貨物 oversize or overweight goods, out-of-gage freight
超限货物等级/超限貨物等級 classification of out-of-gage freight
超限货物检查架/超限貨物檢查架 examining rack for out-of-gage freight
超压密/超壓密 overconsolidation
超音速/超音速 supersonic speed
超音速运输机/超音速飛機 supersonic transport
超远作业/超遠作業 over distance stacking operation
超越概率/超過機率 exceedance probability, probability of exceedance
超越角/超越角,預置角 overshoot angle, overshoot, preset angle
超载工况/意外之操作狀況 overriding operational condition
超载式挡土墙/負超載擋土牆 surcharged wall
超载预压/堆載預壓 surcharge preloading
超载重/超載重 surcharge load
超张拉/超限應力,過度拉伸 over stretching, over tensioning, overstretching
超障高度/障礙許可高度 obstacle clearance altitude, OCA
超折射/超折射 super-refraction
超重吊货/吊货超重 overload of a sling
超重货/逾重貨 heavy-lift cargo
超重货装卸费/逾重貨附加費 heavy-lift charge
超重力波/超重力波 ultra-gravity wave
超重索/起重索 derrick rope
超转离合器/超速離合器 overrunning clutch
超转试车/超速試驗 overspeed test
超自旋/超自旋 super spin
超钻/預鑽 subdrilling
潮波/潮波,潮浪 tidal wave

潮差/潮差　tidal range, tide range
潮差比/潮距率　range rate
潮高/潮高　height of tide
潮高比/潮高比　height rate
潮高差/潮高差　height difference
潮高基准面/潮汐基準面　tidal datum
潮间地/海浦地，低潮地　tidal land, tideland
潮龄/潮齡　tidal age
潮流/潮流　tidal stream, tidal current
潮流表/潮流表　tidal stream table
潮流冲刷/潮流掃洗現象　tidal flush
潮流界/潮流界　tidal current limit
潮流曲线/潮流曲線　current curve
潮流图/潮流圖　atlas of tidal stream, current diagram
潮面/潮面, 潮位　tide level
潮喷混凝土/半濕混凝土　half wet shotcreting
潮期/潮期　duration of tide
潮区界/潮汐界　tidal limit
潮区码头/潮水碼頭　tidal quay
潮湿/濕性　wetness
潮湿类型/潮濕類型　dampness type
潮湿试验/濕度試驗　humidity test
潮时差/潮時差　time difference of tide
潮水船坞/潮港　tidal dock
潮水发电站/潮力發電所　tidal power station
潮水水位/潮水位　tidal water level
潮水涨落/落潮流　ebb and flow
潮土/潮土　moisture soil
潮位/潮位, 潮面　tide level
潮位记录仪/潮位記錄儀　marigraph
潮位偏差/潮位偏差　deviation of tidal level
潮位曲线/潮位記錄圖　marigram
潮位站/檢潮所　tide-gage station
潮汐/潮[汐]　tide
潮汐岸壁式码头/潮水碼頭　tidal quay
潮汐表/潮汐表　tide table
潮汐常数/潮汐常數　tidal constant
潮汐发电站/潮力發電廠　tidal power plant
潮汐观测/潮位觀測　tidal observation
潮汐[海]图/潮汐圖　atlas of tides
潮汐河流/[感]潮河　tidal river
潮汐集中力/潮汐集中力　tide concentrating force
潮汐摄动/潮攝動　tide perturbation
潮汐调和常数/潮汐調和常數　tidal harmonic constant, harmonic constant of tide
潮汐系数/潮汐係數　tidal coefficient
潮汐效率/潮汐效率　tidal efficiency

潮汐信号/潮汐信號　tidal signal
潮汐周期/潮汐週期　tidal period
潮滞/高低潮時差　tidal lag
车场/車場　yard
车次/車次　serial number of bus run
车次表示/列車車次表示　train number indication
车挡/緩衝柱　bumper post
车档表示器/車用緩衝指示器　buffer stop indicator
车道/[單向行]車道　lane
车道方向控制信号/車道方向控制號誌　lane direction control signal
车道分布/車道分布　lane distribution
车道分界线/車道線　lane line, lane marking
车道荷载/車道載重　lane load
车道宽[度]/車道寬度　lane width, roadway width
车道偏移/車道偏移　lane shift
车道平衡/車道平衡　lane balance
车道收费机/車道收費機　lane toll machine
车道通行能力/車道容量　lane capacity
车道系数/車道係數　coefficient of lane
车道线/車道分界線, 交通行動線　traffic line
车道占有率/車道占有率　lane occupancy ratio
车道指示信号/車道指示號誌　lane indicating signal
车道纵梁/車道縱梁　roadway stringer
车底电线管/車底電線管　electric wire conduit underneath the car
车底数/車底數　number of allocated passenger trains
车电分线盒/連接盒, 接線盒　junction box
车顶/車頂　roof
车顶冰箱冷藏车/車頂冰箱冷藏車　overhead brine tank refrigerator car
车顶侧梁/車頂側梁　roof cant rail
车顶端横梁/車頂端橫梁　roof end rail
车顶横梁/車頂橫梁　roof cross beam
车顶弯梁/縱[向]襯梁　carline
车顶纵梁/檁條, 桁條　purline
车端缓冲器/車端緩衝器　end-of-car cushioning device
车队/車隊　platoon
车队核算/車隊核算　vehicle fleet accounting
车吨产量/車噸產量　annual output per vehicle tonnage capacity
车钩复原装置/車鉤復原裝置　coupler centering device
车钩缓冲停止器/車鉤緩衝停止器　device for stopping buffer action
车钩缓冲装置/車鉤緩衝裝置　coupler and draft gear

[车钩缓冲装置]压缩与拉伸/[車鈎緩衝裝置]壓縮與拉伸　coupler and draft gear running-in and running-out
车钩间隙/車鈎間隙　coupler slack
车钩连接线/車鈎連接線　coupling line
车钩轮廓/車鈎輪廓　coupler contour
车钩牵引力/拖桿拉力　tractive effort at coupler, drawbar pull
车钩三态作用/車鈎三態作用　three states of coupler operation
车钩托梁/車鈎托板,車鈎架,聯結器托架　coupler carrier
车钩中心线高度/鈎高　height of coupler center from top of rail, coupler height
车号/車號　number of car
车号抄录电视/車號抄録電視　TV for record vehicle number
车号灯/號數板燈　side number plate lamp
车号员无线电通信/車號員無線電通訊　radio communication for number taker
车架式起落架/車式起落架　bogie landing gear
车间/車間,工場,作坊　workshop
车间底漆/工場防銹底漆　shop primer
车间焊接/廠焊　shop welding
车间净距/行車間距　vehicular gap
车间可换件/車間可換件　shop replaceable unit, SRU
车间维修/車間維護　shop maintenance
车辆/車輛　vehicle
车辆报废/車輛報廢　vehicle scrapping
车辆报废限度/車輛報廢界限　car condemning limit
车辆标记/車輛標記　lettering and marking of car
车辆舱/車輛艙　vehicle hold
车辆长距比/車輛長距比　ratio of car body length to length between truck centers
车辆厂修/車輛廠修　car repair in work
车辆冲击/車輛衝擊　car impact
车辆冲击试验/車輛衝擊試驗　car impact test
车辆出行/車輛行程　vehicle travel
车辆存在监测器/車輛存在監測器　presence monitor
车辆大修/車輛大修　car heavy repair
车辆调拨/車輛調撥　vehicle allotment
车辆定距/車輛定距　length between truck centers
车辆动力学试验/車輛動力試驗　car dynamics test
车辆段/車輛段　car depot, vehicle depot
车辆段检修台位利用率/車輛段檢修臺位利用率　rate of utilization of repair positions in car depot
车辆段修/車輛段修　car repair in depot
车辆分散供电/車輛分散供電　separate power supply system for car
车辆封存/車輛封存　vehicle storing up
车辆辅修/車輛輔修　car auxiliary repair
车辆改造/車輛改造　vehicle remoulding
车辆感应信号/車輛感應號誌　vehicle actuated signal
车辆高度/車輛高度　height of car
车辆高度检测器/車高偵測器　vehicle height detector
车辆更新/車輛更換　vehicle replacement
车辆工作率/車輛工作率　vehicle working rate
车辆公里/車輛公里　car kilometer
车辆构造速度/車輛構造速度　design speed of car, construction speed of car
车辆购置附加费/車輛購置附加費　vehicle purchase additional fee
车辆合理使用寿命/車輛合理使用壽命　vehicle rational service life
车辆横向/車輛橫向　lateral direction of car
车辆互撞/車輛互撞　car collision
车辆换算长度/車輛換算長度　converted car length
车辆换算系数/車輛換算係數　vehicle conversion factor
车辆活塞作用/車輛活塞作用　piston action of moving vehicle
车辆集中供电/車輛集中供電　centralized power supply system for car
车辆计数/交通量調查,交通量觀測　traffic count
车辆计算长度/車輛計算長度　calculated length of car
车辆技术档案/車輛技術檔案　vehicle technical file
车辆技术履历簿/車輛技術履歷簿　technical record book of car
车辆技术使用寿命/車輛技術使用壽命　vehicle technical service life
车辆加速器/車輛加速器　car accelerator
车辆甲板/車輛甲板　car deck, vehicle deck, wagon deck
车辆检测器/車輛偵測器　vehicle detector
车辆检修/車輛檢修　car inspection and maintenance
车辆检修率/車輛檢修率　rate of cars under repair
车辆检修设备/車輛檢修設備　car repair facility
车辆检修停留时间/車輛檢修停留時間　down time for holding car for repairing
车辆检修限度/車輛檢修限度　car repair limit
车辆检修在修时间/車輛檢修在修時間　down time

for car under repair

车辆减速器/車[輛]減速器,軌道制動器,阻車器 car retarder, wagon retarder

车辆交通/車輛交通 vehicular traffic

车辆交直流供电/車輛交直流供電 AC-DC power supply for car

车辆经济使用寿命/車輛經濟壽命 vehicle economic service life

车辆警告指示/車輛警告指示 vehicle warning indication

车辆宽度限制/車輛寬度限制 width limit

车辆模型运动/車輛模型運動 vehicle movement model

车辆年修/車輛年度檢修 car yearly repair

车辆平均长度/車輛平均長度 average length of car

车辆平均技术等级/車輛平均技術等級 mean grade of vehicle technical condition

车辆平均载重/車輛平均載重 traffic average weight

车辆强度试验/車輛強度試驗 car strength test

车辆全长/車輛全長 length over pulling face of coupler

车辆全轴距/車輛全軸距 wheelbase of car

车辆设计规范/車輛設計規範 specification for design of car

车辆使用寿命/車輛使用壽命,車輛耐用年限 vehicle service life

车辆事故损失/車輛事故損失 vehicle accident loss

车辆停放指数/停車配建指標 parking index

车辆停驶/車輛停駛 vehicle lay-off

车辆停驶率/車輛停駛率 vehicle non-working rate

车辆完好率/車輛完好率 vehicle avail ability rate

车辆尾气污染/車輛排氣汙染 vehicle exhaust

车辆修理厂/車輛修理廠 car repair work, workshop wagon

车辆允许噪声标准/車輛容許噪音標準 allowable vehicle noise standard

车辆运行作业计划/車輛運行作業計劃 vehicle operation plan

车辆运营/車輛運營 car operation

车辆运用维修/車輛運用維修 car operation and maintenance

车辆运用限度/車輛運用限度 car road service limit

车辆噪声/機動車輛噪音 vehicle noise

车辆站务费/車輛碼頭費 vehicle terminal charge

车辆折旧/車輛折舊 vehicle depreciation

车辆折旧里程/車輛折舊里程 vehicle depreciation mileage

车辆折旧率/車輛折舊率 vehicle depreciation rate

车辆制检/車輛制檢 car brake examination, car brake inspection

车辆制造厂/車輛製工場 car manufacturing work

车辆中修/車輛中修 car medium repair

车辆轴检/車輛軸檢 car journal and box examination, car journal and box inspection

车辆注册登记/車輛註冊登記 vehicle registration

车辆装备/車輛裝備 vehicle outfitting

车辆装卸修/車輛裝卸修 car repair before loading or after unloading

车辆纵向/車輛縱向 longitudinal direction of car

车辆租赁/車輛租賃 vehicle leasing

车辆最大高度/車輛最大高度 maximum height of car

车辆最大宽度/車輛最大寬度 maximum width of car

车辆最大容许速度/車輛最大容許速度 maximum permissible speed of car

车列/列車組 train set, train unit

车令/車令 engine orders

车令指示器/車令指示器 engine telegraph order indicator

车流/車流,交通流 car flow, vehicle flow, traffic stream

车流返回波/車流反向波 backward wave in traffic flow

车流径路/車流徑路 car flow routing

车流量/車流量 vehicle flowrate

车流起动波/車流啟動波 starting wave in traffic flow

车流调整/車流調整 adjustment of car flow

车流停驶波/車流停駛波 stopping wave in traffic flow

车流组织/車流組織 organization of car flow

车轮/車輪 wheel

车轮抱死/車輪鎖定 wheel lock up

车轮不圆/車輪不圓 wheel out of round

车轮厂/車輪廠 car wheelset repair factory

车轮动平衡仪/車輪動態平衡器 wheel dynamic balancer

车轮滑行/車輪滑行 wheel sliding, wheel skid

车轮滑转/車輪旋轉 wheel spinning

车轮检测器/輪軸偵測器 wheel detector

车轮静平衡检验/車輪靜平衡試驗 car wheel static balance test

车轮空转/車輪空轉 wheel slipping

车轮扣环/車輪扣環 retaining ring of tire

车轮内侧间距/車輪內側間距 back gage

车轮贴靠/車輪貼靠　flanging
车轮形药柱/輪形藥柱　wagon wheel grain
车轮直径/車輪直徑　wheel diameter
车门自动控制/車門自動控制　automatic train door control
车票有效期/客票有效期限　ticket availability
车上给水装置/車上給水裝置　water supply equipment with roof tank
车上交货/車上交貨　free on truck, free on rail
车上水箱/車頂水箱　roof water tank
车身矫正机/車身矯直機　body and frame straightener
车速/車速　speed
车速及延迟调查/速率及停滯調查　speed and delay study
车台/車臺　wagon stage
车体/車身　car body
车体侧倾装置/車體可傾裝置　car body tilting device
车体长度/車體長度　length over ends of body, length of car body
车体骨架/車體骨架　body framing
车体及外部装备密封试验/車體及外部裝備密封試驗　test for sealing of body and external equipment
车体宽度/車體寬度　width over sides of car body
车体内长/車體內長　length inside car body
车体内高/車體內高　height inside car body
车体内宽/車體內寬　width inside car body
车体内中心处高度/車體內中心處高度　height inside car body from floor to roof center
车体弯曲振动试验/車體彎曲振動試驗　test of vibration caused by car body bending
车头间距/[前后]車頭間距　space headway, headway
车头时距/車頭時距,時間車距　time headway, time interval headway
车位/車位　loading lot, unloading lot
车下电气插座/車下電力插座　car power receptacle
车下给水装置/車下給水設備　water supply equipment with lower tank
车下水箱/車下水箱　lower water tank
[车厢门口的]踏板/板呎　board feet
车厢容积/車廂容積　carriage box volume capacity
车行道/車行道,分隔道路　carriageway
车行道边[缘]线/車行道邊緣線　edge line of carriageway
车行道绿化/車行道綠化　driveway greening
车行道中[心]线/行車道中心線　center line of carriageway
车行桥/車行橋　car bridge
车行信号相/車行時相　vehicular phase
车型/車型　model of car, vehicle model, vehicle type
车型分类/車輛分類　vehicle classification
车型检测器/車型檢測器　vehicle type detector
车削/車削　turning
车载地面站/車載地面站　vehicle earth station
车载钢轨涂油器/車載鋼軌塗油器　on-board rail lubricator
车载式颠簸累积仪/車載式顛簸累積儀　vehicular bump-integrator
车站/車站　station
车站班计划/車站班計劃　station shift operating plan
车站办理车数/車站辦理車數　number of inbound and outbound cars handled at station
车站等级/車站等級　class of station
车站电台/車站無線電臺　station radio set
车站分布/車站分布　distribution of stations
车站工作组织/車站工作組織　organization of station operation
车站公共区/車站公眾區　public zone of station
车站广场/車站廣場　station square, station place
车站广场停机坪/車站前廣場,停機坪　terminal apron
车站候车厅/車站大廳　station hall
车站技术作业表/車站技術作業表　station technical working diagram
车站间隔时间/車站間隔時間　time interval between two adjacent trains at station
车站阶段计划/車站階段計劃　station stage operating plan
车站控制/車站控制　station master control
车站控制室/車站控制室　control room of station
车站埋深/車站埋深　depth of station
车站起点里程/車站起點里程　start mileage of station
车站隧道/車站隧道　station tunnel
车站通过能力/車站通過能力　carrying capacity of station
车站信号/車站信號　signaling at station
车站行车工作细则/車站行車工作細則　instructions for train operation at station
车站咽喉/車站咽喉　station throat
车站咽喉通过能力/車站咽喉通過能力　carrying capacity of station throat
车站中心里程/車站中心里程,月臺中點里程车站终点里程/車站終點里程　middle mileage of station, end mileage of station
车站主楼/車站主廈　station main building
车站作业计划/車站作業計劃　station operating plan
车长电台/列車車長電臺　train conductor station
车长阀/守車閥　caboose valve, conductor valve, guard valve
车辙/[車]轍　rut, rutting
车辙试验/車轍試驗,輪跡試驗　wheel rutting test, wheel tracking test
车钟/車鐘　engine telegraph
车钟报警/車鐘警報　engine telegraph alarm
车钟发送器/車鐘發送器　telegraph transmitter
车钟记录簿/車鐘記錄簿　telegraph book, bell book
车钟记录仪/車鐘記錄儀　telegraph logger
车钟接收器/車鐘接收器　telegraph receiver
车种/車種　type of car
车轴/車軸　axle
车轴超声探伤/車軸超音波探傷,車軸超音波檢驗　ultrasonic inspection for axle
车轴齿轮箱/車軸齒輪箱　axle gear box
车轴电磁探伤/車軸磁粉探傷,車軸磁力檢驗　magnetic particle inspection for axle, magnaflux inspection for axle
车轴发电机/車軸發電機　axle generator
车轴发电机控制箱/車軸發電機控制箱　axle generator control box
车轴空心轴驱动/輪對空心軸傳動　quill drive, hollow axle drive
车轴模拟试验台/車軸模擬試驗臺　axle analogy test machine
车轴驱动方式/車軸驅動方式　mode of axle drive
[车轴]弯曲/車軸彎曲　bent axle
[彻]体力/徹體力,物體力,實體力　body force
掣链钩/吊鏈鈎,拉線爪,止鏈爪　devil claw
掣链器/制鏈器,錨鏈扣　deck stopper, chain stopper
掣锚器/止錨器　anchor stopper
掣索器/制索器　rope stopper
撤场/撤回　withdrawal
撤船/撤船　withdrawal of ship
撤防/撤防　unset condition
撤销/取消　cancel
尘暴/塵暴　dust storm
尘密/塵密　dust-tight
尘土/塵土,塵埃　dust
沉船/沈船,船舶殘骸　wreck
沉船残留物/沈船殘留物　wreck remains
沉船残体/難船漂流物　wreckage
沉船打捞/打撈沈船　raising of a wreck
沉船防波堤/沈船防波堤　sunken ship breakwater
沉船浮标/沈箱浮標　wreck marking buoy
沉船勘测/沈船勘測　wreck surveying
沉[床]园/沈[床]園,低地花園,低地庭園　sunken garden
沉垫自升式钻井平台/沈墊自昇式鑽井平臺　mat jack-up drilling platform, mat jack-up drilling unit
沉淀/沈澱　sediment
沉淀池/沈澱池　sedimentation basin, subsiding basin
沉淀管/沈碴管　sediment tube
沉淀柜/澄清櫃　settling tank
沉淀剂/沈澱劑　precipitant
沉淀室/沈澱室　sedimentation compartment
沉浮模态/長過期起伏模態　phugoid mode
沉管法/沈埋法　immersed tunnelling method
沉管灌注桩/沈管場鑄樁　tube-sinking cast-in-situ pile
沉积节理/沈積節理　sedimentation joint
沉积量/沈積量　sediment yield
沉积速度/澱積率,堆積率　deposition rate
沉积物移动/沈碴輸送　sediment transport
沉积岩/沈積岩　sedimentary rock
沉积作用/沈降[作用]　sedimentation
沉降/沈降,沈陷,下沈　settlement
沉降测量/沈陷測定　settlement measurement
沉降差/差異沈陷　differential settlement
沉降池/沈澱池　sedimentation basin, subsiding basin
沉降法/沈澱法　sedimentation method
沉降分析/沈陷分析　settlement analysis
沉降缝/沈降縫　settlement joint
沉降观测/沈陷觀測　settlement observation
沉降海岸/曲折沈陷海岸　ria coast
沉降粒子/析出粒子　precipitate particle
沉降裂缝/沈陷裂縫　settlement crack
沉降时间/沈澱時間　sedimentation period
沉降室/沈降室,沈澱槽　gravity separator, settling chamber
沉降速度/沈降速度　dropping velocity, fall velocity
沉降性固体/沈降性固體　settleable solid
沉降性试验/沈降試驗　settleability test
沉降作用/沈降作用　settlement action
沉井/沈井　open caisson
沉井挡墙/沈箱擋土牆　caisson retaining wall
沉井基础/沈井基礎,開口沈箱基礎　open caisson

foundation
沉井减摩装置/沈井減摩裝置　tube draw bench, tubing machine
沉井刃脚/沈井刃腳,沈箱刃腳　caisson cutting edge, cutting edge of open caisson
沉雷/沈雷　sunken mine
沉埋法/沈埋[工]法　immersed tunneling method, immersed tube method
沉没/沈没　founder, submergence
沉没陆地/淹水地　submerged land
沉没物/沈没物　sunk object
沉泥积层/沈泥積層　silt grade
沉泥系数/淤泥因數　silt factor
沉沙地/沉沙池　silt basin
沉沙箱/集泥箱　silt box
沉陷/下沈　subsidence
沉陷影响范围/沈陷部位　seat of settlement
沉箱/沈箱,潛水箱　caisson
沉箱防波堤/沈箱防波堤　caisson breakwater
沉箱滑道/沈箱滑道　caisson slipway
沉箱基础/[氣壓]沈箱基礎　pneumatic caisson foundation, caisson foundation
沉箱型平台/沈箱平臺　caisson platform
沉渣池/沈砂間　grit compartment
沉子/沈子,沈錘　sinker
沉子纲/沈子綱　ground rope
陈列馆/陳列館,展示館,展覽館　exhibition hall
陈列室/陳列室　showroom
陈雪/萬年雪,雪冠　firn snow
晨光始/黎明之開始　beginning of morning twilight
晨检室/晨檢室　morning-check room
晨雾/晨霧　morning fog
衬板/襯板　linear plate, liner plate
衬层/襯裡　liner
衬底层/底層防水膜　underlay
衬垫/襯墊,墊材,襯材　dunnage, pad
衬垫焊/襯墊焊法　welding with backing
衬枋头/襯枋頭　chenfangtou
衬料/襯料,襯層,內襯　lining
衬砌/襯砌　lining
衬砌变形/襯裡變形　lining deformation
衬砌腐蚀/襯裡腐蝕　lining corrosion
衬砌裂损/襯砌裂損　lining cracking, lining split
衬砌隧道/襯砌隧道　trimmed tunnel
衬套/套筒　sleeve
称职/稱職　professional competence
称量/稱量　weighing mass
称重试验/稱量檢驗　weighing test
称重系统/秤重系統　weighing system
撑材/支桿,支柱　strut
撑杆/撐桿　bracing, boat pole
撑棍/分道管　saddle clip
撑架/支撐式圍堰　braced cofferdam
撑架桥/撐架橋　strutted beam bridge
撑开/撐開　breast off
撑柱/撐柱　shore
成本估计/估價　cost estimation
成本估算/估價　cost estimation
成本核算/成本會計　cost accounting
成本加酬金合同/成本補償合同　cost reimbursement contract, cost-plus-fee contract
成本加固定费用合同/成本加酬契約　cost-plus-fee contract
成本加运费价格/成本與運費　cost and freight, C and F
成本-效益比率/益本比　cost-benefit ratio
成本-效益分析/成本效益分析　cost-benefit analysis
成材/製材,鋸材　sawn timber
成槽流量/造河流量　formative discharge
成层石砌体/層砌工　rangework
成端电缆/成端電纜　formed cable
成对频率/成對頻率,頻率對　paired frequencies
成对运行图/成對運行圖　train diagram in pairs
成分波/成分波　component wave
成拱作用/拱作用　arching, arch action
成件包装货物/成件包裝貨物　packed freight
成交函/成交書　fixing letter, fixture note
成批货/整批貨,大宗貨　lot cargo
成品库/成品庫　final product storage
成品率/成品率　rate of finished product
成品线性排水沟/成品線性排水溝　finished linear drains
成品油船/油品船,成品油[運載]船　product carrier
成熟期/成熟期　ripening period
成套动力装置/整套動力設備　unit power plant
成像光谱仪/圖像頻譜器　imaging spectrometer
成形法/成型法　forming
成组/單元化　unitization
成组货/單元化貨物　unitized cargo
成组立模成型/成組立模成型　vertical cassette form moulding
成组模板/分組鑄模　gang mould
成组运输/成組貨運　unitized transport
成组装车/分組裝車　car loading by groups
诚笃园/誠篤園　Garden of Fidelity
承包/承包　project acceptance, contract, contracting

承包工程/承包工程　contract work
承包工作/承包工作　contracting job
承包商/承建商,建築商　contractor
承保一切险/全險　against all risk
承德避暑山庄/承德避暑山莊　Chengde Imperial Summer Resort
承拉螺栓/連接螺栓　tie bar, tie bolt
承力蒙皮结构/承力蒙皮結構,應力蒙皮結構　stressed-skin construction
承力索/承力索　catenary
承力索弛度/承力索弛度　catenary sag
承力索接头线夹/承力索接頭線夾　catenary splice
承力索终端锚固线夹/承力索終端錨固線夾　termination fitting for catenary
承力筒/承力筒　loaded cylinder
承力系统/承力系統　load supporting system
承磨环/耐磨環　wear ring
承泥板/承泥板　mud bearer
承台/樁帽,載臺　bearing platform, pile cap, platform
承推架/軸承架　bearing beam
承推梁/承推梁　pushed beam
承托/托座　haunch
承压地下水/湧泉地水　artesian ground water
承压井/拘限井　confined well
承压面/平面支承　surface bearing
承压强度/承載強度　bearing strength
承压[水]流/湧泉流　artesian flow
承压水压力/湧泉壓力　artesian pressure
承运/承運　acceptance of consignment
承运船/運送船　carrier
承运货物代理费/承運貨物代理費　freight forwarder agency charge
承运人/運送人　carrier
承运人责任期间/運送人責任期　period of responsibility of carrier
承载鞍/接頭,配接器,轉接器　adapter
承载板/載重板,加載板　bearing plate, loading plate
承载板试验/平板負載試驗　plate loading test
承载比试验/承載比試驗　bearing ratio test
承载力系数/承力係數　coefficient of bearing capacity
承载能力/承載能力,負荷能量　load carrying capacity, bearing capacity, carrying capacity
承载系数检定/承載係數檢定　load factor rating
承载值/承載值　bearing value
承重层/承重層　supporting course
承重构件/承重結構　load bearing member
承重墙/承重牆　load bearing wall, bearing wall
承租人/租傭人　charterer
承租人责任终止条款/租傭人責任留置條款　cesser clause of charterer liability
城邦/城邦　city state
城堡/城堡　castle
城池/城池　chengchi, city fortress, city wall and moat
城郭/城郭　inner and outer city walls
城濠/護城河　city moat, city trench
城隍庙/城隍廟　Temple of City God, Chenghuang Miao
城际交通/都市間交通　intercity traffic
城间道路/城市間道路　interurban road
城建监察/城建監察　urban construction supervision and inspection
城[门]楼/城[門]樓　city gate tower
城内交通/區域內運輸　intraregional transportation
城墙/城牆　city wall
城市/城市,都市　city, urban
城市保护/都市保育,都市保存　urban conservation
城市边缘区/都市外緣　urban periphery, urban fringe
城市变电站/都市變電所　urban electric substation
城市滨水区/臨水區　water front area
城市病/都市病　urban disease
城市布局/都市布置,都市規劃　urban layout
城市承载力/都市承載力　urban carrying capacity
城市橙线/都市橙線　city orange line
城市重建/都市重建　urban reconstruction, city rebuilding
城市出入口公路/都市出入口公路　city approach highway
城市次干路/都市幹線道路,都市次幹線　urban secondary trunk road
城市大气环境保护规划/都市大氣環境保護規劃　urban atmospheric environment protection planning
城市大气环流/都市大氣環流　urban atmospheric circulation
城市导线测量/都市導線測量　urban traverse surveying
城市道路/都市道路,市區道路　urban road
城市道路工程/都市道路工程　urban road engineering
城市道路横坡/[都市道路]橫坡　cross slope
城市道路红线/都市道路紅線　urban road red line building line
城市道路检查井/都市道路檢修孔　urban road

manhole

城市道路交叉口/都市道路交叉口　urban road intersection

城市道路交通设施/都市道路交通設施　urban road traffic facilities

城市道路街沟/都市道路溝渠　urban road ditch

城市道路路基/都市道路路基　urban road subgrade

城市道路路面/都市道路路面　urban road pavement

城市道路绿化/都市道路綠化　urban road green

城市道路面积率/都市道路面積比,都市道路面積率　urban road area ratio

城市道路排水管道/都市道路排水管　urban road drainage pipe

城市道路平曲线/都市道路平面曲線　horizontal curve of urban road

城市道路桥/都市道路橋　urban road bridge

城市道路视距/都市道路視距　sight distance of urban road

城市道路竖曲线/都市道路竖曲線　vertical curve of urban road

城市道路网/都市道路網　urban road network

城市道路网密度/都市道路網密度　density of urban road network

城市道路系统/都市道路系統　urban road system

城市道路系统规划/都市道路系統規劃　urban road system planning

城市道路用地/都市道路用地　land for urban road

城市道路雨水口/都市道路排水溝　urban road gully

城市道路照明/都市道路照明　urban road lighting

城市道路中心线/都市道路中心線　center line of urban road

城市道路纵坡/都市道路縱坡,都市道路經向梯度　longitudinal gradient of urban road

城市等级结构/都市體系階層式結構　hierarchical structure of urban system

城市地理学/都市地理學　urban geography

城市地区/[都]市區　urban area

[城市]地下空间/都市地下空間　urban underground space

城市地质灾害防治/都市地質災害計劃　geological hazard prevention

城市地质灾害防治规划/都市地質災害防治規劃　urban geological disaster prevention planning

城市地质灾害评估/都市地質災害評估　urban geological hazard assessment

城市地质灾害预警/都市地質災害警報　urban geological disaster warning

城市电力工程/都市電力工程　urban eletric power engineering

城市电力系统/都市電力系統　urban eletric power system

城市电信/都市電信　urban telecommunication

城市电信工程系统规划/都市電信工程系統規劃　urban telecom engineering system planning

城市雕塑/都市雕塑　urban sculpture

城市对外交通/都市對外交通,城際運輸,都市間運輸　intercity transportation

城市对外交通规划/城際運輸規劃　external transportation planning

城市发展/都市發展　urban development, city development

城市发展方向/都市發展方向,都市開發方向,都市發展定位　urban development direction, city development orientation

城市发展计划/都市發展計劃　urban development planning

城市发展模式/都市發展模式　urban development pattern

城市发展目标/都市發展目標　urban development goals, city development goal

城市发展战略/都市發展策略　urban development strategy

城市发展政策/都市發展政策　urban development policy

城市防洪/都市防洪　urban flood control

城市防洪工程/[都市]防洪工程　urban flood control engineering, flood control work

城市防洪工程设施规划/都市防洪標準設施規劃　urban flood control facility planning

城市防洪规划/都市防洪規劃　urban flood control planning

城市防空/都市防空　urban air defense

城市防空工程设施规划/都市防空工程設施規劃　urban air defense engineering facility planning

城市防灾/都市防災　urban disaster prevention

城市防震/[都市]防震　urban earthquake hazard protection, earthquake hazard protection

城市防震工程/都市防震工程　urban earthquake prevention engineering

城市仿真/都市模擬　urban simulation

城市废水/都市廢水,城市汙水　municipal waste water

城市分类/都市分類　city classification

城市分区规划/都市區規劃　urban district planning

城市风环境模拟/都市風環境模擬　urban wind environment simulation

城市风廊/都市風廊　urban wind corridor
城市风貌/都市風貌　cityscape
城市辐射力/都市輻射力　urban radiation
城市复兴/都市復興　urban revitalization
城市副中心/副都心　sub-city center
城市腹地/都市腹地　urban hinterland
城市改建/都市再開發,都市再發展　urban redevelopment
城市改建工程/都市再發展工程　urban redevelopment work
城市改造计划/都市改造計劃　town improvement scheme
城市格局/都市型態　urban space pattern
城市更新/都市更新,都市再生　urban renewal, urban regeneration
城市更新单元/都市再生單元　urban regeneration unit
城市更新规划/都市再生規劃　urban regeneration planning
城市更新计划/都市更新計劃　urban regeneration program, urban regeneration action plan
城市工程管线综合/都市工程管線綜合　integrated design for utilities pipeline
城市工程管线综合规划/都市工程管線綜合規劃　urban engineering pipelines comprehensive planning
城市公共服务设施控制指标/都市公共服務設施控制指數　urban public service facility control index
城市公共交通/都市公共交通　urban public transport, urban public transportation
城市公共交通规划/都市公共交通規劃　public transport planning
城市公共交通系统/都市公共交通系統　urban public transportation system
城市公共客运/都市公路客運　urban bus transport
城市公共领域/都市公共領域　urban public realm
城市公共设施/都市公共設施　urban public facility
城市公共设施用地/都市公共設施土地利用　city public facilities land
城市公共艺术/都市公共藝術　urban public art
城市公共中心/都市公共中心　city public center
城市公园/都市公園　city park, urban park
城市公园系统/都市公園系統　urban park system
城市功能分区/都市功能劃分,都市功能區劃　urban functional partition, urban functional district, urban functional zoning
城市供电/都市電力供應,都市供電　urban electricity supply
城市供电电源/[都市]電源,動力源　urban power source, power source
城市供电系统/[都市]供電系統　urban power supply system, power supply system
城市供热/都市供熱,都市熱供應　urban heat supply, municipal heat supply
城市供热工程/都市供熱工程　urban heat supply engineering
城市供热工程系统规划/都市供熱系統規劃　urban heating system planning
城市供热系统/都市供熱系統　district heating system
城市供水/都市供水　urban water supply
城市固体废物污染控制规划/都市固體廢棄物汙染控制規劃　municipal solid waste pollution control planning
城市光污染/都市光汙染　urban light pollution
城市广场/都市廣場　city square
城市规划/都市計劃,都市規劃　urban planning, city planning, town planning
城市规划编制单位资质/都市規劃編製單位資質　certificate of qualification for compilation of urban planning
城市规划标准/都市計劃標準　city planning standard
城市规划法规/都市計劃法制,都市規劃法規,都市計劃法令　legislation for city planning, legislation on urban planning, urban planning legislation
城市规划纲要/都市規劃綱要　city planning outline
城市规划管理/都市計劃管理,都市規劃管理　city planning management, city planning administration, urban planning administration
城市规划管理信息系统/都市規劃管理資訊系統　urban planning management information system
城市规划建设管理/都市規劃建設管理　urban planning and development control
城市规划理论/都市計劃理論　urban planning theory
城市规划区/都市規劃區　city planning area, urban planning area
城市规划实施/都市規劃實施　urban planning implementation
城市规划硕士/都市規劃碩士　Master of Urban Planning
城市规划委员会/都市計劃委員會　urban planning commission
城市规划用地管理/都市規劃用地管理　urban planning land use management, urban planning land use administration

城市规划与设计/都市規劃與設計　urban planning and design
城市规划专业/都市規劃專業　urban planning major
城市规划组织/都市計劃機構　urban planning organization
城市规模/都市規模　city scale
城市轨道交通/都市軌道交通　urban rail transit
城市轨道交通用地/都市軌道交通用地　land for urban rail transit
城市核心/都市中心區　urban core
城市黑线/都市黑線　city black line
城市红线/都市紅線　city red line
城市化/都市化　urbanization
城市化经济/都市化經濟　urbanization economy
城市化水平/都市化水準　urbanization level
城市环境/都市環境　urban environment
城市环境保护/都市環境保護　urban environmental protection, city environmental protection, urban environment protection
城市环境保护规划/都市環境保護規劃　urban environmental protection planning
城市环境规划/都市環境規劃　urban environmental planning
城市环境容量/都市環境容量　urban environmental capacity
城市环境卫生/都市環境衛生　urban sanitation
城市环境污染/都市環境汙染　urban environmental pollution, city environmental pollution
城市环境效应/都市環境效應,都市環境影響　urban environmental effect
城市环境质量/都市環境品質　urban environmental quality, city environmental quality
城市环境质量评价/都市環境品質評估　urban environmental quality assessment, city environmental quality evaluation, city environmental quality assessment
城市环卫工程系统规划/都市衛生工程系統規劃　urban sanitation engineering system planning
城市黄线/都市黃線　urban yellow line, city yellow line
城市活力/都市活力　urban vitality
城市货运交通走廊/都市貨運運輸路廊　urban freight transportation corridor
城市肌理/都市肌理　urban texture
城市基本功能/都市基本機能　fundamental urban function
城市基础设施/都市基礎設施　urban infrastructure
城市基础设施专项规划/都市基礎設施規劃　urban infrastructure planning
城市集中供热/都市供熱　urban central heating
城市给水/都市給水　urban water supply, water supply, municipal water supply
城市给水工程/都市給水工程　water supply engineering
城市计划/都市規劃　urban planning
城市计划调查/都市計劃調查　town planning survey
[城市]建成区/建成區,已建區　built-up area
城市建设管理/都市建設管理　urban construction administration, urban construction management
城市建设用地/都市土地開發　urban developed land
城市建设用地分类/都市建設用地分類,都市建設土地分類　urban construction land classification
城市建设用地供应计划/都市建設用地供應計劃　urban land use supply plan
城市建设用地结构/都市建設用地結構,都市發展用地結構　structure of urban construction land
城市建设用地平衡表/都市建設用地平衡表　urban land use balance sheet
城市建设用地评价/都市建設用地評價　land-use evaluation for urban construction
城市建设用地适宜性评价/都市建設用地適用性評估　applicability assessment of urban land use
城市建筑法规/都市建築規範　urban building code
城市建筑学/都市建築學　urban arthitecture
城市交通/市區交通,都市運輸　urban traffic, urban transportation
城市交通规划/都市交通規劃　city transport planning, city transportation planning
城市交通结构/都市交通結構　urban transport structure, urban transportation mode
城市交通美学/都市交通美學　urban traffic aesthetics
城市交通设计/都市交通設計　city traffic design
城市交通网络规划/都市交通網路規劃　urban traffic network planning
城市交通预测/都市交通預測　urban transportation forecast
城市阶层/都市體系,都市階層　urban hierachy
[城市]街道网/街道網　street network
城市节能技术/都市節能技術　urban energy-saving technology
城市结构/都市結構　urban structure
城市经济/都市經濟　urban economy
城市经济学/都市經濟學　urban economics
城市经营/都市行銷　city marketing
城市景观/都市景觀　cityscape, urban landscape

城市竞争力/都市競争力　urban competitiveness
城市居住区/都市集居　urban settlement
[城市]开放空间/開放空間　open space
城市勘察/都市調査　civic survey, urban exploration
城市抗震工程设施规划/都市地震工程設施規劃　urban earthquake engineering facilities planning
城市抗震减灾规划/都市抗震減災規劃　urban earthquake disaster reduction planning
城市科学/都市[科]學　urban science
城市可持续发展/都市永續發展　urban sustainable development
城市客车/市區公車,城市巴士　city bus
城市客运交通走廊/都市客運運輸路廊　urban passenger transportation corridor
城市客运枢纽/都市客運換乘樞紐　urban passenger transfer hub
城市客运枢纽规划/都市客運換乘樞紐規劃　urban passenger transfer hub planning
城市空间/都市空間　urban space
城市快速道路/都市高速道路,都市高速公路,市區快速道路　urban express way, urban expressway
城市快速公交系统/公車捷運系統　bus rapid transit system, BRT system
城市快速轨道系统/都市快速交通系統　urban rapid rail system
城市快速路/都市高速道路　urban express way
城市扩展/都市膨脹　urban expansion
城市扩展模型/都市擴展模型　city expanding model, city expansion model, urban growth model
城市蓝线/都市藍線　urban blue line, city blue line
城市历史保护/都市保全　urban history conservation
城市历史文化保护/都市歷史文化保護　conservation of urban history and heritage
城市立体交通/都市立體交通　urban multi-level transportation
城市林业/都市林業　urban forestry
城市旅游/都市旅遊　city tourism
城市绿地/都市綠地　urban green space
城市绿地率/都市綠地率　urban green land rate
城市绿地系统/都市綠地系統　urban green space system
城市绿地系统[专项]规划/都市綠地系統規劃　urban green space system planning
城市绿化/都市綠化　urban greening, urban afforestation and greening
城市绿化覆盖率/都市綠地覆蓋率　urban green coverage rate, urban green coverage
城市绿化覆盖面积/都市綠地覆蓋面積　urban green coverage area
城市绿线/都市綠線　boundary line of urban green space, city green line
城市煤气/都市煤氣　city gas, town gas
城市美化/都市美化　urban beauty
城市美化运动/都市美化運動　city beautiful movement
城市美术/都市藝術　civic art, urban art
城市美学/都市美學　urban aesthetics
城市模型/都市模型　urban model
城市能源规划/都市能源綜合規劃　urban energy planning
城市能源结构/都市能源結構　urban energy structure
城市排水/都市排水,下水道[系統]　urban sewerage and drainage, sewerage
城市排水工程/[都市]下水道工程　urban sewerage engineering, sewerage engineering
城市排水系统/[都市]下水道系統,汙水排水系統　urban sewerage and drainage system, sewerage system
城市膨胀/都市爆炸　urban explosion
城市片区/都市區　urban section
城市贫困阶层/都市貧民　urban low-income group
城市评价/都市評估　urban evaluation
城市气候/城市氣候,都市氣候　urban climate
城市区域/城市區域　city region
城市群/都市聚集[區]　urban agglomeration
城市燃气/都市燃氣　urban gas
城市燃气调度/都市煤氣調度　urban gas dispatch
城市燃气工程/都市燃氣工程　urban gas engineering
城市燃气工程系统规划/都市燃氣工程系統規劃　urban gas system planning
城市燃气供应系统/[都市]供氣系統　urban gas supply system
城市燃气门站/都市燃氣門站　urban gas gate station, town border station
城市燃气输配系统/都市煤氣輸配系統　urban gas transmission and distribution system
城市热岛/都市熱島　urban heat island
城市热岛效应/都市熱島[效應]　urban heat island effect
城市热负荷/都市供熱量　urban heating load
城市人口/都市人口　urban population
城市人口规模/都市人口規模　urban population size
城市人口机械增长/都市人口機械增長　urban population mechanical growth
城市人口机械增长率/都市人口機械增長率

mechanical growth rate of urban population
城市人口结构/都市人口結構 urban population structure
城市人口流动/都市人口流動 population floating
城市人口流向/都市集中 population flow
城市人口学/都市人口學 urban demography
城市人口预测/都市人口預測 urban population forecast, urban population projection
城市人口增长/都市人口增長,都市人口成長 urban population growth
城市人口增长率/都市人口增長率 urban population growth rate
城市人口自然增长/都市人口自然成長 urban population natural growth
城市容量/都市容量 urban capacity
城市三角测量/都市三角測量 urban triangulation surveying
城市色彩/城市色彩 city color
城市设计/都市設計 urban design
城市设计导则/都市設計導則,都市設計準則,都市設計指南 urban design guideline
城市设计及其理论/都市設計及其理論 urban design and its theory
城市设计奖励/都市設計獎勵 urban design bonus
城市设计图则/都市設計規範 urban design code
城市社会/都會社區 metropolitan community
城市社会学/都市社會學 urban sociology
城市社会运动/都市社會運動 urban social movement
城市社区/城市社區 city community
城市生态功能区划/都市生態功能區劃 urban ecological functional zoning
城市生态规划/都市生態規劃 urban ecological planning
城市生态环境保护规划/都市生態環境保護規劃 urban ecological environmental protection planning
城市生态基础设施/都市生態基礎設施 urban ecological infrastructure
城市生态平衡/都市生態[系統]平衡 urban ecological balance, balance of city ecosystem
城市生态位/都市生態棲位 urban ecological niche
城市生态系统/都市生態系統 urban ecosystem, urban ecological system
城市生态修复规划/都市生態修復規劃 urban ecological restoration planning
城市生态学/都市生態學 urban ecology
城市生态用地/都市生態土地 urban ecological land
城市声环境模拟/都市音環境模擬 urban acoustic environment simulation
城市史/都市史 history of urban
城市市政隧道/都市公共隧道 urban utility tunnel
城市首位度/都市首位度 urban primacy index
城市竖向规划/都市竖向規劃 urban vertical planning
城市衰退/都市衰退 urban decline
城市水环境保护规划/都市水環境規劃 urban water environmental planning
城市水文学/都市水文學 urban hydrology
城市水污染控制单元/都市水汙染控制單元 urban water pollution control unit
城市水系/都市水系 urban water system
城市水系规划/都市水系規劃 urban river system planning
城市私有房屋/都市私有房屋 urban private housing
城市碳排放/都市碳排放 urban carbon emission
城市碳平衡/都市碳平衡 urban carbon balance
城市碳循环与代谢/都市碳循環與代謝 urban carbon cycle and metabolism
城市特色/都市特色 urban indentity
城市体形环境/都市自然環境 urban physical environment
城市天际线/都市輪廓線 city skyline
城市铁路/城市鐵路 city railway, urban railway
城市停车场/停車場 parking lot
城市停车设施/都市停車設施 urban parking facility
城市停车设施规划/都市停車設施規劃 urban parking facility planning
城市通风廊道/都市通風廊道 urban ventilation corridor
城市通信工程/都市通信工程 urban communication engineering
城市通信系统/都市通信系統 urban communication system
城市土地政策/都市土地政策 urban land policy
城市网格/都市格網 urban grid
城市微气候环境/都市微氣候環境 urban micro climatological environment
城市文化/都市文化 urban culture
城市文脉/都市文脈 urban context
城市问题/都市問題 urban issue
城市污水/都市汙水 sewage
城市污水处理/都市汙水處理 urban sewage treatment
城市[无计划]蔓延/都市蔓延 urban sprawl
城市吸引力/都市吸引力 urban attraction
城市详细规划/都市詳細計劃,都市細部規劃 city

detailed planning, detailed urban planning
城市消防/都市消防,都市火控　urban fire control
城市消防工程/都市消防工程　urban fire protection engineering
城市消防工程设施规划/都市消防工程設施規劃　city fire engineering facility planning
城市新区/都市新區　urban new district
城市信息基础设施/都市資訊基礎建設　urban information infrastructure
城市信息系统/都市資訊系統　urban information system
城市形态/都市形態　urban morphology, urban pattern
城市形体环境/都市自然環境　urban physical environment
城市形象/都市形象　city image
城市性质/都市性質,都市機能　designated urban function
城市蓄涝区/都市蓄澇區　local flooding detention and retention area
城市选址/都市選址　site selection
[城市沿道路]带状发展/帶狀發展　ribbon development
城市研究/都市研究　urban study
城市夜景/都市夜景　urban night scenery
城市意象/都市意象　city image
城市用地/都市土地　urban land
城市用地布局/都市用地布局　urban land-use arrangement, urban land-use layout
城市用地规模/都市用地規模　urban land scale
城市用地平衡/都市用地平衡　urban land-use balance
城市用地评价/都市用地評價　urban land-use evaluation
城市用地竖向规划/都市用地竪向規劃　vertical planning of urban
城市用地选择/都市用地選擇　selection of urban land
城市用电负荷/都市用電負荷,電負載　electricity need load, electrical load, urban electrical load
城市用水/都市用水量　urban water consumption
城市雨水调蓄区/都市雨水調蓄區　urban storm water detention and retention area
城市原型/都市原型　urban prototype
城市愿景/都市願景　urban vision
城市运输/市内運輸　intracity transportation
城市再开发/都市再開發,都市再發展　urban redevelopment

城市再生/城市再生,都市再生　urban regeneration
城市噪声/都市噪音　urban noise
城市噪声污染控制规划/都市噪音汙染控制規劃　urban noise pollution control planning
城市增长边界/都市發展邊界,都市增長邊界　urban growth boundary
城市照明/都市照明　urban lighting
城市支路/都市支線,都市岔路,都市支路　urban branch road, urban service road
城市职能指数/都心機能指數　index of urban function
城市治理/都市治理　urban governance
城市中心/都市中心　city center
城市主干路/都市主幹道,都市主街　urban arterial road, main street, urban trunk road
城市专门化指数/都市中心專業化指數　specialization index of urban center
城市紫线/都市紫線　urban purple line, city purple line
城市综合承载力/都市綜合能力　urban comprehensive capacity
城市综合防灾减灾规划/都市防災工作規劃　urban disaster prevention planning
城市综合交通/都市綜合交通　urban comprehensive transportation
城市综合交通规划/都市綜合運輸規劃　urban comprehensive transportation planning
城市综合交通体系/都市綜合運輸體系　urban comprehensive transportation system
城市综合交通[体系]规划/都市綜合運輸體系規劃　urban comprehensive transportation system planning
城市综合体/城市綜合體　urban complex
城市总体布局/都市空間布局　urban comprehensive layout
城市总体规划/都市總體規劃,綜合性規劃　city master planning, urban master planning, urban comprehensive planning
城市总体规划纲要/都市總體規劃綱要　city master planning outline, master plan outline, urban master planning outline
城市总体规划强制性内容/都市綱要計劃強制性內容　compulsory content of urban master planning
城市总体规划现状调研/都市綱要計劃現址勘查　on-site investigation of urban master planning
城市组团/城市組團,城市群　city group, city cluster
城乡二元结构/城鄉二元結構　rural-urban dual structure
城乡规划/城鄉規劃,市鄉規劃　urban and rural

planning, town and country planning

城乡规划编制/城鄉規劃編製　urban-rural planning making

城乡规划编制机构资质/城鄉規劃編製機構資質　qualification of urban-rural planning making institution

城乡规划编制与审批/城鄉規劃編製與審批　making and approval of urban and rural plan

城乡规划标准/城鄉規劃標準　urban planning standard

城乡规划部门规章/城鄉規劃部門規章　departmental rules on urban and rural planning

城乡规划地方法规/城鄉規劃地方法規　local regulations on urban and rural planning

城乡规划动态监测/城鄉規劃動態監測　dynamic monitoring of urban and rural planning

城乡规划督察/城鄉規劃監督　urban-rural planning supervision

城乡规划督察员制度/城鄉規劃督察員制度　urban and rural planning inspector system

城乡规划法/城鎮計劃法　urban and rural planning law

城乡规划法律责任/城鄉規劃法律責任　legal liability of urban and rural planning

城乡规划公众参与/城鄉規劃民眾參與　public participation of urban-rural planning

城乡规划顾问/城鄉規劃顧問　urban and rural planning consultant

城乡规划管理/城鄉規劃管理　administration of urban and rural planning, urban and rural planning administration

城乡规划管理信息系统/城鄉規劃管理資訊系統　information systems of urban and rural planning

城乡规划行政处罚/城鄉規劃行政處罰　administrative punishment on urban and rural planning

城乡规划行政法规/城鄉規劃行政法規,城鄉規劃行政規範　administrative regulations on urban and rural planning

城乡规划行政复议/城鄉規劃行政複議　administrative review on urban and rural planning

城乡规划行政规章/城鄉規劃行政規章　administrative rules on urban and rural planning

城乡规划行政诉讼/城鄉規劃行政訴訟　administrative litigation on urban and rural planning

城乡规划技术标准/城鄉規劃技術標準　technical standard on urban and rural planning

城乡规划技术标准体系/城鄉規劃技術標準體系　technical standard system on urban and rural planning

城乡规划监督检查/城鄉規劃監督檢查　supervision and inspection of urban-rural planning

城乡规划教育评估/城鄉規劃教育評估　accreditation of urban-rural planning education program

城乡规划课/城鄉規劃課　course of urban and rural planning

城乡规划审批/城鄉規劃許可　urban-rural planning approval

城乡规划实施/城鄉規劃實施　urban-rural planning implementation

城乡规划实施管理/城鄉規劃實施管理　implement management of urban-rural planning

城乡规划实施监督检查/城鄉規劃實施監督檢查　supervision and inspection of urban-rural planning implementation

城乡规划实施评估/城鄉規劃實施評估　evaluation of urban-rural planning implementation

城乡规划司法救济/城鄉規劃司法補償　judicial remedy on urban and rural planning

城乡规划体系/城鄉規劃體系　urban-rural planning system

城乡规划委员会/城鄉規劃編製機制　commission of urban and rural planning

城乡规划效能监察/城鄉規劃效能監察　urban-rural planning implementation supervision and inspection

城乡规划修改/城鄉規劃修改　urban-rural planning modification

城乡规划学/城鄉規劃學　urban and rural planning discipline

城乡规划与设计/城鄉規劃與設計　urban and rural planning and design

城乡规划制定/城鄉規劃編製　urban-rural planning making

城乡规划主管部门/城鄉規劃營建署　urban and rural planning agency

城乡接合部/都市外緣　urban periphery, urban fringe

城乡统筹/統籌城鄉,城鄉發展統籌　balancing urban and rural development, integrated urban and rural development

城乡统筹发展战略/城鄉統籌發展戰略　urban and rural integration development strategy

城乡统筹规划/城鄉一體化規劃　urban-rural integration planning

城乡一体化/城鄉整合　rural-urban integration

城乡用地/城鄉用地,城鄉土地利用,鄉鎮用地　urban and rural land-use, town and country land
城乡用地分类/城鄉用地分類,城鄉土地使用分類　urban and rural land-use classification, town and country land-use classification
城乡用地管理/城鄉土地利用管理　urban and rural land-use administration
城乡用地汇总表/城鄉用地總報表　summary table of urban and rural land-use
城乡用地评定/土地利用評價　land-use evaluation
城乡治理/城鄉治理　urban-rural governance
城厢/城厢　chengxiang, city border area
城镇发展潜力/都市發展潛力　urban development potential
城镇合理规模/都市合理規模　optimal urban scale
城镇化水平/都市化水準　urbanization level
城镇化水平预测/都市化水準預測　projection of urbanization ratio
城镇化速率/都市化速率　speed of urbanization
城镇建设用地/都市建設用地　urban construction land
城镇景观/市鎮景觀　townscape
城镇空间体系结构/都市體系立體結構　spatial structure of urban system
城镇群/城鎮群,都市群　urban group, town and city agglomeration
城镇燃气/城鎮氣體燃料　city gas, town gas
城镇燃气输配系统/城鎮氣體燃料輸配管網　city gas transmission and distribution system
城镇人口预测/都市人口推計　urban population projection
城镇生活垃圾无害化处理率/城鎮生活垃圾無害化處理率　urban living garbage harmless treatment rate
城镇生态敏感性分析/城鎮生態敏感性分析　analysis of city eco-sensitivity
城镇体系/都市體系　urban system
城镇体系规划/城鎮體系規劃　urban system planning
城镇体系职能结构/都市體系功能結構　functional structure of urban system
城中村/都市村　urban village
乘潮水位/乘潮水位　tide riding level
乘警/乘警　train police
乘客候车站台/行人登車島　pedestrian loading island
乘员分系统/乘員子系統　crew subsystem
乘员设备装备间/乘員設備製備室　space-crew equipment preparation room
乘员组训练/組員訓練　crew training
乘坐品质控制/乘坐品質控制　ride quality control
乘坐舒适度/乘車舒適度　riding comfortableness, vehicle ride comfort
盛货帆布袋/載貨帆布袋　canvas cargo bag
程控电话交换机/程式控制系統交換機　stored program controlled telephone switching system
程控交换机房/交換機房　private branch exchange room
程序/程式　program
程序和布置手册/程式和布置手冊　procedures and arrangement manual
程序控制/程式控制　programmed control, process control
程序块谱/區塊譜　program block spectrum
程序脉冲/程式脈衝　program pulse
程序配电/程式配電　program power distribution
程序图/流程圖,流量圖　flow diagram
程序违法/程式性違法　breach of procedural law
程序信号/程式信號　procedure signal
程序引导/應用指示　program designation
程序制导/程式導引　program guidance
程序转弯/程式轉彎　procedure turn
程租船/航程包租　voyage charter
橙色烟号/橙色煙號　orange smoke signal
秤动点/天平動點　libration point
秤杆组件天平/桿秤天平　weigh beam balance
吃水/吃水[量]　draft
吃水标志/吃水標誌　draft mark
吃水差/俯仰差　trim
吃水差比尺/俯仰表　trimming table
吃水差曲线图/俯仰差圖　trim diagram
吃水限制灯/吃水限制號燈　deep draft vessel light
吃水指示系统/吃水指示系統　draft indicating system
螭首/螭首　chishou
池边坐人矮墙/池邊坐人矮牆　seat wall surrounded pool
池塘/池沼,小湖　pool, pond
池座/池座　stall
弛豫方程/鬆弛方程　relaxation equation
弛豫时间/鬆弛時間　relaxation time
弛豫现象/鬆弛現象　relaxation phenomena
驰道/馳道　royal road, ancient drive way
驰振/馳振　galloping
迟发雷管/遲發雷管　delay detonator
迟炸/遲爆炸　late burst

持久强度极限/持久強度極限　stress-rupture limit, long time limit
持久塑性/應力斷裂塑性　stress-rupture plasticity, long time plasticity
持久性有机污染物/持久性有機汙染物　persistent organic pollutant
持水曲线/保水曲線　retention curve
持续常用功率/額定連續常用出力　continuous service rating, CSR
持续功率/持續功率　continuous power
持续牵引力/持續牽引力　continuous tractive effort
持续适航文件/持續適航檔　continuous airworthiness instruction
持续适航性/持續性適航　continuous airworthiness
持续速度/持續速度　continuous speed
持续性加速度/持續性加速度　sustained acceleration
持续性客流/連續性客運交通　continuous passenger traffic
持续运转功率/連續運轉功率限界　power limit for continuous running
持证艇员/持證救生艇員　certificated lifeboat person
尺寸/尺寸　dimension
尺寸界线/尺寸界線　size dimension line
尺寸起止符号/尺寸起止符號　dimension start terminate symbol
尺寸线/尺寸線　dimension line
尺寸效应/尺寸效應　size effect
尺度效应/尺度效應,縮尺效應　scale effect
尺度协调/尺度協調　size coordination
尺度转换/尺度分析　scaling
齿/齒　tooth
齿槽连接/齒槽連接　notch and tooth joint
齿轨[传动]机车/齒軌機車　rack locomotive
齿轨铁路/齒軌鐵路　rack railway, toothed railway
齿轮泵/齒輪泵　gear pump
齿轮齿条式升降机/齒輪齒條昇降機　rack and pinion hoist
齿轮传动[装置]/齒輪驅動　gear drive
齿轮荷载/齒輪載重　gear load
齿轮油/齒輪油　gear oil
齿圈/輪緣　rim
齿条-齿轮/齒條與小齒輪　rack and pinion
赤潮/赤潮　red water, red tide
赤道/赤道　equator
赤道潮汐/赤道潮　equatorial tide
赤道地平视差/赤道地平視差　equatorial horizontal parallax
赤道里/赤道浬　equatorial mile

赤道无风带/赤道無風帶　doldrums
赤道仪/赤道儀　equatorial telescope
赤道坐标系/赤道坐標系統　equatorial system of coordinates
赤经/赤經　right ascension, RA
赤纬/赤緯　declination, Dec
赤纬圈/赤緯平行圈　parallel of declination
赤玉土/赤玉土　Akadama soil
冲便阀/沖洗閥　flush valve
冲程/衝止距,行程　stopping distance, stroke
冲弹丸钻法/衝彈丸鑽法　shots drilling
冲荡/抖動　whipping
冲动-反动式涡轮机/衝動反動渦輪機　impulse-reaction turbine
冲动级/衝動輪級　impulse stage
冲动式汽轮机/衝動式汽輪機,衝動渦輪機　impulse turbine, impulse steam turbine
冲动式透平/衝動式汽輪機,衝動式渦輪機　impulse turbine
冲动式涡轮/衝動式渦輪機,衝動式汽輪機　impulse turbine
冲断层/受壓斷層　thrust fault
冲沟/沖蝕溝　coombe, gulch
冲击/衝擊,碰撞　impact
冲击扳手/衝擊扳手　impact wrench
冲击闭合器/衝擊閉合器　shock closer
冲击波/衝擊波　shock wave
冲击不回零性/衝擊不回零性　balance character of non-return to zero under starting load
冲击电流/衝擊電流,脈衝電流　impulse current
冲击腐蚀/衝擊腐蝕　impingement corrosion
冲击负载/衝擊負載　impact load
冲击高度/衝擊試驗高度　shock height
冲击夯/衝擊夯　shocking rammer
冲击荷载/衝擊載重,突增負載　impulsive load, shock loading
冲击环境/衝擊環境　shock environment
冲击加速度耐受限值/衝擊加速度容許限界　impact acceleration tolerance limit
冲击角/衝擊角　shock angle
冲击接地电阻/衝擊接地電阻　shock ground resistance
冲击冷却/衝擊冷卻　impingement cooling
冲击力/衝擊力　impact force
冲击脉冲/衝擊脈波　shock pulse
冲击敏感性/撞擊靈敏度　impact sensitivity
冲击破碎机/衝擊碎石機　impact crusher
冲击谱/震譜　shock spectrum

冲击谱合成/衝擊譜合成　spectrum synthesis shock
冲击韧度/衝擊韌性　impact toughness
冲击韧度试验/衝擊韌性試驗　impact toughness test
冲击韧度试验仪/衝擊韌性儀器　impact toughness apparatus
冲击式碾压机/夯式壓路機　impact roller
冲击[式]涡轮/衝動式汽輪機,衝動式渦輪機　impulse turbine
冲击式凿岩机/衝擊式鑿岩機　shocking jack hammer
冲击式钻机/衝擊式鑽機　impact-type drill machine, percussion type drill machine
冲击式钻土机/撞擊式鑽探機　percussion boring machine
冲击试验/衝擊試驗[機]　impact test, percussion testing
冲击试验机/衝擊試驗機　shock test machine
冲击试验Ⅰ级/衝擊試驗Ⅰ级,脈衝試驗Ⅰ级　impulse test-class Ⅰ
冲击试验Ⅱ级/衝擊試驗Ⅱ级,脈衝試驗Ⅱ级　impulse test-class Ⅱ
冲击试验Ⅲ级/衝擊試驗Ⅲ级,脈衝試驗Ⅲ级　impulse test-class Ⅲ
冲击损失/衝擊損失　impact loss
冲击塔/衝擊塔　impact tower
冲击误差/衝擊誤差　ballistic error
冲击系数/衝擊係數,衝擊因數,衝量係數　impact factor, coefficient of impact
冲击系数测定/衝擊係數測定　impact factor evaluation
冲击[响应]谱/衝擊[響應]譜　shock response spectrum
冲击性钻杆/助鑽桿　sinker bar
冲击旋转式凿岩机/衝擊旋轉式鑿岩機　shocking rotary jack hammer
冲击因数/衝擊因數　impact factor
冲击与螺旋钻探/外殼内鑽法　shell and auger boring
冲击载荷/衝擊負載　impact load
冲击中心/衝擊力中心　center of impact
冲击钻[机]/頓鑽　percussion drill
冲击钻孔/撞擊式鑽孔　percussion drilling
冲击钻孔机/壓孔機　thrust borer
冲击座/衝擊座　striker, striking casting
冲积岸堤/堤岸,灘肩　berm
冲积层/沖積層　alluvium deposit
冲积河道/沖積河槽　alluvial channel
冲积平原/沖積平原　alluvial plain
冲积坡泉/沖積坡泉　alluvial slope spring
冲积沙/沖積沙　washed sand
冲积扇/沖積扇　alluvial fan
冲积水道/沖積河槽　alluvial channel
冲积土/沖積土[壤]　alluvial soil, alluvium
冲剪破坏/衝剪破壞　punching shear failure
冲量/衝量,力积　impulse
冲砂管/排淤管　scour pipe
冲刷/沖刷　scouring, erosion
冲刷防护/防沖面層　scour protection
冲刷防治/沖刷控制　erosion control
冲刷深度/沖刷深度　scouring depth
冲刷系数/沖刷係數　coefficient of scouring
冲水试验/沖水試驗,射水試驗　hose test
冲送法/沖送法　jet lifter method
冲填土/水力沖填　hydraulic fill
冲突/碰撞　collision
冲突点/衝突點　point of conflict
冲洗/沖洗　wash
冲洗阀/清碴閥　washout valve
冲洗排水槽/反洗排水渠　wash water trough, wash water gutter
冲洗强度/反沖速度,反沖強度　backwash rate
冲洗装置/沖洗裝置　flushing arrangement
冲翼艇/衝翼艇,氣翼艇　ram-wing craft
充磁/磁化　magnetization
充磁开关/激磁開關　pre-exciting switch
充氮阀/充氮閥　nitrogen fill valve
充电/充電　charge
充电保持能力/充電保持能力　charge retention
充电插头/充電插頭　charging plug
充电接受能力/充電接收能力　charge acceptance
充电率/充電率　charging rate, charge rate
充电深度/充電程度　depth of charge, degree of charge
充电效率/充電效率　charge efficiency
充放电板/充放電盤　charging and discharging board, battery charging and discharging panel
充放电制/充放電型　charge and discharge regime
充风位/充風位　charge position
充氦潜水钟/合氦潛水鐘　helium diving bell
充量/填充,裝載　charge
充量系数/占空係數,填充係數,裝載係數　coefficient of charge
充量限制阀/充量限制閥　filling limiting valve
充气避雷器/充氣避雷器　gas filled arrester
充气玻璃/充氣玻璃　aerated glass
充气家具/充氣家具　inflatable furniture

充气结构/充氣結構　pneumatic structure, air inflated structure
充气轮胎式压路机/膠輪輾壓機　pneumatic rubber tired roller
充气石膏板/通氣石膏板　aerated gypsum panel
充气式设备/充氣救生設備　inflated appliance
充气试验/充氣試驗　air test, air charging test
充气维护型光缆/充氣維護型光纜　gas maintenance type optical fiber cable
充气系数/容積效率,體積效率　volumetric efficiency
充塞泡沫塑料打捞/噴以泡沫塑膠浮昇　raising by injection plastic foam
充水装置/充水器　water charger
充氧阀/充氧閥　oxygen fill valve
充氧能力/供氧能量,供氧能力　oxygenation capacity
充液式压力真空安全装置/充液式壓力真空切斷器　liquid-filled pressure vacuum breaker
充油变压器/充油變壓器　oil-filled electrical transformer
充油型光缆/充油型光纜　jelly filled type optical fiber cable
虫媒植物/蟲媒植物　entomophilous plant
重城环套形制/重城環套形制　circular town pattern system
重传/重傳　retransmission
重叠冰/重疊冰,載冰　rafted ice
重叠波/重疊波　overlapped wave
重叠船模/對疊[船]模,重疊模　double model
重叠螺旋桨/重疊型螺槳　overlapping propeller, overlap propeller
重叠区段/重疊部分　overlap section
重叠系数/重疊係數　overlap coefficient
重定向/改向　redirection
重发器模式/重發器模式　repeater mode
重复/重複　repeat, RPT
重复灌溉/重複灌溉　repeating irrigation
重复检查/重複檢查　repeated checking
重复接地/重複接地　iterative earthing
重复利用给水系统/重複利用給水系統　reuse water system
重复启闭预作用自动喷水灭火系统/重複啟閉預作用自動噴水滅火系統　recycling preaction sprinkler system
重复起动程序/重複起動程式　repeated starting sequence
重复使用返回器/重複使用返回器　reusable recoverable capsule
重复使用火箭发动机/重複使用火箭發動機　reusable rocket engine, reusable rocket
重复性/重複性　repeatability
重复运输/重複運輸　reflux of freight, repeated traffic
重复噪声/重複雜訊　repetitive noise
重复振动/再振動,再震實　revibration
重复作用/重複作用　repeated action
重建/重建,復健　rehabilitation
重建计划/重建計劃,再開發計劃　redevelopment plan
重联插座/多装置插座　multiple unit socket
重联机车走行公里/多機牽引走行公里　multi-locomotive running kilometers
重联运行试验/重聯運行試驗　test on coupled operation, test on multi unit operation
重铺路面/路面重鋪,軌道重整　resurfacing
重塑测试/重塑試驗　remoulding test
重塑土样/重塑樣本　remolded sample
重塑指数/重塑指數　remoulding index
重调/重置,復歸　reset
重现期/重現期,回復期,回歸期　recurrence interval, return period
重新安置/遷置,徙置　resettlement
重新定居/遷置,徙置　resettlement
重新定相/重行定相　rephasing
重新定向/再定位　reorientation
重新配合/重新組合　recoordination
重新调整/重新組合　recoordination
重檐/重檐　double eave
重组竹地板/重組竹地板　recombinant bamboo flooring
冲裁/衝切　blanking
冲孔/衝孔,穿孔　piercing, punching
冲孔成桩法/衝孔成樁法　pile by percussion drill method
冲压车间/衝壓庫　pressing and stamping shop
冲压喷气发动机/衝壓噴射發動機　ramjet engine
[冲压式]翼伞/翼傘　parafoil, airfoil parachute
冲抓成孔机/衝抓鏜孔機　impact grab boring machine
冲抓法/衝抓法　percussion and grabbing method
冲桩管线/水沖管路　jetting pipeline
抽舱排泥装置/抽艙排泥裝置　self-emptying installation
抽风机/抽風機　exhauster
抽气/抽氣　bleed
抽气量/抽氣率　bleed air rate
抽气器/空氣抽射器　air ejector

抽气循环/抽氣循環　combustion tap-off cycle
抽汽式汽轮机/抽汽渦輪機　extraction turbine, steam bleeding turbine
抽汽系统/抽汽系統,分汽系統　steam bleeding system
抽水灌溉/抽水灌溉　lift irrigation
抽水机坑/抽水機井　pump pit
抽水井/抽水井　pumped well, pumping well
抽水漏失率/抽水漏水率　pump slip
抽水设备/抽水設備　pumping equipment
抽水蓄能电站/抽蓄式發電廠　pumped storage power station
抽提/萃取,抽出　extraction
抽提试验/抽樣試驗　extraction test
抽条/抽條　article extraction
抽芯铆接/抽芯鉚接　cherry riveting
抽验/抽驗　selective acceptance
抽样方案/抽樣方案,抽樣計劃　sampling scheme
抽样检验/抽樣檢驗,抽樣檢查　sampling inspection
抽样交通调查/交通量抽樣調查　sample traffic survey
抽样可靠性/樣本可信率　sampling reliability
抽样试验/抽樣試驗,抽樣測試,樣品試驗　sample test, sampling test
抽样信度/樣本可信率　sampling reliability
抽液管座/抽液管座　unloading pipe connection
抽真空/抽真空　vacuum-pumping
稠度/稠度　consistency
稠度计/稠度試驗器　consistometer
稠度界限/稠度界限　consistency limit
稠度试验/稠度試驗　consistency test
稠度台试验/流動臺試驗　flow-table test
稠化剂/增稠劑　thickener
筹展接待区/籌展接待室　preparation and reception area
臭气控制/異味控制　odor control
臭味/臭　odor
臭氧/臭氧　ozone
臭氧层/臭氧層　ozonosphere
臭氧发生器/臭氧產生器　ozone generator
臭氧化/臭氧化[作用]　ozonization
臭氧消毒/臭氧消毒　disinfection by ozone
出厂评审/出廠評審　ex-factory review
出厂试飞/交機試飛　delivery flight test
出厂试验/發貨前試驗　predelivery test
出厂证明试验/驗證試驗　certification test
出车时间/出車時間　vehicle line haul hour
出发/駛離岸　put off

出发场/出發場　departure yard
出发港/出發港　port of departure
出发台/起跑板　starting block
出发线/出發線　departure track
出港到港车道边/出港到港車道邊　departure-arrival curb
出港压载水/出港壓艙水　departure ballast
出港引水费/出港引水費　outward pilotage
出界概率/出界概率　out of bound probability
出境交通/外駛交通　outbound traffic
出口/出口　exit
出口报告书/結關報告　report of clearance
出口标志/出口指示　exit sign
出口仓间/出口倉間　out bound compartment
出口段/出口段　outlet section
出口加工区/加工出口區　export processing zone
出口区段/出口區　exit zone
出口损失/出口損失　outlet loss
出口温度分布/出口溫度分布　exit temperature distribution
出口许可/出口許可　export permit
出口许可证/出港許可證　port clearance
出口预告标志/出口預告標誌　advance exit sign
出口匝道控制/出口匝道控制　exit ramp control
出口照明/出口照明　exit lighting
出链长度/放鏈長度　chain scope
出流堰/出水堰　effluent weir
出纳区/出納區　receiving and lending area
出浅力/脫淺力,再浮力　refloating force
出让地价/出讓地價　land leasing price
出入口/出入口　access opening
出入口控制系统/存取控制系統　access control system, ACS
出入口隧道/隧道通道　access tunnel
出入通道/出入道路　access road
出入院大厅/出入院大廳　inpatient register hall
出射光瞳/出射[光]瞳　exit pupil
出生率/出生率　birth rate
出水管/出水管　effluent pipe, outlet conduit
出水口/排水口,出口　outlet, outfall
出水量/出水量　water yield
出水容量/出水容量　outlet capacity
出水总管/出口下水道,放流下水道　outfall sewer
出跳/出跳　projecting step, chutiao
出坞/出塢　undock, undocking
出现/出露　emergence
出行/出行,[短程]旅行,旅遊　travel, trip
出行长度/行程長度　trip length

出行端点/出行端點　trip end
出行端点模型/出行端點模型　trip end model
出行方式/出行方式　traffic mode, transportation mode
出行分布/旅次分布[模式]　trips distribution
出行交换模型/出行交換模型　trip interchange model
出行率/來回程運率　trip rate
出行目的/出行目的　trip purpose
出行生成/旅次產生，旅次發生　trip generation
出行时间/往返時間　trip time
出行吸引/旅次吸引　traffic attraction, transportation attraction
出油阀/輸油閥　delivery valve
出油阀偶件/出油閥偶合件　delivery valve matching parts
出油阀座/輸油閥座　delivery valve seat
出碴/出碴　tunnel muck hauling, mucking and removing
出碴车/出碴車　muck car
出碴作业/出碴作業　mucking out
出站厅/迎客大廳　arrival hall
出站信号机/出發號誌[機]　starting signal
出中继电路/長途去話中繼器，長途去話中繼電路　outgoing trunk circuit
出走/背著走　walkaway
出租船/出租船　chartered ship
出租房屋/租賃房屋　rental housing
出租汽车/出租汽車，計程車　taxi, taxicab
出租汽车客运/出租汽車客運，計程車運輸　taxi transport
出租型住房/租賃房屋　rental housing
出租性工业厂房/出租性工業廠房　rentable industrial building
出租住宅/出租住宅　tenement house
初步测量/初測　preliminary surveying
初步分析报告/早期分析報告　initial analysis report
初步粉碎机/粗軋碎石機　primary crusher
初步辗压/初步輾壓　initial rolling
初步设计/初步設計　preliminary design, preliminary design
初步设计评审/初步設計審查　review of preliminary design
初步运行能力/初始運轉能力　initial operational capability, IOC
初步证据/表面證據　prima facie evidence
初沉污泥/初級汙泥　primary sludge
初次沉淀池/初步沈澱池　primary settling tank
初次检验/初次檢驗　initial survey, original inspection
初次入级/初次入級　initial classification
初澄池/初步澄清池　preliminary clarifier
初给泵/起動泵　priming pump
初级产业/初級工業，第一級產業　primary industry
初见陆地/初見陸地　landfall
初滤排水/初濾排水　filtrate to waste
初凝/初凝　initial setting
初凝时间/初凝時間，始凝時間　initial setting time, age of hardening
初期径流/初期徑流　initial runoff
初期微震/初期微震　preliminary tremor
初期养护/初期養護　initial maintenance
初期雨水/初期徑流　initial runoff
初期支护/前期支撐　primary support
初生化需氧量/初生化需氧量　immediate BOD
初生水/原生水　primitive water
初始报告/初步報告　initial report
初始沉降/初始沈陷　immediate settlement
初始对准/初始校準　initial alignment
初始轨道计算/初步軌道計算　preliminary orbit calculation
初始轨道确定/初步軌道決定　preliminary orbit determination
初始裂纹深度/初始裂縫深度　initial crack depth
初始偏差/初[始]誤差　initial error
初始破坏/初期破壞　incipient failure
初始缺陷/初始不平整瑕疵　initial imperfection
初始时间间隙/初始時間間隙　initial time gap
初始图形交换规范/起始圖形交換規格　initial graphics exchange specification, IGES
初始推力峰/初始推力峰　initial thrust peak
初始温度/起始溫度，初溫　initial temperature
初始应力场/原始應力場　primary stress field
初始预应力/初始預力　initial prestress
初始蒸汽参数/初始蒸汽參變數　initial steam parameter
初始姿态捕获/初始姿態取得　initial attitude acquisition
初始自由容积/初始自由容積　initial free volume
初速减缓装置/初速減緩裝置　slow starter
初碎机/粗碎機　primary breaker
初稳心/初定傾中心　initial metacenter
初稳心半径/初定傾半徑　initial metacentric radius
初稳心高度/初定傾中心在基線以上高度　initial metacentric height above baseline
初稳性/初穩度　initial stability

初稳性高度/初定傾中心高度　initial metacentric height, initial stability height
初样设计/原型設計　prototype design
初样试验/原型試驗,原型測試　prototype test
初样[星]/工程模型　engineering model, EM
除冰系统/除冰系統　deicing system
除冰装置/除冰裝置　deicer
除草机/雜草切除機　weed cutting machine, weed cutter
除草剂/除草劑　herbicide
除尘/除塵　dust removal, dust separation, dust control
除尘器/除塵器　dust separator, dust collector, particulate collector
除尘装置/集塵機,集塵器　dust collector
除臭装置/除臭設備　odor removal
除垢/除垢　descaling
除鳞机/除鱗機　scaler
除砂机/除砂機　sand removing machine
除湿器/消濕器　dehumidifier
除湿[作用]/去潮法　dehumidification
除鼠/滅鼠　deratting
除树机/伐木機　treedozer
除外条款/豁免條款　exemption clause
除污器/[粗]濾器　strainer
除锈/除銹　removing rust, descaling
除雪/除雪,鏟雪　snow removing
除雪车/除雪車,鏟雪車　snow plow
除雪机/除雪機,鏟雪機　snow remover, snow sweeper
除烟[法]/煤煙防治　smoke abatement
除盐/除鹽,淡化　desalination
除盐水/除礦質水　demineralized water
除氧器/除氧器　deaerator
除叶剂/除葉劑　defoliant
除油/祛油　oil removal
除油器/集油器　oil remover
厨房/廚房,茶水間　galley, kitchen
厨房车/廚車　kitchen car
厨园/廚園　kitchen yard
橱窗/櫥窗,陳列窗,展覽窗　show window
处理方法/處理方法　treatment process
处理过程/處理過程　treatment process
处理流程/處理流程　treatment flowsheet
处理器模式/處理器模式　processor mode
处理设备/處理設備　process unit
处理时间/處理時間　processing time
处女航/處女航　maiden voyage

处置废物/廢棄物處理　disposal of wastes
杵环杆/杵環桿　bar with ball and eye, ball-socket bar
杵座鞍子/鞍式鞍部,鞍形鞍部　socket-type saddle
储备/備用　reserve
储备浮力/預[留]浮力　reserve buoyancy
储备功率/備用功率　reserve power
储备排水量/排水量餘裕　displacement margin
储备通行能力/備用容量,備轉容量　reserve capacity
储藏[室]/儲藏室,貯藏室,倉庫　storage, storage room
储存渗透设施/儲存滲透設施　detention-infiltration equipment
储存书库/儲存書庫　basic stack
储存稳定度试验/耐貯性試驗　storage stability test
储风罐/蓄氣器　air reservoir
储料斗/進料斗　storage hopper
储配站/貯氣站　gas holder station
储片机构/儲片機構　film storing mechanism
储气罐/貯氣槽,貯氣箱,煤氣塔　storage tank, gas holder
储气瓶/儲氣瓶　air flask
储气箱/空氣儲蓄器　air container
储水系数/儲水係數　storage coefficient, storativity
储酸室/貯酸室　acid store room
储蓄所/儲蓄銀行　savings bank
储液缸/貯液櫃　liquid container
储液器/貯液器　receiver
储油船/儲油船,貯油船　oil storage tanker
储油间/儲油間　oil storage room
储油平台/儲油平臺　oil storage platform
畜力车/獸力車　animal-drawn vehicle
畜力车道/鄉村路　cart road
畜力剪草机/畜力剪草機　horse lawnmower
畜禽舍建筑/養畜場　livestock house
触变性/觸變性,靜凝性,搖溶性　thixotropy
触变性涂料/膠滯漆　thixotropic paint
触电保安器/電擊保護器　electric shock protector
触发器/觸發器　trigger
触发引信/觸發引信　contact fuze
触发引信灵敏度/觸發引信靈敏度　sensitivity of contact fuze
触礁/觸礁　strike on a rock
触敏控制板/觸摸感應板　touch sensitive panel
触浅掉头/觸淺短迴轉掉頭　turning short round by one end touch the shoal
触损/接觸損害　contact damage
穿地遥测/鑽地遙測　penetrating earth telemetry

穿斗式/穿斗 column and tie-beam construction, chuandou
穿盖弹射/穿蓋彈射 through canopy ejection
穿晶断裂/穿晶破斷 transgranular fracture
穿井/穿井 drived well
穿孔率/穿孔率 perforated percentage
穿入式喷注器/鍵入注射器 inserted injector
穿式结构/穿式結構 through structure
穿束机/穿束機 strand pulling machine
穿梭油轮/梭運油輪,短程往返油輪 shuttle tanker
穿销防爬器/穿銷防爬器 wedged rail anchor
穿越/橫越 crossing
穿越时间/穿越時間 crossing time
传爆系列/炸藥系列,導火藥 explosive train
传爆药柱/傳爆藥柱 booster grain
传播路径/傳播路徑 propagation path
传播深度/分布深度 spreading depth
传播速度/傳播速度 propagation velocity
传播途径/擴散通道 spread channel
传播误差/傳播誤差 propagation error
传达室/傳達室,收發室 gatekeeper room, gateman room, porter room
传导/傳導 conduction
传导发射/傳導發射 conducted emission
传导发射安全系数测量/傳導發射安全因數量測 conduction emission safety factor measurement
传导发射测量/傳導發射量測 conduction emission measurement
传导干扰/傳導介面 conducted interference
传导敏感度/傳導易感受性,傳導靈敏度 conducted susceptibility
传导敏感度测量/傳導靈敏度量測 conduction sensitivity measurement
传导模/波導模態 guided mode
传导无线电噪声/傳導無線電雜音 conducted radio noise
传递标准/傳遞標準,轉移標準 transfer standard
传递窗/傳遞窗 pass box
传递导纳/傳遞動性 transfer mobility
传递刚度/傳遞勁度 carry-over stiffness
传递函数/轉移函數 transfer function
传递矩阵/傳接矩陣,變換矩陣 transfer matrix
传递路由/中轉途徑 transit route
传递弯矩/傳遞彎矩,傳遞力矩 carry-over moment
传递系数/傳遞因數 carry-over factor
传递阻抗/轉移阻抗 transfer impedance
传动/傳動 transmission
传动齿轮/傳動齒輪 transmission gear
传动机构/傳輸裝置 transmission device
传动试验/傳輸測試 transmission test
传动头/打椿砧 driving head
传动系统/傳動系統 driving system
传动轴/傳動軸 transmission shaft
传动轴系/傳動軸系 transmission shafting
传感器/傳感器,感測器,測感子 sensor, pickoff, transducer
传感信息控制/感測控制 sensory control
传力杆/梢桿 dowel bar
传力黏结/傳力黏結 transfer bond
传热/熱傳導,導熱 heat transfer
传热系数/熱傳[遞]係數 heat transfer coefficient
传热阻/抗熱導性,熱阻 heat transfer resistance
传声器/傳聲器,話筒,麥克風 microphone
传声增益/[傳遞]增益 transmission gain
传输/傳輸 transmission
传输继电器/傳輸繼電器 transmitting relay, transmission relay
传输结束信号/傳輸結束信號 end-of-transmission signal
传输时钟/傳送時鐘 transfer clock
传输通道/傳輸通道,傳遞通路,傳輸路徑 transmission path
传输通路/傳輸通道,發送通道 transmission channel
传输网络中心/傳輸網路中心 transmission network center
传输系统/傳輸系統,傳遞系統 transmission system
传输线/傳遞線 transmission line
传输效率/傳輸效率 transmission efficiency
传输性能/傳輸性能 transmission performance
传送同步方式/傳送同步方式 transmission synchronized mode
传送帧/傳送幀 transfer frame
传统村落/傳統村落 traditional village
传统风貌/傳統特色 traditional feature
传统风貌建筑/傳統特色建築 traditional scene building
传统复兴式/傳統復興式 Chinese revival
传统格局/傳統格局 traditional pattern
传统式输送设备/傳統式輸送設備 conventional transfer rig
传统修缮技术/傳統修繕技術 traditional treatment technique of heritage
传统园林建筑/傳統園林建築 traditional garden building
传焰管/傳焰管 interconnector

传氧效率/氧傳輸效率　oxygen transfer efficiency
传真/傳真　facsimile, Fax
传真发送机/傳真發送機　facsimile transmitter
传真机/傳真儀器　facsimile apparatus, Fax
传真接收机/傳真接收器　facsimile receiver
传真收发机/傳真收發兩用機　facsimile transceiver
传真天气图/傳真天氣圖　facsimile weather chart
传质/質量傳遞,質量轉移　mass transfer
船岸间距/船岸間距　bank clearance
船板/船板　planking
船边交货/船邊交貨　alongside delivery, free alongside ship
船边交货条款/船邊交貨條款　sous-palan clause
船表/對時表　hack watch
船[舶]/船,艦　vessel, ship
船舶安全检查/船舶安全檢查　ship safety inspection
船舶安全学/船舶安全工程　vessel safety engineering
船舶安全营运管理/船舶安全營運管理　management for the safe operation of ships
船舶保向宽度/船舶巷道　ship lane
船舶报告系统/船舶報告系統　vessel reporting system
船舶避碰/船舶避碰　ship collision prevention
船舶操纵/船舶操縱　shiphandling
船舶操纵性/船舶操縱性　ship maneuverability
船舶操纵性指数/操縱性能指數　maneuverability indices
船舶常数/船舶常數　ship constant
船舶代理/船舶代理　ship agent
船舶登记/船舶登記　ship registration
船舶抵押贷款/船舶押款　bottomry
船舶抵押合同/船舶抵押契約,船舶貸款保證書　bottomry bond
船舶抵押合同持有人/船舶抵押債券持有人　bottomry bondholder
船舶抵押权/船舶抵押權　ship mortgage
船舶地球站/船舶地面臺,船舶衛星電臺　ship earth station, SES
船舶地球站启用试验/船舶衛星電臺啟用試驗　SES commissioning test
船舶地球站识别码/船舶衛星電臺識別碼　ship earth station identification, SES ID
船舶电气设备/船舶電氣設備,船舶電力裝置　marine electrical equipment, marine electric installation
船舶电台/船舶電臺　ship station
船舶电台表/船舶電臺表　list of ship station

船舶电台群呼识别/船舶電臺群呼識別　group ship station call identity
船舶电台识别/船舶電臺識別　ship station identity
船舶电站/船舶電力設備,船舶發電所　marine electrical power plant, ship power station
船舶电站自动控制装置/船舶電力設備自動控制裝置　automatic control system for marine electric power plant
船舶定线制/船舶定航線制　ship routing
船舶动力装置/船舶動力裝置　marine power plant
船舶动力装置操纵性/船舶動力裝置操縱性　marine power plant maneuverability
船舶动力装置经济性/船舶動力裝置經濟性　marine power plant economy
船舶动力装置可靠性/船舶動力裝置可靠性　marine power plant service reliability
船舶动力装置可维修性/船舶動力裝置可維修性　marine power plant maintainability
船舶动态业务/船舶移動業務　ship movement service
船舶吨位/船噸位　ship tonnage
船舶飞机协作搜寻/船舶飛機協作搜尋　ship-aircraft coordinated search
船舶辅机/船舶輔機　marine auxiliary machinery
船舶辅助观测/輔助船舶觀測　auxiliary ship observation, ASO
船舶改装/船舶改裝　ship conversion
船舶工程/船舶工程　maritime engineering, ship engineering
船舶共有人/船舶共有人　co-owner of ship
船舶供应商/船舶供應商　shipchandler
船舶管理人/船舶管理人　ship husband
船舶管辖权/船舶管轄權　jurisdiction over ship
船舶核动力装置/船用核子動力裝置　marine nuclear power plant
船舶呼号/船舶呼號　ship call sign
[船舶或船货]抵押/[船舶或船貨]抵押　hypothecation
船舶机械通风/船舶機械通風　ship mechanical ventilation
船舶挤靠力/船舶擠靠力　ship breasting force
船舶加速度/船舶加速度　acceleration of ship
船舶检验/船舶檢驗　ship survey
船舶减摇装置/船舶穩定裝置　ship stabilizing gear
船舶交通调查/船舶交通調查　vessel traffic survey, vessel traffic investigation
船舶交通工程/船舶交通工程　vessel traffic engineering

船舶交通管理/船舶交通服務 vessel traffic service, VTS
船舶交通管理系統/船舶交通管理系統 vessel traffic management service, VTMS
船舶交通管理站/船舶交通服務站 VTS station
船舶交通管理中心/船舶交通服務中心 vessel traffic service center, VTS center
船舶交通模擬/船舶交通模擬 ship traffic simulation
船舶經紀人/船舶經紀人 shipbroker
船舶經紀人佣金/船舶經紀人佣金 shipbrokerage
船舶經理人/船舶經理人 ship manager
船舶經營人/船舶營運人 ship operator
船舶靠泊系統/船船靠泊系統 docking system
船舶空氣調節/船舶空調 marine air conditioning
船舶快速性/船舶阻力性能 ship resistance and performance
船舶領域/船舶領域 ship domain
船舶旅客/船舶旅客 ship passenger
船舶配備要求/船舶配備要求 ship carriage requirements
船舶碰撞/船舶碰撞 ship collision
船舶碰撞管轄權/船舶碰撞管轄權 jurisdiction of ship collision
船舶碰撞民事管轄權某些規定的國際公約/關於船舶碰撞事件民事管轄國際公約 International Convention on Certain Rules Concerning Civil Jurisdiction in Matters of Collision
船舶碰撞准據法/船舶碰撞適用法 applicable law of ship collision
船舶起貨設備檢驗簿/船舶貨物裝卸設備登記簿 register of cargo handling gear of ship
船舶氣象報告/船舶氣象報告 ship weather report
船舶全損險/全損險 total loss only
船舶入級和建造規範/船舶入級與建造規範 Rules for Classification and Construction of Ships
船舶所有人/船舶所有人,船東 shipowner
船舶通風/船舶通風 ship ventilation
船舶[通信]業務/船舶[通信]業務 ship business
船舶塗料/船舶塗料 marine paint
船舶推進/船舶推進 ship propulsion
船舶推進軸系/船舶推進軸系 marine propulsion shafting
船舶無線電導航/船舶無線電導航 marine radio navigation
船舶無線電執照/船舶無線電臺執照 ship radio license
船舶系統/船舶系統 ship system, marine system
船舶消防/船舶滅火 ship fire fighting

船舶消防裝置/船用滅火系統 marine fire fighting system
船舶搖蕩/船舶搖盪 ship oscillation
船舶優先權/船舶優先權,海事留置權 maritime lien
船舶優先權和抵押權國際公約/船舶優先權及抵押權國際公約 International Convention on Maritime Liens and Mortgage
船舶油污險/油汙險 oil pollution risk
船舶運動圖/運動圖 maneuvering board
船舶載重量/船舶載重噸位 deadweight tonnage of vessel, deadweight of vessel
船舶噪聲/船舶噪音 ship noise
船舶戰爭險/船舶戰爭險 hull war risk
船舶蒸汽鍋爐/船用蒸汽鍋爐 marine steam boiler
船舶蒸汽機/船用蒸汽機 marine steam engine
船舶證書/船舶證書 ship certificate
船舶證書檢驗簿/船舶證書檢驗記錄簿 ship certificates surveying record book
船舶制冷裝置/船舶冷凍裝置 marine refrigerating plant
船舶軸系/船舶軸系 marine shafting
船舶主機/船舶主機 marine main engine
船舶撞擊力/船舶碰撞力,船舶衝擊力 ship collision force, ship impact force
船舶自動互救系統/自動互助船舶救助系統 automated mutual-assistance vessel rescue system, AMVER
船舶自然通風/船舶自然通風 ship natural ventilation
船舶總流向/船流總向 general direction of traffic flow
船舶租購/光船租購 bareboat charter with hire purchase
船舶租金/船舶租傭金,傭船費 charter hire
船舶租賃/船舶租賃 hiring of ship
船舶阻力/船舶阻力 ship resistance
船舶阻力特性/船體阻力特性 hull resistance characteristic
船側骨架/側肋骨 side frame, side framing
船長/船長,艦長 length
船磁/船磁 ship magnetism
船到岸遇險報警/船與岸間遇險警報 ship-to-shore distress alerting
船到船遇險報警/船與船間遇險警報 ship-to-ship distress alerting
船底板/[鋼]船底外板,船底殼板 bottom plating, bottom plate
船底橫骨/[船]底肋骨 bottom frame

船底横桁/船底橫材　bottom transverse
船底漆/船底漆　bottom paint
船底涂料/船底塗料,船底漆　ship bottom coating, ship bottom paint
船底验平/船底校準　ship bottom alignment check
船底纵骨/［船］底縱肋　bottom longitudinal
船钉/船釘　boat spike
船东/船東,船舶所有人　shipowner
船渡费/船渡費　ferry toll
船队/船隊,艦隊　fleet
船队通信网/船隊通信網　fleet NET
船筏/船艇,載具　craft
船方不负责装卸积载费/裝卸堆裝費自理　free in and out stowed
船方不负装卸费用/裝卸自理　free in and out, FIO
船后螺旋桨试验/［螺槳］船後試驗　behind test, behind ship test of propeller
船级/船級　class of ship
船级标记/船級標誌　ship class mark
船级符号/船級符號　ship class symbol notation
船级社/船級協會,船級機構　register of shipping, classification society, ship classification society
船籍/船籍國　nationality of vessel
船籍港/船籍港　port of registry, home port, port of registration
船架/船架　cradle
船［舰］间横距/船艦間橫距　beam distance between ships
船壳险/船身保險　hull insurance
船宽吃水比/船寬吃水比　beam draft ratio
船龄/船齡　age of ship
船楼端/艛端　break
船模/船模　block model, ship model
船模试验/船模試驗　tank experiment
船模系列试验/船模系列試驗　systematic test of ship model
船模阻力仪/阻力儀　resistance dynamometer
船内驳运/船內轉駁　internal transfer
船内通信设备/船上通信設備　apparatus for on-board communication
船排/船臺,滑道,斜道　slipway, marine railway
船期表/船期表　sailing schedule
船旗歧视/船旗歧視　flag discrimination
船上管理/船上管理　shipboard management
船上通信/船上通信　on-board communications
船上通信电台/船上通信電臺　on-board communication station
船上训练/船上訓練　on-board training
船上训练记录簿/船上訓練記錄簿　on-board training record book
船上油污染应急计划/船上油汙染應急計劃　shipboard oil pollution emergency plan
船身效率/船殼效率　hull efficiency
船首倍角法/艏倍角定位法　doubling angle on the bow
船速分布/航速分配　ship speed distribution
船台/船臺,造船碼頭　building berth, ship building berth
船台标杆线/船臺標桿線　vertical template for hull assembly
船台坡度/船臺坡度,船臺斜度　inclination of building slip, slope of building berth, slope of ways
船台舾装/船臺舾裝　berth outfitting
船台装配/船臺裝配　berth assembly
船体/船體,船身,船殼　hull, ship hull
船体保养/船體保養　hull maintenance
船体变形/船體變形　shipbody deformation
［船体］变形测量系统/變形量測系統　shipbody deformation measurement system
［船体］放样/［船體］放樣　lofting
船体刚度/船體剛性　hull stiffness
船体固有振动频率/船體自然頻率　hull natural frequency
船体回路系统/船體回路系統　hull-return system
船体加工/船體鋼料加工　hull steel fabrication
船体建造工艺/船體建造工藝　technology of hull construction
船体建造公差/船體建造公差　tolerance of hull construction
船体结构/船體結構,船身構造　hull construction, hull structure
［船体零件］号料/船體零件標記　marking of hull parts
船体密性试验/船體密性試驗　tightness test for hull
船体挠度/船體撓度　hull deflection
船体扭转振动/船體扭轉振動　hull torsional vibration
船体强度/船體強度　hull strength
船体下坐/艉坐　squat
船体线型/船形　hull form
船体型表面/船［體］型面　molded hull surface
船体以上高度/［號燈］距船身高度　height above the hull
船体振动/船體振動　ship vibration
船体装配/船體組合　hull assembly
船体姿态角/船體姿態角　shipbody attitude angle

船外除泥/船外除泥　removing mud around wreck
船尾角/船尾角　boat tail angle
船位/船位　ship position, fix
GPS船位/全球定位系統船位　GPS fix
船位报告/船位報告　position report
船位差/船位差　position difference
船位精度/船位精度　accuracy of position, ship position accuracy
船位漂移/船位漂移　drift of ship position
[船位]误差平行四边形/誤差平行四邊形　error parallelogram
[船位]误差三角形/誤差三角形　cocked hat
[船位]误差椭圆/船位誤差橢圓　error ellipse of position
[船位]误差圆/未定的船位圈　circle of uncertainty
船位圆/位置圈　circle of position
船坞/[船]塢, 船渠　basin, dry dock, dock
船坞拖船/港內拖船　dock tug
船坞舾装/船塢舾裝　dock outfitting
船吸效应/船間相互作用　interaction between ships
船舷接管/船舷接管　ship side pipe
船行风速/船行風速　velocity of ship wind
船形灯标/船形燈標　light-float
船型曲线/船用曲線板　ship curve
船型系数/線型係數　coefficients of form
船医/船醫　ship doctor
船艺/船藝　seamanship
船用泵/船用泵　marine pump
船用变压器/船用變壓器　marine transformer
船用柴油/船用柴油　marine diesel oil
船用柴油机/船用柴油機　marine diesel engine
船用齿轮箱/船用齒輪箱　marine gear box
船用厨房设备/船用廚房設備　marine galley equipment
船用电力电缆/船用電力電纜　shipboard power cables
船用阀门/船用閥門　marine valves
船用防火板/船用防火板　marine fire proof panel
船用焚烧炉/船用焚化爐　marine incinerator
船用风机/船用風機　marine-type fan
船用广播设备/船用廣播系統　marine public address system
船用锅炉/船用鍋爐　marine boiler
船用焊条/船用焊條　shipbuilding electrode
船用火灾自动报警装置/船用火災自動警報系統　marine automatic fire alarm system
船用家具/船用家具　marine furniture
船用胶合板/船用合板　marine plywood

船用雷达/船用雷達　marine radar
船用离合器/船用離合器　marine clutch
船用联轴器/船用聯軸節　marine coupling
船用内燃机/船用引擎　marine engine
船用气瓶/船用氣瓶　marine air bottle
船用汽轮机/船用蒸汽渦輪機　marine steam turbine
船用轻柴油/船用輕柴油　marine gas oil
船用全功能焚烧炉/船用多功能焚化爐　marine multifunction incinerator
船用燃气轮机/船用燃氣渦輪機　marine gas turbine
船用射频电缆/船用射頻電纜　shipboard radio-frequency cables
船用生活污水处理装置/船用生活汙水處理系統　marine sewage treatment system
船用条件/船用條件　marine condition
船用通信电缆/船用通信電纜　shipboard telecommunication cables
船用卫生设备/船用衛生設施　marine sanitation device, MSD, marine sanitary fixtures
船用物料/船用物料　marine store
船用蓄电池组/船用蓄電池組　marine storage batteries, marine accumulator batteries
船用液压气动元件/船用液壓氣動元件　marine hydropneumatic components and units
船员/船員　crew
船员定员/船員配額　complement
船员法/海員法　law of mariner
船员名单/船員名單, 船員名冊　crew list
船员室/船員室　crew space, crew room
船员证书/船員證書, 航海人員證書　certificate of seafarer
船员自用物品报关/船員自用物品申請單　crew customs declaration
船闸/船閘　navigation lock, shipping lock
船闸沉箱/船式沈箱門　ship caisson gate
船闸输水门/水閘室　lock paddle
船闸输水系统/船閘輸水系統　filling and emptying system of lock
船闸水头/船閘水頭　lift of lock
船长/船長, 艦長　captain
船长借支/船長借支　advance to captain
船长室/船長室　captain room
船只或排筏的撞击力/船隻或排筏的撞擊力　collision force of ship or raft
船钟/船鐘　clock
船装/船體舾裝　hull outfit, hull outfitting
船姿船位[测量]系统/船姿船位[測量]系統　ship attitude and position measuring system

椽架/椽架　rafter span
椽[子]/椽　rafter
喘振/喘振,波振,湧振　surge, surging, breathe vibration
喘振边界/喘振極限　surge limit
喘振限/喘振限　surging limit
喘振线/喘振線,顫動線　surge line
喘振裕度/喘振裕度,喘振極限,喘振邊界　surge margin
串并联扫描/串并聯掃描　serial and parallel scan
串并联引爆系统/并串聯引爆系統　series-parallel fuzing system
串级调速/梯列控制調速　speed regulation by cascade control
串励电动机/串勵電動機　series excited motor
串联电容补偿装置/串聯電容比較電橋　compensator with series capacitance
串联电阻/串聯電阻　series resistance
串联供水/串聯供水　series water supply
串联驱动/前後傳動　tandem drive
串联扫描/串聯掃描　serial scan
串联式船坞/串聯式船塢　tandem dock
串联式轨道电路/串聯式軌道電路　serially connected track circuit
串联式推进装置/串聯推進系統　tandem propulsion system
串联往复泵/串聯往復泵　reciprocating pump in series
串联系泊装油系统/串列裝卸系統　tandem loading system
串联引爆系统/串聯引爆系統　series fuzing system
串列螺旋桨/串聯螺槳,重疊螺槳　tandem propeller
串列叶栅/串聯葉片　tandem cascade
串扰/串話　cross talk
串行传输/串列傳輸　serial transmission
串行高密度记录/序列高密度記錄　serial high-density recording
串音/串音　crosstalk
串音测试器/串音測試儀,串音計　crosstalk meter
串音衰减/串音衰減,串話衰減　crosstalk attenuation
串音抑制滤波器/串音抑制濾波器　crosstalk suppression filter
窗地面积比/玻地面積比　ratio of glazing to floor area
窗洞口/採光口　daylight opening
窗洞口采光系数/採光口晝光因數　daylight factor of daylight opening
窗函数/窗函數　window function

窗间板/窗間板　pier sheathing
窗井/窗井　window well
窗景/窗景　window garden
窗口/窗口,視窗　window
窗宽修正系数/窗寬修正係數　correction coefficient of window width
窗框/窗框　window sash
窗帘/窗簾　curtain, window curtain
窗帘盒/窗簾盒　curtain box, pelmet box
窗楣/窗楣　brow, lintel
窗墙面积比/窗牆面積比　window to wall ratio
窗式空气调节器/窗型空調　window type air conditioner
窗锁/窗鎖　window sash lock
窗台/窗臺　window sill, window rail
窗台绿化/窗臺綠化　window sill greening
床铺/床[鋪]　bunk
床沙质/床沙質,河床質載　bed material load
床头灯/床燈　berth lamp
床[位]/床　bed
创意城市/創意城市　creative city
吹除/吹洩　blow off, purge
吹除阀/清除閥　sea chest cleaning valve
吹除系统/吹氣系統　purging system
吹除压强/吹洗壓力　purging pressure
吹灰器/吹灰器　soot blower
吹开风/離岸風,陸風　offshore wind
吹拢风/向岸風　onshore wind
吹泥船/駁船卸載式挖泥船　barge unloading dredger
吹气襟翼/吹氣式襟翼　blown flap
吹气式风洞/吹式風洞　blowdown wind tunnel
吹气式风洞能量比/吹式風洞能量比　energy ratio of blowdown tunnel
吹入通风/鼓風換氣　blowing ventilation
吹填/吹填　hydraulic reclamation, hydraulic fill
吹脱塔/汽提塔,脱除塔　stripping tower
吹吸式风洞/吹吸式風洞　blowdown-indraft wind tunnel
吹雪/飄雪　blowing snow
吹引式风洞/吹引式風洞　blowdown-ejection wind tunnel
吹制沥青/吹製瀝青　blown bitumen
垂带/垂帶　chuidai
垂荡/[船身]起伏　heaving
垂钓/垂釣　fishing
垂度/垂度　sag
垂花门/垂花門　festooned gate, chuihuamen
垂脊/垂脊　diagonal ridge for hip roof, chuiji

垂曲修正/垂度改正　correction for sag
垂线间长/垂標間距　length between perpendiculars, LBP
垂线偏差/垂直偏差　vertical deviation
垂线偏角/垂線偏角　deviation of the vertical
垂向冲击/垂直衝擊　vertical impact
垂向棱形系数/垂向稜塊係數　vertical prismatic coefficient
垂向弯曲振动/垂向彎曲振動　vertical flexural vibration
垂向振动/垂向振動　vertical vibration
垂鱼/垂魚　fish-shaped board, chuiyu
垂枝盆景/垂枝盆景　penjing planted with pendulous-tree
垂枝植物/垂枝樹　weeping tree
垂直/垂直,立式　vertical
垂直安定面/垂直安定面　vertical stabilizer
垂直变位/垂直變位　down throw
垂直波束宽度/垂直波束寬度　vertical beam width
垂直补给/垂直整補　vertical replenishment
垂直测试/垂直[發射]試驗　vertical test
垂直磁棒/上昇用磁鐵　vertical magnet
垂直带/垂直分布帶　altitudinal zone, altitudinal belt
垂直带分异/垂直帶分化　vertical zonality differentiation
垂直单向流/垂直單向流　vertical unidirectional airflow
垂直动载荷/垂向動荷重　vertical dynamic load
垂直度调整/垂直度調整　verticality adjustment
垂直-短距起落动力装置/VTOL-STOL 動力設備　VTOL-STOL power plant
垂直发射/垂直發射　vertical launch
垂直发展/立體發展　vertical development
垂直反力/垂直反力　vertical reaction
垂直分布/垂直分布　vertical distribution
垂直工作范围/垂直工作範圍　vertical working range
垂直光弧/垂直弧區　vertical sector
垂直极化/垂直極化　vertical polarization
垂直间隔/垂直隔離　vertical separation
垂直剪切/垂直剪力　vertical shear
垂直角定位/垂直角定位　fixing by vertical angle
垂直角距离/垂直角距離　distance by vertical angle
垂直角位置线/垂直角位置線　position line by vertical angle
垂直结太阳电池/垂直接面太陽電池　vertical junction solar cell
垂直净距/垂直淨距,垂直淨空　vertical distance
垂直能见度/垂直能見度　vertical visibility
垂直排水砂井/垂直排水砂樁　vertical sand drain
垂直起落飞机/垂直起降飛機　vertical take-off and landing airplane, VTOL airplane
垂直切削/垂直切挖　vertical cut
垂直侵蚀/垂直沖蝕　vertical erosion
垂直圈/垂直大圓　vertical circle
垂直上升/垂直上昇　vertical ascent
垂直摄影/垂直[航空]攝影　vertical photography, vertical photographing
垂直升船机/垂直昇船機　vertical ship lift
垂直式阻力动力仪/垂直式阻力動力計　vertical-type resistance dynamometer
垂直丝/十字縱絲　vertical hair
垂直天线/垂直天線　vertical antenna
垂直陀螺/直立陀螺儀　vertical gyroscope
垂直危险角/垂直危險角　vertical danger angle
垂直尾翼/垂直尾翼　vertical tail
垂直线/垂直線,竪線　vertical line
垂直载荷/垂直荷重　vertical load
垂直整体运输/垂直整體運輸　integral vertical transportation
垂直轴阻尼法/垂直軸阻尼法　damped method of vertical axis
垂直总装测试厂房/垂直裝配測試廠房　vertical assembly and test building
捶击/拍底　pounding
锤工/控錘工　hammerman
锤击沉桩法/錘擊沈樁法　pile driving method by hammer
锤击式碎石机/錘式壓碎機　hammer crusher
锤击试验/錘擊試驗,錘擊檢驗　hammer test
锤实法/錘實法　hammering compozer method
锤式冲抓斗/錘式抓斗　hammer grab
锤式破碎机/錘碎機　hammer mill
锤头式起重机/錘式起重機　hammer head crane
锤线/錘線　plumb-bob line
春翻层/春季翻騰　spring overturn
春分点/春分點　vernal equinox
春梢/春梢　spring pin
纯粹主义/純粹主義,純粹派　purism
纯度/純度　purity
纯度对比/純度對比　purity contrast
纯合体/純合子,同接合子　homozygote
纯剪切/純剪　pure shear
纯林/[單]純林,單一樹種林　pure forest
纯气田天然气/純氣田天然氣　field natural gas
纯水/純水　pure water

纯弯曲/純彎曲　pure bending
纯音/純音　pure tone
醇酸类地坪漆/醇酸類地塗層　alkyd floor coating
祠堂/祠堂　memorial hall
瓷质阳极化/瓷質陽極化　electrochemical enamelizing
瓷质砖/瓷磚　porcelain tile
瓷砖壁画/瓷磚壁畫　painted tile mural tablet
磁暴/磁暴　magnetic storm
磁北/磁北　magnetic north
磁测量/地磁测量　magnetic surveying
磁层/磁層　magnetosphere
磁层亚暴/磁層亞暴　magnetospheric substorm
磁差/[地]磁差　magnetic variation
磁场/磁場　magnetic field
磁场模式/磁場模式　magnetic field model
磁场热处理/磁性熱處理　magnetic heat treatment
磁场调速/磁場控制調速　speed regulation by field control
磁场削弱/磁場減弱　field weakening
磁场削弱接触器/磁場削弱接觸器，磁場減弱接觸器　field weakening contactor
磁场削弱系数/磁場削弱係數，磁場減弱係數　coefficient of field weakening
磁赤道/[地]磁赤道　magnetic equator
磁带记录/磁帶錄音　magnetic tape recording
磁[带]记录器/磁帶記錄器　magnetic tape recorder
磁导率/磁導率　magnetic permeability
磁导率测量/磁導率量測　permeability measurement
磁轭/磁軛　yoke
磁方位/磁方位　magnetic bearing, MB
磁粉检测/磁粉探傷[檢查]　magnetic particle testing, magnetic particle flaw detection, magnetic testing
磁粉离合器/磁粉離合器　magnetic particle clutch
磁粉探伤[检验]/磁粉探傷[檢查]　magnetic powder detection
磁粉探伤仪/磁粉探傷儀　magnetic powder flaw detector
磁浮铁路/磁浮鐵路　magnetic levitation railway, maglev railway
磁干扰力矩/磁擾動力矩　magnetic disturbance torque
磁感式沉降标/磁性信號裝置，磁性警報器　magnetic tell tale
磁感应[强度]/磁感應[強度]　magnetic induction
磁感应式车辆检测器/電磁車輛偵測器，電磁車輛感知器　magnetic inductive vehicle detector

磁刚度/磁剛度，磁剛性　magnetic rigidity
磁共振室/磁共振室　magnetic resonance imaging room, MRI room
磁轨制动/電磁[鋼]軌刹車　electromagnetic rail brake
磁过滤电弧沉积/磁過濾電弧沈積　magnetically filter arc deposition
磁航向/磁[航]向　magnetic course, MC, magnetic heading
磁极/磁極　magnetic pole
磁卡收费机/磁卡收費機　magnetic card toll machine
磁卡通行券/磁卡通行券　magnetic card toll pass ticket
磁壳/磁殼　magnetic shell
磁空气动力学/磁[空]氣動力學　magnetoaerodynamics
磁力矩器/磁矩，電磁扭力器　magnetic torquer
磁力起重机/磁力起重機　magnetic crane
磁力探伤/磁力探傷法　magnetic crack detection
磁流体动力推进装置/磁[性]流體動力推進裝置　magneto hydrodynamic propulsion plant
磁流体动力学/磁[性]流體動力學　magnetofluid dynamics
磁路[系统]/磁路　magnetic circuit
磁轮/磁輪　magnet wheel
[磁]罗差/羅經[誤]差　compass error
磁罗经/磁羅經，磁羅盤　magnetic compass
磁罗经校正/磁羅經校正　magnetic compass adjustment
磁罗经指向误差/磁羅經指向誤差　directive error of magnetic compass
磁脉冲加工/磁脈衝加工　magnetic impulse machining
磁敏感性/磁化率　magnetic susceptibility
磁偶极子矩/磁偶極矩　magnetic dipole moment
磁偏吹/磁吹　magnetic blow
磁偏角/磁偏轉　magnetic deflection
磁强计/磁強[力]計　magnetometer
磁倾角/[地]磁傾角　magnetic dip
磁倾角针/地磁俯角針　dip needle
磁倾仪/地磁俯角儀　dip circle
磁扇形/扇形磁場　magnetic sector
磁石电话机/磁石式電話機　magneto telephone set
磁石电话交换机/磁石電話交換臺　magneto telephone switch board
磁石发电机/永磁發電機　magneto
磁试验/磁性試驗　magnetic test

磁试验设备／磁性試驗設備　magnetic test facility
磁通[量]／磁通量　magnetic flux
磁通门罗经／磁通門羅經　flux gate compass
磁稳定／磁穩定　magnetic stabilization
磁向导线／磁向導線　needle traverse
磁卸载／磁卸載　magnetic dumping
磁性／磁性　magnetic property
磁性测裂计／磁探裂器,磁探傷器　magnetic crack detector
磁性合金／磁性合金　magnetic alloy
磁[悬]浮／磁懸浮,磁力懸撐　magnetic suspension, magnetic levitation
磁[悬]浮车辆／磁懸浮車體　maglev vehicle
磁悬浮技术／磁懸浮技術　magnetic suspension technique
磁悬挂天平／磁懸浮天平　magnetic suspension balance
磁亚暴仿真设备／磁亞暴模擬設備　magnetic substorm simulation facility
磁引信／磁引信　magnetic fuze
磁针／磁針　magnetic needle
磁致伸缩换能器／磁致伸縮換能器　magnetostrictive transducer
磁致伸缩效应／磁致伸縮效應　magnetostrictive effect
磁滞／磁滯　hysteresis
磁滞陀螺电机／磁滯陀螺電機　hysteresis gyro motor
磁轴承／磁浮軸承　magnetic bearing
磁轴承反作用动量轮／磁浮軸承反作用動量輪　magnetic bearing reaction momentum wheel
磁轴承飞轮／磁浮軸承飛輪　magnetic bearing flywheel
磁子午线／磁子午線　magnetic meridian
磁阻／磁阻　reluctance
磁坐标系／地磁坐標體系　magnetic coordinate system
次波动／副振動　secondary undulation
次干路／次幹道,次要道路,次要公路　sub-arterial road, secondary road, secondary trunk road
次高级路面／次高級路面　sub-high type pavement, sub-high class pavement
次固结／次壓密,副壓密　secondary consolidation
次级道路／次要道路　minor road, secondary road
次级天文钟／次級天文鐘　hack chronometer
次级限值／二次限度　secondary limit
次间／邊開間　side bay
次梁／次梁　secondary beam
次流／副流　secondary flow
次生孔隙度／次孔隙度　secondary porosity
次生林／次生林,再生林　secondary forest
次生群落／次生群集　secondary community
次生演替／次生演替,次級消長　secondary succession
次生植被／本地植物　secondary vegetation, native vegetation
次声／超低頻音　infrasound
次同步旋转／次同步旋轉　subsynchronous whirl
次谐波／次諧波　subharmonic
次谐波共振响应／次諧波響應　subharmonic response
次要构件／次[要]構件　secondary member
次要控制／次級控制　minor control
次要入口／次要入口　secondary entrance
次要园路／次要園路　secondary garden road
次要种／次要種,輔助樹種　accessory species
次应力／次應力　secondary stress
刺激-反应理论／刺激效應理論　stimulus-response, S-R
刺篱／刺籬　thorny plants hedge
刺网／刺網　gill net
刺网渔船／刺網漁船　gill netter
刺吸式害虫／刺吸式害蟲　suction pest
葱花穹顶／蔥花穹頂　ogee dome
从板／從動件　follower
从动齿轮／從動齒輪　driven gear
从动轮对／從動輪組　driven wheel set
从价／從價　ad valorem
从价运费／從價運費　ad valorem rate
从轮对／從輪對　trailing wheel set
从轮转向架／後轉向架　trailing truck
从签约地法／從簽約地法　lex loci contractus
从事捕鱼的船舶／從事捕鱼中船舶　vessel engaged in fishing
从属故障／從屬故障　dependent fault
从属信号机／從屬信號機　dependent signal
从站／役使電臺,副站　slave station
丛林／叢林　jungle
丛植／叢植,聚植,穴播　bunch planting, group planting, clump planting
粗糙表面／粗糙面　rough surface
粗糙带／粗糙帶　rough strip
粗糙度／粗糙度　roughness
粗糙度阻力／粗面阻力　roughness resistance
粗糙货／粗貨　rough cargo
粗糙系数／粗糙係數,皺度係數　coefficient of rugosity, roughness coefficient
粗[大误]差／總誤差,人爲誤差　gross error

粗滴过渡/粒狀傳遞　globular transfer
粗对准/粗校準　coarse alignment
粗骨料/粗骨料,粗骨材　coarse aggregate
[粗]过滤器/[粗]濾器　strainer
粗化处理/糙化,弄粗糙法　roughening
粗级配/粗級配　coarse gradation
粗级配沥青混凝土/粗級配瀝青混凝土　coarse graded asphaltic concrete
粗集料/粗粒料　coarse aggregate
粗加工/粗面粉刷　rough finishing
粗检漏试验/粗滲漏試驗　gross leak test
粗颗粒物/顆粒物質　coarse particulate matter
粗缆/粗纜,鋼繩　cable
粗粒土/粗粒土壤　coarse grained soil
粗粒土填料/粗粒土壤填料　coarse grained soil filler
粗滤池/粗濾池　roughing filter
粗瞄/粗瞄　coarse aiming
粗磨石/粗磨石　primary grinding stone
粗砂/粗砂　coarse sand
粗石/塊石　rubble stone
粗石集料/粗骨材　rubble aggregate
粗碎机/粗軋碎石機　primary crusher
粗同步法/粗同步法　coarse synchronizing method
粗细集料比/粗細骨材比　ratio of coarse to fine aggregate
粗腰钢轨/帽形軌條　filled rail
粗野主义/粗獷主義,蠻橫主義　brutalism
粗制螺栓/粗糙螺拴　rough bolt
促成栽培/促成栽培　forcing culture
促进剂/促進劑,加速器　accelerator
促凝剂/促凝劑,助凝劑　coagulant
促凝压蒸试验/促凝熱壓膨脹試驗　accelerated setting autoclave test
猝发/突發　burst
攒尖/攢尖,稜錐屋頂　pyramidal roof
窜机油/竄機油　lubricating oil carry-over
窜气/漏氣　blow-by
窜油/抽油　oil pumping
催化点火/催化點火　catalytic ignition
催化剂/催化劑,觸媒　catalyst
催化剂床/催化劑基座　catalyst bed
催化热裂/觸媒裂解　catalytic cracking
催化式肼单组元推进系统/催化式肼單組元推進系統　catalytic monopropellant hydrazine system
催化特性/催化特性　catalysis characteristic
催化氧化器/催化氧化劑　catalytic oxidizer
脆点/脆化點　brittle point
脆点试验/脆點試驗　brittle point test

脆断/脆[性破]裂　brittle fracture
脆化/脆化　embrittle
脆性/脆性　brittleness
脆性材料/脆性材料　brittle material
脆性断裂/脆[性破]裂　brittle fracture
脆性破坏/脆性破壞,脆性損毀　brittle failure
脆性涂层法/脆性塗層法　brittle coating method
淬火/淬火[硬化]　quenching, quench hardening
淬火轨/淬火鋼軌　head hardened rail, quenched rail
淬火尖轨/淬火尖軌　surface-hardened switch rail, quenched switch rail
淬火冷却/淬火,急冷　quenching
淬火冷却开裂/淬火裂痕　quenching crack, quench cracking
淬火冷却起始温度/淬火溫度　quenching temperature
淬火冷却应力/淬火應力　quenching stresses
淬火裂纹/淬火裂紋　quench crack
淬透性/可硬化性　hardenability
淬硬性/淬火性,硬化性　hardening capacity
村规划编制成果/村莊規劃成果　village planning result
村落/農村聚落,鄉村集居　rural settlement
村落景观/村落景觀　village landscape
村民委员会/村民委員會　villager committee
村民小组/村民小組　villager group
村民意愿/村民意願　villager wish
村民自治/村民自治　villager autonomy
村卫生室/鄉村保健診所,鄉村保健站　village health clinic
村镇规划/鄉村規劃　rural planning
村镇建设规划/鄉街建設規劃　constructive program plan of village and town
村镇体系/鄉街體系　town and village system
村镇总体规划/鄉街綜合規劃　comprehensive plan of village and town
村[庄]/村莊,村落　village
村庄规划/村莊規劃　village planning
村庄整治规划/村落整建計劃　village renovation plan
存车搭乘/停車搭乘　park and drive
存车换乘/停車轉乘　park and ride
存车线/存車線　storage siding, storage track
存储器/記憶單位　memory unit
存储转发/存儲轉發,存放及轉送　store and forward
存储转发单元/儲存前管器　store and forward unit
存活率/存活率　probability of survive
存量规划/存貨規劃,庫存規劃　inventory planning

存量建筑/存量建築　stock building
存量土地/存量土地　stock land
存水弯/濾波器,捕捉器,祛水器　trap
存在空间/存在空間　existence space
存在型车辆检测器/存在車輛偵測器　presence vehicle detector
搓板/波形磨损,褶皱　corrugation
措施项目/措施項目　measurement item
错车道/避車彎　passing bay
错车洞/錯車洞,讓車洞　passing bay in tunnel
错乘/錯乘　taking wrong bus, taking wrong train
错缝铺路/錯鋪路　crazy paving path
错口木梁/嚙合木梁　indented girder
错溜/錯溜　miseroute
错排座席/交錯座位　staggered seating
错平结/假平结　granny knot
错台/錯臺　slab staggering
错位交叉/錯位交叉　staggered intersection, offset intersection
错误办理/錯誤辦理　wrong handling
错误处理/故障處理　fault handling
错误关闭信号/錯誤關閉信號　false stopping of a signal
错误解锁/錯誤解鎖　false release
错误开放信号/錯誤開放信號　wrong clearing of a signal
错误锁闭/錯誤鎖閉　false locking
错误显示/錯誤顯示　wrong indication
错型/錯模　shift
错牙接头/錯牙接頭　rail ends unevenness in line or surface
错移/偏位　offset
错油门/[嚮]導閥,導引閥　pilot valve
错运/錯運　misshipment
错装/誤裝　misloading

D

搭边/搭邊　lap
搭架式架设/支架式架設　erection by staging
搭接/搭接　lap joint
搭接长度/搭接長度　lap length
搭接钢板接缝/搭接鋼板接合　lapped steel plate joint
搭接焊/搭焊　lap weld, lap welding
搭接接头/搭接接頭　lap joint, lap connection
搭扣瓦/互扣瓦　interlocking tile
搭铁/搭鐵　electrical ground
搭载费/[搭載]船费　embarkation charge
达到位姿/可達姿勢　attained pose
达·拉格阿医院庭院/達·拉格阿醫院庭院　Hospital Da Lagoa
达拉斯联合银行喷泉广场/達拉斯聯合銀行大廈噴泉廣場　Dallas Fountain Place
达朗贝尔佯谬/達朗白假設　D'Alembert paradox
达朗贝尔原理/達朗白原理　Darren Bell principle
达特[稳定]系统/彈道自動定位複校準系統　directional automatic realignment of trajectory system, DART stabilization system
打道钉机/打道釘機　spike driver
打底焊道/打底焊接　backing weld, backing run
打夯机/打夯機,填塞機　power rammer, ramming machine
打横/船身突橫　broach to
打浆/打漿　beating
打浆机/打漿機　beater
打蜡防水/打蠟防水　paraffin waterproofing
打捞船/救撈船,救難船　salvage ship, rescue ship, salvage and rescue ship
打捞浮筒/打撈浮筒　lifting pontoon
打磨钢轨/波形磨耗　rail grinding
打气式模型/吹氣管　ductube
打入桩/打擊樁,錘擊樁　driven pile
打入阻力/錘入抵抗　driving resistance
打竖井/直井開鑿　shaft sinking
打水砣/打水砣　heave the lead
打药车/噴藥車　pesticide spraying vehicle
打药机/打藥機　pesticide spraying machine
打印机/列印機　printer
打印结束信号/列印結束信號　printing finished signal
打针/打針　give or take an injection
打桩/打樁　pile driving
打桩船/打樁[駁]船　floating pile driving plant, floating pile driver, pile driving barge
打桩锤/打樁錘　pile driving hammer
打桩分析仪/打樁分析儀　pile driving analyzer, PDA
打桩公式/打樁公式　pile driving formula
打桩机/打樁機　pile driver, hammer piling
打桩记录/打樁記錄　driving record
打桩架/打樁架　pile driving frame
打桩落锤/穿心錘　monkey
打桩试验/打樁試驗　pile driving test
大暴雨/傾盆雨　cloud burst
大便收集/糞便收集　feces collection
大潮/大潮　spring tide, high water
大潮平均高潮位/朔望平均高潮位　mean high water springs
大潮升/大潮昇　spring rise, SR
大城市/大都市　metropolis
大城市地区/[大]都會區,都會區域　metropolitan area, metropolitan region
大城市连绵区/[特]大都會　megalopolis
大城市市[中心]区/都會區　metropolitan district
大低潮/大低潮　low water spring tide
大地测量/大地測量　geodetic survey, geodetic surveying
大地电阻率/地電阻率,大地電阻係數　earth resistivity
大地水准面/大地水準面　geoid
大地水准面高度图/大地水準面高度圖　geoidal height map
大地纬度/大地緯度,地理緯度　geodetic latitude
大地位/重力位　geopotential
大地污染/土地汙染　land pollution
大地线/測地線　geodetic line
大地坐标/大地坐標　geodetic coordinate
大地坐标系/大地坐標系　geodetic coordinate system
大定位误差/定位顯著誤差　large location error

大都会中心/都會中心　metropolitan center
大都市交通圈/大都市交通圈　extent of metropolitan communication
大都市区/[大]都會區　metropolitan area
大断面开挖/大斷面開挖　large cross section excavation
大风警报/大風警報　gale warning, GW
大风浪航行工况管理/惡劣氣候航行作業形式管理　heavy weather navigation operating mode management
大风浪中船舶操纵/大風浪中操船　shiphandling in heavy weather
大幅液体晃动力学/大幅液體晃動力學　large-amplitude-slosh liquid dynamics
大副/大副　chief officer, chief-mate
大功率转辙机/高負載轉轍機　heavy duty switch machine
大攻角试验/大攻角試驗　test at high attack angle
大管轮/二管輪　second engineer
大广场/大廣場　great plaza
大规模更新/大規模更新，大型更新　large-scale renewal
大轨缝/大軌縫　excessive joint gap, wide joint gap
大寒日/大寒　great cold
大横杆/鷹架橫木　ledger
大横梁/橫撐　cross bearer
大环比对/大環驗證　major loop validation
大回路演练/大回路演練　full loop exercise, system rehearsal
大角(牧夫 α)/大角(牧夫 α)　Arcturus
大角度机动控制/大角度機動控制　large angle maneuver control
大揭盖清筛机/大揭蓋清篩機　ballast cleaning machine with removed track panel
大街/大街　main street
大街坊/大街坊　superblock
大距/高螺距　high pitch
大孔混凝土/無砂混凝土，無細粒料混凝土　no-fines concrete
大口井/大口井，掘井　dug well, large opening well
大跨度建筑/大跨度建築，長跨度結構　large span building, long span structure
大跨度结构/大跨度結構　large span structure, long span structure
大跨径桥/長跨橋　long span bridge
大浪/洶濤　rough sea
大理石/大理石，大理岩　marble
大粒子/顆粒，粒子　particle

大梁/縱梁　longeron
大量生产/大量生產　quantity production
大量元素养分/大量營養素　macronutrient
大流量加注/大流量[率]裝填　large flow rate filling
大陆架/大陸架，大陸棚　continental shelf
大陆架界线/大陸架界線　continental shelf boundary
大陆坡/大陸斜坡　continental slope
大陆桥/大陸橋　transcontinental railway
大模板/組合模板　large form, gang form
大模板混凝土结构/大範本混凝土結構　large form concrete structure
大木锤/大木槌　wooden maul
大木作/大木作　greater structural carpentry, damuzuo
大幕/舞臺幕布　proscenium curtain
大挠度理论/大撓度理論　large deflection theory
大漆/中國漆　Chinese lacquer, raw lacquer
大气/大氣　atmosphere
大气保暖气体/温室氣體　greenhouse gas
大气保暖效应/温室效應　greenhouse effect
大气边界层风洞/大氣邊界層風洞　atmospheric boundary layer wind tunnel
大气参数检测/大氣參數量測　atmospheric parameter measurement
大气层/大氣層　atmospheric layer
大气潮/大氣潮　atmospheric tide
大气程辐射/大氣路徑輻射　atmospheric path radiation
大气窗口/大氣窗口　atmospheric window
大气辐射/大氣輻射　atmospheric radiation
大气腐蚀/大氣腐蝕　atmosphere corrosion
大气干旱/大氣乾旱　atmospheric drought
大气光谱透过率/大氣光譜透射比　atmospheric spectral transmittance
大气光学厚度/大氣光厚度　atmospheric optical thickness
大气耗损/大氣損耗　atmospheric loss
大气环境/大氣環境　air environment
大气环境容量/大氣環境容量　atmospheric environmental capacity
大气环流/大氣環流　general atmospheric circulation
大气校正/大氣修正　atmospheric correction
大气结构/大氣結構　atmospheric structure
大气静温表/大氣靜溫指示器　static air-temperature indicator
大气静压控制/大氣壓力控制　atmospheric pressure control
大气冷凝器/大氣冷凝器，大氣凝結器　atmospheric

condenser
大气模式/大氣模型　atmospheric model
大气能见度/大氣能見度　atmospheric visibility
大气品位指数/大氣品質指數　atmospheric quality index
大气散射/大氣散射　atmospheric scattering
大气散射效应/大氣散射效應　scattering effect in the atmosphere
大气色散/大氣色散　atmospheric dispersion
大气闪烁/大氣老化　atmospheric scintillation
大气摄动/大氣擾動　atmospheric perturbation
大气式燃烧器/大氣燃燒器　atmospheric burner
大气数据计算机/大氣數據計算機　air data computer
大气衰减/大氣衰減　atmospheric attenuation
大气水/天水, 雨水　meteoric water
大气透明度/大氣透明率　atmosphere transparency
大气透射比/大氣透射率　atmospheric transmittance
大气透射波段/大氣透射[波]段　atmospheric transmission band
大气透射率/大氣傳達量　atmospheric transmissivity
大气湍流/大氣紊流　atmospheric turbulence
大气微量污染控制/大氣微量汙染控制　atmospheric trace contamination control
大气温度表/大氣溫度計　air-temperature indicator
大气污染/大氣汙染　air pollution, atmospheric pollution
大气污染监测/大氣汙染監測　atmospheric pollution monitoring
大气污染物/大氣汙染物　air contaminant
大气污染源/大氣汙染源　source of atmospheric pollution
大气吸收/大氣吸收　atmospheric absorption
大气效应/大氣效應　atmospheric effect
大气选择性散射/大氣選擇性散射　atmospheric selectivity scattering
[大]气压/大氣壓力　atmospheric pressure
大气压力/大氣壓力　air pressure
大气压式采暖装置/大氣壓式採暖裝置　atmospheric pressure steam heating equipment
大气压式暖汽调整阀/大氣壓式暖汽調整閥　vapor regulater
大气噪声/大氣雜訊　atmospheric noise
大气折射/大氣折射　atmospheric refraction
大气质量/大氣質量　air mass, AM
大气质量指数/大氣品質指數　air quality index
大气自净作用/大氣自淨[作用]　atmospheric self-purification

大桥/大[型]橋梁　great bridge, major bridge
大倾角稳性/大傾側角時之穩度　stability at large angle of inclination
大球场/大球場　the Great Ball Court
大石块上钻的炮眼/石塊爆孔　block hole
大使官邸/大使官邸　ambassador residence
大式/大式　dashi-style
大事故/嚴重事故　serious accident
大树/大苗木　large tree
大树移植/大樹移植　big tree transplanting
大数据/大數據　big data
大堂/大廳　lobby
大体积混凝土/大量混凝土　mass concrete
大桶/大桶　hogshead
大头螺栓/螺樁, 無頭螺栓　stud bolt
大头桩/大頭樁　express pile
大雾/濃霧　dense fog
大西洋东区/大西洋東區　Atlantic Ocean Region East
大西洋极锋/大西洋極鋒　Atlantic polar front
大西洋区/大西洋區域　Atlantic Ocean Region, AOR
大西洋西区/大西洋西區　Atlantic Ocean Region West
大芯板/大芯板　blockboard, laminated wood board
大行星/[大]行星　major planet
大型/大呎寸, 大號　large size
大型多钻头钻机/鑽孔機架　drill jambo
大型浮标/高燈芯浮標　high focal plane buoy
大型固定拌和设备/大型固定拌合設備　large fixed batching
大型客车/大客車　large bus
大型矿车/大型礦車　large-scale ore car
大型临时工程/大型臨時工程項目　large-scale temporary project
大型挠性航天器的振动控制/大型撓性飛行器振動控制　large flexible spacecraft vibration control
大型挠性航天器的姿态控制/大型撓性飛行器姿態控制　large flexible spacecraft attitude control
大型墙板/大型牆板　large panel wall
大型全断面清筛机/大型全斷面清篩機　large ballast undercutting cleaner, on-track full section undercutting cleaner
大型屋面板/大型屋面板　large roof slab, large panel roof slab
大型线路机械/大型線路機械　heavy permanent way machine
大型油船/巨型油輪　very large crude carrier, VLCC

大修工程费/大修工程費　major maintenance cost
大修计划/大修計劃　plan of capital repair
大学城/大學城　campus city, university town
大循环运行/大循環運行　full circulation operation
大洋航路/大洋航路　ocean passage
大洋航行/大洋航行　ocean navigation
大洋水深图/大洋水深圖　ocean sounding chart
大腰带/腰梁,中部圍欄　waist rail
大雨/大雨,暴雨　heavy rain
大圆/大圈　great circle
大圆顶点/頂點　vertex
大圆方位/大圓方位　great circle bearing, GCB
大圆分点/大圓中分點　intermediate point of great circle
大圆改正量/半幅合角　half-convergency
大圆海图/大圓海圖　great circle chart
大圆航线/大圓航線　great circle route
大圆航线角/大圓航向角　great circle course angle
大圆航线算法/大圓航法　great circle sailing
大圆航向/大圓航向　great circle course, GCC
大圆距离/大圓距離　great circle distance
大院/大院　dayuan, walled compound
大运量快速交通/大眾捷運　mass rapid transit
大站电气集中联锁/大站繼電器聯鎖　relay interlocking for large station
大中修周期/養護週期　maintenance period
大众运输/大眾運輸　mass transport
大抓力锚/高抓著力錨　high holding power anchor
大庄园/大莊園　manor
大自然交响乐/大自然交響樂　natural symphony
大宗货物/大宗貨物　mass goods, mass freight
呆重锚座/呆重錨座　dead man anchor
代办站/代理[者]　agency
代表性流域/代表性流域　representative basin
代表性试样/代表樣品　representative sample
代表性项目目录/代表性項目表　representative item list
代偿背心/背心　pressure jacket, waistcoat
代理人/代理人　agent
代旗/代旗　substitute flag
代位/代位　subrogation
代位求偿权/代位求償權　right of subrogation
代谢仿真装置/代謝模擬裝置　metabolic simulation device
代谢率/代謝率　metabolic rate
代谢物/代謝產物　metabolite
代用票/代用票　substituting ticket
代用天然气/合成天然氣　substitute natural gas,
SNG
代征地/代徵地　in-site land for public
带板/系板　band plate
带柄道岔表示器/帶柄道岔表示器　switch indicator with level
带缠绕成形/帶繞組　tape winding
带尺/卷尺　measuring tape
带重叠缠绕/帶平面纏繞　tape plane winding
带底座的标志杆/根基標誌　pedestal sign
带顶标浮标/桿形浮標　beacon buoy
带动道岔/帶動道岔　switch with follow up movement
带飞/教練飛行　instructional flight
带盖弹射/帶蓋彈射　ejection with canopy
带钢/帶鋼　band steel, strip steel
带回流线的直接供电方式/帶回流線的直接供電方式　direct feeding system with return wire
带宽/帶寬　band width
带缆口令/帶纜口令　mooring orders
带缆羊角/帶纜羊角　mooring cleat
带缆桩/繫纜樁,繫船柱　bollard, mooring bitt
带缆桩顶端/纜柱頭　bitt head
带缆桩肘板/繫船曲柱,繫船橫支柱　bracket bitt
带链/帶形鏈　band chain
带挠性附件的航天器动力学/柔性附屬構件太空載具動力學　spacecraft dynamics with flexible appendage
带倾斜缠绕/帶傾斜纏繞　tape inclined position winding
带裙鱼尾板/護裙魚尾板,裙部魚尾板　aproned fish plate, fish plate with apron
带筛机/帶式活動篩　belt screen
带式输送机/帶式運送機　belt conveyor, belt conveyer
带式装料机/帶式裝料機　belt loader
带条伞/條帶式降落傘　ribbon parachute
带通滤光片/帶通濾波器　band-pass filter
带土球苗木/帶土球苗木　plants with soil ball, trees with soil ball
带土球移植/帶土球移植　transplanting with root
带外发射/頻帶外發射　out-of-band emission
带谐系数/帶諧係數　zonal harmonic coefficient
带形城市/帶形城市　linear city
带液体晃动的航天器动力学/液體振盪太空載具動力學　spacecraft dynamics with liquid slosh
带有卫星厅的集中式航站楼/帶有衛星廳的集中式航站樓　centralized terminal with remote satellite
带有指廊的集中式航站楼/帶有指廊的集中式航站

楼　centralized terminal with piers, centralized terminal with fingers
带有转运车的集中式航站楼／帶有轉運車的集中式航站樓　centralized terminal with boarding transporter
带罩叶轮／帶罩葉輪　propeller impeller
带植／帶植　belt planting, linear planting
带状地形图／帶狀地形圖,地带地圖　belt topographic map, strip map
带状分布／帶狀分布　zonal distribution
带状公园／帶狀公園　linear park
带状花坛／帶狀花壇　ribbon flower bed
带状接头／接合扁鋼　joint strap
带状矩阵／帶狀矩陣　banded matrix
带状配植／條栽,條作,條狀栽培　strip cropping
贷款偿还能力／貸款償還能力　loan repay ability
待爆／預位,備炸　arming
待爆指令／備炸指令　arming command
待爆状态／備炸狀態　armed condition
待避所／避難地　refuge place
待发段逃逸／待發段逃脱　readied segment escape
待机准备完好率／備用準備　standby readiness
待命可靠度／警備可靠度,警戒可靠度　alert reliability
待命时间／備用時間　standby time, alert time
待修机车／待修機車　locomotive waiting for repair
怠速工况／空轉模式　idling mode
怠速排放污染物／怠速排放汙染物　pollutants of idle speed emission
袋式除尘器／袋[狀過]濾器,濾塵袋　bag filter
袋形线网／袋形線網　pocket type public transport network
袋形走廊／袋形走廊　dead end corridor
袋压成形／袋模塑　bag moulding
袋装仓库／袋裝倉庫　bagged material warehouse
袋装混凝土／袋裝混凝土　sacked concrete
袋装货／袋裝貨　bagged cargo
袋装砂井／袋裝砂井　sand bag well
戴马格接缝／德馬格接縫　Demag joint
担保物权／擔保物權　security interest on property
担架／擔架　litter
单板舵／單板舵,平板舵　single plate rudder
单倍体／單倍體　haploid
单倍体育种／單倍體育種　haploid breeding
单臂掘进机／單旋臂型掘削機　single boom roadheader
单臂受电弓／單臂式集電弓　single arm pantograph
单边带发射／單邊帶發射　single sideband emission, SSB emission
单边带通信／單邊帶通信　single sideband communication
单边带无线电话／單邊帶無線電話　single sideband radiotelephone, SSB RT
单边供电／單邊供電　one way feeding
单边极限环／單邊極限環　single side limit cycle
单边型直线感应电动机／單邊直線感應電動機　single sided linear induction motor
单边装货／單邊裝貨　one side cargo handling
单编结／魯班[單]扣　sheetbend
单侧导坑法／單側導坑法　single side heading method
单侧减速齿轮驱动／單級減速齒輪驅動　single reduction gear drive
单侧[踏面]制动／單側[踏面]制動　single shoe brake
单层／單層　lamina
单层仓库／單層倉庫　single-story warehouse
单层厂房／單層工業廠房　single-story industrial building
单层衬砌／單殼襯砌　single shell lining
单层建筑／單層建築[物]　single-story building
单层筛／單層篩　single deck screen
单层塔／單層塔　single-story pagoda
单差／單差　single difference
单车产量／單車產量　annual output per vehicle
单车道／單車道　single lane
单车核算／單車核算　unit vehicle accounting
单车试验／單車試驗　single car test
单车试验器／單車試驗裝置　single car testing device
单程运输／單程運輸　one way loading transport
单船围网／單船圍網　single boat purse seine
单床间／單人房間　single-bed room
单代号网络图／優先網路圖　precedence network diagram
单道焊／單道焊接　single-pass welding
单底／單底　single bottom
单点定位／單點定位　point positioning
单点接地／單點接地　single point grounding
单点失效／單件失效　single point failure, SPF
单点失效概率／單件失效概率　probability of SPF
单点系泊／單點繫泊　single point mooring, SPM
单点系泊设施／單點繫泊系統　single buoy mooring system
单点系泊装置／單點繫泊裝置　single point mooring unit, SPM unit
单点约束／單點限制　single point constraint

单电动机驱动/單發動機驅動　monomotor drive
单动式泵/單動式抽水機　singleacting pump
单动式桩锤/單動式樁錘　singleacting hammer
单斗挖掘机/單斗挖掘機,動力鏟　power shovel,
　　single bucket excavator
单独操纵继电式电气集中联锁/單獨操縱全電驛聯
　　鎖　individual level type all-relay interlocking
单独操纵作业/人工操作,人工控制　manual
　　operation
单独海损/單獨海損　particular average
单独接地/獨立接地　independent grounding
单独[局部]控制/個別控制　independent control
单独透气管/單通氣孔　individual vent
单独制动阀/單獨司軔閥　independent brake valve
单独仲裁员/單獨仲裁人　sole arbitrator
单独作用/單一作用　single acting
单断/單獨中斷　single break
单飞/單飛　solo flight
单分量天平/單分量天平　single component balance
单幅路/單行路　single carriageway road
单幅式城市道路/單幅式市區道路　one-slab urban
　　road
单杆作业/單吊桿系統　single boom system
单缸功率/單缸功率　power per cylinder
单缸[内燃]机/單缸機　single-cylinder engine
单个脉冲的最小冲量/單個脈衝的最小衝量
　　minimum impulse bit at MEPW
单工/單工[作業],單式　simplex, simplex operation
单工操作/單工作業　simplex operation
单工传输/單工傳輸　simplex transmission
单工无线电通信/單工[機]無線電通訊　simplex
　　radio communication
单栱/單栱　single-tier bracket
单鼓球磨机/單鼓球磨機　single drum ball mill
单管供暖系统/單管供熱系統　one pipe heating
　　system
单管逆变器/單管逆變器　individual inverter
单管设备/單管設備　single-hose rigs
单管压力计/單管測壓計　single tube manometer
单管荧光灯/單管熒光燈　single tube fluorescent
　　lamp
单管制蒸汽热网/單管制蒸汽熱網　one pipe steam
　　heat supply network
单管柱桩/單管樁　monotube pile
单光子发射计算机体层摄影室/單光子發射計算機
　　斷層攝影術,單光子發射體層攝影術　single-
　　photon emission computed tomography room
单轨条式轨道电路/單軌條式軌道電路　single rail
　　track circuit
单轨铁路/單軌[鐵路]　monorail
单轨小车/手車　hand cart
单横队/單横隊　single line abreast
单呼/個別呼叫　individual calling
单回路供电/單電路電力供應,單回路供電電源
　　single circuit power supply
单机运行/單機運行　light locomotive running
单机走行公里/單機走行公里　light locomotive
　　running kilometer
单级废气涡轮增压/單級渦輪增壓　single stage
　　turbocharging
单级腐化/單級腐化　single stage digestion
单级管网系统/單級系統　single stage system
单级火箭/單節火箭　single stage rocket
单级汽轮机/單級蒸汽輪機　single stage steam
　　turbine
单级入轨运载器/單級入軌運載器　single-stage-to
　　orbit launch vehicle
单级闪发/單級閃蒸發　single stage flash evaporation
单级压缩机/單級壓縮機,單階壓縮機　single stage
　　compressor
单甲板船/單層甲板船　single-decked vessel, single-
　　decked ship
单价合同/單價合同　schedule of rates contract, unit
　　rate contract
单肩回交路/單臂交路　single-arm routing
单肩模板/單肩軌枕墊板　single shouldered template
单绞辘/單滑車　single whip
单铰拱桥/單鉸拱橋　single hinged arch bridge
单截面/簡式斷面　single section
单筋/單面鋼筋　single reinforcement
单进路/單進路　single route
单晶高温合金/單晶超合金　single crystal superalloy
单晶硅太阳电池/單晶矽太陽能電池　single
　　crystalline silicon solar cell
单晶叶片/單晶葉片　single crystal blade
单晶铸造/單晶鑄造　single crystal casting
单局制/單局制　single-office system
单卷筒绞车/單筒絞車　single drum winch
单卷筒卷扬机/單筒絞車　single drum winch
单开道岔/單開道岔　simple turnout, lateral turnout
单跨/單跨,單孔　single span
单跨建筑物/單跨建築物　single-bay building
单框筒结构/單框筒結構　frame tube structure
单立管排水系统/單立管系統　single stack system
单粒子多位翻转/單事件多位元翻轉　single event
　　multiple bit upset

单粒子翻转事件/單事件翻轉　single event upset, SEU
单粒子功能中断事件/單事件功能中斷　single event functional interrupt
单粒子烧毁事件/單事件燒毀　single event burnout, SEB
单粒子事件/單粒子事件　single partical event
单粒子事件效应/單事件效應　single event effect
单粒子锁定事件/單事件鎖定　single event latchup, SEL
单粒子硬错误/單粒子硬體錯誤　single hard error
单联滤器/單過濾器　single strainer
单梁式架桥机/單梁架橋機　single beam girder-erecting machine
单列布置/單列布置,單行排列　single row layout arrangement
单流/單流　single current
单流式蒸汽机/單流蒸汽機　uniflow steam engine
单流液力机械传动/單流液壓-機械傳動　hydromechanical drive with inner ramification
单路通道排队/單通道排隊　single channel queue
单轮着陆/單輪落地　one-wheel landing
单脉冲跟踪/單脈波追蹤　monopulse tracking
单脉冲技术/單脈波技術　monopulse technology
单脉冲雷达/單脈衝雷達　monopulse radar
单脉冲雷达跟踪系统/單脈衝雷達追蹤系統　monopulse radar tracking system
单脉冲零深/單脈波零位深度　monopulse null depth
单脉冲天线/單脈波[雷達]天線　monopulse antenna
单锚泊/單錨泊　riding to single anchor
单锚腿储油装置/單錨腿儲油裝置　single anchor leg storage, SALS
单锚腿系泊/單錨腿繫泊　single anchor leg mooring
单锚腿系泊装置/單錨腿錨泊　single anchor leg mooring, SALM
单面铆接/盲铆接　blind riveting
单面托盘/單面托盤　single-deck pallet
单模法/單模法　individual mould system
单模光纤/單模光纖　single-mode optical fiber
单目标/單目標　single purpose
单排球轴承/單排滾珠軸承　single-row ball bearing
单频感应器/單頻感應器　single frequency inductor
单频调制/單頻調製　one-N modulation
单坡/單坡度　one way gradient
单坡屋顶/單坡度屋面　lean-to roof
单墙围堰/單層圍堰　single-wall cofferdam
单曲线/單曲線　simple curve
单缺口斜接头/單缺口斜接頭　single skew notch

单人常压潜水服/大氣壓潛水衣　atmospheric diving suit
单人坐板/工作吊板　bosun chair
单色光/單色光　monochromatic light
单色像差/單色像差　monochromatic aberration
单色谐调/單色諧調　monochromatic harmony
单式不对称道岔/非對稱雙開道岔　unsymmetrical double curve turnout
单式对称道岔/對稱雙開道岔　symmetrical double curve turnout
单式交分道岔/單向交叉橫渡道岔　single slip switch
单式同侧道岔/内方分岔　unsymmetrical double curve turnout in the same direction
单室多推力发动机/單室多推力發動機　single-chamber multistage thrust motor
单室双推力火箭发动机/單室雙推力火箭發動機　single chamber dual thrust rocket engine
单室箱梁/單元箱形梁　single cell box girder
单输入多输出/單輸入-多輸出　single input-multi output
单双工兼容无线电通信/單雙工相容無線電通訊　compatible simplex-duplex radio communication
单索面斜拉桥/單索面斜拉橋,單索面斜張橋　single plane cable stayed bridge, cable stayed bridge with single cable plane
单索索道/單線索道　single rope aerial ropeway
单索抓斗/單索抓土機　single rope grab
单塔式起重机/單柱起重機　monotower crane
单套结/單套結　bowline
单体船/單體船　mono hull ship
单体太阳电池/單太陽能電池　single solar cell
单体太阳电池的有效光照面积/單體太陽電池的有效光照面積　active area of a solar cell
单筒壁灯/單筒壁燈　single cylindrical shade wall lamp
单头缆/單頭纜　single rope
单凸轮换向/單凸輪換向　single cam reversing
单推力室液体火箭发动机/單推力室液體火箭發動機　single chamber liquid rocket engine
单拖/單拖　otter trawling
单拖网船/單桅網漁船　otter trawler
单位/單位　unit
单位暴风/單位暴雨　unit storm
单位产品用水量/單位產品用水量　unit water use
单位成本[承包]合同/單價承包,單價契約　unit-cost contract
单位GDP二氧化碳排放量/單位GDP二氧化碳排放

量　CO_2 emissions per unit of GDP
单位工程/單位工程,單元工程　unit project
单位估价表/標準單價表　standard schedule of unit rates
单位荷载法/單位負載法　unit load method
单位活塞面积功率/單位活塞面積功率　piston unit area power
单位降雨/單位雨量　unit rainfall
单位降雨历时/單位雨量歷時　unit rainfall duration
单位历线综合/單位歷線綜合　unit-hydrograph synthesis
单位流量/單位流量　unit discharge
单位螺线/單位螺線　unit clothoid
单位绿地/單位綠地　unit green area
单位面积排水量/單位面積排水量　unit area drainage discharge
单位面积纤维质量/單位面積纖維重量　fiber weight of unit area
单位GDP能耗/每個GDP單位能源消耗量　energy consumption per unit of GDP
单位能量/能量密度,比能[量]　specific energy
单位容积制冷量/單位氣缸容積冷凍效果　refrigerating effect per unit swept volume
单位剩余功率/比過剩功率　specific excess power, SEP
单位体积功率/單位容積功率　specific volume power
单位推力/比推力　specific thrust
单位迎面推力/單位迎面推力　thrust per frontal area
单位用水量/單位用水量　water duty per unit area
单位有效散射面积/單位有效散射面積　unit effective scattering area
单位造价/單位成本　unit cost
单位轴马力制冷量/單位制動馬力冷凍效果　refrigerating effect per brake horse power
单位阻力/比阻力　unit resistance, specific resistance
单线臂板信号/單線臂[木]式號誌　single wire semaphore signal
单线继电半自动闭塞/單線繼電半自動閉塞　single track all-relay semi-automatic block system
单线缆索/單索　monocable
单线桥/單線橋,單軌橋　single track bridge
单线隧道/單線隧道　single track tunnel
单线铁路/單線鐵路,單軌鐵路　single track railway
单线运行图/單線運行圖　train diagram for single track
单线制/單線系統　single wire system

单向传输/單向傳輸　unidirectional transmission
单向阀/止回閥,防逆瓣　check valve
单向固结/單向壓密　uni-dimensional consolidation
单向过闸/單向通路　one-way transit
单向航路/單向航路　one-way route
单向横列式编组站/單向橫列式編組站　unidirectional transversal type marshalling station
单向混合式编组站/單向混合式編組站　unidirectional combined type marshalling station
单向交通/單向交通　one-way traffic
单向流/單向流　unidirectional airflow
单向配筋/單面鋼筋　single reinforcement
单向[配筋混凝土]板/單向平板　one-way slab
单向通信/單向通信　one-way communication
单向推力墩/單向推力墩　single direction thrusted pier, one-way anti thrust pier
单向纤维复合材料/單向纖維複合材料　unidirectional fibrous composite material
单向性客流/單向性客運交通　unidirectional passenger traffic
单向旋回法/單迴旋法　single turn
单向预浸带/單向預浸帶　unidirectional prepreg tape
单向匝道/單向匝道　one-way ramp
单向自动闭塞/單向自動閉塞　single-directional running automatic block
单向纵列式编组站/單向縱列式編組站　unidirectional longitudinal type marshalling station
单项工程/單項工程　individual project
单项检查/單項檢查　individual check
单项预算/單項預算　individual budget
单相低频交流制/單相低頻[率]交流制　single-phase low frequency AC system
单相电度表/單相電表　single-phase wat-hour meter
单相短路/單相短路　single-phase short-circuit
单相工频交流电力机车/單相工業頻率交流電力機車　single-phase industrial frequency AC electric locomotive
单相工频交流电力牵引/單相工頻交流電力牽引制　single-phase industrial frequency AC electric traction system
单相工频交流制/單相工頻交流制　single-phase industrial frequency AC system
单相供电/單相電力供應　single-phase power supply
单相交流电动车组/單相交流電動車組　single-phase industrial frequency AC motor train unit
单相交流电力机车/單相交流電力機車　single-phase AC electric locomotive
单相交流牵引电动机/單相交流牽引電動機　single-

phase AC traction motor
单相接地/單相接地 one-phase ground, single-phase earthing
单相接线牵引变压器/單相接線牽引變壓器 traction transformer of single-phase connection
单相 V-V 接线牵引变压器/單相 V-V 接線牽引變壓器 traction transformer of single-phase V-V connection
单相流换热/單相流熱傳遞 single-phase flow heat transfer
单相配电/單相電源分配系統 single-phase power distribution system
单相桥式整流器/單相橋式整流器 single-phase bridge rectifier
单相运行保护/單相保護 protection against single-phasing
单效蒸发/單效蒸發 single effect evaporation
单星及多星导航/單星與多星導航 single star and multistars navigation
单行道/單行道,單向街道 one-way street
单行道路/單行道 one-way access, one-way road
单行路/單行道路,單行道 one-way road
单行线/單向交通 one-way traffic
单行线标志/單行線標誌,單行道標誌 one-way sign
单循环液力传动/單循環液壓傳動 single-circuit hydraulic transmission
单叶平转桥/單葉平轉橋,單葉平旋橋 single leaf swing bridge
单叶竖旋桥/單葉竖旋橋,單葉上開橋 single leaf bascule bridge
单一草坪/單一草坪 single lawn
单因子试验/單因子實驗 single factor experiment
单油头/單油頭 single probe
单元/單元 unit, element
单元测试/單元測試 unit test
单元测试楼/單元測試建築 component test building
单元刚度矩阵/單元勁度矩陣 element stiffness matrix
单元校准/單元校準 single unit calibration
单元列车/單元火車 unit train
单元式办公室/單元式辦公室 single-unit office
单元式工厂/單元式工廠 unit factory
单元式住宅/公寓大樓,公寓住宅 apartment building, apartment house
单元探测导引头/單探測歸航器 single-detector homing head
单元探测器/單元偵檢器 single-element detector
单元体设计/模組設計 modular design
单元舾装/單元舾裝 unit outfitting
单元诊断/部件診斷 unit diagnosis
单元制动/軔組,刹車組 brake unit
单元组装/單元組合,小組合 unit assembling
单闸门/單門 single gate
单站触发/單站觸發 single-station triggering
单站定位/單測站定位 mono-station locating
单站制/單站制 single-station system
单胀式蒸汽机/單脹式蒸汽引擎 single expansion steam engine
单胀式蒸汽机车/單脹式蒸汽機車 single expansion steam locomotive
单支点半柔壁喷管/單支點半柔壁噴管 half flexible plate nozzle with single hinge point
单枝防浪堤/單枝防浪堤 single breakwater
单值评价量/單值評價量 single-number quantity
单置信号点/單置信號點 single signal location
单中心城市体系/單中心都市體系 mono-centric urban system
单轴燃气轮机/單軸燃氣輪機 single-shaft gas turbine
单轴稳定平台/單軸穩定平臺 single-axis stable platform
单轴系/單軸系 single shafting
单轴转向架/單軸轉向架 single-axle truck
单轴姿态稳定/單軸姿態穩定 single-axis attitude stabilization
单肘破碎机/單肘碎石機 single-toggle crusher
单株选择法/個體選拔 individual selection
单柱式[桥]墩/單柱橋墩 single columned pier, single shaft pier
单转子摆式罗经/單轉子擺式電羅經 single gyro pendulous gyrocompass
单转子滑片式空压机/單轉子滑片式空壓機 single rotary compressor
单桩/單樁 individual pile, single pile
单桩承载力/獨樁承載力 bearing capacity of pile
单桩锚/獨椿錨碇 single pile anchor
单子叶植物/單子葉植物 monocotyledon
单自由度/單自由度 single degree of freedom
单自由度陀螺仪/單自由度陀螺儀 single-degree-of-freedom gyro
单自由度系统/單自由度系統 single-degree-of-freedom system
单字母信号码/單字母信號碼 single letter signal code
单纵队/單縱隊 single line ahead, single column
单组元喷嘴/單元噴嘴 single-component injector

单组元推进剂/單元推進劑　monopropellant
单组元[推进剂]火箭发动机/單元推進劑火箭發動機　monopropellant rocket engine
单组元推进系统/單元推進系統　monopropellant propulsion system
单作用泵/單動泵　single acting pump
单作用锤/落錘　drop hammer
单作用气动桩锤/單動氣壓樁機　single acting pneumatic hammer
单作用式柴油机/單動式柴油機　single acting diesel engine
单作用压缩机/單動式空氣壓縮機　single acting compressor
单作用油缸/單動式氣缸　single acting cylinder
单作用蒸气桩锤/單動式蒸氣錘　single acting steam hammer
淡化器具/去鹽設備　desalting kit
淡化设备/除鹽器　desalting apparatus
淡季/淡季,非生產季節　off season
淡水/淡水,食水　fresh water
淡水泵/淡水泵　fresh water pump
淡水舱/淡水艙,淡水櫃　fresh water tank
淡水加热器/淡水加熱器　fresh water heater
淡水冷却器/淡水冷卻器　fresh water cooler
淡水滤器/淡水過濾器　fresh water filter
淡水系统/淡水系統　fresh water system
淡水循环泵/淡水循環泵　fresh water circulating pump
淡水载重线/淡水載重線　fresh water load line
淡水注入管/淡水注入管　fresh water filling pipe
弹齿耙/彈齒式耙　spring-tooth harrow
弹带阻力/彈帶阻力　ammunition belt drag
弹道靶/彈道試驗場　ballistic range
弹道表/彈道表　ballistic table
弹道参数/彈道參數　trajectory parameter
弹道测量/彈道測量　trajectory measurement
弹道测量系统/彈道測量系統　trajectory measurement system
弹道函数/彈道函數　ballistic function
弹道极限曲线/彈道極限曲線　ballistic limit curve
弹道偏角/彈道偏轉角　trajectory deflection angle
弹道倾角/彈道傾角　trajectory tilt angle, flight path angle
弹道摄影/彈道攝影　ballistic photography
弹道式再入/彈道重返　ballistic re-entry
弹道相机/彈道攝影機　ballistic camera
弹道学/彈道學　ballistics
弹道诸元/彈道資料　trajectory data
弹道自导段/彈道自導段　self-guided ballistic phase
弹道自控段/彈道自控段　self-controlled ballistic phase
弹道坐标测量/彈道坐標量測　ballistic coordinate measurement
弹街路面/彈街路面　pitching pavement
弹体赋形天线/飛彈整形天線　missile shaping antenna
弹体解耦/飛彈解耦　missile body decoupling
弹体遥测/飛彈遙測　missile body telemetry
弹头气动特性/彈頭氣動特性　aerodynamic characteristic of nose
弹头遥测/彈頭遙測　warhead telemetry
弹头引信/彈頭引信　fuse of warhead
弹托/支承環　sabot
弹药舱/彈藥艙　magazine
弹药转运间/彈藥搬運室　ammunition carrier room, ammunition handling room
蛋鸡舍/蛋雞舍　layer house
氮气吹除/氮氣吹洩　nitrogen blow-off
氮气风洞/氮氣風洞　nitrogen wind tunnel
氮气配气台/氮氣配氣臺　nitrogen gas distribution board
氮气置换/氮氣置換　nitrogen replacement
氮氧化合物/氮氧化物　nitrogen oxide, NOx
氮氧化合物污染/氮氧化物汙染　NOx pollution
当班工长/領班　shift boss
当地交通/地區客運　local transit
当地水位/當地水位　local water level
当地重力加速度/本地引力加速度　local gravitational acceleration
当量比/當量比　equivalent ratio
当量故障率/等效失效率　equivalent failure rate
当量厚度/相當厚度　equivalent thickness
当量空速/等值空速　equivalent airspeed
当量跨距/當量跨距　equivalent span length
当量扩张角/當量發散角　equivalent divergence angle
当量圆直径/當量圓直徑　diameter of equivalent circle
当量轴次/當量軸次　equivalent axles
挡板/阻流板　baffle board
挡板曝气/隔板式曝氣　baffle aeration
挡冰栅/流冰擋　ice guard
挡车器/車用緩衝器　stop buffer
挡风墙/擋風牆　wind-break wall
挡光板/擋板,障板　baffle

挡光筒/擋光筒　baffling barrel
挡浪板/擋浪板　breakwater
挡土墙/擋土牆　retaining wall
挡土墙上分力/擋土牆上分力　component of retaining wall
挡雪台阶/擋雪臺階　snow slip protection step
挡烟板/折煙板　smoke deflector
挡烟垂壁/折煙垂壁　hang wall
挡油设施/擋油設施　oil threshold trapping collection device
挡渣板/浮渣擋板　scum baffle
档案馆/檔案館　archives
档案室/檔案室　archives room
刀把梁/刀把梁　lowered draft sill
刀具/刀具　cutting tool
刀状天线/刀形天線　blade antenna
导板/導板　guide plate
导爆管/導爆管　exploding pipe
导爆索/導爆索,爆炸保險絲　exploding fuse, blasting fuse
导爆线/導火線,引爆索　primacord
导爆药柱/導爆藥柱　lead explosive
导边/導緣,前緣　leading edge
导标/引導示標,導航標誌　leading beacon, leading mark
导程/導程,測[深]錘　lead
导出包络/導出包絡　derived envelope
导出[测量]单位/導出[量測]單位　derived unit of measurement
导出量/導出量　derived quantity
导锤吊架/導錘吊架　hanging leader
导锤轨/導錘軌　false leader
导弹测控系统/飛彈測控系統　missile TT and C system
导弹电控测试装置/飛彈電線束試驗器　missile electrical harness tester
导弹发射架/飛彈發射器　missile launcher
导弹攻击区/飛彈攻擊範圍　missile attack envelop
导弹归零/飛彈歸零　missile zeroin
导弹护卫舰/飛彈巡防艦　guided missile frigate, FFG
导弹快艇/[導向]飛彈快艇　guided missile boat, FAC
导弹离轴发射/飛彈離軸發射　missile offboresight launch
导弹试验场/飛彈試驗靶場　missile test range
导弹卫星跟踪测量船/飛彈衛星跟蹤測量船　missile range instrumentation ship

导堤/突堤,防波堤,導流堤　jetty, training mole
导电轨受电器/導電軌受電器　conductor rail collector
导电率/導電度　electrical conductivity
导电涂层/導電塗層　conductive coating
导电氧化/導電氧化　electric conductive oxidation
导电液体/導電液體　conducting liquid
导洞/導洞　heading, pilot
导洞法/導洞法,導坑法　pilot tunneling method, pilot tunnel method
导洞与层阶法/頂部光進洞開鑿挖掘法　heading and bench tunneling method
导阀/[繇]導閥,導引閥　pilot valve
导风轮/導風輪　inducer
导风罩/導風罩　wind scooper
导杆式柴油打桩锤/導桿式柴油打樁機　guide rod type diesel pile hammer
导管/導管,輸流管　duct, tube, pipe
导管调整器/導管調整器　pipe compensator
导管推进器/導罩螺槳　shrouded propeller, ducted propeller
导管样件/導管樣品　sample tube
导管装置/導管裝置　pipe installation
导轨/滑導,滑軌　sliding guide, slide rail
导轨灯/履帶燈　track-mounted luminaire
导轨式气动凿岩机/鑽岩機　drifter
导轨与悬浮系统相互作用/導槽懸浮系統相互作用　guideway suspension interaction
导航/導航　navigation
GPS导航/全球定位系統導航　GPS navigation
导航比/導航常數　navigation ratio
导航标志系统/導航標誌系統　taxi sign system
导航参数/導航參數,導航變數　navigation parameter
导[航]灯/導航燈,距離燈　range light
导航分系统/導航子系統　navigation subsystem
导航杆/導桿,示向桿　guide rod
导航攻击系统/導航攻擊系統　navigation attack system
导航精度/導航精度　navigation accuracy
导航雷达/導航雷達　navigation radar
导航设备/導航設施　navigational aid, navigation equipment
导航声呐/導航聲納　navigation sonar
导航卫星/導航衛星　navigation satellite, navigational satellite
导航卫星网/導航衛星網路　navigation satellite network

导航线/導航線　leading line
导航信号/導航信號　navigation signal
导火索/導火線,安全引線　blasting fuse, safety fuse
导坑/礦坑引道　heading
导坑法/導坑法,導隧法　pilot tunnel method
导口/導槽入口　entry guide
导框式转向架/導框式轉向架　pedestal truck
导缆孔/[繫船]導索管　mooring pipe
导缆器/導索器　fairleader, fairlead
导缆钳/導索器　chock
导链轮/導鏈器　chain cable fairlead
导梁/架橋導梁,曳進導梁　launching nose
导梁法/推進式架設　erection by launching
导流槽/導槽　flame diversion trough
导流岛/導行島,槽化島　channelization island
导流堤/導流堤　diversion dike, training levee
导流构筑物/導流建築物　diversion structure
导流建筑物/導流建築物,調節建築物　regulating structure
导流流量比/分水比　diversion ratio
导流面/導面　guide face
导流渠/分水渠,分水道,導水路　diversion channel
导流型容积式水加热器/導流型容積式水加熱器　storage heat exchanger of guide flow type
导流叶片/導流片　guide vane
导流罩舵/球形舵　bulb rudder
导流锥/變位錐面　deflection cone
导轮/導輪　guide wheel
导轮对/導輪組　leading truck wheel set
导轮转向架/導輪轉向架　leading truck
导纳电桥/導納電橋　admittance bridge
导频/導頻　pilot frequency
导频放大器/導頻放大器　pilot amplifier
导频无人增音机/導頻無人值守自動增音機　pilot unattended repeater
导曲线/導軌曲線,分岔内方曲線　lead curve
导曲线半径/導軌之曲線半徑　radius of lead curve
导曲线支距/導軌曲線支距　offset of lead curve
导热系数/導熱係數,導熱性　heat conduction coefficient, coefficient of thermal conductivity
导热油沥青熔化装置/導熱油瀝青熔化裝置　asphalt hot oil melter
导水系数/導水係數　transmissivity
导索环/導索環　backet loop
导套/定向套筒　guide sleeve
导体/導體　conductor
导线/導線　traverse, conductor
导线安装曲线/導線安裝曲線　wire installation curve
导线测量/導線測量　traverse survey, traversing
导线穿管敷设/導線穿管敷設　conductor installed enclosed in conduit
导线导轮/導線導輪,攜帶型線盤　wire carrier
导线点/導線點　traverse point
导线反正扣/導線反正扣　wire-adjusting screw
导线立轮/垂直輪　vertical wheel
导线平轮/水平輪　horizontal wheel
导线平轮组/導線平輪組　horizontal wheel assembly
导线调整器/導線調整器　wire compensator
导线网/導線網　traverse net
导线装置/導線裝置　wire installation
导向安全/導向安全　failure to the safe side
导向杆/導桿　guide bar, guided rod
导向滚轮/臺式滾輪　pedestal roller
导向力/導向力　guidance force
导向面伞/導向面傘　guide-surface parachute
导向器/渦輪噴嘴　turbine nozzle
导向器叶片/噴嘴導流片　nozzle guide vane
导向索/導索,扶手索　guide rope, guideline
导向套/定向套筒　guide sleeve
导向系统/導引系統　guidance system
导向线/導線,指令線　guidance line, leading line, alignment guiding line
导向叶片/導葉[片]　guide vane, guide blade
导星/導星　guiding star
导压系数/導壓係數　piezometric conductivity
导叶泵/擴散泵　diffuser pump
导医处/查詢臺,詢問臺,服務中心　information desk, service center
导音频信号/聲頻導頻信號　pilot audio fequency signal
导引方程/導引方程　steering equation
导引律/導引律　guidance law
导引试体/導引試體　pilot specimen
导引头分辨率/歸航器解析度　homing head resolution
导引头盲区/歸航器盲區　homing head blind zone
导引头一体化引信/歸航器綜合引信　integrated fuze with homing head
导引装置/歸航器　homing head
导游解说/導遊解說　tour description and direction
导游图/導遊圖　tourist map
导桩/導樁　pilot pile
岛/[路]島　island
岛架/島架　island shelf
岛礁区航行/多礁水域航行　navigating in rocky

water
岛[式防波]堤/離岸堤　isolated breakwater, offshore breakwater, detached breakwater
岛式挖掘法/島式挖掘法　island process
岛式舞台/圓形舞臺,中心式舞臺　arena stage
岛式站台/島式站臺　island platform
岛园/島園　island garden
岛状冻土/隔離凍土　segregated frozen ground
岛状花境/島狀花境　island border
捣镐/栓塞　packer
捣固/夯實,搗實　tamping
捣固道床/石碴夯實工程　ballast tamping
捣固机械/砸道機,剳道機　tamping machine
倒垛/倒垛　stack transfer
倒塌/倒塌　collapse
到岸价[格]/到岸價格,含保險費與運費之貨價　cost insurance and freight, CIF
到达场/到達場,到達區　receiving yard, arriving yard
到达船/到港船　arrived ship
到达点/到達點　arrival point
到达港/到達港　port of arrival
到达路/到達路　destination railway
到达旅客厅/迎客大廳　arrival hall
到达线/到達線　receiving track, arriving track
到发场/到發場,駛離區　receiving departure yard
到发线/到發線　arrival and departure track
到发线出岔电路/到發線出岔電路　protection circuit with switch lying in receiving departure track
到发线通过能力/到發線通過能力　carrying capacity of receiving departure track
到付运费/到付運費　freight to collect
到港日期/到港日期　date of arrival
到港压载水/抵港壓艙水　arrival ballast
到货通知/到貨通知　arrival notice
到寿件/到壽件　life-limit element
倒车/倒車　backing, astern
倒车操纵阀/倒車操縱閥　astern maneuving valve
倒车冲程/倒車停車距離　reverse stopping distance
倒车舵/倒車舵　flanking rudder
倒车阀/倒車閥　astern guardian valve, astern valve
倒车隔离阀/倒車護閥　astern guarding valve
倒车工况/倒車狀況　astern condition
倒车功率/倒車動力　astern power, backing power
倒车排汽室喷雾器/倒車排氣室噴霧器　astern exhaust chest sprayer
倒车喷嘴/倒車噴嘴　astern nozzle
倒车汽轮机/倒車蒸汽渦輪機　astern steam turbine

倒车燃气轮机/倒車燃氣渦輪機　astern gas turbine
倒车试验/倒車試航　astern trial
倒车装置/倒車裝置　means of going astern
倒丁字挡土墙/倒丁字擋土牆　inverted T type retaining wall
倒飞/倒飛　inverted flight
倒飞油箱/倒飛油箱　inverted flight fuel tank
倒拱式护墙/倒拱式護牆　counter-arched revetment
倒航工况管理/倒航操作形式管理　astern running operating mode management
倒虹吸管/倒虹[吸]管　inverted siphon
倒虹吸涵/倒虹吸涵　inverted siphon culvert
倒计时程序/倒數程式　countdown procedure
倒缆/倒纜　spring
倒流防止器/回流防止器　backflow preventer
倒片室/卷片室　rewind room
倒签提单/倒簽載貨證券　anti-dated bill of lading
倒[数]计时/倒數　countdown
倒拖/倒拖　reverse towing
倒T形材/倒丁字　inverted tee
倒Y形索塔/倒Y型索塔　inverted Y tower
倒影池/倒影池　mirror pool
倒置式屋面/倒置式屋面　inverted roofing
倒转层位/倒轉層位　inverted position
倒转水平/倒式水平儀　invert level
倒座/倒座　opposite house, daozuo
道班/道班　track maintenance gang
道班房/道班房　maintenance gang house
道班养护/道班養路　gang maintenance
道岔/道岔　turnout, switches and crossings
道岔表示/道岔表示　switch indication
道岔表示电源/道岔表示電源　power source for switch indication
道岔表示器/轉轍表示器　switch indicator
道岔侧线/道岔分歧線　branch line of turnout, branch track of turnout, turnout branch
道岔错误表示/道岔錯誤表示　false indication of a switch
道岔定位表示/道岔定位表示　switch normal indication
道岔动作电源/道岔動作電源　power source for switch operation
道岔反位表示/道岔反位表示　switch reverse indication
道岔封锁/道岔封鎖　switch closed up
道岔号数/道岔號數　turnout number
道岔后部理论长度/道岔後部理論長度　rear part theoretical length of turnout

道岔后部实际长度/道岔後部實際長度　rear part actual length of turnout
道岔护轨/道岔護軌　turnout guard rail
道岔基线/道岔基準線　reference line of turnout
道岔绝缘段/道岔絕緣段　insulated switch section
道岔控制电路/道岔控制電路　switch control circuit
道岔控制电源/道岔控制電源　power source for switch control
道岔拉杆/轉轍器拉桿，尖軌拉桿　switch rod, stretcher bar
道岔理论导程/道岔理論導距　theoretical lead of turnout
道岔理论长度/道岔理論長度　theoretical length of turnout
道岔连接杆/道岔連接桿　connecting bar, following stretcher bar
道岔密贴/道岔密貼　switch point closure
道岔配列/道岔布置　switch layout
道岔启动/道岔啟動　switch starting
道岔前部理论长度/道岔前部理論長度　front part theoretical length of turnout
道岔清扫房/道岔清掃房　switch cleaner cabin
道岔区/道岔區　turnout zone
道岔区段/道岔區段　section with a switch or switches
道岔区坡/道岔區坡　gradient within the switching area
道岔全长/道岔全長　total length of turnout
道岔人工解锁/道岔人工解鎖　manual release of a locked switch
道岔熔冰器/轉轍器融雪器，道岔加熱器　switch heater
道岔失去表示/道岔失去表示　loss of indication of a switch
道岔实际长度/道岔實際長度　actual length of turnout
道岔始端/道岔始端　beginning of turnout
道岔数/道岔號數　turnout number
道岔顺序启动/道岔順序啟動　sequential starting of switches
道岔顺序转换/道岔順序轉換　sequential transiting of switches
道岔锁闭/道岔鎖閉　switch point locking
道岔锁闭表示/道岔鎖閉表示　switch locked indication
道岔握柄/轉轍閘柄　switch lever
道岔中途转换/道岔中途轉換　switch thrown under moving car
道岔中心/道岔中心　center of turnout
道岔终端/道岔終端　end of turnout
道岔主线/道岔之主基準線　main line of turnout, main track of turnout, turnout main
道岔柱/道岔柱　turnout mast
道岔转换/道岔轉換　switch in transition
道岔阻力/轉轍阻力　switch resistance
道床/道［碴］床　ballast bed
道床边坡夯实机/道床肩部夯實機　ballast shoulder consolidating machine
道床底碴夯实机/底碴夯實機　subballast consolidating machine
道床夯实/道碴夯實　ballast ramming
道床厚度/道碴深度　thickness of ballast bed, depth of ballast bed
道床宽度/道碴床寬度　width of ballast bed
道床配碴整形/道碴分配整理　ballast distributing and trimming
道床系数/道床係數，道碴係數，碴床係數　ballast coefficient, ballast modulus
道床碴肩/道碴床道肩　shoulder of ballast bed
道床阻力/道床阻力　ballast resistance
道钉/道釘　track spike, rail spike, spike
道钉锤/道釘錘　spike hammer
道观/道觀，道院，道宮　Taoist temple, guan
道肩/跑道肩　runway shoulder
道具室/道具儲藏室，保管室　property room
道口/平交道　grade crossing, level crossing
道口防护无线电通信/平交道保護裝置無線電通訊　radio communication for highway crossing protection
道口护桩/平交道護樁　protective stake at grade crossing
道口监视电视/平交道保監視電視　monitor TV for highway crossing
道口接近区段/平交道接近區段　approach section of a highway level crossing
道口警标/平交道警告標誌　warning sign at grade crossing
道口看守工/平交道看守工　grade crossing watchman, level crossing watchman
道口栏木/平交道欄木　cross barrier at grade crossing
道口平台/平交道平臺　level stretch of grade crossing
道口铺面/平交道鋪面　grade crossing pavement, surface of grade crossing
道口闪光信号/平交道閃光信號　highway level

道 91

crossing flashing signal
道口室外音响器/平交道室外音響器　highway level crossing out door audible device
道口通知设备/平交道通知設備　highway level crossing announcing device
道口信号机/平交道信號機　highway level crossing signal
道口信号控制盘/平交道信號控制盤　highway level crossing signal control panel
道口遥信遥测设备/平交道遥信遥测設備　remote surveillance and telemetering for highway level crossing
道口栅栏/平交道柵欄　side barrier at grade crossing
道口遮断信号/平交道遮斷信號　highway level crossing obstruction signal
道口自动信号/平交道自動信號　automatic level crossing signal
道路/道路　road
道路边界线/街路界線　street line
道路边坡绿化/道路邊坡綠化　road slope greening
道路标高/道路標高　road elevation
道路标识/道路標線　road marking
道路标线漆/標字線漆　road mark paint
道路标志/道路標線　road marking
道路催眠状态/道路催眠狀態　road hypnosis
道路等级/道路分類　road classification
道路断面/道路斷面　road section
道路翻新/補修路　retreading road
道路反光镜/道路反射鏡　road reflecting mirror
道路防护林/道路保安林　road protection forest
[道路]服务水平/服務水準　level of service
道路工程[学]/道路工程[學]　road engineering
道路功能/道路功能　road function
道路广场用地/道路廣場用地　roads and squares
道路横断面/道路橫斷面　road section, road cross-section
道路红线/道路紅線,建築限界,街路界線　road boundary line, street line
[道路]环形交叉/迴轉交叉　gyratory intersection, rotary intersection
道路几何设计/公路幾何設計,公路線形設計　geometric design of highways
道路几何数据收集/道路幾何資料擷取系統　road geometry data acquisition system
道路技术标准/道路技術標準　road technical standard
道路建设/道路施工　road construction
道路建筑/道路施工　road construction
道路建筑限界/道路建築限界,道路建築邊界線　boundary line of road construction
道路交叉/道路交叉　road intersection
道路交叉口/道路會合處　road junction
道路交通/道路交通　road traffic
道路交通标线/道路交通標線　road traffic marking
道路交通法规/道路交通安全法律法規　road traffic law and regulation
道路交通信号/道路交通號誌　road traffic signal
道路经济分析/道路經濟分析　road economical analysis
道路沥青/道路瀝青　road bitumen
道路路边分隔带/側帶　side strip
道路绿地/道路綠地　green space attached to urban road and square
道路绿化/道路植载　road planting
道路面积率/道路面積率　road area ratio
道路面积密度/道路面積率　road area ratio
道路容量/道路容量　road capacity
道路洒水车/灑水車　road sprinkler
道路施工/道路施工　road construction
道路收费系统/道路收費系統　road toll system
道路枢纽/道路會合處　road junction
道路水泥/道路水泥　road cement
道路通车容量/道路容量　road capacity
道路通行能力/道路容量　road capacity
道路网/[公]路網　road network, highway network
道路网密度/[公]路網密度　road network density, density of road network
道路系统/道路系統　approach system, road system
道路线形/道路線向　road alignment
道路养护/養路　road maintenance
道路引导系统/路徑誘導系統　route guidance system
道路用地/道路用地　land for roads
道路用地线/路權用地線　right of way line
道路与交通设施用地/道路與交通設施用地　street and transportation land, land for street and transportation
道路运输/公路運輸　road transport
道路照明/道路照明　road lighting
道路中线车道/中心車道　center line lane
道路中心线/道路中心線　road center line, street center line
道路中央分隔栏/中央分線島　central divider
道路转弯半径/道路轉彎半徑　road turning radius
道面等级号/路面分類號碼　pavement classification number, PCN

道面强度/跑道強度　runway pavement strength
道碴/道碴　ballast
道碴槽/道碴槽　ballast tub
道碴层/道碴層　ballast layer
道碴巢/道碴巢　ballast nest
道碴袋/道碴袋　ballast pocket
道碴电阻/道碴電阻　ballast resistance
道碴轨道/道碴軌道　ballasted track
道碴机械/道碴機械　ballast machine
道碴级配/道碴級配　ballast grading
道碴犁/道碴犁　ballast plow
道碴桥面/鋪碴橋面　ballasted deck, ballasted floor
道碴清筛机械/道碴清篩機　ballast cleaning machine, ballast screening machine
道碴撒铺车/道碴撒布機　ballast spreader
道碴箱/道碴箱　ballast box
德国船级社/德國驗船協會　German Lloyd
LED 灯/LED 光源　LED lamp
灯标/燈標　lighted mark
灯标表/燈塔表　light list
灯标及航标表/燈塔燈標表　light and beacon list
灯标艇/燈標船　beacon boat
灯船/燈[標]船　light boat, light vessel
LED 灯带/LED 燈帶　LED flexible rope light
灯高/燈[距水面]高,塔燈高度　elevation of light, height of light
灯光船/集魚燈船　fishing light boat
灯光导航/燈光導航　light navigation
灯光渡桥/燈光橋　lighting bridge
灯光控制室/燈光室　lighting control room
灯光射程/燈光射程　light range
灯光通信/燈號通信　flashing light signaling
灯光信号/燈光信號,燈火信號　light signal
灯光诱杀/誘蟲燈　light trap
灯光诱鱼/燈光誘魚　lamp attracting
灯光诱鱼船/誘魚燈船　fish luring light boat
灯光照明标志/照明標誌　illuminated sign
灯光转移/燈光轉移　to transfer of lighting indication
灯具/照明器具　luminaire
灯具间/燈具室　lamp room
灯具效率/燈具效率,發光效率,照明器效率　luminaire efficiency
灯具遮光角/燈具遮光角,燈具遮罩角,燈具遮蔽角　shielding angle of luminaire
灯具最大允许距高比/燈具最大允許中高比　maximum permissible spacing height ratio of luminaire
灯室/燈罩,光源　lamp house

灯丝断丝/燈絲斷絲,燈絲燒斷　filament burn-out
灯丝断丝报警/燈絲斷絲報警　alarm for burnout of filament
灯塔/燈塔　lighthouse, beacon
灯塔供应船/燈塔補給船　lighthouse tender
灯柱/街燈柱,路燈柱　lamppost
灯桩/燈[浮]標　light beacon
登岸浮桥/登陸浮橋　landing floating bridge
登岸桥/浮棧橋,浮碼頭　landing stage floating, floating landing stage
登岸证/登岸證　landing permit, shore pass
登舱臂/登艙臂　climbing module arm
登船梯/乘載梯　embarkation ladder
登高/登高　climbing
登机门/登機門　boarding gate
登记长度/登記長度　registered length
登记宽度/登記寬度　registered breadth
登记深度/登記深度　registered depth
登陆港/登陸港　landing harbor
登陆航海勤务/登陸海勤　navigation service for landing
登陆舰/登陸艦艇　landing ship
登陆艇/登陸艇　landing craft
登陆战舰艇/兩棲作戰艦艇　amphibious warfare ships and crafts
登轮检查/登輪檢查　inspection by boarding
登山电缆车/登山電纜車　climbing a mountain cable car
登山运动/登山運動　mountaineering
登艇灯/[艇筏]乘載照明燈,小艇甲板燈　embarkation lamp, boat deck lamp, boat deck light
登艇梯/登艇梯　boarding ladder
登月轨道/登月軌道　lunar landing trajectory
蹬舵/蹬舵　apply rudder
蹬索/鐙,繫索　stirrup
等百分线/等百分線　constant percentage chord line
等变运动/等變運動　uniform varying motion
等参元/等參元　isoparametric element
等潮差线/等潮差線　co-range line
等潮时/等潮時　cotidal hour
等潮时图/等潮圖,同時潮圖　cotidal chart
等潮时线/等潮線　cotidal line
等磁差图/等偏差線,等角線圖　isogonic chart
等磁差线/等偏磁線　isogonic line
等代均布荷载/等效勻布静載荷　equivalent uniform distributed load
等待/等候　waiting
等待程序/等待程式　holding procedure

等待点／等待點　holding point
等待油量／等待油量　holding fuel
等电位联结／等電位聯結　equipotential bonding
等多普勒频率线／等都卜勒頻移線　line of constant Doppler shift
等[方向]角航线／等角線　rhumb-line
等分平衡法／等分平衡法　method of making the rock equational and balanced
等概率误差椭圆／等可能誤差橢圓　equal-probable error ellipse
等高差／等高差　equation of equal altitude
等高法／等高法　equal altitude method
等高面测绘／輪廓[等高線]繪圖　contour mapping
等高圈／等高圈,高度圈　circle of equal altitude, almucantar
等高线／等高線,恆值線　contour line, contour lines
等高线地图／暈色地形圖　layered map
等高[线]距／等高線間距,等高線間隔　contour interval
等高[值]线图／等高線圖　contour map
等光强曲线／等光度曲線　iso-luminous intensity curve
等级公路／等級公路　standard highway, classified highway
等级航道／分級航道　graded fairway
等剂量线／等劑量線　isodose line
等加速度／等加速度　uniform acceleration
等加速运动／等加速度運動　uniform accelerated motion
等价锥热流计算／等價錐熱流計算　heat flux calculation of equivalent cones
等降颗粒／等降粒子　equal-falling particle
等角航线／等角航線　rhumb line route
等角投影／等角投影　equiangular projection
等精度测量／等精度量測　equal precision measurement
等精度曲线／等精度曲線　contours of constant geometric accuracy
等距射影／等距投影法　equidistance projection
等离子弧焊／電漿弧焊[接]　plasma arc welding
等离子[弧]喷涂／電漿噴塗　plasma spraying, plasma coating
等离子加工／電漿加工　plasma machining
等离子清洗／電漿清潔　plasma cleaning
等离子蚀刻／電漿蝕刻[法]　plasma etching
等离子体／等離子體,電漿　plasma
等离子体离子辅助沉积／電漿離子輔助沈積　plasma ion-assisted deposition
等离子体鞘套／電漿鞘　plasma sheath
等离子体射流／電漿噴流　plasma jet
等离子体显示屏／電漿顯示器　plasma display panel, PDP
等离子体湮没改性／電漿浸沒改質　plasma immersed modification
等离子体源离子注入／電漿源離子植入　plasma source ion implantation
等离子体诊断／電漿診斷學　plasma diagnostics
等亮度曲线／等亮度曲線　iso-luminance curve
等量法／等量法　equalizing method
等量高度法／等值高度法　equivalent-altitude method
等烈度线／等震度線　coseismic line
等螺距／定螺距　constant pitch
等面燃烧／中性燃燒,定推力燃燒　neutral burning
等平均有效压力限／平均有效壓力限制　mean effective pressure limit
等强度梁／等強度梁　constant strength beam
等强度设计／等強度設計　design of equal bearing capacity
等倾角法／恆向線法　rhumb line method
等倾斜线／等坡線　contour gradient
等熵管流／等熵管流　isentropic flow in pipe
等熵流动／等熵流動　isentropic flow
等深线／等深線　depth contour, isobath
等深线图／等深線圖,水深圖,海底地形圖　bathymetric map
等时线图／等時間線圖　time contour map
等势线／等勢線,等位線　equipotential line
等视差面／等視差面　surface of equal parallax
等[水]深线／地水等深線　hydroisobath
等水位线／等水壓線　isopiestic line
等速工况／等速模態　cruising mode
等外材／等外材　under grade wood
等外公路／等外公路　substandard highway
等温超塑性锻造／等温超塑性鍛造　isothermal superplastic forging
等温淬火／恆温淬火　isothermal hardening, isothermal quenching
等温锻[造]／等温鍛造　isothermal forging
等温管流／等温管流　isothermal flow in pipe
等温过程／等温過程　isothermal process
等温面／等温面　isothermal surface
等温射流／等温射流　isothermal jet
等温线／等温線　isotherm
等温压缩／等温壓縮　isothermal compression
等稳定设计／等穩定設計　design of equal stability
等响曲线／等響曲線　equal-loudness contour

等效/等效,等值 equivalent
等效安全水平/等效安全 equivalent level of safety
等效超载/等值超载 equivalent surcharge
等效单轮荷载/相當單輪載重 equivalent single wheel load
等效干扰电流/等效擾動電流 equivalent disturbing current
等效荷载法/均布載重法 equivalent load method
等效技术/等效技術 equivalence technique
等效剪切波速/等效剪切波速 equivalent shear wave velocity
等效结点荷载/等效節點荷載 equivalent nodal load
等效矩形应力图/等效矩形應力塊 equivalent rectangular stress block
等效连续A声级/等效持續A加權聲壓位準,等價持續A加權聲壓位準 equivalent continuous A-weighted sound pressure level
等效器/模擬機 simulator, equivalent device
等效全向辐射功率/等效等向輻射功率,全向等效輻射功率 equivalent isotropically radiated power, equivalent isotropic radiated power, EIRP
等效吸声面积/等效吸音面積 equivalent absorption area
等效系统/等效系統 equivalent system
等效线圈/等效線圈 equivalent coil
等效应变/等效應變 equivalent strain
等效应力/等效應力 equivalent stress
等雪[量]线/等雪深線 isochion
等压面/等壓面 isobaric surface, equipressure surface
等压面图/等值圖 contour chart
等压线/等[水]壓線 isobar, isopiestic line
等压线间距/等壓線間距 piestic interval
等雨量线/等雨指數線 isopluvial line
等照度曲线/等照度曲線 iso-illuminance curve
等值/等值,等效,當量 equivalent
等值焦距/等效焦距 equivalent focal length
等值剖面积/等值斷面積 equivalent sectional area
等转矩限/轉矩轉速限制 torque speed limit
凳/長凳 bench, stool
澄清池/固體接觸澄清池 solids contact clarifier
澄清器/澄清器 clarifier
磴道/腳踏石 stone step
低保真度/保真度不高的,非保真的,靈敏度不高的 Lo-Fi
低标准船/次標準船 substandard ship
低播焰性/低度火焰蔓延 low flame spread
低侧音/低側音 low side tone
低层住宅/低層樓房 low-rise house
低潮/低潮 low water, LW
低潮间隙/低潮間隔 low water interval
低潮礁/低潮礁 low water rock
低潮时/低潮時 low water time
低承台桩基/低承臺樁基 embedded footing on piles
低冲击开发/低衝擊開發模式 low-impact development
低磁钢/非磁性鋼 non-magnetic steel, low-magnetic steel
低弹道[飞行]试验/低彈道試驗 low trajectory test
低低潮/較低低潮 lower low water, LLW
低地球轨道/低空[地球]軌道 low earth orbit
低地下水位/泉面低位 phreatic low
低电压保护/低電壓保護 low-voltage protection
低电压释放/低電壓釋放 low-voltage release
低发热值/低發熱值 fuel net calorific value
低发射率颜料/低發射率顏料 low-emittance pigment
低辐射镀膜玻璃/低輻射鍍膜玻璃 low emissivity coated glass
低负荷滴滤池/低率滴濾池 low-rate trickling filter
低高潮/[較]低高潮 lower high water, LHW
低高度梁/低高度梁 shallow girder
低轨道搜救卫星系统/低軌道搜救衛星系統 low Earth orbit SAR satellite system
低轨道搜救卫星系统本地用户终端/低軌道衛星搜救系統地面終端臺 LUT in a LEOSAR system
低滑油压力保护装置/低潤滑油壓跳脫設施 low-lubricating oil pressure trip device
低货位/低貨位 low freight lot
低级路面/低級路面 low level pavement, low class pavement
低极轨道卫星搜救系统/衛星輔助搜救系統 COSPAs-SARSAT system
低极轨道卫星搜救系统信文/衛星輔助搜救系統信文 COSPAs-SARSAT message
低极轨道卫星搜救组织理事会/國際衛星輔助搜救組織理事會 COSPAs-SARSAT council
低价住房/廉價住宅 low-cost housing
低净空标志/低消除標誌 low clearance sign
低空避撞/低空防撞 low-level collision avoidance
低空飞行/低空飛行 low-level flight
低流量观测/低水流量觀測 low flow observation
低率滴滤池/低率滴濾池 low-rate trickling filter
低密度风洞/低密度風洞 low density wind tunnel
低密度烧蚀材料/低密度熔蝕材料 low density ablator

低摩合成闸瓦/低摩擦式合成閘瓦　low friction composite brake shoe
低膨胀高温合金/低膨脹高溫合金　low expansion superalloy
低频干扰防卫度/低頻干擾防衛度　signal to low frequency interference rate
低频燃烧不稳定性/低頻燃燒不穩定　low-frequency combustion instability
低频线振动台/低頻線性振動臺　low-frequency linear vibration table
低频压力/低頻應力　low-frequency stress
低平板挂车/低臺拖車　low bed trailer
低气压试验/低壓試驗　low pressure test
低潜水位/泉面低位　phreatic low
低氢型焊条/低氫焊條　hydrogen controlled electrode, low hydrogen type electrode
低区电梯/低區電梯　low-zone elevator
低热［硅酸盐］水泥/低熱水泥，低熱波特蘭水泥　low heat Portland cement
低热值/低熱值　lower calorific value
低收入住房/低收入住宅建設　low-income housing
低水头/低水頭　lower head
低水位桥/低水位橋　low water level bridge
低速标志/低速號誌　slow speed signal
低速柴油机/低速柴油機　low speed diesel engine
低速风洞/低速風洞　low speed wind tunnel
低速过滤池/低速率漏濾池　low-rate filter
低速流/低速流　low speed flow
低碳产业园区/低碳產業園區，低碳工業園區　low-carbon industrial park
低碳城市/低碳都市　low-carbon city
低碳城市规划/低碳都市規劃　low-carbon urban planning
低碳交通/低碳交通　low-carbon transportation
低碳经济/低碳經濟　low-carbon economy
低碳园林/低碳園林　low-carbon landscape
低湍流度风洞/低紊流度風洞　low turbulence wind tunnel
低洼泉/窪地泉　depression spring
低位通海阀/低位海水吸入閥　low sea suction valve
低位小便器/低位小便器　low-level urinal
低温泵/低溫泵　cryopump
低温测量/低溫量測　cryogenic measurement
低温超导陀螺/低溫超導陀螺儀　cryogenic superconducting gyroscope
低温风洞/低溫風洞　cryogenic wind tunnel
低温腐蚀/低溫腐蝕　low temperature corrosion
低温工况/過冷狀態　worst cold case

低温核供热系统/低溫核反應爐供熱系統　heat supply system based upon low temperature nuclear reactor
低温加注系统/低溫加注系統　cryogenic loading system
低温连接器/低溫連接器　low temperature connector
低温密封/低溫密封　low temperature sealing
低温模拟试验/低溫模擬試驗　simulated cold climate test
低温球阀/低溫球閥　cryogenic ball valve
低温热水地板辐射供暖/低溫熱水地板輻射供暖　low temperature hot water floor radiant heating
低温烧蚀材料试验/低溫燒蝕材料試驗　ablation test of low temperature ablator
低温试验/低溫試驗　low temperature test
低温水/低溫熱水　low temperature hot water
低温推进剂/低溫推進劑　cryogenic propellant
低温推进剂火箭发动机/低溫推進劑火箭發動機　cryogenic propellant rocket engine
低温推进剂贮箱/低溫推進劑箱　cryogenic propellant tank
低温退火钢丝/應力消除鋼線　stress-relieved wire
低温温度传感器/低溫溫度感測器　cryogenic temperature sensor
低温吸附/低溫吸附　cryogenic absorption
低温系统/低溫系統　cryogenic system
低温植物/低溫植物　microtherm
低温砖/次等磚，隔熱磚　soft brick
低限效应/門檻效應，臨限效應　threshold effect
低压/低［氣］壓　low pressure
低压保安阀/低壓安全閥　low pressure safety valve
低压泵/低壓抽水機　low pressure pump
低压舱/低壓艙，低壓室　altitude hypobaric chamber
低压槽/［低壓］槽　trough
低压侧调压/低［電］壓調節　low voltage regulation
低压电路/低電壓電路　low voltage circuit, low tension circuit
低压二氧化碳灭火系统/低壓二氧化碳滅火系統　low pressure carbon dioxide extinguishing system
低压反应离子镀/低壓反應離子鍍　low voltage ion reactive plating
低压管/低壓管　low pressure pipe
低压化学气相沉积/低壓化學蒸汽沈積　low pressure chemical vapor deposition
低压开关设备/低壓開關設備　low voltage switch equipment
低压空气瓶/低壓空氣瓶　low pressure air bottle
低压敏感性检查/低壓易感受性檢驗　hypobaric

susceptibility test
低压钠[蒸气]灯/低壓鈉[光]燈,低壓鈉氣燈 low pressure sodium vapor lamp, low voltage sodium lamp
低压配电室/低壓配電室 low voltage distribution room
低压配电系统/低壓配電系統 low voltage distribution system
低压配电装置/低壓配電裝置 low voltage distribution equipment
低压缺氧检查/低壓缺氧檢查 hypobaric hypoxia examination
低压绕组/低壓繞組,低壓線圈 low voltage winding, low tension winding
低压软管/低壓軟管 low pressure hose
低压调压开关/低電壓分接頭 low voltage tap changer, low tension tap changer
低压透平/低壓渦輪機 low pressure turbine
低压温度舱/減壓溫度室 hypobaric thermal chamber
低压温度试验舱/減壓溫度試驗艙 hypobaric and temperature test chamber
低压压气机/低壓壓縮器 low pressure compressor
低压蒸汽发生器/低壓蒸汽發生器,低壓蒸汽產生器 low pressure steam generator
低压铸造/低壓鑄造 low pressure die casting
低液限粉土/低液限粉土 low liquid limit silt
低液限黏土/低液限黏土 low liquid limit clay
低音风喇叭/低音調氣喇叭 low tone air horn
低音雾笛/霧號器 diaphone
低营养湖/缺養湖泊 oligotrophic lake
低影响开发/低衝擊開發 low-impact development, LID
低真空保护装置/低真空保護設施 low-vacuum protective device
低值易耗品/低值易耗品 low value and easily wornout articles
低阻高效太阳电池/低電阻高效率太陽電池 low resistance high efficiency solar cell
低阻炸弹/低阻力炸彈 low drag bomb
堤岸冲刷/堤岸沖蝕,河岸侵蝕 bank erosion
堤岸种植/堤岸種植 bank planting
堤[坝]/堤 dyke, levee, embankment
堤坝加高/堤防加高 levee raising
堤坝加宽/堤防加寬 levee widening
堤坝决口/決潰 breach
堤坝开闸/穿堤孔口 levee opening
堤坝坡道/堤防坡路 levee ramp
堤道/堤道 causeway
堤防/堤防 levee
堤脚/堤腳 dyke foot
堤内地/堤內地 inner land of levee
堤内坡度/堤內坡度 landside slope
堤内区/堤內低地 protected lowland
堤体/堤體 levee body
堤心/防波堤心 breakwater core
滴点/落點 drop point
滴定/滴定 titration
滴定浓度/滴定濃度,滴定量 titer
滴灌/滴灌,滴水灌溉 drip irrigation, trickle irrigation
滴灌设备/滴灌設備 drip irrigation equipment
滴滤池/滴濾池 coarse-grained filter
滴水/滴水 drip tile
滴水槽/滴水槽 throating
滴水喷头/滴水噴頭 emitter, dripper
滴水兽/承溜口 gargoyle
滴水线/滴水槽 throating
滴头/滴[液]架 dripper
滴油润滑/滴油潤滑 drop lubrication
狄法尔磨耗试验机/杜巴爾磨耗試驗機 Deval abrasion testing machine
狄塞尔循环/狄賽爾循環 Diesel cycle
迪克辐射计/迪克輻射計 Dicke radiometer
迪斯科舞厅/迪斯可舞廳 disco club
敌对进路/衝突進路 conflicting route
敌对信号/敵對信號 conflicting signal
敌我识别系统/敵我識別系統 identification of friend or foe system, IFF
笛号/笛號 whistle signal
抵抗变形/形變抵抗 deformation resistance
抵抗力矩/抗力矩 moment of resistance
抵抗弯矩图/阻力彎矩圖 resistance moment diagram
抵押登记/抵押登記 mortgage registration
抵押契据/抵押契約 mortgage deed
底板/底板 floor, sole plate
底边舱/船底邊艙 bottom side tank
底冰/底冰 bottom ice
底部防热/底部防熱 base heat protection
底部放水管/底部洩放廊道 bottom emptying gallery
底部剪力/基層剪力 base shear
底部剪力法/[基]底層剪力法 base shear method, equivalent base shear method
底部框架-抗震墙砌体结构/底部框架-抗震牆砌體

结构 masonry structure with bottom frame-shear wall
底部流动/基流 base flow
底部试样/海底採樣 bottom sample
底部掏槽/底部炸除 bottom cut
底部斜撑/底斜支撐,底侧支撐 bottom lateral bracing
底部泄水管/底部洩水管 bottom outlet pipe
底部阻力/底面阻力 base drag
底部阻力修正/底端阻力修正 base drag correction
底舱/底[货]艙 lower hold
底舱肋骨/艙肋骨 hold frame
底层流/底層流 bottom current
底堆石/地石堆 ground moraine
底鼓/底鼓 floor heave
底基层/底基層,基層下層 subbase, subbase course
底迹/底跡 bottom tracking
底架/底架,底框 underframe
底架长度/底架長度 length over end sills, length of underframe
底架架承式牵引电动机/底架架承式牽引電動機,底框架承式牽引電動機 underframe mounted traction motor
底架宽度/底架寬度 width over side sills
底脚螺栓/錨螺栓 stone bolt
底流/潛流 undercurrent
底门/底門 bottom door
底盘测功机/車底盤測力計 chassis dynamometer
底盘车/[車]底盤 chassis
底栖生物/底棲生物 benthos
底漆/底漆 prime coat, undercoat paint
底圈/底圈 mud ring
底石/基石 plinth stone
底图/底圖 base map
底土/底土,亞土,下層土 subsoil
底土勘探/基層土探測 subsoil exploration
底拖网/底曳網 bottom trawl
底线/基線 base line
底卸式挂车/底卸式拖車 bottom-dump trailer
底碴/底碴 sub ballast
底炸孔/底炸孔 lifter hole
底质/底質,底料 quality of the bottom, bottom material
底质污染/沈積物汙染 sediment pollution
底阻/底面阻力 base drag
底座基础/放腳基礎 footing foundation
地板创平机/地板創平機 plank floor planer
地板灯/輔助照明 floor light

地板面高度/底板高 height of floor from rail top, floor height
地板面积/地板面積,樓板面積 floor area
地板排水装置/地板排水裝置 floor draining device
地被/地被 ground cover, cover plant
地被植物/地被植物,覆蓋植物 ground cover plant
地标/地標 landmark
地标领航/地標航行 pilotage
地表粗糙度/地面粗糙度,路面粗糙度 surface roughness
地表改变率/地表改變率 rate of change of earth surface
地表径流/直接地表徑流 direct surface runoff
地表径流系数/地表徑流係數 surface runoff coefficient
地表排水/地表排水 surface drainage
地表水/地表水,地面水 surface water
地表水文学/地表水文學 surface water hydrology
地表水质量/地表水品質標準,地面水品質標準 surface water quality standard
地表温度模拟/地面温度模擬 surface temperature simulation
地表植被/地表植被 ground vegetation
地表滞水/地表保水,地面蓄水 surface retention
地表贮藏/地表瀦蓄 surface storage
地波/地波 ground wave
地层/地層 stratum
地层锚杆/地錨 ground anchor
地层-隧道结构相互作用/地下隧道結構交互作用 ground tunnel structure interaction
地层弹性抗力/地層彈性抗力 elastic resistance of ground
地层序列/層序 sequence of strata
地层压力/地面壓力,地壓 ground pressure, stratum pressure
地层支护/支保 ground support
地层柱状图/地層直方圖 column diagram of stratum, graphic log of strata, drill log of stratum
地层走向/地層走向 strike of bed
地产/地產 real estate
地产开发/地產開發 estate development
地秤/磅秤 platform scale
地出/地出 earth-out
地磁/地磁 terrestrial magnetism
地磁场/地磁場 geomagnetic field
地磁赤道/地磁赤道 geomagnetic equator
地磁极/地磁極 geomagnetic pole
地磁力矩/地磁力矩 geomagnetic torque

地磁扰动/地磁擾動　geomagnetic disturbance
地磁图/地磁圖　magnetic chart
地磁指数/地磁指數　geomagnetic index
地带性气候/地帶性氣候　zonal climate
地带性植被/帶狀植被　zonal vegetation
地道/地道　underground path
地电流影响/地電流影響　influence of ground current
地方标准时/地方標準時　local standard time
地方公路/地方公路　local highway
地方恒星时/當地恆星時　local sidereal time, LST
地方交通/地區客運　local transit
地方[平]时/地方平均時　local time, local mean time, LMT
地方时角/當地時角　local hour angle, LHA
地方太阳时/地方太陽時　local solar time
地方铁路/地方鐵路,本地鐵路,地區鐵路　local railway, regional railway, district railway
地方性编组站/本地編組站　local marshalling station
地方性公路/地方公路　local highway
地方性气候/地方性氣候　local climate
地方植物志/地方植物誌　local flora
地栿/地栿　floor tie-beam, difu
地衡风速/地衡風速　geostrophic wind velocity
地积比率/建地比　floor area ratio
地基/地基　foundation, foundation soil
地基变形/地基變形　subsoil deformation
地基沉降/地盤沈陷　settlement of ground
地基承载力/地基承載力,基礎承載能力　bearing capacity of subsoil, subgrade bearing capacity, bearing capacity of foundation
地基承载力特征值/地基承載力標準值　characteristic value of subgrade bearing capacity
地基处理/地基處理,地盤改良,基礎處理　ground improvement, ground treatment, foundation treatment
地基防护工程/地基防護工程　groundwork protection engineering
地基刚度/地基剛度　stiffness of subsoil
地基极限承载力/地基極限承載力　ultimate bearing capacity of ground
地基[加固]处理/地基加固　geotechnical process
地基勘察/地基調查　soil investigation, soil exploration
地基梁/地中梁　ground beam
地基土/地基土　foundation soil, subsoil, subgrade
地基原位测试/地基原位測試　subgrade in-situ test
地基整体破坏/一般性破壞　general failure

地极/地極　terrestrial pole, earth pole
地籍/土地登記簿,魚鱗冊　land register
地价/地價　land cost, land price
地价递减率/地價遞減率　rate of land reduction
地价调查/地價調查　land value survey
地脚螺钉/底腳螺絲　foot screw
地脚螺栓/地腳螺栓,壓緊螺栓,錨螺拴　holding down bolt
地界标志/地界線　property line post
地景/地景　earthscape, land scenery
地径/地徑　ground diameter
地-空-地载荷循环/地-空-地負載循環　ground-air-ground load cycle
地块城市设计/小區都市設計　block scale urban design
地理编号/地形號數　geographic number
地理变种/地理變種　geographical variety
地理分类/地區劃分　geographic sorting
[地理]经度/地理經度　geographic longitude
地理景观/地理景觀　geographical landscape
地理空间建模/地理空間建模　geo-spatial modeling
地理区域群呼/地理區域群呼　geographical area group call
[地理]纬度/地理緯度　geographic latitude
地理信息系统/地理資訊系統　geographic information system, GIS
地理信息遥感数据库/地理資訊遙測資料庫　remote sensing data base of geographical information
地理音/地理音　geophonies
地理坐标/地理坐標,地面坐標　geographic coordinate
地理坐标系/地理坐標系,地面坐標系　geographic coordinate system
地沥青/瀝青,柏油,地瀝青膏　asphalt, land asphalt
地梁/地中梁　ground beam
地梁轨枕/地梁軌枕　ground beam sleeper
地裂/地裂　ground fracturing
地龙墙/地壟牆　sleeper wall
地隆/地脹現象　ground swell
地漏/地面排水,地面洩水　floor drain
地埋灯/地埋燈,埋地燈　underground lamp, buried light
地脉动/微震　micro-tremor
地貌调查/地貌調查　topographic feature survey, geomorphologic survey
地面/地表面　ground surface
地面安全控制/地面安全控制　ground safety control
地面备份星/地面備用衛星　ground spare satellite

地面比冲/地面比衝 ground specific impulse
地面标高/地基高程 ground level
地面部分/地面部分 ground segment
地面部分操作员/地面部分運作者 ground segment operator
地面测量/地面測量 ground survey
地面测试/地面測試 ground test
地面沉降/地盤下陷,地層下陷,地表沈陷 land subsidence, land asphalt
地面沉陷/地層陷落 land subsidence
地面底点/地底點 ground plumb point
地面电台/地面電臺 terrestrial station
地面电源/地面電源 ground electrical power source
地面定线/地面定線 surface alignment
地面仿真试验/地面模擬試驗 ground simulation test
地面分辨率/地面解析度 ground resolution
地面风/地面風 surface wind
地面风载荷/地面風載荷 ground wind load
地面风载荷试验/地面風負載試驗 ground wind test
地面辅助设备/地面支援裝備 ground support equipment, GSE
地面感应器/地面感應器 wayside inductor
地面钢轨涂油器/地面鋼軌塗油器 on-track rail lubricator
地面高/地面高,地盤高 ground height
地面高程/地面高程 ground elevation, land elevation
地面共振试验/接地諧振法 ground resonance test
地面环境/地面環境 ground environment
地面集水时间/流入時間,集流時間 inlet time, concentration time
地面加注阀/地面加載閥 ground loading valve
地面加注系统/地面加載系統 ground loading system
地面径流/地表流 surface flow
地面控制点/地面控制點 ground control point
地面控制点测量/地面控制點測量 ground control point survey
地面控制模式/地面控制模式 ground control mode
地面立体摄影测量/地面立體攝影測量 ground stereo photogrametry
地面流速/地表流速 field velocity
地面隆起/地隆起 land upheaval
地面慢车/地面慢車轉速 ground idle speed
地面瞄准/地面瞄準 ground aiming
地面瞄准总误差/地面瞄準合成誤差 resultant error of ground aiming

地面配电器/地面配電器 ground distributor
地面设备/地面設備 ground equipment, wayside equipment
地面设备状态检查/地面設備狀態檢查 ground support equipment state check
地面摄影像片/地上照相 terrestrial photograph
地面水平测量/地面水平測量 surface levelling
地面搜救处理器/地面搜救處理器 ground search and rescue processor
地面索道/傾斜索道 inclined cableway
地面台/地面臺 ground station
地面[天气]图/地面天氣圖 surface weather chart
地面铁道/地上鐵道 surface railway
地面通信网络/地面通信網路 terrestrial communication network
地面通信系统/地面通信系統 terrestrial communication system
地面推力/地面推力 ground thrust
地面维护设备/地面維護設備 ground maintenance equipment
地面无线电通信/地面無線電通信 terrestrial radio communication
地面效应/地面效應 ground effect
地面效应试验/地面效應試驗 ground effect testing
地面信号/地上號誌,沿線號誌機 ground signal
地面医监台/地面醫學監測臺 ground-based medical monitoring station
地面有速度弹射试验/地面有速度彈射試驗 ground dynamic ejection test
地面雨水径流/雨水徑流 rainwater runoff
地[面]杂波/陸地雜波 land clutter
地面照片/地面攝影 ground photograph
地面真地平/感觀水平面 sensible horizon
地面指挥进近系统/地面管制進場 ground controlled approach system, GCA
地面坐标系/地面軸系 earth-fixed axis system
地皿/地皿 sunken pan
地名标志/地名標誌 place name sign
地名指示标志/地名指示標誌 place identification sign
地排灯/地排燈 floats
地平/地平 horizon
地平穿越/地平穿越 horizon crossing
地平穿越式地球敏感器/地平穿越式地球敏感器 horizon crossing indicator
地平跟踪/地平跟蹤 horizon tracking
地平面/地基高程 ground level
地平视差/地平視差 horizontal parallax

地平坐标系/水平坐標制　horizontal coordinate system
地坪涂料/地面塗料　floor coating
地-气系统辐射收支/地氣系統輻射收支　earth-atmosphere system radiation budget
地球/地球　earth
地球半径/地球半徑　radius of the earth
地球扁率/地球扁率　flattening of earth, earth oblateness
地球捕获/地球獲得　earth acquisition
地球长半轴/赤道半徑　equatorial radius
地球磁层/地球磁層　earth magnetosphere
地球-电离层波导/地球-電離層波導　earth-ionospheric waveguide
地球反照角系数/地球反照角係數　earth infrared radiation factor
地球反照率/地球反照率　earth albedo
地球辐射/地面輻射　terrestrial radiation
地球辐射带/地球輻射帶　radiation belts of the earth
地球辐射收支/地球輻射收支　earth radiation budget
地球角/地球角　earth angle
地球静止轨道/同步軌道　geostationary orbit
地球静止轨道卫星/同步軌道衛星　geostationary orbit satellite
[地球]静止气象卫星/[地球]同步氣象衛星，[地球]定置氣象衛星　geostationary meteorological satellite, GMS
地球静止卫星位置漂移/同步衛星位置漂移　position drift of geostationary satellite
地球空间信息科学/地球空間資訊科學　geo-spatial information science, Geomatics
[地球]内辐射带/[地球]内輻射帶　inner radiation belt of the earth
地球偏心率/地球偏心率　eccentricity of earth
地球屏/接地遮蔽，接地遮罩　earth shield
地球曲率校正/地球曲率訂正　earth curvature rectification
地球-太阳两面角/地球-太陽旋轉角　earth-sun rotation angle
地球太阳信号鉴别/地球太陽信號鑒別　discrimination between the earth and the sun light
地球同步对地观测系统/地球同步觀測衛星　geosynchronous earth observation system, GEOS
地球同步轨道/地球同步軌道　geosynchronous orbit
地球同步轨道卫星/地球同步軌道衛星　geosynchronous orbit satellite
地球同步合成孔径雷达/對地同步合成孔徑雷達　geosynchronous synthetic aperture radar
[地球]同步气象卫星/[地球]同步氣象衛星，[地球]定置氣象衛星　geostationary meteorological satellite, GMS
地球椭球体/地球橢球體　spheroid of earth
地球椭圆体/地球橢圓體　earth ellipsoid, terrestrial ellipsoid
[地球]外辐射带/[地球]外輻射帶　outer radiation belt of the earth
地球位/重力位　geopotential
地球物理勘探/地球物理勘探　geophysical exploration
地球物理勘探船/地球物理探測船　geophysical survey ship, geophysical survey vessel
地球形状/地球形狀　earth shape
地球形状摄动/地球非正球體之擾動　non-spherical earth perturbation
地球圆体/地球球體　terrestrial sphere
地球月球信号鉴别/地球月球信號鑒別　discrimination between the earth and the moon light
地球站/地面站，地球臺，地面電臺　earth station
地球转速单位/地球角速度單位　earth rate unit
地球资源卫星/地球資源衛星　earth resources satellite
地区电话交换机/市内電話交換機　local telephone switching system
地区电话网/市内電話網　local telephone network
地区交通/地區交通，當地交通　local traffic
地区条款/地區條款　local clause
地热/地熱　geothermy
地热发电/地熱發電　geothermal power generation
地热供热系统/地熱供熱系統　heat supply system based upon geothermal energy
地热能/地熱能　geothermal energy
地热梯度/地溫梯度，地熱比降　geothermal gradient
地热学/地熱學　geothermy
地热资源/地熱資源　geothermal resource
地入/地入　earth-in
地上敷设/地面裝置　above ground installation
地上结构/地上構造　superstructure
地上沥青贮仓/地面瀝青儲倉　ground asphalt storage
地生苗/秧苗，幼株　young plant
地速/地速　ground speed
地速偏流表/地速偏流表　ground speed-drift angle indicator
地坛/地壇　Temple of Earth, Di Tan
地天波改正量/地波對天波修正值　ground wave to

sky wave correction
地铁/地下鐵路 underground railway
地铁工程/地鐵工程 subway engineering, metro engineering
地铁隧道/地鐵隧道,地下鐵道隧道 subway tunnel, underground railway tunnel, metro tunnel
地铁站/捷運站 metro station, subway station
地图板显示/地圖顯示器 map display
地图显示器/地圖顯示器 map display
地外生物学/星球生物學 exobiology
地温梯度/地溫梯度,地熱比降 geothermal gradient
地温通过无人增音机/地溫通過無人增音機 unattended repeater with ground temperature compensation and powerpassing
地温折返无人增音机/地溫折返無人增音機 unattended repeater with ground temperature compensation and power feed loop back
地文航海/地文航海術 geo-navigation
地物相机/地形攝影機 terrain camera
地下冰/地冰 ground ice
地下仓库/地下倉庫 underground storehouse
地下测量/地下測量 underground surveying
地下厂房/地下廠房,地下工場 underground workshop
地下车库/地下車庫 underground garage
地下储气/地下儲氣 gas underground storage
地下储油/地下存儲油 underground storage of oil
地下存储核废料/地下存儲核廢料 underground storage of nuclear waste
地下存储液化天然气/地下存儲液化天然氣 underground storage of liquefied natural gas, underground storage of LNG
地下电缆/地下電纜 ground cable
地下电源间/地下電力室 underground power room
地下废水处理/地下廢水處置 subsurface waster water disposal
地下敷设/地下安裝 underground installation
地下工程/地下工程,地下工廠 underground engineering, underground works
地下管廊/地下管廊 underground pipe gallery
地下管线/地下管線 underground pipelines
地下管线间距/地下管線間隔 interval of underground utility
地下管线综合设计/地下管線綜合設計 underground pipelines comprehensive design
地下灌溉/地下灌溉 subirrigation, subsurface irrigation
地下过滤场/地下滲水槽,地下滲水場 subsurface filter
地下害虫/地下害蟲 underground pest
地下河/隱河道,伏流 underground river, buried river, subterranean river
地下机铲/坑内用鏟 underground-shovel
地下建筑/地下建築 underground architecture
地下街/地下街 underground street
地下结构/下部結構,地下構造物 substructure, underground structure
地下截流工程/地下水截流 interception of underground water
地下空间/地下空間 underground space
地下空间设施规划/地下空間設施規劃 underground space facility planning
地下沥青贮仓/地下瀝青儲倉 underground asphalt storage
地下连续墙法/地下連續牆法 underground diaphragm wall method, underground wall method, diaphragm wall method
地下排水沉淀池/地下排水沈澱池 underdrained settling basin
地下排水[系统]/地下排水 subsurface drainage
地下气化/地下煤炭氣化 underground gasification of coal
地下潜蚀/地下侵蝕 subsurface erosion
地下热交换温室/地下熱交換溫室,地下蓄熱溫室 underground heat exchange greenhouse
地下商场/地下商店 underground market
地下渗透/地下滲水 subsurface filtration
地下[式]电站/地下發電廠 underground power station
地下室/地下室 basement
地下室防水/地下室防水 basement waterproofing
地下输电线/地下輸電線 underground transmission line
地下水/地下水 ground water, subsoil water
地下水坝/地水堰 ground water dam
地下水补给/地水進入,含水層補注,地水補注 ground water intake, recharge of aquifer, recharge of groundwater
地下水补给量/地下水補給容量 ground water recharge capacity
地下水储量/地水潴蓄 ground water storage
地下水储量盈亏估计/地水登錄 ground water inventory
地下水存储曲线/地水潴蓄曲線 ground water storage curve
地下水动态/地下水位動態 ground water regime

[地下水]降深/洩降　depression head
地下水径流/地水徑流　ground water runoff
地下水可开采量/地下水可開採量　ground water available yield
地下水控制/地下水控制　ground water controlling
地下水库/地下水水庫　ground water reservoir
地下水亏损/地水降　ground water depletion curve, ground water recession
地下水连通试验/地下水連通性試驗　ground water connectivity test
地下水流/地下流　subsoil flow, subsurface flow
地下水流速/地下水流速　velocity of ground water
地下水漏斗/地下水漏斗　ground water funnel
地下水露头/地下水露頭　outcrop of ground water
地下水面/地下水面　ground water table
地下水面比降/地下水位坡度　water table slope
地下水平均流速/地水平均流速　average velocity of ground water
地下水取水/地水進入　intake of ground water
地下水示踪试验/地下水追蹤劑試驗　ground water tracer test
地下水位/地下水位,地下水面　ground water level
地下水位变动/地下水面漲落　fluctuation of watertable
地下水位等高线/地下水位等高線　watertable contour
地下水位降低/地水下降　phreatic decline
地下水位剖面图/地下水位縱剖　water table profile
地下水位下降/地下水位降落　water lowering
地下水位[线]/地下水面　ground watertable
地下水污染/地下水汙染　ground water contamination
地下水硬度/地下水硬度　ground water hardness
地下水增量/地水增益　ground water increment
地下水准测量/地下水準測量　underground levelling
地下水总矿化度/地下水總礦化度　total mineralization of ground water
地下铁道/地下鐵道,地下電纜管道　subway, metro, underground railway
地下铁道电动车组/地[下鐵]道電動車組　subway motor train unit
地下停车库/地下停車場　underground parking
地下通道/地下道　under crossing, underpass
地下文物埋藏区/地下文物埋藏區,地下遺物,地下考古空間遺物　underground cultural relics buried area, underground archaeological remains, underground area of archaeological remains
地下线标定/地下定線　alignment of underground line
地下消防栓/地下消防拴　underground hydrant
地下蓄热温室/地下蓄熱溫室,地下熱交換溫室　underground heat exchange greenhouse
地下蓄水库/地下水流　ground water basin
地下油罐/地下儲油罐　underground oil tank
地下油库/地下油庫,油盒　oil cellar
地下支撑/架底短柱　ground prop
地下支撑系统/地下系統支援　underground system support
地效飞行器/地面效應載具　ground effect vehicle
地心纬度/地心緯度　geocentric latitude
地心纬度改正量/地心緯度修正　correction of geocentric latitude
地心坐标系/地心坐標系　geocentric coordinate system
地形/地形,地勢　topography
地形岸线测量/地形岸線測量　topographic and coastal survey
地形参考导航系统/地形參照導航系統　terrain referenced navigation system
地形测绘雷达/地面測繪雷達　ground mapping radar
地形测量/地形測量　topographic survey, topographical survey
地形存储/地障存儲　terrain storage
地形改造设计/地形改造設計　topographical reform design
地形跟随/地形追蹤　terrain following
地形跟随雷达/地形追蹤雷達　terrain following radar, TFR
地形回避/地障迴避　terrain avoidance
地形回避雷达/地障迴避雷達　terrain avoidance radar, TAR
地形轮廓/地形輪廓　terrain profile
地形敏感装置/地障敏感裝置　terrain sensing unit
地形匹配/地障比對　terrain matching
地形匹配制导/地形比對導引　terrain matching guidance
地形设计/地形設計　topographical design
地形图/地形圖　topographic map, contour map, topographical map
地形[性]降水/地形降水　orographic precipitation
地形因子/地形因素,地形因子　topographic factor
地形雨/山嶺雨　orographic rain
地形指数/地形指數　topographic index
地学统计/地學統計,地理統計　geostatistics
地役权/地役權　easement

地影时间/黃道時間　ecliptic time
地应力/地[殼]應力　crustal stress
地域生产综合体/地域生產綜合體　territorial production complex
地源热泵系统/地源熱泵系統　ground-source heat pump system
地震波/地震波　seismic wave
地震重现期/地震重現期,地震復發週期　earthquake recurrence period, earthquake return period
地震带/地震帶　earthquake zone, seismic zone
地震地基失效/地震地基失效　seismic failure of foundation
地震动/地震動　ground motion
地震动参数/地震動參數　ground motion parameter
地震动孔隙水压力/地震動孔隙水壓　seismic pore water pressure
地震动土压力/地震動土壓力　seismic earth pressure, earthquake dynamic earth pressure
地震反应/地震反應　earthquake response
地震工程/地震工程[學]　earthquake engineering
地震海啸/地震海嘯　seismic sea wave
地震荷载/地震荷載,地震載重,地震負載　earthquake load
地震基本烈度/地震基本烈度,地震基本強度,基本震度　basic earthquake intensity, basic intensity of earthquake, seismic basic intensity
地震加速度/地震加速度　seismic acceleration
地震勘探/震波探查　seismic prospecting
地震力/地震力　earthquake action, seismic force
地震烈度/地震強度　earthquake intensity
地震区/震區　seismic region, earthquake region, seismic zone
地震设计烈度/地震設計烈度　design intensity of earthquake
地震危险性分析/地震危險性分析　seismic risk analysis
地震危险性评定/地震危險性評定　seismic risk evaluation
地震物探法/地震地球物理勘測　seismic geophysical survey
地震系数/地震係數,震度　seismic coefficient
地震系数法/地震係數法　seismic coefficient method
地震小区划分/地震微分區　seismic microzoning
地震仪/地震儀　seismometer
地震应力/地震應力　earthquake stress
[地震]灾害/地震災難　earthquake disaster
地震震动质量/地震質量　seismic mass
地震震害/地震災害,震災　earthquake damage, seismic hazard
地震震级/地震等級,震級,地震規模　earthquake magnitude
地震周期/地震時間　earthquake period
地震作用/地震作用　earthquake action
地震作用效应/地震作用效應　seismic action effect
地址/地址,位址　address
地质测井/地質測井　geologic logging
地质点/地質觀察點　point of observation, geologic observation point
地质调查/地質調查　geologic survey, geological survey
地质调查船/地質調查船　geological survey vessel, geological survey ship
地质公园/地質公園　geopark
地质景观/地質景觀　geological landscape
地质剖面/地質橫斷面圖　geologic section
地质剖面图/地質縱斷面圖　geologic profile
地质适宜性/地質適宜性　geological suitability
地质图/地質圖　geologic map, geological map
地质图测绘/地質圖測繪　survey and drawing of geological map, surveying and sketching of geological map
地质图例/地質圖例　geologic legend
地质钻机/鑽探機　exploration drill
地掷球场/地擲球場　bocci court
地掷球运动/地擲球運動　bocci sports
地中/地中　earth-center
地中电缆盒/地中電纜盒　underground cable terminal box
地中海系泊法/地中海繫泊法　Mediterranean mooring
地中相移/地中相移　earth-center phase shift
地轴/地軸　earth axis
地转风/地轉風,地衡風　geostrophic wind
地转风速/地轉風速　velocity of geostrophic
帝/帝,北極二,小熊β　Kochab
帝王宫苑/帝王宮苑　imperial palace garden
递减率/減率　declining rate
递降速过滤/遞降速過濾　declining rate filtration
递近递增运价/遞近遞增運價　increasing rate with decreasing distance
递热器/遞熱器　combining chamber
递远递减运价/遞遠遞減運價　decreasing rate with increasing distance
第二产业/第二級產業,二級工業　secondary industry
第二车道/第二車道　second lane

第二喉道/第二喉道,第二喉部　second throat
第二甲板/第二[層]甲板　second deck
第二接近区段/第二接近區段　second approach section
第二离去区段/第二離去區段　second departure section
第二系悬挂/二次懸吊　secondary suspension
第二限度/第二限度　2nd limit
第二循环系统/熱水循環系統　hot water circulation system
第二宇宙速度/第二宇宙速度　second cosmic velocity, escape velocity
第三产业/第三級產業　tertiary industry
第三车道/第三車道　third lane
第三代中速柴油机/第三代柴油機　third generation engine
第三电极/第三電極　third electrode
第三角法/第三角法　third-angle system
第三十最高年小时运量/第三十最高年小時交通量　thirtieth highest annual hourly volume
第三宇宙速度/第三宇宙速度　third cosmic velocity, solar escape velocity
第四纪/第四紀　quaternary era
第五立面/第五立面　fifth facade
第一产业/第一級產業,初級工業　primary industry
第一车道/第一車道　first lane
第一次大修期/第一次大翻修　time to first overhaul
第一第二系弹簧挠度比/第一第二系彈簧撓度比　ratio of spring deflections of primary and secondary suspension
第一段生化需氧量/第一段生化需氧量　first stage BOD
第一喉道/第一喉部　first throat
第一接近区段/第一接近區段　first approach section
第一离去区段/第一離去區段　first departure section
第一系悬挂/一次懸吊　primary suspension
第一限度/第一限度　1st limit
第一循环系统/第一循環系統　heat carrier circulation system
第一印象区/第一印象區　the first impression area
第一宇宙速度/第一宇宙速度　first cosmic velocity, elliptic velocity
第一振型/基本模態　fundamental mode
第一自振周期/基本週期　fundamental period
蒂卡尔国家公园/蒂卡爾國家公園　Tikal National Park
蒂瓦纳科文化的精神和政治中心/蒂瓦納科文化的精神和政治中心　Spiritual and Political Center of the Tiwanaku Culture
颠簸/顛簸,紊流　turbulence
颠簸累积式平整仪/顛簸累積式平整儀　bump-integrator roughometer trailer
颠倒温度计/倒轉溫度計　reversing thermometer
典藏室/簿記室　book-keeping department
典当行/當鋪　pawn shop
典型车速/模式車速　model speed
典型抽样/代表抽樣　representative sample
典型景观/典型景觀　typical landscape
典型气象年/典型氣象年　typical meteorological year, TMY
CP点/CP點,合并點　consolidation point, CP
点播/點播　spaced sowing
点滴腐蚀试验/點滴腐蝕試驗　dropping corrosion test
点对点长途自动接续/點對點長途自動接續　point to point toll automatic dialing
点对点连接/點對點[式]連接　point to point connection
点腐蚀/痕蝕　pitting corrosion
点焊/點焊,點熔接　spot welding, point welding
点焊机/點焊接機　spot welder
点弧/點弧　arc-firing
点火/點火　ignition, lighting
点火边界/點火極限　ignition limit
点火高度/點火高度　ignition altitude
点火能量/點火能　ignition energy
点火器/[火花]點火器,火星塞　ignition plug, igniter, firing unit
点火时串/點火時間序列　ignition time series
点火提前角/點火提早角　ignition advance angle, spark advance angle
点火系统/點火系統　ignition system
点火压力峰/點火壓力峰值　ignition pressure peak
点火延迟/點火延遲,點火遲延　ignition lag, spark lag, ignition delay
点火延迟时间/點火延時　ignition delay time
点火装置/點火裝置,點火器　ignition device
点火姿态/點火姿態　firing attitude
点景牌楼/點景牌樓　naming pailou, decorated archway
点控制/點控制　spot control, isolated signal control
点连式调速系统/點連續式調速系統　point-continued type speed control system
点燃式内燃机/火花點火引擎,引燃機　spark ignition engine
点散射体/點散射　point scatter

点蚀/點蝕，斑蝕，麻點　pitting corrosion, pitting
点式机车信号/點式機車信號　intermittent type cab signaling
点式调速系统/點型式調速器，點型式調節器　point type speed control system
点速度/點速　spot speed
点头振动/上下顛簸　pitching vibration, nodding vibration
点图/點圖型　dot pattern
点污染源/汙染點源　point source of pollution
点样本校验/單點樣本校驗　point sample
点雨量/點雨量　point rainfall
点源污染/點源汙染　point source pollution
点-轴发展理论/點-軸系統理論　pole-axis theory
点状绿地/點狀綠地　green spot
电报电缆浮标/電報電纜浮標　telegraph buoy
电报交换机/轉發電報設備　telegraph switching equipment
电报通信/電報通訊　telegraph communication
电报[通信]网/電報通信網　telegraph network
电报线立标/電報線標桿　telegraph cable beacon
电报学/電報學　telegraphy
电爆阀/電爆閥　electric blasting valve
电波折射修正/無線電折射訂正　radio wave refraction correction
电测井/電檢法　electric logging
电测仪表/電測定儀器　electrical measuring instrument
电铲/電動鏟土機　electric shovel
电池/電池　cell
电池伏安特性曲线/電池伏安特性曲線　V-I characteristic curve of cell
[电池]壳体/外殼,機殼　case, container
电池内阻/電池內電阻　internal resistance of cell
电池容量/電池容量　capacity of cell
电池组/電池[組]　battery
电除尘器/靜電除塵器，靜電集塵器　electrostatic precipitator
电传/電傳　teleprinter exchange
电传飞行控制/電飛操控制　fly-by-wire control
电传机/電傳打字機,打字電報機　teletype
电锤/電錘　electric hammer
电磁摆/電磁擺　electromagnetic pendulum
电磁波/電磁波　electromagnetic wave
电磁波暗室/無線電波回波室　electromagnetic wave anechoic chamber
电磁波测距仪/電磁波測距儀　electromagnetic wave distance measuring instrument

电磁波吸波材料/吸波材料　electromagnetic wave absorber
电磁测量/電磁量測　electromagnetic measurement, EM measurement
电磁场/電磁場　electromagnetic field
电磁场能量/電磁場能量　energy of electromagnetic field
电磁成形/電磁成形　electromagnetic forming
电磁阀/電磁閥　solenoid valve, electromagnetic valve
电磁辐射/電磁輻射　electromagnetic radiation
电磁辐射危害/電磁輻射危害　electromagnetic radiation hazard
电磁干扰/電磁干擾　electromagnetic interference, EMI
电磁干扰测量/電磁干擾量測　electromagnetic interference measurement, EMI measurement
电磁干扰诊断技术/電磁干擾診斷技術　EMI diagnosing technology
电磁环境/電磁環境　electromagnetic environment
电磁环境电平/電磁環境電平　electromagnetic ambient level
电磁环境效应/電磁環境效應　electromagnetic environment effect
电磁换向阀/電磁方向控制閥　solenoid directional control valve
电磁计程仪/電磁計程儀,電磁測程儀　electromagnetic log, EM log
电磁计量室/電磁測量室　electromagnetic measurement room
电磁继电器/電磁繼電器　electromagnetic relay
电磁兼容[性]/電磁相容性　electromagnetic compatibility, EMC
电磁兼容[性]测量/電磁相容性量測　electromagnetic compatibility measurement, EMC measurement
电磁浇注/電磁澆鑄　electromagnetic pouring
电磁接触器/電磁接觸器　electromagnetic contactor
电磁控制罗经/電磁控制電羅經　electromagnetically controlled gyrocompass
电磁离合器/電磁離合器　electromagnetic clutch
电磁流量计/電磁流量計　electromagnetic flow meter
电磁脉冲/電磁脈衝　electromagnetic pulse
电磁敏感度/電磁敏感度　electromagnetic susceptibility
电磁敏感度测量/電磁靈敏度量測　electromagnetic sensitivity measurement, EM sensitivity

measurement
电磁能/放射能,辐射能 radiant energy, radiation energy
电磁屏蔽/電磁遮蔽,電磁遮罩 electromagnetic shield
电磁屏蔽暗室/電磁遮罩暗室 electromagnetic shielding darkroom
[电磁]屏蔽车间/遮罩車間 electromagnetic shielding shop, proof electromagnetic shop
电磁屏蔽室/電磁遮罩室 electromagnetic shield enclosure
电磁屏蔽涂层/電磁遮罩塗層 coating for EM shielding
电磁铁/電磁鐵 electromagnet
电磁铁驱动器/電磁鐵驅動器 magnet driver
电磁吸盘/起重磁鐵 lifting magnet
电磁吸引式系统/電磁吸引式系統 electromagnetic attraction system
电磁悬浮系统/電磁懸掛系統 electromagnetic suspension system, EMS system
电磁引爆引燃安全系数测量/電磁引爆引燃安全係數量測 EM detonation and firing safety factor measurement
电磁诱导检测/電磁感應檢測 magnetic induction inspection
电磁噪声/電磁噪音,電磁干擾 electromagnetic noise
电磁侦车器/電磁偵車器 vehicle magnetic detector
电磁制动器/電磁刹車 magnetic brake
电磁自差/電磁自差 electromagnetic deviation
电磁组件天平/電磁單元天平 electromagnetic unit balance
电导率/導電率,傳導性,傳導度 conductivity
电点火/電點火 electric ignition
电点火头/電點火器 electric igniter
电动臂板电锁器联锁/電動臂板電鎖器聯鎖 interlocking by electric locks with electric semaphore
电动臂板信号机/電動臂[板]式號誌機 electric semaphore signal
电动操舵装置/電動舵機 electric steering gear
电动车组/電聯車 electric multiple unit, motor coach set, electric motor train unit
电动冲击夯/電動衝擊夯 electric shocking rammer
电动传送设备/電動氣動傳送設備 electric motor operated conveyer
电动吊车/電動吊車,電動起重機 electric hoist
电动舵机/電舵機 electric steering engine
电动辅机自动起动装置/電動輔機自動起動裝置 automatic starting installation for electrical motor driven auxiliaries
电动滑道/電動滑道 electric slipway
电动机/電動機,馬達 motor
电动机超速/電動機失控速度,電動機飛逸轉速 runaway speed
电动机车/電動車 electric motor car
电动机独立供电/電動機獨立供電 motor individual power supply
[电动机]起动阻塞控制/起動阻塞控制 start blocking control
电动机特性/電動機特性 motor characteristic
电动机转矩/電動機轉矩 motor torque
电动机转速/電動機轉速 motor speed
电动卷扬机/電動卷揚機,電動絞車 electric hoister, electric winch
电动[力矩]平衡器/電平衡器 electrical balancer
电动膜片式气笛/電動氣笛 motor siren
电动排斥式系统/電動斥力系統 electrodynamic repulsion system, EDRS
电动喷雾器/動力噴霧機 power sprayer
电动起货机/電動起貨機 electric cargo winch
电动气动式/電動氣動式 electro pneumatic type
电动汽车/電動汽車,電動車輛 electric vehicle
电动汽车充电设施/電動車輛充電設施 electric vehicle charging facility
电动汽车充电站/電動汽車充電站 electric vehicle charging station
电动势/電動勢 electric motive force, electromotive force
电动水泵/電動水泵 electric water pump
电动四柱秋千/電動四柱秋千 electrical four-pole swing
电动液压操舵装置/電動液壓操舵系統 electro hydraulic steering system, electro hydraulic steering gear
电动液压传动/電動液壓驅動 electro hydraulic drive
电动液压舵机/電動液力舵機 electro hydraulic steering engine
电动凿岩机/電體鑿岩機 electric jack hammer
电动振动台/電動力振動產生器 electrodynamics vibration generator
电动主机传令装置/電動車鍾 electric engine telegraph
电动转辙机/電動轉轍機 electric switch machine
电镀/電鍍 electroplating, galvanization

电镀厂/電鍍廠　electroplating factory
电镀车间/電鍍車間　electroplating shop
电发火管/電爆裝置　electric squib
电法勘探/電探　electric prospecting
电分段装置/電分段裝置　section point
电杆/電桿　pole
电感式传感器/感應式感測器　inductive pickoff, inductance-type transducer
电感式加速度计/感應式加速計　inductive accelerometer
电感应/電感應　electric induction
电工间/電工場　electrical shop, electrician store
电功率/電功率　electric power, electrical power
电焊钢管/電焊鋼管　arc-welded steel pipe
电焊机/電焊機　electric welding machine
电焊条/電焊條　covered electrode
电航迹线/電航路線　electrical flight path line
电荷传输效率/電荷傳送係數　charge transfer efficiency, CTE
电荷耦合器件/電荷耦合裝置　charge-coupled device, CCD
电荷耦合器件太阳敏感器/電荷耦合元件太陽感測器　charge-coupled device sun sensor, CCD sun sensor
电荷耦合器件星敏感器/電荷耦合裝置星體感應器　charge-coupled device star sensor, CCD star sensor
电荷注入器件星敏感器/電荷注入元件星體感應器　charge injection device star sensor, CID star sensor
电弧点焊/電弧點焊　arc spot welding, arc spot weld
电弧电压/電弧電壓　arc voltage
电弧放电/圓弧放電　arc discharge
电弧风洞/電弧風洞　arc tunnel
[电]弧焊/電弧焊[接],電弧熔接　arc welding
电弧加热器/電弧加熱器　arc heater
电弧钎焊/電弧硬焊　arc brazing
电弧切割/電弧切割　arc cutting, electric cutting
电[化腐]蚀/電流侵蝕,電流腐蝕　galvanic corrosion
电化学保护/電化學防蝕,電解防蝕　electrochemical protection
电化学测量/電化測流法　electrochemical gauging
电化学分析/電化[學]分析　electrochemical analysis
电化学腐蚀/電化[學]腐蝕,電流腐蝕　electrochemical corrosion, galvanic corrosion
电化学加固/電化學加固　electrochemical stabilization
电化学加固土壤/電化學土壤整治　electro chemical treatment of soil
电化学涂层/電化塗膜　electrochemical coating

电化学氧化/電化學氧化,陽極處理,陽極防蝕　anodizing, electrochemical oxidation
电话/電話　telephony, telephone
电话闭塞系统/電話閉鎖系統　telephone block system
电话分组交换网/電話分组交換網　packet switching telephone network
电话机/電話機　telephone set
电话集中器/電話集中器　concentrated telephone unit
电话网/電話網[路]　telephone network
电话线/電話線　telephone line
[电话]用户/電話用戶　telephone subscriber
电火花穿孔/電火花穿孔　spark-erosion perforation
电火花加工/電火花加工　spark-erosion machining, electrical discharge machining, EDM
电火花线切割/電火花線剪切　spark-erosion wire cutting
电击/電擊,電震,觸電　electric shock
电机厂/電機廠　electric generator and motor manufactory
电机集中联锁/電機聯鎖　electro-mechanical interlocking
电机空心轴驱动/空心軸電動傳動　hollow shaft motor drive
电机驱动电梯/電梯,電力昇降機　electric elevator
电机员/電機工程師　electrical engineer
电机转速误差/馬達轉速誤差　motor revolution error
电极/電極　electrode
电极电位/電極電位　electrode potential
电极反应/電極反應　electrode reaction
电极极化/電極之極化　polarization of electrode
电极式加湿器/電極式加濕器　electrode humidifier
电加热/電[加]熱　electric heating
电加热锅炉/電熱鍋爐　electric boiler
电[加]热器/電熱器　electric heater
电加湿器/電加濕器　electric moistening device
电键/電鍵　key
电解厂/電解廠　electrolysis plant
电解车间/電解車間　electrolysis shop
电解腐蚀/電蝕　electrolytic corrosion
电解加工/電解加工　electrochemical machining, ECM, electrolytic machining
电解型腔加工/電解型腔加工　electrolytic forming
电解液/電解液　electrolyte
电解质/電解質　electrolyte
电空传送设备/電動氣動傳送裝置,電動氣動傳送機

电空阀/電動氣動閥　electropneumatic conveyer
电空阀/電動氣動閥　electropneumatic valve
电空接触器/電動氣動接觸器　electropneumatic contactor
电空制动/電動汽動式靭　electropneumatic brake
电空制动电路/電-氣動制動回路　electropneumatic brake circuit, E-P brake circuit
电空制动控制器/電壓氣動制動器,電壓氣動刹車控制器　E-P brake controller
电空制动装置/電-氣動制動裝置　electropneumatic brake equipment
电空转辙机/電動氣動式轉轍機　electropneumatic switch machine
电控罗经/電磁控電羅經　electromagnet control gyrocompass
电缆/電纜,粗纜,纜線　electric cable
电缆摆杆/電纜擺桿　cable swinging rod
电缆标石/電纜標石,電纜標桿　cable marking stake
电缆舱/電纜艙　cable tank
电缆充气维护设备/纜線充氣設備　cable gas-feeding equipment
电缆防火涂料/電纜防火塗料　fire resisting coating for cable
电缆分界室/電纜配電室,電纜配電間,電纜配電房　cable inlet distribution room
电缆浮标/電纜浮標　cable buoy
电缆沟/電纜槽　cable trough
电缆管道/電纜管道　cable duct
电缆夹层/電纜窨　cable vault
电缆进线室/電纜進線室　cable incoming room
电缆井道/電纜豎井,電纜引入井　cable shaft
电缆框/穿線環圍,線孔線圍　cable coaming
电缆排管敷设/電纜排管敷設　laying in duct bank
电缆屏蔽系数/電纜遮罩係數　shielding factor of cable
电缆桥架/電纜托盤　cable tray
电缆蛇形敷设/電纜的蛇形敷設　snaking of cable
电缆伸缩箱/電纜箱　cable box, cable expansion box
电缆束/電纜束　cable harness
电缆竖井/電纜豎井,電纜引入井　cable shaft
电缆松紧指示器/電纜鬆緊指示器,電纜鬆緊計　slack meter, cable slack meter
电缆隧道/電纜隧道,纜道　cable tunnel
电缆套管/纜線套管　cable sleeve
电缆通廊/電纜槽,電纜管道　cable channel
电缆筒/穿線環圍,線孔線圍　cable coaming
电缆网/電纜網　cable net, cable network
电缆系泊浮码头/錨煉固定浮船塢　cable mooring floating dock
电缆线路/電纜線　cable line
电缆障碍探测器/電纜故障探測器　cable fault detector
电缆支架/電纜架　cable bracket
电缆直埋敷设/電纜直埋敷設　cable direct burial laying
电缆转接箱/電纜連接箱　cable connection box
电雷管/電起爆器　electric detonator
电离/電離,游離　ionization
电离层/電離層,游離層　ionosphere
电离层暴/電離層[風]暴　ionosphere storm
电离层辐射测量/電離層輻射量測　ionospheric radiation measurement
电离层模式/電離層模型　ionosphere model
电离层闪烁/電離層閃爍　ionosphere scintillation
电离层吸收/電離層吸收　ionosphere absorption
电离层折射改正/電離層折射修正,游離層折射修正　ionospheric refraction correction
电离层折射校正/電離層折射修正,游離層折射修正　ionospheric refraction correction
电离度/電離度　ionicity
电离辐射/電離[化]輻射,游離輻射　ionizing radiation
电离辐射环境/電離輻射環境　ionizing radiation environment
电力变压器/電力變壓器　power transformer
电力传动方式/電力驅動方式　mode of electric drive
电力传动内燃机车/電[力]傳動機車　diesel-electric locomotive
电力电缆及连接器/電力電纜連接器,供電電纜連接器　power supply cable and coupling
电力调度电话/電力調度電話　power dispatching telephone
电力负荷/電力負載　electric load
电力机车/電力機車　electric locomotive
电力配电箱/電力分配盤　power distribution panel
电力牵引干扰/電力牽引干擾　electric traction interference
电力牵引供电系统/電力牽引供電系統　power supply system of electric traction
电力牵引远动系统/電力牽引遥控系統　electric traction telemechanical system, electric traction remote control system
电力输送线/輸電線　power transmission line
电力推进/電力推進　electric propulsion
电力推进船/電力推進船　electric propulsion ship
电力推进电机间/電力推進馬達室　electrical

propulsion motor room
电力推进装置/電力推進設備 electric propulsion plant
电力拖动/電力驅動 electric drive
电力拖动装置/電力驅動設備 electric drive apparatus
电力线/電力線,輸電線 power line
电力执行机构/電力引動器 electric actuator
电连接器/電連接器,電氣接頭 electrical connector, electric coupler
电连接线夹/電連接線夾 electrically connecting clamp
电量参数/電性参数 electrical parameter
电流/電流 current
电流表/電流表,安培计 ammeter
电流传感器/電流感測器 current sensor
电流互感器/電流比流器 current transformer, CT
电流继电器/電流繼電器,電流替續器 current relay
电流-力特性/電流-力特性 current-force characteristic
电流温度系数/電流温度係數 current temperature coefficient
电流制/電流制 current system
电流制转换开关/電流制轉換開關 current system changeover switch
电路/電路 circuit
电路交换/電路交換,線路交换 circuit switching
电码/電碼 code
电码轨道电路/編碼軌道電路 coded track circuit
电码继电器/電碼繼電器 code relay
电码孔/碼孔 code hole
电码自动闭塞/電碼自動閉塞 automatic block with coded track circuit
电能损耗/能量損耗,有功損耗 energy loss
电能消耗/電力消耗 power consumption
电偶腐蚀/電流腐蝕,電流侵蝕 galvanic corrosion
电耦合系数/電耦合係數 electric coupling coefficient
电抛光/電抛光,電磨光 electropolishing
电平/電平 level
电平表/電平錶 level meter
电瓶车/電瓶車 storage battery car
电瓶车库/電瓶車庫 batter truck room
电起动/電力起動 electrical starting
电-气变换器/電動氣力轉變器,電子氣力轉變器 electro-pneumatic transducer
电气捕鱼/電氣捕魚 electrical fishing
电气电子机电零件/電機電子機電零件 electrical, electronic and electromechanical part

电气合练/電氣裝置預演 electric installation rehearsal
电气化/電氣化 electrification
电气化干扰/電[氣]化干擾 electrification interference
电气化工作/電氣化工作 electrification work
电气化区间/電氣化區段 electrified section
电气化铁路/電[氣]化鐵路 electrified railway
电气火灾监控探测器/電氣火災監控探測器 detector for electric fire prevention
电气火灾监控系统/電氣火災監控系統 alarm and control system for electric fire prevention
电气集中[联锁]/電氣聯鎖裝置 electric interlocking
电气联锁/電氣聯鎖 electrical interlocking
电气路牌闭塞/電氣路牌閉塞 electric tablet block system
电气路牌机/電氣路牌機 electric tablet instrument
电气路签闭塞/電氣路簽閉塞 electric staff system
电气路签机/電氣路簽機 electric staff instrument
电气日志/電機日誌 electrical log book
电气设备/電[氣]設備,電力裝備 electric equipment, electrical equipment
电-气式主机遥控系统/電動氣力遙控系統 electric-pneumatic remote control system for main engine
电气试验/電氣試驗 electric test
电气锁闭/電氣鎖裝置 electric locking
电气系统/電氣系統 electrical system, electric system
电气制动试验/電氣制動試驗 electric braking test
电气总工程师/電機總工程師 chief electrical engineer
电器室/電器室 electric apparatus room
电热玻璃/電加熱玻璃 electric heating glass
电热采暖装置/電加熱設備 electric heating equipment
电热[法]张拉/電加熱預力 electric heat prestressing
电热管/電熱管 tubular electric heating element
电热模拟/電熱模擬 electricityheat analogy
电热融霜/電除霜 electric defrost
电热融霜定时器/電除霜定時器 electric defrost timer
电热式肼单组元推进系统/電熱式肼單組元推進系統 electrothermal monopropellant hydrazine system
电热式沥青加热装置/制热用瀝青電熱裝置 bitumen electrical heating device
电热水器/電熱水器 electric water heater

电热养护/電熱養護,通電養護　electric heat curing, electric curing
电容储能点焊/電容器放電點焊　condenser discharge spot welding
电容器/電容器　capacitor, condenser
电容器室/電容器室　capacitor room
电容式传感器/電容式感測器　capacitive pickoff, capacitance-type sensor
电容式加速度计/電容式加速計　capacitive accelerometer
电容引信/電容引信　capacitance fuze
电熔连接/電熔連接　electrofusion-jointing
电扫描技术/電子掃描技術　electronically scan technology
电扫描天线/電子掃描天線　electronic scanning antenna
电扇/電扇　electric fan
电渗析/電透析,離子電析　electrodialysis
电渗析法/電滲析法,電透析法　electrodialysis process, electrodialysis method
电声控制室/音響控制室　sound control room
电视测量/電視測量　television measurement, TV measurement
电视跟踪/電視跟蹤　television tracking, TV tracking
电视跟踪测量系统/電視追蹤測量系統　television tracking measurement system
电视会议/視訊會議　video conference
电视摄影间/電視照像間　television pick-up house
电视塔/電視塔　television tower
电视台/電視臺　television station
电视、调频广播发射台/電視、調頻廣播發射臺　television and frequency modulation transmitting station, TV and FM transmitting station
电视望远镜/電視望遠鏡　television telescope
电视制导/電視導引　television guidance
电视自动跟踪/電視自動追蹤　television automatic tracking
电枢反应/電樞反應　armature reaction
电枢线圈/電樞線圈　armature coil
电刷/電刷　brush
电刷装置/刷式機構　brush gear
电锁器/電鎖　electric lock
电锁器联锁/電鎖聯鎖　interlocking by electric lock
电台/電臺　station
电台航向/電臺航向　heading of station
电弹簧/電[氣]彈簧　electrical spring
电探/電探　electrical resistivity survey

电梯/電梯,昇降機　elevator
电梯底坑/電梯底[層地]坑　elevator pit
电梯对重/電梯對重　elevator counterweight
电梯缓冲器/電梯緩衝器　elevator buffer
电梯轿厢/電梯車廂　elevator car
电梯井/電梯井　elevator shaft, elevator core
电梯速度/電梯速度　elevator speed
电透析/電透析,離子電析　electrodialysis
电推进/電力推進　electric propulsion
电推进系统/電推進系統　electric propulsion system
电网结构/電力網路構造　power network configuration
电位测量装置/電壓試驗裝置　potential test device
电位分析/電位分析　potentiometric analysis
电位轮/電位輪　potential test wheel
电文格式/信文格式　message format
电文交换/信文交換　message switching
电务维修无线电通信/電務維修無線電通訊　radio communication for maintenance of signal and communication equipment
电线管/電線管,導[線]管　electric wire tube, conduit
电信/電信　telecommunication
电信工程/電信工程　telecommunication engineering
电信机房/電信機房　telecommunication machine room
电信间/電信間　communication booth
电信局/電訊所　telecommunication office
电信局站/通信電臺　telecommunication station
电信专用房屋/電信私營處所　telecommunication private premise
电性试验模型/電性試驗模型　electric test model
电学模拟实验室/電刺激實驗室　electric stimulation laboratory
电压保护水平/電壓保護水準　voltage protection level
电压表/電壓表,伏特計　voltmeter
电压波动/電壓波動　voltage fluctuation
电压传感器/電壓傳感器　voltage sensor
电压电流变换器/電壓電流轉變器　voltage-current transducer
电压过低/電壓過低　voltage below level
电压互感器/電壓互感器,比壓器　voltage transformer, potential transformer, PT
电压畸变/電壓畸變,電壓失真　voltage distortion
电压继电器/電壓繼電器,電壓電驛　voltage relay
电压精度/電壓精度　voltage accuracy
电压偏差/電壓偏差　voltage deviation

电 111

电压调整器/電壓調節器　voltage regulator
电压温度系数/電壓溫度係數　voltage temperature coefficient
电压稳定度/電壓穩定度　voltage stability
电压质量/電壓品質　voltage quality
电压自动补偿装置/電壓自動調節補償器　autoregulation voltage compensator
电压自动调整器/自動電壓調節器　automatic voltage regulator
电液成形/電液成形　electro-hydraulic forming
电液阀/電子液壓閥　electro-hydraulic valve
电液换向阀/電動液力方向控制閥　electro-hydraulic directional control valve
电液式换能器/電動液壓轉變器　electro-hydraulic transducer
电液伺服阀/電動液力伺服閥　electro-hydraulic servo valve
电液伺服机构/電動液力伺服致動器　electric-hydraulic servo actuator
电液转辙机/電液轉轍機　electro-hydraulic switch machine
电液自动找平装置/電子液壓自動平層裝置　electronic-hydraulic automatic leveling device
电引信/電引信　electrical fuze
电影经纬仪/電影經緯儀　cinetheodolite
电影经纬仪跟踪系统/電影經緯儀追蹤系統　cinetheodolite tracking system
电影望远镜/電影望遠鏡　cine telescope
电影院/電影院　cinema
电影制片厂/電影製片廠　motion picture studio
电涌保护器/電湧保護器　surge protective device, SPD
电涌保护器脱离器/電湧保護器脫離器　surge protective device disconnector
电源/電源　power source, power supply
电源变电所/電源變電站　substation of power source
电源变压器/電源變壓器,供電變壓器　supply transformer
电源端子/電源端子　terminal for power supply
电源分系统/電源供應次系統　power supply subsystem
电源控制设备/電源控制設備　power control electronics
电源屏/電源屏　power supply panel
电源室/電氣室　power supply room
电源转换屏/電源轉換屏　power switching over panel
电晕放电试验/電暈試驗　corona test

电渣焊/電熱熔渣焊接　electro-slag welding
电站锅炉/電廠鍋爐,動力廠鍋爐　power plant boiler
电站列车[车组]/電站列車車組　power plant car, power plant train-set
电致伸缩效应/電伸縮效應　electrostrictive effect
电铸/電鑄　electroforming
电铸成形/電鑄成形　electrotyping process
电装/電裝　electric fitting
电子电话交换机/電子電話交換機　electronic telephone switching system
电子对抗/電子反制　electronic counter-measure
电子反对抗/電子反反制　electronic counter counter-measure
电子方位线/電子方位線　electronic bearing line, EBL
电子管/電子管,真空管　valve
电子管振荡器/真空管振盪器　valve oscillator
电子海图/電子海圖　electronic chart
电子海图数据库/電子海圖資料庫　electronic chart data base
电子海图显示与信息系统/電子海圖顯示與資訊系統　electronic chart display and information system, ECDIS
电子航海/電子儀航行　electronic navigation
电子轰击型推力器/電子衝擊推進器　electron bombardment thruster
电子会议系统/電子會議系統　electronic conference system
电子计算机X射线体层摄影室/電子計算機X射線體層攝影室　computed X-ray tomography room
电子计算机制造厂/電子計算機廠　computer factory
电子控制电路/電子控制電路　electronic control circuit
电子控制器/電子控制單元　electronic control unit
电子[设备]海上维修/海上電子維修　electronic maintenance at sea
电子时间引信/電子定時引信　electronic time fuze
电子[式]调速器/電子調速器　electronic governor
电子式压力扫描阀/電子式壓力感測器　electronic-scanned pressure sensor
电子式主机遥控系统/主機電子遙控系統　electronic remote control system for main engine
电子收费系统/電子收費系統　electronic toll system
电子束打孔/電子束穿孔　electron beam perforation
电子束焊/電子束焊　electron beam welding
电子束加工/電子束加工　electron beam machining, EBM
电子束流动显示/電子束流動可視化　electron beam

flow visualization
电子束荧光技术/電子束螢光技術 electron beam fluorescence technique
电子数据交换/電子數據交換 electronic data interchange
电子水平仪/電子水平儀 electrolevel
电子搜索/電子搜尋 electronic search
电子探针/電子探針 electronic probe
电子提单/電子載貨證券 electronic bill of lading
电子调节器/電子調整器 electronic regulator
电子调速器/電子調速器 electronic governor
电子显微镜/電子顯微鏡 electron microscope
电子信息系统机房/電子資訊系統機房 electronic information system room
电子[学]测量/電子量測 electronic measurement
电子巡查系统/電子巡更系統 guard tour system
电子邮件/電子郵件 electronic mail
电子邮件业务/電子郵件業務 electronic mail service
电子元件厂/電子元件廠 electronic component factory
电子战/電子戰 electronic warfare, EW
电子战吊舱/電子戰吊艙 EW pod
电子战飞机/電子戰飛機 electronic warfare airplane
电子侦察/電子偵察 electronic reconnaissance
电子侦察卫星/電子偵察衛星 electronic reconnaissance satellite
电子支援措施/電子支援措施 electronic support measure, ESM
电子资料库系统/電子圖書館系統 electronic library system
电子自动售票系统/電子自動售票系統 automatic electronic ticket system
电子综合显示系统/電子整合顯示系統 electronic integrated display system
电阻带式加热器/電阻帶式加熱器 electric resistance belt heater
电阻点焊/電阻點焊,電阻點熔接 resistance spot welding, resistance spot weld
电阻管式加热器/電阻管式加熱器 electric resistance tube heater
电阻焊/電阻焊接,閃光[對]焊 resistance welding, flash butt welding
电阻勘探法/電探法 electrical prospecting
电阻率/電阻率,電阻係數 electrical resistivity
电阻率测量装置/電阻率試驗裝置 resistivity test device
电阻率法/電阻率法 resistivity method
电阻器/電阻器 resistor
电阻钎焊/電阻硬焊 resistance brazing, resistance soldering
电阻应变仪/電阻[式]應變計,電阻變形計 electric resistance strain gage
电阻制动/電阻刹車 rheostatic brake
店铺/商店 shop
垫板/墊板,承壓板 bearing plate, bearing pad
垫板运输/墊板運輸 pallelalization
垫舱货/填墊貨 dunnage cargo
垫舱物料/墊艙物,墊材 dunnage
垫底货/底艙貨 base cargo
垫冻害垫板/墊凍害墊板 track shimming
垫管底料/墊管底料 equalising bed
垫接接头/托接式接頭 supported joint
垫块/基塊 foot block
垫块法/墊塊法 model pad method
垫块支座/襯墊軸承 pad bearing
垫木/墊木 chock
垫圈/墊圈 filling ring, washer
垫砂起道/鏟斗裝豆碎石填充 measured shovel packing
垫升风扇/墊昇風機 lift fan
垫水/艙底水 tank bottom water
垫碴/道碴墊 ballast packing
殿后舰/殿後船艦 rear ship
殿堂式/殿堂式 palace-type structure, diantang
凋落物/凋落物,枯枝落葉 litter
凋落物层/落葉枯枝層 litter horizon, litter layer
雕塑/雕塑 sculpture
雕塑公园/雕塑公園 sculpture park
雕塑群/雕塑群 sculpture ensembles
吊板/工作吊板,單人吊板 boatswain chair
吊车/吊車,起重機 crane
吊车费/起重機使用費 cranage
吊车荷载/吊車荷載 crane load
吊车梁/起重機行車大梁 crane girder
吊车走道/吊車走道 crane walkway
吊顶/懸吊天花板 suspended ceiling
吊斗/吊斗 skip
吊放回收装置/吊放回收裝置 launch retrieval apparatus
吊放式救生筏/吊放式救生筏,吊桿下水救生筏 davit launched type liferaft, davit launching liftraft
吊杆/吊桿,起重桿,懸桿 derrick boom, suspender, hanger
吊杆安全工作负荷/吊桿安全工作負荷,吊桿安全使用負荷 safe working load, SWL

吊杆叉头/吊桿根　derrick heel
[吊杆]根部滑车/[吊桿]根部滑車　heel block
吊杆架/吊桿架　boom cradle
吊杆跨距/吊桿伸出舷外距離　boom outstretch
吊杆偏角/吊桿偏角,吊桿旋角　slewing angle
吊杆索具/吊桿索具　derrick rigging
吊杆托架/吊桿托架,吊桿承座　derrick rest
吊杆仰角/吊桿俯仰角　boom topping angle
吊杆柱/主柱　king post
吊杆柱平台/主柱突出臺木　kingpost outrigger
吊杆装置/吊桿裝置　derrick, derrick rig
吊杆座/吊桿承座　derrick socket
吊缸/吊缸　lift out piston
吊沟/吊溝　suspended ditch
吊挂架/掛架　pylon
吊环/吊環　suspension ring
吊货杆/吊貨桿　cargo boom
吊货工夹具/吊貨工夾具　hoisting fixture
吊货钩/吊貨鉤　cargo hook
吊货索/吊貨索　cargo sling, cargo runner, cargofall
吊货索环/起吊索具　hoisting sling
吊货索具/吊貨索具　cargo wire runner, cargo purchase rigging
吊货索卷筒/吊貨索卷軸　cargo drop reel
吊货网/吊貨網　cargo net
吊货眼板/吊貨眼板　cargo purchase eye
吊具小车/吊具車　hoisting tool bogie
吊篮/吊籃　lifting cage, lifting car
吊篮吊具/吊籃吊具　lifting cage sling
吊缆/吊纜,吊索　suspension cable
吊梁/吊梁　lifting beam
吊锚/吊錨　cat, weigh
吊锚杆/吊錨桿　anchor crane, anchor davit, cat davit
吊锚滑车/吊錨滑車　cat block
吊锚索具/吊錨索具　cat-chain, cat tackle
吊桥/吊橋　suspension bridge
吊升信号/吊昇信號　hoisting signal
吊索/吊索,懸索　suspension rod
吊艇钩/吊艇鉤　boat lifting hook
吊艇机/小艇吊機,小艇絞車　boat winch
吊艇架/小艇吊架　boat davit
吊艇索/小艇吊索　boat fall
吊艇柱座/凸式套座　pedestal socket
吊艇装置/小艇吊放裝置　boat handling gear
吊弦/吊弦　hanger
吊弦线夹/吊弦線夾　hanger ear
吊柱桁架/吊式桁架　hanging truss

吊装/起重　hoisting
吊装分析/吊裝分析　lifting analysis
钓船/釣船　line fishing boat
钓饵/釣餌　bait
钓竿/釣竿　angle rod
钓竿箱/釣竿盒　fishing rod box
钓鱼区/釣魚區　fishing center
钓鱼塘/釣魚塘　fishing pond
调查表调查/調查表調查　inquiry form survey
调查测绘/調查測繪　survey and drawing of investigation, investigation survey, investigation surveying and sketching
调查坑道/檢查坑　investigation gallery, survey tunnel
调查庭/調查庭　court of survey
调查委员会/調查委員會　board of investigation, board of inquiry
调车/調車　shunting, car marshalling
调车表示器/調車表示器　shunting indicator
调车表示器电路/調車表示器電路　shunting indicator circuit
调车场/調車場　marshalling yard, shunting yard, classification yard
调车费/調車費　dispatch charge
调车呼叫信号音/調車呼叫信號音　shunting calling tone
调车机车/調車[線]機車　shunting locomotive, switcher
调车进路/調車進路　shunting route
调车控制器/調車調度員　shunting controller
调车区/調車區　switching area
调车区电气集中联锁/調車區電氣集中聯鎖　interlocking for shunting area
调车设备/調車設備　marshalling facility, classification equipment
调车事故/調車事故　accident in shunting operation
调车无线电通信/調車無線電通訊　radio communication for shunting
调车线/調車線軌道　shunting track, classification track
调车线始端减速器/調車線始端減速器　tangent retarder
调车信号/調車號誌機　shunting signal
调车信号音/調車信號音　shunting tone
调车作业计划/調車作業計劃　shunting operation plan
调度渡线/調度渡線　dispatching crossover
调度方法/調度方法　dispatching method

调度集中/集中式交通控制　centralized traffic control, CTC
调度集中分机/集中式交通控制分機　field equipment of CTC
调度集中总机/集中式交通控制總機　control office equipment of CTC
调度监督系统/調度監督系統　dispatcher supervision system
调度控制/調度器控制　dispatcher control
调度命令/調度命令　dispatching order, traffic dispatching order, train dispatching order
调度区段/調度區段　train dispatching section, train control section
调度日班计划/調度日班計劃　daily and shift traffic plan
调度日志/調度日誌　dispatching log
调度所/調度所　traffic controller office, dispatcher office
调度所选叫通话箱/調度所選叫通話箱　selective calling and talking box for dispatching office
调机飞行/調機飛行　transfer flight
调水引流/調水引流　water transfer and drainage
掉抢/掉餕　come about
掉头/掉頭,短迴轉　turning around, turning short round
掉头区/迴旋區　swinging area
跌落水/落水　by the board
跌落线/跌落線　drop-off curve
跌水/跌水,水壓降　hydraulic drop, water drop
跌水段/跌水段　drop-down section
迭代/迭代　iteration
迭代法/迭代法　iteration method
叠板弹簧/疊板彈簧,疊片彈簧　laminated spring
叠标/疊標桿　transit beacon
叠层板/積層板,疊合板　laminate
叠层的极限强度/積層板終極強度　ultimate strength of the laminate
叠层太阳电池/堆疊太陽電池　stacked solar cell, cascade solar cell
叠层橡胶支座/板式橡膠支座,板式橡膠支承　laminated rubber bearing
叠氮聚合物推进剂/疊氮聚合物推進劑　glycidyl azide polymer propellant, GAP propellant
叠桁式拱架/疊桁式拱架　double layer truss centering
叠加轨道电路/疊加軌道電路　overlap track circuit
叠片式电弧加热器/疊片式電弧加熱器　Macker type arc heater

叠拼住宅/疊拼住宅　townhouse
叠石/疊石　stones laying
叠压供水/疊壓供水　pressure superposed water supply
叠柱式/層疊式柱式　superimposed order
碟式油分离机/盤形油[水]分離機　disc oil separator
蝶阀/蝶形閥　butterfly valve
丁坝/丁壩　spur dike
丁坝坝头/丁堤首　groyne head
丁苯橡胶/苯乙烯-丁二烯橡膠　styrene butadiene rubber, SBR
丁堤区/丁堤區　groyne field
丁堤体/丁堤體　groyne body
丁钠橡胶/丁納橡膠,布納橡膠　Buna rubber
丁香结/丁香結　clove hitch
丁形离水阀/丁形除水閥　tee trap
丁砖砌法/丁頭砌法　heading bond
丁字尺/丁字尺　T square
丁字接头/丁字接縫　T joint
丁字形交叉/T形交叉　T intersection
顶边舱/[翼]肩艙　top side tank
顶标/頂上標誌　topmark
顶部采光/天窗採光　top daylighting
顶部导坑/頂部導坑　top heading
顶部间隙/竖向淨孔　overhead clearance
顶层刚架/頂層構架　top frame
顶潮流航行/頂潮航行　stem the tide
顶车/頂車　lift one end of car
顶车座/起重器支墊,千斤頂立架　jacking pad
顶灯/吊燈　ceiling lamp
顶点纬度/頂點緯度　latitude of vertex
顶端优势/頂端優勢　top edge
顶风停船/頂風停船　in iron
顶风停住/頂風停住　in stays
顶盖座/頂蓋座　hatch cover seat
顶杆/頂桿　crown bar
顶杆螺钉/昇降螺旋　lifter screw
顶管法/頂管法　pipe jacking method
顶管掘进机/頂管掘進機　pipe jacking tunnelling machine
顶光/頂燈　top light
顶级群落/極頂群落　climax community
顶级望远镜/頂位望遠鏡　top telescope
顶接接头/頂接接頭　tee connection
顶进法/頂進法　jack-in method
顶索绞车/俯仰絞機　topping winch
顶[头]风/頂[頭]風,逆風　head wind
顶[头]浪/頂[頭]浪,逆浪　head sea

顶推/推頂 pushing
顶推操纵缆/推頂操舵纜 pushing steering line
[顶]推船/推[型拖]船 push boat, pusher
顶推船队/推駁船隊 pusher train
顶推法/節塊推進工法 incremental launching method
顶推架/推頂架 pushing frame
顶推设备/頂推設備 incremental launching device
顶推式架设法/頂推法架橋 erection by incremental launching method
顶推柱/推頂柱 pushing post
顶推装置/推頂裝置 pushing gear
顶置气阀式发动机/頂置閥式引擎 valve-in head type engine
顶装法/頂裝法 load on top, LOT
订舱/訂載 booking
订舱单/訂運單 berth note
订租确认书/成交書 fixing letter, fixture note
钉板梁桥/釘板梁橋 pin connected plywood girder bridge
钉结板梁/釘結板梁 nailed plate girder
钉连接/釘結合 nailed joint
钉栓/釘榫 spike dowel
定班运行/定班運行 scheduled run
定边/定向 sense determination
定测/定測,定位测量 location survey, alignment, final location survey
定常空泡/穩定空泡 steady cavities
定常流/穩流 steady flow
定常直线飞行法/定常直線飛行法 steady straight flight method
定程租船/航程包租 voyage charter
定点保持/位置保持 station keeping
定点捕获/定點捕獲 station acquisition
定点精度/定點精度 stationing accuracy
定点停车/定點停車 stopping a train at a target point
定额/定額,限額 norm, quota, rating
定额客票/定額客票 valued ticket
定额赔偿/定額補償 rated compensation
定反位锁闭/定反位鎖閉 normal and reverse locking
定风量空气调节系统/變風量空調系統 constant volume air conditioning system
定光/定光 fixed light
定光灯/定光燈 non-flashing light
定轨精度/軌道決定精度 orbit determination accuracy

定滑轮装置/定滑輪 fixed pulley
定级证书/分級證書 grading certificate
定检公里/定檢公里 running kilometer between predetermined repairs
定检时间/定檢時間 time between predetermined repairs
定角引爆/定角引爆 initiation at fixed angle
定界符/定義符,限制符,限定器 delimiter
定镜差/水平鏡誤差 side error
定距螺桨/定距螺旋槳 fixed pitch propeller
定距瞄准/距離瞄準 range sighting
定距引爆/定矩引爆 initiation at fixed range
π定理/π定理 π theorem
定量测试/定量試驗 quantitative test
定量油马达/固定排量油馬達 fixed-displacement oil motor
定苗/定苗 final singling
定期保险/定期保險 time insurance
定期保养制度/定期保養制度 system of periodical maintenance
定期检查/定期檢查 periodical inspection
定期检修/定期檢修 repair based on time or running kilometer, periodic repair
定期检验/定期檢驗 periodical survey
定期票/定期票 periodical ticket
定期试验/日常試驗,例行測試 routine test
定期维修/定期維修,定期保养,定期維護 regular maintenance, periodic maintenance, routine maintenance
[定期]预防维修/預防保養 preventive maintenance
定期租船/計時雇船,計時租賃 time charter
定日镜/定日鏡 heliostat
定日镜采光器/定日鏡採光器 heliostat daylighting device
定容循环/定容循環,等容循環 constant volume cycle
定时/定時 timing
定时抖动/時序顫動 timing jitter
定时广播/定時廣播 for scheduled broadcast
定时监测/週期監測 periodic monitor
定时喷灌控制器/定時噴灌控制器 timing of sprinkler irrigation controller
定时器/定時器 timer
定时热水供应系统/定時熱水供應系統 fixed time hot water supply system
定时信号/計時信號 timing signal
定时信号控制/定時控制 fixed time control
定时信号控制机/定時控制器 pretimed controller,

timing controller
定位/定位 locating, position fix, positioning
GPS定位/全球定位系统定位 GPS position
定位尺寸/定位尺寸 positioning scale
定位格架/定位格 location grid
定位管/定位臂 registration arm
定位焊/定位點焊, 定位點熔接 tack welding
定位环/定位環 steady ring
定位几何误差因子/定位精度因子 position dilution of precision
定位接点/正常接觸 normal contact
定位锚/定位錨 positioning anchor
定位铆接/定位鉚接 registration riveting
定位器/固定臂 steady arm
定位时间/定位時間 time for positioning
定位索/定位索 registration wire
定位锁闭/定位鎖閉 normal locking
定位调节螺丝/調整螺釘 adjusting screw
定位线夹/定位線夾 steady ear
定位轴线/軸線 axis, axial line
定位柱/定位柱 registration mast
定位桩/定位樁 spud
定位桩架/定位樁架 spud gantry
定位桩台车/定位樁臺車 spud carriage
定位装置/定位裝置 registration device
定线/線路勘定 line location
定线运行/定線運轉 fixed line operation
定向/定向 orientation
定向爆破/定向爆破 directional blasting
定向导航灯/導向燈 directional light
定向共晶高温合金/方向性凝固共晶超合金 directionally solidified eutectic superalloy
定向交通/分向運送法 directional traffic
定向结晶叶片/定向結晶葉片 directional crystallization blade
定向精度/定位精度 orientation accuracy
定向控制/定向控制 control of orientation
定向瞄准/方向瞄準 directional sighting
定向凝固/定向凝固 directional solidification
定向凝固高温合金/方向性凝固超合金 directionally solidified superalloy, DS superalloy
定向上下行驶/分向運送法 directional traffic
定向设计小时交通量/定向設計小時交通量 directional design hourly traffic volume, DDHTV
定向式立交/定向[式]立體交叉, 定向道路交匯 directional interchange
定向天线/定向天線 directional antenna
定向无线电信标/定向無線電示標 directional radio beacon
定向行车道标记/定向行車道標記 directional carriageway marking
定向引爆/定向引爆 directional initiation
定向有机玻璃/定向有機玻璃 oriented organoglass
定向运动/定向運動 directional movement
定向战斗部/定向戰鬥部 directional fragment warhead, aimable fragment warhead
定向照明/指向性照明 directional lighting
定相/定相 phasing
定心冲压机/中心衝孔機 center-punching
定型试验/檢定[合格]測試 qualification test
定性测试/定性試驗 qualitative test
定压点/加壓點 pressurization point
定压方式/補水定壓方式, 加壓方式 pressurization method
定压风缸/定壓風缸 constant pressure reservoir
定压功放/定壓功放 power amplifier with fixed voltage
定压涡轮增压/定壓渦輪增壓 constant pressure turbo-charging
定压循环/定壓循環, 等壓循環 constant pressure cycle
定压增压/定壓增壓, 等壓增壓, 恆壓增壓 constant pressure charging
定压装置/加壓裝置 pressurization installation
定义测量方法/定義量測法 definitive method of measurement
定员/座位容量 seating capacity
定约承运人/契約運送人 contract of carrier
定站客票/定站客票 fixed ticket
定站停靠率/定站停靠率 rate of stops at scheduled bus stops
定值控制/穩定控制 stabilization control
定制/訂製 made-to-order
定置试验/定置試驗 static state test, stationary test, test at standstill
定置网/定置漁網 stationary fishing net
定置渔具/定置漁具 stationary fishing gear
定周期交通信号/固定週期信號 fixed cycle signal
定轴性/定軸性 gyroscopic inertia, orientation stability
定子/定子, 静子 stator
丢失事故/丢失事故 loss accident
东北大学建筑系/東北大學建築系 Department of Architecture in Northeastern University
东大距/東大距 greatest eastern elongation
东方标/東方標 east mark

东方式插花/東方式插花 eastern style of flower arranging
东风波/東風波 easterly wave
东西距/東西距 departure, Dep
东西位置保持/東西向位置保持 east-west station keeping
冬季季节区带/季節性冬期地帶 winter seasonal zone
冬季季节区域/季節性冬期區域 winter seasonal area
冬季施工/冬季施工,冬季建造 cold weather construction, winter season construction
冬季载重线/冬期載重線 winter load line
冬园/冬園 winter garden
冬至点/冬至[點] winter solstice
氡室/氡室 radon chamber
动板/動板 movable plate
动臂起重机/简易起重機 whip crane
动车/動車 motor car
动车组/動車組 motor train unit, motor train set
动程/衝程,行程 stroke
动床/不穩定河槽 unstable channel
动导数/動力導數 dynamic derivative
动导数试验/動態導數試驗 dynamic derivative testing
动方向稳定性/動方向穩定性 dynamic directional stability
动刚度/動態剛性,動態勁度 dynamic stiffness
动高度/動力高度 dynamic height
动观/動觀 in-motion viewing
动航向稳定性/動向穩度 dynamic course stability
动横倾角/動橫傾角 dynamical heeling angle
动横倾力臂/動橫傾力臂 dynamical heeling lever
动横倾力矩/動橫傾力矩 dynamical heeling moment
动基准坐标系/動參考坐標系 moving reference coordinate system
动基座对准/動基座對準 moving alignment
动接点/可動接頭 contact heel, movable contact
动界/動界 arena
动镜差/垂直誤差 perpendicular error
动力车/動力小車 moto-buggy
动力触探试验/動態聲測,動力貫入試驗 dynamic sounding, dynamic penetration test
动力船/動力船舶 power driving vessel
动力锤/動力錘 power hammer
动力打桩公式/動力打樁公式 dynamic pile-driving formula
动力定位/動力定位,動態定位 dynamic positioning

动力段制导/主動段制導 powered phase guidance
动力吨位/動力噸位 power tonnage
动力放大过程线/動力放大過程線 dynamic amplification duration curve
动力飞行段/動力飛行階段 power flight phase
动力固结法/强夯法 dynamic consolidation method, dynamic compaction method
动力锅炉/動力廠鍋爐,電廠鍋爐 power plant boiler
动力夯/機動夯土機 power rammer
动力回动机/動力回動機 power reverse gear
动力活塞/動力活塞 power piston
动力继电器柜/動力繼電器櫃 power plant relay cabinet
动力剪草机/動力剪草機 power lawnmower
动力控制台/動力控制臺 power plant control console
动力冷却/動冷卻 dynamic cooling
动力内接/動力内接 dynamic inscribing
动力黏[滞]度/動力黏度,動黏[滯]度 kinematic viscosity
动力坡度/動量坡度 momentum grade
动力气象学/動力氣象學 dynamic meteorology
动力牵引车/動力手車 power buggy
动力强度/動力強度 dynamic strength
动力三轴试验/動態三軸試驗 dynamic triaxial test
动力射程/動力射程 dynamic range
动力式弯沉仪/動力式彎沈儀 dynaflect
动力试验车/動力測定車 dynamometer car
动力室/動力室 power room
动力探测/動力探測 dynamic sounding
动力特性/動態特性 dynamic characteristics
动力调谐/動力調諧 dynamic tuning
动力调谐陀螺/動力調諧陀螺 dynamic tuned gyroscope
动力调谐陀螺仪/動力調諧陀螺儀,動態調諧陀螺儀 dynamically tuned gyro, DTG
动力土钻/動力式螺旋鑽 power earth auger
动力稳定机/動力穩定車 dynamic track stabilizer
动力涡轮/動力渦輪,動力輪機 power turbine
动力系数/動力係數 coefficient of dynamic force
动力系统/動力系統,電源系統 power system
动力响应/動力反應 dynamic response
动力行程/動力衝程 power stroke
动力学/動力學 dynamics, kinetics
动力学仿真/動力學模擬 dynamics simulation
动力学分析/動力學分析 dynamics analysis
动力学设计/動力學設計 dynamics design
动力学试验/動力學試驗 dynamics test

动力[学]相似性/動力相似性　dynamic similarity
动力循环/動力循環　power cycle
动力增温/動加熱　dynamic heating
动力制动/動力剎車,動力掣　dynamic brake
动力中心/動力中心　power center
动力装置单位质量/動力裝置單位質量　power plant specific mass
动力装置燃油消耗率/動力裝置燃油消耗率　power plant effective specific fuel oil consumption
动力装置生命力/動力裝置壽命　power plant viability
动力装置[有效]热效率/動力裝置[有效]熱效率　power plant effective thermal efficiency
动量/動量　momentum
动量储存能力/動量儲存能力　momentum storage capability
动量法/動量法　momentum method
动量方程/動量方程式　momentum equation
动量分量/分動量　component of momentum
动量交换/動量交換　momentum exchange
动量交换机动/動量交換機動　momentum exchange maneuver
动量交换装置/動量交換裝置　momentum exchange device
动量矩/動量矩　moment of momentum
动量理论/動量理論　momentum theory
动量轮/動量輪　momentum wheel
动量偏置方式/動量偏斜模式　bias momentum mode
动量守恒/動量守恆　conservation of momentum
动量系数/動量係數　momentum coefficient
动量线/動量線　momentum line
动量增益/動量增益　momentum gain
动量转移理论/動量輸送理論　momentum transfer theory
动密封/動態封口　dynamic seal, moving seal
动摩擦/動摩擦　kinetic friction
动摩擦系数/動摩擦係數　coefficient of kinetic friction
动能/動能　kinetic energy
动配合/動配合　movable fit
动平衡/動態平衡,動力平衡,動力均衡　dynamic balancing, dynamical balance, dynamic balance
动平衡试验/動平衡試驗　dynamic balancing test
动倾覆角/動傾覆角　dynamical upsetting angle
动圈式传感器/動圈式感測器　moving coil pickoff, moving coil transducer
动式机器人服务系统/移動式機器人服務系統　mobile robot servicing system, MSS
动视觉敏锐度/動態視覺敏銳度　dynamic visual acuity
动水头/動水頭　kinetic head
动水压线/動水壓力線　operation pressure
动索/動索　running rigging
动态/動態　dynamic state
动态不平顺/動態軌道不整　dynamic track irregularity
动态测力天平/動力天平　dynamic balance
动态测量/動態量測　dynamic measurement
动态测试/動態試驗,動力試驗,操作試驗　dynamic test, operational test
动态长度/動態長度　distance-to-go
动态断裂韧性/動態破裂韌性　dynamic fracture toughness
动态范围/動態範圍　dynamic range
动态分析/動態分析　dynamic analysis
动态公式/動力公式　dynamic formula
动态规划/動線規劃　dynamic programming
动态回弹弯沉/動態回彈彎沈　dynamic rebound deflection
动态模拟/動態模擬　dynamic simulation
动态耦合/動態結合　dynamic coupling
动态平衡阀/動態平衡閥　dynamic hydraulic balancing valve
动态三轴试验/動態三軸試驗　dynamic triaxial test
动态设计/動態設計,動力設計　dynamic design
动态摄影分辨率/動態照相分辨率　dynamic photographic resolution
动态试验/動態試驗　dynamic test
动态弹性模量/動彈性模量　dynamic modulus of elasticity
动态投资/動態投資　dynamic investment
动态图像/動態影像　dynamic image
动态系统/動系統　dynamical system
动态相似律/動力相似律　law of dynamic similarity
动态响应/動態應答　dynamic response
动态响应指数/動態響應指數　dynamic response index, DRI
动态运动/動態運動　dynamic motion
动态照明/動態光線　dynamic lighting
动态诊断/動態診斷　dynamic diagnosis
动态轴重检测器/動態軸重偵測器　dynamic axle weight detector
动态作用/動態作用,動力作用,動態行動　dynamic action
动弯沉/動力撓曲,衝擊撓度　dynamic deflection

动稳[定]性/動穩定性,動穩度　dynamic stability
动稳性力臂/動穩度力臂　dynamical stability lever
动稳性曲线/動穩度曲線　curve of dynamical stability
动物实验室/動物實驗室　animal laboratory
动物通道/動物廊道　animal corridor
动物箱/牲口櫃　cattle container
动物园/動物園　zoo, zoological garden
动休息区/動休息區　dynamic rest space
动压力/動壓力　dynamic pressure
动压气浮陀螺仪/動壓氣浮陀螺儀　hydrodynamic gas bearing gyro
动压强/動壓力　dynamic pressure
动压头/動落差,動高差　dynamic head, kinetic head
动压陀螺电机/動壓陀螺電機　hydrodynamic gas bearing gyro motor
动叶[片]/[轉]動葉片　moving blade
动叶水涡轮/動葉水渦輪　movable blade water turbine
动叶损失/轉動葉片損耗　moving blade loss
动员费预付贷款/動員費預付貸款　advance mobilization loan
动载[荷]/動態負荷,動力負載　dynamic load
动载试验/動力試驗　dynamic test
动载因子/動載因素　dynamic load factor
动植物检疫/動植物檢疫　animal or plant quarantine
动轴/動軸　moving axis
动轴箱/動輪軸箱　driving box
动轴箱平铁/動輪軸箱平鐵　driving box shoe
动轴箱楔铁/動輪軸箱楔　driving box wedge
动作杆/動作桿　throw rod
动作连接杆/動作連接桿　operating rod for driving a switch
动作研究/動作研究　motion study
冻害/凍害,凍傷,凍脹　freezing injury, frost damage, frost heaving
冻害垫板/防凍填隙片　frost heave board, track shim for frost heaving roadbed, frost shim
冻结/凍結　freezing
冻结层上水/凍土表水　superpermafrost water
冻结度/寒凍度　degrees of frost
冻结法/冷凍工法　ground freezing method
冻结高度层/結冰高度　freezing level
冻结核/結冰核　freezing nuclei
冻结货物/凍結貨物　frozen freight
冻结间/冷凍室,冷藏室　freezing room
冻结接头/凍結接頭　frozen joint
冻结流动/凍結流　frozen flow
冻结区/凍土層　freezing zone
冻结深度/冰凍深度　freezing depth
冻结系数/凍結係數　freezing fraction
冻结指数/凍結指數　freezing index
冻融/凍融　frost thawing
冻融[循环]试验/凍融試驗,融凝試驗,解凍及凍結試驗　freezing and thawing test
冻水/凍結水　frozen water
冻原/凍原,苔原　tundra
冻胀/凍脹　frost heaving
冻胀力/凍脹力,冰舉力　frost heaving force
洞/岩洞,洞穴　cave
洞口/洞口　opening, tunnel adit, tunnel opening
洞口段衬砌/洞口段襯砌　lining of tunnel portal section
洞门框/洞門框　tunnel portal frame
洞室药包爆破/洞室藥包爆破　chamber explosive package blasting, chamber blasting
洞穴地段路基/洞穴地段路基　subgrade in cavity zone, subgrade in cavern zone
斗/斗　bearing block, bucket
斗车/斗式裝料機　bucket loader
斗栱/斗栱　bracket set, block and bracket cluster, dougong
斗口/斗口　doukou, timber module
斗轮式挖沟机/斗輪式挖溝機　bucket wheel trencher
斗轮式挖掘机/斗輪[式]挖掘機,犀頭轉輪挖土機　bucket wheel excavator
斗式混凝土布料机/漏斗式混凝土攤鋪機　hopper type concrete spreader
斗式提升机/斗式昇降機,斗昇機,箕斗昇運機　bucket elevator
斗式挖泥船/抓斗挖泥船　grab dredger
抖动/抖動,顫動　jitter
抖动器/顫動器　dither
抖振/抖振,振動　buffeting, buffet
抖振边界/抖振界限　buffet boundary
抖振试验/抖振試驗　buffet test
陡坡涵洞/急傾斜涵洞　culvert on steep grade
陡升速度/陡昇速度　steepest climb speed
都鄙/都鄙　fief
都城/都城,京師,首府　capital city
都市连绵区/都市連綿區,大都會帶,巨大都市帶　metropolitan interlocking region, megalopolis
都市农业/都市農業　urban agriculture
都市区/[大]都會區　metropolitan area
都市圈/[大]都會區　metropolitan area

都邑/[都]邑　du yi, city, capital
毒害工业/毒害工業　noxious industry
毒品车/毒品車　poison car, poisonous goods wagon
毒种/毒種　virus species
独轨铁路/獨軌鐵路,單軌鐵路　monorail railway
独户住宅/獨户住宅　single-family house
独立波/孤立波　solitary wave
独立传动机车/獨立傳動機車　individual drive locomotive
独立电源/獨立電源　independent electric supply
独立工矿区/獨立礦區　independent mining area
独立故障/獨立故障　independent fault
独立基础/獨立基礎,獨立底脚　single footing, pad foundation
独立基脚/獨立基脚,獨立放脚基礎　individual footing foundation
独立控制/獨立控制　isolated control
独立平行进近/獨立平行進場　independent parallel approach
独立平行离场/獨立平行離場　indepenednt parallel departure
独立驱动/單獨驅動　individual drive
独立设计权/獨立設計權　independent design right
独立式挡土墙/懸臂式擋土牆　cantilever retaining wall
独立式低层住宅/別墅　villa
独立式住宅/獨户住房,獨建住宅　detached house, single family house
独立同步方式/獨立同步方式　individual synchronized mode
独立线束铁心/纜心束　independent wire rope core
独木舟/獨木舟　dugout canoe
独塔式斜拉桥/獨塔斜拉橋　stayed bridge with single pylon
独塔斜拉桥/獨塔斜張橋　single pylon cable stayed bridge
读出寄存器/讀取暫存器　readout register
读出时钟/讀出時鐘　readout clock
读卡机/讀卡機　card reader
堵缝/填料接縫　caulking
堵孔/塞孔　plug-hole
堵口堤/堵口堤　closing dike
堵漏/堵漏,損漏防護　leak stopping, leakage protection
堵漏器材/堵漏器材　leak stopper
堵漏水泥箱/水泥堵[漏]箱　cement box
堵漏毯/堵漏毯,防水墊　collision mat
堵塞技术/堵塞技術　choked technique

赌场/賭場,卡息諾　casino
度假村/度假地,休閒地　resort
度假设施/度假設施　resort facilities
度假胜地/假日勝地　holiday resort
度日/度日　degree-day
渡板/渡板　gangway foot plate
渡槽/導水渠道　aqueduct
渡船/渡船　ferry boat, ferry
渡口/渡口　ferry, ferry crossing
渡口安全规则/渡口安全規程　ferry safety regulation
渡口管理/渡口管理　ferry management
渡口管理所/渡口管理所　ferry house
渡轮/渡船,輪渡　ferry boat
渡桥码头/渡橋碼頭　portal bridge
渡线/渡綫　crossover
渡运码头/渡運碼頭　ferry wharf
镀铬/鍍鉻　chrome plating
镀铬缸套/鍍鉻缸套　chrome plated liner
镀铬环/鍍鉻環　chrome-plate ring
镀后处理/鍍後處理　treatment after plating
镀膜/鍍膜　film plating
镀锡铁皮/鍍錫鐵片　tin sheet
镀锌/鍍鋅　galvanization, zinc plating, galvanizing
镀锌板/鍍鋅鋼板　galvanized steel sheet
镀锌钢/鍍鋅鋼　galvanized steel
镀锌钢板/鍍鋅薄鋼板　zinc-coated steel sheet
镀锌钢管/鍍鋅鋼管　galvanized steel tube, galvanized steel pipe
镀锌钢绞线/鍍鋅鋼絲股　galvanized steel wire strand
镀锌钢丝/鍍鋅鋼絲　galvanized steel wire
镀锌焊接钢管/鍍鋅焊接鋼管　galvanized welded steel pipe
镀锌丝/鍍鋅綫　galvanized wire
端板/端板　end plate
端部舱壁/端隔牆　end bulkhead
端部固定/端部固定　encastre
端部塞门/端部塞門　end cock
端承桩/端承樁　point bearing pile
端淬试验/熱處理硬化試驗　jominy test
端电压/端電壓　terminal voltage
端盖/端蓋　end shield
端横梁/端横梁　end floor beam
端接管/短管[節]　pipe nipple
端接焊缝/邊[緣]焊縫　edge weld
端净空/兩端清除　end clearway
端开门箱/端開貨櫃　open end container

端靠式渡船/端靠式渡船　front mooring ferry boat
端梁/端梁　end sill
端裂/端裂　end check
端门/端門　end door
端面/端面　edge
端面燃烧/端面燃燒　end burning
端墙包板/端[牆]板　end sheathing
端墙式洞门/端牆式洞門　end wall tunnel portal
端羟基聚丁二烯推进剂/端羥基聚丁二烯推進劑　hydroxyl terminated polybutadiene propellant, HTPB propellant
端羧基聚丁二烯推进剂/端羧基聚丁二烯推進劑　carboxyl terminated polybutadiene propellant, CTPB propellant
端柱/端柱　end post
短波单边带无线电台/單邊帶短波無線電臺　single side-band short wave station
短波辐射/短波輻射　short wave radiation
短波红外/短波紅外線波段　short wave infrared
短波通信车/短波通信車　short wave radio communication vehicle
短[插]接/短編接　short splice
短撑材/短撑材　kicking piece
短程国际航行/短程國際航程　short international voyage
短程线穹顶/網格圓屋頂　geodesic dome
短程运输路线/短程運輸線　shuttle train line
短定子/短定子　short stator
短吨/短噸　short ton
短峰波/短峰波, 短岸波　short crested waves, short crested wave
短钢索/帽索　cap cable
短轨/短軌　short rail
短轨条/短軌條　shorter rail
短轨枕/短軌枕　shorter tie
短基线干涉仪/短基線干涉儀　short base-line interferometer
短交路/短交路　short routing
短截/短截, 截剪　a short cut, cutting back
短距起落飞机/短距起落飛機　short take-off and landing airplane, STOL airplane
短缆系结/短纜繫結　short line connection
短路/短路, 短接　short circuit, short circuiting
短路电流/短路電流　short circuit current
短路电流密度/短路電流密度　short circuit current density
短路器/短路裝置　short-circuiting device
短路匝式传感器/短路匝式感測器　short circuit turn pickoff
短螺旋成孔机/短螺旋土壤螺鑽機　partial screw earth auger
短期重复性/短期重複性　short term repeatability
短期刚度/短期剛度　short term stiffness
短期频率稳定度/短期頻率穩定度　short term frequency stability
短期稳定性/短期穩定性　short term stability
短期效应组合/短期效應組合　combination for short term action effects
短日[照]植物/短日照植物　short day plant
短声/短[笛]聲　short blast
短时高温强度极限/短時高温强度極限　strength limit of short time in high temperature
短时计数/短期計數　short time count
短时间加速度/短期加速度　short-duration acceleration
短寿命发动机/短壽命發動機　expendable engine
短隧道/短隧道　short tunnel
短榫/短榫　stub tenon
短台拖车/短臺拖車　shot plate-form trailer
短停维护/短停維護　turnover service
短卸/短卸　short-landed, short-delivery
短卸货/短卸貨　short-landed cargo
短枕/短枕　short tie, block tie
短肢剪力墙/短肢剪力牆　short-pier shear wall
短周期模态/短週期模態　short-period mode
短周期摄动/短週期攝動　short periodic perturbation
短周期事故/短週期事故　short period accident
短轴/短軸　minor axis
短装/短裝　short-shipped
段管线/段管線　depot siding
段同步/段同步　segment synchronization
段信号/段信號　segment signal
段修循环系数/段修循環係數　circulating factor of repair in depot
断背曲线/斷脊曲線　broken back curve
断层/斷層　fault
断层泉/斷層泉　fault spring
断层水/斷層水　fault water
断层走向/斷層走向　fault strike
断层阻塞泉/斷層阻塞泉　fault dammed spring
断点/折點　break-point
断缝/破縫, 裂縫　breaking joint
断高/斷高　broken height
断根机/斷根機　increased machine
断轨保障/斷軌保障　broken rail protection
断火/斷火　interruption of firing

断级配／斷級配　gap gradation
断键／斷鍵　broken bond
断阶／斷階　step, planing step
断口检验／斷口檢驗　fracture examination
断口金相学／斷口金相檢驗　fractography
断链／斷鏈　broken chain
断裂／斷裂，破裂　fracture
断裂带／破碎帶，破裂帶，裂隙帶　fractured zone
断裂点／破裂點，破壞點　breaking point
断裂力学／斷裂力學　fracture mechanics
断裂面／破斷面　surface of fracture
断裂剖视图／斷裂剖視圖　braking sectional view
断裂区／破裂區，破裂帶　zone of fracture
断裂韧性／斷裂韌性　fracture toughness
断裂应变／裂斷應變　breaking strain
断裂应力／破裂應力，折屈應力，破斷應力　fracture stress, crippling stress
断裂准则／破裂準則　fracture criterion
断路器／[電路]斷電器　circuit-breaker
断面渐变段／斷面漸變區，橫切面過渡區　transition zone of cross section
断面收缩率／斷[裂]面縮率　reduction of area
断面水平测量／斷面水準測量　section leveling
断面缩减／斷面縮減　contraction of area
断面形状系数／斷面形狀係數　coefficient of sectional form
断桥铝门窗／斷橋鋁門窗　bridge-cut aluminum alloy door and window
断圈嵌环／斷圈嵌環　split thimble
断头路／斷頭路　end breaking road, dead end highway
断续海岸／斷續海岸　broken coast
断续焊／斷續焊法　intermittent welding
断续焊缝／斷續焊縫　intermittent weld
锻锤／鍛錘　forging hammer
锻钢／鍛鋼　forged steel
锻工／控錘工　hammerman
锻工车间／鍛工場　forging shop
锻接／鍛接　forge weld, forging welding, smith welding
锻铝合金／鍛造鋁合金　forging aluminium alloy
锻压车间／鍛壓工場　forging and pressing shop
锻造／鍛造　forging, smithing
锻造比／鍛造比　forging ratio
锻造车间／鍛工場　forging shop
锻造合金／鍛用合金　forging alloy
锻造型曲轴／鍛造曲柄軸　forged type crankshaft
堆场／儲存場　storage yard
堆垛／堆垛　stacking up
堆垛机／堆積機　stacker
堆垛机械／堆垛機械　stowing machinery
堆放／堆積　piling up
堆肥／堆肥　composting, farmyard manure
堆焊／堆焊[接]　build up welding, surfacing
堆货场／堆貨場，堆料場　stock yard, storage yard
堆货荷载／貨載　cargo load
堆积／堆積　accumulation
堆积冰／圓丘冰　hummocked ice
堆积土／堆積土壤　accumulation soil
堆积锥／承接錐　stacking cone
堆料台／堆料臺　roadside material terrace
堆码／裝載　stowage
堆码件／堆積裝具　stacking fitting
堆码能力／堆碼能力　stacking capability
堆码作业／堆碼作業　stacking operation
堆砌圬工／堆砌圬工　uncoursed masonry
堆热功率／反應器熱功率　heat output of reactor
堆石／堆石，填石　fill rock, stone terracing
堆石排水沟／積石排水溝　rubble drain
堆芯／索芯　core
堆装货物／貨櫃貨運　stack-loading freight
堆装试验／堆積試驗　stacking test
队列／編隊　formation
队列方位／編隊方位　formation bearing
队列角／編隊角　formation angle
队列线／編隊線　formation line
队列轴／編隊軸　formation axis
队形变换／隊形變換　changing formation
队形标志灯箱／信號箱　station marker light box
队形长度／隊形長度　length of formation
队形灯／隊形燈　station light
队形宽度／隊形寬度　width of formation
对比度／對比率，反差比　contrast ratio
对比色／對比色　contrast color
对比色突出／對比色突出　contrast colors accent
对称半控桥式整流器／對稱半控橋整流器　symmetric half-controlled bridge rectifier
对称电缆／對稱電纜　symmetrical cable
对称电缆通信／對稱電纜載波通信　symmetrical cable communication
对称灌水／平衡泛水　counter flood
对称进水／對稱浸水　cross flood, symmetrical flooding
对称浸水／對稱浸水　cross flood, symmetrical flooding
对称配光型灯具／對稱配光型照明器具

symmetrical luminaire
对称平衡/對稱平衡 symmetrical balance
对等原则/互惠原则 principle of reciprocity
对地电压/對地電壓 voltage to ground
对地观测卫星/地球觀測衛星 earth observation satellite
对地静止卫星/地球同步衛星,地球静止衛星 geostationary satellite
对地闪击/對地閃擊 lightning flash to ground
对第三者负责的保险/責任保險 liability insurance
对动活塞式内燃机/對衝活塞引擎 opposed-piston engine
对缝焊管/叠缝焊管 butt-welded tube
对活塞式柴油机/對置活塞柴油機 opposed-piston type diesel engine
对讲电话机/電話對講機 intercommunication telephone set
对角撑/對角拉條 diagonal brace
对接舱/對接艙 docking module
对接焊/對接焊接 butt welding
对接接头/對接接頭,半寬接頭 halved joint, butt connection
对接框/對接框 interface frame, mating frame
对接式伸缩装置/對接式伸縮裝置 butt type expansion installation
对景/對景 opposite scenery, view in opposite place
对景图/視圖 view
对开船体/開體船 split hull
对开耙吸挖泥船/對開式耙吸船 splittrail, split-type trailing suction dredger
对空气象广播/飛行氣象資料廣播 VOLMET broadcast
对空潜望镜/對空潛望鏡 altiperiscope
对零表/對零表 alignment zero instrument
对流/對流 convection
对流层/對流層 troposphere
对流层顶/對流層頂 tropopause
对流层折射改正/對流層折射修正 tropospheric refraction correction
对流层折射校正/對流層折射修正 tropospheric refraction correction
对流的/對流的 convective
对流过程/對流程序 convective process
对流换热系数/對流熱傳遞係數 convective heat transfer coefficient
对流冷却/對流冷卻 convective cooling
对流运输/對流運輸,逆流運輸 counter flow transport, cross-haul traffic

对数频率扫描率/對數頻率掃描速率 logarithmic frequency sweep rate
对数增长期/對數式生長期 period of logarithmic growth
对数周期天线/對數週期天線 log-periodic antenna
对水移动/對水移動 making way through water
对拖/雙拖 pair trawling, twin trawling
对外交通/對外交通 external traffic
对外交通用地/對外交通用地 land for external transport, intercity transportation land
对向重叠进路/對向重疊進路 route with overlapped section in the opposite direction
对象的否定/對象的否定 negation of a referent
对应水位/對應水位 corresponding water level
对遇/正對 end on
对遇局面/迎艏正遇情況 head-on situation
对照试验/對照試驗 contrast test
对植/對植 opposite planting, coupled planting, symmetry planting
对置/對置 opposed placed
对置活塞式柴油机/對衝活塞柴油機 opposed piston diesel engine
对中定位/對中定位 pad aligning at the central point
对转螺旋桨/對轉螺槳 contra-rotating propellers
对转涡轮/對轉渦輪 counter-rotating turbine
对准/校準 alignment
对准传递/校準傳遞 alignment transfer
对准误差/對準誤差 alignment error, misalignment
吨税/噸稅 tonnage dues
吨位/[額定]噸位 tonnage, rated tonnage
吨位丈量/噸位丈量 tonnage measurement
墩/墩 blocks, drum shaped seat, pier
墩基[础]/墩基礎 pier foundation
墩帽/[橋]墩帽,墩頂 pier cap, pier coping
墩前壅水/墩前壅水 back-water at pier
墩身/墩身,墩牆 pier body, pier shaft
墩式桥台/墩式橋臺 abutment
墩台防撞/墩臺防撞 collision prevention around pier, pier protection against collision
墩台基础挖验/墩臺基礎挖驗 excavating foundation for checking purpose, foundation examination by excavation
墩台基础钻探/墩臺基礎鑽探 drilling foundation for checking purpose, foundation examination by drilling
墩周冲淤/橋墩沖淤 scouring and depositing around pier

墩柱/墩柱　pier stud
镦粗/鐓鍛,鍛粗　upsetting
镦头锚/鐓頭錨,圓頭錨座　bulb-end anchorage, button head anchorage
蹲配/蹲配　side stones
蹲式便器/蹲式便器　eastern type toilet, squat-across type water closet
逛船/躉船　pontoon
钝边/鈍邊　root face
钝化[作用]/鈍化,降低活性　passivation, deactivation
钝角辙叉/鈍角轍叉　obtuse frog
盾构/[隧道]盾構　tunnel shield, shield
盾构法/盾構法,潛盾工法　shield method
盾构法掘进隧道/盾式開鑿法　shield tunneling
盾构掘进机/盾構掘進機　shield tunnelling machine
盾构切口环/盾構切削環　cutting ring of shield
盾构支承环/盾構支持環　supporting ring of shield
多倍体育种/多倍體育種法　polyploid breeding
多波束测深系统/多波束測深系統　multi-beam sounding system
多层仓库/多層倉庫　multi-story warehouse
多层厂房/多層工業廠房　multi-story workshop, multistory industrial building
多层车站/多層車站　multiple-deck station, multiple-level station
多层次交叉口/多層式交口　multi-level intersection
多层澄清池/多層式澄清池　multiple-tray clarifier
多层叠合结构/夾層結構　sandwich structure
多层隔热材料/多層熱絕緣材料　multi-layer insulation material
多层焊/多層焊接　multi-layer welding
多层建筑/多層建築,多層房屋　multi-story building
多层立交/多層立交　multi-level interchange
多层[立体]交叉口/多層式交叉　multi-bridge intersection
多层施工/多層昇建　multiple-lift construction
多层式进水口/多層式進水口　multi-level intake
多层栈桥/多層棧橋　multiple-deck trestle
多层住宅/多層住宅　multi-story house
多车道/多車道　multiple lanes, multi-lane
多车道道路/多線道路　multi-lane road
多乘员车辆车道/高乘載車道　high occupancy vehicle lane
多重故障/多重故障　multiple fault
多重回声/多重回聲　multiple echo
多重决策程序/多重決策程式　multiple-decision process
多重识别控制/多重識別控制　multi-identification control
多船避碰/多船避碰　multi-ship collision avoidance
多磁铁系统/多磁鐵系統　multimagnet system
多次冲击防护屏/多次衝擊遮罩　multi-shock shield
多次反射回波/多次反射回波　multiple reflection echo
多次磨耗车轮/多次磨耗車輪　multiple wear wheel
多次碰撞/多重碰撞　multiple collision
多次起动火箭发动机/多次起動火箭發動機　multi-start rocket engine, multi-start rocket
多弹头遥测/多頭遙測　multi-head telemetry
多道抗震设防/多道抗震設防　multi-defense system of seismic resistance
多点激振系统/多點振動激發系統　multi-point vibration excitation system
多点连接/多點[式]連接　multi-point connection
多点同步顶推/多點同步頂推　incremental launching construction by multi-point jacking
多点系泊系统/多點繫泊系統　multi-point mooring system
多点约束/多點限制　multi-point constraint
多电流制电力机车/多系統電力機車　multiple system electric locomotive
多电平编码/多級編碼　multi-level encoding
多斗挖掘机/聯斗挖土機,複斗開挖機,複斗挖泥機　multi-bucket excavator
多度/多度　abundance
多度中心/多度中心　abundance center
多段桥[联结]/串接橋　bridges in cascade, multi-rectifier bridge
多分量天平/多分量天平　multi-component balance
多浮筒系泊/多浮筒繫泊　multi-buoy mooring
多浮筒系泊系统/多浮筒繫泊系統　multi-buoy mooring system
多刚体动力学/多剛體動力學　rigid multi-body dynamics
多刚体航天器动力学/多剛體太空載具動力學　dynamics of multiple rigid body spacecraft
多功能传感器/多功能感測器　multi-function transducer
多功能惯性敏感器/多功能慣性感測器　multi-inertial sensor
多功能剧场/多用途劇場　multi-use theater
多功能雷达/多功能雷達　multi-function radar
多功能水平吊具/多功能水平吊索　multi-functional horizontal sling
多功能厅/多功能廳　multi-functional hall

多功能外加剂/多功能外加劑　multi-functional admixture

多功能演播厅/多用途演播室　multi-purpose studio, multi-purpose hall

多功能转椅/多功能轉椅　multi-functional rotating chair

多功能桩架/多功能打樁架　multi-purpose pile frame

多关节结构/關節式結構　articulated structure

多管压力计/多管壓力計　multiple manometer

多管制蒸汽热网/多管制蒸汽熱網　multi-pipe steam heat supply network

多光谱遥感/多光譜遙感　multi-spectral remote sensing

多规合一信息平台/多規合一資訊平臺　multi-regulatory information platform

多户住宅/多户住宅　multi-family house

多滑面滑板/多滑面滑板　multiple bearing type guide

多回路供电/多重電路電力供應　multiple circuit power supply

多机计算机系统/多計算機系統　multi-computer system

多机牵引/多機牽引　multi-locomotive traction

多机牵引无线电通信/多機牽引無線電通信　radio communication for multiple operated locomotive units

多级泵/多級泵　muti-stage pump

多级船闸/多級船閘　multi-chamber lock, lock flight

多级管网系统/多級系統　multi-stage system

多级过滤/多段過濾　multi-stage filtration

多级火箭/多級火箭　multi-stage rocket

多级开伞/多級開傘　multi-stage opening

多级离心泵/多階離心泵　multi-stage centrifugal pump

多级膨胀发动机/複衝程引擎　multiple expansion engine

多级屏障思想/多重障礙觀念　multiple barrier concept

多级闪发/多級閃蒸發　multiple-stage flash evaporation

多级压缩机/多級壓縮機　multi-stage compressor

多级预热给水/多級預熱給水　multi-stage feed heating

多甲板船/多甲板船　multi-decked ship

多浆植物/肉汁植物　succulent plant

多角度交通事故预测法/多工交通事故預測法　multiplex traffic accident prediction method

多结砷化镓太阳电池/多接面砷化鎵太陽電池　multi-junction gallium arsenide solar cell

多结太阳电池/多接面太陽電池　multi-junction solar cell

多进口脉冲转换器/多進口脈波變換器　multi-entry pulse converter

多进口脉冲转换器系统/多進口脈衝變換器系統　multi-entry pulse converter system

多京制/多京制　multi-capital system

多径/多[途]徑　multi-path

多径传播/多[路]徑傳播　multi-path propagation

多径误差/多徑誤差　multi-path error

多局制/多局制　multi-office system

多孔板/多孔板　perforated plate, porous slab

多孔壁/多孔壁　porous wall

多孔材料/多孔物質　porous material

多孔材料喷注器/多孔材料注射器　hard sifter injector

多孔层压材料/多孔積層材料　multi-orifice laminated material

多孔盖板/多孔蓋板　perforated cover plate

多孔混凝土/多孔混凝土　porous concrete

多孔介质/多孔介質　porous medium

多孔排水管/多孔排水管　perforated drain pipe

多孔盘/多孔盤　porous disc

多孔吸声材料/多孔吸音材料　porous absorbing materials

多孔[性]砖/多孔磚,散氣磚　porous brick, perforated brick

多跨建筑物/多跨建築物　multi-bay building

多立克柱式/多利克柱式　Doric order

多联式分体空调机/多聯分體冷氣機　multi-split air conditioning system

多链路/多鏈路,多重連接　multi-link

多路传输数据总线/多工資料匯流排　multiplex data bus

多路复用/多工　multiplex

多路[复用]通信/多路通信,多工通信　multiplex communication

多路交叉[口]/複式交叉　multiway intersection

多路停车控制/多路停車控制　multiway stop control

多路通道排队/多通道排隊　multiple channel queue

多轮压路机/多輪式壓路機　multi-wheel roller

多媒体教室/多媒體[電腦]教室　multimedia classroom

多面临空爆破/多面臨空爆破　open face blasting

多面体投影/多面體投影　polyhedral projection

多模渐变型光纤/多模漸變型光纖　graded index

多模制导/多模導引　multimode guidance
多姆克蜂房接缝/多姆克蜂巢接縫　Domke honeycomb joint
多目标坝/多目標壩　multipurpose dam
多目标测量/多目標量測　multi-target measurement
多目标处理能力/多目標處理能力　multi-target processing ability
多目标跟踪/多目標追蹤　multi-target tracking
多目标规划/多目標規劃　multi-objective planning
多目标水库/多目標水庫　multi-purpose reservoir
多能打桩架/多[功]能打樁架　multiple pile driver tower
多年冻土路基/多年凍土路基　subgrade in permafrost soil zone
多年生植物/多年生植物,宿根植物　perennial plant
多普勒波束锐化/都卜勒敏銳波束　Doppler beam sharpening, DBS
多普勒测速/都卜勒測速　Doppler range rate measurement
多普勒导航系统/都卜勒導航系統　Doppler navigation system
多普勒定位/都卜勒定位　Doppler location
多普勒伏尔/都卜勒特高頻多向導航臺　Doppler VOR, DVOR
多普勒跟踪/都卜勒[頻率]追蹤　Doppler tracking
多普勒计程仪/都卜勒計程儀,都卜勒測程儀　Doppler log
多普勒计数/都卜勒計數　Doppler count
多普勒频移/都卜勒頻移　Doppler shift, Doppler frequency shift
多普勒声呐/都卜勒聲呐　Doppler sonar
多普勒位置信息/都卜勒位置資訊　Doppler position information
多普勒无线电引信/都卜勒無線電引信　Doppler radio fuze
多普勒相移/都卜勒相移　Doppler phase shift
多普勒效应/都卜勒效應　Doppler effect
多谱段扫描仪/多重波譜掃描器　multi-spectral scanner
多式联运/多式聯運　multimodal transportation
多式联运经营人/多式聯運經營人　multimodal transport operator
多式联运提单/多式聯運載貨證券　multimodal transport bill of lading
多视技术/多視技術　multiple-look technique
多室箱梁/多單元箱形梁　multi-cell box girder
多输入多输出/多輸入-多輸出　multiinput-multioutput
多塔斜拉桥/多塔斜張橋　multi-pylon cable stayed bridge
多体船/多[胴]體船　multi-hulled craft, multi-hulled ship
多体控制/多體控制　multi-body control
多体问题/多體問題　multi-body problem
多通道数字记录系统/多通道數字記錄系統　multi-channel digital record system
多推力室液体火箭发动机/多推力室液體火箭發動機　multi-chamber liquid rocket engine
多桅帆船/多桅帆船　barkentine
多卫星链路/多衛星鏈路　multi-satellite link
多线桥/多軌橋　multi-track bridge
多线隧道/多線隧洞　multiple track tunnel
多线铁路/多線鐵路　multiple track railway
多向模锻/多向模鍛　multiple-ram forging, multi-ram forging
多效添加剂/多功能添加劑　multi-purpose additive
多效蒸发/多效蒸發　multiple-effect evaporation
多芯电缆/多芯電纜　multi-core cable
多星共位/多星共位　multi-satillite colocation
多循环液力传动/多循環液壓傳動　multi-circuit hydraulic transmission
多压式汽轮机/多壓渦輪機　multi-pressure turbine
多样性/多樣性　diversity
多样性指数/多樣性指標　diversity index, richness index
多样中心/多樣性中心　diversity center
多叶舵/多葉舵　multi-bladed rudder
多因子试验/複因子試驗　multiple factor experiment
多用浮箱/多功能浮箱　multi-function pontoon
多用户信息插座/多用戶電信插座　multi-user telecom-munication outlet
多用途车/多用途車輛,多用途載具　multi-purpose vehicles, MPV
多用途飞船/多功能太空船　multi-function spacecraft
多用途货船/多用途貨船　general purpose ship, multi-purpose cargo ship, multi-purpose cargo vessel
多用途拖船/多用途拖船　multi-purpose towing ship
多用途渔船/多用途漁船　multi-purpose fishing boat
多用养护车/多用途養護車　multi-use maintenance truck
多余水/過度水,超滲水量　excess water
多余物检查/多餘物質檢查　checking of redundant substance

多余雨量/過度雨量,超滲雨量　excess rainfall
多遇地震/頻繁發生地震　frequently occurred earthquake
多遇地震烈度/多遇地震烈度　intensity of frequently occurred earthquake
多元校准/多元校準　multi-units calibration
多元梁/多元梁　multi element beam
多元论/多元論,多元主義　pluralism
多元探测导引头/多元探測歸航器　multi-detector homing head
多元探测器/多元偵檢器　multi-element detector
多元中心理论/多元中心理論　polycenter theory
多站触发/多站觸發　multi-station triggering
多站交会/多站交叉點　multi-station intersection
多站联用测量系统/多站連接追蹤系統　multi-station joining tracking system
多站制/多站制　multi-station system
多振动台系统/多振動器系統　multi-shaker system
多支承舵/多舵針舵　multi-pintle rudder
多支点半柔壁喷管/多支點半柔壁噴管　half flexible plate nozzle with many hinge point
多支点全柔壁喷管/多支點全柔壁噴管　all flexible plate nozzle with many hinge point
多值性/多值性　ambiguity
多址通信/多接取通信　multiple access communication
多智能体系统/多智慧體系統　multi-agent system
多中心城市体系/多中心都市體系　polycentric urban system
多种流线型翼/多流翼　multiflow wing
多轴车/多軸車　multi-axle car
多轴转向架/多軸式轉向架　multi-axle truck
多专长高级船员/多專長甲級船員　polyvalent officer
多自由度系统/多自由度系統　multi-degree of freedom system
掇山/掇山　piling artificial hill, piled stone hill, hill making
掇山五法/掇山五法　five methods of rock piling
舵/[方向]舵　rudder, vane
舵板/舵板　rudder plate
舵臂/舵臂　rudder arm
舵柄/舵柄　tiller
舵柄连杆/舵柄連桿　tiller tie-bar
舵掣/舵韌,舵制動器　rudder brake
舵承/舵[軸]承　rudder bearing, rudder carrier
舵杆/舵桿　rudder stock
舵杆接头/舵頸接頭　rudder coupling
舵杆扭矩/舵轉矩　rudder torque
舵杆填料函/舵填料函　rudder stuffing box, stuffing box
舵构架/舵肋　rudder frame
舵机/操舵裝置,導片致動器　steering gear, rudder actuator, vane actuator
舵机舱/舵機艙　steering gear room, steering engine room
舵机间/舵機室　steering gear room
舵机追随机构/舵機從動裝置　steering hunting gear
舵角/舵角　helm angle, rudder angle
舵角限位器/舵止器,制舵器　rudder stopper, rudder stop
舵角指示器/舵角指示器　rudder angle indicator, electric rudder angle indicator
舵力/舵力　rudder force
舵链导轮/導滑車　leading block
舵令/舵令　steering order, helm order
舵轮/舵輪　steering wheel
舵面积/舵面積　area of rudder
舵面积比/舵面積比　rudder area ratio
舵钮/舵針承　rudder gudgeon
舵偏角/舵偏角　angle of rudder reflection
舵平衡比/舵平衡面積比　rudder balance area ratio, coefficient of balance of rudder
舵扇/舵柄弧,扇形舵柄　quadrant, rudder quadrant
舵设备/舵裝置　rudder gear, rudder and steering gear
舵头/上部舵桿　rudder head
舵销/舵針　rudder pintle
舵效/舵效　rudder effect
舵压力/舵壓[力]　rudder pressure
舵压力中心/舵[壓]力中心　center of rudder force, center of rudder pressure, rudder pressure center
舵叶/舵葉　rudder blade
舵轴/舵軸　rudder axle
舵轴舵/舵軸兼舵柱型舵　simplex rudder
舵柱/舵柱　rudder post
惰化浓度/惰化濃度　inerting concentration
惰轮/惰輪　idling gear, idler
惰锚/下風錨,不著力錨　lee anchor
惰行泵/惰行泵　idle running pump
惰行阻力/滑行阻力　idle running resistance, coasting resistance
惰性气体/惰性氣體,惰氣　inert gas, IG, rare gas
惰性气体保护[电弧]焊/惰性氣體保護電弧焊,惰氣金屬電弧焊,金屬惰氣電弧焊　inert gas welding, inert gas shielded arc welding

惰性气体发生器/惰氣產生器　inert gas generator
惰性气体鼓风机/惰氣鼓風機　inert gas blower
惰性气体灭火系统/惰性氣體滅火系統　inert gas extinguishing system
惰性气体雾化粉末/惰性氣體霧化粉末　inert gas atomized powder
惰性气体系统/惰性氣體系統　inert gas system, IGS
惰性气体增压系统/惰性氣體加壓系統　inert gas pressurization system
惰性气体窒息灭火系统/惰氣窒火系統　inert gas smothering system
惰转时间/空轉時間　idle time

E

阿房宫/阿房宫　E-Pang Palace
鹅颈槽/鵝頸槽　goose neck tunnel
额定电流/額定電流　rated current
额定电压/額定電壓,正常電壓　rated voltage, normal voltage
额定负载/額定負載　rated load, nominal load
额定工作条件/額定操作條件　rated operating condition
额定光力射程/公稱光程　nominal range
额定流量/額定流量　rated flow
额定起重量/額定載量　rated load weight
额定热负荷/額定熱負荷　rated heat input, rated heat load
额定容量/額定容量　rated capacity
额定输出/額定出力,標定出量　rated output
额定[输出]功率/額定功率　rated output, rated power
额定推力/額定推力　rated thrust, nominal thrust
额定蒸汽温度/額定蒸汽溫度　rated steam temperature
额定蒸汽压力/額定蒸汽壓力　rated steam pressure
额定值/額定值　rated value
额定状态/額定狀態　normal rating
额[枋]/額枋,簷飾綿腳　architrave
扼流变压器/阻抗變換器　impedance transformer
扼流圈/阻流圈,抗流圈　choke
轭架/軛架　yoke
轭式天平/軛鐵天平　yoke balance
恶臭货/惡臭貨　malodorous cargo
恶劣天气/惡劣氣候　heavy weather
颚式碎石机/顎式壓碎機　jaw crusher
恩氏黏度/恩氏黏度,恩格勒黏度　Engler viscosity
儿科预检处/兒科預檢處　pre-examination of paediatric
儿童福利院/兒童福利院　children welfare home, children welfare institute
儿童公园/兒童公園　children park
儿童活动区/兒童活動區　children playing space
儿童乐园/兒童樂園　children paradise
儿童游乐场/兒童遊樂場所,兒童遊戲場　children playground
儿童游乐设施/兒童文娛設備　children play equipment
儿童游戏场地设计/兒童遊戲設計　space design on children game
儿童游戏群体/兒童遊戲群體　play group of children
儿童展厅/兒童展覽館　children exhibition hall
耳房/耳房　side room
耳光室/耳光室　side light room
耳机/耳機　earphone
耳间[听觉]互相关函数/雙耳互相關函數　interaural cross correlation function, IACC function
耳墙/懸臂耳牆　cantilevered wing wall
耳墙式洞门/耳牆式隧道洞門　ear wall tunnel portal
耳墙式桥台/耳牆式橋臺　abutment with cantilevered retaining wall
耳台/耳臺　caliper side stage
二层甲板/中甲板　tween deck
二车/二管輪　second engineer
二冲程柴油机/二衝程柴油機　two-stroke diesel engine
二冲程发动机/二衝程引擎　two-cycle engine, two-stroke engine
二冲程循环/二衝程循環　two-stroke cycle
二次泵冷水系统/二次泵冷水系統　primary-secondary pumps
二次表面镜/第二表面鏡,次面鏡　second surface mirror
二次参数/二次參數,次線線圈參數,副邊參數　secondary parameter
二次场/二次場　secondary field
二次衬砌/二次襯砌　secondary lining
二次电源/二次電源　secondary electrical power source
二次辐射/二次輻射　re-radiation
二次监视雷达/二級監視雷達,次級搜索雷達　secondary surveillance radar, SSR
二次胶接/二次膠合　second bonding
二次空气/二次空氣　secondary air
二次力矩补偿器/二次力矩補償器　the second order moment compensator

二次流损失/二次流損耗　secondary flow loss
二次能源/次級能量　secondary energy
二次能源系统/二次能源系統　secondary power system
二次辗压/二次輾壓　second rolling
二次配电系统/二次配電系統　secondary distribution system
二次喷射/二次噴射　secondary injection
二次碰撞/二次碰撞　secondary collision
二次屏障/次防壁　secondary barrier
二次群/次級團體　secondary group
二次水/外來水,次生水　secondary water
二次损伤/二次損壞　secondary damage
二次污泥/二次下水污泥　secondary sludge
二次污染/二次汙染,二級汙染,次級汙染　secondary pollution
二次污染物/二級汙染物,次級汙染物　secondary pollution
二次相位因子/二次相位因子　secondary phase factor, SPF
二次行程回波/二次回波　second-trace echo
二次压缩/二次壓縮　secondary compression
二次蒸发箱/瞬間蒸發槽　flash tank
二次蒸汽/二次蒸汽　flash steam
二次撞击/次要衝擊　secondary impact
二等三角测量/二等三角測量　second order triangulation
二等三角点/二等三角點　secondary triangulation station
二等水平标点/二等水平標點　second order bench mark
二等水准测量/二等水準測量　second order leveling
二等作图仪/二等作圖儀　second order plotting instrument
二点透视/二點透視　two-point perspective
二分点功率预算/二分點功率預算　power budget during equinox
二副/二副　second officer, second mate
二股流/二股流,次氣流　secondary air
二管轮/三管輪　third engineer
二灰[混合料]/石灰飛灰　lime flyash
二回路/二次回路,副電路,二次電路　secondary circuit
二级保护区/二級保護區　the second class preservation district
二级泵/次級泵　secondary pump
二级标准太阳电池/二級標準太陽電池　secondary standard solar cell
二级沉淀池/二級沈澱池　secondary sedimentation basin
二级处理/二級處理　secondary treatment
二级粉碎机/覆軋碎石機　secondary crusher
二级腐化/二段消化　two stage digestion
二级公路/二級公路　second-class highway
二级轻气炮/二級輕氣炮　two-stage light gas gun
二级水手/普通水手　ordinary seaman, OS
二级无线电电子证书/第二級無線電電子員證書　second-class radio electronic certificate
二级增压/二級增壓　two-stage supercharging
二级注册建筑师/二級註册建築師　grade 2 registered architect
二铰拱桥/二鉸拱橋　two hinged arch bridge
二阶段设计/兩階段設計　two-stage design
二阶理论/二階理論　second order theory
二进制编码/二進制編碼　binary encoding
二力构件/二力構件　two-force member
二列冲动叶轮/雙排衝動葉輪　two-row impulse wheel
二年生植物/二年生植物　biennial plant
二三压力混合机构/二三壓力混合機構　composite two and three-pressure equalizing system
二时更/暮更　dog watch
二手房市场/二手樓市　secondary housing market
二体问题/二體問題　two-body problem
二桅帆船/雙桅帆船　brig, brigantine, schooner
二维弹翼/二維翼　two dimensional wing
二维弹翼试验/二維機翼試驗　two dimensional wing test
二维风洞/二維風洞　two dimensional wind tunnel, two dimensional wind tunnel
二维流/二維流動　two dimensional flow
二维喷管/二維噴嘴　two dimensional nozzle
二维碰撞/二維衝撞　two dimension collision
二位侧/二位側　right side of car
二位端/二位端　A end of car
二位三通换向阀/二位三通方向控制閥　two-position three way directional control valve
二显示自动闭塞/二顯示自動閉塞　two-aspect automatic block
二线扬声/雙線揚聲　two wire loudspeaking
二压力机构/二壓力機構　two-pressure equalizing system
二氧化硫污染/二氧化硫汙染　SO_2 pollution, sulfur dioxide pollution
二氧化氯/二氧化氯　chlorine dioxide
二氧化碳发生器/二氧化碳發生器　CO_2 generator

二氧化碳分压控制／二氧化碳分壓控制　carbon dioxide partial pressure control
二氧化碳还原技术／二氧化碳減少技術　carbon dioxide reduction technique
二氧化碳灭火器／二氧化碳滅火器　carbon dioxide fire extinguisher
二氧化碳浓缩器／二氧化碳濃縮器　carbon dioxide concentrator
二氧化碳气体保护[电弧]焊／二氧化碳氣體保護焊　carbon dioxide gas shielded arc welding
二氧化碳清除／二氧化碳移除　carbon dioxide removal
二氧化碳收集／二氧化碳收集　carbon dioxide collection
二元脉冲电路／二元脈動電路　binary pulse circuit
二元脉冲调宽电路／二元脈衝寬度變調電路　binary pulse width modulation circuit
二至点功率预算／二至點功率預算　power budget during solstice
二轴车／兩軸車　two-axle car
二轴转向架／雙軸轉向架　two-axle truck
二自由度陀螺仪／二自由度迴轉儀　two-degree of freedom gyroscope

F

发包／發包　project offer
发报局／發報局　office of origin
发报台／發信臺　station of origin
发车表示器／發車表示器　departure indicator
发车表示器电路／發車指示電路　departure indicator circuit
发车进路／發車進路　departure route
发车进路信号／發車進路號誌　route signal for departure
发车线路表示器／發車線表示器　departure track indicator
发车信号／出車號誌　departure signal
发车正点率／發車正點率　rate of on time departure
发出／發出　forward
发电／發電　power generation
发电厂／[發]電廠　electric station, power plant
发电厂出电量／電廠出電量　station output
发电厂房／發電廠房　power house
发电厂容量／電廠容量　station capacity
发电车／發電車　generator car
发电轨道车／發電軌道車　power generating rail car
发电机／發電機　generator
发电机电动机系统／列氏電動操作系統　generator-motor system, Ward-Leonard system
发电机房／發電機室　generator room
发电机[控制]屏／發電機控制屏　generator control panel
发电机励磁系统／發電機激磁系統　generator excited system
发电机流速计／發電機式流速計　generator-type current meter
发电机组／發電機組　generating set
发电量／發電量　generated energy
发电室／發電室　power plant compartment
发电用内燃机／發電機引擎　dynamo engine, genset engine
发电站／[發]電廠　electric station, power plant
发电走行两用车／發電自走式車　self-propelled power generating car
发动机比冲／引擎比衝　engine specific impulse, motor specific impulse
发动机舱／引擎室　engine compartment
发动机舱测试工作梯／機艙工作梯　engine compartment checking ladder
发动机初始质量／發動機初始質量　motor initial mass
发动机大修／引擎再製，引擎再造　engine rebuilding, engine remanufacture
发动机反推力／發動機反向推力　engine reverse thrust
发动机飞行试验台／發動機飛行測試臺　engine flight test bed
发动机负推力／發動機負向推力　engine negative thrust
发动机干质／發動機淨重　engine dry mass
发动机高度特性／發動機高度特性　engine altitude characteristic
发动机高空仿真试验／發動機高空模擬試驗　engine test in simulated altitude condition
发动机高空模拟试车台／發動機高空模擬試驗設施　engine high altitude simulated test facility
发动机工作时间／發動機工作時間　engine operating duration, motor action time
发动机关机／發動機熄火　engine cutoff
发动机关机减速性／發動機關機減速性　slow-down time of engine during shutdown transient
发动机管路特性／發動機管路特性　engine line characteristic
发动机混合比／發動機混合比　engine mixture ratio
发动机加速性／發動機加速[性]　engine acceleration performance
[发动机]检修／調準　tune up
发动机减速性／發動機減速性　engine deceleration performance
发动机校准试验／發動機校驗測試　engine calibration test
发动机节流特性／發動機節流特性　engine throttle characteristic
发动机结构完整性大纲／發動機結構整體計劃　engine structure integrity program
发动机结构质量／發動機結構質量　motor structure mass

发动机可靠性/發動機可靠度　engine reliability
发动机可靠性试验/發動機可靠度試驗　engine reliability test
[发动机]累积工作时间/發動機累積工作時間　accumulated duration of engine
发动机六分力试验/發動機六分力試驗　motor six component test
发动机喷管/發動機噴嘴　engine nozzle
[发动机]喷管压力损失/[發動機]噴管壓力損失　nozzle pressure loss
发动机起动/發動機起動　engine starting
发动机起动加速性/發動機起動加速　acceleration time of engine during start transient
发动机清洗机/發動機清洗器,發動機清潔器　engine cleaner
发动机燃尽质量/發動機燃畢質量　motor burnout mass
发动机湿质/發動機濕重　engine wet mass
发动机试车台/發動機測試臺　engine test bed, engine test stand
发动机试验/發動機測試,引擎試驗　engine test
发动机适用性/發動機操作性　engine operability
发动机推力/引擎推力　engine thrust
发动机[推力]架/發動機固定隔框　engine thrust frame
发动机推质比/發動機推力質量比　engine thrust-mass ratio
[发动机]稳定性裕度/發動機安全度　engine stability margin
发动机显示器/發動機顯示器　engine display
发动机性能/發動機性能　engine performance
发动机性能参数/發動機性能參數　engine performance parameter
发动机性能试验/引擎性能試驗　engine performance test
发动机旋转试验/發動機旋轉試驗　motor rotating test
发动机引气系统/發動機供氣系統　engine bleed air system
发动机噪声/發動機雜音　motor noise
发动机诊断仪/發動機分析器　engine analyzer
发动机振动监视系统/發動機振動監視系統　engine vibration monitoring system
发动机质量比/發動機質量分數　motor mass fraction
发动机最大负推力/發動機最大負向推力　engine maximum negative thrust
发光标志/發光標誌　luminous sign

发光顶棚照明/發光頂板照明　luminous ceiling lighting
发光二极管/發光二極體　light emitting diode, LED
发光二极管视频显示屏/發光二極體視訊顯示屏　light emitting diode video display screen, LED video display screen
发光二极管显示屏最大亮度/發光二極體顯示屏最大光度　maximum luminance of light emitting diode screen
发光二极管像素失控率/像素失控率　ratio of out-of-control pixel
发光强度/發光強度　luminous intensity
发光铁道图/明亮軌道展示板　illuminated track diagram
发光效率/發光效率　luminous efficiency
发汗材料/發汗材料　sweat-out material
发黑处理/發黑處理,黑變　blackening
发火顺序/點火順序　firing order
发火性能/點火性　ignition quality
发货区/發貨區　despatch area, delivery area
发货人/發貨人,裝貨人　shipper, consignor
发卡机/發卡機　card sender
发蓝处理/發藍處理　bluing
发码器/發碼器　code sender
发泡/發泡　foaming
发泡剂/發泡劑　foamed agent, foaming agent
PVC发泡木塑/PVC發泡塑膠　PVC foamed plastics
发泡玻璃/發泡玻璃,泡沫玻璃　foamed glass, cellular glass
发泡塑料/有孔塑膠　expanded plastic
发气率/發氣率　rate of gas generation
发热电缆地面辐射供暖/發熱電纜地面輻射供暖　heating cable floor radiant heating
发热量/熱值　heating value
发散冷却/蒸散冷卻,蒸發冷卻　transpiration cooling
发散冷却材料/散發冷卻材料　transpiration cooling material
发散摄影/發散攝影　divergent photographing
发射/發射　emission, launch
发射本领/發射能力　emission capability
发射波谱特征/發射光譜特性　feature of emission spectrum
发射操作队/發射操作隊　launch operating team
发射场/發射場　launch site
[发射场]测试测控数据网/[發射場]測試測控資料網　prelaunching checkout and control data network of launch site
发射场电视监视系统/發射場地電視監控系統

发射场电视监视系统/發射場電視監視系統 launch site television monitor system
发射场故障率/發射場故障率 site fault rate
发射场坪/發射平地 launching level ground
发射场设备更换率/發射場設備更換率 site equipment change rate
发射成功率/發射成功率 launching success rate
发射窗口/發射窗 launch window
发射窗口后沿/發射窗後沿 launch window ending
发射窗口前沿/發射窗前沿 launch window beginning
发射点/發射點 launch point
发射方式/發射方式 launch mode
发射方位[角]/發射方位角 launch azimuth
发射方向/發射方向 launching direction
发射工位/發射工作場所 launching workplace
发射工作队/發射工作隊 launch working team, test group
发射光谱分析/發射光譜分析 emission spectrum analysis
发射轨道/發射軌道 launching trajectory
发射后不管空空导弹/發射後不理空對空飛彈 fire and forget air-to-air missile
发射环境/發射環境 launch environment
发射机/發射機 transmitter
发射计划网络图/發射計劃線路圖 launch plan network chart
发射静止搜救卫星无效报警/發射無效之定置搜救衛星警報 GEOSAR invalid alert transmitted
发射距离/發射距離 launch distance
发射可靠度/發射可靠度 launching reliability
发射控制中心/發射管制中心 launching and control center
发射类别/發射等級 class of emission
发射领导组/發射領導組 launch leading team
发射率/放射率 emissivity
发射频谱/發射光譜 emission spectrum
发射前测试/發射前測試 prelaunch testing
发射勤务保障/發射勤務保障 launching service support
发射勤务塔/發射勤務塔 launching service tower
发射区/發射地區 launch area
发射任务书/發射任務指派檔 mission document
发射任务指挥部/發射任務指揮部 launch mission headquarter
发射日/發射日 launch day
发射时/發射時間 launching time
发射试验/發射試驗 launching test
发射试验大纲/發射試驗大綱 launch experiment outline
发射释放机构/發射釋放機構 launch release mechanism
发射塔/發射塔 launch tower
发射台/發射臺 launch pad
发射台导轨/發射臺軌道 launch pad rail
发射台调平机构/發射臺水平機構 launching pad leveling mechanism
发射台折倒臂/發射臺轉運 launch pad transportation
发射台支承盘/發射臺方位盤 bearing plate for launching pad
发射台支架/發射臺支架 launch pad support
发射台转轨装置/發射臺轉軌裝置 change-over rail mechanism for launch pad
发射逃逸/發射逃生 launch escape
发射逃逸分系统/發射逃生分系統 launch escape subsystem
发射天线/發射天線 transmitting antenna
发射条件/發射條件 launching condition
发射演练/發射操演 launch drill
发射预案/發射預案 launch reserve scheme
发射月/發射月 launch month
发射载荷/發射負載 launch load
发射指挥控制中心/發射指揮管制中心 launch command and control center
发射诸元/發射資料 launch data
发射准备时间/發射準備時間 launch preparation time
发射综合设施/發射區設施 launch complex
发射坐标系/發射坐標系 launching coordinate system
发生炉煤气/發生爐煤氣 producer gas
发生土壤学/發生土壤學 pedology
发送路/發送路 originating railway
发送信道/發報通路 transmit channel
发现概率/檢測機率 detection probability
发信放大器/發信放大器 transmitting amplifier
发信台识别符/發射臺識別符 transmitter identification character
发芽力/發芽力 germination capacity
发芽率/發芽速度, 發芽勢 germination rate
发运/發運 pre departure operation
发展计划/個案發展計劃 development project
发展建议/發展建議 development proposal
发展控制区/發展控制區 development control area
发展轴带/發展軸 development axis
乏力/乏力, 缺乏動力 lack of power

乏汽轮机/排蒸汽渦輪機　exhaust steam turbine
乏汽喷口/廢汽噴嘴　exhaust nozzle
乏汽喷口座/排氣噴嘴座　exhaust nozzle seat
伐木机/伐木機　treedozer
阀动图/閥動圖,祝納氏汽閥圖　valve diagram, Zeuner valve diagram
阀动椭圆图/閥橢圓　valve ellipse
阀杆导承/閥桿導件　valve spindle guide
阀[门]/閥[門],活門,氣門　valve
阀门响应/閥[門]響應　valve response
阀面研磨/閥面研磨　valve lapping
阀式轨道电路/閥式軌道電路　valve type track circuit
阀调整/閥定位　valve setting
阀箱/閥箱,歧管閥,閥櫃　manifold valve, valve chest
阀行程/閥行程　valve travel
阀型避雷器/閥阻式避雷器　valve type arrester
阀装置/閥動裝置,閥動機構　valve gear
筏/筏　raft
筏道/流木道　raftpath, raftway
筏式基础/筏式基礎　raft foundation
筏形基础/筏式基礎　raft foundation
GM法/GM法　Guyon Massonet method
法定测量单位/法定量測單位　legal unit of measurement
法定规划/法定計劃　statutory plan
法定检验/法定檢驗　statutory survey
法定时/法定時　legal time
法尔奈斯庄园/法爾奈斯莊園　Villa Palazina Farnese
法官室/法官室　judge suite
法国船级社/法國驗船協會　Bureau Veritas, BV
法国古典主义建筑/法國古典主義建築　French classical architecture
法国文物建筑保护学派/法國文物建築保護學派　French school of built heritage conservation
法兰键槽/凸緣上之槽孔　slot in flange
法兰连接/凸緣接合　flange joint
法兰西式园林/法蘭西式園林　French style garden
法人组织/法人　incorporation
法向导引/法向導引　normal steering
法向力/法向力,垂直力　normal force
法向应变/法向應變,正向應變　normal strain
法向应力/法向應力,正應力,垂直應力　normal stress
法向轴/垂直軸　normal axis
法院/法院　court house
法院地法/法院地法,審判地法　lex fori
法制计量[学]/法定計量學　legal metrology
发裂/髮裂　hair like crack
发裂纹/[毛]細裂痕　hair crack
发针形曲线/U型曲線　hairpin curve
帆板运动/風帆衝浪運動　windsurfing
帆布/帆布　canvas
帆船/帆船　sailer, sailing boat, sailing ship
帆船码头/遊艇港　yacht harbor
帆船运动/帆船運動　sailing
帆拱/帆拱　pendentive
帆脚杆/帆桁　boom
帆缆间/帆纜庫,索具庫　deck store, hawser store, boatswain store
帆缆箱/帆纜箱　boatswain chest
帆缆作业/帆纜作業　canvas and rope work
帆下角/縱帆踵,吊鋪攀　clew
帆缘索/帆[帳]緣索　bolt rope
翻板/翻板　platform trap door
翻板阀/回流閥,止逆流閥　flap valve
翻车机/傾卸裝置　tipper, tipping plant, dumper
翻地犁/翻地犁　uncovering plough
翻斗铲/翻鏟裝載機　rocker shovel
翻斗车/小型翻斗車,傾倒車　small dumper, tipper, tipover car
翻斗轨道/礦兜導軌　skip track
翻斗卡车/傾卸用無邊車　tipping lorry
翻滚试验/翻滾試驗　tumbling test
翻浆/翻漿　frost boiling
翻浆冒泥/噴泥　mud-pumping
翻修/翻修,檢修,大修　overhaul
翻修路面/軌道重整,路面重鋪　resurfacing
翻修寿命/翻修間時　time between overhauls
凡尔赛宫苑/凡爾賽宮苑　Versailles Palace Park
繁华市区/市中心地區　downtown area
繁殖场/繁殖場　breeding ground, nursery ground
繁殖季节/繁殖期　breeding season
繁殖温室/繁殖溫室　plant propagation greenhouse
反差系数γ/反差係數γ　contrast coefficient γ
反铲挖掘机/反鏟挖掘機,拖鏟機　backhoe excavator, drag shovel
反铲挖土机/反鏟挖土機　backhoe, backacter
反超高/反超高　reverse superelevation, counter superelevation, negative superelevation
反城市主义/反都市主義　anti-urbanism
反充电/反向充電　reverse charge
反垂曲线形拱/垂曲線拱　catenary arch
反磁力系统/反磁性系統　anti-magnetic system

反定位／反定位　push-off mode
反动度／反動度　degree of reaction
反动级／反應級　reaction stage
反动式汽轮机／反動式汽輪機,反動式渦輪機　reaction turbine, reaction steam turbine
反舵角／反舵角　counter rudder angle
反复振动／反復振動　reversal vibration
反复作用／反復動作　reversed cyclic action
反光标识／反光標識　reflecting marking
反光标志／反光標誌　reflecting sign
反光材料／反光材料　retro-reflective material
反光路钮／反光路鈕,反光標鈕　reflecting button, reflector button
反滚转力矩／反向滾轉力矩　anti-rolling moment
反击式破碎机／衝擊碎石機　impact crusher
反击式水轮机／反動式水渦輪　reaction hydraulic turbine
反季节施工／反季節施工　anti-season construction
反桨／螺旋槳反槳　propeller reversing
反接制动／逆流制動　counter-current braking
反馈／反饋　feedback
反馈重发纠错／反饋重發糾錯　error correction by feed-back repetition
反馈式速率陀螺仪／反饋式速率陀螺儀　feedback type rate gyro
反馈系统／反饋系統　feedback system
反雷达涂层／反雷達塗裝　anti-radar coating, radar absorb painting
反力式制动试验台／反擊式刹車試驗器,反動式刹車試驗器　reaction type brake tester
反力涡轮／反動式渦輪　reaction turbine
反流／逆向流動　reverse flow
反流区／逆流區　reversed flow region
反滤层／反濾層,反向濾池,倒濾層　inverted filter, reverse filtration layer, protective filter
反码副帧同步／逆代碼副幀同步　inverse code subframe synchronization
反扭导流片／防扭風板　anti-twist vane
反跑道炸弹／反跑道炸彈　antirunway bomb
反配重／反配重　counter-balancing weight
反气旋／反氣旋　anticyclone
反潜机／反潛機　anti submarine warfare airplane
反潜控制／反潛作戰　anti submarine warfare control
反曲线接点／反曲線接點　point of reverse curve
反射／反射　reflection
反射波谱特征／反射光譜特性　reflectance spectral feature
反射法地震勘探／地震波反射法　seismic reflection method
反射跟踪／雷達追蹤,表皮追蹤　skin tracking
反射光束采光／反射光束採光　reflective beam daylighting
反射红外／反射紅外　reflective infrared
反射计法／反射計法　reflectometer method
反射裂缝／反射裂紋　reflection crack
反射炉／反射爐　reverberatory furnace
反射罗经／反射羅經　reflector compass
反射率／反射率　reflectivity, reflectance, reflective index
反射面／反射面　reflecting surface
反射平板法／反射樣板法　reflection plate method
反射器／反射器　reflector
反射实体观察镜／反射實體觀察鏡　reflection stereoscope
反射实体镜／反射實體鏡　mirror stereoscope
反射式光学系统／反射式光學系統　reflective optical system
反射水准仪／反光式水準儀　reflecting level
反射特性／反射特性　reflectance characteristic
反射系数／反射係數　reflectance coefficient, reflection coefficient
反射型运行／反射式運行　reflected shock operation
反射因子／反射比因子　reflectance factor
反射直角棱镜装置／反射直角稜鏡裝置　reflection right-angle prism device
反射[总]日辐射／反射[全球]太陽輻射,反射日射　reflected global solar radiation
反渗排水井／逆向排水井　inverted drainage well
反渗透／反滲　osmosis reverse, reverse osmosis
反渗透法／反滲透法,逆滲透法　reverse osmosis method, reverse osmosis process
反渗透海水淡化装置／逆滲透[海水淡化]裝置　reverse osmosis device, reverse osmosis desalination device
反视方向角／反視方向角　reverse direction angle
反台阶法／反臺階法　negative benching tunnelling method
反推火箭／後推火箭　retro-rocket
反推力装置／推力反向器　thrust reverser
反推力状态／反推力工作狀態　thrust reversing rating
反推喷管／後推噴嘴　retro-nozzle
反弯点／反曲點,回折點　inflection point
反位接点／反向觸點　reverse contact
反位锁闭／反位鎖閉　reverse locking
反洗／反洗　backwashing

反向/反向,回动 reverse
反向程序/颠倒程式 reversal procedure
反向传播/反向傳播 reverse propagation
反向反射信号/反射層信號 backscattered signal
反向喷管/反[向]推力噴管 reversal nozzle
反向偏压/反向偏壓 reverse bias
反向器/反向器 reverser
反向曲线/反向曲線 reverse curve, curve of opposite sense
反向信道/反向通道 backward channel
反向行车/反向行車 train running in reverse direction
反向应力/反向應力 reversed stress
反向应力构件/相反應力構材 reversal stress member
反T形材/倒丁字形材 inverted tee
反循环钻机/反循環鑽土機 reverse circulation drill
反循环钻孔法/反循環鑽孔法 reverse circulation boring method
反压护道/反壓護道 loading berm, berm for back pressure, counter swelling berm
反[演]分析/反分析 back analysis
反应/反應 response
反应板/反應板 reaction plate
反应槽/反應槽 reaction tank
反应度/反應程度 degree of reaction
反应堆舱/[核子]反應爐艙 reactor room
反应堆周期/反應器週期 reactor period
反应舵/反動式舵 reaction rudder
反应轨/反應軌 reaction rail
反应结合/反應黏合 reaction bond
反应离子蚀刻/反應性離子蚀刻[法] reactive ion etching
反应离子束蚀刻/反應性離子束蚀刻[法] reactive ion beam etching
反应谱/反應譜 response spectrum
反应谱特征周期/反應譜特徵週期 characteristic period of response spectrum
反应器/反應器 reactor
反应时间/反應時間 reaction time
反应系数/反應因數,響應因數 response factor
反照地球敏感器/反照水平感測器 albedo earth sensor, albedo horizon sensor
反照率/反照率 albedo
反装/反裝 left-handed machine
反[作用]力/反作用力 reaction, reaction force
反作用轮/反作用輪 reaction wheel
反作用轮控制/反作用輪控制 reaction wheel control
返工/返工,重做,再製 rework
返还系数/釋放因數 release factor
返航/返航 homeward voyage, return flight
返回/返回,回行 return
返回舱/可回收艙 recoverable module
返回点/返回點 return point
返回段测控/返回段追蹤、遥測和控制 TT and C of return phase
返回段救生/返回段救生 return phase rescue
返回方式/返回模式 return mode
返回分系统/返回分系統 return subsystem
返回高度/返回高度 return altitude
返回轨道/返回軌跡 return trajectory
返回过程/返回過程 return course
返回技术/返回技術 return technique
返回角/返回角 return angle
返回落点控制/返回落點控制 returning site control
返回器/返回式太空艙 recoverable capsule
返回式航天器/返回式太空船 recoverable spacecraft
返回式卫星/可回收衛星,可恢復衛星 recoverable satellite
返回速度/返回速度 return velocity
返回系统/回路系統 return system
返青水/綠色水 green water
返束光导管摄像机/回訊攝影機 return-beam vidicon camera, RBVC
返洗速率/返洗速率 backwashing rate
返修/返修,回修 repair
返修率/返修頻率 shop visit rate
饭店/飯店 restaurant
泛灌渠/泛濫渠 inundation canal
泛光灯/泛光燈,投射燈 floodlight
泛光照明/泛光照明,探照燈 floodlighting
泛滥/泛濫,暴漲 freshet, inundation
泛滥标/洪水位,高潮位標誌,泛水標誌 flood mark
泛水/遮雨板,衛水板 flashing
泛油/泛油,瀝油 bleeding
范艾伦辐射带/範艾倫帶 Van Allen belt
范德瓦耳斯方程/凡得瓦爾方程式 Van der Waals equation
方案比选/方案比較 scheme comparison, route alternative
方案设计/方案設計,概念設計 conceptual design, schematic design
方便旗/權宜船籍 flag of convenience
方差/方差 variance
方差分析/方差分析,變差分析 analysis of variance

方城明楼/方城明樓　square-walled bastion and memorial shrine
N-S 方程/奈威-斯托克方程式　Navier-Stokes equation
PNS 方程/抛物化奈威-斯托克方程式　parabolized Navier-Stokes equation
方钢/方鋼　square steel
方格投影/正方圆柱投影法　square cylindrical projection
方格形道路网/棋盤式街道系統　checkboard street system
方格形道路系统/方格形道路系統　latticed road system
方块图/方塊圖　block diagram
方龙骨/條龍骨　bar keel
方螺纹/方螺紋　square thread
方镁石/方鎂石　periclase
方木/方木,方材　sawn lumber, squared timber, square timber
方头螺钉/大型螺釘,道釘　coach-screw
方艉/平艉　transom stern
方艉端面/艉橫板,艉橫材　transom
方位/方位　bearing, azimuth, orientation
方位标/方位標　azimuth marker, azimuth reference pole
方位标志/方位標誌,方位標記　cardinal mark, bearing mark
方位单元/方位單元　localizer unit
方位等距投影/方位等距投影　azimuthal equidistant projection
方位定位/交叉方位定位　fixing by cross bearings
方位方向/方位方向　azimuth direction
方位分辨力/方位分析度　bearing resolution
方位分辨率/方位分辨率　azimuth resolution
方位基准/方位參考　azimuth reference
方位角/方位角　azimuth, azimuth angle
方位角差/方位角差　azimuth difference
方位角法/方位角法　azimuth method
方位角数字显示仪/方位角數位顯示儀表　azimuth digital display instrument
方位角误差/方位角誤差　azimuth error
方位距离定位/方位距離定位　fixing by bearing and distance
方位瞄准/方位瞄準　azimuth aiming
方位瞄准精度/方位瞄準精度　accuracy of azimuth aiming
方位模糊/方位模糊　azimuth ambiguity
方位取齐/方位校準　azimuth alignment
方位圈/方位圈　bearing circle
方位锁定/方位鎖定　azimuth caging, azimuth locking
方位投影/方位投影　azimuthal projection
方位投影图/天頂投影圖　zenithal chart
方位陀螺/方位陀螺　azimuth gyro
方位[陀螺]仪/定向迴轉儀　directional gyroscope
方位位置线/方位位置線　position line by bearing
方位线/方位線　bearing line
方位线偏角/方位線偏角　grib bearing
方向标志/方向指示標誌　direction sign
方向岛/導向島　directional island
方向电源/方向電源　directional traffic power source
方向舵/方向舵　rudder, yaw rudder
方向分布/定向分布　direction distribution
方向浮标/方向浮標　direction float
方向角/方向角　direction angle
方向控制阀/方向控制閥　directional control valve
方向滤波器/方向濾波器,分向濾波器　directional filter
方向谱/方向[頻]譜　directional spectrum
方向升降舵/方向昇降舵　rudervator
方向稳定性/方向穩定性　directional stability
方向效应/方向效應　direction effect, orientation effect
方向性照明/指向性照明　directional lighting
方向选择/方向選擇　direction selection
方向预告标志/前置方向標誌　advance direction sign
方向指示器/方向指示器　direction indicator
方向转接器/方向轉接器　directional switch
方形沟槽/方形溝槽　square trench
方形系数/方塊係數　block coefficient
方型镉镍蓄电池/矩形鎳鎘蓄電池　rectangular cadmium-nickel battery
方[型]艉/方型艉　square cut stern
方枕器/方枕器　tie respacer
方正轨枕/方形軌枕　tie respacing, squaring of tie
方正石/規則石　regular stone
方琢石/方石　ashlar
坊巷/坊巷　fang xiang, blocks and lanes
芳香花园/芳香花園　fragrant garden
芳香疗法/芳香療法　aromatherapy
芳香园/芳香園　aroma garden
芳香植物/芳香植物　aromatic plant, aromatic herb, scented plant
枋/枋　joist, fang
防白蚁屏障/防白蟻障壁　anti-termite barrier
防爆/防爆　explosion prevention

防爆安全检查系统/防爆安全檢查系統　security inspection system for anti-explosion
防爆波电缆井/防爆波電纜井　anti-explosion cable pit
防爆波活门/衝擊閥門　blast valve
防爆地漏/防爆地漏　blastproof floor drain
防爆电气设备/防爆電氣設備　explosion-proof electrical equipment
防爆防毒化粪池/防爆防毒化糞池　blastproof and gasproof septic tank
防爆设施/防爆設施　blasting protection facility
防爆式风机/防爆風扇　explosion proof fan
防爆系统/防爆系統　fuel detonation suppressant system
防爆型/防爆型　explosion proof type
防冰表面热载荷/防冰熱負荷　heat load of anti-icing
防冰系统/防冰裝置　anti-icing system
防冰液/防凍液　anti-icing fluid
防冰装置/防冰設備　anti-icing equipment
防波堤/防波堤　breakwater, mole
防波堤口门/堤頭口門　breakwater gap
防擦地角/防擦地角　tip back angle
防拆报警/防拆報警　tamper alarm
防拆装置/防拆功能　tamper device
防潮层/防潮層　damp proofing course
防潮林/防潮林　tidewater protection forest
防潮门/防潮門　tide gate
防潮水泥/防水水泥　hydrophobic cement
防潮堰/防潮堰　tide weir
防尘/防塵[處理]　dust-protected, dust prevention, dust control
防尘板/遮塵板,防塵罩　dust guard
防尘板座/防塵座　dust guard seat
防尘车间/避塵車間　dust proof workshop
防尘设施/防塵設施　dustproof facilities
防冲击波闸门/防衝擊波閘門　defense shock wave gate
防喘系统/防波動系統　surge-preventing system
防串装置/防爬器　anti-creeping device
防吹坪/噴流防護墊　blast pad
防弹玻璃/防彈玻璃　bullet resistant glass
防倒立角/防倒立角　nose over angle
防倒塌棚架/防倒塌棚架　collapse-proof shed
防滴型/防滴型　drip proof type
防地震接头/耐震接頭　earthquake-proof joint
防冻水栓/防凍水栓　unfreezable tap
防冻箱/防凍箱　frostproof closet
防风固沙林/防沙林　wind protection and sand fixation forest, wind break and sand fixation forest
防风减灾规划/風災減輕計畫　wind disaster reducing planning
防风拉杆/防風拉桿　wind-proof pull rod
防风林/防沙林　wind protection forest, wind break forest
防风雨的/耐候　weather-proof
防风栅栏/防風柵　wind-break fence
防辐射混凝土/輻射屏蔽混凝土　radiation shielding concrete
防腐处理/防蝕處理,防腐蝕　anti-corrosion treatment, corrosion proofing, corrosion preventing treatment
防腐剂/防腐劑　preservative, antiseptics
防腐木/防腐[蝕]木　anticorrosive wood
防腐木材/防腐木材　preservative-treated wood
防腐室/防腐室　anticorrosive chamber
防腐锌阳极/鋅陽極防蝕　zinc-anode for protection
防寒/防寒　cold protection
防核生化服/核生化防護服　nuclear biological and chemical protective suit, NBC protective suit
防洪/防洪,洪水控制　flood control, control of flood
防洪坝/防洪壩　flood control dam
防洪保护区/防洪保護區　flood protection area
防洪标准/防洪標準　flood control standard, standard for flood control
防洪等级/防洪等級　grade of flood protection
防洪对象/防洪對象　flood protection object
防洪阀/防洪閥　anti-flood valve
防洪水库/防洪水庫　flood control reservoir
防洪预抢工程/防洪預搶工程　precautionary work against flood
防护/防護　protection
防护变压器/防護變壓器　protective transformer
防护波门/防護門　guard gate
防护层使用年限/防護層使用年限　service life of protective layer
防护单元/防護單元　protective unit
防护道岔/防護道岔　protective turnout
防护堵盖/防護罩　protective cover
防护对象/保護對象　protection object
防护服/防護衣　protective clothing, protective suit
防护工程/防護工程　protection engineering
防护货/防護貨　protecting cargo
防护级别/防護級別　level of protection
防护间距/防護間距　protection distance
防护栏杆/防護欄杆　protection railing
防护冷却水幕/防護冷卻水幕　drencher for cooling

protection
防护林/保安林　protection forest
防护林带/防風林緣,林套　shelter belt
防护率/防護比　protection ratio
防护绿地/防護綠地　green buffer, green area for environmental protection
防护滤波器/防護濾波器　protection filter
防护帽/潛水帽　helmet
防护门/防爆炸門　blast door
防护密闭隔墙/防護密閉隔牆　protective airtight partition wall
防护密闭门/防氣密爆炸門　airtight blast door
防护区/保護區　protection area, protected section
防护热板法/防護熱板法　guarded hot plate method
防护热箱法/防護熱箱法　guarded hot box method
防护头盔/防護頭盔　protective helmet
防护信号/防護信號　protection signal
防护型灯具/保護構造照明器具　protected luminaire
防护音响信号/防護音響信號　protecting acoustic signal
防护栅/安全欄,欄柵　guard fence, safety fence
防护罩/護罩,遮罩,屏護　protective cover, shield
防滑层/防滑層　skid resistant course
防滑处理/防滑動處理　anti-skid treatment
防滑甲板涂料/防滑甲板漆　anti-skid deck paint
防滑路面/防滑路面　skid-proof surface
防滑器/防溜裝置　anti-skid device
防滑刹车系统/防鎖死剎車系統　anti-skid brake system
防滑设施/防滑設施　anti-skid facility
防滑条/防滑條　reeding, non-slip step
防滑鞋/防滑鞋　anti-skid shoe
防晃板/防晃擋板　anti-sloshing baffle
防回流装置/回流防止器,回流防止設施　backflow preventer, backflow prevention device
防回弹装置/反回彈裝置　resilience-proof device
防火/防火　fireproof, firebreak
防火玻璃/防火玻璃　fire resistant glass
防火舱壁/防火艙壁　firewall, fireproof bulkhead, fire proof bulkhead
防火窗/防火窗　fire window
防火分隔水幕/防火分隔水幕　water curtain for fire compartment
防火分区/防火區劃,防火區制　fire compartment, fire-zoning
防火风门/防火擋板　fire damper
防火封堵材料/耐火密封材料　fireproof sealing material
防火隔离带/火障　fire barrier
防火计划/防火計劃　fire scheme
防火间距/防火間距　fire separation distance
防火净距/防火距離　fire protection distance
防火卷帘/防火卷簾　fire resisted shutter
防火控制图/火災控制圖　fire control plan
防火林带/防火林帶　fire protection green belt
防火门/防火門,爐門　fire door, fire protection gate
防火幕/防火幕　fire curtain
防火墙/防火牆　firewall, fire protection wall
防火区/防火[地]區　fire prevention district, fire zone
防火涂料/防火漆　fire-retardant paint
防火网/滅焰器,防焰網　flame arrester, flame screen
防火植物带/防火植物帶　living fire break
防技术开启能力/防技術開啟能力　anti-technical open ability
防渐晕滤光片/校正過濾片　anti-vignetting filter
防溅挡板/防濺板　splash plate
防静电工作区/静電放電保護區　electrostatic discharge protected area, EPA
防静电工作台/防静電工作臺　antistatic control worktable
防静电接地电阻/防静電接地電阻　electrostatic grounding resistance
防静电性/抗静電性　static electricity resistance
防空编队与部署/防空編隊與序列　air defense formation and disposition
防空[措施]/防空　air raid precaution
防空工程/防空工程　air defense works, air defense project
防空专业队工程/防空專業隊工程　air defense contingents project
防空转防滑行保护电路/防空轉防滑行保護電路　anti-slip slide protection circuit
防空转防滑行保护装置/防空轉防滑行保護裝置　anti-slip slide protection device
防空转撒砂电空阀/防空轉撒砂電空閥　anti-slip sanding valve
防浪阀/止浪閥　storm valve
防雷等电位联结/雷電防護等電位聯結　lightning protection equipotential bonding
防雷接地/落雷　lightning grounding
防雷区/防雷區域　lightning protection zone, LPZ
防雷装置/避雷裝備,防雷器　lightning protection system, LPS, lightning protection device
防漏/防漏　leak prevention

防磨损换位/索位掉頭　freshen the nip
防目标重入/防目標重入　anti pass-back
防爬器/防爬器,路軌鎖,軌道錨　anti-creeper, rail anchor
防爬支撑/防爬器支撑　anti-creep strut
防破坏能力/防破壞能力　anti destroyed ability
防倾肘板/防撓肘板　tripping bracket
防倾装置/抗搖裝置　anti-toppling device
防区/防禦區　defense area
防区外发射武器/距外武器　stand-off weapon
防热/隔熱,耐熱,抗熱　heat proof
防热层/防熱板　heat shield
防热结构/防熱結構　thermal protection structure
防热漆/防熱漆　heat-resistant paint
防热涂层/熱防護塗層　thermal protection coating
防沙坝/防沙壩　sand protection dike
防沙堤/攔砂壩,攔砂堤　sediment barrier
防沙设施/防沙設施　sand protection facilities
防砂/防砂　sand-drift control, sand protection
防渗铺盖/不透水鋪層　impervious blanket
防渗墙/不透水牆　impervious wall
防渗心墙/不透水心牆,不透水心壁　impervious core
防生物危害实验室/防生物危害實驗室　anti-biohazard laboratory
防牲畜护栏/防牲畜護欄　cattle fence
防蚀/防蝕　corrosion prevention, corrosion protection
防蚀工程/防蝕工程　erosion control work
防暑降温/防暑降溫　cooling temperature
防鼠板/防鼠板　rat guard, anti-rat plate
防鼠挡/防鼠板,防鼠罩　rat guard
防鼠隔栅/防鼠隔柵　anti-rat grille
防水/防水　waterproofing
防水板/防水紙板　waterproof board, waterproof sheet
防水[薄]膜/防水膜　waterproofing membrane
防水材料/防水材料　waterproofing materials
防水层/防水層　waterproof layer, waterproofing
防水的/不透水　waterproof
防水等级/防水等級　classification of waterproof
防水盖布/油帆布　tarpaulin
防水混凝土/防水混凝土　waterproofed concrete, waterproof concrete
防水剂/防水劑　water-repellent admixture, waterproofing agent
防水胶/間苯二酚　resorcinol
防水胶带/防水膠帶　watertight adhesive tape
防水卷材/防水卷材　rolled waterproof material, waterproofing roll roofing
防水林/防水林　forestation against flood
防水砂浆/防水砂漿,防水灰漿　waterproof mortar
防水手电筒/防水手電筒　waterproof electric torch
GCL 防水毯/GCL 防水毯　GCL waterproof layer
防水涂层/防水塗層　waterproof coating
防水涂料/防水塗料　waterproof paint
防水型/防水型　waterproof type
防松装置/抗鬆裝置　anti-slack device
防酸性能/耐酸,抗酸　acid proof, acid resistance
防台锚地/防颱錨地　typhoon anchorage
防坍护墙/防坍護牆　landslide protection wall
防卫空间/防禦空間　defensible space
防污/防汙　anti-fouling
防污隔断阀/防汙隔離閥　anti-pollution isolating valve
防污漆/防汙漆　anti-fouling paint
防污涂料/防汙漆　anti-fouling paint
防雾林/防霧林　fog prevention forest
防锈/防銹　anti-rust, rust proof
防锈漆/防銹漆　anti-rust paint
防锈涂料/防銹漆,防蝕漆　anti-corrosion paint, rust-preventing paint
防锈油/防銹油　rust preventive oil
防眩板/防光眩板　anti-glare panel
防眩屏/防光眩屏　anti-glare screen
防雪/防雪　snow drift control, snow protection
防雪林/防雪林　snow drift prevention forest
防雪设施/防雪裝置　snow protection facilities
防雪树篱/防雪籬　snow protection hedge
防雪栅/防雪籬,雪欄　snow fence, snow guard
防雪障/防雪堤　snow protection bank
防烟/防煙,煙氣控制　smoke control
防烟阀/排煙閘　smoke proof damper, smoke damper
防烟分区/防煙火分隔間　smoke compartment
防烟楼梯间/除煙樓梯間　smoke-prevention stairwell
防烟面具/防煙面具　smoke mask
防盐风林/防鹽風林　salty wind protection forest
防疫站/防疫站　epidemic prevention station
防音绿地/防音綠地　noise proof green space
防淤堤/攔沙壩　sand-blocking dam
防雨棚/防雨棚　rain shelter greenhouse
防灾避难场所/避難處所　evacuation shelter
防灾工程设施/防災工程設施　disaster engineering facilities
防灾公园/防災公園　disasters prevention park, disaster prevention park

防灾规划/防災計劃　disaster prevention plan
防灾据点/防災據點　disasters prevention stronghold, disaster prevention strong hold
防噪间距/防噪間距　anti-noise spacing
防噪设施/防噪音設施　acoustic treatment facilities
防振材料/振動吸收材料　vibration absorption material
防震挡块/防震擋塊　anti-knock block, restrain block
防震缝/防震縫　aseismic joint, earthquake proof joint
防止不完全燃烧装置/防止不完全燃燒裝置　oxygen depletion safety shut off device
防止重复信号/防止重複信號　prevention for repetitive clear of a signal
防止垃圾污染/防止垃圾汙染　prevention of pollution by garbage
防止落石/防止落石　rockfall prevention
防止倾倒废物及其他物质污染海洋公约/防止傾倒廢棄物及其他物質汙染海洋公約　Convention on the Prevention of Marine Pollution by Dumping of Wastes and Other Matters
防止生活污水污染/防止家庭汙水汙染　prevention of pollution by sewage
防止油污染/防止油汙染　prevention of pollution by oil
防撞舱壁/防撞艙壁,防碰艙壁,碰撞隔堵　collision bulkhead, forepeak bulkhead
防撞灯/防撞燈　anticollision light
防撞垫/緩衝板　bumper
防撞墩/防撞墩　crash bearer, anticollision pier
防撞破凌/防撞破淩　breaking up ice run, breaking up ice floe prevent collision
防撞墙/防撞牆　anticollision wall
防坠器/防墜器　falling protector
妨害故障/妨害故障　hindrance fault
房舱布置图/房艙布置圖　cabin plan
房车/房車　house vehicle
房地产/房地產,不動產　estate
房地产抵押/房地產抵押　mortgage of real estate
房地产交易管理/房地產交易管理　administration of real estate transaction
房地产金融/不動產財務　real estate finance
房地产经纪人/房地產代理人　estate agent
房地产开发/房地產開發　real estate development
房地产开发企业/房地產開發企業　real estate development enterprise
房地产开发项目质量责任/房地產開發項目品質保證　quality assurance of real estate development project
房地产开发项目资本金/房地產開發項目自備資金　equity capital for real estate development project
房地产权属登记/房地產權屬登記　real estate ownership registration
房地产市场/房地產市場,不動產市場　real estate market
房地产投资信托基金/不動產投資信託　real estate investment trusts, REITs
房地产项目债务资金/房地產開發項目借貸資金　debt capital for real estate development project
房地产信托/不動產之信託　real estate trust
房地产行政管理/房地產行政管理　real estate administrative management
房地产业/地產業　realty industry
房地产中介服务机构/房地產仲介服務機構　real estate intermediate service agency
房基线/建築線　building line
房价收入比/房價收入比　price to income ratio
房间常数/室常數　room constant
房间声学语言传输指数/房間聲學語言傳輸指數　room acoustics speech transmission index, RASTI
房间吸声量/室吸收　room absorption
房建大修/房建大修　major repair of building and structure
房建检修/房建檢修　inspection and repair of building and structure
房建维修/房建維修　regular maintenance of building and structure
房山石/房山石　Fangshan stone
房屋边线/建築線　building line
房屋检查员/建築稽查員　building inspector
房屋建筑规范/建築規則　building code
房屋界线/建築線　building line
房屋静力计算方案/建築靜應力分析　static analysis scheme of building
房屋设计/建築工程設計　building design
房屋所有权/房屋所有權　home ownership
房屋污水管/建築汙水管　building sewer
房屋征收/房屋徵收　house expropriation
房务部/房管部　housekeeping
仿形铣削/靠模銑切　copy milling, profile milling
仿真发射/模擬發射　simulated launch
仿真飞行/模擬飛行　simulated flight
仿真技术/類比技術　simulation technology
仿真器/模擬器,模擬設施　simulator
仿真失重水槽/模擬失重水槽　water tank of

simulated weightlessness
仿真施矩/模擬加矩　analogous torquing
仿真式太阳敏感器/模擬太陽感測儀　analogue sun sensor
L-G仿真试验/L-G模擬試驗　L-G simulation test
仿真天线/假天線　artificial antenna
仿真线/仿真線,人工線,模擬線　artificial line
仿真信号源/信號模擬器　signal simulator
仿真演练/模擬操演　simulated drill
仿真引导/模擬指示　analog designation
仿真植物/仿真植物　artificial plant
访问/存取　access
访问控制/存取控制　access control
纺锤形浮标/紡錘形浮標　spindle buoy
纺织厂/紡織廠　textile mill
纺织物/紡織品　textile
舫/船庫,艇庫　boat house
放大倍数/放大因數　magnification factor
放大[率]/放大[率]　magnification
放大器/放大器,擴大器,增幅器　amplifier
放电/放電　discharge
放电[倍]率/放電率　rate of discharge, discharging rate
放电灯/放電燈　discharge lamp
放电电流/放電電流,洩漏電流　discharge current
放电加工/放電加工　electro-discharge machining
放电器/放電器　discharger
放电深度/放電深度　depth of discharge
放电特性曲线/放電特性曲線　discharge characteristic curve
放电效率/放電效率　discharge efficiency
放飞标准/飛行核準標準　flight permission criteria
放风阀/釋壓閥　vent valve
放宽静稳定性控制/放寬靜穩定性控制　relaxed static stability control
放气/吹洩　air bleed
放气阀/吹洩閥　blow-off valve, vent valve
放气系统/吹洩系統　blow-off system
放热规律/放熱律　law of heat release
放热率/釋熱率　rate of heat release
放散温度力/放散温度力　destressing, stress liberation
放射部/放射科　department of radiology
放射科/放射科　department of radiology
放射路/放射路,輻射道路　radiated road, radial road
放射路线/放射路線　radial route
放射式绿地带/放射式綠地帶　radial green belt
放射式配电系统/放射形配電系統,輻射形配電系統　radial distribution system
放射线穿透检测/放射線穿透檢測　radial activity inspection
放射线网/輻射式公共交通車站,輻射式公共交通線路網　radial type public transport network
放射形道路系统/放射形道路系統　radiate road system
放射性/放射性　radioactivity
放射性测量/放射性度量　radioactive measurement
放射性沉降/放射[性]沈積　radioactive fallout, radioactive deposition
放射性废水箱/輻射性廢水箱櫃　radioactive waste water tank
放射性废物/放射性廢物　radioactive waste
放射性废物箱/固體輻射性廢棄物儲存箱櫃　radioactive solid waste storage tank
放射性货物/放射性貨物　radioactive goods
放射性流出物/放射性流出物　radioactive effluent
放射性落尘/放射[性]落塵　radioactive fallout
放射性泉/輻射性泉　radioactive spring
放射性示踪剂/放射性示蹤劑　radioactive tracer
放射性同位素/放射性同位素　radioisotope
放射性污染/放射性汙染　radioactivity pollution
放射性物质/放射[性]物質　radioactive substance
放射性云/放射性雲霧　radioactive cloud
放射医学/輻射醫學　radiation medicine
放射状沟施/放射狀溝施　radial trenching fertilization
放射状绿地/放射狀綠地　radiate green space
放射状水系/放射狀水系,輻射狀水系　radial drainage
放水阀/吹洩閥,釋放閥　blow off valve, drain valve
放松/放鬆,鬆弛　slack away, release
放松拉索激振/放鬆拉索激振　vibration excited by cutting off holding rope
放艇安全索/放艇安全索　life rope
放网/投網　shooting net, cast net
放线/放線,定線　setting-out of route, lay out of route, setting out
放行准则/放行準則　exit criteria
放样/放樣　setting out
放样架/放樣架　leading frame
放样间/放樣場　template shop
放映室/放映室　projection room
放油系统/放油系統　defuelling and jettison system
放淤/放淤　colmatage
飞车/飛車,螺槳空車,螺槳空轉　propeller racing, run away

飞椽/飛椽　flying rafter, feichuan
飞扶壁/拱扶垛,飛拱　flying buttress
飞高/裙底氣隙　hover gap
飞机/飛機　airplane, aeroplane
飞机等级数/飛機分類號碼　aircraft classification number, ACN
飞机—发动机一体化/飛機—發動機一體化　aircraft-engine integration
飞机仿真试验/飛機模擬試驗　aircraft simulation test
飞机库/飛機庫　hangar, aircraft hangar
飞机蒙布/飛機織布　aircraft fabric
飞机燃油系统/飛機燃油系統　aircraft fuel system
飞机尾迹/飛機尾跡　aircraft trail
飞机制造厂/飛機製造廠　aircraft manufactory
飞剪[型]艒/飛剪式艒　clipper stem, clipper bow
飞溅/飛濺　spatter
飞溅区/飛濺帶,濺擊帶　splash zone
飞溅区腐蚀/飛濺區腐蝕　splash zone corrosion
飞溅阻力/濺水阻力　spray resistance
飞轮/飛輪,慣性輪　fly wheel
飞轮扫描地球敏感器/機輪掃描地球感測器　wheel scanning earth sensor, wheel scanning horizon sensor
飞轮轴承组件/飛輪軸承組件　fly wheel bearing unit
飞砂/飛砂　blown sand
飞艇/飛艇,飛船　airship
飞行/飛行　flight
[飞行]安全控制系统/飛航安全控制系統　flight-safety control system
[飞行]安全判断准则/飛行安全判斷準則　flight-safety judgment criterion
飞行安全区/飛行安全區　flight-safety region
[飞行]安全自毁判定模式/[飛行]安全自毁判定模式　flight-safety self-destruction determine mode
[飞行]安全自毁系统/[飛行]安全自毁系統　flight-safety self-destruction system
飞行安全走廊/飛行安全走廊　flight-safety channel
飞行包线/飛行包線　flight envelope
飞行包线扩展试飞/飛行包線擴充　flight envelope extension test flight
飞行边界控制系统/飛行邊界控制系統　flight boundary control system
飞行参数记录器/飛行資料記錄器,黑盒子　flight data recorder
飞行测量/飛行量測　flight measurement
飞行颤振试验/飛機翼振顫測試　flight flutter test
飞行程序训练/飛行程序訓練　flight procedure training
飞行方位角/飛行方位角　flight azimuth
飞行高度/飛行高度　flight altitude
飞行高度层/飛行高度,航空空層　flight level
飞行管理系统/飛行管理系統　flight management system
飞行轨迹测量/飛行路徑量測　flight path measurement
飞行后检查/飛行後檢查　postflight check
飞行后医学分析/飛行後醫學分析　postflight medical analysis
飞行后医学监督和保障/飛行後醫學監控與支撐　postflight medical monitoring and support
飞行环境/飛行環境　flight environment, flight environment of vehicle
飞行机构/飛行機構　flying mechanism
飞行计划/飛行計劃　flight plan
飞行甲板/飛行甲板　flying-off deck, flight deck
飞行阶段/飛行階段　mission phase
飞行结果分析/飛行結果分析　flight trial evaluation
飞行可靠度/飛行可靠度　flying reliability
飞行控制系统/飛控系統　flight control system
飞行控制指挥部/飛行控制指揮部　flight control headquarter
飞行力学/飛行力學　flight mechanics
飞行路径角/飛行角　flight path angle
飞行慢车/空中慢車轉速　flight idle speed
飞行模拟器/飛行模擬器,飛行模擬機　flight simulator
飞行品质/飛行品質　flying qualities
飞行品质仿真器/飛行品質模擬器　flying quality simulator
飞行剖面/飛行任務剖面　flight profile, mission profile
飞行气象条件/航空天氣狀況　flight weather condition
飞行器/飛行器　flight vehicle
飞行器的气动构型/飛行器空氣動力外型　aerodynamic configuration of vehicle
飞行器滚摇/飛行器滾搖　vehicle rock
飞行器空气动力学/飛行器空氣動力學　vehicle aerodynamics
飞行器气动特性/飛行載具空氣動力特性　aerodynamic characteristics of vehicle
飞行器姿态/飛行載具姿態　attitude of flight vehicle
飞行签派/飛航派遣　flight dispatch
飞行前规定试验/預先飛行試驗　preliminary

flightrating test, PFRT
飞行前检查/飛行前檢查　preflight check
飞行前医学分析/飛行前醫學分析　preflight medical analysis
飞行前医学检查/飛行前醫學檢查　preflight medical examination
飞行情报/飛航情報　flight information
飞行情报区/飛航情報區　flight information region, FIR
飞行区/飛行區　aircraft movement area
飞行区标志/飛行區標誌　aircraft movement area mark
飞行区等级/飛行區等級　aircraft movement area reference code
飞行任务分析/飛行任務分析　flight mission analysis
飞行任务剖面/飛行任務剖面　flight mission profile
飞行任务训练/飛行任務訓練　flight mission training
飞行时串/飛行時間序列　flight time series
飞行事故/飛行事故　flight accident
飞行事故记录器/失事記錄器,黑盒子　accident recorder
飞行试验/飛行試驗,試飛　flight test
飞行数据辨识/飛行資料識別　identification from flight data
飞行速度/飛行速度　flight velocity
飞行弹射试验/飛行彈射試驗　flight ejection test
飞行稳定性/飛行穩定性　flight stability
飞行信息区/飛航情報區　flight information region, FIR
飞行性能/飛行性能　flight performance
飞行训练/飛行訓練　flight training
飞行遥控机器人服务器/飛行遠程機器人服務器　flight telerobotic servicer, FTS
飞行载荷测量/飛行負載量測　flight load measurement
飞行振动测量/飛行振動量測　flight vibration measurement
飞行指引系统/飛航指引系統　flight director system
飞行中/飛行中　on the fly
飞行中医学分析/飛行中醫學分析　inflight medical analysis
飞行中止标准/飛行中止標準　flight abortion criteria
飞行状态参数/飛行狀態參數　flight status parameter
飞檐/飛檐　cornice
飞重式调速器/配重調速器　weight governor

非安全电路/非安全電路　non-vital circuit
非饱水带/未飽和帶　unsaturated zone
非爆炸危险区域/非危險區,安全區　non-hazardous area
非常荷载/不規則荷載　abnormal load
非常征用权/非常徵用權　right of angary
非潮汐流/非潮流　non-tidal current
非承压地下水/非拘限地水　unconfined groundwater
非承压井/非自流井　non-artesian well
非承重墙/非承重牆　non bearing wall
非触发引信/非觸發引信　noncontact fuze
非单向流/非單向流　non-unidirectional airflow
非等精度测量/非等精度量測　unequal precision measurement
非等弹性力矩/非等彈性力矩　anisoelasticity torque
非点源污染/非點源汙染　non-point source pollution
非电量参数/非電性參數　non-electrical parameter
非定班运行/非定班運行　non-scheduled run
非定常管流/非恆定管流　unsteady flow in pipe
非定常空气动力学/非定常空氣動力學　unsteady aerodynamics
非定常流/不穩定流　unsteady flow
非定向力效应/非定向效應　non orienting force effect
非都市土地/非都市土地　non-urban land
非对称半控桥式整流器/不對稱半控橋整流器　asymmetric half-controlled bridge rectifier
非对称飞行/不對稱飛行　unsymmetrical flight
非对称转捩/非對稱過渡　asymmetric transition
非锋面降水/非鋒面降水　non-frontal precipitation
非共面交会/非共面交會　non-coplanar encounter
非共面转移/異面轉移　non-coplanar transfer
非关键区/非關鍵區　noncritical area
非关联故障/非關聯故障　non-relevant fault
非灌溉期/非灌溉期　non-irrigation period
非规则波/不規則波[浪]　irregular wave
非规整园林/非規整園林　informal garden style
非机动车道/非機動車道　nonmotorized vehicle lane, non vehicle lane, non motor carriageway
非机动车辆/非動力車輛　non-power driven vehicle
非机动车运输/非動力車運輸　non-power driven vehicle transport
非机动船/非動力船,無動力船　non-powered ship, non-power driven vessel
非机械化驼峰/非機械化駝峰　non-mechanized hump
非机械化驼峰设备/非機械化駝峰設備　unmechanized hump yard equipment

非基本经济部门/非基礎經濟部門 non-basic economic sector
非基本职能/非基礎功能 non-basic function
非集合模型/解集模型 disaggregation model
非集中道岔/非集中道岔 locally operated switch
非集中联锁/非集中聯鎖 non-centralized interlocking
非计划性维修/臨時維護,不定期維護 unscheduled maintenance
非计划修理/臨時修理 unscheduled repair
非寄宿制学校/非寄宿學校 nonboarding school
非建设用地/非開發土地 non-development land
非交织交通流/非交織交通流量 non-weaving traffic flow
非接触测量/非接觸量測 noncontact measurement
非接触式传感器/非接觸式傳感器 non-contacting proximity sensor
非结构性破坏/非結構物損壞 nonstructural damage
非金属夹杂/非金屬夾雜物 non-metallic inclusions
非紧坡地段/非緊坡地段 section of unsufficient grade, section of insufficient grade
非进路调车/非進路調車 to hold route for shunting
非进路调车电路/非進路調車電路 circuit to hold a route for shunting
非浸润性液体/非浸潤性液體 nonwetting liquid
非晶材料/非結晶質材料 amorphous materials
非精密进近程序/不精確進場程式 non-precision approach procedure
非静止卫星通信容量/非定置衛星通訊之容量 volume of non-GEOSAR traffic
非居住区/禁[建]區 exclusion area
非聚焦合成天线/未對焦之合成天線 unfocused synthetic antenna
非聚束合成孔径雷达/未聚焦合成孔徑雷達 unfocused SAR
非绝缘锚段关节/非絕緣錨段關節 uninsulated overlap
非绝缘转换柱/非絕緣轉換柱 uninsulated transition mast
非均匀收缩/差别收缩 differential shrinkage
非开放港/未開放港 unopened port
非离子乳化沥青/非離子乳化瀝青 non-ionic emulsified bitumen
非离子型表面活性剂/非離子性表面活性劑 nonionic surfactant
非联锁道岔/非聯鎖開關 non-interlocked switch
非联锁区/非聯鎖區 non-interlocking area
非林地/非林地 non-forestry land

非毛管孔隙度/非微管孔隙率,非微管孔度 non-capillary porosity
非密闭区/非密閉區 airtightless space
非密封源/非密封源 unsealed source
非黏性土/無黏性土壤,非凝聚性土壤 non-cohesive soil
非黏着制动/非黏著式制動 non-adhesion braking
非农业人口/非農業人口 non-farming population
非排水船舶/非排水型船 non-displacement craft
非排土桩/非排土樁 non-displacement pile
非配属机车/未分配機車 unallocated locomotive
非平衡流动/不平衡流 non-equilibrium flow
非平行运行图/非平行運行圖 non-parallel train diagram
非屏蔽平衡电缆/非遮罩平衡電纜 unscreened balanced cable
非破碎波/未碎波浪 non-breaking wave
非破损检测/非破壞檢查 non destructive inspection
非破损试验/非破壞性試驗 non destructive test
非侵染性病害/非侵染性病害 non-infectious disease
非侵入测量/非侵入式量測 non-intrusive measurement
非球面/非球面 aspherical surface
非软化岩石/非軟化岩 unsoftening rock
非渗水土路基/不滲透基土 non-permeable soil subgrade, impervious embankment
非渗透性/不透水性 impervious
非生物因子/非生物因子,無機因子 abiotic factor
非生物资源/非生物資源 non-living resources
非收放型减摇鳍装置/非收放型鰭板穩定器 non-retractable fin stabilizer
非守恒型方程/非守恆型方程式 nonconservative equation
非水密舱壁/非水密艙壁 non-watertight bulkhead
非水密门/非水密門 non-watertight door
非踏面制动/非踏面制動 off tread braking
非弹性体系/非彈性體系 inelastic system
非弹性稳定性/非彈性穩定性 inelastic stability
非铁金属/非鐵金屬 non-ferrous metal
非通航桥孔/非適航跨距 non-avigable span
非同类余度/非同類冗餘 non-congeneric redundancy
非危险区域/非危險區域 non-hazardous areas
非稳态传热/不穩定傳熱 unsteady heat transfer
非物质文化遗产/非物質文化遺產,無形文化遺產 intangible cultural heritage, non-physical cultural heritage
非吸上式注水器/非吸上式注水器 non-attraction injector

非线性电阻器/非線性電阻器　non-linear resistor
非线性规划/非線性規劃　non-linear programming
非线性设计/非線性設計　non-linear design
非线性阻尼/非線性阻尼　non-linear damping
非相参应答机/非同調應答機　non-coherent transponder
非相干散射/非同調散射　non-coherent scattering
非相似余度/不相似冗餘　dissimilar redundancy
非协调元/不相容元　incompatible element
非仪表跑道/無航儀跑道　non-instrument runway
非溢流坝/非溢流壩　non-overflow dam
非营业性运输/自營性運輸　own account transport
非营业站/非操作站　non-operating station
非游览区/非遊覽區　no admittance area
非雨天事故/非雨天事故　dry traffic accident
非预应力钢筋/非預力鋼筋　non-prestressed reinforcement
非约束运行/非約束運行　unconstrained operation
非运用车/非運用車　non-serviceable car, car not for traffic use
非运用车系数/非運用車係數　coefficient of car not in service
非再生式生命保障系统/非再生式維生系統　nonregenerative life support system
非责任故障/非責任故障　non-chargeable fault
非责任事故/非責任事故　non-responsible accident
非增压的/非增壓的　unsupercharged
非增压发动机/吸氣式發動機,吸氧式引擎　aspirated engine, air breathing engine
非振荡非自由参量耗散差分格式/NND 格式　non-oscillatory and non-free-parameter dissipation difference scheme, NND scheme
非整倍体/非整倍數性　aneuploidy
非正规就业/非正規就業　informal employment
非支配机车/非支配機車　undisposal locomotive
非周边地面/核心區位　core region
非周期过渡条件/非週期過渡條件　aperiodic transitional condition
非周期罗经/無週期羅經,立復羅經,安定羅經　aperiodic compass
非周期性干扰力矩/非週期性擾動扭矩　non-periodic disturbing torque
非周向对称布局/周邊不對稱布局　peripheral asymmetric configuration
非自复式按键开关/非自複式接紐開關　non-self-reset push-key switch
非自复式按钮/非自複式按鈕　stick button
非自航船/無動力船　non-powered ship
非自流水/非湧[泉]水　non-artesian water
非自燃推进剂/非自燃推進劑　nonhypergolic propellant
非自燃推进剂火箭发动机/非自燃推進劑火箭發動機　nonhypergolic propellant rocket engine
非自主式敏感器/非獨立式感測器　non-autonomous sensor
菲涅耳反射/弗芮耳反射　Fresnel reflection
菲涅耳面/菲涅耳面,Fresnel 面　Fresnel surface
菲涅耳数/菲涅耳數　Fresnel zone number
肥力等级/土壤肥力等級　fertility grade
肥力评价/土壤肥力評估,土壤肥力分析　fertility evaluation
肥料/肥料　fertilizer
肥水灌溉/施肥灌溉　manuring irrigation
肥土/肥沃土　fertile soil
肥效分析器/肥效分析器　fertilizer analyzer
肺泡通气量/肺泡通氣量　alveolar ventilation volume
废车堆积场/廢車堆積場　auto-wrecking yard
废方处理/廢方處理　waste bank treatment
废品再生工厂/廢品再生工廠　waste-recycling plant
废气锅炉/廢氣熱交換器　exhaust gas heat exchanger
废气净化/排氣淨化　exhaust purification
废气滤清器/廢氣洗滌器　exhaust scrubber
废气排放标准/廢氣排放標準　exhaust emission standard
废气排放塔/廢氣排氣塔　waste gas exhaust tower
废气燃烧器/廢氣燃燒器　waste gas burner
废气涡轮/廢氣渦輪機　exhaust turbine
废气涡轮发电机组/廢氣渦輪發電機組　exhaust turbine generating set
废气涡轮复合系统/廢氣渦輪複合系統　exhaust turbo compound system
废气涡轮增压/廢氣渦輪增壓　turbocharging, exhaust turbocharging
废气涡轮增压柴油机/廢氣渦輪增壓柴油機　turbocharged diesel engine
废弃工程/廢棄工程　abandoned project, abandoned construction work
废弃河道/廢棄河道　abandonded channel
废[弃]污泥/廢汙泥　waste sludge
废弃物/廢棄物　waste
废热/廢熱,餘熱　waste heat
废热回收/廢熱回收　waste heat recovery
废热回收装置/廢熱回收裝置　waste heat recovery plant
废石堆/廢石堆　spoil

废水/廢水,汙水　wastewater
废水出口/廢水出口　wastewater outlet
废水处理厂/廢水處理廠　wastewater treatment plant, wastewater treatment works
废水处理设备/廢水處置設施　wastewater facility
废水处置/廢水處置　wastewater disposal
废水带/廢水帶　wastewater field
[废水的]空气氯化处理/加氯曝氣　aerochlorination
废水二级处理/二級廢水處理　secondary wastewater treatment
废水费/廢水費　wastewater charge
废水分解/廢水分解　wastewater decomposition
废水分析/廢水分析　wastewater analysis
废水灌溉/廢水灌溉　wastewater irrigation
废水回收/廢水回收　wastewater reclamation
废水净化/廢水淨化　wastewater purification, waste water renovation
废水勘察/廢水調查　wastewater survey
废水量/廢水流量　wastewater flow rate
废水率/廢水率　wastewater rate
废水喷射器/廢水噴射器　wastewater ejector
废水收集器/廢水收集器　wastewater collector
废水塘/廢水塘　wastewater lagoon
废水污泥/廢水汙泥　wastewater mud
废水循环/廢水循環　wastewater recycling
废水氧化/廢水氧化　wastewater oxidation
废水状况/廢水狀態　wastewater condition
废水资源化/廢水資源化　reutilization of wastewater
废水组成/廢水成分　wastewater composition
废物处理/廢物處理,廢汙處理　waste treatment
废物处理厂/廢汙處置廠　waste disposal plant
废物处理系统/廢物處理系統　waste disposal system
废物处置/廢物處置　waste disposal
废物收集器/廢物收集器　waste collector
废物收集与管理系统/廢物收集與管理系統　waste collection and management system
废液处理厂/液體廢棄處理工廠,廢液處理工廠　waste liquid treatment station
沸石/沸石　zeolite
沸石滤池/沸石濾池　zeolite filter
沸腾钢锭/未靜鋼錠　rimming steel ingot
沸腾式省煤器/蒸汽節熱器　steaming economizer
沸腾蒸发/沸騰蒸發　boiling evaporation
沸溢性油品/沸溢性油品　boiling spill oil
费率本/價目表,費率規章,收費制　tariff
费用偏差/成本差異　cost variance
费用效果分析/成本效果分析,成本效能分析,成效分析　cost effectiveness analysis, CEA
费用效益分析/成本利益分析　cost benefit analysis, CBA
费油/費油　excessive fuel consumption
分包/分包,外包　subcontracting, sectional contract
分包合同/分包　subcontract
分包人/外包商,轉包商　subcontractor
分包商/外包商,轉包商　subcontractor
分包遥测/分封遙測　packet telemetry
分包制/分包制　partial contract
分贝/分貝　decibel, dB
分辨率/解析度,解像度　resolution
分布/分布,分散　dispersion
分布比/配水比　distribution ratio
分布参数/分布參數　distributed parameter
分布法/分配法　distribution method
分布[钢]筋/分布鋼筋,勻力鋼筋　distribution bar
分布区/分布區　areal
分布区地理学/分布區地理學　areographic geography
分布曲线/分配曲線　distribution curve
分布式关节/分布式關節　distributed joint
分布式光缆温度探测报警系统/分布式光纜溫度探測報警系統　optical fiber distributed temperature detection and alarm system
分布式计算机系统/分布[型]電腦系統,分散式電腦系統　distributed computer system
分布式能源/分散式能源　distributed energy
分布式网络/分布網路　distributed network
分布式遥测系统/分散式遙測系統　distributed telemetry system
分布系数/分布因數　distribution factor
分布中心/分布中心　distribution center
分部工程/分部工程　part project
分部开挖法/分部開挖法　partial excavation method
分舱吃水/艙區劃分吃水　subdivision draft
分舱因数/艙區劃分因數,隔艙因數　factor of subdivision
分舱载重线/艙區劃分載重線,艙間吃水線　subdivision loadline
分层/分層,脫層　layer, delamination, stratification
分层固化/分層成化　multi-shell curing
分层图/暈色地形圖　layered map
分叉道/岔出線　turnout track
分岔/分岔　bifurcation
分岔路/交叉路　intersection leg
分潮/分潮　partial tide
分车带/分車帶,分離帶　diverge separator, dividing

stripe
分车带绿化/分車帶綠化　dividing stripe greening
分车岛/車道分隔島　divisional island
分车道行驶道路/分線道　divided road
分出功率输出装置/輔助功率輸出裝置　power take-off, PTO
分次预加力/再施預力　retensioning
分道交通/分道交通　separate traffic
分道角区/分道角區　gore area
分道通航制/分道通航制　traffic separation schemes, TSS
分点/春秋分點　equinox
分点潮/春秋分點潮,二分潮　equinoctial tide
分点大潮/春秋分大潮　equinoctial spring tides
分电话所/分局電話局,支局電信局　branch telephone office
分动式汽阀/可調活塞閥　adjustable piston valve
分度/分度,刻度　graduation
分段/分段　segmentation, sectioning
分段充电/分段充電　step charge
分段多层焊/間段焊接法　block sequence welding
分段阀/放洩閥　sectioning valve
分段分环结合砌拱/分段分環結合砌拱　laying arch by sections and rings
分段航行/分段航行　sectional navigation
分段减压/分段減壓　split reduction
分段建造法/分段建造法　sectional method of hull construction
分段绝缘器/分段用絕緣子,區隔絕緣體　section insulator
分段曝气/分段曝氣　stage aeration
分段砌拱/分段砌拱　laying arch by sections
分段施工/區段施工　section construction
分段式固体火箭发动机/分段固體火箭發動機　segmented solid rocket motor
分段舾装/分段舾裝　section outfitting
分段验收/分段驗收　sectional acceptance
分段引航/分段領航　sectional pilotage
分段运输/分段運輸　single-segment transportation
分段装配/[船體]分段裝配　section assembly, fabrication
分断电流/切斷電流　breaking current
分断能力/遮斷容量,斷路容量　breaking capacity
分割模型板/裂口墊板　split plate
分割区段/分割軌道電路　cut section
分隔/分離,分流　separation, sever
分隔带/分隔帶,分道區　separation zone
分隔设施/分開設備　separate facilities

分隔式车行道/分隔式車行道　divided carriageway
分隔线/分道線　separation line, division line
分隔行驶公路标志/分隔行駛公路標誌,分示公路區間前置標誌　divided highway sign
分根/分根　split-root
分工承包/分包制　partial contract
分管燃烧室/管狀燃燒室　tubular combustor
分光/分光　splitting
分光镜/分光鏡　beam splitter
分光湿度表/光系濕度計　spectroscopic hygrometer
分号运行图/分號運行圖　variant train diagram
分洪河道/洩洪道　floodway
分环砌拱/分環砌拱　laying arch by rings
分货种运费/[貨別]商品運費　commodity freight
分机/分機　extension
分级/揀分　sorting
分级保护/分級保護,等級保護　grade protection, cascade protection
分级槽/分級機　bowl classifier
分级处理/分段處理　stage treatment
分级滴滤池/多段滴濾池　stage trickling filter
分级关机/分級關機　staged cutoff
分级滑动/逐進性滑動　progressive slide
分级机/分級器　sizer
分级控制/分級控制　step control
分级起动/分級啟動　staged start
分级设备/分級設備　grading equipment
分级调压/分級電壓調整　stepped voltage regulation
分级网[络]/分級網,階層式網路　hierarchical network
分级消化/分段消化　stage digestion
分级卸载/分級卸載　load shedding
分集/分集　diversity
分集接收/分集接收　diversity receiving, diversity reception
分拣作业/分類作業　sorting operation
分检室/分檢室　mail sorting room
分接牵引变压器/抽頭[式]牽引變壓器　tapped traction transformer
分节驳船/組合駁船　integrated barge
分节驳船队/組合駁船隊　integrated barge train
分解/分解　decomposition
分解检查/拆卸檢查　tear down inspection
分界标志/界標　boundary sign
分界点/分界點　train spacing point, intermediate train spacing point
分开的平行运行/隔離平行作業　segregated parallel operation

分开式扣件/分開式[鋼軌]扣件　separated rail fastening, indirect holding fastening
分开式燃烧室/分離式燃燒室　divided combustion chamber
分控/分控　branch console
分类/揀分　sorting
分类保护/分類保護　classification protection
分类折旧率/分類折舊率　classified depreciation rate
分离/分離　segregation
分离点/分離點,分流點　separation point
分离电连接器/分離連接器　separation connector
分离机构/分離裝置　separation device
分离离合器滑行/分離離合器滑行　coasting with clutch disengaged
分离流/分離流　separated flow
分离盘/分離盤　separating disc
分离盆/分離盆　separating bowl
分离破坏/分離破壞　separation failure
分离式立交/分離式立交　grade separation without ramps
分离式立体交叉/立體交叉　separate grade crossing
分离式路基/分離式路基　separated subgrade
分离姿态/分離姿態　separation attitude
分力/分力　component force
分裂/破片　fragmentation
分流/分流　diverging
分流道路/分配道路　distributor road
分流电抗器/分路電抗器　divert shunt reactor
分流电阻器/分路電阻器　divert shunt resistor, shunting resistor
分流交通/分流交通　diverted traffic
分流交通量/轉向交通量　diverging traffic volume
分流套管/分水接管　tapping sleeve
分流堰/溢流堤　deversoir
分流运输/分流運輸　diversion transport
分流制/分流制,分離系統　segregation system, separation system, separate system
分流制排水系统/分流式下水道系統　separate sewer system
分流制污水系统/分流溝管系統　separate sewerage system
分流制下水道/分流式汙水道　sewerage of separate system
分路/分路,并聯,分流器　shunt
分路道岔/分路道岔　branching turnout, branch turnout
分路灵敏度/分流靈敏度　shunting sensitivity
分路效应/分流作用　shunting effect

分罗经/子羅經,羅經複示儀　compass repeater
分模数/分模數　infra-module
分蘖/分蘖　tillers
分配/配送　distribution
分配电箱/分電箱,配電盤　distribution box, distribution board
分配阀/分配閥　distributing valve
分配阀试验台/分配閥試驗臺　distributing valve test rack
分配管/分配管　service header
分配弯矩/分配彎矩,分配力矩　distributed moment
分配值/分配值　allocated value
分批称料器/承重分料機　weigh batcher
分品复接/分品連接　grading
分坡平段/分坡平段,相對平坡度　level stretch between opposite sign gradients, level grade between opposite gradients
分期修建/階段建造　stage construction
分区供水/分區供水　zoned water supply
分区规划/[分]區規劃　district planning
分区式[供暖]系统/分區[供暖]制　zone system
分区所/分區站　section post, SP
分区协调人/分區協調人　sub-area coordinator
分区一般照明/局部化照明　localized lighting
分区中心/次區域中心　subregional center
分权化/分散化,分權化,逆中心化　decentralization
分散/疏散　disperse
分散单元式航站楼/分散單元式航站樓　decentralized unit terminal
分散定居/稀疏集居　dispersed settlement
分散发展/分散開發　dispersed development
分散化/分散化,分權化,逆中心化　decentralization
分散供电方式/分散供電系統　diversified power supply system
分散供热/分散供熱　decentralized heating, decentralized heat supply
分散剂/分散劑　dispersing agent, dispersant
分散结构/分散結構　dispersed structure
分散容器/分散容器　dispersion cup
分散式发电/分散式發電　distributed generation
分散式供水/分散式供水　non-central water supply
分散性客流/分散性客運交通　dispersive passenger traffic
分散性土/分散性土　dispersive soil
分色滤光片/分光濾色片　color separation filter
分数[测量]单位/[量測]分數單位　sub-multiple unit of measurement
分水机/分水機　purifier

分水脊/分水嶺 water parting
分水岭/分水嶺 dividing ridge, watershed
分水线/分水線 water parting
分水堰/分水堰 separating weir
分体式浮船坞/分段浮塢 sectional floating drydock, sectional dock
分通信枢纽/分通信樞紐 sectional communication center
分析模型/分析模型 analysis model
分系统/分系統,子系統 subsystem
分系统测试/子系統測試 subsystem test
分线盒/分配箱 distribution box without protectors
分线盘/分線盤 distributing terminal board
分线盘端子/分線盤端子 terminals on distributing board
分线箱/分線箱 distribution box with protectors
分相回流线/分裂回流線 split return wire
分相绝缘器/分相絕緣器 neutral section insulator
分相装置/中性區間 neutral section
分向车道/分向車道 separated traffic lane
分向电缆盒/分向電纜盒 cable branching terminal box
分项工程/分項工程 item project
分项系数/分項係數 partial factor
分心斗底槽/分心斗底槽 fenxin doudi cao
分型剂/脫模劑 parting agent
分选机/分級器 sizer
分选系数/篩分係數 sorting coefficient
分压供水/分壓供水 separate pressure water supply
分运/分運 partite transport
分载垫圈/分載墊圈 load-distributing washer
分站/配電所,變電所 substation
分支管/分枝管 branch pipe
分支接线/分接 branch connection
分支街道/街道支線 street feeder
分支渠/分枝水路 branch channel
分支点/分枝點 branch point
分支系统/分歧式配管制 branching system
分质供水/分質供水 separate quality water supply
分轴燃气轮机/拼合軸燃氣渦輪機 split-shaft gas turbine
分株繁殖/分株繁殖 division propagation
分转向角/分轉向角 auxiliary deflection angle
分子标记/分子標誌 molecular marker
分子标记辅助育种/分子標記輔助育種 molecular marker assistant selection breeding
分子结构/分子結構 molecular structure
分子筛/分子篩 molecular sieve

分子筛制氧/分子篩製氧 molecular sieve oxygen generation, MSOG
分子污染/分子汙染 molecular contamination
分子育种/分子繁育 molecular breeding
分组交换/分組交換,分封交換 packet switching
分组交换网/分封交換網路 packet switching network
芬克[式]桁架/芬克式桁架 fink truss
酚含量/酚含量 phenol content
酚含量试验/酚含量試驗 phenol content test
酚类化合物/酚化合物 phenolic compound
酚醛泡沫塑料/酚醛發泡塑膠 phenolic foamed plastic
焚烧/焚化,灰化 incineration
焚烧炉/焚化爐 incinerator
粉尘污染/灰塵汙染 dust pollution
粉红[色]噪声/粉紅噪音,粉紅雜訊 pink noise
粉红噪声频谱修正量/粉紅噪聲頻譜修正量 pink noise spectrum adaptation term
粉粒级/坋土成分,沈泥成分 silt fraction
粉料仓/粉料倉 filler bin
粉料秤/粉料秤 filler weigher
粉料计量给料器/粉料定量餵料機 filler metering feeder
粉料撒布机/粉料撒布機 filler spreader
粉煤灰[硅酸盐]水泥/粉煤灰矽酸鹽水泥,卜特蘭粉煤灰水泥 Portland fly ash cement, fly ash Portland cement
粉煤灰混凝土小型空心砌块/粉煤灰混凝土空心砌塊 small hollow block of fly ash concrete
粉煤灰水泥/飛灰水泥 fly ash cement
粉煤灰水泥混凝土/飛灰水泥混凝土 fly ash cement concrete
粉末锻造/粉[末]鍛造 powder forging
粉末高温合金/粉末冶金超合金 powder metallurgy superalloy
粉末货物车/粉末運貨車 powdered goods car
粉末静电喷涂/粉末靜電噴塗 electrostatic powder spraying
粉末铝合金/粉末冶金鋁合金 powder metallurgy aluminium alloy
粉末钛合金/粉末冶金鈦合金 powder metallurgy titanium alloy
粉末冶金合金/粉末冶金合金 powder metallurgical alloy
粉砂级/坋土成分,沈泥成分 silt fraction
粉刷石膏/石膏糊料 gypsum plaster
粉碎拌和机/粉碎拌和機 pulvimixer

粉碎机/碎木機　grinder
粉碎筛/磨碎篩　comminuting screen
粉碎设备/粉碎設備　comminuter
粉体/粉體　pulverulent body
粉土/粉砂　silt
粉[土质]砂/粉砂質砂　silty sand
粉线/墨線　chalk line
粉质黏土/粉質黏土　silty clay
粉状货挂车/粉狀貨掛車　bulk tanker trailer
粉状雪/粉雪　powder snow
粪便泵/穢水泵,汙水泵　sewage pump
粪便处理厂/糞尿處理廠　manure disposal plant
粪便处理站/糞尿處理廠　manure disposal plant
丰满度/肥[瘠]度　fullness
风暴波/暴風波浪　storm wave
风暴潮/暴[風]潮,暴風浪　storm surge, storm tide
风暴扶手/風暴扶手　storm rails
风暴海滩/暴風海灘　storm beach
风暴浪/暴風波浪　storm wave
风暴路径/暴雨途徑　storm lane
风暴中航行/惡劣氣候航行　navigating in heavy weather
风车试验/風車試驗　windmill test
风车状态/風轉　windmilling
风尘环境模拟试验/風塵環境模擬試驗　simulated dust environment test
风挡/風擋　windscreen, wind shield, vestibule diaphram
风挡除雨系统/風擋除雨系統　wind shield rain removal system
风挡防雾系统/風擋防霧系統　wind shield anti-fogging system
风挡缓冲板/風擋緩衝板　vestibule diaphram buffer plate
风挡面板/風擋面板　vestibule diaphram face plate
风道/風道,導氣管,通風管　air duct, air channel
风道式通风/風道通風　ventilation by air passage
风电场/風電場　wind power plant, wind farm
风电场风力发电站/風電場風力發電站　wind farm generating electric power
风电站/風力發電廠　wind power station
风动泵/衝壓氣渦輪　ram-air turbopump
风动混凝土浇筑机/風動混凝土壓送機　pneumatic concrete placer
风动石碴[漏斗]车/風動卸碴車　pneumatic ballast hopper car
风动摇炉装置/氣動搖爐裝置　pneumatic grate shaking rigging

风动凿岩机/氣動鑿岩機,氣力鑿岩機　pneumatic rock drill
风动支架/氣腿　air leg
风洞/風洞　wind tunnel
风洞背景噪声/風洞背景雜訊　background noise of wind tunnel
风洞本体/風洞本體　wind tunnel noumenon, wind tunnel body
[风]洞壁干扰/[風]洞壁干擾　wall interference
风洞测量控制系统/風洞測量控制系統　measurement and control system of wind tunnel
风洞程序控制/風洞程式控制　wind tunnel program control
[风洞]吹风/[風洞]吹風　operating wind tunnel
风洞仿真能力/風洞模擬能力　wind tunnel simulation capability
风洞辅件/風洞附件　accessory of wind tunnel
风洞高速摄影技术/風洞高速攝影技術　high speed photograph application in wind tunnel
风洞工作介质/風洞工作媒質　working medium of wind tunnel
风洞计算机一体化/風洞電腦整合　wind tunnel-computer integration
风洞流场校测/風洞流場校準　flow field calibration of wind tunnel
风洞流量/風洞流率　wind tunnel flow rate
风洞能量比/風洞能量比　wind tunnel energy ratio
风洞气流污染/風洞氣流汙染　stream contamination of wind tunnel
风洞试验/風洞試驗　wind tunnel test
风洞试验模型/風洞試驗模型　model in wind tunnel test
风洞试验数据库/風洞試驗資料庫　wind tunnel test data base
风洞天平/風洞平衡區　wind tunnel balance
风洞压缩比/風洞壓縮比　compression ratio of wind tunnel
风洞运行/風洞操作　wind tunnel operation
风洞自由飞实验/風洞自由飛行實驗　wind tunnel free-flight test
风洞坐标系/風洞坐標系　wind tunnel axis system
风斗/風斗　wind scooper
风干/風乾　air drying
风干木材/風乾材　air dried wood
风干状态/風乾狀態　air dried state
风镐/風鎬　air pick, pneumatic pick
风格派/德斯太爾抽象畫派　De Stijl
风管/[通]風道,[通]風溝,氣道　air duct, duct

风管路调压设备/風管路壓力調節器　air pipeline pressure governor
风管式通风/風管式通風　ventilation by pipes
风海流/風驅流,風生流　wind driven current
风[荷]载/風荷載,風壓載重,風負荷　wind load
风荷载体型系数/風荷載的結構形狀因數　structural shape factor of wind load
风荷载应力/風負載應力　wind load stress
风花/風花圖　wind rose
风化产物/風化産物　weathering product
风化花岗岩/分解花崗石　decomposed granite
风化物/岩石風化土　weathered rock soil
风化系数/風化係數　weathering coefficient
风化作用/風化[作用]　weathering
风机盘管/風機盤管機組　fan-coil unit
风机盘管加新风系统/風機盤管加新風系統　primary air fan-coil system
风机盘管空气调节系统/風機盤管系統　fan-coil air-conditioning system, fan-coil system
风积/風積　aeolian
风积土/風積土　aeolian soil, aeolian deposit
风级/風級　wind scale
风景/風景　landscape
风景保护用地/風景保護用地,風景恢復用地　landscape conservation land
风景地貌/風景地貌　natural geomorphology
风景点建设用地/景區建設用地　scenic spots construction land
风景恢复区/園景地帶,園景區　landscape recovery area
风景林/風景林　landscape forest, ornamental forest
风景林地/風景林地　scenic forest land
风景林荫路/風景林蔭路　landscape avenue
风景旅游城市/風景旅遊城市　scenic tourist city
风景名胜/風景名勝,風景名勝區　famous scenery, famous scenic site
风景名胜公园/風景名勝公園　famous scenic park
风景[名胜]区/風景[名勝]區,風景[地]區　landscape and famous scenery, scenic area
风景名胜区范围/風景名勝區範圍　the range of scenic area
风景名胜区管理局/風景名勝區管理局　landscape and famous scenery administration
风景名胜区管理条例/風景名勝區管理條例　regulations on the management of landscape and famous sceneries
风景名胜区管理委员会/風景名勝區管理委員會　landscape and famous scenery management committee
风景名胜区规划/風景名勝區規劃　scenic area planning, landscape and famous scenery planning
风景名胜区徽志/風景名勝區徽志　landscape and famous scenery emblem
风景名胜区监管信息系统/風景名勝區監管資訊系統　landscape and famous scenery regulation information system
风景名胜区界桩/風景名勝區界樁　boundary stone of landscape and famous scenery
风景名胜区体系规划/風景名勝區體系規劃　landscape and famous scenery system planning
风景名胜区详细规划/風景名勝區詳細規劃　landscape and famous scenery detailed planning
风景名胜区性质/風景名勝區性質　nature of scenic area
风景名胜区综合整治/風景名勝區綜合整治　landscape and famous scenery comprehensive improvement
风景名胜区综合执法/風景名勝區綜合執法　landscape and famous scenery comprehensive law enforcement
风景名胜区总体规划/風景名勝區總體規劃　landscape and famous scenery master plan
风景区道路/風景區道路　park way, scenic area way
风景线/風景線　scenery line
风景学/風景學　scenicology
风景游览区/風景區　scenic resort
风景游赏/風景遊賞　landscape tour
风景游赏用地/風景遊賞用地　landscape tour land
风景园林规划与设计/風景園林規劃與設計　landscape planning and design
风景园林课/風景園林課程　course of landscape architecture
风景资源/風景資源,景觀資源　landscape resources, scenic resources, scenery resources
风景资源调查/風景資源調查　landscape resources evaluation
风景资源评价/風景區評估　scenic area evaluation
风景资源有偿/風景資源有償　compensated use of landscape
风口/風口,空氣孔,通氣口　air port
风缆/抗風纜索　wind cable
风浪/風成浪,風波　wind wave
风浪槽/風成浪槽　wind wave channel
风浪高度/風[成]浪高　wind wave height
风、浪、流试验水池/風、浪、流試驗水槽　wind wave and current tank

风冷/空氣淬火　air quenching
风冷式冷凝器/氣冷式冷凝器　air-cooled condenser
风力发电/風[力發]電　wind power generation, wind power
风力记录仪/風壓計　anemograph, anemobiagraph
风力加速堤/風力加速堤　wind accelerating dike
风力输送/氣力輸送, 氣動輸送　pneumatic conveying, pneumatic transport
风力系数/風力係數　wind coefficient
风裂/風裂　wind shake
风流/風送流　wind current
风流压差/偏流修正角　crab angle
风轮/風機　fan
风玫瑰图/玫瑰風圖, 風頻圖, 風花圖　wind direction diagram, rose diagram of wind direction, wind rose
风媒植物/風媒花植物　anemophilous plant
风幕/空氣幕, 氣簾　air curtain
风能/風能　wind energy
风切变/風切　wind shear
风切变探测系统/風切探測系統　wind shear detection system
风区/受風區　fetch
风沙地段路基/風沙地段路基　subgrade in windy and sandy zone, subgrade in desert
风筛分析试验/風析試驗　air analysis test
风筛机/風析機　air elutriator
风扇/風扇　fan
风扇系统/風扇系統　fan system
风扇整流罩/風扇艙　fan nacelle
风生流/風生流, 風驅流　wind driven current
风时/風時, 吹風延時　wind duration
风蚀/風蝕　wind erosion
风蚀等级/風蝕等級　wind erosion class
风蚀类型/風蝕型態　wind erosion type
风蚀灾害/風蝕災害　wind erosion hazard
风水林/風水林　fengshui forest
风水塔/風水塔　fengshui pagoda
风水学/風水學　fengshui
风速/風速　wind velocity, wind speed
风速表/風速計　anemometer
风速管/畢托[静力]管　Pitot-static tube
风速计/風速[記錄]計　anemograph, anemometer
风速频率图/風速頻率圖　wind velocity diagram
风物/風景觀光　landscape and article
风险/風險　risk
风险等级/風險等級　level of risk
风险分析/風險分析　risk analysis
风向/風向　wind direction
风向标/風向標, 風向儀　wind vane
风向频率/風向頻率　wind direction frequency
风向频率图/風向頻率圖　wind direction frequency diagram
风向指示器/風向指標　wind direction indicator
风汛信号/風訊信號　wind signal
风压/風壓　wind pressure
风压差/風壓差角　leeway angle
风压差系数/風壓差係數　leeway coefficient
风压分布图/風壓分布圖　wind pressure distribution graph
风压高度变化系数/風壓高度變異係數　height variation coefficient of wind pressure
风压横倾力臂/風壓傾側力臂　wind heeling lever
风压横倾力矩/風壓傾側力矩　wind heeling moment
风压继电器/氣壓繼電器　air pressure relay
风压调整器/風壓調整器　manometer regulator
风雨操场/風雨操場　indoor sports hall
风雨密/風雨密　weathertight
风雨密门/風雨密門　weathertight door
风雨密性/風雨密性　weathertightness, weather proofness
风障/風障　wind break
风振系数/風振係數　wind pulse vibration factor
风筝/風筝, 鳶　kite
风筝运动/風筝運動　kite movement
风致摆动/風振動　wind induced oscillation
风阻力/風阻力　wind resistance
风阻力矩/風阻力矩　moment of wind resistance
风阻力系数/風阻力係數　wind resistance coefficient
风嘴/風嘴　wind fairing
枫丹白露宫园/楓丹白露宮園　Fontainebleau Palace Garden
封/封閉, 閉塞, 阻塞　sealing, blocking
封闭湖/閉口湖泊　closed lake
封闭[集装]箱/封閉貨櫃　closed container
封闭交通/封閉交通　close to traffic
封闭井/封閉井　closed well
封闭空间/封閉空間　enclosure space
封闭空间升降平台/密封房間昇降平臺　sealed room elevating operation platform
封闭流域/封閉流域　non-contributing area
封闭楼梯间/封閉樓梯間　enclosed stairwell
封闭母线/金屬封閉母線　metal enclosed busbar
封闭生态系统/封閉式生態系統, 密閉生態系統　closed ecosystem
封闭式钢索/光面鋼索, 密封鋼絲繩　locked coil rope
封闭式楼梯/封閉式樓梯　enclosed staircase

封闭式收费系统/封閉式收費系統　closed toll system
封闭式弹射/封閉型彈射　enclosed ejection
封闭式通风集装箱/封閉式通風集裝箱　closed ventilated container
封闭系统/閉塞系統　closed system
封闭线路作业时间/封閉線路作業時間　work occupation time
封闭轴线/閉合軸線　closed axis
封舱/封艙　closing module
封舱抽水打捞/封艙抽水浮昇　raising by sealing patching and pumping
封舱设备/艙口壓緊裝置　hatch battening arrangement
封舱锁条/鎖緊柄　locking bar
封舱楔/艙口楔　hatch wedge
封舱压条/艙口壓條　hatch batten
封层/封閉層,封閉底漆　seal coat
封存机车/封存機車　locomotive stored up
封底处理/底封　subsealing
封底焊/防漏焊　seal weld, sealing welding
封底焊道/背焊道　sealing run, back weld
封缝料/封縫料　joint sealing compound
封缸/封缸　closing cylinder
封港/封港　embargo
封口/封口　sealing
封漏/止漏　leak stoppage
封锚/封錨　sealing off and covering anchorage
封山育林/封山育林,封山造林　closing the land for reforestation
封山育林区/封山育林區　region closed for afforestation
封锁/封鎖　close up, blockade
封锁地区/封鎖區　blockade zone
封锁区间/封鎖區間　closing the section
封檐板/山牆封檐板　fascia board, barge board
封堰/封堰　sealing weir
封装/封裝,密封　encapsulation
峰包功率/峰包功率　peak envelope power
峰顶/峰頂　hump crest
峰顶调车员室/峰頂調車員室　shunter cabin at hump crest
峰顶平台/峰頂平臺　platform of hump crest
峰顶式/峰頂　peak top
峰段/峰段　crest segment
峰-峰噪声/峰-峰雜訊　peak-to-peak noise
峰峰值/峰對峰值　peak-to-peak value
峰高计算点/峰高計算點　calculate point of hump height
峰荷热源/尖峰負載熱源　peak load heat source
峰量时间/峰量時間　time of peak flow
峰量指示计/峰量指示計　crest-gage indicator
峰隙/距波高度　wave clearance
峰下减速器/峰下減速器　master retarder
峰值/[尖]峰值　peak value
峰值[地面]加速度/尖峰地面加速度　peak ground acceleration
峰值[地面]速度/尖峰地面速度　peak ground velocity
峰值[地面]位移/峰值位移　peak ground displacement, peak displacement
峰值电流/尖峰電流　peak current
峰值电压/峰值電壓　peak voltage
峰值话音功率/尖峰語言功率　peak speech power
峰值检波器/峰值檢測器　peak detector
峰值强度/尖峰強度　peak strength
峰值时间/尖峰時間　peak time
峰值响应/峰值響應　peak response
峰值转矩/峰值轉矩　peak torque
锋/鋒　front
锋面/鋒面　frontal surface
锋面过境/鋒過境　frontal passage
蜂窝夹层结构/蜂巢夾心結構　honeycomb sandwich construction
蜂窝夹层结构胶黏剂/蜂窩夾層結構膠黏劑　honeycomb sandwich structure adhesive
蜂窝结构/蜂巢結構　honeycomb structure
蜂窝器/蜂巢　honeycomb
缝帆工具/縫帆工具　sailmaker tool
缝焊/縫焊接　seam welding
缝合接触面运行/專用接觸面運行　tailored contact surface operation
V缝式太阳敏感器/V縫式太陽敏感器　V slit type sun sensor
缝隙/縫隙,間隙　crack
缝隙腐蚀/間隙腐蝕,隙間腐蝕　interstitial corrosion, crevice corrosion
缝隙水/間隙水　interstitial water
缝隙天线/槽孔天線,槽式天線　slot antenna
佛教寺院/佛寺　buddhist monastery, buddhist temple complex, si
佛理/佛理　Buddhist philosophy
佛罗伦萨宪章/佛羅倫薩憲章　Florence Charter
佛氏铁/校磁鐵棒　Flinders' bar
佛塔/寶塔　pagoda
否定要素/否定要素　negation element

否认/否認,負確認　negative acknowledge, NAK
夫琅和费[谱]线/夫朗和斐[譜]線　Fraunhofer line
孵化器建筑/孵卵器建築　incubation building
孵化厅/孵化場　hatchery
敷网渔船/敷網漁船　square netter
弗劳德数/佛勞數,佛魯德數　Froude number
弗洛尔住宅/弗洛爾住宅　house of Flore
伏尔肯弹性联轴器/福爾幹撓性聯軸節　Vulkan flexible coupling
伏流/伏流　subterranean stream
扶壁/扶壁,支墩　buttress
扶壁式挡土墙/撐式擋土牆　counterfort wall
扶壁式桥台/扶壁式橋臺,撐式橋臺[牆]　counterfort abutment, buttressed abutment, abutment with counterfort
扶臂式挡土墙/[扶]垛式擋土牆　counterfort retaining wall
扶垛/扶壁,支墩　buttress
扶脊木/扶脊木　fujimu
扶贫旅游/扶貧旅遊　pro-poor tourism
扶强材/加勁材,加強材,防撓材　stiffener
扶手/扶手　handrail, handhold, grab iron
扶手栏杆/扶手欄杆　handrail
扶正分析/扶正分析　uprighting analysis
服饰店/成衣配飾件商店　haberdashery
服务半径/服務半徑,導致半徑　service radius
服务标准/服務標準　criterion of service
服务部/服務網點　tourist service point
服务舱/服務艙　service module
服务处所/服務空間　service space
服务公寓/商務住宅　service apartment
服务行业/服務業　service industry
服务航速/航海船速,營運船速　service speed
服务区/服務區,服務圈　service area, service zone
服务区标志/服務區標誌　service area sign
服务人口/服務人口　service population
服务设施/[生活]服務設施　service facilities
服务设施用地/服務設施用地　service facilities site
服务手续费/服務費　service fee
服务水平/服務水準　level of service, LOS
服务水平量度参数/服務水平有效性度量　effectiveness measure of LOS
服务水头/服務水頭　service head
服务隧道/工作隧洞　service tunnel
服务台/接待處　reception desk
服务系统/服務系統　service system
服务性道路/側道,臨街道路　frontage roadway
服务巡逻/服務巡邏　service patrol
服务业/服務業　service industry
服务中心/服務中心　service center
服装厂/服裝廠,被服廠　clothing factory
服装店/服裝店　clothing store
服装风机/服裝通風機　suit ventilator
服装供氧/服裝供氧　suit oxygen supply
服装间/箱房　costume room
服装通风/服裝通風　suit ventilation
服装压力调节器/服裝壓力調節器　suit pressure regulator
氟利昂/氟氯烷冷凍劑　freon
氟塑料/氟基塑膠　fluoroplastic
氟烃树脂/氟碳樹脂　fluorocarbon resin
氟[烃]油/氟[代烴]油　fluorocarbon oil
浮坝/浮壩　floating dam
浮标/浮標,浮筒　buoy, float
浮标系数/浮標係數　coefficient of float
浮标站/校位浮標　station buoy
浮冰/浮冰　floe ice
浮冰群/塊冰　pack ice
浮沉振动/浮沈振動　bouncing vibration
浮充电/浮接充電　floating charge
浮充供电/浮充供電　floating charge power supply
浮船架设/浮船架設　pontoon erection
浮[船]坞/浮[船]塢　floating dock
浮岛/漂浮島嶼　floating island
浮吊/起重船　crane ship
浮动/漂浮　afloat
浮动灯标/燈浮標　floating light, lighted buoy
浮动防碰设备/浮防舷材　floating fender
浮动轨枕/浮置軌枕　pumping dancing sleeper
浮动平台/浮碼頭　floating stage
浮动设备/浮水設備,漂浮設備　floating equipment
浮筏基础/浮式基礎　buoyant foundation
浮放道岔/浮放道岔　sliding point, move switch, superimposed crossing
浮杆/浮桿,測流漂桿　float rod, drifting pole
浮桨/浮槳　buoyant paddle
浮力/浮力　buoyancy
浮力舱/浮力艙　air tank
浮力曲线/浮力曲線　buoyancy curve
浮力调节系统/浮力調節系統　buoyancy regulating system
浮力修正/浮力修正　buoyancy correction
浮码头/浮碼頭　pontoon, floating pier
浮锚/浮錨,海錨　sea anchor, floating anchor
浮囊/浮囊　floatation bag
浮泥/浮泥　floating sludge

浮漂度/漂浮性,浮動性　floatability
浮漂度试验/漂浮性試驗,浮動性試驗　floatability test
浮桥/浮橋　pontoon bridge, floating bridge, bateau bridge
浮石/浮石　pumice, pumice stone
浮式采油[生产]平台/浮式產油平臺　floating oil production platform
浮式沉井基础/浮式沈箱基礎　floating caisson foundation
浮式沉箱靴/浮式沈箱靴　floating caisson shoe
浮式储油装置/浮動型貯油裝置　floating storage unit, FSU
浮式防波堤/浮式防波堤　floating breakwater
浮式码头/浮式碼頭　floating type wharf
浮式起重机/浮式起重機,水上起重機　floating crane, floating derrick
浮式生产储卸油装置/浮式採油貯油及卸油裝置　floating production storage offloading, FPSO
浮式生产储油及卸载设施/浮動型石油生產貯藏及卸載設施　floating production storage and offloading facility, FPSOF
浮式生产储油装置/浮式生產儲油裝置,浮式生產儲油單元　floating production storage unit, FPSU
浮式生产系统/浮式生產系統　floating production system, FPS
浮式输油软管/浮式輸油軟管　floating oil loading hose
浮式蒸发皿/浮蒸皿　floating pan
浮水勺/浮水勺　buoyant bailer
浮水设备/浮水設備,漂浮設備　floating equipment
浮态/浮揚狀態　floating condition
浮体/浮體　floating body
浮筒打捞/用救難浮箱浮昇　raising with salvage pontoons
浮筒号数/浮筒號數　buoy number
浮筒式起落架/浮筒起落架　float gear
浮筒系钩/浮筒繫鉤　buoy hook, buoy shackle
浮筒卸扣/浮筒繫鉤　buoy hook, buoy shackle
浮筒液位计/浮動液位計　float level gage
浮拖网/浮曳網　floating trawl
浮箱/浮箱,浮力艙櫃,躉船　buoyancy tank, pontoon, floating box
浮箱式浮船坞/浮箱式浮船塢　pontoon floating dock
浮箱式坞门/浮式塢門　floating caisson
浮心/浮[力中]心　center of buoyancy
浮心高度/浮心高　height of center of buoyancy
浮心距中距离/縱向浮心與舯距離　longitudinal distance of center of buoyancy from midship
浮心曲线/浮[力中]心曲線　curve of centers of buoyancy
浮心纵向坐标/縱向浮[力中]心　longitudinal center of buoyancy, longitudinal center of flotation
浮液体积补偿器/浮液容積補償器　fluid volume compensator
浮油层取样器/浮油層取樣器　float oil layer sampler
浮油回收船/撈油船　oil skimmer
浮游土采样器/浮游土採樣器　suspended sediment sampler
浮运沉井/浮式沈井　floating caisson
浮运架桥法/浮運架橋法,浮運法架橋　bridge erection by floating method, bridge erection by floating, erection by floating
浮运架设法/浮載架設法　floating erection
浮载重/浮載重　buoyant load
浮渣间/浮渣間　scum space
浮渣室/浮渣室　scum chamber
浮渣收集器/浮渣撤除器　scum collector
浮碴层/浮碴層　layer of scum
浮筑地面/浮動地板　floating floor
浮桩基础/浮式樁基礎　floating pile foundation
浮装/浮載　float-on float-off
浮子/浮子　float
浮子纲/浮繩,浮筒索　float line, buoy rope
符号/符號　symbol
符号关系学/符號關係學　syntactic
符号族/符號族　symbol family
幅移键控/移幅按鍵　amplitude shift keying, ASK
幅域/振幅域　amplitude domain
辐板/輻板　plate, web
辐板径向裂纹/輻板徑向裂紋　radial crack in plate
辐板孔/輻板孔　plate hole, web hole
辐板圆周裂纹/輻板圓週裂紋　circumferential crack in plate
辐合/輻合　convergence
辐合线/輻合線　convergence line
辐亮度/輻射量　radiance
辐流沉淀池/輻射流沈澱池　radial flow sedimentation tank
辐流式汽轮机/徑向流渦輪機　radial flow turbine
辐散/輻散　divergence
辐散线/輻射線　divergence line
辐射/輻射　radiation
辐射测量/輻射量測　radiation measurement
辐射出射度/輻射出射率　radiant exitance

辐射带／輻射帶 radiation belt
辐射带模式／輻射帶模式 radiation belt model
辐射定标装置／輻射校準裝置 radiometric calibration device
辐射对称／輻射對稱 radial symmetry
辐射发射／輻射發射，輻射放射 radiated emission
辐射发射安全系数测量／輻射發射安全因數量測 radiation emission safety factor measurement
辐射发射测量／輻射發射量測 radiation emission measurement
辐射发生器／輻射發生器 radiation generator
辐射法／輻線法 radial method
辐射防护／輻射防護，輻射保護 radiation protection
辐射防热／輻射熱防護 radiative thermal protection
辐射分辨率／輻射解析度 radiometric resolution, radiation resolution
辐射干扰／輻射干擾 radiated interference
辐射供暖／輻射加熱 panel heating, radiant heating
辐射光谱／輻射頻譜 spectrum of radiation
辐射换热系数／輻射傳熱係數 radiative heat transfer coefficient
辐射计法／輻射計法 radiometer method
辐射剂量／輻射劑量 radiation dose
辐射剂量率／輻射劑量率 radiation dose rate
辐射加速器／輻射加速器 radial accelerator
辐射校正／輻射修正 radiant correction
辐射街路／輻射街道 radial street
辐射冷却／輻射冷卻 radiation cooling
辐射敏感度／輻射敏感性，輻射易感受性 radiated susceptibility
辐射敏感度测量／輻射靈敏度量測 radiation sensitivity measurement
辐射敏感性／輻射敏感性，輻射易感受性 radiated susceptibility
辐射敏感元件／輻射靈敏元件 radio-sensitive element
辐射模／輻射模態 radiation mode
辐射能／輻射能，放射能 radiant energy, radiation energy
辐射平衡／輻射平衡 radiometric balance
辐射强度／輻射強度 radiation intensity
辐射热／輻射熱 radiant heat
辐射散热器／輻射器，散熱器 radiator
辐射式道路／輻射道路 radial road
辐射式公路／輻射[狀]公路 radial highway
辐射损伤／輻射損傷，輻射損壞 radiation damage
辐射体／輻射體 radiation body
辐射通量／輻射通量 radiant flux

辐射通量密度／輻射通量密度 radiant flux density
辐射危害／輻射熱害 radiation hazard
辐射温度／輻射溫度 radiation temperature
辐射系数／輻射係數 radiation coefficient
辐射系统／輻射系統 radial system
辐射形流域／輻射狀流域 radial basin
辐射诱变／輻射誘發突變 radiation induced mutation
辐射源／輻射源 radiation source
辐射致冷器／輻射冷凍機 radiative refrigerator
辐射状水系／輻射狀水系，放射狀水系 radial drainage
辐向剪力带／輻射剪力區 radial shear zone
辐照度／照射度 irradiance
辐照监督管／照射檢測管 irradiation inspection tube
辐照食品／照射食品 irradiated food
辐照试验／輻射試驗 irradiation test
辐照装置／輻照裝置 irradiation installation
福尔马肼[浊]度／福爾馬濁度單位 Formazin turbidity unit
福勒襟翼／阜勒氏襟翼 Fowler flap
福利性住房／福利住宅 welfare housing
斧头／斧頭，太平斧 axe
俯冲／俯衝 dive
俯冲波浪／奔波，衝浪 plunging wave
俯冲轰炸／俯衝轟炸 dive bombing
俯[顶]视图／俯[頂]視圖 top view
俯极／下天極 depressed pole
俯视景观／俯視景觀 downward landscape
俯仰程序角／俯仰程式角 pitch program angle
俯仰角／俯仰角，縱搖角 pitch angle
俯仰角速度／俯仰率 rate of pitch
俯仰力矩／俯仰力矩 pitching moment, trimming moment
俯仰姿态／俯仰姿態 pitch attitude
俯仰姿态捕获／俯仰姿態獲取 pitch attitude acquisition
辅柴油机／輔柴油機 auxiliary diesel engine
辅道／輔助道路 auxiliary road
辅锅炉／輔鍋爐，副鍋爐 donkey boiler, auxiliary boiler
辅锅炉自动控制系统／輔鍋爐自動控制系統 auxiliary boiler automatic control system
辅机／輔助機車 assisting locomotive
辅机舱／輔機艙 auxiliary machinery room, auxiliary machinery compartment
辅给水系统／輔給水系統 auxiliary feed line, auxiliary feed system
辅冷凝器循环泵／輔機冷凝器循環泵 auxiliary

condenser circulating pump
辅路/輔助道路,旁路　side road, auxiliary road, relief road
辅汽轮机/輔蒸汽渦輪機　auxiliary steam turbine
辅汽轮机组/輔蒸汽渦輪機組　auxiliary steam turbine set
辅燃气轮机/輔燃氣渦輪機　auxiliary gas turbine
辅助编组站/輔助編組站　auxiliary marshalling station
辅助标线/輔助標線　supplementary marking
辅助标志/輔助標誌　auxiliary sign
辅助操舵装置/輔[助]操舵裝置　auxiliary steering gear
辅助柴油机/輔助柴油機　auxiliary machinery diesel engine
辅助车场/輔助車場　auxiliary yard
辅助承力索/輔助承力索　auxiliary catenary
辅助道路/輔助道路,收集道路,出入道路　collector road, frontage street, subsidiary road
辅助等电位连接/輔助等電位聯結　supplementary equipotential bonding, SEB
辅助等高线/輔助等高線　supplementary contour
辅助电动机/輔助電動機,輔助馬達　auxiliary motor
辅助电路/輔助電路　auxiliary circuit
辅助电路电压表/輔助電路電壓計　auxiliary circuit voltmeter
辅助电路库用插座/輔助電路庫用插座　circuit socket for shed supply
辅助电路库用转换开关/輔助電路庫用轉換開關　auxiliary circuit transfer switch for shed supply
辅助电源/輔助電源　auxiliary electrical power source
辅助动力装置/輔助動力單元　auxiliary power unit
辅助墩/輔助墩　auxiliary pier
辅助发电柴油机/輔助柴油發電機　auxiliary generator diesel engine
辅助发电机/輔助發電機　auxiliary generator
辅助飞行操纵系统/輔助飛行控制系統　auxiliary flight control system
辅助浮船坞/輔助浮船塢　auxiliary floating dock
辅助工程/附屬工程　appurtenant work
辅助功率输出装置/輔助功率輸出裝置　power take-off, PTO
辅助供水水源/輔助水源　supplemental water-supply source
辅助机油泵/輔助[潤]滑油泵　auxiliary lubricating oil pump
辅助机组试验/輔助機組試驗　test on auxiliary machines
辅助基线/輔助基線　auxiliary base line
辅助舰船/輔助艦　auxiliary ship, auxiliary ship and service craft
辅助接触器/輔助接觸器,副接觸器　auxiliary contactor
辅助坑道/輔助坑道　service gallery, service tunnel
辅助梁/輔助梁　floor stringer
辅助炮眼/輔助炸孔　relief hole, reliever, easer
辅助绕组/輔助繞組,附加繞組　auxiliary winding
辅助软管设备/輔助軟管設備　auxiliary hose rigs
辅助设施/輔助設備　auxiliary facility
辅助设施费/輔助設備費　cost of ancillary facility
辅助视图/輔助圖　auxiliary view
辅助书库/輔助書庫　auxiliary stack
辅助所/輔助線路所　auxiliary block post
辅助天气图/輔助天氣圖　auxiliary weather chart
辅助推进系统/輔助推進系統　auxiliary propulsion system
辅助系统/輔助系統　auxiliary system
辅助线/輔助線　assistant line
辅助修理坞/輔助修船塢　auxiliary repair dock
辅助装卸费/輔助裝卸費　auxiliary handling charge
辅助装卸作业/輔助裝卸作業　auxiliary handling operation
辅助装置/輔助設施　auxiliary device
辅助走行公里/輔助走行公里　auxiliary running kilometer
腐臭污水/陳腐廢水　stale wastewater
腐化处理/腐化　septicization
腐坏事故/腐壞事故　decay accident
腐蚀/腐蝕,銹蝕,侵蝕　corrosion
腐蚀产物/腐蝕生成物　corrosion product
腐蚀负荷/腐蝕負荷　corrosion load
腐蚀麻点/腐蝕麻點　corrosion pit
腐蚀磨损/腐蝕耗損　corrosion wear
腐蚀疲劳/腐蝕疲勞,銹蝕疲勞　corrosion fatigue
腐蚀试验/腐蝕試驗,銹蝕試驗　corrosion test
腐蚀速率/腐蝕速率　corrosion rate
腐蚀体系/腐蝕體系,腐蝕系統　corrosion system
腐蚀性分级/腐蝕性分級　corrosiveness classification
腐蚀性物质/腐蝕性物質　corrosives
腐蚀裕量/腐蝕裕度　corrosion allowance
腐熟/腐熟　maturity
腐叶土/腐葉土　rotten leaf soil
腐殖土/腐殖土　muck
腐殖质/腐殖質　humus, humic substances, humics
负承压水头/負湧泉水頭　negative artesian head

负反馈/負反饋　negative feedback
负反馈控制系统/負反饋控制系統　negative feedback control system
负荷/負荷,負載　load
负荷分配/負載分配　load-sharing
负荷开关/負載開關　load break switch, load switch
负荷模拟试验/負荷模擬試驗　simulated load test
负荷曲线/負荷曲線,需量曲線　power load curve
负荷伸展曲线/載重伸長曲線　load-extension curve
负荷试验/負荷試驗　load test
负荷特性/負載特性　load characteristic
负荷系数/負荷因數,負載因數　load factor
负荷限制旋钮/負荷限制旋鈕　load limit knob
负荷指示器/負荷指示器　load indicator
负极/負極　negative electrode
负极柱/負極端子,負端　negative terminal
负加速度/減加速度　negative acceleration
负孔隙水压力/負孔水壓　negative pore water pressure
负摩阻力/負表面摩擦　negative skin friction
负推力持续时间/負推力持續時間　negative thrust duration
负响应区/負響應區　negative response zone
负压阀/負壓閥　negative pressure valve
负压锅炉/負壓鍋爐,抽氣鍋爐　induced draft boiler, suction boiler
负压裤/負壓褲　negative pressure trousers
负压强指数推进剂/負壓指數推進劑　propellant with negative burning rate pressure exponent
负硬度/負硬度　negative hardness
负载/負載,負荷　load
负载电压/有載電壓　on-load voltage
负载试验/負載試驗　loaded test, load test
负载调节器/負載調節器　load governor
负载系数/負載因數,負荷因數　load factor
负责操作人员的职务/負責作業人員之職位　responsible operator position
附壁爬梯/鐵爬梯　step iron
附壁石/附壁石　stone appended to wall
附加常数/附加常數　additive constant
附加车道/輔助車道　auxiliary lane
附加导线/附加導線　additive wire
附加二次相位因子/附加二次相位因子　additional secondary phase factor, ASF
附加费用/附收費用　accessorial charge
附加风缸/輔助風缸　supplementary reservoir
附加耗热量/附加耗熱量　additional heat loss
附加荷载/附加荷載　superimposed load, supplementary load
附加检验/額外檢驗　additional survey
附加力/副[負]載,副載荷　subsidiary load, secondary load
附加偏心距/意外偏心　accidental eccentricity
附加[运]费/附加費　additional charge
附加质量/附加質量　added mass
附加阻力/附加電阻　additional resistance
附角斗/附角斗　fujiaodou
附具摊销费/附具攤銷費　attachment cost
附生植物/附生植物　epitphyte
附属工程/附屬工程　appurtenant work
附属建筑/附樓,附屬房屋　attached building
附属绿地/附屬綠地　attached green space
附属文物/附屬文物　heritage component, subsidiary of cultural relics
附属种/追隨種,衛星種　satellite species
附体/附屬物　appendages
附体激波/附體激波　attached shock wave
附体阻力/附屬物阻力　appendage resistance
附着式混凝土振动器/附著式混凝土振動器　form concrete vibrator
附着式振动器/外部[振]動機　external vibrator
附着水/持著水　held water
附着涡/受束渦旋　bound vortex
附着涡面/受束渦旋面　bound vortex surface
附着系数测定/附著係數測定　traction coefficient measurement
复拌/重拌　remixing
复测法/重複法　repetition method
复层建筑涂料/複合建築塗料　multi-layer coating for architecture
复传力法预应力/複傳力法預應力　prestressing by subsequent bond
复飞/重飛　wave off, go around
复飞点/重飛起始點,誤失進場點　missed approach point
复轨器/復軌器　re-railer, rerailing device
复合[标准]过程线/複合歷線　compound hydrograph
复合材料/複合材料　composite, composite materials
复合材料结构/[整體]複材結構　integral composite structure, composite structure
复合衬砌/複合式襯砌　composite lining, double lining
复合催化效率/组合催化效率　compound catalysis efficiency
复合地基/複合地基　composite subgrade

复合电镀/複合電鍍 composite plating
复合断层/複雜斷層 compound fault
复合肥料/複合肥料 compound fertilizer
复合改性双基推进剂/複合改進雙基推進劑 composite modified double-base propellant, CMDB propellant
复合钢/護面鋼,包層鋼 clad steel
复合管/複合材料管 composite pipe
复合[硅酸盐]水泥/複合矽酸鹽水泥,複合卜特蘭水泥 composite Portland cement
复合家庭/複合家庭 composite family
复合截面加固法/複合截面加固法 structure member strengthening with externally bonded reinforced materials
复合可调整合金镀/複合調變合金電鍍 composition modulated alloy plating
复合冷却/混合冷卻 combined cooling
复合片/複合板 composite sheet
复合生态系统/複合生態系統 composite ecosystem
复合识别/複合識別 combination identification
复合实验室/混合實驗室 composite laboratory
复合式柴油机/複合式柴油機 compound-supercharged diesel engine
复合式混凝土路面/複合式混凝土鋪面 composite type concrete pavement
复合调制雷达引信/複調制雷達引信 multiple modulation radar fuze
复合调制引信/多工調變引信 multiplex modulation fuze
复合推进剂/複合推進劑 composite propellant
复合污染/複合汙染 combined pollution
复合摇臂/複合搖臂 duplicated crank
复合引信/複合引信 combined fuze
复合应力/複[合]應力 compound stress, composite stress, combined stresses
复合增压/複合增壓 compound supercharging
复合指令/複合指令 complex command
复合制导/綜合制導,多重制導,複合導引 combined guidance
复合桩基/樁複合地基 composite foundation pile
复健花园/復健花園 rehabilitative garden
复介电常数/複介電常數 complex dielectric constant
复励电动机/複激電動機 compound excited motor
复励发电机/複激發電機 compound generator
复励阻抗/複激阻抗 compounding impedance
复曲线/複曲線 compound curve
复曲线点/複曲點 point of compound curve, PCC

复色/複色 duplicate color
复色谐调/複色諧調 compound chromatic harmony
复示磁罗经/電導羅經 transmitting compass
复示信号/複示號誌 repeating signal
复示信号机/複示號誌機 repeating signal
复式冲动涡轮机/複式衝動渦輪機 compound impulse turbine
复式挂弹架/複式彈射架 multiple ejection rack, MER
复式夯道机/複式夯道機 multiple-tie tamper
复式桁架/複式桁架 multiple truss, complex truss
复式交叉/多路交叉 compound intersection
复式交叉桁架/雙腹材桁架 double-intersection truss
复式交分道岔/複式交叉轉轍器 double slip switches
复式配水系统/複式配水系統 dual distribution system
复式汽车库/複式汽車庫 compound garage
复式压力级涡轮机/複壓渦輪機 pressure-compounded turbine
复水包装/複水包裝 rehydratable packaging
复水食品/複水食物 rehydratable food
复水饮料/複水飲料 rehydratable beverage
复弹性模量/複數彈性模數 complex modulus of elasticity
复位/重置,復歸 reset
复向期/回復期 reach
复压/再加壓 repressurization
复演程序/重播程式 replay program
复氧系数/再曝氣係數 reaeration coefficient
复用/再[利]用 reuse
复原力臂/扶正力臂 restoring lever, righting lever, righting arm
复原力臂曲线/扶正力臂曲線 righting lever curve, righting arm curve
复原力矩/復原力矩,扶正力矩,回復力矩 restoring moment, righting moment
复原力偶/扶正力偶 righting couple
复原稳性力臂/剩餘扶正力臂 residual righting lever
[复原]摇枕/搖承材 swing bolster
复原装置/定心裝置 centering device
复杂循环燃气轮机/複合循環燃氣渦輪機 complex cycle gas turbine
复涨曲线/復漲曲線 regeneration curve
复壮沟/複壯溝法 rejuvenation ditch
副按键开关组/副按鍵開關組 secondary push-key switch group, secondary key switch set

副坝/副壩　auxiliary dam
副标志/副標誌　counter mark
副标准/次級標準　secondary standard
副产品轻质骨材/副產品輕質骨材　by-product lightweight aggregate
副车钟/副車鐘　sub-telegraph
副堤/縷堤　secondary levee
副对角撑/交叉斜撐　counterbracing
副风缸/輔助貯器,輔助儲器　auxiliary reservoir
副港/二等港　secondary port
副航道/副航道　sub-channel
副机日志/副機日誌　auxiliary engine log book
副交点/輔助交會點　auxiliary intersection point
副阶/副階　attached corridor, fujie
副景/副景　secondary feature
副连杆/輔助連桿　auxiliary connecting rod
副量水计/旁通水表,副量水器　by-pass water meter
副前照灯/副前燈　subhead lamp, dim head light
副热带高压/副熱帶高壓　subtropical high
副热带无风带/副熱帶無風帶,馬緯度　horse latitude
副艏材/副艏材,艏護木,艏牆　apron
副司机/副司機　assistant driver
副台/副臺,役使電臺　secondary station, slave station
副台信号/副臺信號　slave signal
副通气立管/副通氣立管　secondary vent stack, assistant vent stack
副拖缆/副拖纜　auxiliary towing line
副陀螺/輔迴轉儀　auxiliary gyro
副翼/副翼　aileron
副翼反效/副翼反向　aileron reversal
副油箱/副油箱　auxiliary fuel tank, drop tank
副帧/副幀　subframe
副帧同步/副幀同步　subframe synchronization
副帧同步码/副幀同步碼　subframe sync pattern
副中心/副[城市]中心　sub-civic center
副中心城市/副中心都市　sub-center city
副轴/副軸　auxiliary axis
副着陆场/替代登陸位置　alternate landing site
赋形波束天线/型束天線　shaped-beam antenna
赋形座椅/已成型座椅　contoured seat
傅科摆/富可擺　Foucault pendulum
傅里叶变换红外光谱仪/傅利葉轉換紅外光譜儀　Fourier transformation infrared spectrometer
富集作用/富集[作用]　enrichment
富硫酸盐水泥/高硫水泥　supersulphated cement
富锌涂料/富鋅漆　zinc-rich paint
富养植物/富養植物　eutrophic plant, eutrophyte
富营养湖/優養湖泊　eutrophic lake
富营养化/富營養現象,優養　eutrophication
富营养系统/富養系統　eutrophic system
富余水深/餘裕水深　under keel clearance, UKC
富裕压力/安全壓力邊限　safety pressure margin
腹板/腹板,大肋骨,梁腹　web, web plate
腹板折曲/腹板皺曲　web crippling
腹地/腹地　hinterland
腹杆/腹桿,腹材　web member
腹拱/腹拱　spandrel arch
腹筋/腹筋　web reinforcement
腹鳍/腹鰭,腹翅　ventral fin
覆板/二重板,加力板,加強板　doubling plate
覆材甲板/包板甲板,被覆甲板　sheathed deck
覆带防滑板/減速靴　skid shoe
覆盖/覆蓋,遮蔽　cover
覆盖层/覆蓋層　overburden
覆盖防护/覆蓋防護　covered protection
覆盖脉冲干扰/覆蓋脈衝干擾　cover-pulse jamming
覆盖区/覆蓋區[域]　coverage, coverage zone
覆盖区边缘/涵蓋邊緣　edge of coverage
覆盖土层/覆土　earth covering
覆盖物/覆蓋物　mulch
覆盖物分散机/覆蓋物分散機　mulch spreader
覆盖压力/超載壓力　overburden pressure
覆盖植被/覆蓋植被　cover vegetation
覆盆/覆盆　fupen
覆土爆破/泥帽法炸石　mudcapping
覆土法/客土法　borrowed soil, incorporation with extra soil, soils from other places
覆土深度/覆土深度,覆蓋深度　covered depth, covering depth

G

伽辽金法／加勒金法　Galerkin method
伽马分布／加馬分布　gamma distribution
改版图／大改正海圖　large correction chart
改出俯冲轰炸／俯衝拋擲轟炸　dive-toss bombing
改道／改道　gage correction, gaging of track
改航／改航　diversion
改建／房屋重建　building reconstruction
改建地区／改良區　improvement area
改建桥／改建橋　reconstructed bridge
改建铁路／改建鐵路　reconstructed railway
改良曝气法／改良式曝氣　modified aeration
改良土壤树种／改良土壤樹種　soil improving tree species
改善／撫育　improvement
改善级配加固法／機械穩定［處理］　mechanical stabilization
改向性／變向能力　course changing ability
改向性试验／變向能力試驗　course changing ability test
改性加工／改良加工　modification process
改性沥青／改性瀝青　modified bitumen, modified asphalt
改性沥青防水卷材／改性瀝青防水卷材　modified asphalt waterproof membrane
改性双基推进剂／改進雙基推進劑　modified double-base propellant, MDB propellant
改造／再發展　redevelopment
改造方案／整建計劃　rehabilitation plan
改正流速／修正流速　modified velocity
改制气／重組氣　reformed gas
改装／改裝，返廠修改　modification, retrofit
改钻机／改鑽機　drills steel sharpener
钙电极快速测定法／鈣電極快速測定法　calcium electric rapid determination method
钙基润滑脂／鈣基滑脂　calcium grease
钙土植物／鈣土植物，石灰植物　calciphyte
盖板／蓋板　cover plate, covered plate
盖板涵／平板涵　slab culvert
盖板式棚洞／蓋板式棚洞　slab shed tunnel, slab shed gallery
盖度／蓋度　coverage

盖梁／蓋梁　bent cap
盖片／蓋片　cover
盖斯林格弹性联轴器／蓋氏可撓聯結器　Geislinger flexible coupling
盖土机／蓋土機　mounted spreader
概率分布／機率分布　probability distribution
概率航迹区／或然航跡區　probable track area
概率极限状态设计法／概率極限狀態設計法　probabilitic limit state design method
概率密度／機率密度　probability density
概率密度函数／機率密度函數　probability density function
概率模型／機率模式　probabilistic model
概率设计法／機率設計方法　probabilistic design method
概率误差／或然差　probable error
概念规划／概念規劃，構想計劃　concept planning, conceptual plan
概念设计／概念設計，構想設計　concept design
概算定额／概算定額　rating of approximate estimate, rating form for estimate
概位／概略位置　position approximate, PA
干冰／乾冰　dry ice
干舱证书／［貨艙］乾燥證明　dry certificate
干沉降／乾沈降　dry fallout
干稠度混凝土／乾稠度混凝土　concrete of dry consistency
干出高度／出水高度　drying height
干出礁／出水礁石　drying rock
干出滩／潮灘　tidal flat
干船坞／乾［船］塢　graving dock, dry dock
干船坞长度／乾船塢長度　dry dock length
干船坞撑木／乾船塢撐木　dry dock side shore
干船坞注水装置／乾船塢放水設置　dry dock flood device
干捣水泥砂浆／乾搗水泥砂漿　dry tamped cement mortar
干底润滑／乾油槽潤滑　dry sump lubrication
干法缠绕／乾式纏繞　dry winding
干法烟气脱硫法／乾法煙氣脫硫　dry process of flue gas desulfurization

干粉灭火器/乾粉滅火器　powder fire extinguisher
干粉灭火系统/乾粉滅火系統　dry powder fire extinguishing system, powder extinguishing system
干粉炮灭火系统/乾粉炮滅火系統　powder monitor extinguishing system
干涸工程/乾涸工程　land drying
干花插花/乾花插花　dried flower arrangement
干混砂浆/乾混砂漿　dry-mixed mortar
干货/乾貨　dry cargo
干货船/乾貨船　dry cargo ship
干接合/乾接　dry connection
干接头/乾縮縫　dry joint
干进料器/乾式加料機　dry feeder
干浸法/乾浸没　dry immersion
干绝热直减率/乾絕熱線直減率　dry adiabatic lapse rate
干栏/干欄　raised-floor architecture, ganlan
干栏式建筑/干欄式建築　stilt architecture
干裂/乾裂　seasoning crack
干馏/碳化[作用]　carbonization
干罗经/乾羅經　dry compass, dry-card compass
干密度/乾[燥]密度　dry density
干摩擦式轴箱定位装置/乾摩擦式軸箱定位裝置　dry friction type journal box positioning device
干摩擦试验/乾摩擦試驗　dry friction test
干木材/乾木材　dried wood
干喷混凝土/乾噴混凝土,乾式噴射　dry shotcreting
干喷混凝土机/乾噴混凝土機　dry shotcreting machine
干砌石/乾砌石　dry stone wall
干砌石护坡/石護岸　stone revetment
干强度/乾燥強度　dry strength
干球温度/乾球溫度　dry-bulb temperature
干扰/干擾　disturbance, interference, trouble
干扰场强/干擾場強　interference field strength
干扰电压/干擾電壓　interference voltage
干扰度/擾亂程度　degree of disturbance
干扰光/干擾光　obtrusive light
干扰力矩/擾動力矩　disturbance torque
干扰量/干擾量　interference quantity
干扰性沉陷/干擾沈陷　interference settlement
干扰因子/干擾因素　interference factor
干扰影响/擾動影響　disturbing influence
干扰源/干擾源　interference source
干扰云/干擾絲雲　chaff cloud
干扰阻力/干擾阻力　interference drag
干热气候/乾熱氣候　dry hot climate
干容重/乾單位重　dry unit weight

干散货[集装]箱/乾散貨櫃　dry bulk container
干涉/干涉　interference
干涉场/干涉場　interference field
干涉图法/干涉圖技術　interferogram technique
干涉仪/干擾計　interferometer
干涉仪跟踪系统/干涉儀追蹤系統　interferometer tracking system
干湿表/乾濕表,空氣濕度計　psychrometer
干湿分离/乾濕分離　dry wet separation, parting of moisture
干湿计/乾濕計　psychrograph
干湿两用阀装置/乾濕兩用閥裝置　wet and dry pipe valve installation
干湿试验/乾濕試驗　wetting and drying test
干式变压器/乾式變壓器　dry type transformer
干式除尘器/吸塵機　dry dust collector
干式打眼/乾式鑽孔　dry boring
干式缸套/乾式缸套　dry cylinder liner
干式建造法/乾造法　dry construction method
干式交联/乾式交聯　dry type cross-linked
干式水表/乾式水表　dry type water meter
干式通气口/乾式通氣孔　dry vent
干式蒸发器/乾式蒸發器　dry type evaporator
干式自动喷水灭火系统/密閉乾式　dry pipe sprinkler system
干缩/乾[燥收]縮　dry shrinkage, drying shrinkage
干舷/乾舷　freeboard
干舷甲板/乾舷甲板　freeboard deck
干舷漆/乾舷漆　top-side paint
干压砖/乾壓陶瓷磚　dry-pressed tile, powder-pressed tile
干硬稠度灰浆/乾稠度砂漿　mortar of dry consistency
干硬性混凝土/乾硬性混凝土　dry concrete, harsh concrete
干预公海非油类物质污染议定书/油以外物質汙染事故在公海行使干涉議定書　Protocol Relating to Intervention on the High Seas in Case of Pollution by Substances other than Oil
干燥/乾燥　drying
干燥管/乾汽管　dry pipe
干燥混合料/半乾泥漿填塞　dry pack
干燥剂/乾燥劑,催乾劑　drier
干燥-搅拌筒/乾燥攪拌筒　drying mixing drum
干燥类型/乾型　dry type
干燥器/乾燥器,乾燥機　drier, dryer, desiccator
干燥室/乾燥室,乾燥窯　kiln, dry kiln
干燥筒/乾燥器　drier

干蒸汽加湿器／乾蒸汽增濕器　dry steam humidifier
干重／乾重　dry weight
干钻／乾鑽　dry drilling
甘蔗车／甘蔗車　sugar cane car
坩埚炉／坩堝爐　crucible furnace
竿钓／竿　rod
竿钓渔船／竿釣漁船　pole and line fishing boat
杆架式钻／桿架式鑽　mounting bar drill
杆件／桿件，構件　member, bar
杆件缩短损失／桿件縮短損失　loss due to concrete member shortening
杆件弯曲损失／桿件彎曲損失　loss due to bending of concrete member
杆上电缆盒／桿上電纜盒　cable terminal box on a post
杆上工作台／桿上作業臺　pole balcony
杆式液压调速器／槓桿式液壓調速器　lever-type hydraulic governor
杆系结构／桿系結構，骨架結構　rod-type structure, bar structure, skeleton structure
杆状浮标／椿標　spar buoy, pile beacon
赶工／趕工　crashing
感潮河／[感]潮河　tidal river
感潮河段／感潮段，潮達區，潮流河段　tide reaching zone, tidal reach, tidal river reach
感光层／感光層，光敏塗層　photo sensitive coating
感光度／光化度，光化作用，光敏度　actinism, light sensitivity
感光乳胶／照相乳膠　photographic emulsion
感光特性曲线／感光特性曲線　sensitometric characteristic curve, hand D curve
感觉冲突假说／感覺衝突假說　sensory conflict hypothesis
感觉花园／感覺花園，感知園，感官花園　sensory garden
感染性疾病／感染性疾病，傳染性疾病　infectious disease
感染性物质／傳染性物質　infectious substance
感色度／色彩感應度　color sensitivity
感温光缆／熱敏光纜　heat sensitive optical cable
感温式探测器／溫度探測器　thermal detector
感旋光性／光敏度，感光度　photo sensitivity
感压式车辆检测器／感應式車壓偵查器　pressure-sensitive vehicle detector
感烟式探测器／探煙器　smoke detector
感应场引信／感應場引信　induction field fuze
感应传输方式／感應傳輸型，感應傳輸波式　inductive transmission mode

感应船磁／船體感應磁　ship induced magnetism
感应电动机／感應電動機，感應馬達　induction motor
感应加热／[電]感應加熱　induction heating
感应加热淬火／感應硬化　induction hardening
感应觉察／感應感測　induction sensing
感应钎焊／[電]感應硬焊　induction brazing, induction soldering
感应式机车信号／感應式機車信號　inductive cab signaling
感应式列车无线电通信／感應列車無線電通訊　inductive train radio communication
感应同步器／感應同步器　inductosyn
感应线圈／感應線圈，探索線圈　search coil, induction coil
感应信号控制机／車動控制器　traffic actuated controller
感知／感受　perception
感知运动能力／感知運動能力　perceptive-motor performance
橄榄球场／橄欖球場　rugby field
橄榄球运动／[英式]橄欖球　rugby
干管／總管　main pipe
干管水表／幹管水表　main line meter
干流／幹流　trunk stream, main river
干线／幹線　main line, trunk line
干线长途通信／幹線通信，中繼通信　trunk communication
干线长途通信网／幹線通信網　trunk communication network
干线导管／幹繩導管　main line guide pipe
干线调度电话／幹線調度電話　trunk dispatching telephone
干线放线机／放繩機　line casting machine
干线公路／幹線公路　trunk highway, arterial highway, main highway
干线供电／幹線供電　main linely connected power supply
干线会议电话／幹線會議電話，中繼線會議電話　trunk conference telephone
干线客机／幹線運輸機　trunk liner
干线理线机／理繩機　line arrangement machine
干线[排水]系统／下水道幹管　trunk system
干线起线机／卷繩機　line hauler
干线铁路／鐵道幹線　main line railway, trunk railway
干支流交汇水域／主支流匯流區　convergent area of main and branch

冈贝里亚庄园/岡貝里亞莊園　Villa Gamberaia
刚度/剛度,勁度,抗撓性　rigidity, stiffness
刚度法/剛度法　stiffness method
刚度矩阵/剛度矩陣　stiffness matrix
刚架/剛[構]架　rigid frame
刚架拱桥/剛架拱橋　rigid framed arch bridge
刚架桥/剛架橋,剛構橋　rigid frame bridge
刚架式结构/構架結構,框架結構　framed structure
刚架式棚洞/剛架式棚洞　framed shed tunnel, framed shed gallery
刚接节点/固定接頭　rigid joint
刚接梁法/剛性[連]接梁法　rigid connected beam method
刚塑性材料/剛性塑膠材料,硬質塑膠材料　rigid plastic material
刚塑性模型/剛性塑膠模型,硬質塑膠模型　rigid plastic model
刚弹性方案/剛彈性方案　rigid elastic scheme
刚体/剛體　rigid body
刚性/剛性,抗撓性,勁度　stiffness
刚性齿轮驱动/剛性齒輪驅動　solid gear drive
刚性船台/剛式船臺　rigid cradle
刚性挡土墙/不動擋土牆　non-yielding retaining wall
刚性底板/剛性板塊　rigid plate
刚性定位轮对/剛性定位輪對　rigidly positioned wheelset
刚性方案/剛性方案　rigid scheme
刚性防水屋面/剛性防水　rigid water proof roof
刚性固定/剛性固定,完全固定　rigid fixing, fully fixed
刚性航天器动力学/剛體太空載具動力學　rigid spacecraft dynamics
刚性桁架/剛性桁架　rigid truss
刚性横梁法/剛性橫梁法　rigid cross beam method
刚性护栏/勁性護欄　stiff safety fence
刚性基础/剛性基礎　rigid foundation
刚性接口/剛性介面　rigidity joint
刚性结构/剛性結構　rigid construction, rigid structure
刚性救生筏/硬式救生筏　rigid liferaft
刚性联轴器/剛性聯結器　fast coupling
刚性路面/剛性路面　rigid pavement
刚性支承/剛性支承　rigid support
刚性轴系/剛性軸系　stiff shafting
刚性转子/堅固轉子,剛接式旋翼　rigid rotor
刚域/剛性域　rigid zone
钢/鋼　steel

钢板/鋼板　steel plate
钢板护栏/鋼制護欄　steel guardrail
钢板矫平/鋼板平鉋　steel planing
钢板梁桥/鋼板梁橋　steel plate girder bridge
钢板网式空气滤清器/鋼片網式空氣濾清器　steel sheet mesh type air filter
钢板抓/鋼板抓斗　plate grab
钢板桩/鋼板樁　steel sheet pile
钢板桩格型堤岸/艙式隔牆　cellular bulkhead
钢材边缘加工/鋼材邊緣加工　steel edge processing
钢材除锈/鋼材除銹　steel rust removing
钢材剪切/鋼材切割　steel cutting
钢材矫正/鋼材矯正　steel rectification
钢材卷圆/鋼板軋制　steel plate rolling
钢材涂料/鋼材塗料　steel coating
钢材外观检验/鋼材目視檢查　steel visual inspection
钢材弯曲/鋼材彎曲　steel bending
钢材验收试验/鋼材驗收試驗　steel acceptance test
钢材制孔/鋼材衝孔　steel punching
[钢]插板/[鋼]插板　poling plate
钢船/鋼[殼]船　steel ship
钢拱支撑/鋼拱[架]支撐　steel arched support, steel arch support, steel arched timbering
钢构套加固法/鋼構套加固法　structure member strengthening with steel frame cage
钢骨混凝土桥/鋼骨混凝土橋　rolled shape steel reinforced concrete bridge
钢管/鋼管　steel pipe, steel tube
钢管混凝土/鋼管混凝土　concrete filled steel tube
钢管混凝土桥/鋼管混凝土橋　steel pipe encased concrete bridge
钢管结构/鋼管結構　steel tubular structure
钢管桩/鋼管樁　steel pipe pile
钢轨/鋼軌　rail
钢轨擦伤/鋼軌擦傷,車輪空轉灼傷　engine burn, wheel burn
钢轨打标记/鋼軌打標記　branding and stamping of rails
钢轨低接头/鋼軌低接頭　depressed joint, battered joint of rail
钢轨断裂/鋼軌損傷　rail fracture
钢轨对地电位/鋼軌對地電位　rail potential to ground
钢轨肥边/鋼軌肥邊　rail lip, spreading of the rail head
钢轨工作边/鋼軌工作邊,軌距線　gage line, working surface of rail
钢轨基础模量/軌道模數　rail supporting modulus,

钢　167

track modulus
钢轨矫直机/軌條矯直機　rail straightening machine
钢轨接头/鋼軌接頭　rail joint
钢轨接头绝缘/軌條接頭絶緣　rail joint insulator
钢轨接头陷落/軌條接頭陷落　rail joint depression
钢轨接续线/聯軌線　rail bond
钢轨绝缘/鋼軌絶緣　rail insulation
钢轨绝缘不良/鋼軌絶緣不良　bad rail insulation
钢轨拉伸器/鋼軌拉伸器　rail tensor
钢轨连接器/鋼軌接頭結合　rail joint bond
钢轨梁/軌條梁　rail beam
钢轨裂纹/鋼軌破裂　rail crack
钢轨螺栓孔/鋼軌螺栓孔　rail bolt hole
钢轨落锤试验/軌條落錘試驗　drop test of rail
钢轨磨耗限度/軌條磨耗限度　rail wear tolerance
钢轨磨损检查车/鋼軌斷面檢測車　rail profile measuring car
钢轨磨损检查仪/鋼軌斷面磨耗測量器　rail profile gage
钢轨爬行/軌條匍行　rail creeping
钢轨刨边机/鋼軌鉋邊機　rail head edge planing machine
钢轨屏蔽系数/軌道遮罩因數　shielding factor of track
钢轨伤损/鋼軌傷損,鋼軌損傷　rail defects and failures, rail failure
钢轨伸缩调节器/鋼軌伸縮調節器　expansion rail joint, rail expansion device
钢轨锁定/鋼軌扣件鎖定　rail fastening down
钢轨探伤车/鋼軌探傷車　rail flaw detection car
钢轨探伤仪/鋼軌探傷器,鋼軌探傷車　rail flaw detector
钢轨涂油器/鋼軌塗油機　rail lubricator
钢轨推凸机/鋼軌推凸機　rail weld seam shearing machine
钢轨推凸器/鋼軌推凸器　rail shearing device
钢轨位移观测桩/鋼軌位移觀測樁　rail creep indication post
钢轨锈蚀/鋼軌銹蝕　rail corrosion
钢轨压嵌/軌條壓嵌　rail cut
钢轨引接线/鋼軌引接線,駝峰溜放線　track lead
钢轨折断/軌條脆性斷裂　brittle fractures of rail, sudden rupture of rail
钢轨支点弹性模量/鋼軌支點彈性模量　modulus of elasticity of rail support
钢轨桩/鋼軌樁　rail pile
钢轨阻抗/軌道接頭阻抗　rail impedance
钢轨组合辙叉/鋼軌組合轍叉　bolted rigid frog,

assembled frog
钢轨钻孔机/鋼軌鑽孔機　rail drilling machine
钢轨钻孔器/鋼軌鑽孔器　rail drilling tool
钢桁架桥/鋼桁架橋　steel truss bridge
钢桁梁桥/鋼桁梁橋　steel truss girder bridge
钢化玻璃/強化玻璃,回火玻璃　tempered glass
钢化[淬火]玻璃/堅韌玻璃　toughened glass
钢-混凝土组合板/鋼混凝土複合板　steel concrete composite slab
钢-混凝土组合梁/鋼混凝土組合梁　steel concrete composite beam
钢架拱/鋼拱架　steel arch
钢绞线/鋼絲股,鋼索　strand, steel strand
钢结构/鋼[結]構　steel structure
钢结构防火涂料/鋼結構防火塗料　fire resistive coating for steel structure
钢结构加工工艺/鋼結構加工技術　steel structure processing technology
钢筋/鋼筋,鋼條　steel bar, reinforcing steel bar
钢筋保护层测定仪/鋼筋保護層測定儀　cover protectometer
钢筋充分利用点/鋼筋全展點　fully developed point of bar
钢筋电位测量/鋼筋電位測量　bar potential measurement
钢筋电渣压力焊/鋼筋電渣壓力焊　steel bar flux press welding
钢筋电阻率测量/鋼筋電阻率測量　bar resistivity measurement
钢筋对焊/鋼條對焊　steel bar butt welding
钢筋对焊机/鋼條對焊機　steel bar butt welder, steel bar butt welding machine
钢筋镦头机/鋼筋鍛頭機　steel bar header
[钢筋]焊接接头强度试验/熔接接頭強度試驗　welded joint strength test
钢筋混凝土/鋼筋混凝土,強化混凝土　reinforced concrete, steel bar reinforced concrete
钢筋混凝土电杆/鋼筋混凝土水泥桿　reinforced concrete pole
钢筋混凝土管片/鋼筋混凝土砌塊　reinforced concrete segment
钢筋混凝土轨枕/鋼筋混凝土軌枕　reinforced concrete sleeper
钢筋混凝土护栏/鋼筋混凝土護欄　reinforced concrete fence
钢筋混凝土结构/鋼筋混凝土結構　reinforced concrete structure
钢筋混凝土路面/鋼筋混凝土路面,鋼筋混凝土鋪面

reinforced concrete pavement
钢筋混凝土桥/鋼筋混凝土橋 reinforced concrete bridge
[钢筋]混凝土桩/[鋼筋]混凝土樁 reinforced concrete pile
钢筋混凝土组合梁/鋼-混凝土合成梁 steel-concrete composite girder
钢筋机械连接/鋼條機械連接 steel bar mechanical connecting
钢筋冷拔机/鋼筋冷拔機 steel bar dieing drawing machine
钢筋冷镦/鋼筋冷鐓 steel bar button head forging
钢筋冷拉机/鋼條冷拉[拉製]機 bar cold-drawing machine, steel bar cold-drawing machine
钢筋冷压连接/鋼條冷壓連接 steel bar cold press connecting
钢筋理论断点/鋼筋理論斷裂點 theoretical cutoff point of bar
钢筋排列/鋼筋排列 bar arrangement
钢筋气压焊/鋼條氣壓焊 steel bar gas press welding
钢筋气压焊机/鋼條氣壓焊機 steel bar gas press welding machine
钢筋切断机/鋼筋切斷機,切桿機 steel bar cutter, bar cutter, steel bar shears
钢筋水泥船/鋼筋混凝土船 ferro-concrete vessel, reinforced concrete vessel
钢[筋]松弛/鋼材鬆弛 relaxation of steel
钢筋调直机/鋼筋調直機,鋼條矯直機,棒材矯直機 steel bar straightener, bar straightener
钢筋调直切断机/鋼筋調直切斷機 steel bar straightening and shearing machine
钢筋弯箍机/鋼筋彎箍機 stirrup bender
钢筋弯曲机/鋼條彎[曲]機,鋼棒彎[曲]機,彎鋼筋機 steel bar bender, bar bender
钢筋弯折机/彎筋器 bar bender
钢筋网成型机/鋼條網成型機 steel net forming machine
钢筋网喷射混凝土锚杆支护/絲網噴混凝土岩石錨桿支護 wiremesh shotcrete rock bolt support
钢筋网喷射混凝土支护/絲網噴支護 wiremesh shotcrete support
[钢筋]握固长度/錨著長度 grip length
钢筋锈蚀/鋼筋腐蝕,鋼[條]腐蝕 steel bar corrosion, steel corrosion, reinforcement corrosion
钢筋锈蚀测定计/鋼筋鏽蝕測定計 bar corrosion activity indicator
钢筋锈蚀活动性评定/鋼筋鏽蝕活動性評定 bar corrosion activity evaluation
钢筋锈蚀三因素模型/鋼筋鏽蝕三因素模型 three factor model of bar corrosion
钢筋预应力松弛损失/鋼筋預應力鬆弛損失 loss due to tendon relaxation
钢筋约束区/鋼筋約束區 confining region of reinforcement
钢缆索/粗纜,鋼繩 cable
钢梁腐蚀裂纹/鋼橋腐[蝕斷]裂 corrosion cracking of steel bridge
钢梁加固/鋼梁加固 strengthening of steel bridge
钢梁结构试装配/鋼梁結構試裝配 trial steel work fixing
钢梁疲劳损伤/鋼橋疲勞損傷 steel bridge fatigue damage
钢梁应力腐蚀裂纹/鋼橋應力-腐蝕破裂 stress corrosion cracking of steel bridge
钢梁油漆/鋼橋保護塗層 protective coating of steel bridge
钢轮/鋼滾筒 steel drum
钢麻绳/鋼麻合燃索 spring lay rope
钢门窗/鋼門窗 steel door and window
钢模成型/鋼模成型 steel form moulding
钢木组合大梁/鋼木夾合梁 flitch plate girder
钢木组合屋架/鋼木材複合材料屋架 steel timber composite roof truss
钢桥/鋼橋 steel bridge
钢桥就位/鋼橋就位 seating steel bridge on supports
钢桥拼装/鋼橋裝配 assembling of steel bridge
钢丝/鋼絲 steel thread, steel wire, wire-steel
钢丝缠束机/鋼絲纏束機 steel wire strand strapping machine
钢丝冷拔试验/鋼絲冷拔試驗 wire cold drawn test
钢丝牵索/鋼[絲牽]索 wire guy
钢丝三角桩/鋼絲三角樁 triangle wire pile
钢丝绳/鋼絲索 wire rope
钢丝绳冲击钻机/大型鑽孔機 cable drill
钢丝绳剪/切繩器 wire rope cutter
钢丝绳式升降机/導繩式昇降機 guide rope hoist
钢丝绳提升/索吊重 rope hoisting
钢丝束/鋼線束,鋼絞線 bundle of steel wire, bundled steel wires, wire tendon
钢丝束制作/鋼絲束製作 wire grouping
钢丝刷除锈/鋼絲刷清潔 brush cleaning
钢丝网/金屬絲網 wire mesh
钢丝网混凝土板/鋼網混凝土板 wire mesh concrete plate
钢丝网架聚苯乙烯芯板/鋼絲網架聚苯乙烯芯板,GJ板

polystyrene core plate of steel wire rack
钢丝网铺设机/線網鋪設機 wire mesh laying machine
钢丝网水泥船/鋼筋水泥船 ferrocement vessel, ferrocement boat, ferrocement ship
钢塑复合管/鋼塑複合管 steel-plastic composite pipe
钢索护栏/鋼索護欄 cable guardrail
钢索护套/緊張索 guard cable
钢索天线/線天線 wire antenna
钢条/鋼條 steel bar
钢围图/鋼圍圖 steel waling
钢纤维混凝土/鋼纖維混凝土 steel fiber reinforced concrete
钢纤维混凝土结构/鋼纖維混凝土結構 steel fiber reinforced concrete structure
钢纤维混凝土路面/鋼筋混凝土路面 wire reinforced concrete pavement
钢纤维喷射混凝土衬砌/鋼纖維噴射混凝土襯砌 steel fiber shotcrete lining
钢弦式应变计/振動金屬絲應變計 vibrating wire strain gage
钢线/鋼線 steel wire
钢斜拉桥/鋼製斜張橋 steel deck cable stayed bridge
钢芯铝绞线/鋼芯鋁絞線 steel-cored aluminum stranded wire
钢芯铜线/鋼芯銅線 steel-cored copper wire
钢与混凝土组合构件/型鋼混凝土組合結構 steel reinforced concrete composite structural member
钢与混凝土组合梁/鋼-混凝土組合梁 composite steel and concrete beam
钢渣水泥/鋼渣水泥 steel slag cement
钢枕/合成軌枕,組合軌枕 steel tie
钢桩/鋼樁 steel pile
钢钻头/鋼鑽頭 steel bit
缸盖出口废气温度/缸蓋出口廢氣溫度 exhaust temperature at cylinder head outlet
缸径最大磨损/缸徑最大磨損 bore maximum wear
缸套冷却水泵/缸套冷卻水泵 jacket cooling water pump
[缸套]磨损率/缸套磨損率 liner wear rate
港泊图/港圖 harbor plan
港池/港池,盆地 harbor basin
港防/港防 harbor defense
港界/港界 harbor boundary, harbor limit
港口/港口,港[埠] port, harbor
港口暗沙/攔門沙 port bar

港口城市/港口都市 port city
港口电台/港埠電臺 port station
港口费/碼頭費,船席費 berthage
港口服务处/港務接洽處 harbor service kiosk
港口腹地/港口腹地 port hinterland
港口管理/港口管理 port management
港口集疏运交通/港口集疏運交通 port collection and distribution transportation
港口建筑线/碼頭法線 pier head line
港口客运站/水路客運站 port passenger station, waterway passenger station, waterway passenger terminal
港口雷达/港口雷達 harbor radar
港口立交桥/港口立交橋 estuarial crossing
港口陆域/港口陸地區域 port land area
港口区/港區 port district, harbor area, port area
港口设备/港埠設施 port facility
港口设施/港埠設施 port facility
港口使费/貨櫃碼頭費用 terminal charge
港口水域/港口水域 port water area
港口吞吐量/港口[貨物]吞吐量 port cargo throughput, port capacity
港口习惯/港口慣例 custom of port
港口线/臨港線 harbor line
港口营运业务/港埠營運業務 port operation service
港口用地/港區[陸域] land for port
港口租船合同/港口租船契約 port charter party
港内航道/港内航道 harbor fairway
港内水深图/港内水深圖 harbor sounding map
港内速度/港内船速 harbor speed
港区铁路/港區鐵路 port railroad
港湾测量/港灣測量 harbor survey
港湾模型/港灣模型 harbor model
港湾式停车处/港灣式停車處 parking bay
港湾站/港口站 harbour station
港务船/港勤艇 harbour craft, service boat, service craft
港务费/港工捐 harbor dues
港务监督/港務監理 harbor superintendence administration
港务旗/港務旗 port service signal
[港务]杂费/[港務]雜費 petty average
港章/港口規章 port regulations
港址/港址 port site
港作船/港勤船 harbor launch, harbor boat
杠杆原理/槓桿原理 principle of lever
杠杆原理法/槓桿原理法 lever principle method
高保真度/高逼真度,高傳真度 Hi-Fi

高侧窗/縱向天牆　clerestory window
高侧音/高侧音　high side tone
高层厂房/高層工業廠房　high-rise industrial building
高层大气/高層大氣　upper atmosphere
高层建筑/高層建築[物]　high-rise building, tall building
高层建筑风影区/高層建築風影區　wind shadow area of high building
高层汽车库/多層停車庫　high-rise garage
高层云/高層雲　alto-starts
高层住宅/高層住宅　high-rise residential building, high-rise house
高超临速流/高超臨速流　hypercritical flow
高超声速风洞/高超音速風洞,極音速風洞　hypersonic wind tunnel
高超声速激波层/極音速激波層　hypersonic shock layer
高超声速流/極音速流　hypersonic flow
高超声速相似律/超音速相似律　hypersonic similarity law
高潮/高潮,滿潮　high water, high tide, full tide
高潮间隙/高潮間隔　high water interval
高潮礁/高潮礁　high water rock
高潮时/高潮時　high water time
高潮水位线/高潮線　high water line
高承台桩基[础]/高承臺樁基礎,高架樁基礎　high-rise platform pile foundation, elevated footing on piles
高程/高程,標高,高度　elevation, altitude
高处/高處　aloft
高处作业吊篮/高空作業吊籃　aerial work basket
高次谐波频率/高諧頻率　higher harmonic frequency
高弹道[飞行]试验/高彈道試驗　high trajectory test
高灯芯浮标/高燈芯浮標　high focal plane buoy
高[等学]校图书馆/大學圖書館　university library, academic library
高等院校/研究所,機構,學院　university, college, institute
高低潮/[較]高低潮　higher low water, HLW
高低温试验/高低溫試驗　high low temperature test
高低温循环处理/高低溫循環處理　high and low temperature cycling treatment
高低压继电器/高低壓繼電器　high and low pressure relay
高度保持/高度保持　altitude hold
高度表拨正/高度表撥定　altimeter setting
高度差/高度差　altitude difference

高度差法/高度差法　altitude difference method
高度计/高度表　altimeter
高度均衡多边形法/高度均衡多邊形法　height-balance polygons method
高度空穴效应/高度空穴效應,高度空洞效應　altitude-hole effect
高度视差/高位視差　parallax in altitude
高度特性/高度特性　altitude characteristic
高度调整阀/高度控制閥,測高控制閥　leveling valve
高度限制/高度控制　height control
高度限制地区/限高區　height district
高鹅头弯管/鵝頸通風筒　high level bend, swan neck
高尔夫球场/高爾夫球場　golf course
高尔夫球场草坪/高爾夫球場草坪　golf lawn
高尔夫球运动/高爾夫球　golf
高费率货/工資加成貨　penalty cargo
高分辨率红外辐射计/高解紅外輻射計　high resolution infrared radiometer
高分辨率全球大气臭氧测量仪/高解析度全球大氣臭氧測量儀　high resolution global measurement of atmospheric ozone
高分子防水卷材/高分子防水卷材　high polymer waterproof sheet, polymer waterproof sheet
高分子防水片材/高分子防水片材　high polymer water-proof sheet, polymer waterproof sheet
高峰负荷/高峰負載,尖峰負載　peak load
高峰交通[量]/尖峰交通量　peak traffic
高峰[时间]交通流量/尖峰交通流量　traffic peak flow
高峰小时/尖峰小時　peak hour
高峰小时交通量/尖峰小時交通量　peak hour volume
高峰小时系数/尖峰小時係數　peak hour factor, PHF
高峰需水量/高峰需水量　peak demand
高辐射区/高輻射區　high radiation area
高杆灯/高桿燈,高桿照明　high-pole lamp, high mast lighting
高杆照明/高桿照明　high mast lighting
高高潮/較高高潮　higher high water, HHW
高功率室/大功率室　high power room
高硅氧/高矽氧　refrasil
高厚比/高厚比　ratio of height to thickness
高积云/高積雲　alto-cumulus
高级包房卧车/高級包房臥車　superclass corridor compartment type sleeping car

高级惯性参考球/高級慣性參考球,改良型慣性參考球　advanced inertial reference sphere, AIRS
高级沥青路面/高級瀝青路面　high type bituminous surface
高级路面/高級路面　high type pavement, high class pavement
高级微波水汽遥感器/高級微波水汽遙感器　advanced microwave moisture sensor
高级炸药/高速炸藥　high explosive
高技派/高科技　high-tech
高技术产业/高科技產業　high-tech industry
高技术产业开发区/高新技術開發區,高科技產業開發區　high-tech industrial development zone
高技术城/高科技園區　high-tech park
高技术园区/高科技園區　high-tech park
高架仓库/高架倉庫　high rack storage
高架道路/高架道路,高架線　elevated road, elevated line
高架公路/高架公路　elevated highway
高架轨道/高架軌道　elevated rail
高架候车室/高架候車室　crossover waiting room
高架候车厅/架空候車大廳　overhead waiting hall
高架路/高架道路　overhead road
高架桥/高架橋,陸橋,高架道路　viaduct, viaduct bridge
高架索补给装置/高架索補給裝置　highline rig
高架索绞车/高線絞機　highline winch
高架铁路/高架鐵路,懸空鐵道　elevated railway, suspended railway
高架纤维绳传递装置/纜索高線傳遞設備　fiber rope highline rig
高架卸货线/高架卸貨線　elevated unloading track
高架站房/高架站房　crossover station building
高阶电压/高階電壓　high plateau voltage
高阶振型/高階振型　high order mode
高精度测量带/高準確度測量帶　high accuracy measurement corridor
高精度定位系统/高精準定位系統　high precision positioning system
高精度气压发生器/高精度氣壓產生器　high precision air pressure generator
高抗剪铆接/高抗剪鉚接　high antishearing riveting
高抗拉螺栓/高拉力螺栓　high-tensile bolt
高可移动工作台/高可移式工作臺　high removable worktable
高空爆炸/高爆藥　high explosion
高空代偿服/高空代償服　high altitude compensating suit
高空电磁脉冲/高空電磁脈波　high altitude electromagnetic pulse
高空飞行/高空飛行　upper airway flight
高空风/高空風　wind aloft
高空核试验/高空核[子]試爆　high altitude nuclear test
高空火箭发动机/高空火箭發動機　altitude rocket engine
高空减压病/高空減壓病　altitude decompression sickness
高空缺氧/高空性缺氧　altitude hypoxia
高空[天气]图/高空[天氣]圖　upper-level weather chart
高空作业/高空作業　aloft work
高空作业车/高空作業車　aerial work carriage
高空作业平台/高空作業平臺　high altitude operation platform, aerial work platform
高跨比/高跨比　depth span ratio, rise span ratio
高跨比修正系数/高跨校正係數　correction coefficient of height-span ratio
高雷诺数风洞/高雷諾數風洞　high Reynolds number wind tunnel
高肋板/深肋板　depth floor
高篱/高籬　high hedge
高临界流速/上限臨界流速　higher critical velocity
高临界速度/上限臨界流速　higher critical velocity
高磷闸瓦/高磷閘瓦　high phosphor cast iron brake shoe
高岭石/高嶺石　kaolinite
高岭土/高嶺土　kaolin
高炉煤气/鼓風爐氣　blast furnace gas
高炉渣水泥/高爐水泥　blast furnace cement
高铝水泥/高鋁水泥　high alumina cement
高锰钢整铸辙叉/錳鋼岔心　solid manganese steel frog, cast manganese steel frog
高锰酸钾消耗/過錳酸鉀消耗量　potassium permanganate consumed
高敏感性黏土/超敏感性黏土　extrasensitive clay
高摩合成闸瓦/高摩擦式合成閘瓦　high friction composite brake shoe
高能成形/高能率成型　high energy rate forming
高能燃料/高能燃料　high energy fuel
高能束焊接/高能束焊接　high energy density beam welding
高能束加工/高能束加工　high energy beam machining
高浓污泥/濃汙泥　heavy sludge
高频分线盒/高頻分線盒　high frequency terminal

box
高频燃烧不稳定性/高頻燃燒不穩定　high frequency combustion instability
高频通信/高頻通信　HF communication
高频转接段/高頻段　high frequency section
高强度钢/高強度鋼　high strength steel
高强[度]钢丝/高強[度]鋼絲, 硬拉线　hard drawn wire, high strength steel wire, high tensile steel wire
高强[度]螺栓/高強度螺栓, 强力螺栓　high strength bolt
高强度铝合金/高強度鋁合金　high strength aluminum alloy
高强度气体放电灯/高強度氣體放電燈　high intensity discharge lamp, HID lamp
高强钢/高強度鋼　high strength steel
高强钢筋/高強鋼筋　heigh strength bar
高强钢线/高強鋼線　plough wire
高区电梯/高層電梯　high-zone elevator
高容量滤池/高率滴濾池　high-capacity filter
高山草甸风景区/高山草甸風景區, 高山凍原風景區, 高山苔原風景區　alpine tundra landscape spot
高山草甸植物群落/高山草甸植物群落　mesophorbium
高山垫状植被/高山墊狀植被　alpine cushion-like vegetation
高山风景区/高山風景區　alpine scenic spot
高山寒土植物/寒地植物　psychrophyte
高山花卉/高山花　alpine flower
高山滑翔/高山滑翔　mountain glide
高山滑雪/高山滑雪　alpine skiing
高山[流石滩]稀疏植被/高山稀疏植被　alpine talus vegetation
高山旅游/山地旅遊　mountain tourism
高山土壤/高山土　alpine soil
高山植物/高山植物　alpine plant, acrophyte
高山植物群落/高山植物群落　acrophytia
高山植物园/高山植物園　alpine garden
高设花台/高設花壇　raised flower bed
高水河槽/洪水河床　major bed
高水位/特别高潮位　high high water level
高水位池塘/高水位池塘　high water table pond
高水位桥/高水位橋　high water level bridge
高斯积分/高斯積分　Gauss integration
高斯消元法/高斯消去法　Gauss elimination method
高耸结构/高聳結構　tall and slender structure
高速柴油机/高速柴油機　high speed diesel engine
高速车道/快速車道　rapid vehicle lane
高速电镀/高速電鍍　high speed electrodeposition
高速风洞/高速風洞　high speed wind tunnel
高速公路/高速公路　freeway
高速公路服务区/高速公路服務區　highway service area
高速公路服务站/高速公路服務站　highway service area
高速公路监控/高速公路監控　freeway surveillance and control
高速公路收费站/[高速公路]收費站　highway toll station, toll station
高速公路网/公路網　highway network
高速公路主线控制/高速公路主線控制　freeway mainline control
高速构造深度仪/高速構造深度儀　high speed texture meter
高速列车/高速列車　high speed train
高速炮/高速炮　high speed gun
高速燃烧器/高速燃燒設備　high velocity burner
高速摄影机/高速攝影機　high speed camera
高速摄影间/高速攝影間　high speed photography house
高速铁路/高速鐵路　high speed railway
高速艇筏/高速艇筏　high speed craft
高速消化/高速消化　high-rate digestion
高速一维流/高速一維管流　one dimensional high speed flow
高速诱导空气调节系统/高速誘導空調系統　high velocity induction air conditioning system
高台建筑/高臺建築　high-platform architecture, gaotai
高威力炸药/高速炸藥　high explosive
高位水池/高潮潮位　high elevation water tank
高位蓄水/高架蓄水　elevated storage
高温防护涂层/高溫防護塗層　high temperature protection coating
高温腐蚀/高溫腐蝕　high temperature corrosion
高温钢/高溫鋼　calorine steel
高温工况/過熱狀態　worst hot case
高温合金/高溫合金, 超合金　superalloy, high temperature alloy
高温回火/高溫回火　high temperature tempering
高温计/高溫計　pyrometer
高温抗氧化涂层/高溫抗氧化塗層　high temperature oxidation-resistant coating
高温模拟试验/高溫模擬試驗　simulated hot climate test
高温试验/高溫試驗　high temperature test

高温水/高温熱水　high temperature hot water
高温涂层/高温塗層　high temperature coating
高温植物/高温植物　megatherm
高效次氯酸盐/強力次氯酸鹽，漂粉精　high-test hypochlorite
高效活性污泥法/高速活性汙泥法　high rate activated sludge process
高效空气过滤器/高效率空氣微粒過濾器　high efficiency particulate air filter, HEPA filter
高效塑化剂/超增塑劑　superplasticizer
高新科技园区/高新科技園區　high-tech industrial park
高性能船/高性能船　high performance craft
高性能混凝土/高性能混凝土　high performance concrete
高压/高氣壓　high pressure
高压保安阀/高壓安全閥　high pressure safety valve
高压侧调压/高[電]壓調節　high voltage regulation
高压电力电缆/高壓電力電纜　high voltage power cable
高压电路/高壓電路　high voltage circuit, high tension circuit
高压二氧化碳灭火系统/高壓二氧化碳滅火系統　high-pressure carbon dioxide extinguishing system
高压供电/高壓電源[供應器]　high voltage power supply
高压罐车/高壓罐車　high pressure tank car
高压锅炉/高壓鍋爐　high pressure boiler
高压化学气相沉积/高壓化學蒸汽沈積　high pressure chemical vapor deposition
高压机油泵/高壓滑油泵，高氣壓潤滑油泵　high pressure lubricating oil pump
高压[给水]加热器/高壓加熱器　high pressure heater, high pressure feed water heater
高压脊/高壓脊　ridge
高压浸渍/高壓浸漬　high pressure impregnation
高压开关设备/高壓開關設備　high voltage switchgear
高压空气瓶/高壓空氣瓶　high pressure air bottle
高压钠[蒸气]灯/高壓鈉[氣]燈，高壓鈉光燈　high pressure sodium vapor lamp, high voltage sodium lamp
高压配电室/高壓配電室　high voltage distribution room
高压配电系统/高[電]壓配電系統　high voltage power distribution system
高压配电装置/高壓電櫃開關裝置　high voltage cubicle switchboard
高压喷射注浆/高壓噴射注漿法　high pressure jet grouting
高压气瓶/高壓容器　high pressure gas bottle, high pressure vessel
高压气态贮存/高壓氣體儲藏　high pressure gas storage
高压绕组/高壓繞組　high voltage winding, high tension winding
高压软管/高壓軟管　high pressure hose
高压深入供电方式/高壓深入電力供應　high voltage deeping types of electric power supply
高压水冲洗/高壓水冲洗　hydro-blasting
高压水切割/高壓水刀切割　high pressure water jet cutting
高压水射流加工/高壓水噴射切割加工　water jet machining
高压调压开关/高電壓分接頭　high voltage tap changer, high tension tap changer
高压透平/高壓渦輪機　high pressure turbine
高压线/高壓線　high tension line
高压线走廊/高壓[線]走廊　high tension corridor, high-tension line corridor
高压消防给水系统/高壓消防水系統　high pressure fire water system
高压消防系统/高壓消防系統　high pressure fire system
高压压气机/高壓壓縮器　high pressure compressor
高压氧舱/高壓氧氣艙　hyperbaric oxygen chamber
高压氧气系统/高壓氧氣系統　high pressure oxygen system
高压油泵/高壓油泵，燃料噴射泵　high pressure oilpump, fuel injection pump
高压油管/高壓油管　high pressure fuel pipe
高压闸门/高壓閘門　high pressure gate
高压走廊/高壓線路走廊　high voltage line corridor
高G遥测/高G遙測　high G telemetry
高液限黏土/高液限黏土　high liquid limit clay
高音风喇叭/高音調氣喇叭　high tone air horn
高原/高原　plateau
高原气候模拟试验/高原氣候模擬試驗　simulated highland climate test
高站台/高月臺　high platform
高真空/高真空　high vacuum
高枝剪/高枝剪　long pruning shear
高枝锯/高枝鋸　lopper saw
高柱信号机/高頻信號　high signal
高桩承台/高樁承臺　high rise pile cap
高浊度水/超濁水　ultra turbid water

膏体推进剂/膏體推進劑　pasty propellant
膏体[推进剂]火箭发动机/膏體[推進劑]火箭發動機　pasty propellant rocket engine, pasty propellant rocket motor
告警阶段/警戒階段　alert phase
告警系统/警報系統　alarm system
告警线/告警線　alarm line
告警信号/警告信號,警告訊號　warning signal
告警信号电路/警報電路　alarm circuit
戈壁/戈壁　gobi
哥伦比亚咖啡文化景观/哥倫比亞咖啡文化景觀　coffee cultural landscape of Colombia
哥特建筑/哥特式建築　Gothic architecture
搁墩负荷/擱墩負載　block load
搁浅/擱淺　aground
搁浅船/擱淺船　vessel aground
割草机/割草機　lawn mower, mower
割灌机/割灌機　cutting irrigation machine
割炬/火焰截割器　cutting torch
割木法/割木法　conversion of timber
割线模量/正割模數　secant modulus
歌剧院/歌劇院　opera house
阁道/閣道,複道,輦道　fu dao
阁楼/閣樓,頂樓　attic
格斗空空导弹/格鬥空對空飛彈　close combat air-to-air missile
格构/格子　lattice
格构比拟/格架類比　grillage analogy
格构拱/格構拱　trellis arch
格构结构/格狀結構　latticed structure
格构梁/格構框梁,花格[大]梁　latticed girder
格构[式]构件/格狀構件　latticed member
格构柱/柵格柱　latticed column
格林尼治恒星时/格林[威治]恆星時　Greenwich sidereal time, GST
格林尼治平时/格林[威治]平均時　Greenwich mean time
格林尼治时角/格林[威治]時角　Greenwich hour angle, GHA
格林尼治子午线/格林[威治]子午線　Greenwich meridian
格筛/柵篩　grizzly
IRIG-B格式时间码/IRIG-B格式化時間碼　IRIG-B format time code
格特尔特法则/格勞厄脫法則,哥色特法則　Gothert rule
格网航法/方格航法　grid navigation
格网航向/方格航向　grid heading

格网偏差/方格偏差　grid variation
格网坐标系/方格坐標系　grid coordinate system
格栅/格柵,條柵　lattice, rack screen
格栅式风口/通氣格柵　air grill
格栅压路机/格子式滾壓機,條格式壓路機　grid roller
格状排水系统/棋盤式配水制,棋盤式排水制　gridiron system
格子舱盖/格子窗口　grating hatch
格子线/網格線　grid
蛤壳式抓斗/[蚌殼式]抓斗,蛤形抓土器　clamshell bucket, clamshell grab
隔板/隔板,擋板　division plate, baffle
隔爆外壳/防火罩　flameproof enclosure
隔舱填料函/艙壁填料函　bulkhead stuffing box
隔断层/絕緣層,保溫層　insulating course, insulating layer
隔根层/隔根層　root resistant layer
隔火带/防火巷道,防火隔離帶　fire protection strip
隔绝训练/隔離訓練　isolation training
隔框/隔框　bulkhead, frame
隔离/隔離　separated from, isolation
隔离变压器/隔離變壓器　isolating transformer
隔离表/隔離表　segregation table
隔离病房/隔離病院,隔離室　lazaret, isolation ward
隔离层/隔離層　isolation layer
隔离畜舍/隔離畜舍,病畜舍　isolation livestock house
隔离堆焊层/預堆邊焊　buttering
隔离阀/隔離閥　isolating valve
隔离法/隔離法　isolation method, isolating method
隔离观察室/隔離觀察室　isolated observation room
隔离火帽型引信/引體安全型引信　primer-safety fuze
隔离机构/斷續器　interrupter
隔离开关/隔離開關,隔離器　isolating switch, isolator, disconnector
隔离实验室/隔離實驗室　isolation laboratory
隔离体/分離體　free body
隔离体简图/分離體簡圖　free body sketch
隔离网/隔離網　separation net
隔离栅/隔離牆　separation fence
隔离障碍/隔離障礙　sovereignty nuisance
隔离诊室/隔離診室　isolated consultation room
隔离状态/中斷狀態　interrupted condition
隔膜/隔膜,膜[片]　diaphragm, membrane, separator
隔膜式[推进剂]贮箱/隔膜推進劑貯箱　diaphragm

propellant tank
隔票/隔離,析離,分離　segregation, separation
隔汽层/蒸氣防護柵,防濕層　vapor barrier
隔墙/隔間牆,間隔牆　partition wall
隔热材料/隔熱材料,熱絕緣材料　thermal insulation material
隔热层/隔熱層,隔離層,絕熱層　thermal insulating layer, isolation layer, thermal insulation layer
隔热防护层/熱防護層　thermal protection layer
隔热防振屏/後燃器襯裡　afterburner liner
隔热棚车/隔熱棚車　insulated box car
隔热箱/絕熱櫃　insulating container
隔日潮/隔日潮　double day tide
隔声/隔音,聲音絕緣　sound insulation
隔声板/隔音板　insulation board
隔声层/隔音層　soundproof course
隔声道/隔音道　sound isolate road
隔声量/聲音降低指數　sound reduction index
隔声绿化带/隔音綠帶　sound isolate greenbelt
隔声前室/隔聲前室,隔音前室　soundproof front room
隔声墙/隔音壁　sound insulation wall
隔声室/隔聲艙,隔音艙　sound insulating chamber, sound insulation chamber
隔绳/間索　tackline
隔水层/隔水層　water insulation course, aquitard
隔水墙/隔牆,膜壁　diaphragm wall
隔温层/隔溫層,隔熱層　thermal insulation course
隔叶块/隔片,間隔件　spacer
隔音墙/隔音牆　acoustic barrier, noise barrier
隔音室/隔音室　sound-proof chamber
隔油池/隔油井,油脂槽　grease tank, oil separator
隔油器/截油器　grease interceptor
隔振/隔振　vibration isolation
隔振沟/隔振溝　vibration isolate ditch
隔振器/隔振器,隔振體　vibration isolator
隔振体系/減振系統　vibration isolating system
隔振装置/浮置隔振裝置　vibration isolating device
隔震/隔震　seismic isolation
槅扇/槅扇　paneled opening, geshan
镉镍蓄电池/鎳鎘蓄電池　cadmium-nickel storage battery
个别概算/個別概算　individual approximate estimate
个人距离/個人距離　personal distance
个人空间/個人空間,私人空間　personal space
个人示位标/個人示位標　personal locator beacon, PLB
个人通信/個人通信　personal communication

个体防护/個人保護　personal protection
个体交通/個體交通　personal traffic
个体冷却系统/個體冷卻系統　personal cooling system
个体热调节/個體耐熱調節　personal thermal conditioning
个体生态学/個體生態學　autecology
各缸均匀性试验/各缸均勻性試驗　cylinder power equalizing test
各向不等压固结/不等性壓密　anisotropic consolidation
各向同性/各向同性　isotropy
各向同性板/等向性板　isotropic plate
各向同性材料/等向性材料　isotropic material
各向同性湍流/各向同性亂流　isotropic turbulence
各向异性/各向異性,異向性　anisotropy
各向异性板/異向性板　anisotropic plate
各向异性材料/異向性材料　anisotropic material
铬镍合金/克鉻美　chromel
铬酸阳极[氧]化/鉻酸陽極處理　chromic acid anodizing
给定值/調定值　set value
根部半径/根[部]半徑　groove radius, root radius
根部焊道/初層焊道　root pass
根部间隙/根隙　root gap
根部弯曲试验/彎折試驗　root bend test
根插/根插　root cutting
根冠比/根-冠比　root-shoot ratio
根厚/葉根厚度　root thickness
根际/根群區　rhizosphere
根际效应/根圈效應　rhizosphere effect
根接/根接　root grafting
根茎/根莖　tuberous stem
根茎灼烧/根莖灼燒　rhizome burn
根瘤菌/根瘤菌　rhizobia
根施/根施　root fertilizer
根涡/葉根渦旋　root vortex
根系/根系　root system
根弦/根弦　root chord
跟车理论/車輛跟隨理論　car-following theory
跟踪/目標追蹤　tracking
GPS跟踪/全球定位系統追蹤　GPS tracking
跟踪测控系统/追蹤遙測控制系統　tracking telemetering and control system, TT and C system
跟踪点不一致修正/跟蹤瞄準點不一致修正　tracking point inconsistency correction
跟踪方式/追蹤型態　tracking mode
跟踪分系统/追蹤子系統　tracking subsystem

跟踪角加速度/追蹤角加速度　tracking angle acceleration
跟踪角速度/追蹤角速率　tracking angular rate
跟踪接收方式/跟蹤接收方式　tracking-receiving mode
跟踪精度/追蹤準確度　tracking accuracy
跟踪路线/追蹤路線　pursuit course
跟踪视场/追蹤視角　tracking field of view, TFOV
跟踪望远镜/追蹤望遠鏡　tracking telescope
跟踪误差/追蹤誤差　tracking error
跟踪系统/追蹤系統　follow-up system, tracking system
跟踪线/追蹤線　tracking line
跟踪信号中断/追蹤訊號消失　tracking signal blackout
跟踪性能/追蹤性能　tracking performance
跟踪性能设计/追蹤性能設計　tracking performance requirement design
跟踪与数据中继卫星系统/追蹤及資料中繼衛星系統　tracking and data relay satellite system, TDRSS
跟踪站/追蹤站　tracking station
艮岳/艮嶽　Gen Yue Imperial Garden
耕地占补平衡/耕地占補平衡　farmland occupancy and compensation balance
耕种坡限/退耕上限坡度　slope limit for cultivation
耕作[防治]措施/耕作措施　tillage control measure
耕作土壤/耕作土　cultivated soil
更新/更新　renewal
更新改造计划/更新改造計劃　plan of renewal and upgrading
更新意愿/更新意願　regeneration will
更衣室/更衣室　dressing room, locker room
工厂/工廠，製造廠　factory, mill, plant
[工厂]参观走廊/參觀走廊　visitor gallery
工厂化养鸡场/工廠化養雞場　factorial chicken farm
工厂交货/工廠交貨　ex works
工厂控制室/控制室，操縱室　control cabin
工厂绿化/工廠綠化　factory greening, factory gardening
工厂漆/工廠漆　shop coat
工程保险/工程保險　insurance of works
工程报价/工程報價　project quoted price
工程材料/工程材料　engineering material
工程测量/工程測量　engineering surveying
工程场地地震安全性评价/工程場地地震安全性評價　evaluation of seismic safety for engineering site
工程成本/工程費　engineering cost

工程承包/工程承包　contracting of project
工程承包人/建築承包商　building contractor
工程承包商/建築承包商　building contractor
工程承建商/工程承建商　engineering contractor
工程船[舶]/工程船，工作船，作業船　work ship, working ship, engineering ship
工程地质/工程地質　engineering geology
工程地质分区图/工程地質分區圖　engineering geological zoning map
工程地质略图/工程地質素描圖　engineering geologic sketch
工程地质剖面图/工程地質縱斷圖　engineering geological profile
工程地质条件/工程地質條件　engineering geologic requirement, engineering geologic condition
工程地质条件分析/工程地質條件分析　engineering geologic condition analysis
工程地质图/工程地質圖　engineering geological map
工程地质选线/工程地質選線　engineering geologic location of line
工程地质学/工程地質學　engineering geology
工程地质遥感测量/工程地質遙感測量　remote sensing of engineering geology
工程发包/工程發包　contracting out of project
工程[防治]措施/工程管理措施，工程控制辦法　engineering management methodology
工程废水/工程廢水　construction waste water
工程费用/工程費　engineering cost
工程供应商/工程供應商　supplier of engineering
工程管线/工程管線　engineering pipeline
工程管线综合/工程管線綜合　integrated design for utility pipeline, utilities engineering
工程间接费/工程間接費用，工程間接成本　indirect expense of project, indirect cost of project
工程监理/施工監督　supervision of construction, supervision of project
工程监理公司/監理公司　supervision company
工程建设标准/建築工程標準　standard of building construction
工程建设其他费/工程建設其他費　other project cost
工程结算/工程結算　project settlement
工程进度/工程進度　stage of engineering
工程决算/竣工決算　final account of project
工程勘察/工程勘察　engineering investigation and survey
工程控制网/工程控制網　engineering control network

工 177

工程联系单/工程聯繫單　project contact form
工程量计算/工程量計算　measurement of quantities
工程施工无线电通信/工程構造無線電通訊　radio communication for engineering construction
工程受益费/受益費　benefit fee
工程水准测量/工程水準測量　engineering leveling
工程宿营车/工程宿營車　work train with camp cars
工程塑料/工程塑膠　engineering plastic
工程投标/工程投標　bidding for project
[工程]项目例会/[工程]項目例會　engineering project regular meeting
工程岩体/工程岩體　engineering rock mass
工程验收/工程驗收　acceptance of project
工程预备费/工程預備金,工程準備金　reserve fund of project
工程运输/工程運輸　engineering transportation
工程造价/项目成本,工程费　project cost
工程招标/工程招標　calling for tenders of project, calling for tending of project
工程直接费/工程直接費　direct expense of project, direct cost of project
工程质量管理/工程品質控制　engineering quality control
工程质量检验/工程品質檢驗　inspection of engineering quality
工程质量评定/工程品質評定　evaluation of engineering quality
工程质量验收/工程品質驗收　acceptance of engineering quality
工程咨询公司/工程諮詢公司　engineering consulting corporation
[工程]总承包/總承包服務　general contracting
[工程]总承包公司/總承包公司　general contracting company
工地/工地　job site
工地拌和/工地配料,工地配合　job mix
工地焊接/工地焊接,現場焊接　field welding
工地铆钉/工地鉚釘　site rivet
工地漆/工地漆　field coat
工地实习/工地實習　building site practice
工法制度/工法制度　construction method system
工件/工作件　workpiece
工具车间/工具工場　tool making shop
工具分发室/工具分發室　tool distribution room
工具室/工具間　tool room
工具箱/工具箱　work-box
工具中心点/工具中心點　tool center point, TCP
工况报警/狀況警報　condition alarm

工况监视器/狀況偵測器　condition monitor
工况显示器/狀況指示器　condition indicator
工矿机车/工礦機車　industrial and mining locomotive
工料测量师/施工技術員,估算師,估料員　quantity surveyor, QS
工龄探索/壽命探索　age exploration
工频接地电阻/功頻接地電阻　power frequency ground resistance
工期/工期　construction period, construction time limit
工期顺延/工期順延　duration postpone
工期压缩/工期壓縮　duration compression
工期延误/工期延誤　duration delay
工期优化/工期優化　duration optimization
工伤事故/工傷事故　accident on duty
工商业区/經貿地產　trading estate
工头/工頭　ganger
工务段/工務段　track division, track district, track maintenance division
工务房间/工務房間　track office
工务设备台账/工務設備臺賬　technical record of track, bridge and other equipment
工务维修无线电通信/軌道養護無線電通訊　radio communication for track maintenance
工效学/人體工學　ergonomics
工形梁/工形梁,工字梁　I-beam
工序/操作規程,步驟　operation procedure, procedure
工序吨/工序噸　unit operation ton
工业布局/工業分布,產業分布　industrial distribution
工业城市/工業都市,工業城　industrial city
工业城镇/工業市鎮　industrial town
工业厨房/工業廚房　industrial kitchen
工业分散/工業分散　decentralization of industry
工业地产/工業用地　industrial estate
工业地产发展计划/工業區發展計劃　industrial estate development plan
工业废料处理/工業廢汙處理　industrial waste treatment
工业废弃地/工業廢棄土地　industrial wasteland
工业废水/工業廢水　industrial waste drainage, industrial wastewater
工业废物/工業廢汙　industrial waste
工业废渣/工業固體廢棄物　industrial solid waste, industrial waste
工业废渣基层/工業廢料基層　industrial waste base

course, industrial waste base
工业分布/工業分布,產業分布　industrial distribution
工业干扰/工業干擾　industrial interference
工业港/工業港　industrial harbor, industrial port
工业工程/工業工程　industrial engineering
工业固体废物处置利用率/工業固體廢物處置利用率　utilization rate of industrial solid waste disposal
工业锅炉/工業鍋爐　industrial boiler
工业化/工業化　industralization
工业机器人/工業機器人　industrial robot
工业基础类标准/工業基礎類標準　industry foundation class, IFC
工业给水/工業供水　industrial water supply
工业建筑/工業建築物　industrial building
工业密度/工業密度　industrial density
工业企业铁路/專有鐵路　industry railway
工业区/工業區　industrial district, industrial area
工业区道路/工業[區]道路　industrial district road, industrial road
工业区规划/工業區計劃　planning for industrial district
工业去垢剂/工業用清潔劑　industrial detergent
工业圈/工業地帶　industrial belt
工业燃[气用]具/工業煤氣用具　industrial gas appliance
工业人口结构/工業人口結構　industrial population structure
工业通风/工業通風　industrial ventilation
工业污水/工業污水　industrial sewage
工业污水处理/工業廢汙處理　industrial waste treatment
工业物业/工業財產　industrial property
工业性试验/工業性試驗　type approval test
工业需水量/工業生產需水量　industrial water requirement
工业遗产/工業遺產,產業文化資產　industrial heritage
工业用地/工業用地　industrial land
工业用地规划/工業用地規劃　industrial land planning
工业用水/工業用水　industrial water use, industrial water
工业用水水厂/工業水廠　industrial water works
工业余热/工業餘熱　industrial waste heat
工业余热供热系统/工業餘熱供熱系統　heat supply system based upon industrial waste heat
工业站/工業站　industrial station
工业振动/工業振動　industrial vibration
工业支线/工業支線　industrial line
工业专用区/工業專用區　exclusive industrial district, restricted industrial district
工业自动化仪表/工業自動化儀表　industrial process measurement and control instrument
工业作业标准/工業作業標準　industrial performance standard
工艺/工藝,技術　technology, technique, process
工艺补偿/技術補償　technological compensation
工艺参数/工藝參數　technological parameter, process parameter
工艺分离面/工藝分離面　production breakdown interface
工艺美术厂/工藝廠　art and craft factory
工艺美术品店/工藝美術商店　arts and crafts store
工艺性空气调节/工藝性空氣調節　process air conditioning
工艺支架/技術支架　technical support mount
工艺装备/工藝裝備,工具　tooling, process tool
工艺总工程师/首席工藝工程師　chief process engineer
工质/工[作物]質　working substance, working fluid, medium
工字钢桩/工字鋼樁,H形鋼樁　H-section steel pile
工字[形]钢/工字[形]鋼,工形鋼　I-beam steel
工字[形]梁/I形金屬桁梁　I-beam
工字形桩/工字樁　H-pile
工作标准/工作標準　working standard
工作标准太阳电池/工作標準太陽電池　working standard solar cell
工作波长/工作波長　operating wavelength
工作车班/工作車班　vehicle working shift
工作车日/工作車日　working vehicle day
工作持续时间/[工作]歷時　duration
工作点/作業點　operation point
工作电流/工作電流　working current
工作电压/工作電壓,操作電壓　operating voltage
工作负荷/工作負荷　workload
工作过程/工作過程　working process
工作过程参数/工作過程參數　parameter of operation process
工作交换容量/營業[生產]交換容量　operating exchange capacity
工作空间/工作空間　working space
工作面/工作面,作業平面　working plane, working face
工作区布局/工作位置布置　workplace layout

工作日/工作日　working day, WD
工作时间/工作時間　hours of service
工作视场/工作視角　working field of view, WFOV
工作寿命加速试验/工作壽命加速試驗　operating-life accelerated test
工作艇/工作艇,工作船　utility boat, work boat
工作温度/工作溫度,運行溫度　operating temperature
工作行程/工作衝程　working stroke
工作循环/工作循環　working cycle
工作压力/工作壓力　working pressure
工作液/使用溶液　working solution
工作有效度/工作效能　work effectiveness
工作载荷/工作荷載,工作負荷　working load
工作照度试验/工作照度試驗　operating luminance test
工作值/工作值　working value
弓角/弓角　pantograph horn
弓网关系/弓網相互作用　pantograph-contact line relation
公安安全室/警衛室　security room
公安局/公安局,公安部門　public security bureau
公差/公差,容差　tolerance
公称通径/公稱直徑,標稱直徑　nominal diameter
公称压力/公稱壓力　nominal pressure
公称直径/公稱直徑,標稱直徑　nominal diameter
公吨/公噸　metric ton
公共安全系统/公共安全系統　public security system, PSS
公共厕所/公共廁所　public toilet, public lavatory
公共服务/公共服務　public service
公共服务设施/公共服務設施　public service facility
公共管理与公共服务设施用地/公共管理與公共服務設施用地　administrative and public service land use
公共管理与公共服务用地/公共管理與公共服務用地　land for administration and public service
公共和紧急广播系统/廣播和緊急廣播系統　public address and emergency broadcast system
公共呼叫频道/公共呼叫頻道　common calling channel
公共活动中心/公共活動中心　public activity center
公共给水/公共給水　public water supply
公共建筑[物]/公共建築　public building
公共交通/公共交通,公眾運輸　public transport, public transportation
公共交通导向型发展/大眾運輸導向發展　transit-oriented development, TOD
公共交通道路网/公共交通線路網　public transport line network
公共交通道路网密度/公共交通線路網密度　public transport line network density
公共交通覆盖率/公共交通覆蓋率　covered area rate of public transport
公共教学用房/公共教學用房　general teaching room
公共距离/公眾距離　public distance
公共客车票价/公共客車票價　bus ticket price
公共空间/公共空間,公用空間　public space
公共空间私有化/公共空間私有化,公用空間民營化　privatization of public space
公共绿地/公共綠地　public green space
公共绿地定额/公共綠地定額　public green space quota
公共绿地率/公共綠地率　public green space ratio
公共绿地指标/公共綠地指標　public green space norm
公共汽车/公共汽車　bus
公共汽车线路/公車路線　bus route
公共汽车运输/公車運輸　bus transportation
公共汽车站/公車站　bus station
公共汽车终点站/公車終站　bus terminal
公共设施/公共設施,共同設施　common facilities, public facility
公共设施用地/公共設施用地,公共設施保留地　land for public facility, public facilities
公共设施用地规划/公共設施用地規劃　public facilities planning
公共水龙头/公用水栓　public tap
公共停车场/公共停車場　public parking lot
公共投资/公共投資　public investment
公共图书馆/公共圖書館　public library
公共卫生/公共衛生　public health
公共污水系统/公共污水系統　public sewerage
公共信息图形符号/公共資訊圖示符號　public information graphical symbol
公共用水/公共用水　water for public use
公共浴场/公共浴室　public bath
公共自行车/公共自行車　shared bicycle
公共租赁住房/公共租賃住房,租住公屋　public rental housing
公海/公海　high seas
公海海上安全信息/公海海上安全資訊　high seas maritime safety information
公海自由/公海自由　freedom of the open seas
公害/公害　public nuisance

公交[车辆]港湾式停靠站/公車灣式停靠站　bus bay
公交车站/公交車站　bus station, bus stop
公交服务设施/公共交通線路設施,公共交通線路網
　　public transport service facilities
公交网规划/公交線網規劃　transit network
　　planning
公交优先/公交優先　public transport priority
公交[专用]车道/公共汽車專用車道　bus lane,
　　public transport exclusive lane
公开竞标/公開競標　public tender
公开投标/公開投標　public tender
公开招标/公開招標　public tender, competitive
　　tendering, competitive bidding
公里标/公里標　kilometer post
公路/公路,高速通道　highway, public highway
公路标准化美化工程/公路標準化美化工程
　　highway standardized and beautified project
公路病害/公路病害　highway distress
公路残值/公路殘值　highway residual value
公路大修/公路大修　highway major maintenance
公路等级/公路等級　highway classification
公路渡口/公路渡口　highway ferry
公路防护工程/公路防護工程　highway protective
　　engineering
公路服务设施/公路服務設施　highway service
　　facilities
公路附属设施/公路附屬設備　highway
　　appurtenance
公路改善/公路改良　highway improvement
公路改线/公路改線　highway relocation
公路干线系统/公路幹線系統　trunk grid highway
公路工程概算定额/公路工程概算定額
　　approximate estimate norm of highway project
公路工程估算指标/公路工程估算指標　estimate
　　index of highway project
公路工程技术标准/公路技術標準　highway
　　technical standard
公路工程监理/公路工程監理　highway engineering
　　supervision
公路工程学/公路工程學　highway engineering
公路工程预算定额/公路工程預算定額　budgetary
　　norm of highway project
公路功能/公路功能　highway function
公路功能设计/公路功能設計　highway functional
　　design
公路罐车/公路液罐車　road tank vehicle
公路荷载标准/公路荷載標準　highway load
　　standard

公路环境/公路環境　highway environment
公路环境保护设计/公路環境保護設計　highway
　　environmental protection design
公路环境影响评价/公路環境影響評估　highway
　　environmental impact evaluation
公路货运/公路貨運　highway freight transportation
公路基本建设程序/公路基本建設程式　highway
　　capital construction procedure
公路基本容量/公路基本容量　basic highway
　　capacity
公路集装箱中转站/公路貨櫃中轉站　highway
　　container transfer terminal
公路几何设计/公路幾何設計　highway geometric
　　design
公路技术档案/公路技術檔案　highway technical file
公路技术管理/公路技術管理　highway technical
　　administration
公路建设管理/公路建設管理　highway construction
　　administration
公路建设基金/公路建設基金　highway construction
　　fund
公路交叉口/道路交叉口　road crossing
公路交叉口标志/公路交叉號誌　highway crossing
　　signal
公路交通方式/公路交通方式　highway traffic mode
公路交通公害/公路交通公害　highway traffic
　　nuisance
公路交通规划/公路運輸規劃　highway and
　　transportation planning
公路交通监理/道路交通監察　highway traffic
　　supervision
公路景观/公路景觀,公路景色　landscape of
　　highway, highway landscape, vista
公路景观设计/公路景觀設計　highway landscape
　　design
公路勘测规程/公路勘測設計　highway
　　reconnaissance and survey regulation
公路客运/公路客運　highway passenger
　　transportation
公路客运网/公路運輸網路　bus transport network
公路客运站/公路客運站,公路旅客站　highway
　　passenger station, highway bus station
公路里程/公路里程　highway mileage
公路立体交叉/公路立體交叉　highway grade
　　separation
公路路线编号/公路路線編號　code number of
　　highway route
公路路政管理/公路管理局　highway administration

公路绿化/公路綠化　highway greening, highway planting
公路美学/公路美學　highway aesthetics
公路美学设计/公路美學設計　highway esthetics design
公路排水/公路排水系統　highway drainage
公路平面交叉/公路平面交叉　highway grade crossing
公路桥/公路橋,道路橋　highway bridge, road bridge
公路施工管理/公路施工管理　highway construction management
公路施工环境影响/公路建設環境效應,公路建設環境影響　environmental effects in highway construction
公路使用者费用/公路年費　highway user cost
公路使用者效益/公路使用者效益　highway user benefit
公路数据库/公路資料庫　highway data bank
公路隧道/公路隧道　highway tunnel
公路铁路立交/公路鐵路立體交叉　highway railway grade separation
公路通行能力/公路容量　highway capacity
公路透视图/公路透視圖　highway perspective view
公路网/公路網　highway network
公路网规划/公路網規劃　highway network planning
公路网密度/公路網[路]密度　highway network density, density of highway network
公路限界架/公路限界架　highway boundary frame
公路小修[保养]/公路例行維護　highway routine maintenance
公路养护/公路養護　highway maintenance
公路养护质量等级/公路養護品質水準　quality level of highway maintenance
公路用地/公路用地　highway land, right of way, land for national and regional road
公路运输/公路運輸　highway and transportation
公路运输车辆/公路運輸車輛　highway transport vehicle
公路运输车辆管理/公路運輸車輛管理　highway transport vehicle management
公路运输法规/公路運輸法規　highway transport statute
公路运输管理/公路運輸管理　highway transport management
公路运输行业管理/公路運輸行業管理　administration of highway transport industry
公路运输计划/公路運輸計劃　highway transport plan
公路运输经济运距/公路運輸經濟運距　break-even distance for highway transport
公路运输净产值/公路運輸淨產值　net highway transport production output value
公路运输量/公路運輸量　highway transport volume
公路运输行政管理/公路運輸行政管理　administration of highway transport
公路运输总产值/公路運輸總產值　total highway transport production output value
公路灾害/公路災害　highway disaster
公路灾害防治/公路災害防治　prevention and cure against highway disaster
公路造价/公路工程造價　highway construction cost
公路照明/公路照明　highway lighting
公路支挡结构物/公路支擋結構物　highway brace and retaining wall structure
公路支线道路/聯絡道　access road
公路中修/公路中修　highway intermediate maintenance
公路转运/道路轉移　road transfer
公路自然区划/公路自然區劃　highway natural zoning
公墓/公墓　cemetery
公司平均燃料经济性/公司燃油經濟性　corporation average fuel economy, CAFE
公司旗/公司旗　house flag
公私合作/公私營伙伴關係,公私合營,公私合伙　public-private partnership
公铁两用检修车/公路鐵路檢修車　road-railway repairing vehicle
公铁两用桥/公鐵兩用橋,鐵路公路兩用橋　combined highway and railway bridge, combined bridge, combined rail-cum-road bridge
公铁两用线路机械/公鐵兩用線路機械　rail-road permanent way machine
公务车/勤務車　officer car, service car
公务电报/公務電報　service telegram
公务机/公務機　business airplane, executive airplane
公益住房/社會住宅　social housing
公用舱/共用艙　common module
公用乘车证/公用乘車證　service pass
公用处所/公共空間,公用空間　public space
公用道路/公路　public road
公用电话交换网络/公用交換電話網路　public switched telephone network
公用电话网/公用電話網路　public telephone network

公用给水站/公共給水站　public water supply station
公用建筑面积/公用建築面積　common-floorage
公用平台/共用平臺　common platform
公用设施营业网点用地/公用設施營業網點用地　land for municipal utility outlet
公用设施用地/公用設施用地,公用事業用地　public utilities land, land for municipal utility
公用事业/公用事業　public utility
公用数据交换网络/公眾交換數據網路　public switched data network
公用数据网/公用數據網路　public data network
公用水/公用水　public water
公用下水道/公共下水道　public sewer, common sewer
公[有住]房/公共住宅,國民住宅,公屋　public housing
公寓/公寓[住宅]　apartment, tenement building
公寓式办公楼/家庭辦公室,個人及居家辦公室　apartment-office building, small office home office, SOHO
公寓式住宅/公寓住宅　apartment house
公园/公園　park, public park
公园道路/公園道路　park road
公园分布/公園分布　distribution of park
公园规划/公園規劃　park planning
公园间距/公園間距　distance between park
公园类型/公園類型　park type, park category
公园绿地/公園綠地　land for park
公园设施/公園設施　park facility
公园水陆面积比率/公園水陸面積比率　land-water ratio
公园外部效应/公園外部效應　external effect of park
公园系统计划/公園系統計劃　park system plan
公园形式/公園形式　park style
公园最大游人量/公園最大遊人量　maximum visitors capacity in park
公正城市/公正都市　justice city
公证检验/公證檢驗　notarial survey
公证鉴定/公證檢定　inspection by notary public
公证权/公證權　right of notary
公制/公制　metric system
公制粗牙螺纹/公制粗牙螺紋　metric coarse thread
公众参与/公眾參與,公共參與,公民參與　public participation
公众参与技术/公眾參與技術　technology of public participation
公众参与阶梯/公共參與梯子,民眾參與梯子　ladder of public participation
公众监督/輿論監督　public supervision
公众通信/公眾通信　public correspondence
公众通信业务/公眾通信業務　public correspondence service
公装/公裝　finishing and decoration of public building
公租房/公共租賃住房,租住公屋　public rental housing
功/功　work
功率/功率　power
功率储备/功率餘裕　power reserve, power margin
功率储备系数/剩餘動力係數　coefficient of reserve power
功率合成/功率合成　power synthesis
功率换算/功率換算　power conversion
功率密度/功率密度,輸出密度　power density
功率容积比/功率容積比　power-to-volume ratio
功率输入传动装置/功率輸入傳動裝置　power take-in drive
功率提取/輔助功率輸出　power take-off
功率调节系统/功率調節系統　power regulating system
功率因数/功率因數　power factor
功率因数补偿装置/功率因數補償裝置　power factor compensation device
功率预算/功率預算　power budget
功率自动分配/功率自動分配　automatic power apportioning
功能/功能　function
功能材料/機能材料　functional material
功能分区理论/功能分區理論　functional zoning theory
功能复合材料/功能複合材料　functional composite material
功能检查/功能檢查,功能檢驗,功能測試　function inspection, function check
功能检查科/機能實驗室　function laboratory
功能空间/功能空間　functional space
功能区/功能帶　function zone
功能失常/故障　malfunction
功能失灵/功能失效,功能故障　functional failure
功能试验/功能試驗　function test
功能损坏/功能損害　functional damage
功能陶瓷/功能陶瓷　functional ceramics
功能梯度材料/功能梯度材料　functional gradient material

功能图／機能圖　functional diagram
功能性故障／功能故障　functional fault
功能性减速／機能性減速　functional deceleration
功能主义／功能主義　functionalism
功重比／功率重量比　power weight ratio
攻角／攻角，衝角　angle of attack
供电／供電，电力供應　power supply
供电半径／供電半徑　power supply radius
供电臂／供電臂　feeding section
供电臂短路电流／供電臂短路電流　short-circuit current of feeding section
供电臂干扰计算电流／供電臂干擾計算電流　disturbing calculation current of feeding section
供电臂平均电流／供電臂平均電流　average current of feeding section
供电臂瞬时最大电流／供電臂瞬時最大電流　instantaneous maximum current of feeding section
供电臂有效电流／供電臂有效電流　effective current of feeding section
供电臂最大负荷电流／供電臂最大負荷電流　maximum load current of feeding section
供电点／供電點，饋供終端　supply terminal
供电电源／供電電源　power supply source
供电段／供電段　section for power supply
供电方案／供電方案　scheme of power supply
供电分区／供電範圍　power supply area
供电可靠性／供電可靠性　power supply reliability
供电领工区／供電領工區，电力供應領工區　fore work district for power supply
供电网／供電網路　supply network
供电系统／供電系統　electrical power supply system, power supply system, power distribution system
供电线[路]／饋[電]線　feeder, feeder line
供料塔／供料塔　material tower
供暖／供暖　heating
供暖能耗／供熱能量消耗　energy consumed for heating
供暖期度日数／採暖期間日度［數］，供熱期間日度［數］　degree days of heating period
供暖期室外平均温度／採暖期室外平均溫度　outdoor mean air temperature during heating period
供暖热负荷／供熱量，熱負荷　heating load, space heating load
供暖设计热负荷指标／採暖設計熱負荷指標　index of design load for heating of building
供片卷筒／供片卷筒　supply spool
供气／氣體輸送　gas delivery, gas supply

供气调节器／供氣調節器　gas supply regulator
供气调压系统／供氣調壓系統　atmosphere supply and pressure control system
供气系统／氣體供應系統　gas supply system
供气组件／供氣組合件　gas supply assembly
供汽量／供汽量　evaporation capacity for engine
供汽率／供汽率　rate of evaporation for engine
供热／供熱　heat supply
供热半径／供熱半徑　heat range of heat supply service
供热厂／供熱廠　heat-generating plant
供热方式／供熱方式　mode of heat supply system
供热分区／供熱面積　heating areas
供热管道／供熱管道　heat supply pipeline
供热管网／暖氣供應網路　heating network
供热锅炉／供暖鍋爐　industrial boiler, heating boiler
供热介质／熱載體　heating medium
供热介质参数／供熱介質參數　parameter of heating medium
供热能力／供熱容量　heating capacity
供热热源／［供熱］熱源　heat source of heat supply system, heat source
供热系统／供熱系統　heat supply system
供热系统水击／供熱系統水擊　water hammer of heat supply system
供水／給水　water supply
供水工程规划／供水工程計劃　water supply engineering planning
供水管／給水管，送水管　water supply pipe
供水量／供水量，產水量　water output
供水普及率／供水普及率　water supply pervasion
供水设备／給水廠　water supply plant
供水设施／水域設施　water facility
供水系统／供水系統，給水系統　water supply system
供水压力调节器／供水壓力調節器　water supply pressure regulator
供氧高度／供氧高度　oxygen supply altitude
供氧能力／供氧能力　oxygen delivery capacity
供应船／補給船，勤務艦　supply ship, tender
供应设备／供應設備　supply equipment
供应设施用地／供應設施用地　land for provision facility
供油泵／給油泵　oil feed pump
供油提前角／供油提前角　fuel supply advance angle, advance angle of fuel supply
宫城／宮城　gong cheng, palace
宫殿／宮殿　palace
宫苑区／宮苑區　gong yuan area, palace garden area

拱/拱　arch, vault
拱背[线]/拱背，外拱線　extrados
拱波/拱波　two way curved arch tile
拱顶/拱頂　arch crown
拱顶石/拱頂石，頂拱開挖支護　key stone, arch crown block
拱顶输水渠/拱頂輸水渠　corbelled vaulted-roof canal
拱度/拱度　camber, rise
拱腹/拱腹　soffit
拱腹[线]/拱腹[線]　intrados
拱杆/拱勢拉桿　camber rod
拱高/曲弧中高　height of arch
拱涵/拱涵，拱渠　arch culvert
拱架/拱架　arch centering, arch center
拱架卸落/拱架卸載　centering unloading
拱架预压/拱架預壓　preloading centering
拱脚/起拱點　arch springing
拱脚斜块/拱腳斜塊　arch skew block
拱肋/拱肋　arch rib
拱片桥/拱片橋　arch slice bridge
拱砌块/拱石　voussoir, arch stone
拱桥/拱橋　arch bridge
拱桥推力/拱橋推力　bridge thrust
拱曲/拱勢　hog
拱圈/拱圈　arch ring
拱圈封顶/拱圈封頂　closure of arch ring, closing the top of lining
拱圈施工缝/拱圈施工縫　construction joint for arch ring
拱圈应力调整/拱圈應力調整　arch ring stress adjustment
拱上侧墙/拱肩牆　spandrel wall
拱上横墙/拱石坎牆　spandrel cross wall
拱上结构/拱上結構　spandrel structure
拱上立柱/拱肩柱　spandrel column
拱石/拱石　voussoir, arch stone
拱矢/拱高　rise of arch
拱式钢拱架/拱式鋼拱架　steel arch centering
拱推力/拱推力，拱的軸向壓力　arch thrust
拱形明洞/拱形明洞　arch open cut tunnel, arch tunnel without cover, arch gallery
拱形桥台/拱式橋臺　arched abutment
拱形屋架/拱形屋架　arch roof truss, bowstring roof truss
拱形支架/拱形支架　arched timbering
拱形重力坝/拱形重力壩　curved gravity dam
拱券式/拱形構造　arch structure

拱胀/拱脹　blow up
拱轴系数/拱軸係數　arch axis coefficient
拱砖/拱磚　arch brick
拱砖管/拱管　arch tube
拱座/拱形支架，拱臺　arch support, abutment
栱/栱　bracket, bracket-arm, gong
共底/共同艙壁　common bulkhead
共底抽真空/共底抽真空　co-base vacuum-pumping
共电电话机/共電式電話機　common battery telephone set
共电电话交换机/共電式電話交換臺　common battery telephone switch board
共轭赤经/恆星時角　sidereal hour angle, SHA
共轭构造/共軛結構　conjugate structure
共轭压力/共軛壓力　conjugate pressure
共轭轴/共軛軸　conjugate axis
共固化/共成化　co-curing
共晶合金/共晶合金，共熔合金　eutectic alloy
共面交会/共面交會　coplanar encounter
共面转移/同平面轉移　coplanar transfer
共模故障/共模故障，因模式故障　common mode fault
共生/共生　symbiosis
共同安全/共同安全　common safety
共同工作线/操作線　operating line
共同沟/共同溝，管溝　integral pipe trench
共同海损/共同海損　general average, GA
共同海损保险/共同海損支付保險　general average disbursement insurance
共同海损担保/共同海損擔保　general average security
共同海损费用/共同海損費用　general average expenditure
共同海损分摊/共同海損分攤　general average contribution
共同海损分摊保证金/共同海損保證金　general average deposit
共同海损分摊价值/共同海損分攤價值　contributory value of general average
共同海损理算/共同海損理算　general average adjustment
共同海损理算书/共同海損理算書　general average adjustment statement
共同海损时限/共同海損時限　time limit of general average
共同海损损失/共同海損損失　general average loss or damage
共同海损条款/共同海損條款　general average

clause
共同海损牺牲/共同海損犧牲　general average sacrifice
共同海损行为/共同海損行爲　general average act
共同海损总额/共同海損總額　total amount of general average
共同体群体/法人團體　corporate group
共同危险/共同危險　common danger, common peril
共线信令系统/共同通道傳信系統　common channel signaling system
共线自动电话/同線自動電話　party-line automatic telephone
共享空间/分享空間,共用空間,交流空間　sharing space
共享绿地/公享綠地　public open space
共形阵天线/共形陣列天線　conformal array antenna
共因故障/共同原因故障　common cause fault
共用箱/共用箱　cab signal box
共振/共振,諧振　resonance
共振摆/共振擺　resonance pendulum
共振法测桩/共振測樁　resonance inspection for piles
共振频率/共振頻率　resonance frequency
共振筛/共振篩　resonance screen
共振吸声/共振吸音　resonance sound absorption
共轴相关/共軸相關　coaxial correlation
贡院/貢院　examination hall
勾缝/接縫修整　pointing
勾连搭/勾連搭　undulating roof, goulianda
勾头/檐瓦　eave tile
勾头丁坝/勾頭丁壩　bend-ended spur dike
沟边界/溝邊界　ditch-side border
沟槽压路机/邊溝壓實機　trench roller
沟渠氧化/溝渠氧化法　ditch oxidation
沟填法/挖埋法,沈埋工法　trench method
沟通式规划/溝通規劃　communicative planning
沟通性规划/溝通規劃　communicative planning
沟植/溝植　trench planting
沟中边篱/溝中邊籬　hah-hah fence
沟状腐蚀/槽蚀　grooving corrosion, groovy corrosion
钩/鉤　hook
钩车/鉤車　cars per cut
钩吊周期/吊鉤週期　hook cycle
钩耳/鉤耳　coupler pivot lug
钩篙/鉤篙　boat hook
钩肩/鉤角　coupler horn
钩颈/鉤頸　coupler neck
钩阑/鉤闌　railing, goulan

钩螺栓/繫留螺栓,固定螺栓,錨栓　claw bolt, hook bolt, anchor bolt
钩舌/鉤舌,車鉤關節　coupler knuckle
钩舌销/鉤尾銷　knuckle pivot pin
钩身/車鉤柄　coupler shank
钩锁/自動閉鎖　coupler lock
钩锁销/鉤鎖銷　coupler lock lift
钩体/鉤體　coupler body
钩头鞍子/鉤形鞍部　hook-type saddle
钩头正面/鉤頭正面　coupler front face
钩腕外臂/鉤腕外臂　coupler guard arm
钩尾/互鉤尾　coupler tail
钩尾销/車鉤尾銷　draft key
构成主义/建構主義,建構論　constructivism
构架侧梁/架構架側梁　truck side sill
构架端梁/架構架端梁　truck end sill
构架辅助梁/構架輔助梁　truck auxiliary transom
构架横梁/轉向架橫梁　truck transom
构架纵梁/轉向架縱梁　truck longitudinal sill
构件/[結構]構件　member, structural member
构件刚度/構件剛度,構材勁度　stiffness of structural member, member stiffness
构件更换/組件替換　component replacement
构件抗震加固/結構構件抗震加固　seismic retrofit of structural member, seismic strengthening of structural member
构件支撑/構件支撐　member support
构造尺寸/構造尺寸　work size
构造钢筋/構造鋼筋　constructional reinforcement
构造轨缝/構造軌縫　structural joint gap, maximum joint gap structurally obtainable
构造节理/結構縫　structure joint
构造深度仪/構造深度儀　texture meter
构造速度/構造速度　construction speed, design speed
构造应力场/構造應力場　structural stress field, formation stress field
构造柱/構造柱　constructional column, tie column
购物中心/購物中心　shopping center
估价单/估價單　estimate sheet
估算指标/估算指標　preliminary index, index of estimate
估算贮存期/估計貯藏時間　estimated storage life
孤立礁/孤立礁　isolated rock
孤立危险物标志/孤立危險物標誌　isolated danger mark
孤立系统/孤立系統　isolated system
孤赏石/孤賞石　monolith, standing stone

孤植/孤植　specimen planting, isolated planting
孤植树/孤植樹,獨賞樹　singular plant tree
箍筋/箍筋,肋筋　stirrup
古埃及建筑/埃及古代建築　ancient Egyptian architecture
古巴东南第一个咖啡种植园考古风景区/古巴東南第一個咖啡種植園考古風景區　Archaeological Landscape of the First Coffee Plantations in the South-East of Cuba
古代侵蚀/古代侵蝕　ancient erosion
古德曼曲线/古德曼曲線　Goodman diagram
古典园林/古典園林　classical garden
古典主义/浪漫主義　romanticism, romantic classicism
古典主义建筑/古典建築,古希臘與羅馬之建築　classical architecture
古典柱式/古典柱式　classical order of architecture
古分布区/古分布區　paleoareal
古迹公园/古跡公園　historic site park
古建测绘/古建築測繪　ancient building surveying
古罗马城市广场/古羅馬廣場　ancient Roman forum
古罗马建筑/古羅馬建築　ancient Roman architecture
古罗马浴场/古羅馬溫泉浴場　ancient Roman thermae
古生代/古生代　palaeozoic era
古树/古樹　ancient tree
古树复壮/古樹復壯　rejuvenation of ancient tree
古树名木/古樹[名木]　ancient and famous tree, historical tree and famous wood species, famous ancient tree
古树修复/古樹修復　repair of antient tree
古树诊断/古樹診斷　diagnosis of ancient tree
古土壤学/古土壤學　paleopedology
古希腊建筑/古希臘式建築　ancient Greek architecture
古印度建筑/古印度建築　ancient Indian architecture
古植代/古植代　paleophyte
古植物地理学/古植物地理學　paleophytogeography
古植物区系/古植物區系　paleoflora, geoflora
古植物群落分布学/古植物群落分布學　paleophytosynchorology
古植物群落生态学/古植物群落分布學　paleophytosynecology
古植物生态学/古植物生態學　paleophytoecology
古植物学/古植物學,化石植物學　paleobotany
古种子学/古種子學　paleocarpology
谷/[溪]谷　valley

谷密/穀密　grain-tight
谷物/穀類　grain
谷物防动装置/穀類防動裝置　grain fitting
谷物横倾体积矩/穀類體積橫傾力矩　grain transverse volumetric upsetting moment
谷物倾侧力臂/穀類傾側力臂　grain upsetting arm
谷物移动角/穀類移動角　shifting angle of grain
股道空闲/軌道空閒,線路開通　track clear
股道占用/軌道占用　track occupied
骨材标准级配/骨材標準級配　standard gradation of aggregate
骨粉/骨粉　bone meal
骨干树种/骨幹樹種　vital tree species, framework tree species
骨灰寄存处/骨灰寄存處　cinerary casket deposit room
骨-肌/骨骼-肌肉　bone-muscle
骨架/骨架,構架　framing, skeleton
骨架测量/輪廓測量　skeleton surveying
骨架曲线/軀幹曲線　skeleton curve
骨胶/骨膠　bone glue
骨料/骨材,集料　aggregate
骨料采集设备/骨材採集設備　aggregate excavation equipment
骨料混合级配/合成骨材級配　combined gradation of aggregate
骨料级配/骨材級配,集料級配　grading of aggregate
骨料加工设备/骨材處理設備　aggregate processing equipment
骨料筛分机/骨材篩分機　aggregate screen
骨料投配器/骨材配料器　aggregate batcher
骨料咬合力/連鎖聚合力　aggregate interlocking force
钴基高温合金/鈷基高溫合金　cobalt-base superalloy
钴基合金/鈷基合金　cobalt based alloy
鼓风机/鼓風機,吹風機,鼓風扇　blower, forced draft fan
鼓风门测定仪/鼓風門測定儀　blower door equipment
鼓风式燃烧器/空氣噴燈　air blast burner, fun assisted burner
鼓轮/鼓輪　drum
鼓式搅拌机/鼓型拌和機　drum mixer
鼓筒式混凝土搅拌机/滾筒式混凝土攪拌機　drum concrete mixer
鼓形控制器/鼓形控制器,圓筒控制器　drum controller
鼓形位置转换开关/鼓形位置切換開關　drum

position changeover switch
鼓形转子/鼓形轉子,鼓形輪子　drum rotor
鼓座/鼓形石塊　drum
毂径比/轂徑比　hub ratio, hub diameter ratio
毂帽/螺槳帽　propeller cap
固壁喷管/固壁噴管　fixed wall nozzle
固氮能力/固氮能力　nitrogen fixing capacity
固氮作用/固氮作用　nitrogen fixation
固定备用方式/固定備用系統　fixed reservation system
固定冰/堅冰　fast ice
固定布水器/[固]定式分水器　fixed distributor
固定叉心/固定叉心　fixed frog
固定岔心/固定岔心　rigid frog
固定成本/固定成本　fixed cost
固定床/定床　fixed bed
固定的/固定的　stationary
固定电台/基[地]臺　base station
固定吊车/固定起重機　stationary crane
固定杠杆/固定槓桿　truck dead lever
固定高膨胀泡沫灭火系统/固定高脹力泡沫滅火系統　fixed high expansion forth fire-extinguishing system
固定隔墙/固定隔牆　fixed partition
固定含水量法则/固定含水量法則　constant water content law
固定化生物体/固定化生物量　immobilized biomass
固定环/固定光網　fixed reticle
固定环形天线/固定環形天線　fixed loop antenna
固定件/固定裝具　securing fitting
固定距标/距離指標　range marker
固定轮叶水轮机/定葉水渦輪　fixed blade water turbine
固定螺距桨/固定螺距螺槳　fixed pitch propeller, FPP
固定螺栓/夾緊螺絲,調整螺絲　clamping screw
固定锚/繫泊錨,碇泊錨　mooring anchor
固定喷灌器/固定噴灌器　stationary sprinkler
固定桥/固定橋　fixed bridge
固定区/固定區域　non-breathing zone, fixed zone, deformation-free zone
固定式采油平台/固定式產油平臺　fixed oil production platform
固定式挡土墙/固定擋土牆　fixed retaining wall
固定式甲板泡沫系统/固定甲板泡沫系統　fixed deck foam system
固定式内燃机/固定引擎　stationary engine
固定式泡沫灭火系统/固定泡沫滅火系統　fixed foam extinguishing system
固定式起落架/固定式起落架　fixed landing gear
固定式气体灭火系统/固定氣體滅火系統　fixed gas fire extinguishing system
固定式汽阀/固定式活塞閥　rigid piston valve
固定式勤务塔/固定式勤務塔　fixed service tower
固定式挖泥船/固定挖泥機　stationary dredger
固定式装卸机械/固定式裝卸機械　fixed handling machinery
固定数据存储技术/永久資料儲存技術　permanent-data storage technology
固定顺序机械手/固定順序機械手　fixed sequence manipulator
固定探头式星跟踪器/固定頭星體追蹤儀　fixed head star tracker
固定吸式挖泥船/定位吸泥船　fixed suction dredger
固定消防炮灭火系统/固定消防炮滅火系統　fixed fire monitor extinguishing system
固定信号/固定號誌　fixed signal
固定信息标志/固定資訊標誌　fixed message sign
固定旋涡/拘限旋渦　confined eddy
固定压力喷水灭火系统/固定壓力噴水滅火系統　fixed pressure water-spraying forth fire extinguishing system
固定压缩机/固定空氣壓縮機　stationary compressor
固定延时/定時延誤　fixed delay
固定渔网/定骨網　fixed net
固定载荷/固定負荷　dead load
固定支架/固定支座,固定支承　fixed bearing, fixed support
固定支座/固定支座,固定支承　fixed bearing, fixed support
固定轴距/固定軸距　rigid wheelbase, rigid wheel base, fixed wheel base
固定资产/固定資產　fixed assets
固定资产残值/固定資產殘值　scrap value of fixed assets
固定资产大修/固定資產大修　capital repair of fixed assets
固定资产更新改造/固定資產更新改造　renewal and reconstruction of fixed asset, renewal and upgrading of fixed asset
固定资产更新率/固定資產更新率　rate of fixed assets renewal
固定资产投资/固定資產投資　fixed asset investment
固定资产退废率/固定資產退廢率　rate of fixed assets retirement

固定资产原价/固定資產原始價值 original value of fixed assets
固定资产折旧/固定資產折舊 depreciation of fixed assets
固定资金/固定資本 fixed capital
固定自差/固定自差 constant deviation
固定作业程序/現行作業程式 standing operating procedure
固定座位/固定座位 fixed seating
固定座椅/固定座椅 fixed seat
固端拱/固端拱,定端拱 fixed-end arch
固端推力/固端推力,端點推力 fixed-end thrust
固端弯矩/固定端彎矩 fixed moment, fixed-end moment
固化/硬化,成化 curing
固化度/硬化度 degree of cure
固化剂/硬化劑 hardener
固化喷流试验/固化噴射試驗 solidified jet testing
固化条件/成化條件 cure condition
固结/固結,壓實 consolidation
固结比/壓密比 consolidation ratio
固结不排水剪力试验/壓密不排水剪力試驗 consolidated undrained shear test
固结不排水试验/壓密不排水試驗 consolidated undrained test
固结度/固結度 degree of consolidation
固结快剪试验/壓密快剪試驗 consolidated quick shear test
固结快速剪力试验/壓密快速剪力試驗 consolidated immediate shear test
固结慢剪试验/緩速壓密試驗 consolidated slow test
固结试验/固結試驗 consolidation test
固结系数/固結係數 consolidation coefficient, coefficient of consolidation
固结压缩机/壓密器 consolidation press
固结仪/固結計,壓實計 consolidometer
固溶强化/固溶硬化,溶液硬化 solution hardening
固溶热处理/溶液熱處理,溶解熱處理 solution heat treatment
固沙造林/固沙造林 stabilization for sands by afforestation
固沙植物/固沙植物 sand-fixation plant
固态存储器/固態記憶體 solid state memory
固态电路/固態電路 solid state circuit
固碳释氧/固碳釋氧 carbon fixation and oxygen release
固体/固體,固態 solid
固体单位重量/固體單位重 solid unit weight

固体发动机总装厂房/固體推進劑馬達裝配廠房 solid propellant motor assembly building
固体废弃物/固體廢[棄]物 solid waste
固体废弃物处理/固體廢物處理 solid waste treatment
固体废弃物污染/固體廢物汙染 noxious waste pollution, solid waste pollution
固体废弃物循环经济产业园区/固體廢物循環經濟產業園區 recycling park of solid waste treatment
固体废弃物综合利用/固體廢棄物綜合利用 comprehensive utilization of solid wastes
固体浮力材料/固體浮材 solid buoyancy material
固体负荷/固體負荷 solid loading
固体火箭发动机/固體火箭發動機 solid propellant rocket engine
固体火箭推进剂/固體火箭推進劑 solid rocket propellant
固体货站/乾貨整補站 solid cargo station
固体基质/固體基質 solid-substrate
固体径流/沈渣徑流 sediment runoff
固体径流量/沈渣徑流量 sediment yield
固体垃圾焚烧厂/固定廢棄物焚燒廠 solid waste incineration plant
固体垃圾密闭式清洁站/廢棄物密閉式清潔站 closed sanitation station of solid waste
固体垃圾填埋场/一般廢棄物掩埋場 waste landfill
固体垃圾转运站/廢棄物轉運站 waste transfer station
固体垃圾综合处理厂/固定廢棄物處理廠 solid waste treatment plant
固体力学/固體力學 solid mechanics
固体润滑剂/固體潤滑劑 solid lubricant
固体散货/散裝固體貨物 solid bulk cargo
固体散装货物安全操作规则/散裝固體貨物安全實務章程 Code of Safe Practice for Solid Bulk Cargoes
固体声/固載音 solid-borne sound
固体停留时间/固體停留時間 solids retention time
固体推进剂/固體推進劑 solid propellant
固体[推进剂]火箭发动机/固體推進劑火箭發動機 solid propellant rocket engine, solid propellant rocket motor
固体推进剂主曲线/固體推進劑主曲線 master curve of solid propellant
固体压载/固體壓載 solid ballast
固体致冷器/固態冷凍機 solid state refrigerator
固艇索具/艇艄繫纜 boat rope
固有沉陷/固有沈落 inherent settlement

固有畸变/固有畸變　inherrent distortion
固有可用性/固有可用度　inherent availability
固有能力/固有能力　capability
固有频率/固有頻率,自然頻率,自振頻率　inherent frequency, natural frequency, natural frequency of vibration
固有缺陷/固有缺陷　inherent vice
固有色/固有色　inherent color
固有误差/固有誤差　intrinsic error
固有延时/固有遲延　inherent delay
固有振动/自然振動　natural vibration
固有[振动]模态/固有振動模態　natural mode of vibration
固有振动频率/固有振動頻率　natural vibration frequency
固有振动周期/固有振動週期　natural oscillation period
固有贮存期/固有貯藏時間　natural storage life
故障/故障,失效,錯誤　failure, trouble, fault
故障安全/故障安全　fail-safe, fail safe
故障办理/故障辦理　emergency treatment after failure
故障重构/故障重組　failure reconfiguration
故障处置预案/故障處置程式　failure handling program
故障灯/故障號燈　breakdown lights
故障电流/故障電流　fault current
故障定位/故障定位,故障局部化,確定故障點　fault location, fault localization
故障分布/失效分配　failure distribution
故障分析/故障分析,失效分析　failure analysis
故障复原/故障復原　restoration after a failure
故障概率密度/故障機率密度　failure probability density
故障隔离/故障隔離　fault isolation
故障隔离率/故障隔離率　fault isolation rate
故障工龄/失效年限　age at failure
故障工作/故障工作　fail-operation
故障机理/失效機構　failure mechanism
故障积累/故障積累　failure accumulation
故障迹象/故障證據　fault evidence
故障间隔平均时间/平均故障間隔[時間]　mean time between failures
故障检测/故障檢測　fault detection
故障检测率/軟體偵錯率　fault detect rate
故障检测与报警/故障檢測與警報　fault detect and warning
故障检测与辨识/故障檢測與識別　fault detection and identification, FDI
故障检测与排除/故障檢測與排除　fault detection and exclusion, FDE
故障检修/故障檢修,設備保養　corrective maintenance
故障降级/故障降級　fail-passive, degradation
故障率/故障率　failure rate, fault rate
故障模式/失效模式,故障模型　failure mode, fault mode
故障判据/故障準則　failure criteria
故障弱化/故障弱化　fail-soften
故障升级/故障昇級　progression of failure
故障树/故障樹,失效樹　failure tree, failure branch chart, fault tree
故障树分析/失效樹分析　fault tree analysis, FTA
故障数据/故障資料　fault data
故障探测器/故障探測器　fault detector
故障信号/故障信號　fault signal
故障影响/故障影響　fault effect
故障预案/故障對策　fault countermeasure
故障原因/故障原因　fault cause
故障运行/故障操作　failure operation
故障诊断/故障診斷　fault diagnosis
故障[状态]仿真/故障狀態模擬　fault state simulation
故障自动检测/故障自動檢測　automatic failure monitor
顾客活动区/顧客活動區　customer area
锢囚锋/包圍鋒　occluded front
瓜瓣/瓜瓣　scalloped segment
刮板式分粒机/沈澱物分級機　drag-classifier
刮板式混凝土布料机/攔板式混凝土攤鋪機　slat type concrete spreader
刮板式推土机/齒式推土機　rake dozer
刮板输送机/翻板輸送機,板[帶]式運輸機　slat conveyer
刮尺/直尺　straightedge
刮刀/刮刀　scraper
刮泥机/刮汙泥機　sludge scraper
刮伤/刮傷　scoring
刮油环/刮油張圈　scraper ring
刮雨器/擋風雨刷　windshield wiper, windscreen wiper
寡毛类/貧毛類生物　oligochaeta
挂车/拖車　trailer
挂车配比/掛車配比　trailer tractor ratio
挂弹钩/炸彈鉤　bomb shackle
挂断/掛起　hanging up

挂舵臂/半懸舵承架　rudder horn
挂钩牵引功率测定/掛鉤牽引功率測定　drawbar power measurement
挂钩牵引力测定/掛鉤牽引力測定　drawbar pull measurement
挂钩牵引效率测定/掛鉤牽引效率測定　drawbar efficiency measurement
挂号处/掛號處　registration office
挂机状态/掛機　on-hook
挂镜线/掛鏡線條　picture molding
挂靠港/寄泊港　port of call
挂篮/搖臺,托架,吊籃　cradle, basket, traveller
挂梁/掛梁　suspended beam
挂满旗/掛滿旗　full dress
挂瓦室/掛瓦室　journal bearing babbit metal lining room
挂摘钩/掛摘鉤　coupling and uncoupling of hooks
拐角/轉角　corner
拐角导流片/轉向導片　turning vane in corner
关闭设备/船體關閉裝置　hull closure
关闭[水密门窗]/關閉水密[門窗]　dog down
关闭信号/閉合信號　closing signal
关帝庙/關帝廟　Temple of Guan Yu, Guan-di Miao
关封/海關封條　customs seal
关机/關機　cutoff, shutdown
关机点质量/燃盡質量　shutdown point mass, burnout mass
关机方程/關機方程　cutoff equation
关机精度/關機精度　cutoff accuracy
关机余量/關機裕度　allowance for cutoff
关键工程/樞紐工程　key project
关键工序/關鍵性活動　critical activity
关键件/關鍵零件　critical part
关键路线法/要徑法　critical path method, CPM
关键区/關鍵區　critical area
关键软件/關鍵軟件　critical software
关键细节/關鍵細節,重要細節　critical detail
关键因子/關鍵因子　key factor
关键种/關鍵種　key species, keystone species
关节货车/關節貨車　articulated freight car
关节客车/關節客車　articulated passenger car, articulated coach
关节形机器人/關節型機器人　articulated robot
关节坐标系/關節坐標系　joint coordinate system
关口/入境航站,閘道口　gateway
关联故障/關聯故障　relevant fault
关税/關稅　customs duties
关厢/關廂　guanxiang, outer area of city gate

关于在领海和港内使用国际海事卫星船舶地面站的国际协议/在領海及港內使用國際海事衛星船舶地球臺之國際協約　International Agreement on the Use of INMARSAT ship Earth Station within the Territorial Sea and Ports
观测/觀測,觀察　observation
观测船位/觀測船位　observed position, OP
观测船位误差/觀測船位誤差　error of observed position
观测高度/觀測高度　observed altitude
观测高度改正/觀測高度修正　observed altitude correction
观测高塔/觀測高塔　high observing tower
观测柜/窺測油櫃　observation tank
观测经度/觀測經度　observed longitude
观测纬度/觀測緯度　observed latitude
观测预报/觀測預報　tracking condition prediction
观察窗/觀察窗,觀察孔,視察窗　viewport, observation window
观察孔/窺孔　sighting port
观察室/觀察室　observation room
观光/觀光　sightseeing, tourism
观光道路/觀光道路,遊覽路　tour road
观光电梯/觀光電梯　observation elevator, panorama lift
观果植物/觀果植物　plant with ornamental fruits, fruit ornamentals
观花植物/觀花植物　plant with ornamental flowers, flower ornamentals
观景台/觀景臺　sightseeing stand
观赏草/觀賞草　ornamental grass
观赏草坪/觀賞草坪　ornamental lawn
观赏动物/觀賞動物　ornamental animal
观赏果蔬专类园/觀賞果蔬專類園　ornamental fruit and vegetable garden
观赏蕨类/蕨類植物　fern
观赏昆虫类/觀賞昆蟲類　ornamental insect
观赏鸟类/觀賞鳥類　ornamental bird
观赏兽类/觀賞獸類　ornamental beast
观赏温室区/觀賞溫室區　display greenhouse area, display conservatory area
观赏性景观环境用水/觀賞性景觀環境用水　water for aesthetic environment use
观赏园艺学/觀賞園藝學　ornamental horticulture
观赏植物/觀賞植物　ornamental plant
观赏植物嵌合体/花卉嵌合體　chimeras of ornamental plant
观赏植物区/觀賞植物區　ornamental plants area

观演建筑/演藝建築　performing arts building
观叶植物/觀葉植物　foliage plant
观众容量/觀眾容量　audience capacity
观众厅/[大]禮堂,演講廳,演藝廳　auditorium
观众席/觀眾席　spectator seat
官邸/官邸　official residence
官方地图/正式地圖　official map
官方调查/正式調查　official survey
官式/官式　official style
PB 管/PB 管　polybutylene pipe, PB pipe
PE 管/聚乙烯管　polyethylene pipe, PE pipe
PP 管/PP 管　polypropylene pipe, PP pipe
PVC-U 管/PVC-U 管　unplasticized polyvinyl chloride pipe, PVC-U pipe
管板/管板　tube plate
管冰/殼冰　shell ice
管槽/管道,溝道　channel
管槽形药柱/管槽形藥柱　slotted-tube grain
管道/管線　pipeline
管道布置/管線布置　pipe arrangement
管道储气/管道儲氣　gas line packing
管道电缆/管道電纜　duct cable
管道敷设层/管道敷設層　pipe laying course
管道附件/管道附件　pipeline accessories
管道附属设施/管道輔助設備　pipeline auxiliaries
管道灌浆/管道灌漿,導管灌漿　duct grouting
管道间/管道間　pipe room
管道井/管身,管制井筒　pipe shaft
管道摩擦损失/風道摩擦損失　loss due to duct friction
管道排水/管道排水,管式暗溝　pipe drainage
管道式发电站/管路式發電站　conduit type power station
管道运输用地/陸地管線　land for pipeline
管道噪声/導管噪音　duct noise
管道支架/管道支架　pipe trestle
管道支座/管支架　pipe support
管道直饮水净水机房/管道直飲水淨水機房　fine drinking water treatment room
管道直饮水系统/管道直飲水系統　pipe system for fine drinking water
管端喷灌器/管端噴灌器　hose end sprinkler
管风洞/管式風洞　tube tunnel
管沟/[電纜]管道,溝道　channel, pipe duct
管沟敷设/導線管溝敷設　in duct installation
管涵/管涵　pipe culvert
管件/管配件　pipe fitting
管接头/管接頭　pipe joint, tubular joint

管节/管套節　union
管界标/管界標　section sign
管井/管井,鑽井　tubular well, tube well, drilled well
管井水力学/井水力學　hydraulics of well
管卡/管夾,管固定帶　pipe band
管壳式热交换器/殼管式熱交換器　shell and tube heat exchanger
管控型城市设计/管制都市設計　regulatory urban design
管廊/管廊,敷管廊道　pipe gallery
管理程序/管理程式　management program
管理船舶过失/管理船舶過失　default in management of the ship
管理费/一般管理費用　overheads
管理规约/管理規章　management rules and agreements
管理级/管理級　management level
管路/管線　pipeline
管路冲洗/管路沖洗　flushing of pipeline
管路吹除/吹管　blow pipe, line purging
管路附件/管路配件　pipeline fittings
管路特性曲线/管路特性曲線　pipeline characteristic curve
管路图/管線圖　piping drawing
管内工作车/管內工作車　local car to be unloaded
管内客流/管內客流　local passenger flow
管内旅客列车/管內旅客列車　local passenger train
管内装卸率/管內裝卸率　local loading and unloading rate
管棚/管棚　pipe shed, canopy tubes
管棚支护/管棚支護結構　pipe-shed support, pipe-roofing support
管球阻尼器/球管阻尼器　ball-in-tube damper
管渠/管道,導管　conduit
管式护栏/管式護柵　pipe guardrail
管试/管試　tube test
管束式推力室/管狀推力室　tubular thrust chamber
管隧/管道　pipe tunnel
管网/管線網　pipe network, pipeline net
管网灭火系统/管網滅火系統　piping extinguishing system
管系图/管線布置　pipe arrangement
管辖权/行政管轄　jurisdiction
管辖权条款/管轄權條款　jurisdiction clause
管线标/管線標　pipeline mark
管线综合设计/管線綜合設計　integrated design for utility pipeline

管线综合图/管線綜合圖　integral pipeline longitudinal and vertical drawing
管形燃烧室/管形燃燒室,筒形燃燒室　can-type chamber, can-type combustor, tubular combustor
管形支柱/圆管柱　tubular pillar
管涌/管湧,管狀滲蝕　piping
管制标志/管制交通標誌　regulatory traffic sign
管制地带/管制地帶　control zone
管制扇区/管制扇區　control sector
管制移交点/管制移交點　control transfer point
管制值机员/管制值機員　controlling operator
管柱/管柱　tubular column
管柱挡墙/圓柱形軸擋土牆　cylindrical shaft retaining wall
管柱基础/管柱基礎,圓柱樁基礎　colonnade foundation, tubular column foundation, cylinder pile foundation
管状/管狀　tubular shape
管[状]冰/管冰　tube ice
管状电弧加热器/管式電弧加熱器　tube type arc heater
管状药柱/管狀藥柱　tube grain
管子吊架/管吊架　pipe hanger
管子脚手架/管搭腳手架　pipe scaffolding
管嘴量水计/噴嘴式水表　flow-nozzle meter
管嘴流量计/噴嘴式水表　flow-nozzle meter
贯穿辐射/穿降輻射　penetration radiation
贯穿螺栓/貫穿螺栓　through bolt
贯流容量/貫穿能力　breakthrough capacity
贯流式水轮机/管式水渦輪　tubular turbine
贯流式通风机/橫流式風扇　cross-flow fan, tangential fan
贯入度试验/圓錐貫入試驗　cone penetration test
贯入法/滲透法　penetration method
贯入记录/貫入記錄　penetration record
贯入仪/貫入儀　penetration test apparatus
贯索四(北冕 α)/貫索四(北冕 α)　Alphecca
贯通/貫穿　breakthrough
贯通线/貫通線　through track
贯通肘板/全通腋板,貫通托架　through bracket
冠层/林冠,翳蓋　canopy, forest canopy
冠幅/樹冠直徑,冠徑　crown breadth
冠心病监护病房/心臟病監護病房,CCU室　cardiac care unit, CCU
惯导系统机械编排/慣導系統機械編排　inertial navigation system mechanization
惯量椭圆/慣性橢圓　ellipse of inertia
惯性/慣性,惰性　inertia

惯性半径/慣性半徑　radius of inertia
惯性补偿/慣性補償　inertia compensation
惯性测量系统/慣性測量系統　inertial measurement system, IMS
惯性测量装置/慣性量測單元　inertial measurement unit, IMU
惯性传感器/慣性感測器　inertial sensor
惯性导航/慣性導航　inertial navigation
惯性导航系统/慣性導航系統　inertial navigation system, INS
惯性定律/慣性律　law of inertia
惯性法则/慣性律　law of inertia
惯性飞行段/慣性飛行階段　inertial flight phase
惯性积/慣性積　product of inertia
惯性基准坐标系/慣性基準[參考]坐標系　inertial reference frame
惯性技术/慣性技術　inertial technology
惯性矩/慣性矩　moment of inertia
惯性开关/慣性開關　inertia switch
惯性空间三轴稳定/慣性空間三軸穩定　inertial space three-axis stabilization
惯性力/慣性力　inertia force, inertial force
惯性轮/慣性輪　inertia wheel
惯性敏感器/慣性感測器　inertial sensor
惯性耦合/慣性耦合　inertial coupling
惯性耦合控制系统/慣性耦合控制系統　inertial cross-coupling control system
惯性平台/慣性平臺　inertial platform
惯性平台瞄准/慣性平臺瞄準　inertial platform aiming
惯性式制动试验台/慣性式剎車試驗器　inertial type brake tester
惯性试验/慣性試驗　inertial trial
惯性系统/慣性系統　inertial system
惯性延时/慣性遲延　inertial delay
惯性引信/慣性引信　inertial fuze
惯性运转时间/慣性停轉時間　inertial rundown time
惯性增压/慣性增壓　inertia supercharging
惯性制导/慣性導引　inertial guidance
惯性制导系统/慣性導引系統　inertial guidance system, IGS
惯性质量/慣性質量　inertial mass
惯性转头角/慣性轉頭角　overshoot
惯性坐标/慣性坐標　inertial coordinate
盥洗室/盥洗室,廁所　lavatory, toilet, washroom
灌丛/灌叢　shrub
灌封/嵌埋　embedding
灌缝/接縫灌漿　joint grouting

灌溉/灌溉　irrigation
灌溉地区/灌溉區域　irrigation district
灌溉回水/灌溉回水　return flow irrigation
灌溉结构/灌溉結構　irrigation structure
灌溉率/灌溉率　water duty
灌溉面积/灌溉面積　irrigated area
灌溉排水系统/灌溉排水系統　irrigation and drainage system
灌溉强度/灌溉強度　irrigation intensity
灌溉渠道/灌溉渠道　irrigation channel
灌溉水利用系数/灌溉省水效率　water efficiency of irrigation
灌溉隧洞/灌溉隧道　irrigation tunnel
灌溉系统/灌溉系統　irrigation system
灌溉效率/灌溉效率　irrigation efficiency
灌溉[用]水/灌溉水　irrigation water
灌浆/灌漿　slurry penetration, grouting
灌浆材料/灌漿材料，注漿材料　grouting materials, grouting material
灌浆隔墙/灌漿帷牆　grout curtain wall
灌浆盒/灌漿用留洞匣　grout box
灌浆截水墙/灌漿截水牆　grouted cut off wall
灌浆塞/灌漿止水板　grout stopper
灌浆碎石路/灌漿碎石路　grouted macadam
灌浆帷幕/灌漿[隔]幕　grouted curtain, grouting curtain
灌浆压力/灌漿壓力　grouting pressure
灌木/灌木,灌叢　shrub, bush
灌木花境/灌木花境　shrub border
灌木花坛/灌木花壇　shrub bed
灌木林地/灌木材地　shrub land
灌木切割机/割草機,剪枝機　brush cutting machine, brush cutter
灌区/灌溉面積　irrigated area
灌入式碎石路/灌入式碎石路　penetration macadam
灌水均匀系数/布水均匀性　uniformity coefficient of water distribution
灌水泥浆/灌水泥漿　grout cement
灌水器/發射體,發射器　emitter
灌水强度/灌水強度　water application rate
灌水试验/注水試驗　water filling test
灌压浆设备/灌漿設備　grouting equipment
灌注法/灌注法　flooding method
灌注桩/場鑄樁　cast-in-situ pile
灌注桩钻孔机/場鑄混凝土鑽孔機,就地澆鑄混凝土鑽孔機　cast-in-place concrete pile rig
罐车/罐車,槽車　tank car
罐车容积计表/罐車容積計表　tank volume table

罐端板/油罐端板　tank head
罐式集装箱/槽[貨]櫃　tank container
罐体/[水]箱,[油]箱　tank
罐体鞍座/油罐鞍座　tank saddle
罐体长度/罐體長度　length of tank
罐头加工船/罐頭工作船　canning factory ship
罐形浮标/罐形浮標　can buoy
罐装货物/罐車貨物　tank car freight
光/光　light
光斑/斑點　speckle
光饱和/光飽和　light saturation
光饱和点/光飽和點　light saturation point
光标/光標　cursor
光补偿点/光的平準點　light compensation point
光测合作目标/光學追蹤合作目標　optical tracking cooperative target
光测弹性试验装置/光測彈性試驗裝置　photoelastic test installation
光程/光程　optical path
光程长[度]/光徑長度　optical path length
光传飞行控制/光傳飛操控制　fly-by-light control
光传输模式/光傳輸模式　optical transmission mode
光船/空船　bareboat
光船租购/光船租購　bareboat charter with hire purchase
光船租赁/光船租賃　bareboat charter
光船租赁登记/光船租賃登記　bareboat charter registration
光带/光帶　light strip
光带式表示/光帶式表示　stript indication light
光导管采光/光導管採光　light guide daylighting
光导纤维采光/光導纖維採光　optical fiber daylighting
光点式表示/光點式表示　spotted indication light
光电比色分析/光電比色法　photoelectric colorimetry
光电池/光電池　photocell, photoelectric cell
光电导探测器/光[電]導偵測器　photoconductive detector
光电导线/光電導線　photoelectric traverse
光电发射/光電發射　photoemission
光电复合雷达/光電複合雷達　electro-optical combined radar
光电感烟探测器/光電煙塵檢測器　photoelectric smoke detector
光电光度计/光電光度計　photoelectric photometer
光电经纬仪/光電經緯儀　photoelectric theodolite
光电燃气探测器/光電煙道氣探測器　photoelectric

flue gas detector
光电式传感器/光電式傳感器　electro-optical pickoff, photoelec-transducer
光电探测器/光電探測器，光檢波器，光電檢測計　photodetector, photoelectric detector
光电望远镜/光電望遠鏡　photoelectric telescope
光电系统/光電系統　photoelectric system
光电效应/光電效應　photoelectric effect
光电侦察系统/光電偵察系統　electro-optical reconnaissance system
光电准直管/光電準直管　photoelectric collimating tube, photoelectric collimator
光电子/光電子　photoelectron
光度测量/光度測量學　photometry
光度控制系统/光度控制系統　light control system
光伏电池/太陽[能]電池，太陽電池[組]　solar cell, solar battery
光伏电站/光伏電站　photovoltaic plant
光伏探测器/光電偵測器　photovoltaic detector
光伏效应/光伏效應　photovoltaic effect
光辐射/光輻射　light radiation
光功率计/光功率計　optical power meter
光合面积/光合面積　photosynthetic area
光合能力/光合特性　photosynthetic capability
光合时间/光合時間　photosynthetic time
光合作用/光合作用　photosynthesis
光呼吸/光呼吸　photorespiration
光弧/號燈光弧　sector of light
光弧界限/光弧界限　limit of sector
光化学反应/光化學反應　photochemical reaction
光化学过程/光化學過程　photochemical process
光化学烟雾/光化學煙霧　photochemical smoke, photochemical smog
光化学烟雾污染/光化學汙染　photochemical smog pollution
光环境/發光環境　luminous environment
光辉城市/光輝城市，陽光城　radiant city
光接口/光介面　optical interface
光截面火灾探测器/光截面火災探測器　light beam image fire detector
光刻/光刻　photolithography
光控开关/燈光控制系統　sound and light-controlled energy-saving switch
光阑/光闌　diaphragm, stop
光缆/光學電纜，光導電纜，光纖電纜　optical cable, optical fiber cable
光缆接头/光纖接頭　optical fiber cable joint closure
光缆通信系统/光纜通信系統　optical cable communication system
光缆中继站/光纖再生站　optical fiber regeneration station
光缆终接盒/光纜終接盒　fiber optic cable terminating box
光雷达/光雷達　optical radar
光力射程/光照距，光強度視程　luminous range
光连接器/光連接器　optical connector
光亮淬火/光亮淬火　bright quenching, clean hardening
光亮电镀/光亮電鍍　bright plating
[光]亮度/亮度，發光密度　luminance
光亮热处理/輝面熱處理　bright heat treatment
光亮退火/輝面退火　bright annealing, clean annealing, light annealing
光量/燈塔等級　magnitude of light
光面爆破/光面爆破，整修爆炸　smooth blasting
光面钢筋/光面鋼筋，無節鋼筋　plain bar
光面卷筒/光面卷筒　smooth faced drum
光谱/光譜　optical spectrum
光谱测量仪/光譜分析儀　optical spectrum instrumentation
光谱成分/波譜成分　spectral component
光谱法温度测量/光譜溫度量測　spectroscopic temperature measurement
光谱反射特性/光譜反射特性　spectral reflection characteristics
光谱分辨率/光譜解析度　spectral resolution
光谱分析/光譜分析　spectrographic analysis, spectral analysis
光谱辐射通量/[光]譜輻射通量，輻射通量譜　spectral radiant flux
光谱感光度曲线/光譜感受性曲線　spectral sensitivity curve
光谱灵敏度/光譜靈敏度，頻譜靈敏度　spectral sensitivity
光谱滤波/光譜濾波　spectrum filtering
光谱滤波器/光譜濾波器　spectral filter
光谱密度/[光]譜密度　spectral density
光谱特征/光譜特性，光譜符號　spectral feature, spectral signature
光谱响应/頻譜響應，頻譜回應　spectral response
光谱仪/光譜計　optical spectrometer
光谱噪声等效功率/光譜雜訊等效功率　spectral noise equivalent power
光气候/光[照]氣候　light climate
光气候系数/光氣候係數　daylight climate coefficient
光强[度]/光強度，光照強　light intensity

光圈调节[装置]/孔徑定位　aperture setting
光栅/光柵　grating
光栅干涉仪/繞射光柵干涉儀　diffraction grating interferometer
光生电流/光電流　photo-generated current, photocurrent
光生电压/光電壓　photo-generated voltage
光时域反射仪/光時域反射計　optical time domain reflectometer
光适配器/光學適配器　optical adapter
光束角/波束角,波注角　beam angle
光数字段/光數位區間　optical digital section
光衰/光衰　luminous decay
光衰减器/光學衰減器　optical attenuator
光塑性力学/光測塑性學　photoplasticity
光弹性/光彈性　photoelasticity
光弹性试验/光彈性試驗,光彈性分析　photoelastic analysis, photoelasticity test
光弹性仪/光彈儀　photoelastic meter
光探测器/光學偵測器　optical detector
光通量/光通量　luminous flux
光污染/光汙染,光害　light pollution
光纤/光纖　optical fiber
光纤标志/光纖標誌　optic fiber sign
光纤剥除器/光纖剥皮器　optical fiber stripper
光纤测裂计/光纖裂縫感測器　optic fiber sensor for crack monitor
光纤传感器/光纖轉換器,光纖換能器　optical fiber transducer
光纤带宽/光纖帶寬　bandwidth of optical fiber
光纤灯/導光纖維光　fiber optic light
光纤分配架/光纖分配架,光配線架　optical fiber distribution frame
光纤接续损耗/光纖熔接損失　optical fiber splice loss
光纤内流场显示/光纖内流場顯示　internal flow field visualization using optical fiber
光纤切断器/光纖切斷機　optical fiber cutter
光纤融接机/光纖融接機　optical fiber fusion splicing machine
光纤适配器/光纖連接器　optical fiber connector
光纤数字线路系统/光纖數位有線系統　optical fiber digital line system
光纤通信系统/光纖通訊系統　optical fiber communication system
光纤陀螺/光纖陀螺　fiber gyroscope
光线路保护切换设备/光線路保護切換設備　optical line protection switching equipment
光线路终端设备/光線路終端設備　optical line terminal equipment
光心/光心　optical center
光行差/光行差　aberration
光学测距/光學距離測量　optical distance measurement
光学测量/光學量測　optical measurement
光学车间/光學工坊　optical workshop
光学处理器/光處理機　optical processor
光学传递函数/光學傳遞函數　optical transfer function, OTF
光学对中器/光學求心器　optical centering device
光学对准/光學對準,光學校準　optical alignment
光学俯仰传感器/光學俯仰換能器　optical pitch transducer
光学跟踪架/光學[火箭]跟蹤架　optical tracking mount
光学跟踪系统/光追蹤系統　optical tracking system
光学跟踪站/光學追蹤站　optical tracking station
光学机械投影/光學機械投影　optical mechanical projection
光学经纬仪/光學經緯儀　optical theodolite
光学框标/光學框標　optical fiducial mark
光学瞄准/光電瞄準　optical sighting
光学模型/光學模型　optical model
光学实验室/光學實驗室　optical laboratory
光学数字处理器/光學數位處理器　optical digital processor
光学投影/光學投影　optical projection
光学系统/光學系統　optical system
光学显微镜/光學顯微鏡　optical microscope
光学信息处理/光學資訊處理　optical information processing
光学仪器仪表厂/光學儀器廠　optical instrument factory
光学引信/光學引信　optical fuze
光学引信光路角/光學引信光徑角　angle of light path of optical fuze
光学引信视场角/光學引信視野　field of view of optical fuze
光学引信探测角/光學引信探測場　detective field of optical fuze
光学增白/光過濾劑　optical bleach
光学姿态敏感器/光學姿態感測器　optical attitude sensor
光压摄动/太陽輻射攝動　solar radiation perturbation
光诱围网/燈誘圍網　light-purse seine

光源/光源　optical source
光源色/光源色　color of light source
光源寿命/光源壽命　light source life
光再生[中继]段/光再生區段　optical regenerator section
光[再生]中继器/光再生中繼器　optical regenerative repeater
[光]照度/[光]照度,照明度　illuminance
光折射系数/光線折射系數　light refraction coefficient
光轴角/光角　optical angle
光子吸收/光吸收　absorption of the photons
广播电视[发射]塔/無線電發射塔　transmitting tower, broadcasting tower
广播电视工程/廣播電視工程　radio and TV broadcast engineering
广播电视卫星地球站/廣播電視衛星地球站　radio and television satellite earth station
广播电台/廣播電臺,廣播站　broadcasting station
广播分系统/廣播子系統　broadcasting subsystem
广播呼叫/廣播呼叫　broadcast call
广播卫星/廣播衛星　broadcasting satellite
广播星历/廣播天文曆　broadcast ephemeris
广播业务/廣播業務　broadcasting service
广播中心/廣播電臺,廣播站　broadcasting station
广场/廣場　square
广场灯/廣場燈　square lamp, square nightscape lighting
广场控制线/廣場控制線　plaza control line
广场用地/廣場用地　land for square
广角镜头/廣角透鏡　wide-angle lens
广亩城市/廣宇城市　broadacre city
广厅/穿堂　public hall, concourse
广义变分原理/廣義變分原理　generalized variational principle
广义内力/廣義內力　generalized internal force
广义位移/廣義位移　generalized displacement
广域差分 GPS/廣域差分型全球定位系統　wide area differential GPS, WADGPS
广域网/廣域網路　wide-area network, WAN
广域增强系统/廣域[擴增]系統　wide area augmentation system, WAAS
归航/歸航　homing
归位/歸位　bring home
归一变化率/歸一化變化率　normalized rate
归一化探测率/歸一化探測率　normalized detectivity
规避操舵/迴避操舵法　evasive steering
规避航向/迴避航向　evasive course

规避机动/迴避操縱　evasion maneuvre
规程/程序　procedure
规定速度/表定速率　schedule speed
规定值/規定值,給定值　specified value
规范/標準　standard
规范化声压级差/正規化聲壓位準差　normalized sound pressure level difference
规范化撞击声压级/正規化衝擊聲壓位準　normalized impact sound pressure level
规费/規費　stipulated fee
规划/規劃　programming
规划备案/規劃備案　planning record
规划标准/規劃標準　planning standard
规划草案公告/規劃草案公告　announcement of draft plan
规划查询/規劃查詢　planning inquiry
规划程序/規劃程式　planning procedure
规划大纲/規劃綱要　planning outline
规划单元/計劃單元　urban planning unit
规划督察员/規劃檢查員　planning inspector
规划概念/計劃構想　planning concept
规划公示/規劃公示　planning publicity
规划管理程序/規劃管理程式　planning management program
规划管理信息系统/規劃管理資訊系統　information systems of urban planning administration
规划管制区/規劃管制區　planning control zone
规划过程/規劃步驟　planning process
规划机构/規劃機構　planning authority
规划建设发展/計劃發展　planned development
规划建筑线/建築限界,建築定規　construction gage
规划控制单元/規劃控制單元　control unit of planning
规划论证/規劃論證　plan demonstration
规划目标/規劃目標　planning goal
规划年度实施计划/規劃年度實施計劃　annual implementation plan of planning
规划期限/設計時間,計劃期間　planning term, planning period
规划强制性内容/規劃強制性內容　mandatory planning content
规划区[域]/規劃區域　planning region
规划设计条件/規劃設計條件　planning and design brief
规划审查/規劃檢查　planning review
规划审批程序/規劃審批程式　procedure for approval of urban plan
规划审批要点/資格認可關鍵元素　key elements of

qualification approval
规划审议/規劃審議　plan deliberation
规划师/城市規劃者　planner
规划数据标准/規劃資料標準　standard for planning data
规划数据库/規劃資料庫　planning database
规划说明/規劃說明　description of plan
规划说明书/規劃說明書　planning instruction book
规划条件/規劃條件　planning condition
规划条件变更/規劃條件變更　change of the planning conditions
规划条件确定/規劃條件確認　confirmation of planning condition
规划听证/公聽會　public hearing
规划图/規劃[地]圖　planning map
规划图纸/規劃圖紙　diagram of plan
规划委员会/規劃委員會　planning committee
规划文本/規劃文本,規劃條例　planning ordinance, text of plan
规划信息门户/規劃資訊入口網站　planning information portal
规划信息系统/規劃資訊系統　planning information system
规划修改报审程序/規劃修改報審程式　procedure of plan amendment submission
规划许可/規劃許可　planning permit
规划研究/規劃研究　planning study
规划政策/規劃政策　planning policy
规划支持系统/規劃支持系統　planning support system, PSS
规划中线/規劃中心　planning center line
规划助手工具箱/規劃助手工具箱　planning assistance tool box
规线/軌距線,鉚釘線　gage line
规则波/規則波[浪]　regular wave
规则库/規則庫　rule base
规则式园林/整形式園林　formal style garden
规则式种植/正方形植樹　regular planting
规整式道路系统/規整式道路系統　formal road system
规整式园林/規整式園林　formal garden style
硅尘/矽灰　siliceous dust, silica fume
硅尘混凝土/矽塵混凝土　silica fume concrete
硅华/矽華　geyserite
硅化加固/矽化加固　silicification
硅片/矽片　silica sheet
硅砷化镓太阳电池/矽砷化鎵太陽電池　Si-gallium arsenide solar cell

硅[酸]钙板/矽[酸]鈣板　fiber reinforced calcium silicate sheet
硅酸盐砖/矽酸鹽磚　silicate brick
硅太阳电池/矽太陽電池　silicon solar cell
硅酮橡胶/矽酮橡膠　silicone rubber
硅土水泥砂浆/矽酸水泥砂漿　silica cement mortar
硅油/矽油　silicone oil
硅油减振器/矽油減振器　silicon oil damper
硅油弹簧减振器/矽油彈簧減振器　silicon oil spring damper
硅藻土/矽藻土,矽藻岩　diatomite
硅整流器电力机车/矽整流器電力機車　silicon rectifier electric locomotive
硅整流装置/矽整流器裝置　silicon rectifier device
轨撑/軌撐　rail brace
轨道/軌道　track
轨道暗坑/浮枕　loose tie
轨道保持/軌道維護　orbital maintenance
轨道备份星/軌道備用衛星　in-orbit spare satellite
轨道变形/軌道變形　track deformation, track disorder, track distortion
轨道变压器箱/軌道變壓器箱　track transformer box
轨道变阻器/軌道變阻器　track rheostat
轨道标志/軌道標誌　track sign post
轨道捕获/軌道獲得　orbital acquisition
轨道不平顺/軌道不整　track irregularity
轨道参数/軌道參數　orbit parameter, orbital element
轨道残余变形/軌道殘餘變形　track residual deformation, track permanent deformation
轨道舱/軌道艙　orbit module
轨道测量/軌道測量　orbit measurement
轨道测量系统/軌道測量系統　orbit measurement system
轨道长半径/軌道半長徑　semi-major axis of ellipse
轨道长度/軌道長度　track length
轨道电抗器/軌道電抗器　track reactor
轨道电路/軌道電路　track circuit
轨道电路电码化/軌道電路電碼化　coding of continuous track circuit
轨道电路分割/軌道電路分割　cut-section of track circuit
轨道电路分路状态/軌道電路分路狀態　shunted state of track circuit
轨道电路调整状态/軌道電路調整狀態　regulated state of track circuit
轨道电路蓄电现象/軌道電路蓄電效應　storage

effect of track circuit

轨道动力稳定机/軌道動力穩定車　track dynamic stabilizer

轨道动力学/軌道[動]力學　orbit dynamics, track dynamics

轨道段救生/軌道段救生　orbit phase rescue

轨道方向/軌道線型　track alignment

轨道飞行试验/軌道飛行試驗　orbital flight test

轨道改进/軌道調整　orbit correction

轨道改进方法/軌道校正法　orbit correction method

轨道改善/軌道改善　track improvement

轨道更换/軌道更換　renewal of track

轨道鼓出/軌道挫屈　track buckling

轨道鼓出临界温度/軌道挫屈臨界溫度　critical temperature of track buckling

轨道和姿态耦合/軌道和姿態耦合　coupling of orbit and attitude

轨道荷载谱/軌道荷載譜　track load spectrum

轨道横水平校正/軌道橫水平校正　correction of crosslevel

轨道衡线/軌道衡線　weight bridge track

轨道机动/軌道機動　orbit maneuver

轨道机动火箭发动机/軌道操縱火箭發動機　orbit maneuvering rocket engine, orbit maneuvering rocket motor

轨道机械/養路機械　track machine

轨道积分通量/軌道積分通量　orbital integrated flux

轨道几何尺寸容许公差/軌道幾何尺寸容許公差　track geometry tolerance

轨道几何形位/軌道地形學　track geometry

轨道几何状态恶化/軌道幾何狀態惡化　track deterioration

轨道检测/軌道檢查　track inspection

轨道检测设备/軌道量測裝置　track geometry measuring device

轨道检查车/軌道檢查車　track recording car, track inspection car

轨道检查小车/軌道幾何線形測量車　track geometry measuring trolley

轨道交会动力学/軌道交會動力學　orbital rendezvous dynamics

轨道交会对接/軌道會合靠接　orbital rendezvous and docking

轨道交通车辆基地/軌道交通車輛基地　rail transit vehicle base

轨道交通车辆站/軌道交通補給站　rail transit depot

轨道校正/軌道校正　correction of track, orbit adjustment

轨道接触器/軌道接觸器，軌道踏板　track treadle

轨道结构/軌道結構　track structure

轨道控制/軌道控制　orbital control

轨道控制分系统/軌道控制分系統　orbit control subsystem

轨道控制规律/軌道控制律　orbit control law

轨道控制量/軌道控制量　orbit control quantity

轨道控制软件/軌道控制軟體　orbit control software

轨道控制速度增量/軌道控制速度增量　orbit control velocity increment

轨道框架刚度/軌框剛度　rigidity of track panel

轨道缆车/軌道纜車　cableway car

轨道缆车客运站/軌道纜車站　cableway car station

轨道类型/軌道類型　classification of track, track standard

轨道力学/軌道力學　track mechanics, track kinetics

轨道明坑/軌道沈陷　visible pit of track, visible low spot of track, track depression

轨道平车/軌道平車　rail flat car

轨道平均温度/軌道平均溫度　in-orbit average temperature

轨道起重机/軌道起重機　track crane, rail crane

轨道器/軌道載具　orbiter, orbital vehicle

轨道器材修护场/軌道器材修護場　track material repair shop

轨道前后高低/軌道[前後]高低　longitudinal level of rail, track profile

轨道强度计算/軌道強度分析　track strength analysis

轨道倾角/軌道之傾斜　orbit inclination

轨道区域/軌道區　orbital region

轨道确定/軌道決定　orbit determination

GPS轨道确定/全球定位系統軌道決定　GPS orbit determination

轨道设计/軌道設計　trajectory design

轨道生电现象/軌道生電現象　track galvanic effect

轨道失效/路線故障　track failure

轨道施工/軌道鋪設　track construction

轨道寿命/軌道壽命　orbital life

轨道受电变压器/軌道中繼變壓器　track relay transformer

轨道衰变/軌道衰減　orbital decay

轨道衰变模式/軌道衰減模式　orbital decay model

轨道衰减法返回/軌道衰減法返回　orbit decay return mode

轨道水平/軌道水平　track cross level

轨道水平尺/軌道水平尺　track level

轨道瞬时温度/軌道瞬間溫度　in-orbit transient

temperature
轨道送电变压器/軌道送電變壓器　track transformer feed end
轨道碎片/軌道碎片　orbit debris
轨道探伤器/軌條探傷器　rail defect detector
轨道逃生装置/軌道脫離裝置　in-orbit escape device
轨道陀螺罗盘/軌道陀螺羅盤　orbit gyrocompass
轨道弯曲器/千斤頂彎軌器　jack rail-bender
轨道稳定性/軌道穩定性　stability of track
轨道限界/軌道淨空　track clearance
轨道养护标准/軌道整修標準　standards of track maintenance
轨道应力/軌道應力　track stress
轨道预报/軌道預報,軌道預測　orbit prediction
轨道预报误差/軌道預測誤差　orbit prediction error
轨道预示温度/軌道預示溫度　in-orbit predicted temperature
[轨道]运行段测控/[軌道]運行段測控　TT and C of in-orbit phase
轨道质量指数/軌道品質指數　track quality index
轨道中心/軌道中心　track center
轨道中心线/軌道中心線　track center line
轨道周期/軌道週期　orbit period
轨道转移/軌道轉移　orbit transfer
轨道转移火箭发动机/軌道轉移火箭發動機　orbit transfer rocket engine, orbit transfer rocket motor
轨道转运/鐵軌移動　rail transfer
轨底/軌底,鐵路軌座　rail base, rail bottom
轨底崩裂/軌底崩裂　burst of rail base, burst of rail bottom, broken rail base
轨底坡/軌底坡　rail cant
轨顶标高/軌道昇高,軌道高程　track elevation
轨端崩裂/鋼軌裂損　rail end breakage
轨端马鞍形磨损/鋼軌末端沈陷　rail end batter, saddle wear of rail end
轨端削角/軌端去角　rail end chamfering
轨缝/軌縫,軌間隙　rail gap, rail joint gap
轨缝调整/軌縫調整　rail gap adjusting
轨缝调整器/軌縫調整器　rail gap adjuster, rail puller
轨腹上圆弧接触夹板/軌腹上圓弧接觸夾板　head free flat joint bar
轨迹/航跡,軌道　track, TK
轨迹控制/軌跡控制　trajectory control
轨检车评分/軌檢車評分　track evaluation by recording car, evaluation by track inspection car
轨节/軌節　rail link
轨距/軌距　rail gage, track gage
轨距尺/軌距尺,軌距規　track gage, gauging rule
轨距[拉]杆/軌距拉桿,軌撐　gage rod, gage tie
轨距加宽/軌距加寬　gage widening
轨距偏差/軌距偏差　disorder of gage
轨模式混凝土摊铺机/軌模式混凝土攤鋪機　rail form concrete paver
轨排/軌框　track panel, track skeleton
轨钳/軌鉗　rail catch
轨头/鋼軌頭　rail head
轨头波纹磨损/鋼軌波磨,軌條波狀磨耗　corrugation of rail head, rail corrugation
轨头波形磨损/軌頭波形磨損　wave-type deformation of rail head
轨头剥离/軌頭剝離　gage line shelly cracks
轨头侧面磨损/軌頭側面磨損　side wear of rail head
轨头长波浪磨损/軌頭長波浪磨損　long wave undulation of rail head
轨头垂直磨损/軌頭垂直磨損　vertical wear of rail head
轨头垂直劈裂/軌頭縱裂　vertical split of rail head
轨头底面接触夹板/軌頭底面接觸夾板　head contact flat joint bar
轨头掉块/軌頭剝落　spalling of rail head
轨头短波浪磨损/軌頭短波浪磨損　short wave undulation of rail head
轨头发裂/軌頭部乾裂　head checks, hair crack of rail head
轨头非对称断面打磨/鋼軌頭部非對稱斷面打磨　asymmetrical rail head profile grinding
轨头肥边/軌頭肥邊　flow of rail head, lipping of rail head
轨头水平劈裂/鋼軌頭水平裂紋　horizontal split of rail head
轨头微细裂纹/軌頭微細裂紋　detail fracture of rail head
轨头压溃/軌頭壓碎　crushing of rail head
轨头整形/鋼軌頭部整形　rail head reprofiling
轨头总磨损/軌頭總磨損　total wear of rail head
轨下基础/軌下基礎　sub-rail foundation, sub-rail track bed
轨行起重机/軌行起重機　rail crane
轨行式起重机/軌行式起重機　crane on-track, rail-mounted crane
轨行式装运机械/軌行式裝運機械　rail-mounted handling and transportation machine
轨腰/軌腹　rail web
轨腰劈裂/用滾筒輸送時受損之鋼軌　piped rail,

split of rail web
轨枕/軌枕,枕木　tie, cross tie, sleeper
轨枕抽换机/軌枕抽換機　tie replacing machine
轨枕方正/軌枕位置矯正　sleeper respacing
[轨]枕盒/枕盒　crib
轨枕间距/軌枕間距　spacing of sleeper
轨枕接头/軌枕接頭　tie joint, sleeper joint
轨枕螺栓/軌枕螺絲　sleeper-screw
柜/櫃,箱　cabinet
柜式气体灭火装置/櫃式氣體滅火裝置　cabinet gas extinguishing equipment
贵宾席/貴賓席　VIP seat
贵重货/高值貨　valuable cargo
贵重货物/貴重貨[物]　valuable goods, valuable cargo
贵重行包/貴重行李　precious belonging
辊锻/軋機鍛造　roll forging
辊筒式碎石机/輥碎機　roll crusher
辊筒闸门/輥筒式閘門　roller drum gate
辊涂/滾輪式塗漆　roller painting
滚齿/齒輪滾削　gear hobbing
滚点焊/滾點熔接　roll spot welding
滚动共振/滾動共振　rolling resonance
滚动角速度/滾轉率　rate of roll
滚动摩擦/滾動摩擦　rolling friction
滚动摩擦系数/滾動摩擦係數　coefficient of rolling friction
滚动摩阻/轉動阻力　rolling resistance
滚动摩阻系数/滾動抵抗係數　coefficient of rolling resistance
滚动-偏航耦合/滾轉-偏航耦合　roll-yaw coupling
滚动-偏航耦合控制/滾轉-偏航耦合控制　roll-yaw coupling control
滚动桥/輥開橋　rolling bridge
滚动筛/滾動篩　drum screen
滚动式舱[口]盖/滾動式艙口蓋　rolling hatch cover
滚动试验台/滾動試驗臺　rolling rig
滚动圆/滾動圓　tread rolling circle
滚动轴承/滾動軸承,球輥軸承　rolling bearing, ball and roller bearing
滚动轴承故障自动检测/滾動軸承故障自動檢測　automatic roller bearing defect detection
滚动轴承间/滾輪軸承間　roller bearing shop
滚动姿态/滾轉姿態　roll attitude
滚动姿态捕获/滾轉姿態獲取　roll attitude acquisition
滚动阻力测定/滾動阻力測定　rolling resistance measurement
滚动阻力系数/滾動抵抗係數　coefficient of rolling resistance
滚镀/滾鍍　barrel plating
滚翻式舱口盖/單拉[式]艙口蓋　single pull hatch cover
滚浆法/滾漿法　rolling slurry process
滚卷式舱[口]盖/卷動[式]艙口蓋　roll stowing hatchcover
滚轮导缆器/滾子導索器　roller fairleader, roller fairlead
滚轮静线压力测定/滾輪靜線壓力測定　drum static linear pressure measurement
滚轮式钻头/滾齒鑽頭,滾動式鑽頭　roller bit
滚轮摇臂/滾輪搖桿　roller rocker
滚球止推轴承/滾球止推軸承　ball thrust bearing
滚圈/領圈　rolling ring
滚上滚下集装箱叉车/滾上滾下集裝箱叉車　roll on-roll off container fork lift
滚筒式沥青混合料搅拌设备/滾筒式瀝青混合攪拌站　drum mixing asphalt plant
滚弯成形/輥壓成形　roll forming
滚压检验/滾壓檢驗　proof rolling
滚轴支座/滾動軸承,滾子軸承　roller bearing
滚柱式扩管器/擴管器　roller tube expander
滚柱支座/輥軸支承,輥支　roller support
滚柱轴承试验台/滾子軸承試驗臺　roller bearing test stand
滚转角/滾轉角　roll angle
滚转力矩/滾轉力矩　rolling moment
滚转收敛模态/滾轉收斂模態　rolling subsidence mode
滚转速率振荡/滾轉速率振盪　rolling rate oscillation
滚装/滾裝,駛上駛下　roll on-roll off
滚装船/滾裝船,駛上駛下船,轆轆船　drive on-drive off ship, roll on-roll off ship, ro/ro ship
滚装货/滾裝貨　ro/ro cargo
滚装通道设备/滾裝通道設備　ro/ro access equipment
滚装运输/滾裝運輸,駛上駛下運輸,轆轆運輸　roll on-roll off transport
郭/郭　guo, city wall
锅胴/鍋胴　boiler barrel course
锅炉/鍋爐　boiler
锅炉安全阀/鍋爐安全閥　boiler safety valve
锅炉安全装置/鍋爐安全裝置　boiler safety device
锅炉本体/鍋爐[本]體　boiler body, boiler proper
锅炉舱/鍋爐艙,鍋爐間　fire room, boiler room
锅炉点火/鍋爐點火　boiler lighting up

锅炉点火泵/鍋爐點火泵　boiler ignition oil pump
锅炉点火设备/鍋爐點火設備　boiler firing equipment
锅炉额定负荷/鍋爐額定負荷,鍋爐額定蒸發量　boiler rated capacity
锅炉额定容量/鍋爐額定負荷,鍋爐額定蒸發量　boiler rated capacity
锅炉二次鼓风机/鍋爐二次鼓風機　boiler secondary air blower
锅炉房/鍋爐房,鍋爐間　boiler plant
锅炉辅助蒸汽系统/鍋爐輔助蒸汽系統　boiler auxiliary steam system
锅炉附件/鍋爐附件,鍋爐裝具　boiler fittings
锅炉干汽管/鍋爐乾汽管　boiler dry pipe
锅炉鼓风机/鍋爐鼓風機　boiler blower
锅炉过热面积/鍋爐過熱面積　boiler super heating surface
锅炉机组/鍋爐單元　boiler unit
锅炉给水泵/鍋爐給水泵　boiler feed pump
锅炉给水系统/鍋爐給水系統　boiler feed system
锅炉给水止回阀/鍋爐給水止回閥　boiler feed check valve
锅炉借水/鍋爐借水　running at dropping water level
锅炉净效率/鍋爐淨效率　net boiler efficiency
锅炉排污阀/鍋爐放水閥　boiler blow down valve
锅炉排烟温度/鍋爐出口煙溫　boiler outlet gas temperature
锅炉牵条/鍋爐牽條,鍋爐拉條　boiler stay
锅炉牵条管/鍋爐拉條管　boiler stay tube
锅炉牵引力/鍋爐牽引力　boiler tractive effort
锅炉强制循环泵/鍋爐強力循環泵　boiler forced-circulating pump
锅炉燃油泵/鍋爐燃油泵　boiler fuel oil pump, fuel oil boilering pump
锅炉燃油系统/鍋爐燃油系統　boiler fuel oil system
锅炉热平衡/鍋爐熱平衡　boiler heat balance
锅炉热效率/鍋爐熱效率　boiler heat efficiency
锅炉散热面积/鍋爐散熱表面　boiler heat dissipating surface
锅炉受热面/鍋爐受熱面　boiler heating surface
锅炉水冷壁/鍋爐水管壁　boiler water wall
锅炉水强制循环泵/鍋爐強制循環泵　boiler forced circulating pump, boiler water forced circulating pump
锅炉水位/鍋爐水位　boiler water level
锅炉水位表/鍋爐水位計　boiler water gage
锅炉水位调节器/鍋爐水位調整器　boiler water level regulator
锅炉外壳/鍋爐殼,鍋爐襯套　boiler clothing, boiler casing
锅炉效率/鍋爐效率　boiler efficiency
锅炉烟箱/鍋爐煙道　boiler uptake
锅炉引风机/鍋爐誘導通風扇　boiler induced-draft fan
锅炉蒸发加热面积/鍋爐蒸發器加熱表面　boiler evaporative heating surface
锅炉支座/鍋爐鞍座　boiler saddle
锅炉主蒸汽系统/鍋爐主蒸汽系統　boiler main steam system
锅炉自动控制系统/鍋爐自動控制系統　boiler automatic control system
锅炉总效率/鍋爐總效率　total boiler efficiency
锅炉座/鍋爐座　boiler bearer, boiler foundation
锅水/[鍋]爐水　boiler water
锅腰托板/鍋腰托板　waist sheet
国际安全管理规则/國際安全管理章程　International Safety Management Code, ISM Code
国际安全通信网/國際安全通信網　international safety NET
国际标准化组织/國際標準組織　International Organization for Standardization, International Standardization Organization, ISO
国际标准化组织黏度分级/國際標準組織黏度分級　ISO viscosity classification
国际标准环境状态/國際標準組織環境狀況　ISO ambient reference condition
国际标准集装箱/國際標準貨櫃　ISO freight container
国际冰况巡视报告/國際冰況巡邏布告　international ice patrol bulletin
国际参考[地]磁场模式/國際地磁參考場模型　international geomagnetic reference field mode, IGRF mode
国际参考电离层模式/國際參考電離層模型　international reference ionosphere model
国际[测量]标准/國際[量測]標準　international measuring standard
国际城市/國際都市　international city
国际船舶吨位丈量公约/船舶噸位丈量國際公約　International Convention on Tonnage Measurement of Ships
国际船舶载重线公约/國際載重線公約　International Convention on Load Lines, ICLL
国际船舶载重线证书/國際載重線證書　International Load Line Certificate
国际船级社协会/國際船級協會聯合會

International Association of Classification Societies, IACS

国际单位制/國際單位制　International System of Units, SI

国际低极轨道搜救卫星系统计划协定/國際搜救衛星系統計劃協約　International COSPAs-SARSAT Programme Agreement

国际吨位证书/國際噸位證書　International Tonnage Certificate

国际防止船舶造成污染公约/防止船舶汙染國際公約　International Convention for the Prevention of Pollution from Ships, MARPOL

国际防止海洋油污染公约/防止海水油汙染國際公約　International Convention for the Prevention of Pollution of the Sea by Oil

国际防止散装运输有毒液体物质污染证书/國際載運[散裝]有毒液體物質防止汙染證書　International Pollution Prevention Certificate for the Carriage of Noxious Liquid Substance, International Pollution Prevention For the Carriage of Noxious Liquid Substances in Bulk

国际防止生活污水污染证书/國際防止汙水汙染證書　International Sewage Pollution Prevention Certification, ISPP Certification

国际防止油污证书/國際防止油汙證書　International Oil Pollution Prevention Certificate, IOPP Certificate

国际干预公海油污染事故公约/油汙染事故在公海行使干涉國際公約　International Convention Relating to Intervention on the High Seas in Case of Oil Pollution Casualties

国际古迹遗址理事会/國際古跡遺址理事會　International Council on Monuments and Sites

国际海港制度公约与规约/國際海港制度公約與規約　Convention and Stature on the International Regime of Maritime Ports

国际海事委员会电子提单规则/國際海事委員會電子載貨證券規則　CMI Rules of Electronic Bills of Lading

国际海事委员会海运单统一规则/國際海事委員會海運單統一規則　CMI Uniform Rules for Sea Waybills

国际海事卫星/國際海事衛星　international maritime satellite

国际海事卫星船舶地球站/國際海事衛星船舶電臺　International Maritime Satellite Ship Earth Station, INMARSAT SES

国际海事卫星A船舶地球站/國際海事衛星A船舶電臺　INMARSAT A ship earth station

国际海事卫星B船舶地球站/國際海事衛星B船舶電臺　INMARSAT B ship earth station

国际海事卫星C船舶地球站/國際海事衛星C船舶電臺　INMARSAT C ship earth station

国际海事卫星M船舶地球站/國際海事衛星M船舶電臺　INMARSAT M ship earth station

国际海事卫星海岸地球站/國際海事衛星海岸電臺　INMARSAT coast earth station, INMARSAT CES

国际海事卫星陆地地球站/國際海事衛星陸地電臺　INMARSAT land earth station, INMARSAT LES

国际海事卫星网络协调站/國際海事衛星網路協調站　INMARSAT network coordination station

国际海事卫星系统/國際海事衛星系統　international maritime satellite system, INMARSAT system

国际海事卫星移动号码/國際海事衛星行動碼　INMARSAT mobile number

国际海事卫星组织/國際海事衛星組織　International Maritime Satellite Organization, IMSO

国际海事卫星组织公约/國際海事衛星組織公約　Convention on the International Maritime Satellite Organization

国际海事组织/國際海事組織　International Maritime Organization, IMO

国际海事组织公约/國際海事組織公約　Convention on the International Maritime Organization

国际海事组织类号/國際海事組織類號　International Maritime Organization Class, IMO class

国际海事组织危险类别/國際海事組織危險類別　IMO hazard class

国际海员培训、发证和值班标准公约/航海人員訓練、發證及當值標準國際公約　International Convention on Standard of Training Certification and Watch Keeping for Seafarers

国际航标协会/國際燈塔協會　International Association of Light house Authorities

国际集装箱安全公约/國際安全貨櫃公約,安全貨櫃國際公約　International Convention for Safety Container, International Convention for Safe Containers, CSC

国际建筑师协会/國際建築師協會,國際建築師聯合會　International Union of Architects, UIA

国际DSC频率/國際數位選擇呼叫頻率　international DSC frequencies

国际平整度指数/國際平整度指數　international

roughness index, IRI
国际气象组织/國際氣象組織　International Meteorological Organization
国际散装化学品规则/國際散裝化學品章程　International Bulk Chemical Code
国际散装运输液化气体船舶构造和设备规则/國際氣體載運船章程　International Code for the Construction and Equipment of Ships Carrying Liquefied Gases in Bulk
国际时间局/國際時間局　Bureau International de'l Heure
国际式/國際式　international style
国际数字选择呼叫频率/國際數位選擇呼叫頻率　international DSC frequencies
国际水道测量组织公约/國際海道測量組織公約　Convention on the International Hydrographic Organization
国际铁路货物联运协定/國際鐵路貨物聯運協定　agreement of international railway through freight traffic
国际铁路联运/國際鐵路聯運　international railway through traffic
国际铁路联运公约/國際鐵路聯運公約　convention of international railway through traffic
国际铁路协定/國際鐵路協定　agreement of frontier railway
国际通岸接头/國際岸上接頭　international shore connection
国际偷渡公约/處理偷渡人國際公約　International Convention Relating to Stowaways
国际投影图/國際投影圖　international projective chart
国际信号码/國際信號代碼碼組　international signal code
国际信号码组符号/國際信號代碼符號　international code symbol, INTERCO symbol
国际信号旗/國際信號旗　international signal flag
国际信号旗A字硬质复制品/複製硬質國際代碼信號A旗　rigid replica of the International Code flag A
国际信息业务/國際資訊業務　international information service
国际移动卫星组织/國際移動衛星組織　International Mobil Satellite Organization
国际油污防备、响应和合作公约/油汙防備、因應與合作國際公約　International Convention on Oil Pollution Preparedness, Response and Cooperation
国际油污损害民事责任公约/油汙損害民事責任國際公約　International Convention on Civil Liability for Oil Pollution Damage
国际园林景观规划设计行业协会/國際園林景觀規劃設計行業協會　International Landscape Design Industry Association
国际园林师联合总会/國際園林建築師聯合會　International Federation of Landscape Architects, IFLA
国际载重线证书/國際載重線證書　international load line certificate
国际照明委员会标准全晴天空/CIE標準晴天空　International Commission of Illumination standard clear sky
国际照明委员会标准全阴天空/CIE標準陰天空　International Commission of Illumination standard overcast sky
国际照明委员会标准一般天空/CIE標準一般天空　International Commission of Illumination standard general sky
国际咨询工程师联合会/國際顧問工程師聯合會　International Federation of Consulting Engineers, FIDIC
国际自然及自然资源保护联合会/國際自然及自然資源保護聯盟　International Union for Conservation of Nature and Nature Resources
果篱/觀果籬　fruit hedge
果岭草坪/地面高爾夫球場　putting green
果品加工厂/水果加工廠　fruit processing factory
果蔬储藏窖/果蔬儲藏窖　fruit and vegetable storage cellar
果树盆景/果樹盆景　fruit bonsai
果园/果園　orchard
过饱和水/過飽和水　water of supersaturation
过驳/轉駁　lighterage
过超高/過超高　surplus superelevation, excess elevation
过充电/過[量]充電　over charge
过电流/過[量]電流　over current
过电流继电器/過流繼電器　over current relay
过电压/過電壓　over voltage
过电压继电器/過電壓保護　over voltage relay
过顶式装碴机/過頂裝載機　overhead loader
过度城市化/過度都市化　hyper-urbanization
过度开发/過度放牧　over-grazing
过度冷却/過冷　undercooling, under cooling
过度利用/過度利用，過度開發，過度採掘　overexploitation
过度磨损/過度磨損　overwear

过度膨胀/過度膨脹　overexpansion
过度使用土地/過度使用土地　over-use land
过度压实/超夯實,超壓實　overcompaction
过[度]应力/超應力　overstress
过渡舱/過渡艙　entry locker, transfer chamber, transition module
过渡层/過渡層　transition layer
过渡带/過渡[地]帶,過渡區,中間層　transitional zone, transition zone, intermediate belt
过渡导标/疊導標　transit leading mark
过渡电抗器/過渡電抗器　transition reactor
过渡电阻器/過渡電阻器　transition resistor
过渡段/過渡段　transition phase
过渡高/轉換高　transition height
过渡高度/轉換高度　transition altitude
过渡高度层/轉換空層　transition level
过渡工程/過渡工程　transition project
过渡工况/過渡工作情況　transient working condition
过渡阶段/過渡階段　transition period
过渡景观/過渡地貌　transition landscape
过渡孔/過渡孔　transition span
过渡流/轉移流　transition flow
过渡切线/緩和切線　transition tangent
过渡区段/土方過渡區域　transition zone
过渡水深/過渡水深　transitional water depth
过渡照明/過渡照明　transition lighting
过负荷/過[量]負荷,過載,超載　overload
过负载/過[量]負荷,過載,超載　overload
过河标/橫越標　crossing mark
过河点/渡河點　crossing river point
过河管/跨河線　river crossing
过街楼/騎樓　overpass, arcade, qilou
过近地点时刻/過近地點時間　time of perigee passage
过境道路/直達公路　through road
过境公路/直通公路　through highway
过境货/過境貨,轉口貨,接運貨　transit cargo
过境交通/直達交通　through traffic
过境路/過境鐵路　transit railway
过境提单/接運載貨證券　transit bill of lading
过境停机坪/過境停機坪　transit apron
过境运输/過境運輸　transit transport
过境自由公约与规约/過境自由公約與規約　Convention and Stature on Freedom of Transit
过冷/過度冷卻,超冷　supercooling, undercooling, supercool
过冷水滴/過冷水滴　supercooled water droplet

过梁/過梁,門楣　lintel
过量充风/過量充風　overcharge
过量抽水/過量抽水　excessive pumping
过量减压/過度減薄　over reduction
过量空气常数/過量空氣係數　excess air coefficient
过量空气系数/過量空氣係數,過量空氣因數　excess air coefficient, excess air factor
过量石灰法/過量石灰法　excess lime process
过路费/道路費　road toll
过滤/過濾　filtration
过滤材料/透水料　filter material
过滤层/過濾層,過濾器　filter layer, filter, filter course
过滤持续时间/過濾持續時間　period of filter service
过滤介质/濾料　filter medium
过滤井/濾管井　strainer well
过滤面积/過濾面積　filtration area
过滤器/過濾器,濾清器　filter
过滤器堵塞/濾池阻塞　filter clogging
过滤设备/濾水場　filter plant
过滤水/濾過水　filtered water
过滤水池/清水池　filtered water reservoir
过滤效率/過濾效率,濾池效率　filter efficiency
过滤周期/過濾週期,過濾循環　filter run
过密城市/過密城市　over-crowded city
过期提单/過期載貨證券　stale bill of lading
过桥费/過橋費　bridge toll
过热/過熱　over heat, overheating
过热度/過熱度　degree of superheat
过热管/過熱器管　superheater tube
过热器/過熱器　superheater
过热箱/過熱器管集箱　superheater header
过热蒸汽/過熱蒸汽　superheated steam
过热蒸汽室/過熱蒸汽室　superheater chamber
过热组织/過熱組織　overheated structure
过筛材料/過篩材料　screened material
过筛道碴/過篩道碴　screened ballast
过烧/過燒　burning
过烧砖/過燒磚　clinker brick
过剩扬水/過量抽水　excessive pumping
过失速机动/過失速機動　poststall maneuver
过湿类型/過濕類型　excessive dampness type
过试验/超試驗　overtesting
过水断面/過水斷面　discharge flow cross section
过水孔径/橋洩水口　discharge opening of bridge
过水路面/涉水區　ford
过隧费/過隧費,隧道費　tunnel toll
过隧经历时间/過隧經歷時間　duration of tunnel

passage
过滩吃水/淺灘低潮水深　bar draft
过[湍]滩/通過湍流　passing through the rapids
过稳船/高穩度船　stiff ship
过压密黏土/過壓密黏土　over consolidated clay
过夜维护/過夜維護服務　overnight service
过远运输/過遠運輸　excessively long-distance traffic
过载/負載因數,超載　load factor, overload
过载能力/過載能力　overload capacity

过载时间控制/超載時間控制　overload-time control
过载试验/過負荷試驗,超載試驗　overload test
过载脱扣/過載跳脫　overload trip
过载系数/超載因素　overload factor
过载引起的意识丧失/G力昏迷　G-induced loss of consciousness, G-LOC
过早炸/過早爆炸　premature burst
过重装载/過重裝載　supercharge

H

哈德良山庄/哈德良山莊　Hadrian villa
哈密顿原理/漢米頓原理　Hamilton principle
哈斯效应/哈斯效應　Hass effect
[海]岸/海岸　coast
海岸保护/海防　sea coast defense
海岸保护设施/海岸保護設施　coast protection work
海岸带/海岸地帶　coastal zone
海岸带管理权/海岸帶管理權　right of management of coastal strip
海岸地球站/海岸衛星電臺,海岸無線電臺　coast earth station
海岸地球站识别码/海岸衛星電臺識別碼　coast earth station identification
海岸电台/海岸電臺　coast station
海岸电台表/海岸電臺表　list of coast station
海岸电台群呼识别/海岸電臺群呼識別　group coast station call identity
海岸电台识别/海岸電臺識別　coast station identity
海岸工程学/海岸工[程]學　coastal engineering
海岸阶地/海岸臺地　coastal terrace
海岸雷达站/海岸雷達站　coast radar station
海岸砾石/海灘礫石　beach gravel
海岸流/海岸流　nearshore current
海岸侵蚀/海岸侵蝕　coast erosion
海岸区/海岸區,沿岸區　coastal area
海岸台地/海岸臺地　coastal terrace
海岸图/沿海海圖　coast chart
海岸无线电台/海岸無線電臺,海岸衛星電臺　coast earth station
海岸线/海岸線,灘線　shore line
海岸效应/海岸效應　coastal effect
海滨风景区/海濱風景區　seabeach scenic spot
海滨公园/海濱公園　seaside park, seabeach park
海滨海岛类/海濱海島類　seaside and islands type
海冰/海冰　sea ice
海冰密集度/海冰密集度　sea ice concentration
海槽/海槽　trough
海潮/外洋潮　oceanic tide
海船/海船,海輪,遠洋船　sea-going ship, sea-going vessel
海船所有人责任限制国际公约/海船所有人責任限制國際公約　International Convention Relating to the Limitation of the Liability of Owners of Seagoing Ships
海盗/海盜　pirate
海盗行为/海盜行爲　piracy
海道测量学/海道測量學,水文學,水理學　hydrography
海堤/海堤　sea bank, sea dyke
海底电报/海底電報　cable gram
海底电缆/海底電纜,水底電纜,海底纜線　submarine cable
海底电缆传感器/電纜位置測定器　cable position sensor
海底管道/水底管線　submarine pipeline
海底管线/海底油管　submarine pipeline
海底峡谷/海底峽谷　submarine canyon
海底障碍物/海底障礙物　submarine obstacle
海发光/海發光　luminescence of the sea
海风/海風　sea breeze, sea wind
海港/海港　sea port, sea harbor
海沟/海溝　ocean trench
海谷/海谷　sea valley
海关/海關　customs
海关检查区/海關檢查區　customs check area
海积土/海積土　marine soil
海积物/海底沈積物　marine deposit
海岬/海岬　head land
海空两用灯标/海空兩用航行燈　marine and air navigation light
海况/海[面狀]況,海面狀態　sea condition, sea state
海缆登陆站/海纜登陸站　sea cable landing station
海浪干扰抑制/抗海浪干擾　anti-clutter sea
海浪回波/海浪回波　sea echo
海浪预报/波浪預測　wave forecast
海里/[海]浬　nautical mile, n mile
海流/洋流,大洋環流　current, ocean current
海流花/旋潮流圖　current rose
海陆风/海陸風　land and sea breeze
海锚/海錨　sea anchor
海绵/海綿　sponge

海绵城市/海綿城市,海綿都市　sponge city
海面搜寻协调船/海面搜索協調船　surface search coordinator
海面温度/海面溫度　sea surface temperature
海面效应/海面效應　sea effect
海面杂波/海面回波　sea clutter
海面状况/海況　sea state
海难/海上災難　marine disaster
海难救捞船/救撈船,救難船　salvage ship, rescue ship, salvage and rescue ship
海难救助船/救撈船,救難船　salvage ship, rescue ship, salvage and rescue ship
海难救助合同/海難救助契約　salvage contract, salvage bond
海难救助作业/海難救助作業　salvage operation
海平面/海平面　sea level
海平面比冲/海平面比衝量　sea level specific impulse
海平面气压/海平面氣壓　sea level pressure
海平面推力/海平面推力　sea level thrust
海平面修正/海平面校正　sea level correction
海侵/海進　transgression
A1海区/A1海域　sea area A1
A2海区/A2海域　sea area A2
A3海区/A3海域　sea area A3
A4海区/A4海域　sea area A4
海商法/海商法　maritime law, maritime code
海上安全监督/海上安全監督　marine safety supervision
海上安全信息/海上安全資訊,海事安全資訊　maritime safety information, MSI
海上保险/海上保險　marine insurance
海上泊位/海上泊位,海上船席　sea berth
海上补给/海上整補　replenishment at sea, RAS
海上补油站/加油整補站　fueling-at-sea station
海上焚烧/海上焚化　incineration at sea
海上风浪/海上風浪　sea wind wave
海上风险/海上危險　perils of the sea
海上航路标志/海上航標　sea mark
海上核材料运输民事责任公约/海上運載核子物質民事責任公約　Convention Relating to Civil Liability in the Field of Maritime Carriage of Nuclear Materials
海上护送/護航　escorting
海上货物运输法/海上貨物運輸法　Carriage of Goods by Sea, COGSA
海上急救/海上急救　first aid at sea
海上加油/海上加油　FAS
海上加油站/海上加油整補傳送站　FAS delivery station
海上救助/海上救助　salvage at sea, marine salvage
海上救助协调中心/海上搜救協調中心　maritime rescue co-ordination center
海上救助中心/海上救助站　maritime rescue sub-center
海上旅客及其行李运输雅典公约/海上運送旅客及其行李雅典公約　Athens Convention Relating to the Carriage of Passengers and Their Luggages by Sea
海上旅游区/海上旅遊區　sea tourist area
海上平台/海上平臺　offshore platform
海上气象数据/海上氣象數據　marine weather data
海上求生/海上求生　survival at sea
海上识别数字/水上識別碼　maritime identification digits, MID
海上事故/海上事故,海上災難　sea accident, marine disaster
海上书信电报/海上書信電報　sea letter telegram, SLT
海上搜救/海上搜索與救助　marine search and rescue
海上搜救计划/海上搜救計劃　maritime SAR plan
海上速度/海流速率　sea speed
海上拖船/出海拖船　sea going tug
海上维修/海上維修　at sea maintenance
海上卫星无线电导航业务/水上無線電衛星導航業務　maritime radionavigation-satellite service
海上无线电导航业务/海上無線電助航業務　maritime radionavigation service
海上无线电话/海上無線電話　marine radiotelephone
海上无线电书信/海上無線電書信　radio maritime letter
海上询问/海上詢問　maritime enquiry
海上移动选择呼叫识别码/水上行動選擇呼叫識別碼　maritime mobile selective-call identify code
海上移动业务/水上行動業務　maritime mobile service
海上移动业务识别/水上行動業務識別　maritime mobile service identity
海上营救/海難搜救　sea rescue
海上预报/海上預報　marine forecast
海上遇险信道/海上遇險頻道　maritime distress channel
海上运输/海運　maritime transportation
海上蒸汽雾/海面蒸汽霧　sea smoke
海上资历/海勤資歷　sea service

海上自然保护区/海洋自然保護區　marine natural reserves
海上钻井架/海上鑽油臺　drilling rigs at sea
海事报告/海事報告　marine accident report
海事调查/海事調查　maritime investigation
海事法庭/海事法庭　maritime court
海事分析/海事分析　marine accident analysis
海事管辖/海事管轄權　maritime jurisdiction
海事和解/海事和解　maritime reconciliation
海事判例/海事判例　maritime case
海事请求/海事求償　maritime claim
海事诉讼/海事訴訟　maritime litigation
海事索赔责任限制公约/海事求償責任限制公約　Convention on Limitation of Liability for Maritime Claims
海事调解/海事調解　maritime mediation
海事卫星/海事衛星, 航海衛星　maritime satellite
海事援助/海事援助　maritime assistance
海事仲裁/海事仲裁　maritime arbitration
海水/海水　sea water
海水泵/海水泵　sea water pump
海水淡化装置/海水淡化裝置　sea water desalting plant
海水滤器/海水濾器　sea water filter
海水密度/海水密度　sea water density
海水染色标志/海水染色標誌　dye marker
海水染色剂/海水色素　sea coloring agent
海水入侵/海水入侵　seawater intrusion
海水水色/海水水色　sea water color
海水透明度/海水透明度　sea water transparency
海水温度/海水温度　sea temperature
海水系统/海水系統　sea water service system
海水循环泵/海水循環泵　sea water circulating pump
海水盐度/海水鹽度　sea water salinity
海水蒸发器/海水蒸發器　sea water evaporator
海水蒸馏装置/海水蒸餾裝置　sea water distillate plant, sea water distillation plant
海损/海損　average
海损担保函/海損擔保　average guarantee
海损分担保证书/共同海損承諾書　average bond
海损管制示意图/損害管制圖　damage control plan
海损理算人/海損清算人　average adjuster
海损理算书/海損理算書　average statement
海滩/海灘　beach, shore
海图比例尺/海圖比例尺　chart scale
海图标题栏/海圖圖例　chart legend
海图灯/海圖燈　chart lamp, chart table light

海图基准面/海圖深度基準面　chart datum
海图夹编号/海圖夾編號　folio number
海图夹标签/海圖夾標籤　folio label
海图夹目录/海圖夾目錄　folio list
海图卡片/海圖卡　chart card
海图室/海圖室　chart house, chart room
海图桌/海圖桌　chart table
海图作业/海圖作業　chart work
海图作业工具/海圖作業工具　chart work tools
海湾/海灣　gulf
海王星/海王星　Neptune
海峡/海峽　strait, euripus
海峡[渡]船/海峽船　channel steamer, channel ship
海峡桥/狹橋　narrow bridge
海啸/海嘯　tsunami
海啸浪/海嘯波　tsunami wave
海牙规则/海牙規則　Hague Rules
海洋沉积/海洋沈積　oceanic deposit
海洋磁力测量/海洋磁力測量　marine magnetic survey
海洋大气腐蚀/海洋大氣腐蝕　marine atmosphere corrosion
海洋调查/海洋調查　marine investigation
海洋调查船/海洋調查船, 海洋研究船　oceanographic research ship, oceanographic research vessel
海洋定点船/海洋測候船　ocean station vessel
海洋法/航政法　marine law
海洋腐蚀/海洋腐蝕　marine corrosion
海洋工程/海洋工程　oceaneering
海洋工程测量/海洋工程測量　marine engineering survey
海洋观测卫星/海洋觀測衛星　ocean observation satellite
海洋环境/海洋環境　marine environment
海洋环境保护/海洋環境保護　marine environmental protection
海洋环境调查/海洋環境調查　marine environment investigation
海洋监测/海洋監測　marine monitoring
海洋监测船/海洋監測船　ocean monitoring ship
海洋监视/海洋監視　marine surveillance
海洋监视卫星/海洋監視衛星　ocean surveillance satellite
海洋科学技术/海洋科技　marine science and technology
海洋矿物资源/海洋礦產資源　mineral resources of the sea

海洋能/海洋能　ocean energy
[海洋]平台/海域平臺　offshore unit, offshore platform, platform
海洋气象报告/海洋氣象報告　ocean weather report
海洋生态调查/海洋生態調查　marine ecological investigation
海洋生物资源/海洋生物資源　living resources of the sea
海洋水色成像仪/海色成像器　ocean color imager
海洋水文/海洋水文　marine hydrology
海洋天气船/氣象船,海洋測候船　ocean weather vessel
海洋投弃/海洋處置　ocean disposal
海洋卫星/海洋衛星　ocean satellite
海洋污染/海洋汙染,海水汙染　marine pollution
海洋污染物/海洋汙染物　marine pollutant
海洋污染物报告/海水汙染物報告　marine pollutants report
海洋渔业/海洋漁業　marine fishery
海洋云/海洋雲　ocean cloud
海洋噪声/海鳴　sea-noise
海洋重力测量/海洋重力測量　marine gravimetric survey
海洋主权/海洋主權　maritime sovereignty
海洋资源调查/海洋資源調查　marine resources investigation
海涌/觸底湧,激湧　ground swell
海员/航海人員　seafarers
海员通常做法/海員常規　ordinary practice of seaman
海员证/船員證　seaman book
海运单/海運單　seaway bill
海运货/海運貨　sea-borne cargo
海运货物保险/海運貨物保險　maritime cargo insurance
海运界/海運界　marine field
氦封/氦封　helium seal
氦弧焊/氦[氣電]弧焊接,氦氣保護弧焊　heliarc welding, helium arc welding, helium shielded arc welding
氦检漏试验/氦漏試驗　helium leak test
氦气吹除/氦吹洩　helium blow-off
氦气风洞/氦風洞　helium wind tunnel
氦气泡法/氦氣泡法　helium bubble method
氦气配气台/氦氣配氣臺　helium gas distribution board
氦气瓶车/氦氣瓶車　helium bottle truck
氦气瓶库配气台/氦氣瓶配氣臺　gas distribution board of helium bottle depot
氦气置换/氦氣置換　helium replacement
氦深冷板/氦深冷板　helium cryopanel
氦压缩机车/氦壓縮機汽車　helium compressor truck
氦氧潜水/氦氧潛水　helium-oxygen diving
氦质谱检漏/氦質譜探漏　helium mass spectrum leak detection
氦质谱仪检漏系统/氦質譜儀偵檢系統　helium mass-spectrometer detecting system
含肥泥炭盆/含肥泥炭盆　fertile peat pot
含酚废水/酚廢汙　phenol waste
含蜡量/石蠟[含]量　paraffin content
含蜡量试验/含蠟量試驗　paraffin content test
含硫矿泉/含硫泉水,硫泉　sulfur spring
含硫试验/含硫試驗　sulphate test
含氯石灰/漂白粉　chlorinated lime
含泥量/含泥量,汙垢含量　soil content
含泥量试验/含泥量試驗　silt content test
含沙量/沈碴濃度　sediment concentration
含砂的/含砂　gritty
含砂低液限粉土/含砂低液限粉土　sandy silt of low liquid limit
含砂低液限黏土/含砂低液限黏土　sandy clay of low liquid limit
含砂高液限黏土/含砂高液限黏土　sandy clay of high liquid limit
含少量沥青质的岩石/岩瀝青　rock asphalt
含湿量/濕度比　humidity ratio
含水层/含水層,儲水層　water stratum, water bearing strata
含水层水力坡线/含水層水力坡線　hydraulic profile of aquifer
含水地层/含水地層　water bearing ground
含水量/含水量　water content
含水量试验/含水量試驗　water content test, moisture test
含水率/含水率,濕度　percentage of moisture content
含铁水泥/鐵水泥　iron cement
含油舱底水/含油舣水　oily bilge water
含油混合物/含油混合物　oily mixture
含油率/含油率　bitumen content, bitumen rate
焓/焓　enthalpy
焓湿图/濕氣圖,濕度線圖　psychrometric chart
涵道比/旁通比　bypass ratio
涵道尾桨/涵道式尾槳　ducted tail rotor
涵[洞]/涵[洞]　culvert

涵洞八字墙/涵洞翼牆　culvert wing wall
涵洞出水口/涵洞出水口　culvert outlet
涵洞跌水/涵洞水滴　culvert water drop
涵洞洞身长度/涵洞長度　culvert barrel length
涵洞沟床/涵洞溝床　gully bed neighboring to culvert
涵洞进水口/涵洞進水口　culvert inlet
涵洞孔径/涵洞孔徑　culvert aperture, aperture of culvert
涵洞口隆起/涵洞口隆起　culvert end lift
涵洞口铺砌/涵洞口鋪砌　culvert inlet-outlet apron
涵洞一字墙/涵洞一字牆　culvert straight end wall
涵口沉降缝/涵洞沈降縫　settlement joint in culvert
寒潮/寒潮　cold wave
寒冷地区/寒帶　cold zone
寒[洋]流/寒流,冷流　cold current
罕遇地震/大地震　rarely occurred earthquake
罕遇地震烈度/罕遇地震烈度　intensity of seldom occurred earthquake
汉堡规则/漢堡規則　Hamburg Rules
汉普顿王宫/漢普頓王宮　Hampton Court Palace
旱地土壤/旱地土　upland soil
旱季流量/旱天流量　dry weather flow
旱井/乾井　dry well
旱桥/跨線橋　dry bridge
旱生树种/旱生樹種　xerophilous tree species
旱生植物/旱生植物　xerophyte
旱生植物群落/旱生群落　xerophytia
焊层/焊層　layer
焊道/焊珠　bead
焊道下裂纹/焊珠底龜裂　under bead crack
焊点距/焊道間距　weld spacing
焊缝/焊縫,焊道　weld, weld seam
焊缝长度/焊道長度　weld length
焊缝管/疊縫焊管　butt-welded tube
焊缝金属/焊接金屬　weld metal
焊缝强度/熔接強度　weld strength
焊缝区/焊接金屬面積　weld metal area
焊缝轴线/焊接線　axis of weld
焊缝着色试验/焊縫染色試驗　pigment test of welds
焊根/焊根　weld root
焊根裂纹/根部龜裂　root crack
焊工/焊工,熔接工　welding operator
焊轨机/鋼軌焊接機　rail welding machine
焊后处理/焊後處理　postweld treatment
焊后热处理/焊接後熱處理　postweld heat treatment
焊剂/助焊劑,焊藥,熔接劑　welding flux
焊件/焊件　weldment

焊脚/焊腳　leg, weld leg
焊接/焊接[法],熔接　welding, weld
焊接变形/熔接變形　welding deformation
焊接操作/焊接操作　welding operation
焊接操作机/自動操控機　manipulator
焊接长钢轨/焊接長鋼軌　welded long rail
焊接车间/焊接工場　welding shop
焊接程序/焊接程式　welding procedure
焊接电弧/焊接電弧　welding arc
焊接电流/焊接電流　welding current
焊接电源/焊接電源　welding power source
焊接方法/焊接程式　welding procedure
焊接钢管/焊接鋼管　welded steel pipe, welded steel tube
焊接钢轨/焊接軌條　welded rail
焊接钢桥/焊接鋼橋　welded steel bridge
焊接工艺参数/焊接條件　welding parameter, welding condition
焊接机座/熔接機座　welding frame
焊接技术/焊接技術　welding technique
焊接夹具/焊接用夾具　fixture, welding jig
[焊接]接头/焊接接頭,熔接[頭]　welding joint, welded joint
焊接结构/焊接結構　welded structure
焊接[空心]球节点/焊接空心球節點　welded spherical node, welded hollow spherical node
焊接连接/焊接連接　welding connection
焊接裂纹敏感性/焊接裂紋靈敏性　welding crack sensibility
焊接面/焊接區域　welding area
焊接区域/焊接區域　welding area
焊接缺陷/焊接缺陷,熔接缺陷　weld defect, welding defect
焊接式电磁屏蔽室/焊接電磁遮罩室　welded electromagnetic shielding enclosure
焊接式钢轨接续线/焊接聯軌線　welded bond
焊接顺序/焊接順序　welding sequence
焊接速度/焊接速度　welding speed
焊接通电时间/焊接時間　weld time
焊接型曲轴/焊接型曲柄軸　welded type crankshaft
焊接性/焊接性,可焊性　weldability, weldableness
焊接应力/焊接應力,熔接應力　welding stress
焊接辙叉/焊接轍叉　welded frog
焊炬/吹把　torch
焊料/硬焊料　solder, brazing solder
焊前处理/焊前處理　preweld treatment
焊区腐蚀/焊道[晶間]腐蝕　weld corrosion, weld decay

焊条/[被覆]焊條　covered electrode, welding wire, welding electrode
焊条夹持端/焊條裸端　exposed core, bare terminal
焊条压涂机/焊條塗藥機　welding rod extrusion press
焊锡/錫焊　tin solder
焊修钢轨/鋼軌焊補　resurfacing of rail
焊趾/焊[接縫突]趾　toe of weld, weld toe
焊趾裂纹/趾裂痕　toe crack
夯击式压路机/夯壓機　tamping roller
夯实/夯實, 搗實　tamping
夯实道床/夯實道床　ballast ramming, ballast consolidating
夯实机械/道床夯實機　ballast consolidating machine
夯实砂桩法/夯實砂樁法　sand compaction pile method
夯实填土/夯實填土　compacted fill
夯土机/打夯機　tamper
行列编队/行列編隊　line formation
行列式/行列式　row layout, housing in row
行株距/列間距　line spacing
航摆角/平擺角, 偏航角　yaw angle
航班飞行/固定班機　schedule flight
航标/航行標誌, 導航設備　nautical mark, navigation mark, navigational aid
航标表/燈標表　list of lights
航标船/浮標勤務船, 浮標母船, 浮標管理船　buoy tender
航标起重机/燈浮標起重機, 吊航標機　light buoy crane
航标艇/設標艇　dan boat
航测外控点/航測外控點, 航空攝影測量外控點　field control point of aerophotogrammetry
航测选线/航測選線　aerial surveying alignment
航程/航程　distance run, range
航程因子/航程因子　range factor
航次/航次　voyage
航次保险/航次保險　voyage insurance
航次报告/航次報告　voyage report
航次结账单/航次賬單　trip account
航次期租合同/航次計時租船　time charter on trip basis, TCT
航次租船/航次傭船　voyage charter, trip charter
航带设计/起落地帶設計, 單連續航攝帶設計　flight strip design, design of flight strip
航弹伞/航空炸彈傘　aerial bomb parachute
航道/航道　fairway, navigation channel
航道标志/航道標誌　channel marker

航道标准尺度/航道標準尺度　standard dimension of channel
航道测量船/测量船　hydrographic survey ship, hydrographic survey vessel, survey ship
航道灯标/航道燈標　channel light
航道浮标/航道浮標　channel buoy
航道罗盘/航向指示器　course indicator
航道通过能力/航道通過能力　waterway transit capacity
航道弯曲度/航道彎曲度　bend of channel
航段/航線段　route segment
航高/航高, 基数高度　flight level, cardinal altitude
航海保证/航海勤務　nautical service
航海表/航海表　navigation table, nautical table
航海晨昏朦影/航海朦光　nautical twilight
航海法规/海事法規　maritime rules and regulations
航海顾问/航海諮詢　navigation consultant
航海过失/航海過失　nautical fault
航海健康申报书/航海健康申報書　maritime declaration of health
航海科学/航海科學　nautical science
航海模型运动/航海模型運動　navigation model movement
航海气象/航海氣象　nautical meteorology
航海日志/航海日誌, 航泊日誌　log book
航海史/航海史　history of marine navigation, nautical history
航海天文历/航海曆　nautical almanac
航海通告/航行通告　notice to mariners
航海图/海圖　marine chart
航海图书目录/航海圖書目錄　catalog of charts and publications
航海图书资料/航海圖書刊物　nautical charts and publications
航海心理学/航海心理學　marine psychology
航海性能/航海性能　seagoing qualities
航海学/航海學　marine navigation
航海医学/航海醫學　marine medicine
航海仪器/航海儀器　nautical instrument
航海专家系统/航海專家系統　marine navigation expert system
[航海]状态记录系统/[航海]衛星報況系統　state recording system
航弧/船身回擺　sheer
航迹/航跡, 航路　track, flight path, TK
航迹冲程/航跡衝距　track reach
航迹灯/航跡燈　wake light
航迹方位角/航跡方位角　flight path azimuth angle

航迹分布/航跡分布　track distribution
航迹绘算/海圖作業　chart work
航迹积算仪/推算航跡儀　dead-reckoning tracer, DRT
航迹计算/航跡計算　track calculating
航迹角/航跡角　track angle, flight path angle
航迹推算/實際航跡　track made good
航迹坐标系/航線軸系　flight path axis system
航空/航空，飛行　aviation
航空病理学/航空病理學　aviation pathology
航空布雷/航空布雷　airborne mine-laying
航空材料/航空器材　aeronautical material
航空测量/航空測量　aerial survey
航空弹道学/航空彈道學　aeroballistics
航空灯标/地面燈標　aeronautical light beacon
航空地图/航空[地]圖　aeronautical chart
航空电气系统/航空器電力系統,飛機電力系統　aircraft electrical system
航空电子试验机/航空電子裝備試驗臺　avionics test bed
航空电子系统/航空電子系統,空電系統　avionics system
航空电子系统仿真/航空電子系統模擬　avionics system simulation
航空电子学/航空電子學　avionics
航空毒理学/航空毒物學　aviation toxicology
航空发电机/航空發電機　aircraft generator
航空发动机/航空器發動機　aero-engine
航空发动机试验室/航空發動機試驗室　aircraft engine test stand room
航空反辐射导弹/機載反輻射飛彈　airborne anti-radiation missile
航空反潜/空中反潛　airborne antisubmarine
航空反坦克导弹/機載反戰車飛彈　airborne anti-tank missile
航空反星导弹/機載反衛星飛彈　airborne anti-satellite missile
航空港/航空站,[飛]機場　airport, aerodrome
航空工效学/航空生物工學,航空人體工學　aviation ergonomics
航空管制/航空站管制業務,空中交通管制　aerodrome control service, air traffic control
航空航天/航空太空,航太　aerospace
航空航天系统工程/航空航太系統工程　aerospace system engineering
航空护林/航空森林保護　aerial forest protection
航空火箭弹/空用火箭,機載火箭　airborne rocket

航空火力控制系统/機載火力控制系統　airborne fire control system
航空机炮/航空機炮　airborne cannon
航空机枪/航空機槍　airborne machine gun
航空基地/飛行基地　air base
航空胶片感光度/航空底片感光度　aerial film speed
航空救生/航空緊急救生　aviation emergency escapement
航空临床医学/航空臨床醫學　clinical medicine of aviation
航空流行病学/航空流行病學　aviation epidemiology
航空六分仪/航空六分儀　aeronautic sextant
航空母舰/航空母艦　aeroplane carrier, aircraft carrier
航空气候/航空氣候　aviation climate
航空气候分界/航空氣候分界　aviation climate divide
航空气象学/航空氣象學　aeronautical meteorology
航空汽油/航空汽油　aviation gasoline
航空器/航空器,飛機　aircraft
航空器出勤率/飛行出勤率　aircraft serviceability
航空器磁场/航空器磁場　aircraft magnetic field
航空[器]电台/航空電臺　aircraft station
航空器动力装置/飛機動力裝置　aircraft powerplant
航空器告警系统/航空器警告系統　aircraft alerting system
航空器工艺基准系统/飛機製造參考系統　aircraft production reference system
航空器结冰/飛機積冰　aircraft icing
航空器结构完整性/飛機結構完整性　aircraft structural integrity
航空器静电试飞/航空器靜電飛行試驗　flight test of aircraft static electricity
航空器可用度/飛機可用性　aircraft availability
航空器牵连铅垂地面坐标系/航空器連接正交地面軸系　aircraft carried normal earth fixed system
航空器全寿命费用/航空器壽命[週期]成本　aircraft life cycle cost
航空器停机位标志/停機位標線　aircraft stand marking
航空器完好度/飛機完整性　aircraft integrity
航空器性能代偿损失/航空器效能損失　aircraft performance penalty
航空器悬挂物相容性/航空器懸掛物相容性　aircraft-store compatibility
航空器噪声审定/飛機噪音證明書　aircraft noise certification
航空燃料/航空燃料　aviation fuel

航空摄影/航空攝影學,航空攝影術,空照圖　aerophotography, aerial photograph, aerial photography
航空摄影测量/航空攝影測量　aerial photogrametry, aerial photographic surveying
航空摄影机/空用照相機　aerocamera
航空生理学/航空生理學　aviation physiology
航空生理训练/航空生理訓練　aviation physiological training
航空生物动力学/航空生物動力學　aviation biodynamics
航空视频记录系统/機載視頻記錄系統　airborne video recording system
航空水雷/空投水[地]雷　aerial mine
航空水准测量/航空水準測量　aerial levelling
航空危险天气/航空危險天氣　aviation hazard weather
航空卫星通信网/航空衛星　aviation satellite, AVSAT
航空无线电设施/航空無線電設施　air navigational radio facililty
航空武器/航空武器　aerial warfare weapon
航空武器系统/航空武器系統　airborne weapon system
航空线路监视雷达/航空線監視雷達　air route surveillance rader
航空心理学/航空心理學　aviation psychology
航空遥感技术/航空遙測術　aerial remote sensing technique
航空液压油/航空液壓油　aviation hydraulic fluid
航空医学/航空醫學　aviation medicine
航空诱惑弹/空用誘導飛彈　airborne decoy
航空鱼雷/空投魚雷　air-launched torpedo
航空运输/空運　air transportation
航路/航路,航線　passage, route, airway
航路点/航路點,定位點　way point, aeroroute waypoint
航路监视雷达/空中航線監視雷達　aeroroute surveillance radar, ARSR
航路设计图/航路圖　routing chart
航路预报/航線預報　aeroroute forecast
航路指南/航行指南　sailing directions
航路指南补篇/航行指南增補篇　supplement of sailing directions
航片地质判读/空中照片地質判讀　geological interpretation of aerial photograph
航区/航區　flight range
航区合练/航行區域預演　flight range rehearsal

航摄基线/航攝基線　aerophoto base line
航摄像片判读/航空照片判讀　aerophoto interpretation
航速/航速,船速　ship speed
航速燃油消耗量条款/船速與耗油量條款　vessel speed and fuel consumption clause
航速试验/速率試車　speed trial
航速索赔/航速索賠　speed claim
航天/太空飛行　space flight
航天病理学/太空病理學　space pathology
航天材料/太空材料　space material
航天测控技术/太空遙測控制技術　space telemetry and control technology
航天测控通信网/航太測控通信網　communication network for space flight test
航天测控网/航太測控網　space flight TT and C network
航天测控系统/太空飛行 TT & C 系統　space flight TT and C system
航天测控与数据采集/航太測控和數據採集　space tracking and data acquisition
航天测控与数据采集网/航太測控和數據採集網　space tracking and data acquisition network
航天测控中心/航太測控中心　space tracking telemetry and control center
航天测量船/航太測量船　space tracking ship
航天产品的可靠性/太空產品可靠性　reliability of space product
航天产品质量/太空產品品質　quality of space product
航天乘员组/太空組員　space crew
航天代谢/太空新陳代謝　space metabolism
航天地面设备/航太地面設備　space-ground equipment
航天地外生命探索/太空外生命探索　space extraterrestrial life exploration
航天电子学/太空電子學　space electronics
航天动力学/太空動力學　astrodynamics
航天动力因素与救生/太空動力因數與求生　space dynamic factors and survival
航天毒理学/太空毒物學　space toxicology
航天发射场/航太發射場,航天器發射場　space launching site, spacecraft launching complex
航天发射基地/航太發射基底　space launching base
航天发射技术/太空發射技術　space launching technology
航天发射台/航天器發射臺　spacecraft launching-pad
航天发射中心/太空發射中心　space launching

center

航天发射综合设施/航太綜合發射設施 space launching complex

航天返回技术/航太返回技術 space return technology

航天防御/太空防衛 space defense

[航天]飞船/宇宙飛船 spaceship

航天飞机/太空梭,太空飛機 space shuttle, space plane

航天飞机成像光谱仪/太空梭成像頻譜儀 shuttle imaging spectrometer, SIS

航天飞机成像雷达/太空梭成像雷達 space shuttle imaging radar

航天飞机遥控机械手系统/太空梭遙控操作器系統 shuttle remote manipulator system, SRMS

航天飞行环境/空間飛行環境 space flight environment

航天飞行技能训练/太空飛行技能訓練 space flight skill training

航天[飞行]器/太空載具,太空船 spacecraft

航天飞行原理/太空飛行原理 space flight principle

航天服/太空衣 space suit

航天服循环系统/太空衣循環系統 space suit circulation system

航天服压力制度/太空服壓力圖表 space suit pressure schedule

航天跟踪/太空追蹤 space tracking

航天工程/航太工程 space engineering

航天工程系统/航太工程系統 space engineering system

航天工效学/太空生物工學 space ergonomics

航天工业/航太工業 space industry

航天攻击/太空攻擊 space attack

航天骨矿物质脱失/太空骨礦物質損失 bone mineral loss in space

航天骨疏松/太空骨質疏鬆 space bone osteoporosis

航天红细胞量减少/太空紅血細胞質量減少 red blood cell mass reduction in space, red corpuscle mass reduction in space

航天环境仿真设备/太空飛行環境模擬設備 space flight environment simulation facilities

航天环境工程/空間環境工程 space environment engineering

航天环境控制与生命保障系统/太空環境控制與維生系統 space environment control and life support system

航天环境适应性训练/太空環境適應訓練 space environment adaptation training

航天环境医学/太空環境醫學 space environmental medicine

航天机器人/空間機器人 space robot

航天肌肉萎缩/太空肌肉萎縮 muscle atrophy in space

航天计量与测试/太空計量與測試 space metrology and measurement

航天技术/太空科技 space technology

航天驾驶员/太空駕駛員 pilot astronaut, PA

航天科学研究机构/太空研究中心 space research institute

航天控制与导航/太空控制與導航 space control and navigation

航天联合指挥部/航太聯合指揮部 space flight united headquarter

航天免疫学/太空飛行免疫學 space flight immunology

航天内分泌学/太空內分泌學 space endocrinology

航天能源/太空電源 space power source

航天贫血症/太空貧血 space anemia

航天器材料/航天器材料 spacecraft material

[航天器]长期运行管理/長期運轉管理 spacecraft long-term operation management

航天器动力学/航天器動力學 spacecraft dynamics

航天器发射/太空船發射 spacecraft launch

航天器发射场/航天器發射場 spacecraft launching complex

航天器发射前试验/太空船發射前試驗 spacecraft prelaunch test

航天器工程/太空航具工程 spacecraft engineering

航天器环境/太空船環境 spacecraft environment

航天器环境工程/航天器環境工程 spacecraft environment engineering

航天器环境污染/太空船環境汙染 spacecraft environment contaminant

航天器回收系统/航天器回收系統 spacecraft recovery system

航天器火箭联合检查/太空載具火箭聯合檢查 spacecraft-rocket unite check

航天器技术/航天器技術 spacecraft technology

航天器结构动力学/航天器結構動力學 structure dynamics of spacecraft

航天器结构强度/太空航具結構強度 spacecraft structural strength

航天器结构系统/太空船結構系統 spacecraft structure system

航天器内力矩/太空載具內扭距 spacecraft internal torque

航天器热控系统/航天器熱控系統　spacecraft thermal control system
航天器消毒/太空船消毒　spacecraft sterilization
航天器载测控分系统/航天器載測控分系統　spacecraft-borne TT and C subsystem
航天器制造工程/航天器製造工程　spacecraft manufacturing engineering
航天器制造工艺/航天器製造工藝　spacecraft manufacturing technology
航天器转运/太空載具轉移　spacecraft transfer
航天器装配测试厂房/太空船裝配測試廠房　spacecraft assembly and test building
航天器总装厂/太空器裝配廠　spacecraft assembling plant
航天人体测量学/太空人體計測　space anthropometry
航天摄影/太空攝影　space photography
航天神经科学/太空神經科學　space neural science
航天生理学/太空生理學　space physiology
航天生理医学/太空生理醫學　space physiology and medicine
航天生理应激/太空生理壓迫　space physiological stress
航天实施医学/太空作戰醫學　space operational medicine
航天食品/太空食物　space food
航天食品管理/太空食物管理　space food management
航天食谱/太空食譜　space recipe
航天适应综合征/太空適應徵候群　space adaptation syndrome
航天手套/太空手套　space gloves
航天睡袋/太空睡袋　space sleeping bag
[航天]特殊环境适应性/特殊環境適應性　specific environmental adaptability
航天体液调节/太空體液調節　body fluid regulation in space
航天通信/太空通訊　space communication
航天头盔/太空頭盔　space helmet
航天推进/太空推進　space propulsion
航天卫生学/太空衛生學　space hygienics
航天武器/太空武器　space weapon
航天系统/太空系統　space system
航天系统工程/航太系統工程　space system engineering
航天心理学/太空心理學　space psychology
航天心血管失调/太空心血管去適應　cardiovascular deconditioning in space

航天行星探测/太空行星探測　space planetary exploration
航天靴/太空靴　space boots
航天学/航太學，太空航行學　astronautics
航天血液学/太空血液學　space hematology
航天训练仿真设备/太空飛行訓練模擬設備　space flight training simulation facilities
航天遥测/太空遥測　space telemetry
航天遥感/航太遥測　space remote sensing
航天遥感考古/太空遥測考古　space remote sensing for archaeology
航天药剂学/太空藥劑學　space pharmaceutics
航天药理学/太空藥理學　space pharmacology
航天药物/太空藥物　space drugs
航天药物动力学/太空藥物動力學　space pharmacokinetics
航天医监医保设备/太空醫學監測與支撐設備　space medical monitoring and support facilities
航天医师/太空飛行醫生　space flight doctor
航天医学/太空醫學　space medicine
航天医学仿真实验设备/太空醫學模擬實驗設備　space medicine simulation test facilities
航天医学工程/太空醫學工程　space medicine engineering
航天医学工程设施/太空醫學工程設施　space medico-engineering facilities
航天医学数据库/太空人醫學資料庫　space medicine database
航天员/太空人　astronaut, cosmonaut
航天员安全性/太空人安全性　astronaut safety
航天员安全掩体/太空人安全儲倉　astronaut safety bunker
航天员[保健]医师/太空人保健醫生　astronaut care doctor
航天员飞行手册/太空人飛行手冊　astronaut flight handbook
航天员工作能力/太空人作業能力　astronaut work capacity
航天员检疫/太空人檢疫　astronaut quarantine
航天员健康管理/太空人健康照護　astronaut health care
航天员健康状况判断/太空人健康狀態評估　astronaut health state assessment
航天员进舱/太空人進艙　space crew enter spacecraft
航天员决策/太空人決策　astronaut decision-making
航天员生产能力/太空人生產力　astronaut productivity

航天员通信头戴/太空人通信頭戴式耳麥 astronaut communication headsets
航天员系统/太空人系統 astronaut system
航天员心理学评定/太空人心理學評價 astronaut psychological evaluation
航天员选拔/太空人選拔 astronaut selection
航天员选拔标准/太空人選拔標準 astronaut selection criteria
航天员选拔训练中心/太空人選拔訓練中心 astronaut selection and training center, ASTC
航天员训练/太空人訓練 astronaut training
航天员训练大纲/太空人訓練方案 astronaut training program
航天员训练建筑/太空人訓練建築 astronaut training building
航天员药箱/太空人藥箱 astronaut medical kit
航天员医学监督/太空人醫學監控 astronaut medical monitoring
航天员医学监督与保障/太空人醫學監控與支撐 astronaut medical monitoring and support
航天员医学监督中心/太空人醫學監測中心 astronaut medical monitoring center
航天员医学鉴定/太空人醫藥給證 astronaut medical certification
航天员营区/太空人營區 astronaut camp
航天员营养/太空人營養 astronaut nutrition
航天员作息制度/太空人工作休息班期表 astronaut work rest schedule
航天月球探测/太空月球探勘 space lunar exploration
航天运动病/太空動量症 space motion sickness
航天运动病易感性/太空動暈症易感受性 space motion sickness susceptibility
航天运输/太空運輸 space transportation
航天运输系统/太空運輸系統 space transportation system
航天运载器/航太運載火箭 space launch vehicle
航天运载器技术/太空運載器技術 space launch vehicle technology
航天侦察/太空偵察 space reconnaissance
航天指挥中心/太空指揮中心 space command center
航天制导导航和控制/太空導航與控制 space guidance navigation and control
航天着陆场/航太登陸位置 space landing site
航位推算法/航位推測法 dead reckoning
航线/航線,航向,航路 trade route, shipping route, aeroroute
航线间隔/航路間隔 track spacing
航线角/航向角 course angle
航线可换件/飛行線可換件 line replaceable unit
航线设计/航線設計 passage planning
航线式相机/航帶攝影機 strip camera
航线维修/航線[飛行]維護 line maintenance
航向/航向,航線 course, shipping route, heading
航向保持/航向固定 heading hold
航向保持性/航向保持 course keeping, course keeping quality
航向操纵/方向控制 directional control
航向基准/航向參考 heading reference
航向记录器/航向記錄儀 course recording machine, course recorder
航向陀螺/定向迴轉儀 directional gyroscope
航向稳定性/航向穩定性 stability of motion, course stability
航向线/航向線 course line, CL
航向向上/航向向上 course up
航向信标/定位器,信標臺,左右定位臺 localizer
航向自动操舵仪/航向自動操舵裝置 course autopilot
航行安全通信/航行安全通信 navigation safety communication
航行标志/航路標誌 navigation mark
航行波/航跡波,船行浪 ship wave
航行补给船/航行補給船 underway replenishment ship
航行测量/航行測量 measurement during sailing
航行垂直补给/海上垂直補給 perpendicular replenishment at sea
航行灯/航行燈 navigation light, running light, navigation light
航行灯控制器/航行燈指示器 running light indicator, navigation light indicator
航行灯照距测定/航行燈照距測定 determination of range of visibility for navigation light
航行风/航行風 navigation wind, ship wind
航行管理/航管 navigation management
航行横向补给/航行中橫向補給 abeam replenishment at sea
航行计划/航行計劃 navigational plan, sailing plan
航行计划报告/航行計劃報告 sailing plan report
航行警告/航行警告 navigational warning
航行警告[电传]系统/航行警告電傳 navigational telex, NAVTEX
航行警告区/航行警告區 NAVAREA
航行警告区公告/航行區警告通告 NAVAREA

warning bulletin
航行警告区警告/航行警告區之警告　NAVAREA warning
航行警告区业务/航行警告區業務　NAVAREA warning service
航行警告区域协调国/航行警告區域協調人　NAVAREA coordinator
航行警告信号/航行警告信號　navigational warning signal
航行期间/航行期間　term of voyage
航行情报服务/航空資訊服務　aeronautical information service, AIS
航行权/航行權　right of navigation
航行试验/[海上]試航　sea trial
航行速度三角形/速度三角形　velocity triangle
航行信号设备/航行信號設備　navigation signal equipment
航行值班/航行當值　navigational watch
航行纵向补给/海上艉向補給　astern replenishment at sea
航修/航修　voyage repair
航用参考图/非航用海圖　non-navigational chart
航用海图/航海用海圖　navigational chart
航用信号/航用信號　signal nautical
航用行星/導航行星　navigational planets
航运法/航業法　shipping law
航运业务/航運業務　shipping business
航站楼/航站樓　air terminal
航站区/航站區　terminal area
巷道式通风/乾井通風　ventilation by ducts
毫地速/毫地速　milli-earth rate unit
毫米波引信/毫米波引信　millimeter wave fuze
4毫米锁闭/4毫米鎖閉　check 4mm opening of a switch point
毫秒雷管/瞬發雷管　millisecond detonator, instantaneous detonator
毫秒延迟爆破/毫秒延遲爆破　millisecond delay blasting
毫微米/毫微米　millimicron
豪氏桁架/郝威式桁架　Howe truss
好路率/好路率　rate of good level highway
好能见度/能見度良好　visibility good
号灯/號燈　ship light, lights
号灯垂直位置/號燈之垂直位置　vertical positioning of lights
号灯发光强度/號燈照明強度　intensity of lights
号灯间距/號燈間隔　spacing of lights
号灯能见距/號燈能見距　visibility of light

号灯水平位置/號燈水平位置　horizontal positioning of lights
号灯照距测定/航行燈照距測定　determination of range of visibility for navigation light
号笛控制装置/號笛控制器　whistle controller, whistle and siren control system
号笛音响度测定/音響信號聽距測定　determination of range of audibility of sound signal
号锣/鑼　gong
号旗/信號旗　code flag, signal flag
号型/號標　shape
号钟/號鍾　bell
好氧消化/好氧消化　aerobic digestion
耗地作物/耗地作物　crop of depleting soil fertility
耗尽关机/耗盡關機　exhausted cutoff
耗能减震/耗能減震　energy dissipation and earthquake response reduction
耗汽量/蒸汽消耗量　steam consumption
耗汽率/耗汽率　steam rate
耗热定额/熱消耗定額　heat consumption quota
耗热量/耗熱量,熱損失　heat loss, heat consumption
耗热量指标/熱耗指標,熱損失指標　index of heat loss
耗热率/耗熱率　heat rate
耗水量/消耗[水]量　consumptive use, consumptive water use
耗水型植物/耗水型植物　water consumption plant
耗损区/損耗區　wearout region
耗损失效期/損耗失效期　wearout failure period
耗损特性/損耗特徵　wearout characteristics
耗氧量/耗氧量　oxygen consumption
耗油率/單位燃料消耗量,單位耗油量,燃油消耗比　specific fuel consumption
合班教室/合班教室　combined-teaching classroom
合并杆/聯合桿　combination lever
合并舷灯/合并燈,聯合燈　combined lantern
合成标准不确定度/合并不確定度　combined standard uncertainty
合成波高/合成波高　height of wave and swell combined
合成潮/合成潮　resultant tide
合成干涉仪雷达/合成雷達干涉技術　synthetic interferometer radar
合成胶/人造膠　synthetic resin glue
合成孔径侧视雷达/旁觀合成光圈雷達　synthetic aperture side-looking radar
合成孔径长度/合成孔徑長度　length of synthetic

aperture
合成孔径分辨率/合成孔径解析度 resolution of synthetic aperture
合成孔径雷达/合成孔径雷達 synthetic aperture radar, SAR
合成孔径天线/合成孔径天線 synthetic aperture antenna
合成孔径谐波雷达/諧波合成孔徑雷達 harmonic SAR
合成坡度/合成坡度 resultant gradient
合成气/合成氣 synthesis gas
合成清洁剂/合成清潔劑 synthetic detergent
合成树脂乳液砂壁状建筑涂料/合成樹脂乳液砂壁狀建築塗料 sand textured building coating based on synthetic resin emulsion
合成树脂乳液涂料/合成樹脂乳液塗料 synthetic resin emulsion coating
合成树脂瓦/合成樹脂瓦 synthetic resin tile
合成水文学/合成水文學 synthetic hydrology
合成天线/合成天線 synthetic antenna
合成污泥/合成汙泥 synthetic sludge
合成纤维/合成纖維 synthetic fiber
合成纤维混凝土/合成纖維混凝土 synthetic fiber reinforced concrete
合成橡胶水泥/合成橡膠水泥 synthetic rubber cement
合成橡胶支座/合成橡膠支座 elastomeric pad bearing
合成应力/合應力 resultant stress
合成油/合成油 synthetic oil
合乘车辆车道/合乘車輛車道 car pool lane
合格/合格,符合 conformity, compliance
合格安全型设备/合格安全型設備 certified safe type apparatus
合格工程/合格建設工程 qualified project
合格供应商目录/合格供應商清單 qualified supplier list
合格证书/合格證書,符合證書 document of compliance, certificate of conformity, certificate of compliance
合金/合金 alloy
合金棒/合金鋼條 alloy bar
合金淬火轨/合金淬火軌 head hardened alloy steel rail, quenched alloy steel rail
合金电镀/合金電鍍,合金鍍膜 alloy plating
合金轨/合金鋼軌 alloy steel rail
合金铅管/合金鉛管 alloyed-lead pipe
合理施肥/合理施肥 rational fertilization

合理速遣/合理派遣 reasonable despatch
合理运输/合理運輸 rational traffic
合力/合力 resultant, resultant force
合力偶/合力偶 resultant couple
合练/预演,演习 rehearsal, combind training
合练大纲/預演大綱 rehearsal outline
合练[火]箭/合練[火]箭 launching crew training rocket
合练模型/合練模型 rehearsal model
合流/合流 merging
合流交通量/合流交通量 converging traffic volume
合流水量/合流水量 combined sewer flow
合流污水泵站/合流汙水泵站 combined sewage pumping station
合流污水工程系统/合流溝管系統 combined sewerage system
合流制/合流制,合流系統,合流式 combined system
合流制排水系统/合流式下水道系統 combined sewer system
合同/合約,契約 contract
合同费率制/合約運費制 contract freight system
合同管理/合約管理 contract management
合同价/合約價格,包價 contract price
合同评审/合約評審 contract review
合同条件/契約條件 conditions of contract
合同通用条件/合約基本條款 general conditions of contract
合同文件/契約合同 contract documents
合同运输/合同運輸 contract transport
合同专用条件/合約特殊條件 special condition of contract
合造客车/合造客車 composite passenger car, composite coach
合资铁路/合資鐵路 joint investment railway, jointly owned railway
合作伙伴关系/合作夥伴關係 cooperative partnership
合作指数/協同指數 index of cooperation
合座舷灯/合并燈 sidelights combined in one lantern
和玺彩画/和璽彩畫 dragon or phoenix pattern, hexicaihua
河岸/河[川堤]岸 river bank
河岸地/堤外地 riverside land, waterside land
河边/堤外河邊 riverside
河滨公园/河濱公園 riverside park
河槽/河槽,河道 river channel
河槽天然冲刷/河槽天然沖刷 natural scour of

河槽压缩/河槽收縮　channel contraction
河槽淤积/河床填料　channel filling
河潮/河潮　fluvial tide
河川测量/河川測量　river surveying
河川坡度/河川坡度　slope of stream
河床/河床　river bed
河床比降/河床比降　river bed gradient
河床波/河床波　bed wave
河床冲刷/管道冲蝕　channel erosion
河床铺砌/河床鋪砌　river bed paving
河床演变/河床變動　river bed evolution
河床载运/河床載運　bed load transport
河道/河道,水道　water course
河道糙率/渠道糙度　channel roughness
河道调查/河道調查,河川勘測　river survey, river course survey
河道护坡绿化/河道護坡綠化　river slope greening
河道坡度/河川坡度,河川比降　stream gradient
河道侵蚀/河槽侵蝕,河槽銷蝕,溝渠銷蝕　channel encroachment, channel erosion
河道水情预报/河流預測　river forecasting
河道维护/河川維護　river maintenance
河道演变/河床變動　river bed evolution
河道整治/河川治理　channel regulation
河道治理规划/治河規劃　river regulation planning
河堤/堤防,堤岸　levee, river bank
河堤格网工/河堤格網工　hurdle work
河底/河底　river bottom, stream bottom
河调-防护失修/河調-防護失修　disrepair of flow regulating and shore protecting structure, river bank protection out of repair
河港/内河港　river port
河宫/河宫　river palace
河谷耗水量/河谷耗水量　valley consumptive use
河鼓二(天鹰 α)/河鼓二,牽牛[星],牛郎[星](天鷹 α)　Altair
河海测量/河海測量　nautical hydrograph
河湖滨水区/河湖濱水區　waterfront areas of river and lake
河湖生态水量/河湖生態水量　ecological water requirement of river and lake
河口/河口　river mouth, estuary
河口改良/河口改良　river mouth improvement
河口港/河口港　estuary harbour, estuary port, river mouth harbor
河口污染/河口汙染　estuarine pollution
河砾石/河礫　river gravel
channel
河流比降/河川比降,河道坡度,河川坡度　slope of river, comparable horizon of river, stream gradient
河流沉积/河流沈積　fluvial deposit
河流处置/河川處置　river disposal
河流阶地/河岸臺地　river terrace
河流截夺/河奪　river capture
河流流域/流域　river basin
河流水尺/河水尺　river gage
河流卫生/河川環境衞生　stream sanitation
河流袭夺/河流襲奪　river piracy
河[漫]滩/河漫灘[地],洪水平原　flood land, flood plain
河曲地带/曲流带,蜿蜒帶　meander belt
河沙/河砂　river sand
河水涨落/河水漲落　river breathing
河滩路堤/河灘路堤　embankment on plain river beach
河外星系/河外星雲　anagalactic nebula
河系/河川系統　river system
河制系数/河制係數　coefficient of river regime
荷兰滚模态/荷蘭滾模式　Dutch roll mode
核爆中心/核爆炸中心　nuclear explosion center
核测量系统/核子測量系統　nuclear measurement system
核查/查核,查驗,核對　check
核查标准/查核標準　check standard
核磁共振谱仪/核磁諧振譜儀　nuclear magnetic resonance spectrometer
核磁共振陀螺/核磁共振陀螺儀　magnetic resonance gyroscope
核电厂/核能電廠,核能發電站　nuclear power station, nuclear power plant
核电磁脉冲/[核爆]電磁脈波　nuclear electromagnetic pulse
核电磁脉冲敏感度测量/核電磁脈衝量測　nuclear EM pulse sensitivity measurement
核电磁脉冲耦合/核電磁脈衝耦合　nuclear electromagnetic pulse coupling
核电磁脉冲效应/核電磁脈衝效應　effect of nuclear electromagnetic pulse
核电源系统/核能電源系統　nuclear power system
核电站/核能電廠,核能發電站　nuclear power station, nuclear power plant
核动力船/核能動力船,核子動力船　nuclear powered ship
核动力船舶经营人责任公约/核子船舶營運人責任公約　Convention on the Liability of Operators on Nuclear Ships

核动力货船安全证书/核子貨船安全證書 nuclear cargo ship safety certificate
核动力客船安全证书/核子客船安全證書 nuclear passenger ship safety certificate
核动力驱动/核能驅動 nuclear driven
核动力推进装置/核能推進裝置 nuclear propulsion plant
核动力装置/核子動力設備 nuclear power plant
核对数字/核對數位 check digit
核反应堆/核子反應器 nuclear reactor
核反应堆保护系统/核反應器保護系統 reactor protective system
核反应堆控制系统/核反應器控制系統 reactor control system
核反应堆中毒/核子反應器中毒 nuclear reactor poisoning
核辐射/核子輻射 nuclear radiation
核辐射环境/核子輻射環境 nuclear radiation environment
核环境/核環境 nuclear environment
核距/核距 core distance
核裂产物/核分裂生成物 fission products
核能/核能 nuclear energy
核潜艇/核子潛艇 nuclear submarine
核燃料/核燃料 nuclear fuel
核闪光盲/核閃光視盲 nuclear flash blindness
核设施/核設施 nuclear installation
核生存能力/核存活率 nuclear survivability
核试验/核[子]試爆 nuclear test
核推进/核能推進 nuclear propulsion
核心保护范围/核心保護地帶 core conservation zone
核心-边缘理论/中心邊陲理論 center-periphery theory
核心车次/核心車次 scheduled train number
核心机/核心發動機 core engine
核心家庭/核心家族 core family
核心景区/核心[風]景區 core scenic, scenic spot in the heart
核心[区]/核心區,地核,中心地域 core, core area
核心筒/核心筒 core tube, core wall
核心吸引力/核心吸引力 core attraction
核心种质/核心種質 core germplasm
核医学科/核醫[學]科,核醫療學 department of nuclear medicine
核易损性/核易損性 nuclear vulnerability
核子动态湿度密度仪/核子動態濕度密度儀 nuclear moisture and density dynamic meter

核子静态湿度密度仪/核子靜態濕度密度儀 nuclear moisture and density static meter
核子密度湿度测定/核子密度濕度測定 determination of nuclear density moisture
核子湿度密度仪/核子濕度密度儀 nuclear moisture and density meter
盒式天平/盒式天平 box type balance
盒形件/盒形件 box part
盒形梁/盒形梁 box beam
荷载/負荷,負載 load
荷载标准值/荷載標準值 characteristic value of load, standard load
荷载分项系数/負荷部分安全係數 partial safety factor for load
荷载横向分布/負載橫向分布,橫向負載分布 transverse distribution of load, transverse load distribution
荷载平衡法/載重均衡法 load balancing method
荷载设计值/荷載設計值,設計載重,設計荷載 design load, design value of load
荷载试验/帶負荷試驗 loading test
荷载系数/負荷因素,負載因數 load factor
荷载效应/負載效應 load effect
荷载组合/負載組合,載重組合 loading combinations, load combination
赫林格-赖斯纳原理/赫林格-賴斯納原理 Hellinger Reissner principle
褐煤/褐煤 lignite
褐炭/褐炭 lignite
黑玻璃/濾光玻璃 filter glass
黑潮/黑潮 Black stream, Kuroshio
黑洞效应/黑洞效應 black hole effect
黑棉土/黑綿土 black cotton soil
黑球温度/黑球溫度 globe temperature
黑色金属/鐵金屬 ferrous metal
黑色旅游/黑暗旅遊 dark tourism
黑视/黑視 blackout
黑水/黑水 black water
黑体/黑體 black body
黑体辐射/黑體輻射,黑體發射 black body emission
黑体源/黑體源 black body resources
黑体噪声等效功率/黑體雜訊等效功率 black body noise equivalent power
黑匣子/黑盒子 black box
黑匣子剧场/黑匣子劇場 black box theater
黑心可锻铸铁/黑心展性鑄鐵 black heart malleable cast iron
黑障区/黑障區 blackout range

痕迹/跡　trace
恒定风/恆定風　permanent wind
恒定峰值功率输出/可靠尖峰出量　firm peak output
恒定落差率定曲线/定差水位率定曲線　constant-fall rating curve
恒定最大输出/可靠尖峰出量　firm peak output
恒定最高容量/可靠尖峰容量　firm peak capacity
恒功率调速/恆功率調速　speed regulation by constant power
恒功调速比/恆功調速比　speed ratio on constant power
恒[荷]载/静負載,呆負載　dead load
恒流充电/恆流充電,定電流充電　constant current charge
恒流驱动控制/恆流驅動控制　constant current drive control
恒湿器/恆濕器,濕度調節器　humidistat
恒速/恆定速率,等率　constant speed
恒速过滤/恆速過濾　constant rate filtration
恒速恒频交流电源系统/恆速恆頻交流電源系統　constant speed-frequency AC power system
恒速螺桨/恆速螺旋槳　constant speed propeller
恒速驱动装置/恆速傳動裝置　constant speed drive unit
恒速特性曲线/等速特性曲線　characteristic curve at constant speed
恒位线/等方位線　line of equal bearing
恒温恒湿系统/恆溫恆濕系統　constant temperature and humidity system
恒温膨胀阀/調溫膨脹閥,定溫膨脹閥　thermostatic expansion valve
恒温器/恆溫器　thermostat
恒温调节器/恆溫調節器,溫度調節器　thermostat regulator
恒向线/恆向線　rhumb line
恒向线方位/恆向線方位　rhumb line bearing, RLB
恒向线航线算法/恆向線航法　rhumb line sailing
恒星/恆星　star
恒星敏感器/恆星感測器　stellar sensor
恒星日/恆星日　sidereal day
恒星时/恆星時　sidereal time, ST
恒星视位置/恆星視位置　star apparent place
恒星图/星座圖　star chart, star atlas
恒星相机/恆星攝影機　stellar camera
恒星星等/恆星星等　stellar magnitude
恒星月/恆星月　sidereal month
[恒星]周年视差/週年視差　annual parallax
恒压充电/恆壓充電　constant voltage charge

恒压式供应系统/定壓輸給系統　constant pressure feed system
恒载压力线/恆載推力線　dead load thrust line
恒张力带缆绞车/自動張力繫船絞車　automatic constant tension mooring winch
恒张力拖缆机/自動等拉力拖攬機　automatic constant tension towing winch
恒转矩调速/恆轉矩調速　speed regulation by constant torque
珩磨/搪磨,搪光　honing
桁/橫桁,帆桁　yard
桁材/桁,縱梁　girder
桁材深度/縱桁深度　girder depth
桁架/桁架,構架　truss
桁架比拟法/桁架比擬法　truss analogy method
桁架拱桥/桁架拱橋　trussed arch bridge
桁架梁/桁架梁　trussed beam
桁架梁桥/桁架梁橋　trussed beam bridge
桁架桥/桁架橋　truss bridge
桁架式钢结构/桁架式鋼結構　truss type steel structure
桁架式机器人/移程機器人　gantry robot
桁架式系杆拱/桁架繫拱橋　braced tied arch
桁架桅/籠形桅,格式桅　cage mast, lattice mast
桁架支柱/桁架支柱　truss post
桁链吊桥/梁架鏈橋　braced chain suspension bridge
桁梁/縱梁　longeron
桁梁式结构/縱梁結構　longeron structure
桁式木拱架/桁式木拱架　wood truss centering
桁式T形刚构桥/T形桁架剛構橋　T-shaped truss rigid frame bridge
桁条/桁條　stringer
桁拖网/桁拖網　beam trawl
桁拖渔船/舷側拖網船　beam trawler
横波/橫波　transverse wave
横舱壁/橫向艙壁　transverse bulkhead
横侧运动/橫向運動　lateral-directional motion
横撑板/短木條　cross poling
横承力索/橫承懸索　headspan wire
横承力索线夹/橫承力索線夾　headspan wire clamp
横带/橫梁　rail, platband
横担/橫擔,橫臂　cross arm
横荡/橫移　sway, swaying
横道图/直方圖,柱狀圖　bar chart
横电磁波小室/橫電磁波小室　cross electromagnetic wave small room, transverse electromagnetic cell
横动式桥梁/推開橋　traversing bridge
横洞/橫洞,橫向平巷　transverse gallery

横断面/橫斷面,橫切面,[橫]截面 cross section
横断面测量/橫斷面調查,橫剖面量測,橫截面測量 cross section, transverse profile, section profile
横断面设计/橫截面設計 cross section design
横断面图/剖視圖 cross-sectional view
横断面选线/截面選線 cross section method of railway location, location with cross section method, cross section method for location of line
横队/橫隊 line abreast
横舵柄/橫舵柄,[舵]軛 rudder yoke, yoke
横帆/橫帆,方帆 square sail
横帆船/橫帆船 square-rigged vessel
横风/橫風 cross wind
横风航驶/橫戧 reach
横缝/橫向節理 transverse joint
横隔板/橫隔板,隔膜 transverse diaphragm, diaphragm
横骨架式/橫肋系統 transverse frame system, transverse framing system
横管/橫管,水平管 horizontal pipe
横贯斜坡路/橫貫斜坡路 traversing slipway
横轨枕/橫軌枕 transverse sleeper
横滚/滾轉 roll
横滚角/滾轉角 roll angle
横过道/橫過道 transverse aisle
横焊/橫向焊接 horizontal welding, horizontal position welding
横桁闪光信号灯/橫桁閃光信號燈 blinker yardarm
横滑道/橫滑道 broadside slipway
横江轮渡号型/橫江渡輪號標 shape for crossing ferry
横接缝/橫接縫 transversal joint
横截面畸变/橫截面畸變 distortion of cross section
横进水轮机/橫進口水渦輪 cross inlet water turbine
横距/[迴旋]橫距,[迴轉]橫距 transfer
横靠泊位/靠泊船席 alongside berth
横缆/橫纜 breast line
横浪/橫浪,舷浪 beam sea
横梁/橫梁 transverse beam, cross beam
横列式区段站/橫列式編組站 transversal type district station
横流/橫流,側流 cross current, transverse current
横流标/橫流標 cross current mark
横流扫气/橫驅氣 cross scavenging
横漂/橫漂,飄移,漂流 drift, crabbing
横坡/橫坡 cross slope
横剖面/橫剖面,橫截面 transverse section, cross section
横剖面图/橫剖面圖 transverse section plan
横剖线/船體曲面線 body lines
横强度/橫向強度 transverse strength
横倾/傾斜,偏斜,傾側 heel, list
横倾角/橫傾角 angle of heel, angle of list
横倾力矩/傾側力矩 heeling moment
横伸挂车/可調軌拖車 adjustable track trailer
横驶区/橫越區 crossing area
横式幅面/橫式幅面 horizontal sheet style
横试坑/橫試坑 test adit
横甩/橫甩,橫轉 broaching
横通道/橫通道 transverse passage-way
横拖/橫拖 girding
横纹压力/橫紋壓力 compression perpendicular to grain
横稳心/橫定傾中心 transverse metacenter
横稳性/橫向穩度 transverse stability
横系杆/側撐桿,橫支撐 lateral bracing
横向/橫向,橫切 athwartships
横向标记/橫向畫線 transverse marking
横向补给装置/橫向補給裝置 abeam replenishing rig
横向操纵/橫向控制 lateral control
横向操纵偏离参数/橫向控制分離參數 lateral control departure parameter, LCDP
横向承载桩地基系数法/側向力承載樁地基係數法 subsoil reaction modulus method for laterally loaded pile
横向冲击/側向衝擊 lateral impact
横向冲距/橫向衝距 side reach
横向重叠率/橫向重疊率 transverse overlap
横向传播特性/橫向傳播特性 cross propagation characteristic
横向磁棒/橫向磁棒 athwartships magnet
横向磁通直线感应电动机/橫向磁通直線感應電動機 transverse flux linear induction motor
横向导引/橫向導引 lateral steering
横向的/橫向的 transverse
横向吊车机/活動吊車 cherry picker
横向分辨率/橫向解析度 cross-track resolution
横向分布/橫向分布 transverse distribution
横向荷载/橫向載重 transverse loading
横向桁架/側向桁架 lateral truss
横向滑道/橫向滑道 side slipway
横向加劲肋/橫向加勁材 transverse stiffener
横向间断光源/橫向間斷光源 laterally intermittent illuminant

横向间隔/橫向隔離　lateral separation
横向间隙/側向間隙　lateral clearance
横向校平/橫斷面水準測量　cross-levelling
横向拉杆/橫向連桿　lateral connecting rod
横向力/橫向力　transverse force, lateral force
横向力设计/橫力設計　lateral force design
横向力系数测试仪/橫向力係數測試儀　sideway force coefficient routine investigation machine
横向裂缝/橫裂[紋]　transverse crack, transverse fissure
横向摩擦[力]/側向摩擦　side friction
横向排水/橫向排水　transverse drainage
横向排水沟/橫暗渠　cross-drain
横向坡度/橫向坡度　crossfall
横向强度/橫向強度　transverse strength
横向强化/橫向強化　transverse strengthening
横向强制摇荡装置/橫向強制搖擺裝置　transverse forced oscillation device
横向侵蚀/橫向沖蝕　lateral erosion
横向弹性/橫向彈性　lateral elasticity, lateral resilience
横向弹性模量/橫向彈性模數,剪彈性模數　modulus of transverse elasticity
横向弹性系数/橫向彈性模數,剪彈性模數　modulus of transverse elasticity
横向通风/橫向通風,橫流式通風　transverse ventilation, transversal ventilation
横向推力/水平推力　horizontal thrust
横向位移/橫變位　transverse displacement
横向稳定[性]/橫向穩定性　lateral stability
横向下水/橫向下水　side launching
横向悬砌拱法/橫向懸砌拱法　laying arch by transverse overhanging method
横向摇摆/側傾,側移　lateral sway
横向摇摆力/橫向搖擺力　transverse rocking force
横向预应力/橫向預力　transverse prestress
横向振动/橫[向]振動,側向振動　lateral vibration, transversal vibration
横向支撑系统/橫向支撐系統　lateral bracing system
横向支承/橫向支承　lateral support
横向阻力/橫向阻力　lateral resistance
横摇/[船身]橫摇　rolling
横摇变形角/滾轉變形角　roll deformation angle
横摇角/橫摇角,滾轉角　rollling angle, roll angle
横摇扭矩/橫摇力矩　rolling moment, rolling torsional moment
横摇周期/橫摇週期　rolling period

横摇阻尼/橫摇阻尼　rolling damping
横移/側滑　sideslip
横移率/橫移率　rate of transverse motion
横张索/吊架跨索　davit span
横重稳距/橫向定傾高　transverse metacentric height
横轴/橫軸　lateral axis
横轴投影/橫向投影,赤道投影法　transverse projection, equatorial projection
衡重吊桥/開闔橋　counterpoise bridge
衡重式挡土墙/衡重式擋土牆,平衡式擋土牆　balance weight retaining wall, gravity retaining wall with relieving platform, balanced type retaining wall
衡重式桥台/權平衡橋臺　weight balanced abutment
轰炸/轟炸,投彈　bombing
轰炸机/轟炸機　bomber
轰炸雷达/轟炸雷達　bombing radar
轰炸瞄准具/轟炸瞄準器　bombing sight
烘干材/爐乾木材　kiln-dried wood, oven-dried wood
烘干土/爐乾土　oven dry soil
烘干状态/爐乾狀態　oven dry condition
红丹/紅丹漆　red lead paint
红灯/紅燈　red light
红灯时间/紅燈時間　red time
红[黏]土/紅[黏]土　red clay
红壤/紅壤,紅土　red soil
红色旅游/紅色旅遊　red tourism
红色提单/附帶保險載貨證券　red bill of lading
红色信号/紅星信號　red star-signal
红砂岩/紅砂岩　red sandstone
红树林/紅樹林　mangrove forest
红套/紅套　shrink-on
红外比色测量仪/紅外線色溫度計　infrared colorithermometer
红外窗口材料/紅外窗口材料　infrared window material
红外导引头/紅外線歸航器　IR homing head
红外灯阵/紅外線燈陣　infrared lamp arrays
红外地球敏感器/地球紅外線感測器　infrared earth sensor, infrared horizon sensor
红外发射主机/紅外線發射器　infrared transmitter
红外仿真器/紅外線模擬器　infrared simulator
红外仿真试验/紅外線模擬試驗　infrared simulation test
红外辐射测量仪/紅外[線]輻射計　infrared radiometer
红外辐射计定标设备/紅外線輻射計校準設備　infrared radiometer calibration facility

红外辐射率/紅外發射率　infrared emittance
红外辐射器/紅外線散熱器　infrared radiator, IR radiator
红外辐射源/紅外線輻射源　infrared radiation source
红外跟踪测量系统/紅外線追蹤測量系統　infrared tracking measurement system
红外功率密度/紅外線功率密度　infrared power density, IR power density
红外加热笼/紅外線加熱籠　infrared heating cage
红外加热器/紅外線加熱器　infrared heater
红外胶片/紅外線軟片　infrared film
红外焦平面阵列/紅外聚焦平面陣列　infrared focal plane array
红外接收器/紅外[線]接收器　infrared receiver, IR receiver
红外雷达/紅外線雷達　infrared radar
红外扫描仪/紅外[線]掃描器　infrared scanner
红外摄像头/紅外攝影機　infrared camera
红外摄影/紅外線攝影　infrared photography
红外搜索跟踪器/紅外線搜索與追蹤器　infrared search and track device, IRST device
红外探测器/紅外線偵檢器　infrared detector
红外望远镜/紅外[線]望遠鏡　infrared telescope
红外显微镜/紅外[線]顯微鏡　infrared microscope
红外线/紅外線　infrared ray
红外线车辆检测器/紅外線車輛偵測器　infrared vehicle detector
红外线烘干装置/紅處線烘乾裝置　infrared oven stand
红外线加湿器/紅外線加濕器　infrared humidifier
红外线同声传译系统/紅外線同聲翻譯系統　infrared simultaneous interpretation system
红外线再流焊/紅外線回流焊接　infrared reflow soldering
红外线轴温检测所/紅外線軸溫檢測所　infrared journal temperature detection point
红外线轴温探测系统/紅外線軸溫探測系統　infrared journal temperature detection system
红外相机/紅外照相機　infrared camera
红外遥感/紅外遙測,紅外傳感　infrared remote sensing, infrared sensing
红外抑制/紅外抑制　infrared inhibition
红外引信/紅外線引信　infrared fuze
红外隐形材料/紅外隱身材料　infrared stealth material
红外制导/紅外線導引　infrared guidance
红外自动跟踪/紅外[線]自動追蹤　infrared automatic tracking

红线/[邊]界線　boundary line, property line
红星火箭/火箭信號　rocket signal, rocket star signal
红雪松/美國香柏　red cedar
宏观腐蚀/巨蝕　macroetch
宏观交通模型/宏觀交通模型　macro traffic model
宏观组织/巨觀結構　macrostructure
虹吸存水弯/虹吸存水彎　siphon trap
虹吸管气压表/虹吸管氣壓表　siphon barometer
虹吸涵洞/虹吸涵洞　siphon culvert
虹吸雨量计/虹吸雨量計　siphon rainfall recorder
洪泛区/洪泛區　flood plain
洪峰/洪[水]峰　flood peak, peak flood
洪积层/洪積層　diluvium deposit
洪积土/洪積土[壤]　diluvial soil, pluvial soil, diluvium deposit
洪流观测/洪流觀測　flood flow observation
洪水/洪水　flood
洪水标记/洪水位,泛水標誌　flood mark
洪水超蓄/洪水超蓄　flood surcharge
洪水重现期/洪水重現期　return period of flood
洪水调查/洪水調查　flood survey
洪水发生概率/洪水機率　flood probability
洪水泛滥区/洪水泛濫區,洪泛區　flooded area, flooding area
洪水降落系数/退水係數　coefficient of flood recession
洪水径流/洪水徑流　flood run off
洪水流量/洪水量　flood discharge
洪水频率/洪水頻率　flood frequency
洪水曲线/洪水曲線　flood curve
洪水水面/洪水平面　flood plane
洪水位/洪水位　flood level, flood water level
洪水位过程线/洪水位延時曲線　flood level duration curve
洪水吸收/洪水吸收,攔洪　flood absorption
洪水淹没/洪水淹沒　flood inundation on tracks
洪水溢流道/溢流式溢洪道　overflow flood spillway
喉板/喉板　throat sheet
喉部流速/管喉流速　throat velocity
喉部烧蚀率/喉部燒蝕率　throat ablative rate
喉道加热/喉部加熱　throat heating
喉深/喉深　throat depth
喉通面积比/喉通面積比　throat to port area ratio
猴锤/猴錘　monkey gravity hammer
后八字/後八字方向　on the quarter
后板/後罩板　back sheet
后备断路器/備用斷路器　back-up breaker

后部/船尾部　after body
后车架片/後車架　rear frame
后车距离/前後間距,追蹤距離　following distance
后处理/後處理　post-processing
后从板座/後從板座　rear draft lug, rear draft stop
后挡板/後擋板　back shield
后方/後方,向後　astern
后峰锯齿冲击脉冲/後陡鋸齒形衝擊脈波　final peak sawtooth shock pulse
后固化/後硬化,後成化　postcure
后花园/後花園　back yard garden
后缓冲铁/後擋　rear bumper
后接点/後觸點,背觸點　back contact
后冷却器/後冷卻器　after cooler
后掠角/後掠角　sweepback angle
后掠式腰支杆/後掠式腰支桿　swept waist support
后掠翼/後掠翼　sweepback wing, swept wing
后掠翼独立性原理/後掠翼獨立性原則　independence principle of swept wing
后氯化/後氯處理　post-chlorination
后滤池/後過濾器　after filter
后面基地线/後面基地線　rear lot line
后膨胀板/後膨脹板　rear expansion sheet
后评价/後評價　post-assessment
后勤保障分析/後勤支援分析　logistic support analysis
后勤保障科/後勤服務中心　department of logistic service
后勤舱/後勤指令艙　logistics module
后圈/後圈　back coil
后燃/後燃　after-burning
后燃期/後燃期　after burning period
后热/後熱　post heating, postheat
后三点起落架/起落架尾輪　tail wheel landing gear, taildragger
后视/後視　backward sight
后视图/後視圖　rear view
后体/後半段船體　aft body
后庭/後庭　back yard, rear yard
后退/後退　set back
后退信号/後退信號　backing signal
后桅/後桅　aft mast, after mast
后[舞]台/後[舞]臺　back stage
后现代主义/後現代主義　post-modernism
后向反射器/倒反射器,復歸反射器　retroreflector
后向散射/反向散射,背向散射　back scattering
后效冲量/後效衝量　cutoff impulse, thrust decay impulse
后效段/推力衰減段　thrust decay phase
后卸式自卸车辆/後卸車　rear dumper
后行桨叶/後行槳葉　retreating blade
后续舰/後續船艦　follow-up ship
后缘角/後緣角　trailing-edge angle
后缘襟翼/後緣襟翼　trailing-edge flap
后院/後院　rear yard
后院线/後院線　rear yard line
后张[法]/後張法,後拉　post tensioning method
后张法[预应力]混凝土/後拉法預力混凝土　post-tensioned concrete
后张法预应力混凝土结构/後張法預應力混凝土結構　post-tensioned prestressed concrete structure
后张法预应力梁/後張法預應力梁　post-tentioned prestressed concrete girder
后张拉体系/後拉法　post-tensioning system
后张自锚法预应力/後張自錨法預應力　self anchored post-tensioning prestressing
后缀装土机/後綴裝土機　rear mounted loader
厚板/[木]板　plank
厚壁/厚壁　thick wall
厚壁轴承/厚鋼殼型軸承　thick steel shell type bearing
厚度分布/厚度分布　thickness distribution
厚度规/厚度規,測厚規,測隙規　thickness gage
厚钢板/厚鋼板　heavy steel plate
厚壳/厚殼　thick shell
厚膜压力传感器/厚膜壓力換能器　thick film pressure transducer
厚屏蔽/厚遮罩　thick shield
候补航天乘员组/後備飛航組員　backup space flight crew
候场室/休息室　green room
候潮港/淺灘港,淺浪港　bar port, shoaled harbor
候车室/候車室,候車大廳　waiting room, waiting hall, waiting lounge
候车厅/候車大廳,候車室　waiting room, waiting hall, waiting lounge
候机楼/旅客終站　passenger terminal
候机厅/候機室　waiting hall, waiting lounge
候(蛇夫α)/候(蛇夫α)　Rasalhague
候审室/候審室　trial waiting room
候梯厅/電梯間　elevator hall
候选人/候選人　candidate
候诊处/等待區,等候處　waiting area, lounge
呼号/呼號　call sign, CS
呼叫/呼叫,通話　calling, call
呼叫尝试/嘗試性呼叫　call attempt

呼叫点/呼叫點　calling-in-point, CIP
呼叫各电台/呼叫各電臺　CQ
呼叫检查/呼叫檢查　calling check
呼叫信号/呼叫信號,叫通信號　calling signal
呼叫装置/呼叫按鈕　call button
呼救信号/呼救信號　calling help signal
呼气阻力/呼氣阻抗　expiratory resistance
呼损率/電話呼損率　percent of call loss
呼吸代偿障碍/呼吸代償失調　respiratory decompensation
呼吸阀/呼吸閥　breather valve, breathing valve
呼吸器/呼吸器　breathing apparatus
呼吸性货物/呼吸性貨物　respiratory goods
呼吸压力波动/呼吸壓力波動　breathing pressure fluctuation
弧度频率/圓週頻率,週率　radian frequency
弧焊机/電弧焊機　arc welder
弧形闸门/扇形閘門　tainter gate, sector gate
胡海昌-鹫津原理/胡[海昌]-鷲津原理　Hu-Washizu principle
胡克定律/虎克定律　Hook law
胡马雍陵/胡馬雍陵　Humayun tomb
胡同/胡同　hutong, alley
湖滨公园/湖濱公園,濱湖公園　lakeside park
湖池垦殖/湖池墾殖　lake bottom reclamation
湖沥青/湖瀝青　lake asphalt
湖泊/湖泊　lake
湖泊风景区/湖泊風景區　lake round scenic spot
湖泊景观/湖泊景觀　lake view
湖泊类/湖泊類　lake type
湖泊类水体/湖泊類水體　impoundment
湖泊水位-面积曲线/深度面積曲線　depth-area curve
湖相沉积/湖積黏土　lacustrine deposit
蝴蝶架/蝶形架　butterfly type frame
糊泥爆破法/覆土炸碎法　plaster shooting
[互]补色/[互]補色,餘色　complementary color
互不控制复原方式/被叫和主叫用戶雙方拆線　called and calling subscriber release
互感系数/互感係數　mutual inductance coefficient
互感阻抗/互感阻抗　mutual inductive impedance
互功率谱/交叉功率頻譜　cross-power spectrum
互光/變色燈　alternating light
互换/交換　interchange, austausch
互换性/互換性　interchangeability
互惠共生/互利共生　mutualistic symbiosis
互击喷嘴/互擊式噴嘴　unlike-impinging injector element

互见中/互見中　in sight of one another
互见中的船舶/船舶互見　vessel in sight of one another
互连/互連,内連　interconnect
互连条/互連符　inter connector
互调产物/互調產物　intermodulation products
互调干扰/互調干擾　intermodulation interference
互通式立交/交流道　interchange
互通式立交收费站/互換收費站　interchange toll station
互通式立体交叉/交流道　interchange
互引导/互指示　mutual designation
互有责任碰撞条款/雙邊過失碰撞條款　both to blame collision clause
户籍人口/設籍人口　registered population
户内变电所/户内式變電所,屋内變電所　indoor substation
户室比/户室比　plan type rate
户外壁灯/户外壁燈　outdoor wall lamp
户外变电站/屋外變電所　outdoor substation
户外游憩/户外遊憩,户外休閒　outdoor recreation
户外娱乐资源/户外娛樂資源　outdoor recreation resources
户型比/户型比　house type ratio, housing type composition
护岸/護岸　bank protection, bank revetment, shore protection
护岸林/護岸林　stream bank protection forest
护坝/副壩,前壩　counter dam
护背间隔/護背間隔　guard rail face gage
护背距离/護軌與護軌間距離　guard rail face gage, back gage
护壁板/木閘門,木圍堰　cleading
护城河/護城河,城壕　moat
护拱/護拱　back haunch fillet of arch
护轨/護軌　guard rail, check rail
护轨与心轨的查照间隔/鼻軌與護軌内側之間距　guard rail check gage
护角/護角鐵　corner guard
护栏/護欄　guard rail
护理单元/護理室　nursing unit
护轮带/護擋皮帶　guard belt
护轮槛/緣石　kerb, curbing
护面块体/消波塊,砌塊　block, armor block
护面墙/護面牆　facing wall
护坡/護坡,坡面防護　slope protection, revetment, pitching
护坡草坪/斜坡草坪　slope lawn

护[坡]道/護堤, 餞道, 餞堤　berm
护坡砖/護坡磚　slope brick
护墙/護牆, 堤岸襯牆　guard wall, chemise
护墙板/木閘門, 木圍堰　cleading
护热式平板热导仪/護熱式平板熱導計　guarded hot plate conductometer
护士站/護士站　nurse station
护送/船團護航　convoy escort
护坦/護坦, 護床　apron
护套/護套, 護皮　sheath
护筒/護筒　pile casting
护头装置/頭部防護裝置　head guard, head restraint
护尾雷达/機尾預警雷達　tail-warning radar
护卫舰/巡防艦　frigate
护卫艇/護航艇　escort boat
护舷材/護舷材, 碰墊　fender
护翼轮/機身外側垂直輪　outrigger wheel
护栅/欄柵　guard fence
护柱/護柱, 圍護椿　guard post
花车/花車　festooned vehicle
花带/花帶　flower belt
花粉培养/花粉培養　pollen culture
花粉污染/花粉汙染　pollen pollution
花岗石/花岡岩　granite
花岗岩/花岡岩　granite
花格架/花格架　trellis
花灌木/景觀灌木　landscape shrub
花卉/花卉[類]　herb, flower, flowers and plants
花卉疗法/花卉療法　flowers therapy
花架/花架　flower shelf, pergola, trellis
花窖/花窖　flower cellar
花结花坛/花結花壇　knot bed
花径/花徑　flower border
花境/花境　flower border
花境花卉/庭園植物　border plant
花篮梁/花籃梁　ledger beam
花蕾期/芽期　bud period
花篱/花籬　flower hedge
花旗松/洋松　Douglas fir
花水/急浪　rips
花台/花臺　flower-stand
花坛/花壇　flower bed
花坛分界隔板/花壇分界隔板　plastic bed divider
花坛植物/花壇植物　bedding plant
花桶/花桶　flower tub
花纹路/花紋路　pattern path
花药培养/花藥培養　anther culture
花艺设计/插花裝飾　flower design

花园/花園　garden
花园村/花園村　garden village
花园林荫路/花園林蔭路　garden avenue
花园路/公園[大]路　parkway
花园式屋顶绿化/花園式屋頂綠化　gardening roof greening, intensive roof greening
划痕/劃痕, 刮痕　scratch
划桨船/划槳船　row boat
划桨救生艇/搖槳推進救生艇　oar-propelled lifeboat
华白[指]数/韋比指數　Wobbe index, Wobbe number
华版/華版　carved panel
华表/華表　ornamental pillar, huabiao
华栱/華栱　huagong
华伦桁架/沃倫式構架　Warren truss
华清宫/華清宮　Hua-Qing Palace
华盛顿宪章/華盛頓憲章　Washington Charter
华氏阀装置/華氏閥動機構　Walschaerts valve gear
滑板/滑板　skate board
滑冰/滑冰　skating
滑冰场/溜冰場　outdoor ice skating rink
滑冰馆/滑冰館, 溜冰館　indoor ice skating rink
滑车/滑車　block
滑车组/滑車轆轤　tackle
滑床板/滑床板　slide plate, switch plate
滑道/滑道　launching way
滑道末端压力/軌端壓力　way end pressure
滑道逃逸/滑道逃脫　slide escape
滑道摇架/滑道托架　slipway cradle, slipway turn cradle
滑道转盘/滑道轉盤　slipway turntable
滑动船闸门/滑動船閘門　sliding lock gate
滑动带/滑動帶　slip zone
滑动干船坞门/滑動乾船塢門　sliding dry dock gate
滑动关节/滑動接合　sliding joint
滑动门/滑門, 拉門　sliding door
滑动面/滑動[平]面　slide plane, slide surface, slip surface
滑动模板/滑動式範本　slip form
滑动配合/滑動配合　slide fit
滑动破坏/滑動破壞　sliding failure
滑动三脚架/伸縮三腳架　sliding tripod
滑动式沉箱/滑行沈箱　sliding caisson
滑动式盘车机构/滑動式盤車裝置　sliding type barring mechanism
滑动圆弧法/滑動圓弧法　slip circle method
滑动轴承/滑動軸承, 普通軸承　plain bearing
滑动轴承箱/滑動軸承殼　sliding bearing housing

滑阀/滑閥　slide valve
滑阀导程/滑閥導程　lead of slide valve
滑杆/滑動梢　slip bar
滑钩/滑鉤　slip hook, pelican hook
滑轨/滑軌　slide rail
滑轨车/滑軌車　track sled
滑开型裂纹/滑移型裂紋　sliding mode of crack
滑块/滑塊　sliding block, slide, slipper
滑块制动器/塊狀軔, 塊狀刹車　block brake
滑溜测量仪/滑溜測量儀　skidometer
滑轮/頂滑車　head pulley
滑马/吊運車　traveller
滑模/滑動式模板　sliding form, slipform
滑模浇筑混凝土/滑模澆鑄　slipform concreting
滑模式混凝土路缘铺筑机/滑模式混凝土路緣鋪築機　slipform concrete curb paver
滑模式混凝土摊铺机/滑模式混凝土攤鋪機　slipform concrete paver
滑坡/滑坡, 山崩, 地滑　landslide, landslip
滑坡地段路基/滑坡地段路基　subgrade in slide
滑橇式起落架/橇形起落架　skid landing gear
滑升模板/滑動模板　slipform
滑失/滑流　slip
滑水运动/滑水運動　water-skiing
滑塌/滑動, 崩落　slide
滑台/滑臺　expansion shoe
滑翔/滑翔　glide
滑翔场/滑翔場　gliding field
滑翔机/滑翔機　glider
滑翔伞/滑翔傘　gliding parachute
滑翔运动/滑翔運動　gliding movement
滑巷/滑巷　lane slip
滑行/滑行, 滑翔　coasting, taxiing
滑行带/滑行道地帶　taxiway strip
滑行道/滑行道　taxiway
滑行道边灯/滑行道邊燈　taxiway edge light
滑行道标志/滑行道標線　taxiway marking
滑行道距离灯/滑行道距離燈　runway range marker light
滑行道中线灯/滑行道中心線燈　taxiway center line light
滑行灯/滑行[道]燈　taxi light
滑行段/滑行段　coasting-flight phase, cruising phase
滑行工况/滑行工況　coasting mode
滑行距离测定/滑行距離測定　coasting distance measurement
滑行路线/滑行起落航線　taxi circuit
滑行时间/滑行時間　coasting time
滑行试验/滑行試驗, 溜坡試驗　coasting test
滑行水道/滑行水道　taxi channel
滑行艇/滑行[快]艇, 水上快艇, 滑航艇　glider, planing boat
滑行引导标志/滑行導引標誌　taxiing-guidance sign
滑行引导系统/滑行引導系統　taxiing-guidance system, TGS
滑行姿态/滑行姿態　cruising attitude
滑行阻力测定/滑行阻力測定　coasting resistance measurement
滑雪运动/滑雪　skiing
滑移流/滑移流　slip flow
滑油泵/[潤]滑油泵　lubricating oil pump, oil pump
滑油舱/[潤]滑油櫃　lubricating oil tank
滑油加热器/滑油加熱器　lubricating oil heater
滑油间歇净化/滑油間歇淨化, 潤滑油分批淨化　lubricating oil batch purification
滑油净化系统/滑油淨化系統　lubricating oil purifying system
滑油冷却器/[潤]滑油冷卻器　lubricating oil cooler
滑油连续净化/潤滑油連續淨化　lubricating oil pass purification
滑油滤器/[潤]滑油過濾器　lubricating oil filter
滑油热交换器/滑油熱交換器　oil heat exchanger
滑油输送泵/[潤]滑油輸送泵　lubricating oil transfer pump
滑油通风器/油霧分離器　oil vent
滑油系统/滑油系統　lubricating oil system
滑油消耗率/滑油消耗率, 單位耗滑油量, 單位滑油消耗量　specific lubricating oil consumption
滑油泄放柜/滑油洩放櫃　lubricating oil drain tank
滑油泄放系统/滑油洩放系統　lubricating oil drain system
滑油注入管/[潤]滑油注入管　lubricating oil filling pipe
滑轴平开窗/滑軸平開窗　sliding projecting casement window
化肥厂/化肥廠　chemical fertilizer plant
化粪池/化糞池, 腐化槽　septic tank
化感作用/排拒作用, 相剋作用　allelopathy
化工厂/化[學]工廠　chemical plant
化合价/[化合]價　valence
化合物半导体太阳电池/化合物半導體太陽能電池　compound semiconductor solar cell
化合性余氯/結合性餘氯　combined residual chlorine
化石燃料/化石燃料, 礦物燃料　fossil fuel
化石植物/化石植物　fossil plant
化石植物学/化石植物學　fossil botany

化铣结构/化學銑製結構　chemical-milled structure
化学爆炸/化學爆炸　chemical explosion
化学测量/化學量測　chemical measurement
化学沉积/化學沈積,化學沈淬　chemical deposition, chemical sediment
化学除氧/化學除氧　chemical deoxidization
化学处理/化學處理　chemical treatment
化学处理法除锈/金屬防銹預處理　chemical rust removing
化学灯/[指距]化學燈　chemical light
化学电源/電化學電源　electrochemical power source
化学镀[膜]/化學電鍍　chemical plating, electroless plating
化学法预加应力/化學預力法　chemical prestressing
化学反应流/化學反應流　chemical reaction flow
化学反应速率/化學反應速率　chemical reaction rate
化学反应蓄热/化學反應加熱再生　chemical reaction heat regeneration
化学方程式/反應式　reaction formulas
化学方法测定/化學測流　chemical gauging
化学防治/化學防治　chemical control
化学防治法/化學防治法　chemical control method
化学肥料/化學肥料　chemical fertilizer
化学腐蚀/化學腐蝕,化學侵蝕　chemical corrosion
化学灌浆/藥液灌漿　chemical grouting
化学火箭发动机/化學[燃料]火箭發動機　chemical rocket engine, chemical rocket motor
化学计算混合比/化學計量混合比　stoichiometric mixture ratio
化学灭火器/化學滅火器　chemical fire extinguisher
化学能/化學能　chemical energy
化学品仓库/化學材料倉庫　chemical material warehouse
化学品船/化學品船　chemical cargo ship, chemical carrier, chemical tanker
化学气相沉积/化學蒸汽沈積　chemical vapor deposition, CVD
化学气相渗透/化學氣相滲透　chemical vapor infiltration
化学恰当比/化學計算比率　stoichiometric ratio
化学侵蚀/化學侵蝕　chemical attack
化学清洗/化學清洗　chemical cleaning
化学溶液槽/藥品溶液槽　chemical solution tank
化学实验室/化學實驗室　chemistry laboratory
化学推进/化學推進　chemical propulsion
化学污泥/化學汙泥　chemical sludge
化学物添加系统/化學品添加系統　chemical addition system
化学铣切/化學蝕銑　chemical milling
化学纤维绳/合成纖維索　synthetic fiber rope
化学需氧量/化學需氧量　chemical oxygen demand, COD
化学氧发生器/化學氧發生器　chemical oxygen generator
化学氧化/化學氧化　chemical oxidation
化学氧贮存/化學氧儲存　chemical oxygen storage
化学诱变/化學突變誘發,化學物誘變作用　chemical mutagenesis
化学预应力混凝土/化學預應力混凝土　chemical prestressed concrete
化学增压系统/化學加壓系統　chemical pressurization system
化学注浆/藥液灌漿　chemical grouting
化验/化學分析　chemical analysis
化妆室/演出準備室,更衣室,化妝間　dressing room
划定区域交通量调查/劃定區域交通量調查　cordon count study
划界渔业/區劃漁業　demarcated fishery
划线/劃線,標線　layout, laying out, marking
划线机/劃線機　road marking machine
画舫/畫舫　painted pleasure boat
画幅式相机/像框攝影機　frame camera
画廊/藝廊　gallery
话传电报业务/話傳電報業務　voice messaging service
话传用户电报/話傳交換電報　phone telex, PHONETEX
话带传输/聲帶傳輸　voice-band transmission
话路/電話通道　telephone channel
话频/話頻　voice frequency
话务量/話務,電話業務　telephone traffic
话音侧音/話音側音　speech side tone
话音记录器/通話記錄器　voice recorder
话音指令控制系统/語音命令系統　voice command system
还船/還船　redelivery of vessel
还原法/還原法　reduction method
环保产业/環保產業　environmental protection industry
环保植物/環保植物　environment protecting plant
环壁阻力损失/環週損失　annulus drag loss
环槽铆钉铆接/環槽鉚釘鉚接　hooked riveting with lock rivet
环刀取样器/薄管取樣器　foil sampler
环岛/圓環島,環形交叉路,環形交通樞紐　roundabout, rotary island, roundabout island

环动喷灌器/環動噴灌器　circle sprinkler
环封闸门/環封閘門　ring-seal gate
环缝伞/環縫降落傘　ring slot parachute
环缝式喷注器/環縫式噴注器　ring slot injector
环箍钢筋/閉合箍筋　hooping
环管形燃烧室/環筒形燃燒器　can annular type combustor
环焊/環焊　boxing
环化橡胶/環化橡膠　thermoprene
环节多角形/環多角形　link polygon
环境/環境　environment
环境保护/環境保護,環境保育　environmental conservation, environmental protection
环境保护植物/環境保護植物　environmental conservation plant
环境测试舱/環境試驗室　environmental test chamber
环境恶化/環境惡化,環境衰敗　environmental deterioration
环境法律委员会/環境法委員會　Commission on Environmental Law, CEL
环境仿真/環境模擬　environmental simulation
环境分区/環境區　environment zone
环境风险评价/環境風險評估　environmental risk assessment
环境腐蚀/環境腐蝕　environmental corrosion
环境工程/環境工程[學]　environment engineering
环境工艺学/環境技術　environmental technology
环境功能区划/環境功能區劃,環境功能分區　environmental function zoning, environmental functional zoning
环境管理/環境管理　environmental management
环境荷载/環境負荷　environmental load
环境或然论/環境或然論　environmental probabilism
环境技术/環境技術　environmental technology
环境监测/環境監測,環境監視　environmental monitor, environmental monitoring
环境监测船/環境監測船　environmental monitoring ship, environmental monitoring vessel
环境监控系统/環境監視系統　environmental monitoring system
环境经济社会政策委员会/環境經濟社會政策委員會　Commission on Environmental, Economic and Social Policy, CEESP
环境决定论/環境決定論　environmental determinism
环境科学/環境科學　environmental science
环境可能论/環境可能論　environmental possibilism
环境空气质量标准/環境空氣品質　ambient air quality
环境控制畜舍/自動控制環境畜舍　controlled environment livestock house
环境控制和生命保障分系统/環境控制和生命保障分系統　environmental control and life support subsystem
环境控制系统/環境控制系統　environmental control system
环境力矩/環境轉矩　environmental torque
环境伦理/環境倫理　environmental ethics
环境绿化/環境綠化　environmental greening
环境模拟试验/環境模擬試驗　simulated environment test
环境评价/環境評估　environmental assessment
环境热负荷/環境熱負載　environmental heat load
环境认知/環境認知,環境識知,環境知覺　environmental perception, environmental cognition
环境容量/環境容量　environment capacity, environmental capacity
环境色/環境色彩　environmental color
环境色适应/環境色適應　environmental color adaptation
环境设计/環境設計　environmental design
环境设计余量/環境設計安全係數　environment design margin
环境设施用地/環境設施用地　land for environmental facility
环境试验/環境試驗　environmental test
环境适宜性/環境適宜性　environment fitness
环境适应性/環境適宜性　environment fitness
环境舒适度/舒適度　comfort degree
环境损害/環境危害,環境公害　environmental hazard
环境特性/環境特性　environmental characteristics
环境条件/環境條件　environmental conditions
环境卫生设施/環衛設施　environment sanitation facility
环境卫星/環境衛星　environment satellite
环境温度/環境溫度,周圍溫度　ambient temperature
环境污染/環境汙染　environmental pollution
环境污染负荷/環境汙染負荷　environmental pollution load
环境效益/環境效益　environmental benefit
环境效应/環境效應　environmental effect
环境协调区/環境協調區,協調區域　environmental coordination zone, coordination area

环境心理学/環境心理學　environmental psychology
环境行为/環境行爲　environmental behaviour
环境-行为研究/環境-行爲研究　environment-behavior studies
环境学派/環境學派　environmental school
环境压力/環境壓力,周圍壓力,環境緊迫　ambient pressure, environmental stress
环境艺术/環境藝術　environmental art
环境影响评价/環境影響評估　environmental impact assessment, environmental impact evaluation
环境应力/環境壓力　environmental stress
环境应力筛选/環境壓力篩選　environmental stress screening, ESS
环境预示/環境預測　environment prediction
环境园艺学/環境園藝學　environmental horticulture
环境载荷/環境負荷　environmental load
环境噪声/環境噪聲,環境噪音,環境雜訊　environmental noise, ambient noise
环境噪声标准/環境噪音標準　environmental noise standard
环境噪声侧音/環境噪音側音　ambient noise side tone
环境噪声等级分布/環境噪音等級分布　distribution of environmental noise level
环境噪声自动监测系统/環境噪音自動監視系統　environmental noise automatic monitoring system
环境振动/環境振動　environment vibration
环境振动标准/環境振動標準　environmental vibration standard
环境知觉/環境知覺　environmental perception
环境植物学/環境植物學　environmental botany
环境指示者/環境指標　environmental indicator
环境质量/環境品質　environmental quality
环境质量指数/環境品質指標　environmental quality index
环境治疗/環境治療[法]　environmental therapy
环境自净作用/環境自淨作用　environmental self-purification
环壳/環殼　toroid shell
环量/環流　circulation
环裂/輪裂　ring shake, annular shake
环流理论/環流理論　circulation theory
环路电阻/回線電阻,環線電阻　loop resistance
环球航行/環航　circum-navigation
环绕式舞台/環繞式舞臺　stage in the round
环施/環施　ring fertilizer
环索/環索,回頭索　endless rope
环透式结构/環透式結構　cave mode
环卫工程/環境衛生工程　environmental sanitary engineering
环卫停车场/[環境]衛生停車場　sanitation truck parking
环线/環路,環狀公路　loop, belt highway
环向缠绕/環箍纏繞　hoop winding
环向应力/環箍應力　hoop stress
环销/環樺　ring dowel
环行公路/環狀公路　circumferential highway
环行交叉/環形交叉路,環形交通樞紐　roundabout
环形道路/環狀道路　ring road, loop road, circumferential road
环形道路网/環道系統　ring road system
环形道路系统/環形道路系統　circular road system
环形放射式道路系统/環形輻射式道路系統　ring and radial road system
环形供电/環形供電　ring circuit power supply
环形交叉/環狀交叉　rotary intersection, roundabout
环形交路/循環選路　circular routing
环形立交/環形立交　rotary interchange
环形燃烧室/環形燃燒室　annular combustor, toroidal combustion chamber
环形赛道/環形賽道,巡回路線　circuit
环形枢纽/環形樞紐　loop-type junction terminal
环形天线/環形天線　loop antenna
环形天线装调误差/環形天線對準誤差　loop alignment error
环形通气管/環形通氣管　loop vent
环形网[络]/環狀網路　ring network
环形线圈式车辆检测器/環形線圈車輛偵測器　loop vehicle detector
环形线网/環形線網　loop type public transport network
环形匝道/環形匝道　loop ramp
环形止水阀门/環封閘門　ring-seal gate
环形钻架/環狀鑽孔　ring drilling
环氧涂料/環氧塗層　epoxy coating
环氧树脂/環氧樹脂,環養膠　epoxy resin, epoxide resin
环照灯/環照燈　all-round light
环植/環植　circular planting
环状供电/環狀供電　looply connected power supply
环状管网/環狀管網,格狀網路　gridiron network
环状街道/環狀街道　ring street, loop street
环状绿地/環狀綠地　ring shaped green belt
环状绿型/環狀綠型　annular green space
环状天线测向器/環形天線測向儀　loop direction

finder
环状星云/環狀星雲　annular nebula
缓变参数/緩變參數　slow varying parameter, parameter requiring low response
缓冲层/緩衝層,過渡層,中間層　cushion layer, buffer layer
缓冲带/緩衝帶　buffering stripe
缓冲杆/緩衝桿,減震支柱　shock strut, buffer rod
缓冲罐/緩衝櫃,緩衝水槽　surge tank
缓冲护栏/緩衝護欄　cushion guardail
缓冲间/緩衝室　buffer room
缓冲梁/緩衝梁,防撞梁　buffer beam
缓冲绿地/緩衝綠地　buffer green space
缓冲器/緩衝器　buffer
缓冲器反弹/緩衝器反彈　draft gear recoil
缓冲器能量吸收率/緩衝器能量吸收率　rate of energy absorbed by draft gear
缓冲器容量/緩衝器容量　draft gear capacity
缓冲器箱体/緩衝器箱體　draft gear housing
缓冲器行程/緩衝器行程　draft gear travel
缓冲器预紧力/緩衝器預緊力　draft gear initial compression
缓冲器阻抗力/緩衝器阻抗力　draft gear reaction force at rating travel
缓冲区/緩衝[區]　buffer zone, buffer, transition zone
缓冲弹簧/緩衝彈簧　buffer spring
缓冲装置/緩衝裝置　shock absorber
缓冲作用/緩衝作用　cushioning effect
缓动继电器/緩動繼電器,慢动作繼電器　slow-acting relay
缓发中子/遲延中子　delayed neutron
缓放继电器/緩釋繼電器　slow release relay
缓放时间/緩放時間　slow release time
缓和坡度/緩坡　slight grade, flat grade, easy grade
缓和坡段/緩和坡段　transitional grade
缓和区间/緩和區間　transition part
缓和曲线/緩和曲線,過渡曲線,分界曲線　transition curve, easement curve
缓和曲线半径变更率/緩和曲線半徑變更率　rate of easement curvature, rate of transition curve
缓和照明/適應照明　adaptation lighting
缓解波速/緩解波速　release propagation rate
缓解部/緩解部　release portion
缓解阀/排出閥,放洩閥　release valve
缓解停车/緩解停車　stopping at release
缓流/憩流,亞臨速流　slack stream, subcritical flow
缓流航道/憩流航道　slack current channel

缓凝高效减水剂/緩凝高幅度減水摻合物　set retarding superplasticizer
缓凝减水剂/緩凝減水摻合物　set retarding and water reducing admixture
缓凝水泥/緩凝水泥　slow setting cement
缓跑径/緩跑徑,慢跑大道　jogging track
缓坡地段/平緩坡度　section of easy grade, section of gentle slope
缓坡段/緩坡段　transition slope
缓坡缘石/斜緣石　lip curb
缓蚀/緩蝕　corrosion inhibition
缓蚀剂/緩蝕劑,抑制劑,阻止劑　inhibiter, corrosion inhibitor
缓释肥/緩釋性肥料　slow release fertilizer
缓松/緩鬆,回舵　ease
缓吸继电器/緩吸繼電器　slow pick-up relay
缓吸时间/緩吸時間　slow pick-up time
缓圆点/緩圓點　point of spiral to curve, SC
缓直点/緩直點　point of spiral to tangent, ST
幻日/幻日　anthelion
幻通谐振变压器/幻路諧振變壓器　phantom resonant transformer
幻月/幻月　antiselena
换板/換板　changing plate
换侧/換邊　change side of double line
换乘枢纽/換乘樞紐　junction of park and shift
换乘站/轉運站　transfer station, interchange station
换挡/換擋　changeover governor
换档/齒輪換擋,齒輪變速　gear shifting
换地计划/換地計劃　replotting program
换行/換行,饋行　line feed
换件大修/換件大修　component exchange repair
换能器/換能器,轉換器,轉發器　transducer
换能器充磁/轉變器充磁　magnetization of transducer
换能器指向性/轉換器指向性　transducer directivity
换盆机/換盆機　repotting machine
换气/換氣　air change
换气窗/通氣窗　vent window
换气次数/通氣率　ventilation rate
换气过程/換氣過程　scavenging period
换气-压缩行程/驅氣-壓縮衝程　scavenging-compression stroke
换气装置/通氣層,通氣管　breather
换热面积/受熱面積　heating surface area
换热器/熱交換器　heat exchanger
换水孔/換水孔　exchanging water hole
换算吨公里成本/換算噸公里成本　cost of converted

ton-kilometer
换算交通量/車輛折算係數　equivalent traffic volume
换算截面/換算截面　transformed section, converted section
换算均布活载/等代均布動載荷,等效均布動載荷　equivalent uniform live load
换算坡度/相當坡度,等值坡度　equivalent grade
换算图表/換算圖表　conversion chart
换算线路长度/換算線路長度　equivalent track kilometerage
换算箱/二十英尺貨櫃當量　twenty-feet equivalent units, TEU
换算重量/換算重量　converted weight
换算周转量/換算週轉[量]　converted turnover
换算走行公里/換算走行公里　converted running kilometers
换算阻力/換算阻力　converted resistance
换土/換土　replacement of earth, change soil, soil replacement
换土垫层/換土墊層　cushion
换向/逆轉　reversing
换向机构/逆轉裝置　reversing gear, reversing arrangement
换向极铁心/換向極鐵心,間極鐵心　interpole core
换向极线圈/換向極線圈,間極線圈　interpole coil
换向联锁/逆轉聯鎖　reversing interlock
换向片/換向片,整流片　commutator segment
换向起动程序/換向起動程式　reverse starting sequence
换向器/換向器,整流器　commutator
换向时间/換向時間　reversing time
换向试验/逆轉試驗　reversing test
换向伺服器/回動伺服電動機　reversing servomotor
换向限止阀/換向限制閥　standstill detector valve
换向轴/逆轉軸,倒車軸　reversing shaft
换相电抗器/整流電抗器　commutation reactor
换相电容器/換相電容器,整流電容器,加速[響應]電容器　commutating capacitor
换相联结/換相連結　exchange phase connection, phase alternating connection
换药室/病區處置室,醫療室　dressing change room
换帧频率/換幀頻率　frame refresh frequency
换证检验/換證檢驗　renewal survey
换装线/交換裝載線　interchange loading track
换装站/中轉站　transhipment station
荒地/裸露地　barren land
荒漠化/沙漠化　desertification
荒漠土[壤]/荒漠土,沙漠土　desert soil
荒漠植物/沙漠植物　eremophyte
荒野地保护区/荒野地保護區　wilderness area
皇城/皇城,宫城　huang cheng, royal town, imperial city
皇家园林/皇家園林　royal garden, imperial garden
黄白交角/白道斜度　obliquity of the moon path
黄赤交角/黄道斜度　obliquity of the ecliptic
黄道/黄道　ecliptic
黄道带/黄道帶　zodiac
黄极/黄道天極　ecliptic pole
黄金比/黄金比率,黄金分割　golden section
黄金分割/黄金分割,黄金比率　golden section
黄金散射花园/黄金散射花園　gold-scattering garden
黄经/黄經　ecliptic longitude
黄麻填料/麻纖崁縫　jute packing
黄麻填塞/麻纖填塞　jute-stop
黄壤/黄壤　yellow soil
黄石/黄石　yellow stone
黄石国家公园/黄石國家公園　Yellowstone National Park
黄铜/黄銅　brass
黄土/黄土　loess
黄纬/黄緯　ecliptic latitude
黄焰/黄焰　yellow flame
簧上重量/[彈]簧上重量　suspended weight, sprung weight
簧下重量/[彈]簧下重量　non-suspended weight, unsprung weight
晃荡/沖激,晃擊　sloshing
晃动挡板/晃動擋板　slosh barrier
晃动力/晃動力　slosh force
晃动力矩/晃動力矩　slosh torque
晃动力学模型/晃動力學模型　mechanical model of slosh
晃动频率/晃動頻率　slosh frequency
晃动抑制/晃動抑制　slosh suppression
晃动质量/晃動質量　slosh mass
晃动周期/晃動週期　slosh cycle
晃动阻尼/晃動阻尼　slosh damping
晃动阻尼比/晃動阻尼比　damping ratio of slosh
晃击/晃擊,沖激　sloshing
灰度等级/灰度[等級]　gray level, gray scale
灰分[含量]/灰分含量,含灰量　ash content
灰分含量试验/灰分含量測定　ash content test
灰分元素/灰分元素　ash element
灰化作用/灰土化　podsolization

灰浆/灰漿,砂漿,水泥漿　grout
灰浆搅拌机/灰漿攪拌機　mortar mixer
灰浆喷射器/灰漿噴射器　mortar sprayer
灰浆输送泵/灰漿輸送泵　mortar conveying pump
灰阶/灰階　gray scale
灰空间/灰空間　gray space, blur space
灰色/青灰色　grey
灰色控制系统/灰色控制系統　grey control system
灰色系统理论/灰色系統理論　grey system theory
灰视/灰視　greyout
灰水/洗滌水　greywater
灰体/灰體　gray body
灰土/灰土　lime soil
灰土换填夯实法/灰土換填夯實法　method of lime-soil replacement and tamping
灰雾度/霧度　fog
灰线/圓角模　moulding
灰箱/灰盤　ash pan
灰铸铁/灰[口]生鐵　gray pig iron, gray cast iron
挥发分含量/揮發物含量　volatile matter content
挥发分含量试验/揮發物含量試驗　volatile matter content test
挥发性的/揮發性　volatile
挥发性固体/揮發性固體　volatile solid
挥发性酸/揮發酸　volatile acid
挥发性物质/揮散物質　volatile matter
挥发性有机化合物/揮發性有機化合物　volatile organic compound, VOC
挥舞变距耦合系数/揮舞變距耦合係數　pitch-flap coupling coefficient
挥舞铰/翼動鉸　flapping hinge
恢复/恢復,復原,回復　restoration
恢复规程/恢復程式　recovery procedure
恢复力曲线/恢復力曲線　hysteretic curve, restoring force curve
恢复通车/恢復通車　restoring traffic
恢复温度/恢復溫度　recovery temperature
恢复系数/恢復係數　recovery coefficient, coefficient of restitution
辉光放电流动显示/發光放電流動可視化　flow visualization by luminescence
辉绿岩/輝綠岩　diabase
回波/回波　echo
回波损耗/回波損耗,反射波損耗　return loss
回波锁定/回波鎖定　echo lock
回波效应/回波效應　echo effect
回差/[儀表]回差　hysteresis
回车/回车　carriage return
回车场/轉向環道　turn around loop
回车场地/回車場地　turn around space
回车道/回車道　turn around loop
回程/回行衝程　return stroke
回程货/回程貨　return cargo
回程系数/回程係數　return factor
回答脉冲/應答脈衝　reply pulse
回答旗/回答旗,答應旗　answering pendant
回动拉杆/回動拉桿　reverse pull rod
回动手把/回動手把,換向桿,回動桿　reverse lever
回舵/回舵,鬆舵　ease her
回舵阻力/回舵阻力　pull-out resistance
回风/回風　return air
回风道/回風管道　air return duct
回复开关/回復開關　recall switch
回灌井/注水井,補注井　injection well, recharging well
回归保持/遞回保持　recursion keeping
回归潮/回歸潮　tropic tide
回归分析/回歸分析　regression analysis
回归轨道/回歸軌道　recursive orbit, tropical orbit
回归习惯/回歸習性　homing behavior
回归与相关分析/回歸與相關分析　regression and correlation analysis
回火/回火,逆火　flashback, back fire
回火脆性/回火脆性　temper brittleness
回火色/回火色　temper color
回廊/迴廊　cloister, loggia
回力比/反饋比　feedback ratio
回铃音/回鈴音　ring back tone
回流/退潮,逆流　reflux
回流比/回流比　recirculation ratio
回流操作/回流操作　recirculation operation
回流管/回流連接　backflow connection
回流区/回流區,再循環區　recirculation zone, recirculating zone
回流燃烧室/逆流燃燒室　reverse flow combustor
回流扫气/環流掃氣,環狀驅氣　loop scavenging
回流污泥/流回汙泥,回鱗泥　return sludge, returned sludge
回流污染/回流汙染　backflow pollution
回流线/回流線,回[路導]線　return wire
回路时间/回路時間　loop time
回路阻值/回路抵抗值　loop resistance value
回汽刹车/回汽剎車　reverse steam brake
回迁房/迴遷住宅　relocated housing
回热度/回熱器有效性　regenerator effectiveness
回热器/回熱器,再生器　regenerator

回热式汽轮机/回熱式蒸汽渦輪機,再生式渦輪機　regenerative turbine, regenerative steam turbine
回热循环燃气轮机/回熱循環燃氣渦輪機　regenerative cycle gas turbine
回扫时间/返馳時間　flyback time
回砂/回砂　sand sweeping
回砂机/回砂機　sand recovering machine
回升/回昇　come up
回声/回聲　echo
回声测冰仪/測冰儀　ice fathometer
回声测量船/回聲測量船　echo sounding boat
回声测深/回音測深　echo sounding
回声测深仪/回聲測深儀　echo sounder, acoustic depth finder
回收/回收,恢復　recovery
回收方式/恢復模式　recovery mode
回收分系统/回收子系統　recovery subsystem
回收率/採取率　recovery ratio
回收片盒/回收片盒　recovery cassette
回收区/回收區　recovery area
回收伞/回收傘　recovery parachute
回收索/回收索　recovery line
回收型照相侦察卫星/回收型照相偵察衛星　recoverable photo reconnaissance satellite
回收遥测/恢復遙測　recovery telemetry
回输振荡/回輸振盪　return transfer oscillations
回水/還歸水　return water
回水管/回水管　water return pipe
回送空箱/回送空箱　return empty container
回缩/回縮　retraction
回弹/彈回量　spring back
回弹模量/彈能模數　modulus of resilience
回弹曲线/回彈曲線　rebound curve
回弹弯沉/回彈彎沈　rebound deflection
回弹仪/回彈儀,回彈計　rebound tester, Schmidt hammer, resiliometer
回填/回填充　back filling
回填土/回填土　backfill
回填土密实度检验/回填土密實度檢驗　earth fill compactness inspection
回填土压实/回填夯實　backfill compaction
回填压实机/回填夯實機　backfill tamper
回填注浆/背填灌漿　backfill grouting
回头缆/滑索　slip wire, slip rope
回头曲线/反面線圈　switch back curve, reverse loop
回旋[曲]线/迴旋曲線,緩和曲線　clothoid
回旋水域/迴船場,迴翔水域　turning basin
回旋头/迴旋頭　swing head
回旋钻/磨鑽　abrasion drill
回用水/再生水,回收水　reclaimed water
回油阀式喷油泵/溢流閥式噴射泵　spill-valve injection pump
回油孔式喷油泵/布氏噴油泵　Bosch injection pump
回淤强度/沈降強度　sedimentation intensity, sedimentation rate
回折波图/回折波圖　diffracted diagram
回转/迴轉,旋轉,水平轉　rotary, slewing
回转不均匀/迴轉不規律度　cycle irregularity
回转场地/旋轉[磁]場　rotary field
回转[吊杆]绞车/[吊桿]迴旋絞車　slewing winch
回转斗成孔机/迴轉斗成孔機　drilling bucket boring machine
回转横倾角/迴轉傾側　heel on turning
回转迹线/迴旋跡線　turning path
回转流/旋轉流　rotary current
回转罗盘/迴轉式羅盤儀　gyroscopic compass
回转平台/旋轉臺,旋轉盤　turn table
回转起重机/旋轉吊車　rotary crane
回转区域/迴轉圈,旋迴圈,迴旋圈　turning circle
回转区域半径/迴旋圈半徑　turning circle radius
回转式掘削机械/迴轉挖泥機　rotary excavator
回转式空气预热器/迴轉式空氣預熱器,再生式空氣加熱器,迴轉式空氣預熱器　regenerative air heater, rotary air heater
回转式盘车机构/旋轉式盤車裝置　rotary type barring mechanism
回转式起动空气分配器/旋轉式起動空氣分配器　rotary starting air distributor
回转式扫气阀/轉動驅氣閥　rotary scavenging valve
回转式压缩机/旋轉式空氣壓縮機　rotary compressor
回转试验/迴旋試驗　turning trial, turning test
回转误差/轉彎誤差　turn error
回转叶片式制冷压缩机/轉動滑葉冷凍壓縮機　rotary sliding-vane refrigerating compressor
回转仪/迴轉儀　gyroscope
回转直径/迴旋直徑　tactical diameter, steady turning diameter
回转中心/迴轉中心　center of turning circle
回转周期/迴旋週期　turning period
回转轴/旋轉軸　axis of revolution
洄游路线/洄游路線　fishing migration route
毁灭性地震/激震　ruinous earthquake
毁灭性破坏/劇變崩陷　catastrophic collapse

毁伤概率/命中率　kill probability
汇/匯[座]　sink
汇合端/匯合端　merging end
汇合通气管/通氣管頭　vent header
汇接电话所/電話匯接局　tandem telephone office
汇流/沈流　sink flow
汇流标志/匯流標誌　converging sign
汇流排/匯流排　busbar
汇流时间/集流時間　concentration time, time of concentration
汇流条/匯流條,匯流排,母線　busbar
汇水面积/集水面積,集水區,流域　catchment area, water collecting area, drainage area
汇水区流域特征调查/匯水區流域特徵調查　survey of catchment basin characteristic
会车/會車　meeting
会车间隔时间/會車間隔時間　time interval for two meeting trains at station
会馆/會館　guild hall, native place association, huiguan
会客室/會客室,接待室　reception room
会客厅/會客室,接待室　reception room
会签栏/會簽欄　signature column
会让站/會讓站　passing station
会日点/會日點　junction
会所/會所建築　club house, club building
会议电话/會議電話　conferencing call
会议电话分机/會議電話分機　conference telephone subset
会议电话汇接机/會議電話匯接臺　conference telephone tandem board
会议电话总机/會議電話總機　conference telephone central board
会议电视系统/會議電視系統　conference television system
会议调度/會議調度　conference dispatching
会议纪要/會議紀要　meeting minute
会议旅游/會議旅遊　conference tourism
会议室/會議室,研討室　meeting room, conference room
会议厅/會議廳　assembly hall, conference room
会遇/會遇　encounter
会遇率/會遇率　encounter rate
会展中心/會展中心　convention and exhibition center
绘景间/繪景間　painter room
绘图笔/繪圖筆　drawing pen
绘图仪/作圖儀　plotting instrument

绘图纸/繪圖紙　drawing paper
彗星/彗星　comet
彗[形像]差/彗形像差　coma
惠康原理/惠康原理　Whecon principle
惠普尔缓冲屏/惠普爾緩衝屏　Whipple bumper shield
昏影终/曙昏終了　end of evening twilight
浑水冲刷/渾水沖刷　scour with sediment motion
混播草坪/混播草坪　mix-sowing turf
混合/混合,拌合　mixing
混合比/混合比,拌合比　mixture ratio, mixing ratio
混合比调节器/混合比調節器　mixture ratio regulator
混合编队/複列編隊　compound formation
混合材/混合材料　blending material
混合采光/混合採光　mixed daylighting
混合草坪/混合草坪　mixed lawn
混合长度/混合長度　mixing length
混合潮/混合潮　mixed tide
混合池/混合池　mixing basin
混合床离子交换/混床離子交換　mixed bed ion exchange
混合导航系统/混合導航系統　hybrid navigation system
混合电源/混合電源,複合電源　hybrid power source, AC-battery power source
混合定律/混合法則　mixing rule
混合多次冲击防护屏/混合多次衝擊遮罩　hybrid multi-shock shield
混合法/混合法　mixed method
混合废水/組合廢水　combined wastewater
混合功能区理论/混合功能區理論　mixed-use area theory
混合供电制/混合供電制　AC-battery power supply system
混合骨架式/混合肋骨系統　combined frame system, mixed frame system
混合硅酸盐水泥/混合矽酸鹽水泥　mixed Portland cement
混合航线算法/混合航法　composite sailing
混合花境/混合花境　mixed border
混合货/混合貨物,混載貨　mixed cargo
混合交通/混合車流　mixed traffic
混合结构/混合結構　mixed structure
混合料/混合物　mixture
混合料斗式升送机/混合料斗式昇送機　mixture hopper elevator
混合料刮板升送机/混合料刮板昇送機,混合料刮板

輸送器　mixture slat elevator
混合列车/混合列車　mixed train
混合流/混合[潮]流　mixed current, mixed airflow
混合气体保护焊/混合氣體[保護]焊　mixed gas welding
混合器/混合器,調合機　mixer
混合桥面斜拉桥/混合橋面斜拉橋　cable stayed bridge with mixed deck
混合区/混合採訪區　mixed zone
混合砂浆/複合砂漿　composite mortar
混合社区/社會混合社區　mixed community
混合式/混合式　comprehensive style
混合式道路系统/混合式道路系統　combinationi-type road system
混合式防波堤/混合防波堤　compound breakwater
混合式货场/混合式貨場　mixed type freight yard
混合式给水预热装置/混合給水加熱器　mixed feed water heater
混合式凝汽器/混合冷凝器　mixing condenser
混合式配电系统/複合型配電系統　combined type distribution system
混合式热交换器/混合式熱交換器　mixed heat exchanger
混合式收费系统/混合式收費系統　mixed toll system
混合式水加热器/混合式水汽加熱器　vapor and water mixing heater
混合式通风/結合吹通風排氣系統　combination of blowing and exhaust system of ventilation
混合式挖泥机/複式挖土機　compound dredger
混合式园林/混合式園林　mixed garden style, mixed style garden
混合室/混合室　mixing chamber
混合水/結合水　combined water
混合提单/合運載貨證券　omnibus bill of lading
混合调节/混合調節　mixing governing
混合[推进剂]火箭发动机/混合推進劑火箭發動機,混成推進劑火箭引擎　hybrid propellant rocket engine, hybrid propellant rocket motor
混合线圈/混合線圈,拼合線圈　hybrid coil
混合形枢纽/複合型樞紐　combined type junction terminal
混合型花境/混合型花境　hybrid flower border
混合选择法/混合選擇,集團選擇　bulk selection
混合循环/混合[式]循環　mixed cycle, hybrid cycle
混合液/混合液　mixed liquor
混合液力机械传动/混合液力機械傳動　hydromechanical drive with direct step

混合液中的悬浮固体/混合液懸浮固體　mixed liquor suspended solid
混合用地/混合用地　land for mixed use
混合元/混合元素　mixed element
混合照明/混合照明　mixed lighting
混交林/混交林,混合林　mixed forest
混流泵/混流泵　mixed flow pump
混流式水轮机/混流水渦輪　mixing flow turbine
混煤/混煤　mixed coal
混凝/混凝　coagulation flocculation
混凝土/混凝土　concrete
混凝土板路面/混凝土路面板　concrete slab pavement
混凝土保护层/混凝土保護層　concrete cover
混凝土保护层测量仪/混凝土保護層量測儀　concrete cover meter
混凝土泵车/混凝土泵車　concrete pump truck
混凝土泵送法/混凝土澆灌法　concreting by pumping
混凝土表面泌水/混凝土表面泌水　surface weeping of concrete
混凝土布料杆/混凝土塔式機械臂　concrete placing boom
混凝土布料机/混凝土攤鋪機　concrete spreader
混凝土厂/混凝土拌和廠　concrete plant
混凝土沉箱/混凝土沈箱　concrete caisson
混凝土船/混凝土船　concrete ship
混凝土大板结构/混凝土大板結構　large panel concrete structure
混凝土单桩支撑/混凝土單樁支撐　concrete pile support
混凝土电热养生/混凝土通電養護　electric curing of concrete
混凝土垫层/混凝土底板　concrete subslab
混凝土吊斗/混凝土吊斗　concrete lifting bucket
混凝土封底/混凝土封底　bottom sealing by concreting
混凝土构件振动成型机/混凝土構件振動成型機　concrete member jolt moulding machine
混凝土管/混凝土管　concrete pipe
混凝土管桩/混凝土管樁　concrete pipe pile
混凝土轨枕/混凝土軌枕　concrete sleeper, concrete tie
混凝土回弹试验/混凝土回彈試驗　rebound test of concrete
混凝土碱集料反应/鹼性骨材反應,鹼骨料反應,鹼[質]粒料反應　alkali aggregate reaction
混凝土搅拌车/[混凝土]拌和車　truck mixer

[混凝土]搅拌船/混凝土攪拌船,浮動混凝土攪拌站 floating mixer, floating concrete mixer, floating concrete mixing plant
混凝土搅拌机/混凝土攪拌機,混凝土拌合機,混凝土混合機 concrete mixer
混凝土搅拌[卡]车/拌和車 agitating lorry
混凝土搅拌楼/混凝土攪拌樓,混凝土拌和廠 concrete mixing plant, concrete batching and mixing tower
混凝土搅拌设备/混凝土攪拌設備,混凝土拌和廠 concrete mixing plant, concrete agitating equipment
混凝土搅拌[运输]车/車裝混合機,具混凝土泵的攪拌車 concrete mixing and transporting car, truck mixer, transit mixer
混凝土搅拌站/混凝土攪拌站 concrete batching and mixing plant
混凝土接缝密封机/灌縫機,封縫機 concrete joint sealing machine
混凝土结构/混凝土結構 concrete structure
混凝土结构防火涂料/混凝土結構防火塗料 fire resisting coating for concrete structure
混凝土锯/鋸縫機 concrete saw
混凝土空心板成型机/混凝土空心板成型機 concrete hollow slab moulding machine
混凝土块防波堤/混凝土塊防波堤 concrete block breakwater
混凝土块路面/混凝土塊路面 concrete block pavement
混凝土块铺面/混凝土塊鋪面 concrete block pitching
混凝土梁滑模浇筑设备/滑模式混凝土攤鋪機 concrete beam slipform device
混凝土裂纹/混凝土裂縫 concrete cracks
混凝土流动性试验/混凝土流動性試驗 concrete fluidity test
混凝土路面/混凝土路面 concrete pavement
混凝土路面拉毛机/混凝土路面拉伸締卷機 concrete pavement texturing machine
混凝土路面切缝机/混凝土路面切縫機 concrete pavement joint cutting machine, concrete pavement expansion joint cutter
混凝土路面清缝机/混凝土路面清縫機 concrete pavement joint cleaning machine
混凝土路面填缝机/混凝土路面填縫機 concrete pavement joint sealing machine
混凝土路面整平机/混凝土修飾機 concrete finisher
混凝土氯化物含量测量/混凝土氯化物含量測量 concrete chloride content measurement
混凝土抹面机/混凝土面整平機 concrete finishing machine
混凝土耐久性/混凝土耐久性 durability of concrete
混凝土配合比设计/混凝土配合比設計,混凝土配料設計 concrete mix design
混凝土配合料/混凝土配料 batching
混凝土配制强度/混凝土配製強度 concrete confected intensity, concrete mixing strength
混凝土喷射机/混凝土噴射機,混凝土噴製機 concrete spraying machine, shotcrete machine
混凝土砌块/混凝土塊 concrete block
混凝土砌块成型机/混凝土制模機 concrete block moulding machine
混凝土强度超声测量/混凝土強度超音測量 ultrasonic test of concrete strength
混凝土强度等级/混凝土強度等級 strength grade of concrete
混凝土桥/混凝土橋 concrete bridge
混凝土切割机/混凝土切割機 concrete cutting machine
混凝土收缩损失/混凝土收縮損失 loss due to concrete shrinkage
混凝土[输送]泵/混凝土[輸送]泵 concrete pump
混凝土输送塔/混凝土輸送塔 concrete tower
混凝土水平基层/混凝土水平基層 levelling concrete
混凝土摊铺机/混凝土路面攤鋪機,混凝土鋪路機 concrete paver, concrete spreader
混凝土摊铺列车/混凝土聯合鋪路機 concrete paving train
混凝土弹性压缩损失/混凝土彈性壓縮損失 loss due to elastic compression of concrete
混凝土碳化试验/混凝土碳化試驗 concrete carbonation test
混凝土套加固法/混凝土套加固法 structure member strengthening with reinforced concrete jacketing strengthening
混凝土瓦/混凝土瓦 concrete tile
混凝土外加剂/混凝土外加劑,混凝土摻合料 concrete admixture
混凝土外墙板/混凝土外牆板 concrete exterior wall panel
混凝土斜拉桥/混凝土橋面斜張橋 concrete deck cable stayed bridge
混凝土徐变损失/混凝土徐變損失 creep loss of concrete
混凝土养护工艺/混凝土養護工藝 concrete curing technology

混凝土养生/混凝土養護　concrete curing
混凝土折板结构/混凝土折板結構　concrete folded-plate structure
混凝土枕螺栓钻取机/混凝土枕螺栓鑽取機　concrete tie dowel drilling and pulling machine
混凝土振捣机/混凝土震動機　concrete vibrating machine
混凝土振动台/混凝土振動臺,混凝土振動器　concrete vibrating stand, concrete vibrating table, concrete vibration stand
混凝土重力式平台/混凝土重力式平臺　concrete gravity platform
混凝土砖/混凝土磚　concrete block, concrete brick
混凝土转运车/混凝土轉送車　concrete transfer car
混凝土钻孔机/混凝土鑽孔機　concrete drilling machine
混凝土钻孔内窥镜检查/混凝土鑽孔內窺鏡檢查　concrete coring hole inspecting by endoscope
混凝最佳点/混凝最佳點　optimum point of coagulation
混频器/混頻器,混波器　mixer
混砂砾/未篩礫石　unscreened gravel
混水连接/混水直接連接　water mixing direct connection
混水装置/混水裝置　water admixing device
混土器/土壤混合機　soil mixer
混响/交混回響　reverberation
混响场/混響場,回響場　reverberation field
混响声/混響聲　reverberant sound
混响时间/交混回響時間　reverberation time
混响试验/混響試驗,回響試驗　reverberation test
混响室/混響室,混響腔　reverberation chamber
混压式进气道/混壓式進氣道　mixed compression inlet
混杂不清货/混雜不清貨　commixture and unidentifiable cargo
混杂复合材料/混成複合材料　hybrid composite
混杂结构/混合式結構　hybrid structure
混杂纤维复合材料/混雜纖維複合材料　fiber hybrid composite
混装/混裝　mixed loading
混装舱间/共同裝載艙間　compartment loaded in combination
混装船/混載船　combination carrier
混装修理法/混裝修理法　depersonalized repair method
锪削/锪孔　spotting
活顶盖/活頂蓋　removable hatch cover

活顶棚车/活頂棚車　sliding roof box car, sliding roof goods van
活动靶标/活動目標　moving target
活动半径/活動半徑　mission radius
活动布水器/動式分水器　movable distributor
活动地面/活動地面　movable floor
活动吊篮/移動式吊籃　travelling cradle
活动发射台/活動發射臺　mobile launch pad
活动隔墙/可動間壁　movable partition
活动轨迹/活動軌跡　activity track
活动花坛/活動花壇　movable flower bed
活动环/活動光網　moving reticle
活动积温/活動積溫　active accumulated temperature
活动建筑/可動結構　mobile structure
活动解拖钩/[活動]脱鉤　movable relieving hook
活动距标/可變距指標　variable range marker
活动看台/移動架　movable stand
活动空间/活動空間　activity space
活动模架逐跨施工法/活動模架逐跨施工法　segmental span-by-span construction using form traveller
活动模式/活動模式　active mode
活动桥/活動橋,開合橋　movable bridge
活动伸缩缝支座/滑動支承,伸縮支承,伸滑支承　sliding expansion bearing
活动式模板/移動式模板　travelling form
活动式勤务塔/活動式勤務塔　mobile service tower
活动梯步/舷梯活動踏步　feathering step, feathering tread
活动舞台/可變式舞臺　flexible stage
活动物货/牲口貨　livestock cargo
活动堰/活動堰　movable weir
活动载荷/廢物載重　disposal load
活动支架/可動支承　movable support
活动支座/可動支承,活動支承　expansion bearing, movable bearing, movable support
活动中梁底架/活動中梁底架　underframe with sliding center sill, cushioning underframe
活动座席/活動座席　flexible seating
活动座椅/活動座椅　self-folding seat
活度比/活性比　activity ratio
活荷载/活荷載,活動負載,活載重　live load
活荷载应力/活[載重]應力　live stress, live load stress
活力方程/活力方程式　vis-viva formula
活门气检/氣門氣體洩漏檢查　gas leak inspection of valve
活墙棚车/活牆棚車　sliding side box car

活塞/活塞　piston
活塞泵/活塞[式]泵　piston pump
活塞衬套/活塞襯套　piston bush
活塞顶烧蚀/活塞頂燒蝕　piston crown ablation
活塞杆/活塞桿　piston rod
活塞杆填料函/活塞桿填料函　piston rod stuffing box
活塞环/活塞環,活塞圈　piston ring
活塞环搭口间隙/活塞環介面間隙　piston ring joint clearance, piston ring gap clearance
活塞环断裂/活塞環斷裂　piston ring breakage
活塞环磨损监测系统/活塞環磨損監測系統　piston ring wear monitoring system
活塞环黏着/活塞環膠著　piston ring sticking
活塞环平面间隙/活塞環軸向間隙　piston ring axial clearance
活塞冷却喷嘴/活塞冷卻噴嘴　piston cooling nozzle
活塞冷却水泵/活塞冷卻水泵　piston cooling water pump
活塞流反应器/塞流反應器　plug flow reactor
活塞面积/活塞面積　piston area
活塞平均速度/活塞平均速度,平均活塞速度　mean piston speed
活塞取土器/活塞採樣器　piston sampler
活塞裙/活塞裙　piston skirt
活塞式发动机/活塞發動機　piston engine
活塞式压缩机/往復[式]壓縮機　reciprocating compressor
活塞体/活塞體　piston body
活塞头/活塞頭,活塞頂　piston head, piston crown
活塞下部泵气功能/活塞下部泵效應　piston underside pumping effect
活塞销/活塞銷,軸頭銷　gudgeon pin, piston pin
活塞行程/活塞衝程　piston stroke
活塞运动装置失中/活塞連桿裝置欠對準　piston-connecting-rod arrangement misalignment
活塞组件/活塞組件　piston assembly
活牲畜运输船/活牲畜運輸船　live stock carrier
活树亭/活樹亭　arbor, tent arbor
活套结/套馬扣　running bowline
活头丁字尺/活頭丁字尺　shifting T-square
活性固体/活性固體　activated solid
活性水/活性水　active water
活性炭吸附/活性碳吸附　activated carbon adsorption
活性污泥/活性汙泥　activated sludge
活性污泥槽/活化汙泥槽　activated sludge tank
活性污泥法/活性汙泥法,活化汙泥法　activated sludge process
活性污泥荷载/汙泥負載　activated sludge loading
活性指数/活性指數　activity index
活鱼车/活魚車　live fish car
活鱼运输船/活魚[運輸]船　live fish carrier
活载发展均衡系数/活載遞增平衡因數　balancing factor for increasing live load
活载[荷]/活載荷,活動負載,活載重　live load
火车轮渡/火車渡船　train ferry
火车票/列車通行券　train ticket
火车站/火車站,鐵路車站　railway station, train station
火成侵入岩/火成侵入[岩]　igneous intrusion
火床炉/爐箅鍋爐　grate fired boiler, stoker fired boiler
火工矫形/火焰矯正　fairing by flame
火工品检测间/火工品檢測間　ordnance checkout room, pyrotechnics checkout room
火工品贮存库/火工品貯存庫　ordnance warehouse, pyrotechnics warehouse
火工品装配间/火工品裝配間　ordnance assembly room, pyrotechnics assembly room
火管锅炉/火管鍋爐　fire tube boiler
火管式沥青熔化装置/火管式瀝青熔化裝置　asphalt firepipe melter
火花间隙/火花隙,電花隙,火花放電器　spark gap
火化间/火化間　cremation chamber
火箭/火箭　rocket
火箭垂直度/衛星載具垂直度　launch vehicle verticality
[火箭的]控制系统/火箭控制系統　control system of rocket
[火箭的]推进系统/推進系統火箭　propulsion system of rocket
火箭发动机/火箭發動機　rocket engine, rocket motor
火箭发动机高空试验/火箭發動機高空試驗　rocket engine high altitude test
火箭发动机羽流/火箭發動機煙流　rocket engine plume
火箭发射装置/火箭發射器　rocket launcher
火箭滑车/火箭滑車,火箭滑橇　rocket sled
火箭滑车试验/火箭滑道試驗　rocket sled test
火箭降落伞火焰信号/火箭式降落傘照明彈　rocket parachute flare signal
火箭排气噪声/火箭廢氣噪音　rocket exhaust noise
火箭喷口/火箭噴射　rocket jet
火箭牵引/火箭牽引　rocket extract

火箭橇/火箭橇,火箭滑車　rocket sled
火箭橇技术/火箭橇技術　rocket-propelled sled technique
火箭射流/火箭噴射　rocket jet
火箭推进剂/火箭推進劑　rocket propellant
火箭推进系统/火箭推進系統　rocket propulsion system
火箭羽焰试验/火箭煙流試驗　rocket plume test
火警信号/火警警報　fire alarm signal
火炬信号/火炬[信號]　torch
火力发电厂/火力發電廠　steam power plant, thermal power plant
火力发电站/熱力發電所,熱能發電廠　heat power station, thermal power station
火炉供暖/火爐供暖,爐子供暖　stove heating
火帽/火帽　primer
火炮/火炮　artillery
火山/火山　volcano
火山灰/火山灰　trass, volcanic ash
火山灰云/火山灰雲　volcanic ash cloud
火山灰质[硅酸盐]水泥/火山灰質波特蘭水泥,卜特蘭火山灰水泥　Portland pozzolana cement
火山碎屑岩/火山屑岩　pyroclastic rock
火山岩/火山岩　volcanic rock
火山岩屑/火山岩屑　volcanic detritus
火山渣/火山渣　scoria
火险/火險　fire insurance
火箱/火箱,燃燒室　firebox
火箱管板/火箱管板　firebox tube sheet
火星/火星　Mars
火星地质/火星地質　geology of Mars
火星网/火花防止網　spark arrester netting
火星熄灭器/火花防止器　spark arrester
火焰除锈/火焰清除　flame cleaning
火焰传播/火焰傳播　flame propagation
火焰传播速度/火焰[傳播]速度　combustion velocity, flame speed, rate of flame propagation
火焰淬火/火焰硬化　flame hardening
火焰割焊/火焰割焊　flame cutting and welding
火焰管/火管,焰管　flame tube
火焰加热法除锈/火焰加熱法除銹　fire heating rust removing
火焰夹角/火焰夾角　angle between flame central axis and line-of-sight of station
火焰监测器/火焰探測器,火焰偵測器　flame detector
火焰检测系统/火警偵察器系統　fire detection system
火焰喷涂/火焰塗層　flame coating
火焰气刨/火焰開槽　flame gouging
火焰前峰/焰鋒　flame front
火焰切割/火焰截割　flame cutting
火焰衰减/火焰衰減器　flame attenuation
火焰筒/火焰筒　liner
火焰稳定器/火焰維持器　flame holder
火药点火/火藥點火　powder ignition
火药起动器/火藥致動器　explosive actuator
火药起动系统/火藥啟動系統　powder start system
火灾/火災　fire hazard, fire accident
火灾报警探测器/火警探測器　fire detector, detector for fire alarm system
火[灾报]警系统/火[警報]警系統　fire alarm system
火灾警报器/火警警報器　fire alarm, fire alarm sounder
火灾损失/燃燒損失　loss on ignition
火灾探测器安装间距/火警監測器安裝間距　fire detector spacing
火灾探测器保护半径/火災探測器監測半徑　fire detector monitoring radius
火灾探测器保护面积/火災監測保護面積　fire detector monitoring area
火灾危险环境/火災危險環境　fire hazardous atmosphere
伙食冷库/糧食冷凍庫　food stuff refrigerated storage
货泵舱/貨泵室　cargo pump room
货舱/貨艙　cargo hold, cargo compartment, freight compartment
货舱隔离/全艙隔離　separated by a complete compartment or hold from
货舱工作灯/裝卸貨照明燈　cargo lamp, cargo light
货舱鉴定/貨艙檢查　inspection of hold
货舱空气干燥系统/貨艙空氣乾燥系統　cargo hold dehumidification system
货舱口/貨艙口　cargo hatch
货舱容积/貨艙容量　hold capacity, cargo capacity
货差/貨差　freight shortage
货差率/貨差率,誤報率　shortage rate of goods, mistake rate of goods
货场/貨場　freight yard, goods yard
货场监视电视/貨物車場監視電視　monitor TV for freight yard
货车/貨車　freight car, wagon
货车保有量/貨車保有量　number of freight car on hand

货车标记载重量/貨車標記載重量　marked loading capacity of car
货车动态/貨車作業狀態　operation status of truck
货车动载重/貨車動載重　dynamic load of car
货车技术交接所/貨車技術交接所　freight car technical condition handing-over post
货车检修率/貨車檢修率　ratio of freight car under repair
[货车]脚蹬/[貨車]腳蹬　sill step
货车静载重/貨車靜負載,貨車靜荷載　static load of car
货车溜放风阻力/貨車溜放風阻力　rolling car resistance due to wind effect
货车溜放基本阻力/貨車溜放基本阻力　basic rolling car resistance
[货车]门锁/門鎖,門閂　door latch
[货车]内墙板/貨車隔板　lining
货车日产量/貨車日產量　serviceable work-done per car day
货车日车公里/貨車日車公里　car kilometers per car per day
[货车]上侧梁/上弦桿　top chord
[货车]上开门/貨車上開門　upward swing door
货车施封/貨車施封　car seal, wagon seal
货车洗刷所/貨車洗刷所　freight car washing point
[货车]下开门/貨車下開門　downward swing door
[货车]摇枕挡/搖枕擋　column guide
货车运用效率/貨車運用效率　freight car operation efficiency
货车载重量利用率/貨車載重量利用率　coefficient of utilization for car loading capacity
货车站修所/貨車檢修所　freight car repairing point
货车中转距离/貨車中轉距離　average car-kilometers per transit operation
货车周转距离/貨車週轉距離　average car-kilometers in one turnround
货车周转时间/貨車週轉時間　car turnround time
货车装卸安全间距/貨車裝卸安全間距　truck handling safety interval distance
货车装载清单/貨車裝載清單　car loading list
货船/貨船,貨輪　cargo carrier, cargo ship, freighter
货船安全证书/貨船安全證書　Cargo Ship Safety Certificate
货船构造安全证书/貨船安全構造證書　Cargo Ship Safety Construction Certificate
货船设备安全证书/貨船安全設備證書　Cargo Ship Safety Equipment Certificate
货船无线电安全证书/貨船安全無線電證書　Cargo Ship Safety Radio Certificate
货船无线电报安全证书/貨船安全無線電報證書　Cargo Ship Safety Radiotelegraphy Certificate
货船无线电话安全证书/貨船安全無線電話證書　Cargo Ship Safety Radiotelephony Certificate
货到交付/貨到交付　delivery on arrival
货抵押贷款/船貨押貸　respondentia
货垛/堆裝貨物　stack of freight
货港未定租船合同/任務待定傭船契約　open charter
货柜车/圓櫃貨車　tank wagon
货机/貨運機　cargo airplane
货流/貨流　freight flow
货流量/貨流量　freight flow volume
货流图/貨流圖　freight traffic diagram, freight flow diagram
货轮/貨船　cargo ship
货名/貨名　description of goods
货盘/托貨板　cargo pallet
货棚/貨棚,風雨棚　shed, freight shed, goods shed
货票/貨票,運費單　freight bill, way bill, freight invoice
货桥/上貨停機場　loading ramp
货区/貨運站　freight area, goods area
货损/貨損　freight damage
货损率/貨損率　damage rate of goods
货位/貨位　freight lot, freight section, goods section
货物伴生废弃物/貨物所生相關廢棄物　cargo-associated waste
货物包装/商品包装　goods packing
货物标记/貨籤　freight label
货物标志/貨物標誌　goods mark
货物残损单/貨損清單　damage cargo list
[货物]仓库/倉庫　warehouse
货物操作吨/貨物操作噸　tons of cargo handled
货物操作量/貨物操作量　tonnage of cargo handled
货物操作系数/貨物操縱係數　coefficient of cargo handling
货物查询单/貨物追查單　cargo tracer
货物承运/貨物承運　acceptance of freight
货物到达吨数/貨物到達噸數　tonnage of freight arrived
货物到达作业/貨物到達作業　freight operation at destination station
[货物]堆存吨天数/堆存噸天數　storage ton day
货物发送吨数/貨物發送噸數　tonnage of freight despatched
货物发送作业/貨物發送作業　freight operation at

originated station
货物分等运价/貨物分等運價 classified rates for goods
货物换装整理/貨物換裝整理 transhipment and rearrangement of goods
货物积累损伤指数/貨物積累損傷指數 rate of accumulated freight damage
[货物]计费重量/計費重量 charged weight
货物记录簿/液貨記錄簿 cargo record book
货物交付/貨物交付 delivery of freight
货物交接所/貨物交接所 freight transfer point
货物拒收险/貨物拒收險 rejection risks
货物冷藏装置检验/貨物冷凍裝置檢驗 survey of refrigerated cargo installation
货物列车/貨物列車 freight train, goods train
货物列车编组计划/貨物列車編組計劃 freight train formation plan
货物列车检修所/貨物列車檢修所 freight train inspection and service point
货物列车区段检修所/貨物列車區段檢修所 transit freight train inspection and service point
货物列车一般检修所/貨物列車一般檢修所 freight train ordinary inspection and service point
货物列车主要检修所/貨物列車主要檢修所 freight train main inspection and service point
货物流量/貨運量 freight traffic volume
货物流时/貨流量時間 freight traffic time
货物流向/貨物流向 freight traffic direction
货物码头/貨物碼頭 freight wharf
货物配载图/貨物裝載圖,艙位裝載圖,載貨圖 cargo plan
货物品类/貨物品類,商品分類 goods category
货物平安险/單獨海損免責 free from particular average, FPA
[货物]平均堆存天数/平均堆存天數 average storage day
货物平均运程/貨運平均運程 average haul of freight traffic
货物平均运距/貨物平均運距 freight average haul distance
货物清单/運費單 freight list
货物水渍险/水漬險 with average, WA
货物途中作业/貨物途中作業 freight operation en route
[货物]托盘/托板,棧板 pallet
货物托运/貨物托運 consigning of freight
货物移位/貨物移位 cargo shifting
货物运单/運貨證書,提貨單,托運單據 bill of lading, consignment note
货物运到期限/貨物運送期限 freight transit period
货物运价号/運價表號 freight tariff number
货物运价里程/貨物運價里程 tariff kilometerage
货物运价率/[貨物]運費率 freight rate
货物运输/貨物運輸,貨運 freight transport, freight transportation
货物运输变更/貨車交通改道 traffic diversion
货物运输计划/貨物運輸計劃 freight traffic plan
货物运输量/貨運量 freight traffic volume
货物运输系数/貨運交通係數 coefficient of freight traffic
货物运输杂费/貨物運輸雜費 miscellaneous charge for freight transport
货物运送吨数/貨物運送噸數 tonnage of freight transported
货物战争险/貨物戰爭險 cargo war risk
货物站台/貨物月臺 freight platform, goods platform
货物站务费/貨物站務費 freight terminal charge
货物重心的横向位移/貨物重心橫向偏移 lateral shift for center of gravity of goods
货物重心的纵向位移/貨物重心縱向偏移 longitudinal shift for center of gravity of goods
货物周转量/貨物週轉量,貨運週轉量 turnover of freight traffic
货物转向架/貨物轉向架 freight turning rack
货物转向架支距/貨物轉向架支距 distance between centers of freight turning rack
货物装卸/裝卸區 goods handling
货物装卸费/貨物裝卸費 goods handling charge
货物装卸量/貨物裝卸量 loading-unloading volume
货物装卸设备/貨物裝卸設備 cargo gear
货物装载/貨物裝載 cargo-handling and stowage
货油泵/貨油泵 cargo oil pump
货油泵舱管系/貨油泵室管路 cargo oil pump room pipe line
货油舱/貨油艙 cargo oil tank
货油舱管系/貨油艙管路 cargo oil tank pipe line
货油舱气压指示器/貨油艙氣壓指示器 cargo oil tank gas pressure indicator
货油舱清洗装置/洗艙裝置 tank-cleaning plant
货油舱扫舱系统/貨油艙收艙系統 cargo oil tank stripping system
货油舱透气系统/貨油艙通氣系統 cargo oil tank venting system, cargo oil tank venting piping system
货油舱洗舱设备/貨油艙清洗裝置 cargo oil tank

cleaning installation

货油舱洗舱系统/貨油艙洗艙裝置　cargo oil tank cleaning installation, cargo oil tank cleaning system

货油舱油气驱除装置/貨油艙清除有害氣體裝置　cargo oil tank gas-freeing installation

货油阀/貨油閥　cargo oil valve

货油加热系统/貨油加熱系統　cargo oil heating system

货油控制室/貨油控制室　cargo oil control room

货油软管/貨油軟管　cargo oil hose

货油装卸系统/貨油裝卸系統　cargo oil pumping system, cargo oil handing system

货油装卸总管/貨油總管　cargo oil transfer main pipe line, cargo oil main line

货油总管/貨油主管　main cargo oil line

货源/貨源　freight source, freight traffic source

货源调查/貨源調查　freight source survey

货源信息/貨源資訊　information of freight source

货运/貨運　freight

货运波动系数/貨運波動係數　fluctuating coefficient of freight traffic

货运代理人/轉運代理人　forwarding agent

货运调度/貨運調度　dispatching of freight transport

货运调度电话/貨運調度電話　freight dispatching telephone

货运公路/貨運公路　freight road

货运合同/貨運契約　contract of affreightment

货运机车/貨運機車　freight locomotive, goods locomotive

货运及时率/貨運及時率　rate of timely freight

货运交通/貨運交通　freight traffic

货运交通规划/貨運交通規劃　freight transportation planning

货运经济调查/貨運經濟調查　economic investigation of freight traffic

货运拒赔/貨運拒賠　reject of freight claims

货运理赔/貨運理賠　actions for freight claims

货运联运站/貨運聯運站　intermodal freight terminal

货运密度/貨運密度　density of freight traffic

货运签约人/貨運簽約人　freight contractor

货运生产平衡/貨運生產平衡　freight production balance

货运事故/貨運事故　freight traffic accident

货运枢纽站/貨運樞紐站　freight hub terminal

货运索赔/貨運索賠　freight claims

货运索赔时限/貨運索賠時限　period of limitation for freight claims

货运停机坪/貨物裝卸場　cargo apron

货运信息中心/貨運資訊中心　freight information center

货运业务/貨運業務　freight transport business

货运杂费/貨運雜費　miscellaneous fees of goods traffic

货运站/貨運車站, 货［物］站　cargo terminal, freight station, freight depot

货运站码头/貨運碼頭　freight pier

货运站综合作业自动化/貨運站綜合作業自動化　automation of synthetic operations at freight station

货运质量/貨運品質　freight transport quality

货运质量事故频率/貨運品質事故頻率　frequency of freight quality accident

货运质量指标/貨運品質指標　freight quality indicator

货运专线/貨運專線　railway line for freight traffic, freight special line, freight traffic only line

货主/收货人, 收件人, 受託人　owner of freight, shipper

获得位置概率/獲得位置機率　location acquisition probability

获救财产价值/獲救財產價值　value of property salved

霍尔片/霍爾片　Hall plate

霍华德城堡园林/霍華德城堡園林　Howard Castle Garden

霍曼转移/郝曼轉移　Hohmann transfer

豁免/豁免　exemption

豁免证书/豁免證書　exemption certificate

J

几/幾　stand small table
击实试验/壓實試驗,壓實測試　compaction test
击实仪/擊實儀,壓實儀器　compaction test apparatus
机舱/機艙,輪機室　engine room
机舱布置/機艙布置　engine room arrangement
机舱辅机/機艙輔機　engine room auxiliary machinery
机舱集控室/機艙控制室　engine control room
机舱集控台/機艙集中控制臺　centralized control console of engine room
机舱棚/機艙棚,機艙天罩　engine room casing
机舱涂料/機艙塗料　engine compartment coating, engine compartment paint
机舱污水井/機艙舣水　machinery space bilge
机舱应急舱底水阀/機艙應急舣水吸入閥　engine room emergency bilge suction valve
机舱照明系统/機艙照明系統　engine room lighting system
机舱自动化/機艙自動化　engine room automation
机场/機場,航空站,飛行場　airport, aerodrome
机场饱和/機場飽和　aerodrome capacity saturation
机场标高/機場標高　aerodrome elevation
机场参考点/航空站標點　aerodrome reference point
机场大楼/機場大廈　terminal building
机场道面/機場鋪面　airport pavement
机场地面探测设备/機場探測設備　airport surface detection equipment
机场管制塔台/機場管制塔臺　aerodrome control tower
机场监视雷达/機場監視雷達,機場搜索雷達　airport surveillance radar, ASR
机场交通/機場交通　aerodrome traffic
机场界限信号/起落區界線標誌　boundary marker
机场警告/機場警報　aerodrome warning
机场净空/機場淨空　airport clearance, obstacle free airspace
机场陆侧交通/機場陸側交通　airport ground transportation
机场起落航线/飛機場航線　aerodrome traffic pattern
机场容量/機場容量　aerodrome capacity
机场吞吐量/機場吞吐量　handling capacity of an airport
机场用地/機場用地　land for airport
机场预报/機場預報　aerodrome forecast
机场运行设施/機場運行設施　aerodrome operating facility
机场运行最低标准/機場最低飛航限度　aerodrome operating minimum
机场指向标/航空站指示燈　aerodrome-beacon
机场指向灯/航空站指示燈　aerodrome-beacon
机车/機車　locomotive
机车包乘制/機車包乘制　system of assigning crew to designated locomotive
机车保养/機車維修　locomotive maintenance
机车报废/機車報廢　locomotive retirement
机车比率/機車比率　locomotive ratio
机车长度/機車全長　locomotive overall length
机车厂修/機車廠修　locomotive repair in work
机车超重牵引/機車超重牽引　traction for train exceed mass norm
机车车辆厂/機車車輛廠　locomotive and rolling stock factory
机车车辆冲击/機車車輛衝擊　impact of rolling stock
机车车辆共振/機車車輛共振　resonance of rolling stock
机车车辆溜逸/機車車輛失穩　runaway of locomotive or car
机车车辆破损/機車車輛破損　rolling stock damage
机车车辆上部限界/機車車輛上部限界　clearance limit for upper part of rolling stock
机车车辆下部限界/機車車輛下部限界　clearance limit for lower part of rolling stock
机车车辆运用计划/機車車輛運用計劃　rolling stock utilization plan
机车车辆振动/機車車輛振動　vibration of rolling stock
机车乘务制度/機車乘務制度　locomotive crew working system
机车乘务组/機車乘務組　locomotive crew

机车重联电连接器/機車重聯電聯結器，多機牽引電耦合器　multi-locomotive electric coupler

机车出入段作业/機車出入段條件　preparation of locomotive for leaving and arriving at depot

机车出租/機車出租　leased locomotive

机车储备/機車儲備　locomotive reservation, locomotive storage

机车传动效率/機車傳動效率　transmission efficiency of locomotive

机车大修/檢修類別大修理　locomotive overhaul repair, locomotive general overhaul

机车电台/機車電臺　locomotive station

机车调度命令/機車調度命令　locomotive dispatching order

机车定期修/機車定期修　locomotive periodical repair

机车段修/機車段修　locomotive repair in depot

机车分配阀/機車分配閥　locomotive distributing valve

机车感应器/機車感應器　locomotive inductor

机车高度/機車高度　locomotive height

机车公里/機車公里　locomotive kilometer

机车功率/機車功率　locomotive power

机车功率试验/機車功率試驗　locomotive traction power test

机车功率因数测定/機車功率因數測定　measurement of power factor

机车固定轴距/機車固定軸距　locomotive rigid wheel base

机车故障/機車故障　locomotive failure

机车锅炉/機車鍋爐　locomotive boiler

机车集中供电/機車集中供電　locomotive centralized power supply

机车计算重量/機車計算重量　calculated weight of locomotive

机车技术规范/機車技術規範　locomotive technical specification

机车监控记录装置/機車監控記錄裝置　locomotive supervise and record apparatus

机车检修/機車檢車段　locomotive inspection and repair

机车检修段/機車修理廠　locomotive repair depot

机车检修率/機車檢修率　ratio of locomotives under repair

机车检修修程/機車檢修類別　classification of locomotive repair

机车交路/機車交路　locomotive routing

机车接近通知/機車接近通知　approaching announcing in cab

机车紧急放风阀/機車緊急放風閥　locomotive emergency vent valve

机车库/機車庫　locomotive shed

机车宽度/機車寬度　locomotive width

机车临修/機車臨時修理，機車小修　locomotive temporary repair

机车轮乘制/機車輪乘制　locomotive crew pooling system

机车轮周功率曲线/機車輪週功率曲線　locomotive power curve at wheel rim

机车轮周效率/機車輪週功率　efficiency of locomotive at wheel rim

机车履历簿/機車履歷簿　locomotive logbook

机车每轴闸瓦作用力/機車每軸閘瓦作用力　brake shoe force per axle of locomotive

机车能耗/機車能量消耗　locomotive energy consumption

机车黏着重量/機車黏重　locomotive adhesive weight

机车平均牵引总重/機車平均牽引總重　average gross weight hauled by locomotive

机车牵引变压器/機車牽引變壓器　traction transformer of locomotive

机车牵引力/機車牽引力　locomotive tractive effort

机车牵引力曲线/機車牽引力曲線　locomotive tractive effort curve

[机车]牵引梁/牽引梁　draw beam

机车牵引区段/機車牽引區　locomotive tractive district

机车牵引特性/機車牽引特性　locomotive tractive characteristic

机车牵引特性曲线/機車牽引特性曲線　locomotive tractive characteristic curve

机车全周转/機車全週轉　complete turnround of locomotive

机车全周转距离/機車全週轉距離　distance of one complete turnround of locomotive

机车全周转时间/機車全週轉時間　period of one complete turnround of locomotive

机车全轴距/機車全軸距，機車總車軸距　locomotive total wheel base

机车日产量/機車日產量　average daily output of locomotive

机车日车公里/機車日車公里　average daily locomotive running kilometer

机车设备/機車設備　locomotive equipment

机车试运转/機車試運轉　locomotive trial run

机车速度表/機車速度計　locomotive speedmeter
机车随乘制/機車隨乘制　locomotive caboose crew system
机车调速试验/機車調速試驗　test on speed regulation
机车万吨公里能耗/機車萬噸公里能耗　energy consumption per 10000 t·km of locomotive
机车无线电遥控/機車無線電遙控　radio telecontrol for locomotive
机车效率/機車效率　total locomotive efficiency
机车效率测定/機車效率測定　measurement of efficiency of locomotive
机车信号/司機棚號誌　cab signal
机车信号测试区段/機車信號測試區段　cab signaling testing section
机车信号设备/機車信號設備　cab signaling equipment
机车信号作用点/機車信號感應器作用點　cab signaling inductor location
机车需要系数/機車需要係數　coefficient of locomotive requirement
机车验收/機車驗收　acceptance of locomotive
机车用柴油/機車柴油　diesel oil for locomotive
机车用电/機車用電　electricity for locomotive
机车用换算煤/機車用換算煤　converted coal for locomotive
机车用煤/機車用煤　coal for locomotive
机车用润滑剂/機車潤滑劑　lubricant for locomotive
机车预期牵引特性曲线/機車預期牽引特性曲線　predetermined tractive characteristic curve of locomotive
机车运用段/機車運用段　locomotive running depot
机车运用指标/機車運用指標　index of locomotive operation
机车在段停留时间/機車在段停留時間　detention time of locomotive at depot
机车噪声/機車雜訊　locomotive noise
机车振动参数测试/機車振動參數測量　measurements of vibration parameters
机车整备/機車整備工作　locomotive servicing, locomotive running preparation
机车整备能力/機車整備能力　locomotive service capacity
机车整备重量/機車工作重量　locomotive service weight
机车制动机/機車制動裝置　locomotive brake gear
机车制动距离/機車剎車距離　locomotive braking distance
机车制动周期/機車制動時間　locomotive braking period
机车种类/機車[類]型　type of locomotive
机车重量/機車重量　locomotive weight
机车重量分配/機車重量分布　weight distribution of locomotive
机车周转图/機車週轉圖　locomotive working diagram
机车专用设备/機車特殊設備　special equipment for locomotive operation
机车转向架轴距/機車轉向架軸距　locomotive wheel base of bogie
机车自动操纵/機車自動操作　automatic locomotive operation
机车走行公里/機車走行公里　locomotive running kilometer
机车走行线/機車走行線　locomotive running track
机车组装后的检查与试验/機車組裝後的檢查與試驗　inspection and test of locomotive after completion of construction
机床厂/機床廠　machine tool factory
机待线/機待線　locomotive waiting track
机弹干扰/機載飛彈干擾,空射飛彈干擾　aircraft-missile interference
机电工程师/機械工程師　building equipment engineer, mechanical engineer
机动操纵/操縱　maneuver
机动车/機動車輛　motor vehicle
机动车出入口方位线/車輛出入口方位線　vehicle entrance line
机动车道/[機動]車道　driveway, vehicle lane, motor carriageway
机动车辆/機動車[輛],動力車輛　power driven vehicle, motor vehicle, vehicle motor
机动车停车场/機動車停車場　motor vehicle parking lot
机动车停放规划/停車場規劃　vehicle parking planning
机动车运输/動力車運輸　power-driven vehicle transport
机动船/機動船,動力船,自航船　self-propelled vessel, power-driven vessel
机动吹灰机/機動吹灰機　power blower
机动弹头遥测/機動彈頭遙測　maneuverable warhead telemetry
机动点/操縱點　maneuver point
机动渡车船/動力渡船　powered ferry boat
机动跟踪/機動追蹤　maneuver tracking

机动刮平机/[機動]刮平機　motorized grade
机动舰[船]/運轉船　maneuvering ship
机动襟翼/操縱襟翼　maneuver flap
机动救生艇/動力救生艇,馬達救生艇　motor lifeboat
机动螺钉-螺栓搬手/機動螺栓-螺栓搬手　rail screw-bolt power wrench
机动三轮车/馬達三輪車　motor pedicab
机动性/機動性,靈敏性,可操縱性　mobility, maneuverability
机动有轨车/軌道自動車　railcar
机动裕度/操縱餘裕　maneuver margin
机动载荷/操縱負載　maneuver load
机动载荷控制/機動載荷控制　maneuver load control
机帆船/機帆船　motor sailer, power-sail ship
机房工程/機房工程　engineering of electronic equipment plant, EEEP
机高/飛機高度　overall height
机耕道/機耕道　tractor road
机工/機工　motor man
α机构/α機構　α angle mechanism
β机构/β機構　β angle mechanism
机架/機架,框架　frame, headstock
机架定位/機架定位　positioning of engine frame
机库/[飛]機庫,棚廠　hangar
机炉舱/機艙[空間],機器空間,機械室　machinery space
机轮/機輪　wheel
机轮设计载荷/設計輪重　design wheel load
机敏材料/智慧型材料　smart material
机内测试/自設測試　built-in test
机内通话器/對講機　interphone, intercom
机内照明/飛機內照明　aircraft interior lighting
机内自检/機內測試　built-in test, BIT
机炮射速/機炮射速　gun fire rate
机器处所/機艙[空間],機器空間,機械室　machinery space
机器人/機器人　robot
机器人技术实验装置/機器人技術實驗裝置　robot technology experiment device, ROTEX
机器人系统/機器人系統　robot system
机器人学/機器人學　robotics
机器样板/機器樣板　template with machined bushings
机上天线/飛機天線　aircraft antenna
机上维修系统/機上維護系統　on-board maintenance system

机身/機身　fuselage
机身长细比/機身細度比　fuselage fineness ratio
机身最大横截面积/機身最大橫截面面積　fuselage maximum crosssectional area
机体/機體,引擎體　engine block, main frame
机体坐标系/機體坐標系　body coordinate system
机外照明/飛機外照明　aircraft exterior lighting
机务段/機務段　locomotive depot
机务段联系电路/機務段聯繫電路　liaison circuit with a locodepot
机务段运行揭示/機務段運行揭示　running service-bulletin of depot
机务设备通过能力/機務設備通過能力　carrying capacity of locomotive facility
机务维修无线电通信/機務維修無線電通訊　radio communication for maintenance of locomotive
机务折返段/機務折返段　locomotive turnaround depot
机匣处理/機匣處理　casing treatment
机械保温车辆段/機械保溫車輛段　mechanical refrigerator car depot
机械臂板信号机/機械臂板信號機　mechanically operated semaphore signal
机械剥蚀/機械剝露　mechanical denuding
机械不完全燃烧热损失/機械不完全燃燒熱損失　heat loss due to combustibles in refuse
机械操作证/機械操作證　operation certificate of machinery
机械出租/機械出租　renting of machine
机械除锈/機械除銹　mechanical rust removal, mechanical rust removing
机械传动/機械傳動　mechanical transmission
机械传动内燃机车/機械傳動內燃機車　diesel-mechanical locomotive
机械肺/假肺　mechanical lung
机械负荷/機械負荷　mechanical load
机械功/機械功　mechanical work
机械故障/機器故障　failure of machine
机械故障率/機械故障率　failure rate of machinery
机械管理责任制/機械管理責任制　responsibility system of machinery management
机械夯/機械夯實器　mechanical rammer
机械合金化弥散强化材料/機械合金化法散布強化材料　mechanically alloyed dispersion strengthened material
机械合练/機制預演　mechanism rehearsal
机械滑车/機械複滑車,鏈滑車　mechanical purchase, chain block

机械化/機械化,馬達化 motorization
机械化程度/機械化程度 level of mechanization
机械化盾构/機械盾挖法 mechanical shield
机械化驼峰/機械化駝峰 mechanized hump
机械化驼峰设备/機械化駝峰設備 mechanized hump yard equipment
机械集中联锁/機械連鎖,機械聯動 mechanical interlocking
机械技术经济定额/機械技術經濟定額 technical economic quota of machinery
机械技术状况/機械技術狀況 technical condition of machine
机械加工/機械加工 machining, machine finishing
机械加工车间/機械車間 machining shop
机械搅拌/機械攪拌 mechanical agitation
机械接口/機械式介面 mechanical interface
机械接口坐标系/機械式介面坐標系 mechanical interface coordinate system
机械结合/機械結合 mechanical bond
机械框标/機械框標 mechanical fiducial mark
机械冷藏车/機藏式通風冷藏[火]車 mechanical refrigerator car
机械冷藏车组/機藏式通風冷藏[火]車組 mechanical refrigerator car group
机械力除尘器/機械力除塵器 mechanical dust separator
机械利用率/機械運轉率 operation rate of machinery
机械联锁机/機械聯動機 mechanical interlocking machine
机械能/機械能,力學能 mechanical energy
机械耙/機械柵 mechanical rake
机械喷射/機械噴射,無氣噴射 solid injection
机械曝气装置/機械曝氣器 mechanical aerator
机械气阀传动机构/機械致動閥機構 mechanically actuated valve mechanism
机械强度/機械強度 mechanical strength
机械生产定额/機械生產預計額 production quota of machinery
机械施工/機械施工 mechanical execution
机械式立体汽车库/機械式立體汽車庫 mechanical and stereoscopic garage
机械式锚杆/機械式岩石錨桿 mechanical rock bolt
机械式汽车库/機械式汽車庫 mechanical garage
机械式上支撑/機械式上支撐 mechanical top bracing
机械式调速器/機械[式]調速機 mechanical governor
机械式停车库/機械式停車庫 mechanical parking garage
机械式压力扫描阀/機械壓力掃描器 mechanical pressure scanner
机械事故/機械事故 machinery accident
机械事故处理/機械事故處理 accident handling of machinery
机械手/機械手 manipulator
机械损失功率/機械損失功率,機械損耗功率 mechanical loss power
机械锁闭/機械鎖定位置 mechanical locking
机械台班定额/機械臺班定額 rating per machine per team, rating per machine-team
机械天平/機械式天平 mechanical type balance
机械天平动稳定性/機械天平動穩定性 mechanobalance dynamic stability
机械天平恢复力矩/機械天平恢復力矩 mechanobalance restoring moment
机械天平静稳定度/機械天平静穩定度 mechanobalance static stability
机械停修台日/機械停修臺日 suspensive daily shift of machine
机械通风/機械[式]通風 mechanical ventilation, mechanical draft
机械通风装置/機械通風裝置 mechanical ventilation equipment
机械投影/機械投影法 mechanical projection
机械土工/機械土工 mechanical earth work
机械推进救生艇/機械推進救生艇 mechanically propelled lifeboat
机械脱水/機械祛水法 mechanical dewatering
机械挖掘机/機械挖掘機 cable operated excavator
机械完好率/機械完好率 availability rate of machinery
机械维护/機械維護 maintenance of machine
机械维修间隔/機械維修間隔 time interval of machine maintenance and repair
机械维修作业项目/機械維修作業項目 item of machine maintenance and repair
机械[无气]喷射柴油机/無氣噴射柴油機 solid-injection diesel
机械雾化油燃烧器/機械霧化油燃燒器 mechanical atomization oil burner
机械系列/機械系列 series of machine
机械效率/機械效率 mechanical efficiency
机械效益/機械利益 mechanical advantage
机械型谱/機械型譜 model spectrum of machine
机械性能实验室/機械性能實驗室 mechanical

properties laboratory
机械修理/機械修理　repair of machine
机械移栽/機械移栽　machine transplanting
机械引信/機械引信　mechanical fuze
机械预切割法/機械預切割法　mechanical precutting method
机械运转/機器作業　machine operation
机械运转记录/機械運轉記錄　operating record of machine
机械杂质/機械雜質　mechanical impurities
机械噪声/機械噪音　mechanical noise
机械增压/機械增壓　mechanical supercharging, engine-driven supercharging
机械增压柴油机/引擎驅動式增壓柴油機　engine-driven supercharged diesel engine
机械振动/機械振動　mechanical vibration
机械致冷器/機械冷凍機　mechanic refrigerator
机械装卸/機械裝卸　mechanical handling
机械装卸作业比重/機械裝卸作業比重　share of machine handling operation
机械装卸作业量/機械裝卸作業量　machine handling operation volume
机械阻抗/機械阻抗　mechanical impedance
机修车间/維修車間　maintenance and repair shop
机修间/工場　work shop
机要室/機要室　confidential room
机翼/機翼　wing
机翼变弯度控制/可變弧翼控制　variable wing camber control
机翼滚摆/機翼滾擺　wing rock
机翼流试验/機翼流試驗　wing flow testing
机翼面积/機翼面積　wing area
机翼扭转/機翼扭轉　wing twist
机油泵/［潤］滑油泵　lubricating oil pump, oil pump
机油粗滤器/機油粗濾器　lubricating prefilter
机油老化/潤滑油老化　ageing of lubricating oil
机油滤清器/潤滑油過濾器,濾油器　lubricating oil filter, oil filter
机油热交换器/機油熱交換器　lubricating oil heat exchanger
机油稀释/潤滑油稀釋　lub-oil dilution
机油消耗量/油耗,耗油量　oil consumption
机油消耗率/潤滑油消耗比　specific oil consumption
机载动目标检测雷达/空用活動目標檢測雷達　airborne MTD radar
机载动目标指示雷达/空用活動目標顯示雷達　airborne MTI radar
机载防撞设备/機載避撞設備　airborne collision avoidance equipment
机载火控雷达/機載火控雷達　airborne fire-control radar
机载计算机/機載計算機　airborne computer
机载警戒与控制系统/空中警戒與管制系統　airborne warning and control system, AWACS
机载雷达/機載雷達　airborne radar
机载气象雷达/空中氣象雷達　airborne weather radar
机载预警雷达/空用早期警報［預警］雷達　airborne early warning radar
机载侦察雷达/機載偵察雷達　airborne reconnaissance radar
机载制氧/機載製氧系統　on-board oxygen generation, OBOG
机制砂/人工砂　manufactured sand
机柱/柱　column
机装/輪機艙裝　machinery fitting
机组/機組　unit
机组有效效率/機組有效效率　unit effective efficiency
机座/機座,座板,框架　engine bed, engine seat, bed plate
机座找平/定機座水平　leveling of engine bed
矶/磯　rock projecting over water
鸡舍/雞舍　chicken coop
奇偶检验/奇偶校驗　parity check
奇偶校验码/奇偶校驗碼,奇偶檢驗碼　odd-even check code
积差[率]/[累]積差率　accumulated rate
积肥/積肥　collect manure
积肥场/堆肥場　manure yard
J积分/J積分　J-contour integral
积分法/積分法　integration method
积分球/積分球　integrating sphere
积分时间/積分時間　integration time
积分式[测量]仪器/積分[量測]儀器　integrating measuring instrument
积分调节器/積分調整器　integral regulator
积分透镜/積分透鏡　integration lens
积分陀螺仪/積分迴轉儀　integrating gyroscope
积极空间/積極空間,正空間　positive space, active space
积木式电缆填料盒/多管穿線板　multi-cables transit, MCT
积木式家具/積木式家具,組合式家具　combination furniture
积深取样法/積深取樣法　depth integration sampling

积水/積水,過量水　excess water
积水面积/積水面積　ponding area
积算/推算　dead reckoning, DR
积算船位/推算船位　dead reckoning position
积炭/積炭,碳沈積　carbon deposit
积雪/積雪　snow mantle
积雪标杆/積雪標示桿　snow deposit marker post
积雪场/積雪場　snow pack
积云/積雲　cumulus
积载/裝載　stowage
积载因数/積載因數,裝載因數　stowage factor
基本[测量]单位/基本[量測]單位　base unit of measurement
基本测量方法/基本量測法　fundamental method of measurement
基本陈列展厅/基本陳列展廳　basic exhibition hall
基本重复频率/基本重複頻率　basic repetition frequency
基本等级/基本階段　basic grade
基本地下水位/主要地下水面　main water-table
基本方案/基本計劃　basic plan
基本飞行控制系统/基本飛行控制系統　primary flight control system
基本风压/基本風壓　basic wind pressure
基本符号/基本符號　general symbol, basic symbol
基本港/母港　basic port, BP
基本公共服务均等化/基本公共服務均等化　equalization of basic public service
基本轨/道岔主軌　stock rail
基本耗热量/基本耗熱量　basic heat loss
基本恢复修理/修復　recovering repair
基本加热器/基本加熱器　primary calorifier
基本建设计划/基本建設計劃　plan of capital construction
基本建设投资/基本建設投資　capital construction investment
基本建设支出/资本建設支出　capital construction expenditure
基本建筑限界/基本建築限界　fundamental construction clearance, fundamental structure gage
基本交叉间隔/基本交叉間隔　fundamental transposition interval
基本结构体系/基本結構　primary structure
基本进路/基本進路　basic route
基本经济部门/基礎經濟部門　basic economic sector
基本径流/基本徑流　base runoff
基本可靠性/基本可靠度　basic reliability
基本联锁电路/基本聯鎖電路　fundamental interlocking circuit
基本量/基本量　base quantity
基本烈度/基本烈度　basic intensity, zoning intensity
基本模数/基本模組　basic module
基本农田/基本農田　prime farmland
基本农田保护区/基本農田保護區,基本農田儲備　prime reserve farmland, basic farmland reserve
基本票价/基本運價　basic fare
基本热源/基本熱源　base load heat source
基本人口/基準人口　basic population
基本容量/基本容量　basic capacity
基本书库/基本書庫　basic stack
基本水流/基本徑流　base runoff
基本台/主舞臺　main stage
基本通行能力/基本容量　basic capacity
基本图/基準圖　basic map
基本限值/基本極限　basic limit
基本型链路控制规程/基本型鏈接控制程式　basic link control procedure
基本运费/基本運費　basic rate, basic freight
基本运行图/基本運行圖　primary train diagram
基本站台/基本月臺　primary platform
基本折旧率/[基本]折舊率　depreciation rate, basic depreciation rate
基本振型/基諧[振動]模式　fundamental mode, fundamental mode of vibration
基本职能/基本功能　basic function
基本周期/基本週期　fundamental period
基本阻力/基本阻力　basic resistance
基标制/基標制　coordinal marking system
基波/基波,主波　fundamental wave
基层/基層,底層　base course, subbase
基层材料/基層材料　subbase course material
基层村/基層村　basic-level village
基层宽度/底層寬　base width
基层摩擦/基層摩擦　subbase friction
基层排水/基層排水　subbase course drainage
基础/基礎　foundation
基础板/底板　sole plate
基础测绘/基礎測繪　basic surveying and mapping
基础沉降/基礎沈降,地基沈陷,地基下沈　foundation settlement
基础垫层/基礎地盤　foundation bed
基础工程/地基工程　foundation engineering
基础工程学/基礎工程學,地基工程學　foundation engineering, ground engineering
基础工业/基礎工業　basic industry
基础件修理/基礎零件修理　basic part repair

基础结构/基礎結構 base structure
基础连梁/基礎橫梁 foundation tie beam
基础梁/基礎梁 foundation beam
基础隆胀力/基礎脹力 heave force of foundation
基础埋置深度/基礎埋置深度,基礎埋深 embedment depth of foundation, embedded depth of foundation
基础设施/基礎設施 base installation
基础设施网络/基礎設施網路 infrastructure network
基础施工法/基礎施工法 foundation practice
基础选拔/綜合選拔 general selection
基础训练/基本訓練 basic training
基础油/基油 base oil
基础约束/基礎拘束 foundation restraint
基础振动/基礎振動 vibration of foundation
基础制动装置/基本軔基裝置 foundation brake rigging
基础种植/基礎種植 foundation planting
基础资料汇编/實證資料匯編 compilation of investigation data
基床/基床 subgrade bed, formation
基床表层/基床表層 surface layer of subgrade bed, formation top layer, surface layer of subgrade
基床底层/基床底層 bottom layer of subgrade, formation base layer, bottom layer of subgrade bed
基带/基帶 baseband
基带传输/基帶傳輸,基頻傳輸 baseband transmission
基底/基底 foundation base, base
基底剪力/基層剪力 base shear
基底面积/基底面積 building covering area
基底屈服点/基底屈服點 yield of base
基底石/柱腳,柱基 plinth
基底应力扩散/基底應力擴散 stress dispersal beneath footing
基地/基地 plot, site
基地电台/基[地]臺 base station
基地线/基地線 lot line
基点/基點 base point, BP
基点风/四方位風 cardinal winds
基调树种/優勢木 dominant tree
基调音/基調音 keynotes sound
基尔霍夫假设/基爾霍夫假說 Kirchhoff hypothesis
基肥/基肥 basal fertilizer
基高比/基高比 base to height ratio
基坑/基坑 foundation pit
基坑井点排水法/基坑井點排水法 foundation pit well point drainage method
基坑排水/基礎排水 foundation drainage
基坑支护/基坑支護 retaining and protecting for foundation excavation
基面标准图/基面標準圖 dutum chart
基频/基本頻率,最低頻率,一階頻率 fundamental frequency
基期/基期 base period
基区宽度/底層寬 base width
基群/基[本頻帶]群 basic group
基群报警/群警報 group alarm
基群配线架/基群配線架 basic group distribution frame
基色/參考色 reference color
基石/基石,底腳石 base stone, footing stone
基体/基材 matrix
基体拉压强度/基材拉壓強度 tensile or compressive strength of matrix
基体裂纹/基材裂解 matrix cracking
基线/基[準]線 datum line, base line, BL
基线测量/基線測量 base line measurement
基线长度/基線長度 base length
基线高度法/底高法 base altitude method
基线误差/艉線誤差 lubber line error
基线延迟/基線遲延 baseline delay
基线延长线/基線延長 baseline extension
基线制/基線系統 base line system
基线转弯/基本轉彎 base turn
基性岩/基性岩 basic rock
基岩/基岩,地盤岩,岩石底床 bedrock
基岩图/岩石地質圖 solid map
基因资源/遺傳資源 genetic resources
基油/基油 base oil
基于性能的抗震设计/基于性能的抗震設計 performance-based seismic design
基站/基站 index station
基值误差/基準誤差 datum error
基质/基質 substrate
基桩病害检测系统/基樁診斷系統 foundation pile diagnosis system
基桩检测/樁基檢測 testing of pile foundation, pile foundation test
基准地价/基準地價 basic land price
基准分段/基準分段 basic section
基准刚度/基準勁度 reference stiffness
基准航空器/設計航機 datum aircraft
基准舰/基準艦 datum ship
基准量规/基準規 reference gage

基准楼板/基準樓板　reference floor
基准面/基準面　datum level, base plane
基准面层/基準面層　reference cover
基准[燃]气/參考氣體　reference gas
基准燃油低热值/基本燃料低熱值　fundamental fuel lower calorific value
基准收益率/要求報酬率　hurdle rate
基准水平面/基本水平面　standard sea level
基准纬度/基準緯度　standard parallel
基准线/基線,導引線　fiducial line, guide line
基座/基座,基架,底座　base, pedestal
基座坐标系/基座坐標系　base coordinate system
缉私船/緝私船,緝私艇　revenue cutter
畸变/畸變,失真,變形　distortion
畸变波/畸變波,扭曲波　distortional wave
畸变容限/畸變容限　distortion tolerance
畸变图谱/畸變圖譜　distortion pattern
畸变指数/畸變指數　distortion index
激波/震波　shock wave
激波-边界层干扰/激波-邊界層相互干擾　shock wave-boundary layer interaction
激波捕捉法/震波捕捉法　shock capturing method
激波捕捉算法/激波捕獲演算法　shock capturing algorithm
激波层/震波層　shock layer
激波风洞/震波風洞　shock tunnel
激波管/震波管　shock tube
激波光滑处理/震波光滑處理　smooth treatment of shock wave
激波极曲线/震波極圖　shock polar curve
激波膨胀波法/震波展開法　shock expansion method
激波失速/震波失速　shock stall
激波装配法/震波疏移法　shock fitting method
激光表层改性/雷射表面處理　laser surface modification
激光玻璃/雷射玻璃　laser glass
激光测高仪/雷射高度計　laser altimeter
激光测距/雷射測距　laser stadia ranging, electronic distance measurement
激光测距经纬仪/雷射測距經緯儀　theodolite with laser ranging
激光测距器/機載雷射測距儀　airborne laser range finder
激光测距仪/雷射偵距儀　laser rangefinder
激光测速仪/雷射測速儀　laser velocimeter
激光测探仪/雷射測深儀　laser sounder
激光淬火/雷射淬火　laser hardening, laser transformation hardening
激光打孔/雷射光束穿孔　laser beam perforation
激光点火/雷射點火　laser ignition
激光定位测量/雷射定位測量　laser location surveying
激光动平衡/雷射動態平衡　laser dynamic balancing
激光多普勒测速仪/都卜勒雷射測速儀　laser Doppler velocimeter
激光多普勒风速计/雷射都卜勒風速計　laser-Doppler anemometer
激光防护/雷射防護　protection of laser hazard
激光跟踪/雷射跟蹤　laser tracking
激光跟踪测量系统/雷射追蹤測量系統　laser tracking measurement system
激光跟踪照射器/追蹤照射雷射器　tracking illuminator laser
激光光网探测器/雷射螢幕產生器　laser screen generator
激光焊/雷射電阻焊接　laser beam welding
激光化学气相沉积/雷射化學氣相沈積　laser chemical vapor deposition
激光回波率/雷射回波比　laser echo ratio
激光加工/雷射光束加工　laser beam machining
激光角反射体/雷射角反射器　laser corner reflector
激光校靶/雷射瞄準　laser boresight
激光雷达/雷射雷達,光達　laser radar, lidar
激光脉冲重复频率/雷射脈衝往復頻　laser pulse repetition frequency
激光瞄准仪/雷射瞄準儀　laser aiming instrument
激光屏显示/雷射屏顯示　laser-screen method of flow visualization
激光器/雷射二極體　laser diode, LD
激光铅垂仪/雷射鉛垂儀　laser plummet apparatus
激光切割/雷射光束切割　laser beam cutting
[激光]全息玻璃/雷射玻璃　laser glass
激光全息干涉仪/雷射全像干擾計　laser holographic interferometer
激光全息检测/雷射全像術檢驗　laser holography testing
激光全息照相/雷射全像術　laser holography
激光热处理/雷射熱處理　laser heat treatment
激光热导仪/雷射熱導計　laser conductometer
激光熔覆/雷射熔融塗層　laser melting coating
激光散斑/雷射斑點　laser speckle
激光散斑干涉仪/雷射斑點干涉儀　laser speckle interferometer
激光束加工/雷射光束加工　laser beam machining
激光陀螺仪/雷射迴旋儀　laser gyro, laser

gyroscope
激光物理气相沉积/雷射物理氣相沈積　laser physical vapor deposition
激光引信/雷射引信　laser fuze
激光诱导荧光/雷射誘導螢光　fluorescence induced by laser
激光制导/雷射導引　laser guidance
激光装置/雷射裝置　laser device
激光准直/雷射對準　laser alignment
激光准直法/雷射準直法　method of laser alignment
激光准直挠度测量/雷射校準撓度測量　laser alignment deflection measurement
激光准直仪/雷射準直儀　laser collimator
激光自动跟踪/雷射自動追蹤　laser automatic tracking
激光自动找平装置/雷射自動平層裝置　laser automatic leveling device
激活/啟動　activation
激进式规划/激進式規劃　radical planning
激励/激勵,激發　excitation
激励花园/激勵花園,激勵園林　incentive garden
激励[振]频率/激振頻率　exciting frequency
激流装置/激紊裝置　turbulence stimulator
激振/激振動　excitation
激振机/激振機　vibration exciter
激振器/激振器,振動器　vibration excitor, vibration generator
激振试验/激振試驗　exciter test
级/級,等级,级别　level, grade
1级风/1級,軟風　light air
2级风/2級,輕風　light breeze
3级风/3級,微風　gentle breeze
4级风/4級,和風　moderate breeze
5级风/5級,清勁風　fresh breeze
6级风/6級,強風　strong breeze
7级风/7級,疾風　near gale
8级风/8級,大風　gale
9级风/9級,烈風　strong gale
10级风/10級,狂風　storm
11级风/11級,暴風　violent storm
12级风/12級,颶風　hurricane
级间段/級間段　interstate section
级间段铁轮支架车/級間段鐵輪臺車　interstage section iron wheel carriage
级间分离/階段分離　stage separation, staging
级间分离试验/階段分離試驗　stage separation test
A级旅游景区/A級旅遊區　A grade tourist scenic
级配/級配,分级,分等　gradation

级配不良/劣級配　poor grade
级配发路面/級配發路面　pavement by grading method
级配反滤层/級配過濾料　graded filter
级配集料基层/級配碎石基層　graded aggregate base
级配控制设备/級配控制廠　gradation control plant
级配路面/級配路面　graded aggregate pavement
级配曲线/級配曲線　grading curve
级配砂/級配砂　graded sand
级效率/級效率　stage efficiency
极地冰/極冰　polar ice
极[地]轨道/極軌道　polar orbit
极地考察船/極地考察船　polar expedition ship
极端低温/極端低溫　extreme hypothermy
极端高温/極端高溫　extreme hyperthermia
极端工况/極端運行情況　extreme operating condition
极锋/極鋒區　polar front
极冠吸收/極冠吸收　polar cap absorption, PCA
极惯性矩/極慣性矩　polar moment of inertia
极光/極光　aurora
极轨道/極軌道　polar orbit
极轨道卫星业务/極軌道衛星業務　polar orbiting satellite service
极轨气象卫星/極軌道氣象衛星　polar orbit meteorological satellite
极好能见度/能見度極佳　visibility excellent
极化分集/極化分集　polarization diversity
极化误差/極化誤差　polarization error
极距/極距　polar distance
极帽/極冠　polar cap
极片/屏極　plate
极频轨道电路/極頻軌道電路　polar-frequency pulse track circuit
极频自动闭塞/極頻自動閉塞　automatic block with polar frequency impulse track circuit
极谱分析/極譜分析[法]　polarographic analysis
极谱分析室/極譜室　polarography room
极区船/北極冰區船　arctic ship
极区导航/極區導航　polar navigation
极区航行/極區航行　polar navigation
极曲线/極[曲]線　polar, polar curve
极软钢/低碳鋼　dead mild steel
极色/極色　polar color
极少主义/極簡主義　minimalism
极射线/極射線　polar ray
极投影/極心投影　polar projection

极限承载力/極限承載力　ultimate bearing capacity
BMX 极限单车场/小輪自行車極限單車場　BMX bike limit ground
极限的/極限的,最後的　ultimate
极限动倾角/最大動傾角　maximum angle of dynamic inclination
极限分析/極限分析　limit analysis
极限负载/極限負載,極限載荷　limiting load
极限荷载设计/極限載重設計法　ultimate load design
极限横倾力矩/最大傾側力矩　maximum heeling moment
极限环/極限環　limit cycle
极限环角速度/極限環角速率　angular rate of limit cycle
极限间隙/間隙限制,許可限制　clearance limit
极限剪切/極限剪力　ultimate shear
极限精度加工/極限精度加工　limiting accuracy machining
极限开关/極限開關　proximity limit switch
极限抗拉应力/極限張應力　ultimate tensile stress
极限摩擦/極限摩擦　limiting friction
极限磨损/磨耗限度　wear limit
极限扭矩/極限扭矩　ultimate torque
极限平衡分析/極限平衡分析　limit equilibrium analysis
极限强度设计法/破壞強度設計法　ultimate strength design method
极限容量/極限容量　limited capacity
极限蠕变应力/極限潛變應力　limiting creep stress
极限设计/極限設計　limit design
极限使用寿命/極限使用壽命　ultimate life
极限速度/臨界速度,臨界流速　critical velocity
极限条件/極限條件,界限條件　limiting condition
极限弯矩/極限彎矩　ultimate moment
极限误差/極限誤差　limit error
极限压强/極限壓力　ultimate pressure
极限应变/極限應變　ultimate strain
极限应力/極限應力　ultimate stress
极限运动/極限運動　limit movement
极限运动场/極限運動場　extreme sport hall
极限载荷/極限負載,終極負載　ultimate load
极限支承压力/極限支承壓力　ultimate bearing pressure
极限重心高度/臨界重心高度　critical height of center of gravity
极限状态/極限狀態　limit state, ultimate limit state
极限状态法/極限狀態法　limit state method
极限状态方程/極限狀態方程　limit state equation
极限状态设计法/極限狀態設計方法,界限狀態設計法　limit state design method
极性变换/極性變換,反向,倒轉　reversal
极性检查电路/極性檢查電路　polarity checking circuit
极性交叉/極性交叉　polar transposition
极值分布/極值分布　extremal distribution
极重要/極重要　vital
极柱/端子,接線柱　terminal
极坐标法/極坐標法　polar coordinate method
极坐标滑阀图/滑閥極坐標圖　polar slide valve diagram
极坐标机器人/極面機器人　polar robot
即期船/即期船　prompt ship
即期装船/即時裝載　prompt loading
即时位置/現在位置　present position
即时性反应/及時的反應　immediate response
即食食品/即食食物　ready-to-eat food
急救/急救　medical first aid
急救医疗器具/急救醫藥用品　first aid outfit
急救站/急救站,救護站,護理站　first aid station, first-aid station
急救中心/急救中心　emergency center
急流/急流　rapid stream
急流槽/滑槽　chute
急流引水/急流引水　rapid flow diversion
急盘旋下降/盤旋俯衝　dive spiral
急闪光/快速閃光　quick flashing light
急性缺氧检查/急性缺氧檢查　acute hypoxia examination
急运货/急運貨,急裝貨　distress cargo
急诊部/急診部,急診室　emergency department
疾病预防控制中心/疾病管制與預防中心　center for disease control and prevention
棘轮装置/棘輪裝置　ratchet gear
棘爪棘轮机构/棘輪與爪機構　ratchet and pawl mechanism
集尘器/集塵器　dirt collector
集[沉]砂池/沈砂槽　grit catcher
集成建筑/集成建築　integrated building
集电环/滑環　slip ring
集电靴/集電靴　collector shoe
集合点/合并點,CP 點　consolidation point, CP
集合点缆线/合并點纜線　consolidation point cable
集合模型/聚合模型　aggregation model
集会广场/集會廣場　congregation plaza
集建区/集建區,集中建設區　collective buildable zone

集结时间/集結時間　car detention time under accumulation
集结性客流/集合體客運交通,聚合體客運交通　aggregate passenger traffic
集居规模/集居規模　size of settlement
集居类型/集居模式　settlement pattern
集居模式/集居模式　settlement pattern
集聚/聚集　conglomeration, agglomeration
集聚-辐射效应/聚集-輻射效應　concentration-radiation effect
集控室控制/主機控制室控制　engine control room control
集块参数/集塊參數　lump parameter
集料/集料,骨材　aggregate
集料剥落/集料剝落　stripping of aggregate
集料剥落试验/集料剝離試驗　stripping test for aggregate
集料级配/集料級配,骨材級配　grading of aggregate
[集料]亲水系数/親水係數　hydrophilic coefficient
集贸市场/集貿市場,農產品市場　farm product market
集气罐/空氣收集器　air collector
集气圆顶/集氣圓頂　gas dome
集散车道/集散道　collector distributor lane
集散道路/集散道路　collector distributor road
集散式布风器/噴氣擴散器　air jet diffuser
集散厅/穿堂層　concourse
集砂器/集砂設備　grit collector
集渗沟/滲水溝　infiltration ditch
集束炸弹/集束炸彈　cluster bomb unit
集水槽/集水槽　gully
集水池/集水箱　water collection tank
集水沟/集水溝　collecting channel
集水管道/集水管　collecting conduit
集水井/集水井　collecting well, drop pit
集水坑/集水坑　sump
集水口/集水口　gulley
集水区/集水區　gathering ground
集水渠/集水渠　collecting channel
集水渗透检查井/集水滲透檢查井　collect-infiltration manhole
集水时间/集水時間,進水時間,集流時間　inlet time
集水系统/集水系統　collecting system
集体合住宅/集合住宅　collective housing, multiple dwelling
集污舱/貯留艙　holding tank
集鱼灯/集魚燈　fishing lamp
集约发展/密集發展　compact development

集中拌制混凝土/集中式拌和混凝土　central mixed concrete
集中报警系统/網路報警　remote alarm system
集中操纵货油装卸系统/集中操縱貨油裝卸系統　centralized operation cargo oil pumping system
集中道岔/集中道岔　centrally operated switch
集中电源/集中電源　centrally connected power source
集中供电/集中供電　centrally connected power supply
集中供电方式/集中供電系統　centralized power supply system
集中供暖/中央暖氣供應　central heating
集中供热/集中供熱　centralized heating, central heating supply, centralized heat supply
集中供热普及率/集中供熱涵蓋率　popularity rate of centralized heating
集中化修理/集中化設備修理　centralization of repair
集中监测器/集中偵測器　centralized monitor
集中监视系统/中央監視系統　centralized monitoring system
集中建设区/集中建設區,集建區　collective buildable zone
集中控制/集中控制,集控,中心控制　centralized control
集中力/集中力　concentrated force
集中联锁/集中聯鎖　centralized interlocking
集中排水/集中排水　concentrated drainage
集中配料厂/集中配料廠　central batching plant
集中器/集中機,集線器　concentrator
集中热水供应系统/集中熱水供應系統　central hot water supply system
集中式供水/集中供水　central water supply
集中式混凝土拌和厂/集中式混凝土拌和廠　central concrete mixing plant
集中式空气调节系统/中央空調系統,中央空氣調節系統　central air conditioning system
集中式逆变器/集中式逆變器　centralized inverter
集中式网络/集中式網路,中控式網路　centralized network
集中载荷/集中負載,集中荷重　concentrated load
集中质量/集中質量,堆集質量　lumped mass
集重货物/集重貨物　concentrated weight goods
集装袋/[柔性]集裝袋　contain bag, flexible freight container
集装化运输/集裝箱運輸　containerized traffic

集装货/貨櫃裝載貨物　containerized cargo
集装箱/集裝箱,貨櫃　container, freight container
集装箱包箱运价/集裝箱包箱運價　charter rate by number of containers
集装箱舱/貨櫃艙　container hold
集装箱叉车/集裝箱叉車　container fork lift
集装箱车/貨櫃車　container car
集装箱船/貨櫃船　container ship
集装箱导具/貨櫃導具　container guide fitting
集装箱吊架/貨櫃吊架　container lifting spreader
集装箱吊具/貨櫃吊具,貨櫃吊架　container lifting spreader, container spreader, spreader
集装箱堆场/貨櫃場　container yard, CY
集装箱额定质量/集裝箱額定質量　rating of freight container
集装箱服务费/貨櫃服務費　container service charge
集装箱挂车/貨櫃拖車　container trailer
集装箱化率/集裝箱化率　containerization ratio
集装箱货车/集裝箱運輸車　container carrier
集装箱货运站/貨櫃集散站　container freight station, CFS
[集装]箱积载图/[貨物]裝載圖　stowage plan
集装箱建筑/集裝箱建築　container architecture
集装箱空箱运价/集裝箱空箱運價　rate of empty container
集装箱栏板挂车/貨櫃側卸拖車　container dropside trailer
集装箱码头/貨櫃碼頭　container wharf, container pier
集装箱内容积/貨櫃內容積　container volume capacity
集装箱平板挂车/貨櫃平板拖車　container platform trailer
[集装]箱容利用率/貨櫃容利用率　container volume capacity utilizing ratio
[集装]箱容系数/貨櫃容係數　container specific volume capacity coefficient
集装箱维修费/集裝箱維修費　container maintenance charge
[集装]箱位/箱位　container lot
集装箱箱次费/集裝箱箱次費　per container charge
集装箱运输/貨櫃運輸　container transport, freight container traffic
集装箱载重/貨櫃載重量　payload of freight container
[集装]箱载重利用率/貨櫃載重利用率　container load capacity utilizing ratio
集装箱中转费/集裝箱中轉費　container transit charge
集装箱重箱运价/集裝箱重箱運價　rate of loaded container
集装箱专用挂车/貨櫃專用拖車　container flatframe trailer
集装箱装箱单/貨櫃裝櫃圖　container load plan
集装箱装卸机械/貨櫃裝卸機械　container handling machinery
集装箱[装卸]作业区/貨櫃終站基地　container terminal
集装箱自重/貨櫃自重　tare mass of freight container
集装箱自重系数/貨櫃自重係數　coefficient of container dead weight
集装箱自装卸挂车/貨櫃自裝載拖車　self loading container trailer
集总加感/集總加感　lumped loading
瘠土/貧瘠土　infertile soil
几何不变体系/幾何不變體系,幾何穩定系統　geometrically stable system
几何非线性分析/幾何非線性分析　geometric nonlinearity analysis
几何刚度矩阵/幾何[力]勁度矩陣　geometric stiffness matrix
几何惯性导航系统/幾何慣性導航系統　geometric inertial navigation system
几何校正/幾何訂正　geometric correction, geometric rectification
几何可变结构/幾何形不穩定結構　geometrically unstable structure
几何可变体系/幾何可變體系,幾何不穩系統　geometrically unstable system
几何量测量/幾何形狀量測　geometric measurement
几何扭转/幾何扭轉　geometric twist
几何声学/幾何聲學　geometrical acoustics
几何式园林/幾何式園林　geometric garden style
几何稳定性/幾何穩定性　geometric stability
几何相似/幾何相似　geometrical similarity
几何相似船模/幾何相似模型　geometrical similarty model, geometrically similar ship models
[几何]压缩比/壓縮比　compression ratio
挤岔/擠岔　forcing open of the point
挤岔报警/擠岔報警　alarm for a trailed switch
挤轨/軌距加寬度,軌距擴大　gage widening
挤拉成形/拉擠成型　pultrusion process, pultrude
挤密砂桩/壓密沙樁　sand compaction pile
挤奶间/擠乳間,擠乳室　milking parlor
挤切/擠切　dissectible

挤切销/擠切削 dissectible pin
挤塑聚苯板/EPS 板 expanded polystyrene board
挤脱/擠脱 trailable
挤压闭胸盾构/擠壓閉胸盾構 closed squeezing shield, closed extruding shield
挤压混凝土衬砌/擠壓混凝土襯砌 extruding concrete tunnel lining, extruded concrete lining
挤压式供应系统/壓力輸給系統 pressure-feed system
挤压式液体火箭发动机/擠壓式液體火箭發動機 pressure-feed liquid rocket engine
挤压水/壓縮水 water of compaction
挤压涡流/擠壓渦流 extruding swirl
挤压型材/擠壓型材 extruded shape
挤压叶型/擠壓斷面 extruded section
挤压油膜阻尼器/擠壓油膜阻尼器 squeeze oil film damper
挤压铸造/壓擠鑄造 squeeze casting
挤压砖/擠出瓦 extruded brick, extruded tile
给风阀/給風閥 feed valve
给料机/加料機,進料機 feeder
给气比/給氣比 delivery ratio
给气调整阀/壓力調節閥 pressure regulating valve
给水/給水 feed water, water supply, feedwater
给水倍率/給水率 feed water ratio
给水泵房/給水泵房 water pump room
给水处理/給水處理 water supply treatment, feed water treatment
给水处理厂/自來水廠 water treatment plant
给水度/給水度 specific yield
给水阀/給水閥 feed valve, feed water valve
给水风缸/給水風缸 water supply air reservoir
给水工程/給水工程 water supply engineering
给水管/給水管線,供水管 water service pipe, supply line
给水加热器/給水加熱器 feed water heater
给水软化装置/給水軟化裝置 water-softening plant
给水设备/給水設備,給水設施 water supply equipment, water supply facility
给水水源/[給水]水源 water source, water supply source
给水隧洞/給水隧道 water supply tunnel
给水调整阀/給水調整閥 water supply governer valve
给水系统/給水系統,供水系統 water supply system
给水预热装置/給水加熱器 feed water heater
给水站/給水站 water supply station
给水主干管/給水幹管 trunk main

给水装置/給水裝置,供水裝置 feed water rigging, water-service installation
脊骨梁桥/脊柱梁橋 spine girder bridge
脊瓦/脊瓦 ridge tile
计测磁记录器/計測磁記錄器 instrumentation tape recorder
计程包车运价/計程包車運價 charter rate by distance
计程绳/測深線 log line
计程仪/計程儀 log, log line
计程仪读数/計程儀讀數 log reading
计程仪改正率/計程儀修正率 percentage of log correction
计程仪航程/測程儀航程 distance by log
计程仪航速/計程儀航速 speed by log
计费吨公里/計費噸公里 tonne-kilometers charged
计费吨公里成本/計費噸公里成本 cost of charged ton-kilometer
计费里程/計費里程 charged mileage
计费时间/計費時間 chargeable time
计费重量/計費重量 charged weight
计划调度/計劃調度 planned dispatching
计划航迹向/預期航向 course of advance, CA
计划航速/前進速 speed of advance
计划洪水/規劃洪水 project flood
计划换地/計劃換地 suspense replotting
计划内运输/計劃內運輸 planned freight traffic
计划评估法/計擊評核術 program evaluation and review technique, PERT
计划权/規劃權 planning power
计划任务书/計劃任務書 planning assignment
计划外维护/臨時維護,不定期維護 unscheduled maintenance
计划外运输/計劃外運輸 out-of-plan freight traffic, unplanned freight traffic
计划维修/定期維護,週檢 scheduled maintenance
计划预防维修制度/計劃預防維修制度 scheduled preventive maintenance and repair system
计划运输/計劃運輸 planned transport
计价标准/計價標準 charge standard
计件行包/計件行李 piece luggage
计量保证/計量保證 metrological assurance
计量保证体系/計量保證體系 metrological assurance system
计量泵/計量泵 metering pump
计量管理/計量管理 metrological management
计量监督/計量監督 metrological supervision
计量检定规程/計量檢定規程 regulation of

计量器具/量測儀器　measuring instruments
计量确认/計量確認　metrological confirmation
计量室/計量室　metrology room
计量系统/計量收費制　metered system
计量[学]/計量學,度量衡學　metrology
计量与支付/定額付款　measurement and payment
计权/加權　weighting
计权标准化声压级差/加權標準化聲壓位準差　weighted standardized sound pressure level difference
计权标准化撞击声压级/加權標準化衝擊聲壓位準　weighted standardized impact sound pressure level
计权表观隔声量/加權視隔音指標　weighted apparent sound reduction index
计权隔声量/加權聲音降低指數　weighted sound reduction index
计权规范化声压级差/加權正規化聲壓位準差　weighted normalized sound pressure level difference
计权规范化撞击声压级/加權正規化衝擊聲壓位準　weighted normalized impact sound pressure level
A计权声压级/A加權聲壓位準　A-weighted sound pressure level
计权网络/加權網路　weighting network
计日工/計日工　daywork labor
计时/計時,定時　timing
计时包车运价/計時包車運價　charter rate by time
计时记分牌/計分板　scoreboard
计时控制圆盘/計時控制圓盤　time dial
计时设备机房/計時裝置機械室　timing device mechanical room
Z计数/Z計數　Z-count
计算采暖期/計算採暖期　heating period for calculation
计算方位/計算方位　calculated azimuth, computed azimuth
计算风力力臂/計算風壓力臂　calculated wind pressure lever
计算风力力矩/計算風壓力矩　calculated wind pressure moment
计算高度/計算高度　calculated altitude, computed altitude
计算供汽率/計算供汽率　calculated rate of evaporation for engine
计算机辅助避碰/電腦輔助避碰　computer assisted collision avoidance
计算机辅助测量和控制/計算機輔助測量與控制　computer aided measurement and control, CAMAC
计算机辅助测试/電腦輔助測試　computer aided testing, CAT
计算机辅助工程/電腦輔助工程　computer aided engineering, CAE
计算机辅助工艺规程编制/電腦輔助制程規劃　computer aided process planning, CAPP
计算机辅助规划/電腦輔助規劃　computer aided planning
计算机辅助绘图/電腦輔助製圖　computer aided drawing, CA drawing
计算机辅助软件工程/電腦輔助軟體工程　computer aided software engineering, CASE
计算机辅助训练器/電腦輔助訓練機　computer aided trainer, CAT
计算机辅助制造/電腦輔助製造　computer aided manufacturing, CAM
计算机几何建模/電腦幾何建模　computer geometric modeling
计算机教室/電腦教室　computer classroom
计算机绝对坐标/電腦絕對坐標　computer absolute coordinate
计算机控制系统/計算機控制系統　computer control system
计算机零点/電腦零值　computer coordinate zero
计算机流动显示/電腦流動可視化　flow visualization by computer
计算机设计阶段/電腦設計階段　computer design phase
计算机设计图/電腦設計圖　computer design drawing
计算机设计文件/電腦設計檔案　computer design file
计算机实体模型/電腦實體模型　computer solid model
计算机图学/電腦繪圖　computer graphics, CG
计算机网[络]/電腦網路　computer network
计算机网络机房/電腦網[路]控制室　computer network room
计算机系统/電腦系統　computer system
计算机相对坐标/電腦相對坐標　computer relative coordinate
计算机协同设计/電腦協同設計　computer cooperative design
计算机信息系统安全专用产品/電腦資訊系統資料結構　security product for computer information system
计算机遥测/電腦遙測系統　computer telemetry system
计算机优化设计/電腦最佳化設計　computer

optimization design
计算机制图/電腦輔助製圖　computer aided drawing, CA drawing
计算结构力学/計算結構力學　computational structural mechanics
计算空气动力学/計算空氣動力學　computational aerodynamics
计算跨径/計算跨徑　calculated span
计算流体力学/計算流體力學　computational fluid mechanics
计算期/計算期　account period
计算矢高/計算矢高　calculated rise of arch
计算提前角的光学瞄准/前置計算光學瞄準　lead computing optical sight, LCOS
计算纬度/推算緯度　latitude by account
计算误差/計算誤差　error in calculation
计算载荷/設計負載　design load
计算遮断比/計算遮斷比　calculated cut-off
计箱装卸费/計箱裝卸費　handling charge by container number
计心造/計心造　filled-heart method, jixinzao
计重货物/計重貨　weight cargo
计轴自动闭塞/計軸自動閉塞　automatic block with axle counter
记发器/記發器,記錄器　register
记号/記號,標記　marking
记录方式/記錄模式　recording mode
记录式[测量]仪器/記錄式量測儀器　recording measuring instrument
记录台/記錄臺　recording desk
记录制/記錄制　record demand working
记名背书/記名背書　named endorsement
记名提单/記名載貨證券　straight bill of lading
记事灯/記事燈　writing lamp
记忆花园/記憶花園　anamnestic garden
记忆效应/記憶效應　memory effect
记忆音/記憶音　memorial sound
记忆-重发遥测/記憶重播遙測　memory-replay telemetry
记者席/記者席　press seat
纪念地/紀念地　commemorative place
纪念地类/紀念地類　memorial type
纪念公园/紀念公園,生命紀念園區　memorial park, commemorative park
纪念馆/紀念館　memorial museum
纪念林/紀念林　memorial forest
纪念物/紀念物　monument
纪念性建筑/紀念[性]建築　monumental architecture, monumental building
技防/技術保護　technical protection
3S技术/3S技術　RS, GIS, GPS technology, 3S technology
技术安全组/技術安全性群組　technical safety team
技术标准规定/技術標準規定　technical standard order, TSO
技术厂房/技術廠房　technical preparation building
技术尺寸/技術尺寸　technical size
技术档案室/技術檔案室　technical archives room
技术防范/技術保護　technical protection
技术服务/技術服務　technical service
技术改造/技術革新　technical renovation, technical remolding
技术规范/[技術]規範,規格　technical specification, specification
技术检验/技術檢驗　technical checking
技术交底/技術交底　construction technical clarification
技术经济可行性/技術經濟可行性　technoeconomic feasibility
技术经济论证/技術經濟論證　technoeconomic appraisal
技术经济指标/技術經濟指標　technoeconomic indicator
技术设计/技術設計　technical design
技术审查/技術審查　technical examiniation
技术试验卫星/技術試驗衛星　technological experiment satellite
技术试验卫星机械手/技術試驗衛星機械手　engineering test satellite manipulator, technological test satellite manipulator
技术速度/技術速度　technical speed
技术淘汰寿命/技術有效壽命　technologically useful life
技术条款/技術條款　technical specifications
技术通报/技術通報　technical bulletin
技术性试验/技術性試驗　technical test
技术站/技術站　technical station
技术整备/技術整備　technical servicing
技术直达列车/技術直達列車　technical through train
技术指标/技術指標　technical index
技术质量组/技術品質組　technical quality team
技术状态更改控制/型態變更控制　configuration change control
技术状态管理/型態管理　configuration management
技术[准备]区/技術區,[火箭]技術陣地　technical

area

技术准备完好率/技術準備完好率　technical readiness

忌装/忌裝　avoidance of mixed loading

季风/季[候]風,季節風　monsoon, monsoon wind

季节电功率/季節電力　seasonal power

季节航路/季節性航路　seasonal route

季节交通量变化图/季節性交通型態　seasonal traffic pattern

季节期/季節期間　seasonal periods

季节性冻土/季節凍土　seasonal frozen ground

季节性河流/季節性河流,間歇溪流　seasonal river, ephemeral stream

季节性恢复/季節恢復　seasonal recovery

季节性货源/季節性貨源　seasonal freight source

季节性径流/季節性徑流　seasonal runoff

季节性客流/季節性客運交通　seasonal passenger traffic

季节性库容/季節蓄水　seasonal storage

季节性热带区域/季節性熱帶區域　seasonal tropical area

季节性热负荷/季節性負荷　seasonal heating load

季节性维护/季節性維護　seasonal maintenance

季相/季[節]相　seasonal aspect

季相景观/季相景觀　seasonal phenomena

季[雨]林/季風雨林　monsoon forest

剂量率响应/劑量率響應　dose rate response

剂量限值/劑量限度　dose limit

迹流/跡流,伴流　wake

迹线/徑線,路線　path line

既有铁路/既有線路　existing railway

既有线/現有線　existing line

既有线测量/既有線測量　survey of existing railway

继电半自动闭塞系统/繼電半自動式閉鎖系統　all-relay semi-automatic block system

继电并联传递网路/繼電并聯傳遞網路　successively worked parallel relay network

继电并联网路/繼電并聯網路　parallel relay network

继电串联网路/繼電串聯網路　series relay network

继电联锁/繼電聯鎖裝置　relay interlocking

继电器/繼電器　relay

继电器防震架/繼電器防震架　shock absorber base for relays

继电器控制电源/繼電器控制電源　power source for relay control

继电器灵敏度/繼電器靈敏度　relay sensitivity

继电器室/繼電器室　relay room

继电器释放/繼電器釋放　relay released

继电器吸起/繼電器吸動　relay energized

继电器箱/繼電器箱,繼電器櫃　relay case

继电式电气集中联锁/全電驛聯鎖　all-relay interlocking

继动泵/接力水泵　relay pump

继续/繼續操作　carry on

祭坛/祭殿　altar

寄生细菌/寄生菌　parasitic bacteria

寄生植物/寄生植物　parasitic plant

寄宿制托儿所/託兒所　boarding nursery

寄宿制学校/寄宿學校　boarding school

加班飞行/加班飛行　extra schedule flight

加冰所/加冰所　re-icing point

加撑支架/加撑支架　racked timbering

加臭/加臭[劑]　odorization

加大链环/加大鏈環　enlarged link

加顶垂直折合机车天线/竪向荷載合機車天線　vertical loading folded locomotive antenna

加顶圆盘机车天线/轉盤負載機車天線　disc-loading locomotive antenna

加尔佐尼庄园/加爾佐尼莊園　Villa Garzoni

加负荷程序/加載方案　load-up program

加感电缆/加感電纜,負載電纜　loaded cable

加感节距/加感節距,加感線圈間距　loading coil spacing

加感箱/加感箱　loading coil box

加工厂建筑/加工廠建築　fabrication plant building

加工车间/加工車間　processing shop

加工拖网渔船/拖網加工船　factory trawler

加工余量/机制裕度　machine finish allowance, machining allowance

加固/加強,補強　stiffening

加固层/合并層　consolidating layer

加固地基/加固地基　consolidated subsoil, improved foundation, improved ground

加固分配/硬度分配　hardness allocation

加固设计/硬度設計　hardness design

加固天线窗材料/加固天線窗材料　hardened antenna window material

加固注浆/固結灌漿　consolidation grouting

加荷时效/加負載時效,裝載時效　load up ageing

加荷载重/加荷載重　load surcharge

加减速顶/加減速頂　dowty accelerator-retarder

加减速延误/加減速延誤　acceleration-deceleration delay

加筋壳结构/加勁殼　stiffening shell

加筋土/加筋土　reinforced earth

加筋土挡土墙/加筋土擋土牆　reinforced earth

retaining wall, reinforced soil retaining wall
加劲板/加勁板　stiffening plate
加劲壳结构/加勁殼結構　stiffened shell structure
加劲肋/加勁肋,加强肋　stiffener
加劲梁/加勁梁,加強梁　stiffening girder, stiffening beam
加[劲]腋/托肩,拱腰　haunch
加快票/加快票　fast extra ticket
加宽缓和段/加寬緩和區,曲線加寬過渡區　transition zone of curve widening
加宽渐变段/加寬之配合　attainment of widening
加宽转角式交叉口/加寬轉角式交叉口　intersection with widened corner
加力比/昇推比　augmentation ratio
加力牵引坡度/輔助坡　assisting grade
加力燃烧室/後燃器　afterburner
加氯消毒/氯消毒　disinfection by chlorine
加煤机/加煤機　stoker
加密等级/加密等級　secret grade
加气混凝土/加氣混凝土,輸氣混凝土　aerated concrete
加气混凝土板/加氣混凝土板　autoclaved aerated concrete slab
加气混凝土砌块/加氣混凝土砌塊　aerated concrete block
加气剂/加氣劑,輸氣劑　air entraining agent, gas forming admixture
加强/加強,補強　stiffening
加强层/加強層,加強材　reinforcement, story with outrigger and belt member
加强构件/受拉桿件　tension member
加强筋/加強筋　stiffener
加强框/加強框　reinforced bulkhead
加强肋/加強肋　reinforced rib
加强氯丁橡胶板接合/加強氯丁橡膠板接合　strengthened neoprene plate joint
加强线/饋電導線　line feeder
加权残值法/加權留數法　weighted residual method
加权平均/加權平均　weighted average
加权蠕变比/加權潛變比　weighted-creep ratio
加权算术平均值/加權算術平均值　weighted arithmetic average
加权算术平均值的实验标准偏差/加權算術平均值實驗標準離差　experimental standard deviation of weighted arithmetic average
加热/加熱　heating
加热集装箱/加熱集裝箱　heated container
加热水倍率/加熱水率　heating water ratio
加热损失/加熱損失　heating loss
加热损失试验/加熱損耗試驗　heating loss test
加热箱/加熱櫃　heating container
加热型塑料/加熱型塑膠　hot laid plastic
加热蒸汽/加熱蒸汽　heating steam
加湿/增濕[作用]　humidification
加湿器/加濕器,給濕器　humidifier
加速/加速[度],增速　speeding up, acceleration
加速车道/加速車道　acceleration lane
加速顶/加速頂　dowty accelerator
加速度/加速度　acceleration
加速度冲击[响应]谱/加速度衝擊[響應]譜　acceleration shock response spectrum
加速度导纳/加速度導納　entrance
加速度反馈/加速度反饋　acceleration feedback
加速度防护/加速度防護　acceleration protection
加速度分量/加速度分量　component of acceleration
加速度环境/加速度環境　acceleration environment
加速[度]计/加速[度]計,加速儀[表]　accelerometer
加速度计摆轴/加速度計擺軸　pendulous axis of accelerometer
加速度计输出轴/加速度計輸出軸　output axis of accelerometer
加速度计输入轴/加速度計輸入軸　input axis of accelerometer
加速度计坐标系/加速度計坐標系　accelerometer coordinate system
加速度耐力/耐G力　acceleration tolerance
加速度耐力检查/耐G力檢查　acceleration tolerance examination
加速度耐力训练/耐G力訓練　acceleration tolerance training
加速度谱/加速振動譜　acceleration spectrum
加速度性肺萎陷/加速度致成的肺不張症　acceleration atelectasis
加速法/加速法　accelerating method
加速腐蚀试验/加速腐蝕試驗　accelerated corrosion test
加速工况/加速模態　accelerating mode
加速滑行/加速滑行　accelerating-coasting
加速缓坡/加速[緩]坡　easy gradient for acceleration, accelerating grade
加速老化试验/加速老化試驗　accelerated ageing test
加速力/加速力　acceleration force
加速坡/加速坡　accelerating grade, acceleration grade

加速燃气轮机/助力燃氣渦輪機,加力燃氣渦輪機 booster gas turbine
加速任务试车/加速任務試驗 accelerated mission test, AMT
加速试验/加速試驗,加速測試 accelerated test
加速寿命试验/加速壽命試驗 accelerated life test
加速停止距离/加速停止距離 accelerate stop distance
加速-停止距离/加速-停止距離 acclerate stop distance
加速通风/加速通風 accelarated draught
加速推送信号/加速推送信號 humping fast signal
加速性能/加速性能 acceleration performance
加速性能试验/加速度試驗 acceleration test
加速旋回/加速迴旋 acceleration turn
加速因子/加速因子 accelerated factor
加速噪声/加速雜訊 acceleration noise
加速制动阀部/加速制動閥部 accelerated application valve portion
加填料的沥青/和粉瀝青 filled bitumen
加温比/加溫比 temperature rise ratio
加温车/暖氣車 heater car
加温时间/暖機時間 warm-up time
加温套/蒸汽夾套 steam jacket
加温温室/加熱溫室 heated greenhouse
加温运输/加溫運輸 heating transport
加压泵站/輔助[中繼]電臺,昇壓電臺,增壓站 booster station
加压供氧系统/正壓氧氣系統 positive pressure oxygen system
加压过滤/壓力過濾 pressure filtration
加压呼吸/加壓呼吸 pressure breathing
加压溶解气体/加壓溶解氣體 gases dissolved under pressure
加压式燃油系统/封密加壓燃油系統 closed and pressured fuel system
加压头盔/加壓頭盔 pressure helmet
加腋/加腋 haunch
加腋梁/加腋梁 haunched beam
加油吊舱/加油吊艙 refuelling pod
加油平台/加油平臺 refuelling platform
加油艇/加油艇 bowser boat
加油站/加[燃]油站 oil fuel filling station, filling station
加载反力架/加載反力架 reaction frame for loading
加载阶段/載荷階段 loading stage
加载平台/加載平臺 weighted platform
加载设备/裝載設備 loading facilities
加载水箱/加載水箱 water tank for loading
加载速度/裝載速率 loading speed
加载速率/加載率 rate of loading
加载性能/加載性能 loaded performance
加重底镀/加重底板 surcharge base plate
加州承载比试验/美國加州承載比試驗 California bearing ratio test
加州承重比/加州承力比 California bearing ratio, CBR
加注/加注 loading, filling
加注方案/裝載計劃 loading plan
加注管/加油管,注油管 filler pipe
加注合练/加載預演 loading rehearsal
加注后总质量/加注後總質量 loaded-rocket mass, total mass after loading
加注控制室/加載控制室 loading control room
加注控制台/加載控制臺 loading test-control desk
加注前检查/加注前檢查 check before the loading
加注软管/加載柔性軟管 flexible hose for loading
加注升降温/加[負]載昇降溫 loading up-down the temperature
加注信号电缆/加注信號電纜 signal cable for loading
加注信号联试/加注信號聯試 loading signal unite test
加注信号台/加載信號盤 loading signal board
加注信号箱/加注號誌箱 loading signal box
加注压强/加注壓力 filling pressure
加注液位/加注液位 loading liquid level
加注硬管/加載硬管 hard hose for loading
加桩/加樁 additional stake, plus stake
家畜车/運畜[火]車廂 stock car
家具/家具 furniture
家具尺度/家具尺度 furniture scale
家禽车/家禽車 poultry car
家庭过滤器/家庭過濾器 domestic filter
家庭旅馆/家庭旅館 family hotel
家用电器厂/家用電器廠 domestic electric appliance plant
家用过滤器/家用過濾器 household fiter
家用排水管/家庭汙水管 house sewer
家用燃[气用]具/家用燃氣用具 domestic gas appliance
家用洗涤剂/家用清潔劑 household detergent
家装/房屋裝修 finishing and decoration of house
夹板拱架/夾板拱架 centering by clamped planks in arch shape
夹层/夾層 mezzanine

夹层板/夹心板　sandwich plate
夹层玻璃/層合玻璃　laminated glass
夹层结构/夾層結構　sandwich structure
夹层结构材料/夾層材料　sandwich material
夹层结构修补技术/夾心結構修補技術　sandwich construction repair technique
夹城/夾城　jiacheng
夹紧螺钉/夾緊螺絲,調整螺絲　clamping screw
夹景/夾景　vista line
夹具/夾具,緊固具,夾持器　gripgear, jigs and fixtures, gripper
夹片式锚具/夾片式錨具　strand tapered anchorage
夹丝玻璃/烙網玻璃　wired glass
夹心墙/空心牆　cavity wall
夹杂物/夾雜物　inclusion
夹直线/夾直線　intermediate straight line, tangent between curves
甲板/甲板　deck
甲板板/甲板板　deck plate
甲板边板/甲板緣[厚]板　deck stringer
甲板布置图/甲板布置圖,甲板位置圖　deck plan
甲板部/艙面部門　deck department
甲板冲洗管系/甲板冲洗管路系統　deck washing piping system
甲板窗/甲板透光玻璃　deck light
甲板方位角/甲板方位角　deck bearing
甲板防滑涂料/甲板防滑塗料　anti-slip deck paint, anti-skid deck paint
甲板敷料/甲板被覆　deck covering
甲板敷面/甲板被覆　deck covering
甲板高低角/甲板仰角　deck elevation
甲板高度/甲板上高度　altitude above deck
甲板横桁/甲板深橫桁　deck transverse
甲板货油管系/甲板貨油管路　cargo oil deck pipe line
甲板机械/艙面機械　deck machinery
甲板加压舱/船上加壓室　deck compression chamber
甲板间舱/甲板間艙　tween deck cargo space, tween deck space
甲板间肋骨/甲板間肋骨　tween deck frame
甲板结构/甲板結構　deck structure
甲板进水角/甲板浸水角　angle of deck immersion
甲板列板/甲板列　deck strake
甲板排水口/甲板排水孔　deck scupper
甲板漆/甲板漆　deck paint
甲板洒水系统/甲板灑水系統　deck sprinkle system, deck sprinkler system
甲板室/甲板室,甲板房艙　castle, deck house
甲板水封/甲板水封　deck water seal
甲板水排泄管系/甲板水排洩管路系統　deck water piping system
甲板梯/甲板梯　deck ladder
甲板通岸接头/通岸接頭　shore connection
甲板涂料/甲板漆　deck paint
甲板系索耳/艙面繫索扣　deck cleat
甲板线/甲板線　deck line
甲板淹湿/甲板濺濕,甲板上浪　deck wetness
甲板羊角/艙面繫索扣　deck cleat
甲板照明系统/甲板照明系統　deck lighting system
甲板中线/甲板中線　deck center line
甲板纵骨/甲板縱材　deck runer, deck longitudinal
甲板纵桁/甲板縱梁　deck girder
甲板坐标系/甲板坐標系　deck coordinate system
甲级分隔/A級區　A class division
甲烷发酵/甲烷發酵　methane fermentation
甲烷化/甲烷化　methanization, methanation
甲烷菌/甲烷細菌　methane bacterium
岬[角]/岬[角]　headland, cape
假彩色/假彩,假色　false color
假彩色合成/假彩合成　false-color composite
假彩色还原/假彩再現　false-color rendition
假舱壁/組合肋架　assembly frame
假底/[水槽]活動底　false bottom
假缝/假縫　dummy joint
假毂/假轂　dummy propeller boss
假回波/假回波　false echo
假结合/假縫　dummy joint
假绝热直减率/假絕熱傾率　pseudo-adiabatic lapse rate
假模/假模　dummy model
假目标产生器/假目標產生器　false-target generator, FTG
假凝/假凝　false set
假山/假山　artificial hill, rockery
假山工程/假山工程　rockery engineering
假山设计/假山設計　artificial hills design
假山石挡土墙/假山石擋土牆　rock retaining wall
假山石楼梯/假山石樓梯　rock stairway
假山验收/假山驗收　artificial hills acceptance
假山园/假山園　rock garden, Chinese rockery
假台口/假臺口　false proscenium
假线/附加[平衡]網路,補償網路　building-out network
假想出油量/假想油流出量　hypothetical outflow of oil
假信号/鬼信號　ghost signal

假引信/假引信　dummy fuze
假圆筒投影/擬圓柱投影　pseudo-cylindrical projection
假圆锥投影/擬圓錐投影　pseudo-conic projection
假载法/假負載法　pseudo load method
假植/假植　temporary planting
价格调整/價格調整　price adjustment
价格租金比/房價租金比　price to rent ratio
价目/價目　tariff classification
价值评估/價值評估　value assessment
驾驶舱/駕駛艙,座艙　cockpit, flight deck
驾驶操纵能力/駕駛人操縱能力　driving operation ability
驾驶船舶过失/駕駛船舶過失　default in navigation of the ship
驾驶杆/駕駛桿,操縱桿　control stick
驾驶和航行规则/操舵及航行規則　steering and sailing rules
驾驶技能/駕駛技能　driving skill
驾驶技术/駕駛技術　driving technique
驾驶甲板/航海甲板,橋樓甲板　bridge deck, navigation deck
驾驶模拟器/駕駛模擬機　driving simulator
驾驶能力/駕駛能力　driving ability
驾驶盘/駕駛柱,操縱桿　control column
驾驶疲劳/駕駛疲勞　driving fatigue
驾驶适应性/駕駛適應性　driving adaptability
驾驶室/駕駛室,[操]舵房　navigation bridge, wheel house
驾驶室视野试验/駕駛室視野試驗　test for field of vision of driver cab
驾驶室仪表板振动测定/駕駛室儀表板振動測定　vibration measurement of driver cab instrument board
驾驶台/駕駛臺,橋樓　bridge
驾驶台甲板/駕駛臺甲板　bridge deck
驾驶台间通信/船橋間通信　bridge-to-bridge communication
驾驶台控制/指揮臺操縱　bridge control
驾驶台遥控系统/駕駛臺遙控系統　bridge remote control system
驾驶习惯/駕駛習慣　driving habit
驾驶信息/駕駛訊息　driving information
驾驶行为/駕駛行爲　driving behavior
驾驶员/駕駛員,駕駛人　deck officer, pilot
驾驶员操作程序/飛行員操作程式　pilot operation procedure, POP
驾驶员反应时间/駕駛人反應時間　driver reaction time
驾驶员判断时间/駕駛人判斷時間　driver judgement time
驾驶员心理和生理反应/駕駛人心理和生理反應　driver psychological and physiological reaction
驾驶员心理选拔/飛行員心理挑選　pilot psychological selection
驾驶员行为特性/駕駛人行爲模式　driver behavior pattern
驾驶员诱发振荡/飛行員誘導振盪　pilot induced oscillation
驾驶员助手系统/飛行員協助系統　pilot-aid system
驾驶员座位振动测定/駕駛人座位振動測定　vibration measurement of driver seat
驾助/助理船副　assistant officer
架/架子　stand shelf
架板结/跳板結　plank stage hitch
架车/架車　jack up car body
架承式牵引电动机/支架固定牽引電動機　frame mounted traction motor
架空层/架空層　elevated story
架空传输线/架空輸電線　overhead transmission line
架空地线/架空地線　aerial earth wire, overhead earth wire
架空地线屏蔽系数/架空地線遮罩係數　shielding factor of aerial earth wire
架空电缆/架空電纜,架空纜線　overhead power cable, aerial cable
架空吊车/吊運車,天鉤　trolley, sky hook
架空管线/架空管道,高架管道　overhead pipeline, elevated pipeline
架空控制线/架空控制線　overhead control line
架空明线/架空線,明線　open wire
架空索道/架空纜車,吊車纜索　aerial ropeway, track cable
架空通风屋面/通風屋頂　ventilated roof
架空线路/架空線　overhead line
架立钢筋/紮配鋼筋,紮筋　erection bar
架桥机/架橋吊機　bridge erection crane
架桥机架设法/架橋機架設法　erection by bridge girder erecting equipment
架桥设备/架橋設備　bridging equipment
架式举升机/架式昇降機　crossing lift
架修/架修　intermediate repair
嫁接/嫁接　grafting
嫁接刀/嫁接刀　grafting knife
嫁接繁殖/嫁接繁殖　propagation by grafting
嫁接苗/嫁接苗　grafted seedling

嫁接亲和力/嫁接親和力　graft compatibility
尖舭/銳稜舴[線],硬稜舴　hard chine
尖舱肋骨/尖艙肋骨　peak frame
尖齿/爪齒　tine
尖锤/鏨[面]錘　chipping hammer
尖顶/塔尖,尖塔,尖峰　spire
尖顶浮标/雙彎頂部浮標　ogival buoy
尖端对接/錐尖相連　apexes together
尖端杆/尖端桿　front rod of a point
尖端向上/錐尖向上　apex upwards
尖端向下/錐尖向下　apex downwards
尖峰负荷发电厂/尖峰負載發電廠　peak load power station
尖峰加热器/尖峰負荷加熱器　peak load calorifier
尖峰热负荷/尖峰熱負荷　peak heating load
尖峰翼型/尖峰翼形　peaky aerofoil profile
尖拱法封顶/尖拱法封頂　closure by wedging in crown
尖轨/[轍]尖軌,道岔尖軌　switch rail, tongue rail
尖轨保护器/尖軌保護器　switch protector
尖轨补强板/加強筋,鋼筋　reinforcing bar
尖轨长度/尖軌長度　length of switch rail
尖轨动程/轉轍器動程　throw of switch
尖轨跟端/尖軌跟端　heel of switch rail
尖轨护轨/尖軌護軌　switch point guard rail
尖轨尖端/尖軌尖端　actual point of switch rail
尖轨理论尖端/岔心理論交叉點　theoretical point of switch rail
尖塔/尖塔狀　steeple
尖头信号/跳波　blip, spray wave
歼击轰炸机/戰鬥轟炸機　fighter-bomber
歼击机/戰鬥機　fighter
坚韧层/堅韌層　tough way
坚硬围岩/堅硬圍岩　hard surrounding rock
间/間,區　bay
肩/水線肩部　shoulder
监测/監測,監視　monitoring
监测信号/監視信號,監聽信號　monitor signal
监测站/監視站　monitor station
监测植物/監測植物　monitoring plant
监督对象/監督對象　surveillanced object
监督区/監督區　supervised area
监工/指揮員　banksman
监控/監測,監視　monitoring
监控摄像机/港區監視器　surveillance camera
监控试片/監測試片,檢測試片　monitoring coupon
监控中心/監控中心　monitoring and controlling center

监理工程师/監理工程師　supervising engineer
监理工程师代表/監理工程師業務代表,主管工程師業務代表　supervising engineer representative
监舍/囚室,牢房　prison cell
监视雷达/監視雷達　surveillance radar
监视屏/監測屏　monitoring panel
监视器/監視器,顯示器　monitor
监视区/監視區　surveillance area
监视系统/監督系統　supervision system
监视显示系统/監視顯示系統　monitor and display system
监狱/監獄　prison, jail
兼容测试/相容性測試　compatibility test
兼容性/相容性　compatibility
兼性塘/兼性塘　facultative pond
兼性厌氧细菌/兼性菌　facultative anaerobic bacteria
检波/檢波　detection
检波器/檢波器　detector
检测/檢驗　check-out, inspection and measurement
检测单元/檢測單元　monitoring unit
检测器/偵測器,偵檢器　detector
检测性试验/檢測性試驗　detective test
检测仪器/試驗儀表　testing instrument
检测与控制系统/檢測與控制系統　detect and control system
检测质量/檢測質量　proof mass
检查/查核,查驗,核對　check
检查井/人孔,檢修孔,觀測井　manhole, inspection well
检查口/檢查口　check hole, check pipe
检查门/檢查門　access door, inspection door
检查清单/檢查表　check-off list
检查权/搜索權　right of search
检查日期/檢查日期　date of inspection
检察院/檢察院,檢查機關　procuratorate
检潮站/檢潮站　tide chamber
检车电视/檢驗電視　TV for inspection
检错码/偵錯碼,錯誤檢測碼　error detecting code
检定/檢定,驗證　verification
检定结果[不合格]通知书/檢定拒收通知書　rejection notice of verification
检定系统[表]/檢定體系　verification scheme
检定证书/檢定證書　verification certificate
检衡车/檢衡車　weigh bridge test car, track scale test car
检后记录/檢後記錄　postdetection recording
检漏/檢漏,漏檢測,漏失檢查　leak detection
检漏厂房/檢漏廠房　building for leak detection

检漏器/测漏器　leak detector
检漏试验/渗漏试验　leak test
检录处/檢錄處　call area
检票监视电视/檢票監視電視　monitor TV for ticket check
检票口/檢票口　check post
检前记录/預查記錄　predetection recording
检视/視檢　visual inspection
检修不良/檢修不良　not well inspected and repaired
检修范围/檢修範圍　scope of repairing course, scope of repairing
检修工艺规程/檢修工藝規程　technological regulations for repair and inspection
检修机车/檢修機車　locomotive under repairing
检修基本技术条件/檢修基本技術條件　fundamental technical requirements for repair and inspection
检修井/檢查井　inspection chamber
检修停时/檢修停時　standing time under repair
检修限度/檢修限度　locomotive repair limit
检修周期/檢修週期　period of inspection and repair
检修作业程序/檢修作業程式　repair procedure, shop program
检验/檢驗,檢測　inspection
检验报告/檢驗報告　survey report
检验检疫[检查]区/待驗區　quarantine check area
检验批/檢驗批　inspection lot
检验试车/查核試驗　check test
检验证书/檢驗證書　certificate of inspection
检验中心/檢驗中心　inspection center
检疫/檢疫　quarantine
检疫船/檢疫船　quarantine ship, quarantine vessel, quarantine boat
检疫船席/檢疫船席　quarantine berth
检疫浮筒/檢疫浮筒　quarantine buoy
检疫港/檢疫港　quarantine port
检疫码头/檢疫碼頭　quarantine wharf
检疫锚[泊]地/檢疫錨地　quarantine anchorage
检疫证书/檢疫證書　free pratique
减摆器/搖擺阻尼器　shimmy damper
减反射膜/防反射膜　antireflection coating
减负荷程序/減載方案　load-down program
减机运转试验/停機試驗　engine cut off test
减价票/減價票　reduced-fare ticket
减菌效应/減菌效應　bacteria reduction effect
减面燃烧/減面燃燒　regressive burning
减摩剂/抗摩擦劑　antifriction, antifriction composition, anti-wear agent

减轻地震灾害/減輕地震災害　earthquake disaster mitigation
减轻孔/減輕孔　lightening hole
减少交通事故效益/減少交通事故效益　benefit from accidents reducing
减升板/減昇板　lift dumper
减湿[作用]/去潮法　dehumidification
减水/減水　set down, fall
减水剂/減水劑　water reducing agent
减速/減速　slacken speed, slow down, deceleration
减速板/減速板　airbrake, speed brake
减速比/減速比,縮減比　reduction ratio
减速车道/減速車道　deceleration lane
减速齿轮[箱]/減速齒輪,減速裝置　reduction gear
减速顶/減速頂　dowty retarder
减速工况/減速工況　decelerating mode
减速过桥/減速過橋　passing bridge with reduced speed
减速力/減速力　deceleration force
减速器/減速器,阻尼器　retardor
减速器出口速度/減速器出口速度　release speed at retarder
减速器工作状态/減速器工作狀態　retarder in working state
减速器缓解状态/減速器緩解狀態　retarder released
减速器接近限界/減速器接近限界　clearance of retarder
减速器入口速度/減速器入口速度　entrance speed at retarder
减速器制动状态/減速器制動狀態,緩凝器制動狀態　retarder in closed state
减速伞/減速傘,阻力傘　deceleration parachute, brake parachute, drag parachute
减速推送信号/減速推送信號　humping slow signal
减速信号/限值信號　restriction signal
减速炸弹/慢降炸彈　retarded bomb
减推力起飞/減推力起飛　reduced thrust take-off
减温器/減温器,調温器　attemperator
减压/減壓　decompression
减压病/減壓症　decompression sickness
减压阀/減壓閥　pressure reducing valve
减压井/放壓井　bleeder well
减压棱体/減壓棱體　pressure reducing fill
减压器/減壓器　pressure reducer
减压易感性/減壓易感受性　decompression susceptibility
减压中继阀/減壓中繼閥　reduction relay valve
减摇泵/減摇泵　anti-roll pump

减摇控制设备/穩定器控制裝置　stabilizer control gear
减摇鳍装置/鰭板穩定器　fin stabilizer
减摇设备舱/穩定裝備室　stabilizer equipment room
减摇水舱/減搖水艙　anti-rolling tank
减摇装置控制设备/穩度器控制裝置　stabilizer control unit
减载波发射/減載波發射　reduced carrier emission
减噪效应/降噪效應　noise reduction effect
减振措施/減振措施　vibration reducing measure
减振联轴器/減振聯軸節　vibration-absorbing coupling
减振器/減振器,振動吸收器　shock absorber, damper, vibration absorber
减振器试验台/減振器試驗臺　damper test stand
减振指数/減振指數　damping index
减轴运转试验/減軸運轉試驗　shaft cut off test
剪板机/截斷機　guillotine shear, plane shear
剪裁/裁剪　tailoring
剪草机/割草機　lawn mower, mower
剪刀撑/交叉撐條　cross bracing
剪刀式楼梯/剪刀式樓梯,橋式樓梯　scissor stairs
剪接室/視聽編輯室　editing room
剪跨比/剪跨比　shear span ratio
剪力板/剪力板　shear plate
剪力方程/剪力方程式　shear equation
剪力分布/剪力分配　shear distribution
剪力键/抗剪鍵　shear key
剪力铰/剪力塑鉸　shear hinge
剪力流/剪切流　shear flow
剪力器/剪力連接器　shear connector
剪力墙/耐力牆　shear wall
剪力墙结构/剪力牆結構　shear wall structure
剪力枢接/剪力樞接　shear-pin splice
剪力图/剪力圖　shear diagram
剪力销/剪力樞,剪力栓　shear pin
剪力滞后/剪力滯後,剪滯　shear lag
剪面/剪面　shear plane
剪切/剪切,剪割　shearing, shear
剪切边/剪邊　sheared edge
剪切波速测试/切變波速度試驗　shear wave velocity measurement
剪切盒法/箱式剪力試驗　shear box test
剪切滑坍/剪滑動　shear slide
剪切角/剪切角　shearing angle
剪切抗力/抗剪力　shearing resistance
剪[切]模量/剪切模數,切變模數　shear modulus
剪切试验/剪力試驗　shear test, shearing test
剪切速度/剪力速度　shear velocity
剪切弹性模量/剪切彈性模數　shearing elastic modulus
剪切稳定性/受剪穩定度　shear stability
剪切仪/箱式剪力[試驗]儀　box shear apparatus
剪切振动/剪力振動　shearing vibration
剪切滞后/剪力滯後,剪滯　shear lag
剪切中心/剪心　shear center
剪压破坏/剪應力破壞　shear compression failure
剪影照明/剪影照明,背光照明　silhouette lighting
剪应变/剪應變　shear strain, tangential strain
剪应力/剪[切]應力　shear stress, tangential stress
剪胀性/體積膨脹量　dilatancy
简单桁架/簡式桁架　simple truss
简单路面/簡單鋪面　small sett paving
简单式屋顶绿化/簡單式屋頂綠化　extensive roof greening
简单悬挂/簡單懸掛　tramway type suspension equipment
简单循环/簡單循環　simple cycle
简化符号/簡化符號　simplified symbol
简式提单/簡式載貨證券　short form bill of lading
简图用符号/簡圖用符號　symbol for diagram
简谐量/簡諧量　simple harmonic quantity
简谐运动/簡諧運動　harmonic motion
简谐运动周期/簡諧運動週期　period of simple harmonic motion
简谐振动/簡諧振動,諧和振動　simple harmonic vibration
简易补给装置/暫時補給裝置　temporary replenishing rig
简易混凝土搅拌站/簡易混凝土混合場　simple concrete mixing plant
简易驼峰/簡易駝峰　simplified hump
简支边/簡支緣　simple supported edge
简支梁/簡支梁　simply supported beam, simple beam
简支梁桥/簡支梁橋,簡支承桁橋　simply supported beam bridge, simply supported girder bridge
碱脆/鹼性脆化,苟性脆性　caustic embrittlement
碱度/鹼度,鹼性　alkalinity
碱腐蚀/鹼性腐蝕　alkaline corrosion
碱[活性]骨料反应/鹼骨料反應,鹼性骨材反應,鹼[質]粒料反應　alkali aggregate reaction
碱土/鹼土　solonetz
碱性电池/鹼性電池[組]　alkaline battery
碱性集料反应/鹼性骨材反應　alkali-aggregate reaction

碱性土/鹼性土[壤] alkaline soil
碱性土植物/鹼性土壤植物 alkaline soil plant
[碱]煮炉/煮煉 boiling out
见证取样检测/見證取樣檢測 evidential testing
见证取样送样/見證取樣和送檢 witness sampling and delivery
件杂货/零散雜貨 break bulk cargo
间苯二酚胶/間苯二酚 resorcinol
间壁/間壁,隔板 partition
间壁式热交换器/隔道換熱器 recuperator, recuperative heat exchanger
间插等高线/間插等高線 supplementary half interval contour
间断级配/間斷級配 gap grading
间断级配混凝土/越級配混凝土 gap-graded concrete
间断级配集料/越級配粒料,越級配骨材 gap-graded aggregate
间隔/間隔 space
间隔挡板/間隔支牆板 open sheeting
间隔钢筋/交互鋼筋,交替鋼筋 alternating bar
间隔区/間隔區 spacer
间隔铁/間隔鐵 filler, spacer block
间隔铁式尖轨转辙器/間隔鐵式尖軌轉轍器 loose heel switch
间隔制动/間隔制動 spacing braking
间隔最低标准/最低隔離標準 separation minima
间接采光窗/間接採光窗 borrowed light window
间接测量法/間接量測法 indirect method of measurement
间接传动/間接傳動 indirect transmission
间接费/間接成本 indirect cost
间接荷载/間接載重 indirect load
间接换装/間接換裝 indirect transshipment
间接回波/間接回波 indirect echo
间接加热/間接加熱 indirect heating
间接距离测量/間接距離測量 indirect distance surveying
间接冷却式空气冷却器/間接空氣冷卻器 indirect air cooler
间接连接/間接連接 indirect connection
间接排水/間接排水 indirect drain
间接驱动/間接驅動 indirect drive
间接视野/間接視野 indirect field of vision
间接效益/間接利益 indirect benefit
间接照明/間接照明 indirect lighting
间苗/間苗,間拔 thinning, thin out seedling
间色/混色 assorted color

间隙量片/間歇繞組 intermittence wind
间隙效应/間歇效應 slack action
间歇沉降[作用]/斷續沈澱 intermittent sedimentation
间歇供暖/週期式供暖,週期式供熱 intermittent heating
间歇过滤池/間歇濾池 intermittent filter
间歇过滤法/間歇濾過法 intermittent filtration
间歇泉/間歇[噴]泉 geyser, intermittent spring
间歇时间/間歇時間 intermittent time
间歇式反应器/間歇式反應器 batch reactor
间歇式高速摄影机/間歇高速攝影機 intermittent high-speed camera
间歇式交通量观测站/間歇式交通量觀測站 intermittent traffic count station
间歇式沥青混合料搅拌设备/間歇式瀝青混凝土攪拌站 batch asphalt mixing plant
间歇[性]故障/間歇故障,斷續故障 intermittent fault
间歇性灌溉/間歇灌溉 intermittent irrigation
间歇性河流/間歇河川 intermittent stream
间歇因子/間歇性因子 intermittency factor
间歇运动/間歇運動 intermittent motion
间作/間作 intercropping
建地递减率/建地遞減率 rate of areal reduction
建构表达/建構表達 tectonic expression
建群种/建群種 edificator, constructive species
建设场地/建築基地 building site
建设场地开发/地區開發 site development
建设程序/施工程式,施工步驟 construction procedure
建设工程规划许可证/建設工程規劃許可證,建築執照 permit for a planned construction project, building permit
建设工程竣工验收/建設工程竣工驗收 acceptance check of a construction project
建设工程勘察/建設工程勘察 surveying and geotechnical engineering of construction project
建设控制地带/建設控制地帶,建設管制地帶,建設管制區 development control zone, development control area
建设期/工期 construction period, construction time limit
建设期贷款利息/建設期貸款利息 loan interest in construction period
建设投资/工程投資 construction investment
建设项目/建設計劃 construction project
建设项目交通影响评价/建設計劃交通影響分析

transportation impact analysis of construction project
建设许可证/建築執照 building permit
建设用地/建設用地,適建地 construction land
建设用地范围/開發地區範圍 scope of development land
建设用地规划许可证/建設用地規劃許可證 permit for planned use of land for construction, land use permit, planning permit for land use
建设预定线/建設預定線 projected line
建造/建造,建設 construction
建造日期/建造日期 date of built
建造入级/建造入級 constructive classification
建造师/建造師 constructor
建造相应阶段/建造達類似階段 similar stage of construction
建造中船舶权利登记公约/建造中船舶權利登記公約 Convention Relating to Registration of Rights in Respect of Vessels under Construction
建筑/建築[物] building
建筑安装工程费/建安費 construction and installation cost
建筑暗沟/建築地下排水 building subdrain
建筑边坡/建築邊坡 building slope
建筑表达/建築表現 architectural presentation
建筑材料/建築材料,營建材料 building materials, material of construction
建筑材料厂/建築材料廠 building material factory
建筑材料实验室/建築材料實驗中心 building material laboratory
建筑测绘/建物測量 building surveying
建筑策划/建築規劃 architectural programming
建筑承包单位/建築承包商 building contractor
建筑承包商/建築承包商 building contractor
建筑创作/建築創作 architectural creation
建筑大样图/建築大樣圖 architectural detail drawing
建筑地盘/建築基地 building site
建筑地震破坏等级/建築地震破壞等級 grade of earthquake damage to building
建筑法规/建築法[規] building code, building ordinance
建筑反射隔热涂料/建築反射保溫塗料 architectural reflective thermal insulation coating
建筑方案/建築方案 capital programme
建筑方格网/建築方格網格 building square grid
建筑防水污染/建築防水汙染 prevent water pollution for construction

建筑防灾/建築防災 building disaster prevention
建筑风格/建築風格 architectural style
建筑符号学/建築符號學 semiotics of architecture
建筑覆盖率/建蔽率,建築面積比 building coverage ratio
建筑高度/建築高度 building altitude, building height
建筑高度比/建築高度比 building height ratio
建筑高度控制/建築高度控制 building height control
建筑高度区/建築高度區 building height district
建筑隔声/建築隔聲 sound insulation for building
建筑工程费/建造成本,造價,施工費用 construction cost
建筑[工程]机械厂/建築[工程]機械廠 construction machinery factory
建筑工程监理/建築工程監理 construction engineering supervision and control
建筑工程质量/營建工程品質 quality of construction engineering
建筑工人/建築者 builder
建筑功能/建築功能 architectural function
建筑供配电/供配電系統 power supply and distribution in building
建筑构图原理/建築構圖原理 principle of architectural composition
建筑构造/建築結構 architectural construction
建筑构造课/建築構造課 architecture structure
建筑管理规则/建築業管理規則 architectural control
建筑管理体制/建築業管理體制 administration system of building industry
建筑管制/建築管制 building control
建筑光污染/建築光線汙染 light pollution of construction
建筑光学/建築照明 architectural lighting
建筑规划师/實質規劃師 physical planner
建筑规模/建築結構尺寸 building dimension
建筑红线/建築線,地界線,界址線 building line, property line
建筑化夜景照明/建築化夜景照明 structural nightscape lighting
建筑画/建築圖 architectural drawing
建筑环保/建築環境保護 building environment protection
建筑环境模型/建築環境模型 building environment model
建筑活动执业资格制度/建築活動執業資格制度

qualification system for construction activities
建筑机构/建築業組織　organization of building industry
建筑机械/建築機械,施工機械　construction machine
建筑基底面积/建築基面　building base area
建筑基底线/建築基線　building base line
建筑基坑/建築基坑　building foundation pit
建筑给水/建築給水　building water supply
建筑给水排水/建築給水排水　building plumbing system
建筑技术/建築技術　building technology
建筑技术科学/建築技術科學　building technology science
建筑技术课/建築技術課程　course of architectural technology
建筑间距/建築間距　building interval
建筑检查员/建築稽查員　building inspector
建筑交通空间/建築循環空間　circulation space
建筑教育/建築教育　architectural education
建筑节能/建築節能　building energy conservation
建筑结构/建築結構,房屋結構　building structure
建筑结构单元/建築結構單元　building structural unit
建筑结构防微振体系/建築結構防微振體系　micro-vibration control system of structure
建筑经济[学]/建築經濟學　building economics
建筑勘探/建築勘探　building geotechnics
建筑抗震/建築抗震　seismic building, earthquake resistance of building
建筑抗震概念设计/建築抗震概念設計　seismic concept design of building
建筑抗震加固/建築抗震加固　seismic retrofit of building, seismic strengthening of building
建筑抗震鉴定/建築抗震鑑定　seismic appraiser of building, seismic evaluation for building
建筑抗震设防分类/抗震設防類別　seismic fortification category for building construction
[建筑]抗震设计/建築抗震設計　seismic design of building
建筑科学/建築科學　building science
建筑空间/建築空間　architectural space
建筑空间构成/建築空間構成　architectural space composition
建筑空间组合/建築空間組合　architectural space combination
建筑控制高度/建築控制高度　building control high
建筑控制线/建築線　building line

建筑垃圾/建造廢物,建築廢料,建築剩餘　construction waste
建筑垃圾受纳场/建築拆除廢棄物掩埋場　landfill site of construction and demolition waste
建筑垃圾资源化处理厂/建築拆除廢棄物處理廠　recycling-plant of construction and demolition waste
建筑类型/建築物類型　building type
建筑类型学/建築類型學　typology of architecture
建筑理论/建築理論　architectural theory
建筑理论课/建築理論課程　course of architectural theory
建筑历史课/建築歷史課程　course of architectural history
建筑历史与理论/建築歷史與理論　architectural history and theory
建筑美术实习/建築藝術演練　architectural art practice
建筑美学/建築美學　architectural aesthetics
建筑密度/建築密度　building density, building coverage
建筑密度限制区/建築密度限制區　density district
建筑面积/建築面積　floor area
建筑面积比率/建地比　floor area ratio
建筑面积分区/建築面積分區　building acreage zoning
建筑面积毛密度/地板面積毛密度　gross floor area density
建筑面积密度/建築面積密度,地板面積密度　floor area density, density of living floor area
建筑面积指数/建地空間指數,容積指數　floor space index
建筑模数/構建模組　building module, construction module
建筑模型/建築模型　building model
建筑内部得热/建築物熱增益　inner heat gain of building
建筑内部给水系统/建築內部給水系統,建築內部供水系統　interior water supply system of building
建筑排水/房屋排水　building drainage
建筑评价/建築物評估　building evaluation
建筑气候区划/建築氣候區劃　climatic regionalization for architecture, building climate demarcation
建筑气候学/建築氣候[學]　building climatology
建筑全寿命周期/建築全壽命週期　life cycle of building
建筑群/建築群　group of buildings
建筑群配线设备/建築群配線設備　campus

distributor
建筑群主干电缆/建築群主線電纜 campus backbone cable
建筑群子系统/建築群子系統 campus subsystem
建筑热工设计分区/建築熱工設計分區 dividing region for building thermal design
建筑热工学/建築熱力工程 building thermal engineering
建筑热水/建築熱水 building hot water
建筑日照/建築日照 sunshine on building
建筑容积/建築容積 building volume
建筑容积分区/建築容積分區 building bulk zoning
建筑容积区/建築容積區 building bulk district
建筑容积限制/建築容積限制 building bulk restriction
建筑设备/建築設備,施工設備 building equipment, construction equipment
建筑设备工程师/建築設備工程師 building equipment engineer
建筑设备管理系统/建築設備管理系統 management system of building equipment
建筑设备监控机房/建築設備控制室 control room of building equipment
建筑设备监控系统/建築設備監視系統 monitoring system of building equipment
建筑设计/建築設計 architectural design
建筑设计单位/建築設計單位 architectural design institution
建筑设计规范/建築設計規範 code of building design
建筑设计及其理论/建築設計及其理論 architectural design and its theory
建筑设计课/建築設計課程 course of architectural design
建筑设计课程任务书/建築設計任務書 design course program
建筑设计院/建築設計院 architectural design institute
建筑设计主持权/建築設計主持權 design direction right
建筑设计专题教学/建築設計專題教學 architectural design workshop
建筑深度/建築深度 building depth
建筑生物气候图/建築生物氣候圖 building bio-climatic chart
建筑声学/建築聲學 architectural acoustics
建筑师/建築師 architect
建筑师事务所/建築師事務所 architect associate

建筑师执业知识/建築學專業知識 knowledge on architectural profession
建筑师职业道德/建築師職業道德 ethics and conducts of architects
建筑师职业精神原则/建築師職業精神原則 principle of professionalism for architects
建筑施工/建築工程施工 building construction
建筑石膏/煅石膏,燒石膏,熟石膏 building plaster, calcined gypsum
建筑实践课/建築實踐課程 course of architectural practice
建筑史/建築史 architectural history
建筑使用许可/建築使用執照 building occupation permit
建筑体积/建築量體,建築容積 building volume, building bulk
建筑体积比/建築容積比 building bulk ratio
建筑体系/建築體系 building system
建筑图学/建築幾何學 architectural geometry
建筑维护/建築維修,房屋維修 building maintenance
建筑文化/建築文化 architectural culture
建筑五金/建築小五金 architectural hardware, building hardware
建筑物/建築物 building
建筑物放样/建築物放樣 setting out of building
建筑物高度区划/[建築]高度分區管制 height zoning
建筑物耗热量指标/建築物耗熱量指標 index of heat loss of building
建筑物理[学]/建築物理 building physics
建筑物配建停车场设施/建築物配建停車場 building accessorial parking facility
建筑物配线设备/大樓配線設備 building distributor
建筑物区分所有权/建築物區分所有權 building ownership
建筑物入口设施/建築物入口設施 building entrance facility
建筑物体形系数/體形係數 shape coefficient of building
建筑物雨水下水道/建築雨水管 building storm sewer
建筑物轴线放样/建築軸線放樣 setting out of building axes
建筑物主干缆线/建築物主幹纜線 building backbone cable
建筑现象学/建築現象學 phenomenology of architecture

建筑线/建築線　building line
建筑详图/建築大樣　architectural detail
建筑小品/場地美化　site furnishings
建筑信息模型/建築資訊模型　building information model, BIM
建筑行为学/行爲建築學　behavioral architecture
建筑形式/建築形式,建築形態　architectural form
建筑形态构成/建築形態構圖　architectural configuration composition
建筑性能/建築性能　building performance
建筑修缮/建築修繕　building renovation
建筑选址/建設用地指定　building site designation
建筑学/建築學　architecture
建筑学教育宪章/建築教育憲章　Charter for Architectural Education
建筑学硕士/建築碩士　master of architecture
建筑学学科/建築設計原則　architecture discipline
建筑学学士/建築學士　bachelor of architecture
建筑学院/建築學院　school of architecture
建筑学专业教育评估/建築學專業教育評估　architectural education accreditation
建筑业/建築業,營造工業　building industry
建筑业总产值/建築業總產量　total output of building industry
建筑遗产/建築遺產　architectural heritage
建筑艺术/建築藝術　architectural art
建筑艺术课/建築藝術課程　course of architectural art
建筑用地/建築基地　building site
建筑造型/建築造型　architectural image
建筑制品/建築產品　building product
建筑中水/建築中水　reclaimed water system for building
建筑坐标/建築坐標　construction coordinate
建筑坐标系/建築坐標系　building coordinate system
剑石/石筍　stalagmite
健康城市/健康城市　healthy city
健康检查/健康檢查　medical examination
健身房/健身房,體育館,運動室　gymnasium, gym
健身俱乐部/健身中心　fitness center, health club
健身绿道/健身綠道　fitness the greenway
健身设施/健身設施　fitness facilities
健身中心/健身中心　fitness center, health club
健走/走步　walking
健走径/步道　walking path
舰间间隔/船艦間橫距　beam distance between ships
舰间斜距/船艦間斜距　oblique distance between ships
舰间纵距/船艦間縱距　fore-and-aft distance between two ships
舰艇编队队形/艦艇編隊隊形　ship formation pattern
舰艇编队队形要素/船艦編隊隊形要素　elements of ship formation pattern
舰艇编队序列/艦艇編隊序列　order of ship formation
舰艇编队运动/艦艇編隊運動　ship formation movement
舰艇编队运动规则/船艦編隊運動規則　regulations for ship formation movement
舰艇编队转向/艦艇編隊轉向　ship formation course alteration
舰艇相遇圆/船艦相遇圓　ship meeting circle
舰载航空器/艦載機　carrier aircraft, shipboard aircraft
渐变板/引道板　transition slab
渐变段/截錐形部分　tapered section
渐变故障/逐漸故障,漸次失效　gradual failure, gradual fault
渐变曝气/漸減曝氣　tapered aeration
渐进规划/漸進式計劃　incremental planning
渐进式更新/漸進式再生　incremental regeneration
渐进性破坏/漸進性破壞　progressive failure
渐近法/逐步近似法　method of successive approximation
渐近流速水头/漸近流速水頭,漸近流速高差　approaching velocity head
渐近面/漸近面　approach surface
渐近稳定性/漸近穩定性　asymptotic stability
渐缩喷嘴/漸縮噴嘴　convergent nozzle
渐细索/漸細索　tapered end rope
渐晕/漸暈,暈邊現象　vignetting
毽球运动/羽毛球,毽子　shuttlecock
溅落海域/飛濺區　splashdown zone, splashdown area
溅射/濺射　sputtering
溅射沉积/濺射沈積　sputtering deposition
溅射刻蚀/噴濺蝕刻［法］　sputtering etching
溅射式压力传感器/飛濺式壓力換能器　splashing type pressure transducer
溅[雨]击侵蚀/濺出銷蝕　splash erosion
鉴别力[阈]/鑒別閾　discrimination threshold
鉴定过程/鑒定過程　qualification process
鉴定合格/鑒定合格　be qualified
鉴定试飞/評估飛行試驗　evaluation flight test
鉴定试验/鑒定試驗,評定試驗　evaluation test,

qualification test, homologation test
鉴定室/鑒定室　authentication room
键槽/鍵槽　keyway
键合梁/加榫梁　keyed girder
键连接/鍵接　keyed joint
键盘/鍵盤　keyboard
箭-地接口检查/箭-地介面檢查　rocket-ground port check
箭翎线/箭翎線　herringbone track
箭楼/箭樓　archery tower, jianlou
箭上电缆网/箭上電纜網　cable network onboard
箭上跟踪与安全控制系统/箭上追蹤與安全控制系統　onboard tracking and safety control system
箭上遥测天线/箭上遙測天線　telemetry antenna onboard
箭上遥测系统/箭上遙測系統　onboard telemetering system
箭体/火箭體　rocket body
箭体翻转吊具/發射載具翻轉吊索　launch vehicle turning sling
箭体公路运输车/發射載具拖車　launch vehicle trailer
箭体结构/火箭體構造　rocket body structure
箭体水平吊具/發射載具水平吊索　launch vehicle horizontal sling
箭体铁路运输车/發射載具鐵路平臺卡車　launch vehicle railway platform truck, launch vehicle rail transporter
箭体铁轮支架车/發射載具鐵輪臺車　launch vehicle iron wheel carriage
箭体直径/箭體直徑　rocket body diameter
箭体坐标/發射載具坐標　launch vehicle coordinate
箭头绿灯/箭頭綠燈　green arrow light
箭载测控分系统/箭載測控分系統　rocket-borne TT and C subsystem
江河风景区/江河風景區　river landscape district
江河类/江河類　the rivers type
江南园林/江南園林　garden on the Yangtze Delta
江心洲/江心洲　central island
将船撑开/使船橫著離開　breasting the ship apart
浆液搅拌机/灌漿拌和機　grout mixer
缰绳/韁繩　bridle
礓蹉/礓蹉　ramp saw-tooth surface
奖励旅游/獎勵旅遊　incentive tourism
桨/槳　oar
桨盾器/槳盾器　shielded erector
桨根切除/槳根切除　blade root cut-off
桨毂/[螺槳]毂　boss, hub

桨毂空化/毂空化　hub cavitation
桨尖轨迹平面/槳尖軌跡平面　tip path plane
桨距/槳葉間距, 螺旋槳螺距　blade pitch, propeller pitch
桨距表/螺旋槳傾角指示計　propeller pitch indicator
桨距不变平面/槳距不變平面　no-feathering plane
桨轮通气/轉輪式曝氣　paddle-wheel aeration
桨门/槳架　oarlock
桨盘面积/旋翼盤形面積　rotor disk area
桨入水过深/槳入水過深　catch a crab
桨扇发动机/槳扇發動機　propfan engine
桨-涡干扰/渦旋與葉片表面交互作用　blade vortex interaction, BVI
桨叶/槳葉, 輪葉　blade, vane
桨叶摆振/擺振運動　blade lagging, lead-lag motion
桨叶方位角/槳葉方位角　blade azimuth angle
桨叶挥舞/葉片拍動　blade flapping
桨叶搅拌通气机/翼板式曝氣器　paddle aerator
桨叶剖面安装角/槳葉剖面安裝角　blade section pitch
桨叶式太阳电池阵/槳式太陽電池陣　paddle type solar array
桨叶式装载机/葉片式裝載機　paddle loader
桨叶周期变距/槳葉週期變矩　blade cyclic pitch
降测/降測　chaining downhill, drop chaining
降尘/降塵　dustfall
降低出力/降額馬力, 降低額定馬力　derating
降低粉尘浓度/粉塵抑制　dust suppression
降低系数/折減因數　reduction factor
降额/降額馬力, 降低額定馬力　derating
降级/降級, 下坡　degradation, down grade
降交点/降交點　descending node
降解/退化, 退降　degradation
降落场/降落區域, 著陸區域　landing area
降落伞/降落傘　parachute
降落伞信号/降落傘信號彈　parachute signal
降落终速/終端沈降速度　terminal fall velocity
降落锥/傘錐　paracone
降落锥弹射座椅/傘錐彈射座椅　paracone ejection seat
降凝剂/流動點下降劑　pour point depressant
降旗礼/低旗敬禮　dip
降深率/比洩降　specific drawdown
降水径流量/降水剩餘, 超降水　excess precipitation
降水量/降水[量]　precipitation
降水量累积线/降雨累積線　precipitation mass curve
降水渗入系数/降雨滲入係數　rainfall infiltration coefficient

降水头渗透率仪/落水頭滲透計　falling head permeameter
降水-蒸发比/降水蒸發比　precipitation-evaporation ratio
降水蒸发指数/降水蒸發指數　precipitation-evaporation index
降水指数/降水指數　precipitation index
降温/冷卻　cooling
降温池/冷卻槽　cooling tank
降雪/降雪　falling snow
降压电阻/降壓電阻　step down resistance
降压起动/降壓起動　reduced-voltage starting
降压气室/減壓氣室　pressure reducing reservoir
降雨分区/降雨分區　rainfall partition
降雨截留/降雨截流　rainfall interception
降雨径流量/超滲雨量　rainfall excess
降雨历时/[臨界]降雨延時,降雨持續時間　duration of rainfall
降雨模拟装置/模雨計　rainfall simulator
降雨强度/降雨強度　rainfall intensity
降雨强度历时曲线/降雨強度延時曲線　rainfall intensity duration curve
降雨侵蚀力/降雨侵蝕力　rainfall erosivity
降雨区/雨區　rainfall area, hyetal region
降雨入渗/降雨入滲,滲雨深度　rainfall infiltration, rainfall penetration
降雨深度/雨量深度　rainfall depth
降噪量/噪音減量,雜訊降低量　noise reduction
降噪路面/無噪聲路面　reducing noise pavement
降噪系数/噪音減低係數　noise reduction coefficient
交变应力/交變應力,反復應力　alternating stress
交叉导数/交叉導數　cross derivative
交叉道口安全设备/鐵路平交道防護設備　railroad crossing protection device
交叉渡线/剪式橫渡線,交叉道岔,交叉橫渡道岔　scissors crossing, double crossover
交叉放射线网/四通八達的流通網路　criss cross-radial type public transport network
交叉感染/交互傳染,相互傳染　cross-infection
交叉刚度/交叉勁度　cross stiffness
交叉轨迹角/交叉軌跡角　cross track angle
交叉极化反干扰/交叉極化抗干擾　cross polarization ECCM
交叉角/交角,岔道角　intersection angle, crossing angle
交叉口/交點,連絡點　junction
交叉口出口/交叉點出口　intersection exit
交叉口负荷系数/交叉口負荷因素　load factor of intersection
交叉口交通调查/交叉口交通調查　intersection census
交叉口进口/交叉點入口　intersection entrance
交叉口进口道/交叉點引道　intersection approach
交叉口设计/平交道口設計　road crossing design, intersection design
交叉口视距/交叉口視距　sight distance of intersection
交叉口通行能力/交叉口容量　intersection capacity
交叉口延误/交叉口延誤　intersection delay
交叉[跨越]/交叉[通過]　crossing
交叉连接/交叉連接　cross-connect, cross connection
交叉摩阻/交叉路口衝突　intersectional friction
交叉偏差/交叉間隔偏差　deviation from transposition interval
交叉区/交叉區,交叉段　transposition section
交叉曲线/交叉曲線　cross curve
交叉施工/交叉施工　parallel construction
交叉式楼梯/交錯樓梯,疊合式樓梯　intersecting stairs, staggered stairs
交叉疏解/交叉疏解　crossing untwining
交叉线/交叉線,十字線　cross wires
交叉相遇局面/交叉相遇情況　crossing situation
交叉斜撑/交叉拉桿　counterbracing
交叉指数/交叉指數　transposition index
交叉制式/換位制　transposition system
交出空车数/交出空車數　number of empty cars delivered
交出重车数/交出重車數　number of loaded cars delivered
交船/交船　delivery of vessel
交错断续角焊缝/交錯間斷式填角焊縫　staggered intermittent fillet weld
交错铆接/交錯鉚接　staggered riveting
交错排列的磁铁布置/交錯排列磁鐵布置　staggered magnet configuration
交点/交點　intersection point, IP
交点月/交點月　draconitic month
交发日期/交發日期　filing date
交发时间/交發時間　filing time
交分道岔/交叉[橫渡]道岔　slip switch, slip turnout
交付/交貨　delivery
交付试车/提交試車　delivery test
交互挠度定理/交互撓度定理　reciprocal deflection theorem
交互设计/交互設計　interaction design
交互式系统/交互式系統　alternate system

交互式协议/交互式協議　interactive protocol
交换/交換,互换　exchange, switching
交换地设计/交換地設計　design of replotting
交换性离子/可交換離子　exchangeable ion
交会测量/交會測量　intersection measurement
交会对接/交會和對接　rendezvous and docking, RVD
交会法/交會法　method of intersection
交会角/交會角,碰撞角,遭遇角　encounter angle
交会条件/交會條件　encounter conditions
交会信号/交會信號　spill-over signal
交会阻力/交會阻力　medial friction
交货港/交貨港　port of delivery
交接/交接　cross-connect
交接检测/交接檢驗　handing over inspection
交接箱/電纜交接箱,電纜接線箱　cross-connecting box
交接桩/交接樁　delivery-receiving stake
交联剂/交聯劑　crosslinking agent
交联双基推进剂/交聯雙基推進劑　crosslinked double-base propellant, CDB propellant
交流/交流,溝通　communication
交流变频调速/交流變頻調速　A-C speed regulating by frequency variation
交流电动机/交流電動機　alternating current motor
交流电动机软启动/交流電動機軟啟動　soft starting of alternating current motor
交流电动机调速/交流電動機速率控制　speed control of alternating current motor
交流电力推进装置/交流電力推進裝置　AC electric propulsion plant
交流电源/交流供電　alternating current power supply
交流电源屏/交流電源屏　AC power supply panel
交流电站/交流電站　AC power station
交流二元二位继电器/交流二元二位繼電器　AC two element two position relay
交流发电机/交流發電機　alternating current generator
交流感应子发电机/感應式交流發電機　inductor type alternator
交流供电制/交流電源系統　AC power supply system
交流轨道电路/交流軌道電路　AC track circuit
交流换向器电动机/交流換向器電動機　alternating current commutator motor
交流计数电码轨道电路/交流計數電碼軌道電路　AC counting coded track circuit
交流计数电码自动闭塞/交流計數電碼自動閉塞　automatic block with AC counting code track circuit
交流继电器/交流繼電器,交流電驛　AC relay
交流接触器/交流接觸器　AC contactor
交流牵引变电所/交流牽引變電站　AC traction substation
交流牵引电动机/交流牽引電動機　AC traction motor
交流三相三线制/交流三相三線制　AC three-phase three-wire system
交流主发电机/交流主發電機　AC main alternator
交调干扰/交互調變干擾　cross modulation interference
交通/交通　communication
交通安全/交通安全　traffic safety
交通安全评估/交通安全評估　appraisal of traffic safety
交通安全设施/交通安全設施　traffic safety facilities
交通标志/交通標誌　traffic sign
[交通标志中]文字标志/文字標線　word marking
交通产生/交通產生　traffic generation
交通产生单位/交通產生單位　traffic generating unit
交通场站用地/交通場站用地　land for transportation terminal
交通冲突/交通衝突　traffic conflict
交通出入口方位/交通出入口方位,交通出入口位置　exit and entrance position, direction of entry
[交通]出入口数量/[交通]出入口數量　number of entry, exit and entrance amount
交通导向设施/路徑誘導系統　route guidance system
交通导引系统/交通指揮系統　traffic guidance system
交通岛/交通島　traffic island
交通调查/交通調查,運輸調查　traffic survey, traffic census
交通调查表/交通調查表　traffic survey chart
交通发展战略/交通發展策略　transportation development strategy
交通法庭/交通法庭　traffic court
交通方式划分/交通方式劃分　traffic model split
交通方式选择/交通方式選擇　traffic mode choice
交通方式选择模型/交通方式選擇模型　traffic modal choice model
交通防护绿带/交通防護綠地　traffic protective greenbelt
交通仿真/交通模擬　traffic simulation
交通分隔/交通分隔　segregation of traffic

交通分类/交通分類　traffic classification
交通分流/交通分流　traffic diverging
交通分散/交通分散　traffic decentration
交通分析/交通分析　traffic analysis
交通分析图/交通分析圖　traffic analysis drawing
交通服务水平/交通服務水準　transportation service level
交通感应式控制/交通感應控制　traffic responsive control
交通感应信号/交通感應變色號誌　traffic actuated signal
交通干扰/交通干擾　traffic interference
交通隔离墩/交通隔離墩　traffic divided block
交通工程[学]/交通工程　traffic engineering
交通管理费/交通管理費　traffic administration cost
交通管理设施/交通管理設施,交通運輸管理設施　traffic management devices
交通管制标志/交通管制標誌　traffic control sign
交通管制区/交通管制區　traffic control zone
交通广场/交通廣場　traffic square
交通广告/交通廣告　traffic advertisement
交通规划/交通規劃　traffic planning
交通规则/交通規則　traffic rules, traffic regulations, traffic regulation
交通护栏/交通護欄　traffic guardrail
交通汇合/交通匯合　traffic converging
交通计数区划线/區域線　cordon line
交通监控系统/交通控制系統　traffic surveillance and control system
交通监控中心/交通控制中心　traffic surveillance and control center
交通建筑/交通建築　transportation building
交通可达性/交通可達性　traffic accessibility
交通控制/交通管制　traffic control
交通控制区/交通控制區　traffic control area
交通量/交通量　traffic volume
交通量测量仪/交通量計數器　traffic counter
交通量调查/交通量調查,交通流調查　traffic volume survey
交通[量]分配/交通量分配　traffic assignment, traffic volume distribution
交通量估计/交通量估計　traffic volume estimating
交通量观测/交通量觀測,交通量調查　traffic count
交通量计量/交通量測量　traffic volume measurement
交通量修正系数/交通量調整係數　traffic volume adjustment factor
交通量预测/交通量預測,運量預測　traffic volume forecast, traffic volume prognosis
交通流理论/交通流理論　traffic flow theory
交通流量/交通流量　traffic flow
交通流率/交通流[動速]率,交通流量　traffic flow rate
交通流线/交通流線　traffic stream line
交通流线节点/交通流線節點　intersection
[交通]流线图/流線圖　flow line plan
交通路钮/路面標鈕　traffic button
交通密度/交通密度　traffic density
交通面积/交通面積　traffic area
交通模型/交通模型　traffic model
交通频率/交通頻率　frequency of traffic
交通评价/交通影響評估,影響評價　traffic assessment
交通瓶颈/交通瓶頸　traffic bottleneck
交通强度/交通量強度,擁擠度　traffic intensity
[交通]渠化/槽化　channelization
交通容量/交通容量,交通能量　traffic capacity, traffic ability
交通设施/交通設施,運輸設施　transportation facility, traffic equipment, traffic facilities
交通设施容量/運輸設備容量　capacity of transportation facilities
交通设施用地/運輸設施用地　land for transportation facilities
交通生成/旅次產生,旅次發生　trip generation
交通生理学/交通生理學　traffic physiology
交通时相/交通時相　traffic phase
交通事故/交通事故　traffic accident, accident traffic
交通事故地点图/肇事地點圖　accident spot map
交通事故多发地段/經常肇事地點　black spot
交通事故率/交通事故率　traffic accident rate
交通事故隐患/交通隱患　hidden peril of accident
交通事故预测/交通事故預測　traffic accident prediction
交通枢纽/公共交通總站　public transport terminal
交通枢纽用地/交通樞紐用地　land for transportation hub
交通枢纽综合开发/交通樞紐綜合開發,交通樞紐綜合發展　comprehensive development of traffic hub
交通疏导/交通疏導　traffic dispersion
交通特性/交通特性　traffic characteristics
交通艇/交通艇　traffic boat
交通通道/交通通道　traffic aisle
交通统计学/交通統計　traffic statistics
交通网络/交通網路　traffic network
交通违章/裁罰　traffic violation

交通违章者/交通違犯者　traffic violator
交通稳定性/交通穩定性　traffic stability
交通稳静化/交通寧靜區　traffic calming
交通系统/交通系統　traffic system, circulation system
交通系统管理/運輸系統管理　transportation system management, TSM
交通线网优化/交通線網優化　optimization of traffic line and network
交通小区/交通分析小區　transportation analysisunit
交通心理学/交通心理學　traffic psychology
交通信号灯/交通號誌燈,行車管制號誌　traffic signal lamp, traffic control signal
交通信号脱机控制/交通號誌離線控制　traffic signal off line control
交通信息系统/交通資訊系統　traffic information system
交通行为/交通行爲　traffic behavior
交通需求/交通需求　traffic demand
交通需求分析/旅行需求分析　travel demand analysis
交通需求管理/旅行需求管理　travel demand management
交通需要预测/交通需求預測　traffic demand forecast
交通巡逻/交通巡邏　traffic patrolling
交通延误/交通延遲　traffic delay
交通研究/交通研究　traffic study
交通因素/交通因數　traffic factor
交通拥挤/交通擁擠,車輛擁擠　traffic congestion
交通与土地利用一体化/交通與土地利用完整性　transportation and land use integration
交通预测/交通預測　traffic estimation, traffic prediction
交通运输工程/交通工程　traffic engineering
交通运输网/運輸網　transportation network
交通噪声/交通噪音　traffic noise
交通噪声频谱修正量/交通噪聲頻譜修正量　traffic noise spectrum adaptation term
交通噪声评价/交通噪音評估　traffic noise evaluation
交通噪声指数/交通噪音指標　traffic noise index, TNI
交通肇事罪/交通肇事罪　traffic accident crime
交通振动/交通振動　traffic vibration
交通政策/運輸政策　transportation policy
交通指路牌/行车方向標牌　traffic direction block
交通指示[灯]/交通號誌　traffic signal
交通指向钮/行車方向鈕　traffic direction stud
交通终点/交通終點　traffic terminus
交通状况图/交通狀況圖　traffic condition diagram
交通自动调节信号/交通感應變色號誌　traffic actuated signal
交通综合体/交通綜合體　multimode transportation complex
交通走廊/交通走廊,交通路廊　traffic corridor
交通阻塞/交通擁擠　traffic jam
交通组成/交通組成　traffic composition
交通组织/交通組織　traffic organization
交往空间/交往空間　communication space, social space
交越频率/交越頻率　crossover frequency
交织/交織　weaving
交织交通流/交織交通流量　weaving traffic flow
交织角/交織角　weaving angle
交织路段/交織路段　weaving section
交织路段长度/交織區間長　weaving length
交织区/交織區　weaving area
交织区通行能力/交織路段容量　weaving section capacity
交-直-交流传动/交-直流-交[電]驅動　AC-DC-AC drive
交-直流传动/交直流[電]驅動　AC-DC drive
交直流继电器/交直流繼電器　AC-DC relay
郊区/郊區　suburb
郊区城市化/郊區化　suburbanization
郊区道路/郊區道路　suburban road
郊区景观/郊區景觀　suburban landscape
郊区绿地/郊區綠地　suburban green space
郊区绿化/郊區綠化　suburban greening
郊外工业区/郊外工業區　industrial suburb
郊外公园/郊外公園　suburban park
郊外住宅区/郊外住宅區　residential suburb
浇洒道路用水/澆灑道路用水　flushing demand
浇注/澆注,澆鑄　pouring, casting, placing
浇筑/灌鑄　placing
胶层/黏膠層　adhesive layer
胶衬泥泵/膠襯泥泵　rubberized dredge pump
胶焊胶黏剂/焊接黏著劑　weld bonding adhesive
胶合板/膠合板,三夾板,木夾板　plywood
胶合板结构/膠合板結構　plywood structure
胶合接头/膠接接合　glued joint
胶合木板/膠夾木材　glued laminatec timber
胶合木结构/層板膠合結構　glued timber structure
胶合木桥/膠接木橋　glued timber bridge
胶接点焊/焊接點焊　spot-weld bonding, weld

bonding

胶接点焊结构/膠合點焊結構　spotweld bonding structure

胶接接头/膠合節點　bonding joint

胶接结构/膠合[結]構件　bonded structure

胶接绝缘接头/膠黏絕緣接頭,膠接絕緣接合　glued insulated joint

胶接料/黏接[材]料　binding materials, cementitious materials

胶接强度/膠黏強度　adhesive strength

胶接型锚杆/膠黏劑錨桿　adhesive rock bolt

胶接装配/黏著接點裝配　adhesive joint assembly

胶连接/黏附連接　adhesion connection

胶轮推土机/膠輪推土機　tyre dozer

胶铆连接/鉚接　rivet bonding

胶泥防水薄层/膠泥防水薄層　sheet mastic water proofing

胶黏剂/膠膠,黏合劑,膠合劑　adhesive

胶黏土/黏結料　clay binder

胶凝材料/結合劑,黏結劑　binding materials, cementitious materials

胶片/照相軟片,感光底片　photographic film

胶片变形/軟片變形　deformation of film

胶片感光度/底片感光度,軟片速率　film speed

胶片记录/膠片記錄　film recording

胶片解像力/軟片解析度　resolution of film

胶片卷曲/軟片旋度　film curl

胶片判读仪/微膠卷閱讀機　film reader

胶片片基/片基,軟片基底　film base

胶片粘连/軟片內聚　cohesion of film

胶体/膠體物質　colloidal matter

胶体溶液灌浆/膠質灌漿　colloidal grout

胶体推进剂/膠凝推進劑　gelled propellant

胶体[推进剂]火箭发动机/膠體推進劑火箭發動機　gelled propellant rocket engine, gelled propellant rocket motor

胶体推力器/膠體推進器　colloid thruster

胶体稳定性/膠體穩定性　colloidal stability

胶质/膠體物質　colloidal matter

胶状混凝土/膠質混凝土　colloidal concrete

焦点/焦點　focus

焦化厂/煉焦廠　coking plant

焦距/焦點距離　focal length

焦炉煤气/焦爐煤氣,煉焦爐氣　coke-oven gas

焦平面/焦[平]面　focal plane

焦深/焦深[度]　depth of focus

焦外系统/非聚焦系统,無聚焦系統　afocal system

焦叶/焦葉　withered leaf

焦油沥青/焦油　tar

角变形/角變形,角扭曲　angular distortion

角捕获/角捕獲　angle acquisition

角捕获时间/角捕獲時間　angle acquisition time

角撑/隅撐　knee bracing

角灯/牆腳燈　corner lamp

角动量交换式控制/角動量交換控制　angular momentum exchange control

角动量守恒/角動量守恒,角動量不滅　conservation of angular momentum

角动量卸载/角動量卸載　angular momentum dumping, angular momentum desaturation, angular momentum unloading

角度传感器/角度感應器　angular position sensor

角度机构控制系统/角度控制系統　angle control system

角度欺骗干扰/角度欺騙干擾　angle deception jamming

角阀/[折]角閥,肘閥　angle valve

角分辨率/角度解析度　angle resolution

角杆/角桿　angular pole

角钢/角鋼,角鐵　angle steel

角钢镶边接缝/角鋼鑲邊接縫　angle steel edged joint

角钢重量/角鋼重量　angle weight

角跟踪/角追蹤　angle tracking

角跟踪误差/追蹤角偏差　angle tracking error

角跟踪系统/角追蹤系統　angle tracking system

[角]工作范围/工作範圍,作用距離　angle operating range

角焊缝/填角焊道,填角焊接　fillet weld

角脊/角脊　diagonal ridge, jiaoji

角加速度/角加速度　angular acceleration

角加速度生理效应/角加速度生理效應　physiological effects of angular acceleration

角件/櫃角裝置　corner fitting, corner fittings

角-角系统/角-角系統　θ-θ system

角砾/角礫,礫石　angular gravel, gravel

角梁/角梁　corner beam

角裂/角裂　corner break

角楼/角樓　corner tower, jiaolou

角扭曲/角扭曲,角變形　angular distortion

角偏差/角偏差　angular misalignment

角频率/角頻率,圓週頻率,週率　angular frequency, radian frequency

角深/角深　pull

角树[材]/角木　hornbeam

角搜索系统/角搜索系統　angle search system

角速度/角速度　angular velocity
角系数/角度因数　heat humidity ratio, angle factor
角形反射器/角形反射器,雷達波反射器　corner reflector
角形接合钣/角形接合鈑　angle type joint bar
角宿一(室女α)/角宿一(室女α)　Spica
角页岩/角頁岩　hornfels
角隅钢筋/角隅鋼筋,隅角鋼筋　corner steel, corner bar
角隅种植/角隅種植　corner planting
角振动试验/角振動試驗　angular vibration test
角质层蒸腾/表皮蒸散　cuticular transpiration
角柱/角柱,隅角柱,腿柱　corner column, corner post
绞车/絞車,絞機　winch
绞船索/曳網,曳繩,拖索　warp
绞机/牽索絞機　hauling winch
绞缆滚筒/絞纜滾筒　gypsy
绞缆机/絞索絞機　gypsy winch
绞缆绞车/卷索絞機　warping winch
绞缆筒/卷索筒,卷索鼓　warping end, warping head
绞缆移船/絞纜移船　warping the berth
2-1绞辘/大轆轤,二接一轆轤　luff tackle
绞盘/絞盤,起錨機　capstan
绞杀植物/纏勒植物　strangler
铰接板法/横絞鏈連接的平板法　transversely hinge-connected slab method
铰接盾构/鉸接式盾構　articulated shield
铰接节点/鉸接頭　hinged joint
铰接梁法/鉸鏈接梁法　hinge-connected beam method
铰接桥墩/鉸端橋墩　hinged pier
铰接式旋翼/關節式旋翼　articulated rotor
铰接式压路机/鉸接式壓路機　articulated roller
铰接式装油塔/活節裝載塔　articulated loading tower
铰接式自卸车/活節轉向架　articulated truck
铰接塔/關節連接柱　articulated column
铰接塔系泊系统/活節塔繫泊系統　articulated tower mooring system
铰接支座/鉸支點　rounded support
铰接柱/關節連接柱　articulated column
铰孔/絞孔　reaming
铰链力矩/絞鏈力距　hinge moment
铰链力矩导数/絞鏈力距導數　hinge moment derivative
铰链力矩试验/鉸鏈力矩試驗　hinge moment testing

铰链力矩天平/鉸鏈力矩天平　hinge moment balance
铰链力矩系数/鉸鏈力矩係數　hinge moment coefficient
铰链连接/鉸鏈連接　link joint
铰链门/鉸鏈[式]門　hinged door
铰式支座/鉸式支座,關節軸式,肘節軸承　knuckle bearing
铰枢/鉸樞　hinged pin
铰吸式挖泥船/鉸刀吸入式挖泥船　cutter suction dredger, suction cutter dredger
铰支桥墩/鉸支橋墩　rocker pier
铰支座/鉸支[承]　hinged support
矫直/矯直　straightening
矫直钢轨/矯直潰軌　straightening of kinked rail
矫直机/矯直器　straightener, straightening machine
脚蹬/舵磴,方向舵踏板　rudder pedal
脚光/腳燈　foot light
脚手板/腳手板　scaffold board
脚手架/腳手架,工作架,鷹架　scaffold
脚手架支柱/鷹架桿　scaffolding pole
搅拌车/拌送車　agitator truck
搅拌时间/拌和時間　mixing time
搅拌台/拌合平臺　mixing platform
搅拌站/混凝土配料廠　batch plant
搅拌装置/攪拌器　stirring apparatus, mixer
叫号电话/叫號電話　station call
[轿车]车身测量整形机/車身測量整形機　body and frame measure and correct system
轿车运载[半挂]车/汽車[運輸]尾拖車　car carrier semitrailer
校测风洞/校準風洞　calibration wind tunnel
校对人/校閱者　checker
校飞/飛行校準　calibration flight
校飞程序/飛行校準程式　calibration flight program
校飞航路/飛行校準航路　calibration flight route
校零变频器/校零變頻器　zero calibration frequency converter
校零应答机/校零應答機　zero calibration transponder
校频/頻率校準　frequency calibration
校正不足/校正不足　under-correction
校正架/校正裝具,校正臺　calibration rig
校正空速/校正空速　calibrated airspeed
校正龄期/校正齡期　age of correction
校正仪/校正儀　rectifying apparatus
校直/鑿榫　tabling
校中/對中線　centering

校准/校準,定標　calibration
校准电平/校準平準　calibration level
校准杆/校準桿　calibrating lever
校准角/校準角　aligning angle
校准目标/校準目標　calibration target
校准实验室/校正實驗室　calibration laboratory
校准塔/校準塔　calibration tower
校准位姿/校準姿勢　alignment pose
校准证书/校正證書　calibration certificate
较大限制信号/較大限制信號　more restrictive signal
较大允许信号/較大允許信號　more favorable signal
较强涨潮/較強漲潮　lesser flood
较弱落潮/較弱落潮　lesser ebb
教会建筑/教會建築　missionary architecture
教具室/工具間　tool room
教练[导]弹/訓練飛彈　practice missile, training missile
教练机/教練機　trainer, training airplane
教师办公用房/教師辦公室　teacher office
教室/教室　classroom
教学管理用房/教學[管理]辦公室　administrative room
教学海图/教學海圖　instructional chart
教育车/教育車　education car
教育建筑/文教建築物　educational building
教育科研设计用地/教育科學研究土地使用　education and scientific research land use
教育科研用地/教育科研用地　land for education and scientific research
教育设施/教育設施　educational facility
教育园地/教育園地　educational garden
教员台/指導員臺　instructor station
酵母/酵母　yeast
阶地/階地,臺地　terrace
阶段发展/分期發展　stage development
阶段缓解/逐漸釋放　graduated release
阶段提升/階段提昇　graduated increasing
阶段制动/階段制動　graduated application
阶段钻眼/階式鑽孔　bench drilling
阶式边墙/臺階牆壁　stepped wall
阶梯教室/階梯教室　lecture theater
阶梯式涵洞/階梯式涵洞　stepped culvert
阶梯形活塞/階段活塞,塔形活塞　stepped piston
阶梯直达列车/階梯直達列車　through train originated from several adjoining loading points
阶条石/階條石,階沿石　stone slab at platform edge
阶形柱/階梯式柱　stepped column

阶跃操舵/階躍操舵　step steering
阶跃操纵/分步控制,分級控制　step-control
阶跃输入/分段輸入　step input
接/結[合],聯集　join
接岸标/岸標,界標　land mark
接插软线/接插軟線　patch call
接车进路/接車進路　receiving route
接车进路信号机/接車進路號誌　route signal for receiving
接车信号/接車信號　receiving signal
接触变质作用/接觸變質作用　contact metamorphism
接触不良/不良接觸　bad contact
接触测量/接觸量測　contact measurement
接触池/接觸池,接觸槽　contact tank
接触腐蚀/接觸腐蝕　contact corrosion
接触灌浆/接觸面灌漿　contact grout
接触光刻/接觸膠印　contact lithograph
接触觉察/接觸覺察　contact sensing
接触滤池/接觸濾池　contact filter
接触面/接觸面　contact surface
接触器/接觸器,觸頭　contactor
接触热阻/接觸熱阻　thermal contact resistance
接触水平/曝露準位　exposure level
接触网/接觸網　overhead contact line equipment
接触网标称电压/架空接觸線標稱電壓　nominal voltage of overhead contact line
接触网测试车/接觸網測試車　measuring car for overhead contact line equipment
接触网工区/接觸網養路班　maintenance gang for catenary
接触网故障探测装置/接觸網故障探測裝置　fault locator for overhead contact line equipment
接触网架线车/接觸網運輸安裝車　installation vehicle for contact wire
接触网检修车/接觸網檢修車　repairing car for overhead contact line equipment
接触网限界/接觸網限界　clearance limit for overhead contact wire, clearance limit for overhead catenary system, overhead catenary system gage
接触网悬挂/接觸網懸掛　overhead contact line, catenary
接触网支柱/接觸網桅桿　catenary mast
接触网最低电压/架空接觸線最低電壓　minimum voltage of overhead contact line
接触网最高电压/架空接觸線最高電壓　maximum voltage of overhead contact line
接触网作业车/接觸線作業車　operation vehicle for

contact wire
接触稳定法/接觸穩定法　contact stabilization process
接触问题/接觸問題　contact problem
接触线/接觸線　contact wire
接触线弛度/接觸線弛度　contact wire sag
接触线电连接线夹/接觸線電連接線夾　electrically connecting clamp for contact wire
接触线接头线夹/接觸線接頭線夾　contact wire splice
接触线预留弛度/接觸線預定弛度　contact wire pre-sag
接触线终端锚固线夹/接觸線終端錨固線夾　termination fitting for contact wire
接触线最大水平偏移值/接觸線最大水平位移　maximum horizontal displacement of contact wire
接触型离子推力器/接觸型離子推進器　contact ion thruster
接触絮凝/接觸絮凝［作用］　contact flocculation
接地/接地　earth connection, grounding
接地安全棒/接地棒　earthing pole
接地保护放电装置/接地保護放電［裝置］　earth protection discharger
接地报警/接地報警　grounding alarm
接地带灯/著陸區燈　touchdown zone light
接地导体/接地導體　ground conductor
接地地带/落地區　touchdown zone
接地电抗器/接地電抗器　earthing reactor, grounding reactor
接地电流/［接］地電流　earth current
接地电路/接地回路　ground return circuit, earthed circuit
接地电阻/接地電阻,大地電阻　ground resistance, resistance of an earthed conductor, grounding resistance
接地端子/接地線端　grounding terminal
接地和搭接电阻测量/接地和搭接電阻量測　grounding and lapping resistance measurement
接地回流电刷/接地碳刷　earth return brush
接地极/接地電極,接地棒　ground rod, earth bar, ground electrode
接地继电器/接地故障繼電器　earth fault relay
接地检查灯/接地檢查燈　ground detecting lamp
接地开关/接地開關　earthing switch, grounding switch
接地配置/接地配置　grounding arrangement
接地速度/接地速率　touchdown speed
接地网/接地［電極］網　grounding lattice, ground electrode network
接地系统/接地系統　earthing system
接地线/基線,地平線　ground line
接地线夹/接地夾　earth clamp
接点闭合/接點閉合　contact closed
接点断开/接點斷開　contact open
接点系统/接點系統　contact system
接点压力/接觸壓力　contact pressure
接发车进路信号/接發車進路號誌　route signal for receiving-departure
接发车无线电通信/接發車無線電通訊　radio communication for train reception and starting
接发列车/接發列車　train reception and departure
接缝/接縫,接頭,接線　joint, seam
接缝钣调整器/接縫鈑調整器　low joints adjuster
接缝带/合縫帶　joint tape
接缝灌浆/接縫灌漿　joint grouting
接缝及密封材料/填隙料　caulking material
接缝破损/接縫破損　joint failure
接缝止水材料/封縫劑　joint sealer
接杆/接桿　pipe jaw
接管箍/受張套筒　tension sleeve
接合板/護緣板　shin
接合点/分道起點　junction point
接合井/會合井　junction well
接合螺栓/固定螺栓　fitting-up bolt
接户管/接户管,輸送管　inter-building pipe, service pipe
接近表示/趨近指示　approach indication
接近长度/接近長度　approach length
接近发码/接近發碼　coding during train approaching
接近距离/分開距離　separation distance
接近连续式机车信号/接近連續式機車信號　approach continuous cab signaling
接近区段/接近區段　approach section
接近速度/靠近速度　close velocity
接近锁闭/接近鎖定裝置　approach locking
接口/接口,介面　interface
接口控制文件/介面控制檔　interface control document, ICD
接力运输/接力運輸　relay transport
接坪滑行道/接坪滑行道　apron access taxiway
接鞘/接鞘　coupler sheath
接入空车数/接入空車數　number of empty cars received
接闪器/接閃器　air-termination system
接收换能器/接收換能器　receiving transducer
接收机/接收機　receiver

GPS 接收机/全球定位系統接收器　GPS receiver
接收机保护/接收機保護　receiver protection
接收机动态范围/接收機之動態範圍,可接收信號之動態範圍　receiver dynamic range
接收机灵敏度/接收機靈敏度,接收器靈敏度　sensitivity of a receiver, receiver sensitivity
接收机通道合并/接收儀通道合併　receiver channel combination
接收机选择性/接收機選擇性　selectivity of a receiver
接收静止搜救卫星无效报警/接收無效之定置搜救衛星警報　GEOSAR invalid alert received
接收天线/接收天線　receiving antenna
接收系统品质因素/接收系統品質因素　merit factor of receiving system
接收线圈/接收線圈　receiving coil
接收信道/接收通道　receive channel
接收站/接收站,接收電臺　receiving station
接受船/受補船　receiving ship
接受者/感受器　receptor
接穗/接穗　scion
接通率/電話接通率　percent of call completed
接通能力/閉合容量　making capacity
接头夹板/接板,魚尾板　joint bar, splice bar, fish plate
接头夹板螺栓/魚尾[板]螺栓,軌節螺栓　fishbolt
接头联结零件/接頭聯結零件　rail joint accessories, rail joint fastenings
接头螺栓/魚尾板螺栓　track bolt, fish bolt
接头瞎缝/閉接頭,閉熔接　closed joint, tight joint
接头阻力/接頭阻力　joint resistance
接线端子/接線座　connection terminal
接线盒/接線盒,接線箱,開關箱　junction box, connection box, joint box
接续标定法/接續標定法　successive relative orientation
接运重车数/接運重車數　number of loaded cars received
街/街　street
街道/街道　sub-district, street
街道广场绿地/街道廣場綠地　street and square green area
街道家具/街道家具,道路附屬設施　public furniture
街道绿化/街道綠化,街樹栽植　street greening, street planting
街道设施/街道附屬設施,街道家具　street furniture
街道系统/街路系統　street system
街道峡谷/街道峽谷　street canyon
街道照明/街路照明　street lighting
街道装备/街道附屬設施,街道家具　street furniture
街坊绿地/街坊綠地　residential block green belt
街沟/街溝　street gully
街景/街景　streetscape
街廊/街廊　street profile
街面停车/沿街停車　on-street parking
街旁绿地/街頭綠地　roadside green space
街墙/沿街牆　street wall
街区/街區,區塊　block
街区城市设计/區域都市設計　block urban design, district urban design
街头篮球/街頭籃球　street basketball
街外停车处/路外停車場　offstreet parking space
街巷制/街巷制　jie xiang system
街心花园/街心花園　street crossing center garden
街心驻车/中央停車　center parking
孑遗种/殘留種,古老種　relic species, epibiotic species
节/節　knot
节点/節點　node, nodal point
节点板/角牽板　gusset plate
节点舱/節點艙　node module
节点刚度/節點勁度　joint stiffness
节点计算机/節點計算機　node computer
节点式相机/節點照相機　node-point camera
节点详图/節點詳圖　architectural detail drawing
节点支块/接點支塊　angle block
节段施工法/分節施工法　segmental construction method
节段预制拼装法/節段預製拼裝法　segmental precast erection method
节间/節間　panel
节间长度/節間長度　panel length
节流/節流　throttle
节流板/截水板　cut-off plate
节流阀/節流閥　throttle valve
节流特性/節流特性　throttle characteristics
节流调节/節流調速　throttle governing
节流嘴/計量孔　metering orifice
节能/能源節約　save energy, conservation energy
节能灯/省電燈[泡],省電燈管　energy saving lamp
节能率/節能率　energy saving ratio
节能器/節能器　economizer
节事活动/節事活動　festival and special event
节水/節水　water conservation
节水灌溉/節水灌溉　water saving irrigation
节水型园林/節水型園林　water saving landscape

节油率／節油率　fuel saving ratio
节约型园林／資源節約園林　resources saving landscape
节约用电／電氣節能　electric energy saving
节制闸灯／調整閘燈　regulating lock light
杰克逊[浊]度／傑克生濁度計　Jackson turbidity unit
杰森条款／詹森條款，超額條款　Jason clause
拮抗作用／拮抗作用　antagonism
洁净车间／潔淨廠房　clean workshop
洁净度／清潔度，潔淨，淨度　cleanliness
洁净工作服／潔淨工作服　clean working garment
洁净工作台／潔淨[工作]臺，無塵實驗臺　clean bench
洁净煤技术／潔淨煤技術　clean coal technology
洁净能源／清潔能源　clean energy
洁净区／潔淨區，清潔區　clean zone
洁净实验室／潔淨實驗室　clean laboratory
洁净室／潔淨室，無塵室　clean room
洁净推进剂／清潔推進劑　clean propellant
结冰／結冰　icing
结冰气象参数／積冰氣象參數　meteorological parameter of icing
结冰强度／積冰強度　icing intensity
结冰区／結冰區　icing area
结冰信号器／冰偵測裝備　icing signaller, icing detector
结冰云／積冰雲　icing cloud
结点板／角牽板　gusset plate
结点任务控制中心／節點任務管制中心　nodal MCC
结构／結構，構造　structure
结构安全等级／結構安全等級　safety classes of structure
结构侧移刚度／結構側移剛度　lateral displacement stiffness of structure
结构层／構造層　structural floor, structural layer
结构吃水／强度[計算]吃水　scantling draft
结构传热试验／結構熱傳遞試驗　structural heat transfer test
结构动力特性／結構動力分析　dynamic property of structure layer
结构动力特性测试／結構動力特性測試　dynamic property measurement of structure
结构动力学／結構動力學　structural dynamics
结构分析／結構分析　structural analysis
结构分系统／結構分系統　structure subsystem
结构刚度试验／結構勁度試驗　structure stiffness test
结构钢／結構鋼　structural steel

结构高度／結構高度　system height, encumbrance
结构功能主义／結構功能論　structural functionalism
结构规划／結構綱領　structure plan
结构建模／結構建模　structural modeling
结构胶黏剂／結構性黏著劑　structural adhesive
结构静强度试验／結構靜強度試驗　structure static strength test
结构抗震变形能力／結構抗震變形能力　earthquake resistant deformability of structure
结构抗震承载能力／結構抗震承載力　seismic resistant capacity of structure
结构抗震性能／結構抗震性能　earthquake resistant behavior of structure
结构理论／結構理論　theory of structure
结构力学／結構力學　structural mechanics
结构面／結構面　structural plane
结构面粗糙度／結構面粗糙度　structural plane roughness
结构面积／結構面積　structure area
结构面间距／結構面間距　spacing of structural planes
结构模型／結構模型　structural model
结构品级号／結構品級　structural ratings
结构屏蔽／結構遮罩　structural shield
结构强度／結構強度　structural strength
结构墙／結構牆，承重牆　structural wall
结构轻骨料／結構用輕骨材　structural lightweight aggregate
结构屈服／結構屈服　yielding of structure
结构热低压试验／結構熱低壓試驗　structural thermal low pressure test
结构热防护试验／結構熱防護試驗　structural thermal protection test
结构热外压试验／結構熱外壓試驗　structural thermal external pressure test
结构热稳定性试验／結構熱穩定性試驗　structural thermal stability test
结构热振动试验／結構熱振動試驗　structural thermal vibration transfer
结构实体几何表示法／建構固體幾何　constructive solid geometry, CSG
结构[试验]模型／結構測試原型　structure model, SM
结构钛合金／結構鈦合金　structural titanium alloy
结构陶瓷／結構陶瓷　structural ceramics
结构体系抗震加固／結構體系抗震加固　seismic retrofit of structural system, seismic strengthening of structural system

结构体系转换/結構體系轉換　structure system transform
结构图/結構圖　structural drawing
结构完整性/結構完整性　structural integrity
结构系统/結構系統　structural system
结构型密封材料/結構密封膠　structural sealant
结构性破坏/結構損傷,船體損傷　structural damage
结构性种植/結構性種植　structural planting
结构选型/結構選型　selection of structure typology
结构延展性/結構延性　structure ductility
结构优化设计/最優結構設計　optimum structural design, optimized design of structure
结构噪声/結構噪音　structure borne noise
结构振动控制/結構振動控制　structural vibration control
结构振动试验台/結構振動試驗臺　shaking table for structure test, vibrostand
结构重要性系数/結構重要性係數　coefficient for importance of structure
结构总工程师/結構總工程師　chief structural engineer
结构阻尼/結構阻尼　structural damping
结关/結關,出港許可　clearance
结关单/出口結關證書,出航許可證　clearance certificate
结关清单/出口結關單,出港證書　bill of clearance
结果数据处理报告/結果數據處理報告　result data handling report
结合层/拉結層　binding course
结合杆/聯接桿,耦桿　union link, connecting link
结合力/黏著[力],附著[力]　adhesion
结合梁/膠結梁　bonded beam
结合梁桥/組合梁橋　composite beam bridge, composite girder bridge
结合料/黏結劑,黏合劑　binder
结合水/結合水　combined water
结合通气管/結合通氣管　yoke vent pipe
结胶/膠結,結塊　gumming, caking
结晶水/結晶水　water of crystallization
结绳/結繩　tying knot
捷联式惯性测量装置/捷聯式慣性測量裝置　strapdown inertial measurement unit
捷联式惯性导航系统/捷聯式慣性導航系統,固裝式慣性導航系統　strapdown inertial navigation system
捷联式惯性制导/捷聯式慣性導航　strapdown inertial guidance
捷联式惯性制导系统/捷聯式慣性制導系統　strapdown inertial guidance system
捷水道/捷徑航路　short-cut route
截断比/截斷比　cut-off ratio
截断塞门/切換旋塞　cut-out cock
截干/莖插條,枝插　cutting stem
截根/切根　cutting root
截获/截獲　acquisition
截击卫星/攔截衛星　interceptor satellite
截留倍数/截留倍數　interception ratio
截流管/截流汙水管　intercepting sewer, interceptor
截流器/截留計　interceptometer
截流式系统/截流式,截流系統　intercepting system
截面/截面　section
截面法/截切法,斷面法　method of section, sectional method
截面刚度/截面剛度　rigidity of section
截面惯性矩/截面慣性矩,斷面慣性矩,面積的二次矩　second moment of area, moment of inertia
截面回转半径/迴轉半徑　radius of gyration
截面极惯性矩/截面二次軸矩　polar second moment of area, polar moment of inertia
截面面积矩/面積一次矩　first moment of area
截面模量/截面模數,剖面模數,斷面模數　section modulus, modulus of section
截面收缩率/斷[裂]面縮率　reduction of area
截面有效高度/截面有效高度　effective depth of section
截潜水给水系统/截潛水給水系統　phreatic water supply system
截切法/截切法　method of dissection
截水沟/截水溝　intercepting ditch, catch-drain, intercepting drain
截土坝/防砂壩　soil saving dam
截止波长/截止波長　cutoff wavelength
截止电压/截止電壓　cutoff voltage
截止阀/停止閥,截流閥　stop valve, shutoff valve
截止刚度/截止勁度　cutoff rigidity
截止滤光片/截止濾波器　cutoff filter
截止能量/截止能量　cutoff energy
解爆/解爆　remove exploding, disexplosion
解除/解除　release
解除保险指令/警報命令　arm command
解除闭塞/解除閉塞　block cleared
解除限速/解除速限　end of speed limit
解冻指数/融解指數　thawing index
解钩装置/脱接器　uncoupling device
解构主义/解構主義　deconstructivism
解开/解開　cast off

解扩/解擴散 de-spread
解码/解碼,譯碼 decoding, decode
解偶联/解偶聯 uncoupling
解剖室/解剖室 autopsy room
解说/新聞評論 commentary
解锁/解鎖,脱扣 release
解锁按钮盘/解鎖按鈕盤 manual release button panel
解锁电路/解鎖電路 release circuit
解锁进路/解鎖進路 released route
解锁力/解鎖力 releasing force
解体调车/解體調車 break-up of trains
解调/解調[變] demodulation
解吸除氧/解吸除氧 desorption deoxidization
解吸[附作用]/去吸附,脱附 desorption
解析式惯性导航系统/解析慣性航行系統 analytic inertial navigation system
解析余度/解析冗餘 analytic redundancy
解约/解約 canceling
解约日/解約日 canceling date
介电材料/介電材料 dielectric material
介电监控/介電監控 dielectric monitoring
介电强度试验/絕緣強度試驗,介質性能試驗 dielectric test
介电性能/介電性質 dielectric properties
介质/介質 medium
介质强度试验/介質強度試驗 dielectric strength test, dielectric test
介质天线/介質天線 dielectric antenna
介质土/中等土壤 medium soil
界面/介面,接口 interface
界面反应/介面反應 interface reaction
界面滑动接触/介面滑動接觸 sliding contact of interface
界面连续接触/介面連續式接觸 continuous contact of interface
界面排水/介面排水 interface drainage
界面热交换器/介面熱交換器 inter exchanger
界面受剪/介面剪切 interface shear
界限标/界限標 limit mark
界限配筋梁/平衡的加固梁 balanced reinforcement beam
界限偏心距/平衡偏心率 balanced eccentricity
界限[燃]气/界限[燃]氣 limit gas
界限线/界限線 barrier line
借出处/外借部 lending department
借景/借景 borrowed scenery, view borrowing
借土/借土 borrow earth

金刚宝座塔/金剛寶座塔 Vajra Throne pagoda
金刚砂/金剛砂,碳化矽 silicon carbide
金刚石刀具/金剛石切削器 diamond cutter
金刚石切削/金剛石切削 diamond cutting
金工车间/機械工廠 machine shop
金融建筑/金融建築 financial building
金属板幕墙/金屬板幕牆 metal panel curtain wall
金属[材料]/金屬材料 metal materials
金属防锈预处理/金屬防鏽 metal rust proofing
金属腐蚀/金屬腐蝕 metal corrosion
金属覆盖层/金屬覆蓋層 metal coating
金属冠/鎢鋼鑽頭,超硬鑽頭 metal crown
金属滚轴带氯丁橡胶板接缝/金屬滾軸帶氯丁橡膠板接縫 metal roller with neoprene plate joint
金属化/敷金屬 metallization
金属基复合材料/金屬基複合材料 metal matrix composite
金属极弧焊/金屬弧焊接 metallic-arc welding
金属家具/板金家具 metal furniture
金属间化合物/金屬間化合物 intermetallic compound
金属结构/金屬結構 metal structure
金属救生艇/金屬救生艇 metal lifeboat
金属扣合/金屬扣合 tie insert
金属卤化物灯/金屬鹵素燈 metal halide lamp
金属面夹芯板/金屬面夾芯板 metal skinned sandwich panel
金属黏合剂/金屬黏著劑 metal-to-metal adhesive
金属黏合胶/金屬黏著劑 metal-to-metal adhesive
金属喷镀/金屬噴鍍,金屬噴敷 metal spraying
金属片状粗滤器/金屬層片過濾器 metal-edge type strainer
金属铺板/金屬板 metal deck
金属桥/金屬橋 metallic bridge
金属氢化物镍电池/金屬氫化物鎳電池 metal-hydrogen nickel battery
金属热浸镀/金屬熱浸鍍 metal hot dipping
[金属]热浸涂层/熱浸鍍層 hot dip coating
金属蠕变/金屬潛變 creep of metal
金属软管/金屬軟管 metallic hose, flexible metallic conduit
金属刷密封/金屬刷密封 metal brush seal
金属陶瓷/金屬陶瓷 metal ceramic, cermet
金属条/扁鋼 metal strap
金属瓦/金屬瓦 metal tile
金属网/金屬網,鋼絲網 metal mesh
金属纤维/金屬纖維 metal fiber
金属型铸造/金屬模鑄造,永久模鑄造 gravity die

casting, permanent mold casting
金厢斗底槽/金箱斗底槽　jinxiang doudi cao
金相检查/金相檢查　metallographic inspection
金相检验/金相檢驗　metallographic examination, metallographic inspection
金星/金星　Venus
金星地质/金星地質　geology of Venus
金字桁架/金字桁架　simple hanging truss
金字塔/金字塔　pyramid
筋斗/觔斗　loop
襟翼/襟翼　flap
襟翼舵/襟翼舵　flap rudder, flap-type rudder
紧凑城市/緊密城市,集約城市　compact city
紧凑型荧光灯/小型熒光燈　compact fluorescent lamp
紧固件/緊固件,鎖定器,扣件　fastener
紧固螺栓/緊固螺栓　fastening bolt
紧急/緊急　emergency, urgency
紧急报告/緊急信文　urgency message
紧急报警/警报器　emergency alarm
紧急报警装置/緊急警報裝置　emergency alarm switch
紧急部/緊急部　emergency portion
紧急倒车/緊急倒車　back emergency
紧急倒车冲程/緊急停車距離　crash stopping distance
紧急的/緊急的　urgent
紧急断缆工具/緊急斷纜工具　emergency breakaway tools
紧急风缸/緊急風缸　emergency reservoir
紧急复压系统/緊急復壓系統　emergency repressurization system
紧急关闭/緊急關閉　emergency shut-down
紧急关机/緊急關機　emergency cutoff
紧急航行危险报告/緊急航行危險報告　urgent navigational danger report
紧急呼叫/緊急呼叫　emergency call, urgency call
紧急呼叫格式/緊急呼叫格式　urgency call format
紧急回转/緊急迴轉　emergency turn
紧急阶段/緊急階段　emergency phase
紧急警报/緊急警報　emergency warning
紧急局减/緊急局減　quick action
紧急灭火机/緊急滅火機　emergency fire extinguisher
紧急气象危险报告/緊急氣象危險報告　urgent meteorological danger report
紧急强制用车/緊急強制用車　emergency overriding
紧急撒砂/緊急撒砂　emergency sanding
紧急刹车/緊急剎車,緊急軔　emergency brake
紧急示位发信机/應急示位發射機　emergency locator transmitter, ELT
紧急停车按钮/緊急停車按鈕　emergency stop push button
紧急停车装置/應急停車裝置　emergency stop mechanism
紧急停堆/緊急關閉　emergency shut-down
紧急通信/緊急通信　urgency communication
紧急通信程序/緊急通信程式　urgency communication procedure
紧急脱离/緊急脫離　breakaway emergency
紧急危险/立即危險　immediate danger
紧急无线电示位标/應急指位無線電示標　emergency position-indicating radio beacon, EPIRB
紧急无线电示位标识别/應急指位元無線電示標識別　EPIRB identification
紧急响应工作队/緊急應對工作隊　emergency response team
紧急信号/緊急信號　urgency signal, emergency signal
紧急优先等级/緊急優先順序　urgency priority
紧急制动/緊急剎車　emergency braking, emergency application
紧急制动阀/緊急制動閥,車長閥　emergency brake valve
紧急制动信号音/緊急剎車信號音　emergency braking tone
紧急转车道/緊急橫渡線　emergency crossover
紧密结构/緊密結構　tight structure
紧密连接器/緊密連接器　tight lock coupler
紧配合/緊配合　tight fit
紧坡地段/緊坡地段　section of sufficient grade
紧迫局面/彼此接近　close quarters situation
紧迫危险/立即危險　immediate danger
紧线器/索夾　wire grip
紧转配合/緊轉配合　close running fit
紧追权/緊追權　right of hot pursuit
锦玻璃/馬賽克玻璃　glass mosaic
谨慎处理/必要[的]注意　due diligence
尽端式/盡端式　stub-end type
尽端式枢纽/盡頭式樞紐　stub-end type junction terminal
尽端式舞台/盡端式舞臺　end stage
尽端式站台/端末月臺　end platform
尽头式货场/盡頭式貨場　stub-end type freight yard
尽头式货运站/盡頭式貨運站　stub-end freight station

尽头式客运站/盡頭式客運站　stub-end passenger station
尽头线/盡頭綫　stub-end siding
尽头信号机/盡頭信號機　signal for stub-end track
进步式规划/進步式規劃　progressive planning
进场/進場,近場　approach
进场灯/進近燈光　approach light
进场验收/進場驗收　site acceptance
进出站地道/旅客地道　passenger tunnel, platform tunnel
进出站天桥/月臺天橋　platform bridge
进出站线路/進站線路　approach line
进倒车掉头/進退車短迴轉掉頭　turning short round by ahead and astern engine
进动角速度/進動角速度　angular velocity of precession
进动性/進動　precession
进动轴线/前進軸　axis of precession
进度偏差/進度偏差　schedule variance
进风道/進氣導管　air inlet duct
进港航道/進港航道　approach channel, entrance channel
进港信号/港口號誌　approach signal
进化/進化,演化　evolution
进给量/供給　feed
进给装置/給水設備　feeding apparatus
进近窗口/進近窗口　approach aperture
进近灯光系统/進場燈光系統　approach light system
进近面/進近地面　approach surface
进局电缆/引入電纜　entrance cable
进局设备/進局設備　incoming equipment
进口关单/進口[報]關單,進港證書　bill of entry
进口货码头/進口貨碼頭　import wharf
进口许可/輸入許可　import permit
进流段/艙入水段　entrance
进流段长/艙入水段長　length of entrance
进路表/途程表　route sheet
进路表示器/進路表示器　route indicator
进路表示器电路/進路表示器電路　route indicator circuit
进路操纵作业/進路操縱作業　semi-automatic operation by route operation
进路储存器/進路儲存器　route storaging device
进路电路/進路選擇電路　route selecting circuit
进路分段解锁/進路分段解鎖　sectional release of a locked route
进路继电式电气集中联锁/進路全電驛聯鎖　route type all-relay interlocking
进路交叉/進路交叉　crossing of routes
进路解锁/路線解鎖　route release
进路人工解锁/進路人工解鎖　manual route release
进路锁闭/進路鎖定　route locking
进路锁闭表示/進路鎖定表示　route locking indication
进路信号/進路號誌　route signal
进路一次解锁/進路一次解鎖　route release at once
进气道/進氣口,進氣導管　air intake, intake, intake duct
进气道板位-锥位表/進氣道板位-錐位表　inlet ramp-cone position indicator
进气道唇口/進氣道唇　inlet lip
进气道动态畸变/進氣口動態失真　inlet dynamic distortion
进气道动态响应/進氣口動力反應　inlet dynamic response
进气道-发动机相容性/進氣道-發動機相容性　inlet-engine compatibility
进气道辅助进气门/進氣道輔助進氣門　auxiliary inlet door
进气道附加阻力/進氣口附加阻力　inlet additive drag
进气道喉道/進氣道喉部　inlet throat
进气道空气动力学/進氣口空氣動力學　inlet aerodynamics
进气道试验/進氣口試驗　air intake test
进气道外阻/進氣口外部阻力　inlet external drag
进气道稳定裕度/進氣口安全度　inlet stability margin
进气道总压恢复/進氣道總壓恢復　inlet total pressure recovery
进气度/進氣度　gas inlet degree
进气阀/進氣閥　inlet valve, air inlet valve
进气管/進氣管　air inlet pipe
进气壳体/進氣殼體　air intake casing
进气设备/進氣裝置　air inlet unit
进气提前角/進氣提前角　inlet advance crank angle
进气凸轮/進氣閥凸輪　inlet cam
进气温度/進氣溫度　intake-air temperature
进气稳压箱/進氣穩壓箱　air inlet pressure stabilizing chamber
进气涡流/進氣渦流　intake swirl
进气消音器/進氣消音器　intake silencer
进气行程/進氣衝程,吸氣衝程,吸入衝程　suction stroke, intake stroke
进气旋流畸变/進氣旋渦流畸變　inlet swirl flow

distortion
进气压力/進氣壓力,進入壓力　intake pressure
进气压力表/進氣口壓力計　inlet pressure gage
进气滞后角/進氣滯後角　inlet lag crank angle
进气装置/進氣裝置　air inlet unit
进气总温畸变/進氣總溫畸變　inlet total temperature distortion
进气总压畸变/進氣總壓力畸變　inlet total pressure distortion
进汽度/進汽度　degree of admission
进汽余面/蒸汽餘面　steam lap
进入段/進入段　access zone, approach section
进深/進深　depth of building
进水角/浸水角,泛水角　flooding angle
进水口/進水道,取水口,入口　inlet, intake, water-intake
进水口防臭阱/密封陰井蓋　gulley trap
进水量/取水量　quantity of water
进水区/進水區　intake area
进水渠/引水渠　intake channel, inlet channel
进水速度/泛水速度　speed of flooding
进水位/引水水位　intake water level
进速比/前進比　advance ratio
进速系数/前進係數　advance coefficient
进坞/進塢　docking
进坞操纵/進塢操縱　docking maneuver
进相机/進相機　phase advancer
进行信号/進行號誌　proceed signal
进站信号机/進站號誌機　home signal
近岸/離岸　offshore
近岸流/近岸流　inshore current
近岸移动式钻井装置/可動式離岸鑽探平臺　mobile offshore drilling unit, MODU
近滨/近灘　nearshore
近场/近場　near field
近场区/近場區　near field area
近程待爆/短距離備炸　short distance arming
近程监督分区/近程監督分區　directly surveillanced subsection
近程网路/近程網路　directly surveillanced network
近代巴洛克式园林/近代巴洛克式園林　modern Baroque style
近代环境系统/近代環境系統　modern environment system
近地点/近地點　perigee
近地点幅角/近[地]點幅角　argument of perigee
近地点火箭发动机/近地點火箭發動機　perigee kick rocket engine, perigee kick rocket motor
近地点注入/近地點入軌　perigee injection
近地告警系统/貼地飛行警示系統　ground-proximity warning system
近地空间/近地空間　near earth space
近点角/近點角　anomaly
近点月/近點月　anomalistic month
近端串扰/近端串音,近端交叉通話　near-end crosstalk, NEXT
近端串音/近端串音,近端交叉通話　near-end crosstalk, NEXT
近端串音衰减/近端串話衰減,本端串話衰減　near-end crosstalk attenuation
近海/離海　offshore
近海测量/近海測量,離岸測量　offshore survey
近海沉积/近海沈積　offshore deposit
近海岛屿/外圍島嶼,離島　offshore island
近海航行/近海航行　offshore navigation
近海区/離島地區　offshore area
近海渔业/近海漁業　offshore fishery
近海钻井作业/近海鑽探作業　offshore drilling operation
近红外/近紅外[線]　near infrared
近红外相机/近紅外照相機　near infrared camera
近机位/近機停機位　contact aircraft stand, gate stand
近景/近景　nearby view
近耦鸭式布局技术/近耦鴨式布局技術　technique of close coupled canard configuration
近破波/破碎波　breaking wave
近期建设规划/近期建設規劃,近期施工規劃　recent construction planning, short-term plan, short-term plan for development
近区效应/近區域效應　close area effect
近日点/近日點　perihelion
近日点前移/近日點前移　advance of perihelion
近似色谐调/近似色諧調　approximate colors harmony
[近]碎波深/碎波水深　breaking wave depth
近体防护/近體防護　nearby protection
近铁道平交道线/近鐵道平交道線　approach-to-level-crossing marking
近艉/近艉,向艉　aft, abaft
近现代建筑/現當代建築　modern and contemporary architecture
近星点前移/近星點前移　advance of periastron
近因/近因　proximate cause
近炸引信/近發引信,近距信管[引信]　proximity fuze

近障碍物线/近障礙物線　approach-to-obstacle marking
近震/近震　near earthquake
近中天/近中天　ex-meridian
近中天高度改正/折合中天高度　reduction to the meridian
浸焊/浸焊接　immersed solder
浸胶/浸漬　impregnation
浸没燃烧/浸沈燃燒,沈没燃燒　submerged combustion, immersion combustion
浸没式蒸发器/浸没式蒸發器　flooded evaporator
浸泡稳定性试验/浸水穩定度試驗　immersion stability test
浸润面积/浸濕面積　wetted area
浸润线/地水線,泉面線　phreatic line
浸润性液体/浸潤性液體　wetting liquid
浸水/水浸　flood
浸水路堤/浸水路堤　immerseable embankment
浸水试验/浸水試驗　water immersion test
浸压木材/膠合木　compregnated wood
浸压试验/浸壓試驗　immersion compression test
浸沾钎焊/熱浸硬焊　dip brazing, dip soldering
浸种/浸種　seed soaking
浸渍/浸漬　impregnating
浸渍法/注入煉製法　impregnation method
浸渍防腐木材/油浸木材　creosoted timber
浸渍混凝土/浸漬混凝土　impregnated concrete
浸渍金属碳石墨/浸漬金屬碳石墨　carbon-graphite impregnated with metal
浸渍磷酸盐碳石墨/浸漬磷酸鹽碳石墨　carbon-graphite impregnated with phosphate
浸渍钎焊/熱浸硬焊　dip brazing, dip soldering
浸渍时间/均熱時間　soaking time
浸渍树脂碳石墨/浸漬樹脂碳石墨　carbon-graphite impregnated with resin
浸渍无机盐碳石墨/浸漬無機鹽碳石墨　carbon-graphite impregnated with inorganic salt
禁超车区/禁超車區段　non-passing zone
禁伐禁猎区/禁伐禁獵區　region forbidden to tree cutting and hunting
禁飞区/禁航區　prohibited area, forbidden zone
禁航区/禁航區　prohibited area, forbidden zone
禁建区/禁建區　no-build zone
禁令标志/禁制標誌　prohibitory sign
禁溜车停留线/禁溜車停留線　no-humping car storage
禁区/禁區　restricted area
禁渔期/禁漁期　fishing closed season

禁渔区/禁漁區　forbidden fishing zone
禁运/禁運,封港,扣船　embargo
禁运货物/禁運貨物,禁運品　contraband goods
禁止/禁止　prohibitory
禁止标志/禁止標誌　forbidden sign, mandatory forbidding sign, sign mandatory forbidding
禁止超车/禁止超車　no overtaking
禁止超车标志/禁止超車標誌　overtaking prohibited sign
禁止超车区/禁止超車區段　non-passing zone
禁止超车线/禁止超車線　overtaking prohibited marking
禁止船舶通航/禁止船舶通航　embargo on ship
禁止掉头/禁止迴轉　no U-turns
禁止掉头标志/禁止掉頭標誌　no U turn sign
禁止机动车开口线/禁止機動車開口線　prohibition of motor vehicle opening line
禁止建设区/禁區建設區　development-prohibited zone
禁止建筑/禁止建築　prohibition of building
禁止锚泊标/禁泊標誌　anchor prohibited mark
禁止驶入标志/禁止駛入標誌　no entry sign
禁止停车/禁止停車　parking prohibited
禁止停车线/禁止停車線　no parking marking
禁止停放标志/禁止停放標誌　parking ban sign
禁止通行/禁止通行,禁止進入　traffic prohibited, no entry
禁止通行标志/禁止通行標誌　traffic prohibited sign
禁止右转弯标志/禁止右轉彎標誌　no right turn sign
禁止左转弯/禁止左轉　no left turn
禁止左转弯标志/禁止左轉彎標誌　no left turn sign
京畿/京畿　jingji, capital area
经差/經差　difference of longitude
经常维修费/例規修理費[用]　routine repair cost
经幢/經幢　sutra pillar
经典冲击脉冲/經典衝擊脈波　classic shock pulse
经度/經度,經線　longitude
经度改正量/經度修正值　longitude correction
经济车速/經濟速率　economic speed
经济传热阻/經濟熱阻　economic thermal resistance
经济调查/經濟調查　economy survey, economic investigation, economic survey
经济工况/經濟工作狀況　economic working condition
经济功率/經濟功率　economical power
经济航速/經濟船速,經濟速率　economical speed
经济核算/經濟核算　economic accounting

经济[技术]开发区/經濟技術開發區　economic technological development district
经济技术指标/經濟與技術指標　economic and technical indicator
经济净现值/經濟淨現值　economic net present value, ENPV
经济跨径/經濟跨度　economic span
经济林/經濟林　non-timber product forest
经济内部收益率/經濟內部收益率　economic internal rate of return, EIRR
经济评价/經濟評估　economic evaluation
经济区/經濟區　economic region
经济适用房/保障性住房,低收入住宅　affordable housing
经济寿命/經濟壽命　economic life
经济输送容量/經濟輸送容量　economical transmission capacity
经济速度/經濟速[率],儉速　economical speed, economic speed
经济特区/經濟特區　special economic zone
经济通行能力/經濟容量　economical capacity
经济效果/經濟效果　economic effect
经济效益费用比/經濟效益費用比　economic benefit cost ratio, EBCR
经济型旅馆/經濟旅館,快捷旅館　economic hotel
经济巡航状态/經濟巡航狀態　economic cruising rating
经济转速/經濟轉速　economical speed
经流时间/流過期間　flowing through period
经批准的计划/核定之計劃　approved plan
经纬仪/經緯儀　transit
经行时/經行時　time of travel
经验方法/經驗法　empirical method
经验修正法/經驗校正法　experience correction method
经营成本/生产成本,生產費用　operating cost
经营性项目/經營性項目　operating project
经营性用地/經營性用地　profit-oriented land
经营许可证/營業[許可]證　business certificate
惊奇喷泉/驚奇噴泉　surprise fountain
晶间断裂/晶間破裂　intercrystalline fracture, intercrystalline rupture
晶间腐蚀/晶間腐蝕,粒間腐蝕　intergranular corrosion
晶粒度/粒度,粒徑　grain size
晶体材料/晶狀材料　crystalline materials
晶体管/電晶體　transistor
晶须/晶鬚　whisker

晶闸管变流器电力机车/閘流體換流器電力機車　thyristor converter electric locomotive
晶闸管整流器电力机车/閘流體整流器電力機車　thyristor rectifier electric locomotive
晶闸管整流装置/閘流體整流器裝置　thyristor rectifier device
精测临场雷达/精確進入雷達　precision approach radar
精度/精度　precision accuracy
精度分配/精度分配　accuracy distribution, accuracy allocation
精度管理/精度控制　accuracy control
精度鉴定/精度評估　accuracy evaluation
精度校飞/精度飛行校準　accuracy calibration flight
精对准/精校準　fine alignment
精检漏试验/精滲漏試驗　fine leak test
精密车间/精密車間　precision workshop
精密冲裁/精衝　fine blanking, precision blanking
精密导线测量/精密導線測量　precise traverse survey, accurate traverse survey
精密定位业务/精密定位業務　precise positioning service, PPS
精密定线/精密定線　precise alignment
精密伏尔/精密特高頻多向導航臺　precision VOR, PVOR
精密焊/精密熔接　precision welding
精密进近程序/精確進場程式　precision approach procedure
精密进近雷达/精確進場雷達,精確進入雷達　precision approach radar, PAR radar
精密离心机/精密離心機　precision centrifuge
精密离心试验/精密離心測試　precision centrifuge test
精密配磨/精密配磨　precision pair grinding
精密去毛刺/精密去毛刺　precision deburring
精密水准测量/精密水準測量　precise levelling
精密星历/精密天文曆　precise ephemeris
精瞄/精瞄　exact aiming, fine aiming
精明收缩/精明收縮　smart shrinkage
精明增长/精明增長　smart growth
精确制导武器/精準導引彈藥　precision guided munitions
精神疲劳/精神衰弱　mental fatigue
精轧螺纹锚/細線筋錨固　thread bar anchorage
精制螺栓/精製螺栓　finished bolt
精致货/精細貨　delicate cargo
精装修/精裝修　fine fitment
精装修房/全裝修房　fully decorated house

井/井 well
井的干扰/井擾 well interference
井的最大出水量/井最大出水量 maximum capacity of well
井的最大出水能力/井最大出水量 maximum capacity of well
井点法/井點法 well point method
井点回灌/井回抽 well point back pumping
井点排水/井點排水,井點降水法 well point dewatering
井点系统/井點系統 well point system
井干式/井乾式構架 log-cabin construction, jinggan
井函数/井函數 well function
井架/[礦]井架 headframe
井口平台/井口平臺 wellhead platform
井砾石墙/礫壁井 gravel wall well
井水/井水 well water
井水呼吸效率/井水呼吸效率 barometric efficiency of well
井水位过程线/井歷線 well hydrograph
井探/井探,試坑 shaft test, test pitting
井田制/井田制 jingtian system, ancient farming land subdivision system
井筒支架/竪坑撐框 shaft set
井下测量/鑽孔測量 borehole surveying
井字梁/交叉梁,格排梁 cross beam, grillage beam
井字桩/井字型樁,井筒形樁 intersecting parallels pile
肼发动机/肼發動機,聯氨發動機 hydrazine engine
景/景 view, scenery, feature
景点/[觀光]景點 scenic spot, feature spot, view spot
景观/景觀,地景 landscape, scenery
景观保护/景觀保護 landscape preservation
景观尺度/景觀尺度 landscape scale
景观灯/景觀燈 landscape lamp
景观都市主义/景觀都市主義 landscape urbanism
景观多样性/景觀多樣性 landscape diversity
景观格局/景觀格局 landscape pattern
景观规划/景觀規劃 landscape planning
景观环境用水/景觀環境用水 water for scenic environment use
景观建设/地景建設 landscape architecture
景观评价/地景評估 landscape evaluation
景观桥/景觀橋梁 landscape bridge
景观人类学/景觀人類學 landscape of anthropology
景观设计/景觀設計,風景設計,園林設計 landscape design
景观设计师/造園技師,環境美化設計家 landscape architect
景观社会学/景觀社會學 landscape sociology
景观生态学/景觀生態學 landscape ecology
景观视线/影觀視線 landscape view
景观镶嵌体/景觀嵌合體 landscape mosaic
景观效能/景觀效果 landscape efficiency
景观形状指数/景觀形指數 landscape shape index
景观栽植/景觀綠化 landscape planting
景观照明/景觀照明 landscape lighting
景观指数/景觀指數 landscape index, landscape metrics
景框种植/景框種植 planting as enframent
景区/風景區,觀光景點,旅遊勝地 scenic spot, scenic zone
景区地块/景區地塊 scenic spot plot
景群/景群 scenic community, scenic spots group
景深/景深 depth of field
景物/景物,風物 scenery, scenic feature
景象匹配制导/圖像比對導引 image matching guidance
景序/景序 order of sceneries
警标艇/燈標船 beacon boat
警察巡逻/員警巡邏 police patrol
警冲标/警衝標 fouling post
警笛/號笛,警報器 siren
警告/警告 warning
警告标记/警告標線 warning marking
警告信号/警告信號,警告訊號 warning signal
警戒高/警戒高 alert height
警戒区/警戒區 precautionary area
警戒水位/警戒水位 warning stage
警觉/警戒 vigilance
警旗/旗標警報 flag alarm
警示标志/警告標 caution sign
警惕按钮/警惕按鈕 acknowledgment button
警惕手柄/警惕手柄 acknowledgment lever
警惕装置/警惕裝置 vigilance device
警务室/派出所,分駐所 police station
警务站/警衛室 security room
劲性骨架混凝土桥/勁性骨架混凝土橋 skeleton reinforced concrete bridge
径锯/輻射切割 radial cut
径流/徑流 run off
径流面积/徑流面積 run off area
径流侵蚀力/徑流侵蝕力 run off erosivity
径流深/徑流深度 run off depth
径流式水电站[厂]/川流式發電廠 run-of-river type

power station
径流式涡轮/徑向流渦輪[機] radial-flow turbine
径流式涡轮增压器/徑向流渦輪增壓器 radial-flow turbocharger
径流式压缩机/徑向流壓縮機 radial-flow compressor
径流系数/徑流係數,流失量係數 run off coefficient
径流小区/徑流試驗場 run off plot
径流循环/徑流循環 run off cycle
径流雨量/超滲雨量,過度雨量 excess rainfall
径面纹理/板面木紋 quarter grain
径切面/徑[向]切面,徑斷面 radial section
径向锻造/徑向鍛造 radial forging
径向分辨率/徑向解析度 sagittal resolution, radial resolution
径向固结系数/徑向固結係數 radial consolidation coefficient
径向畸变/輻射畸變差 radial distortion
径向加速度/徑向加速度 radial acceleration
径向剪力/輻射剪力 radial shear
径向剪力带/輻射剪力區 radial shear zone
径向精锻/徑向精密鍛造 radial precision forging
径向流/徑向流,輻射流 radial flow
径向球轴承/徑向滾珠軸承 radial-ball bearing
径向位移/徑向位移 radial displacement
径向压力/輻射壓力,包圍壓力 radial pressure
径向支柱/徑向支撐 radial strut
径向柱塞式液压马达/徑向活塞液力馬達 radial-piston hydraulic motor
净安全承载力/淨安全承載力 net safe bearing capacity
净暴雨量/淨暴雨量 net storm rain
净初级生产量/淨初級生產量 net primary production
净吨位/淨噸位 net tonnage, NT
净峰流量/淨高峰流量 net peak flow
净高/淨空高,垂直淨空 vertical clearance
净功率/淨馬力 net horsepower, net power
净灌溉定额/淨用水額,淨用水率 net duty
净化/淨化 purification
净化器/淨化器,清潔器 purifier, cleaner
净化系统/淨化系統 purification system
净化装置/淨化裝置 refining plant
净极限承载力/淨極限承載力 net ultimate bearing capacity
净截面/淨斷面 net section
净空/淨空 clearance
净空道/清除區 clearway

净空高度/淨空高[度] height clearance, air draft
净跨/淨跨度 clear span
净跨径/淨跨度 clear span
净宽/淨寬,水平淨空 horizontal clearance
净区/淨區 clear zone
净人口密度/淨人口密度 net population density
净砂/淨砂 washed sand
净土压力/淨土壓力 net soil pressure
净压头/淨壓頭,有效水頭,有效落差 effective head
净预算/淨預算 net budget
净正抽吸压头/淨正吸水頭 net positive suction head, NPSH
净正吸高/淨正吸入高 net positive suction height
净正吸入压头/淨正吸水頭 net positive suction head, NPSH
净制动率/淨制動率 net braking ratio
竞赛区/競技場 arena, field of play
竞争性谈判/競爭性談判 competitive negotiation
竞争优势/競爭優勢,有利競爭 competitive advantage
敬老院/老人養護中心,老人安養院 nursing home for senior
静/安静 quiet, peaceful, silence
静不稳定结构/靜不穩定結構 statically unstable structure
静导数/靜[態]導數 static derivative
静电除尘器/靜電除塵器,靜電過濾,靜電集塵器 electrostatic precipitator
静电打印机/靜電列印機 electrostatic printer
静电放电/靜電放電 electrostatic discharge, ESD
静电放电干扰测量/靜電放電干擾量測 electrostatic discharge interference measurement
静电放电敏感度测量/靜電放電靈敏度量測 electrostatic discharge sensitivity measurement
静电感应/靜電感應 electrostatic induction
静电[感应]电流/靜電感應電流,靜電誘導電流 electrostatic induced current
静电加速度计/靜電加速度計 electrostatically support accelerometer
静电接地/靜電接地 electrostatic grounding
静电喷涂/靜電噴塗 electrostatic spraying
静电屏蔽/靜電遮罩,靜電遮蔽 electrostatic shielding
静电陀螺仪/靜電陀螺儀 electrical suspended gyro, ESG
静电危害/靜電危害 electrostatic harm
静电泄漏/靜電洩漏 electrostatic leakage
静电悬浮陀螺/靜電支承式陀螺儀 electrostatically

suspended gyroscope
静电噪声/静電雜訊　electrostatic noise
静电支承加速度计/静電支承加速度計　electrostatically suspended accelerometer
静电中和/静電中和　electrostatic charge neutralization
静定/静定　statically determinate
静定反力/静定反力　statically determinate reaction
静定结构/静定結構　statically determinate structure
静定梁/静定梁　statically determinate beam
静定桥梁结构/静定橋梁結構　statically determinate bridge structure
静动组合天平/静動力天平　static-dynamic balance
静观/静觀　in-position viewing
静航向稳定性/静航向穩定性　static course stability
静横倾角/静横傾角　static heeling angle
静回复力矩/静定面積矩　statical moment of area
静基座对准/静基座對準　static-base alignment
静寂时间/死時　dead time
静校精密度/静態校準精密度　static calibration precision
静校准确度/静態校準準確度　static calibration accuracy
静力触探/静力觸探,静力测深法　static sounding, static probing, cone penetration test
静力触探试验/静力觸探試驗,静态贯入试验　static penetration test, cone penetration test, CPT
静力矩/静力面積矩　static moment of area
静力内接/静力内接　static inscribing
静力平衡原理/静力平衡原理　principle of statical equilibrium
静力试验/静力測試　static test
静力学/静力學　statics
静力压拔桩机/静力壓拔椿機　static pile press extractor
静力压路机/静態式壓路機　static roller
静力压桩/静壓椿　static press piling
静力压桩试验/静力壓椿試驗　pile static loading test
静力[载荷]试验/静負載試驗　static load test
静力作用/静態作用　static action
静脉产业园区/静脈產業園區　venous industry park
静密封/静態接封　static seal
静摩擦系数/静摩擦係數　coefficient of static friction
静默时间/静默時間　silence period, SP
静凝聚/静態縮減　static condensation
静配合/静配合　stationary fit
静平衡试验/静[力]平衡試驗　static balance test
静强度试验台/静強度測試架　static strength test rack
静视觉敏锐度/静視覺銳度　static visual acuity
静水/死水　dead water
静水护壁钻孔法/静水護壁鑽孔法　static water head hole boring method
静水力曲线/静水[性能]曲線　hydrostatic curve
静水面/静水面　still water surface
静水弯矩/静水彎[曲力]矩　still water bending moment
静水位/滞留水位　standing water level
静水压力/静水壓力　hydrostatic pressure
静水压力拱形曲线/静水壓拱曲線　hydrostatic arch
静水压力释放器/[静力]释放装置　release device, hydrostatic release unit
静水压线/静壓線　static pressure line
静索/静索,固定索具　standing rigging
静态/静態　static state
静态不平顺/静態軌道不整　static track irregularity, irregularity without load
静态测力天平/静力天平　static balance
静态测量/静態量測　static measurement
静态测试/静態測試,静力测试　static test, at-rest test
静态长度/静態長度　car space
静态地球敏感器/静態地球感測器　static earth sensor, static horizon sensor
静态定位/静態定位　static positioning
静态分析/静態分析　static analysis
静态刚度/静態勁度　static stiffness
静态交通/静態交通　static traffic
静态康乐用地/静態休閒用地　passive recreation area
静态漂移/静態漂移　static drift
静[态]平衡/静力均衡　static balance
静态平衡阀/静態平衡閥　static hydraulic balancing valve
静态柔度/静態柔度　static compliance
静态摄影分辨率/静態照相解像力　static photographic resolution
静态投资/静態投資　static investment
静态温度/静態温度　static temperature
静态轴重检测器/静態軸重偵測器　static axle weight detector
静态作用/静態作用　static action
静稳定性/静穩定性　static stability
静稳定裕度/静穩定裕度,静態穩定界限　static margin, static stability marging
静稳性/静穩度　statical stability

静稳性曲线/静穩度曲線　curve of static stability, statical stability curve, curve of statical stability
静休息区/静休息區　static rest space
静压/静壓力　static pressure
静压沉桩法/静壓沈樁法　pile jacking in method
静压迟滞/静壓遲滯　static pressure lag
静压力拔桩机/静壓力拔樁機　static pressure pile extractor, static pressure pile drawing machine
静压气浮陀螺加速度计/静壓氣浮擺式積分陀螺加速度儀　hydrostatic gas bearing PIGA
静压气浮陀螺仪/静壓氣浮陀螺儀　hydrostatic gas bearing gyro
静压强/静壓力　static pressure
静压调节器/静壓力調整器　static pressure regulator
静压头/静落差　static head
静压箱/調壓室　plenum chamber
静压液浮陀螺加速度计/静壓液浮擺式積分陀螺加速度儀　hydrostatic liquid bearing PIGA
静压液压陀螺仪/静壓液壓陀螺儀　hydrostatic liquid bearing gyro
静叶[片]/定子輪葉,固定葉片　stator blade, stationary blade
静叶损失/固定[葉]片損耗　stationary blade loss
静液挤压/水力擠壓　hydrostatic extrusion
静液压泵/静液力泵　hydrostatic pump
静液压马达/液態馬達　hydrostatic motor
静载/静態負載　static load
静载能力/载重[能]量　dead weight capacity
静载试验/静力試驗,静载重試驗　static test, static loading test
静载应力/静载重應力　dead stress
静噪/消雜音,静音　squelch
静止地球轨道/定置軌道,地球同步軌道　geostationary earth orbit
静止锋/滯留鋒　stationary front
静止搜救卫星通信率/定置搜救衛星通訊比率　GEOSAR traffic ratio
静止搜救卫星系统/定置搜救衛星系統　geostationary SAR satellite system
静止图像可视电话/静止圖像視訊電話　still picture videophone
静止土压力/静止土壓力　earth pressure at rest
静止卫星/静止衛星,定置衛星　geostationary satellite, stationary satellite
静止卫星报警通报时间/定置衛星警報通報時間　time of GEOSAR alert notification
静止卫星轨道/定置衛星軌道　geostationary satellite orbit

静止卫星通信容量/定置衛星通訊容量　volume of GEOSAR traffic
静止卫星业务/定置衛星業務　geostationary satellite service
静止运行环境卫星/定置運作環境衛星　geostationary operational environmental satellite
境内出行/境内出行　local trip
镜框式舞台/鏡框式舞臺　proscenium stage
镜面车削/鏡面車削　mirror turning
镜面反射/鏡面反射　specular reflection
镜面反射采光/鏡面反射採光　specular reflection daylighting
镜面磨削/鏡面輪磨　mirror grinding
镜式伸长计/鏡式伸長計　mirror extensometer
镜像法/鏡像法,影像法　image method
镜像频率干扰/影像頻率干擾　image frequency interference
镜像投影法/鏡像投影法　mirror image projection
镜像支架/鏡像支架　mirror support, image support
纠错码/錯誤更正碼,改错碼,改誤碼　error correcting code
鸠尾榫/鳩尾榫　dovetail tenon
久航速度/最大滯空時間速度　speed for maximum endurance speed
酒吧/酒吧　bar, lounge
酒吧车/餐車,速食車　buffet car
酒店/酒店,旅館,旅社　hotel
旧城/舊城　old city, old town area
旧城改造/舊城改造,都市重建　old city redevelopment
旧城区/老城區　old town
旧件修复成本/舊件修復成本　used parts reconditioning cost
旧路技术改造/舊路技術改造　technical reformation of existing road
旧桥/舊橋,既有橋梁　existing bridge
旧线清除机/舊線清除機　marking cleaning machine
救护车/救護車,流動診療車　ambulance
救护站/救護站,急救站　first aid station
救捞船/救撈船　salvage boat, salvage ship
救生/救生　lifesaving
救生包/求生包　survival kit
救生部署表/救生部署表　boat station bill
救生措施/救生行動　rescue action
救生担架/救生擔架　rescue litter
救生吊带/救生吊帶　rescue sling
救生吊篮/救生吊籃　rescue basket
救生吊座/救生吊座　rescue seat

救生筏/救生筏　liferaft, life raft
救生飞船/救生太空船　rescue spacecraft
救生服/救生衣　immersion suit
救生浮/救生浮具,救生筏　life float
救生浮具浮力试验/救生浮具浮力試驗　buoyancy test for buoyant apparatus
救生浮索/救生浮索　buoyant lifeline
救生杆/救生桿　lifesaving stem
救生器材/救生包,求生包　survival kit
救生圈/救生圈　life buoy
救生圈试验/救生圈浮力試驗　buoyancy test for lifebuoy
救生圈自发烟雾信号/救生圈自發煙霧信號　life buoy self-activating smoke signal
救生伞/救生傘　survival parachute
救生设备/救生設備,救生器具,救生裝備　life saving appliance, life saving equipment
救生设备配备/救生設備配備　carriage of life saving appliances on board
救生设施/救生裝置　life saving appliance
救生食品/生存食物　survival food
救生手册/求生手冊　survival manual
救生属具/救生屬具,救生設備　life saving appliance, life equipment
救生索/救生索,攀手索　life line
救生台/救生站　life saving station
救生艇/救生艇　lifeboat
救生艇乘员定额/救生艇容載量　carrying capacity of lifeboat
救生艇筏/救生艇筏　survival craft
救生艇筏回收装置/救生艇筏回收裝置　survival craft recovery arrangement
救生艇筏手提无线电设备/救生艇用輕便無線電設備　portable radio apparatus for survival craft
救生艇甲板/救生艇甲板　lifeboat deck
救生艇罗经/救生艇用羅經　lifeboat compass
救生艇试验/救生艇試驗　test for lifeboat
救生艇无线电报设备/救生艇無線電報裝置　radiotelegraph installation for lifeboat
救生网/救生網　rescue net
救生信号/救生信號　life saving signal
救生性能包线/安全性能包線　escape envelope
救生衣/救生衣　life jacket
救生衣灯/救生衣燈　life jacket light
救生衣柜/救生衣櫃　life jacket chest
救生衣试验/救生衣浮力試驗　buoyancy test for life-jacket
救生员/救生員　lifeguard

救生钟/救生鍾　rescue bell
救险车/搶修車　wrecker
救援车/搶修車　wrecker
救援队/救援隊　breakdown gang
救援机车/救援機車　breakdown locomotive
救援列车/救援列車　breakdown train, rescue train, relief train
救援列车无线电通信/救援列車無線電通訊　radio communication for train relieving
救援起重机/救援起重機　wrecking crane
救灾通道/救災通道,緊急通道　emergency access, anti-disaster access
救灾物资储备库/救災物資庫　pool of relief supplies
救助报酬/救助報酬　salvage remuneration
救助报酬请求/救助求償　claim for salvage
救助泵/救助泵,救難泵　salvage pump
救助船/救難船　rescue ship, salvage vessel
救助单位/救助單位　rescue unit, RU
救助分中心/救助分中心　rescue sub-center, RSC
救助机构/打撈業務,救難服務　salvage service
救助人/施救者　salvor
救助艇/救難艇　rescue boat
救助协调中心/救難協調中心　rescue coordinator center
救助义务/救助義務　obligation to render salvage service
救助站/庇護所　refuge
就车修理法/就車修理法　personalized repair method
就地拌和/現場拌和　mix-in-place
就地保存/就地保育　in situ conservation
就地灌注法/就地灌注法,現場澆注法　cast-in-place method, cast in situ method
就地灌注桩/現場灌注樁　cast-in-place concrete pile, cast in situ concrete pile
就地浇筑混凝土/場鑄混凝土　cast-in-place concrete
就地控制/就地控制,現場控制　local control
就业/就業　employment
就业结构/就業結構　employment structure
就业率/就業率　employment rate
就业人口/就業人口　employed population
拘留权/扣押權　right of seizure
拘留所/拘留所,觀護所　detention house
拘束船模试验/拘束模型試驗　captive model test
居间障碍物/居間障礙物　intervening obstruction
居民出行/居民出行　personal travel
居民出行调查/居民出行調查　resident trip survey
居民点/安置點,聚落,居留地　settlement point, settlement

居民控制区/居民控制區　resident-command district
居民容量/居民容量　resident capacity
居民选择调查/居民選擇調查　residents choice survey
居委会/居民委員會　neighborhood committee
居住舱[室]/居住艙,房艙,艙室　accommodation, cabin, habitation module
居住单元/住宅單位　dwelling unit
居住分异/住宅分化　residential differentiation
居住混合/雜居地　mixed living
居住建筑/住宅用房屋　residential building
居住空间/居住空間　habitable space
居住绿地/居住區綠地　green space attached to housing estate, residential green space
居住密度/居住密度　residential density
居住区/居住區,住宅[地]區　residential district, residential area
居住区道路系统/居住區道路系統,住宅區道路交通系統　residential traffic system, residential road system
居住区公园/居住區公園　residential district park
居住区规划[设计]/居住區規劃,社區規劃　residential district planning, community planning
居住区过密/過密居住　over dwelling
居住区中心/居民區中心　center of residential area
居住人口密度/住宅人口密度　residential population density
居住使用面积/住宅樓板面積　living floor space
居住问题/住宅問題　housing problem
居住物业/住宅用不動產　residential property
居住[小]区/住宅區　residential community, residential quarter, housing estate
居住小区给水系统/住宅區供水系統,居住區給水系統　residential district water supply system
居住用地/居住用地,自用住宅用地　residential land
居住用地规划/住宅用地規劃　residential land planning
居住状况/居住水準　dwelling condition
居住组团/居住組團,住宅組團　sub-community, housing cluster, housing group
局部比例尺/局部比例尺　local scale
局部舱壁/部分艙壁　partial bulkhead
局部冲刷/局部冲刷,局部侵蝕　local scour, partial scour
局部淬火/局部淬火　selective hardening, localized quench hardening
局部等电位连接/局部等電位連接　local equipotential bonding, LEB
局部电源/局部電源　locally supplied power source
局部封锁/局部封鎖　partial blockade
局部腐蚀/局部腐蝕　localized corrosion
局部共振/局部共振,局部諧振　local resonance
局部故障/局部失效　partial failure
局部减压/局部減壓　local reduction
局部剪切破坏/局部剪壞　local shear failure
局部开挖/局部開挖,部分開挖　partial excavation
局部控制/局部控制　local control
局部控制电路/局端控制電路　local control circuit
局部控制盘/現場控制盤　local control panel
局部模态/局部模態　local mode
局部破坏/局部性破壞,區域性失效　local failure
局部强度/局部強度　local strength
局部屈曲/局部屈曲,局部側潰　local buckling
局部热水供应系统/局部熱水供應系統　local hot water supply system
局部失稳/局部屈曲,局部側潰　local buckling
局部视图/部分視面　partial view
局部受压强度/局部受壓強度　local bearing strength
局部调节/局部調節　localized regulation
局部稳定性/局部穩定性　local stability
局部应变法/局部應變法　local strain method
局部应力/局部應力　local stress
局部应用二氧化碳灭火系统/局部應用二氧化碳滅火系統　local application carbon dioxide extinguishing system
局部约束/部分固定　partially fixed
局部照明/局部照明　local lighting
局部照射/部分照明　partial illumination
局部真空电子束焊/局部真空電子束焊接　local vacuum electron beam welding
局部振动/局部振動　local vibration
局间通信枢纽/局間通信樞紐　communication center between several railway administration
局间直通中继方式/局間中繼電路線　inter office through trunk
局通信枢纽/鐵路管理局通信中心　communication center of railway administration
局线长途通信/鐵路管理局長途通訊　toll communication within railway administration
局线长途通信网/局線長途通信網　railway administration toll communication network
局线调度电话/鐵路管理局調度電話　dispatching telephone within railway administration
局线会议电话/鐵路管理局電話會議　telephone conference within railway administration
局用电缆/局用電纜　central office cable

局域差分 GPS/區域差分型全球定位系統　local area differential GPS, LADGPS
局域网[络]/區域網路，局部區域網路　local area network, LAN
橘瓣状抓斗/橘皮型挖泥斗　orange peel grab
橘皮状表面/橘皮狀面　orange peel
矩量表/矩量表　moment table
矩形板/矩形板　rectangular plate
矩形波导开槽天线/矩形波導開槽天線　slotted rectangular waveguide antenna
矩形窗/矩形窗　rectangular window
矩形截面风洞/矩形風洞　rectangular wind tunnel
矩形梁/矩形梁　rectangular beam
矩形桥墩/矩形橋墩　rectangular pier
矩形通风装置/矩形通風裝置　oblong ejector
矩形柱/矩形柱　rectangular column
矩阵力法/矩陣力法　matrix force method
矩阵势能/矩陣勢能　matrix potential
矩阵位移法/矩陣位移法　matrix displacement method
矩阵信号/矩陣信號　matrix signal
举架/舉架　raising-the-roof method, jujia
举升泊车机/舉昇泊車機　parking lift
举折/舉折　folding-the-roof method, juzhe
举证责任/舉證責任　burden of proof, onus of proof
巨浪/極大浪　very rough sea
巨粒土/巨粗粒土壤　over coarse grained soil
巨石阵/巨石陣　stonehenge
巨型起重机/門式起重機　goliath crane
巨型油轮/巨型油輪，極大型原油輪　very large crude oil carrier, VLCC
拒爆/不發火，不著火　misfire
拒水粉防水粉屋面/拒水粉防水粉屋面　water-proof roofing with water-repellent compound layer
俱乐部/俱樂部　club
俱乐部车/俱樂部車　club car
剧场/劇場，劇院　theater
距变率/距離變動率　rate of distance variation
距离避盲/距離避盲區　avoidance of range blind zone
距离标/距離標　range reference pole
距离捕获/距離捕獲　range acquisition
距离捕获时间/距離獲取時間　range acquisition time
距离测量/距離測量　distance surveying
距离差位置线/距離差位置線　position line by distance difference
距离定位/距離定位　fixing by distances
距离-方位系统/距離-方位系統　p-θ system
距离方向/距離方向　range direction
距离分辨力/距離分解[度]，距離解析度　range resolution
距离分辨率/距離分解[度]，距離解析度　range resolution
距离跟踪/距離追蹤　range tracking
距离和/距離和　range sum
距离和变化率/距離和變化率　range sum rate
距离校零/距離校零　zero range calibration
距离截止/距離截止　range cutoff
距离截止特性/距離截止特性　range cutoff characteristic
距离模糊/距離含糊度　range ambiguity
距离索/距離索　distance line
距离弯曲/距離彎曲　range curvature
距离位置线/距離位置線　position line by distance
距离消模糊/距離不定性　resolution of range ambiguity
距离选择/距離選擇　range selection
距离游动/距離游動　range walk
锯成木材/鋸[成木]材，製材　sawn timber, converted timber
锯齿法/鋸齒法　tooth method
锯齿形码头/鋸齒碼頭　saw tooth type wharf
锯齿形天窗厂房/鋸齒形天窗廠房　saw tooth industry building
锯齿形屋架/鋸齒形屋架　saw tooth roof truss
锯缝/鋸成縫　sawn joint
锯轨机/鋸軌機，鋼軌鋸　rail cutting machine, rail sawing machine
锯末/鋸末，鋸屑　sawdust
聚[氨基甲酸]酯泡沫塑料/聚氨酯泡沫塑膠　polyurethane-foam plastic, PUR-foam plastic
聚氨酯冲裁/聚氨酯遮蔽　polyurethane pad blanking
聚氨酯地坪涂料/聚氨酯敷層，聚尿烷塗層　polyurethane floor coating
聚氨酯泡沫塑料/泡沫聚氨基甲酸乙酯　expanded polyurethane, polyurethane foam
聚氨酯推进剂/聚氨酯推進劑　polyurethane propellant, PU propellant
聚丙烯管/聚丙烯管　polypropylene pipe
聚丙烯筋带/聚丙烯帶　polypropylene belt
聚电解质/聚電解質　polyelectrolyte
聚丁二烯丙烯腈推进剂/聚丁二烯丙烯腈推進劑　polybutadiene acrylonitrile propellant, PBAN propellant
聚丁二烯丙烯酸共聚物推进剂/聚丁二烯丙烯酸共聚物推進劑　polybutadiene acrylic acid copolymer propellant, PBAA copolymer propellant

聚丁烯管/聚丁烯管　polybutylene pipe
聚光灯/聚光燈,閃光燈　spotlight
聚光镜/集光器　collector
聚光太阳电池/聚光太陽能電池　concentrator solar cell
聚光太阳电池方阵/聚光型太陽能電池陣　photovoltaic concentrator solar array
聚光太阳电池组件/聚光型太陽能組件　photovoltaic concentrator module
聚光照明/聚光照明　spot lighting
聚合物改性沥青/聚合物改性瀝青　polymer modified asphalt
聚合物混凝土/聚合物混凝土　polymer concrete
聚合物乳液建筑防水涂料/聚合物乳液建築防水塗料　polymer emulsion architectural waterproof coating
聚合物水泥防水涂料/聚合物水泥防水砂漿　polymer-modified cement compound for waterproofing membrane, polymer-cement waterproofing coating
聚合织物防水层/聚合織物防水層　water proof polymer fabrics
聚集/凝聚,聚結　coalescence
聚焦合成孔径/聚焦合成孔徑　focused synthetic aperture
聚焦合成天线/對焦合成天線　focused synthetic antenna
聚焦装置/焦點調整裝置　focusing device
聚居型居民点/聚居型居民點　inhabited type residential
聚硫推进剂/多硫推進劑　polysulfide propellant, PS propellant
聚落/聚落　settlement
聚氯乙烯管/聚氯乙烯管,PVC 管　polyvinyl chloride pipe
聚束合成孔径雷达/聚點束射合成孔徑雷達　spot beam SAR
聚四氟乙烯/聚四氟乙烯　polytetrafluoroethylene, PTFE
聚四氟乙烯板/聚四氟乙烯板　polyfluortetraethylene plate
聚四氟乙烯支座/聚四氟乙烯支座,聚四氟乙烯支承　polytetrafluoroethylene bearing, PTFE bearing
聚酰胺/聚醯胺　polyamide, PA
聚酰亚胺树脂/聚醯亞胺樹脂　polyimide resin
聚液窝/液體濾閥　liquid trap
聚乙烯沥青装置/聚乙烯瀝青裝置　polyethylene asphalt unit

聚酯树脂/聚酯樹酯　polyester resin
捐赠展厅/捐贈展銷廳　donation exhibition hall
涓流充电/涓流充電,點滴式充電,浮充電　trickle charge
卷/卷,收　furl
卷包式太阳电池/卷包式太陽電池　wrap-around type solar cell
卷边槽钢/滾邊槽鋼　lipped channel
卷边角钢/滾邊角鋼　lipped angle
卷层云/卷層雲　cirrostratus
卷尺/卷尺　measuring tape
卷尺修正/量尺校正　tape correction
卷帆索/卷帆索　brails
卷纲机/［繩］索卷盤,卷繩機　rope reel
卷管机/鋼腱套管導筒機,鋼腱套管卷取機,鋼腱套管絡筒機　tendon duct winding machine
卷积云/卷積雲　cirrocumulus
卷浪/卷入形碎波　plunging breaker
卷帘/滾卷,卷布　rolling
卷门/滾輪移動門　rolling door
卷棚/卷棚　rolled ridge roof
卷片室/卷片室　rewind room
卷杀/卷殺　entasis, juansha
卷绳车/儲放卷盤　storage reel
卷式太阳电池阵/卷式太陽電池陣　roll-up type solar array
卷筒/鼓輪,卷索鼓　hoisting drum
卷筒铺管驳/卷盤駁船　reel barge
卷网机/卷網機　net drum
卷涡/盤蝸　volute
卷跃波浪/奔波,衝浪　plunging wave
卷云/卷雲　cirrus
决策支持系统/決策支援系統　decision support system
决断高/决定高　decision height, DH
决断高度/决定高度　decision altitude, DA
决口/穿堤孔口　levee opening
绝对 GPS/絕對全球定位系統　absolute GPS
绝对标高/標高,絕對高程,海拔　absolute elevation
绝对测量/絕對量測　absolute measurement
绝对定向/絕對定位　absolute orientation
绝对辐射定标/絕對輻射校正　absolute radiometric calibration
绝对辐射热星等/絕對熱星等　absolute bolometric magnitude
绝对刚度/絕對勁度　absolute stiffness
绝对高度/絕對高度　absolute altitude
绝对光谱灵敏度/絕對光譜靈敏度　absolute spectral

sensitivity
绝对光谱响应/絕對光譜響應　absolute spectral response
绝对航高/絕對航高　absolute flying height
绝对基面/絕對基準　absolute datum
绝对计程仪/絕對計程儀,絕對測程儀　absolute log
绝对加速度/絕對加速度　absolute acceleration
绝对加速度反馈/絕對加速度反饋　absolute acceleration feedback
绝对免赔额/自負額　deductible
绝对黏度/絕對黏度,動力黏度,動力黏性　absolute viscosity, dynamic viscosity
绝对湿度/絕對濕度　absolute humidity
绝对视差/絕對視差　absolute parallax
绝对速度/絕對速度　absolute velocity, absolute speed
绝对太阳通量/絕對太陽通量　absolute solar flux
绝对停止信号/絕對停止號誌　absolute stop signal
绝对温标/熱力學溫度標,溫度熱力標　Kelvin scale
绝对温差/絕對溫差　absolute range
绝对温度/絕對溫度　absolute temperature
绝对效率/絕對效率　absolute efficiency
绝对信号/絕對號誌　absolute signal
绝对压力/絕對壓力　absolute pressure
绝对延迟/絕對遲延　absolute delay
绝对运动/絕對運動　absolute motion
绝对转动刚度/絕對旋轉勁度　absolute rotational stiffness
绝对最大弯矩/絕對最大彎力矩　absolute maximum bending moment
绝干/全乾狀態　absolute dry
绝热/絕熱,隔熱　adiabatic
绝热板/隔熱板　insulation board
绝热壁/絕熱壁　adiabatic wall
绝热壁温度/絕熱壁溫　adiabatic wall temperature
绝热材料/絕熱材料　heat insulating material
绝热层/熱絕緣層,隔熱層,保溫層　adiabatic layer, heat insulation layer
绝热递减率/絕熱直減率　adiabatic lapse rate
绝热管流/絕熱管流　adiabatic flow in pipe
绝热过程/絕熱過程,絕熱程序　adiabatic process
绝热集装箱/隔熱式貨櫃　insulated container
绝热壳体/絕熱外殼　insulated case
绝热冷却/絕熱冷卻　adiabatic cooling
绝热流/絕熱流　adiabatic flow
绝热温升/絕熱溫度上昇　adiabatic temperature rise
绝热养护/絕熱養護　adiabatic curing
绝缘板/絕緣板　insulation board
绝缘不良/絕緣不良　bad insulation
绝缘材料/絕緣材料　insulating material
绝缘层/絕緣　insulation
绝缘带/分離帶　insulated strip, insulation strip
绝缘导线/絕緣導線,絕緣導體　insulated conductor
绝缘电缆/絕緣電纜　insulated cable
绝缘电阻/絕緣電阻　insulation resistance
绝缘轨距杆/絕緣軌距拉桿　insulated gage rod
绝缘间隙/絕緣間隙　insulation gap
绝缘接头/絕緣接頭　insulated joint
绝缘楼地面/絕緣地板　insulated floor
绝缘锚段关节/絕緣錨段關節　insulated overlap
绝缘配合/絕緣協調　insulation coordination
绝缘强度/絕緣強度　insulation strength
绝缘梯车/絕緣有梯卡車　insulated ladder trolley
绝缘体/絕緣體　insulator
绝缘鞋/絕緣鞋　insulant shoe
绝缘阳极[氧]化/電絕緣陽極處理　electric insulation anodizing
绝缘转换柱/絕緣轉換柱　insulated transition mast
绝缘子/絕緣子　insulator
绝缘子清洗车/絕緣子清洗車　insulator cleaning car
掘沟机/掘溝機　ditch-scoop excavator
掘进方法/挖掘法　tunneling method
[掘进机]刀盘/刀盤　cutter head
掘进机法/掘進機法　tunnel boring machine method
掘土作业/挖掘　digging
蕨类植物专类园/蕨園　fern garden
军辅船/輔助艦　auxiliary ship, auxiliary ship and service craft
均布荷载/均勻負載　uniform load, distributed load
均方根噪声/均方根噪聲　root mean square noise, RMS noise
均方根噪声电流/均方根噪聲電流,噪聲的有效電流　root mean square noise current
均方根噪声电压/均方根噪聲電壓,噪聲的有效電壓　root mean square noise voltage
均方根值检波器/均方根檢測器　root mean square detector
均方[误]差/均方誤差　mean square error
均分尺寸/均分尺度　equipartition scale, equal dimension scale
均功调节/均衡調節　equalizing regulation
均衡/均衡,平衡,均等　equalization
均衡防护/平衡保護　balanced protection
均衡风缸/均衡貯氣筒　equalizing reservoir
均衡杠杆/平衡桿,均衡梁　equalizing lever
均衡加固/均衡硬化　balanced hardening

均衡拉杆/均衡拉桿　equalizing pull rod
均衡梁/均衡梁,均衡裝置　equalizer
均衡坡度/平衡坡度　balanced grade
均衡速度/均衡速率　balancing speed
均衡系统/均衡系統　equalizing system
均化池/均化槽　equalization tank
均力绳/附平衡錘索　compensating rope
均流电抗器/均流電抗器　sharing reactor
均田制/編户授田　equal-field system, land equal distribution system
均性区/均性區　homogeneous area
均压网/均壓網格　equalizing lattice
均压线/均壓器,均衡器,等化器　equalizer, cable bond
均压轴承/均匀支承　even bearing
均匀沉降/均匀沈落　uniform settlement
均匀的/均匀的　uniform
均匀度/均匀度,均等性　evenness, uniformity
均匀度模数/均一性模數　uniformity modulus
均匀度指数/均匀性指數　evenness index
均匀分布/均匀分布　uniform distribution, regular distribution
均匀化退火/均質化退火　homogenizing annealing
均匀加速度/等加速度　uniform acceleration
均匀系数/均匀係數　coefficient of uniformity, unformity coefficient
均匀性/均匀性　uniformity

均质材料/均質材料,等向性材料　homogeneous materials, isotropic material
均质货/匀質貨　homogeneous cargo
均质片/均質片　homogeneous sheet
均质器/均質機　homogenizer
龟裂/龜裂,裂紋　crazing, alligator crack, fissure
菌根/菌根　mycorrhiza
菌形按钮/菌形路面標鈕　mushroom button
菌形底桩/菌形底樁　mushroom base pile
菌形锚/菌形錨　mushroom anchor
菌形通风筒/菌型通風筒　mushroom ventilator
峻岭/峻嶺　steep mountain
竣工/竣工　completion of construction, completion of works
竣工报告/竣工報告　completion report of construction work
竣工测量/最後測量,最終查勘　final survey
竣工决算/[竣工項目]決算　final settlement of account, final accounts of completed project
竣工日期/完工日期,完成時期　completion date
竣工图/竣工圖　as built drawings
竣工验收/竣工驗收　completion acceptance, final acceptance
竣工验收资料/竣工驗收資料　information on the acceptance of completed project
竣工总平面图/竣工總平面圖　general plan of as-built works

K

咖啡厅/咖啡館　cafe
喀斯特/喀斯特[地區]　karst
喀斯特地段路基/喀斯特地段路基　subgrade in karst zone
喀斯特景观/喀斯特景觀　karst landscape
喀斯特水文学/喀斯特水文學,石灰岩區水文學　karst hydrology
喀音/喀嚦聲　click
卡带/油罐卡帶　tank band
卡丁车赛场/卡丁車賽場　kart racing ground
卡尔曼滤波/卡爾曼濾波　Kalman filtering
卡尔曼滤波器/卡爾曼濾波器　Kalman filter
卡方分布/卡方分配　chi-square distribution, X^2-distribution
卡计法/卡計法　calorimeter method
卡口/卡口,瓶頸段　pass capacity barricade, bottle neck road
卡雷吉奥庄园/卡雷吉奧莊園　Villa Careggio
卡门-钱公式/卡門-錢學森公式　Karman-Tsien formula
卡门涡街/卡門渦列　Karman vortex street
卡塞格林天线/卡塞格林天線　Cassegrain antenna
卡塞格林望远镜/卡塞格林望遠鏡　Cassegrain telescope
卡氏定理/卡氏定理　Castigliano theorem
卡斯特罗花园/卡斯特盧花園　Castello Garden
开杯试验/開杯法試驗　open cup test
开闭比/孔隙率　porosity
开闭式平交道栅/開閉式平交道柵　sliding barrier
开闭所/開閉所,開關站,開關場　switching station, sub-section post, SSP
开标/開標　bid opening, tender opening
开采沉陷/礦穴沈陷　mining subsidence
开舱/開艙　opening modules
开槽壁/開槽牆　slotted wall
开槽机/開槽機　grooving machine
开敞空间/開敞空間,開敞地,開放空間　wide open space, wide space, open space
开敞锚地/敞開錨地,開放錨地,曝露錨地　open anchorage, exposed anchorage
开敞式救生艇/敞式救生艇　open lifeboat
开敞式楼梯/開放式樓梯　open staircase
开敞式卧车/開放式臥車　open type sleeping car
开敞式舞台/露天舞臺　open stage
开船旗/開船旗　blue peter
开底井/開底井　open-ended well
开底泥驳/開底泥駁　hooper barge
开底泥船/開底泥船　hopper mud burge
开底挖泥船/斗式挖泥船　hooper dredger
开发尺度/開發尺度　development scale
开发方案/開發計劃　development project
开发计划/開發計劃　development plan
开发控制/開發控制　development control
开发控制指标/發展管理指標,發展管制指標　development control index
开发强度/發展密度,發展程度　development intensity
开发区/開發區　development zone, development area
开发权转让/發展權移轉　transfer of development right
开放港/開港　open port
开放交通/通車　open to traffic
开放空间/開放空間　open space
开放时间/開放時間　opening time
开放式办公室/開放辦公室　open space office
开放式厨房/小廚房,小膳房　kitchenette
开放式畜舍/開放式養畜場　open livestock house
开放式燃[气用]具/無煙道氣體燃料裝備　flueless gas appliance, unvented type
开放式收费系统/開放式收費系統　open toll system
开放网络/開放網路　open network
开放系统互连/開放系統連結　open system interconnection, OSI
开放信号/話終信號　clearing signal
开缝襟翼/開縫襟翼　slotted flap
开工/開工　starting of construction
开工报告/開工報告　report for starting construction, construction starting report
开沟机/挖溝機[械]　ditcher, trenching machine
开沟平路机/開溝平路機　track shaving machine, ditching and grading machine

开关/開關　switch
开关柜/金屬鎧裝開關　metal enclosed switchgear
开关式控制/開關控制　on-off control
开关调整器/開關調整器　switch-adjuster
开关站/開關站,開閉所,開關場　switching station
开罐器/開罐器　tin opener
开航日期/啟航日期　date of departure
开花草坪/開花草坪　flowering lawn
开环系统/開環系統　open-loop system
开级配/開級配　open gradation
开架书库/開架書庫區　open stack
开架阅览室/開架閱覽室　open shelf reading room
开间/開間　bay
开孔壁/多孔牆　perforated wall
开孔套管井/有孔套管井　perforated casing well
开口/開口　opening
开口比/開孔比　opening ratio
开口端管桩/開口管樁　open end pipe pile
开口断面/開口斷面　open section
开口滑车/開口滑車,活口滑車　snatch block
开口式风洞/開口式風洞　open jet wind tunnel
开口销/開口銷,夾針梢　split pin
开口压力计/開式液壓計　open manometer
开阔海湾/敞灣　open bay
开裂荷载/開裂載重　cracking load
开裂襟翼/分裂式襟翼　split flap
开裂扭矩/開裂扭矩　cracking torque
开裂弯矩/開裂彎矩　cracking moment
开路电压/開路電壓　open circuit voltage
开路式风洞/斷路式風洞　open circuit wind tunnel
开路式轨道电路/開路式軌道電路　open type track circuit
开锚/離岸錨　offshore anchor
开拍/開拍　start photographing
开普勒轨道/Keplar軌道　Keplar orbit
开启查验/開啟查驗　luggage opening for inspection
开启桥/活動橋,[均衡]開合橋　movable bridge, balance bridge
开伞冲击/張傘震動　parachute opening shock
开伞冲击耐力/開傘震動耐力　parachute opening shock tolerance
开伞动载/開傘衝擊　opening shock
开伞速度/開傘速率　opening speed
开式回热循环燃气轮机/開式回熱循環燃氣輪機　open regenerative cycle gas turbine
开式给水系统/開式給水系統　open feed system
开式加注/開式加載　opened loading
开式简单循环燃气轮机/開式簡單循環燃氣輪機　open simple cycle gas turbine
开式冷却水系统/開式冷卻水系統　open cooling water system
开式联合碎石机组/開式碎石機組　open type crushing plant
开式喷油器/開式燃油閥　open type fuel valve
开式燃烧室/開式燃燒室　open combustion chamber
开式热水供应系统/開式熱水供應系統　open hot water system
开式热水热网/開口式熱水熱供應網路　open type hot-water heat-supply network
开式水轮机/開槽式水渦輪　open-flume water-turbine
开式循环/開口循環　open cycle
开式循环燃气轮机/開口循環式燃氣輪機　open cycle gas turbine
开式液压系统/開式液壓系統　open type hydraulic system
开式转注/開式轉注　opened transferring
开水间/開水間　water heater room
开榫眼/榫眼　mortice
开锁时间/開鎖時間　uncaging time
开锁位置/開鎖位置　lockset position of coupler
开停业管理/開停業管理　entry-exit regulation
开通/開通　put into operation
开挖工作面/開挖面　excavated surface, excavation face
开挖面挡土板/胸板　breast board
开往/開往　bound to
开尾销/開口銷　cotter pin
开业报批程序/開業報批程式　entry application and approval procedure
开业条件/開業條件　entry condition
铠装电缆/鎧裝電纜,裝甲電纜　armoured cable
看守所/看守所,拘留所　detain station
勘测设计无线电通信/設計測量無線電通訊　radio communication for survey and design
勘察资质/勘察資質　qualification of surveying and geotechnical engineering
勘探/勘探,探勘　exploration, prospecting
勘探点/勘探點　exploratory spot, exploratory point
勘探孔/勘探孔　exploration hole
勘探线/勘探線　exploratory line
堪培拉建筑教育协议/坎培拉建築教育協議　Canberra accord on architectural education
坎贝尔图/坎貝爾圖　Campbell diagram
坎托罗维奇法/坎托羅維奇法　Kantorovich method
看齐角/校準角　aligning angle

看台/觀眾看臺 spectator stand, bleacher
康复花园/專類康復花園,醫療花園 healing garden
康复性景观/康復景觀 therapeutic landscape
康复[医学]科/復健科 rehabilitation department
康复医院/康復醫院 rehabilitation hospital
康索尔/康蘇 Consol
康索兰/康蘇蘭 Consolan
抗爆单元/抗轟炸單元 anti-bomb unit
抗冰加强/抗冰加強 ice strengthening
抗剥落剂/抗剝落劑 anti-stripping agent
抗侧力刚度/側向勁度 lateral stiffness
抗侧力体系/抗側力體系 lateral resisting system
抗冻性/抗凍性 frost resistant
抗风稳定性/抗風穩定性,空氣動力穩定性 wind resisting stability, wind resistant stability
抗风系杆/抗風梁 wind beam
抗风压性能/風壓載重抗逆性 wind load resistance performance
抗风支撑/抗風支撐,風撐 wind bracing
抗风植物/抗風植物,耐風植物 wind resistant plant
抗风柱/抗風柱 wind-resistant column
抗浮设防水位/抗浮設防水位 groundwater level for prevention of upfloating
抗浮桩/抗拔樁 uplift pile
抗辐射加固/輻射加固,輻射硬化 radiation hardening
抗辐射加固器件/輻射加固零件 radiation hardened component
抗旱性/抗旱性 drought resistance
抗核加固/核硬化 nuclear hardening
抗荷动作/抗G動作 anti-G maneuver
抗荷服/抗G衣 anti-G suit
抗荷装备/抗G裝備 anti-G equipment
抗滑明洞/抗滑明洞 anti-skid-type open cut tunnel, anti-skid-type tunnel without cover, anti-skid-type gallery
抗滑稳定性/抗滑穩定[性] stability against sliding
抗滑桩/抗滑樁 spud for antislip, antislide pile, countersliding pile
抗火/耐火 fire-resisting
抗挤出稳定性/抗擠出穩定性 stability against forcing out during train buckling
抗剪力/抗剪力 shearing resistance
抗剪连接件/剪力連接器 shear connector
抗剪强度/抗剪強度 shear strength
抗G紧张动作/抗G緊張動作 anti-G strain maneuver, AGSM
抗浸服/防浸水衣 anti-immersion suit

抗静电地板/抗靜電地板,耗散靜電地板 static resistant floor
抗拉强度/抗拉強度,拉伸強度,抗張強度 tensile strength
抗拉试验曲线/抗拉試驗曲線 tensile test curve
抗老化剂/抗老化劑 anti-ager
抗涝性/抗澇性 flooding resistance
抗力/抵抗力,阻力 resistance
抗力分项系数/抵抗力分項係數 partial safety factor for resistance
抗裂加强钢筋/抗裂鋼筋,防裂鋼筋 anti-crack reinforcement
抗裂性/裂縫阻抗 crack resistance
抗硫酸盐硅酸盐水泥/耐硫酸鹽波特蘭水泥 sulfate resisting Portland cement
抗磨剂/抗磨劑 anti-friction composition, anti-wear agent
抗扭强度/抗扭強度 torsional strength
抗扭塑性截面模量/扭矩塑性斷面模數 plastic torque modulus of section
抗侵蚀材料/抗侵蝕材料 erosion resistant material
抗倾覆安全系数/抗翻安全因數 factor safety against overturning
抗倾覆稳定性/抗傾覆穩定性,抗翻穩定 stability against overturning
抗扰度/抗擾度 immunity to interference
抗蠕变钛合金/抗蠕變鈦合金 creep-resistant titanium alloy
抗乳化度/脫乳化數 demulsification number
抗闪燃/抗燃 flash resistant
抗折强度/破裂強度 rupture strength
抗渗性/不滲透性,不透水性 impermeability
抗脱轨稳定性/抗出軌穩定性 stability against derailment
抗弯强度/彎曲強度 bending strength
抗污染植物/抗汙染植物 anti-pollution plant, pollution resistant plant
抗谐鸣边/抗諧鳴邊 anti-singing edge
抗压强度/抗壓強度 compressive strength
抗压稳定度/抗壓穩定度 stability against crushing
抗盐植物/抗鹽植物 salt resistant plant
抗氧化剂/抗氧化劑 oxidation inhibitor
抗氧化抗腐蚀剂/抗氧化抗腐蝕劑 anti-oxidant anti-corrosion additive
抗液化措施/抗液化措施 anti-liquefaction measure, liquefaction defense measure
抗雨蚀涂层/防雨水腐蝕塗層 rain erosion resistant coating

抗震措施/抗震措施　seismic measure
抗震等级/抗震等級　seismic grade
抗震概念设计/耐震概念設計　conceptual seismic design
抗震构造措施/抗震構造　detail of seismic design
抗震规范/防震規則　aseismic code
抗震基础/耐震基礎　earthquake-proof foundation
抗震计算方法/抗震計算方法　seismic analysis method, seismic calculation method
抗震减灾规划/防震減災規劃　earthquake disaster reduction planning
抗震结构/耐震結構　earthquake resistant structure
抗震结构整体性/抗震結構整體性　integral behavior of seismic structure
抗震墙/抗震牆,地震構造牆　seismic structural wall, earthquake resistant wall
抗震设防/抗震設防　earthquake fortification, seismic fortification
抗震设防标准/抗震設防標準,抗震設防水準　earthquake fortification level, seismic fortification criterion
抗震设防烈度/抗震設防烈度　earthquake fortification intensity, seismic fortification intensity
抗震设防区划/地震設防區劃　earthquake fortification zoning
抗震设计/地震設計　seismic design, aseismic design, earthquake resistant design
抗震试验/抗震試驗　earthquake resistant test, seismic test
抗震危险地段/地震危險區域　dangerous area to earthquake resistance
抗震性能评价/抗震性能評估　earthquake resistant performance assessment
抗震支撑/抗震支撐　seismic brace
抗撞能力/衝擊抗力　impact resistance
[考工记]营国制度/[考工記]營國制度　Kaogongji city planning formulation
考古遗址公园/考古遺址公園　archaeological park
考机/考機　general inspection for the whole machine
靠把/護舷材,碰墊　fender
靠泊/靠泊　alongside
靠船撞击力/寄泊衝擊力　berthing impact
靠近加油装置/靠近加油裝置　close-in fueling rig
靠码头/靠[泊]碼頭　alongside berth wharf
靠模弯曲试验/折曲試驗　guide bend test
靠天田/看天田　rain-fed paddy field
靠右行驶/靠右行駛　keep right
靠雨水稻田/看天田　rain-fed paddy field

靠左行驶/靠左行駛　keep left
柯帕卡帕那海滨大道/柯帕卡帕那海濱大道　Aterro de Copacapana
科尔多巴耶稣会牧场和街区/科爾多巴耶穌會牧場和街區　Jesuit Block and Estancias of Córdoba
科技工业园区/科學工業園區　science technology industrial park
科技活动室/科技實驗室　science and technology laboratory
科技园区/科技園區　science and technology park
科里奥利刺激效应/柯氏刺激效應　Coriolis stimulation effect
科里奥利惯性传感器/柯氏慣性感測器　Coriolis inertial sensor
科里奥利加速度生理效应/柯氏加速度生理效應　Coriolis acceleration physiological effects
科里奥利力/科氏力,自轉偏向力　Coriolis force
科林斯柱式/科林斯柱式　Corinthian order
科潘考古遗址公园/科潘考古遺址公園　Copan Archaeological Park
科潘玛雅遗址/科潘瑪雅遺址　Maya Site of Copán
科潘卫城/科潘衛城　Acropolis of Copán
科普活动室/科普活動室,大眾科學活動室　popular science activity room
科氏[加速度]修正/柯氏修正　Coriolis acceleration correction
科学保护区/科學保護區　protection area for scientific research
科学城/科學城　science city
科学共同体/科學共同體　community of science
科学技术馆/科學工藝博物館　science and technology museum
科学价值/科學價值　scientific value
科学景观论/科學景觀論　scientific landscape theory
科学实验建筑/實驗樓　laboratory building
科学卫星/科學衛星　scientific satellite
科学研究图书馆/科學研究圖書館　research institutional library
科学园区/科學園區　science park
颗粒度/顆粒性　granularity
颗粒度试验/粒度試驗　grain size test
颗粒收集器/顆粒收集器　particulate trap
颗粒污染/顆粒汙染　particle contamination
颗粒圆性/顆粒圓性　roundness of particle
颗粒增强复合材料/顆粒強化複合材　particulate reinforced composite
颗粒组成/顆粒級配　grain composition
颗料排放物/排放顆粒　particulate emission

壳/殼　shell
壳管式冷凝器/殼管式冷凝器　shell-and-tube condenser
壳管式热交换器/殼管式交換器　shell-and-tube heat exchanger
壳式泵/殼形抽水機　shell pump
壳式牵引变压器/外鐵式牽引變壓器　shell-type traction transformer
壳体薄膜理论/薄膜殼理論　membrane theory of shell
壳体边界效应/殼層邊緣效應　edge effect of shell
壳体后裙/殼體後裙　aft skirt of case
壳体基础/殼體基礎　shell foundation
壳体绝热层/外殼絕緣　case insulation
壳体黏结式药柱/壁結藥柱　case bonded grain
壳体前裙/殼體前裙　forward skirt of case
壳体式太阳电池阵/殼體太陽電池陣　body-mounted type solar array
壳型铸造/殼模鑄造　shell mold casting
可搬式沥青混合料搅拌设备/可搬式瀝青混合料攪拌設備　movable asphalt mixing plant
可搬式稳定土厂拌设备/可移動穩定土廠拌站　movable stabilized soil mixing plant
可编程序数据采集器/可編程式數據採集器　programmable data logger
可编程遥测/可程式遙測　programmable telemetry
可编程遥测系统/可程式遙測系統　programmable telemetry system
可编程只读存储器/可程式唯讀記憶體　programmable read only memory
可变标志/變數符號　variable sign
可变波束引信天线/可變波束引信天線　variable-beam antenna of fuze
可变成本/變動成本　variable cost
可变的/變動的　variable
可变光阑/可變光圈　variable diaphragm
可变荷载/可變荷載,可變負載,變載　variable load, variable action
可变换的集装箱船/可變換貨櫃船　convertible container ship
可变加速度/變加速度　variable acceleration
可变螺距螺旋桨/[可]變螺距螺槳,可控螺距螺槳　controllable-pitch propeller
可变排气阀关闭机构/可變排氣閥關閉機構　variable exhaust valve closing device
可变喷油正时机构/可變噴油定時機構　variable injection timing mechanism
可变稳定性飞行控制/可變穩定飛行控制　variable stability flight control
可变限速标志/可變限速標誌　variable speed-limit sign
可变限速控制/可變速限控制　variable speed-limit control
可变向车道/調撥車道　reversible lane
可变向中心车道线/可變向中心車道線　reversible center lane line
可变信息标志/資訊可變標誌　changeable message sign
可变压缩比/可變壓縮比　variable compression ratio
可变载荷/變動負荷,變動負載　variable load
可变作用/可變作用　variable action
可测量/可量測量　measurable quantity
可测星等/可測量星等　measurable magnitude
可插车空档/可插車空檔　acceptance gap
可拆链环/拆合環　detachable link
可拆式钻头/可換鑽頭　detachable bit
可拆卸式电磁屏蔽室/模組化電磁遮罩室　modular electromagnetic shielding enclosure
可沉降固体/沈降性固體　settleable solid
可持续城市/永續性都市　sustainable city
可持续技术/可持續技術　sustainable technology
可持续建筑/永續建築　sustainable architecture
可持续性/持續性,永續性　sustainability
可持续性设计/永續設計　sustainable design
可重复使用防热材料/可重複用熱防護材料　reusable thermal protection material
可重组技术/可重組技術　reconfigurable technology
可处理性/可處理性　treatability
可达可用性/實際[達成]可用度　achieved availability
可达性/可達性,易達性,可及性　accessibility
可倒转柴油机/可逆轉柴油機　reversible diesel engine
可调头交叉口/可調頭交叉口　turn crossing
可钉地板/可釘地板　nailable floor
可懂串音/可解串音　intelligible crosstalk
可懂度/可懂度,可解度,清晰度　intelligibility
可动活荷载/移動載重　movable load
可动心轨辙叉/可動式岔心　movable point frog
可动翼轨辙叉/可動翼軌辙叉,移動翼辙叉　movable wing frog
可动圆柱形支座/球滾支承　spherical roller support
可读性/易讀性,可辨識性　legibility
可锻铸铁/展性鑄鐵　malleable cast iron
可更换单元/更換單元　replaceable units
可灌筑性/灌築性　placeability

可航半圆/可航半圓　navigable semicircle
可航性/可航性　navigableness
可航最浅水深/航行最低水深　controlling depth
可互换部件/可互換配件　interchangeable parts
可及性/可達性　reachability
可加工性/可加工性　workability
可检出钻头/可檢出鑽頭　detectable bit
可见的/可見的　visible
可见度因素/可見度因素　visibility attribute
可见光/可見光　visible light
可见光伪装/可見光偽裝　visual camouflage
可见光遥感/可見光遥測　visible spectral remote sensing
可见痕迹/可見痕跡　visible trace
可见信号/視覺號誌　visible signal
可见性伤害/可見性傷害　visible harm
可浸长度/可浸長度　floodable length
可居住面积/生活空間　living space
可靠度基准期/可靠度基準期　reliability datum period
可靠概率/可靠概率　probability of survival
可靠寿命/可靠壽命　reliable life
可靠性/可靠性,可靠度　reliability
可靠性保证大纲/可靠度保證大綱　reliability assurance program
可靠性分配/可靠度分配　reliability allocation
可靠性工作计划/可靠度計劃書　reliability program plan
可靠性监控/可靠性監控,可靠度監控　reliability monitoring
可靠性框图/可靠度方塊圖　reliability block diagram
可靠性模型/可靠度模型　reliability model
可靠性设计/可靠性設計　reliability design
可靠性试验/可靠性試驗,可靠度試驗,可靠度測試　reliability test
可靠性维修性/可靠度及維修度　reliability and maintanability, r and m
可靠性维修性合同参数/可靠度及維修度合約參數　r and m contractual parameter
可靠性维修性使用参数/可靠度及維修度作業參數　r&m operational parameter
可靠性验证/可靠度驗證　reliability verification
可靠性验证试验/可靠度驗證試驗　reliability verification test
可靠性预计/可靠度預測　reliability prediction
可靠性增长/可靠度成長　reliability growth
可靠性增长管理/可靠度成長管理　reliability growth management
可靠性增长试验/可靠度成長試驗　reliability growth test
可靠性指标/可靠性指標,可靠度指數　reliability index
可控被动水舱式减摇装置/可控被動水艙穩定系統　controllable passive tank stabilization system
可控电磁铁/可控電磁鐵　controlled electromagnet
可控硅变流机组/閘流體換流器,閘流體換流組　thyristor converter set
可控硅励磁系统/閘流體勵磁系統　thyristor excited system
可控减速顶/可控減速頂　dowty controllable retarder
可控扩散叶型/可控擴散翼形　controlled diffusion airfoil
可控螺距螺旋桨/可控螺距螺槳,可變螺距螺槳　controllable-pitch propeller
可控气氛热处理/控制氛圍熱處理　controlled atmosphere heat treatment
可控桥式整流器/可控橋式整流器　controlled bridge rectifier
可控涡设计/可控渦設計　controlled vortex design
可控相复励磁系统/可控相之補償複激系統　controllable phase compensation compound excited system
可控自励恒压装置/可控自激等電壓設施　controllable self-excited constant voltage device
可能发电/可能發電　possible power generation
可能碰撞点/可能碰撞點　possible point of collision, PPC
可能容量/可能容量　possible capacity
可能通行能力/可能通行能力　possible capacity
可能最大洪水/可能最大洪水　probable maximum flood
可能最大降水/可能最大降水　probable maximum precipitation
可逆式水泵轮机/可逆泵水渦輪　reversible pump turbine
可逆助力机械操纵/有回力助力操縱系統　reversible boosted mechanical control
可弃压载/可棄壓載　droppable ballast
可燃毒物元件/可燃有毒元素　burnable poison element
可燃性薄雾/可燃薄霧　flammable mist
可燃性气体/可燃氣體　flammable gas
可燃性物质/易燃材料　flammable material
可燃性液体/可燃液體,易燃液體　flammable liquid
可溶性/可溶性　solubility

可溶性树脂含量/可溶樹脂含量 soluble resin content
可熔性/可熔性 fusibility
可识别性/可辯認性，辨識率 recognizability
可视电话/視訊電話，電視電話 videophone
可视电话机/可視電話機 videophone set
可视化/視覺化 visualization
可视杂物/可視雜物 visible sundries
可探测性/檢測能力 detectability
可躺座椅/靠椅 reclining seat
可替代旅游/另類旅遊 alternative tourism
可调安定面/可調水平安定面 adjustable horizontal stabilizer
可调拐肘/可調曲柄 adjustable crank
可调光圈/可調孔徑 adjustable aperture
可调混响室/音質室 acoustical room
可调进气道/可變幾何形狀的進氣道 variable geometry inlet
可调螺距桨/可控距螺槳 controllable pitch propeller, CPP
可调螺距桨控制系统/可控距螺槳控制系統 controllable pitch propeller control system, CPP control system
可调牵引变频器/可調變頻器 variable frequency convertor
可调式灯具/可調照明器具 adjustable luminaire
可调压载水舱/可變壓載艙 variable ballast tank
可调延时/可調遲延 adjustable delay
可调叶片/可調葉片 adjustable vane
可听距离/聞距 range of audibility
可听声/可聽聲音 audible sound
可听[声音]信号/聽覺號誌 audible signal
可透过的/可透的 pervious
可脱水污泥/可脱水汙泥 drainable sludge
可弯式尖轨转辙器/彈性岔尖 flexible switch
可吸入颗粒物/可吸入顆粒物 inhalable particle of 10 μm or less, PM10
可卸螺旋桨叶/可卸螺槳片 loose propeller blade
可卸硬件/可卸儀品 loose hardware
可信性/可信性 dependability
可行性论证/可行性研究 feasibility study
可行性研究/可行性研究 feasibility study
可修复产品/可修復產品 repairable item
可压缩流体/可壓縮流體 compressible fluid
可压缩性/[可]壓縮性 compressibility
可氧化盐/可氧化鹽[類] oxidizable salt
可移式泵/移动式泵 portable pump
可移式灯具/手提式燈具，可搬型照明器具 portable luminaire
可移式风机/可攜式風扇 portable fan
可用材/實用級木材 utility grade wood
可用超载/容許負載因數 permissible load factor
可用功率/可用動力 available power
可用区域/使用區 use district
可用推力/可用推力,有效推力 available thrust
可用性/可用性,可用度,有效性 availability
可再生能源/再生能源 renewable energy, renewable resources
可照时数/可能日照時間 possible sunshine duration
可折顶篷/可折頂篷 foldable canopy
可支付住房/保障性住房,低收入住宅 affordable housing
可贮存推进剂/可貯存推進劑 storable propellant
可贮存推进剂火箭发动机/可貯存推進劑火箭發動機 storable propellant rocket engine
可转挂架/旋轉掛架 rotating pylon
可转管接头/可轉管接頭 victaulic joint
可转静叶/可調靜葉片,可變定子葉片 variable stator blade
可追溯性/可追溯性,溯源性 traceability
克拉佩龙方程/克拉伯隆方程式 Clapeyron equation
克莱蒙特庄园/克萊蒙特莊園 Villa of Claremont
克鲁格襟翼/克魯格襟翼 Krueger flap
克努森数/克努森數 Knudsen number, Kn
刻槽/刻槽 carving groove
刻度板/刻度板 scale plate
刻度防锈饮水杯/有刻度之防銹飲器 rustproof graduated drinking vessel
刻度线/分度線 graduation mark
刻痕钢丝/刻痕鋼絲,齒痕鋼絲 indented wire, corrugated wire, indented steel wire
刻痕螺栓/齒紋螺栓 indented bolt
刻痕器/開槽器 notcher
刻蚀/浸蝕 etching
客舱/客艙 passenger cabin
客舱旅客/房廂乘客 cabin passenger
客舱门/客艙門 passenger door
客车/客車 bus, passenger car, carriage
[客车]摆门/客車擺門 spring butt rocking door
客车保有量/客車保有量 number of passenger cars on hand
客车调度/客車調度 bus dispatching
客车定员/客車定員 rated passenger number
[客车]隔门/中隔門 partition door
客车技术整备所/旅客列車技術整備所 passenger train technical servicing point

[客车]脚蹬/[客車]腳蹬　entrance door step
[客车]脚蹬门/腳蹬門　vestibule entrance door
客车客座利用率/客車客座利用率　percentage of passenger seats utilization per car
[客车]门锁/門鎖　door lock
[客车]内墙板/客車內牆板　panel
客车配属辆数/客車配屬輛數　number of allocated passenger cars
客车平均日车公里/客車平均日車公里　average car-kilometers per car-day
[客车]上侧梁/客車上側梁　cant rail
客车洗车线/客車洗車線　washing siding for passenger vehicle
[客车]摇门/擺動門　swing door
客车运行周期/大客車運行週期　bus run cycle
客车整备库/客車整備庫　coach servicing shed
客车整备所/客車整備所　passenger car servicing depot
客车正班率/客車正班率　rate of on schedule bus runs
客车轴温报警/客車軸溫報警　passenger car journal temperature warning
客船/客船　passenger vessel, passenger ship
客船安全证书/客船安全證書　Passenger Ship Safety Certificate
客房/客房,貴賓室　guest room
客货车厂段修规程/客貨車廠段修規程　regulation for passenger-freight car repair in factory-depot
客货船/客貨船,客貨輪　passenger-cargo ship
客货共线铁路旅客车站/客貨共線鐵路旅客車站　mixed traffic railway station
客货运混合线路/客貨運混合線路　railway line for mixed passenger and freight traffic
客货运站/客貨運站　mixed passenger and freight station
客流/客流,客運量　passenger traffic, passenger flow
客流调查/客流調查　passenger flow investigation
客流量/客流量　passenger flow volume
客流图/客流圖　passenger traffic diagram, passenger flow diagram
客流预测/客流預測　passenger flow forecast
客票/客票　passenger ticket
客室/乘客室　passenger room, passenger compartment
[客室]通道/通道,走道　aisle, gangway
客厅/客廳,大餐廳　saloon, living room
客厅车/轎車,豪華客車　saloon car

客土法/客土法　borrowed soil, incorporation with extra soil, soils from other places
客位/客位　rated seat
客源/客源　passenger source
客源地/觀光地區　tourist source region
客源市场/客源市場　tourist source market
客运班期/公共汽車時刻表　bus schedule
客运包车票/客運包車票　charter bill
客运单证/客運單證　document of passenger transport
客运动态记录单/客運運行記錄　bus running record
客运机车/客運機車　passenger locomotive
客运监视电视/客運監視電視　monitor TV for passenger service
客运交通/客運交通　passenger traffic
客运拒赔/客運拒賠　reject of passenger claim
客运理赔/客運理賠　actions for passenger claim
客运码头/渡船碼頭,旅客碼頭　ferry jetty, passenger wharf
客运密度/客運密度　passenger traffic density
客运设备/旅客設施　passenger facility
客运事故/客運交通事故　passenger traffic accident
客运室/客運室　passenger service office
客运索赔/客運索賠　passenger claim
客运索赔时限/客運索賠時限　period of limitation for passenger claim
客运业务无线电通信/旅客服務無線電通訊　radio communication for passenger service
客运站/客運[車]站　passenger station
客运站站务工作量/客運終站工作負荷　passenger terminal work load
客运质量管理/旅客運輸品質管理　quality management of passenger transport
客运专线/客運專線,旅客列車專線　special line for passenger train, passenger special line, passenger traffic only line
客运专线铁路旅客车站/客運專線鐵路旅客車站　passenger railway station
客栈/客棧,小旅館　inn
客站货场无线电通信/客站貨場無線電通訊　station and freight yard radio communication
啃边/邊緣故障　edge failure
坑槽/壺穴,坑洞　pot holes
坑道自稳时间/坑道自穩時間　self-stabilization time of tunnel
坑内爆炸/坑内爆炸　undermining blast
坑式腐蚀/痕蝕　pitting corrosion
坑探/試坑　pit test

坑洼/路面坑洞　pot-hole
空爆/氣爆　atmospheric explosion, air burst
空爆引信/空爆炸引信　airburst fuze
空舱运费/空艙運費　deadfreight
空侧/空側，空邊　airside
空车调整/空車調整　adjustment of empty car
空车行程/空車行程　deadhead mileage
空车直达列车/空車直達列車　through train with empty car
空车走行率/空車走行率　percentage of empty to loaded car kilometers
空船重量/空船重量，輕載重量　light weight
空船重量分布/空船重量分布　light weight distribution
空档/空檔　stop short
空地导弹/空對地飛彈　air-to-ground missile
空斗墙/竪砌磚空心牆　rowlock cavity wall
空房/空屋　vacant house
空分设备厂/氣體分離設備廠　oxygenerator factory
空风洞运行/空風洞操作　empty wind tunnel operation
空负荷试验/無負載試驗，空載試驗　no-load test
空负荷运行/無負荷運轉　no-load running, no-load operation
空腹大梁/空腹梁　open-frame girder
空腹拱/空腹拱，列柱拱　open-spandrel arch
空腹拱桥/空腹拱橋，空拱肩拱橋　open spandrel arch bridge
空腹桁架/空腹桁架　Vierendeel truss
空腹梁/韋廉迪梁　open web girder, Vierendeel girder
空隔舱/堰艙　cofferdam
空滑比/滑翔比　gliding ratio
空化/空化，空腔作用　cavitation
空化螺旋桨/空化螺槳　cavitating propeller
空化数/空化數　cavitation number
空[货]车/空車　empty car, empty wagon
空间/外太空　space, outer space
空间[波]传播方式/空間波傳播波型　space-wave propagation mode
空间尺度/空間尺度　space scale
空间磁场/空間磁場　space magnetic field
空间地质学/空間地質學　space geology
空间点火试验/空間點火試驗　space ignition test
空间定向/空間定向能力　spatial orientation
空间定向障碍/空間迷向　spatial disorientation
空间动力学模型/空間動態模型　spatial dynamics model

空间段/太空段　space segment
空间段提供者/太空部分提供者　space segment provider
空间对接动力学/空間對接動力學　space docking dynamics
空间法/太空法　space law
空间仿真/空間模擬　space simulation
空间飞行程序/[太空]任務程式　space mission program
空间分辨率/空間解析度　spatial resolution
空间分集/空間分集　space diversity
空间分异/空間差異化　spatial differentiation
空间辐射/太空輻射　space radiation
空间辐射环境/太空輻射環境　space radiation environment
空间格局/空間模式　spatial pattern
空间隔离/空間區隔　spatial segregation
空间隔离法/空間隔離法　distance interval method
空间跟踪/太空追蹤　space tracking
空间构架/立體構架　space frame
空间管制/空間管制　spatial regulation
空间规划/空間規劃　space planning, spatial planning
空间核电源/太空核動力　space nuclear power
空间桁架模型/空間桁架模型　space truss model
空间化学/空間化學　space chemistry
空间环境/太空環境　space environment
空间环境报警/空間環境警報　space environment warning
空间环境仿真/空間環境模擬　space environment simulation
空间[环境]仿真器/空間[環境]模擬器　space environment simulator
空间环境模式/空間環境模型　space environment model
空间环境生物学/太空環境生物學　space environmental biology
空间环境试验/空間環境試驗　space environment test
空间环境效应/空間環境效應　space environment effect
空间环境预报/空間環境預報　space environment forecast
空间火箭发动机/太空火箭發動機　space rocket engine, space rocket motor
空间计量模型/空間計量經濟模型　spatial econometric model
空间监视网/太空監視網　space surveillance network

空间监视系统/太空監視系統　space surveillance system
空间间隔法/空間間隔法　space-interval method
空间交会/太空會合　space rendezvous
空间节点/空間節點　space node
空间结构/立體結構　space structure, spatial structure
空间近视/太空近視　space myopia
空间景观模型/空間景觀模型　spatial landscape model
空间句法/空間句法　space syntax
空间决策支持系统/空間決策支持系統　spatial decision support system
空间科学/太空科學　space science
空间可达性/空間可達性　space accessibility
空间粒子辐射/空間粒子輻射　space particle radiation
空间滤波/空間濾波　space filtering
空间模式/空間模式　spatial pattern
空间频率/空間頻率　spatial frequency
空间平均速度/空間平均速率,區間平均速率　space mean speed
空间燃料电池系统/太空燃料電池系統　space fuel cell system
空间容量/空間容量　space capacity
空间绅士化/空間仕紳化,空間縉紳化　spatial gentrification
空间神经生物学/空間神經生物學　space neurobiology
空间生命科学/空間生命科學　space life science
空间生态位/生境生態位　spatial niche
空间实验操作训练/空間實驗運轉訓練　space experiment operation training
空间实验室/太空實驗室　space laboratory
空间数据/空間資料　spatial data
空间数据模型/空間資料模型　spatial data model
空间所有权/空權　air right
空间探测/太空探測　space exploration
空间探测器/太空探測器　space probe
空间探测卫星/太空探測衛星　space exploration satellite
空间天文观测/空間天文觀測　space astronomical observation
空间天文学/太空天文[學]　space astronomy
空间投入产出模型/空間投入產出模型　spatial input-output model
空间推进法/空間推移法,空間搜尋法　space marching method
空间外热流/空間熱通量　space heat flux
空间网络分析/空間網路分析　space network analysis
空间围合/空間圍合　space enclosure
空间无线电通信/太空無線電通信　space radio communication
空间物理探测/空間物理探測　space physics exploration
空间物理学/太空物理學　space physics
空间物体/太空目標　space object
空间系统/太空系統　space system
空间行为/空間行爲　spacial behavior
空间压缩/時空壓縮　compression of time and space
空间遥令/太空遙令　space telecommand
空间艺术/空間藝術　architectural art, space art
空间诱变/空間誘變　space mutation
空间运动/空間運動　space motion
空间站/太空站　space station
空间站发射/太空站發射　space station launch
空间站遥控机械手系统/太空站遙控操作器系統　space station remote manipulator system, SSRMS
空间织补/空間織補　space darning
空间指向误差/空間指向誤差　space pointing error
空间制氧/空間制氧　space oxygen generation
空间秩序/空間次序,收穫地域順序,收穫地點順序　spatial order
空间轴线/空間軸　space-axis
空间注记/空間注記　space note
空间自由飞行器机械手/空間自由飛行體機械手　space free flight unit manipulator
空舰导弹/空對艦飛彈　air-to-ship missile
空降兵/傘兵部隊　parachute troops
空空导弹/空對空飛彈　air-to-air missile, AAM
空冷/氣冷　air cooling
空灵/空靈　spaciousness, airiness
空陆水联运集装箱/空陸水聯運集裝箱　air-surface container, air-intermodal container
空泡/氣泡　cavity
空[泡腐]蚀/空[泡沖]蝕,孔蝕　cavitation erosion, cavitation corrosion
空炮眼/無藥孔　unloaded hole, unloaded basting hole
空铺地面/增高地板　raised flooring
空气包/空氣包　tank dome
空气冲洗/氣洗　air wash
空气抽除装置/抽氣器　air extractor, air exhauster
空气处理系统/空氣處理系統　air treatment system
空气吹淋室/空氣射叢　air shower

空气锤/[空]氣錘 air hammer, pneumatic hammer
空气动力/氣動力 aerodynamic force
空气动力不稳定性/空氣動力不穩定 aerodynamic instability
空气动力特性/氣動特性 aerodynamic characteristics
空气动力稳定性/氣動穩定性 aerodynamic stability
空气动力系数/空氣動力係數 aerodynamic coefficient, air dynamic coefficient
空气动力学/空氣[動]力學 aerodynamics, aeromechanics
空气断路器/空氣斷路器 air circuit-breaker
空气分配器/空氣分配器 air distributor
空气分配系统/空氣分配系統 air distribution system
空气浮力修正系数/空氣浮力修正係數 air flotation correction coefficient
空气干燥器/空氣乾燥器,風乾器 air dryer
空气管/空氣管 air pipe
空气管头/空氣管頭 air pipe head
空气过滤/空氣過濾 air filtration
空气过滤器/空氣過濾器,空氣濾清器 air filter
空气加热器/空氣加熱器 air heater
空气间层/空氣間隔 air space
空气间隙/空氣間隙 air gap
空气净化/空氣淨化 air cleaning
空气净化器/空氣淨化器 air cleaner
空气净化装置/空氣淨化裝置 air purification unit
空气控制装置/氣動控制裝置 pneumatic control device
空气冷却器/空氣冷卻器 air cooler
空气流量计/量氣計 air meter
空气螺旋桨/空氣螺槳 air screw, air propeller
空气马达/氣動馬達 air motor
空气幕沉井法/空氣幕沈井法 air curtain method for sinking caisson
空气幕法下沉沉井/空氣幕法下沈沈井 sinking open caisson by injected air curtain
空气泡法/氣泡法 air bubble method
空气配气台/空氣分配臺 air distribution board
空气喷射式/空氣噴射式 air injection type
空气清洗/氣提 air stripping
空气渗透/空氣滲漏 air leakage
空气声/空氣音 airborne sound
空气声隔声频谱修正量/空氣音隔音頻譜修正量 spectrum adaptation term for air-borne sound insulation
空气湿度/空氣水分 air moisture

空气-水系统/空氣-水系統 air-water system
空气调节/空氣調節,空調 air conditioning
空气调节机房/空氣調節機房 air handling unit room
空气调节系统冷负荷/空氣調節系統冷卻負載 air conditioning system cooling load
空气调节装置/空氣調節設備 air conditioning equipment
空气调节装置蒸发器/空調器蒸發器 air conditioning evaporator
空气温度/氣溫 air temperature
空气污染/空氣汙染 air pollution
空气污染控治/空氣汙染防治,空氣汙染管制 air pollution control
空气雾化喷嘴/鼓風霧化器 air blast atomizer
空气雾化油燃烧器/噴氣霧化油燃燒器 air atomizing oil burner
空气箱/水密空氣箱 watertight aircase
空气消耗量/空氣消耗量 air consumption
空气消耗率/空氣消耗率,單位耗[空]氣量 specific air consumption
空气悬浮粒子/空浮粒子 airborne particle
空气循环冷却系统/空氣循環冷卻系統 air cycle cooling system
空气压缩机/空氣壓縮機 air compressor
空气压缩机室/空氣壓縮機室 air compressor room
空气扬析/風析 air elutriation
空气养护/空氣養護 air curing
空气预冷装置/空氣預冷器 air precooler
空气预热器/空氣預熱器 air preheater
空气预热装置/空氣預熱器 air preheater
空气源热泵/空氣源熱泵 air source heat pump
空气再生器/空氣再生器 air regenerator
空气再循环系统/空氣再循環系統 air recycle system
空气真空两用制动装置/空氣真空兩用制動裝置 air and vacuum dual brake equipment
空气制动/空中減速,氣刹[車] air brake
空气制动试验/空氣制動試驗 test on air brake
空气制动装置/氣壓制動裝置 air brake equipment
空气质量/氣團 air mass
空气主断路器/空氣主斷路器 line air-blast circuit-breaker
空气贮存器/容氣器 air receiver
空气自动控制装置/空氣自動控制裝置 automatic air control device
空气阻力/空氣阻力 air resistance
空腔作用/空腔作用,空化 cavitation

空勤人员医学选拔/空勤組人員醫學選拔 medical selection of aircrew
空勤组/空勤人員 aircrew
空区/空邊,空側 airside
空权/空權 air right
空燃比/空氣燃油比 air-fuel ratio
空射弹道导弹/空射彈道飛彈 air-launched ballistic missile, ALBM
空射巡航导弹/空射巡弋飛彈 air-launched cruise missile, ALCM
空速/空速 air speed
空速表/空速表 air speed indicator
空速马赫数表/空速馬赫數指示器 air speed Mach number indicator
空态测试/空態測試 as-built test
空天飞机/太空飛機 aerospace plane
空调度日数/冷卻度日 cooling degree day
空调管路系统/空氣調節管路系統 air conditioning pipe system
空调净化/空氣調節淨化 air conditioning purge
空调净化牵引车/空氣調節淨化牽引機 air conditioning cleaned tractor
空调客车/空氣調節客車 air conditioned passenger car, air conditioned coach
空调连接器/空氣調節連接器 air conditioning connector
空调连接器支架/空氣調節連接器支架 air conditioning connector support mount
空调软管/空氣調節軟管 air conditioning hose
空调蒸发器/空調器蒸發器 air conditioning evaporator
空投/空投 air drop
空投设备/空投設備 droppable equipment
空位/空艙 void space
空细胞法/空細胞法 empty-cell process
空箱里程/空箱里程 empty container mileage
空想社会主义城市规划/烏托邦社會主義 utopian urban planning
空心板/空心板,中空樓板 hollow slab
空心板桥/空心板橋 hollow slab bridge
空心玻璃砖/空心玻璃塊 hollow glass block
空心[车]轴/空心軸 tubular axle, hollow axle, hollow shaft
空心村/空心村 hollow village
空心螺栓/螺桿套管 bolt sleeve
空心黏土砌块/空心黏土磚 hollow clay block
空心[桥]墩/空心橋墩 hollow pier
空心叶片/空心葉片 hollow blade

空心支墩坝/空心重力壩 hollow gravity dam
空心重力坝/空心重力壩 hollow gravity dam
空心砖/空心磚 hollow brick
空压机/空氣壓縮機 air compressor
空压机电动机/壓縮空氣電動機 air compressor motor
空压机自动控制/空壓機自動控制 air compressor auto-control
空运/空運 air transportation
空载/空載,無載 no-load, zeroload, bareload
空载吃水/輕載吃水 light draft, light draught
空载电压/無負載電壓 no-load voltage
[空载]电压降低装置/減壓裝置 voltage reducing device
空载流量/無載流量,空轉流量 no-load discharge
空载排水量/空載排水量 light displacement
空载试验/空載試驗,無負載試驗 no-load test
空载水线/輕載水線 light water line
空载特性/無載特性 no-load characteristic
空载运行/無負荷運轉 no-load running, no-load operation
空载状态/輕載船況 light condition
空战/空戰 air combat
空置率/空置率,空閒率,空房率 vacancy rate
空中对准/空中校準 in-flight alignment
空中回收/空中回收 aerial retrieval
空中加油机/空中加油機 tanker airplane
空中加油系统/空中加油系統 tanker refuelling system
空中交通/空中交通,飛航 air traffic
空中交通服务/飛航業務 air traffic service, ATS
空中交通管理/飛航管理 air traffic management, ATM
空中交通管制/飛航管制 air traffic control, ATC
空中交通流量管理/飛航流量管理 air traffic flow management
空中劫持/空中劫機 aerial hijack
空中起动边界/空中起動邊界 airstart boundary
空中摄影地图/攝影地圖,照相地圖 photomap
空中受油系统/空中受油系統 aerial refuelling system
空中索道/空中索道,架空索道 aerial ropeway, aerial cableway
空中探鱼/空中探測魚群,飛行探測魚群 aerial scouting
空中停车/空中停車 engine-off in flight
空中停车率/空中停車率 in-flight shutdown rate
空中营救/空中搜救 air rescue

空中应急放油/空中棄油　in-flight fuel jettison
空中走廊/空中走廊　air corridor
空重/空重　empty weight, bare weight, tare weight
空重车制动装置/空重車調整裝置　empty and load brake equipment
空重车转换塞门/空重車轉換塞門　empty and load changeover cock
空转轮/滾子　idler
空转转速/惰速率　idle speed
空走距离/空走距離　idling stopping distance
空走时间/空走時間　idling braking time
孔板送风/開孔送風　perforated air supply
孔道灌浆/管道灌漿,導管灌漿　duct grouting
孔径/口徑,光圈　aperture
孔径比/孔徑比,口徑比　aperture ratio
孔径光阑/孔徑光闌　aperture stop
孔口加药槽/孔口加藥槽　orifice feed tank
孔雀(孔雀α)/孔雀十一(孔雀α)　Peacock
孔隙/空隙　void space
孔隙比/孔隙比,空隙比　void ratio
孔隙气压力/孔氣壓力　pore air pressure
孔隙水/孔隙水　void water
孔隙[水]压力/孔隙水壓力　pore water pressure
孔隙水压力仪/孔隙水壓力計　pore water pressure cell, pore water pressure meter
孔隙水压系数/孔隙水壓係數　pore water coefficient
孔隙压力消散/孔隙水壓力消散　pore pressure dissipation
孔压静力触探试验/孔壓測量圓錐貫入試驗　cone penetration test with pore pressure measurement
空白/空白　blank
空白背书/空白背書　endorsement in blank
空白定位图/作業圖　plotting chart
空白提单/空白載貨證券　open bill of lading
空地率/空地率　vacant ratio, open space ratio
空地区域/空地區　vacancy area
空格桥面/網格橋面　grid deck
空距/液面上距　ullage
空距尺/液面計　ullage scale
空隙比/氣隙比　air-void ratio
空隙度/孔隙度,孔隙率　porosity, porosity percentage of void
空隙率/空隙量　void content
控温运输/控温運輸　transport under controlled temperature
控制棒导管/操縱桿導管　control rod guide tube
控制棒驱动机构/操縱桿驅動機構　control rod drive mechanism

控制爆破/控制爆破　controlled blasting
控制泵/控制泵　control pump
控制变压器/控制變壓器　control transformer
控制标高/控制標高,控制水準　control elevation, control level
控制部位转换开关/控制站換向開關　control station change-over switch
控制测量/控制測量　control surveying
控制程序/控制程式　control program
控制单元/控制單位　control unit
控制点/控制點　control point, controlling point
控制点测量/控制點測量　control point surveying
控制点坐标/控制點坐標　control coordinate point
控制电机/控制電機,控制電氣機器　control electric machine
控制电缆连接器/控制電纜連接器　control cable coupling
控制电路/控制電路　control circuit
控制电路库用插座/控制電路庫用插座　control circuit socket for shed supply
控制电源/控制電源　control source
控制电源电流表/控制電源電流表　control supply ammeter
控制电源电压表/控制電源電壓計　control supply voltmeter
控制电源隔离开关/控制電源隔離開關　isolating switch for control supply
控制对象/控制對象,受控對象　controlled object
控制阀/[鞽]導閥,導引閥　pilot valve
控制仿真/控制模擬　control simulation
控制符号/管制符號　control symbol
控制高程/控制高程　control elevation
控制工程/控制工程　dominant project
控制机构/操縱機構　control mechanism
控制继电器/控制繼電器,控制電驛　control relay
控制进入的公路/進出管制公路　limited access highway
控制精度/控制精度　control accuracy
控制力矩/控制扭矩　control torque
控制力矩陀螺/控制力矩陀螺系統　control moment gyroscope, CMG
控制流量/支配流量　dominant discharge
控制律/控制律　control law
控制盘/控制盤,控制板　control panel
控制器/控制器　controller, regulator
LED控制器/LED控制器　LED controller
控制区/管制區,受控區域　controlled area
控制区间/控制斷面　control section, controlling

控制试验/管制試驗　control test
控制室/控制室,操縱室　control house, control cabin
控制室操纵屏/控制室操縱板　control room maneuvering panel
控制水平/控制基準　level of control
控制索/控制索　bridle rope
控制塔/控制塔　control tower
控制台/控制臺　console
控制台单元/控制臺單元　control desk element
控制台室/控制[臺]室　control room of station, control room
控制涡流式[直流]扫气/控制漩流趨氣　controlled swirl scavenging
控制系统/控制系統,操縱系統　control system
控制系统模型/控制系統模型　control system model
控制箱/控制箱　control box
控制信号/控制信號　control signal
控制信号检波器/控制信號檢波器,控制信號探測器　control signal detector
控制信息/控制資訊　control information
控制型居民点/控制型居民點　command type residential
控制性详细规划/控制性詳細規劃,控制性細部規劃,細部控制性規劃　detailed regulatory planning
控制性详细规划编制成果/控制性詳細規劃編製成果　products of regulatory detailed planning
控制翼弹头/控制翼彈頭　nose with control wing
控制用空气压缩机/控制用空氣壓縮機　control air compressor
控制增稳系统/控制增益系統　control augmentation system
控制轧制/控制輥軋　controlled rolling
控制站/控制站,控制室　control station
控制指标/控制指數　control index
控制中心报警系统/控制中心報警系統　control center alarm system
控制周期/控制週期,控制循環　control cycle
控制字符/控制字元　control character
口粮/口糧　food ration
扣板/角牽板　gusset plate
扣板式扣件/扣板式鋼軌扣件　pinch plate rail fastening
扣车条件/扣車條件　specified condition for detaining car
扣船/扣留船舶　detention of ship
扣件/軌條扣件,鋼軌扣件,鋼軌扣結裝置　rail fastening
扣件扣压力/扣件扣壓力　toe load of fastening
扣留/扣船,禁運,封港　embargo
扣押船舶/扣押船舶　arrest of ship
枯草层/枯草層　hay layer
枯水季/枯水季　dry season
枯水期/枯水期　dry spell
枯水位/低水位　low water level
骷髅墙/骷髏牆　skull wall, Tzompantli
库场通过能力/庫場貨物週轉量　turnover capacity of storage space
库场作业/庫場作業　storage area operation
库房/庫房,儲藏庫　stock room, storage room
库检/庫檢　examination in depot
库仑土压力理论/庫倫土壓力理論　Coulomb earth pressure theory
库容曲线/[蓄水]容量曲線　storage-capacity curve, capacity curve
库容演算/瀦蓄量演算　storage routing
库塔-茹科夫斯基定理/庫塔-賈克[夫]斯基定理　Kutta-Joukowski theorem
库塔-茹科夫斯基条件/庫塔-賈克[夫]斯基條件　Kutta-Joukowski condition
库址/水庫位置　reservoir site
挎/挎　match
跨度/跨度,跨距　span
跨河桥/跨河橋　river crossing bridge
跨间桥墩/中堅橋墩　standing pier
跨接梁/多支點分荷梁　spreader beam
跨径长/跨距長度　span length
跨境遗产/跨界遺產　transboundary property, cross-border heritage
跨距中点/中央跨孔　center span
跨孔法/跨孔法　cross hole method
跨区客流/區域間客運量　inter-regional passenger traffic
跨声速凹坑/穿音速沈降　transonic dip
跨声速风洞/穿音速風洞　transonic wind tunnel
跨声速流/穿音速流　transonic flow
跨声速面积律/穿音速面積律　transonic area law
跨索系固眼板/跨索儲放眼板　spanwire storage padeye
跨线桥/跨線橋　flyover, overpass bridge, overcrossing
跨越杆/跨越桿　cross-over pole
跨运车/跨載機　straddle carrier
跨中/中央跨孔　center span
跨装/跨載　straddle

块根/塊根　tuberous root
块茎/塊莖　tuber
块料路面/鋪塊路面　block pavement
块石/塊石,巨礫　angular boulder, block stone, boulder
块石拱桥/塊石拱橋　block stone arch bridge
块石基层/泰爾福式基層　Telford base
块石基础/塊石基礎　rubble foundation
块石排水沟/積石排水溝　rubble drain
块式连接件/塊型連接器　block-type connector
块式制动器/塊狀軔,塊狀刹車　block brake
块状绿地/塊狀綠地　green plot
块状生石灰/生石灰,石灰塊　lump lime
快餐店/速食店　fast food restaurant, refreshment store
快动继电器/速動繼電器,速動電驛　quick-acting relay
快剪试验/快剪試驗　quick shear test
快捷旅馆/快捷旅館,經濟旅館　economic hotel
快看显示/快看顯示　quick-look display, quick display
快裂乳化沥青/速斷乳化瀝青　quick breaking emulsified bitumen
快滤池/快沙濾池　rapid sand filter, rapid filter
快滤池滤率/快濾池濾率　rapid sand filter rating
快滤滤筛/快濾濾篩　rapid filter strainer
快门/快門　shutter
快门效率/快門效率　shutter efficiency
快凝液体沥青/快乾液態瀝青　rapid curing liquid asphalt
快砂滤/快濾　rapid sand filtration
快升速度/最良上昇率　best rate climb speed
快速充电/快速充電　fast charge
快速存储记录器/快速擷取記錄器　quick access recorder
快速道路/快速道路,高速道路,高速公路　express way, express road
快速阀/速動閥　quick action valve
快速傅里叶变换/快速富氏轉換　fast Fourier transform, FFT
快速傅里叶变换分析仪/快速傅立葉轉換分析儀　fast Fourier transform analyzer
快速个人公共交通/個人捷運系統　personal rapid transit
快速公共交通系统/捷運系統　rapid transit system
快速公共汽车交通/快速公交　bus rapid transport
快速公共运输/捷運路線　rapid transit
快速固结试验/快速壓密試驗　quick consolidated test
快速减压/快速減壓　rapid decompression
快速减压舱/快速減壓艙　rapid decompression chamber
快速接头/快速接頭,快釋接頭　quick release coupling, quick coupling
快速路/高速道路,高速公路　express way, expressway
快速凝固/快速凝固　rapid solidification
快速凝固材料/快凝材料　rapidly solidified material
快速凝结/閃凝,瞬凝　flash set
快速射击/快射　snap shot, SS
快速式水加热器/直熱式換熱器　instantaneous heat exchanger, instantaneous water heater
快速试验/快速試驗　prompt test
快速稳定装置/快速固定設施　fast settling device
快速响应喷头/快速反應灑水噴頭　fast response sprinkler
快速性/快速性　speedability
快速闸门/閘門　stop gate
快速转辙机/快速開閉轉轍機　quick-acting switch machine
快图设计/快速設計　fast design
快吸继电器/快吸繼電器　quick pick-up relay
快硬硅酸盐水泥/快硬矽酸鹽水泥　rapid hardening Portland cement
快硬硫铝酸盐水泥/快硬硫鋁酸鹽水泥　rapid hardening sulphoaluminate cement
宽带干扰/寬頻干擾　broadband interference
宽带随机振动/寬帶隨機振動　broadband random vibration
宽带信道/寬頻帶通道　wideband channel
宽轨铁路/寬軌鐵路　broad-gage railway
宽混凝土轨枕/寬混凝土軌枕　broad concrete tie
宽跨比/寬跨比　width span ratio
宽频带磁记录器/寬[頻]帶磁帶錄影機　wideband tape recorder
宽深比/寬深比　breadth depth ratio
宽限期/寬限期　period of grace
宽限日期/寬限日期　days of grace
宽翼缘/寬翼緣　wide flange
狂浪/高浪　high sea
狂涛/狂濤　very high sea
矿藏/礦產資源　mineral resources
矿床顶部/礦床頂部　oxidised zone
矿粉/礦粉　mineral powder
矿港/礦港　mine harbor
矿化度/礦化度　mineralization degree

矿化作用/礦質化　mineralization
矿井气/礦井氣,礦山氣體　mine drainage gas, mine gas
矿井水/礦場用水　mine water
矿料/礦物骨材　mineral aggregate
矿棉/礦渣綿　slag wool
矿泉水/礦質水　mineral water
矿砂船/礦砂船　ore carrier
矿砂-石油船/礦砂與油兼用船　ore-oil carrier
矿山法/礦山法　mine tunneling method, mining method
矿山机械厂/礦山機械廠　mining machinery plant
矿山罗盘/礦用羅盤　miner compass
矿山隧道/採礦隧道　mining tunnel
矿山铁路/礦山鐵路　mine railway
矿石车/礦車　ore car
矿物掺和料/礦物混合物　mineral admixture
矿物燃料/礦物燃料,化石燃料　fossil fuel
矿物颜料/礦質顏料　mineral pigment
矿物油/礦[物]油　mineral oil
矿业资源型城市/礦業都市,礦業城　mining city
矿油船/礦砂與油兼用船　ore-oil carrier
矿渣道碴/礦渣路床　slag ballast
矿渣[硅酸盐]水泥/卜特蘭高爐水泥,卜特蘭爐渣水泥　Portland blast-furnace-slag cement
矿渣基层/礦渣基層,熔渣基層　slag base
矿渣棉/礦渣綿　slag wool
矿渣水泥/爐渣水泥　slag cement
矿渣砖/爐碴磚　slag brick
矿质营养/礦質營養,無機營養　mineral nutrition
框坝/框壩,籠壩　crib spur
框标/框標,照準標　collimating mark, fiducial mark
框架/框架,環架　gimbal, frame, skeleton
框架挡土墙/框式牆　crib wall
框架飞轮/懸掛式飛輪　gimbaled flywheel
框架拱/構架拱　framed arch
框架-核心筒结构/框架-核心筒結構　frame-core wall structure
框架-剪力墙/框架剪力牆　frame shear wall
框架-剪力墙结构/框架-剪力牆結構　frame-shear wall structure
框架结构/框架結構　frame structure
框架式星跟踪器/懸掛式星體追蹤儀　gimbaled star tracker
框架误差/水平環誤差　gimballing error
框架箱/框架貨櫃　skeletal container
框架堰/活動架堰　frame weir
框架栈道/構架棧橋　frame trestle
框架-支撑结构/框架加支撐結構　frame-bracing structure
框架自锁/環架鎖定　gimbal lock
框景/框景　enframed scenery
框式家具/模式家具　frame-type furniture
框筒/框架筒　frame-tube
框支剪力墙/框支剪力牆　frame supported shear wall
亏舱/堆貨餘隙,貨載空隙　broken stowage, broken space
亏舱率/堆貨餘隙率　ratio of broken space
亏油率/虧油率　fuel deficit ratio
魁星楼/魁星樓　kuixinglou
馈电电流/饋電電流　feeding current
馈电线路/饋電線　feeder line
馈线链路/饋線鏈路　feeder link
昆山石/崑山石　Kunshan stone
捆绑结构/捆綁式結構　strap-on structure
捆绑[式]火箭/捆綁式發射載具　strap-on launch vehicle
捆包货/捆包貨　baled cargo
捆扎/捆紮　strapping
扩爆药柱/擴爆藥柱　auxiliary booster grain
扩大/擴大　enlargement
扩大初步设计/擴大初步設計　enlarged preliminary design, expanded preliminary design
扩大基础/展式基礎　spread foundation
扩大模数/擴大模數　expanded module
扩底桩/擴底鑽孔樁,鑽孔擴底灌注樁　under reamed pile
扩建/擴建　building expansion
扩径旋压/擴徑旋壓　expanding, bulging
扩孔/擴孔　core drilling
扩频/擴散頻譜,展頻　spread spectrum
扩频通信/擴散頻譜通信,展頻通信　spread spectrum communication
扩频信号/擴散頻譜信號　spread spectrum signal
扩散/擴散,疏散　diffusion, dispersal
扩散边界层/擴散境界層　diffusion boundary layer
扩散场距离/擴散距離　diffuse field distance
扩散工艺/擴散技術　diffusion technique
扩散焊/擴散焊接　diffusion welding
扩散火焰/擴散焰　diffusion flame
扩散连接/擴散結合法　diffusion bonding
扩散钎焊/擴散焊接,擴散硬焊　diffusion brazing
扩散声场/擴散聲場　diffuse sound field
扩散式燃烧器/擴散式燃燒器　diffusion flame burner, spreading-flame burner

扩散退火/擴散退火　diffusion annealing
扩散系数/擴散係數,擴散度　diffusion coefficient, diffusivity
扩声系统/擴音系統　sound reinforcement system
扩束装置/擴束裝置　parallel beam expand device
扩压段/擴散段　diffuser
扩压器/擴散器　diffuser
扩音柱/擴音柱　speaking post in yard
扩音转接机/擴音轉接機　control set for sound amplifying in yard
扩展不确定度/膨脹不確定度　expanded uncertainty
扩展方形搜寻/擴展方形搜索　expanding square search
扩展基础/展式基礎　spread foundation
扩展裂纹/速移裂紋　running crack
扩张激波管/擴張性震波管　expanding shock tube
扩张区/擴張區　expanding area
括纲/收縮綱　purse line
阔大货物/闊大貨物　exceptional dimension freight
阔大货物限界/闊大貨物限界　clearance limit for freight with exceptional dimension, clearance limit for oversize commodities
阔叶林/闊葉[樹]林　broad-leaved forest
阔叶树/闊葉樹　broad-leaved tree
阔叶植物/闊葉植物　broad-leaf plant

L

垃圾/垃圾　garbage
垃圾驳船/垃圾駁船　garbage lighter
垃圾产生量/垃圾產生量　amount of waste generated
垃圾处理/垃圾處理,垃圾處置　refuse treatment, refuse disposal, garbage disposal
垃圾处理场/垃圾處置場　garbage disposal plant
垃圾船/垃圾船,垃圾艇　garbage boat
垃圾发电站/垃圾焚燒發電廠　waste incineration power plant
垃圾分类收集/垃圾收集　sorted refuse collection
垃圾倾倒区/垃圾傾倒區　dumping ground
垃圾清扫船/垃圾清除船　garbage cleaning ship
垃圾清运/垃圾收集　waste collection, refuse collection
垃圾渗滤液/垃圾滲濾液　refuse percolation liquor
垃圾收集点/垃圾收集點　waste collecting station
垃圾收集系统/垃圾收集系統　garbage collection system
垃圾填埋场/垃圾掩埋場　landfill
垃圾箱/垃圾箱　dustbin
垃圾运送槽/垃圾斜槽　garbage shoot, garbage chute
垃圾[转运]站/垃圾轉運站,垃圾中轉站　refuse transfer station, waste station
垃圾资源化/垃圾資源化　reutilization of solid waste
拉拔检验/棒材拉拔檢查　bar drawing inspection
拉板式轴箱定位装置/拉板式軸箱定位裝置　tie-plate type journal box positioning device
拉槽/拉槽　pull trough, trench excavated
拉铲挖掘机/拖斗挖土機　dragline excavator
拉铲挖土机/拖式括土機　drag scraper
拉撑/拉條,支撐線,撐臂　brace
拉出/拉出錨鏈　rouse out
拉出绞车/拉出絞機　outhaul winch
拉出值/斜罩,翼差　stagger
拉到顶/滿懸　close up
拉底/拉底　steady base
拉丁十字形/縱長十字　Latin cross
拉杆/拉桿,縴桿,牽桿　tie bar, pull back on the stick, tension bar

拉杆底座/拉桿底座　bracket base
拉杆式轴箱定位装置/拉桿式軸箱定位裝置　tie-rod type journal box positioning device
拉杆[压管]/拉桿[壓管]　upper cantilever
拉缸/拉缸,氣缸刮削,活塞刮削　cylinder scoring, cylinder scraping, piston scraping
拉格朗日观点/拉格朗日觀點　Lagrange viewpoint
拉沟/開槽溝　slotting
拉钩检查距离/拉鉤檢查距離　car spacing for uncoupled inspection
拉筋/繫索　lacing wire
拉紧索具/拉緊索具　set up rigging
拉进/拉進錨鏈　rouse in
拉进绞车/拉進絞機　inhaul winch
拉开/曳開　haul away
拉开桥/拉開橋　pull-back drawbridge
拉抗试验图/抗拉試驗圖　tension test diagram
拉力/拉力　tension
拉力试验/張力試驗　tension test
拉力桩/張力樁　tension pile
拉毛/拉毛　broom-finish
拉模板/起模板　draw plate
拉模成型/拉模成型　pulling form moulding
拉钮/拉鈕　pull-out button
拉平控制律/拉平控制律　control law of flareout
拉伸荷载/抗拉載重　tensile load
拉伸试验/拉伸試驗　tensile test
拉伸压延成形/張伸成形　stretch-draw forming
拉索结构/拉索結構　guyed structure
拉索式塔架/拉索塔,張索塔　guyed tower
拉索塔/拉索塔,張索塔　guyed tower
拉索桩/繫拉樁　stay pile
拉条/拉條,牽索　stay
拉瓦尔喷管/拉瓦噴嘴　Laval nozzle
拉弯/伸展彎曲　stretch bending
拉弯成形/拉彎成形　stretch-wrap forming
拉线/拉線,拉桿　guy wire, stay wire, stay wire
拉线器/索夾　wire grip
拉削/拉削　broaching, pull broaching
拉形/拉伸成形　stretch forming
拉压刚度矩阵/拉壓勁度矩陣　tensile compressive

stiffness matrix
拉压支座／壓縮張拉支承　tension compression bearing
拉延／拉延　drawing
拉制无缝钢管／無縫鋼管　solid-drawn steel pipe
喇叭天线／漏斗形天線，角形天線　horn antenna
喇叭形进水口／喇叭進水口　bellmouth inlet
喇叭形立交／喇叭形交流道　trumpet interchange
喇叭形尾水管／喇叭形尾水管　hydrancone draft tube
喇叭形直井／喇叭形直井　morning glory shaft
喇嘛塔／喇嘛塔　lama pagoda
蜡封接穗／蠟封接穗　wax seal scion
蜡石／雪花石膏　alabaster
来自／由……來　bound from
来自信号／本臺　Delta Echo, DE
兰金应力状态／蘭金應力狀態　rankine state of stress
兰石／蘭石　lan stone
兰氏平衡器／蘭氏均衡器　Lanchester balancer
兰特庄园／蘭特莊園　Villa Lanterns
拦洪容量／攔洪容量　flood absorption capacity
拦洪水库／滯洪水庫　retarding reservoir
拦截／攔截　interception
拦截攻击／攔截攻擊　intercept attack
拦石墙／攔石牆　stone cut off wall, stone falling wall
拦索／攔索，吊貨控索　bull-rope
拦湾坝／攔門沙壩　bay mouth bar
拦污栅／攔汙柵　trash rack
拦阻钩／捕捉鈎　arresting hook
拦阻索／攔截索　arresting cable
拦阻网／攔截網　arresting barrier
拦阻装置／制動機構　arresting mechanism
栏板挂车／欄板式全掛車　dropside trailer
栏杆／欄杆　railing, balustrade
栏杆柱／欄杆柱，橋頭欄柱　newel post
栏式缘石／欄式緣石　barrier curb
阑额／闌額　vertically positioned architrave, lan'e
蓝脆／藍脆性　blue shortness
蓝钢／藍牌鋼　blue steel
篮球场／籃球場　basketball court
篮球运动／籃球　basketball
篮状种植器／籃狀種植器　basket container
篮子[号型]／籃形號標　basket shape
揽货／攬貨　solicitation
缆／[大]纜，大索　hawser
缆车道／傾斜索道　inclined cableway
缆道挖掘机／索道式挖土機　cableway excavator
[缆]回松／緩緩放鬆　come up
缆绳周径／纜繩週長　circumference of rope
缆索／纜索　hawser, cable
缆索吊装法／纜索吊裝　erection with cableway
缆索防擦垫／纜索防擦墊　mooring mat
缆索卷车／纜索卷車　rope storage reel
缆索起重机／纜索起重機，鋼索吊車　cable crane
缆索散开室／纜索散開室　steel cable splay chamber
缆索铁路／纜索鐵路　cable railway
缆桩／雙繫纜樁　bitts, bollard
廊／廊　porch, gallery, lang
廊道／廊，通道　gallery
廊桥／廊橋　corridor bridge
廊柱园／廊柱園　peristyle garden, patio
朗格尔梁／朗格式梁　Langer girder
朗格尔式桥／朗格式橋　Langer bridge
朗热利耶指数／蘭氏指標　Langelier index
浪高／波高　wave height
浪花／碎浪　breakers
浪击落水／浪擊落水　washed overboard
浪级／波浪等級　wave scale
浪溅区／飛濺帶，濺擊帶　splash zone
浪漫主义／浪漫主義　romanticism, romantic classicism
浪谱分析仪／浪譜分析儀　wave spectra analyzer
浪损／浪損　damage caused by waves
浪向／浪向　sea direction
浪涌保护／突波保護　surge protection
捞缆钩／撈纜機　cable grapnel
捞雷船／撈雷船　torpedo recovery ship
劳动地域分工／勞動區域劃分　regional division of labor
劳动定额／勞動[平均]定額　labor norm, labor ratings
劳动工资管理／勞動工資管理　labor wage management
劳动工资计划／勞動需求的工資計劃　plan of labor and wages
劳动管理／勞動管理　labor management
劳动平衡／勞動力平衡　labor force balance
劳瑞模型／勞里模式　Lowry model
劳氏海事周报／勞氏海事週報　Lloyd Weekly Casualty Report
劳斯汉姆公园／勞斯漢姆公園　Rousham Park
老虎窗／屋頂採光窗，天窗　dormer
老化／老化　ageing, weathering
老化试验／老化試驗　ageing test
老炼／預燒　burn-in

老年人居住建筑/老年人居住建築物，老年人居住房屋 residential building for the senior citizen
老年人设施/老年人設施 facility for the elderly
老年住宅/長者住屋 senior housing
老人(船底α)/老人(船底α) Canopus
烙铁钎焊/鐵錫焊 iron soldering
乐跑活动/樂跑活動 happy running activity
勒脚/護牆腳 plinth
勒诺特尔式园林/勒諾特爾式園林 Le Notre style garden
雷达/雷達 radar
[雷达避碰]试操纵/試操縱 trial maneuvering
雷达标绘/雷達測繪 radar plotting
雷达标校/雷達校準 radar calibration
雷达波束导引装置/雷達波束導引裝置 radar beam-riding guidance device
雷达波吸收结构/雷達吸收結構 radar absorbing structure, RAS
雷达测高计/雷達高度計 radar altimeter
雷达测距器/雷達距離器 radar ranger
雷达测量网/雷達觀測網 radar instrumentation network
雷达测速器/雷達測速器，雷達速率計 radar speedometer
雷达导航/雷達導航 radar navigation
雷达发射机/雷達發射機 radar transmitter
雷达反射率/雷達反射率 radar reflectivity
雷达反射器/雷達反射器 radar reflector
雷达分辨率/雷達解析度 radar resolution
雷达跟踪/雷達追蹤 radar tracking
雷达跟踪站/雷達追蹤站 radar tracking station
雷达海图/雷達海圖 radar chart
雷达回波/雷達回波 radar returns
雷达回波箱/雷達回波箱 radar echo-box
雷达监控/雷達監控 radar monitoring
雷达检测/雷達檢測 radar inspection
雷达间隔/雷達隔離 radar separation
雷达截面[积]/雷達截面積 radar cross section, RCS
雷达进场控制/雷達降落管制 radar approach control
雷达立体观测/雷達立體觀測 radar stereo-viewing
雷达临场指挥/雷達降落管制 radar approach control
雷达模拟器/雷達模擬機 radar simulator
雷达散射计/雷達散射計 radar scatterometer
雷达识别/雷達識別 radar identification
雷达视向/雷達視向 radar look-directions
雷达搜索/雷達搜索 radar search
[雷达]天线罩/天線[外]罩，雷達罩 radome
雷达桅/雷達桅 radar mast
雷达物探法/雷達物探法 radar geophysical survey
雷达陷阱/雷達陷阱 radar trap
雷达信标/雷達信標，雷[達示]標 radar beacon, racon
雷达性能监视器/雷達性能監測器 radar performance monitor
雷达遥感/雷達遙測 radar remote sensing
雷达遥感卫星/雷達遙測衛星 radar remote sensing satellite
雷达引导/雷達引導 radar vectoring
雷达引航图/雷達導航圖 radar navigation chart
雷达引信/雷達引信 radar fuze
雷达应答器/雷達詢答器 radar transponder
雷达罩防静电涂层/雷達罩抗靜電塗層 anti-static coating for radome
雷达侦察系统/雷達偵察系統 radar reconnaissance system
雷达指向标/雷達航標 ramark
雷达最大作用距离/雷達最大效程 maximum radar range
雷达最小作用距离/雷達最小效程 minimum radar range
雷德伯恩体系/雷德伯恩體系 Redburn principle
雷德蒸汽压力/瑞德蒸汽壓 Reid vapor pressure
雷电保护接地/雷電保護接地 lightning protective ground
雷电冲击电流/閃[電]衝擊電流 lightning current impulse
雷电放电敏感度测量/雷電放電靈敏度量測 thunderstreak discharge sensitivity measurement
雷电干扰/雷電干擾 lightning interference
雷电流/雷電流 lightning current
雷管/雷管 detonator
雷光/雷光 thunderlight
雷击/雷擊 lightning stroke
雷击点/雷擊點 point of strike
雷击电磁脉冲/雷電電磁脈衝 lightning electromagnetic pulse, LEMP
雷康/雷[達示]標 racon
雷锚/雷錨 mine anchor
雷诺比拟关系式/雷諾類比關係式 Reynolds analogy relation
雷诺方程/雷諾方程 Reynolds equation
雷诺数/雷諾數 Renold number
雷诺数修正/雷諾數修正 Reynold number

correction

雷诺应力/雷諾應力 Reynold stress

雷氏黏度/雷氏黏度 Redwood viscosity

雷雨/雷雨 thunder storm

雷阵雨/雷陣雨 thunder-shower

垒球场/壘球場 softball field

垒球场草坪/壘球場草坪 softball field turf

垒球运动/壘球 softball

累积加注量/累積加注量 accumulated filling throughout

累积损伤法则/累積損傷律 cumulative damage rule

累积通量/累積通量 fluence

累积延时/累積遲延 cumulative delay

累计当量轴次/累計當量軸次 accumulative equivalent axle

累计式[测量]仪器/累計式[量測]儀器 totalizing measuring instrument

累年值/累年值 normals

肋板/底肋板 floor

肋板桥/肋板橋 ribbed slab bridge

肋钢丝/肋鋼 rib steel

肋拱桥/肋拱橋 ribbed arch bridge

肋骨/肋骨 frame

肋骨拱/肋架拱頂 ribbed vault

肋骨号数/肋骨編號 frame number

肋骨框架/肋骨圈 frame ring

肋距/肋骨間距 frame space, frame spacing

肋片式蒸发器/鰭面蒸發器 finned-surface evaporator

肋腋板/肋腋板 slab with haunched ribs

A类标准不确定度/A類不確定度 type A standard uncertainty

B类标准不确定度/B類不確定度 type B standard uncertainty

类别群体/類別群體 category group

A类部分预应力混凝土/A型部分預力混凝土 type A partially prestressed concrete

B类部分预应力混凝土/B型部分預力混凝土 type B partially prestressed concrete

A类机舱/甲種機艙空間 machinery space of category A

A类机器处所/甲種機艙空間 machinery space of category A

Ⅰ类进近着陆运行/Ⅰ類進近著陸運行 category Ⅰ precision approach and landing operation

Ⅱ类进近着陆运行/Ⅱ類進近著陸運行 category Ⅱ precision approach and landing operation

Ⅲ-A类进近着陆运行/Ⅲ-A類進近著陸運行 category Ⅲ-A precision approach and landing operation

Ⅲ-B类进近着陆运行/Ⅲ-B類進近著陸運行 category Ⅲ-B precision approach and landing operation

Ⅲ-C类进近着陆运行/Ⅲ-C類進近著陸運行 category Ⅲ-C precision approach and landing operation

类属性故障/類屬故障 generic fault

类似色/類似色 analogy color

A类有毒液体物质/A類有毒液體物質 category A noxious liquid substance

B类有毒液体物质/B類有毒液體物質 category B noxious liquid substance

C类有毒液体物质/C類有毒液體物質 category C noxious liquid substance

D类有毒液体物质/D類有毒液體物質 category D noxious liquid substance

棱拱/穹棱拱頂,兩筒正交相貫穹頂 groin vault

棱镜望远镜/折光望遠鏡 prismatic telescope

棱镜直角器/直方稜鏡 prism square

棱条/鑲板條 panel strip

棱形系数/稜形係數,[縱向]稜塊係數 prismatic coefficient

棱[柱体]槽蓄/稜柱蓄積 prism storage

棱柱体抗压强度/稜柱耐壓強度 prismatic compressive strength

棱柱型关节/柱狀關節 prismatic joint

冷拔/冷拔,冷拉伸 cold drawing

冷白色光/冷白光 cold white light

冷拌法/冷拌法 cold mixing method

冷备份/冷備份 cold spare

冷藏车/冷藏車 refrigerator car

冷藏船/冷藏船,冷凍船 cold storage boat, refrigerator ship, refrigerated vessel

冷藏挂车/冷藏全掛車 refrigerated trailer

冷藏货/冷藏貨 refrigeration cargo

冷藏货舱/冷藏貨艙,冷凍貨艙 refrigerated cargo hold

冷藏货车/冷藏車輛 refrigerated vehicle

冷藏货条款/冷凍貨條款 refrigerated cargo clause

冷藏货物/冷凍貨物 refrigerated cargo, freezable freight

冷藏加温车/冷凍暖氣車 refrigerator and heater car

冷藏间/冷凍室,冷房 refrigerated space, refrigerated room

冷[藏]库/冷[藏]庫,冷凍庫 cold store, refrigerating chamber

冷藏箱/冷凍貨櫃 reefer container, refrigerated container
冷藏运输/冷凍運輸 refrigerated transport
冷窗/冷窗 cold window
冷床/冷床 cold bed
冷吹运行/冷吹操作 cold blow-off operation
冷脆/冷脆性 cold brittleness
冷岛效应/冷島效應 cool island effect
冷等离子体/冷離子體,冷電漿 cold plasma
冷底子油/冷底子油 adhesive bitumen primer
冷冻板冷藏车/冷凍板冷藏車 freezing-plate refrigerator car
冷冻货/冷凍貨 frozen cargo
冷冻机厂/冷凍機廠 refrigerator manufactory, refrigerating machine factory
冷冻机油/冷凍油 refrigerator oil
冷冻间/冷凍室 refrigerated chamber
冷冻站/冷凍站 refrigeration station, refrigeration plant room
冷风机/冷氣機 air cooling machine
冷风机组/冷卻裝置 self-contained cooling unit, cooling unit
冷锋/冷鋒 cold front
冷缝/冷縮縫 cold joint
冷高压/冷高壓 cold high
冷工作业/冷作 cold work
冷固化/冷固化,冷定型 cold setting
冷光阑/冷光闌 cold stop
冷氦连接器/冷氦連接器 cold helium connector
冷氦连接器支架/冷氦連接器支架 cold helium connector support mount
冷氦热交换器/冷氦熱交換器 heat exchanger of cold helium
冷害/寒害,冷傷 cold injury
冷黑[背景]/冷黑[背景] cold black
冷滑/冷滑 cold-running
冷季型草/喜冷牧草 cool-season grass
冷季型草坪草/善冷草坪草 cool-season turfgrass
冷剂泵/冷媒泵 refrigerating medium pump
冷加工变形钢筋/冷彎竹節鋼筋 cold worked deformed bar
冷间/冷[藏]房 cold room
冷接/冷縮縫 cold joint
冷紧比/冷緊比,冷緊係數 coefficient of cold-pull
冷紧系数/冷緊係數,冷緊比 coefficient of cold-pull
冷紧张/冷緊張 cold strain
冷浸/冷浸泡 cold soak
冷阱/冷阱 cold trap

冷空间补偿/冷空間補償 cold space compensation
冷库/冷藏倉庫 refrigerated warehouse
冷拉/冷拉 cold stretching
冷拉钢筋/冷拉鋼筋 cold stretched steel bar
冷拉[钢]丝/冷拉鋼線 cold-drawn wire
冷拉率/冷拉率 cold drawn rate
冷拉率控制张拉/冷拉率控制張拉 prestressing by cold drawn rate
冷料输送机/冷集料輸送機 cold aggregate conveyer
冷裂/冷[破]裂 cold cracking
冷磨合/冷磨合 cold breaking in
冷凝/冷凝,縮合,凝結 condensation
冷凝锅炉/冷凝式鍋爐 condensing boiler
冷凝器/冷凝器,冷卻器,冷卻裝置 condenser
冷凝器风道/冷凝器風道 condenser air concentrator
冷凝器真空度/冷凝真空 condenser vacuum
冷凝热交换器/冷凝熱交換器 condensate and heat exchanger
冷暖对比/冷暖對比 contrast between cold and warm color
冷盘管/冷卻盤管,冷卻螺形管 cooling coil
冷喷流试验/冷噴射試驗 cold jet testing
冷平流/冷平流 cold advection
冷屏/冷遮罩 cold shield
冷铺法/冷鋪法 cold laid method
冷铺混合料/冷鋪拌和物 cold laid mixture
冷铺细粒地沥青/石屑冷拌瀝青 fine cold asphalt
冷漆画线机/冷漆劃線機 cold paint road marking machine
冷起动/冷起動 cold start
冷起动试验/低溫啟動試驗 cold start test
冷气团/冷氣團 cold air mass
冷气系统/冷氣系統 pneumatic system, cold gas system
冷气增压系统/冷氣加壓系統 cold gas pressurization system
冷桥/冷橋 cold bridge
冷却/冷卻 cooling
冷却板/冷卻板 cold plates
冷却倍率/冷卻[速]率 cooling rate
冷却法/冷卻法 cooling method
冷却风扇/冷卻風扇,多葉送風機 cooling fan
冷却货物/冷卻貨物 cooled freight
冷却间/驟凍室 chilling room
冷却室/冷卻室 cooling room
冷却水/冷卻水 cooling water
冷却水倍率/冷卻水率 cooling water ratio
冷却水泵/冷卻水泵 cooling water pump

冷却[水]管/冷卻管,冷凝管　cooling pipe, condenser tube
冷却塔/冷卻[水]塔　cooling tower
冷却塔循环水泵房/冷卻塔循環水泵房　pump room for circulating water of cooling tower
冷却温差/冷卻範圍　cooling range
冷却系统/冷卻系統　cooling system
冷却叶片/冷卻葉片　cooling blade, cooled blade
冷却液循环泵/冷卻劑再循環泵　coolant recirculation pump
冷热源设备/冷熱源設備　refrigerating machine chiller
冷色/冷色,寒色　cool color, cold color
冷色表/冷色表　cold color appearance
冷色光/冷光　cold light
冷水泵/冷水泵　cold water pump
冷水器/水冷卻器　water chiller
冷水事故/冷水事故　cold-coolant accident
冷缩/冷收縮　temperature shrinkage
冷缩缝/冷縮縫　cold joint
冷缩配合/收縮配合　shrinkage fit
冷态起动/冷車起動,冷溫起動　cold starting
冷停堆/冷關閉　cold shut-down
冷弯轻钢结构/冷彎輕鋼結構　cold-formed steel framing system, light gage framing system
冷弯试验/冷彎曲試驗　cold bent test
冷弯效应/冷作效應　effect of cold work, effect of cold bending
冷弯型钢/冷彎型鋼　cold formed steel
冷应激/冷應力　cold stress
冷用筑路焦油/冷用路面柏油　cold applied road tar
冷油器/油冷[卻]器　oil cooler
冷源/散熱劑,除熱裝置,熱沈　heat sink
冷轧钢筋/冷軋鋼筋　cold rolled steel bar
冷铸铁轮/冷硬鑄鐵輪,硬面鑄鐵輪　chilled cast iron wheel
冷作/冷作　cold work
冷作用具/鏨子　cold set
离岸/駛離岸　put off
离岸价格/離岸價格,發貨地價格　free on board, FOB
离岸风/離岸風,陸風　offshore wind
离岸流/離岸流,裂流　rip current
离壁衬砌/離壁式襯砌　separate lining
离泊/離泊　clearing from alongside, unberthing
离地间隙测定/離地間隙測定,離地淨空測定　ground clearance measurement
离风/離風　off the wind

离浮筒/離浮筒　clearing from buoy
[离港]出海/出海　put to sea, stand out to sea
离轨/脱軌　deorbit
离轨段/脱軌階段　deorbit phase
离合机构/離合機構　engaging and disengaging gear
离合器/離合器　clutch
离合器操纵装置/離合器操縱機構　clutch operating device
离合器滑转/離合片動　clutch slippage
离解/解離　dissociation
离解度/離解度　dissociaty
离码头/離碼頭　leaving wharf
离去表示/離去表示　departure indication
离去区段/離去區段　departure section
离散化技术/離散式技術　discretization technique
离散选择模型/離散選擇模型　discrete choice model
离散指数/散布指数　dispersion index
离水格子/離水格子　floor rack
离水速度/離水速度　get-away speed
离体保存/離體保存　in vitro conservation
离体培养/體外培養,玻璃器內培養　in vitro culture
离析/析離,偏析　segregation
离线/離線　contact loss
离线测试/離線測試　off-line test
离线率/離線率　contact loss rate
离心包覆/離心包覆　centrifugal coating
离心成型/離心成型　centrifugally spinning moulding
离心持水当量/離心含水當量　centrifuge moisture equivalent
[离心]分油机/油水離心分離器　centrifugal oil separator
离心钢筋混凝土管/離心式鋼筋混凝土管　centrifugal reinforced concrete pipe
离心惯性力矩/離心慣性力矩　centrifugal inertia moment
离心混凝土/離心混凝土　centrifugal concrete
离心混凝土桩/離心式混凝土樁　centrifugal concrete pile
离心机/離心機　centrifuge
离心浇注/離心澆鑄法　centrifugal casting, centrifugal pressure casting
离心离合器/離心離合器　centrifugal clutch
离心力/離心力　centrifugal force
离心喷嘴/離心噴嘴　swirl injector
离心式斗式提升机/離心式斗昇機　centrifugal bucket elevator
离心式风机/離心式壓縮機　centrifugal compressor
离心式机油滤清器/離心式濾油器　centrifugal oil filter

离心式喷注器/離心注射器 centrifugal injector
离心[式水]泵/離心泵 centrifugal pump
离心式水分离器/離心式分水器 centrifugal water separator
离心式通风机/離心風扇 centrifugal fan
离心[式]压缩机/離心[式]壓縮機 centrifugal compressor
离心式制冷压缩机/離心冷凍壓縮機 centrifugal refrigerating compressor
离心脱水/離心脫水 centrifugal dewatering
离心铸铁管/離心式鑄鐵管 centrifugal cast iron pipe
离心铸造/離心鑄造 true centrifugal casting, centrifugal casting
离焰/火焰熄滅 flame lift, lifting
离轴准直拼装式系统/離軸準直模組式系統 off-axis collimated modular system
离轴准直系统/離軸準直系統 off-axis collimated system
离子镀/離子鍍 ion plating
离子镀膜/離子鍍膜 ion film plating
离子感烟探测器/電離煙塵檢測器 ionization smoke detector
离子化静电消除器/離子化靜電消除器 ionizing static eliminator
离子交换/離子交換 ion exchange
离子交换除盐/離子交換法淡化 ion exchange process of desalination
离子交换膜燃料电池/離子交換膜燃料電池 ion exchange membrane fuel cell
离子交换软化/離子交換軟化 ion exchange softening
离子束沉积/離子束沈積 ion beam depositing
离子束辅助沉积/離子束輔助沈積 ion beam assisted depositing
离子束辅助渗镀/離子束輔助滲鍍 ion beam assisted intermingling depositing
离子束混合/離子束混合 ion beam mixing
离子束加工/離子束加工 ion beam machining
离子束溅射/離子束濺射 ion beam sputtering
离子束溅射沉积/離子束濺射沈積 ion beam sputter depositing
离子束蚀刻/離子束蝕刻[法] ion beam etching
离子束增强沉积/離子束增強沈積 ion beam enhanced depositing
离子推力器/離子推進器 ion thruster, ion jet
离子显微镜/離子顯微鏡 ion microscope
离子注入/離子注入,離子植入[法] ion implantation
梨形丁坝/梨形丁壩 pear-ended spur dike
犁式除雪机/V型除雪機 V type snow plough
犁式稳定土搅拌机/鏵犁穩定土拌和機 blade plough soil stabilizer, blade plough stabilized soil road-mixer
篱恒种植/籬恆種植 fence planting
礼拜寺/清真寺 mosque
礼制建筑区/禮制建築區 lizhi building area
里程碑/里程碑 mile stone, kilometer stone
里程标/里程標 mileage post, mile post
里程表/里程表 distance table
里程计/里程計 opisometer
里茨法/李茲法 Ritz method
里坊/里坊 block system, lifang
里坊制/里坊制 traditional neighbourhood unit system
里弄/里弄 linong, hutong, alley
里氏震级/芮氏地震[規模] Richter magnitude
里兹纳指数/雷茲納指數 Ryznar index
理发店/理髮室 barber shop
理化检验/理化檢驗 physical and chemical examination
理货/理貨 tallying of cargoes, tally
理货员/理貨員,記算員 tallyman
理疗科/理療科,理療部 physiotherapy department
理论比冲/理論比衝 theoretical specific impulse
理论弹道/理論彈道 theoretical trajectory
理论空气动力学/理論空氣動力學 theoretical aerodynamics
理论空气量/理論空氣量 theoretical air
理论力学/理論力學 theoretical mechanics
理论燃烧温度/理論燃燒溫度 theoretical combustion temperature
理论热循环/理論熱循環 theoretical heat cycle
理论容量/理論容量 theoretical capacity
理论特征速度/理論特徵速度 theoretical characteristic velocity
理论推力系数/理論推力係數 theoretical thrust coefficient
理论弯沉系数/理論偏轉係數 theoretical deflection coefficient
理论修正法/理論校正法 theoretical correction method
理论烟气量/理論煙道氣量 theoretical quantity of flue gas
理论运价/理論運價 theoretical rate
理网机/理網機 net shifter

理想城市/理想都市　ideal city
理想桁架/理想桁架　ideal truss
理想结构/理想結構　ideal structure
理想流体/理想流體　ideal fluid
理想气体/理想氣體　perfect gas, ideal gas
理想速度/理想速度　ideal velocity
理想弹塑性材料/理想彈性材料　perfect elastoplastic material
理想系统/理想系統　ideal system
理想循环/理想循環　ideal cycle
理性过程规划/理性製程規劃　rational process planning
理性主义/理性主義　rationalism
锂二氧化硫电池/鋰二氧化硫電池　lithium-sulfur dioxide cell
锂金属硫化物电池/鋰金屬硫化電池　lithium-metal sulfide cell
锂离子蓄电池/鋰離子電池　lithium-ions battery
锂亚硫酰氯电池/鋰亞硫醯氯電池　lithium-thionyl chloride cell
力/力　force
力臂调节器/力臂調節器　automatic gear ratio changer
力的传递/力之傳遞性　transmission of force
力的合成/力之合成　composition of forces
力发生器/力發生器　forcer
力法/力法　force method
力-功率反传/力-功率反饋　force-power feedback
力矩包络线/力矩包絡線　moment envelope
力矩电机/扭力馬達　torque motor
力矩迭代法/彎矩迭代法　moment iteration method
力矩反馈试验/力矩回饋試驗　torque feedback test
力矩分配法/力矩分配法,彎矩分配法　moment distribution method
力矩马达/扭力馬達　torque motor
力矩平衡器/力矩調整器　moment compensator
力矩器/扭矩[產生]器　torquer
力锚/著力錨　riding anchor
力偶/力偶　couple of force
力偶臂/偶力臂　arm of couple
力偶分量/偶力分量　component of couple
力平衡式压力传感器/力平衡式壓力轉換器　force-balance type pressure transducer
力平行四边形/力平行四邊形　parallelogram of forces
力谱小时/力譜小時　spectrum hours
力三角形/力三角形　triangle of forces
力系/力系　system of forces

力学测量/力學量測　mechanical measurement
力学环境/力學環境　mechanical environment
力学实验室/力學實驗室　mechanics laboratory
历年平均不保证时/歷年平均不保證時　unassured hour for average year
历史城区/歷史城區　historic district, historic urban area
历史地段/歷史地段,歷史性市區　historic district, historic area
历史地段保护/歷史遺址保護　conservation of historic site
历史风貌/歷史景觀　historic townscape
历史古迹区/歷史古跡區　historical relics area
历史洪水位/歷史洪水位　historic flood level
历史环境/歷史環境　historic environment
历史环境要素/歷史環境因素　historic environment element
历史纪念物/歷史遺產　historical monument
历史价值/歷史價值　historical value
历史建筑/歷史建築　historical building
历史名城/歷史名城　famous historical city
历史名园/歷史名園　historical garden and park
历史圣地类/歷史聖地類　the historic holy land type
历史文化保护区/歷史文化保護區　historic preserved area, conservation district of historic site, historic conservation area
历史文化街区/歷史文化街區　historic and cultural area, historic conservation area
历史文化名城/歷史[文化]名城　historic and cultural city, historic city
历史文化名城保护规划/歷史名城保護規劃　conservation planning of historic city
历史文化名城规划/歷史文化名城規劃　historic city planning
历史文化名村/歷史文化村落,古村落　historic and cultural village, historic village
历史文化名村规划/歷史文化名村規劃　historic village planning
历史文化名街保护规划/歷史街區保護規劃　historic street preservation planning
历史文化名镇/歷史文化名鎮,歷史城鎮　historic and cultural town, historic town
历史文化名镇规划/歷史文化名鎮規劃　historic town planning
历史性城市景观/歷史性都市景觀　historic urban landscape, HUL
历史音/歷史音　historical sound
历史植物地理学/歷史植物地理學　historical plant

geography
历书/曆書,天文曆 almanac
历书时/曆書時 ephemeris time
立板条/道碴墊高 boxing up
立标/標桿 pole beacon, beacon
立标塔/指標塔 beacon tower
立方体强度/立方體強度 cube strength
立方体试块/立方試塊 test cube
立缝/站缝 standing seam
立管/立管,昇導管 vertical pipe, riser, stack
立柜式空气调节器/自給式空調 self-contained air conditioner
立桨/擧槳 toss oars
立交桥/立交橋 overpass, over crossing, grade separation bridge
立接制/無遲緩立即處理接續制 no-delay demand working
立面标记/障礙物體標線 object marking
立面图/立面圖,前視圖 elevation
立式泵/垂直泵 vertical pump
立式的/立式,垂直 vertical
立式风洞/立式風洞 vertical wind tunnel
立式幅面/立式幅面 vertical sheet style
立式锅炉/立式鍋爐 vertical boiler
立式内燃机/立式引擎 vertical engine
立体测图仪器/立體作圖儀 stereoscopic plotting instrument
立体测微仪/立體測微器 stereomicrometer
立体车库/立體車庫 stereo-garage, multi-layer garage
立体电影院/立體電影院 stereophonic cinema
立体分段/立體分段 three-dimensional unit
立体构成/立體構成 stereoscopic composition
立体桁架结构/空間桁架 spatial truss structure
立体花坛/立體花壇 mosaiculture
立体环行交叉/立體圓環道 bridged rotary intersection
立体交叉/立體交叉,立體交口 grade-separated junction, grade separation
立体结构/空間結構 spatial structure
立体跨线设施/立體跨線設施 crossover facility
立体绿化/立體綠化,垂直綠化 vertical greening, vertical planting
立体模型/立體模型 stereoscopic model
立体摄像机/立體照相機 stereocamera
立体摄影/立體攝影 stereophotographing
立体摄影测量/立體攝影測量 stereo triangulation, stereo photogrammetric survey
立体摄影机/立體照相機 stereocamera
立体摄影[术]/立體攝影術 stereophotography
立体停车位/立體停車位 stereoscopic parking space
立体像对/立體像對 pair of stereoscopic pictures, stereopair
立位耐力/正坐性耐力 orthostatic tolerance
立位耐力检查/正坐性耐力檢查 orthostatic tolerance examination
立项/立項 project initiation and approval
立缘石/直立緣石 vertical curb
立爪式装岩机/立爪式裝岩機 vertical claw rock loader
立柱/柱 column
立柱式交通标志/柱式交通標誌 post traffic sign
立柱式托盘/立式托盤 post pallet
立转窗/立懸轉窗 vertical pivot casement
立姿自导弹射座椅/垂直定位彈射座椅 vertical seeking ejection seat
励磁变压器/勵磁變壓器,激磁變壓器 excitation transformer
励磁变阻器/磁場變阻器 field rheostat
励磁电流表/激勵電流表 excitation ammeter
励磁电路/勵磁電路,激勵電路 energizing circuit
励磁机/勵磁機,激磁機 exciter
励磁接触器/勵磁接觸器 excitation contactor
励磁绕组/勵磁繞組 excitation winding
励磁整流装置/勵磁裝置 excitation rectifier device
利物浦伯肯海德公园/利物浦伯肯海德公園 Birkenhead Park
利物浦塞弗顿公园/塞夫頓公園 Sefton Park
利益相关者/利益相關者,利害關係人 stakeholder
利用船体作负极回路的直流单线系统/直流單線船體負極回路系統 negative hull-return DC single system, negative hull-return DC single-wire system
利用频度/利用頻度 usage frequency
利用系数/利用因數,照明因數 utilization factor
沥青/瀝青,柏油 asphalt, bitumen, pitch
沥青薄膜防水层/瀝青膜防水塗層 water proof asphalt membrane
沥青保温罐/瀝青保溫罐 asphalt tank with heating device
沥青泵/瀝青泵 asphalt pump
沥青表面处治/瀝青表面處理 bituminous surface treatment
沥青玻纤瓦/瀝青漬玻璃纖維瓦板 asphalt shingle made from glass felt
沥青秤/瀝青秤 asphalt weigher
沥青抽提仪/瀝青抽提儀 bitumen extractor

沥青稠度/瀝青稠度　bitumen consistency
沥青储罐/瀝青儲槽　asphalt storage tank
沥青道床/瀝青道床　asphalt cemented ballast bed
沥青覆盖层碎石路/護面碎石路　coated macadam
沥青改性剂/瀝青改性劑　asphalt modifier
沥青贯入式路面/瀝青貫入式路面，瀝青貫入碎石路面　bituminous penetration pavement
沥青灌浆/瀝青灌注　asphalt grouting
沥青罐车/瀝青罐車　asphalt truck
沥青滚平机/瀝青鋪築機　asphalt finisher
沥青含量/瀝青含量　asphalt content, asphaltenes content
沥青护石层/瀝青護石屑　coated chipping
沥青混合料/瀝青混合料　bituminous mixture
沥青混合料搅拌设备/瀝青混料拌合裝置　asphalt mixing plant
沥青混合料再生拌和设备/瀝青混合料再生拌和設備　asphalt mixture recycling mixing plant
沥青混凝土混合料/瀝青混凝土混合料　bituminous concrete mixture
沥青混凝土搅拌工厂/瀝青拌和廠　asphalt plant
沥青混凝土路面/瀝青混凝土路面，瀝青混凝土鋪面　bituminous concrete pavement, asphalt concrete pavement
沥青混凝土铺筑机/瀝青混凝土鋪築機　asphalt concrete finisher
沥青混凝土摊铺机/鋪瀝青機，瀝青鋪築機　asphalt paver
沥青混凝土摊铺机试验/瀝青混凝土攤鋪機試驗　asphalt paver test
沥青基层/瀝青底層　black base
沥青基防水涂料/瀝青基防水塗料　asphaltic base waterproof coating
沥青加热设备/熱拌瀝青廠　hot asphalt plant
沥青胶砂/瀝青膠砂　asphalt mastic
沥青胶砂防水层/瀝青膠砂防水塗層　water proof asphalt mastic
沥青流量计/瀝青流量計　asphalt flow meter
沥青路面/瀝青路面　bituminous pavement, asphalt pavement
沥青路面红外线加热器/瀝青鋪面紅外[線]加熱器　asphalt pavement infrared heater
沥青路面火焰加热器/瀝青路面火焰加熱器　asphalt pavement flame heater
沥青路面加热机/瀝青鋪面加熱器　asphalt pavement heater
沥青路面加热器/瀝青面燙板　asphalt surface heater
沥青路面就地再生机/瀝青鋪面原位回收機　asphalt pavement in situ recycling machine
沥青玛蹄脂碎石路面/瀝青瑪蹄脂碎石路面　stone mastic asphalt pavement
沥青喷布机/瀝青灑布機　asphalt sprinkler
沥青喷洒机/瀝青噴灑機　asphalt sprayer
沥青铺面排水沟/瀝青邊溝　asphalt gutter
沥青铺面天沟/瀝青邊溝　asphalt gutter
沥青铺筑机/瀝青鋪築機　asphalt finisher
沥青清漆/瀝青溶液　bituminous solution
沥青熔化加热装置/瀝青熔化加熱裝置　asphalt melting and heating device
沥青乳化机/瀝青乳化機　bitumen emulsifying machine
沥青乳化设备/瀝青乳化設備　bitumen emulsifying plant
沥青乳剂灌浆/包殼防滲法　shell-perm process
沥青乳面层/瀝青乳面層　fog-coat
沥青乳液/瀝青乳液，水柏油　bituminous emulsion
沥青洒布机试验/瀝青灑布機試驗　asphalt distributor test
沥青洒布宽度测定/瀝青灑布寬度測定　distribution width measurement
沥青洒布量测定/瀝青灑布量測定　asphalt distribution measurement
沥青砂/瀝青砂，砂拌瀝青　sand asphalt, asphalt sand
沥青砂浆/瀝青膠泥　asphalt mortar, asphalt cement
沥青石屑/瀝青石屑　asphalt chip
沥青碎石混合料/瀝青碎石混合料　bituminous macadam mixture
沥青碎石路面/瀝青碎石路[面]　bituminous macadam pavement, asphalt macadam
沥青摊铺机/瀝青灑布機　asphalt spreader
沥青土壤/瀝青穩定土壤　asphalt soil
沥青稳定处理/瀝青穩定處理　bituminous stabilization
沥青稀浆/瀝青糊　asphalt slurry
沥青稀浆封层/瀝青糊封閉層，瀝青糊封閉底漆　asphalt slurry seal coat
沥青稀释油/快溶油　flux oil
沥青纤维管/瀝青纖維管　pitch fiber pipe
沥青油/瀝青稀釋油　asphaltic oil
沥青罩面/瀝青塗面層　asphalt overlay
沥青纸/油毛紙　bituminised paper
沥青贮仓/瀝青儲倉　asphalt storage
例行复述/例行複述　routine repetition
例行呼叫/例行呼叫　routine calls
例行试验/例行測試，日常試驗　routine test

例行维护/例行維修,例行保養　routine maintenance
砾类土/礫質土,礫[石]土　gravelly soil
砾砂/礫砂　gravelly sand
砾石/礫石,石礫　gravel
砾质土/礫質土,礫[石]土　gravelly soil
粒度/單位尺度　unit size
粒度分类/粒徑分類法　grain size classification
粒度累积曲线/粒徑累積曲線　grain size accumulation curve
粒化高炉矿渣粉/礦渣微粉　ground granulated blast furnace slag
粒径/粒徑,粒度　grain size
粒径分布曲线/粒徑分布曲線　grain size distribution curve
粒径分析/粒徑分析,粒度分析,粒級分析　granular metric analysis, grain size analysis
粒径曲线/粒度曲線　grain size curve
粒料/粒狀物質　granular material
粒料改善土路/粒料改善土砂道　aggregate treated earth road
粒料空隙率/粒料空隙率　void of mineral aggregate
粒料路面/粒料路面　granular pavement
粒料稳定土基层/集料穩定土基層　aggregate stabilized soil base
粒玄岩/粗粒玄武岩　dolerite
粒雪/砂雪　granular snow
粒子分离器/粒子分離器　particle separator
粒子辐射/粒子輻射　particle radiation
粒子辐射损伤/粒子輻射損害　particle radiation damage
粒子辐照试验/粒子輻照試驗　particle irradiation test
粒子图像测速/質點影像速度儀　particle image velocimetry
粒子云/粒子雲　particle cloud
连/連接　connect
连带责任/連帶責任　joint and several liability
连岛沙洲/繫岸砂洲　tombolo
连动脱钩装置/連動脫鉤裝置　simultaneous disengaging unit
连杆/連[接]桿　connecting rod
连杆比/連桿比　connecting rod length-crank radius ratio
连杆长度/連桿長度　length of connecting rod
连杆衬套/連桿瓦　connecting rod bush
连杆盖/連桿蓋　connecting rod cap
连杆校正器/連桿對準器　connecting rod aligner
连杆螺母/連桿螺母　connecting rod nut
连杆螺栓/連桿螺栓　connecting rod bolt
连杆驱动/連桿傳動　rod drive
连杆体/連桿體　connecting rod body
连杆轴承镗床/連桿對準承缸機　connecting rod bearing boring machine
连杆轴瓦/連桿軸瓦　connecting rod bearing shell
连拱作用/連續拱效應　continuous arch effect
连挂速度/接合速率　coupling speed
连接/連接,接駁　connection
连接板/連接板　connecting plate
连接补给/連接整補　connected replenishment
连接点/連接點　junction point
连接方式/連接模　connection mode
连接杆/連接桿　pipe link
连接公海/與公海相通　connected with the high seas
连接件/連接裝具,結合件　connecting fitting, connector
连接角钢/連接角鋼　connection angle
连接拉杆/制動缸槓桿拉桿　cylinder lever connecting rod
连接缆/連接線　connecting line
连接链环/連接鏈環　lugless joining shackle, connecting link, joining link
连接器/連接器　coupler
连接器件/連接硬體　connecting hardware
连接桥/連橋　cross structure
连接箱/連接箱,接線箱,分線箱　connecting box
连接卸扣/連接[接]環　joining shackle, connecting shackle
连梁/連梁　coupling wall-beam
连通管/内部連接管　interconnecting pipe
连系梁/繫梁　tie beam
连续波/連續波　continuous wave
连续波测量雷达/連續波儀表級雷達　continuous wave instrumentation radar, CW instrumentation radar
连续波多普勒引信/連續波都卜勒引信　continuous wave Doppler fuze, CW Doppler fuze
连续波激光雷达/連續波雷射雷達　continuous wave laser radar, CW laser radar
连续波激光引信/連續波雷射引信　continuous wave laser fuze, CW laser fuze
连续波雷达/連續波雷達　continuous wave radar
连续波雷达跟踪系统/連續波雷達追蹤系統　continuous waves radar tracking system
连续补加/連續補加　continuous topping
连续沉箱/牆式沈箱　wall caisson
连续倒塌/連續塌陷　progressive collapse

连续堤/連續堤 continuous levee
连续底座/連續基腳 continuous footing
连续电流/連續電流 continuous current, permanent current
连续方程/連續方程式 continuity equation, equation of continuity
连续感/連續感 sense of continuity
连续刚构桥/連續剛構橋 continuous rigid frame bridge
连续拱桥/連拱拱橋 continuous arch bridge
连续供暖/連續供暖 continuous heating
连续供氧流量调节器/連續供氧流量調節器 constant oxygen flow regulator
连续构件/連續構件 continuous member
连续灌溉/續灌 continuous irrigation
连续焊缝/連續焊接 continuous weld
连续桁架/連續桁架 continuous truss
连续基础/連續基腳 continuous footing
连续级配/連續級配 continuous grading
连续计算命中点/連續計算撞擊點 continuously computed impact point, CCIP
连续计算命中线/連續計算撞擊線 continuously computed impact line, CCIL
连续计算投放点/連續計算釋彈點 continuously computed release point, CCRP
连续加注/連續加載 continuous loading
连续监测/連續偵測 continuous monitor
连续结构/連續結構 continuous structure
连续介质/連續介質 continuous medium, continuum, continuum medium
连续空间/連續空間 continuous space
连续力学/連體力學 continuum mechanics
连续梁/連續梁 continuous beam
连续梁桥/連續梁橋 continuous beam bridge, continuous girder bridge
连续路径控制/連續路徑控制 continuous path control
连续路面/薄層鋪面 sheet pavement
连续爬升法/直接爬昇法 continuous climbing method
连续配筋混凝土路面/連續配筋混凝土路面,連續鋼筋混凝土鋪面 continuously reinforced concrete pavement, continuous reinforced concrete pavement
连续砌拱/連續砌拱 laying arch continuously
连续墙法/隔牆法 diaphragm wall method, slurry wall method
连续桥面/連續橋面 continuous deck
连续绕片/連續繞組 continuous wind

连续日/連續自然日 consecutive days, running days
连续式风洞/連續性風洞 continuous wind tunnel
连续式风洞能量比/連續式風洞能量比 energy ratio of continuous tunnel
连续式轨道电路/連續軌道電路 continuous track circuit
连续式机车信号/連續式機車信號 continuous type cab signaling
连续式交通量观测站/連續式交通量觀測站 continuous traffic count station
连续式沥青混合料搅拌设备/連續瀝青混凝土混合設備 continuous asphalt mixing plant
连续式调速系统/連續型調速器 continued type speed control system
连续数据系统/連續資料系統 continuous data system
连续索道/連續索道 continuous ropeway
连续系统/連續系統 continuous system
连续性/連續[性] continuity
连续性交通流/連續交通流量 continuous traffic flow
连续性模型/持續演進模式 continuity model
连续性原理/連續性原理 principle of continuity
连续运动/連續運動 continuous motion
连续值守/連續守值 continuous watch
连续铸造/連續鑄造 continuous casting
连续自检/連續自我測試 continuous self test
连作/連作 continuous cropping
帘式混凝土块/簾式混凝土塊 curtain block
莲花式柱/蓮飾柱 lotus column
莲蓬式喷注器/蓮蓬式噴頭,非撞擊射流噴嘴 showerhead injector
联暗光/聯頓光 group occulting light
联动补给装置/聯動補給裝置 housefall rig
联动触发信号/邏輯程式基本信號 basic signal for logical program
联动反馈信号/聯動反饋信號 feedback signal from automatic equipment
联动交通信号/聯動交通信號 coordinated traffic signals
联动控制/連鎖控制 coordinated control
联动控制信号/聯動控制信號 control signal for automatic equipment
联动脱钩装置/聯動脫鉤裝置 simultaneous disengaging gear
联杆操作补给装置/聯桿操作補給裝置 burton rig
联管燃烧室/環管燃燒室 cannular combustor
联轨站/分歧站,會合站 junction station

联合厂房/聯合廠房　workshop under one roof
联合船位/混合定位　combined fix, CF
联合动力装置/複合式動力裝置　combined power plant
联合国船舶登记条件公约/船舶登記條件聯合國公约　United Nations Convention on Conditions for Registration of Ships
联合国国际货物多式联运公约/國際貨物多式聯運聯合國公約　United Nations Convention on International Multimodal Transport of Goods
联合国国际贸易运输港站经营人赔偿责任公约/國際貿易終端站營運人責任聯合國公約　United Nations Convention on the Liability of Operators of Terminals in International Trade
联合国海洋法公约/聯合國海洋法公約　United Nations Convention on the Law of the Sea
联合国气候变化框架公约/聯合國氣候變化框架公約　United Nations Framework Convention on Climate Change
联合国生物多样性公约/聯合國生物多樣性公約　United Nations Convention on Biological Diversity
联合桁架/组合桁架　compound truss
联合基础/聯合基腳　combined footing, combined foundation
联合集尘截断塞门/聯合集塵截斷塞門　combined dirt collector and cut-out cock
联合救助协调中心/聯合救助協調中心　associated rescue coordination center
联合设计专题/聯合設計專題　joint design studio
联合投标/聯合投標　joint ventures bidder
联合挖泥机/聯合挖泥機　combined dredger
联合运输/協調聯運　intermodal transport
联合战术信息分发系统/聯合戰術情報分配系統　joint tactical information distribution system, JTIDS
联机控制/連線控制,在線控制　on-line control
联机诊断/線上診斷　on-line diagnostics
联检/聯檢　joint inspection
联结层/聯結層,瀝青路面的中間層　binder course
联立式住宅/連棟住宅　row house, terrace house, townhouse
联络线/聯絡線,連接線　linking up line, order wire
联排式住宅/連棟住宅　row house, terrace house, townhouse
联片供热/聯片供熱,集中供熱　group heating
联闪光/聯閃光　group flashing light
联试程序/集成測試程式　integration test program
联锁/聯鎖　interlocking

联锁道岔/聯鎖道岔　interlocked switch
联锁电路/聯鎖電路　interlocking circuit
联锁机构/聯鎖裝置　interlock arrangement, interlocking gear, interlocking device
联锁区/聯鎖區　interlocking area
联锁设备/聯鎖設備　interlocking equipment
联锁图表/聯鎖圖表　interlocking chart and table
联锁箱/轉轍電路控制器　point detector
联锁箱联锁/點檢測器聯鎖　interlocking by point detector
联锁桩/嚙合樁　interlocking pile
联调仿真器/整合測試模擬器　integration test simulator
联系电路/聯絡電路　liaison circuit
联系梁/繫梁　tie beam
联运货/聯運貨　through transport cargo, through cargo
联运提单/聯運載貨證券　through bill of lading
联轴器/聯結器　coupling
廉价房屋/廉價住宅　low-cost housing
廉租房/廉租房　low-rent housing
练习生/實習生,學徒　apprentice
炼钢厂/鋼廠　steel plant
炼苗/幼苗鍛煉　seedling hardening
炼制品/精煉品　refined products
链/鏈　cable, chain
链板给料机/板式給料機　slat feeder
链缠锚/錨障　foul anchor
链传动/鏈傳動　chain drive
链船/鏈船　chain boat
链斗式挖沟机/鏈斗式挖溝機　chain bucket trencher
链斗式挖掘机/鏈斗式挖掘機　chain bucket excavator
链斗式挖泥船/梯斗式挖泥船　ladder bucket dredger
链斗式挖泥机/梯斗戽泥機　elevator dredger
链斗卸车机/鏈斗卸車機　unloading machine with chain bucket
链斗装车机/鏈斗裝載機　loading machine with chain bucket
链斗装置/鏈斗裝置　bucket arrangement
链接电缆/聯絡電纜　link cable
链节/[錨鏈]節,錨鏈長度　length of chain cable, shot
链锯/鏈鋸　chain saw
链路管理/鏈接管理　link management
链路控制规程/鏈接控制程式　link control procedure
链路设计/鏈接設計　link budget
链路协议/鏈接協定　link protocol

链轮/鏈輪　gypsy wheel, sprocket
链式起重机/鏈式起重機　chain hoist
链式输送机/鏈條輸送機　chain conveyor
链式水尺/帶形水尺　tape gage
链条滑车/鏈滑車　chain block
链条战斗部/連續桿戰鬥部　continuous rod warhead
链条张紧机构/緊鏈器　chain tightener
链形悬挂/鏈形懸掛　overhead contact line with catenary, longitudinal suspension
链抓力/鏈抓著力　holding power of chain
链子钩/螺旋聯結器　screw coupling
良好船艺/良好船藝　good seamanship
良好级配/良級配　well graded
良好锚地/良好泊錨地　sung anchorage
良好能见度/能見度甚佳　visibility very good
良种繁育/栽培變種　cultivar maintenance
凉亭/涼亭,露臺　gazebo, garden pavilion
梁垫/承梁枕　bolster
梁端缓冲梁/梁端緩衝梁　auxiliary girder for controlling angle change
梁腹/腹板,大肋骨　web
梁高/梁高　beam depth, girder depth, depth of girder
梁拱/拱高,弧高　camber
梁内导管空隙真空加压试验/梁内導管空隙真空加壓試驗　duct void examination by vacuum pressure test
梁桥/梁橋,桁橋　beam bridge, girder bridge
梁式承台/格子梁　grillage girder
梁式钢拱架/梁式鋼拱架　steel beam centering
梁式楼板/梁式樓板　beam and slab floor
梁式起重机/梁式起重機　beam crane
梁式桥/梁式橋　girder bridge, beam bridge
梁腋/托肩,拱腰　haunch
梁肘板/梁肘板,梁腋板　beam knee
梁柱结构/梁柱結構,梁桿結構　beam and column structure
梁座/梁座　beam seat
量测站/置儀點　instrument station
量程/量程,量測範圍　span
量杆/量桿　metering rod
量片辊/計量轆　metering roller
量筒/量筒　measuring cylinder
量隙规/餘隙規　clearance gage
量雪标杆/雪橇　snow stake
量雪桩/雪橇　snow stake
粮仓/糧[食倉]庫,穀倉　granary, grain depot, grain storage
粮库/糧[食倉]庫,穀倉　granary, grain depot, grain storage
粮食加工厂/糧食加工廠　grain processing plant
粮食库/糧食庫,給養艙　provision store, provision room
两半角[转向]法/兩半角轉向法　method of altering course by two half angles
两层独立公寓/複層公寓,樓中樓　maisonette
两层式机械汽车库/兩層式機械汽車庫　two story mechanical garage
两船间距/兩船間距　ship clearance
两次混凝/兩次混凝　double coagulation
两点检查/兩點檢查　released by checking two sections
两端约束梁/束制梁　constrained beam
两段造船法/兩船段建造法　two-part hull construction
两管制水系统/雙管式水系　two-pipe water system
两级管网系统/兩級系統　two stage system
两级喷射系统/兩級噴射系統　two-step injection system
两级增压柴油机/兩級增壓柴油機　two-stage supercharged diesel engine
两脚插头/兩腳插塞　two-pin plug
两阶段设计/二階段設計　two-step design, two-phase design
两栖植物/兩棲植物　amphiphyte
两栖作战舰艇/兩棲作戰艦艇　amphibious warfare ships and crafts
两索套/雙肢吊索　two-leg sling
两系悬挂/兩級懸掛　two-stage suspension
两相短路/兩相短路　two-phase short-circuit
两相流/二相流　two-phase flow
两相流换热/二相流熱傳遞　two-phase flow heat transfer
两相燃烧/兩相燃燒　two-phase combustion
两相位信号/雙時相號誌　two-phase signal
两用渠道/兩用管道,雙目標管道　dual-purpose canal
两自由度陀螺仪/雙自由度陀螺儀　two degree-of-freedom gyro
亮度/亮度,發光率　luminance, brightness, brilliance
亮度对比/亮度對比　luminance contrast
亮度范围/亮度範圍　brightness range
亮度分析/光度分析　photometric analysis
亮度计/亮度計,光度計　photometer, luminance meter
亮[度]温度/亮度溫度　brightness temperature

亮度纵断面/亮度縱斷面[圖] luminance profile
[量的]数值/[量的]數值 numerical value of a quantity
[量的]约定真值/[量的]約定真值 conventional true value of a quantity
[量的]真值/[量的]真值 true value of a quantity
量纲/量綱,量的因次 dimension of a quantity
量纲分析/量綱分析,因次分析 dimensional analysis
量纲为1的量/量綱爲1的量 quantity of dimension one
量化/量[子]化 quantization, digitization, quantizing
量化单位/量子化單位 quantization unit
量累积曲线/流量累積曲線 discharge mass curve, flow mass curve
量调节/變流量調節,可變流量控制 variable flow control
[量]值/[量]值 value of a quantity
量值传递/量值傳遞,量值傳播 dissemination of the value of a quantity
量制/量系統 system of quantities
量子效率/量子效率 quantum efficiency
疗养地/休養地 health resort
疗养公园/療養公園 sanatorium park
疗养花园/療養花園 restorative gardens
疗养院/療養院,勒戒所 sanatorium
檪檐枋/檪檐枋 liaoyanfang
料槽/料槽 trough
料场调查/料場調查 materials field investigation
料斗/料斗 hopper
料石/料石,方石,修琢石 ashlar, dressed stone
料石拱桥/方石拱橋 ashlar arch bridge
料石墙/塊石牆 rubble wall
瞭头/在艏瞭望 look-out on forecastle
瞭望/瞭望 look-out
瞭望车/瞭望車 observation car
瞭望窗/觀察窗,視察窗 observation window
瞭望台/桅桿[瞭]望臺 crow nest
列板/列板,板列 strake
列车/列[車] train
列车保留/列車保留 train stock reserved
列车闭路电视/列車有線電視 cable TV on train
列车编成辆数/列車編成輛數 number of cars in a train
列车编组顺序表/列車編組順序表 train consist list, train list
列车编组站/列車編組站 train make up station
列车标志/列車標記 train marker
列车车次/列車編號 train number

列车车底需要数/列車車底需要數 number of passenger train set required
列车冲击力/列車衝擊力 impact force of train
列车出发正点率/列車出發正點率 percentage of punctuality of train despatched to total train
列车带电平均电流/列車帶電平均電流 average current of charging train
列车带电运行时分/列車行車時間 train running time on load
列车等级/列車等級 train class
列车等线/列車等線 train waiting for a receiving track
列车颠覆/列車傾覆 train overturning
列车调度电话/列車調度電話 train dispatching telephone
列车动力学/列車動力學 train dynamics
列车防护/列車防護 train protection
列车防护无线电通信/列車防護無線電通訊 radio communication for train protection
列车分离/列車分離 train separation
列车公里/列車公里 train kilometer
列车供电电路/列車供電電路 power supply circuit for train
列车供电绕组/列車供電繞組 train coach supply winding
列车管/列車管 train pipe
列车管压差/列車管壓差 train pipe pressure gradient
列车广播/列車廣播 broadcasting for train
列车横向摇摆力/列車橫向搖擺力 lateral swaying force of train
列车活塞作用/列車活塞作用,車輛活塞作用 piston action of train
列车活载/列車活載 live load of train
列车加开/列車加開 running of extra train
列车接近报警器/列車接近警告裝置 train approach warning device
列车接近传感器/列車接近感測器 train approaching sensor
列车接近告警无线电通信/列車接近告警無線電通訊 radio communication for warning of train approaching
列车进路/列車路線 train route
列车客座利用率/列車客座利用率 percentage of passenger seats utilization per train
列车空气动力学/列車空氣動力學 train aerodynamics
列车空隙作业时间/列車空隙作業時間 working

time between trains
列车扣除系数/列車扣除係數　coefficient of train removal
列车拉伸/列車拉伸　train running out
列车离心力/列車離心力　centrifugal force of train
列车旅客无线电话/列車旅客無線電話　passenger radiotelephone on train
列车密度/班次密度　train density
列车平均电流/列車平均電流　average current of train
列车平均载客人数/列車平均載客人數　average number of passengers carried per train
列车平均总重/列車平均總重　average train gross weight
列车牵引力/列車牽引力　tractive force of train
列车去向/列車去向　train destination
列车确报/列車確報　train list information after departure
列车确报电报/列車確報電報　train out report telegraph
列车事故/行车事故　train accident
列车速度检测仪/列車速度監視裝置　train speed monitoring device
列车停运/列車停運　withdrawal of train
列车尾部防护/列車尾部防護　train rear end protection
列车尾部风压反馈/列車尾部風壓反饋　train rear end air pressure feedback
列车尾追/列車尾追　train tail collision
列车位置表示/列車位置表示　train position indication
列车无线电调度通信/列車無線電調度通信　radio dispatching communication for train
列车无线电调度系统/列車無線電調度系統　train radio dispatching system
列车无线电调度转接分机/列車無線電調度轉接分機　transfer branch set for radio train dispatching
列车无线电调度总机/列車無線電調度總機　office equipment for radio train dispatching
列车无线电通信/列車無線電通訊　train radio communication
列车无线电通信系统/列車無線電通信系統　train radio communication system
列车压缩/列車運轉　train running in
列车业务无线电通信/列車服務無線電通訊　radio communication for train service
列车有效电流/列車有效電流　effective current of train

列车与线路相互作用/列車與線路相互作用　track-train interaction
列车预报/列車預報　train list information in advance
列车员/列車乘務員　train attendant
列车员室/列車員室　attendant room
列车运缓/列車運緩　train running delay
列车运行表/列車運行圖　train diagram
列车运行控制系统/列車運行控制系統　train operation control system
列车运行时刻表/班次時刻表,行車時刻表　timetable
列车运行调整/列車運行調整　train operation adjustment
列车运行图/列車運行圖　train diagram
列车运行线/列車運行線　train path
列车运行正点率/列車運行正點率　percentage of punctuality of train running to total train
列车运转曲线/列車運行曲線　train operation curve
列车长/列車乘務長　train conductor
[列车]折叠/折疊　jack knifing
列车正面冲突/列車衝撞　train collision
列车制动/列車制動　train braking
列车制动简易试验/列車制動簡易試驗　train brake simplified test
列车制动力/列車制動力　braking force of train
[列车制动]溜放试验/列車制動溜放試驗　coasting braking test
列车制动全部试验/列車制動全部試驗　train brake overall test
列车制动试验器/列車制動試驗器　train brake tester
列车重量标准/列車重量標準　railway train load norm
列车自动控制装置/列車自動控制裝置　automatic train control device
列车自动调速/列車自動調速　automatic train speed regulation
列车自动停止装置/列車自動停止裝置　automatic train stop device
列车自动限速/列車速度自動監督　automatic train speed restriction
列车自动运行/自動列車運轉　automatic train operation
列车纵向动力/列車縱向動力　longitudinal dynamic force of train
列检/列檢　train examination
列检无线电通信/旅客列車無線電通訊　radio

communication for train inspection
列头柜/列頭櫃　array cabinet
列植/列植　linear planting
列置/列置　row placed
列柱法/列柱[法]　columniation
劣质燃料/劣質燃料　inferior fuel
烈度表/震級　intensity scale
烈士纪念公园/烈士紀念公園　martyr memorial park
猎户座/獵户座　orion
猎雷舰/獵雷艦　mine hunter
猎雷舰艇/獵雷艦，獵雷艇　mine hunter
猎潜艇/驅潛艇　submarine chaser
裂变产物/核子分裂產物　fission product
裂变能/分裂能　fission energy
裂变中子/分裂中子　fission neutron
裂冰[作用]/裂冰[作用]　calving
裂缝/裂縫，裂紋，缺陷　crack, flaw
裂缝[分布]图/裂紋圖形，裂縫樣式　crack pattern
裂缝灌注/裂縫灌注　crack grouting
裂缝间距/裂縫間距　crack spacing
裂缝控制/裂縫控制　crack control, cracking control
裂缝控制等级/裂縫控制等級　classes for cracking control
裂缝宽度/裂縫寬度　crack width
裂缝宽度限值/裂縫開口限值　limit of crack opening
裂缝声发射检测/裂縫聲發射檢測　crack detecting by acoustic emission
裂缝土/裂紋黏土　fissured clay
裂化气/裂煉氣，裂解氣　cracked gas
裂化燃料油/裂化燃料油　cracked fuel oil
裂环连接/裂環接合　split ring connection
裂解处理/分開處理　split treatment
裂流/裂流，離岸流　rip current
裂纹/裂紋，裂痕，裂縫　crack
裂纹扩展寿命/裂紋擴展壽命　crack propagation life
裂纹扩展速率/裂痕成長率　crack growth rate
裂纹扩展阻力/抗裂紋擴展性　crack growth resistance
裂纹敏感性/裂縫敏感度　crack sensitivity
裂纹试验/破裂試驗　cracking test
裂纹探测仪/探傷儀　crackmeter
裂纹形成寿命/裂縫孕育期間　crack initiation life
裂纹形状因子/裂紋形狀因子，裂痕形狀因數　crack shape factor
裂纹张开位移/裂縫開口寬度　crack opening displacement, COD
裂隙/裂隙　crack, fracture, fissure

裂隙带/破碎帶　fractured zone
裂隙模型/裂隙模型　model of fissuration
裂隙黏土/裂紋黏土　fissured clay
裂隙泉/裂縫泉　fracture spring
裂隙水/裂隙水　fissure water
裂隙硬黏土/裂隙硬黏土　stiff fissured clay
裂线定理/裂線定理　fractureline theorem
邻避设施/鄰避設施　NIMBY facility
邻道干扰/鄰接波道干擾　adjacent channel interference
邻角/鄰角　adjacent angle
邻近色/鄰近色　adjacent color
邻居密度/鄰里密度　neighborhood density
邻里/鄰里　neighborhood
邻里单位/鄰里單位　neighborhood unit
邻里单位理论/鄰里單位理論　theory of neighborhood unit
邻里公园/鄰里公園　neighborhood park
邻里关系/鄰里關係　neighborhood relationship
邻里社区/鄰里社區　neighborhood community
邻里修复/社區重建，社區復建　community rehabilitation
邻里中心/鄰里中心　neighborhood center
邻图索引/鄰接海圖索引　index of adjoining chart
邻线干扰/鄰線干擾　interference from neighboring line
林窗/林窗　forest gap
林带/林帶　forest belt
林地/林地，森林地區　wood land
林分/林分，植物群叢　stand
林分改造/林分改造　stand improvement
林分结构/林分構造　stand structure
林分密度/林分密度　stand density
林分组成/林分組成　stand composition
林冠盖度/林冠密度　density of leaf canopy
林冠线/樹冠層　crown canopy
林间隙地/林間隙地　open space in woodland
林间小道/林間小道　path in woodland
林木引种/林木引種　introduction of exotic species
林木种子/森林樹木種子　forest tree seed
林区道路/林道　forest road
林下空间/林下空間　forest space
林下种植/林下種植　underwood planting
林相/林相　forest form
林相图/林相圖　stock map, stand map
林业/林業　forestry
林[业用]地/林[業用]地　forestry land
林荫大道/林蔭大道，林蔭大街　boulevard

林荫路/林蔭路　mall
林荫停车场/林蔭停車場　tree-lined parking lot
林缘线/林緣線　forest margins line
林植/造林，栽植造林，林業林　forest planting
临床选拔/臨床選拔　clinical selection
临检权/臨檢搜索權　right of visit and search
临街道路/銜接道路　frontage road
临街面/臨岸線　frontage
临界邦德数/臨界邦德數　critical Bond number
临界闭伞速度/臨界閉傘速率　critical closing speed
临界表面/臨界表面　critical surface
临界车道/臨界車道　critical lane
临界出水量/臨界流量　critical discharge
临界初稳性高度/臨界初定傾[中心]高度　critical initial metacentric height
临界舵角/臨界舵角　stalling rudder angle
临界风速/臨界風速　critical wind speed
临界干扰力矩/臨界擾動力矩　critical disturbance torque
临界高度/臨界高度　critical height
临界含盐量/臨界鹽量　critical dissolved salt
临界荷载/臨界荷載，臨界負載　critical load
临界间隙/臨界間隙　critical gap
临界角/臨界角　danger angle, critical angle
临界净正抽吸压头/臨界淨有效吸水頭　critical net positive suction head
临界开伞动压/臨界開傘動態壓力　critical parachute open dynamic pressure
临界开伞高度/臨界開傘高度　critical parachute open altitude
临界开伞速度/臨界開傘速度，臨界開傘速率　critical opening speed, critical parachute open speed
临界空化数/臨界空化數　critical cavitation number
临界孔隙比/臨界空隙比　critical void ratio
临界裂纹深度/臨界裂縫深度　critical crack depth, crack depth at fracture
临界流量/臨界流量　critical discharge
临界马赫数/臨界馬赫數　critical Mach number
临界密度/臨界密度　critical density
临界面/臨介面　critical plane
临界浓度/臨界濃度　critical concentration
临界坡度/臨界坡度　critical slope, critical grade
临界牵引力/臨界牽引力　critical tractive effort
临界倾覆力臂/臨界翻覆力臂　critical capsizing lever
临界倾覆力矩/臨界翻覆力矩　critical capsizing moment
临界倾角/臨界傾角　critical inclination
临界深度水表/臨界水深管制計　critical depth water meter
临界实验/臨界試驗　criticality test
临界速度/臨界速度，臨界速率　critical speed
临界通量/臨界通量　critical flux
临界温度/臨界溫度　critical temperature
临界舷角/臨界相對方位　critical relative bearing
临界压力比/臨界壓力比　critical pressure ratio
临界压曲荷载/臨界縱向彎曲載荷　critical buckling load
临界应力/折屈應力　crippling stress
临界值/臨界值　critical value
临界转速/臨界速率，共振轉速　resonance speed, critical speed
临界状态/臨界狀態　critical state, critical condition
临界阻尼/臨界阻尼　critical damping
临界阻尼值/臨界阻尼值　critical damping value
临空面/自由面　free surface, free face
临空墙/防爆炸隔間牆　blastproof partition wall
临射检查/放飛前檢查　prelaunch inspection
临时便线/臨時便線　shoofly
临时灯/臨時燈　provisionary light
临时堆放区/臨時堆放區　temporary stacking area
临时高压消防给水系统/臨時高壓消防給水系統　temporary high-pressure fire water system
临时工程/臨時工程，臨時項目　temporary works, temporary project
临时合同/草約　provisional contract
临时检验/臨時檢驗，臨時檢查　occasional survey
临时建设/臨時工程　temporary construction
临时建筑物/臨時建築　temporary building
临时看台/臨時支座　temporary stand
临时路标/臨時標記　temporary marker
临时旅客列车/臨時旅客列車　extra passenger train, additional passenger train
临时设施/臨時設施　temporary facilities
临时通告/臨時通告　temporary notice
临时围墙/工地圍籬　hoarding
临时围堰/臨時圍堰　temporary cofferdam
临时无灯浮标/臨時無燈浮標　temporary unlighted buoy
临时无线电信标业务/臨時無線電示標業務　temporary radio beacon service
临时线路/臨時線路　temporary track
临时修理/臨時修理，小修　temporary repair
临时许可/臨時放行　provisional release
临时用地/臨時用地　temporary land use, temporary site
临时展厅/臨時展覽室　temporary exhibition hall

临时支撑/撑柱支撑　shoring
临时支护/臨時支架　temporary support
临时桩/臨時樁　temperary pile
临水土戗/臨水戧堤　waterside banquette
临险抢护/緊急修復,應急修理　emergency rush engineering, emergency repair
临修线/臨修線　temporary repair siding
淋水试验/淋水試驗　water pouring test
磷化/磷酸鹽處理　phosphating
磷化铟太阳电池/磷化銦太陽電池　indium phosphide solar cell
磷酸电解质燃料电池/磷酸電解質燃料電池　phosphoric acid electrolyte fuel cell
鳞茎/鱗莖,球根　bulb
檩/檩　purlin, lin
檩条/檩[條],桁條　purline, purlin
灵壁石/靈壁石,靈璧石　Lingbi stone
灵壁石/靈壁石,靈璧石　Lingbi stone
灵活厂房/靈活廠房　flexible workshop
灵敏部分/敏感元件　sensitive element
灵敏度/靈敏度,敏感度　sensitivity, sensibility
灵敏度比/靈敏度比　sensitivity ratio
灵敏度时间控制/靈敏度時間控制,靈敏度時控　sensitivity-time control, STC
灵敏黏土/靈敏性黏土　sensitive clay
灵敏阈[值]/靈敏閾值　sensitive threshold
灵巧引信/智慧型引信　smart fuze
灵台/靈臺　Ling Tai platform garden
灵囿/靈囿　Ling You hunting garden
灵沼/靈沼　Ling Zhao water garden
铃流/環流,環形電流　ring current
凌波性/凌波性　seakindliness
凌[日]/淩[日]　transit
陵墓/墓地　graveyard
陵寝类/陵寢類　mausoleum type
菱形编队/菱形編隊　diamond formation
菱形号型/菱形號標　diamond shape
菱形交叉/菱形道岔　diamond crossing
菱形立交/菱形交流道,鑽石形交流道　diamond interchange
菱形翼型/菱形翼形,雙楔翼形　double wedge aerofoil profile
零/零　zero
零部件制造人批准书/零組件製造者核準書　parts manufacturer approval
零层端子/零層端子　terminals of layer zero of a relay rack
零磁差线/無磁偏線　agonic line

零担办公车/零擔辦公車　office car for peddler train
零担仓库/零擔倉庫　scattered freight storehouse
零担货物/零擔貨物　less-than-carload freight
零担[货物]运输/零擔貨物運輸　less-than-carload transport
零担货物中转站/零擔貨物中轉站,零擔運費中轉站　less-than-carload freight transhipment station, part-load transhipment station
零担货运站/零擔貨運站　less-than-carload terminal
零担运价/零擔運價　less-than-carload rate
零点误差/零點誤差　zero error
零动量方式/零動量模式　zero momentum mode
零动量系统/零動量系　zero momentum system
零断面/零截面　zero section
零方向/零方向　zero direction
零高程/零高程　zero elevation
零功率实验/零功率實驗　zero-power experiment
零过载飞行/失重飛行　zero-g flight
零件检验分类/零件檢驗分類　inspection and classification of part
零件明细表/零件明細表　parts list
零件清洗机/零件清洗機　part washer
零件修理/零件修理　part repair
零-零弹射/零-零彈射　zero-zero ejection
零能耗建筑/零級能量建築　zero energy building
零排污/零排汙　zero blowdown
零偏/零偏　zero offset
零漂/零點漂移　zero drift
零平衡接收机/迪克接收機　zero-equilibrium receiver, Dicke receiver
零燃油重量/無油重量　zero fuel weight
零升力/無昇力　zero lift
零升力角/零昇力[攻]角　zero lift angle
零升力矩/零昇力力矩　zero lift moment
零升阻力/零昇力阻力　zero lift drag
零湿度指数/零濕度指數　zero moisture index
零时化/零時化　zeroed time
零时基点/零時基準點　zero time reference
零售商店/零售店　retail store
零速度面/零速度面　zero-velocity surface
零速度轴/無速軸　axis of zero velocity
零位测量方法/零位量測法,量測衡消法　null method of measurement
零位测试/零測試　zero testing
零位调节/零位調整　zero adjustment
零下温度/零下溫度　subzero temperature
零序电流互感器/零序比流器　zero-sequence current transformer

零序电流继电器/零[相]序繼電器　zero-sequence current relay
零液位/零液位　zero liquid level
零应力轨温/零應力軌温　stress free rail temperature
零载试验/零載重試驗　zero load test
零值误差/零值誤差　zero error
零值星历表/零值星曆表　null ephemeris table
零重力/零重力　zero gravity
零姿态/零姿態　zero attitude
岭/嶺,[山]脊,隆起緣　ridge
领班/領班,工頭　foreman
领海/領海　territorial water, territorial sea, marine belt
领海基线/領海基線　baseline of territorial sea
领航/領航　navigation
领事馆/領事館　consulate
领事签证发票/領事簽證發票　consular invoice
领域/領地,地區,分據　territory
领域性/領域性,勢力圈　territoriality
另有相反的规定除外/除另有明文規定外　except otherwise herein provided
溜冰场/溜冰場,滑冰場　ice rink, outdoor ice skating rink
溜车不利条件/溜車不利條件　unfavorable condition for car rolling
溜车方向/溜車方向　rolling direction
溜车有利条件/溜車有利條件　favorable condition for car rolling
溜放部分/滾放部分　rolling down section
溜放调车/溜放調車　fly-shunting, coasting, jerking
溜放进路自动控制/溜放進路自動控制　automatic switching control of humping yard by route
溜放速度/滑跑速率　rolling speed
溜放速度自动控制/溜放速度自動控制　automatic rolling down speed control
溜放线/滾放線　group lead track
溜泥槽/滑槽　chute
刘易斯数/劉易斯數　Lewis number
留榍/留榍　leave some
留置权/留置權　right of lien, lien
流杯渠/流杯渠　liubeiqu
流冰/流冰,漂冰　ice floes, drift ice, ice drift
流场/流場　flow field
流场测量/流場測量　flow field survey
流场品质/流場品質,氣流參數,流動特性　flow quality, flow field quality
流场相似/流場相似　flow field similarity

流程图/流程圖　flow chart, flow diagram
流出/漫溢,溢出　spill
流出物/流出物　effluent
流刺网/流刺網　drift net
流刺网振网机/流刺網振網機　drift net shaker
流动分离/流動分離　flow separation
流动空间/流動空間　flowing space
流动类型/流型　pattern of flow
流动人口/流動人口　floating population
流动水分点/注動水分點　flow moisture point
流动台试验/轉臺試驗　flow table test
流动图像数字化/流動圖像數位化　digitalization of flow picture
流动显示/流場觀察,流場可視化　flow visualization
流动装载机/機動裝載機　mobiloader
流动资金/流動資金,營運資金　working capital, current capital, liquid fund
流动资金周转/流動資金週轉　turnover of current capital
流固耦合/流固耦合　fluid-solid coupling
流管/流線管　stream tube
流函数/流函數　stream function
流滑/崩潟　flow slide
流化床锅炉/流動床[燃燒]鍋爐　fluidized bed firing boiler, fluidized bed boiler
流化床离子交换/流體化床離子交換　fluidized bed ion exchange
流化剂/流化劑　fluidizer agent
流径/流徑　flow path
流量/流量,通水量　flow discharge
流量变换器/流水傳遞器　flow transmitter
流量表/流量計　flowmeter
流量过程线/流量延時曲線　flow duration curve
流量计/流量計,流速計　flow meter
流量控制/流量控制　flow control
流量控制阀/流量控制閥　flow control valve
流量-历时曲线/延時面積曲線　duration area curve
流量面积/流量面積　discharge area
流量调节阀/流量調節閥,流量控制閥　flow control valve
流量图/流量圖　discharge diagram
流量系数/流量係數　flow coefficient, discharge coefficient
流量总和曲线/流量總和曲線　integrated flow curve
流料箱/前槽　head box
流黏土/液性黏土　quick clay
流谱/流型,流動型式　flow pattern
流砂/流砂,漂沙　quick sand, drift sand

流水/流水　flowing water
流水孔/排洩孔　drain hole
流水压力/流水壓力,水流壓力　flowing water pressure, pressure of water flow
流速/流速　current velocity
流速杆校正数/測速桿校正　velocity rod correction
流速计/速度計,測速器　velometer, velocity meter
流速继电器/流量繼動機　flow relay
流速水头系数/流速水頭係數　velocity head coefficient
流态床热处理/流體化床熱處理　heat treatment in fluidized bed
流态混凝土/連混凝土　flowing concrete
流态条件/砂流條件　quick condition
流态显示/流態顯現　flow visualization
流体/流體　fluid
流体动力学理论/流體動力學理論　hydrodynamics theory
流体黏性/流體黏度　viscosity of fluid
流体特征/流體特徵　characteristic of fluid
流体质点/流體質點　fluid particle
流通过程运输/流通過程運輸　transport in circulation
流网渔船/流網漁船　drift fishing boat, drift netter, drifter
流网作业/流網捕魚　drift fishing
流纹岩/流紋岩　rhyolite
流线/流線　stream line
流线弯曲效应/流線曲率效應　stream line curvature effect
流线型车体/流線型車體　streamlined car body
流线型舵/流線型舵　hydrofoil rudder, stream line rudder
流向/流向　current direction, direction of current
流向探头/流向探針　flow direction probe
流星/流星　meteor
流星体/流星體　meteoroid
流星体模式/流星體模式　meteoroid model
流型/流型,流動型式　flow pattern
流压差/漂移角,流偏角,偏流角　drift angle
流域/[河川]流域　river basin, drainage basin
流域保护/水域保護　water territory protection
流域补给/流域補注　basin recharge
流域产水量/流域出水量　drainage basin yield
流域迟滞/流域延時　basin lag
流域分界线/分水線　drainage divide
流域灌溉/池式灌溉　basin irrigation
流域规划/流域規劃　river basin planning
流域开发/流域開發　river basin development
流域漏失/流域漏失　watershed leakage
流域渗漏[量]/流域漏失　watershed leakage
流域指数/流域指數　basin index
流域滞时/流域延時　basin lag
流域综合开发/流域綜合開發　integrated river basin development
流云顶/雲頂　cloud top
流值/流量值　flow value
流阻/流阻　flow resistance
琉璃瓦/釉面磚　glazed tile
硫分/硫含量　sulfur content
硫黄胶泥/硫磺灰泥　sulfur plaster
硫黄锚固/硫磺錨固,硫磺水泥砂漿錨定　sulphur cement mortar anchor, sulphur cement mortar anchorage
硫黄泉/硫泉　sulphur spring
硫黄石山要塞国家公园/硫磺石山要塞國家公園　Brimstone Hill Fortress National Park
硫侵蚀/硫腐蝕　sulphur corrosion
硫泉/硫磺泉　sulphurous spring
硫酸根离子/硫酸根離子　sulphate ion
硫酸钠法/硫酸鈉法　sodium sulphate method
硫酸盐还原菌/硫酸鹽還原菌　sulfate reducing bacteria
硫酸阳极[氧]化/硫酸陽極處理　sulfur acid anodizing
硫细菌/硫[細]菌　sulfur bacteria
硫循环/硫循環　sulfur cycle
硫质黏土/硫孔黏土　solfataric clay
馏程/蒸餾範圍　distillation range
六分仪/六分儀　sextant
六分仪高度/六分儀高度　sextant altitude
六分仪交会法/六分儀交會法　method of intersection by sextant
六分仪校正/六分儀校正　sextant adjustment
[六分仪]器差/儀器[誤]差　instrument error
六分仪误差/六分儀誤差　sextant error
[六分仪]指标杆/[六分儀]指臂　index arm of sextant
六氟化硫断路器/六氟化硫斷路器,SF_6斷路器　sulfur hexafluoride circuit-breaker
六孔探头/六孔探頭　six holes probe
龙骨/龍骨,托梁　keel, joist
龙骨墩/中心墩　keel block
龙骨式机器人/脊椎式機器人　spine robot
龙骨线/龍骨線　keel line
龙骨翼板/龍骨翼板列,A板列　garboard strake

龙骨坐垫/龍骨坐墊　dock keel
龙卷风/龍卷風　tornado
龙门式吊运车/跨載車線　straddle truck
龙门桅/龍門柱　goal post
龙舟运动/龍舟運動,賽龍舟　dragon boat competition
笼型异步电动机/籠型非同步電機　squirrel-cage asynchronous motor
隆起/[砂]脹　bulking
隆起地基/膨脹地　swelling ground
娄宿三(白羊α)/婁宿三(白羊α)　Hamal
娄宿一(白羊β)/婁宿一(白羊β)　Sheratan
楼板/樓板　floor plate, slab, floor
楼层/樓層　floor, story
楼层剪力/層剪力　story shear force
楼层配线设备/樓層配線設備　floor distributor
楼盖/樓蓋　floor system
楼盖构造/樓面構造　floor construction
楼阁/樓閣　multi-storied building
楼阁式塔/樓閣式塔　multi-storied pagoda in louge style
楼廊/樓廊　two-storied gallery, gallery house
楼面地价/樓面地價　land price per floor area, land value per unit floorage
楼面面积指数/建地空間指數,容積指數　floor space index
楼梯/樓梯,扶梯　stairs
楼梯间/樓梯間　staircase
楼梯栏杆/樓梯欄杆　railing balustrade
楼梯平台/樓梯平臺　stair landing
楼梯望柱/橋頭欄柱,欄杆柱　newel post
楼座/樓座,陽臺　balcony, upper circle
漏报警/滲漏警報　leakage alarm
漏爆概率/漏爆概率　miss burst probability
漏乘/漏乘　missing a bus, missing a train
漏电保护/對地漏電保護　earth leakage protection
漏斗/漏斗　hopper
漏斗车/漏斗車　hopper car
漏斗门风手动传动装置/漏斗門風手動裝置　pneumatic-manual hopper door operating device
漏斗棚架法/漏斗棚架法　hopper-shed support tunnelling method
漏斗式溢洪道/直井式溢洪道　glory hole spillway
漏斗式柱头/大頭柱頂　flared column head
漏浆/滲漏　leakage
漏解锁/漏解鎖　missing release
漏景/漏景　leaking through scenery
漏率/[滲]漏率　leak rate
漏气/漏氣　blow-by
漏气量/漏氣量　gas leak quantity
漏气率/漏氣率　gas leak rate
漏气损失/洩漏損失　leakage loss
漏水/漏水　water leakage
漏水含水层/滲漏含水層　leaky aquifer
漏水检查/漏水調查　water waste survey
漏水口/排水孔　scupper
漏水率/漏水率　rate of leakage
漏水试验/漏水試驗　leakage test
漏水田/漏水田　leaking paddy field
漏损和破损/漏損和破損　leakage and breakage
漏损检测/漏損檢查　examination of leakage and breakage
漏锁闭/漏鎖閉　missing locking
漏泄电流/漏電流　leakage current
漏泄模/洩漏模　leaky mode
漏泄同轴电缆/漏洩同軸電纜　leaky coaxial cable
漏泄同轴电缆传输方式/漏洩同軸電纜傳輸方式　transmission mode with leaky coaxible cable
漏炸/未起爆　non-initiation
漏指令/漏指令　missed command
漏指令概率/漏指令概率　missed command probability
漏装/漏裝　neglected loading
炉舱棚/鍋爐艙棚,鍋爐艙圍壁　boiler room casing
炉撑/爐撐　stay
炉床/爐箄　grate
炉床面积/爐箄面積,爐格面積　grate area
炉底灰/爐底灰　furnace bottom ash
炉口/爐口　fire hole
炉门/爐門,防火門　fire door
炉内软水/鍋爐內軟化水　water softened in boiler
炉内脱硫法/爐內脫硫法　desulfurization in the boiler
炉膛/爐膛　furnace
炉膛容积/爐內容積　furnace volume
炉外软水/鍋爐外軟化水　water softened out of boiler
炉灶/爐灶　range
炉渣/爐碴　furnace clinker
炉渣粉/爐碴粉　quenched blast furnace slag
炉中钎焊/爐內硬焊,爐錫焊　furnace brazing, furnace soldering
栌斗/櫨斗　cap block, ludou
卤代烷灭火系统/鹵碳滅火系統　halocarbon extinguishing system
卤化物灭火系统/海龍滅火系統　halon fire

extinguishing system
卤素查漏仪/鹵素測漏器　halogen leak detector
卤素灯/金屬鹵素燈　metal halide lamp
卤钨灯/鹵鎢燈　tungsten halogen lamp
鲁班经/魯班經　Classic of Luban, Luban Jing
陆标/岸[上目]標　landmark
陆标船位/地文定位　terrestrial fix, TF
陆标定位/岸標定位　fixing by landmark
陆侧/陸側,陸邊　landside
陆地地球站/衛星陸上電臺　land earth station, LES
陆地地球站时分多路复用信道/衛星陸上電臺分時多工頻道　LES TDM channel
陆地电台/陸上[電]臺　land station
陆地机场/飛行場　airfield
陆地卫星/陸地衛星　land satellite
陆地贮材/陸地瀦蓄　land storage
陆风/陸風　land breeze
陆封/陸閘　land lock
陆基导航系统/陸基導航系統　ground-based navigational system
陆界/陸界,陸圈　geosphere
陆区/陸邊,陸側　landside
陆圈/陸圈,陸界　geosphere
陆上移动卫星业务/陸上行動衛星業務　land mobile-satellite service
陆生植物/陸生植物　terrestrial plant
陆线费/陸線費　land-line charge
陆用发动机/陸用引擎　land engine
陆用式/陸用式　land type
陆源沉积/造陸堆積物　terrigenous deposit
录音电话机/錄音電話機　recording phone set
录音棚/錄音室　recording studio, recording room
录音室/錄音室　recording studio, recording room
鹿沼土/鹿沼土　deer bog soil
路拌法/路拌法　road mixing method
路拌机械试验/路拌機械試驗　road mixing machine test
路拌式稳定土搅拌机/穩定土拌和機　soil stabilizer, stabilized roadmixer
路边车道/緣側車道　curb lane
路边公园/路邊公園　roadside park, street park
路边花坛/路邊花壇　roadside flower bed
路边停车/路旁停車　side parking, curb parking
路边停车场/路邊停車處　kerb parking space
路边种植/路邊種植,路旁植樹　roadside planting
路标/道路交通標誌　road sign
路槽/路槽　road trough
路槽排水/基層排水　subbase course drainage

路侧带/路邊地帶　curb side strip
路侧发展/路旁發展　roadside development
路侧广播/路旁無線電廣播　roadside radio broadcasting
路侧摩阻/路緣摩擦　marginal friction
路产/路産　highway property
路岛端/路島端　approach nose
路堤/路堤,堤防　embankment
路堤边坡/路堤邊坡　side slope of embankment, fill slope
路堤填料/路基填料　embankment fill material, embankment filler, filling material of embankment
路段通行能力/路段容量　road section capacity
路幅/路幅　roadway
路拱/路拱　crown, road crown
路拱曲线/路拱曲線　crown curve, camber curve
路滑标志/路滑標誌　skid sign
路基/路基　subgrade, road bed, formation subgrade
路基边沟/路基邊溝　side ditch of subgrade
路基边坡/路基邊坡　side slope of subgrade
路基病害/路基損害　subgrade defect, subgrade lesion
路基承载板测定/路基承載板測定　determination of bearing slab of subgrade, bearing slab method for subgrade testing, bearing plate test on subgrade
路基冲刷/路基侵蝕　subgrade erosion
路基冲刷防治/路基沖刷防護,路基侵蝕防護　subgrade erosion protection
路基防护/路基防護　subgrade protection
路基工程/路基工程　subgrade engineering
路基含水量/路基含水量　subgrade moisture content
路基横断面/路基橫段面　subgrade cross-section
路基机械/路基機械　subgrade machine, machine for roadway work
路基挤起/路基擠起　subgrade bulge, subgrade squeeze out
路基加固/路基加固　subgrade strengthening
路基精整机/路基精整機　subgrade fine trimmer
路基临界高度/路基臨界高度　critical height of subgrade
路基面/路基面　subgrade surface, formation
路基面宽度/路基面寬度　width of the subgrade surface, formation width
路基面修整机/路基整形機　subgrader
路基排水/路基排水　subgrade drainage
路基强度/路基強度　subgrade strength
路基设计/路基設計　subgrade design
路基设计高程/路基設計標高　design elevation of

subgrade
路基松软/路基軟點　soft spot of road bed
路基土/路基土壤　subgrade soil
路基稳定性/路基穩定性　subgrade stability
路基下沉/路基沈降　subgrade settlement
路际串音/通道間干擾　inter-channel crosstalk
路肩/路肩　road shoulder
路肩高程/路基面,施工基面　formation level, shoulder level
路肩缺口/路肩缺口　shoulder gap
路径/路徑　path
路径重复精度/路徑反復精度　path repeatability
路径加速度/路徑加速度　path acceleration
路径精度/路徑準確度　path accuracy
路径衰减校准/航道衰減校正　path attenuation correction, PAC
路径速度/路徑速度　path velocity
路径速度波动量/路徑速度變動　path velocity fluctuation
路径速度重复精度/路徑速度反復精度　path velocity repeatability
路径速度精度/路徑速度準確度　path velocity accuracy
路宽/路寬　road width
路况/路況　highway condition
路况登记/路況登記　highway condition registration
路况调查/路況調查　highway condition investigation, road condition survey
路况检查/路況檢驗　highway condition inspection
路况巡视/路況巡視　highway condition patrol
[路面]凹坑/路面坑洞　pot-hole
路面板/路面板　pavement slab
路面板唧泥/路面板唧泥　slab pumping
路面边线/路面邊線　border-line marking
路面变形/路面變形　surface deformation
路面标线/路面標線　pavement marking, road marking
路面病害摄影组合仪/路面病害攝影組合儀　photographic road survey group
路面补强/路面補強,路面強化　pavement strengthening
路面补强设计/路面加固設計　pavement strengthening design
路面沉陷/路面沈陷　pavement depression
路面粗糙度/路面粗糙度,地面粗糙度　surface roughness
[路面]单向排水/單向排水　single slope drainage
路面垫层/路面墊層　bed course of pavement

路面调查/路面調查　pavement investigation
路面定期调查/路面定期調查　pavement periodical investigation
路面翻修/路面翻修　pavement recapping
路面工程/路面工程　pavement engineering
路面管理系统/鋪面管理系統　pavement management system, PMS
路面滑溜/路面滑溜　surface skidding
路面积水/路面積水　surface gathered water
路面基层/鋪路基礎　base course of pavement
路面激光测试仪/路面雷射測試儀　laser road surface tester
路面加热机/路面加熱器　road heater
路面检测评价系统/路面檢測評價系統　pavement monitor and evaluation system
路面接缝间距/縫距　joint spacing
路面结构/路面結構,鋪面結構　pavement structure
路面结构设计/路面結構設計　pavement structure design
路面结构组合设计/路面結構組合設計　pavement structural composition design
[路面]抗滑试验/防滑試驗　anti-skid test
路面抗滑性能/路面抗滑性能　pavement skid resistance condition, PSRC
路面快速加载试验机/線式加速載入　accelerated loading facility, ALF
路面宽度/路面寬度　pavement width
路面宽度变化路段标志/路寬變更線　pavement-width transition marking
[路面]裂缝度/裂縫度　cracking ratio
[路面]裂缝率/裂紋率　cracking rate
路面面层/路面面層　surface course of pavement
路面摩擦系数/地面摩擦系數,表面摩擦係數　surface friction coefficient
路面排水/路面排水　pavement drainage
路面疲劳寿命/路面疲勞壽命　fatigue life of pavement
路面平整度/地面平坦度,表面平坦度　surface evenness
路面平整度测定仪/測面儀,測平儀　viameter, profilometer
路面评价/鋪面評估　pavement evaluation
路面评价模型/路面綜合評價模型　pavement evaluation model
路面破损率/路面損害率　pavement damage ratio
路面铺装率/路面鋪裝率　paved ratio
路面强度/鋪面強度　pavement strength
路面清扫机/路面清掃機　pavement sweeping

machine
路面曲率仪/路面曲率儀 surface curvature apparatus
路面设计/路面設計 pavement design
路面使用质量指标/路面使用品質指數 pavement operating quality index
[路面]双向排水/雙向排水 double slope drainage
路面松散/路面損壞,路面鬆弛 ravelling, surface loosening
路面随机调查/路面隨機調查 pavement random investigation
路面特性/路面特性 pavement characteristics
路面透水度测定仪/路面透水度測定儀 surface permeameter
路面文字标记/路面文字標記 pavement lettering marking
路面铣削机/路面銑削機,鉋路機 pavemill
路面线纹/路面線紋 score line
路面再生/鋪面再生 pavement recycling
[路面]凿开/打除 chiselling
路面整修机/道路整面機 road finisher
路面状况指数/路面狀況指數 pavement condition index
路名标志/路名標誌 marking designation
路内人员伤亡/路內人員傷亡 casualty of railway man, on-duty casualty
路牌/路牌,標牌 tablet
路牌闭塞/路牌閉塞系統 tablet block system
路牌携带器/路牌傳遞袋 tablet pouch
路牌自动授收机/路牌自動授收機 automatic tablet exchanger
路旁绿化带/路側綠帶 roadside green belt
路签/路簽 train staff
路签灯/路簽燈 train staff lamp
路签授受器/路簽授收機 staff exchanger, tablet exchanger
路签携带器/路簽攜帶器,路簽傳遞器 staff pouch
路签自动授收机/路簽自動授收機 automatic staff exchanger
路堑/路塹 cutting, road cutting
路堑边坡/路塹邊坡 cutting slope, side slope of cut
路堑平台/路塹平臺 platform of cutting, berm in cutting
路堑石方爆破/路塹石方爆破 rock cutting blasting, rock blasting in cut
路堑式明洞/路塹式明洞 cut-type open cut tunnel, cut-type tunnel without cover, cut-type gallery
路容/路容 highway appearance

路上停车点/露天停車場 road parking lot
路外人员伤亡/路外人員傷亡 casualty of non-railway man, not on-duty casualty
路外停车/路外停車 offstreet parking
路网密度/路網密度 density of road network
路网容量/路網容量 road network capacity
路网性编组站/路網性編組站 network marshalling station
路线测量/路線測量,路線勘查 route survey
路线计算机辅助设计/路由電腦輔助設計 route computer aided design
路线控制点/路線控制點 control point of route
路线连续性/路線連續性 route continuity
路线平面图/路線平面圖 route plan
路线三维空间设计/路線三維空間設計 route three dimensional space design
路线设计/路線設計 route design
路线线形/路線線形 route alignment
路线优化设计/路線最佳設計 route optimum design
路线增设/路線增設 track expansion
路线障碍/路線障礙 track obstruction
路线指示标志/路線指示標誌 road identification sign
路用机车/路用機車 locomotive of service train, service locomotive
路用加热柏油/路用加熱柏油 hot applied road tar
路用列车/路用列車 railway service train
路缘标示/缘石標線 curb marking
路缘带/[車行道]路緣帶 marginal strip
[路]缘石/路緣[石],緣石 curb
路障/路障,障礙 roadblock
盝顶/平屋頂,平塔頂 truncated roof
露出/露出量 emergence
露地花卉/露地花卉 outdoor flower
露点[温度]/露點 dew-point temperature
露骨/裸面 bare surface
露瞄栅楼板/透空樓板 open floor
露台/露臺,平臺 terrace
露台绿化/露臺綠化 terrace greening
露天仓库/露天倉庫 open air repository, open air depot, open storage
露天堆场/露天堆場 open stacking yard
露天堆货场/露天堆貨場 open freight storage
露天甲板/露天甲板 open deck
露天甲板空间/露天甲板空間 open deck space
露天开采/露天開採 strip mining
露天烤炉/露天烤爐 open barbecue
露天音乐台/露天音樂臺 outdoor music stand

露天游泳场/露天游泳場　outdoor playground
露营地/露營地　camping site
闾里/閭里，鄰里，鄰居　lv li, Chinese traditional neighborhood
旅次车种/旅次車種　mode of trip
旅馆式办公楼/旅館式辦公樓　service office building
旅馆式公寓/商務住宅　service apartment
旅居车/旅居掛車　motor caravan
旅客/旅客，乘客　passenger
[旅客]安检区/安檢區　security check area
旅客波动系数/旅客波動係數　passenger number fluctuation coefficient
旅客车站专用场地/旅客車站專用場地　surrounding area of a train station
旅客乘车系数/旅客乘車係數　coefficient of passenger travelling by trains
旅客乘降所/旅客乘降所　passenger stop point
旅客到达人数/旅客到達人數　number of passenger arrived
[旅客]登机桥/空橋　boarding bridge
旅客发送人数/旅客發送人數　number of passenger despatched, number of passenger originated
旅客分流/旅客分流　passenger separation
[旅客]航站楼/旅客終站大廈　passenger terminal building
旅客换乘/旅客換乘　passenger transference
[旅]客机/客機　passenger airplane
旅客捷运系统/旅客捷運系統　automated people mover, APM
旅客快车/旅客快車　fast passenger train
旅客列车/旅客列車　passenger train
旅客列车包车制/旅客列車包車制　responsibility crew system of passenger train
旅客列车包乘制/旅客列車包乘制　assigning crew system of passenger train
旅客列车编组/旅客列車編組　passenger train formation
旅客列车车底周转时间/旅客列車週轉時間　turnround time of passenger train set
旅客列车乘务制度/旅客列車車務制度　crew working system of passenger train
旅客列车乘务组/旅客列車車務人員　passenger train crew
旅客列车检修所/旅客列車檢修所　passenger train inspection and service point
旅客列车轮乘制/旅客列車輪乘制　crew pooling system of passenger train
旅客列车直达速度/旅客列車直達速度　through speed of passenger train
旅客流量/客運量　passenger traffic volume
旅客流时/旅客流時　passenger traffic time
旅客流向/旅客流向　passenger traffic flow direction
旅客疲劳时间/旅客疲勞時間，乘客疲勞時間　passenger fatigue time
旅客票价/[旅]客票價　ticket price, passenger fare
旅客平均运程/旅客平均乘距，乘客平均乘距　average journey per passenger
旅客平均运距/旅客平均運距　passenger average haul distance
旅客起居设备/旅客起居設備　passenger accommodation
旅客权利/旅客權利　right of passenger
旅客人公里成本/旅客人公里成本　cost per passenger kilometer
旅客日发送量/旅客日發送量　daily dispatched passenger number
旅客伤亡/旅客傷亡　passenger casualty
旅客特别快车/特別快車　express train
旅客问讯电视/旅客問訊電視　TV for passenger information service
旅客一条龙服务/旅客一條龍服務　bus streamlined service
旅客意外伤害/旅客意外傷害　passenger unexpected injury
旅客意外伤害保险/旅客意外傷害保險　insurance of passenger unexpected injury
旅客运输/旅客運輸，旅客載運　passenger transport, carriage of passenger
旅客运输计划/客運交通規劃　passenger traffic plan
旅客运输量/客運交通量　volume of passenger traffic
旅客运输杂费/旅客運輸雜費　miscellaneous charges for passenger transport
旅客运输质量/旅客運輸服務品質　bus service quality
旅客运送人数/旅客運送人數　number of passengers transported
旅客站房/旅客站房　passenger station building
旅客正运率/旅客正運率　passengers transport regularity rate
旅客直达特别快车/旅客直達特別快車　through express train
旅客周转量/客運週轉量　turnover of passenger traffic
旅客最高聚集人数/旅客最高聚集人數　maximum gathered passenger number, maximum number of

passengers in peak hours
旅行评估/旅行評估 trip assessment
旅行社/旅行社 travel agency
旅行速度/走行速率 travelling speed, commercial speed
旅游/觀光 sightseeing, tourism
旅游策划/旅遊規劃,觀光規劃 tourism plan
旅游产品/旅遊産品 tourism product
旅游产品体系/旅遊産品體系 tourism product system
旅游产业/觀光産業,觀光事業 tourism industry
旅游城市/遊覽城市,觀光都市 tourist city
旅游持续时间/旅次時間 trip duration
旅游船/遊覽船,觀光船 excursion boat, excursion vessel, tourist ship
旅游村/旅遊度假村 tourist village, tourist resort
旅游地产/旅遊房地産 tourism real estate
旅游地理/旅遊地理 tourism geography
旅游地质/旅遊地質 tourism geology
旅游点/旅遊服務站 tourist service station
旅游度假区/旅遊度假區,觀光度假區,觀光勝地 tourism and resort zone, tourist resort
旅游发展规划/旅遊發展規劃 tourism development plan
旅游服务/旅遊服務 travel service
旅游服务基地/旅遊服務基地 tourism service base
旅游服务区/旅遊服務區 tourist service area
旅游服务设施/觀光服務設施 tourism service facilities
旅游服务质量评定/旅遊服務評估 evaluation of travel service
旅游服务质量认证/旅遊服務資格檢定 travel service certification
旅游购物/觀光購物 tourism and shopping
旅游管理/觀光管理 tourism management
旅游规划/旅遊[區]規劃 tourism planning, tourism plan
旅游规划设计资质/旅遊規劃設計資質 qualification on tourism planning and design
旅游交通/旅遊交通 tourist transportation
旅游节事/旅遊節事 tourism festival
旅游经济开发区/旅遊經濟開發區 tourism economic development zone
旅游客车/小型遊覽車 sight-seeing bus, touring bus
旅游客车票价/旅遊客車票價 tourist bus ticket price
旅游客源市场/客源市場構成 tourism source market
旅游列车/觀光火車 tourist train
旅游目的地/旅遊目的地 tourism destination
旅游区/旅遊區,休閒區 tourism area
旅游区详细规划/休閒區細部計劃 tourism area detailed plan
旅游区总体规划/休閒區總體規劃,休閒區總平面圖 tourism area master plan
旅游散客/旅遊散客 individual traveler
旅游商品/旅遊商品 tourism commodities
旅游设施/旅遊設施 tourist facilities
旅游团队/觀光團隊 tourism team
旅游小城镇/旅遊小城鎮 tourist town
旅游形象/旅遊形象 tourism image
旅游娱乐/旅遊休閒 tourist recreation
旅游镇/旅遊鎮 tourist service town
旅游住宿/旅遊接待設施 tourist accommodation
旅游资源/旅遊資源,觀光資源 tourism resources
旅游资源调查/觀光資源調查 tourism resources survey
旅游资源分级/觀光資源評等 tourism resources rating
旅游资源分类/觀光資源分類,旅遊資源學分類 tourism resources classification
旅游资源评价/旅遊資源評價 evaluation of tourism resources
旅游综合体/旅遊綜合體 tourism complex
铝板/花鋁板 aluminum sheet
铝单板/鋁片 aluminum sheet
铝粉漆/鋁漆 aluminum paint
铝蜂窝复合板/鋁蜂窩[複合]板 aluminum honeycomb composite panel
铝管/鋁管 aluminum pipe
铝合金/鋁合金 aluminum alloy, aluminum alufer
铝合金板/鋁合金板 aluminum alloy sheet
铝合金衬塑管/鋁合金襯塑管 aluminum alloy liner plastic pipe
铝合金管/鋁合金管 aluminum alloy pipe
铝合金门窗/鋁合金門窗 aluminum door and window
铝基复合材料/鋁基複合材料 aluminum matrix composite
铝基轴承合金/鋁基軸承合金 aluminum base bearing metals
铝锂合金/鋁鋰合金,鋰鋁合金 aluminum lithium alloy
铝镁合金/鋁鎂合金 aluminum magnesium alloy
铝青铜/鋁青銅 aluminum bronze

铝热焊/鋁熱熔接法,發熱劑熔接法　aluminothermit welding
铝塑复合板/鋁塑[複合]板　aluminum-plastic composite panel
铝塑复合管/鋁塑複合管　aluminum-plastic composite pipe, aluminum polyethylene composite pressure pipe
铝钛合金/鋁鈦合金　aluminum titanium alloy
铝铜合金/鋁銅合金　aluminum copper alloy
履带传动/聯行墊鐵板　crawler track
履带轨距/軌道中心距離　track-center distance
履带护板/履帶防護板　track protection
履带平挖机/履帶平挖機　crawler-mounted gradall
履带式布缆机/履帶式布纜機　liner cable laying machine
履带式铲土机/履帶鏟土機,履帶機動鏟　crawler-mounted power shovel, crawler shovel
履带式单斗挖掘机/履帶式單斗挖掘機　crawler single bucket excavator
履带式沥青混凝土摊铺机/履帶式瀝青攤鋪機　crawler type asphalt paver
履带[式]起重机/履帶式起重機　crawler crane, caterpiller crane
履带式牵引车/齒軌牽引車　tracklaying tractor
履带式推土机/履帶推土機　crawler-mounted bulldozer
履带式拖拉机/履帶式牽引車　crawler tractor
履带式挖掘机/履帶式挖掘機　crawler excavator, caterpillar excavator
履带式稳定土搅拌机/履帶式穩定土拌和機　crawler soil stabilizer, crawler stabilized soil road mixer
履带式行进装置/聯行墊鐵板　crawler track
履带式液压凿岩台车/履帶式液壓鑿岩臺車　crawler hydraulic bench drill
履带式桩架/履帶式樁架　crawler pile frame
履带式装载机/履帶式裝載機　crawler loader
履约保证/履約保證　performance security
履约保证金/履約保證[金]　performance bond
履约担保/履約保證　performance security
律师室/律師辦公室　lawyer room
率定槽/率定槽　rating flume
绿波带/綠波帶　green wave band
绿道/綠道　green way
绿灯时差型式/綠燈時差型式　offset pattern
绿灯时间/綠燈時間　green time
绿地/綠地　green space
绿地标准/綠地標準　open space standard
绿地布局/綠地布局　green space layout
绿地规划程序/綠地規劃程式　planning procedure of the green space
绿地可达性/綠地可達性　accessibility of greenspace
绿地类型/綠地類型　type of green space
绿地率/綠地率　green space ratio, greening rate, ratio of green space
绿地面积/綠地面積　green area
绿地区/綠地區　green district
绿地围挡/綠地擋板　green barrier
绿地系统/綠地系統　green space system, open space system
绿地效果/綠地效果　green space effect
绿地用水/綠帶灑水　green belt sprinkling, green plot sprinkling
绿地与广场用地/綠地與廣場[用地]　green space and city square, land for park and square
绿地资源/綠地資源　green space resources
绿雕塑/綠雕塑　green sculpture
绿化/綠化　greening, planting
绿化布置图/綠化布置圖　green layout planning
绿化带/綠帶　green belt
绿化废弃物/植物垃圾　botanic waste
绿化覆盖率/[都市]綠化覆蓋率,綠地覆蓋率　green coverage ratio, percentage of greenery coverage, greenery coverage ratio
绿化覆盖面积/綠化覆蓋面積,綠化覆蓋率,綠地覆蓋面積　green coverage, green coverage area
绿化隔离带/綠化隔離帶　green insulated belt
绿化隔离区/綠化隔離區　green buffering zone
绿化工程/綠化工程　plant engineering
绿化工程师/綠化工程師　greening engineer
绿化里程/綠化里程　planting mileage, greening mileage
绿化用有机基质/綠化有機介質　greening organic media
绿化植物废弃物/綠葉廢棄物　greenery waste
绿化种植土壤/綠化種植土壤　planting soil for greening
绿廊/綠廊　xystus
绿篱/綠籬,樹籬　hedge, living fence
绿篱植物/綠籬植物　hedge plant
绿篱机/綠籬機　hedge trimmer
绿量/綠量　green capacity
绿泥石/綠泥石　chlorite
绿墙/綠牆　green wall
绿色GDP/綠色GDP,綠色國內生產毛額　green GDP

绿色革命/綠色革命　green revolution
绿色建筑/綠建築　green building
绿色交通/綠色運輸　green transport
绿色街道/綠色街道　green street
绿色通道/綠色通道,快通道　fast channel
绿色照明/綠色照明　green light, green lighting
绿闪光/綠閃光　green flash
绿污泥/新汙泥　green sludge
绿信比/綠信比　split, green ratio
绿星信号/綠星信號　green star-signal
绿岩/輝綠凝灰岩　greenstone
绿荫区/綠蔭區　shade tree section
绿藻[纲]/綠藻類　chlorophyceae
绿洲花园/綠洲[花]園　oasis garden
绿洲效应/冷島效應　cool island effect
氯氨处理/氯氨處理　chlorine-ammonia treatment
氯氨法/氯氨法　chlorine-ammonia process
氯胺化/氯胺化　chloramination
氯丁橡胶/氯丁橡膠　polymeric chloroprene rubber
氯酚/氯酚　chlorophenols
氯化/氯化[作用]　chlorination
氯化硫酸亚铁/氯化硫酸亞鐵　chlorinated copperas
氯化物含量沿深度分布测量/氯化物含量沿深度分布測量　chloride content depth profile measurement
氯化橡胶漆/氯化橡膠漆　chlorinated rubber paint
氯化折点/折點氯處理　break-point chlorination
氯化指数/氯化物指標　chloride index
氯离子/氯離子　chlorine ion
滤饼/汙泥塊　filter cake
滤波电抗器/濾波電抗器　filter reactor
滤波电路/濾波[器]電路　filter circuit
滤波电容器/濾波[器用]電容器　filter capacitor
滤波器/濾波器　filter
滤布/濾布　filtering cloth
滤层/濾層　filter layer
滤尘器/濾塵器　dust filter
滤尘效果试验/濾池效率試驗　test on filter efficiency
滤尘止回阀/濾塵止回閥,濾氣止回閥　strainer check valve
滤池底/濾池底　filter bottom
滤池负荷/濾池負載　filter loading
滤池积水/滴濾池積水　filter ponding, filter pooling
滤池集水沟/濾池集水溝　underdrain of filter
滤池筛/濾池篩　strainer head
滤出水/濾出液　filtrate
滤床/濾床　filter bed

滤床过滤/深度過濾　depth filtration, deep bed filtration
滤毒室/濾毒室　gas-filtering room
滤管堵塞/濾管堵塞　blinding of strainer
滤光片/濾[光]片　filter
滤光系数/濾色鏡係數　filter factor
滤进水/過濾進水　filter influent
滤膜/過濾膜　filter film
滤器自动清洗/過濾器自動清洗　automatic filter cleaning
滤水车/濾水車　filter car
滤水柜/濾水櫃　water filter tank
滤水渠/濾池管廊　filter gallery
滤速/濾率　filter rate
滤油器/淨油機　oil purifier
滤油设备/濾油設備　oil filtering equipment
峦顶式/山頂式　mountain top
卵石/卵石,礫石　cobble, pebble, gravel
卵石床加热器/卵石床加熱器　pebble-bed heater
卵石道碴/礫石道碴　gravel ballast
卵石海岸/石子灘　shingle beach
卵形缓和曲线/卵形緩和曲線　egg-shaped clothoid
乱石基础/拋石基礎,堆石基礎　riprap foundation
乱石墙/塊石牆　rubble wall
乱水/亂水　broken water
乱显示/亂顯示　false indication
伦敦格林尼治公园/倫敦格林尼治公園　Greenwich Park
伦敦海德公园/倫敦海德帕克公園　Hyde Park
伦敦肯辛顿园/倫敦肯辛頓園　Kensington Garden
伦敦绿园/倫敦綠園　Green Park
伦敦摄政王公园/倫敦攝政王公園　Regent Park
伦敦圣·詹姆斯公园/倫敦聖·詹姆斯公園　St James Park
伦敦引航公会/英國導航協會　Trinity House London
轮动起重机/輪動起重機　wheeled tractor crane
轮渡/輪渡,渡船,渡輪　ferry
轮渡引线/輪渡斜引道　ferry slip
轮渡栈桥/輪渡棧橋　ferry trestle bridge
轮渡站/輪渡站　highway ferry station, ferry station
轮对/輪對　wheelset, wheel pair
轮对存放场/輪對存放場　wheelset storing yard
轮对动平衡检验/輪組動平衡試驗　wheelset dynamic balance test
轮对横动量/輪對橫動量　lateral play of wheelset
轮对内侧距/輪緣外面間之距離　distance between backs of wheel flanges

轮箍／輪箍　tire, tyre
轮箍厚度／輪箍厚度　tire thickness
轮毂／輪轂，螺旋桨毂　hub, wheel hub
轮毂长度／輪轂長　hub length
轮毂厚度／輪轂厚度　hub thickness
轮毂孔／輪轂孔　wheel hub bore
轮毂孔直径／輪轂孔直徑　hub bore diameter
轮毂破裂／輪轂破裂　burst hub
轮毂松动／輪轂鬆動　wheel loose on axle
轮毂直径／螺轂直徑　hub diameter
轮灌／輪灌　rotational irrigation, rotation of irrigation
轮轨关系／輪軌關係，輪軌相互作用　wheel-rail relation, wheel-rail interaction
轮轨接触应力／輪軌接觸應力　rail-wheel contact stress
轮轨游间／輪軌遊間　clearance between wheel flange and gage line
轮滑场地／輪滑場地　roller skating field
轮滑运动／輪滑運動　roller skating movement
轮机工程／輪機工程　marine engineering
轮机管理／輪機管理　marine engineering management
轮机日志／輪機記事簿　engine room log book
轮机员／輪機員　engineering officer
轮机长／輪機長　chief engineer
轮迹横向分布系数／輪跡橫向分布係數　coefficient of wheel tracking transverse distribution
轮廓标线／輪廓標線　delineation line
轮廓灯／整補輪廓燈　contour light
轮廓线／輪廓線　border line
轮廓照明／輪廓照明　contour lighting
轮碾机／輪型滾壓機　wheel roller
轮盘／圓盤　disc
轮盘破裂转速／輪盤破裂轉速　disc burst speed
轮生枝／輪生枝　verticillate branch
轮式铲土机／輪動鏟　wheeled tractor shovel
轮式拖拉机／膠輪牽引機，輪式牽引車　wheel type tractor, wheeled tractor
轮式挖沟机／輪式挖溝機　wheel type trencher
轮胎拆装机／輪胎拆裝機　tire changer
轮胎翻新率／輪胎翻新率　tyre recapping rate
轮胎接触面积／輪胎接地面積　tyre contact area
轮胎式单斗挖掘机／輪式單斗挖掘機　wheel type single bucket excavator
轮胎式沥青混凝土摊铺机／輪式瀝青攤鋪機　wheel type asphalt paver
轮胎式起重机／輪[胎]式起重機，膠輪起重機　wheel crane, rubber tired crane, rough-terrain crane
轮胎式推土机／輪式推土機　wheel bulldozer
轮胎式挖掘机／膠輪挖掘機　pneumatic tyred excavator
轮胎式稳定土搅拌机／輪式穩定土拌和機　wheel type soil stabilizer, wheel type stabilized soil road mixer
轮胎式装载机／輪式裝料機　wheel loader
轮胎摊提率／輪胎攤提率　tyre depreciation rate
[轮胎]拖印／輪胎滑行　tyre skid
轮胎挖掘机／輪形挖土機　wheel excavator
轮胎行驶里程定额／輪胎行駛里程定額　tyre mileage rating
轮胎压路机／膠輪壓路機，氣胎壓路機　pneumatic tyred roller, tyre roller, tyred roller
[轮胎]压印／輪胎磨損　tyre scuff
轮胎噪声／輪胎噪音　tyre noise
轮辋／輪輞　wheel rim
轮辋宽度／輪輞寬度　rim width
轮辋辗出／輪輞輾出　spread rim
轮辋烧伤／輪輞燒傷　burnt rim
轮心／車輪中心　wheel center
轮型转子／葉輪轉子　blade wheel rotor
轮修／輪修　alternative maintenance
轮椅坡道／輪椅坡道　ramp for wheelchair
轮椅通道／輪椅通道　passage for wheelchair
轮椅席位／輪椅席位　seat for wheelchair
轮缘／[車輪]輪緣，[車輪]凸緣　rim, wheel flange
轮缘槽／輪緣槽　flange clearance, flangeway
轮缘垂直磨耗／輪緣垂直磨耗　vertical flange
轮缘高度／輪緣高度，凸緣高度　flange height
轮缘厚度／輪緣厚度　flange thickness
轮缘喷油器／輪緣潤滑器　flange lubricator
轮载重／輪載重　wheel load
轮重减载率／輪重減載率　rate of wheel load reduction
轮周功率／輪週輸出功率　output power at wheel rim
轮周牵引力／輪週牽引力　tractive effort at wheel rim
轮助／助理輪機員　assistant engineer
轮转向／輪轉向　wheel turn
轮装盘形制动／輪裝盤形制動　wheel-mounted disc brake
轮作／輪作　crop rotation, rotation of cropping
轮座／輪座　wheel seat
罗北／羅經北　compass north
罗差／羅差　compass deviation
罗差补偿／羅差補償　compass deviation compensation

罗城/羅城　luo cheng, center town
罗茨鼓风机/旋式送風機　Root blower
罗方位/羅經方位　compass bearing, CB
罗方向/羅經方位　compass bearing, CB
罗汉床/羅漢床,坐臥兩用床　platform, daybed
罗航向/羅[經航]向　compass course, CC, compass heading
罗经点/羅經點　compass point
罗经柜/羅經針箱　compass binnacle
罗经花/圖上羅經　compass rose
罗经基点/四向基點,四方　cardinal point
罗经甲板/羅經甲板　compass deck
罗经校正浮标/校正羅經浮標　compass buoy
罗经盘/羅經盤　compass card
罗经盆/羅經碗　compass bowl
罗经液体/羅經液體　compass liquid
罗经座/羅經座　binnacle
罗兰/羅遠儀　Loran
罗兰 A/羅遠 A 導航系統　Loran-A
罗兰 C/羅遠 C　Loran-C
罗兰表/羅遠表　Loran table
罗兰船位/羅遠定位　Loran fix
罗兰 C 告警/羅遠 C 警報　Loran-C alarm
罗兰-惯性导航系统/羅遠-慣性導航系統　Loran inertial navigation system
罗兰海图/羅遠海圖　Loran chart
罗兰 A 接收机/羅遠 A 接收機　Loran-A receiver
罗兰 C 接收机/羅遠 C 接收機　Loran-C receiver
罗兰天地波识别/羅遠天地波識別　identification of Loran ground and skywaves
罗兰位置线/羅遠位置線　Loran position line
罗马美迪奇庄园/羅馬美迪奇莊園　Villa Medici
罗马券柱式/羅馬券柱式　Roman arch and order
罗马式建筑/羅馬式建築,羅曼式建築　Romanesque architecture
罗马水道/羅馬水道　viaduct, Roman waterway
罗盘/羅盤,羅經　compass
罗盘标度盘/羅盤儀　dial compass
罗斯福纪念园/羅斯福紀念園　Franklin D. Roosevelt Memorial
罗望子树/羅望子樹　tamarind tree
逻辑阀/邏輯閥　logical valve
逻辑信道/邏輯通道　logical channel
逻辑诊断/邏輯診斷　logistic diagnosis
螺杆泵/螺泵　screw pump
螺杆式空气压缩机/螺桿壓縮機,螺旋式空壓機　screw air compressor, screw compressor
螺杆式制冷压缩机/螺桿式冷凍壓縮機,螺旋式冷凍壓縮機　screw type refrigerating compressor, screw type refrigeration compressor
螺桨式流速计/螺槳式流速計　propeller currentmeter
螺桨式水轮机/螺槳式水渦輪　propeller water turbine
螺桨调速器/螺旋槳調速機　propeller speed governor
螺距/螺距　pitch
螺距比/節圓直徑比　pitch ratio
螺距规/螺距規　thread pitch gage
螺距角/螺距角　pitch angle
螺距角指示器/螺距角指示器　pitch angle indicator
螺孔裂纹/螺栓孔裂痕　bolt hole crack
螺栓/螺栓　bolt
螺栓扳手/螺栓扳手　track wrench
螺栓孔加强/螺栓孔加強　bolt hole cold-working strenthening
螺栓孔削角/螺栓孔去角　bolt hole chamfering
螺栓连接/螺栓連接,螺栓接頭,螺栓接合　bolted connection, bolted joint
螺栓螺纹钉/螺栓螺紋釘　bolt-screw spike
螺栓扭角终拧法/螺栓扭角終擰法　bolt final twisting by twist angle method
螺栓扭矩终拧法/螺栓扭矩終擰法　bolt final twisting by torque method
螺栓球节点/螺栓球節點　bolted spherical node
螺栓塞焊/螺栓塞焊　bolt embedded welding
螺栓示功扳手/螺栓示功扳手　bolt wrench with indicator
螺丝端杆锚具/螺絲錨座　thread anchorage
螺纹/螺紋　thread
螺纹板牙/螺紋模　threading die
螺纹道钉/螺釘　screw spike
螺纹钢筋/螺紋鋼筋,竹節鋼筋　deformed bar, spiral reinforcing bar
螺纹角/螺紋角　angle of thread
螺纹接头连接/活管套接頭　union joint
螺纹空心铆接/螺旋空心鉚接　hollow riveting with screw
螺纹塞规/螺紋塞規　thread plug gage
螺线板/渦曲線板　spiral rule
螺线试验/蝸旋試驗　spiral test
螺旋板载荷试验/螺旋板載荷試驗　screw plate loading test
螺旋缠绕/螺旋繞組,波繞組　spiral winding
螺旋分级机/渦式分級器　spiral classifier
螺旋风管/螺旋風管,螺旋導管　spiral duct

螺旋钢筋/螺旋[鋼]筋　spiral reinforcement, helical reinforcement
螺旋桨/螺[旋]槳　screw propeller, propeller
螺旋桨敞水效率/螺槳單獨效率　open water propeller efficiency
螺旋桨沉深/螺槳深沈　propeller submergence
螺旋桨船/螺槳船　propeller ship, screw ship
螺旋桨风扇/螺旋槳扇　propeller fan
螺旋桨横向力/螺槳橫向力　sidewise force of propeller
螺旋桨滑流/螺槳跡流　propeller slipstream
螺旋桨进距比/螺旋槳前進比　propeller advance ratio
螺旋桨浸深比/螺槳浸深比　immersion ratio of propeller
螺旋桨浸深横向力/螺槳浸深橫向力　transverse force of propeller submergence
螺旋桨静平衡/螺槳靜平衡　propeller statical equilibrium
螺旋桨流/螺槳流　screw current
螺旋桨盘面积/螺槳盤面積　area of propeller disc
螺旋桨平面/螺槳平面　propeller plan
螺旋桨特性/螺槳特性　propeller characteristic
螺旋桨特性曲线/推進器特性曲線　characteristic curve of propeller
螺旋桨推力/螺槳推力　thrust of propeller
螺旋桨推入力/安裝螺槳壓擠力　propeller fitting force
螺旋桨推入量/安裝螺槳壓擠量　propeller pull-up distance
螺旋桨尾流/螺槳尾流,[螺槳]艉流　slip stream, propeller race
螺旋桨轴/艉[管]軸　propeller shaft, stern shaft, screw shaft
螺旋桨转矩/螺槳轉矩　torque of propeller
螺旋桨转速/螺槳轉速　revolution speed of propeller
螺旋桨锥孔研配/螺轂孔研配　scraping of propeller boss
螺旋桨纵倾角/後傾角　rake angle, rake angle of propeller
螺旋扣/緊索螺釘　rigging screw
螺旋模态/螺旋模態　spiral mode
螺旋喷射桩/旋噴樁　auger injected pile
螺旋曲线/螺形曲線　spiral curve, clothoid curve
螺旋式除雪机/螺旋式除雪機　screw snow remover
螺旋式混凝土布料机/螺旋式混凝土攤鋪機　screw type concrete spreader
螺旋式流速计/螺旋式流速計　screw current meter
螺旋式清洗机/螺旋式清洗機　screwed washer
螺旋试验/蝸旋試驗　spiral test
螺旋输送机/螺旋輸送機,螺旋運送機,渦式輸送機　screw conveyer, worm conveyer, spiral conveyer
螺旋输送器/螺旋式輸送機　helical conveyor
螺旋水轮机/螺旋式水渦輪　spiral water turbine
螺旋弹簧/螺旋彈簧　coil spring, helical spring
螺旋梯/螺旋梯　screw stage
螺旋天线/螺旋天線　helical antenna
螺旋推进器船/螺槳推進船　screw propeller ship
螺旋线/螺形曲線,介曲線,蝸線　spiral curve, spiral
螺旋销卸扣/鬆緊螺扣　screw shackle
螺旋卸车机/螺旋卸車機　spiral unloading machine
螺旋形散布机/螺旋式撒布機　helical screw spreader
螺旋压力机/螺[旋]壓機　screw press
螺旋桩/螺旋樁　screw pile
螺旋钻/螺旋鑽　screw drill, helical auger
螺旋钻孔机/鑽土器　earth borer
螺柱焊/柱焊,嵌柱焊接　stud welding
裸船体/裸船殼　naked hull, bare hull
裸点/光禿點　bare spot
裸根苗/裸根苗[木],裸根實生苗　bare rooted seedling, bare root seedling
裸根苗木/裸根幼木　bare rooted sapling
裸根移植/裸根移植　bare root transplanting
裸拱卸架/裸拱卸架　unloading bare rib, unloading bare ring
裸焊条/焊條　bare electrode
裸露山体绿化/裸露山體綠化　exposed hill pits greening
裸露药包爆破/外部裝藥爆破　adobe blasting, contact blasting
裸岩/明礁　exposed rock
裸置管道/裸置管路　unburied pipeline
裸装货[物]/裸裝貨[物]　naked goods, nude cargo
裸子植物/裸子植物[類]　gymnosperm
洛可可式园林/洛可哥式園林　Rococo style garden
洛朗丹庄园/洛朗丹莊園　Villa Laurentin
洛杉矶磨耗试验机/洛杉磯磨耗試驗機　Los Angeles abrasion testing machine
洛杉矶磨损试验/洛杉磯磨耗試驗　Los Angeles abrasion test
洛杉矶先锋派/洛杉磯先鋒派　Los Angeles avant-garde
洛氏硬度/洛氏硬度　Rockwell hardness
洛氏硬度试验/洛氏硬度試驗　Rockwell hardness test
洛阳宫/洛陽宮　Luoyang Palace

洛泽式桥/洛澤式橋　Lohse bridge
落潮/落潮,退潮　falling tide
落潮持续时间/退潮持續期,退潮延時　duration of ebb, duration of ebb tide
落潮历时/落潮期　duration of fall
落潮流/退潮流　ebb stream, ebb current
落潮流强度/退潮最大速率　ebb strength
落潮水道/退潮水道　ebb channel
落潮滩/落潮灘　beach at ebb tide
落尘/落塵　fallout
落穿试验/落穿試驗　drop penetration test
落锤/落錘　drop hammer
落锤打桩机/落錘打樁機　drop hammer pile driver
落锤夯/落錘夯　drop weight rammer
落锤式夯实器/落錘式夯實器　drop-ram compactor
落锤式弯沉仪/落錘式彎沈儀　falling weight deflectometer, FWD
落锤试验/落重試驗　drop test
落锤心棒/落錘軸　axle of drop hammer
落道/落道　under cutting of track, lowering of track
落点/落點　impact point
落点参数/落點參數　impact parameter
落点测量/落點測量　impact point measurement
落点横向偏差/落點橫向偏差　impact lateral deviation
落点选择/落點選擇　impact selection
落点预报/落點預測　impact prediction
落点纵向偏差/落點縱向偏差　impact longitudinal deviation
落墩/坐墩　lying on the keel block

落管试验/落管試驗　drop tube test
落后角/偏向角　deviation angle
落梁/落梁　lowering of girder
落旗致敬/落旗致敬　dip to
落区/碰撞面積　impact area, drop zone
落石/落石　rock fall
落石槽/落石槽　stone falling channel, trough for catching falling rock
落石冲击力/落石衝擊力　impact force of falling stone
落塔/落塔　drop tower
落塔试验/落塔試驗　drop tower test
落物激振/落物激振　vibration excited by dropping weight
落下/落下　drop down
落下孔车/落下孔車　well-hole car
落下式冲击试验机/落下式衝擊試驗機　drop shock test machine
落压比/落壓比　blowdown ratio
落压式供应系统/落壓式供應系統　blowdown feed system
落压式推进系统/衝壓推進系統　blowdown propulsion system
落叶阔叶林/落葉闊葉林,夏绿林　deciduous broad-leaved forest, summer green forest
落叶阔叶树/闊葉樹種　deciduous broad-leaved tree
落叶绿篱/落葉綠籬　deciduous hedge
落叶乔木/落葉樹　deciduous tree
落叶针叶树/落葉針葉樹　deciduous conifer
落叶植物/落葉植物　deciduous plant

M

麻布袋/麻布袋　burlap bag
麻将室/麻將室　mahjong room
麻面/表面麻坑　surface pockmark
麻醉科/麻醉科,麻醉部　anesthesiology department
麻醉室/麻醉室　anesthesia room
马道/馬道　riding track
马格努斯力/馬格納斯力　Magnus force
马格努斯力矩/馬格納斯力矩　Magnus moment
马格努斯天平/馬格納斯天平　Magnus balance
马赫波/馬赫波　Mach wave
马赫角/馬赫角　Mach angle
马赫数/馬赫數　Mach number
马赫数保持/馬赫數維持　Mach hold
马赫数表/馬赫表　Mach meter
马赫数均方根误差/馬赫數均方根誤差　root-mean-square error of Mach number
马赫数控制/馬赫數控制　Mach number control
马赫数配平/馬赫數配平　Mach trim
马赫数无关原理/馬赫數無關原理　Mach number independence principle
马赫数最大偏差/馬赫數最大偏轉　maximum deflection of Mach number
马赫-曾德尔干涉仪/馬赫-岑得干涉儀　Mach-Zehnder interferometer
马赫锥/馬赫錐　Mach cone
马厩/馬廄,馬舍　stable, dag, horse barn
马克斯抽象园林/馬克斯抽象園林　R.B. Marx abstract garden
马口/馬口　excavation of side wall at intervals
马口铁/馬口鐵皮,鍍錫鐵片　tin sheet
马力限制器/馬力限制器　horsepower limiter
马丘比丘历史保护区/馬丘比丘歷史保護區　Historic Sanctuary of Machu Picchu
马丘比丘宪章/馬丘比丘憲章　Charter of Miachu Picchu, The Charter of Machu Picchu
马舍/馬舍　horse barn
马氏体等温淬火/麻回火　martempering
马术场/馬術場　equestrian field
马术运动/馬術運動　equestrian
马斯诺需求层次理论/馬斯洛需求層次,馬斯洛需要層級　Maslow hierarchy of need

马蹄涡/馬蹄形渦旋　horseshoe vortex
马蹄形断面/馬蹄形斷面　horseshoe-shaped section
马蹄形钩/U形鉤　clevis
马蹄形曲线/馬蹄形曲線,回頭曲線　horseshoe curve
马戏场/馬戲場,競技場　circus
马歇尔工程热层模式/馬歇爾工程熱氣層模式　Marshall engineering thermosphere model
马歇尔劲度/馬歇爾勁度　Marshall stiffness
马歇尔稳定度/馬歇爾穩定度　Marshall stability
马歇尔稳定度试验/馬歇爾穩定度試驗,馬歇爾穩定性試驗　Marshall stability test
玛达玛花园/瑪達瑪花園　Villa Madama
玛雅建筑/馬雅建築　Mayan architecture
码/電碼　code
P码/P碼　precision code, P code
码垛/擁積作用　piling up
码分隔制/碼分隔制　code division system
码分制多路遥测/碼分多工遙測　code division multiplexing telemetry
IRIG-B码接口终端设备/IRIG-B碼介面終端設備　IRIG-B-code interface terminal equipment
码速率/位元率　bit rate
码速调整/碼速調整　code rate justification
码同步/位元同步　bit synchronization
码头/碼頭　wharf, dock, pier
码头岸壁/碼頭岸壁　quay wall wharf
码头费/碼頭費,船席費　berthage
码头工人/碼頭裝卸工人,裝卸工　stevedore
码头护木/碼頭護木　camel
码头起重机/碼頭起重機　wharf crane
码头收货单/碼頭埠單　dock warrant
码头引道/碼頭引道　approach to ferry
码头引桥/碼頭橋臺引道　bridge approach to ferry
码头闸门槛/塢檻　dock sill
码头装卸能力/碼頭裝卸能力　stevedoring capacity
码相位/碼相位　code phase
码型发生器/圓形產生器　pattern generator
码元同步/符號同步　symbol synchronization
码组校验/塊校驗,塊檢驗　block check
码组结束信号/[數據]組末信號　end-of-block signal

码组起始信号/碼組起動信號　start-of-block signal
埋弧焊/潛[弧]焊,潛溶焊　submerged arc welding, embedded arc welding, submerged-melt welding
埋弧自动焊/潛焊法　union-melt welding
埋积谷/埋積谷　wastefilled valley
埋缆机/埋纜機　cable burying machine
埋入长度/埋入長度　embedment length
埋设深度/埋設深度,埋置深度　laying depth, buried depth
埋深/堤基深度　depth of embedment, depth of tunnel, embedment depth
埋式接缝/埋式接縫　buried joint
埋艏/埋艏,艏潛　plough-in
埋条/埋條　bury, planting by bury
埋条繁殖/壓條繁殖　laying propagation
埋头铆钉/埋頭斫平鉚釘　countersunk and chipped rivet
埋头铆接/埋頭鉚接,埋頭鉚釘　flush riveting, countersunk rivet
埋置式桥台/埋置式橋臺,埋入式橋臺　buried abutment, embedded abutment
霾/霾　haze
麦康奈尔螺旋线/麥康奈爾螺旋線　McConnell curve
麦科马克格式/馬科馬可法　MacCormack scheme
脉冲/脈衝　impulse, pulse
脉冲比冲/脈衝比衝　pulsed specific impulse
脉冲编码调制/脈衝編碼調製　pulse code modulation
脉冲变压器/脈衝變壓器　pulse transformer
脉冲操纵/脈衝控制　pulse-control
脉冲测量雷达/脈衝測量雷達　pulse instrumentation radar
脉冲充电/脈衝充電　pulse charge
脉冲重复频率/脈衝複現頻率,脈波重現頻率　pulse repetition frequency
脉冲当量/脈衝當量　pulse equivalency
脉冲等离子弧焊/脈衝電漿弧焊[接]　pulsed plasma arc welding
脉冲等离子体推力器/脈衝電漿推進器　pulsed plasma thruster
脉冲点焊/脈衝點焊　pulsed spot welding, multipleimpulse welding
脉冲点火/脈衝點火　pulse firing
脉冲电镀/脈衝電鍍　pulse plating
脉冲多普勒技术/脈衝式都卜勒技術　pulsed Doppler technology
脉冲多普勒雷达/脈衝都卜勒雷達　pulse Doppler radar
脉冲多普勒频谱/脈衝都卜勒頻譜　pulse Doppler spectrum
脉冲多普勒引信/脈衝都卜勒引信　pulsed Doppler fuze
脉冲风洞天平/脈衝風洞平衡區　pulse wind tunnel balance
脉冲固体火箭发动机/脈衝固體火箭發動機　pulse solid rocket engine
脉冲激光沉积/脈衝雷射沈積　pulsed laser deposition
脉冲激光雷达/脈衝雷射雷達　pulse laser radar
脉冲激光引信/脈衝雷射引信　pulse laser fuze
脉冲继电器/脈衝繼電器　impulse relay
脉冲宽度/脈衝寬度　pulse width
脉冲雷达/脈衝雷達　pulse radar
脉冲雷达引信/脈衝雷達引信　pulsed radar fuze
脉冲模拟调制/類比脈衝調變　pulse analog modulation
脉冲喷气发动机/脈衝式噴射發動機　pulse jet engine
脉冲燃烧/脈衝燃燒　pulse combustion
脉冲上升时间/脈衝上昇時間　pulse rise time
脉冲声/脈衝音　impulsive sound
脉冲施矩/脈衝施矩　pulsed torquing
脉冲式风洞/脈衝式風洞　impulse wind tunnel
脉冲式轨道电路/脈衝軌道電路　pulse track circuit
脉冲式火箭发动机/脈衝火箭發動機　pulse rocket motor
脉冲式太阳仿真器/脈衝太陽模擬器　pulse solar simulator
脉冲式涡轮增压/脈衝渦輪增壓　pulse turbocharging
脉冲数字调制/數位脈衝調變　pulse digital modulation
脉冲下降时间/脈衝下降時間　pulse drop-off time
脉冲响应/脈衝響應,衝激響應　impulse response
脉冲压缩/脈衝壓縮　pulse compression
脉冲压缩技术/脈衝壓縮技術　pulse compression technology
脉冲压缩雷达/脈衝壓縮雷達　pulse compression radar
脉冲氩弧焊/脈衝氬弧焊　argon shielded arc welding-pulsed arc
脉冲阳极[氧]化/脈衝陽極處理　pulse anodizing
脉冲再平衡/脈衝再平衡　pulse rebalance
脉冲增压/脈衝增壓　pulse charging
脉冲转换器增压/脈衝轉換器增壓　pulse converter supercharging

脉冲自动闭塞/脈衝自動閉塞 automatic block with impulse track circuit
脉8定位系统/脈8定位系統 pulse 8 positioning system
脉动磁场/脈動磁場 pulsating magnetic field
脉动空泡/脈動空泡 pulsating cavity
脉动压力/脈動壓力 pulsating pressure
脉动应力/脈動應力 pulsating stress
脉流牵引电动机/脈動電流牽引電動機 pulsating current traction motor
脉码调制终端机/脈衝碼調變終端機 PCM terminal
脉线/痕線 streak line
蛮横主义/蠻橫主義,粗獷主義 brutalism
满舱货/整船貨 full cargo
满舱满载/完全滿載 full and down
满潮/滿潮,高潮 high water, high tide, full tide
满潮位围堰/滿潮位圍堰 full tide cofferdam
满城/滿城 man cheng, manchu quarter
满磁场/滿載磁場,全磁場 full field
满舵/滿舵 hard over
满舵舵角/滿舵角 hard over angle
满帆通风/滿帆逆戧 full and bye
满负荷/容量載 capacity load
满月/滿月,望月 full moon
满载/滿載 capacity load
满载舱/滿載艙間 filled compartment
满载吃水/滿載吃水 load draught, loaded draft
满载吃水线证书/載重線證書 load line certificate
满载货/滿載貨 full and complete cargo
满载排水量/滿載排水量 full load displacement
满载容积/滿載容積 heaped volume
满载水线/滿載水線,載重水線 load waterline
满载水线长/載重水線長 load waterline length
曼彻斯特编码/曼徹斯特編碼法 Manchester encoding
曼格勒变换/Mangler轉換 Mangler transformation
漫步路/步道,小徑 trail
漫地径流/漫地徑流 overland run-off
漫灌/淹灌 flood irrigation
漫洪/片層洪水 sheet flood
漫射器/漫射器,散射器 diffuser
漫射天光/漫射天光 diffuse skylight
漫射照明/漫照,擴散照明 diffused lighting
漫水桥/漫水橋,過水橋,潛橋 overflow bridge, submersible bridge, submergible bridge
漫游/漫遊 panning
漫游机器人/漫遊機器人 rover
慢车道/慢車道 low speed vehicle lane, slow-vehicle lane
慢车状态/慢車工作狀態 idling rating
慢剪试验/慢剪試驗 slow shear test
慢裂乳化沥青/慢裂乳化瀝青 slow breaking emulsified bitumen
慢滤池/慢濾法 slow sand filter, slow filter, slow sand filtration
慢凝液体沥青/慢凝液態瀝青 slow curing liquid asphalt
慢闪光/慢閃光 slow flash light
慢速车混入率/慢車混合率 slow vehicle mixed rate
慢行标志/慢行標誌 slow sign
慢行城市/慢城 slow city
慢行交通/非機動車運輸 non-motorized transportation
慢行交通规划/非車輛化運輸規劃 non-motorized transportation planning
慢行牌/慢行牌 yellow board, speed indicator
慢行系统/慢行交通系統 slow-traffic system
慢转阀/慢轉閥 slow turning valve
慢转起动程序/慢轉起動程式 slow turning starting sequence
芒塞尔体系/孟色耳[色]系統 Munsell system
忙时串杂音/忙時串雜音,忙時串雜訊 busy hour crosstalk and noise
忙音/忙音,占線音 busy tone
盲板法兰/管口蓋板 blind flange, blank flange
盲道/盲道 side walk for the blind
盲发/盲發 blind sending
盲港/盲港 blind harbor
盲沟/盲溝,暗溝,隱式溝塹 blind gully, blind drain, blind ditch
盲沟设计/盲溝設計 blind ditch design, blind drain design
盲孔/盲孔 blind hole, non-penetrated hole
盲区/盲區 blind zone, blind area
盲人公园/盲人公園,盲人花園 park for the blind, blind garden, garden for the blind
盲人花园/盲人花園,盲人公園 park for the blind, blind garden, garden for the blind
盲文地图/盲文地圖 braille map
盲文站牌/盲文站牌 braille bus-stop board
盲向/盲向 blind direction
猫眼/貓眼 cat eyes
猫爪结/貓爪結 cat paw
毛玻璃/毛玻璃,磨砂玻璃 frosted glass, ground glass
毛刺/毛口 burr

毛洞/無襯砌隧道　rough tunnel, unlined tunnel
毛尔伸缩装置/茂爾伸縮裝置　Mauer expansion installation
毛管/毛管　lateral
毛管虹吸作用/毛管虹吸作用　capillary siphoning phenomenon
毛管张力/毛細管張力　capillary tension
毛接法/毛接法　coarse joining method
毛巾杆/手巾架　towel hanging rod, towel rail
毛毛雨/毛毛雨　drizzle
毛坯/毛坯,胚料　blank
毛坯房/毛坯房,初裝飾房　roughcast house
毛石/毛石,片石　rubble
毛石集料/粗骨材　rubble aggregate
毛石砌体/亂石壘　rubble masonry
毛石墙/塊石牆　rubble wall
毛细管喷注器/毛[細]管注射器　capillary injector
毛细管水/毛細作用水　funicular water, water of capillarity
毛细水/毛細管水　capillary water
毛细水上升高度/毛細水上昇高度　capillary water height, capillary height rise
毛毡花坛/毛氈花壇　carpet bed
茅亭/茅亭　thatched pavilion
锚/錨　anchor
锚冰/錨冰　anchor ice
锚泊/錨泊,錨碇　anchoring
锚泊船/錨泊船　anchored vessel
锚泊定位/錨泊定位　anchor moored positioning
锚泊浮窗/錨[位浮]標　anchor buoy
锚泊距离/錨泊距離　anchorage distance
锚泊偏荡/錨泊橫搖　yawing in anchoring
锚泊区/碇泊區域　mooring area
锚泊设备/錨泊設備　anchoring equipment
锚泊状态/錨泊　anchoring, anchored condition
锚出水/錨出水　anchor in sight, clear of water
锚床/錨床　anchor bed, bill board
锚垂直/錨垂直　anchor up and down
锚灯/錨[泊]燈　anchor light
锚地/錨[泊]池　anchorage, anchorage area
锚地防护/錨地防護　defense of anchorage
锚地海图/泊地海圖　anchorage chart
锚垫板/錨碇板　anchor plate
锚垫圈/間隙調整墊圈　washer shim
锚碇/錨碇,錨地,錨座　anchorage
锚碇板/錨碇板　anchor plate
锚碇板式桥台/錨定式板樁岸壁橋臺　anchored bulkhead abutment
锚碇钢腱/錨碇鋼腱　anchored tendon
锚[碇]跨/錨跨　anchor span
锚碇体/錨碇塊　anchor body, anchor block
锚碇桩/錨樁,樁錨　anchor pile, pile anchor
锚锭板式挡土墙/錨碇板式擋土牆　anchored bulkhead retaining wall
锚端链节/轉環,[錨鏈]外短節　swivel piece, outboard shot
锚段/張力長度　tension length
锚段关节/錨段關節　overlap
锚墩/錨墩　anchor pier
锚杆/石栓,錨定螺栓　rock bolt
锚杆长度/螺栓長度　bolt length
锚杆挡墙/錨桿擋土牆　anchored bolt retaining wall, anchored retaining wall by tie rods, anchored retaining wall
锚杆抗力/螺栓抗力　resistance of bolt
锚杆式挡土墙/錨桿式擋土牆　tie rod anchored retaining wall
锚杆支护/錨桿支護　anchor bolt support, rock bolt support
锚更/錨更　anchor watch
锚固变形/錨碇滑動　anchorage slip
锚固长度/錨碇長度　anchorage length
锚固定板/錨碇墊板　anchoring plate
锚固强度/結合強度,黏附力　anchoring strength
锚固区/錨固區[域],錨定區　anchorage zone
锚固桩/繫拉樁　stay pile
锚固装置/錨定裝置,錨定設施　anchor fitting
锚横杆/錨桿　anchor stock
锚环/錨環　jew harp
锚机舱/錨機室　windlass room
锚架/錨架　anchor rack
锚结/漁人扣　fisherman bend
锚具/錨具　ground tackle, anchorage
OVM锚具/OVM錨具　oriental cone anchorage
VSL锚具/VSL錨具　VSL anchorage
XM锚具/XM錨具　X-typed anchorage
YM锚具/YM錨具　Y-typed anchorage, post tensioning strand group anchorage
锚具变形损失/錨頭變形損失,錨固變形損失　loss due to anchorage deformation
锚具温差损失/錨具溫差損失　loss due to anchorage temperature difference
锚跨/錨跨　anchor span
锚缆/錨纜,錨索　anchor hawser, anchor rope
锚缆标记/錨纜標誌　cable mark
锚离底/錨離地　anchor aweigh

锚链/錨鏈　anchor chain
锚链舱/錨鏈艙　chain locker
锚链钩/錨鏈鉤　chain hook
锚链管/錨鏈管,錨鏈筒　chain pipe, naval pipe
锚链绞缠/纏鏈　fouling hawse
锚链孔盖/錨鏈孔蓋　buckler
锚链轮/[嵌]鏈輪　wildcat, cable lifter
锚链内端/錨鏈內端　bitter end
锚链收短/錨鏈收短　anchor at short stay
锚链筒/錨鏈筒　hawse pipe
锚链转环/轉環　swivel
锚梁/錨定梁　anchor girder
锚令/錨令　anchoring orders
锚啮入性/錨嵌入性　anchor penetration
锚球/錨球　anchor ball
锚圈套/錨圈套　anchor loop
锚设备检验/錨與錨設備檢驗　survey of anchor and chain gear
锚式板桩/錨扣板樁　anchor sheetpiling
锚栓/錨栓　anchor bolt
锚索/錨索,錨纜,開傘掛索　anchor cable
锚索用捻绳/正絞股索　cable-laid rope
锚塔/錨墩塔　anchor tower
锚头/錨頭　anchor head
锚位/錨位　anchor position, AP
锚卸扣/錨接環　anchor shackle
锚穴/[嵌]錨穴,錨龕　anchor recess
锚柱/錨柱　anchor mast
锚抓力/錨抓著力　anchor holding power, holding power of anchor
锚抓重比/錨抓著力與重量比　anchor holding power to weight ratio
锚爪/錨爪,錨掌　anchor fluke, fluke
锚爪袭角/攻角,切水角　angle of attack
锚桩/錨樁　anchor pile
锚座/錨座,錨定插座　anchor socket, socket
卯酉圈/卯酉圈　prime vertical, PV
铆锤/打鉛錘　caulking hammer
铆钉/鉚釘　rivet, riveting
铆钉表/鉚釘表　rivet list
铆钉加热/鉚釘加熱　rivet heating
铆钉连接/鉚接連接　riveted connection
铆钉炉/鉚釘加熱器　rivet heater
铆钉试验/鉚釘檢驗　rivet test
铆钉套环/鉚釘盔　rivet collar
铆钉头模/鉚釘鎮　rivet snap
铆钉头型/鉚釘頭型　bucking tool, pedestal riveter
铆工/上鉚　holder-up

铆接/鉚接[法],鉚釘接合　riveting
铆接钢桥/鉚接鋼橋　riveted steel bridge
铆接结构/鉚接結構　riveted structure
铆接试验/鉚接試驗　riveting test
冒顶/落磐　roof fall
冒进信号/冒進信號　overrunning of signal
冒口/冒口　gate riser, riser
贸易航线/貿易航線　trade route
贸易集镇/貿易集鎮　market town
帽木/橫支材　capping piece
梅花瓣飞行试验/葉形飛行試驗　clover leaf flight test
梅氏曲线/梅氏曲線　May curve
梅雨/梅雨　plum rain, Meiyu
煤槽/煤艙　fuel space, coal bin
煤车/煤車　coal car
煤当量/煤當量　standard coal, coal equivalent
煤的工业分析/煤工業分析　proximate analysis of coal
煤的固定碳/煤固定碳　fixed carbon of coal
煤的灰分/煤灰分　ash content of coal
煤的挥发分/煤揮發分　volatile of coal
煤的全硫分/煤總硫量　total sulfur of coal
煤的元素分析/煤[炭]元素分析　elemental analysis of coal, ultimate analysis of coal
煤粉锅炉/粉煤鍋爐　pulverized coal fired boiler
煤粉机车/煤粉機車　pulverized coal locomotive, fine coal locomotive
煤粉燃烧器/煤粉燃燒器　pulverized coal burner
煤焦油/煤焦油,煤溚　coal tar
煤库/煤斗,煤倉　coal store, coal house, coal bunker
煤矿沉陷/礦穴沈陷　mining subsidence
煤沥青/煤瀝青　coal tar
煤气机车/煤氣機車　gas fired locomotive
煤水车/煤水車,補給船　tender
煤水车转向架/煤水車轉向架　tender truck
煤水机车/煤水機車　tender locomotive
煤屑跑道/煤渣跑道　cinder track
煤油发动机/煤油引擎　kerosene engine
煤质分析基准/煤分析基準　basis for coal analysis
霉菌孢子/真菌孢子　fungal spore
霉菌试验/黴菌試驗　mould test, fungus test
每车平均吨位/每車平均噸位　average tonnage per vehicle
每车平均客位/每車平均客位　average seats per vehicle
每吨海里燃油消耗量/每噸海里燃油消耗量　fuel consumption per ton n mile

每分钟转数/每分鐘轉數　revolution per minute
每克驾驶杆力/單位 g 值桿力　stick force per gram
每克升降舵偏角/每克昇降舵角　elevator angle per gram
每厘米吃水吨数/每公分吃水噸數　tons per centimeter immersion, TPC
每厘米纵倾力矩/每公分俯仰差力矩　moment to change trim per centimeter, TPC
每升燃料作业量测定/每公升燃料作業量測定　determination of production quantity per litre fuel consumption
每延米重量/每延米重量　load per meter of track
每周检查/每週檢查　weekly inspection
美国标准协会感光度/美國標準協會感光度,美國標準協會軟片速率　American Standards Association film speed, ASA speed
美人靠/美人靠　chair-back balustrade
美容院/美髮部,美髮室,美髮院　beauty salon
美术馆/美術博物館,藝術博物館,文化藝廊　art museum, art gallery
美术教室/美術教室　atelier, art room
镁合金/鎂合金　magnesium alloy
镁锂合金/鎂鋰合金　magnesium lithium alloy
镁铝合金/鎂鋁合金　magnesium aluminum alloy
镁铁氧体/鎂鐵氧體　magnesium ferrite
门/門　door
门槽/門槽　dock gate channel
门窗侧柱/竪條　jamb post
门到门/戶到戶　door to door
门到门运输/及門運輸　door to door transport
门斗/門斗　enclosed entrance porch
门垛/門墩　door pier
门滑轮/門滑輪　door guide roller
门禁社区/門禁社區　gated community
门槛/門檻　door sill
门槛水深/門檻水深　water depth on sill, lock significant depth
孔宽度/門洞寬度　width of door opening
门口效应/閘門效應　gate effect
门库/閘門室　gate chamber
门框/門框　door frame
门框墙/門框牆　door frame wall
门廊/門廊　porch, portico
门亮子/氣窗,頂窗　transom window
门楣/門楣,過梁　lintel
门桥/門狀構架　portal frame
门塞法/孔底法　doorstopper method
门扇/門扇　door leaf

门式吊机/起重龍門,門架　gantry
门式刚架/門狀構架　portal frame
门式交通标志/門式交通標誌　overhead traffic sign
门式铺轨排机/門式鋪軌排機　track panel laying gantry crane
门式起重机/門式起重機,高架起重機　gantry crane, transtainer
门樘/門框　door frame
门厅/門廳,門廊　entrance hall, anteroom, lobby
门卫种植/門衛種植　guard planting
门位/門口　parking gate
门形索塔/門形索塔　portal framed tower
门簪/門框橫木　pin at doorhead
门诊部/門診部　outpatient department
门诊手术室/門診手術室　outpatient operating room
门柱/門柱　door post
闷顶/閣樓　loft
萌发/萌發　germination
萌芽/萌芽　bud
蒙布式结构/蒙布式結構　cloth-skin structure
蒙皮/蒙皮　skin
蒙皮拉伸成形/蒙皮拉伸成型　skin stretch forming
蒙气差/折光差　refraction
蒙特卡罗方法/蒙地卡羅法　Monte Carlo method
蒙脱石/蒙脱石,蒙脱土,微晶高嶺石　montmorillonite
蒙脱土/蒙脱土,蒙脱石,微晶高嶺石　montmorillonite
孟克力矩/孟克力矩　Munk moment
孟莎式屋顶/孟莎式屋頂　mansard roof
弥散强化/分散強化,散布強化　dispersion strengthening
弥散强化复合材料/分散強化複合材料　dispersion strengthening composites
弥散系数/彌散係數　dispersion coefficient
弥散圆/散光圈　circle of confusion
迷彩涂层/彩繪塗層　coating with pattern painting
迷彩伪装色/眩眼偽裝圖　dazzle camouflage schemes
迷宫绿篱/迷宮綠籬　labyrinth hedge
迷宫式密封/迷宮密封,迷宮環,止漏環　labyrinth seal
迷宫式汽封/迷宮追緊,曲徑填封　labyrinth packing
迷航/迷航　strayed
迷园/迷園　labyrinth
迷阵/迷陣　maze
糜棱岩/壓碎岩,磨爛岩　mylonite
米波引信/公尺波引信,米波引信　meter wave fuze
米轨铁路/一公尺軌距鐵路　meter-gage railway

米勒花园/米勒花園　Miller garden
米泽斯屈服准则/米賽斯屈服準則　Mises yield criterion
泌水性/析水性,釋水性　bleeding
密闭厂房/封閉式廠房　enclosed industrial factory
密闭阀/密閉閥門,氣密閥　airtight valve
密闭隔墙/氣密隔間牆　airtight partition wall
密闭门/氣密門　airtight door
密闭区/密閉區　airtight space
密闭式燃[气用]具/密閉式燃[氣用]具　balanced flued gas appliance, direct vented type, sealed gas burning appliance
密度/密度,濃度　density
密度比冲/密度比衝　density specific impulse
密度分区[管制]/密度區劃　density zoning
密度高度/密度高度　density altitude
密度试验/密度試驗　density test
密度温度系数/實密度-温度修正係數　true density-temperature correction coefficient
密封/密封,封結　seal
密封材料/密封材料　sealing materials
密封舱/密封艙室　sealed module, sealed cabin
密封膏/密封膠,密封劑　sealant
密封镉镍蓄电池/密封鎳鎘蓄電池　sealed cadmium-nickel battery
密封甲板阀/封密甲板閥　hermetic deck valve
密封胶黏剂/密封膠,密封劑　sealant
密封结构/密封結構　seal structure
密封绝热养护/絶熱養護,巨積養護　mass curing
密封铆接/密封鉚接　sealing riveting
密封屏障/密封屏障　confinement barrier
密封圈/密封環,止漏環　seal ring
密封式人井盖板/閉式窨井蓋,閉式人孔蓋　tight manhole cover
密封水系统/水封系統　seal water system
密封条三维伸缩装置/密封帶三維伸縮裝置　three dimension expansion installation with sealing strip
密封性/密封性　leakprofness
密封源/密封[放射]源　sealed source
密封蒸汽系统/封閉蒸汽系統　sealing steam system
密封装置/密封裝置,密封設備　seal
密级配/[致]密級配　dense gradation
密级配沥青混凝土/密級配瀝青混凝土　dense grade asphalt concrete
密集聚居地/密集居住區　compact settlement
密集毛管带/密集毛管帶　closed capillary zone
密集区域/密集區域　density district
密集书库/密集書庫　compact stack

密接式车钩/密貼連結器　tight-lock coupler
密肋楼板/密肋樓板,肋形板　ribbed slab, waffle slab
密肋楼盖/密肋樓蓋　rib floor
密林/密林　midwood
密码/密碼　cipher, cipher code
密码电话学/密語電話　ciphony
密码器/密碼器　cipher device
密切距离/密切距離　intimate distane
密实材料/夯實材料　compact material
密实混凝土/致實混凝土　dense concrete
密室试验/密封試驗　cell test
密贴尖轨/密貼尖軌　closed switch rail, close contact between switch point and stock rail
密贴调整杆/道岔密貼調整桿　adjustable switch operating rod
密檐塔/密檐塔　densely-placed eaves pagoda
密钥/鍵密碼　cryptography key
密语/密語　secret language
蜜源植物/蜜源植物　nectariferous plant
免除处所/免除丈量空間,免丈空間　excluded spaces
免除证书/豁免證書　exemption certificate
免费行包/免費行包　free of charge luggage
免费运送/免費運送　carriage free
免维护蓄电池/免維護蓄電池　maintenance-free battery
免予灭鼠证书/除鼠豁免證書　derating exemption certificate
面/[施工]面　face
面板/面板　face plate
面板切斜连接/短角鐵連接　clip connection
面层/[護]面層,表塗層　topcoat, surface course, armor layer
面层加固法/面層加固法　masonry strengthening with mortar splint
面光桥/面光橋　forestage lighting gallery
面缓冲区/面環域　buffer area
面积比/面積比　area ratio
面积对比/面積對比　contrast of color area
面积加权平均分辨率/面積加權平均解析度　area weighted average resolution, AWAR
面积律/面積法則　area rule
面扩展目标/面擴展目標　area extensive target
面目标效应/水面目標效應　surface target effect
面漆/面塗　top coat
面散射/地面散射　area scattering
面水平测量/面水平測量　area levelling
面水准/面水準　area levelling

面污染源/面汙染源　area pollution source
面向比特协议/位元導向式協定　bit-oriented protocol
面向字符协议/字元導向式協定　character-oriented protocol
面元法/小板法　panel method
面源污染/分散性汙染,非點源汙染　diffused pollution
面碴/上層道碴　top ballast
面罩/面罩　helmet shield, mask, helmet
面阵[列]探测器/面陣列偵檢器　area array detector
面砖/面磚　facing brick
苗木/苗木,植株　nursery stock, planting stock
苗木包装材料/苗木包裝材料　nursery stock package materials
苗木规格/苗木規格　seedling standard
苗圃/苗圃　nursery
瞄准/瞄準,照準　aiming
瞄准标杆/瞄準標桿　aiming pole, aiming post
瞄准点/瞄準點,照準點　aiming point
瞄准吊舱/外掛靶包　targeting pod
瞄准方位角/瞄準方位角　aiming azimuth
瞄准棱镜/校準稜鏡　alignment prism
瞄准线/瞄準線,視線　line of sight
瞄准信号控制仪/瞄準信號控制儀表　aiming signal control instrument
庙宇/禪寺,寺廟　monastery, temple
灭活/滅活　inactivation
灭火花电路/滅火花電路　spark extinguishing circuit
灭火级别/防火等級　fire rating
灭火浓度/滅火濃度　flame extinguishing concentration
灭火器/滅火器　extinguisher, fire extinguisher
灭火水压力/消防水壓　fire pressure
灭火系统/制火系統　fire suppression system
灭火装置/滅火裝備　fire extinguishing appliance
灭菌处理/殺菌處理　germicidal treatment
灭菌器/滅菌器　sterilizer
灭鼠证书/除鼠證明書　derating certificate
民船/民用船　civil ship
民船禁航/禁止民船出港　civil embargo
民航医学/民用航空醫學　civil aviation medicine
民居/民居　vernacular dwelling
民俗风情类/民間習俗　folk-custom type
民俗旅游/族群觀光　ethnic tourism
民俗园/民俗園　folklore garden, folklore village
民宿/民宿　bed and breakfast, B and B
民用车辆/民用車　civilian vehicle

民用晨昏朦影/民用朦光　civil twilight
民用飞机/民航機　civil airplane
民用航空/民用航空,民航　civil aviation
民用航空器适航性/民航適航性　civil aircraft airworthiness
民用建筑/民用建築物　civil building
民政建筑/民政建築　civil affairs building
民族风俗风景区/民族風俗風景區　scenic spot of minority custom
民族植物学/民族植物學　ethnobotany
敏感度/靈敏度,易感受性　susceptibility, degree of sensitivity
敏感度门限/敏感度門限　susceptibility threshold
敏感系数/靈敏度係數　sensitivity coefficient
敏感性分析/敏感性分析,靈敏度分析　susceptivity analysis, sensitivity analysis
敏感植物/敏感植物　sensitive plant
敏感装置/感測裝置　sensing device
敏捷性/敏捷性　agility
名宦祠/名宦祠　memorial hall for renowned official
名木/名木　famous tree
名牌/銘牌　name plate
名牌折扣店/名牌折扣店　outlets
名义攻角/名義攻角　nominal angle of attack
名义应力/標稱應力　nominal stress
名义应力法/標稱應力法　nominal stress method
明暗光/頓光　occulting light
明步楼梯队/明步樓梯隊　stairs without barricade
明洞/明挖隧道,洞廊　open cut tunnel, tunnel without cover, gallery
明洞门/塹式明洞　open-cut-tunnel portal, gallery portal
明度/明度　brightness
明度对比/亮度對比,亮度反襯　brightness contrast
明度基调/明度基調　lightness motif
明火地点/明火地點　open flame site
明给注油器/顯給滑潤器　sight-feed lubricator
明间/明間,中心橋跨　central bay
明礁/露礁　rock uncovered, uncovered rock
明轮/明輪　feathering paddle wheel, paddle wheel
明轮推进器船/明輪船　paddle wheel vessel
明桥[板]面/透空橋面,透空樓板,空架肋板　open floor, open deck, ballastless deck
明渠/明渠　open channel, open culvert
明渠排水/明溝排水　gutter drainage, open channel drainage
明渠演算/明渠演算　open channel routing
明式家具/明式家具　Ming dynasty furniture

明视觉/明視覺,白天视力　photopic vision
明适应/光適應,亮適應　light adaptation
明堂/明堂　mingtang
明挖法/明挖法,明挖回填法　open cut method, cut and cover method
明挖基础/明挖[擴大]基礎　open cut foundation, open excavation foundation
明挖隧道/明挖隧道　open cut tunnel
明晰度/透明度,清晰度　clarity
明线通信/明線通信　open wire communication
明语/明語　plain language
鸣笛标/鳴笛標誌,司機鳴笛標　whistle-requesting mark, whistle board
冥王星/冥王星　Pluto
冥想花园/冥想花園　meditative gardens, contemplative garden
命中概率/命中概率　hit probability
摹拓室/摹拓室　carving room
模场直径/模態場直徑　mode field diameter
模度体系/模度體系　modulor system
模糊度/模糊度　ambiguity
模糊度解析/不明確訊息解析　ambiguity resolution
模糊距离/模糊距離　ambiguity range
模糊空间/模糊空間　gray space
模糊效应/模糊效應　blurring effect
模件式脉冲转换增压/模組脈衝轉換增壓　modular pulse converter supercharging
模块/模組,模件　module
模块式/模組式　modules planting
模量比/模數比　modulus ratio
模拟/模擬　simulation
模拟地震振动试验/模擬地震振動試驗　simulated ground motion test
模拟地震振动台试验/模擬地震振動臺試驗　pseudo-earth-quake shaking table test
模拟飞行/模擬飛行,飛行模擬　simulated flight, flight simulation
模拟分析/模擬分析　simulation analysis
模拟控制信号/模擬控制信號　analog control signal
模拟模型/類比模式　analog model
模拟器/模擬器,模擬設施　simulator
模拟器病/模擬動暈症　simulator sickness
模拟失重训练/模擬失重訓練　simulated weightlessness training
模拟式测量仪器/類比量測儀器　analogue measuring instrument
模拟试验/模擬試驗　simulated test, simulation test, analogue test
模拟视频监控系统/類比視訊監測系統　analog video surveillance system
模拟视频信号/模擬視頻信號　analog video signal
模拟微波中继通信/類比微波中繼通訊　analog microwave relay communication
模拟遥控/模擬遥控　analog telecommand
模式/模式,方式　mode
S模式应答器/雷達辨證系統　mode S transponder
模式语言/模式語言　pattern language
模数/模數　module
模数化网络/模數化網路　modular network
模数协调/模數協調　modular co-ordination
模数转换/類比數位轉換　analogue-to-digital conversion, AD conversion
模-数转换器/模擬-數位轉換器　analog-to-digital converter
模态/模態　mode shape
模态辨识/模態識別　modal identification
模态叠加/模態叠加　mode superposition
模态分析/模態分析,模式分析　modal analysis
模态刚度/模態勁度　modal stiffness
模态平衡/模態平衡　modal balancing
模态试验/模態試驗　modal test
模态特性/模態特徵　mode characteristics
模态有效质量/模態有效質量　modal efficient mass
模态质量/模態質量　modal mass
模态综合/模態綜合　modal synthesis
模纹花坛/模紋花壇,毛毯花壇　carpet flower bed, pattern flower bed
模线/模線　lofting
模型车/模型車　traveller form
模型车间/模型工場　pattern shop
模型分析/模型分析　model analysis
模型[火]箭/模型火箭　model rocket
模型空间/模型空間　model space
模型理论/模型理論　model theory
模型试验/模型試驗　model test
模型支架/模型掛架　model support
模型自由飞试验/模型自由飛行試驗　model free-flight test
膜分离法/薄膜分離法　membrane separation process
膜过滤/薄膜過濾　membrane filtration
膜结构/薄膜結構　membrane structure
膜结构用膜材料/電解質膜材料　membrane material for membrane structure
膜冷却/膜冷卻　liquid film cooling
膜式空气弹簧/膜式空氣彈簧　diaphragm type air

spring
膜式水泵/[薄膜式]隔離泵　diaphragm pump
膜式水冷壁/薄膜壁　membrane wall
膜选择性/透膜選擇度　membrane selectivity
摩擦/摩擦[力]　friction
摩擦板/摩擦板　friction plate
摩擦电流/摩擦電流　frictional working current
摩擦焊/摩擦焊,摩擦熔接法　friction welding
摩擦结合式高强度螺栓/高強螺栓　high strength friction grip bolt
摩擦力/摩擦力　friction force, frictional force
摩擦联结器/摩擦離合器　frictional clutch
摩擦式减振器/減震器,錨鏈制止器　snubber
摩擦式离合器/摩擦離合器,摩阻離合器　friction clutch
摩擦损失/摩擦損失　frictional loss
摩擦系数/摩擦係數　friction coefficient
摩擦系数测定仪/摩擦試驗機　friction tester
摩擦型锚杆/摩擦型岩石錨桿　friction rock bolt
摩擦圆分析法/摩擦圓分析法　friction circle analysis
摩擦制动/摩擦制動　friction braking
摩擦桩/摩擦樁　friction pile
摩擦阻力/摩擦阻力　frictional resistance, friction drag
摩擦阻尼/摩擦阻尼　frictional damping
摩托车/摩托車,機動腳踏車　motor cycle
摩托艇运动/摩托艇運動　motor movement
摩振腐蚀/磨[耗腐]蚀　fretting corrosion
摩阻流速/摩擦速度　friction velocity
磨粉机/磨粉機　pulverizer
磨缝机/磨縫機　concrete joint grinder, joint grinder
磨光/磨光,抛光　polishing
磨光层/封層　flush coat
磨光石/研磨石　abraded stone
磨轨车/磨削鋼軌車　rail grinding car, rail grinding coach
磨轨机/磨軌機　rail grinding machine
磨轨列车/軌道研磨列車　rail grinding train
磨耗板/耐磨護板　wearing plate
磨耗层/磨耗層　wearing course
磨耗度/抗磨性　abrasiveness
磨耗试验/磨耗試驗　abrasion test
磨耗限度/磨損極限　limit of wear
磨耗型踏面/磨耗型踏面　worn profile tread
磨合/磨合,試車,適配運轉　running-in, breaking-in
磨合维护/磨合維護　running-in maintenance
磨料磨损/磨料磨損　abrasive wear
磨气门机/閥面磨光機　valve refacer

磨气门座机/磨氣門座機,閥座磨床,氣門座研磨機　valve seat grinder
磨肉机/磨肉機　meat mill
磨砂玻璃/磨砂玻璃,毛玻璃　frosted glass, ground glass
磨蚀疲劳/磨蝕疲勞　fretting fatigue
磨蚀试验机/磨耗試驗機　abrasion test machine
磨碎/研磨　grinding
磨损/磨損,損耗,磨耗　wearing, wear
磨损过程/磨損過程　wear process
磨损率/磨耗率　wear rate
磨损试验/磨耗試驗,耐磨試驗　wear test
磨损限值/磨耗容許量　wear allowance
磨削/輪磨,磨光　grinding
磨钻机/磨鑽機　bits grinders
磨钻器/鑽頭磨銳機　drill sharpener
蘑菇石/蕈狀岩,菌狀岩　mushroom rock
蘑菇亭/蘑菇亭　mushroom pavilion
蘑菇形结构/菌形構造　mushroom construction
蘑菇形开挖法/蘑菇形開挖法　mushroom-type tunnelling method
抹光/光製　finishing
抹灰接头/填縫接頭　plaster joint
抹浆/抹漿　browning plaster
抹面砂浆/抹面灰漿　finishing mortar, mortar for coating, decorative mortar
抹芽/疏芽　bud picking
末端环/鏈端環,尾環　end link
末端链节/船内端錨鏈節　inboard end chain
末端卸扣/端接環　end shackle
末端再加热空气调节系统/終端再加熱空調系統　terminal reheat air conditioning system
末端执行器/末端作用器　end-effector
末端执行器耦合装置/末端作用器耦合裝置　end-effector coupling device
末端治理/末端治理　terminal treatment
末区/末區　end area, down range
末叶片/最後葉片　final blade
末制导/終端導引　terminal guidance
没水深度/没水深度　depth of flooding water
莫尔包线/莫爾包線　Mohr envelope
莫尔-库仑定律/莫爾庫侖定律　Mohr Coulomb law
莫尔屈服准则/莫爾屈服準則　Mohr yield criterion
莫尔斯码/莫[爾]斯電碼,Morse 碼　Morse code
莫尔斯码雾号/莫[爾]斯碼霧號　Morse code fog signal
莫尔圆/莫爾圓　Mohr circle
莫氏信号灯/莫氏信號燈　Morse signal light

莫卧儿花园/莫臥兒花園　Mughul Gardens
墨卡托海图/麥卡托海圖　Mercator chart
墨卡托算法/麥卡托航法　Mercator sailing
墨卡托投影/麥卡托投影法　Mercator projection
模板/模型,範本　formwork, form
模板端头/範本止塊　form stop
模板间/放樣場　template shop
模板台车/範本臺車　formwork jumbo
模锻/模鍛,落錘鍛造　die forging, drop forging
模内淬火成形/模内淬火成形　die quench-forming
模压成形/壓模成形法,熱壓法　compression molding
模样/模型　pattern
模样[火]箭/原型火箭　prototype rocket
模样[星]/模型[星]　mockup
模筑衬砌/模築襯砌　moulded lining
母材/母材　parent metal, base metal
母车/母車　car with axle generator
母线/母線　generating line
母线电压/母線電壓　bus voltage
母岩/母岩　parent rock
母株/母料　parent stock
母子式渔船/母子式漁船　mother-ship with fishing dory
木坝/木造壩　wooden dam
木板船/木板船　planking ship
木板梁/木板梁　wooden plate girder
木板桥/木板橋　plank bridge
木背板/木背板　timber lagging
木本花卉/木本植物　woody flower plant
木变石/矽化木　silicified wood
木材船/木材[運載]船　lumber cargo ship
木材防腐法/木材防腐法　preservative for timber
木材港/木材港　lumber harbour, timber harbour
[木材]浸渍防腐法/飽和細胞法　full-cell process
木材品种/樹種　wood species
木材条款/木材條款　timber clause
木材载重线/載木載重線,裝載木材載重線　timber load line
木材制品/木材製品　timber products
木衬板/木襯砌　wood lining
木撑架桥/木撐架橋　timber strut framed bridge
木船/木船　wooden ship, wooden vessel
木槌/大搥,木夯　beetle
木钉/木釘　wooden nail
木工车间/木工工作室　carpentry shop
木工活/木工　carpenter work
木工间/木工庫　carpenter store

木夯/木夯,大搥　beetle
木桁架桥/木桁架橋　wooden truss bridge
木滑轮/木滑輪　wooden block
木混凝土合成梁/木料混凝土合成梁　wood-concrete-composite beam
木建筑/木構造　wooden construction
木匠/木匠　carpenter
木结构/木結構,木構造　timber structure, wood structure
木块路面/木塊路面　plank pavement
木块芯板/木塊芯板　blockboard
木块[砖]/木塊　wooden block
木梁桥/木梁橋　wooden beam bridge
木门窗/木門窗　wood door and window
木排/木排,木筏　log raft, wood raft
木排架桥/木排架橋　timber trestle bridge
木前枕/木支護　wooden strut
木桥/木橋　timber bridge, wooden bridge
木纤维/木纖維　wood fiber
木屑跑道/木屑跑道　sawdust runway
木星/木星,邱比特　Jupiter
木堰堤/木造壩　wooden dam
木造码头/木造碼頭　wood pier
木栈桥/木棧橋,木架橋　wooden trestle
木枕/木枕　wooden tie
木枕防腐/木枕防腐　preservation of wooden tie
木枕防裂装置/防止割裂裝置　anti-splitting device
木枕刻痕/枕木刻切加工　incising of wooden tie
木枕削平机/枕木削正機　wooden sleeper adzing machine
木枕预钻孔/枕木預鑽孔　preboring of wooden tie, preboring of spike hole
木枕钻孔机/木枕鑽孔機　wooden tie drilling machine
木支撑/木支撐　timbering support
木质人造板/人造木板　man made wood board
木质纤维/木纖維　wood fiber
木桩/木椿　timber pile
木桩校正法/椿校法　peg adjustment method
木桩锚碇/木椿錨碇　timber pile anchorage
目标/目標,靶　target
目标捕获/目標獲得　target acquisition
目标打靶控制/目標射擊　target shooting
目标定位/目標定位　target positioning
目标仿真/目標模擬　target simulation
目标仿真器/目標模擬器　target simulator
目标跟踪器/目標跟蹤儀　target tracker
目标进入角/視角,相關方位角　aspect angle

目标录取/目標獲得　target acquisition
目标模型/目標模型　target model
目标强度/目標強度　target strength
目标散射特性/目標散射特性　target scattering characteristics
目标识别/目標認定　target recognition
目标缩比模型/目標縮比模型　target scaled model
目标锁定/目標鎖定　target lock-on
目标探测装置/目標探測裝置　target detecting device
目标特性测量/目標特徵測定　target signature measurement
目标信息/結果資訊　object information
目标值/目標　goal
目标指向编程/目標導向程式設計　goal directed programming
目标状态估计器/目標狀態估計器　target state estimator
目测/目測　visual measurement, visual inspection, visual observation
目测方位/目測方位　visual bearing
目的地码/目的地碼　destination code
目的港/目的港　port of destination
目的港船上交货/船上交貨　ex ship
目的港码头交货/碼頭交貨　ex quay, ex pier, ex wharf
目的制动/目的制動,目的刹車　target braking
目镜/目鏡　ocular
目录厅/目錄廳　catalog room
目视飞行/目視飛行　visual flight
目视飞行规则/目視飛航規則　visual flight rules, VFR
目视飞行规则的直线进近/目視飛航直線進場　straight-in approach
目视分辨率/可見解析度　visible resolution
目视告警装置/目視告警裝置　visual alerting device
目视检查/目視檢查,目視檢驗　visual check, visual inspection
目视鉴别率/目視鑒別率　visual resolution
目视进场下滑道指示系统/目視進場滑降指示系統　visual approach slope indicator system
目视进近坡度灯光系统/目視進場滑降指示燈系統　visual approach slope indicator light system
目视气象条件/目視飛行氣象條件　visual meteorological condition, VMC
目视助航设施/目視助航設施　navigational visual aid
沐浴水箱/沐浴水箱　ablution tank
苜蓿叶形立交/苜蓿葉形交流道,四葉形交流道　clover leaf interchange
苜蓿叶形立体交叉/四葉形交流道　clover leaf interchange
牧场/牧場　pasture
牧场草坪/牧場草坪　meadowy land
钼高速钢/鉬高速鋼　molybdenum high speed steel
墓地/墓地　graveyard
墓园/墓園,墳地　cemetery garden, tomb garden, cemetery
墓葬/陵墓　tomb
幕墙/簾牆　curtain wall
穆曼-科尔格式/穆曼-科爾格式　Murman-Cole scheme

N

纳米技术/奈米技術　nanotechnology
纳斯卡和朱马纳草原的线条图/納斯卡和朱馬納草原的線條圖　Lines and Geoglyphs of Nasca and Pampas de Jumana
纳维-斯托克斯方程/奈威-斯托克方程式　Navier-Stokes equation
钠和钒含量/鈉釩含量　sodium and vanadium content
钠基润滑脂/鈉基滑脂　sodium grease
钠硫电池/鈉硫電池　sodium-sulfur battery
奈伏泰斯/航行警告電傳　navigational telex, NAVTEX
奈伏泰斯电文编号/航行警告電傳信文編號　NAVTEX message numbering
奈伏泰斯紧急警告/航行警告電傳緊急警告　NAVTEX vital warnings
奈伏泰斯日常警告/航行警告電傳例行警告　NAVTEX routine warnings
奈伏泰斯优先电文/航行警告電傳優先信文　NAVTEX priority message
奈伏泰斯重要警告/航行警告電傳之重要警告　NAVTEX important warning
奈奎斯特频率/奈奎斯特頻率　Nyquist frequency
奈良真实性文件/奈良真實性檔　Nara Document on Authenticity
耐波性/耐波性能,耐海性,凌海性　seakeeping performance, seakeeping quality
耐波性衡准/耐海性準則　criteria of seakeeping qualities
耐波性试验/耐海性試驗　seakeeping test
耐波性试验水池/耐海性試驗水槽　seakeeping tank
耐潮绝缘材料/抗濕絕緣材料　moisture resistant insulating material
耐冻性/耐凍性　freezing tolerance
耐冻炸药/低凍炸藥　low-freezing explosive
耐冻植物/耐凍植物　freezing-tolerant plant
耐毒性/耐毒性　toxic tolerance
耐辐射涂层/耐輻射塗層　radiation resistant coating
耐腐蚀轨/耐腐鋼軌　corrosion resistant rail
耐高热接缝料/耐高熱接縫料　jet seal
耐高热设施/耐高熱設施　jet blast

耐根穿刺防水层/耐根穿刺防水層　root resistant waterproof layer
耐寒树种/耐寒樹種　winter hardy tree species
耐寒性/耐寒性,耐寒力　cold hardiness, frost hardiness
耐寒植物/耐寒植物　hardy plant
耐旱性/耐旱性　drought tolerance, desiccation tolerance
耐旱植物/耐旱植物　drought enduring plant, drought-tolerant plant
耐航试验/耐航試驗　seaworthiness test
耐候钢/耐候鋼　weathering steel
耐候性胶黏剂/防潮黏著劑　weatherproof adhesive
耐回转能力/旋轉容量　rotative capacity
耐火/耐火　fire-tight, fire resistant, fire-resisting
耐火材料/耐火材料,耐火物　refractory material, refractories
耐火等级/耐火等級　fire resistance rating
耐火电缆/耐火電纜,抗燃電纜　fire-resisting cables, fire resistant cable
耐火度/耐火度,耐火性　refractoriness
耐火构造/耐火構造　fire-resisting construction
耐火混凝土/耐火混凝土,防火混凝土　refractory concrete, fireproof concrete
耐火极限/耐火極限　extreme limit of fire resistance
耐火救生艇/防火救生艇　fire protected lifeboat, fire-resistant lifeboat, fire protected lifeboat
耐火黏土/[耐]火泥,燒磨土　chamotte, chamot, fireclay
耐火砂浆/耐火灰漿,耐火墁料　refractory mortar
耐火性/耐火性　fire resistance
耐火植物/耐火植物,抗火性植物　pyrophyte
耐火砖/[耐]火磚,燒磨土磚　chamotte brick, firebrick
耐碱玻璃纤维/耐鹼玻璃纖維　alkali-resistant glass fiber
耐碱植物/耐鹼植物　alkalifast plant
耐久极限/持久極限　endurance limit
耐久性设计/耐久性設計　durability design
耐久[性]试验/耐久性試驗,耐久性測試　durability test, endurance test

耐久性系数/耐性因數　durability factor
耐冷限/耐寒性　cold tolerance
PC 耐力板/PC 耐力板　PC resistant board
耐力铆钉/耐力鉚釘　stress rivet
耐磨钢轨/耐磨鋼軌,超班鐵軌條　sorbite rail
耐磨轨/耐磨鋼軌　wear resistant rail
耐磨性/耐磨耗性　wear resistance
耐磨硬度试验仪/抗磨硬度儀器　wear hardness testing apparatus
耐磨装置/耐擦器　chafing gear
耐逆性/應激耐受力　stress tolerance
耐热材料/耐熱材料　heat resisting material
耐热钢/耐熱鋼　heat resisting steel, heat resistant steel
耐热限/耐熱性　heat tolerance
耐湿植物/耐濕植物　damp tolerant plant
耐蚀钢/耐蝕鋼　chemical resistant steel, corrosion resistant steel
耐蚀铝合金/抗蝕鋁合金　corrosion resistant aluminium alloy
耐酸混凝土/耐酸混凝土　acid resisting concrete
耐酸砂浆/耐酸灰泥　acid resisting mortar
耐酸植物/耐酸植物　acid proof plant
耐温性/耐溫性　temperature toleration
耐污染物种/耐性種,耐陰種　tolerant species
耐污性/耐汙性　pollution tolerance
耐压壳体/壓力殼　pressure hull
耐压壳体进水/壓力殼浸水　flooding of pressure hull
耐压试验/壓力試驗　pressure test
耐压性/耐壓性　barotolerancy
耐盐碱植物/耐鹽鹼植物　saline-alkali tolerant plant
耐盐性/耐鹽性,抗鹽性　salt tolerance, salinity tolerance
耐盐植物/耐鹽植物　haloduric plant, salt-tolerant plant
耐氧性/耐氣性　aerotolerant
耐荫植物/耐陰植物　shade-enduring plant
耐荫树种/耐陰樹種　shade-tolerant tree species
耐坠毁性/墜機保全能力,經摔性　crashworthiness
耐坠毁座椅/耐撞座椅　crashworthy seat
南北位置保持/南-北位置保持　north-south station keeping
南大西洋辐射异常/南大西洋輻射異常　South Atlantic radiation anomaly
南方标/南方標　south mark
南方松/南方松　southern pine
南河三(小犬 α)/南河三(小犬 α)　Procyon
南极/南極　south pole
南极光/南極光　aurora australis
南极星座/南極星座　octans
南门二(半人马 α)/南門二(人馬 α)　Rigil Kent
南水北调/南水北調　south to north water transfer
南天极/南天極　south celestial pole
难降解有机物/難分解有機物　refractory organics
难燃烧体/難燃組分,難燃材料　difficult-combustible component
难熔合金/耐火合金　refractory alloy
难熔金属高温抗氧化涂层/耐火材料高溫抗氧化塗層　high-temperature oxidation-resistant coating for refractory
难行车/難行車　hard rolling car
难行线/難行線　hard running track
[难船]漂浮物/遇難船漂浮物　flotsam
囊式空气弹簧/膜盒式空氣彈簧　bellow type air spring
囊式贮箱/囊式貯箱　bladder propellant tank
挠度/撓度,撓曲　deflection
挠度横向分布/撓曲橫向分布　transverse distribution of deflection
挠度横向分布测量/撓度橫向分布測量　transversal distribution measurement of girder deflection
挠度计/撓度計　deflectometer
挠度理论/撓度理論　deflection theory
挠度曲线/撓度曲線　deflection curve
挠度限制器/撓度限制器　deflection limiter
挠度裕量系数/撓度裕量係數　coefficient of spring deflection reservation
挠曲/拱勢　hog
挠曲变形/彎曲變形　flexure deformation
挠曲刚度/抗彎剛度　flexural rigidity
挠曲钢筋/彎鋼筋　bend bar
挠曲钢筋束/彎折鋼腱　draped tendon
挠性固定/彈性連接　flexible fixing
挠性航天器动力学/撓性太空載具姿態動力學　flexible spacecraft dynamics
挠性加速度计/撓曲加速度計,轉矩加速度表　flexure accelerometer
挠性接头/豬尾式接頭　pigtail
挠性罗经/撓性電羅經　flexibility gyrocompass
挠性陀螺仪/撓性迴轉儀　flexibility gyroscope
挠性支承/撓性支承　flexure suspension
挠性轴系/撓性軸系　flexible shafting
挠性转子/柔性轉子　flexible rotor
闹市区/市中心　downtown
内包装/貨物內裝　inner package

内保温/内保温　internal thermal insulation
内波/内波,潜波　internal wave
内补偿法/内補償法　method of internal compensation
内部安全检查/内部安全稽核　internal safety audits
内部测试设备/内部測試設施　internal test facility
内部查看/內部檢查　interior examination
内部单元/内部單元　internal element
内部防雷装置/内部雷擊防護系統　internal lightning protection system
内部过电压试验/内部過電壓試驗　test on internal overvoltage
内部空气系统/内部氣流　internal air system
内部裂纹/内部裂紋　internal crack
内部区段/内部區域　interior zone
内部收益率/内部報酬率　internal rate of return, IRR
内部稳定性/内穩定[性]　internal stability
内部震动/内部震動　pervibration
内侧车道/快車道　fast lane
内侧轴系/内軸　inner shafting, inner shaft
内插翼/内插翼　gross wing
内衬不锈钢复合钢管/内襯不銹鋼複合鋼管　stainless steel lined composite steel pipe
内衬铜复合钢管/内襯銅複合鋼管　copper lined composite steel pipe
内城/内城區　inner city
内城复兴/内城復興　inner city revival
内窗/内窗　internal window
内底/内底　inner bottom
内底板/内底板　inner bottom plating, inner bottom plate
内底边板/二重底緣板,舥緣板　margin plate
内底横骨/副肋骨　reversed frame
内底结构图/内底結構圖　inner bottom construction plan
内底纵骨/内底縱材　inner bottom longitudinal
内电磁脉冲/内部電磁脈衝　internal electromagnetic pulse
内顶板/天花板　ceiling
内定标器/内校準器　internal calibrator
内端墙/内端牆　inside end wall
内方位元素/内方位元素　elements of interior orientation
内防波堤/内防堤　inner breakwater
内伏牛顿流理论/嵌式牛頓流理論　embedded Newtonian flow theory
内港船席/内港船席　inside berth

内港航线/内港航道　inner route
内港锚地/内港錨地　inner anchorage
内功/内功　internal work
内功率/内功率　internal power
内构架转向架/内構架轉向架　inside-frame truck
内海/内海　internal sea, inner sea
内河船/内河船,内陸水域船　inland ship, inland vessel, river boat
内河分级航区/分級航區　graded region
内河航标/内陸水道助航標誌　inland waterway navigation aids
内河航道图/内水航道圖　chart of inland waterway
内河航行/内河航行　inland navigation
内河航行规则/内河航行規則　inland rules
内河航行基准面/内水航行海圖深度基準面　chart datum for inland navigation
内河航运/内陸水運　inland water transportation
内河引航/内水領航　inland waterway navigation and pilotage
内河引航图/内水引水圖　pilot chart of inland waterway
内活塞/内活塞　inner piston
内火箱/内火箱　inside firebox, inner firebox
内火箱顶板/内火箱頂板　crown sheet
内进汽/内側進汽蒸汽機　inside admission
内径比/内淨徑比　inside clearance ratio
内径千分尺/内分釐卡,内測微計　inside micrometer
内净空断面/内淨空斷面　inner section
内聚破坏/膠合體失效　cohesive failure
内孔燃烧/内孔燃燒　internal bore burning
内窥镜/内視鏡　endoscope
内涝防治系统/内澇防控體系　local flooding prevention and control system
内力/内力　inner force, internal force
内力重分布/内力重分布　redistribution of internal force
内流空气动力学/内部氣動力學　internal aerodynamics
内流式涡轮/内流水渦輪　inward flow turbine
内陆还箱站/内陸還箱站　inland container depot
内陆水/陸地水　inland water
内陆水道/内陸水道　inland waterway
内陆水运/内陸水運　inland water transportation
内陆站/内陸倉庫　inland depot
内门/内門　internal door
内摩擦/内摩擦　inner friction
内摩擦角/内摩擦角　internal friction angle, angle of internal friction

内摩擦系数/内摩擦係數　internal friction coefficient
内能/内能　internal energy
内黏聚力/内黏聚力　internal cohesion
内啮合齿轮沥青泵/内嚙合瀝青泵　inside gear asphalt pump
内排水/内［部］排水　internal drainage
内平开下悬窗/内平開下懸窗　tilting and turning sash
内墙/内牆　internal wall
内倾/船舷内傾　tumble home
内燃动车组/柴油客車廂組　diesel coach set
内燃机车/内燃機車，柴油機車　diesel locomotive, internal combustion locomotive
内燃机船/内燃機船　motor vessel, MV
内燃机动力装置/内燃機動力設備　internal combustion engine power plant
内燃牵引干扰/内燃牽引干擾　diesel traction interference
内燃凿岩机/内燃鑿岩機　motor jack hammer
内热源/内熱源　internal heat source
内渗水/下滲水　infiltration water
内时统/内計時系統　inside timing system
内式应变天平/内部應變規式平衡儀　internal strain gage balance
内水/内水　internal waters
内梯/油罐内梯　manhole ladder
内天井式住宅/内天井式住宅　inner-patio housing
内透光照明/内透光照明　lighting from interior light
内舾装/室裝　accommodation outfitting
内线航道/内線航道　inside passage
内效率/内效率　internal efficiency
内斜轴系/漸縮軸系　converging shafting
内旋/内旋，内［向旋］轉　inboard turning, inward turning
内压式进气道/内壓式進氣道　internal compression inlet
内压试验/内壓試驗　internal pressure test
内烟筒/内煙筒　stack extension
内檐装修/内檐裝修，内裝修工程　interior finish work
内营力地质作用/内營力地質作用，地質内營力作用　endogenic geological process
内应力/内應力　internal stress, interior stress
内匝道/内匝道　interior loop, inner loop
内在渗透/内在滲透率　intrinsic permeability
内在预力/内在預力　internal prestress
内止点/内止點　inner dead point, inner dead center
内置式平面轴承/内置式平面軸承　inboard plain bearings
内置遮阳中空玻璃制品/内置遮陽中空玻璃製品　sealed insulating glass unit with shading inside
内纵梁/内縱梁　interior beam, interior stringer
内走廊/内走廊　inside corridor
能工作时间/可操作時間　up time
能耗制动/動力剎車，動力制軔　dynamic braking
能见地平/視水平線　visible horizon
能见度/能見度，可見度，視程　visibility
能见度不良/能見度不良　visibility poor
能见距/能見距　range of visibility
能力测试/能力試驗　proficiency testing
能力储备系数/儲備量係數　coefficient of reserved capacity
能［量］/能［量］　energy
能量法/能量法　energy method, method energy
能量方程/能量方程　energy equation
能量峰面/能量峰面　energy front
能量高度/能量高度　energy height
能量管理系统/能源管理系統　energy management system
能量耗散/能量耗散，消能　energy dissipation
能量平衡法/能量均衡法　energy-balance method, energy-budget method
能量释放率/能量釋放率　energy release rate
能量守恒定律/能量守恆律　law of conservation of energy
能［量］输送/能量輸送　energy transport
能量调节阀/能量調節閥　capacity adjusting valve
能量吸收/能量吸收　energy absorption
能量系数/能量係數　energy coefficient
能量原理/能量原理　energy principle
能谱/能譜　energy spectrum
能源/能源　energy sources
能源供应密度/能源供應密度　energy supply density
能源渐变线/能量比降線　energy gradient line
能源林/能源林　energy forest
能源品位/能量級　energy grade
能源强度/能量強度，能源密集度　energy intensity
能源梯级利用/能源逐級利用　energy cascade use
能源植物/能源植物　energy plant
尼尔森式洛泽梁桥/尼爾森體系洛澤式橋　Nielsen type Lohse bridge
尼尔森体系桥/尼爾森體系橋　Nielsen system bridge
尼曼斯花园/西薩塞克斯郡，西蘇塞克斯郡　Nymans Garden
尼特拉芒炸药/硝銨火藥　nitramon

尼亚加拉大瀑布/尼加拉瀑布　Niagara Falls
泥泵/挖泥泵　dredge pump
泥驳船/泥駁船　hopper barge, mud barge, mud lighter
泥舱容积/泥艙容量　hopper capacity
泥车/出碴車　muck car
泥灰结碎石路面/泥灰結碎石面　clay-lime bound macadam
泥[浆]泵/泥漿泵　mud pump, slurry pump, dredging pump
泥浆护壁钻孔法/泥漿護壁鑽孔法　slurry hole boring method
泥浆套沉井法/泥漿套沈井法　slurry jacket method for sinking caisson
泥浆套法下沉沉井/泥漿套法下沈沈井　sinking open caisson by slurry coating
泥结碎石路面/泥結碎石面　clay bound macadam
泥流/泥流　mud flow, solifluction
泥泉/泥泉　mud spring
泥沙含量/沈滓值　sediment charge
泥沙径流/泥渣徑流　sediment runoff
泥沙控制/沈渣控制　sediment control
泥沙浓度/載運濃度　transport concentration
泥沙起动流速/泥沙起動流速　sediment moving incipient velocity
泥沙输移能力/沈渣載運能力　sediment transport competency
泥石流/泥石流，土石[混]流　debris flow, earth flow, mud and rock flow
泥石流地段路基/泥石流地段路基　subgrade in debris flow zone
泥石流流域/土石流集水域　catchment basin of debris flow
泥水盾构/泥漿盾構　slurry shield
泥水匠/粉刷工　plasterer
泥炭/泥炭　peat
泥炭土/泥炭土，泥沼質土壤　peat soil
泥炭藓/泥炭蘚屬，水蘚屬　sphagnum
泥炭压制播种饼/泥炭壓制播種餅　peat seeding pellet, peat seeding starter
泥箱/泥箱　mud box
泥岩/泥岩，間隔土　mud stone
泥毡层/泥氈　mud blanket
泥沼地区路基/泥沼地區路基　subgrade in bog soil zone, subgrade in morass region, subgrade in swampland
铌基合金/鈮基合金　niobium based alloy
铌钛铝化合物/鈮鈦鋁介金屬　niobium titanium aluminide
霓虹灯/霓虹燈，氖燈　neon lamp
拟动力试验/擬動力試驗，擬動態試驗　pseudo dynamic test
拟静力试验/僞静力試驗　pseudo-static test
逆变器/變流器，反向器　inverter
逆城市化/逆都市化，反都市化　deurbanization
逆电流试验/逆流試驗　reverse current test
逆断层/逆斷層　fault reverse
逆风/逆風　foul wind, contrary wind
逆风航驶/逆戧　by the wind
逆功率保护/逆功率保護　reverse power protection
逆功率试验/逆功率試驗　reverse power test
逆合成孔径雷达/逆合成孔徑雷達，反向合成孔徑雷達　inverse synthetic aperture radar, ISAR, inverse SAR
逆火/逆火，回火　flashback, back fire
逆流/逆流，退潮　reflux
逆流靶/逆流靶　counter flow range
逆流船/逆流船　upstream vessel
逆流截止阀/止回閥　non-return valve
逆流燃烧/逆流式燃燒　counter-flow combustion
逆流再生/逆流再生　counter current regeneration
逆螺线试验/逆蝸旋試驗　reverse spiral test
逆挠理论/逆撓度理論　theory of reciprocal deflection
逆时针旋转/逆時針旋戧，左向旋轉　left-hand rotation
逆时针转动/逆時針旋轉　counter-clockwise rotation
逆水/逆流　up stream
逆向拆除分析/逆向拆除分析　retrogressive analysis for bridge erection
逆向牵引/逆向牽引　backward haulage
逆向渗透法/逆滲透法，反滲透法　reverse osmosis process
逆行轨道/逆行軌道　retrogressive orbit
逆压梯度/逆向壓力梯度　adverse pressure gradient
逆增益干扰/逆增益干擾　inverse gain jamming
逆筑法/逆築工法　top down construction method
腻子/油灰，補土　putty
年差/年磁差　magnetic annual change
年第三十位最大小时交通量/年第三十位最大小時交通量　annual thirtieth highest hourly traffic volume
年度检验/歲驗　annual survey
1978年海员培训、发证和值班国际公约/一九七八年航海人員訓練、發證及當值標準國際公約　International Convention on Standard of Training,

Certification and Watching keeping for seafarers, 1978
年耗热量/年熱能消耗量　annual heat consumption
年耗水量/年耗竭率　annual depletion rate
年洪水序列/年洪峰序列,年洪水級數　annual flood series
年交通形式/年交通量型　yearly traffic pattern
年径流[量]/年徑流量　annual runoff
年均温差/年平均温差　annual mean temperature difference
年龄结构/年齡結構　age structure
年龄塔/年齡塔　pyramid of age
年平均日交通量/年平均每日交通量　annual average daily traffic, AADT, annual average daily traffic volume
年容量/年容量　annual capacity
年游客量/年遊客量　annual number of tourists
年最大小时交通量/年最大小時交通量　annual maximum hourly traffic volume
黏层/黏層　tack coat
黏度/黏度　viscosity
黏度分级/黏度分級　viscosity classification
黏度计/黏度計　viscosimeter, viscometer
黏度试验/滯度試驗　viscosity test
黏度-温度图/黏度-温度[曲線]圖　viscosity-temperature diagram
黏度指数/黏性指數　viscosity index
黏度自动控制系统/黏度自動控制系統　viscosity automatic control system
黏附/黏附,黏著　adhesion
黏垢/黏泥　slime
黏胶/黏液　viscose
黏接结构/膠合[結]構件　bonded structure
黏结/膠合　gluing, adhesive-bonding
黏结长度/錨著長度　grip length
黏结的预应力筋/黏裹鋼腱　bonded tendon
黏结钢腱/成束鋼腱　boundled tendon
黏结滑移/握裹滑移　bond slip
黏结力/黏著力　cohesion
黏结力试验/黏著力檢驗　cohesion test
黏结石膏/黏結石膏　gypsum binder
黏结应力/黏合應力　bond stress
黏粒部分/黏土成分　clay fraction
黏粒粒级/黏土成分　clay fraction
黏塑性/黏塑性　viscoplasticity
黏弹性/黏彈性　viscoelasticity
黏弹性材料/滯彈性材料　viscoelastic material
黏弹性理论/黏彈性理論　viscoelasticity theory

黏弹性性能/滯彈現象　viscoelastic behaviour
黏弹性阻尼器/黏彈阻尼器　viscoelastic damper
黏土/黏土　clay soil
黏土灌浆/黏土灌漿　clay grouting
黏土矿床/黏土層　clay deposit
黏土矿物/黏土礦物　clay mineral
黏土炮泥/黏土封口　clay tamping
黏土取样器/黏土取樣器　clay sampler
黏土瓦/黏土瓦管　clay tile
黏土质砂/黏土質砂　clayey sand
黏性底层/黏性次層　viscous sublayer
黏性干扰/黏性干涉　viscous interference
黏性干扰参数/黏性干擾參數　viscous interaction parameter
黏性激波层方程/黏性震波層方程式　viscous shock-layer equation
黏性流动/黏性流動　viscous flow
黏性[流]空气动力学/黏性流動空氣動力學　viscous flow aerodynamics
黏性流体/黏性流體　viscous fluid
黏性土/黏[結]性土　cohesive soil
黏性系数/黏度係數　coefficient of viscosity, viscosity coefficient
黏性压差阻力/黏滯壓力阻力　viscous pressure drag
黏性阻力/黏性阻力　viscous resistance
黏性阻尼/黏滯阻尼,阻滯　viscous damping
黏压阻力/黏性壓差阻力　viscous pressure resistance
黏质粉土/黏質粉土　clayey silt
黏质土/黏土質土壤　clayey soil
黏着力/黏著[力],附著[力]　adhesion
黏着牵引力/黏著牽引力　adhesive tractive effort
黏着系数/黏著係數　adhesion coefficient
黏着限/黏著限度,黏限　sticky limit
黏着制动/黏著制動　adhesion braking
黏着重量利用系数/黏重利用因數,黏重利用率　adhesive weight utility factor
捻度/撚度　amout of twist
捻缝/撚縫　caulking, calk
捻距/絞線股長　length of lay
辗钢车轮/軋製鋼輪　wrought steel wheel, rolled steel wheel
辗环/車環軋　ring rolling
碾米厂/碾米廠　rice milling plant
碾压/滾壓實　rolling, rolling compaction
碾压坝/滾壩　rolling dam
碾压法/輾壓　compaction by rolling
碾压混凝土/壓實混凝土　rolled concrete
碾压混凝土路面/碾壓混凝土路面　rolling

compacted concrete pavement, RCCP
碾压机/壓路機　roller
碾压速度/滑跑速率　rolling speed
碾压填土/輾壓填土　rolled fill
碾压土坝/輾壓土壩　rolled earth dam
碾玉装/碾玉裝　nianyuzhuang
鸟瞰图/鳥瞰圖　bird eye view
鸟类保护区/鳥類保護區　bird sanctuary
鸟笼/鳥籠　bird cage, bird coop
鸟舍/鳥舍　bird cottage, nestle box
鸟浴/鳥浴　bird bath
鸟撞/鳥擊　bird strike
尿收集袋/尿收集袋　urine collection bag
镍铬耐热合金/鎳鉻合金　nichrome
镍铬钛[耐热]合金/鎳鉻立克[耐熱合金]　nimonic alloy
镍基高温合金/鎳基超合金　nickel-base superalloy
镍基合金/鎳基合金　nickel based alloy
镍铝化合物/鎳鋁介金屬　nickel aluminide
凝固点/凝固點,凝結點　solidification point, solidifying point
凝灰岩/凝灰岩　tuff
凝结/凝結　setting
凝结核/凝結核　condensation nucleus
凝结激波/凝結震波　condensation shock
凝结潜热/凝縮潛熱　latent heat of condensation
凝结时间/凝結時間　setting time
凝结水/冷凝液　condensate
凝结水回收率/冷凝液採收率　condensate recovery percentage
凝结水回收系统/凝結水回流系統　condensate return system
凝结水箱/冷凝槽　condensate tank
凝结作用/凝結作用　pozzolana action
凝聚/凝聚　cohesion, coagulation
凝聚剂/凝聚劑　coagulant
凝聚力/凝聚力,凝結力　cohesion
凝聚作用/凝聚作用　retentive
凝汽器/凝汽器　condenser
[凝汽器]冷却面积/冷卻面　cooling surface, condenser cooling surface
凝汽式汽轮机/凝汽式汽輪機,凝汽渦輪機,凝汽式蒸汽渦輪機　condensing turbine, condensing steam turbine
凝视导引头/起動歸航器　staring homing head
凝视阵列/凝視陣列　staring array
凝水泵/凝水泵　condensate pump
凝水系统/凝水系統　condensate system
凝水再循环管路/凝水再循環泵　condensate recirculating pipe line
牛顿理论/牛頓理論　Newtonian theory
牛乳处理间/[牛]乳處理廠　milk house
牛腿/托架,支托　bracket, corbel
牛形底桩/瘤根樁　button-bottom pile
牛眼环/牛眼環　bull eye ring
扭杆式加速度计/扭轉加速度計　torsional accelerometer
扭杆式速率陀螺仪/扭式速率陀螺儀　torsion type rate gyro
扭杆弹簧/扭力棒彈簧　torsion bar spring
扭剪式高强度螺栓/扭剪式高強度螺栓　torshear type high strength bolt
扭矩/扭矩,轉[力]矩　torque, torsional moment
扭矩表/扭矩計,扭矩儀　torque indicator
扭矩-扭角曲线/扭矩-扭轉角曲線　torque-torsional angle curve
扭矩弹簧/扭轉彈簧　torque spring
扭矩转换器/扭矩變換器　torque converter
扭力/扭力,扭轉　torsion
扭力扳手/扭力扳手,轉矩扳手　torque spanner, torque wrench
扭力计/扭力計,轉矩計　torsional meter
扭曲/扭曲,扭轉　twisting, distortion, twist
扭锁/扭轉鎖定器　twist lock
扭[振]共振/扭轉共振　torsional resonance
扭振减振器/扭轉振動減振器　torsional vibration damper
扭转/扭轉,扭力　torsion
扭转半径/扭轉半徑　radius of tortion
扭转动作/扭轉作用　twist action
扭转刚度/扭轉勁度　torsional stiffness
扭转角/扭[轉]角　angle of twist
扭转疲劳裂纹/扭轉疲勞裂痕　torsional fatigue cracks
扭转强度/抗扭強度　torsional strength
扭转屈曲/扭轉挫曲　torsional buckling
扭转试验/扭力試驗　torsion test
扭转振动/扭轉振動　torsional vibration
扭转中心/扭[轉中]心　center of twist
纽约高线公园/紐約高線公園　High Line Park of New York City
纽约中央公园/保護區中心區　Central Park of New York City
钮头/鉚釘頭　button head
农产品储藏库/農產品庫房　agro-products storage building

农村道路/鄉道　village road
农村地区/鄉村地區,農村區域　rural area
农村发展/農村開發　rural development
农村公共设施用地/鄉村公共設施用地　rural public facility land
农村环境卫生/鄉村環境衛生　rural sanitation
农村集市/農村集市,草市　rural market
农村给水/農村給水　rural water supply
农村建设用地/鄉村建設用地　rural construction land
农村节能炉窑/農村節能爐窯　rural fuel saving stove and kiln
农村经营性建设用地/農村經營性建設用地　rural operating construction land
农村能源建筑/鄉村能源建築物　rural energy building
农村人口/鄉村人口　rural population
农村社区/農村社區,鄉村社區,田園社區　rural community
农机具维修站/農機具維修站　agricultural machine repair station
农机站/農機站　farm machinery station
农具棚/農業工具房　agricultural tool shed
农林复合生态系统/農林複合生態系統　integral agroforestry ecosystem
农林复合系统/農業森林學　agroforestry
农林用地/農林用地　agricultural and forestry land
农贸市场/集貿市場,農產品市場　farm product market
农田防护林/農田防護林,農田保安林　farmland shelterbelt
农田排水/農田排水　agricultural drain
农田排水沟/農田排水溝　agricultural drain
农药残效期/農藥殘效期　pesticide residual effect period
农药厂/農藥廠　pesticide plant
农业带/農業地帶　agricultural belt
农业服务中心/農業研究中心　agricultural service center
农业合作社/農業合作社　agricultural cooperation
农业机/農業飛機　agricultural airplane
农业机械厂/農業機械廠　agricultural machinery plant
农业建筑/農業建築　agricultural building
农业排水/農田排水　agricultural drain
农业排水沟/農田排水溝　agricultural drain
农业气象站/農業氣象站,農業氣象室　agrometeorological station
农业区/農業區　agricultural district
农业区划/農業區劃　agricultural zoning
农业生产设施用地/農業生產設施用地　agricultural production facility land
农业生态学/農業生態學　agroecology
农业土壤学/實用土壤學,土壤生態學　edaphology
农业用地/農地　agricultural land
农用仓库建筑/農場倉庫建築物　farm store building
农用船/農用船　agricultural vessel
农用地/農業用地　farmland
农用地转用/農地變更　farmland conversion
农用人工气候设施/農用人工氣候設施　artificial climate control installation for agriculture
农用运输汽车/農用運輸汽車　agricultural truck
农作物蒙尘/農作物蒙塵　crops covering by dust
浓差电池腐蚀/濃差電池腐蝕　concentration cell corrosion
浓度/濃度,密度　density
浓缩/濃縮　concentration
浓缩倍数/濃縮倍數　cycle of concentration
浓缩池/濃縮槽　thickener
浓缩器/濃縮器　concentrator
努塞特数/紐賽數,奴塞數　Nusselt number
怒涛/怒濤　precipitous sea
女儿墙/女兒牆,欄杆　parapet wall
暖锋/暖鋒　warm front
暖锋降水/暖鋒降水　warm front precipitation
暖机/暖機　warming-up
暖机蒸汽系统/暖機蒸汽系統　warming-up steam system
暖季型草/暖帶　warm-season grass
暖季型草坪草/暖季草坪草　warm-season turfgrass
暖流/暖流　warm current
暖棚/暖棚,塑膠溫室　shed, plastic house
暖平流/暖平流　warm advection
暖气团/暖氣團　warm air mass
暖汽端阀/列車閘管端閥　train pipe end valve
暖汽软管/暖汽軟管　heater hose
暖汽软管连接器/暖汽軟管連接器　heater hose coupler
暖汽支管/暖汽支管　heater branch pipe
暖汽主管/暖汽主管　heater train pipe
暖色/暖色　warm color
暖色表/暖色表　warm color appearance
暖色光/暖光　warm light
暖体假人/暖體假人　thermal manikin
挪威船级社/挪威驗船協會　Det Norske Veritas, NV

O

欧拉方程/歐拉方程式　Euler equation
欧拉观点/歐拉觀點　Euler viewpoint
欧拉荷载/尤拉負載　Euler load
欧拉临界力/歐拉臨界力　Euler critical force
欧拉数/歐拉數,尤拉數　Euler number
欧姆接触/歐姆接觸　ohmic contact
欧洲风景公约/歐洲風景公約　European Landscape Convention
欧洲建筑遗产宪章/歐洲建築遺產憲章　European Charter of the Architectural Heritage
呕吐袋/嘔吐袋　seasickness bag
偶发噪声/偶發噪音　sporadic noise
偶极子/偶流　doublet
偶极子流/偶極子流　doublet flow
偶然故障/隨機故障　random fault
偶然荷载/偶然荷載　accidental load, accidental action
偶然失效期/偶然失效期　chance failure period
偶然误差/偶差　accidental error
偶然作用/偶然作用　accidental action
耦合/耦合　coupling
耦合模态/耦合模態　coupled mode
耦合运动/耦合運動　coupling motion
耦合振动/耦合振動　coupled vibration, coupling vibration
耦合装置/聯結裝置　coupling device

P

爬轨/爬軌 climb on rail
爬碱/爬鹼 electrolyte creepage
爬模/爬模,昇模 climbing shuttering, climbing form
爬坡车道/爬坡車道 climbing lane
爬坡车道标志/爬坡車道標誌 climbing lane sign
爬坡性能试验/爬坡性能試驗 climbing ability test
爬山廊/爬山廊 sloping gallery
爬升/爬昇 climb
爬升角/爬昇角 angle of climb, climbing angle
爬升距离/爬昇距離 climbing distance
爬升率/爬昇率 rate of climb, climbing rate
爬升模板/爬模,昇模 climbing shuttering, climbing form
爬升时间/爬昇時間 climbing time
爬升梯度/爬昇梯度 climbing gradient
爬升限制重量/爬昇限制重量 climb limiting weight
耙斗装料机/刮土裝載機 scraper loader
耙斗装载机/刮土裝載機 scraper loader
耙式分级机/栅式分級機 rake classifier
耙式分离器/栅式分級機 rake classifier
耙吸挖泥船/耙吸挖泥船 trailing suction hopper dredger
耙吸装置/耙吸設施 drag and suction device
帕拉第奥券柱式/帕拉第奧母題,帕拉迪奧母題 Palladian motive
帕伦克古城和国家公园/奇特旺國家公園 Pre-Hispanic City and National Park of Palenque
拍岸浪/拍岸浪,潑岸浪 surf
拍击/拍擊 pounding
拍卖船舶/拍賣船舶 auction of ship
拍频/拍頻,差頻 beat frequency
排斥力/排斥力 repulsion force
排出阀/排出閥,排放閥 discharge valve
排出流/排出流 discharge current
排出流横向力/排流橫向力 transverse force of discharge current
排出水处置/放流水處置 effluent disposal
排出压头/流出落差 discharge head
排队规则/排隊規則 queue rule
排队理论/排隊論 queue theory
排队论/編序理論,鵠候理論 queuing theory

排筏/木排,木筏 log raft, wood raft
排放标准/流出物標準 effluent standard
排放管/排放器 eductor
排放集管/排洩歧管 discharge manifold
排放口/排水口,出口 outlet
排放浓度/流出物濃度 effluent concentration
排放条件/排洩條件 conditions of discharge
排放污染/排氣污染 exhaust emission, exhaust pollution
排放性能/排放性能 emission performance
排风道/排風管道 air exhausting duct
排风机房/排風機房,排風機室 exhaust fan room
排风机通风/排風機通風,抽風機通風 ventilation by exhaust fan
排风竖井/排風竖井 blowing-out shaft
排管/排管 tube rake
排汗冷却效率/出汗冷卻效率 cooling efficiency of sweating
排架/排架 bent frame, bent
排架式满布木拱架/排架式滿布木拱架 full span wooden bent centering
排架式桥墩/椿排架橋墩,排架椿墩 pile bent pier
排架桩墩/排架椿墩,椿排架橋墩 pile bent pier
排架桩基础/椿排架基礎 pile bent foundation
排距/行距 row spacing
排涝/排水 drainage, water drainage
排涝桥/排澇橋 flood relief bridge
排练厅/排練室,排演室 rehearsal room
排链/錨艙排列錨鏈 tiering
排列进路/排列進路 route setting
排流速度/退卻流速 velocity of retreat
排流线圈/排流線圈 drainage coil
排泥管/輸泥管,輸泥倉 dredge pipe, line mud pipe
排泥管接岸装置/排泥管接岸裝置 shore connecting plant
排泥机具/排泥設施 soil discharging facility
排泥沙喷射泵/泥漿噴射器 silt ejector
排泥设备/排泥設施 soil discharging facility
排气背压/排氣背壓,排氣反壓力 exhaust back pressure
排气槽/通氣孔,通氣口 air vent

排气冲量/排氣衝量　exhaust impulse
排气道/排氣[導]管　exhaust duct
排气阀/排氣閥　exhaust valve
排气阀液压旋转系统/排氣閥液壓轉動系統　hydraulic exhaust valve rotation system
排气风机/排氣機,抽風機　exhaust fan
排[气]风扇/排風機,抽風機　exhaust fan
排气管/通氣管,通風管　vent pipe
排气净化器/排氣用淨化器　exhaust purifier
排气颗粒/排氣顆粒　exhaust particulate
排气壳体/排氣外殼　exhaust hood, exhaust casing
排气口/排氣口　exhaust port
排气门/排氣閥　exhaust valve
排气速度/排氣速度,排出速度　exhaust velocity
排气凸轮/排氣凸輪,排氣轢　exhaust cam profile
排气温度/排氣温度　exhaust temperature
排气温度表/排氣温度表　exhaust gas thermometer
排气系统/排氣系統　exhaust system
排气箱/排氣箱　exhaust box
排气消声器/排氣消音器　exhaust muffler
排气行程/排氣衝程　exhaust stroke
排气压力表/排氣壓力表　exhaust gas pressure gage
排气烟度/排煙濃度　exhaust smoke density
排气有害成分/毒性排氣成分　poisonous exhaust composition
排气噪声/排氣噪音　exhaust noise
排气支管/排氣支管　exhaust branch pipe
排气装置/排氣裝置　exhaust unit
排气总管/排氣歧管　exhaust manifold
排气组件/排氣組件　gas deflation assembly
排汽/排汽　exhaust steam
排汽室/排氣室　exhaust chest
排汽系统/排汽系統　exhaust system, exhaust steam system
排汽余面/排汽餘面　exhaust lap
排球场/排球場　volleyball court
排砂阀/排砂閥　scour valve
排水板/排水板　drainage board
排水板法/排水板法　sheet drainage
排水泵站/排水泵站　drainage pumping station, drainga pumping
排水不良/排水不良　poor drainage
排水槽/排水道　drainage channel
排水船/排水型船　displacement ship
排水定额/排水定額　wastewater flow norm
排水法/排洩法　draining method
排水工程/排水工程　water drainage works, drainage works, wastewater engineering
排水沟/排水溝,下水溝　drainage ditch, drain ditch
排水管/排水管　drainage pipe
排水剪切试验/排水剪力試驗　drained shear test
排水口/排水口　wash port, drain opening
排水量/排水量　displacement, drainage discharge
排水量曲线/排水量曲線　displacement curve
排水能力/排水性能,排水能量　drainage ability, water discharge capacity
排水平衡/排水平衡　drainage equilibrium
排水情形/排水情形　drained condition
排水区/排水區域　drainage area
排水砂垫层/排水砂墊層　drainage sand mat, sand filled drainage layer, drainage sand blanket
排水设备/排水設施　drainage appliance
排水设计/排水設計　drainage design
排水设计暴雨强度/排水設計暴雨強度　intensity of rainstorm in drainage design
排水设计重现期/排水設計頻率　drainage design frequency
排水设施/排水設施,廢水設施　wastewater facility, drainage facility
排水试验/排水試驗　drained test
排水系统/排水系統,廢水系統　drainage system, sewer system
排水型船/排水型船　displacement ship
排水制度/下水道系統　sewer system
排土桩/排土樁,打入樁　displacement pile
排污/排汙　blowdown
排污阀/底部吹洩閥,沖放閥　blowdown valve
排污费/汙水費　sewage charge
排污口/廢水放流口　wastewater outfall
排泄/排放　discharge
排泄系统/放氣系統　bleed system
排序/順序排列　ordination
排衙石/排衙石　guard stone
排烟/排煙　smoke extraction
排烟道/排煙窗　smoke vent
排烟阀/排煙閥門　smoke exhaust damper
排烟机房/排煙室　smoke exhaust room
排烟口/煙出口　smoke outlet
排烟热损失/排煙熱損失　heat loss due to exhaust gas
排烟数/煙值　smoke number
排盐/排鹽　elimination
排盐泵/衝放泵　blow down pump
排盐量/排鹽率　brine rate
排油阀卸载作用/排油閥油路減壓,排油閥油路卸載　delivery valve line retraction

排油监控系统/洩油監控系統　oil discharge monitoring and control system, oil discharge monitoring system
排油监控装置/洩油偵控系統　oil discharge monitoring and control system
排油控制/排油管制　control of discharge of oil
排障器/排障器　pilot, life guard
牌坊/牌坊　memorial archway, paifang
派出所/派出所　local police station
潘萨住宅/潘薩住宅　House of Pansa
攀岩运动/攀岩　rock climbing
攀缘绿化/攀緣綠化　climber greening
攀缘式/攀緣式　climbing planting
攀缘植物/攀緣植物, 纏繞植物　climbing plant
盘车/盤車, 起動　bar the engine, barring
盘车机构/盤車裝置　barring mechanism, barring gear
盘车联锁装置/盤車聯鎖裝置　turning gear interlocking device
盘管/盤管　coil
盘脚桩/底盤式樁　disc pile
盘面比/盤面比　disc ratio
盘山路/盤山路　switch back
盘式曝气器/盤式曝氣器　tray aerator
盘头铆钉/盤頭針頭, 平頭鉚釘　pan head rivet
盘线装置/卷線機, 盤繩機　line winder
盘型制动/盤式刹車, 圓盤軔　disc brake
盘旋/盤旋　turn
盘旋法/盤旋法　method of turns
盘旋进近/繞場進場　circling approach
判读/判讀　identification, interpretation
判决值/決策值　decision value
旁瓣回波/旁[波]瓣回波　sidelobe echo
旁瓣抑制/旁[波]瓣抑制　sidelobe depression
旁承/邊軸承, 側支座　side bearing
旁承承载/滾邊軸承負載　side bearing loading
旁承间隙/旁承間隙　side bearing clearance
旁承载荷/滾邊軸承, 輥式側支座　load on side bearing
旁承支重转向架/滾邊軸承轉向架, 輥式側支座轉向架　side bearing truck
旁道/替代道路　relief road
旁桁材/側縱梁　side girder
旁进式人孔/側入人孔　side entrance manhole
旁流水/側流　side stream
旁路/旁通管　bypass pipe
旁内龙骨/側內龍骨　side keelson
旁视雷达/側視雷達　side-looking radar, SLR

旁通阀/旁通閥　by-pass valve
旁通调节/旁通調節, 旁路調節　by-pass governing, by-pass control
旁弯/旁彎　sidewise bending
旁压试验/壓力計試驗　pressure meter test, PMT
抛单锚/拋單錨　coming to a single anchor
抛放弹/子彈, 彈藥筒, 彈殼　cartridge
抛盖弹射/拋蓋彈射　canopy jettison ejection
抛光/拋光, 磨光　polishing
抛落式救生艇/自落式救生艇　free fall lifeboat
抛锚/拋錨　breakdown on the way, let go anchor
抛锚掉头/拋錨短迴轉掉頭　turning short round with anchor
抛锚试验/錨[泊]試驗　anchor test, anchoring trial, anchoring test
抛起锚口令/錨令　anchoring orders
抛弃/拋棄, 投棄　jettison
抛射体运动/拋射運動　motion of a projectile
抛绳回收袋/射索回收袋　shot line return bag
抛绳设备/拋繩器　line throwing appliance
抛石防护/拋石保護　riprap protection
抛石基床/拋石機床, 塊石基礎　rubble base, rubble-mound foundation
抛石挤淤/拋石擠淤　throwing stones to packing sedimentation, packing up sedimentation by dumping stones
抛石理波/拋石理波　grading of rock mound
抛坍爆破/拋坍爆破　collapse blasting
抛填/拋填　dumping fill
抛艉锚/拋後錨　anchor by the stern
抛物面/拋物曲面　parabolic surface
抛物面天线/拋物面天線　parabolic antenna
抛物线穹顶/拋物形拱頂　parabolic vault
抛物线状薄壳/拋物形薄殼　parabolic shell
抛掷爆破/拋擲爆破　throwing blasting, pin-point blasting
抛掷清扫车/拋擲清掃車　abandon sweeper
跑场道/交通廊道　access gallery
跑道/跑道　runway
跑道边灯/跑道邊燈　runway edge light
跑道标志/跑道標誌　runway marking
跑道道面/跑道鋪面　runway surface
跑道端安全地区/跑道頭安全區　runway end safety area
跑道进出滑行道/跑道進出滑行道　runway access taxiway
跑道末端灯/跑道頭辨識燈　runway end identification light

跑道容量/跑道容量　runway capacity
跑道入口/跑道入口　runway threshold
跑道入口灯/跑道入口指示燈　runway threshold light
跑道视程/跑道視程　runway visual range, RVR
跑道限制重量/跑道限制重量　runway limiting weight
跑道中线灯/跑道中心線燈　runway center line light
跑马场/跑馬場,賽馬場　race course
跑偏/跑偏　pulling to one side
跑台/跑步機　treadlemill
泡沫玻璃/泡沫玻璃,發泡玻璃　foamed glass, cellular glass
泡沫分离/泡沫分離　foam separation
泡沫混凝土/泡沫混凝土,起泡混凝土　foamed concrete, foam concrete
泡沫聚苯乙烯/泡沫聚苯乙烯　foamed polystyrene
泡沫矿渣/多孔爐碴,膨脹爐碴　foamed slag
泡沫沥青装置/泡沫瀝青裝置　foam asphalt unit
泡沫灭火器/泡沫滅火器　foamite extinguisher, foam fire extingusher
泡沫灭火系统/泡沫滅火系統　foam fire extinguishing system
泡沫-水雨淋灭火系统/泡沫-水雨淋系統　foam-water deluge system
泡沫塑料/泡沫塑膠,氣泡塑膠　foamed plastic, cellular plastic
泡沫橡胶/泡沫橡膠,氣泡橡膠　foamed rubber
炮风洞/炮風洞　gun tunnel
炮架/炮架　gun rest, carriage
炮口功率/炮口功率　muzzle power
炮身窗护板/炮擋,炮圍　gun shield, gun port shield
炮塔/炮塔,角塔　turret
炮眼布置/鑽孔配置　drilling pattern, hole placement
炮眼导向架/鑽孔定位支架　hole director
炮眼扩孔/孔底擴大　chambering
炮眼深度/井眼深度　borehole depth
炮眼直径/井徑　borehole diameter
胚培养/胚培養　embryo culture
胚乳培养/胚乳培養　endosperm culture
胚状体/不定胚　embryoid
陪都/陪都　peidu, auxiliary capital
培根型燃料电池/培根燃料電池　Bacon type fuel cell
培养/培養　incubation
培养基/培養基　culture medium
赔偿率/賠償率　rate of freight compensation
赔付线/給價界線　pay line
佩恩希尔公园/佩因斯希爾莊園　Painshill Park
佩里公园/派利公園　Paley Park
佩特沃思府邸/佩特沃斯莊園,佩特沃恩住宅　Petworth House
配餐间/配膳室　pantry
配电/配電　distribution, distribution of electricity
配电变压器/配電變壓器　distribution transformer
配电电器/配電電器　distributing apparatus
配电柜/配電櫃,配電箱,分線盒　distribution box, electric power distribution cabinet
配电距离/分布距離　distribution distance
配电开关/配電開關　distribution switch
配电盘/配電盤,配電板,控制板　distribution panel, distribution board, switch board
配电屏/饋電盤,饋電屏　feeder panel
配电系统/配電系統　distribution system
配电箱/配電箱,分線盒　distribution box
配电站/配電站　power distribution station
配箍率/配箍率　stirrup ratio
配光曲线/發光強度分布曲線,測光曲線　luminous intensity distribution curve, photometric curve
配合比/配合比　mix proportion
配合比设计/配比設計　design of mix proportion
配合件/配合件　matching member
配合件标记/裝配標記　match-marking
配件互换修/配件互換修　repair with interchangeable component
配建设施/服務設施　service facility
配筋/鋼筋排列　bar arrangement
配筋率/鋼筋比　reinforcement ratio, steel ratio
配筋砌体/配筋砌體　reinforced masonry
配筋砌体结构/配筋砌體結構　reinforced masonry structure
配筋砖砌体/加筋砌磚工　reinforced brickwork
配景/配景　objective view
配料槽/調劑室　dosing tank
配料车间/混凝土配料廠　batch plant
配料机/分配器　dispenser
配料给料装置/配料給料裝置　aggregate feeder unit
配料设备/調劑設備　dosing device
配平/配平　trimming
配平攻角/配平攻角　trim angle of attack
配平角/俯仰角　trim angle, angle of trim
配气定时/閥動定時　valve timing
配气管道/配氣管道　gas distribution pipeline
配气间/配氣站　gas distribution room
配气门站/[配氣]門站　gate station of gas

distribution network
配气相位/配氣相位 valve timing
配气站/配氣站,氣體分輸站 gas distribution station, gas distributing station
配汽机构/配汽機構,配汽設施 steam distribution device
配汽调整/配汽調整 steam distribution adjustment
配色/配色 color matching
配色系统/配色系統 color matching system
配饰/屬具,附屬品 accessory
配属机车/分配機車 allocated locomotive
配水池/配水池,配水庫 distributing reservoir
配水干管[渠]/配水主管 distributing main
配水管/配水管 distributing pipe, water distribution pipe
配水管网/配水管網,配水系統 water distribution system, water distribution network
配水面积/配水面積 distributing area
配送支管/配水支管 distributing branch
配线电缆/分配電纜,分配線 distribution cable
配音室/配音室 dubbing room
配碴整形机/配碴整形機 ballast distributing and regulating machine
配置轴/序列軸 disposition axis
配重/配重 counter weight, mass-balance weight
配重箱/壓重箱,壓載箱 ballast box
配装类/裝載種類 stowage category
喷播式/噴播式 spray-seeding planting
喷潮/噴潮 tidal blow
喷点/噴點 sprinkler site
喷管摆动力矩/噴管擺動力矩 nozzle swing moment
喷管摆动速率/噴管擺動速率 nozzle swing rate, nozzle slew rate
喷管摆心/噴管擺心 nozzle pivot point
喷管摆心漂移/噴管擺心漂移 nozzle pivot point drift
喷管半扩张角/噴管半擴張角 nozzle divergence half angle
喷管冲质比/噴嘴衝質比 impulse to mass ratio of nozzle
喷管初始扩张角/噴嘴初始擴張角 nozzle initial divergence angle
喷管底阻/噴管底阻 nozzle base drag
喷管堵盖打开压强/噴管堵蓋打開壓強 nozzle closure opening pressure
喷管段/噴嘴組 nozzle section
喷管[面积]扩张比/噴嘴面積擴散比 nozzle area expansion ratio
喷管[面积]收缩比/噴嘴面積收縮比 nozzle area contraction ratio
喷管名义马赫数/噴管名義馬赫數 nominal Mach number of nozzle
喷管膨胀比/噴嘴膨脹比 nozzle expansion ratio
喷管潜入比/噴嘴潛沒比 submergence ratio of nozzle
喷灌/噴灌,噴灑灌溉 sprinkler irrigation, spray irrigation
喷灌电磁阀/噴灌電磁閥 sprinkler irrigation solenoid valve
喷灌覆盖面/噴灌覆蓋面 sprinkler coverage
喷灌器/固定噴灌器 stationary sprinkler
喷灌系统/噴灌系統 sprinkler irrigation system
喷溅抑制槽/噴濺抑制槽 groove type spray suppressor
喷溅阻力/濺水阻力 spray resistance
喷浆层/噴漿襯砌 gunite lining
喷浆机/水泥噴槍 concrete injector, cement gun
喷浆挖掘法/沖挖法 jet cutter method
喷口送风/噴口送風 nozzle outlet air supply
喷口位置表/噴嘴位置顯示 nozzle position indicator
喷淋设备/噴水系統,噴灑系統 sprinkler system
喷淋式热交换器/噴霧式熱交換器 spray type heat exchanger
喷淋蒸发式冷凝器/噴灑蒸發冷凝器 spray evaporative condenser
喷流试验/噴射試驗 jet testing
喷流噪声/噴氣噪音 jet noise
喷锚衬砌/噴射錨栓襯砌 shotcrete bolt lining
喷锚构筑法/噴錨支護法 shotcrete bolt construction method
喷锚支护/噴錨支承 shotcrete and rock bolt support
喷泥作用/噴泥作用 mud pumping action
喷漆/噴漆 spray painting, spraying lacquer
喷漆房/噴漆棚 spray booth
喷气发动机/噴射發動機 jet engine
喷气发动机驱动风洞/噴射[發動]機驅動風洞 jet-driven wind tunnel
喷气发动机[叶片]调制效应/噴射發動機調制效應 jet engine modulation effect, JEM effect
喷气反作用控制系统/噴射反應控制系統 jet reaction control system
喷气脉冲/噴氣脈衝 jet pulse
喷气燃料/噴射機燃油 jet fuel
喷气式除雪机/噴氣式除雪機 air jet snow remover
喷气推进/噴射推進 jet propulsion
喷气推进船/噴氣推進船,噴氣推進艇 air jet

propelled boat, air jet ship
喷气推进器/噴射推進器 jet propeller, jet propulsion unit
喷气姿态控制/噴氣姿態控制 gas jet attitude control
喷枪/噴[液]槍 spray gun, spray lance
喷泉/噴泉 fountain
喷泉控制系统/噴泉控制系統 fountain control system
喷泉设备/噴水池裝置 fountain equipment
喷燃器/燃燒器,燃燒爐 burner
喷洒除草机/除草機 weed killing machine, weed killer
喷洒方式/噴霧形狀 spray pattern
喷洒灌溉/噴灑灌溉 sprinker irrigation
喷洒沥青/瀝青灑布 asphalt distribution
喷洒装置/噴灑裝置,撒布器 sprinkler
喷砂/噴砂 sand blast, sand blasting
喷射/噴射 jetting
喷射泵/噴射泵 jet pump, jet dredge pump
喷射泵挖泥船/噴射式挖泥船 jet ejector dredger
喷射成形/噴射成形 spray process, spray forming
喷射成形材料/噴射成形材料 spray formed material
喷射处理/噴砂處理 blasting
喷射动量/噴射動量 eject momentum
喷射法除锈/噴射法除銹 shot rust removing
喷射钢纤维混凝土/鋼纖維噴射混凝土 steel fiber shotcrete, steel fiber reinforced shotcrete
喷射过渡/噴灑狀傳遞 spray transfer
喷射混凝土/噴射混凝土,噴凝土 shotcrete
喷射混凝土衬砌/噴射混凝土襯砌 shotcrete lining
喷射混凝土粉尘/噴製混凝土塵 shotcrete dust
喷射混凝土回弹/噴射混凝土回彈 rebound of shotcrete
喷射混凝土机械手/噴射混凝土機械手 shotcrete manipulator
喷射混凝土锚杆支护/噴製混凝土錨定螺栓支座 shotcrete rock bolt support
喷射混凝土修理/噴射混凝土修理 shotcrete repair
喷射混凝土支护/噴射混凝土支護 shotcrete support
喷射能/噴射能 jet energy
喷射器/噴射器 eductor
喷射式污水排水器/壓氣污水抽送機 pneumatic sewage ejector
喷射运输机/噴射輸送機 jet conveyor
喷射装置/噴射裝置 jet bubbler

喷施/噴施 spraying fertilizer
喷水池/噴水池 fountain pool
喷水管布置/噴水管布置 piping schema
喷水冒砂/沙沸,沙湧 sand boil
喷水泉/噴水泉 spring geyser
喷水推进/噴水推進,噴射推進 waterjet propulsion, jet propulsion
喷水推进船/噴水推進船,噴射推進船 hydrojet propelled ship, waterjet vessel, hydrojet boat
喷水推进器/噴水推進器 waterjet propulsor
喷水推进燃气轮机/噴水推進燃氣渦輪機 waterjet propulsion gas turbine
喷头工作压力/噴頭工作壓力 sprinkler operating pressure
喷头流量/噴頭流量 sprinkler flow rate
喷头射程/噴頭射程 sprinkler pattern radius
喷涂/噴塗 spray painting, spraying, spray coating
喷涂包覆/噴塗布,噴塗層 spraying coating
喷涂发泡/噴塗層發泡 spray coating foaming
喷涂陶瓷密封环/噴塗陶瓷封環 spraying-ceramic seal ring
喷丸/噴丸[處理],噴[射鋼]珠除銹,珠[粒噴]擊 shot blasting, grit blasting
喷丸成形/珠擊成型 shot peen forming
喷丸机/噴珠除銹機 shot blaster, shot blast chamber, shot blast machine
喷雾喷灌器/噴霧噴灌器 mist sprinkler, spray head sprinkler
喷雾器/噴霧器 sprayer
喷雾自控系统/噴霧自控系統 automatic mist control system
喷焰衰减/噴焰衰減 plume attenuation
喷油泵/噴油泵 fuel injection pump
喷油泵传动装置/噴油泵傳動機構 injection pump transmission mechanism
喷油泵驱动齿轮/噴射泵驅動齒輪 injection pump drive gear
喷油泵凸轮/噴油泵凸輪 injection pump cam
喷油持续角/噴油持續角 continuous injection angle
喷油定时/噴油定時 injection timing
喷油规律/噴油規律 law of injection
喷油器/噴油器,燃油噴射器 fuel injector
喷油器冷却泵/燃料噴射閥冷卻泵 fuel injection valve cooling pump
喷油器滤芯/噴油器濾芯 injector filter core
喷油器启阀压力/燃油閥開啟壓力 fuel valve opening pressure
喷油器试验台/噴油器試驗設備 injector testing

equipment
喷油速率/噴油速率 injection rate
喷油提前角/噴油提前角 fuel injection advance angle, injection advance angle
喷油压力/噴射壓力 injection pressure
喷油正时/噴油定時 injection timing
喷油嘴滴漏/噴油嘴滴漏 nozzle dribbling
喷油嘴偶件/噴射器嘴偶合件,噴油嘴噴嘴偶合件 injector nozzle matching parts
喷油嘴针阀/噴嘴針閥 nozzle needle valve
喷油嘴针阀体/噴嘴針閥體 nozzle needle valve body
喷注/噴注 jetting
喷注器/注射器 injector
喷嘴/噴嘴,噴口 nozzle
喷嘴阀/噴嘴閥 nozzle valve
喷嘴环/噴嘴環,噴管環 nozzle ring
喷嘴流量计/管嘴計 nozzle meter
喷嘴式沥青乳化机/噴嘴式瀝青乳化機 nozzle bitumen emulsifying machine
喷嘴试验器/噴射器試驗裝置 nozzle tester
喷嘴室/噴嘴室,噴箱 nozzle box, nozzle chamber
喷嘴调节/噴嘴調節 nozzle governing
喷嘴组/噴嘴塊 nozzle block
盆地/盆地 basin
盆花花卉/盆栽 potted plant
盆花生产/盆花生產 potted flower production
盆景/盆景 miniature landscape, penjing, bonsai art
盆景花坛/盆景花壇 penjing flower bed
盆景配件/盆景配件 penjing accessories
盆景盆体/盆景盆體 penjing pot
盆景土/盆景土 pot mixture for penjing
盆景艺术/盆景藝術 penjing art
盆景园/盆景園 penjing garden, bonsai garden, miniature landscape
盆景植物/盆景植物 penjing plant
盆式拌和机/盆式拌合機 pan type mixer
盆式橡胶支座/盆式橡膠支座,盆式橡膠支承 pot rubber bearing
盆式支座/盆式支座 pot bearing
盆形燃烧室/盆形燒燒室 bowl shaped combustion chamber
盆栽/盆栽,盆景 potting, bonsai
盆栽灌水系统/盆栽灌水系統 pot watering system
盆栽花坛/盆栽花壇 potted flower bed, basined flower bed
盆栽机/盆栽機 potting machine
盆栽试验/盆栽試驗 pot culture experiment
砰击/波擊 slamming

砰击载荷/波擊負荷 slamming load
棚车/箱車 box car, covered goods wagon
棚洞/棚洞 shed tunnel
棚户区/棚戶區 shanty area
棚架绿化/棚架綠化 trellis greening
棚屋/儲藏庫 covered storage, storage shed
棚屋护板/木板擋牆 camp sheathing
硼铝复合材料/硼鋁複合材料 aluminum boron composite
硼碳高温合金/硼碳高溫合金 boron-carbon superalloy, BC superalloy
膨润土/皂土 bentonite
膨润土处理/皂土處理 bentonite treatment
膨胀/漲脹 swelling
膨胀比/膨脹比 expansion ratio
膨胀波/膨脹波 expansion wave
膨胀多变指数/膨脹多方指數 polytropic index of expansion
膨胀管/伸縮管 expansion pipe
膨胀柜/膨脹櫃 expansion tank
膨胀-换气行程/膨脹-驅氣衝程 expansion-scavenging stroke
膨胀混凝土/膨脹混凝土 expansive cement concrete, expansive concrete
膨胀剂/膨脹劑 expanding admixture, expansion agent, expansive agent
膨胀节/膨脹接頭,伸縮接頭 expansion joint
膨胀矿渣/膨脹熔碴,有孔熔碴 expanded slag
膨胀力/膨脹力 swelling force
膨胀量/膨脹量 swelling amount
膨胀裂缝/膨脹裂縫 expansion crack
膨胀螺栓/膨脹螺栓 expansion bolt
膨胀铆钉/膨脹鉚釘 expansion rivet
膨胀黏土/膨脹黏土 expanded clay
膨胀试验/膨脹試驗 swelling test
膨胀水泥/膨脹[性]水泥 expansive cement, expanding cement
膨胀水箱/膨脹箱櫃 expansion tank, expansion drum
膨胀土地区路基/膨脹土地區路基 subgrade in swelling soil zone
膨胀系数/膨脹係數 coefficient of expansion
膨胀行程/膨脹衝程 expansion stroke
膨胀性黏粒/膨脹性黏土 expansive clay
膨胀性黏土/膨脹性黏土 expansive clay
膨胀性岩石/膨脹岩 expansive rock, swelling rock
膨胀循环/膨脹循環 expander cycle
膨胀压力/膨脹壓力 swelling pressure

膨胀页岩/膨脹頁岩　expanded shale
膨胀珍珠岩/膨脹珍珠岩　expanded perlite
膨胀蛭石/膨脹蛭石,層脹蛭石　exfoliated vermiculite, expanded vermiculite
膨胀终点温度/膨脹終點溫度　expansion terminal temperature
膨胀终点压力/膨脹終點壓力　expansion terminal pressure
碰垫/碰墊,護舷材　fender
碰角/碰撞角　collision angle
碰撞保险/碰撞保險　collision insurance
碰撞点/碰撞點　point of collision, PC
碰撞护栏/減速輔助器　crash barrier
碰撞警报/碰撞警報　collision warning
碰撞开关/碰撞開關,碰擊開關　impact switch
碰撞力/衝力　impulsive force
碰撞速度/碰撞速度　collision speed
碰撞危险/碰撞危機　risk of collision
批次/批　lot, batch
批发商店/批發店　wholesale store
批判的地域主义/批判的地域主義　critical regionalism
批注清单/批註清單　remark list
坯料/坯料,毛坯　billet, blank
劈拉强度/劈拉強度　split tensile strength, split strength
劈离砖/劈離磚,劈裂磚,劈開磚　split tile
劈裂/劈開　splitting
劈裂试验/分裂試驗　splitting test
劈裂注浆/劈裂灌漿　fracture grouting
劈相机/分相器　Arno converter, phase splitter
劈相机故障隔离开关/分相器故障隔離開關　fault isolating switch for phase splitter
皮带称重装置/輸送皮帶秤　conveyer belt scale
皮带打滑/皮帶滑動　belt slip
皮带给料机/帶式進料機　belt feeder
皮带输送机/帶式裝料機　belt loader
皮革厂/製革場　fur and leather factory, leather ware factory, tannery
皮划艇航道/皮劃艇航道　kayak channel
皮划艇运动/皮劃艇運動　canoe-kayak, canoeing
皮托管/皮托管,皮氏管　Pitot tube
皮托静压管/動靜壓管　Pitot static tube
毗连区/鄰接區　contiguous zone
铍合金/鈹合金　beryllium alloy
疲劳/疲勞　fatigue
疲劳承载能力/疲勞承載能力　fatigue capacity
疲劳断裂/疲勞破壞　fatigue failure

疲劳范围/疲勞範圍　fatigue range
疲劳荷载/疲勞負載　fatigue load
疲劳极限/疲勞極限,持久限界,疲勞限界　endurance limit, fatigue limit, endurance limit
疲劳裂纹/疲勞裂紋　fatigue cracking
疲劳裂纹扩展速率/疲勞裂痕成長率　fatigue crack growth rate
疲劳破坏/疲勞破壞　fatigue failure
疲劳破损/疲勞破壞　fatigue failure
疲劳强度/疲勞強度　fatigue strength
疲劳设计/疲勞設計　fatigue design
疲劳试验/疲勞試驗,耐久試驗　fatigue test
疲劳寿命/疲勞壽命　fatigue life
疲劳限度/疲勞[極]限　fatigue limit
疲劳载荷谱/疲勞負載譜　fatigue load spectrum
疲劳总寿命/疲勞總壽命　total fatigue life
匹配/配合,相配　matching
匹配检查/匹配檢查　matching check
匹配滤波器/匹配濾波器　matched filter
匹配试验/配對試驗　matching test
辟雍/璧雍　imperial academy
偏摆/船身回擺　sheer
偏差/偏差　deviation
偏荡/縱橫搖盪,[艚艉]平擺　yawing
偏度/偏度　skewness
偏二甲肼铁路运输车/偏二甲肼鐵路搬運車　UDMH railway tank transporter
偏光显微镜/偏光顯微鏡　polarizing microscope
偏航/偏航　off course, leeway, yawing
偏航角/偏航角　track angle error, yaw angle
偏航角速度/偏航率　rate of yaw
偏航距离/偏航距離　cross track distance
偏航力矩/偏航力矩　yawing moment
偏航修正角/預測角　prediction angle
偏航姿态/偏航姿態　yaw attitude
偏航姿态捕获/偏航姿態獲取　yaw attitude acquisition
偏畸变/偏移失真　bias distortion
偏极继电器/偏極繼電器　polar biased relay
偏角/偏角,折角　deflection angle, angle of deflection
偏角法/偏角法　deflection angle method
偏近点角/偏近點角　eccentric anomaly
偏缆灯/拖帶邊燈　towing side light
偏流/偏流　drift
偏流角/偏流角,流偏角,漂移角　drift angle
偏流修正/偏流修正　drift correction
偏食/偏食,偏蝕　partial eclipse

偏析/偏析,析離　segregation
偏斜张量/軸差應力　deviator stress
偏心传动装置/偏心機構　eccentric gear
偏心杆/偏心桿　eccentric rod, eccentric lever
偏心距[离]/偏心距[離]　eccentricity, eccentric distance
偏心距增大系数/偏心放大係數　magnifying coefficient of eccentricity
偏心率/偏心率,偏心度　eccentricity
偏心曲拐/偏心曲柄　eccentric crank
偏心受压/偏心壓力　eccentric compression
偏心受压法/偏心壓力法　eccentric compression method
偏心受压柱/偏心[壓力]柱　eccentrically compressed column
偏心显示/偏心顯示　off-centered display
偏压衬砌/偏壓襯砌　unsymmetrically loading lining eccentrically compressed lining
偏移/偏位,偏差,偏壓　offset, bias
偏振/偏振,極化　polarization
偏振光/偏振光　polarized light
偏[振]光镜/偏光鏡　polariscope
偏振滤光片/偏極化濾鏡　polarizing filter
偏振片/偏振片,偏光片　polaroid
偏置/偏壓,偏差　bias
偏置动量控制/動量偏斜控制　momentum bias control
偏置动量系统/動量偏斜系統　momentum bias system
偏置动量姿态控制系统/動量偏斜姿態控制系統　momentum bias attitude control system
偏置控制能力/偏斜控制能力　control bias capability
偏置稳定性/零偏穩定性　bias stability
偏中值/偏中值　misalignment value
偏转副翼/偏轉副翼　rudderon
偏转仪/磁向偏差測算儀　deflector
片筏基础/筏式基礎,席式基礎　raft foundation
片光流态显示/片光流場顯現　light-sheet flow visualization
片间平均电压/換向片間電壓　mean voltage between segments
片间最高电压/換向片間最高電壓　maximum voltage between segments
片理/片理　schistosity
片区供热系统/區域供熱系統　district heating system
片石/片石,毛石　rubble
片石基础/片石基礎　rubble foundation

片蚀/層[狀腐]蚀　layer corrosion
片式离合器/盤形離合器　disc clutch
片体/雙體船的半船體　demihull
片状空化/片狀空化　sheet cavitation
漂浮/漂浮　afloat
漂浮式防波堤港/浮式防波體　floating harbour
漂浮式管线/浮式輸泥管　floating pipeline
漂浮式下水/漂浮下水,自由浮離下水　floating launching, float-free launching
漂浮物/漂浮物,漂流物　drifter, floating substance, floating object
漂浮烟雾信号/浮[式發]煙信號　buoyant smoke signal
漂浮植物/漂浮植物　fluitante
漂航/漂流　drifting
漂角/漂移角,流偏角,偏流角　drift angle
漂流杆/測流漂桿,浮桿　drifting pole, float rod
漂流角/偏流修正角　crab angle
漂流瓶/測流瓶　drift bottle
漂流物/漂流物　derelict
漂流渔船/流網漁船　drift fishing boat, drift netter, drifter
漂石/漂礫,巨礫　boulder
漂心/浮面中心　center of flotation
漂心距中距离/縱向浮面中心與舯距離　longitudinal distance of center of flotation from midship
漂移/漂移,偏移　drift
漂移角/航偏角　angle of drift
漂移量/漂移量　drift value
漂移率/漂移率　drift rate
漂移修正/偏流修正　drift correction
漂白粉/漂白粉　chlorinated lime
票货分离/票貨分離　separation of waybill from shipment
票据传送设备/票據傳送設備　classification list conveyer system
撇缆/撇纜　heaving line
撇缆活结/撇纜索活結　heaving line slip knot
撇缆枪/撇纜槍,射繩槍,拋繩槍　line throwing gun
撇缆绳/撇纜繩,引纜繩　hauling line, heaving line
撇渣/撇除物　skimming
拼/拼　assemble
拼车货/拼車貨　less than truck load, LTL
拼合式/拼合式　split type
拼合轴燃气轮机/拼合軸燃氣渦輪機　split-shaft gas turbine
拼接/對接　butting
拼接板/拼接板,编接板　splice plate

拼贴城市/拼貼城市　collage city
拼箱/拼箱　mixed stuffing
拼箱货/不滿櫃貨物,拼裝櫃　less than container load, LCL
拼装式衬砌/裝配式襯砌　precast lining
拼装式桥墩/拼裝式橋墩　assembly pier, pier constructed with precast units
贫腐水性生物/貧腐水性生物　oligosaprobien
贫化/貧化　depletion
贫混凝土/貧乏混凝土　lean concrete
贫混凝土基层/貧混凝土基層　lean concrete base
贫民区/貧民區,貧民窟　slum area
贫民区改造/貧民窟清除　slum clearance
贫树脂区/樹脂貧區　resin starved region
贫养植物/貧營養植物　oligotrophic plant
贫营养化/貧養化　oligotrophication
频爆式推土机/頻爆式推土機　blasting bulldozer
频标/頻率標準　frequency standard
频带/頻帶　frequency band
频道/頻道　channel, spectral channel, frequency channel
频道空闲信号/頻道空閒信號　path free signal
频道切换阈值/頻道交換閾值　threshold for channel switching
频道选择器/頻道轉換開關,通道轉換開關,通道選擇器　channel selector
频度/頻度,頻次　frequency
频度中心/頻率中心　frequency center
频发噪声/頻發噪聲　frequent noise
频分复用/頻率分隔多路傳輸　frequency division multiplex
频分制多路遥测/頻分多工遙測　frequency division multiplexing telemetry
频分制多路遥测系统/頻分多工遙測系統　frequency division multiplex telemetry system
频率/頻率,週率　frequency
频率标准/頻率標準　frequency standard
频率表/頻率表　frequency list
频率定点切换/定點頻率開關　fixed-point frequency switching
频率反应谱/頻率反應譜　frequency response spectrum
频率分辨率/頻率解析度　frequency resolution
频率分布/頻率分布　frequency distribution
频率分隔制/頻率分隔制　frequency division system
频率分集/頻率分集　frequency diversity
频率分集雷达/頻率分集雷達　frequency diversity radar
频率跟踪切换方式/頻率跟蹤開關模式　frequency tracking switching mode
频率混淆/頻率混疊　frequency aliasing
频率基准系统/頻率基準系統　reference frequency system
频率捷变/頻率敏捷性　frequency agility
频率偏差/頻率偏差值　frequency offset
频率漂移率/頻漂率　frequency drift rate
频率容限/頻率容許差度　frequency tolerance
频率扫描/頻率掃描　frequency scanning
频率图/頻率圖　frequency diagram
频率稳定度/頻率穩定度　frequency stability
频率响应函数/頻率響應函數　frequency response function
频率选择/頻率選擇　frequency selection
频率仪/頻率記錄器　frequency recorder
频率指配/頻率指配　frequency assignment
频率准确度/頻率準確度　frequency accuracy
频谱/頻譜　frequency spectrum
频谱纯度/頻譜純度　spectrum purity
[频谱]发射率/頻譜發射率　spectrum emissivity
频谱特性/頻譜特徵　spectrum character
频谱特性测量/頻譜特性量測　spectral characteristic measurement
频闪灯/閃光燈　strobe light
频闪效应/運動錯覺效果　stroboscopic effect
频移键控/移頻鍵控,移頻按鍵[制]　frequency shift keying, FSK
频域/頻[率]域　frequency domain
频域分析/頻域分析　frequency domain analysis
频组方式/頻群方式　frequency group mode
频组选择器/群[波]頻率選擇器　group frequency selector
品系/品系　strain
品质/品質　character
品质因数/品質因數　quality factor, Q factor
品种/[栽培]品種　cultivar
品种权/品種權　variety right
品种群/[群]組　group
品种退化/品種退化　degeneration of cultivars
品字形导坑法/品字形導坑法　top and twin-side bottom heading method
乒乓球台/乒乓球臺　table tennis table
乒乓球运动/乒乓球　table tennis
平岸流量/平岸流量　bankful discharge
平板玻璃/平板玻璃　sheet glass, flat glass
平板测量器/平板測量器　kit for plane tabling
平板地板/平肋板　flat floor

平板挂车/平板拖車　platform trailer, flat trailer
平板结构/平板構造　flat slab construction
平板龙骨/平板龍骨　plate keel
平板千斤顶/平頭千斤頂,扁千斤頂　flat jack
平板式[混凝土]振捣器/板式振動器,板式振動機　plate vibrator
平板式混凝土振动器/塑性混凝土路面振動整實器　plate concrete vibrator
平板式组件/平板型模組　flat plate module
平板拖车/平板車　flat-bed trailer
平板仪/平板儀　plane table
平板载荷试验/平板載荷試驗,載重板試驗　load plate test, plate loading test
平板照相测量/平板照相測量　plane-table photogrammetry
平板振动压实机/平板式振動壓實機　plate-vibrating compactor
平板支座/平板支座,平板載重　plate bearing
平波电抗器/平滑電抗器,濾波電抗器　smoothing reactor
平舱/平艙,扒平　trimming
平舱费/平艙費　leveling charge
平插座/平式套座　flush socket
平车/平車　flat car
平吃水/縱平浮　even keel
平赤道/平赤道　mean equator
平地机/平土機　grader
平地升送机/平地昇送機　elevation grader
平调/平調　flat regulation
平顶铆钉/平頭鉚釘　flat head rivet
平方和的平方法/平方和之平方根法　square root of sum of squares method, SRSS
平方律补偿/平方律補償　square-law compensation
平飞速度/水平飛行速度　level flight speed
平缝/平緩節理　flat joint
平钢板/扁鋼板　flat steel plate
平根数/平根數　mean element
平轨器/彎軌器　rail bending tool, rail bender
平焊/平焊[接]　flat welding, flush weld, flat position welding
平衡/平衡　equilibrium
平衡表法/平衡表法　balance table method
平衡潮理论/潮汐平衡原理　equilibrium theory of tide
平衡锤/平衡錘,均衡錘　elevator counterweight, balance bob
平衡电缆/平衡電纜　balanced cable
平衡舵/平衡舵　balanced rudder, balance rudder

平衡阀/均衡閥,均壓閥　balanced valve
平衡方程/平衡方程式　equation of equilibrium
平衡杆/均衡桿　balance bar
平衡拱/平衡臂式拱,均衡臂式拱　balanced arch
平衡含水量/平衡含水量　equilibrium moisture content
平衡活塞/均衡活塞,均壓活塞　dummy piston
平衡流动/平衡流　equilibrium flow
平衡扭转/平衡扭轉　equilibrium torsion
平衡配筋率/均衡鋼筋比　balanced steel ratio
平衡坡度/平衡坡度,自然坡度　equilibrium slope
平衡式浮船坞/平衡式浮船塢　balanced type floating dock
平衡试验/平衡試驗　balancing test
平衡水库/調節水池　balancing reservoir
平衡水温/均衡水溫　balanced water temperature
平衡速率/均衡速率　balancing speed
平衡弹簧/均衡彈簧　balance spring
平衡通风/平衡通風　balanced draft
平衡土方工程/平衡土工,均衡土工　balanced earthwork
平衡土方量/平衡土工,均衡土工　balanced earthwork
平衡陀螺仪/平衡迴轉機　balanced gyroscope
平衡弯矩/均衡彎矩　balancing moment
平衡箱/均衡箱　balance box
平衡悬臂施工/平衡懸臂工法　balanced cantilever construction
平衡悬浇法/平衡懸臂現場澆鑄法　cast-in-place balancing cantilever method
平衡悬拼法/平衡懸拼法　precast balancing cantilever method
平衡重/衡重,配重　counterweigh
平护木/平護木　horizontal fender
平滑表面/平滑面　smooth surface
平黄道/平黄道　mean ecliptic
平甲板船/平甲板船　flush deck vessel, flush deck ship
平江图/平江圖　ping jiang tu, historic Suzhou city map
平桨/平槳　bank the oars
平交道/平交道　level crossing
平交道标志/平交道標誌　level crossing sign
平结/平結　reef knot
平截面假定/平截面假設　plane cross section assumption
平近点角/平近點角,平均近點離角　mean anomaly
平均包装容积/平均包裝容積　average bale capacity

平均波高/平均浪高 mean wave height
平均波浪/平均波 mean wave
平均波浪周期/平均波浪週期 mean wave peroid
平均层数/平均層數 average number of floors
平均潮差/平均潮差 mean tidal range
平均潮面/中潮海平面 half-tide level
平均潮位/平均潮位 mean tide level
平均车日行程/平均車日行程 average vehicle daily travel
平均车数/平均車數 average number of vehicles
平均车速/平均速率 average speed
平均吃水/平均吃水 mean draft
平均传热系数/平均傳熱係數 mean heat transfer coefficient
平均大潮低潮/大潮平均低潮位 mean low water springs tide
平均大潮低潮面/朔望平均低潮位 mean low water springs
平均大潮高潮/平均大潮高潮位 mean high high water spring tide
平均低潮间隙/平均低潮間隙 mean low water interval, MLWI
平均低低水位/平均小潮低潮位 mean low low water level
平均低水位/平均低水位 mean low water level
平均电压/平均電壓 average voltage
平均辐射温度/平均輻射溫度 mean radiant temperature
平均高潮/平均高潮位 mean high water
平均高潮间隙/平均高潮間隙 mean high water interval, MHWI
平均工作气隙/平均操作氣隙 mean operating air gap
平均故障间隔时间/平均故障間隔時間,故障前平均時間 mean time interval between failures, mean time before failure, MTBF
平均海面/平均海平面 mean sea level, MSL
平均海面季节改正/平均海平面季節性變更 seasonal change in mean sea level
平均海平面/平均[海]水位 mean sea level
平均机械损失压力/平均機械損失壓力 mean mechanical loss pressure
平均几何弦/平均幾何弦長 mean geometric chord
平均减速度/平均減速度 average retardation rate
平均经度/平均經度 mean longitude
平均空档深度/平均空檔深度 average void depth
平均空气动力弦/平均氣動弦 mean aerodynamic chord

平均控制/平均數管制 average control
平均每吨容积/平均每噸容積 average per ton
平均气动弦长/平均氣動弦 mean aerodynamic chord
平均曲率半径/平均曲率半徑 mean radius of curvature
平均任务持续时间/平均任務持續時間 mean mission duration time, MMDT
平均日交通量/平均日交通量 average daily traffic volume, average daily traffic, ADT
平均日流量/平均日流量 average daily flow, ADF, mean daily flow
平均日用水量/平均日耗[水]量 average day consumption
平均深度/均深 mean depth
平均失效发生时间/平均失效時間 mean time to failure, MTTF
平均时间有效率/平均時間有效率 mean time effective rate
平均时用水量/平均時用水量 average hourly water consumption
平均寿命/平均壽命 average life
平均输出光功率/平均輸出光功率 average optical output power
平均水位/中水位 mean water
平均速点/平均速點 mean velocity position
平均透过率/平均透射率 mean transmissivity
平均推力/平均推力 average thrust
平均纬度/平均緯度 mean latitude
平均无故障工作时间/平均無故障時間,平均故障間隔時間 mean time between failures, MTBF
平均误差/平均誤差 mean error
平均吸声系数/平均吸音係數,平均吸音率 average sound absorption coefficient
平均修复时间/平均修復時間,平均修護時間 mean repair time, mean time to repair, MTTR
平均压力计/平均壓力計 mean pressure meter
平均压强/平均壓強 average pressure
平均叶宽/平均葉寬 mean blade width
平均叶宽比/平均葉寬比 mean blade width ratio
平均应力/平均應力 mean stress
平均有效压力/[制动]平均有效壓力,有效平均壓力 brake mean effective pressure, effective mean pressure, mean effective pressure
平均值检波器/平均值檢波器 average detector
平均指示压力/平均指示壓力,指示平均有效壓力 indicated mean effective pressure, mean indicated pressure

平均自由程/平均自由行程,平均自由徑　mean free path
平均总吨位/平均總噸位　average total tonnage
平均总客位/平均總客位　average total seats
平均纵坡/平均梯度　average gradient
平均最大负荷/平均尖峰負載　average peak load
平均最低水位/平均最低水位　mean lowest water level
平均最高水位/平均最高水位　mean highest water level
平开窗/豎鉸鏈窗　side-hung window, casement window
平开门/平開式門　side-hung door
平孔排水/平孔排水　horizontal hole drainage
平离/平離　leaving bodily
平流/憩流,憩潮　slack water
平流层/平流層,同溫層　stratosphere
平流层紫外成像光谱仪/平流層紫外成像光譜儀　ultraviolet stratospheric imaging spectrometer, USIS
平流沉淀池/平流沈澱池　horizontal flow sedimentation tank
平流池/水平流池　horizontal-flow basin
平流区域/憩流區域　slack water area
平路机/道路整面機　road finisher
平面舱壁/平面艙壁　plane bulkhead
平面测量/平面測量　plan surveying, planimetric surveying
平面缠绕/平面纏繞　planar winding
平面传感器/平面感應器,平面探針　flat-surface sensor, flat-surface probe
平面调车场/平面調車場,平面調配場　flat marshalling yard
平面分段/平面分段　flat section
平面工艺/平面技術　planar technique
平面构成/平面構成　plane composition
平面股钢丝绳/扁平股索　flattened strand rope
平面交叉/平面交叉[口],平交道　at-grade intersection, level crossing, grade crossing
[平面]交叉口/交叉路口　intersection, crossing, junction
平面结构/平面結構　plane structure
平面控制点/水平控制點　horizontal control point
平面框架/構架平面　frame plane
平面力系/同平面力系　co-planar forces
平面磨床/磨面機　surface grinder
平面三角形/平面三角形　plane triangle
平面设计/平面設計　plane design

平面示意图/平面圖,草圖　plan sketch
平面图/平面圖　plane chart, plan
平面位置显示器/平面位置指示器　plane position indicator, PPI
平面无线电调车信号/平面無線電調車信號　radio operated signal for level shunting
平面线形/平面線形　horizontal alignment
平面压路机/平面壓路機　flat roller
平面掩星角/平面掩星角　planar osculating angle
平面摇摆振动/摇晃振動　rocking vibration
平面应变/平面應變　plane strain
平面应力/平面應力　plane stress
平面运动/[同]平面運動　plane motion, co-planar motion
平面运动机构试验/平面運動機構試驗　planar motion mechanism test, PMM test
平面阵天线/平面式陣列天線　planar array antenna
平面直角坐标/平面直角坐標　plane rectangular coordinate
平辗/光輪壓路機　smooth-wheel roller
平坡式/平坡式　tiny slope style
平棋/平棋　flat coffered ceiling, pingqi
平曲线半径/水平曲線半徑　radius of horizontal curve
平曲线横净距/平面曲線橫淨距　lateral clear distance of horizontal curve
平曲线极限最小半径/平面曲線極限最小半徑　ultimate minimum radius of horizontal curve
平曲线加宽/曲線加寬　curve widening
平曲线最小半径/最小平面曲線半徑　minimum radius of horizontal curve
平曲线最小长度/平面曲線最小長度　minimum length of horizontal curve
平时/平均時　mean time
平时封锁/平時封鎖　pacific blockade
平视显示器/平視顯示器　head-up display
平台/平臺,陽臺,露臺　platform, terrace
平台导电滑环/平臺導電滑環　platform slipping ring
平台电子箱/平臺電子箱　platform electronic assembly
平台基座/平臺基礎　platform base
平台[集装]箱/平臺貨櫃,平板[貨]櫃　platform container
平台计算机制导/平臺電腦制導　platform-computer guidance
平台甲板/平臺甲板　platform deck
平台减震器/平臺隔振器　platform vibration isolator
平台开闭锁检查/平臺開閉鎖檢查　platform switch

lock check
平台罗经/平臺羅經　stabilized gyrocompass
平台内框架/平臺内環架　platform inner gimbal
平台式惯性导航系统/平臺式慣性導航系統,萬向架慣性導航系統　gimbaled inertial navigation system, platform inertial navigation system
平台式惯性制导系统/平臺式慣性導引系統　platform inertial guidance system
平台式龙门架/平臺式移動起重機　platform gantry
平台式起重机/平臺式吊重機　platform hoist
平台伺服回路/平臺穩定回路　platform servo-loop, platform stabilized loop
平台推进剂/平臺推進劑　plateau propellant, mean-burning propellant
平台外框架/平臺外環架　platform outer gimbal
平台外罩/平臺外罩　platform cover
平台卸载电机/平臺卸載電機　unload motor of platform
平台形海滩/平臺海灘　step type beach
平台转运/平臺轉移　platform transfer
平台坐标/平臺坐標　platform coordinate
平台坐标系/平臺坐標系　platform coordinate system
平太阳/平[均]太陽　mean sun
平太阳日/平均太陽日　mean solar day
平太阳时/平均太陽時　mean solar time
平滩水位/平灘水位　flood land line water level
平头钉/平頭釘　flat-headed nail
平头焊接/點焊　tack weld
平头铆钉/平頭鉚釘　flat-head rivet
平托盘/平臺板　flat pallet
平瓦/平瓦,無楞瓦,板瓦　plain tile
平纬航向/平緯航向　parallel course
平稳电压/穩定電壓　steady voltage
平稳性指标/平穩性指標　riding index
平屋顶/屋頂平臺　flat roof
平屋面种植/屋頂平臺綠化　flat roof greening
平巷/側導坑　side drift
平行导坑/平行進風平巷　parallel heading
平行渡线/平行[橫]渡線　parallel crossover
平行钢丝束/平行鋼絲股索　parallel wire strand
平行光/準直光　collimated light
平行航线搜寻/平行航線搜索　parallel track search
平行滑行道/平行滑行道　parallel taxiway
平行接近/平行接近　parallelism approach
平行接近法/平行接近法　parallel approach method, constant bearing navigation
平行进路/平行進路　parallel route
平行坑道/平行橫坑　parallel adit
平行码头/平行碼頭　parallel wharf
平行锚/一字力錨　riding one point anchors
平行渠/側運渠　side canal
平行圈/平行圈,緯圈　parallel circle
平行停车/縱向停車　longitudinal parking
平行系统/平行系統　parallel system
平行运行图/平行運行圖　parallel train diagram
平行中体/平行舯體　parallel middle body
平行舯体/平行舯段　parallel body
平型双头夹板/扁形接頭板,平接條板　flat joint bar
平旋/水平螺旋　flat spin
平旋恢复/水平螺旋復原　flat spin recovery
平旋桥/[平]旋橋,平轉橋　swing bridge
平旋推进器/擺線推進器,垂直翼螺槳　cycloidal propeller, Voith Schneider Propeller, VSP
平压阀/平壓閥　surge relief valve
平移壳/平移殼　translational shell
平原地区选线/平原地區選線　location in plain region, plain location
平原区/平原區　plain terrain
平缘石/平緣石　flush curb
平扎/平纏　flat seizing
平整冰/平整冰　level ice
平整度/平整度　level up degree
平直翼/直翼　straight wing
平周期/平均週期　mean period
平转桥/平轉橋,[平]旋橋　swing bridge
平装容量/裝載能量　struck capacity
平坐/平坐　subsidiary construction level, pingzuo
评标/評標　evaluation of bids, tender evaluation
评价参数/評價指標　evaluation parameter
评价制度/評估方式　evaluation system
评图/計劃審議　review of design
评议室/審查室　review room
苹果曲线/蘋果形曲線　apple curve
屏蔽/屏蔽,屏護　shielding, screening
屏蔽变压器/遮罩變壓器　reduction transformer
屏蔽层/簾幕　screen
屏蔽电缆/遮罩電纜　shielded cable
屏蔽结构/遮蔽結構　shielding structure
屏蔽平衡电缆/遮罩對稱電纜　screened balanced cable
屏蔽式电热偶/遮蔽式電熱偶　shielded thermocouple
屏蔽室屏蔽效能测量/遮罩室遮罩效力量測　shielding efficacy measurement of shielding room
屏蔽体/遮罩,鎧裝,保護裝置　shield

屏蔽系数/遮蔽因數,遮罩因數　shielding factor
屏蔽效能/遮罩效率　shield effectiveness
屏风/屏風　folding screen
屏石/屏石　screen stone
瓶颈路段/瓶頸段　bottle neck road
瓶颈效应/瓶頸效應　bottleneck effect
瓶式泥沙采样器/瓶式土樣器　bottle silt sampler
瓶饰/瓶飾　garden vase
瓶组气化站/瓶組氣化站　vaporizing station of multiple cylinder installation
坡比值/坡比值,邊坡坡度,邊坡值　grade of side slope
坡差/坡差　gradient difference
坡长限制/坡長限制　grade length limit
坡道标志/坡道標誌　slope sign
坡道段/坡段　gradient section
坡道式汽车库/坡道式汽車庫　ramp garage
坡道阻力/梯度阻力,爬坡阻力　gradient resistance
坡地/坡地　slope land
坡顶/坡頂,坡肩　top of slope
坡度/坡度,斜度,梯度　grade, gradient, slope
坡度标/斜坡標　grade post
坡度[代数]差/坡度[代數]差　algebraic difference between adjacent gradients
坡度牵出线/坡度牽出線　draw-out track at grade
坡度损失/坡度損失　loss in grade
坡度图/坡度圖　slope gradient map
坡度折减/坡度折減　compensation of gradient, gradient compensation, grade compensation
坡段/坡段,斜坡區間　grade section
坡段长度/斜坡區間長度　length of grade section
坡积土/坡積土　slope wash soil, slope wash
坡脚/坡腳　toe of slope, toe of side slope
坡脚圆/坡趾圓　toe circle
坡口角/槽角　groove angle
坡口面/開槽面　groove face
坡口面角度/斜角　bevel angle
坡面防护/坡面防護　slope protection
坡面景观/邊坡景觀　slope landscape
坡面径流/薄層流　sheet flow
坡桥/坡橋　bridge on slope
坡屋顶/斜屋頂　pitched roof
坡屋顶绿化/坡屋面種植　slope roof greening
泊松比/帕松比　Poisson ratio
泼水试验/澆水試驗　pouring water test
迫导向径向转向架/迫導向徑向轉向架　forced-steering radial truck
迫降/迫降　ditch, forced landing
破冰船/破冰船　icebreaker
破冰体/擋冰板,流冰擋　ice apron, ice-breaking cutwater, ice guard
破冰[型]艏/破冰型艏　icebreaker stem, icebreaker bow
破波波深/碎波水深　breaking wave depth
破波阻力/碎波阻力　wave breaking resistance
破布/破布　rags
破舱水线/浸水吃水線　flooded waterline, flood waterline
破舱稳性/破損穩度,受損穩度　damaged stability, flooding stability
破断强度/裂斷強度　breaking strength, BS
破封/啟封　break a seal
破坏/破壞,損壞　failure
破坏包线/破壞包絡線　failure envelope
破坏荷载/破壞荷載,破壞負荷　failure load
破坏率/損壞率　damage ratio
破坏面/破壞面　failure surface
破坏强度/破斷強度　breaking strength
破坏区/破壞區　failure zone
破坏条件/破壞情形　failure condition
破坏形式/損壞模式　failure mode
破坏性故障/破壞性故障　destructive fault
破坏性试验/破壞性試驗　destruction test, destructive test
破坏应力/破壞應力　breaking stress
破坏载荷试验/損壞負載試驗　failure load test
破坏准则/破壞準則　failure criterion
破键/斷鍵　broken bond
破裂线/切斷線　cutting-plane line
破碎波/碎波,碎浪　breaker
破碎化指数/破碎化指數　fragmentation index
破碎机/錘承　bucker
破碎炮/破碎炮　broken cannon
破损安全结构/破損安全結構　fail safe structure
破损阶段设计法/破損階段設計法　plastic stage design method
破损试验/破壞性測試　destructive test
破折线/碎波線　breaking line
剖面构造/形貌重建　profile construction
剖面形态/剖面形態　profile morphology
剖视图/剖視圖,斷面圖　sectional view, cross-sectional view
扑救场地/撲救場地　fire fight venue
扑翼机/撲翼機　ornithopter
铺草皮/鋪草皮　sodding
铺草皮块草坪/鋪草皮塊草坪　sodding lawn

铺[道]渣/圍堰工　coffering
铺地园/鋪地園　paved garden
铺轨机/鋪軌機械　track laying machine
铺轨列车/鋪軌列車　track laying train
铺砌/砌石,鋪石　pitching
铺砌法路面/鋪砌法路面　pavement by pitching method
铺砂/撒砂　sanding
铺砂法试验/鋪砂法試驗　sand patch test
铺砂机/鋪砂機　gritter
铺设角/層角　ply angle
铺湿砂养护/濕砂養護　wet-sand curing
铺石花坛/鋪石花壇　paved bed
铺首/門環　door knocker
铺贴式/鋪貼式　paste planting
铺碴/鋪道渣　ballasting
铺碴机/道碴撒布機　ballast spreader
蒲福风级/蒲福風級　Beaufort wind scale
普遍腐蚀/全面腐蝕　general corrosion
普遍呼叫/普通呼叫　general call to all station
普查型侦察卫星/普查型偵察衛星　area monitoring reconnaissance satellite
普拉特桁架/普拉特式桁架　Pratt truss
普朗克辐射体/浦朗克輻射體　Planck radiant body
普朗特-格劳特法则/普朗特-格勞厄脫法則　Prandtl-Glauert rule
普朗特-迈耶流/普朗特-邁耶爾流動　Prandtl-Meyer flow
普朗特数/普朗特數,蒲朗多數,蘭特數　Prandtl number
普拍枋/普拍枋　architrave horizontally positioned, pupaifang
普通操作员证书/普通值機員證書　general operator certificate
普通船员/乙級船員　rating
普通大潮高潮/大潮高水位　high water level ordinary spring tide
普通粉刷/普通粉刷　ordinary plaster
普通[硅酸盐]水泥/普通矽酸鹽水泥,普通卜特蘭水泥　ordinary Portland cement
普通焊接钢管/普通焊接鋼管　non-galvanized steel pipe
普通混凝土/普通混凝土　ordinary concrete
普通混凝土小型空心砌块/普通混凝土小型空心砌塊　normal concrete small hollow block
普通货船/傳統船　conventional ship
普通减水剂/減水外加劑　water reducing admixture
普通教室/普通教室　ordinary classroom
普通客票价/普通客票價　ordinary ticket price
普通捻/普通搓索,正絞線　ordinary lay, regular lay
普通砂浆/普通砂漿　ordinary mortar
普通旋压/[普通]旋壓　conventional spinning
普通运价/普通運價　general rate
谱方法/波譜法　spectral method
谱辐射强度/譜強度　spectrum intensity
谱辐照度/譜輻照度　spectrum irradiance
谱估计/譜估計　spectrum estimate
谱密度/譜密度　spectral density
谱密度矩阵/譜密度矩陣　spectral density matrix
谱线数/譜線數　number of spectral line
瀑布/瀑布　waterfall
瀑布风景区/瀑布風景區　waterfall scenic spot

Q

七管连接器/七管連接器　seven pipe connector
七孔探头/七孔探頭　seven holes probe
七专/七專　seven-special parts
期满日/期滿日,失效日　expiry date
期票/期票　promissory note
期望车速/需要速率　desired speed
期限条款/期限條款　duration clause
欺骗干扰/欺騙式干擾　deception jamming
齐退/全體倒劃　stern all
其他观光用地/其他觀光用地　other tourist sites
其他绿地/其他綠地　other green space
奇基托斯耶稣传教区/奇基托斯耶穌會傳教場所　Jesuit Missions of the Chiquitos
奇琴伊察古城/奇琴伊察古城,前西班牙的奇琴伊察城　Pre-Hispanic City of Chichen-Itza
奇西克府邸/英國百靈頓伯爵大屋　Chiswick House
奇异摄动法/奇異擾動,奇異微擾　singular perturbation
歧管连接器/歧管連接器　manifold connector
脐带/臍索　umbilical
脐带电缆/臍索電纜　umbilical cable
脐带式生命保障系统/臍帶式維生系統　umbilical life support system
脐带塔/臍索塔　umbilical tower
畦沟/田溝　field drain
畦灌/畦灌　border irrigation
骑道/馬道　riding track
骑楼/騎樓　overpass, arcade, qilou
骑马/騎馬　horse riding
棋牌室/棋藝室　chess room
棋盘式道路系统/棋盤式道路系統　gridiron road system
棋盘线网/棋盤線網　chessboard type public transport network
棋院/棋院　chess academy
旗杆/旗桿　flag staff
旗柜/旗箱　flag locker, flag chest
旗号通信/旗號通信　flag signaling
旗箱/旗箱　flag locker, flag chest
鳍/鰭,翅　fin
鳍轴/鰭軸　fin shaft

企鹅服/企鵝服　penguin suit
企口缝/槽口,嵌槽　tongue and groove joint, rabbet
企业自备车/私人汽車　private car
启动点/啟動點　actuation point
启动器/啟動器　starter
启动时间/起轉時間　run-up time
启动信号/啟動訊號　actuation signal
启动阈/啟動閾　actuation threshold
启阀压力/噴射啟動壓力　injection start pressure
启航港/出航港　port of sailing
启线压力可调式喷油器/壓力控制式燃油閥　pressure-control fuel valve
启用试验/啟用試驗　commissioning test
起爆/引爆　ignition, detonation, firing
起爆机/爆破機　blasting machine
起爆器/引爆裝置　firing device
起爆药包/引爆藥包　primer cartridge
起爆引信/爆炸導火線　detonating fuse
起爆炸药/起爆炸藥　detonated dynamite
起拨道机/起軌撥軌機　track lifting and lining machine
起拨道器/起軌撥軌器　track lifting and lining tool
起草/製圖　drafting
起草皮机/起草皮機　stubble plough
起潮力/引潮力　tide generating force
起道/軌道起高,起軌,軌道抬昇　raising of track, track lifting
起道钉机/道釘拔出器　spike puller
起道机/起道機　track lifting machine
起道器/小型千斤頂　rail jack, track jack
起点站/起點站　origin station
起吊接头/起吊接頭　hanger fitting
起动/起動,開動　starting, start
起动按钮/起爆鍵　firing key
起动变扭器/起動變扭器　starting torque converter
起动电键/起爆鍵　firing key
起动电流/起動電流　starting current
起动电路/起動電路,觸發電路　starting circuit
起动电容器/起動電容器　starting capacitor
起动电阻器/起動電阻器　starting resistor
起动故障报警/起動故障警報　start failure alarm

起动[过程]电流/起動電流　starting current
起动[过程]转矩/起動轉矩,起動扭矩　starting torque
起动环境/起動環境　start ambient condition
起动缓坡/起動緩坡,起動平緩坡道　flat gradient for starting
起动机/起動機　starter
起动机油泵/起動機油泵　starting lubricating oil pump
起动继电器/起動繼電器　starting relay
起动加速器/起動加速器　starting accelerator
起动加速试验/起動加速度試驗　starting and acceleration test
起动结束信号/起動結束信號　start finished signal
起动空气分配器/起動空氣分配器　starting air distributor
起动空气瓶/起動氣瓶　starting air reservoir
起动空气切断/起動空氣切斷　starting air cut off
起动空气系统/起動空氣系統　starting air system
起动空气总管/起動空氣歧管　starting air manifold
起动控制阀/起動控制閥　starting control valve
起动联锁/起動聯鎖　starting interlock
起动盲区/起動盲區　start-up blind-zone
起动牵引力/起動牽引力　starting tractive effort
起动事故/起動事故　start-up accident
起动试验/起動試驗　starting test
起动凸轮/起動凸輪　starting cam
起动系统/啟動系統　start system
起动性能/起動性能　starting performance
起动压力/起動壓力　starting pressure
起动压力峰/起動尖峰壓力　start peak pressure
起动延迟/起動延滯,啟步延緩　starting delay
起动载荷/起動負載　starting load
起动注油注水/起動注給　priming
起动转速/引擎起動轉速　starting engine speed
起动装置/起動裝置,起動設施　starting device
起动阻力/起動阻力,出發阻力　starting resistance
起飞/起飛　lift-off, take-off
起飞触点/起飛接觸　lift-off contact
起飞滑跑距离/起飛滾行距離　distance of take-off run
起飞距离/起飛距離　take-off distance
起飞决断速度/決定起飛速度　take-off decision speed
起飞绝对时/起飛絕對時間　take-off absolute time
起飞离地速度/起飛速率　take-off speed, lift-off speed
起飞零点/起飛零點　lift-off zero, take-off zero

起飞爬升面/起飛爬昇面　take-off climb surface
起飞漂移/起飛偏移　lift-off drift
起飞漂移量测量/起飛偏移量測　take-off drift measurement
起飞平衡场长/平衡跑道長度　take-off balance field length
起飞托盘/起飛支承板　lift-off support plate
起飞相对时/起飛相對時間　take-off relative time
起飞压板/起飛夾條　lift-off claming strip
起飞预报/起飛預報　take-off forecast
起飞质量/起飛質量　take-off mass
起飞重量/起飛重量　take-off weight
起伏/起伏　heave
起伏周期/漲落週期　cycle of fluctuation
起航与加速工况管理/起動與加速操作形式管理　starting and accelerating operating mode management
起货机/吊貨[絞]機　cargo winch
起货机平台/絞機臺　winch platform
起货绞车/吊貨[絞]機　cargo winch
起货设备/吊貨設備,貨物昇降機　cargo lift, cargo lift equipment, cargo lifting equipment
起货设备吊重试验/貨物裝卸設備安全限試驗　proof test for ship cargo handling gear
起货设备定期检验/貨物裝卸設備定期檢驗　periodical survey of cargo gear
起货索具/吊桿索具　derrick rigging
起居舱室/起居艙,住艙　living quarter, accommodation
起居处所/起居艙空間　accommodation space
起居甲板/起居艙甲板,住艙甲板　accommodation deck
起居设备/起居設備　accommodation
起居室/起居室　living room
起落航线/機場航線　traffic pattern
起落架落震试验/起落架拋投試驗　landing gear drop test
起落绞车/起吊絞機　hoisting winch
起落装置/起落架　landing gear, undercarriage
起锚/起錨　cat, weigh
起锚船/拋錨艇　anchor boat
起锚机/[起]錨機　windlass, anchor windlass
起锚设备/起錨裝置　anchor gear
起锚完毕/起錨完畢　anchor is up
起锚[系缆]绞盘/起錨絞盤,起錨機　anchor capstan
起苗/起苗　lifting of seedling
起皮/剝離　peeling
起讫点调查/起訖點交通調查,起點終點調查,旅次起讫研究　origin destination survey, OD survey, origin destination study
起砂/條紋　sand streak
起始电平/初始電平　starting level, initial level
起始电压/初始電壓　initial voltage
起始段测控/初始階段追蹤,遙測和指令站　TT and C of initial phase
起始断裂/初始破裂　fracture initiation
起始搜寻点/起始搜索點　commence search point
起始液位/初始液位　initial liquid level
起竖/豎立　erection
起竖厅/起豎廳　erecting hall
起停次数/啟停時間　start-stop time
起艇绞车/小艇絞車,小艇吊機　boat winch
起网/曳網　hauling net
起网机/曳網機　net hauler, net winch
起网机组/曳網系統　net hauling system
起压/電壓建起　voltage build-up
起源中心/起源中心　origin center
起止式/起動停止型　start-stop type
起止信号/起止信號　start-stop signal
起止信号发生器/起止信號發生器　start-stop signal generator
起止信号畸变测试器/起止信號畸變測試器　start-stop signal distortion tester
起重/起重　lifting stone
起重驳/吊桿駁船　lighter derrick
起重船/起重[工作]船,水上起重機　derrick barge, crane ship, floating crane
起重船打捞/起重船起吊　lifting by floating crane
起重钢丝绳/吊重索　hoisting rope
起重横梁/底梁,地板梁,地楞橫梁　jacking floor beam
起重机/起重機,吊車　crane
起重机结构/起重機結構　crane structure
起重机[起重]臂/起重機臂　crane boom
起重机三角架/起重機三角架　shear legs
起重机伸距/起重機伸距　crane radius
起重量/起重能力　hoisting capacity
起重码头/起重碼頭　heavy lifting wharf
起重设备/吊車裝備　hoisting equipment
起重桅/吊桿桅　derrick mast
起重运输机械荷载/運輸式起重機荷載　crane and transporter load
起重直升机/吊重直昇機　crane helicopter
起重柱/吊桿柱　derrick post
起重装置/起重機　lifting gear
起皱/皺紋　wrinkles

起座压力/洩氣壓力　popping pressure
气泵/氣控式抽水　pneumatic pump
气闭头/氣閉頭　gas-tight block
气尘云/氣塵雲　gas-dust cloud
气氮加热系统/氣氮加熱系統　gaseous nitrogen warm-up system
气道/導氣管,通風管　air duct
气垫/氣墊　air cushion, cushion
气垫船/氣墊船　air cushion vehicle, ACV
气垫飞行器/氣墊載運工具　air cushion vehicle
气垫式起落架/氣墊起落架　air cushion landing gear
气垫式凿岩机/氣墊式鑽支　air-leg drill
气动补偿/氣動平衡　aerodynamic balance
气动导数/氣動彈性導數　aerodynamic derivative
气动仿真/氣動力模擬　aerodynamics simulation
气动放大器/氣力放大器　pneumatic amplifier
气动幅伞/氣動幅傘　aerodynamical panel parachute
气动功率放大器/氣動功率放大器　pneumatic power amplifier
气动合力/氣動合力　aerodynamic resultant
气动技术应用/氣動技術應用　application of aerodynamic technology
气动加热/氣動加熱　aerodynamic heating
气动控制台/氣動控制臺　pneumatic console
气动控制系统/氣動控制系統　pneumatic control system
气动快速脱落连接器/氣動快速脫落連接器　pneumatic quick-disconnect coupling
气动力布局/空氣動力布局　aerodynamic configuration
气动力减速器/空氣動力減速裝置　aerodynamic decelerator
气动力矩/氣動扭矩　aerodynamic torque
气动[力]中心/氣動力中心　aerodynamic center
气动扭转/氣動扭曲　aerodynamic twist
气动炮/氣動迫擊炮　air-actuated mortar
气动倾卸车/氣壓傾卸車　air dump car
气动热力学/氣動熱力學　aerothermodynamics
气动热弹性/氣熱彈性力學　aerothermo-elasticity
气动热载荷/氣動熱負載　aerothermal load
气动塞式喷管/氣動栓塞噴嘴　pneumatic plug nozzle
气动声学/空氣聲學　aeroacoustics
气动声学设计/空氣聲學設計　aero acoustic design
气动式污水排水器/壓氣汙水抽送機　pneumatic sewage ejector
气动弹性剪裁/氣動彈性裁剪　aeroelastic tailoring
气动弹性力学/氣動彈性[力]學　aeroelasticity,

aeroelastics
气动弹性试验/氣動彈性效應 aeroelastic effect test
气动调节器/氣力調整器 pneumatic regulator
气动稳定/氣動穩定 aerodynamic stabilization
气动稳定性/氣動穩定性 aerodynamic stability
气动岩石破碎机/氣動岩石破碎機 pneumatic rock breaker
气动隐形技术/氣動隱身技術 aerodynamic stealth technique
气动载荷/氣動負載 aerodynamic loading
气动凿岩机/氣動鑿岩機,氣力鑿岩機 pneumatic rock drill
气动噪声/氣力噪音,空氣動力噪音 aerodynamic noise
气动阻尼/氣動阻尼 aerodynamic damping
气阀间隙/閥餘隙 valve clearance
气阀升程/閥昇程 valve lift
气阀升程图/閥昇圖 valve lift diagram
气阀锁夹/閥鍵 valve key
气阀正时/閥動定時 valve timing
气封/氣封 gas seal
气浮加速度计/氣浮加速度計 gas-bearing accelerometer
气浮支承/氣體懸浮 gas suspension
气干材/氣乾木材 air-dried timber, air-seasoned timber
气缸/氣缸 cylinder
气缸常数/氣缸常數 cylinder constant
气缸窜气/氣缸漏氣 cylinder blow-by
气缸盖/缸蓋,缸頭 cylinder cover, cylinder head
气缸盖螺母/氣缸蓋螺母 cylinder head nut
气缸盖螺栓/缸頭用螺樁 cylinder head stud
气缸工作容积/衝程容積 stroke volume
气缸[冷却]水套/缸套 cylinder jacket
气缸起动阀/氣缸起動閥 cylinder starting valve
气缸容积/氣缸容積 cylinder volume, working medium volume
气缸套/氣缸内襯套,缸套 cylinder jacket, cylinder liner
气缸体/[氣]缸體 cylinder block
气缸头温度表/氣缸頭溫度計 cylinder head thermometer
气缸油/氣缸油 cylinder oil
气缸油输送泵/氣缸油輸送泵 cylinder oil transfer pump
气缸油注油量/氣缸油注量 cylinder oil dosage
气缸油注油率/單位氣缸耗油量 specific cylinder oil consumption
气缸直径/氣缸直徑,[氣]缸内徑 cylinder bore, cylinder bore diameter
气缸注油器/氣缸潤滑器 cylinder lubricator
气缸总容积/氣缸總容積 cylinder total volume
气缸最大容积/最大衝程容積 maximum stroke volume
气缸最小容积/最小衝程容積 minimum stroke volume
气割/焰割 gas cutting
气管连接器/氣管式連接器 air tube connector
气氦系统/氣氦系統 gaseous helium system
气焊/[燃氧]氣焊 gas welding, oxyfuel gas welding
气焊接头/氣焰焊接頭 gas welded joint
气候/氣候 climate
气候变化/氣候變化,氣候變遷 climatic change
气候分区/氣候區劃 climate zoning
气候航线/氣候航路 climate routing
气候环境/氣候環境 climate environment
气候极值/氣候極[端]值 climatic extreme
气候区/氣候帶 climate zone
气候试验/氣候試驗 climate test
气候调节/氣候調節 climatic regulation, climate regulation
气候因子/氣候因子 climatic factor
气环/氣密漲圈 gas ring
气孔/氣孔 blowhole, stoma, stomata
气孔导度/氣孔導度 stomatal conductance
气孔蒸腾/氣孔蒸散 stomatal transpiration
气孔阻力/氣孔阻力,氣孔抵抗 stomatal resistance
气力离合器/氣力離合器 air clutch
气力输送机/氣動輸送機,壓氣輸送機 air conveyer, pneumatic conveyor
气力输送装置/壓氣輸送機 pneumatic conveyor
气力提升泵/吸泥泵 air lift mud pump
气流/風送流 wind current
气流穿透深度/射流深度 flow penetration depth
气流吹袭/風爆 windblast
气流动态品质/氣流動態品質 flow pulsation quality
气流方向均匀性/流向均匀性 flow direction uniformity
气流流型/氣流組織 air pattern
气流偏角修正/氣流偏角修正 flow deflection angle correction
气流稳定性/流動穩定性 flow stability
气流组织/風量分配,配風 air distribution, space air diffusion
气流坐标系/氣流軸系 air-path axis system
气门/氣門,閥[門],活門 valve

气门导管/閥導 valve guide
气门横臂/閥橫臂,閥橫撐 valve cross arm
气门升程/閥昇程 valve lift
气门弹簧/閥彈簧 valve spring
气门挺柱/氣門挺桿,閥挺桿 valve tappet
气门推杆/閥推桿 valve push rod
气门旋转机构/氣門旋轉機構,閥旋轉機構 valve rotating mechanism
气门摇臂/閥搖桿 valve rocker
气门座/閥座 valve seat
气密/氣密 airtight
气密框/壓力隔艙 pressure bulkhead
气密试验/氣密[性]試驗 airtight test, air tightness test
气密限制层/密封層 encapsulating layer
气密性/氣密性,氣密度 air tightness
气密性检查/氣體洩漏檢查 gas leak inspection
气密性能/氣密性 air permeability performance
气密[性]试验/氣密試驗,密性試驗 tightness test, airtightness test
气敏查漏仪/氣敏查漏儀 gas-sensitive leak detector
气膜冷却/液膜冷卻 film cooling
气泡/氣泡 blister, bubble
气泡检漏/氣泡檢漏 leak detection by bubble
气泡流动显示/氣泡流場顯現 bubble flow visualization
气泡六分仪/氣泡六分儀 bubble sextant
气泡水准仪/氣泡水準器 air bubble level
气瓶库/氣瓶庫房 gas bottle depot
气瓶气检/氣瓶氣體洩漏檢查 gas leak inspection of bottle
气瓶组/氣瓶組 gas bottle set
气球/氣球 balloon
气球运动/氣球運動 balloon movement
气球载落舱试验/球載落艙試驗 balloon-borne drop capsule test
气溶胶/氣態膠體,懸浮微粒 aerosol
气塞/通氣孔塞 vent plug
气蚀/孔蝕,空蝕,空泡化腐蝕 cavitation erosion, cavitation, cavitation corrosion
气蚀比转速/氣蝕比轉速 cavitation specific angular speed
气蚀裕度/空蝕裕度 cavitation allowance
气水比/氣水比 air water ratio
气态燃料/氣體燃料 gaseous fuel
气提/氣提 air stripping
气体保护[电弧]焊/氣體[遮護]金屬電弧焊接 gas metal arc welding, GMAW, gas shielded arc welding
气体捕集器/防氣彎 gas trap
气体测试仪/氣體試驗器 gas tester
气体处理厂/氣廠 gas plant, processing plant
气体的相对密度/氣體相對密度 relative density of gas, specific density of gas
气体分配器/氣體分配器 gas distributor
气体加工厂/氣廠 gas plant, processing plant
气体灭火防护区/氣體滅火保護區 protected area of gas fire extinguishing
气体灭火系统/氣體滅火系統 gas fire extinguishing system
气体浓度测量仪/氣體濃度測量儀 gas concentration measurement instrument
气体起动系统/氣體啟動系統 gas start system
气体燃料/氣體燃料 gaseous fuel
气体溶解系数/溶氣係數 gas-solubility coefficient
气体渗碳/氣體滲碳 gas carburizing
气体污染物/氣體汙染物 gaseous pollutant
气体压缩机车/氣體壓縮機汽車 gas compressor truck
气体运输船/氣體載運船 gas carrier
气体置换/氣體置換 gas replacement
气体状态方程/氣體狀態方程式 gas state equation
气调库/氣調庫,氣冷庫 air-conditioned cold store
气团/氣團 air mass
气腿式凿岩机/氣腿式鑿岩機 air-rider jack hammer
气味货/氣味貨 odorous cargo
气温/氣溫 air temperature
气温年较差/年溫差 annual temperature range
气温日较差/日溫差 daily temperature range
气温直减率/氣溫遞減率 temperature lapse rate
气析计/氣析計 air siltometer
气隙磁通密度/氣隙磁通密度 air gap flux density
气隙-力特性/氣隙-力特性 distance-force characteristic
气相沉积/蒸氣沈積[法] vapor deposition
气相再流焊/汽相回流焊接 vapor phase reflow soldering
气象保障系统/氣象支援系統 meteorological support system
气象报告/氣象報告 meteorological bulletins, meteorological report
气象传真接收机/氣象傳真接收機 weather facsimile receiver
气象电文/氣象信文 meteorological messages
气象定线/天氣定航 weather routing
气象服务/氣象服務 meteorological service

气象辅助业务/氣象輔助業務 meteorological aids service
气象观测/氣象觀測 meteorological observation
气象回波/氣象回波 meteorology echo
气象监视台/氣象守視臺 meteorological watch office
气象检测器/天氣預報器 weather detector
气象景观/氣象景觀 meteorological diversity scenery
气象警告/氣象警告 meteorological warning, MET warning
气象雷达/氣象雷達 meteorological radar
气象能见度/氣象能見距 meteorological visibility
气象收集中心/氣象滙集中心 meteorological collecting center
气象台/氣象臺 meteorological station
气象图/氣象圖,天氣圖 meteorological chart, weather chart, weather map
气象卫星/氣象衛星 meteorological satellite
气象信息/氣象資訊 meteorological information
气象要素/氣象要素 meteorological element
气象要素图/氣象圖 meteorological chart
气象预报/氣象預報 meteorological forecast, meteorological prevision
气象站/氣象站 meteorologic station
气象资料/氣象資料 meteorologic data, meteorological data
气象自记仪/自記氣象計 meteorograph
气旋/氣旋 cyclone
气旋波/氣旋波 cyclonic wave
气旋风/氣旋風 cyclonic wind
气旋生成/氣旋生發 cyclogenesis
气旋消散/氣旋消散 cyclolysis
气压表/氣壓表,氣壓計 barometer
气压沉箱基础/氣壓沈箱基礎 pneumatic caisson foundation
气压盾构/空氣壓盾構 air pressed shield, shield with air pressure
气压高度表/膜盒高度表 aneroid altimeter
气压焊/氣[焰]壓焊 oxyacetylene pressure welding, gas-pressure welding
气压给水/氣壓給水 pneumatic water supply
气压计/氣壓計 barograph
气压喷射器/氣控式噴射器 pneumatic ejector
气压趋势/氣壓趨勢 barometric tendency
气压刹车系统/氣動剎車系統 pneumatic brake system
气压试验/空氣壓力試驗 air pressure test
气压系统/壓力系統 pressure system
气压信号/壓氣信號 pneumatic signal
气压性损伤/氣壓性傷害 barotrauma
气压引信/氣壓引信 barometric fuze
气液减震器/液氣壓避震器 pneumatic-hydraulic shock absorber
气翼船/氣翼艇 aerofoil boat
气翼艇/氣翼艇,衝翼艇 ram-wing craft
气硬性/氣冷硬化,空氣硬化 air hardening
气硬性胶凝材料/氣冷硬化黏結劑 air hardening binder
气硬性水泥/氣硬水泥 non-hydraulic cement
气源车/氣源汽車 air source truck
气源系统/送風系統,供氣系統 air supply system
气源站/氣體供應站 gas supply station
气闸舱/氣閘艙 airlock module
气闸室/氣閘,氣障 air lock
气胀[救生]筏/充氣救生筏 inflatable liferaft
气胀救生衣/充氣救生衣 inflatable lifejacket
气胀设备/充氣設備 inflatable appliance
气枕压强/氣墊壓強 gas cushion pressure
气阻/汽鎖,汽封 vapor lock
弃船/棄船 abandonment of ship
弃船[救生]演习/棄船演習 abandon ship drill
弃船信号/棄船信號 abandon ship signal
弃链器/釋纜器 cable releaser
弃流设施/棄流設施 initial rainwater removal equipment
弃土/荒地 waste
弃土堆/廢土[石]堆 waste bank, bankette, spoil bank
弃土反耕/棄土反耕 waste bank refarming
弃碴/岩屑 muck, spoil, waste rock
汽车/汽車,機動車輛 motor vehicle, automobile
汽车安全检测线/汽車安全檢測線 vehicle safety inspection and test line
汽车安全性/車輛安全 vehicle safety
汽车百车公里油耗/車輛百公里耗油量 vehicle fuel consumption per hundred kilometers
汽车百吨公里油耗/車輛百噸公里耗油量 vehicle fuel consumption per hundred ton-kilometers
汽车不良技术状况/車輛不良技術狀況 bad technical condition of vehicle
汽车操纵轻便性/汽車操縱輕便性 easiness of vehicle control
汽车操纵稳定性/車輛操縱穩定性 vehicle handling stability
[汽车]侧滑试验台/側滑檢測臺 side slip tester
[汽车]车轮定位仪/車輪定位儀 wheel alignment

meter
汽车大修/汽車大修　vehicle major repair
汽车大修返修率/汽車大修返修率　return rate of vehicle major repair
汽车大修费用定额/汽車大修成本定額　cost quota of vehicle major repair
汽车大修间隔里程/汽車大修間隔里程　average mileage between vehicle major repairs
汽车大修理费用/汽車大修理費用　vehicle overhaul cost
汽车大修平均在厂车日/汽車大修平均在廠車日　average days in plant during major repair of vehicle
汽车大修平均在修车日/汽車大修平均在修車日　average days during major repair of vehicle
汽车代用燃料/車輛替代燃料　alternative motor fuels
汽车底部自动清洗机/汽車底部自動清洗機　automatic underbody washer
汽车地磅/汽車裝卸臺　truck-weighing platform, truck weighbridge
汽车电磁波干扰/汽車電磁干擾　automobile electromagnetic interfere
汽车调头转盘/運貨車轉臺　truck turntable
汽车定期维护/車輛定期維護　vehicle periodic maintenance
汽车动力性/車輛動態品質　vehicle dynamic quality
汽车高速公路/高速公路　highway
汽车工作能力/車輛工作能力　working ability of vehicle
汽车故障/汽車故障　vehicle failure
汽车管理系统/車輛管理系統　vehicle management system
汽车合理使用/車輛合理使用　vehicle rational utilization
汽车合理拖载/汽車合理拖載　vehicle rational towing load
汽车货运装卸站/汽車貨運裝卸站　motor transport handling station
汽车机动性/車輛機動性　vehicle mobility
汽车极限技术状况/車輛極限技術條件　limiting technical condition of vehicle
汽车技术经济定额/車輛駕駛技術經濟定額　techno-economic rating for vehicle operation
汽车技术状况/車輛技術狀況　technical condition of vehicle
汽车技术状况变化规律/車輛技術狀況變化規律　trend of change of vehicle technical conditions
汽车技术状况参数/車輛技術狀況參數　parameters of vehicle technical condition
汽车加气站/汽車加油[加氣合建]站　gas filling station, automobile gas filling station
汽车驾驶/汽車駕駛　automobile driving
汽车检测/汽車檢測　vehicle inspection and test
汽车检测站/車輛檢測站　vehicle inspection and test station
汽车节能/車輛節約能源　vehicle energy saving
汽车节能装置/車輛節能裝置　fuel saving device
汽车节油技术/車輛節油技術　vehicle fuel saving technique
汽车经济车速/車輛經濟速率　vehicle economical speed
汽车经济性/車輛經濟性　vehicle economy
汽车举升机/車輛昇降機　car lift
汽车空箱行程/汽車空箱行程　vehicle empty container mileage
[汽]车库/車庫,停車間　garage, indoor parking
汽车列车/拖曳車組　tractor trailer combination
汽车零件磨损/車輛部件磨損　wear of vehicle parts
汽车轮渡/汽車輪渡,車輛渡輪,車輛渡船　car ferrying, automobile ferry, car ferry
汽车旅馆/汽車旅館　motel, motor inn, motor hotel
汽车门式自动清洗机/閘門式自動清洗機　gate type automatic car washer
汽车耐久性/車輛耐久性　vehicle durability
汽车能量利用率/車輛能量利用因數　vehicle energy utilization factor
汽车能量平衡/車輛能量平衡　vehicle energy balance
汽车排放分析仪/車輛廢氣分析儀　vehicle exhaust analyser
汽车排放物/車輛[廢氣]排放　vehicle emission
[汽车]排气分析仪/排氣分析器,廢氣分析器　exhaust gas analyzer, emission analyzer
汽车平均技术速度/車輛平均技術速度　vehicle average technical speed
汽车起重机/汽車式起重機,起重車　auto crane, truck crane
[汽车]前大灯试验仪/前大燈試驗儀　head light tester
汽车清洗机/洗車機　car washer
汽车燃料利用率/車輛燃料利用因數　vehicle fuel utilization factor
汽车燃料消耗定额/車輛燃料消耗定額　vehicle fuel consumption rating
汽车容载量/車輛裝載量　vehicle load carrying capacity

汽车使用/車輛駕駛　vehicle operation
汽车使用方便性/車輛使用方便性　vehicle utilization conveniency
汽车使用可靠性/車輛操作可靠度　vehicle operational reliability
汽车使用强度/車輛使用强度　vehicle operation intensity
汽车使用条件/車輛駕駛條件　vehicle operation condition
汽车使用效率/車輛運用效率　vehicle operation efficiency
汽车使用性能/汽車使用性能　vehicle operation performance
汽车式起重机/起重[機]卡車　truck crane, automobile crane, autocrane
汽车速度表试验台/速率計試驗臺　speedometer tester
汽车损耗/車輛磨損　vehicle wear-out
汽车停车规则/汽車停車規則　parking rule
汽车通过性/車輛通過　vehicle passability
汽车挖掘机/鏟土車　truck shovel
汽车完好技术状况/車輛完好技術狀況　good technical condition of vehicle
汽车维护/車輛維護　vehicle maintenance
汽车维护场/車輛保養場　vehicle maintenance depot, vehicle maintenance yard
汽车维护定位作业法/車輛維護定位作業法　method of vehicle maintenance on universal post
汽车维护方法/車輛維護方法　vehicle maintenance method
汽车维护工程/車輛維護工程　vehicle maintenance engineering
汽车维护工艺/車輛維護技術　vehicle maintenance technology
汽车维护工艺过程/車輛維護技術程式　vehicle maintenance technological process
汽车维护规范/汽車維護規範　vehicle maintenance norm
汽车维护级别/車輛維護等級　vehicle maintenance grade
汽车维护类别/車輛維護分類　vehicle maintenance classification
汽车维护流水作业法/車輛維護流水作業法　flow method for vehicle maintenance
汽车维护生产纲领/車輛維護生產計劃　production program of vehicle maintenance
汽车维护站/車輛保養站　vehicle maintenance station
汽车维护周期/車輛維護間隔　interval between vehicle maintenances
汽车维护作业/汽車維護作業　operation of vehicle maintenance
汽车维修/車輛維修　vehicle maintenance and repair
汽车维修费用定额/車輛維護成本定額　cost quota of vehicle maintenance and repair
汽车维修工具/車輛維修工具　instrument of vehicle maintenance and repair
汽车维修工艺设备/車輛維修工藝裝備　technological equipment of vehicle maintenance and repair
汽车维修平均费用/車輛維修平均成本　average cost of vehicle maintenance and repair
汽车维修平均工时/車輛維修平均工時　average man-hour of vehicle maintenance and repair
汽车维修企业/車輛維修企業　vehicle maintenance and repair enterprise
汽车维修网点/車輛維修網點　vehicle maintenance and repair network
汽车维修性/車輛維護性　vehicle maintainability
汽车维修指标/車輛維修指標　vehicle maintenance and repair indices
汽车维修制度/車輛修理制度　vehicle maintenance and repair system
汽车污染/汽車汙染　vechile emissions pollution
汽车小修/汽車現場修理　vehicle current repair
汽车小修频率/汽車現場修理頻率　frequency of vehicle current repair
汽车行驶平顺性/車輛行駛平順性　vehicle running smoothness
汽车修理/車輛修理　vehicle repair
汽车修理厂/汽車修理工廠　vehicle repair plant
汽车修理定位作业法/汽車修理定位作業法　vehicle repair on universal post
汽车修理方法/汽車修理方法　vehicle repair method
汽车修理工艺/車輛修理工藝　vehicle repair technology
汽车修理工艺过程/汽車修理技術程式　vehicle repair technological process
汽车修理技术标准/汽車修理技術標準　vehicle repair technical standard
汽车修理类别/車輛修理分類　vehicle repair classification
汽车修理流水作业法/汽車修理流導法　flow method for vehicle repair
汽车修理生产纲领/車輛修理生產計劃　production program of vehicle repair

汽车修理站/汽車修配廠　motor repair shop, car repair pit
汽车运行工况/汽車營運模式　vehicle operational mode
汽车运价构成/汽車運價構成　formation of motor transport tariff
汽车运价管理体制/汽車運價管理體制　motor transport rate management system
汽车运价率/汽車運價率　motor transport tariff rate
汽车运价体系/汽車運價體系　motor transport tariff system
汽车运输/汽車運輸　motor vehicle transport
汽车运输边际成本/汽車運輸邊際成本　motor transport marginal cost
汽车运输车辆大修折旧/汽車運輸車輛大修折舊　motor transport vehicle overhaul depreciation
汽车运输车辆费用/汽車運輸車輛費用　motor transport vehicle cost
汽车运输车型成本/汽車運輸車型成本　motor transport cost by vehicle type
汽车运输沉落成本/汽車運輸沈落成本　motor transport sunk cost
汽车运输成本/汽車運輸成本　motor transport cost
汽车运输成本范围/汽車運輸成本範圍　motor transport cost scope
汽车运输成本分析/汽車運輸成本分析　motor transport cost analysis
汽车运输成本计算单位/汽車運輸成本會計單位　motor transport cost accounting unit
汽车运输成本计算对象/汽車運輸成本會計對象　motor transport cost accounting object
汽车运输成本降低额/汽車運輸成本降低額　motor transport cost reduction amount
汽车运输成本降低率/汽車運輸成本降低率　motor transport cost reduction rate
汽车运输成本结构/汽車運輸成本結構　motor transport cost structure
汽车运输成本控制/汽車運輸成本控制　motor transport cost control
汽车运输成本项目/汽車運輸成本項目　motor transport cost item
汽车运输船/車輛運輸船　pure car carrier, PCC
汽车运输单车成本/汽車運輸單車成本　motor transport unit vehicle cost
汽车运输辅助生产成本/汽車運輸輔助生產成本　motor transport auxiliary production cost
汽车运输机会成本/汽車運輸機會成本　motor transport opportunity cost
汽车运输计划成本/汽車運輸計劃成本　motor transport planned cost
汽车运输企业成本/汽車運輸企業成本　motor transport enterprise cost
汽车运输预测成本/汽車運輸預測成本　motor transport forecast cost
汽车运输运营成本/汽車運輸運營成本　motor transport operation cost
汽车运输站场设施/汽車運輸站場設施　terminal and yard facilities of motor transport
汽车运输装卸成本/汽車運輸裝卸成本　motor transport handling cost
汽车运输综合成本/汽車運輸綜合成本　motor transport comprehensive cost
[汽车运输]总站/聯合車站　union station
汽车运行材料/車輛運行材料　vehicle operational consumption materials
汽车运用工程/汽車運輸工程　automobile transportation engineering
汽车载箱行程/汽車載箱行程　vehicle payload-container mileage
汽车诊断/車輛診斷　vehicle diagnosis
汽车诊断站/車輛診斷臺　vehicle diagnostic station
汽车制造厂/汽車製造廠　automobile factory, motor factory
汽车中修/汽車中修　vehicle medium repair
汽车重量利用系数/車輛重量利用係數　vehicle weight efficiency
汽车重箱行程/汽車重箱行程　vehicle loaded container mileage
汽车专项修理厂/汽車專項修理廠　specialty vehicle repair shop
汽车状况监控/車輛狀態監控　vehicle condition monitoring
汽车综合诊断线/汽車綜合診斷線　vehicle general inspection and diagnosis line
汽车总成修理厂/汽車總修理工廠　unit repair plant
汽车钻机/鑽車　drill truck
[汽车]最小转弯半径/最小迴轉半徑　minimum turning radius
汽笛/汽笛，號笛　whistle
汽阀/活塞閥　piston valve
汽封/汽封　steam seal, steam seal gland
汽封系统/渦輪汽封系統　turbine steam seal system
汽缸/汽缸　cylinder
汽缸鞍/汽缸鞍　cylinder saddle
汽缸珩磨机/缸筒搪磨機　cylinder honing machine
汽缸后盖/後缸蓋　back cylinder head

汽缸排水阀/汽缸自動排水閥　cylinder drain valve
汽缸牵引力/汽缸牽引力　cylinder tractive effort
汽缸前盖/汽缸前蓋　front cylinder head
汽缸套/汽缸襯筒　cylinder bushing
汽耗量/蒸汽消耗量　steam consumption
汽耗率/汽耗率　specific steam consumption, steam rate
汽化氨电热系统/汽化氨電熱系統　vaporizing ammonia electrothermal system
汽化油灶/汽化油灶　vaporizing oil range
汽机鼓/[蒸]汽鼓　steam drum
汽轮鼓风机/渦輪鼓風機　turbo-blower
汽轮机/汽輪機,蒸汽渦輪機　steam turbine
汽轮机厂/汽輪機廠,蒸汽渦輪機廠　steam turbine manufactory
汽轮机车/渦輪機車,燃氣輪機車　turbine locomotive
汽轮机船/蒸汽渦輪機船,汽船　steam turbine ship
汽轮机单缸运行/蒸汽渦輪機單缸運轉　steam turbine single-cylinder operation
汽轮机级/蒸汽渦輪機級　steam turbine stage
汽轮机-燃气轮机联合装置/蒸汽與燃氣渦輪複合推進裝置　combined steam-gas turbine propulsion plant
汽轮机外特性/蒸汽渦輪機外特性　external characteristic of steam turbine
汽轮机油/輪機滑油　turbine oil
汽室/蒸汽室,蒸汽櫃　steam chest, valve chest
汽室套/汽櫃襯套　steam chest bushing
汽-水冲击/汽-水衝擊　steam water shock
汽水共腾/汽水共腾　priming
汽-水换热器/汽-水換熱器　steam water heat exchanger
汽水阻力/壓力降　pressure drop
汽油/汽油　gasoline
汽油机/汽油機,汽油引擎　petrol engine, gasoline engine
砌拱支架/砌拱支架,拱腹架　soffit scaffolding
砌块举重器/砌塊舉重器　segment erector
砌块砌体/砌塊砌體　block masonry
砌块砌体结构/砌體結構　block masonry structure
砌石/抛石護床　stoning, stone masonry
砌石护坡/塊石鋪面　pitched work
砌体/層砌工　rangework
砌体结构/砌體結構,石工結構　masonry structure
砌筑墙/砌築牆　masonry wall
砌筑砂浆/圬工灰漿　masonry mortar
砌筑水泥/墁砌水泥　masonry cement

砌砖工/泥瓦匠　bricklayer
器具通气管/衛生器具通氣管　fixture vent
憩流/憩流,憩潮　slack water
千板岩/千枚岩　phyllite
千层石/千層石　melaleuca stone
千分表/針盤量軌　dial gage
千斤顶/千斤頂　jack
千斤顶法封顶/千斤頂法封頂　closure by jacking and sealing off crown
千斤索/跨索,俯仰頂索,吊桿頂索　span rope, topping lift
千斤索绞车/吊桿頂索絞車　topping lift winch
千斤索具/跨索具　span ringging
千斤座/[桅頂]俯仰滑車座　topping bracket
千粒重/千粒重　the 1000 grain weight
千人指标/千人指標　standard of per thousand people
千柱建筑群/千柱建築群　Grupo de las Mil Columnas
扦插繁殖/扦插繁殖　cutting propagation
迁村并点/遷村并點　relocation and amalgamation of village
迁地保存/域外保育,移地保育　ex situ conservation
迁入移民/移入者　immigrant
迁移植物/遷移植物　migrant plant, migratory plant
钎杆/鑽鋼　drill steel
钎焊/[硬]焊,銅焊　brazing, soldering
钎焊合金/銅焊合金　brazing alloy
钎探/桿測　rod sounding
钎探检验/釺探檢驗　pin exploration
牵出线/[調車]拖上線　switching lead, shunting neck, lead track
牵出线改编能力/牽出線改編能力　resorting capacity of lead track
牵手桩/牽手樁　hand pile
牵索/索索,控索　guy, inhaul line
牵条螺栓/牽條螺栓　stay bolt
牵引/牽引,拖曳　towing, traction, drag
牵引变电所/牽引變電所　traction substation, TSS
牵引变电所标称电压/牽引變電所標稱電壓　nominal voltage of traction substation
牵引变流器/牽引變流器　traction convertor
牵引变频器/牽引變頻器　traction frequency convertor
牵引变压器/牽引變壓器　traction transformer
牵引车/曳引車　tractor
牵引车及挂车/貨櫃拖車　tractor and trailer
牵引电动机/牽引電動機　traction motor

牵引电动机隔离开关/牽引電動機隔離開關 traction motor isolating switch
牵引电动机供电制式/牽引電動機供電系統 traction motor power supply system
牵引电机电流表/牽引電動機電流表 traction motor ammeter
牵引电机电压表/牽引電動機電壓計 traction motor voltmeter
牵引电抗器/牽引電抗器,牽引反應器 traction reactor
牵引电路/牽引電路 traction circuit
牵引定数/牽引定數 tonnage rating, tonnage of traction
牵引方式/牽引方式 mode of traction
牵引杆/牽引桿,曳引桿,拉桿 draw bar
牵引功率比油耗测定/牽引功率比油耗測定 specific drawbar power fuel consumption measurement
牵引钩/牽引鈎 hauling hook
牵引荷载/牽引載重 tractive load
牵引回流电路/牽引回流電路 traction return current circuit
牵引回流轨/牽引回流導電軌 traction return current rail
牵引降压混合变电所/牽引降壓混合變電站 combined substation
牵引力/牽引力 tractive force
牵引力模数/牽引力模數 tractive effort of modulus
牵引链条/制動鏈 drag chain
牵引梁/牽引梁 draft sill
牵引逆变器/牽引逆變器,牽引反相器 traction invertor
牵引热工试验/牽引熱力學試驗 traction and thermodynamic test
牵引刹车/牽引刹車 towing brake
牵引式铲运车/牽引鏟土機 tractor shovel
牵引式刮土平地机/拉式平土機 pull-grader
牵引式刮运机/牽引式刮運機 tractor drawn scraper
牵引试验/牽引[馬力]試驗 draw bar test, traction test
牵引索/拉拖索 trailing cable
牵引网/牽引網 traction electric network
牵引网阻抗/牽引網供電阻抗 impedance of traction electric network
牵引线/拉線 staying wire
牵引载荷/牽挽重量 load hauled
牵引-制动位转换开关/电力-制動轉換開關 power-brake changeover switch

牵引种类/牽引種類 kind of traction, category of traction
牵引装置/牽引機構 draw gear
牵制力/牽制力 holdback force
牵纵拐肘/擒縱器 escapement
铅垂地面坐标系/正交地面軸系 normal earth-fixed coordinate system
铅垂点三角测量/垂直點三角測量 plumb point triangulation
铅垂弹性/鉛垂彈性 vertical elasticity, vertical resilience
铅垂线偏差/垂線偏差 plumb-line deviation
铅锤/測[深]錘 lead, hand lead
铅锤视准测量/測深鉛錘視準測量 plumb-bob collimation
铅基白合金轴承/鉛基白合金軸承 lead base white metal bearing
铅基轴承合金/鉛基軸承合金 lead base bearing alloy
铅粒/鉛粒 particulate lead
铅酸蓄电池/鉛酸性蓄電池 lead-acid storage battery
铅橡胶支座/鉛橡膠支承 lead rubber bearing
签发日期/簽發日期 date of issue
签证处/簽證處 visa department, visa section
前八字/前八字方向 on the bow
前滨/前灘 foreshore
前处理/前處理,預處理 pre-processing
前窗/前排玻璃窗 front window
前垂板/通風道擋板 draft plate
前从板座/前從板座 front draft lug, front draft stop
前导舰/前導船艦 leading ship
前端壁/前端壁 front bulkhead
前端设备/前端設備 front-end device
前帆/前帆 fore sail
前方/前方,向前,正車 ahead
前方让路标志/前方讓路標誌 yield ahead sign
前方视野/前方視野 field of front vision
前方停车标志/前面停止通行信號 stop ahead sign
前方信号标志/前方信號標誌 signal ahead sign
前后吃水不当/前後吃水不當 out of trim
前后风压差/前後風壓差 false gradient
前后轮距/輪距 wheel base
前后轴载重/前後軸載重 tandem axel load
前缓冲铁/前保險槓 front bumper
前接点/前觸點,動合接點 front contact
前进波/前進波 progressive wave
前景/前景 front view

前景音/前景音　foreground sound
前掠角/前掠角　sweep forward angle
前掠翼/前掠翼　sweep forward wing
前轮摆振/前輪擺振　nose wheel shimmy
前面基地线/前面基地線　front lot line
前起落架/前起落架　nose landing gear
前墙/前牆　front wall, breast wall
前轻后重法/前輕後重法　method of making the front part of rock lighter than the back part
前倾[型]艄/斜艄　raked stem, raked bow
前圈/前圈　front coil
前群/前群　pregroup
前三点起落架/前三點起落架　tricycle landing gear
前上方控制板/前置面板　up front control panel
前视红外系统/前視紅外儀　forward-looking infrared system, FLIR
前体/艄部　fore body
前厅/前廳,門廳,通廊　vestibule
前庭/前庭,前院　front yard, forecourt
前庭功能不对称假说/前庭功能不對稱假說　vestibular function asymmetry hypothesis
前庭功能检查/平衡功能檢查　vestibular function examination
前庭功能训练/平衡功能訓練　vestibular function training
前投影/前投影機　front screen projection
前桅/前桅　fore mast
前向纠错/前向偵錯　forward error correction
前向纠错方式/前向偵錯方式　forward error correction mode, FEC
前行舰/正前方船　forward ship
前行桨叶/前進槳葉　advancing blade
前悬装土机/前懸裝土機　front mounted loader
前檐幕/前檐幕　fore-proscenium curtain
前翼/前翼　canard
前缘半径/前緣半徑　leading edge radius
前缘缝翼/前緣縫翼　leading edge slat
前缘襟翼/前緣襟翼　leading edge flap
前缘锯齿/前緣鋸齒　leading edge sawtooth
前缘缺口/前緣缺口　leading edge notch
前缘吸力/前緣吸力　leading edge suction
前缘下垂/前緣下垂,翼前下垂　leading edge droop
前院/前院　front court forecourt
前院线/前院線　front yard line
前照灯/前燈,頭燈　head lamp, head light
前置标志/前置標誌　advance sign
前置放大器/前置放大器　pre-amplifier
前置机/前端處理器　front-end processor

前置站/前置站　front station
前置指路标志/前置方向標誌　advance direction sign
前轴负荷测定/前軸負荷測定　front axle load measurement
钳夹车/鉗夾車　schnabel car
钳口板/齒形接縫板　jaw plate
钳形梁/鉗形梁　schnabel
潜冰/地下冰　subsurface ice
潜[防波]堤/潛堤,水下防波堤,潛壩　submerged breakwater, submerged dyke
潜孔钻机/潛孔鑽機　diving drill
潜流/潛流,埋没河川　undercurrent, buried stream
潜热/潛熱　latent heat
潜热蓄热/潛熱加熱再生　latent heat regeneration
潜入喷管/潛没噴嘴　submerged nozzle
潜式分水工程/潛式分水工程　submerged flow diversion work
潜式进水口/潛式進水口　submerged crib
潜式溢洪道/潛式溢洪道　submerged spillway
潜水/潛水　diving
潜水泵/潛水泵,深水泵,潛式抽水機　immersion pump, submersible pump, diving pump
潜水病/潛水病　diver paralysis
潜水舱/潛水艙　submerged diving chamber
潜水导索/潛水導索　diver descending line
潜水电泵/潛水電泵　electric diving pump
潜水电话/潛水電話　diving telephone
潜水服/潛水服,潛水衣　diving suit
潜水高水位/泉面高位　phreatic high
潜水工作船/潛水工作船,潛水支援船　diving boat, diving support vessel
潜水供气系统/潛水供氣系統　gas distribution system for diver
潜水减压/潛水減壓　decompression of diving
潜水器/潛水器,潛水載具　submersible vehicle, submersible
潜水器母船/潛水器母船　mother ship of submersible
潜水设备/潛水設備　diving equipment
潜水施工/潛水作業　diver work
潜水手语/潛水手語　diver sign language
潜[水]艇/潛[水]艇,潛艦　submarine
潜水头盔/潛水頭盔　diver helmet
潜水位变化周期/泉面週期　phreatic cycle
潜水位下降/泉面下降　phreatic decline
潜水靴/潛水靴　diver boots
潜水员/潛水員,潛水人　diver
潜水支援船/潛水支援船,潛水工作船　diving boat,

diving support vessel
潜水钟/潛水鍾　diving bell
潜水装具/潛水器具　diving apparatus
潜水钻机/潛水鑽機,水下鑽機　underwater rig, diving drill machine
潜艇操纵/潛艇操縱　submarine handling
潜艇操纵强度/潛艇操縱強度　submarine maneuvering strength
潜艇操纵性/潛艇操縱性　submarine maneuverability
潜艇反操纵性/潛艇反操縱性　submarine adverse maneuverability
潜艇航行状态/潛艇航行狀態　submarine proceeding state
潜艇救生船/潛艇救難艦　submarine rescue vessel, submarine rescue ship
潜艇均衡/潛艇均衡　submarine trimming
潜艇母舰/潛艇母艦　submarine depot ship
潜艇平行上浮/潛艇平行上浮　submarine trimmed surfacing
潜艇平行下潜/潛艇平行下潛　submarine trimmed diving
潜艇起浮/潛艇上浮　submarine surfacing
潜艇水面航行状态/潛艇水面航行狀態　submarine surface proceeding state
潜艇水下航行状态/潛艇水下航行狀態　submarine proceeding state underwater
潜艇速浮/潛艇急浮　submarine quick surfacing
潜艇速潜/潛艇急潛　submarine quick diving
潜艇通气管航行状态/潛艇通氣管航行狀態　submarine proceeding state with snorkel
潜艇下潜/潛艇下潛　submarine diving
潜艇相对上浮/潛艇相對上浮　submarine relative surfacing
潜艇相对下潜/潛艇相對下潛　submarine relative diving
潜艇巡航状态/潛艇巡航狀態　submarine cruising state
潜艇鱼雷发射装置/潛艇魚雷發射管　torpedo launcher for submarines
潜望镜/潛望鏡　periscope
潜望六分仪/潛望六分儀　periscope sextant
潜越/潛越　passing underneath
潜在故障/潛在故障　potential fault
潜在缺陷/潛在缺陷　latent defect
潜在通路分析/潛在通路分析　sneak circuit analysis
潜在渔业资源/潛在的漁業資源　potential fisheries resources
潜在蒸发/潛在蒸發[量]　potential evaporation

潜在蒸散/潛在蒸發散[量],可能蒸發散量　potential evapotranspiration, PET
潜在状态/潛在狀態　sneak condition
浅成岩/半深成岩　hypabyssal rock
浅地表排水/地下排水　subsurface drainage
浅放电/淺放電　shallow discharge
浅井/淺井　shallow well
浅孔爆破/淺孔爆破　shallow hole blasting
浅浪登陆/淺浪登陸　landing through surf
浅埋隧道/淺埋隧道,淺層隧道　shallow tunnel, shallow-depth tunnel, shallow burying tunnel
浅水波/淺水波　shallow water wave
浅水潮/淺水潮　shallow water tide
浅水码头/淺水碼頭　shallow water wharf
浅水系数/淺化係數　shoaling coefficient
浅水效应/淺水效應　shallow water effect
浅水与窄航道航行工况管理/淺窄水道航行操作模式管理　shallow and narrow channel navigation operating mode management
浅水作用/淺化　shoaling
浅滩标志/淺灘標誌　shoal indicator
浅震/淺層地震　shallow shock
欠超高/欠超高　deficient superelevation
欠电流继电器/欠流電驛[器]　under-current relay
欠电压继电器/欠壓電驛[器]　under-voltage relay
欠固结土/欠固結土　underconsolidated soil
欠频/欠頻　under-frequency
欠试验/欠試驗　undertesting
欠挖/欠挖　underbreak
欠稳船/低穩度船　tender ship
欠压/欠壓　under-voltage
欠压试验/欠壓試驗　under-voltage test
欠折射/次折射　sub-refraction
堑顶/塹頂　top of cutting slope
嵌板/鑲板　panel board
嵌缝/填料接縫　caulking
嵌缝法/角隅填密法　filleting
嵌缝膏/填隙化合物,斂縫填料　caulking compound, sealant
嵌缝工具/填縫工具　caulking set
嵌缝石膏/嵌縫石膏　joint gypsum
嵌固边缘/固定邊緣　fixed edge
嵌合体/嵌合體　chimera
嵌花式路面/瑪賽克鋪面,馬賽克鋪面　mosaic pavement
嵌接/嵌接　scarfing
嵌入式灯具/嵌入型照明器具　recessed luminaire
嵌锁法路面/嵌鎖法路面　pavement of Macadam

construction
嵌条/鑲板條　panel strip
嵌线/鑲板條　panel strip
嵌岩桩/嵌岩樁　socketed pile
抢风/迎風　close haul
强拆/強拆　forced releasing
强电干扰/強電干擾　high voltage interference
强度/強度　intensity, strength
强度规范/強度規範　strength specification
强度极限/強度極限　strength limit
强度试验/強度試驗,壓力試驗,耐壓試驗　strength test, pressure test
强度准则/強度準則　criterion of strength
强风化岩石/強風化岩　highly weathered rock
强横梁/強力梁,大梁　web beam
强化阶段/強化階段　strain hardening range
强化木地板/強化木地板　laminated flooring with paper impregnated thermosetting resin
强化群呼/強化群呼　enhanced group call, EGC
强化试验/強化試驗　intensified test
强化系数/強化係數　coefficient of intensification
强击机/攻擊機　attack airplane
强剪弱弯/強剪弱彎　strong shear capacity and weak bending capacity
强界面/強介面　strong interface
强肋骨/大肋骨　web frame
强力滑油系统/強力潤滑油系統　forced lubricating oil system
强力甲板/強度甲板　strength deck
强逆流/強逆流　strong head current
强酸值/強酸值　strong acid number, SAN
强行通过/強行通過　forced passage
强胸横梁/抗拍梁　panting beam
强胸结构/抗拍結構　panting arrangement
强涌/強湧　high swell
强制打捞/強制打撈沈船　compulsory removal of wreck
强制急速工况/強制空轉模式　forced idling mode
强制返回/強制返回　forced return
强制滤速/強制濾速　forcing filter rate
强制内接/強制內接　compulsory inscribing
强制式混凝土搅拌机/強制式混凝土攪拌機　forced concrete mixer
强制式混凝土搅拌设备/強制混凝土拌和設備　forced concrete mixing plant
强制式搅拌机/強制拌和機　forced mixer
强制式稳定土搅拌设备/強制穩定土廠拌設備　forced stabilized soil mixing plant

强制通风/強制通風　forced draught
强制脱落机构/強制脫離　forced disengagement
强制性交通流/強制交通流量　forced traffic flow
强制性控制指标/強制性控制指數　mandatory control index
强制旋转拌和机/強制旋轉拌和機　forced circulation mixer
强制循环锅炉/強制循環鍋爐　assisted circulation boiler, forced circulation boiler
强制引航/強制引航　mandatory pilotage, compulsory pilotage
强制招标/強制招標　compulsory tender
强制振动/強制振動　forced vibration
强轴/長軸　major axis
强柱弱梁/強柱弱梁　strong column and weak beam
墙/牆,壁　wall
墙板/牆板　wall panel
墙板压筋/牆板壓筋　flute or rib on sheathing
墙衬/牆襯面　wall lining
墙顶封口/牆頂封口　seal at the top of wall
墙梁/牆[托]梁　wall beam
墙面布光灯/牆面布光燈　wall washer
墙面交接线/內圖廊線　neat line
墙面绿化/牆面綠化　wall greening
墙面线/牆面線　wall surface line
墙裙/護牆板　dado
墙园/牆園　wall garden
墙纸/牆紙　wall paper
墙趾/趾牆　wall toe
墙踵/牆踵　wall heel
蔷薇园/薔薇園,玫瑰園　rose garden
抢救监护室/急診危重病房　emergency intensive care unit, EICU
抢救室/急診[搶救]室　emergency treatment room
抢滩/搶灘　beaching
抢修工程/搶修工程　rush repair work
抢妆室/搶妝室　quick dressing room
强迫导向循环/強迫導向循環　forced guided circulation
强迫发汗冷却/強迫發汗冷卻　forced transpiration cooling
强迫通风式电动机/強制通風式電動機　force ventilated motor
强迫循环/強制循環,壓流循環　forced circulation
强迫振动/強制振動　forced vibration
强迫振动法/強制振動法,強制振盪法　forced oscillation method
戗堤/坡臺　berm

戗脊/戧脊　diagonal ridge for gable and hip roof, qiangji

跷板式桨毂/順槳毂　seesaw hub, feathering hub

锹拌/鏟拌　spading

敲缸/柴油機爆震　piston slap, diesel knock, knock

敲渣锤/鑿[面]錘　chipping hammer

乔木/喬木,樹木　tree, arbor

乔木层/喬木層,喬木帶　tree layer, tree stratum

桥侧人行道/橋側人行道　bridge sidewalk

桥渡勘测设计/跨線橋設計測量　survey and design of bridge crossing

桥墩/橋墩　pier, bridge pier

桥墩分水尖/橋墩分水尖　pier break water

桥墩尖端分水桩/橋墩分水樁　starling

桥墩局部冲刷/橋墩局部沖刷　local scour around pier

桥规/橋[形]規,橋形軸規　bridge gage

桥规值/橋形規值　bridge gage value

桥涵/橋涵　bridge and culvert

桥涵标/橋通路標,橋[梁開]啟標誌　bridge opening mark, bridge mark

桥涵顶入法/橋涵頂入法　jacking in method of culvert or subsurface bridge

[桥涵]拱圈/拱環　arch ring

桥涵扩孔/橋涵擴孔　opening enlargement of bridge and culvert

桥涵水文/橋涵水文　hydrology of bridge and culvert

桥基沉降观测/橋基沈降觀測　bridge foundation settlement observation

桥基冲刷/橋基沖刷　scouring at bridge foundation

桥基稳定性评定/橋基穩定性評定　bridge foundation stability evaluation

桥孔压缩/橋通路收縮　bridge opening contraction

桥[梁]/橋[梁],公路橋　bridge

桥梁安装监测/橋梁架設監測　bridge erection monitoring

桥梁安装容许误差/橋安裝容許誤差　bridge erection tolerance

桥梁编号/橋編號　bridge numbering

桥梁标/橋梁標　bridge post

桥梁标准活载/橋梁標準活載　standard live load for bridge

桥梁标准设计/橋梁設計標準　standard design of bridge

桥梁病害诊断/橋梁病害診斷　bridge defect diagnosis

桥梁病害整治/橋梁病害整治　bridge fault repairing

桥梁测试车/橋梁測試車　bridge testing laboratory vehicle

桥梁承载能力/橋梁負載能力　load carrying capacity of bridge

桥梁承载能力极限状态/橋梁承載能力極限狀態　ultimate limit state of bridge carrying capacity

桥梁道碴槽/橋梁道碴槽　ballast trough

[桥梁]动力响应试验/動力響應試驗　bridge response to forced vibration

桥梁动载试验/橋梁動荷試驗　bridge dynamic loading test

桥梁墩台防撞/橋梁墩臺防撞　collision prevention of pier and abutment

桥梁翻新/橋梁翻新　bridge retrofitting

桥梁方案设计/橋梁概念設計　bridge conceptual design

桥梁概率极限状态设计法/橋梁概率極限狀態設計法　probabilistic limit state design method of bridge

桥梁工程学/橋梁工學　bridge engineering

桥梁管理系统/橋梁管理系統　bridge management system

[桥梁]合龙/[橋梁]合攏　closure, closure of bridge structure

桥梁荷载谱/橋梁荷載譜　bridge load spectrum

桥梁荷载系数设计法/橋梁負載因數設計法　load factor design method of bridge

桥梁横向刚度/橋梁側向剛度　lateral rigidity of bridge

桥梁护轨/橋梁防護欄　guard rail of bridge

桥梁护木/橋梁護木　guard timber of bridge

桥梁基础/橋基　foundation of bridge, bridge foundation

桥梁极限状态设计/橋梁界限狀態設計　limit state design of bridge

桥梁计算机辅助设计/橋梁電腦輔助設計　computer aided design for bridge, CAD for bridge

桥梁技术档案/橋梁技術檔案　bridge technical file

桥梁加固/橋梁加固　bridge strengthening

桥梁监测系统/橋梁監視系統　bridge monitoring system

桥梁检查/橋梁檢查　bridge inspection

桥梁检查规则/橋梁檢查規則　bridge inspection regulation

桥梁检查类别/橋梁檢查類別　bridge inspection category

桥梁检查周期/橋梁檢查週期　bridge inspection cycle

桥梁检定承载系数/橋梁檢定承載係數　rated load-

bearing coefficient for bridge, rated load-bearing coefficient for bridge as compared with standard live loading
桥梁检定试验/橋梁評級試驗　bridge rating test
桥梁建筑高度/橋梁建築高度　construction height of bridge
桥梁建筑限界/橋梁建築限界　bridge construction clearance, bridge structure gage
桥梁铰刀/橋式鉸刀　bridge reamer
桥梁结构安装控制/橋結構安裝控制　bridge structure erection control
桥梁结构可靠度/橋結構可靠度　reliability of bridge structure
桥梁结构设计/橋梁結構設計　bridge structure design
桥梁静载试验/橋梁靜載重試驗　bridge static loading test
桥梁抗震加固/橋梁抗震加固　bridge aseismatic strengthening
桥梁抗震设计/橋梁耐震設計　aseismatic design of bridge
桥梁抗震稳定性/橋梁抗震穩定　aseismatic stability of bridge
桥梁空间结构/橋梁空間結構　space structure for bridge
桥梁孔径不足/橋梁孔徑不足　unsufficient span of bridge
桥梁栏杆/橋欄杆　bridge railing
桥梁脉动测量/橋梁脈動測量　bridge pulsation measurement
桥梁美学/橋梁美學　bridge aesthetics
桥梁模型风洞试验/橋梁模型風洞試驗　bridge model wind tunnel test
桥梁模型试验/橋梁模型試驗　bridge model test
桥梁耐久性/橋梁耐久性　bridge durability
桥梁挠度/橋梁撓度,橋梁撓曲　deflection of bridge span
桥梁挠度曲线/橋梁撓曲曲線　bridge deflection curve
桥梁疲劳剩余寿命/橋梁疲勞剩餘壽命　fatigue residual life of bridge
桥梁疲劳剩余寿命评估/橋梁疲勞剩餘壽命評估　evaluating fatigue residual life of bridge
桥梁平面结构/橋梁平面結構　plane structure for bridge
桥梁评价系统/橋梁評估系統　bridge evaluation system
桥梁破坏/橋梁破壞,大橋垮塌,橋梁垮塌　bridge collapse
桥梁破损/橋梁破損　bridge failure
桥梁浅基/橋梁淺基礎　shallow foundation of bridge, unsafe depth foundation of bridge
桥梁浅基防护/橋梁淺基防護,橋淺基保護　bridge shallow foundation protection, unsafe depth foundation protection
桥梁全长/橋全長　total length of bridge, overall length of bridge
桥梁容许应力设计/橋梁容許應力設計　allowable stress design of bridge
桥梁上部结构/橋梁上部結構　superstructure of bridge
桥梁上拱度/橋梁上拱度　camber of bridge span
桥梁设计/橋梁設計　bridge design
桥梁施工/橋梁工程　bridge construction
桥梁实验车/橋梁試驗車　bridge test car
桥梁使用能力极限状态/橋梁使用極限狀態　serviceability limit state of bridge
桥梁试运行荷载/橋梁試運行荷載　test run loading for bridge
桥梁数据库/橋梁資料庫　bridge data bank
桥梁水毁/橋梁水毀　bridge disaster by flood
桥梁通知设备/橋梁通知設備　bridge announciating device
桥梁细部设计/橋梁細部設計　bridge detail design
桥梁下部结构/橋梁下部結構　substructure of bridge
桥梁限载/橋梁限載　bridge load limit
桥梁验收荷载试验/橋梁驗收載荷試驗　bridge acceptance loading test
桥梁养护/橋梁養護　bridge maintenance
桥梁优化设计/橋梁優化設計,橋梁最佳設計　optimum design of bridge
桥梁遮断信号/橋梁遮斷信號　bridge obstruction signal
桥梁振型分析/橋梁振型分析　bridge vibration mode analysis
桥梁自振频率/橋梁固有頻率　self-excited vibrational frequency of bridge span, natural frequency of bridge span
桥梁自振频率测量/橋梁自振頻率測量　bridge natural frequency measurement
桥梁自振周期/橋梁自振週期　natural vibration period of bridge
桥梁总宽度/橋梁全寬　total width of bridge
桥梁总体规划/天橋全面規劃　bridge overall planning

桥梁最大横向振幅/橋梁最大橫向振幅 maximum lateral amplitude of bridge
桥楼/橋樓 bridge
桥门架/橋門構架 portal frame
桥门架效应/橋門構架效應 portal frame effect
桥面/橋面 bridge deck
桥面板/橋面板 deck slab, bridge deck slab
桥面标高/橋面標高 deck elevation, elevation of bridge deck
桥面单点加载装置/橋面單點加載裝置 single point loading device on deck
桥面荷载/橋面荷載 loading of bridge
桥面横坡/橋面橫向坡度 deck transverse slope, transverse slope of bridge deck
桥面结构/橋面結構 deck structure
桥面净空/橋面淨空間距,橋面板淨空 clearance above bridge deck, horizontal and vertical clearance above bridge deck
桥面净宽/橋面淨寬 width above bridge floor
桥面宽度/橋面寬度 bridge deck width
桥面排水/橋面排水 bridge deck drainage
桥面排水系统/橋面排水系統 deck drainage system
桥面平整度测定仪/橋面平整度測定儀 travelling beam testing device for deck surface irregularity
桥面铺装/橋面鋪裝 deck pavement, bridge deck pavement
桥面伸缩缝/橋面伸縮接合 deck expansion joint
桥面伸缩装置/橋面伸縮裝置 deck expansion installation
桥面系/橋面系 bridge deck system
桥面系统/橋面系統 bridge floor system
桥面纵坡/橋面縱坡 deck profile grade
桥名/橋名 bridge name
桥前壅水/橋前壅水 backwater in front of bridge
桥前壅水高度/橋前壅水高度 backwater height in front of bridge, top water level in front of bridge
桥上人行道/橋上人行道 sidewalk on bridge
桥式吊车/橋式起重機,高架移動起重機 overhead traveling crane
桥式联结器/橋式聯結器 bridge fitting
桥式码头/橋式碼頭 bridge type wharf
桥隧病害整治/橋隧損害修理 damage repair for bridge and tunnel, repair bridge and tunnel fault
桥隧大修/橋隧大修 major repair of bridge and tunnel, capital repair of bridge and tunnel
桥隧改造/橋隧加積,橋隧昇級 upgrading of bridge and tunnel
桥隧经常保养/橋隧定期保養 regular maintenance of bridge and tunnel
桥隧屏蔽系数/橋隧遮罩因數 shielding factor of bridge and tunnel
桥隧守护电话/橋隧守護電話 bridge and tunnel guarder telephone
桥隧巡守/橋隧巡邏 bridge and tunnel patrolling
桥隧巡守工/橋隧巡守工 bridge and tunnel watchman, bridge and tunnel patrolling man
桥隧养护/橋隧養護,橋隧保養 maintenance of bridge and tunnel
桥隧综合维修/橋隧綜合維修 comprehensive maintenance of bridge and tunnel structure
桥塔/橋塔 bridge pylon, bridge tower
桥台/橋臺,橋墩 abutment, bridge abutment
[桥]台后回填/橋臺後回填 back filling behind abutment
桥体绿化/橋體綠化 overpass greening
桥头堡/橋頭堡 bridge head
桥头搭板/橋頭引道板 bridge end transition slab, transition slab, approach slab
桥头回填设计/橋頭回填設計 bridge end backfilling design
桥头绿化/橋頭綠化 bridgehead greening
桥头引道/橋臺引道 bridge approach
[桥头]锥坡/錐坡 conical slope
桥位/橋位 bridge site, bridge location
桥位地形图/橋位地形圖 topographic map of bridge site
桥位勘测/橋位測量 bridge site survey
桥位平面图/橋位平面圖 plan of bridge site
桥位选择/橋址選擇 bridge site selection
桥下净空/橋下淨空 navigable clearance of bridge, clearance under span, underneath clearance
桥下一般冲刷/橋下一般沖刷 general scour at bridge opening
桥形接线/橋接 bridge connection
桥型/橋式 bridge type
桥枕/橋梁枕木 bridge tie, bridge sleeper
桥址断层活动性评定/橋址斷層活動性評定 fault activity evaluation of bridge site
桥址水文观测/橋位水文觀測 hydrologic observation at bridge site, hydrologic observation of bridge site
桥址稳定性评定/橋址穩定性評定 bridge site stability evaluation
桥轴线/橋梁軸線 bridge axis
桥轴线测量/橋軸線測量 survey of bridge axis
桥轴线纵剖面/橋軸線縱剖面 profile of bridge axis

桥柱灯/橋柱燈　bridge pier light
翘度/翹度　wash-back, set-back
翘曲/翹曲　warpage, warping
撬棍/撬桿　lining bar, claw bar
撬落危石/鬆石坍落　scaling down loose rock
切变角/剪切角　shearing angle
切变线/剪切線　shear line
切除残损物/切除殘骸　cutting away wreck
切点/切點　point of tangency, PT
切断/切斷　make dead
切断面/切斷面　cutting plane
切断音响按钮/切斷音響按鈕　button for cut-off an audible signal
切断装置/關斷裝置　shutoff device
切缝机/切縫機　joint cutter
切割/切割　cutting
切割机/切割機　road cutting machine
切割顺序/切割順序　cutting sequence
切割线/切割線　cutting line, line of cut
切花保鲜/切花保鮮　cut flower preservation
切花花卉/切花,插花　cut flower
切花生产/切花產量　cut flower production
切花园/切花圈　cut flower garden
切换到使用重油位置/切換使用重油　switching over to heavy oil
切换阀/輸送閥　transfer valve
切角/切角　cutting corner
切口脆性/缺口脆性　notch brittleness
切缆机/切纜機　cable cutter
切泥刀/切泥刀　clay knife
切片机/切片機　slicing machine
切筛/切篩　cutting screen
切线长[度]/切線長度　tangent length
切线反作用力/切線反力　tangential reaction
切线模量/切線模數　tangent modulus
切线弹性模数/切線彈性模數　tangent modulus of elasticity
切线支距法/切線支距法　tangent offset method
切向分辨率/切向解析度　tangent resolution
切向分量/切線方向分量　tangential component
切向畸变/正切畸變差　tangential distortion
切向加速度/切線加速度　tangential acceleration
切向应力/切線應力　tangential stress
切削/切削　cutting
切削速度/切削速度　cutting speed
切楔法/切楔法　tangent-wedge method
切斜端/切角端　snip end
切叶机/切葉機　foliage cutter

切锥法/切錐法　tangent-cone method
侵染性病害/傳染性病害,感染性病害　infectious disease
侵入限界绝缘/侵入限界絕緣　insulated joint located within the clearance limit
侵入种/侵入種　invading species
侵蚀/侵蝕,浸蝕　erosion, aggressiveness, fretting
侵蚀风景/侵蝕景觀　destructional landscape
侵蚀过程/侵蝕過程　erosion process
侵蚀率/侵蝕率　erosion rate
侵蚀燃烧/剝蝕燃燒　erosive burning
侵蚀土地/侵蝕地　eroded land
侵蚀土壤/侵蝕土壤　eroded soil
侵蚀土壤剖面/侵蝕土壤剖面　eroded soil profile
侵蚀形态/侵蝕地形　erosion form
侵蚀性自由二氧化碳/侵蝕性自由二氧化碳　aggressive free carbon dioxide
侵蚀循环/侵蝕循環　cycle of erosion
侵蚀压强峰/剝蝕壓力峰值　erosive pressure peak
侵蚀灾害/侵蝕災害　erosion hazard
侵蚀周期/侵蝕循環　cycle of erosion
侵蚀作用/侵蝕作用　erosion action
亲代/親代　parental generation
亲和力/親合力　affinity
亲水平台/親水平臺　waterside platform
亲水性/親水性　hydrophilicity
亲水性集料/親水集料,親水骨料　hydrophilic aggregate
亲子活动/親子活動　parent-child activity
亲子旅游/親子旅遊　filial tourism
禽舍/禽舍　poultry house
勤务电话/公務電話,業務電話　service telephone
勤务区/後勤支援區　logistic support area
勤务塔/勤務塔　service tower
揿钮接头/鉚釘錘頭　snap
青黄石/青黃石　qinghuang stone
青年旅社/青年旅館　youth hotel
青少年活动区/青少年活動區　youngsters activities area
青少年活动中心/青少年活動中心　youth center
青石/青石,藍石　blue stone
青铜/青銅　bronze
青铜焊/銅焊　bronze welding
青铜条/青銅條　bronze strip
青瓦/小青瓦　blue roofing tile, grey roofing tile
青云片/青雲片,青雲石,慶雲石　qingyun stone
青砖/青磚　grey brick
轻便铁道/輕便鐵路　light railway

轻舱壁/屏隔艙壁,隔間艙壁　screen bulkhead, partition bulkhead
轻柴油/輕柴油燃料　light diesel fuel
轻柴油输送泵/輕柴油輸送泵　light diesel oil transfer pump
轻浮货物/輕浮貨物,輕量貨物　light goods, light and bulk freight
轻浮行包/輕便行李　light luggage
轻钢龙骨/輕鋼龍骨　light steel keel
轻工业/輕工業　light industry
轻工业区/輕工業區　light industrial district
轻骨料/輕[質]骨材　lightweight aggregate
轻骨料混凝土/輕骨料混凝土,輕[質]集料混凝土　lightweight aggregate concrete
轻骨料混凝土外墙板/輕集料混凝土外牆板　lightweight aggregate concrete exterior wall panel
轻骨料混凝土小型空心砌块/輕骨料混凝土小型空心砌塊　lightweight aggregate concrete small hollow block
轻轨道/輕便軌道　tramway
轻轨交通/輕軌捷運　light rail transit
轻轨交通桥/捷運交通橋　rapid transit bridge
轻轨铁路/輕軌[鐵路],輕便鐵路　light railway, light rail
轻合金/輕合金　light alloy
轻合金船/輕合金船　light alloy ship
轻滑配合/輕滑配合　easy slide fit
轻交通/輕交通　light traffic
轻浪/小浪　slight sea
轻泡货/輕貨　light cargo, bulky cargo
轻气炮/輕氣炮　light gas gun
轻微破坏/輕微損失,輕傷害　slight damage
轻雾/中霧　moderate fog
轻型/輕型　low-duty
轻型吊杆/輕型吊桿　light derrick boom
轻型钢结构/輕型鋼結構　lightweight steel structure
轻型轨道车/輕型軌道車　light rail motor car, light motor trolley
轻型护卫舰/輕型巡防艦　corvette
轻型击实试验/土壤標準壓實試驗法　Proctor compaction test
轻型肋板/減輕孔肋板　lightened floor
轻型桥台/輕型橋臺　light abutment
轻型砂轮机/輕型砂輪機　light grinder
轻压配合/輕壓配合　light press fit
轻制沥青/摻合瀝青,塗料柏油　cutback asphalt
轻质隔墙条板/內牆板　lightweight panel for partition wall
轻质灰泥/輕質灰漿　lightweight plaster
轻质混凝土/輕量混凝土　lightweight concrete
轻质炼制品/輕質精煉品　light refined products
轻质燃料油/輕燃料油　light fuel oil
轻质陶瓷砖/輕質磁磚　light-ceramic tile
轻质土/輕鬆土　light soil
轻质砖/輕質磚　lightweight brick
轻转配合/輕轉配合　easy running fit
氢脆/氫脆化,氫脆性　hydrogen embrittlement
氢能/氫能　hydrogen energy
氢镍蓄电池/氫鎳蓄電池　hydrogen-nickel battery
氢排气自动脱落连接器支架/氫排氣自動脫落連接器支架　hydrogen vent auto-disconnect coupler support mount
氢气排放塔/氫氣排氣塔　gas hydrogen exhaust tower
氢气泡法/氫泡法　hydrogen bubble method
氢气燃烧池/氫氣燃燒池　gas hydrogen combustion pool
氢氧焊/氫氧焊接,氫氧熔接　oxy-hydrogen welding
氢氧排气自动脱落连接器/氫氧排氣自動脫落連接器　hydrogen-oxygen vent auto-disconnect coupler
氢氧切割/氫氧截割　oxy-hydrogen cutting
氢-氧燃料电池/氫氧燃料電池　hydrogen-oxygen fuel cell
氢致破裂/氫脆裂　hydrogen induced cracking
倾差仪/傾差儀　heeling error instrument, heeling adjustor
倾倒污染/傾倒汙染　damping pollution
倾点/流[動]點　pour point
倾斗式雨量器/翻斗雨量計　tipping bucket rain gage
倾翻稳定性试验/傾翻穩定性試驗　overturning stability test
倾废/廢[棄]物傾倒　dumping of wastes
倾覆/傾覆　overturn, capsize
倾角/斜度　slope
倾角仪/傾角計,測斜儀　inclinometer
倾析试验/顆粒洗滌試驗　decantation test
倾斜/傾斜　tilting
倾斜板/懸板　hang plate
倾斜断层/傾斜斷層,傾向斷層　dip fault
倾斜分类/傾斜分類　slope sorting
倾斜拱法/傾斜拱法　dipping ring method
倾斜角度试验机/傾斜角度試驗機　overturn angle tester
倾斜搅拌机/傾式拌和機　tilting mixer
倾斜校正/坡度改正　slope correction
倾斜流/傾斜流　slope current

倾斜盘/旋轉盤,滑盤 swashplate
倾斜试验/傾側試驗 inclining experiment, inclining test
倾斜台/傾斜試驗臺 tilt table
倾斜叶片/傾斜葉片 dihedral vane, lean blade
倾斜仪/傾斜儀 clinometer, tiltmeter
倾斜转弯技术/傾斜轉彎技術 bank to turn technique
倾斜自差/傾側自差 heeling error, heeling deviation
倾卸式货车/傾卸載土車 tipping wagon
清舱/清艙 clearing modules
清舱设备/清艙設施 tank cleaning facilities
清铲/鏨平 chipping
清[冲]洗槽/冼砂池 wash water tank
清除水雷船/掃雷船 vessel engaged in mineclearance operation
清除水雷作业/掃雷作業 mineclearance operation
清除坍方/清除坍方 removing landslide
清创室/清創室 debridement room
清缝器/清縫器 joint cleaner
清根/背縫鏨淨,背縫鏨平 back chipping
清工部工程做法/清工部工程做法 Qing Engineering Manual for the Board of Works by the Ministry of Public Works, Qing Gongbu Gongcheng Zuofa
清洁船体螺旋桨特性曲线/潔淨船體螺槳特性曲線 clean hull propeller curve
清洁货/潔淨貨 clean cargo
清洁区/清潔區[域] clean area, airtight space
清洁生产/清潔生產 cleaner production
清洁提单/清潔提單,無批註載貨證券 clean bill of lading
清洁压载泵/清潔壓艙水泵 clean ballast pump
清洁压载舱/清潔壓艙水艙 clean ballast tank, CBT
清洁压载舱操作手册/清潔壓艙水艙操作手冊 clean ballast tank operation manual
清洁压载水/清潔壓艙水 clean ballast
清解锚链/清解錨鏈 clearing hawse
清净分散剂/清潔分散劑 detergent additive, dispersant additive
清理边沟/清溝 ditch cleaning out
清漆/清漆,亮光漆 varnish
清扫口/清掃,清除口 cleanout
清筛道床/清篩道碴 ballast cleaning
清式家具/清家具 Qing dynasty furniture
清式营造则例/清式營造則例 Qing Structural Regulations, Qingshi Yingzao Zeli
清水冲刷/清水冲刷 scour without sediment motion

清水混凝土/清水面混凝土 fair-faced concrete
清算收入/清算收入 clearing revenue
清尾[车]时间/消除時間 clearance time
清晰度/清晰度,可解度 definition, intelligibility, articulation
清晰区/透明區域 clear zone
清洗/清潔 cleaning
清洗法/清洗方法 cleaning method
清洗和熏蒸费/清洗和熏蒸費 cleaning and steaming charge
清洗试验/清洗試驗 washing test
清洗装置/清洗裝置 washing equipment
清泄配气台/清洩供氣臺 cleaning-drain gas distribution board
清泄软管/清洩軟管 cleaning-drain flexible hose
清岩机/道碴装載機,石碴裝載機 ballast loader
清淤/疏浚,浚渫,濬深 dredging
清真寺/清真寺 mosque
情景规划/情境規劃 scenario planning
情侣泉广场/情侶泉廣場 Fuente de los Amantes
晴空颠簸/晴空亂流 clear air turbulence, CAT
晴空指数/晴空指數 clearness index
晴天方向系数/晴天方向係數 orientation coefficient of clear day
晴天工作日/晴天工作日 weather working day, WWD
晴通雨阻公路/好天氣高速通道 fine weather highway
晴雨通车公路/全天候高速通道 all-weather highway
请求权/請求權,求償權 right of claim
请求数据传送/請求資料轉換 request data transfer
穹顶/拱頂,穹隆,圓頂 dome, vault
穹棱/穹稜,拱肋,交叉拱 groin
丘陵地段选线/丘陵地選線 hilly land location, location of line on hilly land
秋分/秋分 autumnal equinox
秋分大潮/秋分大潮 autumnal equinoctial spring tide
秋千/秋千 swing
秋色/秋色 fall color, autumn color
秋色叶植物/秋色葉植物 autumn leaf plant
秋色植物/秋色植物 colored autumn foliage
秋梢/秋梢 autumn shoots, autumn growth
球鼻[型]艏/球[形]艏 bulbous bow
球场/球場 ball court
球场灯/球場燈 stadium light
球阀/球閥 globe valve

球根花卉/球根花卉　flowering bulb
球根花境/球根花境　bulb flower border
球根园/球根園,鱗莖園　bulb garden
球根植物/球根植物　bulbous plant
球根种植器/球根種植器　bulb planter
球茎/球莖　corm
球壳/球殼　spherical shell
球面/球面　sphere surface
球面滚柱轴承/球面滾子軸承　spherical roller bearing
球[面像]差/球面像差,球面收差　spherical aberration
球面支座/球形軸承,球面軸承　spherical bearing
球面直角坐标/球面直角坐標　spherical rectangular coordinate
球膜式建筑/球膜式建築　geodetic construction
球磨碎机/球磨碎石機　ball mill crusher
球墨铸铁管/球墨鑄鐵管　ductile iron pipe
球体[号型]/球形號標　ball shape
球头/鉚釘頭　button head
球窝[关]节/球窩關節　ball and socket joint
球窝喷管/球窩噴管　ball-socked nozzle
球窝轴承/球窩軸承　ball and socket bearing
球芯折角塞门/球式角旋塞　ball type angle cock
球形分杈管/球形分枝管　spherical branch
球形浮标/球形浮標　spherical buoy
球形滚子轴承/球面滾子軸承　spherical roller bearing
球[形]接头/球接頭　ball joint
球形壳体/球殼　spherical shell
球形[扩脚]桩/球根樁　bulb pile, pile bulb
球形气瓶/球形氣瓶　spherical gas bottle
球形燃烧室/球形燃燒室　spherical combustion chamber
球形柔性桨毂/球形柔性螺旋槳轂　spheriflex hub
球形投影/球狀投影法　globular projection
球形艉/球形艉　bulbous stern, bulb stern
球形心盘/球形心盤　spherical center plate
球形应力/球形應力　stress bulb
球形支座/球面軸承,球支承　spherical bearing, ball support
球形轴箱定位装置/球形軸箱定位裝置　ball type journal box positioning device
区段/段,區域　district
区段列车/區段列車　district train
区段锁闭/區段鎖定裝置　section locking
区段通信/區段通信　division communication
区段小运转列车/區段小運轉列車　district transfer train
区段遥控/區段遙控　remote control for a section
区段占用表示/區段占用表示　section occupancy indication
区段站/區段站　district station
区段征收/區段徵收　zone condemnation
区号/區號　zone letter
区划/分區制,分區布局　zoning
区划法规/分區使用管制規則　zoning ordinance
区划规则/分區規則　zoning regulation
区划条例/分區規則　zoning regulation
区划图/土地分區圖　zoning map
区间/區間,區域　section
区间闭塞/區間閉塞　section blocked
区间电话/旁軌電話　track-side telephone
区间电话转接机/旁軌電話交換裝置　track-side telephone switching device
区间封锁/區間封鎖　section closed up
区间货/區間貨　local cargo
区间空闲/區間空閒　section cleared
区间联系电路/區間聯繫電路　liaison circuit with block signaling
区间速度/總旅行速率　overall travel speed
区间隧道/區間隧道　running tunnel
区间通过能力/區間通過能力　carrying capacity of the block section
区间信号/區間信號　wayside signaling
区间占用/區間占用　section occupied
区界交通调查/區界交通調查　cordon traffic survey, cordon count
区内调查/區內調查　internal study
区内交通/區內交通,當地交通　intra-zone traffic, local traffic
区内客流/區域內客運量　intra-regional passenger traffic
区配电板/區配電板,分段配電板　section board
区时/區[域]時　zone time, ZT
区位分布模型/區位分布模式　location distribution model
区位[理]论/區位理論　location theory
区域/區[域],範圍　region, area
区域报警系统/本地報警系統　local alarm system
区域差异/區域差異　area differentiation, regional difference
区域城市/區域都市　regional city
区域尺度/區域尺度　regional scale
区域导航/區域導航,區域航行　area navigation
区域地质/區域地質學　regional geology

区域发展/區域發展　regional development
区域非均衡发展/區域不均衡發展　uneven regional development
区域覆盖/區域覆蓋　local-mode coverage
区域公用设施用地/區域公用設施用地　land for regional public infrastructure
区域公园/區域公園　regional park
区域供暖/區域供熱　district heating, urban district heating, regional heating
区域供热/區域供熱　district heating, urban district heating, regional heating
区域供热锅炉房/區域供熱鍋爐房　regional heating plant
区域供水系统/區域供水系統,區域給水系統　regional water supply system
区域管治/區域治理　regional governance
区域规划/區域規劃,區域計劃　regional planning, regional plan
区域规划委员会/區域計劃委員會　regional planning commission
区域锅炉房供热系统/區域供暖設備供熱系統　heat supply system based upon heating plant
区域化进程/區域化進程　region-based urbanization
区域环境/區域環境　regional environment
区域给水系统/區域給水系統,區域供水系統　regional water supply system
区域间公路/區域間公路　inter regional highway
区域检查/區域檢查　zonal-installation inspection
区域交通设施用地/區域運輸基本建設,區域運輸基本設施　land for regional transportation infrastructure
区域竞争力/區域競争力　regional competitiveness
区域开发/區域發展　regional development
区域空间管制/區域空間管制　regional spatial control
区域联盟/區域結盟　regional alliance
区域马太效应/區域發展馬太效應,區域發展錦上添花效應　Matthew effect of regional development
区域码/地區碼　area code
区域排水系统/區域污水溝管系統　regional sewerage system
区域热力站/區域熱力站　branch line thermal substation
区域生态学/區域生態學　regional ecology
区域试验/區域試驗　localized experiment
区域外向度/區域外向度　regional export-oriented degree
区域位置图/位置平面圖　location plan
区域协调/區域協作　regional coordination
区域协调人/區域協調人　area coordinator
区域协作/區域協同,區域互助　regional cooperation
区域性编组站/區域[性]編組站　regional marshalling station
区域性洪水/區域性洪水　regional flood
区域性作业模式/區域性作業模式　local mode of operation
区域一体化/區域整合　regional integration
区域预报/區域預報　area forecast
区域运价/區域運價　zoning rate
区域运输/區域間運輸　interregional transportation
区域再加热空气调节系统/區域再熱空調系統　zone reheat air conditioning system
区域整体论/區域整合　regional integration
区域政策/區域政策　regional policy
区域治理/區域治理　regional governance
区域中心/區域中心　regional center
区域主义/區域主義　regionalism
区域总人口/區域總人口　regional total population
区中心/地區中心　district center
曲柄/曲柄　crank
曲柄半径/曲柄半徑,曲柄推程　crank radius, crank throw
曲柄臂/曲柄臂　crank web, crank arm
曲柄臂间距/曲臂間距　crank spread
曲柄连杆比/曲柄半徑與連桿長比　crank radius-connecting rod length ratio
曲柄销/曲柄[軸]銷　crank pin
曲尺/木工用拐尺　carpenter square
曲格形梁桥/曲格形梁橋　curved grillage girder bridge
曲棍球场/曲棍球場　hockey ground
曲棍球运动/曲棍球運動　hockey movement
曲径式密封/曲折填函蓋　labyrinth gland
曲廊/曲廊,之字形廊　zigzag veranda
曲梁/曲梁　curved-beam
曲梁式转向架/曲梁式轉向架　curved-beam truck
曲流/全蜿蜒　full meander
曲流地带/曲流帶,蜿蜒帶　meander belt
曲率/曲率,曲度　curvature, degree of curvature
曲率半径/曲率半徑　radius of curvature
曲率摩擦系数/曲率摩擦係數　coefficient of friction curvature
曲面版/曲版　curved plate
曲面分段/彎曲段　curved section
曲面模型/曲面模型　surface model
曲桥/曲橋　zigzag bridge

P-S-N 曲线/P-S-N 曲線　P-S-N curves
S-N 曲线/S-N 曲線　S-N curves
曲线板/曲線板,雲形板　irregular French curve
曲线标/曲線標　curve post
曲线长/曲線長度　curve length
曲线超高/曲線超高　curve superelevation, cant, elevation of curve
曲线出岔道岔/曲線軌道道岔　turnout from curved track
p-y 曲线法/p-y 曲線[法]　p-y curve method
曲线计/曲線丈量器　curvimeter
曲线尖轨/曲線尖軌　curved switch
曲线控制点/曲線控制點　curve control point
曲线内轨/曲線內軌　inside rail of curve
曲线内接/曲線內接　inscribed to curve
曲线拟合/曲線擬合,曲線貼合　curve fitting
曲线拟合法/曲線擬合法　curve fitting method
曲线桥/曲[線]橋　curved bridge
曲线设定法/曲線測設　curve setting
曲线隧道/彎曲隧道　curved tunnel
曲线通过/曲線運行　curve negotiating
曲线通过试验/曲線通過試驗　curve negotiation test
曲线箱梁桥/曲箱梁橋　curved box girder bridge
曲线运动/曲線運動　curvilinear motion
曲线折减/曲線坡度折減率,曲線補正　compensation of curve, curve compensation
曲线辙叉/曲線轍叉　curved frog
曲线整正/曲線調整　curve adjusting
曲线正矢/曲線正矢　curve versine
曲线中点/曲線中點　midpoint of curve, MC
曲线阻力/曲線阻力,彎道阻力　curve resistance
曲折长度/蜿蜒長　meander length
曲折机动/曲折操縱　zigzag maneuvre
曲折盘旋弯道/連續彎路　winding road
曲轴/曲[柄]軸　crankshaft
曲轴红套滑移/曲柄軸短縮滑移　crankshaft shrinkage slip-off
曲轴减振器/曲軸減震器　crankshaft vibration damper
曲轴疲劳断裂/曲柄軸疲勞破壞　crankshaft fatigue fracture
曲轴平衡块/曲柄平衡塊　crankshaft counter balance
曲轴平衡重/曲柄軸衡重　crankshaft counterweight
曲轴箱/曲[柄]軸箱　crankcase
曲轴箱爆炸/曲柄軸箱爆炸　crankcase explosion
曲轴箱防爆门/曲[柄]軸箱防爆門　crankcase explosion relief door, crankcase explosion proof door, explosion-proof door of crankcase
曲轴箱呼吸器/曲軸箱通氣管　crankcase breather
曲轴箱排放物/曲軸箱排放物　crankcase emissions
曲轴箱扫气/曲柄軸箱掃氣　crankcase scavenging
曲轴箱透气管路/曲[柄]軸箱通氣管　crankcase vent pipe
曲轴正时齿轮/曲軸定時齒輪　crankshaft timing gear
曲轴转角/曲柄角　crank angle
驱动程序/驅動程式　drive program
驱动器/致動器　actuator
驱动式调节阀/平衡式調節閥　actuated type control valve
驱动型控制系统/驅動控制系統　drive control system
驱动元件滑转率测定/驅動元件滑轉率測定　driving element slipping rate measurement
驱气/清除[有害]氣體,消除油氣　gas-freeing
驱气系统/貨油艙清除油氣裝置　cargo oil tank gas-freeing installation, gas freeing
驱逐舰/驅逐艦　destroyer
屈服/屈服,降伏　yield, yielding
屈服点/屈服點,降伏點　yield point
屈服函数/屈服函數　yield function
屈服荷载/屈服載重　yield load
屈服极限/屈服極限,降伏極限　yield limit
屈服铰/屈服鉸　yield hinge
屈服破坏荷载/挫屈破壞負荷　failure load by buckling
屈服强度/屈服強度,降伏極限,屈服應力　yield limit, yield strength
屈服曲线/降伏曲線　yield curve
屈服条件/屈服狀況　yield condition
屈服弯矩/屈服[力]矩　yield moment
屈服应力/屈服應力,屈服強度,降伏極限　yield limit, yield stress
屈服支撑/屈服支承　yield support
屈服准则/屈服準則　yield criterion
屈曲/屈曲,壓曲　buckling
屈肢症/關節氣脹痛,沈箱症,屈痛　bends
趋肤深度/趨膚深度　skin depth
趋势分析/趨向分析　trend analysis
趋势型着陆预报/趨勢降落預報　tend type landing forecast
趋同适应/趨同適應　convergent adaptation
趋异适应/系枝適應　divergent adaptation
渠槽糙度/渠槽糙度　roughness of channel
渠槽渐变段/渠槽轉變段　channel transition
渠道/溝渠,線槽,管道　channel, canal

渠化/槽化 channelization
渠化标线/渠化標線 channelizing marking
渠化交叉口/槽化交叉口 channelized intersection
渠化交通/渠化交通 channelized traffic, channelization traffic
曲艺场/曲藝場,書場 story-telling house
取蜜车间/蜂採館 honey house
取石心钻/取石心鑽 rock core boring
取水构筑物/水集取工程 water intake works
取水塔/進水塔 intake tower
取送调车/取送調車 taking-out and placing-in of cars
取土场/借土場 borrowing area
取土坑/借土坑 borrow pit
取土区/借土場 borrowing area
取消闭塞/取消閉塞 to cancel a block
取消进路/取消進路 to cancel a route
取雪样器/採雪器 snow sampler
取样/取樣,採樣 sampling
取样管/取樣筒 sampling tube
取样器/取樣器,取樣管 sampling probe
取样勺/取樣杓 sampling spoon
去垢油/清潔油 detergent oil
去极化/去極化[作用] depolarization
去禁溜线信号/去禁溜線信號 shunting signal to prohibitive humping line
去流段/舭出水段 run
去流段长/舭出水段長 length of run
去氯剂/去氯劑 antichlors
去污系统/除汙系統 decontamination system
去线性调频[脉冲]/去線性調頻 de-chirping
去应力退火/應力消除退火,應力消除熱處理 stress relief heat treatment, stress relieving, stress relief annealing
去滞曲线/去磁作用曲線,退磁作用曲線,祛磁效應曲線 demagnetisation curve
圈层式发展/圈層式發展 ring-layer development
圈梁/圈梁,環梁 ring beam
全变差下降格式/全變差下降格式,TVD 格式 total variation decreasing scheme, TVD scheme
全补偿链形悬挂/全補償鏈形懸掛設備 auto-tensioned catenary equipment
[全部]解体修复/[全部]解體修復 disassembly of heritage
全部控制进入/完全出入管制 full control of access
全部缆绳松掉/各纜鬆開 cast of all lines
全部容量/總數 all told
全部照射/全部照明 full illumination

全彩控制器/全彩控制器 full color controller
全彩色发光二极管显示屏/全色發光二極體顯示器 full-color light emitting diode panel
全车动式感应控制器/完全交通控制 full traffic-actuated controller
全车动式信号/全自動交通行動標誌 full traffic-actuated signal
全车振动试验台/重車振動試驗臺 full car vibration test rig
全程[飞行]试验/全程試驗 full range test
全程式调速器/可變調速器 variable speed governor
全尺寸风洞/全尺寸風洞 full scale wind tunnel
全充电态/全充電態 fully-charge condition
全船报警装置/通用警報 general alarm
全电波暗室/反射室 anechoic enclosure
全电飞机/電力飛機 electric aircraft
全叠片机座/全疊片機座 full-laminated frame
全动垂尾/全動尾翅 all moving fin
全动平尾/全動式水平安定面 all moving tailplane
全动视力/全動視力 vision with both driver and object moving
全断面道床夯实机/全斷面道床夯實機 full section ballast consolidating machine
全断面掘进法/全斷面開挖法 full face excavation method
全断面开挖法/全斷面掘進機 full face tunneling method, full-face tunnelling method
全反射/全[内]反射 total internal reflection
全分配制会议电话/全分散式會議電話 conference telephone of full-distribution system
全风化岩石/完全風化岩 completely weathered rock
全封闭救生艇/全圍蔽救生艇 totally enclosed lifeboat
全封闭式电动机/全封閉式電[動]機 totally enclosed motor
全封闭式制冷压缩机/全封閉冷凍壓縮機 hermetically sealed refrigerating compressor unit
全浮动式活塞销/全浮動式活塞銷 full floating gudgeon pin
全浮动式轴承套筒/全浮動式套筒 fully-floating sleeve
全负荷/全負荷 full load
全负荷工况/全負荷工況 full load mode
全感应式信号控制/全感應式信號控制 fully-actuated signal control
全功率辐射计/全功率輻射儀 total power radiometer
全固形物/全固態量 total solid matter

全挂车/全拖车　full trailer
全挂汽车列车/全拖车组　full trailer train
全焊钢桥/全焊鋼橋　all welded steel bridge
全红信号/全紅信號　all red signal
全厚翻修/全厚翻修　full depth resurfacing
全厚式沥青路面/全厚瀝青鋪面　full depth asphalt pavement
全呼/一般呼叫　general calling
全回转式架梁起重机/全迴轉式架梁起重機　full circle girder erecting crane
全回转推进器/全向螺槳　all-direction propeller
全集装箱船/全貨櫃船　full container ship
全价票/全價票　full price ticket
全降区标志/全降區標誌　full landing area mark
全金属客车/全金屬客車　all metal passenger car, all metal coach
全景/全景,[概]视图　panorama, general view
全景电影院/全景電影院,環幕影院　panoramic cinema
全景畸变/全景畸變差　panoramic distortion
全景式相机/全景照相機　panoramic camera
全聚焦合成孔径雷达/全聚焦合成孔徑雷達　fully focused SAR
全开位置/全開位置　full open position of coupler
全空气系统/全空氣系統　all-air system
全宽仰堰/全寬仰堰　suppressed rectangular weir
全连续性/全連續性　full continuity
全面计划/全面計劃　overall planning
全面开挖/全面開挖　full face cutting
全面起道捣固/路線起道　out-of-face surfacing
全面质量管理/全面品質管理,全面品質控制　total quality control, TQC, total quality management
全能法测图/全能法測圖　universal photo
全气压盾构/全氣壓盾構　all-round pressurized shield
全潜船/全潛船　underwater ship
全强度/全強度　full strength
全球变暖/全球暖化　global warming
全球城市/全球城市,全球都市　global city
全球城市区域/全球城市區域　global city region
全球城市体系/全球都市體系　global urban system
全球城市网络/全球城市網路　global urban network
全球导航卫星系统/全球導航衛星系統　global navigation satellite system, GNSS
全球定位系统/全球[衛星]定位系統　global positioning system, GPS
全球定位系统-惯性组合导航/全球定位系統慣性整合導航　GPS-inertial integrated navigation
全球定位系统-惯性组合制导/全球定位系統慣性整合導引　GPS-inertial integrated guidance
全球覆盖/全球覆蓋　global-mode coverage
全球覆盖方式/全球覆蓋模式　global coverage mode
全球轨道卫星导航系统/全球軌道衛星導航系統　global orbiting navigation satellite system, GLONASS
全球海上遇险安全系统区域/全球海上遇險及安全系統區域　GMDSS area
全球海上遇险[和]安全系统/全球海上遇險及安全系統　global maritime distress and safety system, GMDSS
全球航行警告业务/全球航行警告業務　world wide navigational warning service, WWNWS
全球化/全球化　globalization
全球生产网络/全球生產網路　global production network
全球生态学/全球生態學　global ecology
全球通信系统/全球通信系統　global communication system
全区合练/全區預演　rehearsal of all region
全曲流/全蜿蜒　full meander
全权限飞行控制/全權飛行控制　full authority flight control
全燃联合动力装置/组合燃氣渦輪機　combined gas turbine and gas turbine power plant, COGOG
全热换热器/全熱換熱器　air-to-air total heat exchanger, enthalpy exchanger
全任务航天训练仿真器/全任務空間飛行訓練模擬機　full-mission space flight simulator
全日潮/週日[單]潮,一日潮　diurnal tide, single day tide
全日热水供应系统/全日熱水供應系統　all day hot water supply system
全日制托儿所/全託託兒所　full-time nursery
全色胶片/全色[軟]片　panchromatic film, pan film
全视图/全景,[概]视图　panorama, general view
全寿命试车/全壽命試車　full life test
全顺砌式/順磚式砌合　stretcher bond
全松/鬆脫　by the run
全速后退/全速後退　back full
全速势方程/全速勢方程式　full potential equation
全损/全損　total loss
全套管成孔机/全套管搪孔機　full casing tube boring machine
全套管钻机/全套管鑽機　all casing drill
全体/全體,全部,總計　total
全天候飞行/全天候飛行　all weather flight

全推力器姿态控制系统/全推力姿態控制系統　all thruster attitude control system
全挖式断面/全挖式斷面　full cut section
全位势方程/全位方程式,全勢方程式　full potential equation, generalized potential equation
全位置焊/軌道電弧焊　orbital arc welding
全息摄影术/全像攝影　holography
全息照相/全息照相　holograph
全系列/全序列　full series
全向导航/全向導航　omnirange navigation
全向导缆器/全向導索器　omnidirectional fairleader
全向天线/全向輻射天線,非定向天線　omnidirectional antenna
全向推进器/全向推進器　all direction propeller, Z propeller
全向无线电测距/萬向無線電測距　omnidirectional radio range
全向无线电信标/萬向無線電示標　omnidirection radio beacon
全相参动目标指示/全相動目標顯示　all coherent moving target indicator
全压服/全壓衣　full pressure suit
全淹没灭火系统/全淹沒滅火系統　total flooding extinguishing system
全验/全驗　overall acceptance
全预应力/全預應力,全施預力　full prestressing, full prestress
全预应力混凝土/全施預力混凝土　fully prestressed concrete
全员劳动生产率/全員勞動生產率　all-personnel labor productivity
全圆周方位角/全圓方向角　whole circle bearing
全载波发射/全載波發射　full carrier emission
全帧/全架　major frame
全姿态捕获/全姿態獲取　global attitude acquisition
全自动汽车检测系统/自動車輛檢測系統　computerized vehicle inspection system
全组合曲轴/全組合曲軸　full built-up crankshaft
泉/泉　spring
泉瀑/泉瀑　spring and water fall
泉水/泉水　spring water
缺火/不著火,無效發射　misfiring
缺口/間隙　gap
缺口敏感系数/缺口敏感係數　sensitivity factor of notch
缺口敏感性/缺口敏感度　notch sensitivity
缺省值/內定值,既定值　default value
缺素症/植物要素缺乏症狀　nutrient-deficiency symptom
缺陷/缺陷,缺點　defect
缺陷工程/缺陷工程　defect project, drawback project
缺陷责任期/缺陷責任期,維修責任期　defects liability period
缺陷责任终止证书/缺陷責任終止證書　defect liability release certificate
缺陷桩/缺陷樁　defective pile
缺氧/缺氧,減氧　oxygen deficiency, oxygen debt
缺氧警告/缺氧警報　hypoxia alarm
缺氧耐力/缺氧耐力　hypoxia tolerance
缺员/缺額　short handed
缺圆拱木/缺圓拱木　segmental arch timber
雀降/雀降　flared landing
雀替/雀替　sparrow brace, queti
确定的事故/可信事故　credible accident
确定设计法/確定性設計方法　deterministic design method
确定性过程/確定程式　deterministic process
确定性模型/確定性模型　determinacy model
确定性系统/決定系統　deterministic system
确定性效应/確定性效應　deterministic effect
确定性振动/確定振動　deterministic vibration
确定证据/確定證據　conclusive evidence
确认/確認,回應　validation, acknowledge, ACK
确认遇险报警收妥/確認收妥遇險警報　acknowledgement of distress alert
确信位置/經確定之位置　resolved position
阙/闕　gate tower, que
裙板/裙板,護裙,副舺材　skirt plate, apron
裙房/墩座牆　podium
裙式给料器/護裙式加料器　apron feeder
裙筒/裙筒　apron shell
群波/群波,波群　group of waves, group wave
群岛水域/群島海域　archipelago sea area
群岛通过权/群島間通過權　right of passage between archipelagoes
群放大器/群放大器,組合放大器　group amplifier
群呼广播业务/群呼廣播業務　group call broadcast service
群解调器/群解調器,群調解器　group demodulator
群决策支持系统/團體決策支持系統,群體決策支援系統　group decision support system
群控电梯/群控電梯　group elevator
群落/群落,群集,群聚　community, coenosium
群落地段/植物群叢,林分　stand
群落地理学/群落地理學　syngeography

群落动态/群落動態　community dynamics
群落动态学/群落動態學,動態群落學　syndynamics
群落发生演替/動態演替,動態消長　syngenetic succession, succession of syngenesis
群落生境/群落小區,生存小區　biotope
群落生态学/群集生態學　community ecology
群落镶嵌/嵌鑲型群集　community mosaic
群速[度]/[波]群速度,群速　group velocity
群体大小/族群大小　population size
群调制器/群調製器　group modulator
群同步/群組同步　group synchronization
群植/群植,集植,組植　group planting, mass planting
群众集会区/群眾集會區　mass meeting square
群众绿化/群眾绿化　mass planting movement
群转接站/轉接站　group through-connection station
群桩/群樁,樁群　pile group, group of piles
群桩折减系数/群樁折減因數　reduction factor of pile group
群桩作用/群樁作用　group pile action

R

燃点/燃[烧]点,[点]火点,引燃點 inflammable point, fire point, burning point
燃点试验/燃點試驗 burning point test
燃耗/燒盡,燒光,燒完 burn-up
燃喉面积比/燃喉面積比 burning surface to throat area ratio
燃具试验/燃氣設備試驗 gas appliance test
燃料/燃料 fuel
燃料包壳/燃料包蓋 fuel cladding
燃料舱/燃料艙 bunker
燃料测试仪/燃油試驗器 fuel tester
燃料低位发热量/燃料淨熱值 fuel net calorific value
燃料电池/燃料電池 fuel cell
燃料附加损耗/燃料消耗量增大 fuel penalty
燃料高位发热量/燃料總發熱值 fuel gross calorific value
燃料晃动干扰力矩/燃料晃動干擾力矩 disturbance torque by the fuel slosh
燃料烧毁/燒毀,燒壞 burn-out
燃料烧尽/燒毀,燒壞 burn-out
燃料脱硫法/燃料脫硫 fuel desulfurization
燃料系数/耗油係數 fuel coefficient
燃料消耗量/燃料消耗量,燃油消耗量 fuel consumption
燃料消耗试验/燃料消耗試驗 fuel consumption test
燃料油/燃料油,重油 bunker oil, fuel oil
燃料油输送泵/燃油輸送泵 fuel oil transfer pump
燃料元件/燃料元素 fuel element
燃煤独立温水采暖装置/燃煤溫水採暖裝置 coal burning heater type hot water heating equipment
燃煤锅炉/燃煤鍋爐 coal burning boiler, coal firing boiler
燃煤机车/燃煤機車 coal fired locomotive
燃煤温水锅炉/燃煤溫水鍋爐 coal burning heater
燃气爆炸/瓦斯爆炸,氣爆 gas explosion
燃气表/煤氣表,氣體表 gas meter, flow meter
燃气侧全压损失/燃氣側全壓損失 total pressure loss for gas side
燃气储存/儲氣 gas storage
燃气舵/氣體導片 gas rudder
燃气额定压力/額定氣體壓力 gas rated pressure
燃气发生器/氣體發生器,氣體產生器,燃氣發生爐 gas generator
燃气发生器混合比/氣體產生器混合比 gas generator mixture ratio
燃气发生器循环/氣體發生器循環 gas generator cycle
燃气阀/氣閥 gas valve
燃气辐射管/燃[燒煤]氣輻射管 gas fired radiant tubes
燃气工业炉/工業煤氣爐 industrial gas furnace
燃气管道/氣體管道 gas pipeline, gas line
燃气管网系统/配氣系統 gas distribution system, gas network
燃气锅炉/煤氣鍋爐 gas boiler
燃气互换性/燃氣互換性 interchangeability of gases
燃气计量/煤氣測量 gas metering
燃气加热器/燃氣加熱爐 gas-fired heater
燃气降温器/爐氣冷卻器 gas cooler
燃气轮机/燃氣渦輪機,氣輪機,氣渦輪 gas turbine
燃气轮机车/燃氣輪機車 gasturbine locomotive
燃气轮机船/燃氣渦輪機船 gas turbine ship
燃气轮机动力装置/燃氣渦輪機動力設備 gas turbine power plant
燃气排送机/排氣機 exhauster
燃气气化率/氣化率 gasification rate
燃气气源/氣體源 gas source
燃气热水器/燃氣加熱器 gas heater
燃气输送干线/煤氣傳送線 gas transmission line, gas main
燃气调压器/[煤]氣壓調節器 gas pressure regulator, governor
燃气调压箱/燃氣調節器 gas regulator box
燃气停留时间/燃氣持久時間 gas stay time
燃气涡轮/燃氣渦輪機,氣輪機,氣渦輪 gas turbine
燃气涡轮发动机/氣渦輪發動機 gas turbine engine
燃气需用量/煤氣需用量 gas demand, gas load
燃气压力/氣體壓力 gas pressure
燃气压力调节/氣體壓力調節 gas pressure regulation
燃气压缩机/氣體壓縮機 gas compressor

燃[气用]具/煤氣用具　gas appliance
燃气灶/煤氣爐　hotplate, gas cooker
燃气-蒸汽联合循环发电厂/燃氣-蒸汽聯合循環發電廠　combined gas and steam turbine cycle power plant
燃烧不稳定性/燃燒不穩定　combustion instability
燃烧产物/燃燒生成物　combustion product
燃烧过程/燃燒過程　combustion process
[燃烧]过量空气系数/過量空氣因數　excess air factor, excess air ratio
燃烧剂/燃燒劑　fuel
燃烧剂光电传感器/燃料光電感測器　fuel photoelectric sensor
燃烧剂过滤器/燃料過濾器　fuel filter
燃烧剂加注口支架/燃燒劑加注口支架　fuel filling port support mount
燃烧剂加注连接器/燃料加載連接器　fuel loading connector
燃烧剂加注软管/燃料加載軟管　fuel loading flexible hose
燃烧剂加注系统/燃料加注系統　fuel loading system
燃烧剂料流量/燃油流率　fuel flow rate
燃烧剂溢出连接器/燃料溢流連接器　fuel overflow connector
燃烧剂溢出软管/燃料溢流軟管　fuel overflow flexible hose
燃烧剂运输车/燃料搬運車　fuel transporter
燃烧率/燃燒率　combustion rate, rate of combustion, rate of firing
燃烧面积/燃燒面積　burning surface area
燃烧模化准则/燃燒模化準則　combustion scaling rule, combustion simulation criteria
燃烧器/燃燒器　combustor, burner
燃烧器喷口/燃燒器嘴　burner tip, burner port
燃烧器调节比/燃燒器調節比　turndown ratio
燃烧区/燃燒區　combustion zone
燃烧势/燃燒勢　combustion potential
燃烧室/燃燒室　fire combustion chamber, combustion chamber
M燃烧室/M燃燒室　M combustion chamber
燃烧室特征长度/[燃燒室的]特性長度　characteristic chamber length
燃烧室外壳/燃燒室外殼　combustor outer casing
燃烧室压力不稳定度/燃燒室壓力不穩定度　combustion chamber pressure roughness
燃烧室压强/燃燒室壓力　combustion chamber pressure
燃烧速度/燃燒速度　combustion velocity

燃烧体/可燃材料　combustible
燃烧稳定性/燃燒安定性　combustion stability
燃料消耗率/單位燃料消耗量,單位耗油量,燃油消耗比　specific fuel consumption
燃烧效率/燃燒效率　combustion efficiency
燃烧噪声/燃燒噪音　combustion noise
燃烧终点压强/燃燒終壓[力]　burning final pressure
燃烧自动控制/自動燃燒控制　automatic combustion control
燃速温度敏感系数/燃燒率溫度敏感性　temperature sensitivity of burning rate
燃速系数/燃燒率係數　burning rate coefficient
燃速压强指数/燃燒率壓力指數　burning rate pressure exponent
燃通面积比/燃通面積比　burning surface to port area ratio
燃压衰减时间/燃燒室壓力衰減時間　chamber pressure decay time
燃油/燃油　fuel oil, oil fuel
燃油泵/燃油泵　fuel pump
燃油驳运系统/燃油轉駁系統　fuel oil transport system
燃油舱/燃油艙,燃油櫃　fuel oil tank
燃油沉淀柜/燃油沈澱櫃　fuel oil settling tank
燃油粗滤器/燃油預濾器　fuel prefilter
燃油独立温水采暖装置/燃油溫水採暖裝置　oil-burning heater type hot water heating equipment
燃油废气组合式锅炉/廢氣燃油複合式鍋爐　composite oil-fired exhaust gas boiler, composite oil-exhaust gas fired boiler
燃油柜/燃油櫃,燃油艙　fuel oil tank
燃油加热器/燃油加熱器　fuel oil heater
燃油精滤器/燃油精密過濾器　fuel precision filter
燃油净化系统/燃油淨化系統　fuel oil purifying system
燃油均化器/燃油均化器　fuel oil homogenizer
燃油流量表/燃油流量表　fuel flow meter
燃油流量计/燃料消耗計　fuel consumption gage
燃油滤器/燃油過濾器　fuel oil filter
燃油黏-温图/燃油黏度溫度圖　fuel oil viscosity-temperature diagram
燃油浓度分布/燃料濃度分布　fuel concentration distribution
燃油[气]热水机组/燃油[氣]熱水機組　burning oil gas hot water heaters
燃油日用柜/燃油日用櫃　fuel oil daily tank
燃油输送泵/燃油輸送泵,燃料供給泵　fuel oil transfer pump, fuel feed pump

燃油温水锅炉/燃油溫水鍋爐　oil-burning heater
燃油雾化喷嘴/燃油噴霧器　fuel atomizer
燃油系统/燃油系統　fuel oil system
燃油箱/燃油箱,燃料箱　fuel tank
燃油消耗量/燃油消耗量,燃料消耗量　fuel consumption
燃油泄放系统/燃油洩放系統,燃油排洩系統　fuel oil drain system
燃油油量表/燃油油量表　fuel quantity meter
燃油预热图/燃油預熱圖　fuel oil preheating chart
燃油注入管/燃油注入管　fuel oil filling pipe
燃油装置/燃油裝備組　oil fuel unit
燃油总管/油路　fuel manifold
燃轴/燃軸　severe hot box
染毒区/染毒區　airtightless space, infected area
染色效应/染色,著色,顯色　coloration
壤土/壤土　loam soil
壤中流/中間流　interflow
让车道/避車道　passing place
让车道标志/讓車道標誌　passing bay sign
让路标志/讓路標誌　yielding sign
让路船/讓路船舶,避讓船　give-way vessel
让路线/讓路線　give-way marking
扰动/擾動　disturbance
扰动力/激振力　exciting force
扰动速度势/擾盪流速勢　perturbation velocity potential
扰动土/擾動土,變形土　disturbed soil
扰动土样/擾動土樣,擾動樣本　disturbed sample, disturbed soil sample
扰动样品/擾動樣本　disturbed sample
扰流板/擾流板,擾流條　spoiler
扰流片/擾流板,擾流條　spoiler
绕航/變更航程　deviation
绕航变更报告/變更航程報告,偏航報告　deviation report
绕射/繞射　diffraction
绕射力/繞射[波]力　diffraction force
绕行标志/迂回標誌　detour sign
绕行道路/繞越道路　bypass
绕行地段/繞行地段　detouring section, round section
绕一道/繞轉　round turn
绕一圈/繞轉　round turn
绕越交通/繞越交通　bypassing traffic
绕住/繞住　catch a turn
惹草/惹草　leaf-patterned board, recao
热拌法/熱拌法　hot mixing method

热拌和料/熱拌料　hot mixture
热备份/熱備份　hot spare
热泵/熱泵　heat pump
热泵供热系数/熱泵性能係數　annual heat pump coefficient of performance
热泵类型/熱泵類型　form of heat pump
热泵热水供应系统/熱泵熱水系統　heat pump hot water system
热泵制热系数/熱泵制熱係數　heat pump coefficient of heating performance
热边界层/熱邊界層　thermal boundary layer
热变质作用/熱變作用　thermal metamorphism
热补偿/熱膨脹補償　compensation of thermal expansion
热测量/熱量測　thermal measurement
热层/熱氣層　thermosphere
热沉/熱沈,除熱裝置,散熱劑　heat sink
热成像导引头/熱像歸航器　IR image homing head, thermal image homing head
热成形/加熱成形　hot forming
热冲击/熱衝擊,熱震　thermal shock
热处理/熱處理　heat treatment
热处理车间/熱處理車間　heat-treating shop
热处理钢轨/硬頭軌條　heat-treated rail
热处理钢筋/熱處理鋼筋,熱處理鋼條　heat tempering bar, heat-treating bar, heat-treated steel bar
热处理软化法/熱處理軟化法　hot process softening
热传导/熱傳導　heat conduction
热传递系数/熱傳[遞]係數　heat transfer coefficient
热窗/熱窗　heat window
热脆/熱脆性　hot shortness
热带淡水载重线/熱帶淡水載重線　tropical fresh water load line
热带低压/熱帶低壓　tropical depression
热带风暴/熱帶風暴　tropical storm
热带辐合带/熱帶輻合地帶　intertropical convergence zone, ITCZ
[热带]高山矮曲林/矮林　elfin forest
热带气旋/熱帶氣旋　tropical cyclone
热带气旋雨/熱帶氣旋雨　tropic cyclonic rainfall
热带区带/熱帶地帶　tropical zone
热带扰动/熱帶擾動　tropical disturbance
热带雨林/熱帶雨林　tropical rain forest
热带载重线/熱帶載重線　tropical load line
热带植物园/熱帶植物園　tropical plants garden
热刀/熱刀　heat knife
热导率/熱傳導性　heat conduction coefficient,

thermal conductivity
热岛效应/熱島[效應] heat island effect, thermal island effect
热等静压/熱[等]壓 hot isostatic pressing, heat isostatic pressing
热等静压扩散焊/熱等靜壓擴散焊接 heat iso-hydrostatic diffusion welding
热电厂/熱電站 cogeneration power plant
热电厂供热系统/熱電廠供熱系統 heat supply system based upon heating power cogeneration plant
热电池/熱電池 thermal battery
热电动势/熱電動勢 thermo electromotive force
热电堆探测器/熱電堆偵檢器 thermopile detector
热电冷联产/冷熱電聯供 cogeneration of heat power and cool, combined cooling heating and power
热电联产/熱電聯產 cogeneration of heat and electricity, heat and power cogeneration
热电流/熱電流 thermocurrent
热电偶/熱電偶 thermocouple
热电式空气调节器/熱電式空調器,半導體空調 thermal electric type air conditioner, semi conductor air conditioner
热动力式疏水器/熱動力式疏水器 thermodynamic type steam trap
热堵塞/熱阻流 thermal choking
热镀锌/鍍鋅 galvanization, galvanizing
热惰性/熱慣性,熱慣量 thermal inertia
热惰性指标/熱慣性指標 index of thermal inertia
热反射层/熱反射層 heat-reflecting layer
热防护系统试验/熱防護系統試驗 thermal protection system test
热分析/熱分析 thermal analysis
热风采暖装置/熱風加熱器 hot air heating equipment
热风供暖/熱風供暖 warm-air heating
热风供暖系统/熱風供暖系統,暖氣加熱系統 warm-air heating system, hot-air heating system
热风幕/熱風幕,熱空氣幕 warm-air curtain
热辐射/熱輻射 thermal radiation
热腐蚀/熱腐蝕 hot corrosion
热负荷/熱負載,供熱量 thermal load, heating load
热负荷图/熱負載圖 heating load diagram
热负荷延续时间图/熱負載持續曲線 heating load duration graph
热负荷指数/韋比指數 Wobbe index, Wobbe number
热干化/熱乾 heat drying

热工摄像术/熱敏複印法 thermography
热工试验室/熱工[程]實驗室 heat engineering laboratory, thermal science laboratory
热功当量/熱功當量 mechanical equivalent of heat
热固性树脂/熱固性樹脂 thermosetting resin
热固性树脂复合材料/熱固性樹脂複合材料 thermosetting resin composite
热固性塑料/熱固性塑膠 thermosetting plastic
热挂/熱堵塞 thermal blockage
热管/熱管 heat pipe
热灌法/熱灌法 hot penetration method
热耗率/耗熱率 heat rate
热核能/熱核能 thermonuclear energy
热红外/熱紅外 thermal infrared
热滑/熱滑 hot-running
热化/熱化 thermalization
热化系数/熱化係數 coefficient of thermalization, thermalization coefficient
热化学烧蚀/熱化學燒蝕 thermochemical ablation
热混合料贮仓/熱拌圓穀倉 hot mix silo
热机/熱機 heat engine
热剂焊/發熱焊接,鋁熱焊接 thermit welding
热继电器/温度繼電器,温度電驛 thermal relay
热交换器/熱交換器 heat exchanger
热交换器加热气体增压系统/熱交換器加熱氣體加壓系統 heated gas-heat exchanger pressurization system
热交换站/熱交換站 heat exchanger room
热校测风洞/熱校準風洞 thermo-calibration wind tunnel
热接缝/熱接縫 hot joint
热节/高熱點 hot spot
热结构材料/熱結構材料 thermal structure material
热解重力分析/熱重分析 thermogravimetric analysis
热紧张/熱緊張 heat strain
热浸/熱浸 thermal soak
热浸镀/熱浸鍍 hot dipping
热井/熱井 hot well, cascade tank
热绝/熱絕,隔熱 thermal insulation
热开关/熱電門 thermal switch
热控带/熱控制膠合劑塗層 thermal control adhesive coating
热控[制]分系统/熱[量]控制分系統 thermal control subsystem
热矿泉/熱礦泉 thermomineral spring
热扩散系数/熱擴散係數,熱擴散率,熱擴散度 thermal diffusivity
热老化试验/熱老化試驗 thermal ageing test

热离子转换器/熱離子換能器　thermionic converter
热力除氧/熱力除氧　thermo-deaeration
热[力]继电器/溫度繼電器,溫度電驛　thermal relay
热力膨胀阀/熱力膨脹閥　thermostatic expansion valve
热力入口/用户熱力入口　consumer heat inlet
热力失调/熱失調　thermal misadjustment
热力网/熱力網　heat supply network
热力学定律/熱力學定律　law of thermodynamics
热力学能/内能　internal energy
热力学温标/熱力學溫度標,溫度熱力標　thermodynamic temperature scale
热力抑制压头/熱力抑制水頭　thermodynamic suppression head, TSH
热力站/供熱熱力站　heat substation, thermal substation
热料仓/熱料倉　hot aggregate bin
热料提升机/熱集料昇降機　hot aggregate elevator
热料振动筛/熱集料振動篩　hot aggregate vibrating screen
热裂/熱裂[煉],高溫龜裂　hot cracking, hot tearing, thermal cracking
热裂解气/熱裂化氣　thermally cracked gas
热裂纹/熱裂縫　thermal crack
热流/熱流　heat flow
热流计/熱流計　heat flow meter
热流密度/熱流密度,熱通量　heat flux per unit time, heat flux
热脉冲测定法/熱脈衝測定法　heat impulsive method
热媒/加熱介質　heat medium
热面点火/表面點火　surface ignition
热敏电阻/熱阻[半導]體　thermistor
热敏电阻探测器/熱阻偵檢器　thermistor detector
热敏记录仪/熱敏感記錄器　heat-sensitive recorder
热膜风速仪/熱膜風速表　hot film anemometer
热磨合/熱磨合　hot breaking in
热模锻/熱模鍛　hot die forging
热能/熱能　thermal energy, heat energy
热盘管/加熱盤管,加熱旋管　heating coil
热喷流试验/熱噴射試驗　hot jet testing
热喷能/熱噴能　thermal jet energy
热喷涂/熱噴塗　thermal spraying
热膨胀模成形/熱膨脹模成形　thermal expansion molding
热膨胀系数/熱膨脹係數　thermal expansion coefficient

热疲劳/熱疲勞　thermal fatigue, heat fatigue
热疲劳裂纹/熱疲勞裂痕　heat fatigue cracking
热平衡/熱平衡　heat balance, thermo balance
热平衡试验/熱平衡試驗　thermal balance test, heat balance test
热屏蔽/熱遮蔽　thermal shielding
热铺法/熱鋪法　hot laid method
热漆画线机/熱漆劃線機　hot paint road marking machine
热起动寿命试验/熱啟動壽命試驗　hot start life test
热气烘干/熱氣乾燥　hot-air seasoning
热气机动力装置/史特靈引擎動力設備　Stirling engine power plant
热气溶胶灭火装置/熱氣溶膠滅火裝置　condensed aerosol fire extinguishing device
热气融霜/熱氣除霜　hot gas defrost
热气系统/熱氣體系統　hot gas system
热强度/耐熱強度　thermal strength
热桥/熱電橋　thermal bridge
热容量/熱容[量]　thermal capacity, heat capacity
热熔连接/熱溶接頭　fusion-jointing
热蠕变/熱潛變　thermal creep
热射风洞/熱射風洞　hotshot tunnel
热 X 射线/熱 X 射線　thermal X-ray
热伸长/熱膨脹　thermal expansion
热身场地/準備活動區　warming up area
热声环境/熱聲環境　thermoacoustic environment
热失控/熱耗散,熱散逸　thermal run away
热失稳/熱失穩　thermal run away
热湿比/熱濕比　heat humidity ratio
热湿交换/熱濕傳遞　heat and moisture transfer
热式研磨机/熱式研磨機　hot miller
热试验/熱試驗　thermal test
热[试验]模型/熱模型　thermal model, TM
热室/熱室　hot cell
热释电探测器/熱電檢知器　pyroelectric detector
热舒适通风/熱舒適通風　thermal comfort ventilation
热舒适性/熱舒適　thermal comfort
热舒适指标/熱舒適指標　thermal comfort index
热水泵/熱水泵　hot water pump
热水储水箱/熱水儲水槽　hot water storage tank
热水供暖/熱水暖氣法　hot water heating
热水供暖系统/熱水加熱系統　hot water heating system
热水供热系统/蒸汽熱供應系統　steam heat supply system
热水供应热负荷/熱水供應熱負載　hot water

heating load
热水柜/熱水櫃,熱水箱　hot water tank
热水锅炉/熱水鍋爐　hot water boiler
热水井/熱井　hot well
热水器/水加熱器　water heater
热水热网/熱水熱網路　hot water heat supply network
热水循环泵/熱水循環泵　hot water circulating pump
热塑划线机/熱塑劃線機　thermoplastic road marking machine
热塑性铺地板/熱塑膠板　thermoplastic tile
热塑性树脂复合材料/熱塑性樹脂複合材料　thermoplastic resin composite
热塑性塑料/熱塑性塑膠　thermoplastic, thermoplastic plastic
热损[失]/熱損失　heat loss
热[态]起动/熱起動　hot start, hot starting
热停堆/熱關閉　hot shut-down
热图技术/熱測繪技術　thermo-mapping technique
热弯试验/熱彎試驗　hot bent test
热网/熱網,供熱網路　heat supply network
热网布置/熱網布置　layout of heat supply network
热网计算/熱網計算　calculation of heat network
热网水力计算/熱網水力計算　hydraulic calculation of heat supply network
热网水压图/熱網水壓圖　pressure diagram of heat supply network
热稳定食品/熱穩定性食物　thermostabilized food
热稳[定]性/熱穩定性,熱安定性,耐熱性　thermostability, heat stability
热污染/熱汙染　thermal pollution
热线风速仪/熱線[式]風速計　hot wire anemometer
热像图/熱像　thermal image
热效率/熱效率　thermal efficiency
热循环/熱循環　thermal cycle
热循环试验/熱循環試驗　thermal cycling test
热压/熱壓　hot pressing, heat pressure
热压釜成形/熱壓釜成形　autoclave moulding
热压焊/熱壓焊接　thermocompression bonding
热盐水融霜/熱鹽水除霜　hot brine defrost
热液蚀变/熱水變質　hydrothermal alteration
热影响区/熱影響[域]　heat-affected zone
热应力/熱應力,熱緊迫　thermal stress, heat stress
热应力指标/熱應力指數　heat stress index
热用户/熱用戶　heat consumer
热预算法/熱收支法　heat-budget method
热源/熱源　heat source
热源井/熱源井　heat source well
热载荷/熱負載　thermal load
热轧变形钢筋/熱軋竹節鋼筋　hot rolled deformed bar
热轧钢筋/熱軋鋼條　hot rolled bar, hot rolled steel bar
热轧氧化皮/軋鋼鱗片　mill scale
热轧异型钢筋/熱軋竹節鋼筋　hot rolled deformed bar
热障/熱障　thermal barrier
热真空舱/熱真空艙　thermal vacuum chamber
热真空试验/熱真空試驗　thermal vacuum test
热值/熱值,發熱量　calorific value, heat value
热指标/熱指數　heat index
热指数/熱指數　heat index
热轴/熱軸　hot box
热装/收縮配合,紅套　shrinkage fit, shrinkage fitting
热阻/熱[電]阻　thermal resistance, heat resistance
热阻系数/熱阻係數　thermal resistance coefficient
热钻孔/高熱鑽孔　thermic boring
人车分流/人車分流,人車分行　separation of pedestrian and vehicular circulation
人动视力/人動視力　vision with driver moving
人防/人員防護　personnel protection
人防地下室/人防地下室　civil air defense basement
人防口部/人防口部　air defense gateway
人防围护结构/人防圍護結構　surrounding structure for air defense
人防信号室/防情訊號房　signal room for civil air defense
人感系统/人爲感覺系統　artificial feel system
人工材料/人工材料　artificial materials
人工操纵/人工操縱　manned
人工促进更新/人促更新　artificial measures promoting regeneration
人工岛/人工島　artificial island
人工捣实/手夯　hand tamping
人工地平/人工水平儀　artificial horizon
人工电报机/人工電報機　manual telegraph set
人工电话所/人工電話局　manual telephone office
人工电子带/人工電子帶　artificial electron belts
人工防治/人爲防治　artificial control
人工防治病虫害/人工防治病蟲害　artificial prevention and control of plant diseases and insect pests
人工分路/人工分路　manual shunt
人工辐射带/人工輻射帶　artificial radiation belt

人工干燥木材/人工乾燥木材　artificially seasoned wood
人工港/人工港　artificial harbor
人工更新/人工更新　artificial reforestation
人工骨料/人造集料,人造骨材　artificial aggregate
人工航槽/浚深水道　dredged channel
人工湖/人工湖　artificial lake
人工环境/人造環境,人爲環境　man made environment, artificial environment
人工混交林/人工混交林　mixture plantation
人工降低地下水位/人工降低地下水位　artificial dewatering, lowering of underground water
人工降雨/人工降水,人造雨　artificial precipitation
人工降雨装置/人工降雨器,降雨模擬器　rainfall simulator
人工接地体/人工接地極　manual grounding electrode
人工解锁/人工解鎖,手動釋放　manual release
人工解锁表示/人工解鎖表示　manual release indication
人工控制/人工控制,手動控制　manual control
人工林/人工林　forest plantation, man-made forest
人工煤气/人造煤氣　manufactured gas
人工密度法/人工密度法　artificial density method
人工黏性/類黏度　artificial viscosity
人工胚乳/人工胚乳　artificial endosperm
人工气候室/人工氣候室　phytotron
人工桥基/人造壩座　artificial abutment
人工群落/人造群集　artificial community
人工燃气/人造煤氣　manufactured gas
人工溶漢港/人工浚漢港　excavated artificial harbour
人工砂/碎砂　crushed sand
人工山丘/人工山丘　artificial knoll
人工生态系统/人工生態系統　artificial ecosystem
人工湿地/人工濕地,人造濕地　artifical wetland, constructed wetland
人工时效[处理]/人工老化　artificial aging
人工水道/人工水道　artificial watercourse
人工通风/人工通風　artifical ventilation
人工脱粘/人工脱裂　stress release boot, stress relief flap
人工压浆处理/人工水泥膠結　artificial cementing
人工压缩法/人工壓縮因數法　artificial compressibility method
人工用户电报业务/人工電報交換業務　manual telex service
人工鱼礁/人工魚礁　fish shelter

人工越控装置/人工越控裝置　manual override system
人工照明过渡/人工照明過渡　artificial lighting transition
人工植物群落/人工植物群落　man-made planting habitat, man-made phytocommunity
人工制造纹理/漆成紋理　graining
人工智能/人工智慧　artificial intelligence
人工智能语言/人工智慧語言　artificial intelligent language
人工种皮/人工種皮　artificial seed coat
人工种质资源/人工遺傳資源　artificial genetic resources
人工种子/人工種子　artificial seed
人工转换/人工轉變,人工轉變　artificial transition
人工转换/人工轉變,人工轉變　artificial transition
人机功能分配/人機功能分配　man-machine function allocation
人-机-环境系统工程/人-機-環境系統工程　man-machine-environment system engineering
人机交互/人機交互作用　man-machine interaction
人机接口/人機介面　man-machine interface
人机调节系统/人機處理系統　man-machine processing system
人-机通信系统/人-機通信系統　man-machine communication system
人机在环仿真/人機在環模擬　man-in-loop simulation
人居/人類聚落　human settlement
人居环境/人類居住環境,人類居住區　human settlement, human habitat
人居环境科学/人居環境科學　science of human settlements
人均城市建设用地/人均都市建設用地,人均城鎮建設用地　per capita urban construction land, urban development land per capita
人均城市建设用地标准/人均都市建設用地標準　per capita urban construction land scale standard
人均城市建设用地面积/人均都市建設用地面積　urban development land area per capita
人均单项城市建设用地/人均單項都市建設用地　single-category urban development land per capita
人均单项城市建设用地面积/人均單項都市建設用地面積　single-category urban development land area per capita
人均道路面积/人均道路面積　road area per capita
人均公共管理与公共服务用地/人均公共管理與公共服務用地　administration and public services

land per capita
人均公共绿地率/人均公共綠地率　per capita public green space ratio
人均公共绿地面积/人均公共綠地面積　per capita public green area
人均公园绿地/人均公園綠地　park land per capita
人均公园绿地面积/人均公園綠地面積　per capita green and park area
人均交通设施用地/人均交通設施用地　street and transportation land per capita
人均居住用地/人均自用住宅用地　residential land per capita
人均绿地/人均綠地面積　green space per capita
人均消费/每人消費量　consumption per capita
人孔/人孔,進入孔　manhole, access opening, manway
人孔盖/人孔蓋　manhole cover
人口/人口　population
人口百岁图/年齡錐體,年齡[金字]塔　age pyramid
人口参数/人口參數　population parameter
人口当量/人口當量　population equivalent
人口的社会增长/人口社會增加　social increase of population
人口分布/人口分布　population distribution
人口构成/人口組成　population composition
人口及劳动力安置/人口與勞動力安置　population and labor resettlement
人口结构/人口結構　population structure
人口净密度/居住淨密度　net residential density
人口[毛]密度/人口密度,居住密度　population density, residential density
人口年龄构成/年齡組成　age composition
人口迁移增长/人口成長與遷移　population growth from migration
人口容量/人口容量　population capacity
人口社会增长率/人口社會增加率　rate of social increase of population
人口疏解/人口分散　population decentralization, decentralization of population
人口预测/人口預測,人口推計　population projection, population estimating, population forecast
人口增长/人口成長　population growth
人口增长率/人口成長率,人口增加率　population growth rate, rate of population increase
人口增长趋势/人口成長趨勢　growth trend of population
人口自然增长/人口自然增加　natural increase of population
人口自然增长率/人口自然增加率,自然成長率　natural growth rate, rate of natural increase of population
人口总密度/總人口密度　gross population density
人类工程学/人身工程,人體工程　human engineering
人类生态环境/人類生態環境　human ecological environment
人类生态学/人類生態學　human ecology
人力车/人力車　man-drawn vehicle
人力渡车船/手開渡船　manually operated ferry boat
人力防范/人員防護　personnel protection
人力应急操舵试验/人力緊急操舵試驗　manual emergency steering test
人力应急起锚试验/人力緊急起錨試驗　manual emergency anchoring test
人力装卸/人力操縱　manual handling
人流量/人流量　visitors flowrate
人流疏散道路/人流疏散道路　crowd evacuating road
人命救助/生命救助費　life salvage
人群荷载/人群荷載,行人負載　pedestrian load
人身净化/人身淨化　body cleaning
人身伤亡赔款限额/人身傷亡責任限制　limit of liability for personal injury
人体测量学/人體計測[學]　anthropometrics, anthropometry
人体尺度/人體尺度　scale of human body
人体离心机/人體離心機　human centrifuge
人体热感觉/人體熱感覺　human thermal sensation
人为肥力/人爲肥力　anthropogenic fertility
人为干扰/人爲干擾　human disturbance
人为故障/人爲故障　human failure
人为侵蚀/人爲侵蝕　anthropogenic erosion
人为演替/人爲植被　anthropogenic vegetation
人文景观/人文景觀,人爲景觀　cultural landscape, human landscape
人文声景/人爲音景　culture soundscape
人文植物学/人文植物學　humanistic botany
人行道/人行道,步道　pedestrian path, sidewalk
人行道板/人行道板　side walk slab
人行道荷载/步道載重　sidewalk loading
人行道绿化/人行道綠　sidewalk greening
人行道托架/人行棧道　sidewalk bracket
人行道线/人行道線　sidewalk marking
人行地道/人行地下道　pedestrian underpass
人行过街横道/行人穿越道　pedestrian crossing,

crosswalk line
人行横道/人行横道,行人穿越道　cross walk, pedestrian crossing
人行桥/人行[陆]橋,陸橋　foot bridge, pedestrian bridge
人行隧道/行人隧道　pedestrian tunnel
人行天桥/人行天橋,人行陸橋　over crossing, pedestrian bridge, pedestrian overpass
人行通道/通道　passage
人用气闸/人孔閘　man lock
人员定位标/人員定位示標　personnel locator beacon
人员净化用室/人身淨化用室　room for cleaning human body
人员可靠性/人員可靠度　human reliability
人员落水/人員落水　man overboard
人员能力损失/人員能力損失　loss of personnel capability
人员失误/人爲錯誤　human error
人员掩蔽工程/人員掩蔽工程　personnel shelter works
人员掩蔽所/人員掩蔽所　hiding-place for personnel
人员因素/人爲因素　human factor
人造板幕墙/人造板材幕牆　artificial panel curtain wall
人造宝石/人造寶石　artificial stone
人造草坪/人造草坪　artificial turf
人造大理石/人造大理石　artificial marble
人造地球卫星/人造地球衛星　artificial earth satellite
人造花插花/人造插花術　artificial flower arrangement
人造极光/人造極光　artificial aurora
人造集料/人造集料,人造骨材　artificial aggregate
人造假山石/人造假山石　artificial stone, man made stone
人造胶/合成黏著劑　synthetic adhesive
人造轻骨料/人造輕質骨材　artificial lightweight aggregate
人造沙滩/人造沙灘　artificial nourished beach
人造石[材]/人造石　artificial stone, imitation stone
人造饰面板/人造裝飾板　artificial decorative board
人造天体/人造天體　artificial celestial body
人造卫星/人造衛星　artificial satellite
人造文化石/人造文化石　artificial culture stone
人造污泥/配製汙泥　artificial sludge
人造雾/人工霧　artificial fog
人造纤维绳/人造纖維繩索　synthetic rope

人造纤维渔网/人造纖維漁網　synthetic fishing net
人造行星/人造行星　artificial planet
人造雪崩/人造雪崩　artificial snow slide
人造重力/人造重力　artificial gravity
人字撑架体系/人字形系統　herringbone system
人字队/V形隊　V-shaped formation
人字栱/人字栱　inverted V-shaped bracket, renzigong
人字构架/人字頂構架　gable frame
人字门槛/人字閘檻　mitre sill
人字坡/人字坡　double spur grade
人字式坞门/人字式塢門　two-gate caisson, mitre caisson
人字桅/人字桅,雙腳桅　bipod mast
人字屋架/三角形屋桁　gable roof truss
人字形排水沟/導水溝　chevron drain
人字形排水系统/人字形排水系統　herringbone drainage system
刃脚/切緣削邊　cutting edge
认航灯标/認航燈標　indentification beacan
认星/識星　star identification
认证/驗證　certification
认知地图/認知圖　cognitive map
认知空间/認知空間　cognitive space
认知模式/認知模式　cognitive pattern
任务计算机/任務計算機　mission computer
任务可靠性/任務可靠度　mission reliability
任务控制中心/任務管制中心　mission control center, MCC
任务控制中心服务区/任務管制中心服務區　MCC service area
任务剖面/任務剖面　mission profile
任务时间/任務時間　mission time
任务维修性/任務維護度　mission maintainability
任务要求/任務要求　mission requirement
任务专家/任務專家　mission specialist, MS
韧度试验/破斷試驗　rupture test
韧性/韌性,韌度　toughness
韧性城市/彈性都市　resilient city
日本式盆景/日本式盆景　Japanese style penjing, bonsai
日变化系数/日變異係數,日變動因數　daily variation coefficient, daily variation factor
日标/日間助航標誌,晝標　day mark
日常检查/定期檢查,常規檢查　routine inspection
日常清洁卫生管理/日常清潔衛生管理　daily sanitation and hygiene management
日常生活圈/日常生活圈　range of daily life

日常维修/日常保養　current maintenance
日常优先等级/日常優先順序　routine priority
日潮/[全]日潮　diurnal tide
日潮不等/週日差　diurnal inequality
日出/日出　sun rise
日地关系/日地關係　solar-terrestrial relationship
日高峰系数/日高峰係數　peak hour factor
日光温室/太陽能溫室　solar greenhouse
日光信号镜/日光信號鏡　daylight signaling mirror
日光仪/量日儀　heliometer
日晷/日晷　sundial
日晷投影/日晷投影　gnomonic projection
[日]环食/[日]環食　annular eclipse
日间人口/日間人口,晝間人口　day time population
日降雨量/日[降]雨量　daily precipitation, daily rainfall
日交通量变化图/每日交通量型　daily traffic pattern
日界线/日界線　date line, calendar line
日冕/日冕　corona
日冕物质抛射/日冕品質拋射　coronal mass emission
日没/日没　sun set
日内瓦公海公约/日内瓦公海公约　Geneva Convention on the High Seas
日内瓦领海和毗连区公约/日内瓦領海與鄰接區公約　Geneva Convention on Territorial Sea and Contiguous Zone
日平均用水量/日平均用水量　daily mean water-consumption
日球/日圈　heliosphere
日食/日食　solar eclipse
日坛/日壇　Temple of Sun, Ri Tan
日调节水池/調節潴蓄,堰蓄　regulator storage, storage regulator
日要车计划/日要車計劃　daily car requisition plan
日用淡水泵/日用淡水泵　daily service fresh water pump
日用柜/日用櫃　service tank, daily tank
日用燃油泵/日用燃油泵　daily service fuel oil pump
日游客量/日遊客量　daily tourist amount
日月摄动/日月攝動　sun-moon perturbation
日照/日照　sunshine
日照百分率/日照百分率　percentage of sunshine
日照标准/日照標準,日光標準　daylight standard, insolation standard
日照分析/日照分析　sunlight analysis
日照间距/日照間距　minimum building distance for sunlight, sunshine interval, daylight standard
日照间距系数/日照間距係數　coefficient of sunshine spacing
日照时数/日照時間,日照延時　sunshine duration
容差分析/容差分析　tolerance analysis
容错/容錯　tolerance fault, fault-tolerance, fault tolerant
容错供电/容錯電力供應　fault tolerant electrical power supply
容积/容積　volume
容积泵/排量式泵　positive displacement pump
容积吨/容積噸,呎碼噸　measurement ton
容积分区/容積分區　bulk zoning
容积负荷/體積負荷　volumetric loading
容积货物/容積貨[物],呎碼貨　measurement cargo
容积率/容積率,建地比　floor area ratio, plot ratio
容积率奖励/容積率獎勵　FAR award
容积率调整/容積率調整　FAR adjustment
容积配合/容積配合　volume mix
容积曲线/容積曲線　capacity curve
容积式热交换器/容積式熱交換器,蓄熱式水加熱器　storage heat exchanger, storage water heater
容积式水加热器/蓄熱式水加熱器,容積式熱交換器　storage heat exchanger, storage water heater
容积式压缩机/容積式壓縮機　positive displacement compressor
容积效率/容積效率,體積效率　volumetric efficiency
容积絮凝/容積絮凝　volume flocculation
容量/容量　capacity
容量曲线/容量曲線,體積曲線　capacity curve, volume curve
容器苗/容器苗　container seedling, plants of container
容器育苗/容器苗圃　container nursery
容热强度/容熱強度　volumetric heat intensity
容水量/[土壤]持水量　water capacity
容许沉降量/容許沈降量,許可沈陷　allowable settlement, permissible settlement
容许承载力/容許承載力　allowable bearing capacity, allowable bearing pressure
容许冲刷/容許沖刷　allowable scour
容许荷载/容許載重　allowable load
容许回弹弯沉值/容許回彈彎沈值　allowable rebound deflection value
容许开采量/容許開採量　permissible yield
容许磨损/容許磨損　permissible wear
容许强度检定/容許強度檢定　working stress rating
容许土压力/土壤許可承壓力　permissible soil pressure

容许误差/容許誤差 tolerance error, admissible error
容许信号/容許信號 permissive signal
容许应力/容許應力 permissible stress, allowable stress
容许应力设计法/容許應力設計法 allowable stress design method
容许运输期限/容許運輸期限 permissive period of transport
容许振动值/允許振動值 allowance value of vibration
容许注水深度/容許淹水深度 allowable flooding depth
容载比/容載比 capacity-to-load ratio
溶剂/溶劑 solvent
溶剂提取/溶劑提煉法 solvent extraction
溶剂型木器涂料/溶劑型木器塗料 solvent based wooden-ware coating
溶剂型涂料/溶劑塗層,溶劑塗膜 solvent-thinned coating
溶解度/溶[解]度 dissolubility, solubility
溶解度试验/溶解度試驗,溶性試驗 dissolubility test
溶解固体/溶解性固體 dissolved solid, dissolved matter
溶解固形物/溶解[性]固體 dissolved solid, dissolved matter
溶解泉/溶解泉 solution spring
溶解物/溶解物 dissolved matter
溶解氧/溶氧 dissolved oxygen
溶解与润湿结合/溶解與潤濕膠合 dissolution and wetting bond
溶解质总量/總溶解固體 total disolved solid
溶气罐/溶解氣罐 dissolving air tank
溶蚀/沖蝕,潰蝕 erosion
溶陷/溶陷 melt sinking
溶氧纵分布曲线/溶解氧縱分布曲線 dissolved oxygen profile
熔池/熔[化]池 molten pool
熔滴/熔滴 globule
熔点/熔點 melting point
熔断器/熔斷器,熔線,保險絲 fuse
熔断器断丝/保險絲熔斷 fuse burn-out
熔断器断丝报警/熔斷器斷絲報警 fuse break alarm
熔敷金属/熔著金屬,堆積金屬 deposition metal, deposited metal
熔敷顺序/熔著順序 built up sequence
熔敷速度/熔著速度 deposition rate
熔敷效率/熔著效率,堆積效率,澱積效率 deposition efficiency
熔焊/熔焊,熔接 fusion welding
熔焊桥丝/焊接橋 welded bridge
熔合区/熔融帶 zone fusion
熔核/焊塊 nugget
熔化穿孔/熔穿鑽 fusion piercing
熔化极惰性气体保护焊/惰性氣體遮護金屬焊[接] metal inert-gas welding
熔化极脉冲氩弧焊/氣體遮護金屬電弧焊 gas metal arc welding-pulsed arc
熔化潜热/熔合潛熱 latent heat of fusion
熔模石膏型铸造/熔模石膏型鑄造 plaster molding for investment casting
熔模铸造/熔模鑄造,包模鑄造,失蠟鑄造 investment casting, fusible pattern molding, lost-wax molding
熔融碳酸盐燃料电池/熔融碳酸鹽燃料電池 molten carbonate fuel cell
熔融盐电池/熔鹽電解池 molten-salt electrolyte cell
熔深/熔解深度 depth of fusion, penetration
融合体布局/融合體布局 blended configuration
融霜储液器/除霜接受器 defrost receiver
融雪洪水/融雪洪水 flood of melted snow, snow-water flood
融雪剂危害/融雪劑危害 snowmelt agent hazards
冗余/冗餘 redundancy
冗余度/冗餘度 degree of redundancy
冗余反力/贅[餘]反力 redundant reaction
冗余信息/冗餘資訊 redundant information
冗余支撑/贅餘支承 redundant support
冗余作用力/贅[餘]力 redundant force
柔壁喷管/柔板噴嘴 flexible plate nozzle
柔度/柔度 flexibility, compliance
柔度法/柔度法 flexibility method
柔度矩阵/柔度矩陣 flexibility matrix
柔韧性/柔性,柔度 flexibility
柔顺性/順從性 compliance
柔性衬砌/柔性襯砌 flexible lining
柔性底板/撓性板 flexible plate
柔性底层/柔性底層 soft ground floor
柔性动力学/柔性動力學 flexible dynamics
柔性墩/柔性橋墩 flexible pier
柔性多体动力学/柔性多體動力學 flexible multibody dynamics
柔性防水屋面/柔性防水屋面 flexible water proof roof
柔性护栏/撓性護欄 flexible safety fence

柔性基础/柔性基礎　flexible foundation
柔性降级/工作可靠但性能下降　graceful degradation
柔性接口/柔性介面　gentle joint
柔性结构/柔性結構　flexible structure
柔性路面/柔性路面,柔性鋪面　flexible pavement
柔性喷管/撓性噴嘴　flexible joint nozzle, flexible bearing nozzle
柔性墙/撓性擋土牆　flexible wall
柔性[桥]墩/柔性橋墩　flexible pier
柔性毡/柔性氈　flexible felt
柔性支承/柔性支承　flexible support
柔性支持板/柔性撐板　flexible stay plate
柔性制造单元/柔性製造單元　flexible manufacturing cells, FMC
柔性制造系统/彈性製造系統　flexible manufacturing system, FMS
柔性转子/柔性轉子　flexible rotor
肉厚分数/肉厚度分數　web fraction
肉鸡舍/肉雞舍　broiler house
肉库/肉庫　butchery
肉类加工厂/肉加工廠,肉聯廠　meat product plant
肉眼检查/肉眼檢查　macroscopic test
茹科夫斯基定理/賈克斯基定理　Joukowsky theorem
蠕变/蠕變,潛變　creep, crawl
蠕变疲劳/蠕變疲勞　creep fatigue
蠕滑/蠕動　creep
乳白玻璃/乳色玻璃　milky glass
乳儿室/嬰兒室　infant room
乳化/乳化　emulsification
乳化剂/乳化劑　emulsifying agent, emulsifier
乳化沥青/乳化瀝青　emulsified bitumen
乳化燃料/乳化燃料　emulsified fuel
乳化油/乳化油　emulsifying oil
乳胶漆/乳膠漆,乳化漆　emulsion paint
乳胶体/乳膠體　emulsoid
入船坞设施/入塢設備　docking accommodation
入轨参数/軌道進入參數　parameters at injection
入轨点/軌道進入點　injection point
入轨[段]测控/入軌段追蹤、遙測和指令　TT and C of injection phase
入轨精度/軌道進入精度　orbit injection accuracy
入轨误差/軌道進入誤差　injection error
入轨姿态/入軌姿態　injection attitude
入户管/入口管,供給管　inlet pipe
入级/入級,船級　classification
入级检验/船級檢驗　classification survey

入级证书/船級證書　classification certificate
入境交通/入境交通　inbound traffic
入口/入口,門口　entrance
入口段/入口段　lead in section
入口控制/通路或出入口管制　access control
入口平台/入口平臺　entrance platform
入口坡道/出入引道　access ramp
入口匝道控制/入口匝道控制　entrance ramp control
入侵/入侵　invasion
入侵报警系统/入侵警報系統　intruder alarm system, IAS
入侵波/侵入波　send wave
入侵探测器/入侵探測器　intruder detector
入侵植物/入侵植物　invasive plant
入侵种/入侵種　invasive species
入射波/入射波　incident wave
入射光瞳/入射[光]瞳　entrance pupil
入射角/入射角,攻角,投射角　incident angle, angle of incidence
入射热流法/入射熱通量法　incident heat flux method
入射余角/低伸角度　grazing angle
入渗池/入滲池　infiltration pool
入渗井/滲濾井　infiltration well
入渗率/下滲率,取水率　intake rate
入网/上網　log in
入坞设备/入塢設備　docking accommodation
入中继电路/入中繼電路　incoming trunk circuit
入住率/建築使用率,建築占用率　occupancy rate
软波导/撓性導波管　flexible waveguide
软错误/軟性錯誤,軟性誤差　soft error
软氮化/軟氮化　soft nitriding
软导线/軟導線　flex lead
软点火/軟點火　soft ignition
软电缆/柔性[電]纜　flexible cable
软定位器/軟定位器　pull-off arm
软管/軟管　hose
软管灯/管燈照明　tubular lighting
软管固定架/油管固定柵架　hose tie rack
软管喷嘴/軟管噴嘴　hose nozzle
软横跨/軟橫跨[懸掛]　head span suspension
软化/軟化　softening
软化点/軟化點　softening point
软化点试验[环球法]/軟化點試驗　softening point test ringball method
软化水/軟化水　softened water
软化系数/軟化係數　coefficient of softness,

softening coefficient
软化岩石/軟化岩　softening rock
软件安全性/軟體安全性　software safety
软件故障/軟體故障　software fault
软件可靠性/軟體可靠性　software reliability
软件维护/軟體維護　software maintenance
软件质量保证/軟體品質保證　software quality assurance
软景库/軟景庫　drop storage
软聚氯乙烯管/塑化聚氯乙烯管線　plasticized polyvinyl chloride pipe, PVC-P pipe
软卷帘/卷簾式　roller blind
软颗粒含量试验/軟顆粒含量試驗　soft grain content test
软练砂浆强度试验/塑性灰漿強度試驗　plastic mortar strength test
软模成形/可撓模具成型　flexible die forming
软木材/軟木　softwood
软黏土/軟黏土　soft clay
软判决/軟式決定　soft decision
软钎焊/軟焊,錫焊　soldering
软钎料/軟焊料,焊錫　solder
软弱地基/軟弱路基,軟弱基層土　soft ground, poor subsoil
软弱围岩/軟弱圍岩　weak surrounding rock
软式传动机构/軟式傳動機構　cable pulley system
软水/軟水　soft water
软水与净水/軟水與純水　water softened and purified
软梯/軟梯,繩梯　rope ladder
软铁球/軟鐵球　soft-iron sphere
软土/軟土　soft soil, mollisol
软土地区路基/軟土地區路基　subgrade in soft soil zone, subgrade in soft clay region
软卧车/軟臥車　cushioned berth sleeping car, upholstered couchette
软岩/軟[質]岩　soft rock
软油箱/軟油箱　bladder fuel tank
软着陆/輕落地　soft landing
软质聚氨脂泡沫塑料/軟質聚氨酯泡沫塑膠　flexible polyurethane foams
软质岩石/軟弱岩石　weak rock
软座车/軟座車　cushioned-seat coach, upholstered-seat coach
锐角辙叉/銳角轍叉,硬角叉心　end frog, acute frog
瑞利-里茨法/雷里・李茲二氏法　Rayleigh Ritz method
瑞利散射/雷萊散射　Rayleigh scattering
闰秒/閏秒　leap second
闰年/閏年　leap year
闰日/閏日　leap day
闰月/閏月　leap month
润滑剂/潤滑劑　lubricant
润滑系统/潤滑系統　lubrication system
润滑油/潤滑油　lubricating oil
润滑脂/[潤]滑脂　lubricating grease, grease
润湿角/潤濕角　wetting angle
弱的/弱的　weak
弱电场区/弱電場區　weak electric field area
弱电分接箱/弱流電纜分線箱　weak current cable branch box
弱电竖井/弱電竖井　communication shaft
弱电小间/弱電小間　communication chamber
弱风化岩石/弱風化岩　moderately weathered rock
弱界面/弱介面　weak interface
弱链环/弱鏈　weak link
弱势群体/弱勢團體　vulnerable groups
弱势群体需求/弱勢群體需求　needs of vulnerable group
弱酸值/弱酸值　weak acid number
弱弹簧示功图/弱彈簧示功圖　weak spring diagram
弱涌/弱湧　weak swell
弱轴/短軸　minor axis
弱阻尼/不足阻尼,欠阻尼　underdamping

S

洒水车/灑水車,灑水器　street sprinkler, sprinkler
洒水短管/灑水短管　spraying tube
洒水系统/噴水系統,噴灑系統　sprinkler system
洒水装置/噴水裝置　sprinkler installation
撒播/撒播　broadcast sowing
撒布/撒布　spreading
撒砂阀/撒砂閥　sanding valve
撒砂机/撒砂機　sand spraying machine
撒砂器/撒砂器　sanding sprayer
撒砂装置/撒砂裝置　sanding device
撒砂装置试验/撒砂裝置試驗,鋪砂裝置試驗　test on sanding gear
萨巴蒂循环/定壓定容混式循環　Sabbath cycle
萨迈帕塔考古遗址/薩邁帕塔考古遺址　Fuerte de Samaipata
萨奈克效应/Sagnac 效應　Sagnac effect
塞尺/餘隙規　clearance gage
塞钉式钢轨接续线/插頭接線　plug bond
塞焊[缝]/塞孔熔接,塞孔焊接　plug weld, plug welding
塞入门/平拉門　plug door
[塞入门]导轮/塞入門導輪　door guide wheel
塞式量热计/塞孔熱量計　plug calorimeter
塞式喷管/栓塞噴嘴　plug nozzle
塞式喷管火箭发动机/栓塞噴嘴火箭發動機　plug nozzle rocket engine
赛车场/賽車場,跑道　racing circuit, racetrack
赛道/賽道,跑道　track
赛马场/賽馬場,跑馬場　race course
赛马场草坪/賽馬場草坪　racecourse lawn
赛氏黏度/色博黏度　Saybolt viscosity
赛艇/競賽艇　runner boat, racing boat
赛艇航道/賽艇航道　rowing channel
赛艇运动/賽艇　rowing
三[层]金属轴承/三[層]金屬軸承　tri-metal bearing
三层筛/三層式篩　triple deck screen
三层网架/三層柵極　triple layer grid
三差/三差　triple difference
三岔路口/三道交叉　three-way intersection
三车道道路/三車道道路,三幅路　three-lane road, triple carriageway road
三次抛物线曲线/三次拋物線曲線　cubic parabola curve
三大件转向架/三件式轉向架　three-piece truck
三岛型船/三島型船　three island vessel
三等三角测量/三等三角測量　third order triangulation
三等三角点/三等三角點　third order triangulation station
三点法/三點法　three point method
三点检查/三點檢查　released by checking three sections
三点透视/三點透視　three point perspective
三防涂料/三防塗料　three-resistance coating
三分之一最大波/三分之一最大波　one-third maximum wave
三幅式城市道路/三幅式都市道路　three-slab urban road
三副/三副　third officer, third mate
三杆分度器/三臂定位器　three-arm protractor, station pointer
三缸星形发动机/三缸星形引擎　y-engine
三拐曲轴/三拐曲軸　three-thrown crank shaft
三管轮/三管輪　fourth engineer
三合院/三合院　courtyard house with three building, sanheyuan
三基色荧光灯/三色帶螢光燈　three-band fluorescent lamp
三级保护区/三級保護區　third class preservation district
三级处理/三級處理　tertiary treatment
三级公路/三級公路　thrid class highway
三级管网系统/三級系統　three stage system
三级作图仪/三級作圖儀　third order plotting instrument
三角板/三角板　triangle plane
三角波/三角波　pyramidal wave
三角测量/三角測量　trigonometric survey, triangulation
三角插塞/三腳插塞　three-pin plug
三角顶标/三角頂標　triangle top mark
三角定位法/三角定位法　triangulation location

三角高程测量/三角高程測量　trigonometric leveling
三角坑/三角坑　twist
三角木块/接點支塊　angle block
三角皮带/三角皮帶　v-beet
三角区分法/三角區分法　triangular division method
三角锁/三角鏈　triangulation chain
三角形过程线/三角形歷線　triangular hydrograph
三角形三(南三角α)/三角形三(南三角α)　Atria
三角形枢纽/三角形樞紐　triangle-type junction terminal
三角形屋架/三角形屋架　triangular roof truss
三角靴/三角靴　triangular shoe
三角眼板/三角眼板　triangular plate
三角翼/三角翼　delta wing
三角洲/三角洲　delta
三角锥网架/三角椎體網架　triangular pyramid space grid
三角坐标土壤分类法/三角坐標土壤分類法　triangular soil classification system
三铰拱/三鉸拱　three-hinged arch
三铰拱桥/三鉸拱橋　three-hinged arches bridge
三脚架/三腳架　tripod
三脚桅/三腳桅　tripod mast
三阶段设计/三階段設計　three-step design, three-phase design
三开道岔/三開道岔　symmetrical three throw turnout, three way turnout
三立管排水系统/三立管排水系統　drainage waste and vent stanch system
三联泵/三缸泵　triplex pump
三轮压路机/三輪壓路機,三輪滾壓機　three wheel roller
三绕组变压器/三卷線變壓器　three-winding transformer
三三脚法/三三腳法　method of three tripod
三声速风洞/三音速風洞　trisonic wind tunnel
三索套/三肢吊索　three leg sling
三体艇/三[胴]體船　trimaran
三体问题/三體問題　three-body problem
三通阀/三通閥　three-way valve, triple valve
三通管/三通管,丁字管　tee branch
三通接头/三通接頭　t-junction
三头开关/三向道岔　three-throw switch
三弯矩方程/三力矩公式　three moment equation
三维打印/三維列印　three dimension printing, 3DP
三维风洞/三維風洞　three dimensional wind tunnel
三维告警/三維警報　three dimensional warning
三维固结/三向壓密　three dimensional consolidation

三维流/三維流動　three dimensional flow
三维扫描/3D掃描　3D scanner
三维弹翼/三維翼　three dimensional wing
三维制导系统/三維導引系統　three dimension guidance system
三位四通换向阀/三位四通方向控制閥　three-position four way directional control valve
三弦桥/三弦桁架橋　three-chord bridge
三显示自动闭塞/三顯示自動閉塞　three-aspect automatic block
三向固结/三向壓密　three dimensional consolidation
三向石英复合材料/三向石英纖維強化複合材　three-direction quartz fiber reinforced quartz composite
三向石英增强二氧化硅复合材料/三向石英纖維強化二氧化矽複合材　three-direction quartz fiber reinforced SiO_2 composite
三向碳-碳/三向碳-碳　3-directional C-C
三向网架/三向網格　three way latticed grid
三向预应力/三維預力　three dimension prestressing
三相点/三相點　triple point
三相短路/三相[對稱]故障　three-phase symmetrical fault
三相反向变流机/三相變流機　three-phase inverter
三相供电/三相電源　three-phase power supply
三相交流牵引电动机/三相交流牽引電動機　three-phase AC traction motor
三相配电/三相配電　three-phase power distribution system
三相桥式整流器/三相橋式整流器　three-phase bridge rectifier
三相三绕组接线牵引变压器/三相三繞組牽引變壓器　traction transformer of three-phase three winding connection
三相四线制/三相四線制　three-phase four-wire system
三相信号/三時相號誌　three-phase signal
三相异步电动机/三相異步電動機　three-phase asynchronous motor
三压力机构/三壓力機構　three-pressure equalizing system
三翼钻头/三翼鑽頭　3-wing bit
三用液压挖掘机/萬能整土機　gradall
三元脉冲电路/三元脈動電路　ternary pulse circuit
[三]原色/原色,基[本]色　primary color
三胀式蒸汽机/三段膨脹蒸汽機　triple expansion steam engine
三轴剪切试验/三軸剪切試驗　triaxial shear test

三轴剪切仪/三軸剪力儀　triaxial shear equipment
三轴强度/三軸強度　triaxial strength
三轴试验/三軸試驗　triaxial test
三轴稳定平台/三軸穩定平臺　three-axis stable platform
三轴压力圆筒/三軸壓力圓筒　triaxial cell pressure cylinder
三轴压路机/三軸壓路機　three-axle tandem roller
三轴仪/三軸試驗機　triaxial apparatus
三轴应力/三軸應力　triaxial stress
三轴转向架/三軸式轉向架　three-axle truck
三轴姿态稳定/三軸姿態穩定　three-axis attitude stabilization
三柱块体/鼎型塊　tribar
三锥形钻头/三錐形鑽頭　triconebit
三字点/中間點　intermediate point
三字母信号码/三字母信號碼　three letter signal code
三组元推进剂/三元推進劑　tripropellant
三组元[推进剂]火箭发动机/三元推進劑火箭發動機　tripropellant rocket engine
三作用千斤顶/三動千斤頂　triple acting jack
伞舱/傘艙　parachute bay
伞系/傘系統　parachute system
伞衣/[降落伞]傘衣　parachute canopy
伞衣呼吸/傘衣呼吸　canopy breath
伞衣织物/傘衣織物　fabric for parachute canopy
伞衣织物透气量/傘衣織物透氣量　canopy fabric porosity
伞翼机/翼傘　parawing
散仓/散倉　decentralized stockroom
散点石/散點石　scattered stone
散货/散裝貨　bulk cargo
散货船/散裝貨船　bulk cargo ship, bulk carrier
散货捆包/大包捆　bundling of bulk
散焦星图像/散焦星圖像　defocused star image
散客/散客　foreign independent tourist
散料仓/散裝儲藏庫　bulk storage, bulk material warehouse
散射/散射　scattering
散射辐射/漫射輻射　diffuse radiation
散射计/散射計　scatterometer
散射锚泊系统/分散錨泊　spread anchoring system
散射系泊定位钻井船/分散繫泊定位鑽探船　spread moored drilling ship
散射系数/散射係數　scattering coefficient
散射正交截面/散射截面　scattering cross section
散射[浊]度/濁度　nephelometric turbidity unit
散植/散植　scattered planting, loose planting
散置/分插　interspersed
散装谷物捆包/散裝穀類捆包　bundle of bulk grain
散装货条款/散裝貨條款　bulk cargo clause
散装货物/散裝貨[運],散裝產品　bulk cargo, bulk goods, bulk freight
散装容积/散裝容積　bulk capacity, grain capacity
散装时危险物质/散裝時危險物質　materials hazardous in bulk
散装水泥车/散裝水泥車　bulk cement car
散波/發散波　divergent wave
散步区/散步區　pedestrian space
散发火花地点/散發火花地點　sparking site
散开纵队命令/疏開編隊　column open order
散流器送风/擴散式空氣補充　diffuser air supply
散热管/散熱器,輻射器　radiator
散热器/散熱器,輻射器　radiator
散热器供暖/散熱器供暖　radiator heating
散热器供暖系统/散熱器採暖系統　radiator heating system
散热器恒温控制阀/散熱器溫控閥　thermostatic radiator valve
散热损失/熱之散逸　heat dissipation
桑拿浴室/桑拿浴室　steam bathroom, sauna bathroom
桑托斯杜蒙特机场花园/桑托斯杜蒙特機場花園　Garden of Santos Dumont Airport
缫丝厂/繅絲廠　silk reeling mill
扫舱泵/殘油泵,收艙泵　stripping pump
扫舱总管/收艙總管　stripping main line
扫海/掃海　bed sweeping
扫雷队形/掃雷隊形　mine-sweeping formation
扫雷航海勤务/掃雷航海勤務　mine-sweeping navigation service
扫雷舰艇/掃雷艇　minesweeper
扫雷具/掃雷具　sweep
扫描/掃描　sweep, scan
扫描重叠率/掃描重疊係數　scanning overlap coefficient
扫描地球敏感器/掃描地球感測器　scanning earth sensor, scanning horizon sensor
扫描电镜/掃描電子顯微鏡　scanning electron microscope
扫描多通道微波辐计/多頻道微波掃描輻射計　scanning multi-channel microwave radiometer
扫描范围/掃描範圍　scanning range
扫描飞轮/掃描飛輪　scan flywheel
扫描角/掃描角　scanning angle

扫描角监控器/掃描角監控器　scan angle monitor
扫描式激光引信/掃描雷射引信　scanning laser fuze
扫描视场/掃描視野　scanning field of view, SFOV
扫描速率/掃描速率　scanning rate
扫描微波辐射计/掃描微波輻射計　scanning microwave radiometer
扫描微波频谱仪/掃描微波分光計　scanning microwave spectrometer, SCAMS
扫描线校正器/掃描線校正器　scan line corrector
扫描效率/掃描效率　scanning efficiency
扫描影像/掃描圖像　scan-image
扫气/驅氣　purge
扫气泵/回油泵　scavenging pump
扫气泵扫气/鼓風機驅氣　blower scavenging
扫气口/驅氣孔　scavenging air port
扫气系数/掃氣係數　coefficient of scavenging
扫气箱/驅氣箱，驅氣接收器　scavenging air receiver, scavenging air manifold, scavenging box
扫气箱着火/驅氣箱著火　scavenging box fire
扫气效率/驅氣效率　scavenging efficiency
扫气压力/掃氣壓力，驅氣壓力　scavenging pressure
扫气压力燃油限制器/驅氣空氣壓力燃油限制器　scavenging air pressure fuel limiter
扫砂机/掃砂機　sand sweeping machine
扫雪机/雪犁　snow plow
色饱和度/色飽和[度]　color saturation
色表/色表　color appearance
色彩/色彩　color
色彩表情/色彩表現　color expression
色彩对比/色對比　color contrast
色彩感觉/色[感]覺　color sensation
色彩构成/色彩合成　color composition
色彩肌理/色彩紋飾　color texturing
色彩三要素/色彩三要素　three key elements of color
色彩体系/色彩系統　color system
色彩象征/顏色象徵　color symbol
色彩心理/色彩心理　color psychology
色带/色帶　ribbon
色灯电锁器联锁/色燈電鎖器聯鎖　interlocking by electric locks with color-light signal
色灯信号机/色燈式號誌[機]，彩色燈號　color-light signal
色调/色調　hue
色度/色度，色品　chromaticity
色度测量/色度測量學　colorimetry
色度计/色度計　colorimeter
色度图/色度圖　chromaticity diagram

色分辨率/色鑒別率，鑒色本領　chromatic resolving power
色感/色感　color sense
色光/彩光　colorful light
色卡/[標準]色紙，色片　color chip
色块/色塊　lumps of color
色立体/[彩]色立體　color solid
色流法/色流法　coloration flow method
色谱分析/色譜分析　chromatographic analysis
色散/色散，波散　dispersion
色散常数/色散常數　chromatic dispersion constant
色温/色溫[度]　color temperature
色相/色表　color appearance
色相对比/色相對比　contrast of color appearance
色相环/色相環　hue circle
色[像]差/色像差　chromatism, chromatic aberration
色性/顏色特徵　color character
色叶植物/色葉植物　colored foliage
森林/森林　forest, sylva
森林保护/森林保護[學]　forest protection
森林动物/森林動物　forest animal
森林分布图/森林圖，林相圖　forest map
森林风景区/森林風景區　forest scenic spot
森林覆盖率/森林覆蓋率　forest coverage rate, forest coverage, percentage of forest cover
森林公园/森林公園　forest park
森林环境/森林環境　forest environment
森林群落/森林群落　forest community
森林生态系统/森林生態系[統]　forest ecosystem
森林铁路/森林鐵路　forest railway
森林土壤/森林土壤　forest soil
森林永续利用/森林永續利用　sustained yield of forest
森林资源/森林資源　forest resources
杀伤区/致死區　lethal zone
沙包强垒/砂包工事　bagwork
沙尘暴/沙暴　sand storm
沙发/沙發　sofa
沙害/沙害　sand hazard
沙狐球室/沙狐球室，沙壺球室　shuffleboard room
沙壶球室/沙狐球室，沙壺球室　shuffleboard room
沙脊/沙畦　sand ridge
沙坑/沙坑　bunkers
沙龙/沙龍　salon
沙漠/沙漠　desert
沙丘/沙丘　sand dune
沙丘固定/沙丘固定　dune fixation
沙生植被/沙地植被　psammophytic vegetation

沙生植物/砂生植物,沙地植物　psammophyte
沙障/沙壩　sand barrier
沙质跑道/撒砂軌道　sand track
沙洲/沙洲,淺灘　shoal
纱/紗,線股　yarn
纱幕/紗幕　veil curtain
刹车距离/刹車距離　braking distance
刹车控制系统/刹車控制系統　brake control system
刹车力矩/制動扭矩　brake torque, braking torque
刹车能量/刹車能量　brake energy
刹车能量限制重量/刹車能量限制重量　brake energy limiting weight
刹车速度/刹車速度　brake speed
刹车压力/刹車壓力,韌壓力　brake pressure
刹车压力表/制動氣壓表　brake pressure gage
砂泵/混水礫泵　gravel pump
砂捕集器/截砂池　sand interceptor
砂槽模型/砂箱模型　sand box model
砂道碴/砂壓載　sand ballast
砂害/漂砂,飛砂　sand blockade, sand drift
砂浆/砂漿,水泥漿　grout
砂浆稠度仪/砂漿稠度儀　mortar consistency tester
砂浆垫层/砂漿敷面　mortar layer
砂浆灌注/砂漿灌注　mortar injection
砂浆速凝剂/砂漿速凝劑　mortar plasticiser
砂胶灌缝施工法/抛石膠漿法　sand-mastic method
砂井/砂樁,砂滲排水　sand well, sand drain
砂井排水法/砂滲法　sand drain method
砂类土/砂質土[壤]　sandy soil
砂砾/砂礫石　sand gravel
砂率/[含]砂率　sand ratio, sand of percentage
砂滤/砂濾　sand filtration
砂轮/盤輪　disc wheel
砂石车/砂石車　gravel car
砂石跑道/砂石跑道　gravel track
砂[土]/砂[土]　sand soil, sand
砂土液化/砂土液化　sand liquefaction
砂纹/條紋　sand streak
砂箱/砂箱　sand box
砂箱墩/砂[箱]墩　sand block, block with sand box
砂型铸造/砂模鑄造　sand casting process, sand mold casting
砂岩/砂岩　sand stone
砂胀比/砂脹比　sand expansion ratio
砂质粉土/砂質粉土　sandy silt
砂质土壤/砂質土[壤]　sandy soil
砂桩/砂樁　sand pile
筛层磨碎机/篩屑磨碎機　screening grinder
筛层切碎机/篩屑切碎機　screening shredder
筛层脱水/篩屑脱水　screening dewatering
筛点移动/節點移動　joint translation
筛分/篩分,篩選　sieve analysis, screening
筛分机械/篩分機,篩選機,搖篩機　sieving machine
筛网/篩網　screen
筛选/篩選,過篩,篩除　screening
筛选砾石/篩選礫石　screened gravel
晒场/曬場　drying yard
晒砖/曬磚坯　sun-dried brick
山地苔藓林/山地苔藓林　montane mossy forest
山地自行车/登山車　mountain bike
山洞式锚碇/山洞式錨碇　anchor in rock gallery
山花/山花　tympanum
山脊/[山]脊,嶺,隆起緣　ridge
[山]脊线/[山]脊線　ridge line
山口/山口　mountain pass
山岭区/山嶺地區　mountain terrain
山岭隧道/山嶺隧道,山嶽隧道　mountain tunnel
山坡被覆工程/山坡保護工程　hillside covering work
山坡地开发/山坡地開發　hillside development
山坡防护林/山坡防護林,護坡林　slope protection forest
山坡工程/山坡工程　hillside work
山坡线/山坡線　hillside line
山坡栅栏工程/山坡柵欄工程　hillside fence work
山墙/山牆,人字牆　pediment, gable wall
山区/山嶺區　mountainous region
山区公路/山區公路　mountain highway
山区河谷选线/山區河谷選線　mountain and valley region location, location of line in mountain and valley region
山区河流/山區河流　mountain river
山区铁路/山區鐵道　mountain railway
山泉水给水系统/泉水給水系統　spring water supply system
山石材料/山石材料　stone materials
山石器设/山石器設　mountain stone set
山水盆景/山水盆景　landscape bonsai
山水审美/山水審美　landscape aesthetic
山头构架/人字頂構架　gable frame
山岳景观/山嶽景觀　mountain landscape, alpine landscape
山岳类/山嶽類　mountain type
山岳雨/山嶺雨　orographic rain
山樟木/樟木　camphor wood
山字钩/雙鉤　double hook
山字块体/鼎型塊　tribar

舢板/舢板　sampan
闪点/闪[燃]點,引火點,著火點　flash point
闪点试验/閃點試驗　flash point test
闪电电磁感应/雷電磁感應　lightning electromagnetic induction
闪电电涌/雷電突波,雷電過電壓　lightning surge
闪电电涌侵入/雷電波侵入　lightning surge on incoming service
闪电感应/雷電感應　lightning induction
闪电静电感应/雷電靜電感應　lightning electrostatic induction
闪电试验/閃電試驗　lightning test
闪发室/急驟蒸發室　flash chamber
闪发蒸发/急驟蒸發　flash evaporation
闪光/閃光　flash, flashing
闪光[灯]标/閃光標桿　flashing beacon
闪光电源/閃光電源　flashing power source
闪光对焊/閃電對焊,閃電對頭焊接　flash butt welding
闪光对接焊接头/閃電對焊接　flash butt welded joint
闪光复位/閃爍復位　flicker reset
闪光信号/閃光信號　flashing signal, flashing light signal
闪光运转/閃光運轉　flashing operation
闪光装置/閃光裝置　flashing feature
闪耀光栅/炫耀光柵　blazed grating
闪耀角/閃耀角　blazed angle
扇拱/扇形拱頂,扇形穹頂　fan vault
扇形/扇形　sector
扇形齿板/扇形齒輪,扇形體　quadrant
扇形冲沙闸门/弧形沖淤閘門,級式排水閘門　segmental sluice gate
扇形拉索/扇形拉索　fan type stay cable
扇形理论/扇形理論,扇狀理論　sector theory
扇形锚头/扇形錨碇　fan type anchorage
扇形面积/扇形面積　sectorial area
扇形排水系统/扇形排水系統　fan system
扇形搜寻/扇形搜索　sector search
扇形艉/扇形艉　fantail stern
扇形泄水闸门/弧形沖淤閘門,級式排水閘門　segmental sluice gate
扇形闸门/扇形閘門　tainter gate, sector gate
扇形支架/扇形支架　fan type support
扇翼/整形片　glove vane
伤害调查/損害調查　damage survey
伤流/溢液現象,泌液現象　bleeding exudation
伤亡率/傷亡率　casualty rate
商场/商場　shop, store
商船/商船　commercial ship, merchant ship
商船旗/商船旗　merchant ship flag
商船搜救手册/商船搜救手冊　merchant ship search and rescue manual
商店/商店　shop, store
商品房/商品房,商品住宅　commodity housing, commodity house
商品房公用建筑面积分摊/商品房公用建築面積　apportionment of common-floorage
商品房市场/商品房市場　commodity housing market
商品房现售/商品房現售　spot sale of commodity house
商品房销售价格/商品房銷售價格　sale price of commodity house
商品房销售面积/商品房銷售地區　sale area of commodity house
商品房预售/商品房預售　advance sale of commodity house
商品有机肥料/商品有機肥料　commodity organic fertilizer
商务办公区/商務區　business district
商务检查电视/商務檢查電視　TV for railway commerce inspection
商务纠纷/商業糾紛,商事糾紛　commercial dispute
商务楼层/商務樓層　business floor
商务旅馆/商務酒店,會議型酒店　convention hotel, conference hotel, business hotel
商务写字楼/商務寫字樓　business office building
商务用地/商務用地　land for business facility
商务园/商業園　business park
商务中心/業務中心　business center
商业城市/商業城　commercial city
商业发射/商業發射　commercial launch
商业服务网点/民用設施　commercial facilities
商业服务业设施用地/商業服務業設施用地　commercial and business land, land for commercial and business facility
商业建筑/商業建築　commercial building
商业街/商業街,商店街　shopping street
商业金融用地/商業金融土地利用　commercial and financial land use
商业区/商業區　commercial district, commercial area, shopping district
商业用地/商業用地　land for commercial facility
商业中心/商業中心　commercial center
商业中心地/商業廣場　market place

商用车辆运行管理系统/商車營運系統管理系統　commercial vehicle operation management system, CVOM
商用汽车/商用車輛,營業車輛　commercial vehicle
商用物业/商業財產　commercial property
商载/有效载荷,有效负载,酬載　payload
商住楼/商住樓　business-living building
商住用地/商住用地　residential and commercial land
熵/熵　entropy
熵层/熵層　entropy layer
熵吞/熵吞　entropy layer swallowing
上鞍/上鞍　tank anchor
上拌下贯式路面/上拌下貫式路面　penetration macadam with coated chip
上玻璃釉法/上釉法　vitreous
上部的/上部　upper
上部结构/上層結構　superstructure
上部转动/上部轉動　upper motion
上层建筑/上層建築,船艛建築　superstructure
上层建筑甲板/船艛甲板　superstructure deck
上层建筑整体吊装/上層建築整體吊裝　lifting and mounting complete superstructure
上层滞水水面/暫棲地水位　perched water table
上承式桁架/上承式桁架　deck truss
上承式桥/上承式橋,上托橋　deck bridge
上单翼/高翼　high wing
上挡墙/上擋土牆　top retaining wall
上导坑法/上導坑法　top-heading method
上顶岩床/上頂岩床　negative confining bed
上舵承/上舵承,舵系上部　upper bearer, rudder carrier
上反角/上反角　dihedral angle
上防跳台/上防跳臺　top operation anticreep ledge
上风岸/上風岸　weather shore
上风船/上風船　vessel to windward
上风舵/上風舵　down helm
上风满舵/上風滿舵　hard up
上风锚/上風錨　weather anchor
上风舷/上風舷,迎風舷　weather side, windward side
上浮/上浮　surfacing
上甲板/上甲板　upper deck
上界解/上限解法　upper bound solution
上开窗/上開窗　uplifting window
上空隙/上部淨空　upper clearance
上跨式立交/立體交叉　overpass
上拉杆/上拉桿　top rod
上林苑/上林苑　Shang Lin Yuan
上面级/上面級　upper stage
上面级发动机/上面級發動機　upper stage rocket engine, upper stage rocket motor
上挠度/反撓度,向上彎,翹起　camber
上排污阀/液面吹洩閥　surface blow off valve, surface blowdown valve
上盘微动螺丝/上盤微動螺絲　upper plate slow motion screw
上旁承/上旁承　body side bearing
上平联/縱向上平聯　top lateral bracing
上坡/上坡　up-grade
上墙板/上牆板　cornice sheathing
上轻下重法/上輕下重法　method of lowering the center of gravity of rocks
上清液/上澄液　supernatant, supernatant liquor
上升滨线/隆起海岸　shoreline of emergence
上升风/上昇風,上坡風　anabatic
上升管/昇導管　riser
上升海岸/隆昇海岸　coast of emergence
上升流/湧昇流　upwelling
上[升]流式接触澄清池/上向流接觸澄清池　upflow contact clarifier
上升时间/上昇時間　time of rise
上桅/上桅　topgallant mast
上位规划/上位規劃　upper level plan
上下导洞法/上下導坑法　top and bottom pilot tunneling method
上下视差/縱視差,Y視差　Y parallax, vertical parallax
上弦/上弦,頂弦　first quarter, top chord, upper chord
上限定理/上限定理　upper bound theorem
上限理论/上限定理　upper bound theorem
上限流线/上限流線　upper boundary flow line
上限越界/上限越界　off-normal upper
上心盘/車體中心板　body center plate
上行/開往　bound to
上行船/上行船　up-bound vessel
上行方向/上行方向　up direction
上行行程/上行衝程　upward stroke
上仰/上仰　pitch-up
上仰轰炸/上仰轟炸,上仰投彈　loft bombing
上游/上游　upper reach
上游坡面/上游坡度　upstream slope
上游隧洞/引水隧道　headrace tunnel
上圆盘/上圓盤　upper circle
上止点/[往復機]上死點　top dead center, top dead point, upper dead center

上中天/上中天　upper meridian passage, upper transit
上中天潮/顺潮,直接潮　direct tide, fair tide
上作用车钩/上作用式車鉤　top operation coupler
烧毁热负荷/燒盡熱通量　burn-out heat flux
烧结骨料/燒成骨材　burnt aggregate
烧结式镉镍蓄电池/燒結式鎳鎘蓄電池　sintered type cadmium-nickel battery
烧结瓦/燒結瓦,陶瓦　fired roofing tile
烧结砖/燒結磚,耐火磚　clinker brick, firing brick, fired brick
烧尽热负荷/燒盡熱通量　burn-out heat flux
烧球式柴油机/半柴油機　semidiesel
烧伤/燒傷　burning
烧蚀/燒蝕,熔蝕　ablation
烧蚀材料/熔蝕材料　ablative material, ablator
烧蚀防热/燒蝕防熱　ablative thermal protection
烧蚀防热材料/熔蝕熱防護材料　thermal-protect ablation material
烧蚀厚度/燒蝕厚度　recession thickness, ablation thickness
烧蚀率/熔蝕速率　ablating rate
烧蚀耦合计算/燒蝕耦合計算　ablation coupling calculation
烧蚀速度传感器/燒蝕速率換能器　ablation rate transducer
烧蚀图像/燒蝕圖像　ablation pattern
烧制车间/爐子間　furnace room
烧制骨材/燒製骨材　pelletized type aggregate
梢根比/翼縮比,漸縮比　taper ratio
梢厚/葉尖厚　blade tip thickness
梢隙/葉尖間隙　blade tip clearance
梢弦/翼尖弦長　tip chord
梢间/梢間　final bay
稍松/稍鬆,打住　check
少筋梁/少筋梁　low-reinforced beam
少筋微弯板/少筋微彎板　under reinforced slab with slightly curved bottom
少烟推进剂/少煙推進劑　reduced smoke propellant
蛇航制动/循環操舵停船法　rudder circling stop
蛇炮眼爆破/鑽內孔碎石法　snakeholing
蛇纹石棉/溫石棉,石棉絨　chrysotile asbestos
设备摆放区/設備配製區　equipment preparation area
设备报废/設備報廢　equipment scrapping
设备残值/設備殘值　remanent value of equipment
设备舱/裝備艙　equipment bay
设备层/設備層　mechanical floor
设备尺度/設備尺度　equipment scale
设备电缆/設備電纜　equipment cable
设备定期维护/設備定期維護　equipment periodic maintenance
设备封存/設備封存　equipment storing up
设备更新/設備更新　equipment replacement
设备购置费/設備費　equipment cost
设备故障/設備故障　breakdown of equipment
设备管理/設備管理　equipment management, facility management
设备机房/機房,機械室　machine room
设备基础/設備基礎　equipment foundation
设备基组/設備基組　foundation set
设备交接单/設備接收單　equipment receipt
设备耐冲击电压额定值/設備耐衝擊電壓額定值　rated impulse withstand voltage of equipment
设备配套/設備配套　coordinative composition of equipment
设备停用/設備停用　equipment out of use
设备状态参数/裝備狀態參數　equipment status parameter
设备总工程师/設備總工程師　chief mechanical and plumbing engineer
设备租赁费用/設備租金　equipment rental cost
设防烈度/設防烈度　fortification intensity
设计暴雨/設計暴雨　design storm
设计变更/設計改變　design change
设计标高/設計標高　design elevation
设计波/設計波　design wave
设计补偿/設計補償　design compensation
设计潮位/設計潮位　design tide level
设计车辆/設計車輛　design vehicle
设计车速/設計車速　design speed
设计吃水/設計吃水　designed draft
设计地震动参数/設計地震動參數　design parameter of ground motion, design ground motion parameter
设计点-非设计点/設計點-非設計點　design-offdesign points
设计方案审查/設計審查,設計審核　design review
设计分离面/設計分離面　initial breakdown interface
设计俯冲速度/設計俯衝速率　design diving speed
设计概算/設計概算,初步估算　approximate estimate of design, budgetary estimate of design
设计高程/設計標高　design elevation
设计高水位/設計高水位　design high water level
设计公司董事长/設計公司董事長　chairman of design corporation

设计规范/設計規範 design specification
设计航速/設計航速 design speed
设计洪水过程线/設計洪水過程線,設計洪水歷線 designed flood hydrograph, design flood hydrograph
设计洪水频率/設計洪水頻率 design flood frequency
设计基本地震加速度/設計基本地震加速度 design basic acceleration of ground motion
设计基准/設計基準,設計準則 design norm, design datum
设计基准期/設計基準期 design reference period
设计极限载荷/設計極限負載 design limit load
设计鉴定/設計評估,設計評價 certification of design, appraisal of design
设计交通量/設計交通量 design traffic volume
设计阶段/設計階段 design phase, design stage
设计竞赛/設計競賽 design competition
设计沥青含量/設計瀝青含量 design asphalt content
设计流量/設計流量 design flow, design discharge
设计流速/設計流速[度] design current velocity, design velocity of flow
设计轮压/設計輪重 design wheel load
设计挠度值/設計撓度值 design deflection value
设计年限/設計[使用]壽命 design life
设计排水量/設計排水量 designed displacement
设计评审/設計審核,設計審查 design review
设计剖面/設計剖面 design profile
设计洽商/設計洽商 design negotiation
设计前期/預設計 pre-design
设计强度/設計強度 design strength, design intensity
设计热负荷/設計供熱量 design heating load
设计人/設計師 designer
设计任务书/設計任務書 design assignment statement
设计[使用]年限/設計使用年限 design life, design working life
[设计]视点/設計觀點 design objective point
设计输出/設計輸出 design output
设计输入/設計輸入 design input
设计水量/設計水量 designed duty of water
设计水位/設計水位 design water level, design water stage
设计水线/設計水線 designed waterline
设计速度/設計速率 design speed
设计通行能力/設計容量 design capacity
设计纬度/設計緯度 designed latitude

设计系统/設計系統 design system
设计限值/設計限值 limiting design value
设计小时供热量/最大時供熱 maximum hourly heat supply
设计小时耗热量/設計小時耗熱量 maximum hourly heat consumption
设计小时交通量/設計小時交通量 design hourly traffic volume, design hourly volume, DHV
设计预算/詳細概算 detailed estimate
设计院院长/設計院院長 director of design institute
设计载荷/設計負載 design load
设计载荷试验/設計負載試驗 design load test
设计贮存期/設計貯藏時間 designed storage life
设计准则/設計準則 design criteria
设计资质/設計素質 design qualification
设计总负责人/設計總負責人 chief designer
设立国际油污损害赔偿基金国际公约/設立油汙損害國際賠償基金國際公約 International Convention on the Establishment of an International Fund for Compensation for Oil Pollution Damage
设施容量/設施容量 facility capacity
设施栽培/設施栽培 facility cultivation
设置条件/置位條件 set condition
社/社 community, she
社会车辆/社會車輛 social vehicle
社会城市/社會都市 social city
社会地理网络/社會地理網路 social geographical network
社会调查/社會調查 social survey
社会福利设施用地/社會福利設施用地 land for social welfare facility
社会福利用地/社會福利土地利用 social welfare land use
社会隔绝/社會隔離 social isolation
社会规划/社會規劃,社會計劃 social planning
社会规划者/社會規劃師 social planner
社会基础设施费用/社會資本支出 social overhead cost
社会结构/社會結構 social structure
社会距离/社會距離 social distance
社会空间混合/社會空間混合 social space mix
社会空间极化/社會空間極化 social spatial polarization
社会空间结构/社會空間結構 social space structure
社会流动/社會流動 social mobility
社会区分析/社會地域分析 social area analysis
社会生活噪声/社區噪音 community noise
社会投资/社會投資 social investment

社会形态学/社會形態學 social morphology
社会性别角色/社會性別角色 social gender role
社会需求评估/社會需求評估 social needs assessment
社会需要/社會需求 social need
社会影响评价/社會影響評價 social impact assessment
社会增加率/社會增加率 social increase rate
社稷坛/社稷壇 Altar of Land and Grain
社区/社區,社群 community
社区参与/社區參與 community participation
社区参与程度/社區參與程度 degree of community participation
社区发展/社區發展 community development
社区发展计划/社區發展計劃 community development plan
社区服务/社區服務,公共服務 community service
社区改良/社區改良 community improvement
社区更新/社區再生 community regeneration
社区公园/社區公園 community park
社区规划/社區規劃,居民區規劃 community planning
社区规划师/社區規劃師 community planner
社区[活动]中心/社區活動中心 community activity center, community recreation center
社区建设/社區營造 community construction
社区教育设施/社區教育設施 community educational facility
社区结构/社區結構 community structure
社区看护/社區保健 community care
社区设计/社區規劃,居民區規劃 community planning
社区设施/社區設施 community facility, community facilities
社区设施标准/社區設施標準 community facility standard
社区设施规划/社區設施規劃 community facility planning
社区设施计划/社區設施計劃 community facility plan
社区生活/共同[社會]生活 community life
社区卫生服务站/社區健康營造中心 community health center
社区卫生服务中心/社區健康營造中心 community health center
社区协商/社區協商,社區談判 community negotiation

社区行动/社區行動 community action
社区影响评价/社區影響評估 community impact evaluation
社区治理/社區治理 community governance
社区自主权强化/社區賦權,社區培力,社區增能 community empowerment
社区组织/社區組織 community organization
射程/射程 range
射程关机/射程關機 range cutoff
射灯/頂篷燈,聚光燈,探照燈 ceiling down light, spotlight
射电辐射/無線電輻射 radio emission
射电六分仪/無線電六分儀 radio sextant
射钉机/釘槍 nail gun, nailer
射击场/射擊場,靶場 shooting range, firing range
射击瞄准具/瞄準器 gunsight
射箭场/射箭場 archery field
射流/射流,噴射 jet
射流喷头/射流噴頭 fluidics sprinkler
射流通风/射流通風 longitudinal ventilation with jetblower
射流纵向通风/射流縱向通風 ventilation by force draft
射频/射頻,無線電頻率 radio frequency
射频干扰/無線電頻率干擾 radio frequency interference, radio interference
射频敏感器/射頻感應器 radio frequency sensor
射树灯/射樹燈 plant spot light
射水沉桩法/射水沈樁法 pile jetting method
射水抽水器/射水抽水器 water ejector
射水打桩机/沖水式打樁機 water jet pile driver
X射线/X射線 X-ray, X-radiation
X射线辐射/X射線輻射 X-ray radiation
X射线光刻/X射線刻板術 X-ray lithography
射线检测/放射線透過檢查,放射線檢驗 radiographic testing, RT
X射线检查/X射線檢查 X-ray examination
X射线结晶学/X光結晶學 X ray crystallography
射线探伤/放射線透過檢查,放射線檢驗 radiographic testing, RT
X射线探伤厂房/X射線偵測廠房 X-ray detection building
射线探伤室/射線探傷室 ray inspection machine room, ray flow detector room
X射线探伤仪/X射線探傷儀 X-ray detector
射线透照检查/放射線檢查 radiographic inspection
X射线照相检验/X射線照相檢驗 X-ray photo detection

射线照相探伤/放射線檢查　radiographic inspection
涉水池/涉水池　wading pool
涉水驾驶/涉水駕駛　fording drive
涉水踏步/涉水踏步　wading step
涉外区/涉外區　district for foreign mission
摄动/攝動,微擾　perturbation
摄动计算/微擾計算　perturbation calculation
摄氏零度等温线高度层/攝氏零度等溫線　0℃ isothermal level
摄影测量/[航空]攝影測量　photogrammetry
摄影测量坐标系/攝影測量坐標系　photogrammetric coordinate system
摄影分辨率/攝影解析度　photographic resolution
摄影机/攝影機　camera
摄影基线/攝影基線,主點基線　photographing base, photo-base
摄影鉴别率/攝影解析度　photographic resolution
摄影经纬仪/攝影經緯儀　phototheodolite
摄影面/攝影面　camera surface
摄影棚/照相部　photograph studio
摄影频率/攝影頻率　photographic frequency
摄影业务/攝影業務　photographing work
摄影影像/照片影像　photographic image
摄影轴/攝影軸　camera axis
摄影坐标系/攝影坐標系　photographic coordinate system
申报/申報,陳報　declaration
伸长率/百分伸長率　percentage elongation
伸出的支架/伸出的支架　outstanding leg
伸出式舞台/深展示舞臺,三面式舞臺　thrust stage
伸顶通气管/煙囪排煙道　stack vent
伸缩板/伸縮板　expansion plate
伸缩铲挖掘机/伸縮鏟挖掘機　telescopic boom excavator
伸缩缝/伸縮縫,脹縫　expansion joint
伸缩滚轴/伸脹滾子　expansion roller
伸缩接头/[套筒]伸縮接頭　dresser coupling, telescopic joint, expansion joint
伸缩裂缝/膨脹裂縫　expansion crack
伸缩器/補償器,調整器　compensator
伸缩区/伸縮區　breathing zone
伸缩式减摇鳍装置/伸縮式鰭板穩定器　retractable fin stabilizer
伸缩式凿岩机/頂鑽　stoper
伸缩台/伸縮臺　run-out extension
伸缩套管/套筒伸縮管　telescope pipe
伸缩运动/伸縮運動　fore and aft motion
伸张面积/伸展面積　expanded area

参宿七/參宿七　Rigel
参宿四(猎户α)/參宿四(獵戶α)　Betelgeuse
砷化镓太阳电池/砷化鎵太陽電池　gallium arsenide solar cell
深舱/深艙　deep tank
深舱肋骨/深肋骨　deep frame, deep tank frame
深层风化/深層風化　deep-seated weathering
深层搅拌桩/深層攪拌樁　deep mixed pile
深层流/深水流　deep current
深层压实/深震法　deep compaction
深成岩/深成岩　abyssal rock, deep-seated rock, plutonic rock
深度比/深度比　depth ratio
深度处理/高級處理　advanced treatment
深度记录器/測深計　depth recorder
深度净化处理/深度處理　advanced water treatment
深度-面积曲线/深度面積曲線　depth-area curve
深度千分尺/深度測微計　micrometer depth gage
深度指示器/深度指示表　depth indicator
深度自动操舵仪/深度自動操舵裝置　depth autopilot
深放电/深度放電　deep discharge
深海分区/深海分區　benthic division
深井水泵/深水泵,深井泵　deep well pump
深空/深太空　deep space
深空探测与跟踪系统/深空探測與追蹤系統　deep space detecting and tracking system
深空网/空間追蹤網　deep space network
深空遥测/深空間遙測　deep space telemetry
深孔爆破/深孔爆破　deep hole blasting
深冷处理/低溫處理　subzero treatment, cryogenic treatment
深梁/深梁　deep girder, deep beam
深埋隧道/深埋隧道,深挖隧道　deep buried tunnel, deep tunnel, deep-depth tunnel
深盆辐板/深盆形輪板　deep dish wheel plate
深潜救生艇/深潛救生艇,深潛救難艇　deep submergence rescue vehicle, deep submersible rescue vehicle, DSRV
深潜器/深潛器　bathyscaphe, deep diving submersible
深潜系统/深海潛水系統　deep diving system
深切河/下切河道　incised river
深熔焊/深透焊接　deep penetration welding
深熔焊条/熔渣鋜電銲條深入電極棒　deep penetration electrode
深水波/深水波　deep water wave
深水航路/深水航路　deep water way

深水码头/深水碼頭　deep water pier
深水抛锚/深海拋錨　deep sea anchoring
深水拖网/深水拖網　deep water trawl
深水坞/深水港池　deep water dock
深水炸弹/深水炸彈　depth charge
神道/神道　Shinto
神经机能测定/神經功能測定　nerve function measurement
审定人/校核者,核準者　approving authority
审核人/會計檢查官,查賬員　auditor
审听室/審查室　review room
审讯室/偵訊室　interrogation room
甚长波通信/甚長波通信　very long wave communication
甚低频通信/特低頻通信　VLF communication
甚高频紧急无线电示位标/特高頻應急指位無線電示標　VHF emergency position-indicating radiobeacon
甚高频全向信标/特高頻多向導航臺　VHF omnidirectional radio range
甚高频全向信标-测距器/特高頻全向信標測距設備　VHF omnidirectional radio range-distance measuring equipment
甚高频全向信标-战术空中导航系统/特高頻全向導航臺-戰術導航判讀系統,特高頻多向導航臺-戰術導航判讀系統　VHF omnidirectional radio range-tactical air navigation system, VORTAC
甚高频通信/特高頻通信　VHF communication
甚高频无线电测向仪/特高頻無線電測向儀　very high frequency radio direction finder, VHF RDF
甚高频无线电话设备/特高頻無線電話裝置　VHF radiotelephone installation
甚高频无线电设备/特高頻無線電裝置　VHF radio installation
渗出泉/濾泉　filtration spring
渗出压/擠水壓力　exudation pressure
渗氮/滲氮,氮化　nitriding, nitrogen case hardening
渗钒/滲釩　vanadizing
渗管/漏洩管　leaky pipe
渗灌/滲灌　infiltrating irrigation
渗井/滲流井　seepage well, leaching well
渗径/流徑　flow path
渗流/滲流　seepage flow, porous flow
渗流面/滲流面　seepage surface
渗流水/滲流水　seepage water
渗流压力/滲流壓力　seepage pressure
渗漏/滲漏,滲出,外滲　bleeding, exfiltration
渗漏试验/漏洩試驗　leakage test

渗漏水/滲漏水　fugitive water
渗漏系数/滲漏係數,漏水係數　leakage factor
渗漏蓄水层/滲漏含水層　leaky aquifer
渗滤坑/排水盲坑　soakaway
渗钼/滲鉬　molybdenumizing
渗铍/滲鈹　berylliumizing
渗渠/集水滲渠　infiltration gallery
渗入法/滲入法　infiltration method
渗入量/滲流入　influent seepage
渗入水/下滲水　infiltration water
渗水暗沟/暗溝,盲溝　blind drain
渗水井/透水井　filter well
渗水坑/排水盲坑　soakaway
渗水试验/現場滲透度試驗　in situ permeability test
渗水隧洞/滲水隧道　leak tunnel, permeable tunnel
渗水土路基/透水路堤　permeable soil subgrade, pervious embankment
渗水压/擠水壓力　exudation pressure
渗碳/滲碳[法]　carburization, carburizing, cementation
渗透管排放系统/滲透排水管網　infiltration drainage pipe system
渗透计/下滲計　infiltrometer
渗透检测/滲透檢測　penetrant testing, PT, penetrant flaw detection
渗透检查井/滲透檢查井　infiltration manhole
渗透力/滲透力,滲流力　osmotic force, seepage force
渗透率/滲透率,浸透性,浸水率　permeability, percolation rate
渗透破坏/滲透破壞　seepage failure
渗透弃流井/滲透棄流井　infiltration-removal well
渗透设施/浸滲設備　infiltration equipment
渗透试验/滲透試驗　permeability test
渗透试验仪/滲透試驗儀器　infiltration testing apparatus
渗透水/滲流水　seepage water
渗透探伤/滲透探傷,滲透檢測　penetrant flaw detection, penetrant testing, penetrant flaw detection
渗透系数/滲透係數　permeability coefficient
渗透雨水口/滲透雨水進入口斗　infiltration rainwater inlet
渗锌/滲鋅　sheradizing
升板/昇板　lift slab
升板结构/昇板結構　lift slab structure
升测/昇測　chaining uphill
升沉测量系统/浮沈測量系統　heaving measurement

system
升程/上昇行程　rise travel
升船机/昇船機,船舶昇降機　ship elevator, shiplift
升功率/升功率　volume power
升华[作用]/昇華　sublimation
升降带/起降地帶　take-off and landing strip
升降舵/昇降舵　elevator
升降舵固持/昇降舵操縱固定,昇降機操縱固定　elevator control fixed
升降舵松浮/昇降舵操縱自由　elevator control free
升降副翼/昇降舵補助翼　elevon
升降工作梯/昇降梯　elevating ladder
升降口/昇降口　companion way
升降门堰/昇降門堰　lift gate weir
升降平台/昇降[機平]臺,上昇平臺　lift platform, lifting table
升降桥/直昇橋　lift bridge, vertical lifting bridge
升降式舱盖/吊式艙蓋　lift hatch cover
升降式支承架/伸出式船臺　telescopic cradle
升降速度表/爬昇指示器　rate-of-climb indicator
升降台/昇降臺　lift
升降系统/頂舉系統　jacking system
升降装置/起重機　lifting gear
升交点赤经/昇交點黃經　right ascension of ascending node, longitude of ascending node
升力/昇力　lift force
升力发动机/昇力發動機　lift engine
升力风扇/墊昇風機　lift fan
升力干扰/昇力干擾　lift interference
升力面理论/昇力面理論　lifting surface theory, lift surface theory
升力曲线/昇力曲線　lift curve
升力式再入/昇力式再入　lift reentry
升力系数/昇力係數　lift coefficient
升力线理论/昇力線理論　lifting line theory, lift line theory
升力线斜率/昇力曲線斜率　slop of lift curve, slope of lift curve
升力阻尼/昇力阻尼　lift effect damping
升流式凝结/上向流混凝　upflow coagulation
升坡/上坡　up-grade
升启桥/上開橋　rolling bascule bridge
升水速率/昇水速率　rising rate
升限/昇限　ceiling
升压泵/增壓泵,加力泵　booster pump
升压器/增壓器,助力器　booster
升压伺服器/增壓伺服馬達　booster servomotor
升运式铲运机/昇運式鏟運機,昇降式刮土機　elevating scraper
升致波阻/昇力誘波阻力　wave drag due to lift
升致阻力/昇力誘發阻力　drag due to lift
升阻比/昇阻比　lift-drag ratio, lift to drag ratio
生产测试船/生產測試船　production test ship
生产储油船/生產儲油船　production storage tanker
生产的火灾危险性分类/生產的火災危險性分類　fire rating of produce
生产废水处理/工業廢水處理　industrial waste water treatment
生产工艺热负荷/處理熱負載　process heating load
生产过程运输/生產過程運輸　transport in production process
生产率测定/生產能力測定　productive capacity measurement
生产绿地/生產綠地　productive plantation area
生产污水/生產汙水　productive waste water
生产性保护/生產性保護　productive protection
生产许可/生產許可,生產容許　production permit
生产许可证/製造許可證　production certificate
生产用水/生產用水,工業用水　process water
生产周转期/產品週轉　production turnaround
生成设计/生成設計　generative design
生存空间/生活空間　living space
生存[能]力/存活性,存活率　survivability
生存训练/求生訓練　survival training
生地/生地　raw land
生废水/新汙水　fresh wastewater
生根剂/生根劑　rooting agent
生活出行/日常生活出行　daily life trip
生活废弃物/生活廢棄物,家庭廢棄物　domestic waste
生活废水/生活汙水,家庭廢水　domestic wastewater, sanitary wastewater
生活废水系统/生活廢水系統　domestic wastewater system
生活福利建筑/福利設施　welfare facility
生活给水系统/生活水系統　domestic water supply system
生活间/生活間　employee welfare facility
生活垃圾/生活廢棄物,家庭廢棄物　domestic waste
生活垃圾收集站/垃圾站　garbage station
生活排水/生活排水　sanitary waste, domestic drainage
生活排水系统/生活排水系統　domestic drainage system
生活热水热交换间/熱水供暖室　hot water heating room

生活污水/生活汙水,民生汙水,家庭汙水　domestic sewage, sewage, sanitary sewage
生活污水标准排放接头/穢水標準排洩接頭　sewage standard discharge connection
生活污水处理/生活汙水處理　domestic sewage treatment
生活污水处理装置/穢水處理裝置　sewage treatment plant, sewage treatment unit
生活污水管道/汙水管　sanitary sewer
生活污水柜/穢水櫃　sewage tank
生活污水排泄系统/穢水管路系統　sewage piping system
生活污水系统/生活汙水處理系統　domestic sewage system
生活污水贮存柜/生活汙水儲存櫃　sewage holding tank
生活型/生活型,生活形相　life form
生活饮用水/飲用水　drinking water, potable water
生活用水/生活用水　living water use, domestic water
生活用水量/家庭用水量　domestic consumption
生活用水系统/生活用水系統　domestic water system
生活杂用水/非飲用水　non-drinking water, non potable water
生景/生景　biological scenery
生境/生[活環]境　habitat
生境岛屿化/棲地島嶼　habitat islanding
生境多样性/棲所多樣性　habitat diversity
生境分离/生境隔離,棲所分隔　habitat segregation
生境管理区/生境管理區　habitat management area
生境片断化/棲地碎裂　habitat fragmentation
生境破碎[化]/棲地碎裂　habitat fragmentation
生境适宜度指数/棲地適宜性指數　habitat suitability index, HSI
生理干旱/生理乾旱　physiological drought, physiological aridity
生理机能测定/生理機能測定　physiological function measurement
生理耐受限值/心理容許限界　physiological tolerance limit
生理疲劳/生理疲勞　physiological fatigue
生理效应/生理效應　physiological effect
生理需要/生理需要,生理需求　physiological need
生命维持系统/維生系統　life support system
生命线工程/生命線工程　lifeline engineering
生命支持系统/生命支援系統　life support system
生命周期/生命週期,壽命週期　life cycle

生漆/中國漆　Chinese lacquer, raw lacquer
生起/生起　concave front façade profile, shengqi
生石灰/生石灰　quick lime
生态/生態學　ecology
生态安全格局/生態安全格局　ecological security pattern
生态保护/生態保育　ecological conservation
生态保护区/生態保護區　ecological reserve
生态补偿/生態補償　ecological compensation
生态补偿机制/生態補償機制　mechanism of ecological compensation
生态承载力/生態系統承載力　carrying capacity of human ecological system
生态城市/生態都市　eco-city
生态城市规划/生態都市規劃　eco-city planning
生态袋/生態袋　ecological bag
生态分布/生態分布　ecological distribution
生态风险评价/生態風險評估　ecological risk assessment
生态复合体/生態複合體　ecological complex
生态隔离带/生態隔離帶　ecological isolation belt
生态功能/生態功能　ecological function
生态功能区划/生態功能區劃　ecological function zoning
生态过渡带/生態過渡區,生態交會區　ecotone
生态环境/生態環境　ecology environment
生态缓冲区/生態緩衝區　ecological buffer area
生态恢复/生態恢復　ecological recovery
生态价值/生態值　ecological value
生态建筑/生態建築　ecological building, ecological architecture
生态交错带/植物群落交會地帶,兩種植物漸換地帶,兩群植物漸換地帶　ecotone
生态金字塔/生態金字塔,生態層塔　ecological pyramid
生态绝灭/生態絕滅　ecological extinction
生态可塑性/生態可塑性　ecological plasticity
生态廊道/生態廊道　ecological corridor
生态旅游/生態旅遊　ecotourism
生态敏感度分析/生態靈敏度分析　ecological sensitivity analysis
生态木/生態木　greener wood
生态平衡/生態平衡,生態均衡　ecological balance
生态圈/生態圈　ecosphere
生态适宜度/生態適宜性　ecological suitability degree
生态塘/生態塘　eco pond
生态条件/生態條件　ecological condition

生态退化/生态退化 ecological degeneration
生态危机/生态危機 ecological crisis
生态位/生態席位 niche
生态位重叠/生態席位重疊 niche overlap
生态位宽度/生態席位廣度 niche breadth, niche width
生态系统/生態系 ecosystem
生态系统承载力/生態系承載力 ecosystem carrying capacity
生态系统多样性/生態系多樣性 ecosystem diversity
生态系统服务功能/生態系服務 ecosystem service
生态系统服务价值/生態系統服務價值 value of ecosystem service
生态系统管理委员会/生態系統管理委員會 Commission on Ecosystem Management, CEM
生态系统健康评价/生態系統健康評價 ecosystem health evaluation
生态系统生态学/生態系生態學 ecosystem ecology
生态系统稳定性/生態系穩定性 ecosystem stability
生态效益/生態效益 ecological benefit
生态型/生態[類]型 ecotype
生态[型]护岸/生態護岸 ecological revetment, ecological embankment
生态修复/生態恢復,生態復育 ecological restoration
生态因子/生態因子 ecological factor
生态园林/生態園林 ecological landscape architecture
生态灾害/生態災害,生態災難 ecological disaster
生态足迹/生態足跡 ecological footprint
生铁/生鐵 pig iron
生土/生土,原土 raw soil
生土建筑/生土建築 earthen building
生土结构/生土建築 earth construction
生污泥/新汙泥 green sludge
生物舱/生物太空艙 biological module, biocapsule
生物处理/生物處理 biological treatment
生物带/生物[分布]帶 life zone
生物多样性/生物多樣性 biodiversity
生物多样性保护/生物多樣性保護 biological diversity protection
生物反馈/生物回饋 biofeedback
生物防治/生物防治 biological control
生物[防治]措施/生物防治措施 biological control measures
生物防治法/生物防治法 method of biological control
生物固沙/生物固砂 sand consolidation with biologic

生物节律/生物節律,生物週期 biorhythm, biological rhythm
生物景观类/生物園林型 biological landscape type
生物量/生物量 biomass
生物滤池/生物濾器,生物濾床 biological filter
生物膜法/生物膜法 biomembrane process
生物培养室/生物學實驗室 biological culture laboratory
生物气/生物氣 biogenic gas
生物区系/生物區,生物相 biota
生物圈/生物圈 biosphere, ecosphere
生物圈保护区/生物圈保護區 biosphere protection area
生物群落/生物群落,生物群集 biocoenosis, biocommunity
生物入侵/生物入侵 bioinvasion
生物生命保障系统/生物維生系統 biological life support system
生物声学/生物聲學 bioacoustics
生物实验室/生物實驗室 biology laboratory
生物塘/生物池塘 biolotical pond
生物卫星/生物衛星 biological satellite, biosatellite
生物修复/生物修復,生物復育 bioremediation
生物氧化塘/生物池塘 biolotical pond
生物遥测/生物遙測 biotelemetry
生物医学遥测/生醫遙測 biomedical telemetry
生物因子/生物因子 biotic factor
生物音/生物音 biological sound
生物制品厂/生物製品廠 biotechnology manufactory, bioengineering manufactory
生物质能/生質能[量] biomass energy
生物资源/生物資源 living resources
生效日/生效日 effective date
生育率/生育率 fertility rate
生长季/生長季 growing season
生长量/生長量 the growth
生长率/生長率,生長速度 growth rate
生长期/生長期 growth period, growing period
生长势/生長勢 growth potential
生长衰减期/生長衰減期 period of declining growth
生长习性/生長習性 growth habit
生长效率/生長效率 growth efficiency
生长型/生長型,生活型 growth form
生长锥/生長錐 increment borer
声爆/音爆 sonic boom
声标志/聲音標記 sound mark
声波/聲波,音波 acoustic wave, sound wave
声波试验/音波試驗 sonic test

声波探测/音波探测　sonic prospecting
声场/聲場,音場　sound field
声场不均匀度/聲分布　sound distribution
声道/聲道　sound channel
声发射测量系统/聲發射系統　acoustic emission system
声发射检测/聲波發射測試　acoustic emission testing, acoustic emission inspection
声反馈/聲反饋,聲回授　acoustic feedback
声反射系数/聲反射係數　sound reflection coefficient
声感式车辆检测器/音波感知器　sound-sensitive vehicle detector
声感式侦车器/感應式車輛偵音器　vehicle sound sensitive detector
声功率/聲功率　sound power
声功率级/聲功率位準　sound power level
声号通信/音響通信　sound signaling
声环境/聲[音]環境　sound environment, acoustic environment
声环境实验室/聲環境試驗艙　sound environment test chamber
声级/聲級,音級　sound level
声级计/聲級計,噪音計,音強度計　sound level meter
声景地图/音響風景　soundscape map
声景生态学/音景生態學　soundscape ecology
声聚焦/聲聚焦　sound focus
声力电话[机]/聲力電話　sound powered telephone
声码器/聲碼器　vocoder
声呐/聲納　sonar
声呐[导流]罩涂料/聲納罩塗料　sonar dome coating, sonar dome paint
声呐电缆绞车/聲納電纜絞車　sonar cable winch
声疲劳/噪音疲勞　acoustic fatigue
声疲劳试验/噪音疲勞試驗　acoustic fatigue test
声屏障/音障,噪音屏障,隔音牆　sound barrier, noise barrier
声屏障插入损失/噪音屏障介入損失　insertion loss of noise barrier
声腔/聲腔　acoustic cavity
声强/聲強,聲音強度　sound intensity
声强级/聲強位準,音強位準　sound intensity level
声桥/聲橋　sound bridge
声生态学/聲生態學　acoustic ecology
声舒适度/聽覺舒適[度]　acoustic comfort
声速/聲速,音速　speed of sound, sonic speed
声速校准/音速校準　sound velocity calibration
声速误差/音速誤差　sound velocity error
声透射系数/聲透射係數　sound transmission coefficient
声线/聲[射]線　sound ray
声线跟踪法/聲線軌跡法　sound ray tracing method
声响信号/音響信號,聽覺信號　audible signal, sound signal
声信号/音響號誌　acoustic signal
声学/聲學　acoustics
声学比/聲強比,聲波比　acoustic ratio
声学测量/聲學量測　acoustic measurement
声学空间/聲學空間　acoustic space
声学设计/聲學設計,聲學計算　acoustic design
声学实验室/聲學實驗室　acoustics laboratory
声学探测/音響測距法　acoustic surveying
声压/聲壓,音壓　sound pressure
声压级/聲壓位準,聲壓度　sound pressure level
声压级差/聲壓位準差　sound pressure level difference
声掩蔽/聲掩蔽　sound masking
声音标记/音標　soundmark
声音景观/音景　sound scape
声音漫步/音景漫步　sound walk
声音事件/音源　sound event
声音形态学/聲音形態學　sound morphology
声音意像/音像,聲像　sound image
声引信/聲引信　acoustic fuze
声影区/聲影區　sound shadow region
声源/聲源,音源　sound source
声源功率/聲源功率　power of sound source
声闸/聲鎖　sound lock
声障/音障　sonic barrier
声罩/聲罩　acoustical shell
声振环境/聲振環境　vibroacoustic environment
声阻抗/聲阻抗　acoustic impedance
牲畜家禽挂车/運畜拖車　livestock trailer
牲畜运输船/牲口運輸船　livestock carrier
牲口箱/牲口櫃　cattle container
绳/繩,纜,索　rope
绳车/卷盤　reel
绳的弯曲部/繩[索]套,回頭索　bight
绳度整正曲线计算器/繩度整正曲線計算器　string lining computer, string-line calculator
绳结/繩結　bends and hitches
绳扣/繩[索]套,吊索,吊鏈　sling, bight
绳路/繩路,塞繩電路　cord circuit
绳栓/繩鉤　rope lug
绳索/繩索　cordage
绳梯/繩梯,軟梯　rope ladder
绳头插接/反插接　backsplice

绳头结/倒纽結　crown knot
绳头卸扣/鋼絲索扣　bulldog grip
绳系卫星/繫繩衛星　tethered satellite
绳系卫星动力学/繫繩衛星動力學　tethered satellite dynamics
绳正法整正曲线/繩正法整正曲線　string lining of curve
绳锥结/椎套結　marline spike hitch
省道/省道,省幹線公路　provincial trunk highway
省干线公路/省幹線公路,省道　provincial trunk highway
省级风景名胜区/省風景名勝區　provincial landscape and famous scenery
省煤器/省煤器,省熱器　economizer
省水船闸/省水閘　water saving lock, thrift lock
圣奥古斯丁考古公园/聖阿古斯丁考古公園　San Agustin Archaeological Park
圣城卡拉尔-苏培/卡羅爾-蘇沛聖城　Sacred City of Caral-Supe
圣何塞广场公园/聖何塞廣場公園　San Jose Plaza Park
圣·克里斯多巴尔住宅庭院/[墨西哥]聖克里斯托巴爾　San Cristobal
圣路易斯历史中心/聖路易斯歷史中心　Historic Center of Sao Luís
圣莫尼卡学派/聖莫尼卡學派　Los Angeles avant-garde, Santa Monica School
圣维南原理/聖凡南原理　Saint-Venant principle
盛行风/盛行風　prevailing wind
剩磁/剩磁　residual magnetism
剩磁矩/剩餘磁矩　residual magnetic moment
剩磁偶极子/殘餘磁偶　residual magnetic dipole
剩余动稳性/剩餘動穩度　residual dynamical stability
剩余功率/剩餘電力,過剩電力　surplus power
剩余核辐射/剩餘核輻射　residual nuclear radiation
剩余降水/降水剩餘,超降水　excess precipitation
剩余视差/殘存縱視差　residual parallax
剩余寿命/殘餘壽命　residual life
剩余水压/餘水壓　residual water pressure
剩余污泥/剩餘汙泥,過剩[活性]汙泥　excess activated sludge, excess sludge, surplus sludge
剩余液位/剩餘液位　residual liquid level
剩余自差/剩餘自差　remaining deviation
剩余阻力/剩餘阻力　residuary resistance, residual resistance
失火警报/火警警報　fire alarm
失火自动报警系统/自動火警警報系統　automatic fire alarm system
失火自动报警与探测系统/自動火警警報與探火系統　automatic fire alarm and fire detection system
失机概率/失機概率　miss launch opportunity probability
失控/失控　out of control
失控船/操縱失靈船　vessel not under command
失控灯/[船]操縱失靈號燈　not under command light
失落的世界建筑群/失落的世界建築群　lost world complex
失去联锁/失去聯鎖　loss of interlocking
失事船舶/遭難船,破船　wrecked ship
失水率/水分散失速率　rate of water loss
失水事故/冷卻水損失事故　loss of coolant accident
失速/失速　speed loss, stall
失速颤振/失速顫振　stall flutter
失速攻角/失速角　stall angle
失速警告/失速警示　stall warning
失速警告系统/失速警示系統　stall warning system
失速偏离/失速離場　stall departure
失速速度/失速速率　stall speed
失速迎角/失速攻角　stall angle of attack
失调/失調,失配,不適應　maladjustment
失吸现象/失吸現象　suction loss
失效/失效,故障　failure
失效报告、分析与纠正措施系统/失效報告、分析與改正行動系統　failure reporting, analysis and corrective action system, FRACAS
失效分析/失效分析,故障分析　failure analysis
失效概率/失效概率　probability of failure
失效机理/失效機構　failure mechanism
失效率/失效率　failure rate
失效模式/失效模式,故障模式　failure mode
失效模式、效应及后果分析/故障模式及影響分析　failure mode and effect analysis, FMEA, failure mode effect and criticality analysis
失效模式、影响与危害度分析/失效模式效應及重要性分析　failure mode, effect and criticality analysis, FMECA
失效模式与影响分析/失效模式及效應分析　failure mode and effect analysis, FMEA
失效日/失效日,期滿日　expiry date
失效影响/故障效應　failure effect
失重/失重　weightlessness
失重对抗措施/失重防範措施　weightlessness countermeasures
失重仿真/失重模擬　weightlessness simulation

失重仿真试验/失重模擬試驗　weightlessness simulation test
失重生理效应/失重生理效應　weightlessness physiological effect
失重试验飞机/抛物線飛行試驗飛機　parabolic flight test aircraft
诗条石/詩條石　poem-engraved stone slab
施放烟幕机动/施放煙幕操縱　smoke screen laying maneuvre
施肥/施肥　fertilization
施肥量/施用量，散布量　application rate
施肥喷灌器/施肥噴灌器　combined feeder and sprinkler
施工/工程執行　execution of work
施工便桥/施工[臨時]便橋　temporary bridge for construction, service bridge
施工步道/檢修通道，貓道，窄道　catwalk
施工测量/施工測量　construction survey, construction surveying
施工产值/施工產值　construction output value
施工场地布置/施工總布置圖　layout of construction site
施工调查/施工勘察　construction investigation
施工方案/施工方案　arrangement and method for construction, statement of arrangement and method for construction
施工防护/施工防護　construction protection
施工防护无线电通信/施工防護無線電通訊　radio communication for protection of construction
施工妨碍/施工妨礙　construction interference
施工废弃物/建造廢物，建築廢料，建築剩餘　construction waste
施工封闭线路/施工封閉線路　line occupation for works
施工复测/施工複測　construction repetition, repetive survey, construction repetition survey
施工工艺流程/施工過程　construction technology process, construction process
施工管理/施工管理　construction management
施工规范/施工規範　construction specification
施工合同条款/工程合約條款，承攬書條款　construction contract term
施工荷载/施工荷載　construction load, constructional loading, site load
施工机械利用率/營造機械利用率　utilization ratio of construction machinery
施工机械排放物/施工機械排放物[量]　construction machine emission
施工机械完好率/營造機械完好率　ratio of construction machinery in good condition
施工机械噪声/施工機械噪音，施工機械雜訊　construction machinery noise
施工机械振动/施工機械振動　construction machinery vibration
施工计划/施工計劃　construction plan
施工计划管理/施工計劃管理　planned management of construction
施工进度管理/施工項目時間管理　construction project time management
施工进度计划/進度時間表，進度規劃圖表　programme, progress plan, progress schedule
施工决算/最終結算　final settlement, final account
施工控制网/施工控制網　construction control network
施工利润/施工利潤　construction profit
施工路段交通管理/施工段交通管理　construction section traffic management
施工区通行能力/施工區通行能力　construction section capacity
施工日志/工程日誌　engineering construction log
施工设备/施工設備　construction equipment
施工水位/施工水位，工作水位　construction water level, construction level, working water level
施工索/鋼索架設法　cable erection
施工通风/施工通風　construction ventilation
施工图/施工圖，工作圖　working drawing, working diagram
施工图设计/施工圖設計　construction drawing design, construction detail design, working drawing design
施工图设计交底/施工圖設計交底　hand over of working drawing
施工图审查/施工圖審查　working drawing review
施工图实习/工作實踐演練　working drawing practice
施工图预算/施工圖預算　construction drawing budget, working drawings based estimate, budget of construction drawing project
施工现场/工地　job site
施工现场管理/施工現場管理　construction site management
施工项目管理/施工項目管理　construction project management
施工形象进度/施工形象進度　construction figure progress, figurative progress of construction work
施工许可/施工許可　working license for

construction
施工验收/施工驗收　delivery-receiving acceptance
施工预算/建築預算　construction budget
施工准备/施工準備　construction preparation
施工总工期/施工總時間　total time of construction, total construction time
施工组织方案/施工組織方案　construction scheme
施工组织设计/施工組織設計　preparation of construction plan
施工坐标系/施工坐標系　construction coordinate system
施救浮索/營救浮環　buoyant rescue quoit
施特鲁哈尔数/史屈霍數　Strouhal number
湿拌砂浆/濕拌砂漿　wet-mixed mortar
湿材/未乾燥木材　unseasoned timber
湿舱/濕艙　wet chamber
湿底润滑/濕油槽潤滑　wet sump lubrication
湿地/濕地　wetland
湿地公园/濕地公園　wetland park
湿地生态学/濕地生態學　wetland ecology
湿地推土机/沼澤地堆土機　swamp bulldozer
湿度/濕度,濕性　humidity, wetness
湿度表/濕度表　hygrometer
湿度计/濕度計　hygrograph
湿度控制/濕度控制　humidity control
湿度密度关系/濕度密度關係　moisture-density relationship
湿法/濕法　wet process
湿法缠绕/濕式纏繞　wet winding
湿法烟气脱硫/濕法煙氣脱硫　wet process of flue gas desulfurization
湿法养生/潤濕處理　moist curing
湿化试验/濕化試驗　slaking test
湿接头/濕接頭　wet joint
湿井/濕井　wet well
湿空气/濕空氣　damp air
湿连接/濕接　wet connection
湿密重/濕密度　wet unit weight
湿面积/浸水面　wetted surface
湿喷混凝土/濕噴混凝土　wet shotcreting
湿喷混凝土机/濕噴混凝土機　wet shotcreting machine
湿喷砂除锈/濕噴砂[除鏽],濕噴砂法　wet sand blasting
湿碰湿/濕式積層　wet on wet
湿气/濕氣　wet
湿球黑体温度指数/綜合溫度熱指數　wet bulb globe temperature index

湿球温差/濕球溫差　approach
湿球温度/濕球溫度　wet bulb temperature
湿球温度计/濕球溫度計　wet bulb thermometer
湿热灭菌器/濕熱滅菌器　moist heat sterilizer
湿热气候/濕熱氣候　wet hot climate
湿热试验/濕熱測試　humidity-heat test
湿热效应/熱液效應　hydrothermal effect
湿容重/濕密度　wet unit weight
湿润剂/防濕劑　wetting agent
湿森林/濕潤林　moist forest
湿生树种/濕生樹種　hygrophilous tree species
湿生植物/濕生植物　hygrophyte
湿绳校正/濕垂線校正　wet line correction
湿式除尘器/濕式除塵器,濕式收塵器　wet dust collector, wet separator, wet dust scrubber
湿式缸套/濕式缸襯[套]　wet cylinder liner
湿式潜水器/濕式潛水器　wet submersible
湿式燃烧法/濕燃法　wet combustion
湿式筛分/濕式篩分　wet screening
湿式水表/濕式水表　wettype water meter
湿式氧化法/濕式氧化法　wet oxidation process
湿式凿岩/濕式鑿岩　wet boring for rock, wet drilling for rock
湿式凿岩机/濕鑽　wet drill
湿式自动喷水灭火系统/濕式噴水系統　wet pipe sprinkler system
湿试样/濕試樣　wet sample
湿损事故/濕損事故　wet damage accident
湿态强度/濕態強度　wet strength
湿污泥/濕汙泥　wet sludge
湿陷性[黄]土/濕陷性[黄]土　collapsed loess, collapsible soil
湿养护/濕養護,濕治　wet curing
湿周/濕周　wetted perimeter
十倍频程/十進位　decade
十进制时间码/BCD 時間碼　binary coded decimal time code, BCD time code
十六烷值/十六烷值　cetane number
十字板剪力仪/十字板剪刀儀　vane shear apparatus
十字板剪切试验/十字板切試驗,十字片鑽剪力試驗　vane test, vane shear test
十字[带]缆桩/十字形繫樁　cross bitt
十字横丝/十字横線　horizontal hair
十字脊屋顶/十字脊屋頂　cross ridge roof
十字架二(南十字α)/十字架二(南十字α)　Acrux
十字交叉/四路交叉　four-way intersection
十字接头/十字接頭　cross joint, cross shaped joint
十字节点板/十字形角牽板　cruciform gusset plate

十字路口/十字路口　cross intersection, cross road
十字木/橫擔木　cross timber
十字片钻/十字片鑽　vane auger
十字头/十字頭　crosshead
十字头扁销/十字頭鍵　crosshead key
十字头滑块/十字頭履　crosshead slipper, crosshead shoe
十字头式柴油机/十字頭型柴油機　crosshead type diesel engine
十字头圆销/十字頭銷　crosshead pin
十字形/十字形　cross
十字形交叉/十字形交叉　cross road
十字形枢纽/十字形樞紐　cross-type junction terminal
十字轴/十字軸,橫軸　cross axis
十字准线/十字線,交叉線　cross wires
石岸/石岸　rock bank
石板/小方塊石　sett
石板桥/石板橋　stone slab bridge
石板瓦/瓦板岩　roofing slate, stone slate
石碑/石碑　stone tablet, stele, stone monument
石标/石標　stone marker
石材防护剂/石材防護劑　stone protectant
石材幕墙/石材幕牆　natural stone curtain wall
石材硬度/石材硬度　hardness of stone
石场弃渣/採石場廢料　quarry waste
石灯笼/石燈籠　stone lantern
石凳/石凳　stone bench
石堤/石堤　stone levee, stone dyke
石洞/石洞,石窟　stone cavern, stone cave
石方爆破/岩礁爆破　rock blasting
石舫/石舫,船庫,艇庫　stone boat, boat house
石膏/石膏　gypsum
石膏基自流平材料/石膏基自動水平材料　gypsum based self-leveling materials
石膏空心条板/石膏空心條板　gypsum panel with cavity
石膏砌块/石膏塊　gypsum block
石膏室/石膏室　plaster room
石工/石工　stoneman
石拱/石拱　stone arch
石花台/石花臺　stone flower bed
石灰/石灰　lime
石灰粉/石灰粉　lime powder
石灰粉煤灰砂砾基层/石灰粉煤灰砂礫石基層　lime flyash sand gravel base course, lime flyash sand gravel base
石灰粉煤灰碎石基层/石灰粉煤灰碎石基層　lime flyash crushed stone base course, lime flyash crushed stone base
石灰粉煤灰土基层/石灰粉煤灰土基層　lime flyash soil base
石灰膏/石灰膏　lime putty, lime paste
石灰含量测定法/石灰含量測定法　method for determining the lime content
石灰火山灰水泥/石灰火山灰水泥　lime pozzolana cement
石灰砂浆/石灰砂漿　lime mortar
石灰砂桩/石灰砂樁　lime sand pile
石灰石/石灰石,[石]灰岩　limestone
石灰刷白/石灰粉刷　lime wash
石灰土基层/灰土基層　lime soil base, lime soil base course
石灰稳定底层/石灰穩定底層　lime stabilized base
石灰性土/石灰土　calcareous soil
石灰岩/[石]灰岩,石灰石　limestone
石灰桩/石灰堆　lime pile
石矶/石磯　rocky ledge
石匠/石工　stoneman
石窟/石窟,岩洞　grotto, shiku
石块铺路面/石塊鋪面　stone block paving
石砾/石礫,礫石　gravel
石砾海滩/石礫海灘　pebble beach
石料分级/石料分級　stone classification
石料裹覆试验/石料蓋覆試驗　stone coating test
石料加速磨光仪/石料加速磨光儀　accelerated stone polishing tester
石料路面/石道　stone pavement
石料磨光值/石料磨光值　polished stone value, polished value
石料磨光值试验/石料磨光值試驗　polished stone value test
石料摊铺机/石料攤鋪機　aggregate paver
石料统一法/石料統一法　method of unifying the rock materials
石榴木/石榴木　pomegranate wood
石笼/石籠,蛇籠　gabion
石米/石米　granolithic
石棉/石棉　asbestos
石棉板/石棉板　asbestos board
石棉管/石棉管　asbestos pipe
石棉灰/石棉灰　asbestos ash
石棉绳/石棉繩　asbestos cord, asbestos rope
石棉水泥瓦/石棉水泥瓦,石棉浪瓦　asbestos cement tile, asbestos cement sheet
石棉瓦/石棉瓦　asbestos tile

石棉衣/石棉衣　asbestos clothing
石棉纸/石棉紙　asbestos paper
石墨/石墨　graphite
石墨电阻加热器/石墨電阻加熱器　graphite resistance heater
石墨防热材料/石墨熱防護材料　thermal protection graphite material
石墨化/石墨化　graphitization
石墨铝复合材料/石墨鋁複合材料　aluminum graphite composite
石墨密封环/石墨封環　graphite-seal ring
石漆/石漆　mineral varnish
石砌护坡/鋪石　stone pitching
石砌体/石砌體　stone masonry
石砌体结构/石結構　stone masonry structure
石桥/石橋　stone bridge
石生植物/岩生植物　lithophyte, rock plant
石水钵/石水鉢　stone water bowl
石笋/石筍　stalagmite
石亭/石亭　stone pavilion
[石]象生/[石]象生　stone tomb statuary
石屑/石片,碎屑　chip
石屑撒布机/屑片撒布機　chip spreader
石英摆式加速度计/石英擺式加速度儀　quartz pendulous accelerometer
石英玻璃/石英玻璃,矽玻璃　quartz glass, vitreous silica
石英陶瓷/石英陶瓷　quartz-ceramics
石英压力传感器/石英壓力測感器　quartz pressure sensor
石油/石油　petroleum
石油伴生气/伴產氣　associated gas
石油沥青/石油瀝青,石油柏油　petroleum asphalt, asphalt, petroleum bitumen
石质基础/石質基礎　soling
石作/石作　stone work, masonry
时变变形/時間相關的變形　time-dependent deformation
时变化系数/[小]時變化係數　per hour change coefficient, hourly variation coefficient, hourly variation factor
时标/定時記號　timing mark
时不变性/時間不變性　time invariance
时程分析法/時程分析法,歷時法　time history method, time history analysis method
时分多路传输遥测系统/分時多址遙測系統　time division multiplex telemetry system
时分多路电报设备/分時多工電報設備　time division multiplex telegraph equipment
时分复用/分時多工,時域多工　time division multiplexing, time division multiplex, TDM
时分制多路遥测/分時多工遙測　time division multiplexing telemetry
时号/對時信號,報時信號　time signal
时基/時基　time base
时基[信号]发生器/時基[信號]發生器　time base generator
GPS 时间/GPS 時間　GPS time
时间表/時量計　hour meter
时[间]差/時差　time difference, equation of time
时间程序指令/時間程式指令　time-program command
时间尺度/時間尺度　temporal scale
时间带宽[乘]积/時間帶寬積,時間-頻寬乘積　time-bandwidth product
时间-断面积图/時間-面積圖　time-area diagram
时间对数拟合法/對數時間法　logarithm of time fitting method, logarithm of time method
时间分辨率/時間解析度　time resolution
时间分隔/時間分割　time division
时间分隔制/分時制　time division system
时间格局/時間模式　temporal pattern
时间固结曲线/時間壓密曲線　time consolidation curve
时间关机/關機時間,停機時間　time shutdown
时间基准系统/計時參考系統　time reference system
时间计/時量計　hour meter
时间继电器/時間繼電器,延時繼電器,定時繼電器　time-delay relay, time relay
时间间隔/時間延遲,時滯　time lag
时间间隔法/時間間隔平均法,隔時法　time interval method
时间校正/時間校正　time calibration
时间结构/時間結構　temporal structure
时间进度表/進度表　time schedule
时间历程/時間歷史　time history
时间历程复现/時間歷史重複　time history duplication
时间流量曲线/時間流量曲線　time-discharge curve
时间面积集流图/時間-面積-集流圖　time-area-concentration diagram
时间-面积值/時面值　time-area value
时间频率测量/時間頻率量測　time and frequency measurement
时间平方根拟合法/時間方根調整法　square root of

time fitting method
时间平均速度/時間平均速率 time mean speed
时间水位曲线/時間水位曲線 time stage curve
时间统一系统/計時系統 timing system
时间相关法/時間相關法 time-dependent method
时间修正/時間修正 time correction
时间序列/時間序列,時間級數 time series
时间选择/時間選擇 time selection
时间延迟积分器件/時間延遲積分設備 time-delay integration device, TDI device
时间引信/定時引信 time fuze
时间占有率/時間佔有率 time occupancy ratio
时角/時角 hour angle, HA
时距曲线/時間距離曲線 time distance curve
时空格局/時空格局 spatial and temporal pattern
时空结构/時空結構 temporal-spatial structure
时频调制/時間頻率調變 time frequency modulation
时频相调制/時間頻率相位調變 time frequency phase modulation
时区号/時區標號 zone description, ZD
时区图/時區圖 time zone chart
时圈/時圈 hour circle
时统分站/時統分站 timing substation
时统设备/計時設備 timing equipment
时统信号控制台/計時信號控制面板 timing signal control panel
时统中心站/時統中心站 center timing station
时隙/時槽 time slot
时限继电器/緩動繼電器 time-lag relay
时效[处理]/時效處理,加齡,歷時硬化 aging, time limitation, time effect treatment
时效裂纹/時效裂紋 aging crack
时效硬化/時效硬化 age hardening
时序/時序,時間順序 time sequence
时延修正/時間延遲校正 time-delay correction
时域/時域 time domain
时滞/時滯,時延 time lag, time delay
时钟花坛/時鐘花壇 flower clock
识别/識別 identify, ID
识别板/銘牌 name plate
识别器/識別器 identifier
识别数据/識別數據 identification data
识别信号/識別信號 identity signal
识别字副帧同步/識別字副幀同步 identification subframe synchronization, ID subframe synchronization
实测弹道/測定彈道 measured trajectory
实测图/實測圖 measured drawing, surveyed map

实尺放样/實尺放樣 full scale lofting
实地调查/野外調查 field investigation
实腹拱/實腹拱,填腔拱 spandrel-filled arch, solid spandrel arch
实腹拱桥/實腹拱橋,實心拱橋 spandrel-filled arch bridge, solid arch bridge
实腹式柱/實腹式柱 solid webbed column
实际曝光时间/實際曝光時間 real exposure time
实际承运人/實際運送人 actual carrier
实际航迹向/實際航跡方向 actual track
实际航速/對地速度 speed over ground
实际交通容量/實際交通容量 practical capacity
实际排水量/實際排水量 actual displacement
实际全损/實際全損 actual total loss
实际通行能力/實際交通容量 practical capacity
实际循环/實際循環 actual cycle, non-ideal cycle
实肩拱/實腹拱,填腔拱 spandrel-filled arch, solid spandrel arch
实践/實務 practice
实况记录/檔記錄 document recording
实况记录系统/即時記錄系統 live recording system
实肋板/實體肋板 solid floor
实木地板/實木地板 solid wood flooring, solid flooring
实木复合地板/嵌木地板,嵌木細工 parquet, wood composite floor
实木家具/木製家具 wooden furniture
实生苗/苗木,[種子]苗 seedling
实生选种/籽苗選擇 seedling selection breeding
实施/實施執行 implementation
实施规划/實施規劃 implementary plan
实施计划/實施計劃 action plan
实施型城市设计/建設性都市設計 implementation oriented urban design
实施性施工组织设计/實施性施工組織設計 design for practical construction organization, practical design for construction scheme, operative construction organization design
实时操作软件/即時操作軟體 real-time operation software
实时测量/即時測量 real-time measurement
实时处理计算机/即時處理計算機 real-time processing computer
实时处理精度/即時處理精度 real-time processing accuracy
实时打印/即時列印 real-time print
实时弹道计算/即時彈道計算 real-time ballistic calculation

实时弹道相机/即時彈道攝影機　real-time ballistic camera
实时方式/實時模式　real-time mode
实时仿真/即時模擬　real-time simulation
实时分析/即時分析　real-time analysis
实时记录/即時記錄　real-time recording
实时交通控制/實時行車調度　real-time traffic control
实时留迹记录/即時軌跡記錄　real-time track recording
实时落点计算/即時落點計算　real-time impact calculation
实时输出/即時輸出　real-time output
实时数据处理/即時資料處理　real-time data processing
实时通信管理程序/即時通信管理程式　real-time communication management program
实时网络管理程序/即時網路管理程式　real-time network management program
实时系统软件/即時系統軟體　real-time system software
实时显示/即時顯示　real-time display
实时遥测/即時遙測　real-time telemetry
实时应用软件/即時應用軟體　real-time application software
实时指令/即時指令　real-time command
实时智能管理系统/即時智能管理系統　real-time intelligent patch cord management system
实体/實體　entity
实体安全/實體安全性　physical security
实体防范/實體防護，實體保護　physical protection
实体规划/實質規劃　physical planning
实体积比率/實積[百分]率　solid volume percentage
实体结构/實體結構　solid structure
实体模型/實體模型　solid model
实体墙/剛性側壁，實心壁　solid wall
实体[桥]墩/實體橋墩　solid pier
实体式码头/實體碼頭　solid wharf
实体违法/實體違法　breach of physical law
实物分隔带/實體分離器　physical separator
实物计划/實質計劃　physical plan
实物量具/實物量具　material measure
实习船/訓練船　training vessel, training ship
实习生/實習生，學徒　apprentice
实线/實線　full line
实线用户/實線用戶　real line subscriber
实效伴流/有效跡流　effective wake
实效重量/虛質量　virtual mass

实心板/實心板　solid slab
实心腹板/實體腹板　solid web
实心护木/實心護木　solid fender
实心轴/實心軸　solid shaft
实心砖/實心磚　solid brick
实芯绝缘电缆/實芯絕緣電纜　solid dielectric cables
实训楼/職業培訓室，專業訓練室　professional training workshop
实验标准偏差/實驗標準離差　experimental standard deviation
实验储存室/[物品]儲藏室　storage room
实验剧院/實驗劇場　experimental theater
实验空气动力学/實驗空氣動力學　experimental aerodynamics
实验力学/實驗力學　experimental mechanics
实验流域/實驗流域　experimental basin
实验室/實驗室　laboratory
实验室化验报告/實驗室分析報告　laboratory analysis report
实验室模拟试验/實驗室模擬試驗　laboratory simulation test
实验填土/實驗填土　experimental banking
实验修正法/實驗校正法　experiment correction method
实用荷载/使用載重　service load
实用类飞机/實用類飛機　airplane in utility category
实战程序/作戰程式　operational program
实制动距离/實制動距離　actual stopping distance
实制动时间/實制動時間　actual braking time, instantaneous application time, IAT
实轴/實軸　solid axis
实作训练/實作訓練　practice training
拾震器/地聲檢知器　geophone
食虫植物/食蟲植物　insectivorous plant
食品残渣收集器/食品殘渣收集器　foods debris taper
食品厂/食品製造廠　food product factory
食品店/[食品]雜貨店　grocery store
食品加热装置/食物加熱設備　foods heat unit
食堂/小餐廳，自助餐廳　canteen, cafeteria
食梯/送菜昇降機　dumbwaiter
食物垃圾/食物廢棄物　food wastes
食物链/食物鏈　food chain
食物网/食物網　food web
食物诱杀/食物誘殺　food bait
食叶[性]害虫/食葉[性]害蟲　leaf-feeding insect, defoliator
食用菌房建筑/食用菌建築　edible fungus building

食用植物/食用植物 food plant
蚀耗极限/蝕耗極限 corroded limit
炻瓷砖/炻瓷磚 stoneware porcelain tile
炻质砖/炻質磚 stoneware tile
史迹保护区/紀念物保護區 historic preservation district
史密斯效应/史密斯效應 Smith effect
史前建筑/史前時代建築 pre-historic architecture
矢高/拱高 rise of arch
矢跨比/矢跨比 rise span ratio
矢量/矢[量],向量 vector
矢量场/向量場 vector field
矢量图/向量圖 arrow diagram
矢量显示/向量顯示 vector display
使船停住/拋錨停航 bring to
使馆/大使館 embassy
使神号机械臂/賀密士機器手臂 Hermes robot arm, HERA
使用荷载/使用載重 service load
使用后评价/用後評估 post occupancy evaluation
使用环境谱/使用環境譜 service environment spectrum
使用检查/營運檢驗 service inspection
使用可用性/操作有效度 operational availability
使用率/使用強度 use intensity
使用面积/使用面積 net floor area, usable area
使用前大纲/使用前計劃 prior-to-service program
使用权混合/使用權混合 mixed right of use
使用试飞/使用試飛 operational flight test
使用试验/運用試驗,運作試驗,實用試驗 service test
使用寿命/使用壽命,有效壽命,使用期限 useful life, service life
使用限度/操作限制 operation limit
使用一种燃油船舶/使用一種燃油船 one-fuel ship
使用重量测定/任務重量測定 operating weight measurement
使用周期/操作週期 operating cycle
使用状态挠度限值/使用狀態撓度限值 deflection limit for serviceability
使用准备完好率/操作備用度 operational readiness
始发港/始航港 port of origin, port of sailing
始发者/創始者 originator
始发直达列车/[鐵道]始發直達列車 through train originated from one-loading point
始航向/起程航向 initial course
驶出/駛出 put out
驶出路外事故/掉線事故 run-off road accident

驶出匝道/出口坡道 exit ramp
驶帆船/揚帆行駛之船舶 vessel under sail
驶风/小艇駛帆 boat sailing
驶离/駛離 put away
驶入匝道/入口坡道 entrance ramp
驶向海岸/駛向海岸 stand into land
示差扫描量热仪/示差掃描熱量分析儀 differential scanning calorimeter
示功阀/指示閥 indicator valve, indicator cock
示功图/示功圖 indicator diagram
P-V 示功图/P-V 示功圖 P-V indicated diagram
P-Φ 示功图/P-Φ 示功圖 P-Φ indicated diagram
示功图丰满系数/示功圖豐滿係數 fullness coefficient of indicator diagram
示教编程/示教程式設計 teach programming
示教盒/示教盒 teach pendant
示教再现机器人/重現型機器人 playback robot
示警柱/交道警告標誌 warning post
示位标/示位標 position indicating mark
示温涂料/熱感應漆 temperature sensitive paint
[示值]误差/[示值]誤差 error of indication
示踪气体测定仪/示蹤氣體測定儀 tracer gas instrument
世界保护区委员会/世界保護區委員會 World Commission on Protected Areas, WCPA
世界城市/世界都市 world city
世界分布/世界分布 cosmopolitan distribution
世界气象组织/世界氣象組織 World Meteorological Organization
世界时/世界時 universal time, GMT
世界卫生组织/世界衛生組織 World Health Organization, WHO
世界无线电行政大会/世界行政無線電會議 World Administrative Radio Conference
世界遗产/世界遺產 world heritage
世界遗产核心区/世界遺產核心地帶 world heritage core zone, boundary of the nominated property
世界遗产缓冲区/世界遺產緩衝區 world heritage buffer zone
世界遗产名录/世界遺產名錄 World Heritage List, List of the World Heritage
[世界遗产]预备清单/[世界遺產]預備清單 Tentative Lists of the World Heritage
世界种/世界種,廣布種 cosmopolitan species, cosmopolite species
世界自然保护联盟/世界自然保護聯盟 International Union for Conservation of Nature and Natural Resources

世界自然基金会/世界自然基金會 World Wide Fund for Nature
世界自然与文化遗产/世界自然與文化遺産 World Natural and Cultural Heritage
世界坐标系/世界坐標系統 world coordinate system, WCS
市/市 city
市[场]/市場,商業廣場 market, market place
市场导向型区位/市場型區位 market oriented location
市场失效/市場失靈 market failure
市场营销/行銷 marketing
市花/市花 city flower
市际交通/城際交通,都市間交通 intercity transportation, intercity traffic
市郊/市郊,郊外 outer city
市郊交通/郊區通信業務 suburban traffic
市郊客车/市郊客車 suburban passenger car, suburban coach
市郊客流/郊區客流量 suburban passenger flow
市郊旅客列车/市郊列車 suburban passenger train
市郊铁路/郊區鐵路 suburban railway
市民代表参与/市民代表參與 citizen representative participation
市民化/市民化 citizenization
市区/[都]市區 urban area
市区重建计划/都市更新計劃 urban renewal plan
市区重建区/都市更新區 urban renewal area
市区公园/都市公園 urban park
市区隧道/都市隧道 urban tunnel
市容/市容,城鎮風貌 townscape
市树/市樹 city tree
市域/市域,市行政區 administrative region of a city
市域城镇体系规划/市域城鎮體系規劃 urban system planning of municipal administrative area
市域规划/都市區域規劃 city regional planning
市镇规划/市鎮計劃 town plan
市政工程管线规划/公用事業管線規劃 utilities pipelines planning
市政工程[学]/市政工程 municipal engineering
市政公用设施用地/市政公用設施用地 land for municipal utilities
市政公园/普通公園 municipal park
市政基础设施/市政基礎設施 municipal infrastructure
市政建筑/市政設施 municipal facility
市政厅/市政大廳 municipal hall
市政中心/市政中心 civic center

市中心[区]/市中心[區] central area
市中心商业区/市中心商業區 downtown
L式浮船坞/L式浮船塢 L shaped floating dock
势流/勢流 potential flow
势能/勢能,位能 potential energy
势能梯度/勢能坡比降 potential gradient
事故/事故,失事 incident, accident
事故报告/意外事故報告,損傷報告 casualty report, CASREP, accident report
事故处理/事故處理 settlement of accident, accident settlement
事故地点档案/肇事位置檔案 accident location file
事故地点图/肇事地點圖 accident spot map
事故调查/失事調查 accident investigation
事故分析/事故分析 accident analysis
事故记录/意外事故記錄 accident record
事故救援/事故救援 accident rescue
事故率/失事率 accident rate
事故赔偿/事故賠償 accident indemnity
事故树分析/故障樹分析 fault tree analysis
事故死亡率/交通死亡率 death rate of accident
事故通风/事故通風,緊急通風 emergency ventilation
事故通风系统/應急通風系統 emergency ventilation system
事故污染/事故汙染,意外汙染 accidental pollution
事故信号/事故信號 accident signal
事故信息管理/事故資訊管理 accident information management
事故修理/損害修理 damage repair
事故易发地点/事故易發地點 accident black spot
事故隐患/事故威脅 accident threat
事故预测/事故預測 accident forecast
事故预防/[意外]事故預防 accident prevention, prevention of accident, accident averting
事故预防措施的检查/事故預防檢查 check for prevention of accident
事故闸门/閘門 stop gate
事故照明/應急照明,應急燈 emergency lighting
事故状态的接触网最低电压/事故狀態的接觸網最低電壓 minimum voltage of overhead contact line at accident condition
事故资料/事故數據 incident data
事后复演/事後重演 post-mission replay
事后校零/事後校零 post-mission zero calibration
事后数据处理/事後資料處理 post-mission processing
事后维护/事後維護 maintenance after failure

事后修理/事後修理　repair after failure
事件树分析/事件樹分析　event tree analysis
事前校零/事前校零　pre-mission zero calibration
事前修理/事前修理　repair before failure
事实推定过失/事實推定過失　factual presumption of fault
事务员/事務員　purser
事务长/勤務長　chief steward
事先试验/預試法　pretesting
饰面排版/設施排字　facing typesetting
饰面型防火涂料/飾面型防火塗料　finishing fire retardant paint
饰面砖/面磚　facing brick
试拌/試拌　trial mix
试车/試車　engine trial
试车[火]箭/試車[火]箭　captive-test rocket
试舵/操舵裝置試驗　test the steering gear
试飞员/試飛員　test pilot
试航速度/試航船速　trial speed
试航条件/試航條件　sea trial condition
试件/試件,試樣,試片　test specimen, specimen, test piece
试件修整器/試體修整器　specimen trimmer
试坑/試[驗]坑,試井　test pit, trial pit
试行装配/臨時組合　tentative assembly, temporary assembly
试验/試驗,測試　test
试验保障方案/試驗保障方案　experiment ensure plan
试验报告/試驗報告　test report
试验舱/實驗艙　laboratory module
试验车/試驗[汽]車　test car
试验出水量/試量　tested capacity
试验段/風洞測試區　test section
试验段菱形区/風洞測試菱形區　diamond region of test section
试验负荷/安全載重,安全負荷　proof load, PL
试验杆/試線桿　test pole
试验工况/試驗運行情況　operating condition of test
试验[规范和标准]取舍/試驗裁剪　test tailoring
试验环道/試驗環道　test loop road
试验机/實驗型飛機　experimental aircraft
试验假人/試驗假人　testing dummy
试验架/測試架　test rack
试验件/試驗品　test article
试验路/試車跑道　test road
试验模型/試驗模型　test model
试验剖面/試驗剖面　test profile

试验[燃]气/試驗煤氣　test gas
试验设备/試驗設施,測試設施　test facility
试验室试验/實驗室試驗　laboratory test
试验台座/試驗臺　testing bed, testing stand
试验载荷/試驗載重　test load
试样/試樣,試件,樣品　test specimen, specimen, sample
试样分流器/試樣分流器,分樣器　sample splitter
试样[火]箭/試飛火箭　flight-test rocket
试样设计/試樣設計　flight-type design
试衣间/試穿室　fitting room
试桩/試樁,反應堆　test pile
视比重试验/視比重試驗　apparent specific gravity test
视差/視差　parallax
视差杆/視差尺　parallax bar
视差角/星位角　parallactic angle
视差三角形/視差三角形　parallactic triangle
视差移位/視差位移　parallactic displacement
视场/視場,視野　field of view, field of vision, FOV
视场光阑/視野闌,視野限度　field stop
视场角/視場角,視野角　angle of field, angle of view, looking angle
视赤道坐标/視赤道坐標　apparent equatorial coordinates
视赤纬/視赤緯　apparent declination
视出没/視出没　apparent rise and set
视错觉/視錯覺　visual illusion
视地平/視海平線　apparent horizon
视顶距/視天頂距　apparent zenith distance
视反转试验/眼球反向旋轉測試　ocular counter rolling test
视风/視風　apparent wind
视风速/船行風速　velocity of ship wind
视高度/視高度　apparent altitude
视加速度/視加速度　apparent acceleration
视角/視角　visual angle
视景系统/視覺系統　visual system
视距三角形/視距三角形,視覺三角形,視線三角形　sight triangle
视觉/視覺　vision
视觉残像/視覺殘像,視覺後像,視覺暫留　visual photogene
视觉干扰/視覺不協調　visual intrusion
视觉告警/視覺警報　visual warning
视觉功效/視覺性能　visual performance
视觉航标/目標輔助設備　visual aid
视觉敏锐度/視覺[敏]銳度,視覺靈敏度　visual

acuity

视觉色彩补偿/視覺色彩補償,视色錯覺 visual color atone

视觉适应/視覺適應 visual adaptation

视觉通信/視覺通信 visual signaling

视觉信号/視覺信號,視覺號誌 visual signal

视觉走廊/視覺走廊,景觀廊 visual corridor

视觉作业/視覺作業,視覺工作 visual task

视口/視埠 viewport

视力识别/視力識別 visual identification

视力适应性/視力適應性 adaptation of vision

视密度/觀測密度 observed density

视敏度/視覺[敏]銳度,視覺靈敏度 visual acuity

视频安防监控系统/視訊安防監控系統 video surveillance and control system, VSCS

视频传输/視訊傳輸 video transport

视频放大器/視訊放大器 video amplifier

视频分配器/視訊分配器 video distributor

视频火灾探测报警系统/視訊火災安全監控 video fire detection, VFD

视频监控/視訊監控 video monitoring

视频监控系统/視訊監控系統 video monitoring system

视频解码器/視訊解碼器 video decoder

视频拼接显示屏/視訊顯示屏拼接,視訊拼接顯示牆 video display screen together

视频切换器/影像控制器 video switcher

视频探测/視訊檢波 video detection

视频显示屏单元/視訊顯示屏單元 video display screen unit

视频显示屏系统工程/視訊顯示系统工程 video display system engineering

视频线/視訊線 video line

视频信号丢失报警/視訊信號丟失報警 video loss alarm

视频主机/視訊控制器 video controller

视-前庭失匹配/視-前庭失匹配 oculo-vestibular disconjugation

视情检修/替代翻修 inspection and repair only as necessary, IROAN

视情维护/基於狀態的維護 condition-based maintenance

视情维修/視情維修,按需維修 on-condition maintenance

视情修理/視情修理 repair on technical condition

视速度/視速度 apparent velocity

视太阳/視太陽,真太陽 apparent sun

视[太阳]时/視[太陽]時 apparent solar time

视位置/视位 apparent position

视线/視線,照準線,瞄準線 sight line, line of sight

视线不良弯道/視線不良彎道 blind curve

视线角/視[線]角 angle of sight

视线角速度/視線角速率 line-of-sight rate

视线设计/視線設計 sight line planning

视线通廊/視覺走廊,景觀廊 visual corridor

视线障碍物/視線障礙物 sight obstruction

视野/視野,視場 field of view, field of vision, FOV

视在大地导电率/視在大地導電率 apparent earth conductivity

视在单位能耗/視在單位能耗 specific apparent energy consumption

视在功率/視[在]功率 apparent power

视在质量/視質量 apparent mass

视重/視重 optical weight

视周期/視週期 apparent period

视准点/視準點 sighted point

适伴流螺旋桨/適跡[流]螺槳 wake-adapted propeller

适地适树/適地適樹 planting according to the environment, matching species with the site

适耕性/土壤適耕性 workability of soil

适海性/適航性 seaworthiness

适航吃水差/適航俯仰差 seaworthy trim

适航规章/適航條例 airworthiness regulation

适航能力/適航性 seaworthiness

适航批准标签/適航核準掛籤 airworthiness approval tag

适航性/①適航性,②適空性 ①seaworthiness, ②airworthiness

适航证/適航證書 airworthiness certificate

适航指令/適航指令 airworthiness directive

适合度/適合度,適應性 fitness

适货/適於運貨 cargo worthiness

适筋梁/少筋梁 under reinforced beam

适居性/可居住性 habitability

适拖/適拖 tow worthiness

适箱货/適箱貨 container load freight

适淹礁/平水礁 rock awash

适宜建设区/適宜建設區 development-appropriate zone, suitable construction area

适宜水面面积/適宜水域面積 suitable water area

适宜水面面积率/適宜水域面積率 suitable water area ratio

适宜种/適宜種 preferential species

适应/適應 adaptation

适应式规划/適應性規劃 adaptive planning

适应性/適應性,適應力 adaptability
适用航速/適用船速 operating ship speed
适用纬度/適用緯度 operating latitude
适用性/適用性 serviceability
适游天数/適遊天數 applicable travel day
适于当值/適於當值 fitness for duty
适运水分限/適運水分限 transportable moisture limit
CCU 室/CCU 室,心臟病監護病房 cardiac care unit, CCU
CT 室/CT 攝影室 computed X-ray tomography room, CT room
SPECT 室/SPECT 室 single-photon emission computed tomography room, SPECT room
室内布线/屋内配線 house wiring
室内测试/實驗室測試 indoor test, laboratory test
室内陈设/内部陳列 interior display
室内反射光增量系数/反射增量係數 increment coefficient due to interior reflected light
室内花卉/室内花卉 indoor flower
室内花园/室内花園 indoor garden
室内计算温度/室内計算溫度 indoor calculated temperature
室内净高/室内淨高 net storey height, floor to ceiling height
室内静电电位/室内靜電電壓 inner electrostatic voltage
室内康乐/戶外遊憩 indoor recreation
室内绿化/室内綠化 indoor greening
室内排水管存水弯/存水彎 house trap
室内攀岩/室内攀石 indoor rock climbing
室内气候/室内氣候 indoor climate
室内热环境/室内熱環境 indoor thermal environment
室内色彩设计/色彩設計 indoor color design
室内设计/室内設計 interior design
室内设计师/室内設計師,屋内設計者 interior designer
室内声学/室内聲學 room acoustics
室内土工试验/室内土壤試驗類 laboratory soil tests
室内养蜂场/養蜂場 bee house
室内允许噪声级/室内容許雜訊級 indoor permission noise level
室内植物/室内植物 house plant
室内装饰/室内裝修 interior decoration
室内装饰植物/室内裝飾植物 ornamental houseplant

室外防盐雾扬声器/室外防鹽霧揚聲器 anti-salt-fog outdoor-speaker
室外供配电/室外電力供應 outdoor power supply
室外管道/室外配管 outdoor piping
室外计算温度/室外計算溫度,露天計算溫度 outdoor calculated temperature
室外建筑挡光折减系数/室外建築擋光折減係數 light loss coefficient due to obstruction of exterior building
室外临界照度/室外臨界照明 exterior critical illuminance
室外平均散射照度/天空照度 sky illuminance
室外人工岩场攀岩/室外人工岩場攀岩 artificial outdoor climbing-rock climbing
室外声柱/戶外聲柱 outdoor column sound
室外音响/室外音響 outdoor speaker
室外展场/戶外展區 outdoor exhibition area
室温控制器/室用恆溫器 room thermostat
室形指数/室形指數,房間指標 room index
室宿一(飞马 α)/室宿一(飛馬 α) Markab
释放/釋放,鬆開 release
释放时间/釋放時間 drop away time
释放源/釋放源 source of release
释放值/始釋值 release value
收报局/收報局 office of destination
收报人/收信人 addressee
收报台/收信臺 station of destination
收发货标志/發貨標記,運輸標誌,嘜頭 shipping mark
收发开关/收發開關 T-R switch
收发室/收發室,傳達室 gatekeeper room, gateman room, porter room
收发天线隔离度/收發天線隔離 isolation between transmitting and receiving antenna
收放式起落架/收放式起落架 retractable landing gear
收费车道检测器/收費車道偵測器 toll lane detector
收费车道信号灯/收費車道信號燈 toll lane signal lamp
收费处/收費處 cashier
收费岛/收費島 toll island
收费道路/收費道路,收費公路 toll road
收费公路/收費公路,收費道路 toll road
收费管理/收費管理 toll administration
收费广场/收費廣場,收費區 toll plaza
收费卡门/關卡 toll gate
收费棚/收費棚 toll canopy
收费桥/收費橋 toll bridge

收费桥梁/收費橋　toll bridge
收费区/收費區段　fare zone
收费弹性/收費彈性　toll elasticity
收费亭/收費所　toll booth, toll house
收费通行券/通行券　toll pass ticket
收费显示器/收費顯示器　toll display
收费站/收費站　toll station
收费制式/收費制式　toll mode
收费中心/收費中心　toll center
收好锚/收錨固定　secure the anchor
收回/救回　retrieval
收回赔偿/收回賠償　reclaim of compensation
收货待运提单/候裝載貨證券　received for shipment bill of lading
收货单/收貨單　mate receipt
收货区/收貨區　receiving area
收货人/收貨人,受貨人,受貨單位　consignee
收集效率/收集效率　collection efficiency
收桨/收槳　boat the oars
收紧/歸位　bring home
收拉绞辘/收繫轆轤　bowsing tackle
收敛计/收斂計　convergence gage
收敛角/收束角　convergent angle
收敛-扩张喷管/斂散噴嘴　convergent-divergent nozzle
收敛转弯法/繞緊轉彎法　wind-up turn method
收锚/收錨　housing anchor
收受设施/收受設施　reception facilities
收束摄影/收束攝影　convergent photographing
收缩/收縮　shrinkage, cissing
收缩比/收縮比　contraction ratio
收缩补偿混凝土/收縮補償混凝土　shrinkage-compensating concrete
收缩段/收斂段,縮颈部分　contraction section
收缩断面/脈縮　vena contracta
收缩激波管/漸縮震波管　converging shock tube
收缩裂缝/收縮裂縫　contraction crack, shrinkage crack
收缩试验/收縮試驗　shrinkage test
收缩损失/縮小損失　contraction loss
收缩系数/約束係數　contraction coefficient
收缩限度/收縮限制,縮限　shrinkage limit
收缩余量/收縮裕度　shrinkage allowance
收妥/收到　acknowledge
收信放大器/收信放大管,接收放大器　receiving amplifier
收鱼船/收魚船　fish buying boat
收碴机/收碴機　ballast recollecting machine

手柄/[手]柄　handle, knob
手操舵装置/手操舵裝置,笨舵　hand steering gear
手铲匝道/手鏟匝道　shovel packing
手持火焰信号/手持火焰信號,手把火焰信號　hand flare, hand fire signal
手持式变形仪/輕便型撓度儀　portable deflectometer
手持式应变仪/變形測定器　portable deformeter
手持式凿岩机/掌上型鑿岩機,手提鑿岩機　hand held rock drill, portable rock drill, jack hammer drill
手持烟火信号/手持火焰信號　hand flare, hand fire signal
手电筒/手電筒　electric torch
手钓/手釣　hand line
手动泵/手搖泵　hand pump, manual pump
手动测试/人工測試　manual test
手动点火/手工點火　manual ignition
手动跟踪/手動跟蹤　manual tracking
手动火灾警报器/手動火災警報系統　manual fire alarm system, manual fire alarm sounder
手动火灾警报装置/手動火災警報系統　manual fire alarm system, manual fire alarm sounder
手动机械天平/手動機械天平　hand operated mechanobalance
手动截止阀/手動截止閥　manual shutoff valve
手动模式/手動模式　manual mode
手动膨胀阀/手動膨脹閥　hand expansion valve
手动水泵/手動水泵　hand water pump
手动调压/人工電壓調節器　manual voltage regulation
手动调整/人工調整　manual setting
手动消防炮灭火系统/手動消防炮滅火系統　manual-controlled fire monitor extinguishing system
手斧/手斧　hatchet
手纲/手綱　sweep line
手工除锈/手工[敲鏟]除銹　hand cleaning, handtool cleaning, hand rust removing
手工焊/人工焊接,手動熔接　manual welding
手工夯实/手夯　hand tamping
手工铆接/手打鉚釘　manual rivet
手工数据输入编程/人工數據輸入程式設計　manual data input programming
手工整修机/墁面工具　hand finisher
手弧焊/金屬被覆電弧焊　shielded metal arc welding, SMAW
手糊成形/手糊製成型　hand lay-up
手机/手機　handset

手绞盘/滚式千斤顶,辊式千斤顶　jack roll
手孔/手孔,手洞　hand hole
手铆/人工铆钉　hand rivet
手旗通信/手旗通信　signaling by hand flags, semaphore signaling
手起动/手起动　hand starting
手球/手球　handball
手球场/手球場　handball court
手术部/手術部　operation department
手术洗涤室/手術洗滌室　scrub up
手术准备室/準備室　preparation room
手提电动捣固机/可攜式電動夯土機　portable electric tamper
手提风动捣固机/可攜式氣動搗固機　portable pneumatic tamper
手提内燃捣固机/可攜式內燃搗固機　portable gasoline-powered tamper
手提式磁力探伤仪/輕便型磁探傷儀　portable magnetic flaw detector
手提式灭火器/輕便滅火器　portable fire extinguisher
手推剪草机/手推剪草機　hand lawnmower
手推式构造深度仪/手推式構造深度儀　minitexture meter
手信号/手動操作號誌　hand signal
手形爪/握爪　gripper
手摇卷扬机/手動卷揚機　manual hoist
手摇钻/手鑽　hand auger
手制动机/手靭,手刹车　hand brake
手制动链轮/手動制動鏈輪　hand brake chain wheel
手制动曲拐/手動制動曲拐　hand brake bell crank
手钻取土机/手鑽　hand auger
守车/守車　caboose, brake van, guard van
守恒力/保守力　conservative force
守恒系统/守恆系統　conservative system
守恒型方程/守恆型方程式　conservation equation
守护船/待命船　standby ship
守时/記時　time keeping
守位浮标/示位置浮標　watch buoy
首部枢纽/井口控制裝置　control head
首次检查期/初次檢查期　preliminary inspection period
首航/處女航　maiden voyage
首区/首區　head area, up range
首位城市法则/首要[型]都市法則　law of the primate city
首位型城市体系/首位型都市體系　urban system with dominating city

首摇/平擺　yaw
首要条款/首要條款　paramount clause
艏/艏　bow
艏标志/艏標誌　heading marker
艏波/艏波　bow wave
艏部/艏部　fore body
艏部结构/艏結構　bow construction, stem structure
艏沉/艏俯　dipping, trim by bow
艏吃水/艏吃水　draught forward, forward draught, forward draft
艏垂线/艏垂標　fore perpendicular, forward perpendicular, FP
艏导缆孔/艏導索樁,分水艏板　bow chock
艏倒缆/前倒纜　fore spring
艏灯/艏燈　head light
艏舵/艏舵　bow rudder
艏钩篙/掌篙手　bow hook
艏横缆/頭腰纜　bow breast
艏尖舱/艏尖艙,前尖艙　fore peak, fore peak tank
艏尖舱泵/艏尖艙手動泵　head pump, fore peak pump
艏尖舱壁/艏艙壁　fore peak bulkhead
艏缆/艏纜　head line
艏离/艏先離　leaving bow first
艏楼/艏樓　forecastle
艏楼甲板/艏樓甲板　forecastle deck
艏落/艏落　dropping
艏锚/艏錨,大錨,主錨　bow anchor, bower
艏锚绞车/艏部定位絞車　bow position winch
艏门/艏門　bow door
艏门跳板/艏大門跳板　bow ramp
艏碰垫/艏碰墊　bow pudding
艏旗杆/艏旗桿　jack staff
艏翘/艏部上翹變形　cocking up of forebody
艏倾/艏俯　dipping, trim by bow
艏上浪/覆浪,[甲板]上浪　green water
艏艉导标/艏艉標　head and stern mark
艏艉锚泊/艏艉碇泊　mooring head and stern
艏艉线/艏艉線　fore-and-aft line
艏舷/艏　bow
艏舷浪/艏側浪　bow sea
艏向/艏向　heading, Hdg
艏向后倒缆/艏向後倒纜　forward back spring leading aft, head aft spring
艏向上/艏向上　head up
艏斜浪/艏側浪　bow sea
艏斜桅/艏斜桅　bowsprit
艏斜桅支索/艏斜桅拉索　bobstay

舷摇/艉摇[艉艉]平摆　yawing, yaw motion
艉摇变形角/艉摇變形角　yaw deformation angle
艉支架/艉支架,艉托臺　fore poppet
艉踵/艉材跟部　forefoot
艉柱/艉柱,艉材　stem
寿命/壽命　lifetime, life
寿命初期/壽命起點　beginning of lifetime, BOL
寿命单位/壽命單位　life unit
寿命末期/壽命終結　end of lifetime, EOL
寿命剖面/壽命剖面圖　life profile
寿命试验/壽命試驗　life test
寿命周期/壽命週期,生命週期　life cycle
寿命周期费用/壽命週期費用　life cycle cost
寿命周期费用分析/壽命週期費用分析　life cycle cost analysis
受电端/受電端　receiving end
受电弓/集電弓　pantograph
受电弓标称电压/集電弓標稱電壓　nominal voltage at pantograph
受电弓电空阀/集電弓閥　pantograph valve
受电弓隔离开关/集電弓隔離開關　pantograph isolating switch
受电弓滑板/弓頭　pantograph pan
受电弓空气动力效应/集電弓氣動效應　aerodynamic effect of pantograph
受电弓气缸/導電弓氣缸　pantograph cylinder
受电弓上抬力/集電弓上衝斷層　pantograph upthrust, pantograph static contact force
受电弓试验/集電弓試驗　pantograph test
受电器/受電器,集電器　current collector
受电靴装置/觸靴裝置　shoegear
受风舷/上風舷,迎風舷　windward side
受话器/收話機　receiver
受话人付费电话/受話人付費電話　collect call
受控对象/受控對象,控制對象　controlled object
受控生态生命保障系统/控制生態下的維生系統　controlled ecological life support system
受拉荷载/抗拉載重　tensile load
受理点/接收點　receiving point
受力件焊缝/受力件焊縫　strength weld
受力体/受力體　loaded body
受力图/力圖　force diagram
受迫对流/強迫對流,強制對流　forced convection
受迫振动/強制振動　forced vibration
受迫振动互谱分析/受迫振動互譜分析　forced vibration cross spectrum analysis
受热面/受熱面　heating surface
受晒因子/受曬因子　percent time in sunlight

受弯构件/抗彎構材,抗彎構桿　flexural member
受弯屈曲/彎曲挫曲　flexural buckling
受污染水/汙染水　polluted water
受限射流/受限射流　jet in a confined space
受压钢筋/受壓鋼筋　compression bar
受压区高度/壓力區深度　depth of compressive zone
受压翼缘/受壓翼緣　compressive flange
受载期/到港期限,許可裝卸日數　laydays
狩猎场/狩獵場　hunting ground
授标/授予合約　award of contract
授时/時間傳遞　time transfer
售后服务/售後服務　after-sales service
售货区/售貨區　sales area
售票处/售票區　ticket office, booking office
兽医站/獸醫站　veterinary station
书场/書場,曲藝場　story-telling house
书法教室/書法活動室　calligraphy classroom
书房/書房　study room
书架层/書架層　stack layer
书架通道/通道,走道　aisle
书库/書庫　stack-room
书面联络法/書面聯絡法　written liaison method
书体/字體,字型　font
书院/書院　college, academy
枢接/樞接　pin connection
枢纽/終端　terminal
枢纽机场/樞紐機場　hub airport
枢纽联络线/終端連接線　terminal connecting line
枢纽小运转列车/樞紐小運轉列車　junction terminal transfer train
枢纽遥控/樞紐遙控　remote control of a junction terminal
枢纽迂回线/終端迂回線　terminal roundabout line
枢纽直径线/樞紐直徑線　diametrical line of junction terminal
枢心/樞心,轉向軸心　pivoting point
枢轴摩擦/樞軸摩擦　pivot friction
梳式接缝/梳式接縫　steel comb joint
梳形板/梳形板　comb plate, comb joint
梳妆架/柵架　comb rack
舒勒调谐/舒勒調諧　Schuler tuning
舒勒原理/舒勒原理　Schuler principle
舒适性空气调节/適宜空氣調節　comfort air conditioning
疏草/薄草　thin grass
疏伐/疏伐　thinning
疏干系数/耗竭係數　dewatering coefficient, depletion coefficient

疏剪/疏剪　thin-out cut
疏浚/疏浚,浚渫,濬深　dredging
疏浚标志/疏浚標誌　dredging mark
疏浚工程/疏浚工程　dredging engineering
疏浚区/疏浚區　dredged area
疏林/疏林　open forest
疏林草地/疏林草地　open forest grassland, lawn with woodland
疏林地/疏林地　open forest land
疏密度/疏密度　degree of closing
疏散标志灯/疏散標誌燈　escape sign luminaire
疏散导流标志/疏散導流標誌　evacuation guiding strip
疏散道路/緊急通路　emergency access
疏散滑梯/逃生滑梯　escape chute
疏散用地/避難區　evacuation area
疏散照明/避難照明,逃生照明　escape lighting
疏散指示标志/疏散指示標誌　evacuation indicator sign
疏水/排洩　drain
疏水泵/排水泵　drain pump, drainage pump
疏水管/排洩管　drain pipe
疏水器/祛水器,蒸汽阱　trap, steam trap, drain valve
疏水系统/排洩系統　draining system
疏水箱/排洩櫃　drain tank
疏松/巨觀縮孔　macroshrinkage
疏松结节/死節　unsound knot
疏松木节/死節　unsound knot
疏透结构/稀疏矩陣　sparse structure
疏枝/分枝　branches
输出步距角/輸出步長　output step size
输出单位/輸出單位　output unit
输出阀/輸出閥　delivery valve
输出复位时钟/輸出重定時鐘　output reset clock
输出信号/輸出信號　output signal
输出轴/輸出軸[承]　output axis, output shaft
输电[线路]塔/輸電線鐵塔　transmission tower, transmission line
输配电系统/輸配電系統　electrical power transmission-distribution system
输片机构/傳送機構　transport mechanism
输片张力控制系统/張力控制機構　film transportation tensile control mechanism
输气管道/傳輸管道　transmission pipeline
输气管道工程/輸氣管道工程　gas transmission pipeline engineering
输气压力/配水壓力　distribution pressure

输入单位/輸入單位　input unit
输入速率/輸入速率　input rate
输入轴/輸入軸,控制軸　input axis, input shaft
输沙量/沈碴流量　sediment discharge
输沙浓度/載運濃度　transport concentration
输水/輸水　water-conveyance
输水管/輸水管,輸送管　delivery pipe, water pipe
输水渠/輸水渠　conveyance canal
输水损失/輸水損失　conveyance loss
输送能力/運輸能力,交通容量　traffic capacity
输送式起重机/輸送起重機　transportal crane
输液室/輸液室　infusion room
输油平台/輸油平臺　transfer platform
输油系统/輸油系統　fuel transfer system
输鱼槽/輸魚槽　fish channel
输运性质/輸送性質　transport property
输纸孔/導孔,輸送孔　feed hole
蔬菜留种网室/蔬菜繁殖溫室　vegetable propagating house
蔬菜码头/蔬菜碼頭　vegetable wharf
熟地/熟地　cultivated land
熟练/熟練　proficiency
熟石灰/熟石灰,消石灰　slaked lime, hydrated lime
熟土/疏軟土　mellow soil
熟悉培训/熟悉訓練　familiarization training
蜀柱/蜀柱　short post, shuzhu
鼠患检查/鼠患檢查　inspection of rat evidence
鼠笼式电动机/鼠籠式電動機　squirrel-cage motor
束筒/框筒束　bundled tube
束筒结构/束筒結構　bundled tube structure
束柱/集墩　clustered pier
树池保护格栅/樹池保護格栅　tree grate
树池坐凳矮墙/樹池坐凳矮牆　seatwall-surrounded planting
[树]干/樹幹　trunk
树干包裹/樹幹包裹　package the trunk
树干保护套栏/樹幹保護套欄　tree guard
树干式配电系统/分散式配電系統　decentralized distribution system
树干涂白/樹幹塗白　put the trunks painted white
树高/樹高　tree height
树根桩/樹根樁　root pile
树冠垂直投影/樹冠垂直投影　vertical projection of a tree
树冠灯/樹冠燈　canopy light
树冠覆盖面/樹冠覆蓋面　tree canopy
树冠截留/樹冠截留　crown interception
树龄/樹齡　age of the tree

树木固定/樅樹形固定　tree fixing
树木配植/樹木配植　arrangement of trees and shrubs
树木推倒机/拔根機　tree cutter
树木学/樹木學　dendrology
树木育种/林育種　tree breeding
树棚/樹棚　living-tree pergola
树皮/樹皮　bark
树皮灼烧/樹皮灼燒　bark burn
树墙/攀架　espalier
树上穿越/樹上穿越　tree traversal
树形网[络]/樹狀網路　tree network
树堰/樹堰　tree weir
树枝状管网/樹分枝管線網　tree-branch pipeline, branch-off pipeline network
树脂传递模成形/樹脂轉注成形　resin transfer molding
树脂含量/樹脂含量　resin content
树脂基复合材料/樹脂基複合材料　resin matrix composite
树脂胶合板/膠合夾板　resin-bonded plywood
树脂型锚杆/樹脂型岩石錨桿　resin anchor bolt
树脂淤积/脂囊　resin pocket, pitch pocket
树种调查/樹木調查工作　tree survey
树种规划/樹種規劃　tree planning
树种选择/樹種選擇　choice of tree species
树桩盆景/樹樁盆景　penjing planted with old dwarf-trees
竖杆/竖桿,垂直構件　vertical member
竖桁/竖桁　vertical girder
竖加劲肋/垂直加勁條　vertical stiffener
竖井/竖井　shaft, vertical shaft
竖井垂线钢丝/吊直線　shaft plumbing wire
竖井跌水式溢洪道/直井式溢水道　drop inlet spillway
竖井加高/上挖直井　shaft raising
竖井联系测量/竖井聯繫測量　shaft connection survey
竖井式溢洪道/直井式溢洪道　glory hole spillway
竖井下沉/直下沈井法　sinking shaft
竖井钻进/鑽孔法鑿井　shaft drilling
竖立式结构/竖立式結構　upright mode
竖流式凝结/上向流混凝　upflow coagulation
竖琴形拉索/竖琴形拉索　harp-type stay cable
竖曲线/竖曲線,縱曲線　vertical curve
竖曲线最小长度/竖曲線最小長度　minimum length of vertical curve
竖向布置图/竖向布置圖,竖向規劃　vertical planning
竖向地震系数/竖向地震係數　vertical seismic coefficient
竖向分区/垂直分帶　vertical division zone
竖向规划/竖向規劃,竖向布置圖　vertical planning
竖向排水/垂直排流　vertical drainage
竖向设计/竖向設計　vertical design
竖向预力/竖向預力　vertical prestress
竖旋桥/竖旋橋,上開橋　bascule bridge
竖直位移/垂直位移　vertical displacement
竖直循环式机械汽车库/竖直循環式汽車庫　vertical circular garage
竖轴式水轮机/直軸水渦輪　vertical shaft water turbine
数据/數據,資料　data
数据报告/數據報告　data report
数据采集/數據採集,數據獲取,資料收集　data acquisition
数据采集系统/數據獲取系統　data acquisition system
数据处理系统/資料處理系統　data processing system
数据传输分系统/資料傳輸次系統　data transmission subsystem
数据传输速率/資料傳輸率　data transmission rate
数据传输系统/資料傳輸系統　data transmission systems
数据传送率/數據轉送率,資料轉送速率　data transfer rate
数据传送设备/資料傳送裝備　data transfer equipment, DTE
数据电话机/數據電話　dataphone
数据电路/數據電路,資料電路　data circuit
数据电路终端设备/資料電路終端設備,資料電路終接設備　data circuit terminating equipment, DCTE
数据分配计划/數據配送計劃　data distribution plan
数据分组交换网/數據分組交換網,分封交換資料網路　packet switching data network, data packet switching network
数据复用器/數據多工器,資料多工器　data multiplexer
数据复原单元/數據復原單元　data recovery unit
数据管理分系统/數據處理次系統　data handling subsystem
数据合理性检验/資料合理性測試　data reasonableness test
数据记录器/數據記錄器　data logger
数据交换中心/資料交換中心　data exchange center

数据库使用率/數據庫使用率　database availability ratio
数据库有效率/數據庫有效比率　database effectiveness ratio
数据链路/數據鏈路,資料鏈,資料連結　data link
数据率/資料速率　data rate
数据滤波/數據濾波　data filtering
数据平滑/資料平滑　data smoothing
数据收集分系统/資料收集子系統　data collection subsystem
数据通信/數據通信,數據通訊,資料通信　data communication
数据通信网/數據通訊網路,資料通信網　data communication network
数据网[络]/數據網路,資料網路　data network
数据线路终端/數據線路終端設備　data circuit terminating equipment
数据信道/數據通道　data channel
数据信号速率/資料發信號率,資料發送率　data signaling rate
数据修正/資料校正　data correction
数据压缩/數據壓縮　data compression
数据预处理/資料預處理　data pre-processing
数据站/數據站,資料站　data station
数据中继卫星/數據中繼衛星　data relay satellite
数据终端设备/數據終端設備,資料終端設備　data terminal equipment, DTE
数据注入/資料注入　data loading, data injection
数据综合处理/合成資料處理　synthetic data processing
数据总线规约/資料匯流協定　data bus protocol
数控加工/數控加工　numerical control machining
数控平面运动拖车/數控平面運動拖車　computerized planar motion carriage, computer controlled planar motion carriage
数量性状/數量性狀　quantitative charactor
数量指标/數量指標　quantitative index
数-模转换/數位-類比轉換器　digital-to-analogy conversion
数-模转换器/數位-模擬轉變器　digital-to-analogy converter
数学放样/數學放樣　mathematical lofting
数值法/數值法　numerical method
数值分析/數值分析　numerical analysis
数值高程模型/數值高程模型　digital elevation model, DEM
数值积分/數值積分　numerical integration
数值孔径/數值孔徑　numerical aperture

数字编码选呼/數位脈衝編碼選擇呼號　selective call with digital pulse coding
数字城市/數位都市　digital city
数字城市规划/數位都市規劃　digital urban planning
数字处理器/數位處理器　digital processor
数字传输/數位通信　digital communication
数字地面模型/數位地形模型　digital terrain model
数字地球/數位地球　digital earth
数字电话网/數位電話網路　digital telephone network
数字电路终接设备/數位電路終接設備,數位電路終端設備　digital circuit terminating equipment, DCTE
数字电视系统/數位電視系統　digital television system
数字仿真/數位模擬　digital simulation
数字复接设备/數位複用設備,數位多路轉換設備　digital multiplex equipment
数字复用/數位多工　digital multiplexing
数字复用设备/數位複用設備,數位多路轉換設備　digital multiplex equipment
数字高程模型/數位高程模型　digital elevation model, DEM
数字光学处理器/數位光處理器　digital light processor, DLP
数字化管理系统/數位化管理系統　digital management system
数字化景区/數位化風景區　digital scenic spot
数字景观/數位景觀　digital landscape
数字开关/數位開關　digital switch
数字录像设备/數位視訊記錄器　digital video recorder, DVR
数字滤波器/數位濾波器　digital filter
数字拼读法/數位拼音　figure of mark pronunciation
数字旗/數字旗　numeral flag
数字式测量仪器/數位量測儀器　digital measuring instrument
数字式地图系统/數位地圖系統　digital map system
数字式多谱段扫描仪/數位化多重波譜掃描器　digital multi-spectral scanner
数字式航空电子信息系统/數位空電資訊系統　digital avionics information system, DAIS
数字式太阳敏感器/數位太陽感測器　digital sun sensor
数字视频/數位視訊　digital video
数字视频监控系统/數位視訊監測系統　digital video surveillance system
数字数据传输网/數位資料傳輸網路　digital data

transmission network
数字图像／數位影像　digital image
数字图像处理系统／數位影像處理系統　digital image processing system
数字图像压缩／數位視訊壓縮　digital compression for video
数字网／數位網路　digital network
数字微波通信系统／數位式微波通信系統　digital microwave communication system
数字微波中继通信／數位微波中繼通信　digital microwave relay communication
数字无线系统／數位無線電系統　digital radio system
数字显示／數位顯示　numeric display
数字显示器／數位顯示器　digital display
数字显示装置／數位顯示裝置　digital display unit
数字线性调频[脉冲]／數位線性調頻[脈衝]　digital chirp
数字信号控制器／數位信號控制器　digital signal controller
数字选择呼叫／數位選擇呼叫　digital selective calling, DSC
数字选择呼叫设备／數位選擇呼叫裝置　digital selective calling installation
数字选择呼叫系统／數位選擇呼叫系統　digital selective calling system
数字引导／數位指示　digital designation
数字有线系统／數位有線系統　digital line system
刷盒／刷盒　brush box
刷坡／開挖邊坡　slope cutting
刷涂／毛刷塗裝　brush plating
刷握／刷握　brush-holder
刷新频率／刷新頻率　refresh frequency
耍头／耍頭　decoratively nosed timber, shuatou
衰减／衰減　attenuation
衰减倍数／減幅倍數　damping factor
衰减常数／衰減常數　attenuation constant
衰减区／衰減區　decay area
衰落／衰落[現象]　fading
衰退／退水　recession
衰退常数／退水常數　recession constant
衰退距离／衰減距離　decay distance
摔跤／摔跤，[中國式]摔角　wrestling
甩竿钓／甩竿釣，蚊鉤釣　fly fishing
甩挂运输／甩掛運輸　trailer pick-up transport
甩客／甩客　denial of passenger
甩油盘／甩油盤　slinger ring atomizer
栓钉／螺樁　stud

栓固能力／栓固能力　restraint capability
栓焊钢桥／栓焊鋼橋，螺栓和焊接鋼橋　bolted and welded steel bridge, welded and high strength bolted steel bridge
栓接／螺栓連接　bolting
栓接钢桥／栓接鋼橋　bolted steel bridge
双班运行／雙班運行　two shifts run
双板舱壁／雙層艙壁　double bulkhead, double plate bulkhead
双半结／雙半套結　two half-hitches
双绑／帶雙[纜]　double up
双绑系牢／各纜打雙　double up and secure
双倍密度记录／雙密度記錄　double density recording
双壁钢围堰钻孔基础／雙壁鋼圍堰鑽孔基礎　double walled steel cofferdam and bored foundation
双壁钢围堰钻孔桩基础／雙壁鋼圍堰鑽孔樁基礎　double walled steel cofferdam and bored pile foundation
双臂受电弓／雙臂式集電弓　double arm pantograph
双边带／雙邊帶　double side-band, DSB
双边供电／雙邊供電　two way feeding
双边极限环／雙邊極限環　two side limit cycle
双边型直线感应电动机／雙邊直線感應電動機　double sided linear induction motor
双波段火灾探测器／雙波段火災偵測器　double wave band fire detector
双侧壁导洞法／雙側壁導坑法　twin side heading method
双侧减速齿轮驱动／雙級減速齒輪驅動　double reduction gear drive
双侧倾卸车／兩側傾卸車　double side tipping wagon
双侧[踏面]制动／抱軔　clasp brake
双层船壳／雙層船殼　double hull
双层床离子交换／雙層床離子交換　stratified bed ion exchange
双层道路／雙層道路　double deck road
双层的／雙層　two ply
双层底／[二]重底　double bottom
双层底舱／[二]重底艙　double bottom tank
双层电梯／雙層昇降機　double deck elevator
双层渡车船／雙層結構渡船　double deck ferry boat
双层钢围囹／雙層鋼圍囹　double walled steel waling
双层公路／雙層式公路　dual type highway
双层轿车平车／雙層轎客車　double deck sedan car
双层客车／雙層客車廂　double deck passenger car, double deck coach, bi level coach
双层廊／雙層廊　gallery house
双层滤池／雙層濾池　two layer filter

双层滤料滤池/雙層濾料池　dual media filter
双层滤网/雙層濾過器　double strainer
双层桥/雙層橋　double deck bridge
双层网格防护屏/雙層網格防護屏　mesh double bumper shield
双层网架/雙層網格　double layer grid
双差/雙差　double difference
双潮/雙潮　double tide
双车道/雙車道　double lane, dual lane
双车道道路/雙車道道路　two lane road
双程运输/雙程運輸　two way loading transport
双重交叉桁架/雙腹材桁架　double intersection truss
双重绝缘棒式绝缘子/雙重絕緣棒式絕緣子　double strut insulator, double rod insulator
双重控制/雙重控制　dual control
双重密封人井盖/人孔口複式封蓋　double seal manhole cover
双重作业/雙重作業　double freight operations
双出口涡壳式水轮机/雙出口水渦輪　double discharge spiral water turbine
双船干坞/雙船乾塢　double ships dry dock
双船围网/雙船圍網　double boat purse seine
双床间/雙人房　double bed room
双垂尾/雙直尾翅　twin vertical fin
双刀开关/複式轉轍器　double switch
双电压制电力机车/雙電壓電力機車　dual voltage electric locomotive
双吊联合作业/雙吊桿作業　union crane service
双动式打桩机/雙動式打樁機　double acting pile driver
双端荧光灯/雙端螢光燈,直管熒光燈　straight tubular fluorescent lamp
双断/雙斷　double break
双二进制编码/雙二進制編碼　duobinary encoding
双方责任/雙方責任　dual responsibility
双方责任碰撞/雙邊過失碰撞　both to blame collision
双防波堤/雙枝防波堤　double breakwater
双风管空气调节系统/雙風管空調系統　dual duct air conditioning system
双浮标寄船碇/雙浮標寄船碇　double buoys mooring
双幅车行道/雙向分隔道路　dual carriageway
双幅路/複式行車道路　dual carriageway road
双幅式城市道路/雙幅式城市道路　two-slab urban road
双杆吊货装置/雙吊桿作業系統　union purchase system
双杆作业/雙桿固定合吊裝置　union purchase system
双干管式[制]/雙線制　two-main system
双干管系统/雙幹管配水劑　double-main system
双缸抽水机/雙缸式抽水機　duplex cylinder pump
双工[操作]/雙工操作,雙工運行,雙工[作業]　duplex, duplex operation
双工传输/雙工傳輸　duplex transmission
双工管理程序/雙工制管理程式　duplex management program
双工计算机系统/雙工計算機系統　duplex computer system
双工无线电通信/雙工無線電通訊　duplex radio communication
双挂汽车列车/雙掛車組　double trailer train
双管供暖系统/雙管供暖系統　two pipe heating system
双管设备/雙管設備　double hose rig
双管荧光灯/雙管螢光燈　double tube fluorescent lamp
双管制蒸汽热网/雙管蒸汽熱網　two pipe steam heat supply network
双轨条式轨道电路/雙軌軌道回路　double rail track circuit
双滚筒提升机/雙筒吊曳機　double drum hoist
双航道运河/雙向道運河　two lane canal
双横队/雙橫隊　double line abreast
双户住宅/雙戶住宅　two family dwelling
双环盲板法兰/眼鏡型盲凸緣　spectacle blank flange, spectacle blind flange
双黄线/雙黄線　double amber lines
双回路风洞/雙回流風洞　double return wind tunnel
双回路供电/雙回路供電電源,雙回路電力供應　double circuit power supply
双机单轴式/雙機單軸系統　twin engine single-shaft system
双机牵引/雙機牽引　double locomotive traction
双机系统/雙機系統　dual system
双机组/雙機組　two unit
双基地雷达/雙基地雷達　bistatic radar
双基推进剂/雙基推進劑　double base propellant, DB propellant
双级过滤/二段過濾　two stage filtration
双级压缩/兩階壓縮　double stage compression
双肩回交路/雙臂交路　double arm routing
1-1 双绞辘/雙索絞車　double purchase winch
双铰拱/二鉸拱　two hinged arch
双脚桅/雙腳桅,人字桅　bipod mast

双节点振动/雙節點振動　two noded vibration
双截门/雙截門　double leaf door
双筋截面/雙鋼筋斷面　doubly reinforced section
双进路/雙方路線　either route
双镜头相机/雙鏡攝影機　twin camera
双卷筒绞车/雙筒絞車　double drum winch
双卷筒卷扬机/雙卷筒卷揚機　double drum winch, twin drum winch
双开道岔/複式道岔　double turnout
双壳船/雙殼船　double hulled ship, double skin ship
双[孔]隧道/雙孔隧道,眼鏡型隧道　twin tunnel
双框架飞轮/雙懸掛式飛輪　double gimbaled flywheel
双拉杆桩/雙拉桿版樁　double tie rods sheet pile
双力矩/雙力矩　bi-moment
双立管排水系统/雙堆疊系統　dual stack system
双联泵/雙缸泵　duplex pump
双联浮子/雙浮球　twin float
双联杠杆/曲拐槓桿機構　toggle linkage
双联滤器/複式過濾器　duplex strainer
双联平车/雙聯平車　twinned flat car
双联曲柄/二拐曲柄　two throw crank
双链式悬索桥/雙鏈式懸索橋　double chain suspension bridge
双链形悬挂/複式鏈形懸掛　compound catenary equipment
双梁式架桥机/雙梁架橋機　double beam girder-erecting machine
双列布置/雙列布置　double row layout arrangement
双列圆盘耙/雙[動]盤耙　double disc harrow, double action disc harrow
双流/雙[電]流,交直流　double current
双流程过热器/雙通道過熱器　two pass superheater
双流汽轮机/雙流渦輪機　divided flow turbine, double flow steam turbine
双流液力机械传动/雙流液壓-機械傳動　hydromechanical drive with outer ramification
双路供电/雙路供電,雙重供電　duplicate supply, two circuit feeding
双轮荷载/雙輪負載,雙輪裝載　dual wheel loading
双轮压路机/串聯式滾壓機　tandem roller
双轮振动压路机/兩輪振動壓路機　tandem vibratory roller
双马[来酰亚胺]树脂/雙馬來亞醯胺樹脂　bismaleimide resin, BMI resin
双锚系泊/雙錨泊船　two anchor mooring
双面调车信号机/雙面調車號誌機　signal for shunting forward and backward

双面焊/雙面焊接接合　welding by both side
双面坡口/雙面槽　double groove
双面托盘/雙層貨盤　double deck pallet
双模式火箭发动机/雙模式火箭發動機　dual mode rocket engine
双模式推进系统/雙模態推進系統　dual mode propulsion system
双纽钢线/雙紐鋼線　double headed wire
双纽线/雙紐線　lemniscate, single headed wire
双排板桩围堰/複牆式圍堰　double wall cofferdam
双拼住宅/半獨立式住宅　semi-detached house
双频测速仪/雙頻測速儀　dual frequency range rate instrumentation
双频感应器/兩倍頻率感應器　double frequency inductor
双频率制电力机车/雙頻電力機車　dual frequency electric locomotive
双坡/雙坡　double way gradient
双腔起落架/雙腔起落架　landing gear with two stage shock absorber
双桥驱动/前後傳動　tandem drive
双曲扁壳/雙曲扁殼　double curvature shallow shell
双曲拱桥/雙曲拱橋　two way curved arch bridge, two way curved arch tile
双曲面/雙曲面　hyperboloid surface
双曲抛物面壳/雙曲拋物面殼　hyperbolic paraboloid shell
双曲线波/雙曲線波　hyperbolic wave
双曲线导航系统/雙曲線導航系統　hyperbolic navigation system
双曲线位置线/雙曲線位置線　hyperbolic position line
[双曲线]远程导航系统-C/長程導航系統-C　long range aid to navigation system C
双燃料柴油机/雙燃料柴油機　dual-fuel diesel engine
双燃料发动机/雙燃料引擎　dual-fuel engine
双刃的/雙刃的　two edged
双色导引头/雙色歸航器　dual color homing head
双扇形系统/雙扇形系統　two sector system
双绳空中索道/雙線索道　double rope aerial cableway
双绳抓斗/雙索抓斗　double rope grab
双试验段风洞/雙試驗段風洞　duplex wind tunnel
双室风缸/雙室減壓缸　two compartment reservoir
双梳式接缝/雙梳式接縫　double steel comb joint
双输运石机/雙輪運石機　turnarocker
双速电动机/雙速電動機　two speed motor

双索吊送传递法/雙索吊送傳遞法　burton method of transfer
双索具/雙肢索　double sling
双索面斜拉桥/雙刃面板斜張橋　double plane cable stayed bridge
双塔斜拉桥/雙塔斜張橋　double pylon cable stayed bridge
双态罗经/雙態羅經　double state compass
双套结/兜腰稱人結，腰結　bowline on the bight
双套设备/雙套設備　duplication of equipment
双体船/雙［胴］體船，雙體或三體船　twin hull ship, catamaran
双体渡车船/雙體渡船　twin ferry boat
双通道光学引信/雙通道光學引信　bichannel optical fuze
双筒壁灯/雙筒壁燈　double cylindrical shade wall lamp
双筒起重机/雙筒吊曳機　double drum hoist
双筒望远镜/雙筒遠望鏡　binoculars
双头钢轨/雙頭軌條　double headed rail
双头螺栓/兩頭尖釘　stud, double pointed nail
双头螺纹/雙頭螺紋　two start screw
双头木螺钉/螺絲梢　dowel screw
双凸轮换向/雙凸輪換向　double cam reversing
双推单溜/雙推單溜　single rolling on double pushing track
双推进器/雙螺槳　twin propellers
双推力火箭发动机/雙推力火箭發動機　dual thrust rocket motor
双推双溜/雙推雙溜　double rolling on double pushing track
双拖渔船/雙拖［網］漁船　two boat trawler, bull trawler
双桅帆船/雙桅帆船　brig, brigantine, schooner
双艉鳍/雙艉鳍　twin skeg
双位/雙位　two position
双位式调节器/雙位開關調整器　on-off two position regulator
双位式信号机/二位式號誌　two position signal
双纹锉/雙向齒銼刀　double cut file
双线笔/雙頭上墨筆　railroad pen
双线臂板信号机/雙線臂［木］式號誌　double wire semaphore signal
双线插入段/雙軌道插入段　double track interpolation
双线继电半自动闭塞/雙線繼電半自動閉塞　double track all-relay semi-automatic block system
双线架空索道/雙索纜道　twin cable ropeway

双线桥/複線橋，雙軌橋　double track bridge
双线圈结构/雙線圈結構　two coil configuration
双线隧道/雙線隧道，複線隧道　double track tunnel, twin track tunnel
双线铁路/複線鐵道　double track railway
双线运行图/雙線運行圖　train diagram for double track
双线制/雙線制，雙線系統　two wire system
双向测速/雙向測速　two way range rate measurement
双向传输/雙向式傳輸　bidirectional transmission
双向反射比因子/雙向反射率因子　bidirectional reflection factor
双向风缸/雙作用油缸　two way cylinder
双向过闸/雙向通行　two way transit
双向航路/雙向航路　two way route
双向桁架/雙向桁架　two-direction truss
双向横列式编组站/雙向橫列式編組站　bidirectional transversal type marshalling station
双向混合式编组站/雙向混合式編組站　bidirectional combined type marshalling station
双向交替通信/雙向交替通訊　two way alternate communication
双向交通/雙向道［路］　two way traffic, two way road
双向路/雙向道［路］　two way traffic, two way road
双向甚高频无线电话设备/雙向特高頻無線電話　two way VHF radiotelephone apparatus
双向通道/兩向街道　two way street
双向同时通信/雙向同時通信　two way simultaneous communication
双向网架/雙向網格　two way latticed grid
双向先合后断触点/雙向先合後斷觸點　two way make-before break contact
双向信标/雙向示標　two course beacon
双向行车/雙向道　two way traffic
双向预应力/二維預力　two dimension prestressing
双向匝道/雙向匝道，雙向坡道　two way ramp
双向载波捕获时间/雙向載波捕獲時間　two way carrier acquisition time
双向止回阀/雙向止回閥　double non-return valve, double check valve
双向自动闭塞/雙向自動閉塞　double direction running automatic block
双向纵列式编组站/雙向縱型式編組站　bidirectional longitudinal type marshalling station
双星定位卫星/雙星定位衛星　dual positioning satellite

双行码头/雙行碼頭　twin pier
双悬臂式架桥机/雙懸臂梁架橋機　double cantilever girder-erecting machine
双旋翼共轴式直升机/同轴直昇機　coaxial helicopter
双旋翼交叉式直升机/同步交叉式雙旋翼直昇機　synchropter
双旋翼纵列式直升机/縱列雙旋翼直昇機　tandem helicopter
双叶平转桥/雙葉平轉橋,雙葉平旋橋　double leaf swing bridge
双叶竖旋桥/雙葉竪旋橋,雙葉上開橋　double leaf bascule bridge
双圆弧翼型/雙曲翼形剖面　biconvex aerofoil profile
双胀式蒸汽机/複膨脹式蒸汽機　compound expansion steam engine
双支承舵/雙支承舵　double bearing rudder
双肢剪力墙/耦合剪力牆　coupled shear wall
双肢柱/聯肢柱,組合柱　coupled column
双职高级船员/雙專長甲級船員　dual purpose officer
双周分潮/半月潮　fortnightly tide
双轴强度/雙軸強度　biaxial strength
双轴速率陀螺仪/雙軸速率陀螺儀　double axis rate gyro
双轴稳定平台/雙軸穩定平臺　two axis stable platform
双轴系/雙軸系　twin shafting
双轴应力/雙軸應力　biaxial stress
双肘式碎石机/雙肘碎石機　double toggle crusher
双主应力/雙軸應力　biaxial stress
双柱/對柱　accouplement
双柱式[桥]墩/雙柱型橋墩　two columned pier, two shaft pier
双转子摆式罗经/雙轉子擺式羅經　twin gyro pendulous gyrocompass
双锥头合钉/雙錐頭合釘　double cone dowel
双缀条/交叉雙連格條　double latticing, double lacing bar
双子金字塔建筑群/雙子金字塔建築群　twin pyramid complexes
双子叶植物/雙子葉植物　dicotyledons, dicots
双自旋稳定/雙自旋穩定　dual spin stabilization
双自旋姿态控制系统/雙自旋姿態控制系統　dual spin attitude control system
双字母信号码/雙字母信號碼　two letter signal code
双纵队/雙縱隊　double column
双组空气抽逐器/雙組空氣抽射器　two element air ejector
双组元喷嘴/雙元噴嘴　two component injector element
双组元推进剂/雙元推進劑　bipropellant
双组元[推进剂]火箭发动机/雙元推進劑火箭發動機　bipropellant rocket engine
双组元推进系统/雙元推進劑推進系統　bipropellant propulsion system
双作用泵/雙動泵　double acting pump
双作用气动桩锤/雙動氣壓樁機　double acting pneumatic hammer
双作用汽缸/雙動汽缸　double acting cylinder
双作用千斤顶/雙動千斤頂　double acting jack
双作用式发动机/雙動[動力]機　double acting engine
双作用蒸汽桩锤/雙動汽錘　double acting steam hammer
双作用蒸汽打桩机/雙動蒸汽打樁機　double acting steam pile driver
霜点/霜點　frost point
霜冻渗透程度/凍結深度　frost penetration degree
霜害/霜害,凍害　frost injury, frost damage
水/水　water
水安全/水安全　water security
水泵接合器/二重聯接,叉形頭聯接　siamese connection
水泵排水/抽出排水　pumping drainage
水泵体/主泵外殼　pump casing
水泵站/抽水站　water pumping station
水表/水表,水位計　water meter, water gage
水表负载系数/水表負載因數　water meter load factor
水簸箕/水簸箕　drainage dustpan, splash block
水舱式减摇装置/減摇水艙穩定系統　anti-rolling tank stabilization system
水舱涂料/水艙塗料　water tank coating
水槽/水槽　water channel, water trough
水产养殖/水産養殖　aquaculture
水产养殖场/海洋牧場　aquafarm
水产资源/水産資源　fishery resources
水车/水紡車　Chinese wheel, water-mill
水池/水池　pool
水尺比读数/水尺比讀數　specific gage reading
水尺关联/水尺關聯　gage correlation
水尺检量/測量水尺　draught survey
水冲沉桩/射水打樁　water-jet piling, hydraulic jet piling
水冲法/沖水法　water jetting

水处理/水處理　water treatment
水锤/水鎚　water hammer
水锤作用/水鎚作用　hydraulic hammer action
水淬[高炉]矿渣/粒狀爐碴　granulated blast furnace slag
水当量/含水當量　water equivalent
水道/水道,航道　channel, euripus
水道测量/水道測量,海道測量　hydrographic survey
水道测量家/海道測量師　hydrographer
水道学者/海道測量師　hydrographer
水的硬度/水硬度　water hardness
水滴轨迹/水滴軌跡　water droplet trajectory
水滴遮蔽区/水滴陰影區　droplet shadowed zone
水滴撞击参数/水滴撞擊參數　droplet impingement parameter
水底电缆/水底電纜　subaqueous cable
水底隧道/水底隧道　subaqueous tunnel
水底植物/底棲植物　benthophyte, submerged plant
水电开发/水力開發　hydropower development, water power development
水电站隧洞/水電站隧道　hydropower tunnel
水电站站址/水力發電位址　water power site
水动力/流體動力　hydrodynamic force
水动力力矩/流體動力力矩　moment of hydrodynamic force
水动力系数/流體動力係數　hydrodynamic force coefficient
水动阻力/水阻力　water resistance
水洞/水洞　water tunnel
水阀/水閥　bid valve
水法/水利法　water law
水分离器/水分[離]器　water separator
水分配/配水　water distribution
水分配器/水分配機　water dispenser
水分/含水量　water content
水分测定/含水量試驗　water content test, moisture test
水分短缺/缺水　water shortage
水分亏缺/缺水量　water deficit
水分利用效率/水分利用效率　water use efficiency
水分凝结/水生成　hydrogenesis
水分平衡/水分平衡,水量平衡,水收支　water balance, water equilibrium, water budget
水分缺失/水分缺乏　moisture deficiency
水分适量/水分適量　moisture adequacy
水分梯度/水分梯度　moisture gradient
水分调整/水分校正　moisture adjustment
水分胁迫/水分逆境　water stress

水[分]循环/水循環　water cycle
水分移动/水分移動,濕漲現象　moisture movement
水封/水封　water seal
水封高度/封彎　trap seal
水封井/水封井　trapped well
水封式漏水口/水封式排水口　water seal scupper
水工法/濕造法　wet construction method
水工构造物/水工建築物　hydraulic structure
水工建筑物/水工建築物　hydraulic structure
水工隧洞/水工隧洞　hydraulic tunnel
水垢沉淀物/水垢沈積　scale deposits
水鼓/水鼓　water drum
水管锅炉/水管鍋爐　water tube boiler
水管理系统/水管理系統　water management system
水管配件/管配件,管接頭　pipe fitting
水柜/水槽,水箱　water tank
水柜阀/水櫃閥　tank valve
水柜机车/水櫃機車　tank locomotive
水果船/青果船　fruit carrier
水过滤器/濾水器　water filter
水害/水災　flood damage, washout
水害断道/水災斷道　railroad break down due to flood, line blockade due to flood
水害复旧/水災復舊工作　restoration work for flood damage, restoration of flood-damaged structures
水害抢修/水災搶修　rush repair of flood damage to open for traffic
水合热/水合熱　heat of hydration
水鹤/水鶴　water crane
水鹤表示器/水鶴指示器　water crane indicator
水滑现象/水滑現象　hydroplaning phenomena
水化/水化　hydration
水化热/水合熱　heat of hydration
水环境/水環境　water environment
水环境容量/水環境容量　water environment capacity
水回收/水回收　water reclamation
水毁/水災　flood damage, washout
水火成形/水火成形　flame and water forming
水击/水鎚　water hammer
水结碎石路面/水結碎石面　water bound macadam
水解/水解　hydrolysis
水解槽/水解槽　hydrolytic tank
水解性氮/水解氮　hydrolyzable nitrogen
水浸仿真试验/浸水模擬試驗　water-immersion simulation test
水经济/水經濟　water economy
水景/水域風景　water scenery, water feature

水景观/水體景觀 water landscape
水景水处理机房/水景水處理室 water treatment room for waterscape
水景园/水景園 water garden
水净化器/水昇華器 water sublimator
水均衡方程式/水文方程式 hydrologic equation
水库/水庫 impounding reservoir
水库发电厂/水庫式發電廠 reservoir type power plant
水库路基/水庫路基 subgrade in reservoir, embankment crossing reservoir
水库入流过程线/水庫進水歷線 reservoir inflow hydrograph
水库调洪演算/水庫演算 reservoir routing
水库位置/水庫位置 reservoir site
水库淤积/水庫沈澱 reservoir sedimentation
水廊/水廊 corridor on water
水雷/水雷 sunken mine, mine
水雷式代换水舱/水雷補重櫃 mine compensating tank
水雷危险区/水雷危險區 areas dangerous due to mines
水冷/水冷卻 water cooling
水冷柴油机/水冷式柴油機 water-cooled diesel engine
水冷却应变天平/水冷卻應變天平 water-cooled strain gage balance
水冷式冷凝器/水冷冷凝器 water-cooled condenser
水力半径/水力半徑 hydraulic radius
水力冲填坝/淤填壩 hydraulic-fill dam
水力充填/水力填土法,淤填法,灌水填築法 slushing, hydraulic filling
水力粗糙/水力粗糙 hydraulically rough
水力发电/水力發電 hydro-electric power
水力发电厂/水力發電廠 hydropower plant
水力发电计划/水力發電總方案 hydro-electric scheme
水力发电开发/水力發電開發 hydro-electric power development
水力发电站/水力發電所 hydropower station, hydro-electric power station
水力防波堤/水力防浪堤 hydraulic breakwater
水力工况/水力狀況 hydraulic regime
水力光滑/水力光滑 hydtaulically smooth
水力计算/水力計算 hydraulic computation
水力开发地点/水力發電位址 water power site
水力勘察/水力發電調查 water power survey
水力模拟/液壓模擬 hydraulic analogy

水力摩阻/水力摩擦 hydraulic friction
水力喷射器/水力噴射器 hydraulic ejector
水力劈裂/水力壓裂 hydraulic fracturing
水力侵蚀/水[侵]蝕,水冲蚀 water erosion
水力射流泵/水力噴射器 hydraulic ejector
水力失调/水力失調[度] hydraulic misadjustment
水力挖掘/沖水挖土法 hydraulic excavation
水力挖土/沖水挖土法 hydraulic excavation
水力稳定性/水力穩定性 hydraulic stability
水力效率/液力效率 hydraulic efficiency
水力演算/水力演算 hydraulic routing
水力资源/水力資源 water power resources
水利风景区/水利風景區 water conservancy scenic area
水利经济分析/水經濟分析 hydroeconomic analysis
水利用/利用水 water utilization
水帘洞/水簾洞 water curtain cave
水量分布/配水 water distribution
水[量]平衡/水量平衡,水分平衡,水文平衡 water balance
水量平衡法/水均衡法 water balance method
水量调节阀/水量調整閥 water regulating valve
水龄学/水齡學 hydrochronology
水流导向/水流導向 current deflecting
水流力/水流力 current force
水龙带/水龍帶 fire hose
水陆交错带/植物群落交會地帶,兩種植物漸挨地帶,兩群植物漸挨地帶 ecotone
水陆两用飞机/水陸兩用飛機 amphibian
水路/航道 water-route
水路客运站/水路客運站 port passenger station, waterway passenger station, waterway passenger terminal
水轮发电机/水渦輪發電機 hydraulic turbine generator
水落管/降水口,流水口 down spout, drain spout
水媒植物/水媒植物,適水植物,喜水植物 hydrophilous plant
水煤浆/煤水漿 coal water slurry, coal water mixture
水煤气/水煤氣 water gas
水密/水密 watertight
水密舱壁/水密艙壁 watertight bulkhead, bulkhead resistant to water
水密舱室/水密艙區 watertight compartment
[水密]分舱/[水密]艙區劃分 watertight subdivision
水密肋板/水密肋板 watertight floor
水密门/水密門 watertight door

水密完整性/完整水密　watertight integrity
水密型/水密型　watertight type
水密性能/水密性能　watertightness performance
水面/水面　water surface
水面饱和水汽压/水面平衡蒸汽壓　water surface equilibrium vapor pressure
水面比降/水面比降,水面坡度　water surface gradient, slope of water surface
水面高程/水面高程　water level elevation
水面航行/水面航行　surface navigation
水面机场/水上機場　seadrome
水面溅落/濺落　splashing
水面坡度/水面坡度　slope of water surface
水面上升/水面上昇　up-surging
水面下降/水面下降　down-surging
水面战斗舰艇/水面艦艇　surface craft, surface combat ship
水灭火系统/噴水滅火系統　water fire extinguishing system
水磨石/水磨石　terrazzo, terrazzo concrete
水磨石机/水磨石機　terrazzo grinder
水魔术/流水魔術　water magic
水幕系统/手動灑水裝置　drencher system
水能开发/水力開發　hydropower development, water power development
水泥/水泥　cement
水泥安定性试验/水泥堅固性試驗　cement soundness test
水泥刨花板/水泥鉋花板,水泥木屑板　cement-bonded particleboard
水泥标号/水泥標號　cement mark
水泥衬里管道/水泥襯裡管　cement lining pipe
[水泥的]含碱量/含鹼量　alkali content
水泥分散剂/水泥擴散劑　cement dispersing agent
水泥灌浆/水泥灌漿　cement grouting, injection cement
水泥混凝土/水泥混凝土　cement concrete
水泥混凝土标号/水泥混凝土標號　cement concrete mark
水泥混凝土混合料/水泥混凝土混合料　cement concrete mixture
水泥混凝土路面/水泥混凝土路面　cement concrete pavement
水泥混凝土配合比/水泥混凝土配合比例　proportioning of cement concrete
水泥基自流平材料/水泥基自動水平材料　cement-based self-leveling materials
水泥加固/水泥穩定法　cement stabilization

水泥孔隙比/水泥空隙比　void cement ratio
水泥路面/混凝土路面　concrete pavement
水泥木丝板/水泥木絲板　wood wool cement board
水泥木屑板/水泥木屑板,水泥鉋花板　cement-bonded particleboard
水泥砂浆/水泥砂漿　cement mortar
水泥输送泵/水泥泵　cement pump
水泥碎石拌和法/水泥碎石拌和法　cement macadam mix method
水泥榫接/水泥榫接[法]　cement joggle
水泥榫块/水泥榫塊　cement mortar key
水泥筒仓/水泥儲倉　cement silo
水泥涂料/水泥漆　cement paint
水泥土基层/水泥土基層　cement-soil base course, cement-soil base
水泥瓦/水泥瓦　cement tile
水泥用量/水泥含量　cement content
水泥针状体/水泥針狀體　cement bacilluse
水泥砖/水泥磚　cement block
水盘/水盤　drip pan
水炮灭火系统/水炮滅火系統　water monitor extinguishing system
水培/[大規模]水耕　hydroponics
水喷雾灭火系统/噴水滅火裝置　water spray extinguishing system
水平安定面/水平安定面,水平穩定器　horizontal stabilizer
水平搬运机械/水平搬運機械　horizontal handling machinery
水平板/水平盤　horizontal plate
水平波束宽度/水平波束寬度　horizontal beam width
水平测试/水平試驗　horizontal test
水平测试工作梯/水平測試工作梯　horizontal checking ladder
水平层/水平面基層　leveling course
水平单向流/水平單向流　horizontal unidirectional airflow
水平地震系数/水平地震係數　horizontal seismic coefficient
水平舵/橫舵　horizontal rudder
水平发射/水平發射　horizontal launch
水平反应/水平反力　horizontal reaction
水平反作用/水平反力　horizontal reaction
水平工作范围/水平工作範圍　horizontal working range
水平光弧/水平弧區　horizontal sector
水平合线/主水平線　horizon trace

水平横撑/水平撑構　horizontal bracing
水平衡方程式/水文方程式　hydrologic equation
水平轰炸/水平投彈　horizontal bombing
[水平]滑台/[水平]滑臺　horizontal slip table
水平基点/水平基點　original bench-mark
水平基准/水平參考　horizontal reference
水平极化/水平[偏]極化　horizontal polarization
水平加劲肋/水平加勁條　horizontal stiffener
水平夹材/水平夾材　sash brace
水平夹角位置线/水平角位置線　position line by horizontal angle
水平剪力/水平剪力　horizontal shear
水平角定位/水平角定位　fixing by horizontal angle
水平井/橫井　horizontal well
水平净距/水平間距　horizontal clearance
水平孔口/水平孔口　horizontal orifice
水平缆线/水平電纜　horizontal cable
水平面/水平面　horizontal surface
水平[面]投影/地平投影法　horizon projection
水平取齐/水平校準　horizontal alignment
水平散水/水平護床　horizontal apron
水平速调装置/球窩水平儀　quick-leveling head
水平调整/水平調整　leveling-up
水平推力/水平推力　horizontal thrust
水平陀螺仪/水平陀螺儀　horizontal gyro
水平弯曲振动/水平彎曲振動　horizontal flexural vibration
水平尾翼/水平尾翼　horizontal tail
水平像片/水平像片　horizontal photograph
水平楔切/水平楔形爆炸　horizontal wedge cut
水平仪/水準儀　level
水平整体运输/水平整體運輸　integral horizontal transportation
水平直线加速法/水平直線加速法　level straight acceleration method
水平直线减速法/水平直線減速法　level straight deceleration method
水平指示灯/海平面指示燈　horizon indicating lamp
水平轴/水平軸　trunnion axis
水平轴阻尼法/水平軸阻尼法　damped method of horizontal axis
水平肘板/水平肘板　horizontal bracket
水平状态显示器/水平狀態顯示　horizontal situation display
水坡升船机/水坡昇船機　water slope
水气比/水氣比　water-air ratio
水汽压/水汽壓　water vapor pressure
水枪/水沖機　hydraulic giant

水球运动/水球運動　water polo sport
水渠/水槽　water channel, water trough
水圈/水圈,水界　hydrosphere
水热蚀变/熱水變質　hydrothermal alteration
水溶性酸/水溶性酸　water-soluble acids
水溶性碳测试/溶碳試驗　water-soluble carbon test
水溶性涂料/水漆　water-based paint
水软化/軟水法　water softening
水润滑/水潤滑　water lubricating
水砂混合体/水滓混合物　water sediment mixture
水上巴士/水上巴士　water bus
水上部分破损/水線上損害　above water damage
水上飞机/水上飛機　seaplane
水上飞机起飞滑行/水上飛機起飛滑行　seaplane take-off taxiing
水上飞机水动性能/水上飛機水動力性能　seaplane hydrodynamic performance
水上飞机着水滑行/水上飛機著水滑行　seaplane landing taxiing
水上航速/水面速[率]　surface speed
水上合拢/水上合攏　afloat joining ship sections
水上迫降/水上迫降　ditching
水上通信/水上通信　marine communication
水上运动/水上運動　water sport
水上运动场/水上運動場　aquatic sport waters
水上运输/水上運輸　marine transportation, water carriage
水上助航标志系统/浮標系統　buoyage system
水上作业/海上作業　operation at sea
水深/水深　depth of water
水深测量/水深測量　bathymetric survey
水深临关系曲线/深度流速曲線　depth velocity curve
水深信号/水深訊號　water signal
水深信号标/水深信號標誌　depth signal mark
水生花卉/水生花　water flower
水生生态系统/水生生態系統,水域生態系　aquatic ecosystem
水生植物/水生植物　hydrophyte, aquatic plant
水生植物园/水生植物園　aquatic plant garden
水声调查船/水聲調查船　underwater acoustic research ship, underwater acoustic research vessel
水声对讲机/水聲對講機　hydrophone intercommunicator
水声反声材料/水下反音材　underwater acoustic reflection material
水声透声材料/水下透音材　underwater acoustic transmission material

水声吸声材料/水下吸音材 underwater acoustic absorption material
水石盆景/水石盆景 rock and water penjing
水手刀/水手刀 jack-knife
水手长/水手長 boatswain, bosun
水输处理系统/水傳輸處理系統 water carriage system
水刷石/汰石子 granitic plaster, washed granolithic plaster
水栓/水栓 tap post
水-水换热器/水-水熱交換器 water-water heat exchanger
水损/海[水漬]損 sea damage
水塔/[高架]水塔 water tower, elevated water tank
水塘/水塘 pond
水套/水[夾]套 water jacket
水体/水體,水質[體] water body
水体富营养化/水體富營養化 water eutrophication
水体污染/水[質]汙染 water pollution
水体质量/水質 water quality
水体自净/水體自淨 self-purification of water body
水体自净能力/水自淨作用 water self-purification
水田/水田 ponding paddy field
水田土壤/水田土 paddy field soil
水听器/水聽器,接收換能器 receiving transducer
水头/水頭 water head
水头损失/水頭損失,壓頭損失 head loss
水头梯度/地下水位比降 water table gradient
水土保持/水土保持 soil and water conservation, soil and water preservation, erosion control
水土保持措施/水土保持措施 soil and water conservation measure
水土保持工程/水土保持工程 soil and water conservation engineering
水土保持规划/水土保持規劃 soil and water conservation planning
水土保持区划/水土保持區域規劃 soil and water conservation regionalization
水土保持塑料网/水土保持塑膠網 erosion control plastic net
水土保持效益/水土保持效益 soil and water conservation benefit
水土流失/水土流失 soil and water loss, erosion loss
水网地区/水網地區 dense waterway net region
水网密度指数/水系密度指數 water system density index
水委一/水委一 Achernar
水位/水位 water level
水位表/水位計,水位指示器 water level indicator, water level gage
水位尺规/水位標尺,量水標 graduated staff gage
水位关系/水位關係 stage relation
水位计/水標尺 stage gage
水位记录仪/水位記錄儀,水位計 level recorder, water level recorder
水位历时曲线/水位延時曲線 duration curve of water level
水位-流量关系/水位流量關係 stage-discharge relation
水位-流量曲线/水位流量曲線 stage-discharge curve
水位坡尺/坡尺 inclined gage
水位突降/水位急降 sudden drawdown
水温控制器/水温調整器 water temperature regulator
水文测量/水文調查,水文勘測 hydrologic survey, hydrological survey
水文测量基准面/測水基點 hydrographic datum
水文测验断面/觀測斷面 hydrometric section
水文测站/流量站 discharge site
水文等值线图/地水同變圖 hydroisopleth map
水文地质参数/水文地理參數 hydrogeological parameter
水文地质调查/水文地質調查 hydrogeological survey, hydrogeologic survey
水文地质图/水文地質圖 hydrogeological map
水文地质[学]/水文地質學 hydrogeology
水文调查船/水文調查船 hydrological survey ship, hydrological survey vessel
水文动态/流況 hydrological regime
水文断面/水文斷面 hydrologic sectional drawing, hydrologic section, hydrologic cross section
水文分析/水文分析 hydrologic analysis
水文过程/水文程式 hydrologic process
水文年度/水文年 hydrological year
水文图/水文圖 hydrological map
水文系统/水文系統 hydrologic system
水文学/水文學,水理學 hydrography, hydrology
水文演算/水文演算 hydrologic routing
水文预报/水文預報,水文預測 hydrological forecasting
水文站/水文站 hydrologic station
水文资料/水文資料 hydrologic data
水稳性/水穩定性 water stability
水污染/水[體]汙染 water pollution, water body

pollution

水污染防治厂/水汙染防治廠 water pollution control plant

水污染治理/水汙染控制,水汙染防治,水汙染管制 water pollution control

水务管理/水務管理 water management

水雾喷头/噴霧嘴,[噴霧]噴嘴 spray nozzle

水洗分析/水洗分析 washing analysis

水系统/水系統 water system

水系型式/排水型態 drainage pattern

水下爆破/水中爆炸 submarine blasting, underwater blasting

水下爆破切割/水下爆切 underwater explosive cutting

水下爆炸试验水池/水下爆炸試驗水槽 underwater explosion tank

水下泵/沈水泵 underwater pump

水下侧面积/水下側[向]面積 lateral underwater area

水下测量作业/水下測量作業 submarine survey work

水下储油罐/水下儲油櫃 underwater oil storage tank

水下弹道测量/水下彈道測定 underwater ballistic measurement

水下倒车/水下倒車 submerged running astern

水下灯/水下彩燈,水柱燈,水中照明 subaqueous lamp, underwater light

水下逗留时间/水下續航力 submerged endurance

水下焊接/水中焊接 underwater welding

水下航行/水下航行 underwater navigation

水下混凝土浇筑/水中灌置混凝土 underwater concreting, underwater concrete pouring

水下机器人/水下機器人 underwater robot

水下基床夯实/水下河床夯實 underwater bed tamping

水下基床整平/水下河床整平 underwater bed leveling

水下监视电视/水下監視電視 monitor TV underwater

水下监听站/水下監測站 underwater monitoring station

水下浇筑混凝土法/水中灌置混凝土 underwater concreting

水下胶黏剂/水下膠黏劑 underwater adhesive

水下阶段减压法/水下階段減壓 underwater stage decompression

水下居住舱/水下居住艙,水下起居艙 underwater habitat

水下黏合/水下黏合 underwater adhesion

水下抛锚/水下抛錨 submerged anchor dropping

水下起锚/水下起錨 submerged anchor weighing

水下切割/水下切割,水中切割 underwater cutting

水下摄影机/水中攝影機 underwater camera

水下生产系统/海底石油生產系統 subsea production system

水下声标/水下聲標 underwater sound projector

水下隧道/水下隧道,水底隧道 subaqueous tunnel, underwater tunnel

水下弹射/水下彈射 underwater ejection

水下推土机/水中推土機 underwater bulldozer

水下文化遗产/水下文化遺產 underwater cultural heritage

水下系泊装置/水下繫泊設施 underwater mooring device

水下悬浮/水下懸浮 underwater hovering

水下旋回/水下迴旋 underwater turning

水下音响信号/水中音響信號 submarine sound signal

水下游览船/水下遊覽船,水下觀光船 tourist submersible, underwater sightseeing boat

水下游览艇/觀光潛艇 tourist submersible

水下障碍物/水下障礙物 sunken danger

水下钻岩机/水中鑿岩機 underwater rock drill

水下作业船/水下作業船 underwater operation ship

水下作业灯/水下作業燈 submerged lamp

水下作业机械/水下作業機械 underwater operating machine

水下作业站/水下工作站 underwater working station

水线/水線 waterline

水线长/水線長度 waterline length

水线面/水線面 water plane

水线面积/水線面積 area of water plane

水线面系数/水線面[積]係數 waterplane coefficient

水线漆/水線漆 boot-topping paint

水线区腐蚀/水線區腐蝕 boot-topping corrosion, waterline zone corrosion

水箱间/水箱間 water tank room

水箱验水阀/水箱驗水閥 water tank test cock

水榭/水榭 waterside pavilion

水星/水星 Mercury

水星地质/水星地質 geology of Mercury

水性木器涂料/水性木器塗料 water-based woodenware coating

水性涂料/水性塗料 waterborne coating

水循环系统/水循環系統　water circulation system
水压/水壓　water pressure
水压舱/水壓艙　water ballast hold
水压机车间/水壓機工場　hydraulic press shop
水压计程仪/水壓計程儀　pitometer log
水压试验/水壓[力]試驗　hydrostatic test
水压图/壓力圖　pressure diagram
水压引信/水壓引信　hydrostatic fuze
水压载/水壓載　water ballast
水翼艇/水翼船　hydrofoil boat, hydrofoil craft
水银槽/水銀盤　mercury bath
水应用/利用水　water utilization
水硬性/水凝性　hydraulicity
水硬性胶凝材料/水硬性黏料，水力結合器　hydraulic binder
水域/水域　water area
水域控制线/水域控制線　controlling line for water area
水缘/水岸　water front
水源/水源　water source
水源保护/水源保護　water source protection, protection of water sources
水源保护区/[飲用水]水源保護區　water source protection area
水源地/水源地　water source site
水源涵养林/水源涵養保安林　water conservation forest
水源林/水源林　head-water forest
水源热泵/水源熱泵機組　water source heat pump unit
水源选择/水源選擇　water sources selection
水运/水輸送　water carriage
水运经济学/海運經濟學　shipping economics
水运系统/水運系統　waterborne system
水再生技术/水再生技術　water regeneration technique
水闸/暗渠閘門　clough
水蒸发器/水蒸發器　water evaporator
水蒸气保护电弧焊/蒸汽保護電弧焊　steam shielded arc welding
水蒸气分压力/蒸汽分壓　partial vapor pressure, partial pressure of water vapor
水蒸气渗透/蒸汽滲透　vapor permeation
水质/水質　water quality
水质标准/水質標準　water quality standard, water standard
水质控制/水質控制　water quality control
水质稳定处理/水質穩定處理　water quality stabilization treatment
水质污染/水[質]汙染　water pollution
水质阻垢缓蚀处理/水質阻垢緩蝕處理　water quality treatment of scale-prevent and corrosion-delay
水中粪生链球菌群/糞便鏈球菌　fecal streptococci
水柱/水柱　water column
水柱测量雷达/水柱儀表級雷達　water column instrumentation radar
水准标尺/水準標尺　leveling staff
水准测量/水準測量，高程測量　leveling survey, differential leveling
水准点/水準點，基準標誌　benchmark, BM
水准点高程测量/基平　benchmark leveling
水准偏差/水準偏差　disorder of cross-level
水准器/氣泡水準儀　bubble level
水准式测角仪/水準式測角儀　level type angle gage
水准仪/水準儀，液位計　level gage, level
水资源/水資源　water resources
水资源规划/水資源規劃　water resources planning
水资源开发利用率/水資源利用率，水資源利用因數　utilization ratio of water resources
水族馆/水族館　aquarium
水阻/水阻力　water resistance
税金/税金　taxation
睡莲池/睡蓮池　water-lily pool
顺岸码头/順岸碼頭，堤岸　parallel wharf, quay
顺坝/順壩　longitudinal dike, longitudinal dam
顺风/順風，尾風　favorable wind, tail wind, following wind
顺风航驶/順風航駛　running free
顺风航行/乘風航行　scudding
顺风换舷/轉向迎風行駛　wearing
顺风涨潮/順風漲潮　wind ward fload
顺桨/螺旋槳順槳　propeller feathering
顺浪/順浪，從浪　following sea
顺浪航行/順浪航行　running with the sea
顺列式枢纽/順列式樞紐　longitudinal arrangement type junction terminal
顺流/順流　favorable current
顺流船/順流船　downstream vessel
顺流掉头/順流掉頭　turning short round with the aid of current
顺坡/緩和段　run-off elevation
顺时针旋转/順時針旋轉　clockwise rotation
顺水/下游　down stream, lower reach
顺纹压力/順紋壓力　compression parallel to grain
顺向重叠进路/順向重疊進路　route with overlapped

section in the same direction
顺行轨道/順行軌道 progressive orbit
顺序测试/順序試驗,系列試驗 sequence testing
顺序单频编码/順序單頻編碼 sequential single frequency code
顺序阀/順序閥 sequence valve
顺序拼装分析/順序拼裝分析 progressive analysis for bridge erection
顺压梯度/[順向]壓力梯度 favorable pressure gradient
顺应式结构或系统/順應式鑽油臺 compliant structures or systems
顺筑法/自底向上建築法 bottom-up construction method
顺砖砌法/順磚式砌合 stretcher bond
瞬变工况/暫態運行情況 transient operating condition
瞬变热流法/暫態熱通量法 transient heat flux method
瞬变现象/過渡現象 transient phenomenon
瞬发临界事故/瞬發臨界事故 prompt critical accident
瞬间干燥机/速乾機 dryer flash
瞬时沉降/即時沈陷 immediate settlement
瞬时单位线/瞬時單位歷線 instantaneous unit hydrograph
瞬时分路/瞬時分路 instantaneous shunt
瞬时分路不良/瞬時分路不良 instantaneous loss of shunting
瞬时根数/瞬態根數 transient elements
瞬时故障/瞬息故障,短暫故障 transient fault
瞬时过载/瞬時過載 momentary overload
瞬时荷载/瞬時載重 transient loading
瞬时空气速度/瞬時空氣速度 instantaneous air speed
瞬时孔隙压力/瞬時孔隙壓力 instantaneous pore pressure
瞬时流量/瞬時流量 instant flow rate
瞬时凝结/瞬凝,閃凝 flash set
瞬时热状态/暫態熱狀態 transient thermal behavior
瞬时视场/瞬間視角 instantaneous field of view, IFOV
瞬时调速率/瞬時速度變動率 instantaneous speed change rate
瞬时效应/暫態效應 transient effect
瞬时应变/瞬時應變 instantaneous strain
瞬时中心/瞬時中心 instantaneous center
瞬时轴线/瞬軸 instantaneous axis

瞬时最大风/瞬時最大風 instantaneous maximum wind
瞬态/瞬時狀態,過度狀態,暫態 transient mode, transient state, instantaneous state
瞬态表面温度探头/暫態表面溫度探測器 transient surface temperature probe
瞬态波试验/暫態波試驗 transient wave test
瞬态测量/瞬態量測 instantaneous measurement
瞬态冲击试验/暫態衝擊試驗 transient shock test
瞬态传热/瞬時熱轉移 transient heat transfer
瞬态电流/暫態電流 transient current
瞬态反应/暫態反應 transient response
瞬态性能/暫態性能 transient performance
瞬态振动/暫態振動 transient vibration
瞬态振动环境/暫態振動環境 transient vibration environment
瞬态中子/瞬發中子 instantaneous neutron
朔望高潮/朔望高潮 high water full and change
朔望月/朔望月 synodical month
司法建筑/法院建築 judicial building
司法权/行政管轄 jurisdiction
司机/司機 driver
司机操纵台/司機操縱臺 driver desk
[司机]反应距离/駕駛人反應距離 driver reaction distance
[司机]感觉反应距离/駕駛人認識反應距離 driver perception-reaction distance
[司机]感觉反应时间/駕駛人認識反應時間 driver perception-reaction time
司机及助手劳动生产率/司機及助手勞動生產率 productivity of driver and assistant
司机控制器/司機控制器 driver controller
司机模拟操纵装置/司機模擬操縱裝置 simulator for driver train-handling
[司机]判断时间/駕駛人判斷時間 driver judgement time
[司机]识别距离/駕駛人識別距離 driver decipherment distance
司机室/駕駛室,運轉室 driver cab
司机室工作条件检查/駕駛室工作條件檢查 check on working condition in the driver cab
司机室空调装置/駕駛室空調器 driver cab air conditioner
司机室取暖电炉/駕駛室電熱器,駕駛室電爐 driver cab electric heater
司机室热风装置/駕駛室暖風器 driver cab air heater
司机运转报单/司機運轉報單 driver service-report,

driver log
司机座椅/司機座椅　driver chair
司炉/司爐　fireman
司太立合金/史帝田合金，鈷鉻鎢合金　Stellite
丝绸之路/絲綢之路　the Silk Road
丝带式转子组件/絲帶式轉子組件　filament rotor assembly
丝网印刷/網印　screen printing
私家园林/私家園林，私家花園　private garden
私立学校/私[立學]校　private school
私密性/私密性，隱私　privacy
私人空间/私用空間　private space
私塾/私塾　private school
私营铁路/私有鐵道，專用鐵道　private railway
私用助航标/私用助航標　private aid to navigation
私有码头/私有碼頭　private wharf
斯柯特接线牵引变压器/斯柯特接線法牽引變壓器，斯柯特連接繞組牽引變壓器　traction transformer of Scott connection
斯坦顿数/斯坦頓數　Stanton number, St
斯特林致冷器/史特靈冷凍機　Stirling refrigerator
斯图海德园/斯圖海德園　Stourhead Park
斯陀园/斯托景觀花園　Stowe Landscape Gardens
撕开型裂纹/撕開裂紋　tearing mode of crack
死胡同/此路不通　no through road
死区/死空間，死帶　dead space, dead band, dead zone
死区段/死區，無電段　dead section
死水/死水　dead water
死头街道/死頭街道　dead-end street
死亡率/死亡率　death rate
四层交叉口/四層交叉道　four-level crossing
四车道/四車道，四幅路　four-lanes, quadri carriageway road
四冲程柴油机/四衝程柴油機　four-stroke diesel engine
四冲程内燃机/四衝程引擎　four cycle engine, four-stroke engine
四冲程循环/四衝程循環　four cycle, four-stroke cycle
四冲程压缩/四衝程壓縮　four-stage compression
四重积/四重積　the four-fold plot
四等三角测量/四等三角測量　fourth order triangulation
四等三角点/四等三角點　fourth order triangulation station
四点方位/四點方位　four point bearing
四点检查/四點檢查　released by checking four sections
四幅式城市道路/四幅式市區道路　four-slab urban road
四钩吊链/四肢吊索　four-leg sling
四管制水系统/四管制水系統　four-pipe water system
四合院/四合院　courtyard house with four building, siheyuan
四级公路/四級公路　fourth-class highway
四极质谱仪/四極質譜儀　quadruple mass-spectrometer
四角锥网架/四角錐網架　square pyramid space grid
四铰管涵/四鉸管涵　quadri-hinge-pipe culvert
四脚锥体/菱形塊　tetrapod
四开木材纹理/板面木紋　quarter grain
四旁植树/四面栽植　four-side tree planting
四频组方式/四頻組方式　four-frequency group mode
四维/四維　four dimension, 4D
四维空间/四維空間　four dimensional space
四维制导系统/四維導引系統　four dimension guidance system
四显示自动闭塞/四顯示自動閉塞　four-aspect automatic block
四线铁路/雙複線　quadruple track
四线扬声/四線揚聲　four wire loudspeaking
四向碳-碳/四向碳-碳　4-directional C-C
四向停车/四通停車　four way stop
四氧化二氮铁路运输车/四氧化二氮鐵路搬運車　nitrogen tetroxide railway tank transporter
四叶式交通布置/四葉形交叉　clover-leaf crossing
四用广播机/四功能播講裝置　four-function public address equipment
四肢约束装置/四肢限動裝置，手腳固定裝置　limb restraint
四轴车/四軸車　four-axle car
四轴平台/四軸平臺　four-axis platform
寺庙园林/寺廟園林，寺觀園林　monastery garden, temple garden
寺院/寺廟，禪寺　monastery, temple
伺服/伺服　servo
伺服步距角/伺服步長　servo step size
伺服电[动]机/伺服電動機，伺服馬達　servomotor
伺服高度表/伺服高度表　servo altimeter
伺服机构/伺服機構　servomechanism
伺服控制单元/伺服控制系統　servo control unit
伺服马达/伺服馬達，伺服電動機　servomotor
伺服疲劳试验机/伺服疲勞試驗機　servo fatigue

testing machine
伺服气动弹性/伺服氣動彈性　servo aeroelasticity
伺服试验/伺服試驗　servo test
伺服系统测试仪/伺服機構試驗器　servomechanism tester
伺服型加速度计/伺服加速度計　servo accelerometer
伺服转台/伺服控制平臺　servo table
饲料储存处/貯料倉　feed storage
饲料加工间/農場内的飼料加工　feed processing plant
松柏园/松柏園　conifer garden
松柏植物/松柏類,針葉樹　conifer
松弛/鬆弛法　relaxation
松弛压力/鬆弛壓　relaxation pressure
松出/鬆出　pay out
松掉/鬆掉　cast loose
松动/鬆開　loosening
松动爆破/鬆動[岩石]爆破　loosening blasting, blasting for loosening rock
松杆/自由駕駛桿　stick-free
松紧螺栓/鬆緊螺絲　turning buckle
松开/鬆開,放鬆　ease off
松配合/鬆配合　loose fit
松铺厚度/鬆鋪厚度　loose laying depth
松铺系数/鬆鋪係數　coefficient of loose laying
松散/鬆散　surface loosening
松散保护层/鬆散保護層　loose protection course
松散压力/鬆散壓力　loosening pressure
松套伸缩接头/套筒伸縮接頭　dresser coupling, sleeve expansion joint
松土除草机/鬆土除草機　cultivator
松土机/鬆土機,破土犁　scarifier, ripper
松针土/松針土　pine needle mulch
松装密度/視密度,表觀密度　apparent density
送电端/送電端　feed end
送风道/供氣管道　air delivery duct
送风机房/送風機室　supply fan room
送风竖井/送風竖井　blowing-in shaft
送风器/吹風機,鼓風機,增壓器　blower
送话器/[送]話筒　transmitter
送受分开电路/送受分開電路　sending and receiving separated circuit
送丝机构/供線機　wire feeder
送丝装置/供[焊]線裝置　wire drive feed unit
送网管/送網管,輸網管　net carrying pipe
送桩/送椿　pile follower
送桩器/送椿器　long dolly

搜查证/搜查令狀　search warrant
搜救程序/搜救程式　search and rescue procedure
搜救重发器接收天线/搜救重發器接收天線　SARR receive antenna
搜救单元/搜救單位　search and rescue unit
搜救雷达应答器/搜救雷達詢答器　search and rescue radar transponder
搜救区/搜救區　search and rescue region, SRR
搜救任务协调员/搜救任務協調人　search and rescue mission coordinator, SRMC
搜救卫星辅助跟踪/搜救衛星輔助追蹤,衛星輔助搜救追蹤系統　search and rescue satellite aided tracking
搜救卫星系统/搜救衛星系統　search and rescue satellite system
搜救协调通信/搜救協調通信　search and rescue coordinating communication, SAR coordinating communication
搜救协调中心/搜救協調中心　rescue coordination center, RCC
搜救业务/搜救業務　search and rescue service, SAR service
搜救中继器/搜救中繼器,搜救重發器　search and rescue repeater
搜索/搜索,搜尋　search
搜索测频法/搜索測頻法　scanning frequency measurement
搜索测向法/搜索測向法　scanning direction finding
搜索功能/搜尋功能　search function
搜索机动/搜索策略　search maneuvre
搜索视场/搜索視野　FOV of search
搜索线/搜索線　sweep
搜寻半径/搜索半徑　search radius
搜寻方式/搜索方式　search pattern
搜寻航线/搜索航跡　search track
搜寻基点/搜索基點　search datum
搜寻遇险船舶空间系统/搜索遇險船舶太空系統　space system for search of distress vessels
苏式彩画/蘇式彩畫　Suzhou style pattern
苏伊士运河吨位/蘇彝士運河噸位　Suez canal tonnage
苏伊士运河探照灯/蘇彝士運河探照燈　Suez canal search light
苏伊士运河专用吨位证书/蘇彝士運河噸位證書　Suez Canal Special Tonnage Certificate
苏州园林/蘇州園林　Suzhou traditional garden
素混凝土/無筋混凝土　plain concrete
素混凝土结构/無筋混凝土結構　plain concrete

structure
素填土/素填土 plain fill
素枕/素枕 untreated wooden tie
速闭舱盖/快速開閉艙蓋 quick acting hatch cover, quick closing hatch cover
速闭阀/快閉閥 quick closing valve
速闭装置/快速關閉設施 quick action closing device
速变参数/速變參數 fast varying parameter, parameter requiring high response
速差制信号/速差制信號 speed signaling
速长比/速長比 speed length ratio
速度/速度,速率 velocity, speed
速度比/速度比率 velocity ratio
速度边界层/速度邊界層 velocity boundary layer
速度变化/速率變化 speed variation
速度差/速差率 speed difference
速度场/速度場 velocity field
速度传感器/速率感測器,轉速感測器 speed sensor
速度导纳/速率導納 mobility
速度地震仪/地震速度計 velocity seismograph
速度分布/速度分布,速度分散,流速分布 velocity distribution, velocity dispersion
速度分量/速度分量,分速度 component of velocity, velocity component
速度关机/速度關機 velocity cutoff
速度合成/速度合成 velocity complex
速度级/速度級 velocity stage
速度记录仪/速度記錄器 tachograph
速度继电器/速率繼電器,轉速繼電器,速率電驛[器] speed relay
速度降/速度降 speed drop
速度降旋钮/降速鈕 speed drop knob
速度均匀性/速度均匀性 velocity uniformity
速度控制范围/速度控制範圍 speed control range
速度控制系统/速率控制系統 speed control system
速度模糊/速度模糊 velocity ambiguity
速度剖面/速度剖面 velocity profile
速度谱/速度振譜 velocity spectrum
速度欺骗干扰/速度欺騙干擾 velocity deception jamming
速度三角形/速度三角形 velocity triangle
速度设定值/速度設定值 speed setting value
速度势/速度[位]勢,流勢 velocity potential
速度特性/速度特性,速率特性 velocity characteristic, speed characteristic
速度图法/速度圖解法 hodograph method
速度误差/速度誤差 speed error
速度误差表/速度誤差表 speed error table
速度误差校正器/速度誤差校正器 speed error corrector
速度系数/速度係數 velocity coefficient
速度限制/速率限制,速限 speed limit
速度型压缩机/渦輪壓縮機,輪機壓縮機 turbo-compressor
速度阻滞/速度阻滯 speed deceleration
速度坐标系/速度坐標系 velocity coordinate system
速高比/速高比 velocity to height ratio
速高比计/速高比計 velocity to height meter
速降/速降 downhill
速降场地/速降場地 downhill site
速率积分陀螺仪/速率積分陀螺儀 rate integrating gyro
速率捷联式惯性制导系统/速率捷聯式慣性制導系統 rate strap-down inertial guidance system
速率距离曲线/速率距離曲線 speed distance curve
速率累积曲线/速率累積曲線 speed accumulation curve
速率陀螺/速率陀螺儀 rate gyroscope
速率转台/速率轉檯 rate table
速率阻尼/速率阻尼 rate damping
速凝/速凝 rapid curing
速凝剂/快凝劑,催凝劑 flash setting admixture, accelerator
速潜/緊急下潛 quick diving
速遣/派遣 despatch
速生树/速生樹 fast growing tree
速脱扣/速脱扣 quick release buckle
速效钾/有效鉀 available potassium
宿存/宿存的,殘存的 persistent
宿根花卉/宿根花卉 perennial root flower, perennial flower
宿根花境/宿根花卉花境 perennial border
宿根园/宿根園 perennial garden
宿舍/集體宿舍 dormitory
宿舍区/宿舍區,住宅區 dormitory area
宿营车/供列車乘務員用的臥鋪車 dormitory car
塑钢门窗/塑鋼門窗 unplasticized polyvinyl chloride door and window, PVC-U door and window
塑化剂/塑化劑 plasticizer
塑胶跑道/塑膠跑道 synthetic track, synthetic surfaced track
塑料/塑膠 plastic
塑料层板/疊合塑膠板 laminated plastic
塑料地板/塑膠地板 plastic floor
HDPE塑料管/HDPE塑膠管 HDPE plastic tube
PE塑料管/PE塑膠管 PE plastic tubing

PPR 塑料管/PPR 塑膠管　PPR plastic tubing
PVC 塑料管/PVC 塑膠管　PVC plastic tubing
UPVC 塑料管/UPVC 塑膠管　UPVC plastic tubing
塑料家具/塑膠家具　plastic furniture
塑料垃圾袋/塑膠垃圾袋　plastic garbage bag
塑料苗木桶/塑膠苗木桶　plastic nursery can
塑料棚/塑膠溫室　plastic house, plastic greenhouse
塑料艇/塑膠艇　plastic boat
塑料涂层/塑膠塗料　plastic coating
塑料温室/塑膠溫室　plastic house, plastic greenhouse
塑料植草格/塑膠植草格　plastic grass grid
塑料轴瓦头/塑膠軸瓦頭　plastic wearing end for plain bearing
塑铝管/鋁塑複合管　plastic-aluminum-plastic pipe, PAP pipe
塑木/塑化木　plastic wood
塑山/塑山　molding hill, man-made rockwork
塑石/塑石,人造石　artificial stone, man-made rockery
塑限/塑[性下]限,塑性限度　plastic limit, PL
塑限试验/塑限試驗　plastic limit test
塑性/塑性　plasticity
塑性波/塑性波　plastic wave
塑性断裂/塑性破壞　plastic fracture
塑性断面模量/塑性斷面模數　plastic section modulus
塑性焊接/塑性焊接　plastic welding
塑性混凝土/塑性混凝土,塑膠混凝土,石膏混凝土　plastic concrete
塑性铰/塑性鉸　plastic hinge
塑性铰线/塑性鉸線　plastic hinge line
塑性理论/塑性理論　theory of plasticity
塑性理论设计/塑性設計　plastic design
塑性流幅/塑性流量範圍　plastic flow range
塑性密封材料/塑性密封材料　plastic sealant
塑性模量/塑性模數　plastic modulus
塑性平衡状态/塑性平衡狀態　state of plastic equilibrium
塑性区尺寸/塑性區尺寸　plastic zone size
塑性屈服/塑性降伏　plastic yielding
塑性土/塑性土壤　plastic soil
塑性弯矩/塑性力矩　plastic moment
塑性位势/塑性位能　plastic potential
塑性限度/塑性限度　plastic limit
塑性形变记录仪/塑性測定器　plastograph
塑性形变理论/塑性變形理論　plastic deformation theory

塑性应变/塑性應變　plastic strain
塑性增量理论/增量塑性理論　incremental theory of plasticity
塑性指数/塑性指標　plastic index, plasticity number
溯源性/溯源性,可追溯性　traceability
酸度/酸度,酸性　acidity
酸度计/酸鹼度計,pH 計　pH meter
酸腐蚀/酸腐蝕　acid corrosion
酸碱度[值]/酸鹼值,pH 值　pH value
酸土植物/酸土植物　oxylophyte, oxyphile
酸洗/酸洗,浸洗　pickling, acid pickling, dipping
酸洗车间/酸洗車間　pickling shop
酸性电池/酸性電池[組]　acid battery
酸性钢/酸性鋼,矽爐鋼　acid steel
酸性泥炭沼泽/酸沼,矮叢沼,雨養深泥沼　moor
酸性土/酸性土　acid soil
酸性土植物/嗜酸植物,喜酸植物　acidophilous plant
酸性岩/酸性岩　acidic rock
酸雨/酸雨　acid rain
酸值/酸值,酸價　acid value
随边/殿緣　trailing edge
随车调查/隨車調查　on-vehicle survey
随车观测法/隨車觀測法　moving observer method
随车液压起重臂/隨車液壓起重臂　escort hydraulic arm
随车装卸机械/隨車裝卸機械　escort handling machinery
随船工程师/任務工程師　mission engineer
随船入坞货/船塢貨　dock cargo
随船医生/任務醫生　mission doctor
随动/伺服　servo
随动跟踪/伺服追蹤　servo tracking
随动控制/追蹤控制,追隨控制　follow-up control
随动速度/追蹤速度　follow-up speed
随动系统灵敏度/隨動系統靈敏度　sensitivity of follow-up system
随工验收/隨工驗收　acceptance following construction, follow-up acceptance
随机/隨機　stochastic
随机变量/隨機變數,序率變數　random variable, stochastic variable
随机抽样/隨機抽樣,隨機採樣　random sampling, random sample
随机动态规划/序率動態規劃　stochastic dynamic programming
随机方法/序率法　stochastic method
随机工具/隨機工具　tool attachment
随机故障/隨機故障,隨機失效　random failure,

random fault
随机过程/機率過程,機率程式　probabilistic process, stochastic process
随机码引信/隨機碼引信　random code fuze
随机模型/隨機模型,機率模式　stochastic model
随机漂移率/隨機漂移率　random drift rate
随机谱/隨機譜　random spectrum
随机取样法/隨機取樣法　method of random sampling
随机水文学/隨機水文學　stochastic hydrology
随机系统/隨機系統　stochastic system
随机线性规划/隨機線性規劃　stochastic linear programming
随机性效应/機率性效應　stochastic effect
随机游动角/隨機遊走角　random walk angle
随机振动/隨機振動　random vibration
随机振动环境/隨機振動環境　random vibration environment
随机振动试验/隨機振動試驗　random vibration test
随浪/順浪,從浪　following sea
随挖随盖法/明挖覆蓋[工]法,先塹後蓋法　cut and cover method
随意组合方石板路/隨意組合方石板路　flag stone path paved at random
岁差/歲差　precession
碎冰/碎冰　brash ice
碎冰机/碎冰機　ice crusher
碎冰山/碎冰山　berg-bit
碎波波高/碎波波高　breaking height
碎波波高指数/碎波波高指數　breaking height index
碎波点/碎波點　wave breaking point
碎波水深指数/碎波水深指數　breaking depth index
碎浪海面/三角波近海　short sea
碎砾石/碎礫石　crushed gravel
碎落台/碎落臺　stage for heaping debris
碎片云/碎片雲　debris cloud
碎片增长率/碎片成長率　debris growing rate
碎肉机/碎肉機　meat chopper
碎石厂/碎石廠　crushing plant
碎石道碴/碎石道碴　stone ballast
碎石分级/碎石分級　crusher-run
碎石灰尘/碎粉　crusher dust
碎石机/破碎機,軋碎機,壓碎機　crusher, granulator, stone crusher
碎石基层/碎石底層　macadam base
碎石路面/碎石路面　gravel pavement
碎石设备/碎石設備　crushed-stone equipment
碎石压路机/碎石路輾壓機　macadam roller
碎土器/土塊粉碎器　soil shredder
碎岩船/碎岩船　rock breaker boat
隧道/隧道　tunnel
隧道报警装置/隧道報警裝置,隧道報警設備　tunnel warning installation, tunnel warning equipment
隧道边墙/隧道邊牆,隧道側牆　tunnel side wall
隧道标/隧道標　tunnel post
隧道冰害/隧道凍害　frost damage in tunnel, freezing damage in tunnel
隧道测量/隧道測量　tunnel survey, tunnel surveying
隧道长度/隧道長度　length of tunnel
隧道衬砌/隧道襯砌,隧道襯壁　tunnel lining
隧道衬砌模板台车/隧道襯砌範本臺車　working jumbo for tunnel lining, tunneling shutter jumbo for tunnel lining
隧道出口/隧道洞口　tunnel exit
隧道底板/隧道底板,隧洞底部　tunnel floor
隧道底鼓/隧道底板隆起　tunnel floor heave
隧道地表沉陷/隧道地面沈陷　tunnel ground subsidence, ground surface subsidence over tunnel, surface settlement
隧道地中位移/隧道地中位移　tunnel surrounding mass deflection
隧道电话系统/隧道電話系統　tunnel telephone system
隧道顶板/隧道洞頂　tunnel roof
隧道顶线/隧[道]頂線　tunnel top line
隧道洞口投点/隧道洞門投點　horizontal point of tunnel portal, geodetic control point of portal location of adit
隧道洞门/隧道門,隧道口　tunnel portal
隧道洞内控制测量/隧道洞內控制測量　intunnel control survey
隧道洞身/隧道安全口　tunnel trunk
隧道洞外控制测量/隧道洞外控制測量　outside tunnel control survey
隧道断面轮廓/隧道斷面輪廓　tunnel contour
隧道断面收敛/隧道斷面收斂　tunnel cross section convergence
隧道对角变形/隧道對角變形　tunnel diagonal deformation
隧道防火措施/隧道防火措施　measures against tunnel fire
隧道防排水/隧道防排水　tunnel water handling
隧道防水/隧道防水　tunnel waterproofing, waterproofing of tunnel

隧道防灾设施/隧道防災設施　tunnel anti-disaster facilities, tunnel anti-disaster equipment, disaster prevention facility of tunnel
隧道非破损探查/隧道非破壞檢測　non destructive investigation of tunnel
隧道改建/隧道改建工程　tunnel reconstruction
隧道工程/隧道工程,隧道開鑿　tunneling
隧道工程学/隧道工程[學]　tunnel engineering
隧道功率分配器/隧道功率分配器　power divider in tunnel
[隧道]拱顶/拱頂,頂拱　crown
隧道拱顶下沉/隧道拱頂下沈,隧道頂拱沈陷　tunnel arch top settlement, tunnel roof settlement
[隧道]拱圈/隧道拱圈　arch, tunnel arch
隧道供电系统/隧道供電系統　tunnel power supply system
隧道管/管式隧道　tunnel pipe
隧道贯通/隧道貫通,通過地道　tunnel through, tunnel holing-through
隧道贯通面/隧道貫通面　tunnel through plane
隧道贯通误差/隧道貫通誤差　tunnel through error
隧道广播系统/隧道播音系統　tunnel broadcasting system
隧道横断面/隧道橫斷面　tunnel cross section, tunnel section
隧道火灾/隧道火災　tunnel fire hazard
隧道火灾监测/隧道火災監測　tunnel fire monitoring
隧道激光导向/隧道雷射導向　tunnel alignment by laser
隧道级别/隧道級別　tunnel class
隧道监控量测/隧道監控量測,隧道監控測量　tunnel monitoring measurement
隧道监控中心/隧道行控中心　tunnel operation control center
隧道建筑限界/隧道建築限界　tunnel construction clearance, tunnel structure gage, construction clearance of tunnel
隧道交通监测系统/隧道交通監控系統　tunnel traffic monitoring system
隧道进口/隧道洞口　tunnel entrance
隧道净断面/隧道淨空間距,隧道餘隙　tunnel clearance, inside crosssection of tunnel
隧道净空/隧道淨空間距,隧道餘隙　tunnel clearance, inside crosssection of tunnel
隧道掘进法/隧道鑿進法　tunnel driving method
隧道掘进机/隧道鑽鑿機,潛盾機　tunnel boring machine, TBM

隧道开挖/隧道開挖　tunnel excavation
隧道勘测/隧道勘察　tunnel reconnaissance
隧道口净空/淨空高度　portal clearance
隧道漏水/隧道漏水　tunnel leak
隧道落底/隧道落底　under cut of tunnel
隧道埋深/隧道埋置深度　buried depth of tunnel, embedment depth of tunnel
隧道埋置深度/隧道埋置深度　buried depth of tunnel, embedment depth of tunnel
隧道模板/隧道模板　tunnel form
隧道内亮度水平/隧道內亮度水準　luminance level in the tunnel interior
隧道内轮廓位移/隧道內輪廓位移　displacement of inner contour of tunnel
隧道排气污染/隧道排放汙染　tunnel discharge pollution
隧道排水设备/隧道排水設施　tunnel drainage facility
隧道坡度折减/隧道坡度折減　compensation of gradient in tunnel, compensation grade in tunnel
隧道群/隧道群　tunnel group
隧道入口区亮度/隧道洞口亮度　tunnel entrance brilliance
隧道弱电场区/隧道弱電場區　weak electric field area in tunnel
隧道射流式通风/隧道射流式通風　tunnel efflux ventilation, tunnel injector type ventilation
隧道摄影车/隧道攝影車　tunnel photographing car
隧道施工防尘/隧道施工防塵　tunnel construction dust controlling
隧道施工通风/隧道施工通風　tunnel construction ventilation, construction ventilation of tunnel
隧道适宜亮度/隧道適宜亮度　suitable brilliance in tunnel
隧道水平变形/隧道水平變形　tunnel horizontal deformation
隧道坍顶/隧道落磐　tunnel roof fall
隧道套拱/隧道套拱　cover arch of tunnel
隧道挑顶/隧道挑頂　top picking of tunnel
隧道通风/隧道通風　tunnel ventilation
隧道通风帘幕/隧道通風簾幕,風障　ventilation curtain
隧道通风试验/隧道通風試驗　tunnel ventilation test
隧道通知设备/隧道通知設備　tunnel announciating device
隧道挖掘机/隧道挖掘機　tunnel excavator
隧道瓦斯爆炸/隧道氣體爆炸,隧道氣爆　gas explosion in tunnel, tunnel gas explosion

隧道瓦斯泄出/隧道瓦斯洩出　gas emission in tunnel
隧道围岩分级/隧道圍岩分類　classification of tunnel surrounding rock
隧道艉/隧[道]艉　tunnel stern
隧道消防系统/隧道防火系統,隧道滅火系統　tunnel fire protection system, tunnel fire fighting system
隧道信号/隧道[防護]信號　tunnel signal
隧道压浆/隧道壓漿　pressure grouting of tunnel
隧道仰拱/隧道仰拱　tunnel invert
隧道养护/隧道維護　tunnel maintenance
隧道用柴油机车/隧道用柴油機車　tunnel diesel locomotive
隧道运营通风/隧道運營通風　permanent ventilation of tunnel
隧道照明/隧道照明　tunnel lighting, tunnel illumination
隧道遮断信号/隧道遮斷信號　tunnel obstruction signal
隧道支撑/隧洞支撐　tunnel support
隧道中继器/隧道中繼器　tunnel repeater
隧道周边位移/隧道周邊位移　tunnel perimeter deflection
隧道注浆止水/隧道注漿止水　tunnel water sealing by injection
隧道专家系统/隧道專家系統　expert system of tunnel
隧道装载机/隧道裝載機　tunnel loader
隧道纵断面/隧道縱斷面　tunnel profile
隧道纵轴线/隧道縱軸線　tunnel axis
隧洞全断面掘进/全斷面開鑿　tunnel full face driving
损管器材/損害管制設備　damage control equipment
损管设备室/損管設備室　damage control equipment room
损害赔偿/損害賠償　compensation for damage
损耗/損益　loss
损坏区/破壞區　failure zone
损伤/損傷,損壞,損害　damage
损伤容限设计/容損設計　damage tolerance design
损伤事故/損失事故　damage accident
损失水线面面积/損失水線面面積　lost waterplane area
损失系数/損失係數　coefficient of loss
榫接/榫接[頭]　butt laying, tenon joint
榫卯/榫卯　mortise-and-tenon joint, sunmao
榫舌/榫舌　joint tongue
榫眼/榫眼　mortice
梭式矿车/接駁車,短程運輸車　shuttle car
梭[行矿]车/接駁車,短程運輸車　shuttle car
缩比模型试验/縮尺模型試驗　scale model test
缩尺/收縮尺　shrinkage rule
缩尺比/標度比　scale ratio
缩短渡线/縮短渡線　shortened crossover
缩短轨/縮短軌　standard shortened rail, fabricated short rail
缩短里程效益/縮短里程效益　benefit from distance shortening
缩短装置/縮短裝置　shortening device
缩帆/縮帆　reef
缩放/調焦　zooming
缩缝/收縮縫　contraction joint
缩减尺寸/尺寸減縮　size reduction
缩剪/縮剪　shrink shear
缩结/縮短結　sheep shank
缩景/縮景　miniature scenery, abbreviated scenery
缩径旋压/縮頸旋壓　necking in spindown
缩轮压路机/縮輪壓路機　retractable wheel roller
缩片机/縮圖儀　reduction printer
缩位地址/簡址　abbreviated address
缩小百分率/縮小百分率　percentage reduction
缩小型居民点/縮小型居民點　shrink type residential
缩小仪/縮圖儀　reduction printer
索鞍/[電]纜鞍,絞纜盤　cable saddle
索铲挖土机/拖索挖機　dragline
索道/索道,纜道　cableway, ropeway
索道客运站/索道站　cableway station
索道运输车/輸送索道　cableway transporter
索多边形/索線多邊形　string polygon
索股/索股　strand
索桁架/纜索桁架　cable truss
索夹/繩夾,[電]纜夾　cable clamp, cable band
索结构/纜索結構　cable structure
索具/索具　rigging
索力测定计/索力測量設備　cable tension measurement device
索力测量/索力測量　cable force measurement
索力控制/索力控制　cable force control
索赔/索賠,理賠,債權　claim
索赔代理证书/代位求償書　letter of subrogation
索平面/索面　cable plane
索式结构/纜索結構　cable structure
索塔/索塔　cable support tower
索头环/鋼索接眼　rope socket

索星/尋星　star finding
索星卡/尋星盤,辨星儀　star identifier, star finder
索引符号/指標符號　index symbol
索引图/索引圖,目録示圖　index chart
锁闭/鎖定,閉鎖　locking
锁闭电路/鎖定電路　locking circuit
锁闭杆/鎖止桿　locking rod
锁闭力/鎖緊力　locking force
锁闭系统/鎖定系統　locking system
锁定/鎖定　caging
锁定轨温/鎖定軌温　fastening-down temperature of rail
锁定开关/鎖定開關　key lock switch
锁定时间/鎖定時間　caging time
锁缝/折贴　crimp
锁结式集料/馬克當碎石,同粒徑碎石　macadam aggregate
锁紧中心销/鎖定中心銷　locking center pin
锁相技术/鎖相技術　phase lock technique
锁相晶体振荡器/鎖相晶體振盪器　phase locked crystal oscillator
锁轴试验/鎖軸試驗　shaft locked test

T

他励电动机／他勵電動機　separately excited motor
塌方／塌落　collapse, cave in
塌方落石报警器／滑坡警告裝置　land slide warning device
塔式高层住宅／塔式高層住宅　apartment of tower building
塔式搅拌楼／塔式拌合設備　tower-type batch plant
塔式搅拌站／塔式拌合設備　tower-type batch plant
塔式起重机／塔式起重機,塔式吊車　tower crane, column crane
塔式天平／錐狀天平　pyramidal balance
塔式住宅／塔式[高層]住宅　tower housing, apartment of tower building
塔斯干柱式／托斯卡納式　Tuscan order
塔索式挖掘机／塔式開挖機　tower excavator
塔体／塔體,塔身　tower body
塔头／塔頭　tower head
塔下建筑／塔下建築　tower skirt building
榻／坐臥兩用床,羅漢床　platform, daybed
踏板／踏板　tread, tread board
踏步／臺階　footstep
踏步立板／樓梯竪板　riser
踏勘／踏勘,勘查　reconnaissance, walk over survey, site reconnaissance
踏面／[輪]踏面,輪距,輪接觸面　landing pitch, tread, wheel tread
踏面剥离／踏面剥蝕　shelled tread
踏面擦伤／踏面擦傷　flat sliding, tread slid flat
踏面基点／踏面基點　tread taping point
踏面磨耗／踏面磨損　tread wear
踏面清扫器／踏面清掃器　tread cleaner
踏面外形／胎面輪廓　tread contour, tread profile
踏面制动／踏面制動　tread brake
踏面锥度／踏面錐度　tread conicity
踏青／郊遊,遠足　outing
胎架／組合模架　assembly jig
胎模成型／胎模成型　socket form moulding
胎模锻／胎模鍛　loose tooling forging, open die forging
台班使用费／臺班使用費　working day cost
台仓／臺倉　understage

台唇／舞臺前區　forestage
台地／臺[地],階[地]　terrace, stage, tableland
台地园／臺地園　terrace garden
台风／颱風　typhoon
台风警报／颱風警報　typhoon warning, TW
台风路径／颱風路徑　typhoon track
台风眼／颱風眼　typhoon eye
台风振动／颱風振動　typhoon vibration
台后填方／涵背回填　filling behind abutment
台基／土臺,基礎,無柱底基　stereobate
台架模拟试验／臺模擬試驗　bench simulation test
台架式集装箱／臺架式集裝箱　platform-based container
台架试验／臺架試驗,試[驗]臺試驗　bench test, testing-bed test, stand test
台间联络线／業務線,座席間中繼線　interposition trunk
台阶／臺階,踏板　steps, original mark bench
台阶灯／踏板燈　step light
台阶法／臺階法,臺階式挖土　benching tunneling method, bench cut
台阶开挖法／臺階工法　bench cut method
台阶式／階段式　terraced style
台阶式洞门／臺階式隧道洞門　bench tunnel portal
台阶式挖土／臺階式開挖　benching
台卡／迪凱　Decca
台卡船位／迪凱船位　Decca fix
台卡导航仪／迪凱導航儀　Decca navigator
台卡海图／迪凱海圖　Decca chart
台卡活页资料／迪凱活頁數據　Decca data sheet
台卡计／相位計　decometer
台卡链／迪凱鏈　Decca chain
台卡位置线／迪凱位置線　Decca position line
台口／舞臺前部,幕前部分　proscenium
台口式断面／臺口式斷面　benched section
台口式路基／臺口式路基　benched subgrade
台链／鏈[條]　chain
台帽／[橋]臺帽　abutment cap, abutment coping
台明／臺明　salient part of foundation, taiming
台球室／撞球室　billiard room, billiard parlor
台身／臺身　abutment body, body of abutment

台式天平/平臺天平,臺秤　platform balance
台塔/舞臺塔　fly tower
台体/穩定元素　stable element
台位利用系数/臺位利用係數　utility factor of the position
台榭/臺榭　high-platform building, taixie
抬高角/抬高角　correction angle due to the force of gravity
抬高水位/堰高　heading up
抬梁式/梁柱結構　post-and-beam construction, tailiang
抬前轮速度/抬前輪速率　rotation speed
抬运/抬運　stone carrying
太湖石/太湖石　Taihu stone
太空/外太空　space, outer space
太空碎片/太空垃圾　space debris
太空碎片防护/太空垃圾防護　protection of space debris
太空碎片仿真/太空垃圾模擬　simulation of space debris
[太空]碎片分布模式/碎片分布模型　debris distribution model
太空碎片环境/太空垃圾環境　space debris environment
太空碎片碰撞动力学/太空碎片碰撞動力學　impact dynamics of space debris
太空碎片通量/太空垃圾通量　flux of space debris
[太空]碎片通量模式/碎片通量模型　debris flux model
[太空]碎片危害/碎片危害　debris hazard
[太空]碎片质量分布/碎片質量分布　distribution of debris mass
太庙/太廟　Imperial Ancestral Temple, Tai Temple
太平斧/太平斧,斧頭　axe
太平间/太平間,停屍間　mortuary
太平洋区/太平洋區域　Pacific Ocean Region, POR
太阳/太陽　sun
太阳保护/太陽防曬　sun protection
太阳捕获/太陽獲得　sun acquisition
太阳常数/太陽常數　solar constant
太阳赤纬角/太陽赤緯角　solar declination angle
太阳出现敏感器/太陽出現感應器　sun presence sensor
太阳电池板/太陽能電池板　solar cell panel
太阳电池等效电路/太陽能電池等效電路　equivalent circuit of solar cell
太阳电池底板/太陽電池底圖　solar cell basic plate
太阳电池伏安特性曲线/太陽電池伏安特性曲線　V-I characteristic curve of solar cell
太阳电池温度/太陽電池溫度　solar cell temperature
太阳电池-蓄电池系统/太陽電池-蓄電池系統　solar array-battery system
太阳电池阵/太陽電池陣列　solar cell array
太阳电池阵初期功率/太陽電池陣初期功率　solar array power at the BOL
太阳电池阵额定功率/太陽電池陣額定動力　rated power of solar array
太阳电池阵面积比功率/太陽電池陣的面積比功率　area to power ratio of solar array
太阳电池阵面积利用率/太陽電池陣的面積利用率　area utilization of solar array
太阳电池阵末期功率/太陽電池陣末期功率　solar array power at the EOL
太阳电池阵驱动机构/太陽能電池陣列驅動　solar array drive, SAD
太阳电池阵实际效率/太陽電池陣實際效率　practical efficiency of solar array
太阳电池阵速率稳定度/太陽能電池陣列速率穩定性　solar array rate stability
太阳电池阵效率/太陽電池陣效率　efficiency of solar array
太阳电池阵翼/太陽電池陣翼　solar cell array wing
太阳电池阵重量比功率/太陽電池陣重量比功率　weight to power ratio of solar array
太阳电池组件/太陽能電池模組　solar cell module
太阳电池组件面积/太陽能電池模組面積　solar cell module area
太阳电磁辐射/太陽電磁輻射　solar electromagnetic radiation
太阳定标器/太陽校驗器　solar calibrator
太阳方位表/太陽方位表　sun azimuth table
太阳方位角/太陽方位角　solar azimuth angle
太阳仿真器/太陽模擬器　solar simulator
太阳仿真试验/太陽模擬試驗　solar simulation test
太阳风/太陽風　solar wind
太阳辐射/太陽輻射,日射　solar radiation
太阳辐射防护/太陽輻射防護　protection of solar radiation
太阳辐射角系数/太陽輻射係數　solar radiation factor
太阳辐射能/太陽能　solar energy
太阳辐射稳定/太陽輻射穩定　solar radiation stabilization
太阳辐射吸收系数/太陽輻射吸收係數　solar radiation absorbility factor
太阳辐射压干扰力矩/太陽輻射擾動力矩　solar

radiation disturbance torque
太阳辐照度/太陽輻射度　solar irradiance
太阳辐照量/太陽輻照,太陽能輻射　solar irradiation
太阳高度/太陽高度　solar altitude
太阳高度角/太陽高度角,太陽仰角　solar elevation, solar altitude angle
太阳跟踪器/太陽追蹤器　sun tracker
太阳光伏能源系统/光壓型太陽能源系統　solar photovoltaic energy system
太阳光谱/太陽光譜　solar spectrum
太阳光谱辐照度/太陽光譜輻照度　solar spectrum irradiancy
太阳黑点/太陽黑點　solar spot
太阳黑子/太陽黑子,日斑　sunspot
太阳红外辐射/太陽紅外線輻射　solar infrared radiation
太阳活动性/太陽活動　solar activity
太阳角/太陽角　sun angle
太阳可见光辐射/太陽可見輻射　solar visible radiation
太阳粒子辐射/太陽粒子輻射　solar particle radiation
太阳粒子事件/太陽粒子事件　solar particle event
太阳罗经/日規　sun compass
太阳敏感器/太陽感測儀　sun sensor
太阳能/太陽能　solar energy
太阳能保证率/太陽能指數　solar fraction
太阳能灯/太陽能燈　solar energy lamp
太阳能发电/太陽能發電　solar power generation
太阳能发电厂/太陽能發電廠　solar power plant
太阳能供暖/太陽加熱　solar heating
太阳能光电转换/太陽能光電轉換　solar photovoltaic conversion
太阳能光伏电站/太陽能光伏電站　solar photovoltaic power plant
太阳能光伏发电/太陽能光伏電池　solar photovoltaic electric power generation
太阳能集热器/太陽能集熱器　solar collector
太阳能沥青熔化装置/太陽能瀝青熔化裝置　asphalt solar energy melter
太阳能热发电站/太陽能熱力發電廠　solar heat power plant
太阳能热水供应系统/太陽能熱水系統　solar water heating system
太阳能热水器/太陽能熱水器　solar water heater
太阳能推进/太陽能推進　solar propulsion
太阳日/太陽日　solar day
太阳射电辐射/太陽無線電發射　solar radio emission
太阳X射线/太陽X射線　solar X-ray
太阳时/太陽時　solar time
太阳时角/太陽時角　solar hour angle
太阳视直径/太陽視直徑　solar apparent diameter
太阳同步保持/太陽同步保持　sun-synchronous keeping
太阳同步轨道/太陽同步軌道　sun-synchronous orbit
太阳同步轨道卫星/太陽同步軌道衛星　sun-synchronous orbit satellite
太阳吸收率/太陽能吸收比　solar absorptance
太阳系/太陽系　solar system
太阳系化学/太陽系化學　chemistry of the solar system
太阳耀斑/太陽閃焰,日閃焰　solar flare
太阳耀斑质子/太陽閃焰質子　solar flare proton
太阳宇宙线/太陽宇宙線　solar cosmic ray
太阳指向三轴稳定/太陽指向三軸穩定　sun-pointing three-axis stabilization
太阳质子效应/太陽質子效應,太陽質子事件　solar proton event
太阳周年视运动/太陽週年[視]運動　solar annual apparent motion
太阳紫外辐射/太陽紫外輻射　solar ultraviolet radiation
太阴半日潮/太陰半日潮　lunar semidiurnal tide
太阴全日潮/太陰日週潮　lunar diurnal tide
太阴日潮/太陰日潮　lunar diurnal tide
钛钒合金/鈦釩合金　titanium vanadium alloy
钛钙型焊条/鹼基氧化鈦系焊條　lime titania type electrode
钛合金/鈦合金　titanium alloy
钛基复合材料/鈦基複合材料　titanium matrix composite
钛铝钒合金/鈦鋁釩合金　titanium aluminum vanadium alloy
钛铝合金/鈦鋁合金　titanium aluminum alloy
钛铝化合物/鈦鋁介金屬　titanium aluminide
钛锌板/鋅銅鈦合金板　zinc-copper-titanium alloy sheet
泰姬陵/泰姬陵,泰吉・瑪哈爾陵　Taj Mahal
泰加林/泰加林,泰加群落　taiga, boreal coniferous forest
泰山石/泰山石　Taishan stone
坍方/坍方,山崩　landslide
坍落度试验/坍度試驗,流動度試驗　slump test
坍落度圆锥筒/坍度錐　slump cone

坍落扩展度/坍落擴展度　slump flow
坍塌/坍塌　sloughing
摊铺/鋪面　paving
摊铺拌和机/鋪面拌和機　paving mixer
摊铺材料压实度试验/攤鋪材料壓實度試驗　paved material compaction test
摊铺厚度/增填厚度　lift thickness
摊铺厚度测定/攤鋪厚度測定　paving depth measurement
摊铺宽度测定/攤鋪寬度測定　paving width measurement
摊铺路面平整度试验/攤鋪路面平整度試驗　paved surface evenness test
摊铺整修机/鋪整平面機　laying and finishing machine
摊铺作业试验/攤鋪作業試驗　paving operation test
滩角/齒形海岸　beach cusp
滩宽/灘寬　beach width
滩涂围垦/潮［淺］灘　tidal bank
谈话室/談話室　talk room
弹钩/滑鉤　slip hook, pelican hook
弹簧补偿器/彈簧張力器　spring tensioner
弹簧道钉/彈簧道釘　elastic rail spike
弹簧垫圈/彈簧墊圈　spring washer
弹簧动挠度/彈簧動載撓度　dynamic spring deflection
弹簧防爬器/彈簧防爬器　spring rail anchor
弹簧分离机构/彈簧分離裝置　spring separation device
弹簧刚度/彈簧勁度　spring stiffness
弹簧静挠度/彈簧靜［荷］載撓度　static spring deflection
弹簧口盖/彈簧口蓋　spring cover
弹簧螺栓/彈簧螺栓　spring bolt
弹簧摩擦式缓冲器/彈簧摩擦式緩衝器　spring friction draft gear
弹簧片式加速度计/彈簧板加速度計　plate spring accelerometer
弹簧柔度/彈簧撓性　spring flexibility
弹簧式减振器/彈簧防震器　spring damper
弹簧托板/簧板　spring plank
弹簧托梁/彈簧托梁　spring plank carrier
弹簧悬挂装置/彈簧懸置　spring suspension
弹力继电器/彈簧式繼電器　spring-type relay
弹［挠］性联轴器/撓性聯結器　flexible coupling
弹射程序控制装置/彈射程序控制裝置　ejection sequence control unit
弹射杆/彈射器活塞　piston ejector ram, ejector piston
弹射轨迹/彈射軌跡　ejection trajectory
弹射回收/彈射回收　ejecting recovery
弹射机构/彈射機構　ejection mechanism
弹射加速度/彈射加速度　ejection acceleration
弹射救生/彈射救生，彈射求生　ejection escape, ejection survival
弹射力/彈射力　catapulting force
弹射试验机/彈射試驗飛行器　ejection test vehicle
弹射损伤/彈射傷　ejection injuries
弹射逃逸/噴射逃脫　ejection escape
弹射座舱/彈射座艙　ejectable cockpit, ejection capsule
弹射座机构/彈座機構　ejection seat mechanism
弹射座椅/彈射座椅　ejection seat
弹塑性断裂力学/彈［性］塑性破壞力學　elastic-plastic fracture mechanics
弹塑性分析/彈塑性分析　elasto-plastic analysis
弹塑性模型/彈塑性模型　elasto-plastic model
弹塑性弯曲/彈塑性彎曲　elasto-plastic bending
弹塑性系统/彈塑性系統　elasto-plastic system
弹条式扣件/彈性桿扣件　elastic rod rail fastening
弹性/彈性　elasticity
弹性凹模深压延/可撓衝模深引伸　flexible die deep drawing
弹性半无限地基/彈性半無限地基　elastic semi-infinite foundation
弹性波/彈性波　elastic wave
弹性层状体系理论/彈力層系統理論　elastic layer system theory
弹性车轮/彈性輪　elastic wheel
弹性齿轮驱动/彈性齒輪驅動　resilient gear drive
弹性地基/彈性基礎　elastic foundation
弹性地基梁/彈性基礎梁　beam on elastic foundation
弹性地基梁比拟法/彈性基礎梁比擬法　analogy method for beam on elastic foundation
弹性垫板/彈性墊板　resilient tie plate
弹性定位轮对/彈性定位輪對　elastically positioned wheelset
弹性方案/彈性方案　elastic scheme
弹性方程/彈性方程式　elastic equation
弹性分析/彈性分析　elastic analysis
弹性荷载/彈性負載　elastic load
弹性荷载法/彈性載重法　elastic load method
弹性荷重/彈性載重　elastic weight
弹性后效/彈性餘效，彈性滯後　elastic hysteresis, elastic aftereffect
弹性环销/彈性環榫　spring-ring dowel

弹性极限/彈性極限,彈性限界,彈性限度　elastic limit
弹性挤开/彈性擠開　gage elastically widened, elastic squeeze-out
弹性简单悬挂/彈性簡單懸掛　stitched tramway type suspension equipment
弹性建筑涂料/彈性建築塗料　elastomeric wall coating
弹性抗力/彈[性]阻力　elastic resistance
弹性扣件/彈性鋼軌扣件　elastic rail fastening
弹性理论/彈性理論　elastic theory
弹性联轴器/彈性聯軸器,彈性聯軸節　elastic coupling, resilient shaft coupling
弹性链形悬挂/垂直訂線懸鏈　stitched catenary equipment
弹性梁支承法/彈性支承梁法　elastic supported beam method
弹性流体动力润滑/彈性流體動力潤滑　elasto-hydrodynamic lubrication
弹性密封材料/彈性封閉層　elastic sealant
弹性模量/彈性模量,彈性係數,彈性模數　modulus of elasticity, elastic modulus
弹性模量试验/彈性模數試驗　elastic modulus test
弹性模数/彈性模數　elastic modulus
弹性旁承/彈性邊軸承　elastic side bearing
弹性区域/彈性範圍　elastic range
弹性设计/彈性設計　elastic design
弹性收缩/彈性收縮　elastic shrinkage
弹性弯曲/彈性彎曲　elastic bending
弹性稳定/彈性穩定　elastic stability
弹性系数/彈性係數　coefficient of elasticity
弹性现象/彈性[現象]　springing
弹性线法/彈性線法　elastic line method
弹性应变/彈性應變　elastic strain
弹性应变能/彈性變形能　elastic strain energy
弹性支承/柔性支承　flexible support
弹性支承边/彈性支承邊　elastically supported edge
弹性支承连续梁法/彈性支承連續梁法　elastically supported continuous girder method
弹性支承梁/彈性支承梁　elastically supported beam
弹性支座/彈性支座　elastic support
弹性止挡/彈性搖枕縱向擋　elastic bolster guide
弹性滞后/彈性遲滯　elastic hysteresis
弹性中心/彈性中心　elastic center
弹性轴承/彈性體軸承,彈性體支承　elastomeric bearing
坦丹札学派/坦丹劄學派　La Tendenza
炭化/碳化[作用]　carbonization

炭化炉煤气/蒸[乾]餾氣體　retort gas
炭化木材/炭化木材　thermo-modified wood
炭精避雷器/碳避雷器　carbon arrester
探槽/探槽　exploratory trench, test trench
探测/探查　detection
探测率/偵測率　detectivity
探测器/偵測器,偵檢器　detector
探测器量子效率/偵檢器量子效率　detective quantum efficiency, DQE
探测器一致性/偵檢器一致　detector conformity
探测器驻留时间/偵檢器照射目標時間　dwell time of detector
探测区域/探測範圍　detection zone
探测时间常数/偵檢器時間常數　time constant of detector
探测视场角/檢測視場角　detective field of view angle
探测系统/探火系統　detecting system
探测元件/偵測元件　detective cell
探查坑道/測量隧道　survey tunnel
探管仪/探管器　pipe locator
探井/探井　exploratory pit, test pit, exploratory shaft
探空火箭试验/探空火箭試驗　sounding rocket test
探伤/探傷　crack detection
探伤器/探傷器　defectoscope
探伤室/探傷儀室　flaw detector room
探伤仪/探傷器　defectoscope
探险游乐场/探險遊樂場　adventure ground
探照灯/探照燈　searchlight
探照式色灯信号机/探照燈信號　searchlight signal
碳氮共渗/滲碳氮化法　carbonitriding
碳当量/碳當量　carbon equivalent
碳钢轨条/碳鋼軌條　carbon steel rail
碳固存/碳固存　carbon sequestration
碳固定/固碳作用　carbon fixation
碳弧焊/碳[極電]弧熔焊　carbon arc welding
碳化硅/碳化矽,金剛砂　silicon carbide
碳化硅-碳化硅复合材料/碳化矽纖維強化碳化矽基複合材　silicon carbide fiber reinforced silicon carbide matrix composite
碳化木/碳化木　carbide wood
碳化深度酚酞试验/碳化深度酚酞試驗　carbonation depth by phenolphthalein test
碳化砖/碳化磚　carbonated lime brick
碳化作用/碳酸化作用　carbonation
碳环式密封/碳精墊圈,碳精迫緊圈　carbon ring gland

碳汇/碳匯　carbon sink
碳获取/碳獲取　carbon acquisition
碳库/碳庫　carbon pool, carbon stock
碳贸易/碳交易　carbon trade
碳排放交易计划/碳排放交易計劃　emissions trading scheme, ETS
碳石墨耐磨材料/碳石墨耐磨材料　wear resistance carbon-graphite material
碳素钢/碳鋼　carbon steel
碳酸化器/碳酸化器　carbonator
碳-碳复合材料/碳-碳複合材料　carbon-carbon composite, C-C composite
碳-碳化硅复合材料/碳纖維強化碳化矽基複合材　carbon fiber reinforced silicon carbide matrix composite
碳纤维/碳纖維　carbon fiber
碳纤维复合材料/碳纖維複合材料　carbon fiber composite material
碳纤维增强塑料/碳纖維強化塑膠　carbon fiber reinforced plastics
碳循环/碳循環　carbon cycle
碳氧平衡/碳氧均衡　carbon and oxygen balance
碳源/碳源　carbon source, carbon sequestration
碳足迹/碳足跡　carbon footprint
汤姆孙定理/湯木生定理　Thomson theorem
蹚测/涉水測量　wading measurement
蹚水测量/涉水測量　wading measurement
唐纳花园/唐尼花園　Donnell Garden
唐纳喷泉/唐納噴泉　Tanner Fountain
镗缸机/搪缸機　cylinder boring machine
镗孔/搪孔　boring
镗削/搪孔　boring
糖浆船/糖蜜船　molasses tanker
掏槽/掏槽,炸心鑽孔　cut, cut hole
掏槽炮眼/切孔　cut hole
掏底开挖/掏底開挖　cut the vertical earthwork bottom
掏箱/拆櫃　unstuffing
逃生/逃出　escape
逃生窗/太平窗　escape window
逃生方法/逃生方法　means of escape
逃生门/太平門　exit door, escape door
逃生通道/逃生通道,安全通道　escape trunk
逃逸/逃脫　escape
逃逸参数注入/逃脫資料注入　escape data injection
逃逸舱/逃脫艙　escape capsule
逃逸飞行器/逃脫飛行器　escape vehicle
逃逸告警/逃脫告警　escape warning
逃逸火箭/逃脫火箭　escape rocket
逃逸火箭发动机/逃脫火箭發動機　escape rocket motor
逃逸塔/逃脫塔　escape tower
逃逸塔落区/逃脫塔降落區　impact area of escape tower
逃逸塔装配测试厂房/逃逸塔裝配測試廠房　escape tower assembly and test building
陶瓷避雷器/陶瓷避雷器　ceramic arrester
陶瓷防热瓦/陶瓷絕緣瓦　ceramic insulation tile
陶瓷基复合材料/陶瓷基質複合材料,纖維強化陶瓷基複合材　ceramic matrix composite, fiber reinforced ceramic composite
陶瓷锦砖/陶瓷錦磚　ceramic mosaic
陶瓷绝缘/陶瓷絕緣　ceramic insulation
陶瓷马赛克/陶瓷錦磚　ceramic mosaic
陶瓷密封环/陶瓷封環　ceramic-seal ring
陶瓷黏合剂/陶瓷黏合劑,陶瓷接著劑　ceramic adhesive
陶瓷砖/瓷磚,磁磚　ceramic tile
陶管滤池集水系统/陶管濾池集水系統　tile filter bottom
陶罐/黏土釜　clay pot
陶粒/陶粒,燒結骨料,輕骨材　ceramsite, sintered aggregate, haydite
陶粒集料/燒脹黏土粒料　expanded clay aggregate
陶器/陶器　crockery
陶土砖/黏土磚　clay brick
陶瓦/陶瓦,燒結瓦　fired roofing tile
陶艺馆/陶藝室　ceramic studio
陶质砖/陶質磚　fine earthenware tile
淘空/淘空　scouring
淘析器/析離器　elutriator
套/套　house unit
套班运行/套班運行　package run
套车/套筒伸縮　telescoping
套房/套[房]　suite
套钩角铁/連繫角鐵　hitch angle
套管/套筒　sheath
套管敷设/下套管　casing installation
套管管靴/套管靴　drive shoe
套管护壁钻孔法/套管護壁鑽孔法　casing hole-boring method
套管铰环/套管鉸環　sleeve with clevis and ring
套管连接/套筒接合　sleeve joint
套管式冷凝器/二管冷凝器　double-pipe condenser
套管钻机/套管鑽機　drill machine with casing
套环/牛眼圈,纜索嵌環　thimble

套接管/臼塞接頭管　socket pipe
套孔法/套鑽法　over coring method
套式锚碇/套式錨碇　loap anchorage
套筒扳手/方頭起子,方頭螺絲把　box spanner
套筒联轴器/套筒聯結器　sleeve coupling
套线/套線,重疊線路　overlapping line
套线道岔/三線式道岔　mixed gage turnout
套箱围堰/套箱圍堰　precast-boxed cofferdam
套型/戶型　dwelling unit type
套种/間植　interplanting
特奥蒂瓦坎/特奧蒂瓦坎　Pre-Hispanic City of Teotihuacan
特别保护区/特別保護區　specially protected areas
特别工业区/特種工業區　special industrial district
特别工作灯/整補作業燈　task light
特别观摩室/特別觀摩室　inspection room for very important person
特别检验/特別檢驗　special survey
特别培训/特別訓練　special training
特别提款权/特別提款權　special drawing right, SDR
特别业务费/特別費用　special charge, SC
特藏书库/特藏書庫　special stack
特长隧道/特長隧道　super long tunnel
特大城市/特大都市,巨大都市　mega-city
特大城市地区/巨型都市區　mega-city region
特大的/特大　king-size
特大高度/特高高度　very high altitude
特大桥/特大橋,特大型橋梁　grand bridge, super major bridge
特等卧室/特等臥室　superclass bedroom, superclass sleeping compartment
特定地点服务业/特定位置服務　specific location service
特定符号/特殊符號　specific symbol
特定航次/指定航程　voyage specified
特定意图区/特定意圖區　specific design district
特定运价/特別運費　special rate
特高频测向仪/特高頻測向儀　VHF direction finder, VHF DF
特高频通信/超高頻通信　UHF communication
特级保护区/特級保護區　special grade preservation district
特急操纵/緊急操縱　crash maneuvering
特技飞行/特技飛行　aerobatic flight
特技类飞机/特技類飛機　airplane in aerobatic category
特解/特別解　particular solution

特快加快票/特快加快票　express extra ticket
特雷斯卡屈服准则/崔斯卡降伏準則　Tresca yield criterion
特立尼达和洛斯因赫尼奥斯山谷/特立尼達和洛斯因赫尼奧斯山谷　Trinidad and the Valley de los Ingenios: Palacio Brunet and the Palacio Cantero, The central park
特色景观旅游名镇/特色景觀旅遊名鎮　characteristic landscape tourism town
特殊[备用]电力/可靠電力　non-firm power
特殊重复频率/特殊重複頻率　specific repetition frequency
特殊单立管排水系统/特殊單立管排水系統　special single stack drainage system
特殊地貌类/特殊地貌類　special terrain type
特殊地质/特殊地質　special geology
特殊工业/特殊工業　special industry
特殊功能选拔/特殊功能選拔　special function selection
特殊荷载/特殊荷載　particular load
特殊环境学/特殊環境學　ectology
特殊教育学校/特殊教育學校　special education school
特殊强制办法/特殊強制方法　special mandatory method
特殊情况/特殊狀況　special circumstances
特殊区域/特別海域　special area
特殊燃料贮存区/特種燃料貯存室　special fuel storage zone
特殊摄动/特殊攝動　special perturbation
特殊试验/特殊試驗　special test
特殊条件下的路基/特殊條件下的路基　subgrade under special condition
特殊土/特殊土　special soil
特殊土路基/特殊土路基　subgrade of special soil
特殊用地/特殊用地,特定目的事業用地　land for special use, specially-designated land
特型喷管/特型噴管　contoured nozzle
特性/特性　characteristic
特性畸变/特性畸變　characteristic distortion
特性试验/特性試驗　characteristic test
特性数/示性數　characteristic number
特性指标/性能指數　performance index
特性阻抗/特性阻抗　characteristic impedance
特许飞行证/特別飛行許可　special flight permit
特许件/豁免件　waiver
特异景观风景区/特異景觀風景區　specific natural scenes area

特因耐力选拔/特殊因素耐性選拔　specific factor tolerance selection
特有种/特有種,固有種　endemic species
特征长度/特徵長度　characteristic length
特征寿命/特徵壽命　characteristic life
特征速度/特徵速度　characteristic velocity
特征速度因子/特徵速度修正因子　correction factor for characteristic velocity
特征线法/特徵線法,特性法　characteristics method, method of characteristic
特征向量/特徵向量　characteristic vector, eigenvector
特征造型/特徵模型　feature modeling
特征值/特徵值,固有值　characteristic value, eigenvalue
特征种/特徵種　characteristic species
特置/特置　specially placed
特种车辆活载/特種車輛活載　special live load, live load of special type wagon
特种车辆货物运输/特種車輛貨物運輸　special truck transport
特种车辆运价/特種車輛運價　rate for special purpose vehicle
特种处所/特種空間　special category space
特种断面尖轨/特種斷面尖軌　special heavy section switch rail, tongue rail made of special section rail, full-web section switch rail
特种断面尖轨转辙器/特殊道岔尖軌轉換器　switch rail of special section
特种钢/特殊鋼　special steel
特种工程结构/特種工程結構　special engineering structure
特种公园/特種公園　special park
特种挂车/特種掛車　special trailer
特种货/特種貨　special cargo
特种货物/專用運輸貨車　special goods
特种货物运价/特種貨物運價　rate for special goods
特种加工/非傳統加工　non-traditional machining
特种旅游/特種旅遊　special travel
特种水泥/特種水泥　special cement
特种业务/特種業務　special service
特种业务客船协定/特殊貿易客船協約　Special Trade Passenger Ships Agreement
特种业务旅客/特殊貿易旅客　special trade passenger
特种用户/特種用户　special subscriber
特种载货汽车/特種車　special truck
特种证书/特種證書　special certificate

特重交通/特高運量　very heavy traffic
藤本植物/藤[本植物]　vine, liana
藤壶/海生介　barnacle
藤家具/藤家具　rattan furniture
藤木/藤木　climbing tree
藤蔓类花卉/藤蔓類花卉　climbing flower
梯/梯[子],梯形物　ladder
梯道/梯道　stairway
梯道布置/梯道與通道布置　stairway and passage way arrangement
梯度/坡度,斜度,漸差度　gradient
梯度分析/梯度分析　gradient analysis
梯度风/梯度風　gradient wind
梯段/梯階　flight
梯队/梯隊　echelon formation
梯级结/梯級結　ratline hitch
梯式挖沟机/梯式挖溝機　ladder type trencher
梯式挖掘机/梯式開挖機　ladder excavator
梯线/梯形線　ladder track
梯形牌/梯形板　trapezoidal board
梯形屋架/梯形屋架　trapezoidal roof truss
梯形箱梁/梯形箱梁　trapezoidal box girder
踢脚/裙板　skirt
踢面/樓梯豎板　riser
提词间/提示箱　prompter box
提单/提單,載貨證券　bill of lading, BL
提单背书/載貨證券之背書　endorsement of bill of lading
提单持有人/載貨證券持有人　holder of bill of lading
提单转让/轉讓載貨證券　transfer of bill of lading
提货单/提貨[通知]單　delivery order
提拉窗/豎拉窗扇　vertical sliding sash
提前换发率/提前換發率　unscheduled engine removal rate
提前角/前置角,投彈角　lead angle
提取/萃取,抽出　extraction
提取空箱/提取空箱　pick up empty container
提升阀/提動閥　poppet valve
提升高度/提昇高度,起吊高度　lifting height, hoisting height
提升滑轮组/起重滑車　lifting block
提示标志/提示信號　prompt sign
提示盲道/提示盲道　warning blind sidewalk
体充电/大電流充電　bulk charging
体积比储水系数/比蓄水率　specific storativity
体积变化/體積變化　volumetric change
体积电阻/體積電阻　volume electrical resistance,

volume resistance
体积力/積體力 body force
体积模量/容積模數 volume modulus
体积温度系数/容積穩定修正係數 volume-temperature correction coefficient
体积系数/容積換算係數 volume conversion coefficient
体积压缩系数/體積壓縮係數 coefficient of volume compressibility
体积装填分数/體積裝填分數 volumetric loading fraction
体目标效应/延伸目標效應 extended target effect
体内环境/内在環境 internal environment
体内减速器/内部減速器 inner reduction gearbox
体内预应力/内傳力法預加應力 prestressing with bond
体能训练/身體健適訓練 physical fitness training
体散射/體散射 volume scattering
体外预应力/體外預應力 external prestressing
体外预应力索/體外預應力索 external prestressing tendon
体外震波碎石机室/體外衝擊波碎石術 extracorporeal shock wave lithotripsy room, ESWL room
体涡/前機身渦旋 body vortex
体细胞无性系变异/體細胞克隆變異 soma clonal variation
体形系数/形狀因數 shape factor
体验旅游/經驗本位觀光 experience-based tourism
体验园/體驗花園 enabling garden
体液沸腾/體液沸騰 ebullism
体液转移/體液轉移 body fluid shift
体育场/體育場,運動場 stadium, arena, athletic field
体育公园/體育園區 sports park
体育馆/體育館,健身房 gym, gymnasium, sports hall
体育建筑/體育設施 sports building
体育器材厂/體育器材廠 sporting equipment factory
体育设施/體育設施,運動設施 athletic facility, sports facility
体育用地/體育用地,體育土地利用 sports land, land for sport
体育运动区/體育運動區 sports activities area
体育中心/體育中心 sports center
体轴坐标系/體軸坐標系 body-axis coordinate system
剃齿/齒輪刮光 gear shaving

替代参数/替代參數 surrogate parameter
替代测量方法/量測替代法 substitution method of measurement
替代件/替代零件 substitute parts
替代设备/交替設施 alternating device
替换定理/替代定理 replacement theorem
替换设备/替换設備 spare attachment
天波/天波 sky wave
天波改正量/天波修正量 sky wave correction
天波延迟/天波延遲 sky wave delay
天波延迟曲线/天波延遲曲線 sky wave delay curves
天车/橋式起重機,高架移動起重機 overhead traveling crane
天池风景区/天池風景區 crater lake scenic spot
天赤道/天球赤道 celestial equator
天船三(英仙α)/天船三(英仙α) Mirfak
天窗/天窗,天光 skylight
天窗架/天窗架 skylight frame
天敌/天敵 natural enemy
天底[点]/天底[點] nadir
天底偏角/天底角 off-nadir angle, angle of view from nadir
天地对接试验/天地整合測試 space-ground integrating test
天-地通信/空對地通信 space-ground communication
天-地通信系统/空間地面通信系統 space-ground communication system
天电干扰/天電干擾,大氣干擾 atmospheric interference
天顶/天頂 zenith
天顶距/天頂距 zenith distance
天顶亮度/天頂亮度 zenith luminance
天顶投影/天頂投影法 zenith projection, zenithal projection
天沟/天溝,邊溝,洩水槽 gutter, overhead ditch, intercepting ditch
天极/天極 celestial pole
天际线/天際線,地平線 skyline
天津四(天鹅α)/天津四(天鹅α) Deneb
天井/天井 patio
天景/天景 sky scenery
天空光/天光,天窗 skylight
天空辉光/天空照亮 sky glow
天空喇叭/天空喇叭 sky horn
天空漫射辐射/天空漫射 diffuse sky radiation
天空遮挡物/天空遮擋 obstruction

天空状况/天空狀況　sky condition
天狼(大犬α)/天狼(大犬α)　Sirius
天幕/天幕,天遮　awning, cyclorama
天幕光/天幕光　back-cloth light
天幕帘/天遮簾[幕]　awning curtains
天幕索/天遮索　awning rope
天平/天平　balance
天平不回零性/天平非零準位　balance character of non-return to zero
天平测力/空氣動力天平量測　aerodynamic balance measuring
天平动/天平動　libration
天平动校[准]/天平動態校準　dynamic calibration of balance
天平动阻尼/天平動阻尼　libration damping
天平干扰/天平干擾　interaction of balance system
天平校准参考中心/天平校準中心　calibration center of balance
天平静校[准]/天平静態校準　static calibration of balance
天平力矩参考中心/天平力矩參考中心　moment reference center of balance
天平室/天平室　balance room
天平组测力/天平測量　balances measuring
天平坐标系/天平坐標系　balance axis system
天气/天氣　weather
天气报告/天氣報告　weather report
天气船/氣象觀測船　weather vessel, weather ship
天气符号/天氣符號　weather symbol
天气公报/天氣公報　weather bulletin
天气过程/天氣過程　synoptic process
天气图/天氣圖　synoptic chart, synoptic weather chart, synoptic weather map
天气现象/天氣現象　weather phenomena
天气形势/綜觀[天氣]大勢　synoptic situation
天气学/天氣學　synoptic meteorology
天气预报/天氣預報　weather forecast
天桥/天橋　connecting bridge, over bridge
天球/天球　celestial sphere
天囷一(鲸鱼α)/天囷一(鯨魚α)　Menkar
天然博物馆/天然博物館　natural open museum
天然材料/天然材料　natural materials
天然稠度试验/天然稠度試驗　natural consistency test
天然堤/自然堤　natural levee
天然地基/天然地基,天然路基　natural subsoil, natural foundation, natural ground
天然地下水位/天然地下水面　natural groundwater table
天然公园/天然公園　natural park
天然拱/天然拱　natural arch
天然骨料/天然骨材　natural aggregate
天然含水量/自然含水量　natural water content
天然荷载/自然載重　natural load
天然纪念物/天然紀念物　natural monument
天然建筑石材/天然建築石材　natural building stone
天然矿泉水/礦質水　mineral water
天然沥青/天然瀝青　natural asphalt, gilsonite
天然林/天然林,自然森林　natural forest
天然能源/初級能源,原生能源　primary energy
天然黏合剂/天然膠著劑　natural adhesive
天然气/天然[煤]氣　natural gas
天然气采集系统/天然氣採集系統　gathering system of natural gas
天然气储量/天然氣蘊藏量　reserves of natural gas
天然气井/天然氣井　natural gas well
天然气田/天然氣田　natural gas field
天然轻骨料/自然輕骨材,天然輕質粒料　natural lightweight aggregate
天然砂/天然砂,自然砂　natural sand
天然石材/天然寶石　natural stone
天然水/自然水　natural water
天然水道/天然水道　natural watercourse
天然文化石/天然文化石　natural culture stone
天然稳定化处理/乾燥法,氣候處理　seasoning
天然演变冲刷/自然沖刷　natural scour
天然源/天然源　natural source
天然重度/自然密度　natural density
天水网/天水網　hydrometeorologcial network
天坛/天壇　Temple of Heaven, Tian Tan
天堂图景/天堂圖景　paradise imagery
天体/天體[星]　celestial body, heavenly body
天体出没/天體出沒　rise and set of celestial body
天体高度/天體高度　celestial altitude
天体罗经/日規　sun compass
天体视运动/天體視運動　celestial body apparent motion
天体与太阳角距/天體與太陽之角距　elongation
天王星/天王星　Uranus
天文潮/天文潮汐　astronomical tide
天文晨昏朦影/天文曦光　astronomical twilight
天文船位/天文定位　astronomical fix, AF
天文导航/天文導航,太空導航　celestial navigation
天文导航系统/天文導航系統　celestial navigation system
天文定位/天體定位　celestial fixing

天文定向/天文定向　astronomical orientation
天文观测/测天　celestial observation
天文观象台/天文臺,觀象臺　observatory
天文馆/天文館,天文臺　planetarium
天文-惯性组合导航/天文-慣性整合導航　celestial-inertial integrated navigation
天文-惯性组合制导/天文-慣性整合導引　celestial-inertial integrated guidance
天文航海/天文航海　celestial navigation
天文经度/天文經度　astronomical longitude
天文罗盘/天文羅盤　celestial compass
天文三角形/天文三角形　astronomical triangle
天文纬度/天文緯度　astronomical latitude
天文卫星/天文衛星　astronomy satellite
天文钟/天文鐘,船鐘　chronometer
[天文钟]日差/天文鐘日差率　chronometer rate, daily rate
天文钟误差/天文鐘誤差　chronometer error, CE
天文子午圈/天文子午圈,天文子午線　astronomical meridian
天文子午线/天文子午線,天文子午圈　astronomical meridian
天文坐标/天文坐標　astronomical coordinate
天线/天線　antenna
天线安装角/天線安裝角　antenna setting angle
天线窗防热盖板/天線窗熱遮蔽蓋板　antenna window thermal shielded cover plate
天线单元/天線[單]元　antenna element
天线电缆耦合测量/天線電纜耦合量測　antenna cable coupling measurement
天线电子消旋/天線電子消自旋　electronic despin for antenna
天线定向机构/天線指向裝置　antenna pointing mechanism
天线定向系统/天線指示系統　antenna pointing system, APS
天线方向[性]图/天線輻射圖形,天線場形　antenna pattern
天线方向[性]图设计/天線輻射圖形設計,天線場形設計　antenna pattern design
天线机械消旋/天線機械消旋　mechanical despin for antenna
天线开关/天線開關　antenna switch
天线视角/天線視角　antenna look angle
天线调谐/天線調諧　antenna tuning
天线温度/天線溫度　antenna temperature
天线效应/天線效應　antenna effect
天线罩波瓣畸变/天線罩波瓣畸變　pattern distortion caused by radome
天象纪要/天文現象　phenomena
天象图/天象圖　sky diagram
天象仪/天象儀,星象儀　planetarium
天轴/天軸　celestial axis
添加剂/添加劑　additive
添加剂法/添加劑法　additive method
添注漏斗/[艙口]灌斗　feeder
田间持水量/田間容水量　field moisture capacity
田间排水沟/田溝　field drain
田间渗透系数/野外滲透係數　field coefficient of permeability
田间试验/田間試驗,野外試驗　field experiment
田间滞水带/田間容量帶　field capacity zone
田径场/田徑場　athletics, track field
田径馆/室內體育館,室內體育場　indoor athletics stadium
田谐系数/田諧係數　tesseral harmonic coefficient
田园城市/田園都市,花園都市　garden city
填板/填料板　filler plate
填舱货/補充貨載　berth cargo
填充货/填充貨,填隙貨　filler cargo
填充脉冲/填充脈衝　filler pulse
填充墙/填充牆　filler wall, infilled wall
填充式结构/填充式結構　filling-up structure
填充物/填充劑,填料　filler
填充线/填充線　interstitial wire
填充因数/填充因數　fill factor, curve factor
填缝/堵縫　joint filling
填缝板/接合板　joint plate
填缝板接缝/填縫密封板　joint with sealing plate
填缝[材]料/填縫料　joint sealing materials, joint filler
填缝机/封縫機　joint sealer
填缝料破损/填縫料故障　joint filler failure
填海辟地/填海造地　land reclamation
填海造陆/填海造地　sea reclamation
[填]角焊/填角熔焊,填角焊接　fillet welding
填空货/填空貨　short stowage cargo
填料/填[充]料　packing
填料分类/填料分類　classification of filling material
填铆接缝/填鉚接縫　fillering
填塞袋/塞孔袋　tamping bag
填塞物/填塞物,堵塞物　stemming
填石排水沟/石盲溝　stone-filled drain
填土/填土　fill earth
填土地基/填地地基　filled-up ground
填隙货/填隙貨,填充貨　filler cargo

填筑式堤坝/填壩　fill type dam
条播/條播,行播　sowing in line
条分法/切片法　method of slice
条缝型风口/條形送風口　slot outlet, slot diffuser
条幅式摄影机/航帶攝影機　strip camera
条件电源/條件電源　conditional power source
条件电源屏/條件電源屏　conditional power supply panel
条件黏度/條件黏度　conditional viscosity
条图显示/直方圖顯示　bar chart display
条形基础/條形基礎,條形基腳　strip foundation, strap footing, strip footing
条形畦田灌溉/帶形灌溉　strip irrigation
调风器/調氣器　register
调峰气/調峰氣　peak load gas, standby gas, peak-shaving gas
调幅/調幅,振幅調變　amplitude modulation
调光器/調光器,減光器　dimmer
调轨机车/調車線機車　shunting engine
调和分析/調和分析　harmonic analysis
调和平均数/調和平均數　harmonic mean
调和漆/調和漆　mixed paint
调洪水库/防洪水庫　flood-control reservoir
调节/調節　regulation
调节板/調節板　regulating plate
调节棒/調整桿　regulating rod
调节池/調節池　regulating pondage
调节电阻器/調節電阻[器]　regulating resistor
调节阀流量特性/調節閥流量特性　flow characteristics of regulating valve
调节放大器/調節放大器　regulating amplifier
调节轨/調節軌　buffer rail
调节级/調節級　governing stage
调节井/調節井　regulating well
调节器/調節器,控制器,操縱器　governor, regulator, controller
调节水池/調節水池　regulating reservoir
调距桨传动/可控距螺槳傳動　controllable pitch propeller transmission
调宽调频控制/脈寬脈波調變控制　pulse width-pulse frequency modulation control
调理器/調理器,調理槽　conditioner
调梁设备/調梁設備　beam straightening equipment
调频/調頻　frequency modulation
调频边带引信/調頻邊[頻]帶引信　frequency modulation sideband fuze, FM sideband fuze
调频测距引信/調頻測距引信　frequency modulation ranging fuze, FM ranging fuze
调频轨道电路/調頻軌道電路,頻率調變軌道電路　frequency-modulated track circuit
调频记录/調頻記錄　frequency modulation recording, recorder
调频雷达/調頻雷達　frequency-modulated radar
调频无线电引信/調頻無線電引信　frequency modulation radio fuze, FM radio fuze
调频液体阻尼器/調諧液體阻尼器　tuned liquid damper, TLD
调频质量阻尼器/調頻質量阻尼器,調質阻尼器　tuned mass damper, TMD
调平误差/調平誤差　leveling error
调坡/調坡　adjusting gradient
调伸长度/懸伸　overhang
调试/除錯　debugging
调速泵组供水/調速泵組供水　governor pump unit water supply
调速电动机/調速馬達　adjustable-speed motor
调速阀/調速閥　speed regulating valve
调速方式/調速方式　mode of speed control
调速器/調速器,節速器　speed governor
调速器驱动齿轮/調速器驅動齒輪　governor drive gear
调速设备/調速設備　speed control device
调速伺服机构/調速伺服機構　speed-governing servomechanism
调速特性/調速特性　speed regulating characteristic, speed-governing characteristic
调速系统/調速系統　speed-governing system
调速装置/速度控制器　speed controller, speed control device
调温服/調溫服　thermo-conditional suit
调谐/調諧　tune
调谐速度/調諧速度　tuned speed
调谐因子/調諧因子　tuning factor
调谐质量阻尼器/調頻質量阻尼器,調質阻尼器　tuned mass damper, TMD
调心轴承/搖動支承　tilting bearing
调压阀/壓力調節閥　pressure regulating valve
调压方式/電壓調整模式　voltage regulation mode
调压井/平壓塔　surge tank
调压开关/電壓調整變換器　voltage regulation changer
调压器/調壓器　pressure regulator
调压牵引变压器/調整牽引變壓器　regulating traction transformer
调压绕组/調壓繞組,調節繞組,調整繞組　regulating winding

调压站/整壓站　regulator station
调整/調整　adjustment
调整阀/調節[器]閥　regulator valve
调整轨缝/調整軌間隙　adjusting of rail gaps
调整流速/修正流速　modified velocity
调整路拱/調整路拱　adjusting crown
调整片/調整片　tab
调整片法/調整片法　trim tab method
调整片效应机构/配平效應機構　trimming effect mechanism
调整式规划/調整式規劃　adjustment planning
调整试飞/調整試飛　development flight test
调整总概算/調整總概算　adjusted sum of approximate estimate
调制/調制,調變　modulation
调制传递函数/調制轉換函數,調變轉移函數　modulation transfer function, MTF
调制解调器/調制解調器,數據機,調變解碼器　modem, modulator-demodulator, MODEM
调制盘/截波器　reticle
调制速率/調制率,調變率　modulation rate
调质/淬火及回火,淬火與回火　quenching and tempering
调准/校準　alignment
挑梁式/懸梁式　suspending-beam structure
挑檐/挑檐　overhanging eaves
眺望台/眺望臺　prospect deck
跳板/跳板,著陸板　ramp, gang board, diving board
跳板门/登陸跳板,登陸舌門　ramp door
跳板台/跳板著陸架　brow landing
跳车激振/跳車激振　vibration excited by truck jumping from threshold on deck
跳轨/跳軌　jump on rail
跳频扩频/跳頻展開頻譜　frequency hopping spread spectrum
跳频通信/跳頻通信　frequency hopping communication
跳棋/跳棋　checker
跳伞塔/跳傘塔　parachute tower
跳伞台/跳傘臺　parachute unit
跳伞训练/跳傘者訓練　jumper training
跳伞运动/跳傘運動　skydiving
跳时扩频/跳時展頻　time hopping spread spectrum
跳水池/跳水池　diving pool
跳[水]台/跳臺　diving platform
跳台滑雪/跳高滑雪　ski jumping
跳弹/跳彈　ricochet
跳弹极限角/跳彈極限角　ricochet limit angle

跳线/跳線,跨接線　jumper
跳跃负载/跳躍載重　saltation load
跳周/跳週　cycle skipping
贴壁式/貼壁式　espalier planting
贴地飞行/貼地飛行　nap-of-the-earth flight
贴附射流/貼附射流　wall attachment jet
贴合面/接合面　faying surface
贴面砖/面磚　facing brick
贴膜玻璃/貼膜玻璃　film-mounted glass
贴体坐标系/邊界契合坐標系統　body-fitted coordinate system
贴线率/貼線率　near-line rate
铁磁吸力/鐵磁吸引力,強磁吸引力　ferromagnetic attraction force
铁道/鐵道,鐵路　railway, railroad
铁道车辆/鐵路車輛　railway vehicle, railway car
铁道科学/鐵道科技　railway science
铁道牵引动力/鐵路牽引動力　railway traction power, railway motive power
铁道通信/鐵路通訊　railway communication
铁粉焊条/鐵粉系焊條　iron powder type electrode
铁粉水泥/鐵粉水泥　iron powder cement
铁活/鐵製品　ironwork
铁基高温合金/鐵基高溫合金　iron-based superalloy
铁基合金/鐵基合金　iron-based alloy
铁拉登特罗国家考古公园/鐵拉登特羅國家考古公園　National Archeological Park of Tierradentro
铁梨木/鐵梨木　lignumvitae
铁梨木轴承/鐵梨木軸承　lignumvitae bearing
铁路/鐵路,鐵道　railway, railroad
铁路保价运输/鐵路保價運輸　value-insured rail traffic
铁路保险运输/鐵路保險交通　insured rail traffic
铁路财务/鐵路財務　railway finance
铁路财务成果/鐵路財務成果　railway financial result
铁路财务状况/鐵路財務狀況　railway financial condition
铁路测量/鐵路測量　railway survey
铁路长期计划/長期鐵路規劃　long-term railway plan
铁路长途电话网/鐵路長途電話網　railway long distance telephone network
铁路长途字冠/鐵路長途冠號　prefix number for railway toll call
铁路道口/平交口　grade crossing, grade intersection
铁路道口标志/鐵路交叉標誌　railway crossing sign
铁路的连带责任/鐵路連帶責任　joint responsibility

of railway

铁路等级/鐵路等級,鐵道等級　railway classification, class of railway

铁路地区电话/鐵路市內電話　railway local telephone

铁路电视/鐵路電視　railway TV

铁路短波通信/鐵路短波通信　short wave communication for railway

铁路法/鐵路法　Railway Law

铁路防护林/鐵路防護林　railway protection forest

铁路防护无线电通信/鐵路防護無線電通訊　radio communication for railway protection

铁路感应无线电通信/鐵路感應無線電通訊　inductive radio communication for railway

铁路干线机车/鐵道幹線機車　railway trunk line locomotive

铁路高速运输/鐵路高速運輸　railway high speed traffic

铁路告警无线电通信/鐵路警告無線電通訊　radio communication for railway warning

铁路工程地质遥感/鐵路工程地質遙測　remote sensing of railway engineering geology

铁路公安无线电通信/鐵路公安無線電通訊　radio communication for railway public security

铁路固定资产/鐵路固定資產　railway fixed asset

铁路涵洞/鐵路涵洞　railway culvert

铁路航空勘测/鐵路航空測量　railway aerial surveying

铁路航空摄影测量/鐵路航空攝影測量　railway aerial photogrammetry

铁路环境污染/鐵路環境保護　railway environmental protection

铁路货物运输/鐵路貨運　railway freight traffic

铁路货物运输规程/鐵路貨運交通規章　regulations for railway freight traffic

铁路货运/鐵路貨運　railway freight transportation

铁路货运组织/鐵路貨運組織　railway freight traffic organization

铁路机车车辆限界/鐵路機車車輛限界　rolling stock clearance for railway, vehicle gage

铁路计划/鐵路計劃　railway plan

铁路技术/鐵路技術　railway technology

铁路技术改造/鐵路技術改造　technical reform of railway, technical renovation of railway, betterment and improvement of railway

铁路技术管理规程/鐵路技術管理規程　regulations of railway technical operation

铁路建设基金/鐵路建設基金　railway construction fund

铁路建筑长度/全國鐵路建築里程　construction length of railway

铁路建筑界限/鐵路建築界限　railroad construction clearance

铁路建筑限界/鐵路建築限界　railway construction clearance, structure clearance for railway, railway structure gage

铁路勘测/鐵路偵察　railway reconnaissance

铁路客运枢纽/鐵路換乘樞紐　passenger railway transfer hub

铁路客运站/鐵路車站,火車站　railway station, train station

铁路客运组织/鐵路客運組織　railway passenger traffic organization

铁路列车编组站/配車站,調車站　train-assembly station

铁路路基/鐵路路基　railway subgrade

铁路路网规划/鐵路路網規劃　railway network planning

铁路旅客运输/鐵路客運[業務]　railway passenger traffic, railway passenger transportation

铁路旅客运输规程/鐵路客運業務規章　regulations for railway passenger traffic

铁路绿化/鐵路綠化　railway greening, railway planting

铁路轮渡/鐵路輪渡　railway car ferry

铁路年度计划/鐵路年度計劃　annual railway plan

铁路平板车/鐵路平臺卡車　railway platform truck

铁路平交道口/鐵路交[叉]口　railway crossing

铁路桥/鐵路橋,鐵道橋　railway bridge

铁路曲线/鐵路曲線[板]　railway curve

铁路枢纽/鐵路樞紐　railway junction terminal

铁路数据交换系统/鐵路數據交換系統　railway data exchange system

铁路隧道/鐵路隧道　railway tunnel

铁路条例/鐵路條例　railway code

铁路弯道/鐵路曲線　railway curve

铁路网/鐵路網　railway network, railroad network

铁路微波中继通信/鐵路微波繼電器通信　microwave relay communication for railway

铁路无线电通信/鐵路無線電通訊　railway radio communication

铁路无线电遥控/鐵路無線電遙控　radio telecontrol for railway

铁路无线电中继通信/鐵路繼電器無線電通訊　relay radio communication for railway

铁路系统/鐵路系統　railway system

铁路线/鐵路線　railway line, railroad line
铁路新线建设/鐵路新線建設　newly-built railway construction
铁路信号/鐵路號誌　railway signaling, railway signal
铁路行车组织/鐵路行車組織　organization of train operation
铁路行车组织规则/鐵路行車組織規則　rules for organization of train operation
铁路选线/鐵路選線,鐵路定線　railway location, approximate railway location, location of railway route selection
铁路移动无线电通信/鐵路移動通信,鐵路行動通信　railway mobile communication
铁路应急短波通信/鐵路應急短波通信　short wave communication for railway emergency
铁路用地/鐵路用地　land for railway, railway land use
铁路运价/鐵路運價表　railway tariff, railway rate
铁路运输/鐵路運輸　railway transportation, railway traffic
铁路运输安全/鐵路運輸安全　safety of railway traffic
铁路运输车/鐵路運輸車　rail transporter
铁路运输调度/鐵路運輸調度　railway traffic control, railway traffic dispatching
铁路运输管理/鐵路[管理]局　railway transport administration
铁路运输经济/鐵路運輸經濟　railway transport economy
铁路运输利润/鐵路運輸利潤　railway traffic profit
铁路运输全员劳动生产率/鐵路運送勞動生產力　labor productivity of railway transport
铁路运输质量管理/鐵路運輸品質控制　quality control of railway transportation
铁路运输周转基金/鐵路運輸週轉資金　railway traffic turnover fund
铁路运输组织/鐵路運輸組織　railway traffic organization
铁路运营/鐵路營運,鐵路營運　railway operation
铁路运营长度/鐵路營運里程　operating length of railway
铁路运营信息系统/鐵路營運資訊系統　railway operation information system
铁路站场/鐵路車場　railway yard
铁路站内电话/鐵路車站電話　railway station telephone
铁路支架车/鐵路臺車　rail carriage

铁路职工数/鐵路職工數　number of railway staff and workers
铁路重载运输/鐵路重載運輸　railway heavy haul traffic
铁路主要技术条件/鐵路主要技術條件　main technical standard of railway, main technical requirement of railway
铁路专用线/鐵路專用線　railway special line
铁路转运/鐵路轉移　railway transfer
铁铝化合物/鐵鋁介金屬　iron aluminide
铁摩辛柯梁/提摩盛科梁　Timoshenko beam
铁模/型砧　swage
铁桥/鐵橋　iron bridge
铁丝篮/鐵絲籃　wire basket
铁网栅/鐵網柵　wire mesh hurdle
铁细菌/鐵細菌　iron bacteria
铁艺/鐵工,鍛工　blacksmith
厅堂式/廳堂式　mansion-type structure, tingtang
汀步/汀步　stepping stone on water surface, stepping stone on water
听觉告警/聽覺警報　auditory warning
听觉空间/聽覺空間　aural space
听觉信号/聽覺號誌　audible signal
听觉阈/聽閾　hearing threshold
听力实验室/聽力實驗室　listening laboratory
烃/烴,碳化氫　hydrocarbon
亭/亭　pavilion
亭桥/亭橋　pavilion bridge, bridge pavilion
庭荫树/遮陰樹,多蔭的樹,行道樹　shade tree, courtyard tree, shady tree
庭园/庭園　courtyard garden
庭院/庭院　courtyard
庭院灯/園燈　garden light, garden lamp
停泊测量/繫泊測量　measurement during mooring
停泊处/碇泊所　harborage
停泊费/碇泊費,船舶滯留費,入港稅　groundage
停泊轨道/停駐軌道　parking orbit
停泊值班/碇泊值班　harbor watch
停潮/平潮　water stand
停车/停車,停轉　parking, shutdown
停车饱和度/停車飽和度　degree of parking saturation
停车标志/停車指示標　stop sign
停车泊位数/停車泊位數,停車容量　parking capacity, number of parking lots
停车场/停車場,停車區,停車坪　parking space, car park, parking area
停车场标志/停車場標誌　parking lot sign

停车场车位利用率/停車使用率　parking turnover rate
停车场绿地/停車場綠地　car park green space
停车车道/停車道　parking lane
停车车辆总数/停車累積數　parking accumulation
停车车位/停車位[置]　parking set, parking space
停车车位短缺/停車位不足　parking deficiency
停车车位供应量/停車位供應　parking supply
停车车位过剩/停車位過剩　parking surplus
停车车位需要/停車位需求　demand for parking spaces
停车持续时间/停車延時,停車時間　parking duration
停车冲程/慣性停車距離　inertial stopping distance
停车带/停車地帶　parking strip
停车道/停止道,跑道餘道　stopway
停车调查/停車調查　parking study
停车防护/停車防護　stopping train protection, standing train protection
停车费/停車費　parking fee
停车分区/停車分區　parking regulation zone
停车港/港灣式停車處　parking bay
停车管理计划/停車管理計劃　parking management program
停车规则/停車規則　parking regulation
停车换乘/停車轉乘　park and ride
停车计划/停車規劃　parking plan
停车计时器/停車計時器,靠泊表　parking meter
停车库/停車庫　parking garage
停车库管理系统/停車場管理系統,停車區管理系統　parking lots management system
停车楼/[多層停]車庫　parking building
停车率/停車率,車位配比　parking rate, parking ratio
停车牌/停車信號,紅信號牌　red board, stop indicator
停车器/阻止裝置　stopping device
停车容量/停車容量　parking capacity
停车视距/[車輛]停車視距　stopping sight distance, vehicle stopping distance sight
停车位/停車位,停車棚　parking stall, parking space
停车线/[車輛]停止線　stop line
停车线标志/停止線　stop line marking
停车线延误/車輛停止線延滯　stop line delay
停车信号/停止信號　stop signal
停车需求量/停車需求　parking demand
停车延误/停車延誤　stop delay
停车周转/停車週轉　parking turnover

停储长度/儲藏期限　storage length
停船冲程/正[慣性]滑行距離,縱向衝距　head reach
停船滑道/船架滑道　marine railway
停船试验/停船[性能]試驗　stopping test
停船性能/停船性能　stopping ability
停电/停電　power failure
停堆深度/停堆深度　shutdown depth
停放车位标线/停車位標線　parking space limit marking
停放刹车/停駐刹車,停車閘　parking brake
停机角/地面角　ground angle
[停]机坪/停機坪　apron
停机坪标志/停機坪標線　apron marking
停靠站/公[共汽]車站　bus stop
停拉/停曳　avast hauling
停留车辆/守候車輛　waiting vehicle
停驶车日/停駛車日　vehicle non-working day
停业报批程序/停業報批程式　exit application and approval procedure
停用/停用,停播　outage
停油位置/停供位置　cut-out position
停止/停止,停車　stopping, stop
停止道/停止道　stop way
停滞水/停滯水　stagnant water
停滞压力/停滯壓力　stagnation pressure
停驻制动/停車刹車　parking braking
停租/停租　off-hire
艇/小艇,船艇　craft, boat
艇底塞/艇底塞　boat plug
艇吊钩/吊鉤　lifting hook
艇筏乘员定额/艇筏乘載量　carrying capacity of craft
艇筏配员/救生艇筏人員配額　manning of lifecraft
艇滑架/艇滑道　boat skate
艇系紧带/小艇扣帶　boat gripe
艇甲板/小艇甲板　boat deck
艇碰垫/小碰墊,繫船椿　dolphin
艇首缆/艇首索　bow painter, painter
艇天幕/小艇天遮　canopy
艇下水装置/小艇下水設施　boat launching appliance
艇长/司艇　coxswain
艇罩/艇罩　boat cover
艇座/小艇座　boat chock
通报表/通報表　traffic list
通报速率/通報速率　telegraph rate
通播/廣播,播講　public address, broadcast
通播发射台/通播發射臺　collective broadcast sending station, CBSS

通播接收台/通播接收臺　collective broadcast receiving station, CBRS
通车里程/通車里程　mileage open to traffic
通车期限/通車期限　time limit for opening to traffic
通道/通道　alleyway, passage
[通道]交叉耦合/交叉耦合　cross coupling
通风/通風,換氣　ventilation
通风车/通風棚車　ventilated box car
通风道/通風管　ventilation stack
通风方式/通風式　ventilation type
通风服/通風服　ventilation suit, ventilation garment
通风[干燥]储粮仓/通風糧庫　ventilated grain depot
通风隔热/通風減熱　heat reduction by ventilation
通风管[道]/通風管,換氣管　ventilation pipe, ventilation piping
通风耗热量/通風熱損失　ventilation heat loss
通风机/通風機,風扇　ventilating set, ventilating machine
通风机电动机/鼓風電動機　blower motor
通风机室/風扇室　fan room
通风监测/通風監測　ventilation monitoring
通风降温/通風降溫　ventilation cooling
通风净化系统/空氣通風淨化系統　air ventilation and purification system
通风口/通氣孔　vent
通风冷却试验/通風冷卻試驗　test on ventilation and cooling
通风量/通風量,通氣率　ventilation volume, ventilation rate
通风帽/通風帽　ventilating cowl
通风器/通風器,通風機　ventilator
通风设备/通風設備　ventilation equipment, ventilation device
通风设计/通風設計　ventilation design
通风式电动机/通風式電動機　ventilated motor
通风塔/通風塔　ventilation tower
通风头盔/通風頭盔　ventilation helmet
通风系统/通氣系統　vent system
通风效率/通風效率　ventilation efficiency, drafting efficiency
通风与空调机间/通風與空氣調節機室　ventilation and air-conditioning room
通风运输/通風運輸　ventilated transport
通风支管/分道通氣機　branch vent
通风装置/通風裝置,通風機,通風設備　aerator, ventilation installation, drafting apparatus
通风阻力/通風損失　draft loss
通风作业/通風　ventilating

通过按钮电路/通過按鈕電路　through button circuit
通过场/通過場　transit yard
通过轨道总重/通過隧道額定載荷重　million gross tonnes, MGT
通过进路/通過路線,基線　through route
通过能力/通過能力　carrying capacity
通过能力限制区间/通過能力限制區間　restriction section of carrying capacity
通过时间/經過時間　passage period
通过式货场/通過式貨場　through-type freight yard
通过式客运站/通過式客運站　through-type passenger station
通过信号机/閉塞號誌機　block signal
通过型车辆检测器/通道車輛偵測器　passage vehicle detector
通过最小曲线半径/曲線通過最小半徑　minimum radius of curvature negotiable
通海阀/通海閥,海水[吸入]閥　sea suction valve, sea valve
通海阀箱/海底門　sea chest
通海接头/通海裝置　sea connection
通海旋塞/海底旋塞　seacock
通航分道/航行巷道　traffic lane
通航河道/可通航河道,適航河道　navigable river, navigation river
通航净空/通航淨空　navigable clearance, navigational clearance
通航流速/通航流速　navigable current velocity
通航期/通航期　navigation period
通航桥孔/可航橋孔,適航跨距　navigable span, navigable bridge-opening
通航水体/通航水道　navigation water
通航水位/[最低]通航水位　navigation water level, NWI
通航水域/適航水域　navigable waters
通话计数器/通話計次器　message register
通话命令/呼叫程式　calling order
通话请求/呼叫請求　calling request
通话锁闭/呼叫鎖閉　calling block
通话完毕/呼叫完畢　over
通廊式住宅/廊式公寓　corridor apartment, corridor house
通量/通量　flux
通流部分/通流部分　flow passage
通路/出入口,進入口,路徑　access, path
通路串杂音防卫度/通路串雜音防衛度　channel signal to crosstalk and noise ratio

通路固有杂音/通道基本雜波,通道基本噪聲 channel basic noise
通路净衰耗/通路淨損失 channel net loss
通路频率特性/通道頻率特性 channel frequency characteristic
通路线性/通路線性 channel linearity
通路振幅特性/通道振幅特性 channel amplitude characteristic
通路振鸣边际/通道振鳴邊限 channel singing margin
通气壁/通風壁 ventilating wall
通气孔隙度/通氣細孔率 aeration porosity
通气立管/通氣直管 vent stack
通气模型/通風模型 ventilating model
通气箱/空氣儲蓄器 air container
通气支管/分道通氣機 branch vent
通勤/通勤 commuting
通勤距离/通勤距離 commuting distance
通勤类飞机/通勤類飛機 airplane in commuter category
通商航海条约/通商航海條約 treaty of commerce and navigation
通商口岸/條約港 treaty port
通视浑浊度仪/通視渾濁度儀 all-through turbidimeter
通视能见度检验仪/通視能見度檢驗儀 all-through visibility tester
通视区/通視區 visible zone
通透性混凝土/透水混凝土 permeable concrete
通信/通信,通訊 communication
通信处理机/通訊處理機 communication processor
通信、导航和识别综合系统/通信、導航與識別綜合航空電子設備 integrated communication navigation and identification, ICNI
通信端站/長途電話終端站 terminal toll office
通信分系统/通訊次系統 communication subsystem
通信记录/通信記錄簿 communication log
通信接口/通信介面 communication interface
通信控制处理机/通信控制處理機 communication control processor
通信控制器/通信控制器,通信控制裝置 communication control unit, communication controller
通信控制字符/通信控制字元,通訊控制字元 communication control character
通信盲区/通信盲區 communication blind district
通信闪光灯/通信閃光燈 flashing light for signaling
通信设备制造厂/通信設備製造廠 communicating manufactory
通信枢纽/通信樞紐,通信中心 communication center
通信网/通信網路 communication network
通信网管理系统/通訊網路管理系統 communication network management system
通信网络系统/通信網路系統 communication network system
通信卫星/通信衛星,通訊衛星 communication satellite
通信协议/通信協定,通訊協定 communication protocol
通信询问/通信詢問 traffic enquiry
通信业务量/業務通報量 traffic
通信站/通訊站 communication station
通信、指挥、控制与情报系统/通信、指揮、控制與情報系統 communication, command, control and intelligence system
通信转发器/通信轉發器 communications transponder
通信子网/通信子網 communication subnet
通信总枢纽/通信總樞紐 master communication center of railway whole administration
通行能力/運輸能力,交通容量 traffic capacity
通行能力指数/通行能力指數,能力指標 capacity index
通行权/通行權 right of passage
通行信号/通過信號 passage signal, through signal
通行信号标/通航標誌 traffic mark
通用泵/通用泵,常用泵 general service pump
通用测试设备/通用測試設施 general test facility
通用的/通用的,萬用的 universal
通用电动机/交直流兩用馬達 universal motor
通用符号/通用符號 common symbol
通用硅酸盐水泥/普通卜特蘭水泥 common Portland cement
通用航空/普通航空 general aviation
通用货车/通用貨車 general purpose freight car
通用机场/普通專用機場 general airport
通用集装箱/通用集裝箱 general purpose container
通用设计图/標準設計圖 standard design drawing
通用实验室/通用實驗室 general laboratory
通用型集装箱叉车/通用型貨櫃叉車 universal container fork lift
通用证书/通用證書 general certificate
通知方/通知方 notify party
通知音/告警音 warning tone
同步/同步,起伏一致 in step, synchronization

同步变压器/同步變壓器,自整角變壓器 synchronous transformer
同步传输/同步傳輸 synchronous transmission
同步电动机/同步電動機,同步馬達 synchronous motor
同步电机/同步機 synchronous machine
同步发电机/同步發電機 synchronous generator
同步感应电动机/同步感應電動機 synchronous induction motor
同步高速摄影机/同步高速攝影機 synchronous high-speed camera
同步技术/同步技術 synchronization technique
同步检波/同步檢波,同步偵測 synchronous detection
同步检波器/同步檢波器,同步檢測器 synchronous detector
同步交通事故预测法/同時交通事故預測法 simultaneous traffic accident prediction method
同步控制器/同步控制器 synchronous controller
同步器/同步器,協調器 synchronizer, synchro
同步器旋钮/同步器旋鈕 synchronizer knob
同步时间/同步時間 synchronization time
同步[式]系统/同步系統,同亮系統 synchronous system, simultaneous system
同步通信/同步通訊 synchronous communication
同步陀螺电机/同步陀螺電機 synchronous gyro motor
同步卫星/同步衛星 synchronous satellite
同步指示灯/同步指示燈 synchro light
同步指示器/同步儀 synchroscope
同步转速/同步轉速 synchronous speed
同步阻抗/同步阻抗 synchronous impedance
同侧下锚/同側下錨 same-side anchor
同层排水/同層排水 same-floor drain
同程式系统/同程式系統 reversed return system
同方向列车连发间隔时间/同方向列車連發間隔時間 time interval for two trains despatching in succession in the same direction
同类色/同類色 congener color
同粒径骨料/同粒徑骨材 one-sized aggregate
同频单工无线电通信/同頻單工無線電通訊 same-frequency simplex radio communication
同频干扰/同頻干擾 same-frequency interference
同频干扰区/同頻干擾區 same-frequency interference area
同声传译控制室/同聲傳譯室,同聲翻譯室 simultaneous interpretation booth
同时对比/同時對比 contrast of contemporary color

同位素示踪剂/同位素示蹤劑 isotopic tracer
同位素室/同位素室 radioisotope unit
同文电报/同文電文 common text message
同向曲线/同向曲線 same direction adjacent curve
同心圆带/同心圓帶 concentric zone
同心圆理论/同心圓理論 concentric zone theory
同形替代/同位置換 isomorphous substitution
同形投影/等積投影[法] homographic projection
同一的/同一的 uniform
同一责任制/同一責任制 uniform liability system
同意按钮盘/同意按鈕盤 agreement button panel
同源多倍体/同源多倍體 autopolyploid
同源校准/同源校準 same source calibration
同震线/等震度線 coseismic line
同质货物/同類貨[物] homogeneous cargo
同质结太阳电池/同質結太陽電池 homojunction solar cell
同轴电缆/同軸電纜,同軸[電]線 coaxial cable, coaxial line
同轴电缆通信/同軸電纜通信 coaxial cable communication
同轴发电机/共軸發電機 integral shaft generator
同轴开槽天线/開槽同軸天線 slotted coaxial antenna
同轴式喷注器/同轴式注射器 concentric tube injector
同轴投影系统/同軸投影系統 on-axis projection system
桐油/桐油 China wood oil, tung oil
铜包钢线/包銅鋼線 copper-clad steel wire
铜材/銅材料 copper materials
铜管/銅管 copper pipe
铜合金/銅合金 copper alloy
铜基轴承合金/銅基軸承合金 copper base bearing metals
铜镍合金/銅鎳合金 copper nickel alloy
铜铅轴承/銅鉛軸承 copper-lead bearing
铜线/銅線 copper wire
统舱/統艙 steerage
统长甲板/連續甲板 continuous deck
统计矩/統計矩 statistical moment
统计上的一致性/統計均一性 statistical uniformity
统计声学/統計聲學 statistical acoustics
统计水文学/統計水文學 statistical hydrology
统计同质性/統計齊一性 statistical homogeneity
统计推论/統計推論 statistical inference
统计误差/統計誤差 statistical error
统计诊断/統計診斷 statistical diagnosis

统计自由度/統計自由度　statistical degrees of freedom
统一S波段/統一S波段　unified S-band, USB
统一S波段测控系统/統一S波段遥測控制系統　USB tracking telemetering and control system
统一船舶碰撞或其他航行事故中刑事管辖权某些规定的国际公约/關於碰撞或其他航行事件之統一刑事管轄國際公約　International Convention for the Unification of Certain Rules Relating to Penal Jurisdiction in Matters of Collision or Other Incidents of Navigation
统一船舶碰撞某些法律规定的国际公约/船舶碰撞法律統一規定國際公約　International Convention for the Unification of Certain Rules of Law with Respect to Collision between Vessels
统一对水上飞机的海难援助和救助及由水上飞机施救的某些规定的国际公约/救助與撈救海上航空器及由航空器施救之統一規定國際公約　International Convention for the Unification of Certain Rules Relating to Assistance and Salvage of Aircraft or by Aircraft at Sea
统一国有船舶豁免某些规定的国际公约/國有船舶豁免權統一規定國際公約　International Convention for the Unification of Certain Rules Concerning the Immunity of State-owned Ships
统一海船扣押某些规定的国际公约/統一海船假扣押規定國際公約　International Convention for the Unification of Certain Rules Relating to the Arrest of Seagoing Ships
统一海难援助和救助某些法律规定公约/海上救助及撈救統一規定公約　Convention for Unification of Certain Rules of Law Relating to Assistance and Salvage at Sea
统一收费系统/統一收費系統　unified toll system
统一土壤分类法/統一土壤分類法　unified soil classification system
统一推进系统/綜合推進系統　unified propulsion system, integrated propulsion system
统一眩光值/統一眩光值　unified glare rating, UGR
桶/桶　barrel
桶式喷雾器/噴灑槽　tank sprayer
桶形浮标/桶狀浮標　barrel buoy
桶装仓库/桶裝倉庫　barreled material warehouse
桶装沥青熔化装置/桶裝瀝青熔化裝置　asphalt barreled melter
筒/筒　trunk
筒拱/筒形拱頂，半圓形拱頂，圓筒形穹窿　barrel vault

筒钩/筒鈎　can hook
筒壳/桶形殼　barrel shell
筒式柴油打桩锤/筒式柴油打樁錘　tubular diesel pile hammer
筒体结构/筒體結構　tube structure
筒瓦/筒瓦　semi-circular tile
筒形变薄旋压/管形旋壓　tube spinning, tube flow forming
筒形活塞式柴油机/筒狀活塞型柴油機　trunk piston type diesel engine
筒中筒/筒中筒　tube in tube
筒中筒结构/筒中筒結構　tube in tube structure
筒子板/門窗側板　jamb lining
偷渡/偷渡者　stowaway
偷心造/偷心造　stolen-heart method, touxinzao
头戴送受话器/頭戴收話器　head set
头低位倾斜/頭低位傾斜　head down tilt, HDT
头高位倾斜/頭高位傾斜　head up tilt, HUT
头盔瞄准具/頭盔瞄準器　helmet-mounted sight
头盔显示器/頭盔顯示器　helmet-mounted display
头尾对换/首尾顛倒換索　end for end
头尾相撞/追撞　rear end collision
投标/投標，競價　bidding
投标保证金/押標金保證　bid bond
投标保证书/投標保證書　tender security
投标担保/押標金保證　bid bond
投标价/投標價格　bidding price, tender price
投标截止期/投標截止時間　deadline of bid
投标截止时间/投標截止期限　deadline for submission of tenders
投标人须知/投標人須知　instruction to bidder, instruction to tenderer
投标书/投標書，出價標單　bid, tender
投标书有效期/投標書有效期　bid validity
投标邀请书/招標書　invitation to bid
投弹斜距/投彈斜距　release slant range
投弹圆/投射圓　release circle
投放/投放　delivery
投放试验/投放試驗　jettison testing
投光灯/聚光燈　spot lamp
投铆钉手/投鉚釘手　rivet catcher
投配比/配量比　dosing ratio
投弃/投棄，抛棄　jettison
投入运行/投產運行　commissioning
投物伞/投物傘　cargo parachute
投影/投影，投射　projection
投影灯/投影燈　projective lamp
投影断链/投影斷鏈　projection of broken chain

投影面/投影面,投影圖　projection surface, plane of projection
投影面积/投影面積　projected area
投影面积比/投影面積比　projected area ratio
投掷式干扰机/消耗性電子亂真器　expendable jammer, EJ
投资估算/投資估算　investment estimation
投资回收期/投資回收期　repayment period of investment, payback period, repayment period of capital cost
投资检算/投資檢算　checking of investment
投资利润率/投資報酬[率]　return on investment, ROI
投资效果/投資效益　effect of investment
透波材料/透電磁波材料　electromagnetic wave transparent material
透波结构/透波結構　transparent structure
透层/透層　prime coat
透风结构/通風結構　ventilating structure
透景线/透景線　perspective line
透镜/透鏡,聚波器　lens, redirecting cover glass
透镜式色灯信号机/透鏡式色燈號誌機　multi-lenses signal
透镜天线/透鏡天線　lens antenna
透空式防波堤/透水防波堤　open type breakwater, permeable breakwater
透空式码头/横棧橋碼頭　open type wharf
透明材料/玻璃質材料　vitreous material
透明传送/透明傳送　transparent transfer
透明工作方式/透明工作方式　transparent operation mode
透明雷达反射涂层/透明雷達反射塗膜　transparent radar reflection coating
透膜损效/透膜損效　membrane poisoning
透平式压缩机/渦輪壓縮機　turbo-compressor
透气孔/氣孔　air hole
透射比/透射比,傳遞率　transmittance
透射率/透射率,透射係數　transmissivity
透射密度/透射密度　transmissive density
透射系数/透射係數　coefficient of transmission, transmission coefficient
透视图/透視[平]圖　perspective view, perspective drawing, perspective plan
透视图检验/透視圖檢查　perspective examination
透水底土层/透水性基層土　pervious subsoil
透水地面/透水地面　permeable floor
透水丁坝/透水丁壩　permeable spur
透水度试验/透水度試驗　pervious test

透水井/透水井　filter well
透水沥青/大孔隙瀝青混合料　porous asphalt
透水路堤/透水路堤　permeable embankment, pervious embankment
透水路面/透水性路面　permeable pavement
透水磨耗层/透水磨耗層　pervious wearing course
透水性/透水性　water permeability
透水性沥青路面/通透性瀝青路面　permeable bituminous pavement
透水折流坝/透水丁堤　permeable groyne
透水砖/透水磚　permeable brick
凸窗/凸窗　bay window
凸肚/凸肚狀　entasis
凸焊/凸出焊接　projection welding
凸块压路机/凸塊壓路機　padfoot roller
凸轮/凸輪　cam
凸轮间隙/凸輪間隙　cam clearance
凸轮控制器/凸輪控制器　cam controller
凸轮位置转换开关/凸輪位置切換開關　cam position changeover switch
凸轮轴/凸輪軸,突輪軸　camshaft
凸轮轴正时齿轮/凸輪軸正時齒輪　camshaft timing gear
凸模/衝頭　punch
凸形竖曲线/凸形豎曲線　convex vertical curve
凸缘/凸緣,翼緣　flange
凸缘联轴器/凸緣連接器　flanged coupling
突变/突變,變種　mutation
突出的普遍价值/突出的普遍價值　outstanding universal value of heritage
突堤/抛石突堤,防波堤　mole
突发差错/叢發錯誤　burst error
突发传输/叢發傳輸　burst transmission
突发环境事件/環境緊急　environmental emergency
突发噪声/突發噪音　burst noise
突扩扩压器/突擴擴散器　dump diffuser
突码头/突堤,碼頭,棧橋　jetty
突泥/突泥　projecting mud soil
突起分隔带/高架式分隔帶　raised separator
突然故障/突發失效　sudden failure
突然倾斜/[船]突傾側　lurch
突水/突水,噴水　gushing water
图案矮篱/圖案矮籬　pattern dwarf hedge
图案花坛群/大花壇,花圃　parterre
图斑比对/圖模式比對　graph pattern comparison
图标/圖像,圖符　icon
图表/圖表　chart
图底关系/圖形背景　figure-ground

图号/圖號　chart number
图解/圖解法　graphical solution
图解导线测量/平板導線測量　graphical traversing
图解静力学/圖解靜力學　graphic statics
图库/圖形程式館　graphics library
图框/圖框　drawing frame
图例/圖例,圖説　legend
图面代号/圖紙大小　drawing sheet size
图上作业法/圖上作業法　graphic dispatching method
图书馆/圖書館　library
图书外借处/圖書外借　books lending
图像处理/影像處理　image processing
图像放大/影像擴大　image magnification
图像分辨力/圖象分解力,圖象清晰度　picture resolution
图像判读/照片判讀　photo interpretation
图像匹配制导/圖型比對導引　pattern matching guidance
CCD图像切换仪/CCD影像順序換景器　CCD image sequential switcher
图像清晰度/圖象清晰度,圖象分解力　picture definition
图像识别/影像識別　image recognition
图像数据格式/視訊資料格式　video data format
图像数据压缩/影像資料壓縮　image data compression
图像通信系统/影像通信系統　image communication system
图像退化/影像退化　image degradation
CCD图像显示仪/CCD影像顯示器　CCD image display instrument
图像镶嵌/圖像拼接　image mosaic
图像型火灾自动报警系统/圖像型火災探測系統　video-based fire detection system
图像增强/影像增強　image enhancement
图像质量/圖象品質　image quality, picture quality
图形标志/圖示符號　graphical sign, graphical symbol
图形符号/圖示符號　graphical sign, graphical symbol
图形数据结构/圖形資料結構　graphic data structure
图形条件/圖形條件　figure condition
图纸幅面/圖的大小　drawing size
图纸会审/圖紙會審　dawings reviewing
图纸空间/圖紙空間,布局空間　paper space
徒步/徒步旅行　hiking
徒步出行/徒步出行　pedestrian trip
徒手画/徒手畫,草圖　freehand drawing
徒长枝/徒長枝　turion
涂层/塗層　coating, paint
涂层退化/塗層退化　coating degradation
涂层污染/塗層汙染　coating contamination
[涂层]吸收发射比/[塗層]吸收發射比　ratio of solar absorptance to emittance
涂层性能/塗層特性　property of coating
涂底漆/刷底漆　priming
涂料/塗料,塗層　coating material, coating, paint
涂料喷射机/噴漆器　paint sprayer
涂料施工/塗裝,塗刷,塗漆　coating, painting
涂料弹涂机/塗料彈射器　paint catapult
涂煤油试验/煤油試驗　kerosene test
涂膜/塗膜　film
涂膜防水材料/覆膜防水材料　coated waterproof materials
涂漆/塗漆,塗刷　painting
涂漆面积/油漆面積　painting area
涂装/塗裝,塗刷,塗漆　coating, painting
涂装车间/塗裝工場　painting shop
屠宰厂/屠場　butchery
土崩/土塌,坍方　earth fall
土层/土層[位]　soil layer, soil horizon, soil stratum
土层剖面/土壤剖面　soil profile
土地保护/土地保護　land conservation
土地财政/土地財政　land finance
土地测量/土地測量　land survey
土地出让/土地[使用權]出讓　land leasing
土地出让金/土地出讓金　land price for sale
土地处理[使用]/土地處理,土地處置法　land disposal, land treatment
土地储备/土地準備　land reserve
土地登记/土地登記簿,魚鱗册　land register
土地二级开发/土地二級開發　secondary land development
土地分割/土地分割　dividing a lot
土地分类/土地分類,土地分等　land classification
土地分区图/土地分區圖　zoning map
土地复垦/新生地　reclaimed land
土地改良/土地改良　land accretion, land improvement
土地改良区/土地改良區　land improvement district
土地[功能]分区图/土地分區圖　zoning map
土地管理/土地管理,地政　land administration, land management
土地划拨/土地劃撥,土地分派,土地無償撥用　land assignment

土地荒漠化/土地荒漠化,土地沙漠化　land desertification
土地混合使用/土地混雜利用　mixed use of land
土地集体所有制/土地集體所有[制]　collective ownership of land
土地价格/地價　land cost, land price
土地交易/土地交易　land transaction
土地开发/土地開發　land development
土地开发管理/土地開發管理　land development administration, management of land development
土地利用/土地利用,土地使用　land use
土地利用调查/土地使用調查　land use survey
土地利用规划/土地使用計劃　land use planning, land use plan
土地利用类型/土地利用類型　land use type
土地利用率/土地利用比　ratio of land use
土地利用模型/土地使用模型　land use model
土地利用图/土地使用圖　land use map
土地利用协调/土地利用協調　land use coordination
土地利用预测模型/土地利用預測模式　land use forecast model
土地利用总体规划/土地利用總體規劃　land use master planning
土地流转/土地流轉　land circulation
土地庙/土地廟　Temple of Land God, Tudi Miao
土地批租/土地批租,土地使用權有償轉讓　leasehold of land
土地平整/整地　land grading, land leveling
土地平整测量/土地平整測量　surveying for land leveling
土地使用控制/土地使用管制,土地用途管制　land use control
土地使用期/土地租佃期　land tenure
土地使用权/土地使用權　right of land usage, land use right
土地使用性质/土地使用性質　land use property
土地使用与交通交互模型/土地利用與交通交互模型　land use and transport interaction model
土地市场/土地市場　land market
土地所有权/土地所有權　ownership of land, land ownership
土地调整/土地重畫　land readjustment
土地投机/土地投機　land speculation
土地退化指数/土地退化關係　land retirement index
土地细分/土地分割,土地分畫　land subdivision
土地闲置/土地閒置　land vacancy
土地盐碱化/土地鹽鹼化　land salinization
土地一级开发/土地一級開發　primary land development
土地拥有权/土地所有權　land ownership
土地用途/用地性質　purpose of land use
土地用途分区/土地利用分類　classification of land use
土地用途管制/土地用途管制,土地使用管制　land use control
土地用途限制/使用限制　use restriction
土地再细分规范/細分規則　subdivision regulations
土地增值/土地增值　land increment, land value increment
土地增值税/土地增值稅　land value increment tax
土地占有期/土地租佃期　land tenure
土地征收/土地徵收　compulsory land acquisition, expropriation
土地征用/土地徵用,土地取得　land acquisition, land requisition
土地政策/土地政策　land policy
土地转让/土地轉讓　land transfer
土地资源/土地資源　land resources
土丁坝/土丁壩　earth spurdyke
土动力性质测试/土動力特性試驗　dynamic property test for soil
土斗车/出碴車　muck car
土方调配/土方調配　cut fill transition
土方调配图/土方變遷圖　cut fill transition diagram
土方工程/土方工程　earth work
土方累积图/土方平衡圖,土方分配圖,累積曲線　mass diagram
土方[量]计算/土方計算　mass-calculation
土方平衡/土方平衡,平衡土方　earthwork balance, equal of cut and fill
土方图/土方圖　earthwork drawing, earthwork planning
土方运距曲线/運土量曲線　mass-haul curve
土干效应/土乾效應　soil drying effect
土工处理/土工技術方式　geotechnical process
土工格栅/地工格網　geogrid
土工合成材料/土工合成材料　geosynthetics
土工膜/地工薄膜　geomembrane
HDPE 土工膜/HDPE 地工薄膜　HDPE geomembrane
土工学/土工技術　geotechnique
土工织物/地工織物　geotextile
土骨架/土壤構架　soil skeleton
土基承载能力/土基承受力　subsoil bearing capacity
土基干湿类型/土基乾濕類型　subsoil moistness classification

土结构共同作用/土壤結構交互作用　soil structure interaction
土块打碎机/土塊粉碎器　soil shredder
土力学/土壤力學　soil mechanics
土粒比重/土粒子比重　specific gravity of soil grain
土粒密度/土粒密度　soil particle density
土路/土砂道　earth road
土路肩/土路肩　earth shoulder
土木工程[学]/土木工程[學]　civil engineering
土牛拱架/土牛拱架　earthen centering
土坯砖/土磚,磚坯　adobe
土球移植/土球移植　ball transplanting
土壤/土壤　soil
土壤饱和含水量/土壤飽和含水量　saturated soil water content
土壤保持/土壤保育　soil conservation
土壤保持措施/土壤保持措施　soil conservation practice
土壤保持分区/水土保持分區　soil conservation division
土壤保持规划/土壤保持規劃　soil conservation planning
土壤保持区/土壤保育區　soil conservation district
土壤保持效益/土壤保持效益　soil conservation benefit
土壤保护/土壤保護　soil protection
土壤比热/土壤比熱　soil specific heat
土壤比重/土壤比重　soil specific gravity
土壤变形/土壤變形　soil deformation
土壤测勘图/土壤測量圖　soil survey map
土壤成因分类/土壤形成分類　soil classification by formation
土壤垂直带谱/土壤垂直帶譜　spectrum of soil vertical distribution
土壤垂直地带性/土壤垂直地帶性　soil vertical zonality
土壤垂直分布/土壤垂直分布　soil vertical distribution
土壤地带性/土壤地帶性　soil zonality
土壤地理[学]/土壤地理學　soil geography
土壤调查/土壤調查,土壤探測　soil survey, soil exploration
土壤动物学/土壤動物學　soil zoology
土壤发生/土壤化育　soil genesis
土壤发育/土壤發育　soil development
土壤肥力/土[壤]肥力　soil fertility
土壤肥力分级/土壤肥力分級　soil fertility grading
土壤肥力监测/土壤肥力監測　soil fertility monitoring
土壤肥力图/土壤肥力圖　soil fertility map
土壤分布/土壤分布　soil distribution
土壤分类/土壤分類　soil classification
土壤分类法/土壤分類法　soil classification system
土壤分析/土壤分析　soil analysis
土壤分析化学/土壤分析化學　soil analytical chemistry
土壤覆盖/土壤覆蓋,土被　soil mulch
土壤改良/土壤改良　soil amelioration, soil improvement, soil amendment
土壤改良材料/土壤改良材料　soil amendment materials
土壤改良剂/土壤改良劑　soil conditioner, soil amendment
土壤概查/土壤概查,土壤普查　generalized soil survey
土壤概图/土壤普查圖　generalized soil map
土壤耕作/土壤耕作　soil tillage
土壤工程分类/土壤工程分類　engineering classification of soil
土壤管理/土壤管理　soil management
土壤含水量/土壤含水量　soil water content
土壤含盐量/土壤鹽含量　soil salt content
土壤滑动/土壤蠕動,土壤潛移　soil creep
土壤化学/土壤化學　soil chemistry
土壤环境/土壤環境　soil environment
土壤环境保护/土壤環境保護　soil environment protection
土壤环境容量/土壤環境容量　soil environment capacity
土壤环境质量/土壤環境品質　soil environment quality
土壤环境质量评价/土壤環境品質評估　soil environment quality assessment
土壤缓冲能力/土壤緩衝能力　soil buffering ability
土壤混合样/土壤混合樣　soil mixture sample
土壤坚实度/土壤硬度　soil hardness
土壤碱度/土壤鹼度　soil alkalinity
土壤碱化作用/土壤鹽鹼化　soil alkalization
土壤鉴定/土壤鑒別　soil identification, identification of soil
土壤胶体/膠質土　soil colloid
土壤搅拌机/土壤混合機　soil mixer
土壤结构/土壤結構,土壤構造　soil structure
土壤景观/土壤地景　soil landscape
土壤净化/土壤淨化　soil purification
土壤绝对含水量/土壤絕對含水量　soil absolute

water content
土[壤颗]粒/土[壤顆]粒 soil particle
土壤可溶盐/土壤可溶性鹽 soil soluble salt
土壤可蚀性/土壤可蝕性 soil erodibility
土壤空气/土壤空氣,土中空氣 soil air
土壤孔隙/土壤孔隙空間 soil pore space
土壤孔[隙]度/土壤孔隙度 soil porosity
土壤矿物/土壤礦物 soil mineral
土壤矿物学/土壤礦物學 soil mineralogy
土壤力度分级取样/均質試樣 fractional sampling
土壤立地/土壤立地,土痕遺址 soil site
土壤利用/土壤利用 soil utilization
土壤利用图/土壤利用圖 soil utilization map
土壤粒组分类/粒度土壤分類 soil classification by grain
土壤流失/土壤流失 soil loss
土壤流失估算/土壤流失量估算,土壤流失量推估 soil loss estimation
土壤密度/土壤密度 soil density
土壤摩擦阻力/土壤摩擦力 friction soil
土壤黏性/土壤黏性 cohesion of soil
土壤评价/土壤評價 soil evaluation, soil assessment
土壤剖面/土壤剖面 soil profile
土壤普查/土壤普查 general detailed soil survey
土壤侵蚀/土壤侵蝕 soil erosion
土壤侵蚀程度/土壤侵蝕程度 soil erosion degree
土壤侵蚀带/土壤侵蝕帶 soil erosion zone
土壤侵蚀方式/土壤侵蝕形態 soil erosion pattern
土壤侵蚀分类/土壤侵蝕分類 soil erosion classification
土壤侵蚀分区图/土壤侵蝕分區圖 soil erosion division map
土壤侵蚀景观/土壤侵蝕景觀 soil erosion landscape
土壤侵蚀类型/土壤侵蝕類型 soil erosion type
土壤侵蚀类型图/土壤侵蝕類型圖 soil erosion type map
土壤侵蚀强度/土壤侵蝕強度 soil erosion intensity
土壤侵蚀区划/土壤侵蝕區劃 soil erosion regionalization
土壤侵蚀小区/土壤侵蝕小區 soil erosion plot
土壤侵蚀因素/土壤侵蝕因數 soil erosion factor
土壤侵蚀指标/土壤侵蝕指數 soil erosion index
土壤侵蚀综合治理/土壤侵蝕綜合治理 comprehensive control of soil erosion
土壤区划/土壤區劃 soil regionalization
土壤区划图/土壤區劃圖 soil regionalization map
土壤取样点/土壤取樣點 soil sampling point

土壤圈/土壤圈 pedosphere
土壤全氮/土壤全氮 soil total nitrogen
土壤全钾/土壤全鉀 soil total potassium
土壤全磷/土壤全磷 soil total phosphorus
土壤全盐量/土壤全鹽量 soil total salt
土壤容积/土壤容積 soil volume
土壤容重/土壤容重,土壤顆粒密度 volume weight of soil, soil bulk density
土壤三相/土壤三相 three phases of soil
土壤渗透系数/土壤透過係數 permeability coefficient of soil
土壤渗透性/土壤滲透率 soil permeability
土壤生态系统/土壤生態系統 soil ecosystem
土壤生态学/土壤生態學 soil ecology
土壤生物量/土壤生質量 soil biomass
土壤生物学/土壤生物學 soil biology
土壤收缩/土壤收縮 shrinkage of soil
土壤水分/土壤水 soil water, soil moisture
土壤水分保持/土壤水分留存 soil moisture retention
土壤水分常数/土壤含水常數 soil moisture constant
土壤水分张力/土壤水分張力 soil moisture tension
土壤水分状况/土壤水分境況 soil water regime, soil moisture regime
土壤水平地带性/土壤水平地帶性 soil horizontal zonality
土壤水平分布/土壤水平分布 soil horizontal distribution
土壤酸度/土壤酸度,土壤酸性 soil acidity
土壤酸度计/土壤酸度計 soil acidity meter
土壤酸度探测器/土壤酸度探測器 pH-value computer
土壤酸化作用/土壤酸化 soil acidification
土壤酸碱度/土壤酸鹼度,土壤 pH 值 soil acidity and alkalinity, soil pH value
土壤探查/土壤探測 soil exploration
土壤添加剂/土壤添加劑 soil additive
土壤通气性/土壤通氣 soil aeration
土壤图/土壤分布圖,土壤示性圖 soil map
土壤退化/土壤退化,土壤劣化 soil degradation
土壤微生物/土壤微生物 soil microorganism, soil microbe
土壤微生物量/土壤微生物量 soil microbial biomass
土壤微生物学/土壤微生物學 soil microbiology
土壤温度/土壤溫度,土溫 soil temperature
土壤稳定剂/土壤安定劑 soil stabilizer

土壤污染/土壤汙染　soil pollution
土壤污染监测/土壤汙染監測　soil pollution monitoring
土壤污染指数/土壤汙染指標　soil pollution index
土壤物理[学]/土壤物理[學]　soil physics
土壤吸力/土吸力　soil suction
土壤系统分类/土壤分類[學]　soil taxonomy
土壤现场鉴别/土壤野外鑒別法　soil field identification
土壤相对含水量/土壤相對含水量　soil relative water content
土壤详查/土壤詳細調查　detailed soil survey
土壤详图/土壤詳圖　detailed soil map
土壤消毒/土壤消毒　soil disinfection
土壤信息系统/土壤資訊系統　soil information system, SIS
土壤形成/土壤形成,土壤生成　soil formation
土壤形态学/土壤形態[學]　soil morphology
土壤学/土壤科學　soil science, agrology
土壤压实/土壤夯實　soil compaction
土壤盐渍度/土壤鹽度　soil salinity
土壤颜色/土壤顏色　soil color
土壤遥感/土壤遙測　soil remote sensing
土壤液化/土壤液化　soil liquefaction
土壤有机质/土壤有機質,土壤有機物　soil organic matter
土壤 pH 值/土壤 pH 值,土壤酸鹼度　soil acidity and alkalinity, soil pH value
土壤制图/土壤製圖　soil cartography
土壤制图单元/土壤製圖單位,土壤測繪單位　soil mapping unit
土壤质地/土壤質地　soil texture
土壤质地剖面/土壤質地剖面　soil texture profile
土壤资源/土壤資源　soil resources
土壤资源调查/土壤資源調查　soil resources investigation
土壤资源评价/土壤資源評價　soil resources evaluation, soil resource assessment
土壤自净功能/土壤自淨功能　soil self-purification function
土壤自然安息角/土壤自然安息角　soil natural angle of repose
土山/土山　earth-piled hill, artificial mound
土石成分调查/土石組成調查　survey of soil and rock composition
土[石]方/土[石]方　earth volume
土石方平衡/土方平衡　equal of cut and fill
土[石]方体积图/土石方體積圖　volume diagram of earth-rock work
土石分类/土石分類　classification of soil and rock
土石物理力学性质/土石物理機械性能　physical and mechanical property of soil and rock
土体抗震稳定性/土壤抗震稳定性　seismic stability of soil
土体蠕动/土壤蠕動,土壤潛移　soil creep
土围堰/土圍堰　earth cofferdam
土楔/土楔　soil wedge
土星/土星　Saturn
土压力/土壓力　earth pressure
土压力盒/土壓計　earth pressure cell, earth pressure gage
土压力系数/土壓係數　coefficient of earth pressure
土压平衡盾构/土壓平衡式潛盾　earth pressure balanced shield, EPBS
土样/土樣,樣本　soil sample, sample
土样试验/土壤試驗　soil test
土圆锥仪/土圓錐儀　soil cone penetrator
土源/土源　topsoil source
土质调查/土質調查　soil survey, geotechnical investigation
土质勘探/土壤探測　soil exploration
土质隧道/土質隧道　tunnel in earth, earth tunnel
土质条件/土壤狀態　soil condition
土著种/自生種,鄉土種　indigenous species, native species
土钻/土鑽　earth drill
湍急河流/驟漲河川　flashy stream
湍流/擾流,紊流,亂流　turbulence, turbulent flow
湍流斑/紊流斑塊　turbulent spot
湍流边界层/紊流邊界層　turbulent boundary layer
湍流分离/紊流分離　turbulent separation
湍流管烧蚀试验/紊流管燒蝕試驗　ablation testing in turbulence pipe
湍流模型/亂流模式　turbulence model
湍流强度/亂流強度　turbulence intensity
湍流球/紊流球　turbulence sphere
湍流数值计算/紊流數值計算　numerical computation of turbulent flow
湍流速度/紊流速　turbulent velocity
团队旅游/團體旅遊　group travel
团聚体结构/團聚結構　aggregate structure
推测承载力/推測承力　presumption bearing capacity
推测领航/推測導航　dead reckoning navigation
推出试验/壓出試驗　push out test
推船/推船　pusher, pushboat
推导式质量计/推導式質量計　extract type mass

fluxmeter
推定全损/推定全損　constructive total loss
推峰速度自动控制/推峰速度自動控制　automatic control for humping speed
推杆/推桿　push the stick forward, push the column forward
推荐航线/推薦航路　recommended route
推荐速度/勸導速率　advisory speed
推进舱/動力裝置艙　propulsion module
推进电机/推進電機　propulsion electric machine
推进分系统/推進分系統　propulsion subsystem
推进风洞/發動機風洞　propulsion wind tunnel
推进风机/推進風機　propulsive fan
推进机组/推進裝置　propulsion units
推进剂/推進劑　propellant
推进剂方块/推進劑塊　propellant block
推进剂供应系统/推進劑供給系統　propellant feed system
推进剂管理系统/推進劑控制系統　propellant management system, propellant control system
推进剂管理装置/推進劑管理裝置　propellant management device
推进剂和材料兼容性/推進劑和材料相容性　material compatibility with propellants
推进剂化验/推進劑化學分析　propellant chemical analysis
推进剂混合比/推進劑混合比　propellant mixture ratio
推进剂加泄管/推進劑進-出管　propellant fill-drain lines
推进剂加注流量/推進劑加載流量［率］　propellant loading flow rate
推进剂加注流速/推進劑加載流速　propellant loading flow velocity
推进剂加注设备/推進劑裝填設備　propellant loading equipment
推进剂加注温度/推進劑加載溫度　propellant loading temperature
推进剂利用系统/推進劑利用系統　propellant utilization system, PUS
推进剂流量/推進劑流率　propellant flow rate
推进剂燃烧时间/推進劑燃燒時間　propellant burning time
推进剂燃烧速率/推進劑燃燒率　propellant burning rate
推进剂药柱/推進劑藥柱　propellant grain
推进剂液面传感器/推進劑水位感測器　propellant level transducer

推进剂液面指示器/推進劑液位指示器　propellant level indicator
推进剂增压系统/推進劑加壓系統　propellant pressurization system
推进剂蒸发/推進劑蒸發　propellant evaporation
推进剂贮存库/推進劑倉庫　propellant storage depot
推进剂贮箱/輔助燃料箱　propellant tank
推进剂转注间/推進劑轉注間　propellant transfusing room
推进器/推進器,螺槳　propulsor, propeller
推进器柱/螺槳柱　propeller post
推进式/推進式　push type
推进特性/推進特性　propulsion characteristic
推进系数/推進係數　propulsive coefficient
推进系统/推進系統　propulsion system
推进效率/推進效率　propulsive efficiency
推进装置/推進設備,推進設施　propelling plant, propulsion device
推拉窗/推拉窗　horizontal sliding sash
推拉门/拉門,滑門　sliding door
推拉下悬窗/推拉下懸窗　double tilting sliding sash
推理机/推理機　inference engine
推力/推力,側向壓力　thrust, thrusting force, propulsion force
推力百分比表/推力百分比表　percentage-thrust indicator
推力标定/推力標定　thrust calibration
推力测量耙/推力測量耙　thrust measurement rake
推力环/推力［軸］環　thrust collar
推力减额因数/推力減少因數　thrust deduction factor
推力控制系统/推力控制系統　thrust control system
推力块/推力墊,止推墊,推力履片　thrust pad, thrust shoe
推力面/推力面　thrust surface
推力盘/推力［軸］環　thrust collar
推力平衡/推力平衡　thrust balance
推力器/噴射機　thruster, jet
推力矢量控制/推力向量控制　thrust vector control, TVC
推力室/推力室　thrust chamber
推力室比冲/推力室比衝　thrust chamber specific impulse
推力室阀/推力室閥門　thrust chamber valve
推力室混合比/推力室混合比　thrust chamber mixture ratio
推力室面积收缩比/推力室面積收縮比　thrust chamber area contraction ratio

推力室推力/推力室推力　chamber thrust
推力收回角/推力回减[轉速]角　thrust cutback angle
推力调节器/推力調節器　thrust regulator
推力系数/推力係數　thrust coefficient
推力线/推力線　line of thrust, thrust line
推力线横移/推力線偏移　thrust line eccentricity
推力线偏斜/推力線偏差　thrust line deviation
推力线调整/推力線調整　thrust line adjustment
推力仪/推力計　thrust meter
推力质量比/推力重量比　thrust mass ratio, thrust to mass ratio
推力终止/推力終止　thrust termination
推力终止时间/推力終止時間　thrust termination time
推力终止压强/推力終止壓力　thrust termination pressure
推力轴/推力軸　thrust shaft
推力轴承/推力軸承　thrust bearing
推力轴轴承/推力[軸]承,止推[軸]承　thrust block, thrust bearing
推力转向发动机/推力轉向發動機　thrust-vectoring engine
推煤机/推煤器　coal pusher
推扫/推掃式　push broom
推送调车/推送調車　push-pull shunting
推送坡度/推送坡度　helper grade
推送速度/推峰速度　pushing speed
推送小车辆/推送小車輛　propelling trolley
推送信号/推送信號　start humping signal
推算船位/估計船位　estimated position, EP
推算航程/實際距離,終結距離　distance made good
推算航迹向/估計航向　estimated course
推算航速/實在速率,終結速率　speed made good
推算经度/估計經度　estimated longitude
推算始点/出航點,出發點　departure point
推算纬度/估計緯度　estimated latitude
推土铲运机/推土機　scraper dozer
推土机/推土機,鏟泥車　bulldozer
推土[机]设备/土工設備　earth-moving equipment
推雪铲/刮雪板　snow blade
推压机构/推壓機構　dipper crowding gear
推移荷载/掃流[負]載　tractional load
推移质/河床質載　bed material load
推移质输沙率/河床質載率　bed load rate
推重比/推重比,推力重量比　thrust to weight ratio, thrust weight ratio
退潮/退潮,落潮　falling tide

退磁/退磁,消磁,去磁　demagnetization
退格/退位　back space
退关/退貨　shut out
退关货/退關貨　shut-out cargo
退化/退化,變質　degeneration, retrogression, regression
退化林/衰退林　degraded forest
退化生态系统/退化生態系　degraded ecosystem
退火/退火　annealing
退桨/反劃　back water
退水过程线/退水歷線　recession hydrograph
退水曲线/退水曲線　recession curve
退线距离/反測距離　set back distance
退行性滑动/退行性滑動　reprogressive slide
吞吐量/吞吐量　throughput
囤顶/囤頂　shallow vaulted roof
托儿所/託兒所,幼稚園,幼兒園　nursery, kindergarten
托管架/艉托架　aft poppet, stinger
托换技术/托換基礎,支撐　underpinning
托架/托架,船架,支撐桁架　bracket, cradle, supporting truss
托脚/托腳　inclined strut, tuojiao
托老所/託老所　the senior center
托梁/[窗下牆的]托梁　spandrel girder, spandrel beam, joist
托列莫利诺斯国际渔船安全公约/托里莫列路斯漁船安全國際公約　Torremolinos International Convention for Safety of Fishing Vessels
托盘/托[貨]板,棧板　pallet
托盘货/托板貨　palletized cargo
托盘运输/貨盤運輸　pallet traffic
托斯卡纳庄园/托斯卡納莊園　Villa Pliny at Toscane
托运/托運[貨物],發貨　consignment
托运计划/托運計劃　consignment plan
托运人/托運人　consignor, shipper
托运行包/托運行李　consigned luggage
托运行李/托運貨物　registered luggage
托座/托架　bracket
拖材结/曳索套結　timber and half hitch
拖车/拖車　trailer
拖车式移动试验车/拖車式移動試驗車　trailer-typed mobile laboratory vehicle
拖车营地/拖車營地　trailer camps
拖船/拖船　tow boat, towing vessel, tug boat
拖带长度/拖帶長度　length of tow
拖带灯/拖航[號]燈　towing light

拖带责任/拖帶責任　liability of towage
拖动电动机/拖動馬達　drive motor
拖动试验/牵引試驗　towing test
拖动阻力测定/拖動阻力測定　towing resistance measurement
拖钩/拖[缆]鉤　towing hook
拖挂式筑路机/斜鏟推土機　tilt dozer, trailbuilder
拖挂运输/拖曳運輸　tractor trailer transport
拖挂重量/拖掛重量　trailing load
拖航合同/拖船合約　towage contract
拖拉机钻机/牵引式鑽孔機　tractor drill
拖拉架设法/推進工法　launching method
拖缆/拖纜,拖索　towrope, towing line
拖缆承架/拖索承梁　towing beam
拖缆弓架/拖纜拱架　towing arch
拖缆机/拖纜絞機　towing winch
拖缆绞车/拖纜絞機　towing winch
拖缆限位器/拖纜限位器　stop posts for towline
拖缆桩/拖纜樁,拖纜柱　towing bitt
拖轮费/拖船費　tug hire
拖锚/拖錨　dragging anchor
拖锚航行/拖錨航行　dredging
拖锚滑行/拖錨溜行　clubbing
拖式铲运机/拖式鏟運機　towed scraper
拖式沥青混合料摊铺机/拖式瀝青攤鋪機　towed asphalt paver
拖式平地机/拖式平地機,平土機　towed grader
拖式羊足碾/拖式羊足碾　towed sheep-foot roller
拖式振动压路机/拖式振動壓路機　towed vibratory roller
拖网/拖網　trawl
拖网浮标/拖網浮標　trawl buoy
拖网渔船/拖網漁船　trawler
拖网作业/拖網作業　trawl fishing, trawling
拖曳船队/拖曳船隊　towing train
拖曳弓架/拖纜拱架　towing arch
拖曳航速/拖曳船速　towing speed
拖曳缆索/拉拖索　trailing cable
拖曳犁土机/拖曳犁土機　wheel-mounted towed-type ripper
拖曳设备/拖曳設備　towing gear
拖曳水池/船模試驗槽　towing tank
拖曳作业工况管理/拖曳作業方式管理　towing operating mode management
拖运率/拖運率　trailer ton km ratio
拖滞/拖移　dragging
拖桩/拖纜樁　towing post
脱靶点/脱靶點　miss point

脱靶方向/脱靶方向　miss direction
脱靶距离/誤差距離　miss distance
脱层/脱層　delamination
脱氮/脱氮,除氮　nitrogen removal
脱档/脱檔　spontaneous out of gear
脱档滑行/脱檔滑行　coasting in neutral
脱钩点/分離點,分流點　separation point
脱钩链段/鵜嘴形滑脱鉤鏈段　senhouse slip shot
脱轨/脱軌,出軌　derailment
脱轨表示器/脱軌標誌　derail indicator
脱轨器/脱軌器　derailer
脱机故障检测/離線故障檢測　off-operational fault detection
脱碱/脱鹼作用　dealkalization
脱焦油/除溚　tar removal
脱壳裂纹/殼狀裂紋　shelly crack
脱扣/跳脱　trip
脱扣线圈/跳脱線圈　tripping coil
脱扣装置/跳脱設施　trip device
脱磷/除磷　phosphorus removal
脱硫/脱硫　desulfurization
脱氯剂/去氯劑　antichlors
脱落插头/脱落插頭　umbilical plug
脱落插座/脱落插座　umbilical socket
脱落电连接器/臍帶連接器　umbilical connector
脱模油/模板用刷油　mould oil
脱萘/脱萘　naphthalene removal
脱皮/脱皮　scaling
脱气/除氣　deaeration
脱浅/脱淺,再浮　refloat
脱水/脱水　water removal, dehydration
脱水机/脱水機　dehydrator
脱体激波/分離震波　detached shock wave
脱体涡/洩渦,旋渦脱落,旋渦分離　shed vortex, detached eddy, body-shedding vortex
脱网/下網　log out
脱险口/逃生窗口　escape scuttle
脱线修/脱線維護　offline maintenance
脱鞋器/脱鞋器　skate throw-off device
脱氧剂/除氧劑,還原劑　deoxidizer
脱叶/剪葉,落葉,採葉　defoliation
脱叶剂/除葉劑　defoliant
脱粘/脱結　debonding
脱轴试验/脱軸試驗　shaft disengaged test
驮道/騎馬專用道　bridle path
陀罗北/電羅經北　gyrocompass north
陀罗差/電羅經誤差　gyrocompass error
陀罗方位/電羅經方位　gyrocompass bearing, GB

陀罗航向/電羅經航向　gyrocompass course, GC
陀螺磁罗经/電磁羅經　gyro magnetic compass
陀螺磁罗盘/陀螺磁羅盤　gyro magnetic compass
陀螺地平仪/陀螺地平儀　gyro horizon
陀螺电机/陀螺電機　gyro motor
陀螺电机工作电流/陀螺電機工作電流　operating current of gyro motor
陀螺翻滚试验/陀螺翻滾試驗　gyro tumbling test
陀螺浮油/陀螺液　gyro fluid
陀螺力矩/陀螺儀扭矩　gyro torque
陀螺力矩反馈试验/陀螺力矩回饋試驗　gyro torque rebalance test
陀螺力偶/迴轉偶力　gyroscopic couple
陀螺六分仪/電動水平六分儀　gyro sextant
陀螺罗经室/電羅經室　gyrocompass room, gyro compass room
陀螺罗盘/陀螺羅盤,迴轉羅盤　gyrocompass
陀螺罗盘对准/陀螺羅盤校準　gyrocompass alignment
陀螺漂移/迴轉儀漂移　gyro drift
[陀螺]漂移不定性/陀螺儀漂移不定性　uncertainty of gyro drift
陀螺漂移率/陀螺儀漂移率　gyro drift rate
陀螺球/陀螺球　gyro sphere
陀螺式减摇装置/陀螺穩定器　gyro scopic stabilizer
陀螺输出轴/陀螺儀輸出軸　output axis of gyro
陀螺输入轴/陀螺儀輸入軸　input axis of gyro
陀螺伺服试验/陀螺伺服試驗　gyro servo test
陀螺体/陀螺穩定儀　gyrostat
陀螺稳定性/陀螺儀穩定性　stability of gyroscope
陀螺效应/陀螺效應,迴轉效應　gyro effect
陀螺[仪]/陀螺儀,迴轉儀　gyroscope, gyro
陀螺转子/陀螺儀轉子　gyro rotor
陀螺自转轴/陀螺儀旋轉軸　spin axis of gyro
陀螺坐标系/陀螺坐標系　gyro coordinate system
驼峰/駝峰　camel hump, hump
驼峰电气集中/駝峰電氣聯鎖裝置　electric interlocking for hump yard
驼峰调车/駝峰調車　humping
驼峰调车场/駝峰調車場　hump yard
驼峰调车场头部/駝峰調車場頭部　hump yard classification throat
驼峰调车场尾部/駝峰調車場尾部　tail throat of a hump yard
驼峰调车机车无线电遥控/駝峰調車機車無線電遙控　radio telecontrol of locomotive for shunting at hump
驼峰复示信号机/駝峰信號轉發器　humping signal repeater
驼峰高度/駝峰高度　hump height
驼峰机车遥控/駝峰機車遙控　remote control of hump engine
驼峰机械修理室/駝峰機械修理室　hump mechanics repair room
驼峰解体能力/駝峰分解能力　break-up capacity of hump
驼峰连接员室/駝峰連接員室　couper cabin at hump crest
驼峰溜车方向/駝峰滾動方向　rolling direction of hump
驼峰溜放部分/駝峰溜放部分　rolling section of hump
驼峰溜放控制系统/駝峰溜放控制系統　humping control system
驼峰溜放线/駝峰溜放線　hump lead, rolling track of hump
驼峰推送部分/駝峰推送部分　pushing section of hump
驼峰推送线/駝峰推送線　pushing track of hump
驼峰无线电调车信号/駝峰無線電調車信號　radio shunting signal at hump
驼峰信号/駝峰信號　humping signal
驼峰信号机/駝峰號誌機　hump signal
驼峰迂回线/駝峰迂回線　round about line of hump
驼峰纵断面/駝峰縱斷面　hump profile
椭球面/橢球面　ellipsoid surface
椭球体/橢球體　ellipsoid
椭圆摆线波/橢圓餘擺線波　elliptic trochoidal wave
椭圆极化/橢圓極化　elliptical polarization
椭圆抛物面壳/橢圓拋物面殼　elliptic paraboloid shell
椭圆弹簧/橢圓彈簧　elliptic spring
椭圆艉/橢圓艉　elliptical stern
椭圆形截面风洞/橢圓形風洞　elliptic wind tunnel
椭圆形天文台/橢圓形天文臺　El caracol
椭圆余弦波/橢圓函數波,淺海波　cnoidal wave
拓宽/加寬[作用]　widening
拓宽路口式交叉口/加寬型交叉口　flared intersection
拓扑学理论/拓撲學理論　topologic theory
拓展运动/拓展運動　expand the movement

W

挖沟/挖溝 trench excavation
挖沟机/挖溝機,掘溝機 trencher, trench cutting machine
挖沟起重器/溝用千斤頂 trench jack
挖掘/挖掘 digging
挖掘铲/土鏟 scoop
挖掘机/挖掘機,挖土機 excavator, excavating machine
挖坑机/挖坑機 drilling machine
挖孔灌桩法/挖孔灌樁法 installing pile shaft by excavation
挖孔桩/挖孔樁 cast in situ pile by excavation, dug pile
挖泥船/挖泥船 dredger
挖泥船自控程序/挖泥船自控程式 automated control system of dredging process
挖泥工具/挖泥設施 dredging facility
挖泥机/挖泥機 dredge machine
挖树机/掘墼機 tree digging machine
挖探/挖探 excavation prospecting
挖填/挖填調配 excavation and filling
挖土/挖土 earth excavation
挖土铲/黏土挖掘機 clay digger
挖土用架空索道/開挖用索道 excavating cableway
洼地泉/窪地泉 depression spring
蛙式夯/蛙式夯 electric frog rammer
蛙跳式涡/跳蛙渦旋 leap-frogging of vortice
瓦/瓦 roof tile, tile
瓦法园/誠篤園 Garden of Fidelity
瓦斯爆炸/瓦斯爆炸,氣爆 gas explosion
瓦斯浓度/氣體密度 gas density, gas consistency
瓦斯突出/瓦斯突出 gas projection
瓦斯治理/氣體控制 gas control
瓦子/瓦子 culture and community center, wazi
瓦作/瓦作 tilework and roofing
外板/外板,船殼板 shell plate
外板展开/外板展開 shell plate development
外板展开图/外板展開圖 shell expansion plan
外保温/外保溫 external thermal insulation
外补偿法/外補償法 method of outer compensation
外部参照/外參考 external reference

外部测试设备/外部測試設施 external test facility
外部导电部分/裝置外可導電部分 extraneous conductive part
外部防雷装置/外部雷擊防護系統 external lightning protection system
外部过电压试验/外因過電壓試驗 test on external overvoltage
外部空间/室外空間 outdoor space
外部设备/外部裝置 external device
外部效应/外部性 externality
外部振捣器/外部[振]動機 external vibrator
外侧车道/外側車道 near side lane, kerb lane, nearside lane
外侧分隔带/外側分隔帶 outer separator
外侧坡度/外側坡度 outer slope
外侧轴系/外側軸 outer shaft, outer shafting
外测数据处理/追蹤數據處理 tracking data processing
外测[信息]仿真/追蹤模擬 tracking information simulation
外层空间/外太空 space, outer space
外窗/外窗 external window
外弹道测量/外彈道測量 exterior trajectory measurement
外弹道测量系统/外彈道測量系統 exterior trajectory measurement system, trajectory tracking system, exterior ballistic measuring system
外动力地质作用/地質外營力作用 exogenic geological process
外端门/外端門 gangway door
外端墙/外端牆 outside end wall
外方位元素/外方位元素 elements of exterior orientation
外功/外功 external work
外挂物/機外掛載 external store
外挂物管理系统/外掛載管理系統 store management system
外挂物试验/外掛載試驗 external stores testing
外观检查/外觀檢查,外部檢查 observation check, exterior check
外海渔业/外海漁業 off-sea fishery

外涵加力燃烧室/外涵加力燃燒室　duct burner
外航路/外航路　offshore tracks
外火箱/外火箱　outside firebox, outer firebox
外[火箱]顶板/外[火箱]頂板　roof sheet
外基线测距/視距測距　stadiametric ranging
外加电流阴极保护/外加電流陰極防蝕　impressed current cathodic protection
外加剂/外加劑,添加劑,摻和劑　additive, admixture
外界可导电部分/裝置外可導電部分　extraneous conductive part
外进汽/外邊進氣　outside admission
外径比/外淨空比　outside clearance ratio
外径千分尺/外分釐卡,外測微計　outside micrometer
外距/外距,矢距　external distance
外壳/外殼　case, enclosure
外廓线/船體側面[圖]　profile
外来入侵种/外來入侵種　alien invasive species
外来植物/外來植物,引入的植物,外地植物　exotic plant
外来种/外來種　alien species, exotic species, allochthonous species
外廊式/外廊式建築　veranda style
外力/外力　external force
外梁/外梁　outside girder
外露可导电部分/外露導電體　exposed-conductive part
外露翼/外露機翼　exposed wing
外锚地/外海錨地　outer anchorage
外门/外[部]門　external door
外面/外側面　outside face
外啮合齿轮沥青泵/外齒輪瀝青泵　outside gear asphalt pump
外排水/外流水系,明溝排水　external drainage
外牵索/外牵索　outhaul line
外墙/外牆,外堤　external wall
外墙内保温系统/外牆內保溫系統　thermal insulation system inside external wall
外墙外保温系统/外牆保溫板　thermal insulation system outside external wall
外倾/舷緣外傾　flare
外燃机/外燃機　external combustion engine
外沙坝/外沙洲　outer bar
外沙堤/外沙洲　outer bar
外射投影/外投影法　external projection
外伸梁/外伸梁　overhanging beam
外渗/外滲　exfiltration

外施电压/外施電壓　applied voltage
外时统/外計時系統　outside timing system
外式应变天平/外部應變規式平衡儀　external strain gage balance
外事用地/外事用地　land for foreign affair
外特性/外部特性　external characteristics
外湾/敞灣　open bay
外围保护地带/外圍保護區劃設　perimeter protection zone
外围地区/外圍區　outlying area
外围设备/周邊設備　peripheral equipment
外物吞咽/外物吞嚥　foreign object ingestion
外舾装/艙面艤裝　deck outfit, deck outfitting
外舷/外擋,舷外　outboard
外显反应/外顯反應　overt response
外相参动目标指示/外相動目標顯示　externally coherent moving target indicator
外斜轴系/外斜軸系　diverging shafting
外形吃水/外形吃水　navigational draft
外形尺寸测定/外形尺寸測定　overall dimension measurement
外形设计/形態設計　configuration design
外旋/外旋,往外轉　outward turning
外压式进气道/外壓式進氣道　external compression inlet
外压试验/外壓試驗　external pressure test
外烟筒/煙囪,煙管道　smokestack, chimney
外延工艺/外延技術　epitaxy technique
外延生长过程/外延過程　epitaxial process
外檐装修/外檐裝修　exterior finish work
外业控制/實測控制　field control
外移桩/外移樁　shift out stake, stake outward, offset stake
外应力/外應力　exterior stress
外闸门/外閘門　outer head
外支式挡土墙/外支式擋土牆　buttressed type retaining wall
外植体/外植體　explant
外止点/外止點　outer dead point, outer dead center
外置式圆柱滚子轴承/外置滾子軸承　outboard roller bearings
外置轴承/船外軸承　outboard bearing
外锥面/陽錐　male cone
外纵梁/外縱梁　exterior beam, exterior stringer
外走廊/外走廊　outside corridor, running board
弯沉盆/偏斜盆地　deflection basin
弯沉试验/撓度試驗　deflection test
弯沉系数/偏轉係數　deflection coefficient

弯沉仪/撓度計　deflectometer
弯沉值/彎沈值　deflection value
弯道标志/彎道標誌　curve sign
弯管/彎管　pipe bending
弯管机/彎管機　pipe bender
弯矩/彎[曲力]矩　bending moment, moment of flexure
弯矩钣/力矩板　moment plate
弯矩包[络]图/彎力矩圖包絡線　bending moment envelope
弯矩面积定理/彎矩面積定理,力矩面積定理　moment-area theorem
弯矩塑性重分布/彎矩塑性重分配　plastic redistribution of moment
弯矩图/彎矩圖　bending moment diagram, moment diagram
弯矩轴/彎[矩]軸　bending axis
弯拉强度/彎拉強度　flexural tensile strength
弯拉应变/彎拉應變　flexural tensile strain
弯拉应力/彎拉應力　flexural tensile stress
弯扭屈曲/扭轉彎曲挫曲　torsional flexural buckling
[弯]扭叶片/扭葉片,扭轉槳葉　twisted blade
弯起钢筋/彎起鋼筋,曲折鋼筋　bent-up bar
弯曲/彎曲　bending, flexure
弯曲度/彎曲度　tortuosity
弯曲刚度/抗彎剛度　flexural rigidity
弯曲刚度矩阵/彎曲勁度矩陣　bending stiffness matrix
弯曲钢筋/彎鋼筋　bend bar
弯曲抗压强度/彎曲抗壓強度　flexural compressive strength
弯曲疲劳破裂/彎曲疲勞破裂　bending fatigue cracks
弯曲疲劳试验/重複彎曲試驗　repeated bending test
弯曲试验/彎曲試驗　bending test
弯曲头锥/彎曲錐　bent cone
弯曲稳定性/彎曲穩定度　bending stability
弯曲振动/彎曲振動　bending vibration
弯头[水力]损失/彎曲損失　knee loss
弯形止阀/彎閥　bend stop valve
弯支杆/彎支桿　bent sting
蜿蜒宽/蜿蜒寬　meander width
完成宅地/完成宅地　through lot
完工检验/完工檢查　inspection after construction, final inspection
完好车率/完好車率　vehicle availability rate
完好车日/完好車日　available vehicle-day
完全重复使用运载器/多次使用太空載具　complete reusable space vehicle
完全处理/完全處理　complete treatment
完全二次型方根法/完整二次項組合法　complete quadric combination method, CQC
完全防洪/完全防洪　complete flood control
完全仿真/完全模擬　complete simulation
完全混合反应器/完全混合反應器　complete mix reactor
完全膨胀/完全膨脹　full expansion
完全气体/完全氣體,理想氣體　perfect gas
完全燃烧/完全燃燒　complete combustion
完全收缩/全收收縮　complete contraction
完全失效/完全失效　complete failure
完全弹性体/完全彈性體　perfectly elastic body
完全退火/完全退火　dead soft annealing, complete annealing, full annealing
完全小学/國民小學　elementary school
完全氧化/完全氧化　total oxidation
完全溢流/完全溢流　perfect overflow
完全预混[式]燃烧/完全預混[式]燃燒　pre-aerated combustion
完全预混式燃烧器/預混燃燒器,無焰燃燒器　premixed burner, pre-aerated burner
完全运行能力/完全運作能力　full operation capability
完全运行状态/完全運作狀況　full operational status
完善性监测台/整合監視器　integrity monitor
完整构架/完整構架　perfect frame
完整货/滿載貨　completing cargo
完整街道/完整街道　complete street
完整稳性/完整穩度　intact stability
完整性控制/完整性控制　integrity control
玩具厂/玩具[工]廠　toy making factory
晚点/計劃進度落後　behind schedule
晚点表示/晚點表示　delaying time indication
碗式搅拌机/碗式拌和機　bowl mixer
万能道尺/萬能道尺　universal rail gage
万能杆件/萬能桿件　fabricated universal steel member, universal member
万能绘图仪/萬能作圖儀　universal plotting instrument
万能试验机/萬能試驗機　universal testing machine
万能支撑器/萬能儀,通用儀器　universal support apparatus
万向导缆器/萬向導纜器　universal fairleader
万向架/萬向吊架,恆平框架　gimbal mounting, gimbal table
万向接头/萬向接頭　universal joint

万向接头式桨毂/萬向接頭螺旋槳轂　gimbaled hub
万向联轴器/萬向聯結器　universal coupling
万向轴驱动/萬向軸驅動　cardan shaft drive
万用的/萬用的，通用的　universal
万有特性/萬有特性　universal characteristic
万有引力常数/萬有引力常數　universal gravitational constant
腕/腕　wrist
腕臂/懸臂，懸桁，肱臂　cantilever
腕臂底座/伸臂底座　cantilever base
王城/王城　wang cheng, royal city
王畿/王畿　wang ji, royal city area
王良四(仙后 α)/王良四(仙后 α)　Schedar
王良一(仙后 β)/王良一(仙后 β)　Caph
网吧/網吧　internet bar, cybercafe
网板/網板　otter board
网板架/網板架　trawl gallow
网侧电路/網側電路　circuit on side of overhead contact line
网侧电压表/網側電壓表　voltmeter on side of overhead contact line, overhead side voltmeter
网船/網船　net boat
网档间距/網間距　distance between twin trawl
网点/網格點　grid
网格/網格模塊　reseau, graticule mesh, grid module
网格法/網格法　grid method
网格分析/網路分析　network analysis
网格化城市管理/網格化都市管理　city-grid management
网格结构/細胞狀結構，管狀結構　cellular structure
网格雷诺数/網格雷諾數　cell Reynolds number
网格生成技术/網格產生技術　grid generation technique
网关/閘道器　gateway
网架/空間網架　space truss, space grid
网架结构/網架結構　space truss structure, space grid structure
网壳/網殼　latticed shell, reticulated shell
网壳结构/網殼結構　latticed shell structure, reticulated shell structure
网孔盆/網孔盆　mesh pot
网裂/網裂，網狀裂縫　net-shaped crack
网络/網路　network
网络操作系统/網路作業系統　network operation system
网络地面/網路地板　network ground
网络管理/網路管理　network management

网络互连/網路互連　interoperation
网络计划技术/網路規劃技術　network planning technique
网络进度计划/網路進度計劃　construction project schedule network diagram
网络控制中心/網路控制中心　network control center
网络图/網路圖　network diagram
网络协调站/網路協調電臺　network coordination station, NCS
网络协调站到陆地球站信令信道/網路協調電臺與陸上衛星電臺之信號頻道　NCS-LES signaling channel
网络协调站到网络协调站信令信道/網路協調電臺間之信號頻道　NCS-NCS signaling channel
网络协调站共用时分多路复用信道/網路協調站共用分時多路頻道　NCS common TDM channel
网球场/網球場　tennis court
网球场草坪/網球草坪　tennis court turf
网筛/孔篩　mesh screen
网位仪/網位儀　net monitor
网纹钢板/格紋板　grid steel plate
网形网[络]/網型網路　mesh network
网衣/網片　netting
网状河流/辮狀河川　braided river
网状配筋砌体/方格網配筋磚砌體　mesh reinforced masonry
网状责任制/網狀責任制　network liability system
往返性客流/往返性客運交通　round trip passenger traffic
往复泵/往復泵　reciprocating pump
往复惯性力矩平衡器/蘭氏均衡器　Lanchester balancer
往复给料机/往復式給料機，往復式饋送器　reciprocating feeder
往复式发动机/往復機，往復式引擎　reciprocating engine
往复式风钻/往復式鑽孔機　reciprocating drill
往复式压缩机/往復[式]壓縮機　reciprocating compressor
往复式制冷压缩机/往復冷凍壓縮機　reciprocating refrigeration compressor, reciprocating type refrigeration compressor
往复式转舵机构/往復式操舵装置　reciprocating type steering gear
旺季/運輸旺季　peak season
望景楼花园/麗城花園　Belvedere Garden
望远镜方位仪/望遠鏡照準儀　telescopic alidade

望柱/欄杆小柱,扶手支柱　baluster
危房改造/危房改造　dilapidated house reconstruction
危害度分析/關鍵分析　criticality analysis
危害度类别/關鍵類別　criticality category
危机处理和人的行为/危機處理及行爲管理　crisis management and human behavior
危桥/危橋　bridge in danger
危险/危險,危害　hazard, danger spot
危险半圆/危險半圈　dangerous semicircle
危险标志/危險物品標誌,危險標記　dangerous mark, hazard sign
危险等级/危害程度　hazard level
危险电文/危險消息　danger message
危险分析/危害分析,冒險分析　hazard analysis
危险固体废物/危險固體廢物　hazardous solid waste
危险海岸/危險海岸　dangerous coast
危险货[物]/危險貨物,危險貨品　dangerous goods, dangerous cargo, dangerous freight
危险货物包装标志/危險貨物包裝標誌　package mark for hazardous goods, labels for packages of dangerous goods
危险货物报告/危險貨物報告　dangerous goods report
危险货物锚地/危險貨物錨地　dangerous cargo anchorage
危险接近/迫在眉睫的危險　imminent to danger
危险津贴/危險津貼　danger money
危险品/危險貨物　dangerous cargo
危险品库/危險材料倉庫　hazardous material storage, hazardous material warehouse
危险品清单/危險貨物清單　dangerous cargo list
危险区[域]/危險區[域]　hazardous areas, danger area, dangerous area
危险水域/航行危險水域　foul water
危险天气通报/危險天氣通報　hazardous weather message
危险[物]/危險　danger
危险物质存放区/危險物品區,危險品庫房　dangerous substance area
危险线/危險線　hazard marking
危险象限/危險象限　dangerous quadrant
危险信标/危險燈號　hazard signal
危险性故障/關鍵性故障,致命故障　critical fault
危险影响/危險影響　dangerous influence
危岩/危岩　overhanging rock, hanging rock
威力系数/功率係數　power coefficient
威廉逊旋回法/威廉生掉頭法　Williamson turn

威尼斯宪章/威尼斯憲章　Venice Charter
微波/微波　microwave
微波测距系统/微波測距系統　microwave ranging system
微波大气探测辐射计/微波大氣探測成像輻射計　microwave atmospheric sounding radiometer
微波辐射/微波輻射　microwave radiation
微波辐射计/微波輻射計　microwave radiometer
微波全息雷达/微波立體照相雷達　microwave hologram radar
微波散射计/微波散射計　microwave scatterometer
微波探测装置/微波探測裝置　microwave sounding unit, MSU
微波通信/微波通信網,微波網路　microwave communication
微波通信车/微波通信車,微波通訊車　microwave communication vehicle
微波通信楼/微波電信大樓　microwave telecommunication building
微波统一系统/微波統一系統　unified microwave system
微波吸收材料/微波吸收材料　microwave absorbing material
微波遥感/微波遙測　microwave remote sensing
微波遥感器/微波遙測器　microwave remote sensor
微波引信/微波引信　microwave fuze
微波站/微波中繼站,微波電驛站　microwave relay station
微波着陆系统/微波降落系統　microwave landing system, MLS
微波着陆系统覆盖/微波降落系統覆蓋　microwave landing system coverage
微差测量方法/微差量測法　differential method of measurement
微处理器/微處理機　micro processor
微穿孔板消声器/微穿孔板消聲器　micropunch plate muffler
微带天线/微帶天線　microstrip antenna
微带天线阵/微帶天線陣列　microstrip antenna array
微电子工厂/微電子工廠　microelectronic manufactory
微动磨损疲劳/磨蝕疲勞　fretting fatigue
微动同步器/微同步器　microsyn
微分法测图/微分法測圖　differential photo
微分求速/微分求速　velocity derived by differential
微分调节器/微分調整器　derivative regulator
微风化岩石/微風化岩　slightly weathered rock

微幅波/小振幅波　small amplitude wave
微耕机/微耕機　mini-tiller
微观腐蚀/微刻蚀　microetch
微观交通模型/微觀交通模型　micro-traffic model
微灌/微灌　microirrigation
微灌系统/細霧噴灌系統　microirrigation system
微光摄像机/微光攝像機　camera used in low-light level
微机/微電腦　microcomputer
微机-继电式电气集中联锁/繼電式電氣集中聯鎖　microcomputer-relay interlocking
微机控制系统/微電腦控制系統　microcomputer control system
微机控制主机遥控系统/微電腦遙控主機系統　microcomputer remote control system for main engine
微机联锁/微機聯鎖　microcomputer interlocking
微加工/微製造技術　micro-manufacturing technology
微进给/微量進給,微量送料　microfeed
微晶玻璃/微晶玻璃,玻璃陶瓷　glass-ceramics, glass ceramics, sitall
微晶玻璃陶瓷复合砖/玻璃陶瓷　glass-ceramics and ceramics combined tile
微孔滤网/微孔濾篩　micro-strainer
微孔塑料/氣泡塑膠　cellular plastic
微浪/静海,浪静　calm sea, rippled sea
微粒物/粒子,質點,顆粒　particles
微量/微量　trace
微量天平/微量天平　microbalance, low load balance
微量元素/微量元素,痕量元素　micro-element, trace element
微量元素养分/微量營養素　micronutrient
微裂缝/微裂紋　micro-crack
微流星防护服/微星際石防護服　micrometeoroid protection garment
微流星仿真器/微隕石模擬器　micrometeorite simulator
微流星体/微星際石　micrometeoroid
微滤器/微孔濾篩　micro-strainer
微喷带/微噴帶　microspray tape
微喷灌/微灌溉　microspray irrigation
微喷头/微型噴霧器　microjet, microsprayer, minisprinkler
微气候/微氣候,小氣候　microclimate
微气象学/小氣象學　micrometeorology
微切削加工/微機械加工　micromachining
微倾水准仪/微傾水平儀　tilting level

微丘区/丘陵地　rolling terrain
微区试验/微區試驗　micro-plot experiment
微生态学/狹域生態學　microecology
微生物活性/微生物活性　microbial activity
微生物胶膜/微生物膠膜　zoogleal matrix
微生物控制/微生物控制　microbiological control
微生物膜/微生物黏膜　microbial film
微生物区[系]/微生物　microbiota
微生物污染控制/微生物汙染控制　microbial contaminant control
微束等离子弧焊/微束電漿弧焊[接]　micro-plasma arc welding
微缩复制图/縮微[複製]本,縮微副本　microcopy
微缩图书阅览室/縮微圖書閱覽室　microfilm reading room
微弯板/微彎板　slab with slightly curved bottom
微弯板组合梁桥/微彎板組合梁橋　composite shell slab and I-beam bridge
微卫星/微衛星　micro-satellite
微污染/微量汙染　micropollution
微污染物/微量汙染物　micropollutant
微细加工/微加工,微型裝配　microfabrication
微型底栖生物/微底棲生物　microbenthos
微型惯性测量装置/微型慣性量測單元　micro inertial measurement unit, MIMU
微型机械加速度计/微機械加速度計　micromechanical accelerometer
微型机械陀螺仪/微型機械陀螺儀　micromechanical gyro
微型盆景/微型盆景　micro-bonsai
微型桩/微型樁　mini-pile
微循环改造/微循環轉換　microcirculation transformation
微烟推进剂/低煙推進劑　low smoke propellant
微振动/微動　micro-vibration
微振动控制/微震動控制　micro-vibration control
微正压锅炉/增壓鍋爐　pressurized boiler
微重力/微重力　microgravity
微重力试验/微重力試驗　microgravity test
微组装/微裝配　micromounting
韦伯数/韋伯數　Weber number
违法建设/違法建設　illegal construction
违法建设查处/違法建設查處　investigating and punishing the illegal construction
违法占地/非法占房　illegal occupation of land
违禁[物]品/違禁品　prohibited articles
违约/違約　default
违章建筑/違章建築,違法營造,違建　illegal

building
违章排放/違規排洩　discharge in violation of regulations
违章行为/違規事項　violation
围蔽处所/圍蔽空間　enclosed spaces
围壁/圍壁　trunk bulkhead
围堤/圍堤，月堤　polder dyke, circle levee
围海[湖]造田/堤圍區　polder
围护结构/建築物外殼　building envelope
围护结构传热系数/建築物外殼傳熱係數　overall heat transfer coefficient of building envelope
围护墙/圍[護]牆　enclosure wall
围栏/圍欄　railing around coping of pier or abutment
围墙/界牆　boundary wall
围裙高度/氣裙昇高度　skirting rise, skirt depth
围裙救生圈/圍裙救生圈　breech buoy
围网/圍網,巾著網　purse seine
围网渔船/圍網漁船,巾著網漁船　seiner, purse seiner
围网作业/旋網漁業　surrounding fishing
围压层/拘限層,局限層　confining bed, confining layer, confining stratum
围岩/圍岩　surrounding rock
围岩分类/圍岩分級　surrounding rock classification
围岩稳定/圍岩穩定度,圍岩穩定性　stability of surrounding rock, surrounding rock stability
围岩压力/圍岩壓力　surrounding rock pressure, pressure of surrounding rock
围岩自承能力/圍岩自承能力　surrounding rock self-supporting capacity, self-supporting capacity of surrounding rock
围岩自稳能力/圍岩自穩能力　self-stabilization capacity of surrounding rock
围堰/圍堰　cofferdam
围油栏/攔油索　oil fence, oil boom
桅/桅　mast
桅灯/桅[頂]燈　mast light, mast head light, masthead light
桅顶横杆/桅頂橫桿　crosstree
桅杆/桅桿　mast, guyed mast
桅杆[式]起重机/桅桿[式]起重機,人字起重機,吊桿式起重機　mast crane, derrick crane
桅杆涂料/桅桿塗料　mast coating
桅冠/桅頂　truck
桅冠灯/桅冠燈　truck light
桅横杆/橫桁,帆桁　yard
桅肩/桅上固定具　outrigger
桅设备/桅檣設備　mast and rigging

桅套/桅跟帆套　boot
桅柱/下桅　lower mast
维持平均照度/維持平均照度　maintained average illuminance
维蒂住宅/維蒂住宅　House of Vetti
维护/維護[服務],保养　maintenance, maintenance service, servicing
维护保养废弃物/維護保養所生廢棄物　maintenance waste
维护标志/修護標誌　maintenance sign
维护系数/維護因數,維持因數　maintenance factor
维护系统/保養制度　maintenance system
维卡稠度仪/維卡儀　Vicat apparatus
维氏变位图/維利奧圖　Williot diagram
维氏硬度试验/鑽頭硬度試驗　diamond pyramid hardness test
维斯比规则/威斯比規則　Visby Rules
维特鲁威建筑三原则/維脫魯維三原理　Vitruvius three principles
维修/維修,維護　maintenance
维修不良/維修不良　not well maintained
维修厂/修理廠　workshop
维修车/檢修車　maintenance car
维修车间/貨櫃保養廠,修護工場　maintenance shop
维修大纲/維護計劃　maintenance program
维修放行/維護放手　maintenance release
维修工程/維護工程　maintenance engineering
维修工时/維護工時　maintenance man-hour
维修工时率/維護率　maintenance ratio
维修级别/維護水準　maintenance level
维修鉴别性/維護辨別　maintenance distinguishing
维修可达性/維護可達性　maintenance accessibility
维修前平均使用时间/平均修復間隔時間　mean-time-to-repair
维修时间/維護時間　maintenance time
维修事件/維護事件　maintenance event
维修性/可維修[維護]性,維護性,維護度　maintainability, maintenability
维修性保证/可維修性保證　maintainability assurance
维修性保证大纲/可維修性保證計劃　maintainability assurance program
维修性分配/維護度分配　maintainability allocation
维修性分析/維護度分析　maintainability analysis
维修性工作计划/維護性工作計劃　maintainability program plan
维修性管理/維護度管理　maintainability management

维修性模型/維護度模型　maintainability model
维修性预计/維護度預測　maintainability prediction
维修周期/維修週期　maintenance cycle
维修作业/維護活動　maintenance activity
维也纳分离派/維也納分離派　Vienna secession, Viennese secession
伪彩色发光二极管显示屏/偽彩色發光二極體顯示器　pseudo-color light emitting diode panel
伪彩色图像处理/偽彩色圖像處理　pseudo-color picture treatment
伪动力试验/偽動力試驗　pseudo-dynamic test
伪方位投影/擬方位投影　pseudo-azimuthal projection
伪静力试验/偽靜力試驗　pseudo-static test
伪距/偽距　pseudo-range
伪码侧音混合测距/虛擬碼側音混合測距　hybrid pseudorandom code and side tone ranging
伪码测距/偽隨機碼測距　pseudorandom code ranging
伪速率增量控制/偽速率增量控制　pseudo-rate increment control
伪随机码/擬隨機碼　pseudorandom code
伪随机码调频引信/偽隨機碼調頻引信　pseudorandom code frequency-modulated fuze
伪随机码调相引信/偽隨機碼調相引信　pseudorandom code phase-modulated fuze
伪随机码调制引信/偽隨機碼調變引信　pseudorandom code modulation fuze
伪随机码引信/偽隨機碼引信　pseudorandom code fuze
伪随机脉位引信/偽隨機脈位引信　pseudorandom pulse position fuze
伪卫星/偽衛星,偽訊號　pseudolite, pseudo satellite
伪星捕获概率/偽星獲得機率　probability of false star acquisition
伪[噪声]码/偽雜訊碼,PN 碼　pseudo-noise code
伪装/偽裝　camouflage
伪装材料/偽裝材料　camouflage material
伪装技术/偽裝技術　camouflage technology
伪装商船/偽裝商船　decoy ship, Q-ship
伪装涂料/偽裝漆　camouflage paint
伪装网/偽裝網　camouflage net
伪锥误差/假性角錐誤差　pseudo-coning error
尾巴电缆/連接電纜,短截電纜　stub cable
尾撑/尾桁架　tail boom
尾灯/尾燈　tail lamp
尾端加温管路系统/尾段加溫管路系統　tail section heating line system
尾端加温控制台/尾段加溫配氣控制臺　tail section heating gas distribution console
尾端加温器/尾段加熱器　tail section heater
尾段/尾段,尾部　rear section, tail section
尾滚筒/艉滾筒　stern roll, stern barrel
尾迹/尾跡　trail
尾桨/尾旋翼　tail rotor
尾景/尾景　terminal feature
尾框/車鉤軛　coupler yoke
尾流/尾流,航跡流　trailing wake, wake
尾流阻塞效应/尾流阻塞效應　wake blockage effect
尾轮/尾輪　tail wheel
尾喷管/排氣噴嘴　exhaust nozzle
尾喷口/排氣噴口　exhaust nozzle exit
尾橇/尾橇　tail skid
尾随车距离/前後間距,追蹤距離　following distance
尾随涡/尾渦流　trailing vortex
尾随行驶/尾隨行駛　following at a distance
尾索/尾索　tail rope
尾拖网/尾拖網　stern trawl
尾拖渔船/艉拖網漁船　stern trawler
尾旋/[尾]螺旋,自旋　spin, tail spin
尾旋风洞/自旋風洞,螺旋風洞　spin wind tunnel
尾翼/尾翼組,尾翅　tail unit, empennage, rear fin
尾翼包装箱吊具/尾翼封裝吊索　tail package sling
尾支杆/探臂式支架　support sting
纬差/緯差　difference of latitude
纬度/緯度　latitude
纬度改正量/緯度修正值　latitude correction
纬度渐长率/緯度漸長比　meridional parts, MP
纬度渐长率差/緯度漸長比數差　difference of meridianal parts, DMP
纬[度]圈/緯度平行圈　parallel of latitude
纬度误差/緯度誤差　latitude error
纬度误差校正器/緯度誤差校正器　latitude error corrector
纬度效应/緯度效應　latitude effect
纬度因数/緯度因數　latitude factor
纬圈/緯圈,平行圈　parallel circle
纬线/緯度平行圈　parallel of latitude
委付/委付　abandonment
委内瑞拉草原/委内瑞拉草原　Venezuelan grassland
萎蔫/凋萎　wilting
萎蔫点/枯萎點　wilting point
萎蔫系数/枯萎係數　wilting coefficient
艉/船尾　stern
艉[部]接近法/艉接近法　astern approaching method

艉部结构/艉段結構　stern construction, stern structure
艉吃水/艉吃水　aft draft, aft draught
艉垂线/艉垂標，後垂標　aft perpendicular, AP
艉灯/艉燈　sternlight
艉风/艉風　wind aft
艉封板/艉封板，艉橫板　stern transom plate
艉管螺母/艉軸管環首螺帽　stern-tube nut
艉管密封装置/艉軸封　stern shaft seal, stern shaft sealing
艉管轴承/艉軸套軸承　stern-tube bearing
艉横缆/艉橫纜　stern breast
艉横梁/艉梁　transom beam
艉滑道/艉斜道，艉坡道　stern ramp
艉滑轮/艉槽輪　stern sheave
艉机型船/艉機型船，艉機艙船　engined aft, stern engined ship
艉迹/艉跡　back track
艉尖舱/艉[尖]艙　aft peak tank, aft peak
艉尖舱壁/艉艙壁　after peak bulkhead
艉尖舱舱壁/艉尖艙壁　aft peak bulkhead
艉阱/艉凹艙　cockpit
艉缆/艉纜　stern line
艉肋板/艉肋板　transom floor
艉离/艉先離　leaving stern first
艉龙骨墩/[吊桿]跟部滑車　heel block
艉楼/艉樓，艉艛　poop
艉楼甲板/艉艛甲板　poop deck
艉落/艉驟降　tipping
艉锚/艉錨　stern anchor, poop anchor
艉锚绞车/艉錨絞車　stern position winch, sternline winch
艉门/艉門　stern port
艉门跳板/艉門跳板　stern ramp
艉膨出部/艉膨出部　bossing
艉旗杆/艉旗桿　ensign staff
艉鳍/分水踵艉鳍　deadwood skeg
艉翘/艉部上翹變形　cocking up of after body
艉倾/艉俯　trim by stern
艉升高甲板船/高艉主甲板船　raised quarter-deck vessel
艉舷/艉部　quarter
艉舷浪/艉側浪　quartering sea
艉向后倒缆/艉向後倒纜　stern aft spring
艉向前倒缆/艉向前倒纜　stern forward spring
艉斜浪/艉側浪　quartering sea
艉斜跳板/艉斜跳板　quarter ramp
艉支架/艉托架　aft poppet, stinger
艉踵/艉踵　aft foot
艉轴/艉[管]軸　propeller shaft, stern shaft, screw shaft
艉轴承/艉軸承　stern bearing
艉[轴]管/艉軸套　stern tube
艉轴管滑油/艉軸管潤滑油　stern tube lubricating oil
艉轴管密封装置/艉軸管密封裝置　stern tube sealing
艉[轴]管填料函/艉軸管填料函　stern tube stuffing box
艉轴管轴封泵/艉軸管軸封油泵　stern tube sealing oil pump
艉轴架/艉軸架，螺槳支架　propeller strut, propeller shaft bracket, shaft bracket
艉轴架轴承/艉軸支架軸承　strut bearing
艉柱/艉柱　stern post
艉柱底骨/舵跟材　sole piece
鲔钓船/鮪釣船　tuna long liner
鲔钓母船/鮪釣母船　tuna mother ship
卫生泵/衛生[水]泵　sanitary pump
卫生单元/衛生單元　sanitary unit
卫生防护标准/衛生防護標準　public health standard
卫生防护距离/衛生防護距離　health protection zone
卫生防护绿化带/衛生防護綠化帶　green belt for health protection
卫生工程学/衛生工程學　sanitary engineering
卫生间/盥洗室　toilet, lavatory
卫生器具/衛生器具　plumbing fixture, fixture
卫生器具当量/衛生器具單位　fixture unit
卫生设备系统/衛生設備系統　plumbing system
卫生设施/衛生設施　health service
卫生水系统/衛生系統　sanitary system
卫生水压力柜/壓力衛生水櫃　sanitary pressure tank
卫生所/衛生所，保健中心　health center
卫星/衛星　satellite
卫星标准频率和时间信号业务/衛星標準頻時信號業務　standard frequency and time signal satellite service
卫星测绘/衛星測繪　satellite surveying and mapping
卫星测距导航/衛星測距導航　satellite ranging navigation
卫星测控网/衛星測控網　satellite TT and C network
卫星测控系统/衛星測控系統　satellite TT and C system

卫星测控中心/衛星控制中心　satellite control center
卫星测试操作控制台/衛星試驗控制臺　test operation console for satellite
卫星测试程序/衛星測試程式　satellite test sequence
卫星测试技术流程/衛星測試技術流程　technical sequence for satellite test
卫星测试设备/衛星檢測裝備　checkout equipment for satellite
卫星测试语言/衛星測試語言　satellite test language
卫星城[市]/衛星城[市]　satellite city
卫星城镇/衛星市鎮　satellite town
卫星充电/衛星充電　satellite charging
卫星船位/衛星定位　satellite fix
卫星搭载环境试验/衛星搭載環境試驗　satellite piggyback environment test
卫星导航/衛星導航,衛星航法　satellite navigation
卫星导航系统/衛星導航系統　satellite navigation system
卫星导航仪/衛星導航儀　satellite navigator
卫星地面电源/衛星地面動力供應　ground power supply for satellite
卫星地球资源勘探/衛星地球資源探測　satellite earth resources exploration
卫星地质/衛星地質　geology of satellite
卫星电位/衛星電位　satellite potential
卫星电文/衛星信文　satellite message
卫星电性等效器/衛星電性等效器　satellite electric simulator
卫星电性能测试/衛星電性能測試　electrical property test of satellite
卫星多普勒导航/衛星都卜勒導航　satellite Doppler navigation
卫星多普勒定位/衛星都卜勒定位　satellite Doppler positioning
卫星发射/衛星發射　satellite launch
卫星发射中心/衛星發射中心　satellite launching center
卫星返回程序/衛星返回程式　satellite return program
卫星仿真飞行程序/衛星模擬飛行程式　simulated satellite flight program
卫星仿真负载/衛星模擬負載　satellite simulation load
卫星仿真器/衛星模擬器　satellite simulator
卫星放电/衛星放電　satellite discharging
卫星分系统/衛星子系統,衛星組成結構　satellite subsystem
卫星分系统电性能测试/衛星子系統電性能測試　electrical property test of satellite subsystem
卫星分系统设计/衛星子系統設計　satellite subsystem design
卫星覆盖区/衛星覆蓋區　satellite coverage
卫星工程/衛星工程　satellite engineering
卫星工作寿命/衛星工作壽命　satellite operating lifetime
卫星功率特性/衛星馬力特性　satellite power characteristic
卫星构形/衛星分布圖,衛星配置圖　satellite configuration
卫星观测系统/衛星測量　satellite observatories
卫星广播/衛星廣播　satellite broadcasting
卫星广播业务/衛星廣播業務　broadcasting-satellite service
卫星轨道/衛星軌道　satellite orbit
卫星轨道高度/衛星軌道高度　satellite orbital altitude
卫星轨道寿命/衛星軌道壽命　satellite orbital lifetime
卫星海上移动业务/衛星水上行動業務,水上行動衛星通信業務　maritime mobile satellite service
卫星海洋监视/衛星海洋監視　satellite ocean surveillance
卫星环境/衛星環境　satellite environment
卫星基频/衛星基頻　satellite fundamental frequency
卫星加注厂房/衛星加注廠房　satellite loading building
卫星紧急无线电示位标/衛星應急指位無線電示標　satellite emergency position-indicating radiobeacon
[卫星]历书/[衛星]曆書　satellite almanac
卫星链路/衛星鏈路　satellite link
卫星密封容器吊具/衛星密閉容器吊索　satellite sealed container hoisting tool, satellite sealed container sling
卫星面积质量比/衛星面積質量比　satellite area-mass ratio
卫星模装/衛星模型化　satellite mock up
卫星配重/衛星配重　satellite counterweight
卫星平台/衛星平臺　satellite platform
卫星普查/衛星普查　satellite area monitoring
卫星气象观测/衛星氣象觀測　satellite meteorological observation
卫星气象业务/衛星氣象業務　meteorological-satellite service
卫星热平衡试验/衛星熱平衡試驗　thermal balancing test of satellite

卫星热设计/衛星熱設計　satellite thermal design
卫星热真空试验/衛星熱真空測試　satellite thermal vacuum test
卫星设备连接/衛星設備連接　satellite equipment connecting
卫星设计寿命/衛星設計壽命　satellite design lifetime
卫星摄动轨道/衛星攪動軌道　satellite disturbed orbit
卫星摄动运动/衛星攪動　satellite perturbance motion
卫星摄影/衛星照相術　satellite photography
卫星食/衛星食　satellite eclipse
卫星搜救跟踪系统/衛星輔助搜救追蹤系統，搜救衛星輔助追蹤　search and rescue satellite aided tracking
卫星搜索与救援/衛星搜救　satellite search and rescue
卫星停放平台/衛星支架　satellite stand
卫星通信/衛星通信，衛星通訊　satellite communication
卫星通信地面站/衛星通訊地面站　satellite telecommunication earth station
卫星同步控制器/衛星同步控制器　satellite synchronous controller
卫星网络/衛星網路　satellite network
卫星无线电测定业务/衛星無線電測定業務　radio determination-satellite service
卫星系统/衛星系統　satellite system
卫星系统测试软件/衛星系統測試軟體　satellite system test software
卫星系统工程/衛星系統工程　satellite system engineering
卫星系统软件/衛星系統軟體　satellite system software
卫星信息流/衛星資訊流　satellite information flow
[卫星]星历/衛星曆表　satellite ephemeris
卫星星历表/衛星曆表　satellite ephemeris
卫星星座/衛星星座　satellite constellation
卫星遥测/衛星遙測　satellite telemetry
卫星遥感/衛星遙測　satellite remote sensing
卫星遥感测量/衛星遙測量測　satellite remote sensing
卫星遥感系统/衛星遙測系統　satellite remote sensing system
卫星移动业务/衛星行動業務　mobile-satellite service
卫星应用/衛星應用　satellite application
卫星云图/衛星雲圖　satellite cloud picture
卫星运行程序/衛星作業程式　satellite operation program
卫星在轨测试交付可靠度/衛星在軌測試交付可靠度　reliability of satellite in orbit test
卫星整流罩/衛星整流罩　satellite fairing
卫星质量特性/衛星質量特徵　satellite mass characteristic
卫星专用测试设备/衛星專用檢測設備　special checkout equipment for satellite, SCOE
卫星转发海上安全信息/衛星轉發之海上安全資訊　maritime safety information via satellite
卫星转发器/衛星轉頻器　satellite transponder
卫星转运/衛星傳送　satellite transfer
卫星装配测试厂房/衛星裝配測試廠房　satellite assembly and test building
卫星姿态/衛星姿態　satellite attitude
卫星自主导航/衛星自主導航　autonomous navigation of satellite
卫星自主性/衛星自主性　satellite autonomy
卫星综合控制台/衛星綜合控制臺　general console for satellite
卫星总测设备/衛星綜合檢測設備　overall checkout equipment for satellite, OCOE
卫星总体布局/衛星總平面圖，衛星總設計圖　satellite general layout
卫星总体设计/衛星總體設計　satellite system design, satellite overall design
卫星总装/衛星程式集　satellite assembly
未包装货/未包裝貨　non-packed cargo
未包装货物/散裝貨物　unpacked goods
未被平衡离心加速度/未被平衡離心加速度　unbalanced centrifugal acceleration
未标名暗礁/未列名礁石　uncharted rock
未衬砌隧道/無襯砌隧道　rough tunnel, unlined tunnel
未定位警报/未能定位之警報　unlocated alert
未风化岩石/未風化岩石　fresh rock
未过滤水/未濾水　unfiltered water
未过筛沙/山砂　pit sand
未焊透/不焊透　incomplete penetration
未加劲悬索桥/無加勁吊橋　unstiffened suspension bridge
未检出差错/未檢出錯誤　undetected error
未结硬的混凝土/未凝混凝土　fresh concrete
未精测的等高线/近似等高線　approximate contour line
未精测的等深线/近似等深線　approximate depth

contour
未开发地区/未發展地區　undeveloped area
未来主义/未來主義　futurism
未来主义城市规划/未來主義都市規劃　futurist urban planning
未列名货/未列名貨　not otherwise specified, NOS cargo
未钎透/不完全穿透　incomplete penetration
未入级的/未入級　unclassified
未修正结果/未修正結果　uncorrected result
未央宫/未央宮　Wei Yang Palace
未预见水/無費用水　unaccounted for water
未知量/未知量　unknown
未指定区域/未指定地　unspecified area
位变率/方位變動率　rate of bearing variation
位差修正角/位差修正角　correction angle due to parallax
位能/位能,勢能　potential energy
位势高度/地勢高度　geopotential height
位同步/位同步　bit synchronizing
位序-规模法则/等級大小法則　rank-size rule
位移导纳/動態柔度,敏納　receptance
位移地震仪/變位地震儀　displacement seismograph
位移法/位移法,變位法　displacement method
位移谱/位移振譜　displacement spectrum
位移曲线/排水量曲線　displacement curve
位移速度/位移速度　displacement velocity
位移元/位移元素　displacement element
位置/位置,部位　location
位置保持窗口/定點保持窗口　station-keeping window
位置标志/位置標誌　location sign
位置灯/位置燈　position light
位置捷联式惯性制导系统/位置捷聯式慣性制導系統　position strap-down inertial guidance system
位置坡降/位置坡降　positional gradient
位置试验/位置試驗　position test
位[置水]头/位置水頭,勢差,位[置高]差　position head, potential head
位置稳定性/位置穩定性　positional stability
位置误差/位置錯誤　position error
位置线/位置線　line of position, LOP, position line
位置线标准差/位置線標準誤差　position line standard error
位置线梯度/位置線梯度　gradient of position line
位置信号码/位置信號碼　position signal code
位置需求/區位要求　locational requirement
位置增益/位置增益　position gain

位置指示器/位置指示器　notch indicator
位置转换开关/位置切換開關　position changeover switch
位姿/姿勢　pose
位姿超调量/姿勢超越量　pose overshoot
位姿重复精度/姿勢反復精度　pose repeatability
位姿到位姿控制/姿勢到姿勢控制　pose to pose control
位姿精度/姿勢準確度　pose accuracy
位姿精度漂移/姿勢準確度漂移　drift of pose accuracy
位姿稳态时间/姿勢穩定時間　pose stabilization time
温备份/溫備份　warm spare
温差/溫差　temperature difference, temperature range
温差发电器/熱變換器　thermoelectric power generator
温差修正系数/溫差修正係數　modified temperature difference factor
温床/溫床　hot bed
[温带]高山矮曲林/高山矮曲林　krummholz
温带气旋/溫帶氣旋　extratropical cyclone
温度报警钟/溫度報警鐘　temperature alarm
温度边界层/熱邊界層　thermal boundary layer
温度变化/溫度變化　temperature change
温度波幅/溫度幅度　temperature amplitude
温度补偿/溫度補償　temperature compensation
温度场/溫度場　temperature field
温度冲击试验/溫度衝擊試驗　temperature shock test
温度传感器/溫度感測器　temperature sensor
温度带/溫度帶,溫度區　temperature zone
温度分辨率/溫度解析度　temperature resolution
温度改正/溫度改正　correction for temperature
温度高度/溫度高度　temperature altitude
温度荷载/溫度負載　temperature load
温度恢复系数/溫度恢復係數　temperature recovery coefficient
温度计/自記溫度計　thermograph
温度继电器/溫度繼電器,溫度開關,熱動繼電器　temperature switch, temperature relay
温度控制/溫度控制　temperature control
温度控制屏/紅外線控制覆板　temperature controlled shroud
温度控制系统/溫度控制系統　temperature control system
温度力/溫度應力　temperature stress

温度力峰/温度應力峰　temperature stress peak
温度上升/温度上昇　temperature rise
温度适应/温度適應　thermal adaptation
温度收缩/温度收縮　temperature shrinkage
温度衰减/温度衰減　temperature damping
温度梯度/温度梯度,熱梯度　thermal gradient, temperature gradient
温度调节/温度控制　temperature control
温度调节阀/温度調節閥,温度控制閥　temperature regulating valve, temperature control valve
温度调节器/温度調節器,温度控制器　thermoregulator
温度效应/温度效應　temperature effect
温度巡检箱/温度巡檢箱　temperature scanning unit
温度循环/温度循環　temperature cycle
温度循环试验/温度循環測試　temperature cycling test
温度应力/熱應力　heat stress, thermal stress
温度与湿度控制系统/温度與濕度控制系統　temperature and humidity control system
温度自补偿/温度自補償　temperature self-compensation
温度自动控制/自動温控　automatic temperature control
温度作用/温度作用,熱作用　thermal action, temperature action
温和地区/温帶　temperate zone, warm zone
温控阀/温度控制閥　temperature control valve
温控涂层/熱控制塗層　thermal control coating
温控系统/控温系統　temperature controlling system
温暖/温暖　warm
温起动/暖起動,暖開機　warm start
温泉度假/礦泉療養勝地　spa resort
温泉风景区/温泉風景區　hot spring scenic spot
温泉群落/温泉群落　thermium
温泉水疗中心/水療中心　spa center, hydrotherapy center
温升/温度上昇　temperature rise
温湿度/温濕度　temperature and humidity
温石棉/温石棉　chrysotile asbestos
温室/温室　greenhouse
温室覆盖/温室覆蓋　greenhouse covering
温室花卉/温室花卉　greenhouse flower
温室气候控制器/温室氣候控制器　greenhouse climate controller
温室气体/温室氣體　greenhouse gas
温室设备/温室設備　greenhouse equipment
温室生态系统/温室生態系　greenhouse ecosystem
温室效应/温室效應　greenhouse effect
温室植物/温室植物　greenhouse plant
温水采暖装置/温水採暖裝置　hot water heating equipment
文本/本文,原文,正文　text
文昌宫/文昌宮　Wenchang Temple
文化公园/文化公園　cultural park
文化广场/文化廣場　cultural plaza
文化和自然混合遗产/文化與自然遺產　mixed cultural and natural heritage
文化活动区/文化活動區　cultural activities area
文化建筑/文化館　cultural building
文化景观/文化景觀,文化地景　cultural landscape
文化景观感知/文化景觀感知　cultural landscape perception
文化景观遗产/文化景觀遺產　cultural landscape heritage
文化旅游/文化觀光業　cultural tourism
文化名城/文化名城　famous cultural city
文化设施用地/文化設施用地　land for cultural facility
文化生态保护区/文化生態保育區　cultural ecological conservation area
文化线路/文化線路　cultural route
文化休憩公园/文化休憩公園　cultural and recreation park
文化遗产/文化遺產　cultural heritage
文化遗产干预/文化遺產干預　intervention of heritage
文化遗址/文化遺址　ancient cultural relic
文化娱乐建筑/文化休憩建築　cultural and recreation building
文化娱乐用地/文化娛樂土地利用　cultural entertainment land use
文化中心/文化中心　cultural center
文件传真机/文件傳真機　document facsimile apparatus
文教区/文教[科研]區　institutes and colleges district, education and research district
文具用品店/文化用品商店　stationary store
文脉/情境[脈絡],語境　context
文脉环境/文脈環境　contextual environment
文脉主义/文脈主義　contextualism
文秘室/文秘室　secretarial office
文庙/文廟　Temple of Confucius, Wen Miao
文丘里流量计/文氏[流量]計　Venturi meter
文丘里管/文氏管　Venturi tube
文丘里量水槽/文氏渡槽　Venturi flume

文物保护单位/文物保護單位，官方保護組織 officially protected monument and site, officially protected entity
文物保护单位保护范围/文物保護單位保護範圍 area of protection for a site protected
文物保护单位建设控制地带/文物保護單位建設控制地帶 area for control of construction around a site protected
文物保护范围/文物保存範圍 cultural relic protection scope
文物保护工程/文物保護 protection of cultural relics
文物保护规划/文物保護規劃 conservation master plan
文物调查/文物調查 identification and investigation of heritage
文物古迹/古跡，文物，文化遺産 historic monument and site, cultural relics, heritage site
文物古迹残损/文物古跡殘損 damage and deterioration of heritage
文物古迹防护加固/文物古跡防護加固 physical protection and strengthening of heritage
文物古迹环境治理/文物古跡環境治理 treatment of heritage setting
文物古迹日常保养/文物遺産定期保養 regular maintenance of heritage
文物古迹现状修整/文物古跡現狀修整 minor restoration of heritage
文物古迹用地/文物古跡用地 land for heritage
文物古迹原址重建/文物古跡原址重建 reconstruction of heritage
文物古迹重点修复/文物遺産規模修復 major restoration of heritage
文物价值/文物價值 heritage value, value of cultural relics
文物建筑/古跡建築 listed building
文物四有/文物四有 four legal prerequisites
文物整理室/文物室 cultural relics arrangement room
文艺复兴建筑/文藝復興[時期的]建築 Renaissance architecture
文艺复兴庄园/文藝復興莊園 Renaissance style villa
文字符号/字母符號 letter symbol
纹理统一法/紋理統一法 method of unifying the rock veins
纹影法/紋影技術 schlieren technique
纹影干涉仪/紋影干涉計 schlieren interferometer
纹影仪/紋影儀 schlieren system
吻合索/吻合索 concordant tendon
吻合效应/重合效應 coincidence effect
紊流/紊流，擾流 turbulence, turbulent flow
紊流探测器/紊流探測器 turbulence detector
稳定/穩定 stabilization
稳定板/穩定鰭 stabilizer fin, stabilizing fin
稳定保护层/穩定保護層 stabilized protection course
稳定材料基层/穩定材料基層 stabilized material base
稳定池/穩定池 stabilization lagoon
稳定的/穩定的 steady
稳定地区/穩定地區 stable area
稳定电阻器/穩定電阻器 stabilizing resistor
稳定段/穩定室 settling chamber
稳定法路面/穩定法路面 pavement by stabilized process
稳定跟踪距离/穩定追蹤範圍 stable tracking range
稳定工况试验/穩流工況試驗 steady state test
稳定光源/穩定光源 stabilized light source
稳定化处理/安定化處理 stabilizing treatment, stabilizing
稳定回路/穩定回路 stabilized loop
稳定回转阶段/穩定迴旋階段 steady turning period
稳定剂/穩定劑，安定劑 stabilizer
稳定减速伞/穩定傘，阻力傘，引導傘 drogue parachute
稳定交通流/穩定交通流量 stable traffic flow
稳定拉起法/穩定拉起法 steady pull-up method
稳定平台/穩定平臺 stable platform
稳定器/穩定器 stabilizer
稳定燃烧/穩定燃燒 stable combustion
稳定燃烧边界/燃燒穩定極限 combustion stability limit
稳定热状态/穩定熱狀態 steady thermal state
稳定时间/安定時間 settling time
稳定输出/可靠出量 firm output
稳定数/穩定數 stability number
稳定索/穩定索 steadying line
稳定塘/穩定池，生物池塘，氧化池 stabilization pond
稳定土厂拌设备/穩定土廠拌站 stabilized soil mixing plant
稳定土基层/穩定土基層 stabilized soil base course, stabilized soil base
稳定土路面/穩定土路面 stabilized soil pavement
稳定土摊铺机/穩定土攤鋪機 stabilized soil paver
稳定位置/調定位置 settling position

稳定[污]水流/穩定放流水　stable effluent
稳定系数/穩定係數　stability coefficient
稳定系统测试/穩定系統測試　stabilization system test
稳定下降/穩定下降　steady descent, steady state descent
稳定型种群/穩定人口　stable population
稳定性/穩定性,安定性　stability
稳定性安全系数/穩定度安全係數　safety factor of stability
稳定性测试/穩定性試驗　stability test
稳定性故障/穩定故障　stable fault
稳定性量测仪/穩定計　stabilometer
稳定性坡度/穩定性坡度　stabilized slope
稳定性条件/穩定條件　stability condition
稳定性研究/穩定研究　stability investigation
稳定仪/穩定計　stabilometer
稳定运行工况/穩定運轉工況,穩定工作狀況　steady running condition
稳定转弯法/穩定轉彎法　steady turn method
稳钩/穩鉤　stabilize hook
稳[恒]定流/恆流　stationary current
稳弧剂/電弧穩定劑　arc stabilizer
稳环时间/光網穩定時間　reticle stabilizing time
稳燃器/穩燃器　stabilizer
稳索/牽索　guy
稳索眼板/牽索眼板　guy eye
稳态/穩[定狀]態　steady state
稳态比冲/穩態比衝　steady state specific impulse
稳态测量/穩態量測　steady state measurement
稳态传热/穩定傳熱　steady heat transfer
稳态反应/穩態應答　steady state response
稳态功耗/穩態功率消耗[量]　steady state power consumption
稳态寿命/穩態壽命　steady state life
稳态太阳仿真器/穩態太陽模擬器　steady solar simulator
稳态性能/穩態性能　steady state performance
稳态振动/穩態振動　steady state vibration
稳心/定傾中心　metacenter
稳心半径/定傾半徑　metacentric radius
稳心高度/定傾[中心]高度　metacentric height
稳心曲线/定傾中心曲線圖　metacentric diagram, locus of metacenters
稳性衡准数/穩度基準數　stability criterion numeral
稳性力臂/穩度力臂　stability lever
稳性力矩/穩度力矩　stability moment
稳性消失角/穩度消失角　angle of vanishing stability, vanishing angle of stability
稳压层/穩壓空間　plenum space
稳压电源/穩壓電源　voltage stabilized power source
稳压器/穩壓器,電壓穩定器,電壓安定器　voltage stabilizer
稳压驱动控制/驅動電壓控制　voltage drive control
问题/問題　problem
问题分析/問題分析　problem analysis
问题趋势分析/問題趨向分析　problem trend analysis
问讯处/查詢處,詢問臺,服務臺　information desk, information office, inquiry office
嗡鸣/蜂鳴,顫振　buzz
瓮城/甕城　barbican, wengcheng
涡道/渦街　vortex street
涡格法/渦格法　vortex lattice method
涡管/渦[流]管　vortex tube
涡核/渦旋核　vortex core
涡街/渦街　vortex street
涡量/渦旋,渦動　vorticity
涡流/渦流　swirl
涡流发生器/渦旋產生器　vortex generator
涡流激振/旋渦激振　vortex-excited oscillation
涡流检测/渦流檢驗　eddy current testing
涡流强度/渦流強度　strength of vortex
涡流式力矩器/渦[電]流扭矩產生器　eddy current torquer
涡流室式柴油机/渦流室式柴油機　swirl-chamber diesel engine
涡流室式燃烧室/旋渦式燃燒室　swirl-combustion chamber
涡流效应/渦流剝離效應　vortex shedding effect
涡流运动黏度系数/渦動滯度係數　coefficient of eddy kinematic viscosity
涡流制动/渦流制動器,渦流刹車　eddy current brake
涡流阻力/興渦阻力　eddy making resistance
涡轮泵/渦輪泵　turbopump
涡轮泵比功率/渦輪泵比功率　turbopump power density
涡轮泵系统循环效率/渦輪泵系統循環效率　turbopump system cycle efficiency
涡轮发电机/渦輪發電機,渦式發電機　turbo-generator
涡轮风扇发动机/渦扇發動機　turbo-fan engine
涡轮功率/輪機功率,渦輪動力　turbine power
涡轮鼓风机/渦式鼓風機　turboblower
涡轮[机]/渦輪機　turbine

涡轮机车/氣渦輪機車　turbine locomotive
涡轮进口温度/渦輪進氣溫度　turbine inlet temperature
涡轮可变几何形状喷嘴装置/渦輪可變幾何形狀噴嘴裝置　variable geometric turbine nozzle device
涡轮冷却器/渦輪冷卻裝置　cooling turbine unit
涡轮螺旋桨发动机/渦槳發動機　turbo-prop engine
涡轮喷气发动机/渦噴發動機　turbo-jet engine
涡轮膨胀比/渦輪膨脹比　expansion ratio of turbine
涡轮驱动/渦輪驅動　turbo
涡轮入口废气温度/渦輪入口廢氣溫度　exhaust temperature at turbine inlet
涡轮入口废气压力/渦輪入口廢氣壓力　exhaust pressure at turbine inlet
涡轮式环形交叉/渦式環行道交叉　turbine-type rotary intersection
涡轮式曝气/渦輪式曝氣　turbine aeration
涡轮室/渦輪室　turbine room
涡轮效率/渦輪效率　turbine efficiency
涡轮压比/汽輪機壓力比　turbine pressure ratio
涡轮增压器/渦輪增壓器,渦輪增壓機　turbo-charger, turboblower
涡轮轴发动机/渦輪軸發動機　turbo-shaft engine
涡轮转速/渦輪轉速　turbine speed
涡面/渦面　vortex surface sheet
涡黏性[度]系数/渦滯係數　coefficient of eddy viscosity
涡破裂/渦裂　vortex bursting
涡升力/渦流昇力　vortex lift
涡声/渦聲　vortex sound
涡丝/渦絲　vortex filament
涡线/渦[旋]線　vortex line
涡旋/渦旋,渦流　vortex
涡旋层/渦層　vortex layer
涡旋发生器/渦旋產生器　vortex generator
涡致振动/渦流振動　vortex induced vibration
沃尔什遥测/沃爾什遙測　Walsh telemetry
卧城/居住型市鎮　dormitory town, bedroom town
卧床实验/臥床休養實驗　bed rest experiment
卧床实验设备/臥床休養實驗設備　bed rest experiment facilities
卧具储藏室/寢具儲存室　linen locker
卧铺客车/臥鋪客車　motor coach sleeper
卧铺票/臥鋪票　berth ticket
卧式内燃机/臥式引擎　horizontal engine
卧室/臥室　bedroom, sleeping compartment
握杆/定桿　control stick fixed
握杆控制/握桿控制　hands-on throttle and stick, HOTAS
握裹长度/握裹長度　bond length
握索结/扶手索結　manrope knot
握住/挽住　hold
乌斯马尔古镇/烏斯馬爾古鎮　Pre-Hispanic Town of Uxmal
乌头门/烏頭門　wutoumen
乌托邦城市规划/烏托邦都市規劃　utopian urban planning
圬工拱/圬工拱　masonry arch
圬工拱桥/圬工拱橋,砌體拱橋　masonry arch bridge
圬工梁裂损/圬工梁裂損　cracking of concrete and masonry beam
圬工桥/圬工橋　masonry bridge
污底/積垢　fouling
污底螺旋桨特性曲线/汙船體螺槳特性曲線　fouled hull propeller curve
污底热阻/積垢熱阻　fouling resistance
污垢/汙垢　fouling, scale
污垢热阻/汙垢熱阻　fouling resistance
污垢抑制/汙垢抑制　fouling inhibition
污秽货/汙穢貨　dirty cargo
污径比/徑流比值　ratio of runoff
污泥/汙泥,淤泥　sludge
污泥层/汙泥浮層　sludge blanket
污泥沉积/汙泥沈積　sludge deposit
污泥[沉积]堆/汙泥堤　sludge bank
污泥沉降比/汙泥沈降比　sludge settling ratio
污泥池/汙泥塘　sludge lagoon
污泥处理/汙泥處理　sludge treatment
污泥处理厂/汙泥處理廠　sludge treatment plant
污泥处置/汙泥處置,汙泥處理　disposal of sludge, sludge disposal
污泥床/汙泥床　sludge bed
污泥焚化/汙泥焚化　sludge incineration
污泥复氧/汙泥再曝氣　sludge reaeration
污泥干化/汙泥乾化,汙泥乾燥　sludge drying
污泥干化床/汙泥乾化床　sludge drying bed
污泥干燥器/汙泥乾燥機　sludge dryer
污泥固体物/汙泥固體　sludge solid
污泥管/排泥管　sludge pipe
污泥柜/油泥櫃,油泥艙櫃,汙油[泥]櫃　sludge tank
污泥过滤机/汙泥過濾器　sludge filter
污泥减量/汙泥減縮　sludge reduction
污泥接种/汙泥接種　sludge seeding
污泥龄/汙泥齡　sludge age
污泥密度指数/汙泥密度指數　sludge density index
污泥浓缩/汙泥濃縮　sludge thickening

污泥泡涌/汙泥泡湧　sludge foaming
污泥膨胀/汙泥蓬鬆　sludge bulking
污泥清除机/汙泥清除機　sludge-stripping machine
污泥容积指数/汙泥體積指數　sludge volume index
污泥收集器/集泥器　sludge collector
污泥淘洗/汙泥清洗　sludge elutriation
污泥调理/汙泥調節,汙泥調質　sludge conditioning
污泥脱水/汙泥脱水　sludge dewatering
污泥脱水液/脱離汙泥液　sludge liquor
污泥消化/汙泥消化　sludge digestion
污泥消化池/汙泥消化槽　sludge digestion tank, sludge digestion chamber
污泥消化气体/汙泥消化氣體　sludge digestion gas
污泥循环/汙泥回流　sludge circulation
污泥压滤/汙泥壓濾　sludge press filtration
污泥真空过滤/汙泥真空過濾　sludge vacuum filtration
污染/汙染　pollution
污染波/汙染波　wave of pollution
污染超限/汙染超限　over limit pollution
污染程度/汙染度　degree of pollution
污染等级/汙染等級　class of contamination
污染负荷/汙染負載　pollutional load
污染控制/汙染管制　pollution control
污染类别/汙染類別　pollution category
污染浓缩池/汙泥濃縮槽　sludge thickener
污染区/汙染區　contaminated area
污染事故/汙染事故　contamination accident
污染物/汙染物　pollutant
污染物排放总量控制/汙染物排出控制總量　total amount control of pollutant discharge
污染系数/汙染係數　pollution coefficient
污染消除/除汙,汙染防治　abatement pollution
污染源/汙染源　pollution source, cause of pollution
污染源分布/汙染源分布　pollutant source distribution
污染指数/汙染指數,汙染指標　contamination index, pollution index
污水/汙水　sewage
污水泵/汙水泵　sewage water pump, sewage pump
污水泵房/廢水泵室　wastewater pump room
污水泵站/汙水抽水站　sewage pumping station
污水舱/舭水艙　bilge tank, bilge water tank
污水厂出水/處理汙水排洩　effluent sewage
污水处理/汙水處理,汙水處置,廢水處理　sewage treatment, wastewater treatment, sewage disposal
污水处理厂/汙水處理廠,廢水處理廠　wastewater treatment plant, sewage treatment plant

污水处理构筑物/汙水處理構築物　sewage treatment structure
污水[处理]率/汙水費率　sewage rate
污水处理设备/汙水處理設備　sewage treatment plant
污水处理站/汙水處理場　sewage treatment station
污水道/通水小孔　limber
污水道盖板/通水道蓋板　limber board
污水二级处理/汙水二級處理　secondary treatment of sewage
污水干管/汙水總管　main sewer
污水工程/汙水工程　sewage work
污水沟管系统/汙水溝管系統　sanitary sewerage system
污水管[道]/汙水管,下水道　sewer, sanitary sewer
污水管干线/下水幹管　trunk sewer
污水管进口/汙水管進口　house inlet
污水管渠/汙水管　sewage sewer
污水灌溉/汙水灌溉,廢水灌溉　sewage irrigation, wastewater irrigation
污水柜/舭櫃,舭水艙　bilge tank
污水井/汙水井,舭水井　bilge well
污水净化沼气池/汙水淨化沼氣池　methane tank-biofilter sewage purification system
污水坑/滲水坑　leaching cesspool
污水滤池/滲水坑　leaching cesspool
污水排除规划/汙水排除規劃　sewage drainage planing
污水排放/處理汙水排洩　effluent sewage
污水排吸装置/舭水抽排裝置　bilge pumping arrangement
污水水流/流出河川,汙水放流河川　effluent stream
污水污泥/汙水汙泥　sewage sludge
污水系统/汙水系統,廢水系統,舭水系統　sewage system, wastewater system, bilge system
污水一级处理/汙水初步處理　primary treatment of sewage
污水再生利用/廢水再用,廢水複用,廢水回用　wastewater reuse
污水支管/汙水支管　lateral sewer
污水[滞流]沉淀池/貯留池　detention tank
污水自动排除装置/舭水自動排除設施　bilge automatic discharging device
污水总管/下水幹管　trunk sewer
污洗室/汙洗室　sluice room
污压载水/不潔壓艙水　dirty ballast
污液舱/汙油[水]櫃　slop tank
污油泵/汙油泵　sludge pump

污油舱/汙油櫃　dirty oil tank
污油水/汙油水　slop
污油水舱/汙油[水]櫃　slop tank
污浊空气/汙濁的空氣　stale air
钨极惰性气体保护焊/氣體遮蔽鎢弧焊,氣體遮護鎢弧焊　TIG welding, gas tungsten arc welding
钨极脉冲氩弧焊/鎢極脈衝氫弧焊　argon tungsten pulsed arc welding
钨丝灯/鎢絲燈　tungsten filament lamp
屋顶/屋頂,天棚,頂部　roof
屋顶花园/屋頂花園　roof garden
屋顶绿化/屋頂綠化　roof greening
屋顶螺栓/屋頂螺栓　roof bolt
屋顶通风机/動力頂通風器　power roof ventilator
屋顶雨水口/屋頂排水槽　roof drain
屋顶种植荷载/屋頂種植荷載　roof planting load
屋盖/屋頂[系統]　roof system, roof
屋盖支撑/屋頂支撐　roof bracing
屋盖支撑系统/屋架支撐系統　roof bracing system
屋基石/屋基石　foundation stone
屋架/屋架　roof truss
屋面/屋面[料]　roofing
屋面板/頂板　roof plate, roof board, roof slab
屋面保护层/屋面保護層　roof protective course
屋面防水/屋面防水　roof water proofing
屋面梁/屋頂梁　roof girder
屋面排水/屋面排水系統　roof drainage system
屋面无组织排水系统/屋面無組織排水系統　roof non-organized drainage system
屋面有组织排水系统/屋面有組織排水系統　roof organized drainage system
[屋]檐/屋檐　eave
无表水栓/無表水栓　non-metered tap
无冰区/無冰區　ice free
无彩色/無彩顏色,非彩色　achromatic color
无侧限抗压强度/無側限抗壓強度　unconfined compression strength
无侧限抗压强度试验/無圍壓縮強度試驗　unconfined compression strength test
无侧限压力试验/無側限壓縮試驗　unconfined compression test
无岔区段/無岔區段　section without a switch
无潮点/無潮點　amphidromic point
无潮港/無潮港,閉口港　non-tidal harbor
无潮区[域]/無潮區[域]　non-tidal compartment, amphidromic region
无潮汐河流/無潮河川　non-tidal river
无窗厂房/無窗廠房　windowless factory building

无导框式转向架/無導框式轉向架　non-pedestal truck
无灯标志/無燈標誌　unlit mark
无舵雪橇滑道/無舵雪橇滑道　luge
无方向性信标/無方向性示標,全方位信標　non-directional beacon, NDB
无纺布伸缩装置/非織物伸縮裝置　non-woven fabrics expansion installation
无纺土工织物/無紡土工織物　nonweaven geotextile
无分隔带道路/未分隔道路　undivided road
无缝钢管/無縫[鋼]管　seamless steel pipe, seamless steel tube
无缝线路/無接頭軌道　continuously welded rail track, jointless track
无副力矩钢索/無副力矩鋼索　concordant cable
无杆锚/無桿錨,山字錨　stockless anchor
无公害农药/無公害農藥　non-polluted pesticide
无功负荷/無功負載　wattless load
无功功率/無功功率　reactive power, wattless power
无功功率自动分配装置/無功功率自動分配裝置　automatic distributor of reactive power
无光浮标/無燈浮標　unlighted buoy
无规噪声/無規[則]噪聲,[散]亂雜音,雜亂噪聲　random noise
无轨电车/無軌電車　trolleybus
无轨运输/無軌交通　trackless transportation
无害地段/無害地段　harmless district
无害通过权/無害通過權　right of innocent passage
无机房电梯/無機房電梯　machine-roomless elevator, elevator without engine room
无机非金属材料/無機非金屬材料　inorganic nonmetallic materials
无机肥料/礦物肥料　mineral fertilizer
无机结合料/無機黏結劑　inorganic binder
无机土/無機土壤　inorganic soil
无级的/無段　stepless
无级调速/無段調速　stepless speed regulation
无级调压/無級調壓　stepless voltage regulation
无极灯/無電極燈　electrodeless lamp
无极继电器/中性繼電器,中和電驛　neutral relay
无极荧光灯/無電極熒光燈泡　electrodeless fluorescent lamp
无间隙牵引杆/無間隙牽引桿　slackless drawbar
无铰拱桥/無鉸拱橋,固端拱橋　hingeless arch bridge, fixed-arch bridge
无铰式旋翼/無鉸旋翼　hingeless rotor
无筋混凝土/無筋混凝土　plain concrete
无居民区/無居民區　uninhabited district

无绝缘轨道电路/無接頭軌道電路　jointless track circuit
无菌室/無菌室　bacteria-free room
无菌手术室/無菌手術室　bioclean operating room
无壳套桩/無殼樁　uncased pile
无控制点镶嵌图/無控制像片圖　uncontrolled mosaic
无缆系结/無纜索連結　non-line connection
无缆系结装置/無纜繫結裝置　ropeless linkage
无缆遥控潜水器/無纜遙控潛水器　untethered remotely operated vehicle
无浪/無風，浪静　calm
无力点/無力點　point of zero pressure
无连接方式/無連接模式　connectionless mode
无梁楼板/無梁樓板　flat slab floor, flat floor
无梁楼板结构/無梁樓板構造　flat slab construction
无梁楼盖/無梁樓蓋　flat slab floor
无量纲变量/無因次變數，無維度變數　dimensionless variable
无锚碇钢腱/無錨碇鋼腱　non-end-anchored tendon
无冒口铸造/無冒口鑄造　head-free casting
无模糊作用距离/明確性作用距離　un-ambiguity operating range
无黏结的预应力筋/未鍵結鋼腱　nonbonded tendon
无黏结预应力钢丝束/無黏裹鋼腱　unbounded tendon
无黏结预应力混凝土/無黏結預應力混凝土　unbonded prestressed concrete
无黏结预应力混凝土结构/無黏結預應力混凝土結構　unbonded prestressed concrete structure
无喷管发动机/無噴嘴火箭發動機　nozzleless rocket motor
无喷管固体火箭发动机/無噴嘴固體火箭發動機　nozzleless solid rocket motor
无破碎侵彻/無破碎穿降　no-disruptive penetration
无铺位旅客/艙面旅客　deck passenger
无气喷射/無空氣噴射　airless injection
无人航天器/無人太空船　unmanned spacecraft
无人驾驶飞行器/無人飛行載具，無人［飛］機　unmanned aerial vehicle
无人看守灯塔/無人看守燈塔　unwatched light
无人潜水器/無人潛水器　unmanned submersible
无人增音机/無人中繼器　unattended repeater
无人值班/無人當值　unattended, unmanned
无人［值班］机舱/無人當值機艙空間，無人化機艙　unattended machinery space, unmanned machinery space
无熟料水泥/無熟料水泥　cement without clinker

无刷交流发电机/無刷交流發電機　brushless AC generator
无刷直流发电机/無刷直流發電機　brushless DC generator
无刷直流力矩电机/無刷直流轉矩電動機　brushless DC torque motor
无水石膏/無水石膏　anhydrite
无水碳酸钠/碳酸鈉，蘇打灰　soda ash
无塑性转变温度/無延性轉變溫度　nil-ductility transition temperature
无损检测/非破壞試驗　nondestructive test, nondestructive testing, NDT
无损检验/非破壞性檢驗，非破壞檢查，非破壞試驗　nondestructive inspection, NDI, nondestructive testing
无损探伤/非破壞性探傷，不破壞檢驗，非破壞性檢驗　nondestructive flaw detection, nondestructive testing
无调中转车/無調中轉車　transit car without resorting
无调中转车停留时间/無調中轉車停留時間　detention time of car in transit without resorting
无头铆钉铆接/無頭鉚釘鉚接　slug riveting
无土栽培/無土栽培　soilless culture
无尾布局/無尾布局　tailless configuration
无尾飞机/無尾翼飛機　tailless airplane
无限竞争性招标/公開招標　public tender
无限翼展机翼/無限翼展機翼　infinite span wing
无线电报/無線電報　radiotelegram
无线电报警信号/無線電警報信號　radio alarm signal
无线电报设备/無線電報裝置　radiotelegraph installation
无线电报学/無線電報術　wireless telegraphy
无线电报员/無線電人員　radio officer, radio personnel
无线电报自动报警［器］/無線電報自動警報［器］　radiotelegraph auto-alarm
无线电操作员/無線電操作人員　radio operator
无线电测定/無線電測定術　radio determination
无线电测定电台/無線電測定電臺　radio determination station
无线电测定业务/無線電測定業務　radio determination service
无线电测距/無線電測距　radio distance-measuring, radio distance-measurement
无线电测量/無線電量測　radio measurement
无线电测向/無線電測向，無線電尋向　radio

direction-finding
无线电测向电台/無線電探向電臺,無線電定向臺 radio direction-finding station
无线电测向仪/無線電測向儀 radio direction finder
无线电测向仪自差/無線電測向儀自差 radio direction finder deviation
无线电传输型侦察卫星/無線電傳遞偵察衛星 radio transmission reconnaissance satellite
无线电大圆方位/無線電大圓方位 radio great circle bearing
无线电导航/無線電導航 radio navigation
无线电导航陆地电台/陸上無線電導航電臺 radio navigation land station
无线电导航台/無線電信標臺 radio beacon station
无线电导航图网/無線電導航網路圖 radio navigational lattice
无线电导航业务/無線電導航業務 radio navigation service
无线电导航移动电台/行動無線電導航電臺 radio navigation mobile station
无线电调车信号/無線調車號誌機 radio shunting signal
无线电定位法/無線電定位 radio position fixing
无线电定位陆地电台/陸上無線電定位電臺 radio location land station
无线电定位[术]/無線電定位[術] radio location
无线电定位移动电台/行動無線電定位電臺 radio location mobile station
无线电方位/無線電方位 radio bearing
无线电方位位置线/無線電方位位置線 radio bearing position line
无线电干扰/無線電干擾 radio interference, radio disturbance
[无线电]干扰测量仪/無線電干擾測試儀器 radio interference meter
无线电干涉仪/無線電干涉儀,電波干涉儀 radio interferometer
无线电高度表/無線電高度表 radio altimeter
无线电跟踪系统/無線電跟蹤系統 radio tracking system
无线电规则/無線電規則 radio regulation
无线电航标/無線電設備 radio aid
无线电航行警告/無線電航行警告 radio navigational warning
无线电话报警信号发生器/無線電話警報信號產生器 radiotelephone alarm signal generator
无线电话呼叫/無線電話呼叫 radiotelephone call
无线电话设备/無線電話裝置 radiotelephone installation
无线电话学/無線電話術 radio telephony
无线电话业务/無線電話業務 radiotelephone service
无线电话遇险频率/無線電話遇險頻率 radiotelephone distress frequency
无线电话员/無線電話務員 radiotelephone officer
无线电机车信号/無線電機車信號 radio locomotive signal
无线电集群通信系统/無線電聚集通信系統 radio aggregation communication system
无线电接力系统/無線電中繼系統 radio relay system
无线电经纬仪/無線電經緯儀 radio theodolite
无线电静默/無線電静止,無線電寂靜 radio silence
无线电罗盘自差/無線電羅盤誤差 radio compass error
无线电免检电报/無線電檢疫信文 radio pratique message
无线电气象业务/無線電氣象業務 radio weather service
无线电时号/無線電對時信號 radio time signal
无线电室/無線電室 radio room
无线电台/無線電臺 radio station
无线电台日志/無線電日誌 radio log
无线电台守候状态/無線電臺守候狀態 radio set in stand-by state
无线电探空仪/無線電探空儀,雷送 radiosonde
无线电通信/無線電通信 radio communication
无线电通信业务/無線電通信業務 radio communication service
无线电雾信号/無線電霧警信號 fog signal radio
无线电舷角/無線電相對方位 relative bearing of radio
无线电信标电台/無線電示[標電]臺 radio beacon station
无线电信标机/無線電信標,無線電[指]示標 radio beacon
无线电信标站/無線電信標臺 radio beacon station
无线电信号/無線電訊號 radio signal
无线电信号表/無線電信號表 list of radio signals
无线电遥测/無線電遙測術 radio telemetry
无线电遥控/無線電遙控 radio telecommand
无线电业务/無線電業務 radio service
无线电引信/無線電引信 radio fuze
无线电用户电报/無線電電報交換 telex over radio, TOR
无线电用户电报电文/無線電傳電報 radiotelexogram

无线电用户电报呼叫/無線電傳呼叫　radio telex call
无线电用户电报书信/無線電交換電報書信　radio telex letter
无线电用户电报业务/無線電電報交換業務　radio telex service
无线电噪声/無線電噪音,無線電雜音　radio noise
无线电真方位/無線電真方位　radio true bearing, RTB
无线电值守/無線電當值　radio watch
无线电指向标/無線電[指]示標,無線電信標　radio beacon
无线电制导/無線電導引　radio guidance
无线话筒/無線變送器　wireless transmitter
无线校零/無線校零　radio zero calibration
无线线路/無線電鏈　radio link
无线寻呼机/無線尋呼機　radio paging set
无效果-无报酬/無效無償　no-cureno-pay
无效运输/無效運輸　ineffective traffic
无心磨削/無心輪磨　centerless grinding
无信号交叉口/無信號控制交叉口　nonsignalized crossing
无信号控制交叉口/非號誌化路口　unsignalized intersection
无形损耗/無形損耗　intangible wear
无形资产/無形資產　intangible assets
无性系选种/無性繁殖選擇　clonal selection breeding
无旋流/無旋流　irrotational flow
无压供水泵/隔膜式泵　spout-delivery pump
无压锅炉/常壓熱水鍋爐　atmospheric hot water boiler
无压力涵洞/無壓力涵洞　inlet unsubmerged culvert, nonpressure culvert
无压隧洞/無壓力隧道　nonpressure tunnel
无烟推进剂/無煙推進劑　smokeless propellant
无焰燃烧器/無焰燃燒器,預混燃燒器　premixed burner, pre-aerated burner
无摇动台式转向架/無摇動臺式轉向架　truck with no swing bolster
无摇枕转向架/無枕梁式轉向架　bolsterless truck
无叶式扩压器/無葉擴散器　vaneless diffuser
无翼桥台/直線橋臺　straight abutment
无因次变量/無因次變數,無維度變數　dimensionless variable
无因次图线/無因次單位圖　non-dimensional unit graph
无用发射/無用發射　unwanted emission
无用能/無用能　unavailable energy

无用信号/干擾信號,不需要的信號　unwanted signal
无油抽气系统/無油抽氣系統　oil free pumping system
无油润滑空气压缩机/無油潤滑空氣壓縮機　oil free air compressor
无源定位/無源定位　passive location
无源探测/被動探測,被動偵察　passive detection
无约束结构/放鬆結構　released structure
无载波雷达/無載波雷達　impulse radar
无载[荷]弦/無載弦　unloaded chord
无载起动电空阀/無載起動電動氣壓閥　no-load starting electro-pneumatic valve
无噪声打桩技术/無噪音打樁技術　noiseless piling technique
无噪声路面/無雜訊路面　noiseless pavement
无碴轨道/無道碴軌道　ballastless track
无碴桥面/無道碴橋面　ballastless deck
无碴无枕梁/無碴無枕梁　girder without ballast and sleeper
无障碍厕所/無障礙廁所　barrier-free lavatory
无障碍厕位/無障礙廁位　barrier-free toilet cubical
无障碍电梯/無障礙電梯　barrier-free lift
无障碍交通设施/無障礙交通設施　barrier-free transit facilities
无障碍客房/無障礙客房　barrier-free guest room
无障碍淋浴间/無障礙淋浴間　barrier-free shower room
无障碍盆浴/無障礙浴室　barrier-free bath room
无障碍入口/無障礙入口　barrier-free entrance
无障碍设计/無障礙設計,可及性設計　accessible design, barrier-free design
无障碍设施/無障礙設施　disabled facilities
无障碍通道/易達的路線　accessible route
无障碍系统/無障礙系統　barrier-free system
无障碍住房/無障礙住房　barrier-free residence
无支架施工/無腳手架進行建築　erection without scaffolding
无中梁底架/無中梁底架　underframe without center sill
无轴承式旋翼/無軸承旋翼　bearingless rotor
无阻尼的/無阻尼　undamped
无阻尼振动/無阻尼振動　undamped vibration
无阻尼自由振动/無阻尼自由振動　undamped free vibration
无钻杆反循环钻机/無桿反循環鑽土機　rodless reverse circulation rig
五彩遍装/五彩遍裝　wucai bianzhuang

五车二(御夫 α)/五車二(禦夫 α)　Capella
五单位数字保护电码/五單位數字電碼　protected 5-unit numerical code
五花山墙/五花山牆　stepped gable wall
五角棱镜/五稜鏡　pentagonal prism
五孔探头/五孔探頭　five holes probe
五人制足球/室内的五人制足球　indoor football
五日 BOD/五天生化需氧量　five-day BOD
五日生化需氧量/五天生化需氧量　five-day BOD
五通塞门/五路旋塞　five-way cock
五岳庙/五嶽廟　Temple of the God of the Five Great Mountains, Wuyue Miao
五子棋/五子棋，聯珠棋　gobang chess
午圈/上子午線　upper branch of meridian
伍德布里奇接线牵引变压器/伍德布里奇接線牽引變壓器　traction transformer of Wood Bridge connection
庑殿/廡殿　hip roof, wudian
武器吊舱/武器吊艙　weapon pod
武术/武術　martial arts
武[术]馆/武術館　Wushu gymnasium
武装直升机/武裝直昇機，攻擊直昇機　attack helicopter
舞池/舞池　dancing floor
舞蹈教室/舞蹈室　dance room
舞龙运动/舞龍運動　dragon dance movement
舞狮运动/舞獅運動　lion dance movement
舞台/舞臺　stage
舞台灯光/舞臺燈光，舞臺照明　stage illumination, stage light
舞台监督室/舞臺監督室　stage manager room
舞台塔/舞臺塔　fly tower
舞厅/舞廳　ballroom
坞底/塢底　dock floor, dock bottom
坞墩/塢墩　docking block
坞坎/塢檻　dock sill
坞口/塢口　dock entrance
坞龙骨/駐塢龍骨　docking keel
坞门/塢門　caisson, dock gate
坞内标校/塢內標校　calibration in dock
坞内检验/入塢檢驗　docking survey
坞墙/浮塢牆　wing wall
坞室/塢室　dock chamber
坞首/塢首　dock head
坞修/塢修，進塢檢修　docking repair, dock repair
物标能见地平距离/物標水平視距　distance to the horizon from object
物动视力/物動視力　vision with object moving

物候/物候學,[生物]季節學,花曆學　phenology
物候监测/物候監測　phenology detection
物候谱/物候生態譜系　phenoecological spectrum
物候现象/物候現象　phenological phenomenon
物化法/物化程式　physico-chemical process
物理爆炸/物理爆炸　physical explosion
物理防治/物理防治　physicial control
物理风化作用/物理性風化　physical weathering
物理机械防治法/物理機械防治法　physical and mechanical method of prevention and cure
物理勘探/物理探查　physical prospecting
物理起动/物理起動　physical start-up
物理气相沉积/物理氣相沈積　physical vapor deposition, PVD
物理实验室/物理實驗室　physics laboratory
物理性分解/物理性分解　physical disintegration
物联网/物聯網　internet of things
物料单/物料單　stores list
物料净化/物料淨化　supplies purify
物料净化用室/物料淨化用室　room for cleaning material
物流仓储用地/物流倉儲用地　logistics and warehouse land use, land for logistics and warehouse
物流中心/物流中心　logistics center
物探/地球物理探查法　geophysical prospecting
物体色/物體色　object color
物业/物業　property
物业服务费/物業管理費　property management fee
物业服务企业/物業管理企業　property management enterprise
物业管理/物業管理　estate management, property management
物质更新/物質更新　physical regeneration
物质结构/實質結構　physical structure
物质性通道/物理性可入　physical access
物种/[物]種　species
物种存续委员会/物種生存委員會　Species Survival Commission, SSC
物种多样性/物種多樣性，種歧異度　diversity of species, species diversity
物种丰富度/物種豐[富]度　species richness
物种管理区/物種管理區　species management area
物种均匀度/物種[均]匀度　species evenness
物资管理/物資管理　material handling, goods handling, material management
误[报]警/誤警,假警報　false alarm
误爆概率/誤爆機率　wrong burst probability

误比特率/位元錯誤率　bit-error rate
误操作报警器/誤操作警報[器]　wrong operation alarm
误差补偿/誤差補償　error compensation
误差传播/誤差傳遞　error propagation
误差分离/誤差分離　error separation
误差函数/誤差函數　error function
误差积分/誤差積分　error intake, error integral
误差理论/誤差[理]論　theory of error
误差模型/誤差模型　error model
误差模型辨识/誤差模型識別　error model identification
误差曲线/誤差曲線　error curve
误差特性统计/誤差特性統計　error characteristic statistics
误差圆半径/誤差圓半徑　errorcircular radius
误发遇险警报/假遇險警報　false distress alerts
误交付/誤交付　delivery mistake
误码测试仪/錯誤[率]測試器　bit error tester, code error tester
误码率/位元錯誤比　bit-error ratio
误期赔偿费/遲延之約定損害賠償　liquidated damages for delay
误卸/誤卸　mislanded
误用故障/誤用故障　misuse fault
误指令/誤差指令　error command
误指令概率/誤差指令概率　error command probability
误字率/字元錯誤率,詞錯誤率　word-error ratio, character-error rate
误走交通/誤走交通　wrongway trafffic
误组率/字組錯誤率　block-error rate
雾/霧,靄　fog, mist
雾泊/霧中拋錨　anchoring in fog
雾滴/霧瀝　fog drip
雾笛/霧笛　fog whistle
雾害/霧害　fog pollution
雾化/霧化　atomization
雾化杯/霧化筒　atomizing cup
雾化程度/霧化程度　degree of mist
雾化金属粉末/霧化金屬粉　atomized metal powder
雾化轮/霧化輪　atomizing wheel
雾化喷射沉积/噴霧[霧化]沈積　spray atomization and deposition
雾化器/霧化器　atomizer
雾检测器/測霧儀　fog detector
雾角/霧角　fog horn
雾警报/霧警報　fog warning
雾雷/霧雷　fog siren
雾锣/霧鑼　fog gong
雾情信号/霧信號　fog signal
雾信号器/霧號　nautophone
雾中航行/霧航　navigating in fog
雾中抛锚/霧中拋錨　anchoring in fog

X

西班牙式园林/西班牙式園林　Spanish style garden
西餐厅/西餐廳　western restaurant
西大距/西大距　greatest western elongation
西方标/西方標　west mark
西方古典园林/西方古典園林　western classical garden
西方式插花/西方式花卉擺放　western style of flower arranging
西雅图高速公路花园/西雅圖高速公路花園　Freeway Park in Seattle
西雅图煤气厂公园/西雅圖煤氣廠公園　Gas Works Park in Seattle
吸波材料电磁特性测量/波吸收材料電磁特性量測　EM characteristics measurement of wave-absorption materials
吸波结构/吸波結構　absorbent structure
吸波室/消音室,回音室　anechoic chamber
吸波性能/吸波性能　absorber performance
吸尘车/[真空]吸塵器　vacuum sweeper
吸出式通风/排氣式通風系統　exhaust system of ventilation
吸顶灯具/頂燈,天花板燈[具]　ceiling luminaire, surface mounted luminaire
吸浮力/吸力,引力　attraction lift force
吸附/附吸,吸著　sorption
吸附等温线/等温吸附線　adsorption isotherm
吸附过程/吸附過程　adsorption process
吸附剂/吸附劑　adsorbent
吸附类攀缘植物/吸附類攀緣植物,吸附類繞攀植物　adsorption of climbing plant
吸附水/吸附水　adsorption water
吸附作用/吸附[作用]　adsorption
吸井/吸引井　suction well
吸力/吸力　suction
吸流变压器/吸流,變壓器　booster transformer, BT
吸流变压器供电方式/吸流變壓器供電方式　booster transformer feeding system
吸能机构/能量吸收器　energy absorber
吸泥泵/吸泥泵,抽泥泵　air lift mud pump, dredge pump
吸泥管/吸入管　suction pipe
吸起时间/吸合時間,啟動時間　pick-up time
吸起值/吸合值,始動值　pick-up value
吸气流率峰值/吸氣期最大氣流　peak volume of inspiratory flow rate
吸气式烟雾探测火灾报警系统/吸氣式煙霧探測火災報警系統　aspirating smoke detection fire alarm system
吸气行程/吸入衝程　suction stroke
吸气阻力/吸氣阻力,吸氣阻抗　inspiratory resistance
吸入流/吸流　suction current
吸入水/入滲水　water of infiltration
吸入压力调节阀/吸入壓力調整閥　suction pressure regulating valve
吸入压头/吸引水頭,吸入高度　suction head
吸上式注水器/吸上式注水器　attraction injector
吸上线/吸上線　boosting cable
吸声/吸音,聲音吸收　sound absorption
吸声材料/吸音材料　sound absorption materials
吸声尖劈/楔形吸收器　wedge absorber
吸声量/等效吸音面積　equivalent absorption area
吸声室/隔音室,聽力測驗室　acoustic chamber
吸声系数/吸音係數,吸聲係數　sound absorption coefficient
吸湿水/沾濕水,附著水　hygroscopic water
吸湿物质/吸濕物　hygroscopic substance
吸湿性货物/吸濕性貨物　humidity absorbing goods
吸收/吸收[作用]　absorption
吸收波段/吸收光譜帶　absorption bands
吸收材料/吸收材　absorbent material
吸收发射比/吸收發射率　absorption-emissivity ratio
吸收光谱/吸收光譜　absorption spectrum
吸收剂/吸收劑　absorption agent, absorbent
吸收率/吸收率,吸收性　absorptivity, absorptance, specific absorption
吸收热流法/吸收熱通量法　absorbed heat flux method
吸收式制冷机/吸收式冷凍裝置　absorption-type refrigerating machine
吸收损耗/吸收損耗　absorption loss
吸收系数/吸收係數　absorption coefficient

吸收制冷/吸收冷凍　absorption refrigeration
吸收装置/吸收器　absorber
吸水高度/吸水高度　suction height
吸水井/吸引井　suction well
吸水坑/吸水坑,吸[水]井　suction pit
吸水率试验/吸水率試驗　water absorptivity test
吸水膨胀/吸液膨脹　imbibition
吸水石/吸水紙　absorbent paper
吸水性/吸水[率]　water absorption
吸扬[式]挖泥船/抽吸式挖泥船,泵吸挖泥船,吸管式挖泥船　pump dredger, suction dredger
吸扬挖沙船/泵砂挖泥機　sand pump dredger
吸引交通量/吸引交通量　absorbed traffic volume
吸引距离/吸引距離　attractive distance
吸引圈/吸引圈　attractive circle
吸油口加热盘管/货油吸入加熱盤管　cargo oil suction heating coil
吸鱼泵/吸魚泵　fish pump
吸着/吸著,附吸　sorption
吸着水/附著水　adsorbed water
汐/汐　evening tide
希波丹姆规划模式/希波丹姆規劃模式　Hippodamus planning system, Hippodamus planning
希腊十字形/四臂長度相等的十字架　Greek cross
析像管星敏感器/析像管星體傳感器　image dissector tube star sensor, IDT star sensor
牺牲阳极/陽極耗蝕　sacrificial anode
牺牲阳极保护/耗蝕性陽極防護　sacrificial anode protection
牺牲阳极电保护/陽極耗蝕保護　sacrificial anode protection, cathodic protection with sacrificial anode
牺牲阳极利用效率/犧牲陽極利用效率　utilization coefficient for sacrificial anode
牺牲阳极阴极保护/犧牲陽極陰極保護,耗蝕性陽極防護,陽極耗蝕保護　sacrificial anode cathodic protection, galvanic anode protection, cathodic protection with sacrificial anode
稀薄空气动力学/稀薄氣體空氣動力學　rarefied aerodynamics
稀薄气流/稀薄氣體流　rarefied gas flow
稀薄气体力学/稀薄氣體力學　rarefied gas mechanics
稀浆封层/漿料封層　slurry seal
稀浆封层机/瀝青糊封口機　asphalt slurry seal machine
稀释处置/稀釋處置法　disposal by dilution
稀释剂/稀釋劑　diluent

稀释系数/稀釋因數　dilution factor
稀树草原/稀樹草原,疏林草原　savanna
稀土[元素]化学热处理/稀土元素化學熱處理　chemical heat treatment with rare earth element
稀有气体/鈍氣,惰性氣體　inert gas, rare gas
稀有植物/稀有植物　rare plant, unusual plant
稀有种/稀有種,罕見種　rare species
舾装/舾裝　hull fittings, outfitting
舾装码头/舾裝碼頭　fitting-out quay
舾装设备/艙面及住艙舾裝品　outfit of deck and accommodation
舾装数/舾裝數,屬具數,船具規號　equipment number
锡基白合金衬层/錫基白金襯層　tin-base white-metal linings
溪涧/[河]流　stream
溪坑石/溪坑石　stream stone
溪流/溪,小河　rivulet
熄火/熄滅　extinction of a flame, quenching of a flame, flame failure
熄火安全装置/熄火安全裝置　flame failure device, flame safeguard
熄火滑行/熄火滑行　coasting with engine off
嬉水园/親水公園　water park
习惯用水/習慣用水　habitual water use
习惯装卸速度/依慣例快速處理　customary quick despatch, CQD
席别灯/席別燈　car class indicating lamp
洗舱/洗艙　washing
洗舱泵/洗艙泵,巴特華斯泵　tank cleaning pump, Butterworth pump
洗舱机/洗艙機　tank washing machine
洗舱口/洗艙開口　tank washing opening
洗舱水/洗艙水　tank washing water
洗池/洗滌槽,水槽　sink
洗涤间/洗滌[間]　washery
洗涤器/清洗器,擦洗器,清除器　scrubber
洗涤塔/洗滌塔　washing tower, washer, scrubber
洗涤油/清潔油　detergent oil
洗罐棚/洗罐棚　tank washing shed
洗罐设备/洗罐設備　tank washing equipment
洗罐线/洗罐線　tank washing siding
洗罐站/洗罐站　tank washing point
洗流时差/洗流時差　lag of wash
洗炉/洗爐　washing boiler
洗炉堵/洗爐塞　washout plug
洗面间/洗滌室　washing room, washing compartment

洗面器/洗盆　wash basin
洗墙灯/洗牆燈,壁燈　halogen down lights, wall lamp, wall washer
洗染店/洗染店　laundering and dyeing shop
洗砂机/洗砂機　grit washer
洗手池/洗盆　wash basin
洗手间/盥洗室　toilet, lavatory
洗手器/洗手機　wash bowl
洗碗水/洗盤水　dishwater
洗消间/洗消間,除汙室　wash and disinfectant house, decontamination room
洗衣房/洗衣房,洗衣間　laundry
洗印厂/電影洗印廠,洗印車間　film laboratory
铣槽/銑削槽　milling groove
铣槽式推力室/銑槽式推力室　milling fluted thrust chamber
铣削/銑切　milling
喜马拉雅条款/喜瑪拉雅條款　Himalaya Clause
戏剧场/小劇場,戲院　playhouse
戏台/戲臺　stage, xitai
系泊/繫泊　berthing
系泊驳船/繫泊小艇　mooring lighter
系泊浮筒/繫船浮筒,錨位浮標　anchorage buoy, mooring buoy
系泊工况管理/繫泊作業管理　mooring operating mode management
系泊绞车/繫船絞車　mooring winch
系泊绞盘/繫船絞盤　mooring capstan
系泊锚/繫泊錨,碇泊錨　mooring anchor
系泊设备/繫泊設備　mooring equipment
系泊设备试验/繫泊裝置試驗　mooring arrangement test
系泊设施/碇泊設施　mooring facility
系泊试验/繫泊試車　mooring trial, dock trial
系泊旋转接头/繫船轉環　mooring swivel
系泊状态/繫泊狀態　moored condition
系船浮[筒]/繫船浮筒,繫泊浮筒　mooring buoy
系船绞盘/繫船絞盤　mooring pull
系船码头/繫船碼頭　mooring wharf
系船设备/錨泊及繫泊設備　anchoring and mooring equipment
系船索/繫船韁索,叉索　bridle
系船柱/繫船柱　mooring post
系船桩/繫船樁,小碰墊　dolphin
系浮标的投海货物/附有浮標之投海貨物　lagan
系浮筒/繫浮筒　securing to buoy
系浮筒索/浮筒索　buoy rope
系杆拱/繫拱　tied arch

系杆拱桥/繫[桿]拱橋　bowstring arch bridge, tied arch bridge
系拱杆/繫拱　tied arch
系缆活结/繫纜活結　slip racking
系缆具/繫纜具　mooring fittings
系缆力/繫泊力　mooring force
系缆[索]/繫纜,繫泊[纜]索　mooring line
系缆桩/繫船樁　mooring bitt
系列遗产/系列遺產　serial properties, serial heritage
系留气球/繫留氣球　captive balloon
系留试验/静態試驗　captive test
系索耳/繫索扣　cleat
系索羊角/繫索扣　cleat
系艇杆/繫艇桿　boat boom
系统/系統,制度,體系　system
系统安全性/系統安全　system safety
系统标称电压/標稱系統電壓　nominal system voltage
系统捕获时间/系統獲取時間　system acquisition time
系统操作测试/系統操作測試　system operability test
系统操作图/系統流程圖　system flow chart
系统测试/系統測試　system test
系统抽样法/系統抽樣　systematic sampling
系统电磁兼容性试验/系統電磁相容性試驗　EMC test of systems
系统电磁脉冲/系統感生電磁脈衝　system-generated electromagnetic pulse
系统反应时间/系統反應時間　system reaction time
系统故障/系統故障　system fail
系统观察/系統觀測　systematic observation
系统管理计算机/系統管理計算機　system management computer
系统规划/系統規劃　systematic planning
系统集成/系統整合　system integration
系统鉴定/系統驗證　system certification
系统接口/系統介面　system interface
系统可靠性/系統可靠性　system reliability
系统可维修性/系統維護度,系統維持性　system maintainability
系统联试/系統整合測試　system integration test
系统锚杆/系統錨桿　system anchor bolt
系统漂移率/規律性漂移率　systematic drift rate
系统评价/系統評估　system evaluation
系统软件/系統軟體　system software
系统设计/系統設計　system design

系统试验/系统測試　system test
系统误差/系統誤差　systematic error
系统响应/系統回應　system response
系统效能/系統有效度　system effectiveness
系统信息/系統資訊　system information
系统性故障/系統性故障　systematic fault
系统余度/系統邊際　system margin
系统植物学/系統植物學　systematic botany, plant systematics
系统总噪声级/系統總噪音級　system total noise level
系线法/繫線法　tie-line method
系住/繫住　bend on
系桩拉力/繫纜[樁]拖力,繫船柱拉力　bollard pull
细编穿刺碳-碳/細編穿刺碳-碳　fine weaving pierced fiber carbon
细部测量/細部測量　detail surveying
细长梁/細長梁　slender beam
细长体理论/細長[體]理論　slender body theory, slender theory
细度/[精]細度　fineness
细度模数/細度模數,細度模量　fineness modulus
细骨料/細骨材,細集料　fine aggregate
细级配/細級配　fine gradation
细集料/細集料,細骨材　fine aggregate
细节/細節,詳圖　detail
细节疲劳额定强度/詳細疲勞強度　detail fatigue rating
细节设计/細部設計　detail design
细菌过滤器/濾菌器　bacteria filter
细颗粒物/細顆粒物　fine particulate matter
细粒土/細粒土壤　fine grained soil
细粒土填料/細粒土壤填料　fine grained soil filler
细料清洗机/細料清洗機　fine material screw washer
细流/低流量　low water flow
细木工板/細木工板,芯塊膠合板　blockboard, laminated wood board
细沙/細沙　fine sand
细炻砖/細炻磚　fine stoneware tile
细水雾灭火系统/細水噴霧滅火系統　water mist fire suppressing system
细牙螺纹/細牙螺絲,密螺紋　fine thread
细则/施行細則,準則　regulation
细琢石路面/細琢石道　dressed stone pavement
隙缝波导天线/槽嵌波導天線,開槽波導天線　slotted waveguide antenna
瞎火/失效飛彈,不發彈　dud
峡谷/峽谷　canyon

峡谷风景区/峽谷風景區　valley scenic spot
狭长流冰区/狹長流冰　stream ice
狭航道效应/局限水域效應　restricted water effect
狭口/狹口　narrow entrance
狭水道/狹[窄]水道　narrow channel
狭水道操纵/狹水道中操縱　maneuvering in narrow channel
狭水道航行/狹水道航行　navigating in narrow channel, channel navigation
下凹控制/切角控制　notching control
下半旗/下半旗　flag at half mast
下部转动/下部轉動　lower motion
下沉海岸/沈陷海岸　coast of subsidence
下沉速度/沈落速度　subsidence velocity
下沉庭院/中央下沈庭院　sinking courtyard
下承式桥/下承橋,穿式橋　through bridge
下垂/下垂,下降　drooping
下单翼/低翼　low-wing
下挡墙/下擋土牆　lower retaining wall
下导轮/下導輪　lower tumbler
下垫面/[下]伏面　underlying surface
下舵承/下舵承　neck bearing
下二层甲板/下方中甲板　lower tween deck
下反角/下反角　anhedral angle
下防跳台/下防跳臺　rotary operation anticreep ledge
下风岸/下風岸　lee shore
下风船/下風船　vessel to leeward
下风满舵/下風滿舵　hard down
下风舷/下風舷,下風側　lee side
下峰信号/下峰信號　down hump trimming signal
下纲/沈子綱,腳繩,踏索　foot line
下滑/下滑,滑翔　glide
下滑信标/滑降臺,滑降坡度　glide slope
下击暴流/下爆流　downburst
下甲板/下甲板　lower deck
下降/下降　descent
下降风/頹風　katabatic
下降管/降水管　downcomer tube, downcomer
下界/下界　lower bound
下界流线/下界流線　lower boundary flow line
下开窗/下開窗　dropping window
下拉荷载/下拉荷載　downdrag
下临界流速/下限臨界流速　lower critical velocity
下锚段衬砌/下錨段襯砌　anchor-section lining
下面级/下面級　lower stage
下木层/林下植物,下層叢薄　undergrowth
下坡/下坡　downhill grade
下坡道防护电路/下坡道防護電路　protection circuit

for approaching heavy down grade
下潜平台／下潛平臺　submersible platform
下墙板／下牆板　wainscot sheathing
下渗区／下滲區　infiltration area
下渗水面积／下滲區　infiltration area
下视显示器／下視顯示器　head down display
下水／下水　launching
下水驳／下水駁船　launching barge
下水车／下水船架　launching cradle
下水道底部／下水道底部　sewer bottom
下水道检查井／下水道窨井，下水道人孔　sewer manhole
下水道配件／下水道附屬設備　sewer appurtenance
下水道气体／下水道氣　sewer gas
下水道区／下水道區　sewerage district
下水日期／下水日期　date of launching
下水设备／下水設備　launching appliance
下水站／下水站　launching station
下水重量／下水重量　launching weight
下水装置／下水裝置　launching arrangement
下套管钻孔／套管鑽孔　cased borehole
下体负压／下半身負壓　lower body negative pressure, LBNP
下体负压试验／下半身負壓試驗　lower body negative pressure test
下卧层／下臥層，下伏岩層　underlying stratum, substratum
下洗／下洗流　downwash
下洗修正／下洗流修正　downwash correction
下洗诱导速度／下洗誘導速度　downwash induced velocity
下弦／下弦[桿]　last quarter, bottom chord, lower chord
下限／下界　lower bound
下限越界／下限越界　off-normal lower
下心盘／下心盤　truck center plate
下行／由……來　bound from
下行船／下行船　down-bound vessel
下行方向／下行方向　down direction
下行行程／下行衝程　downstroke
下翼缘／下翼緣　lower flange
下游／下游　down stream, lower reach
下止点／下死點　lower dead center, bottom dead center, bottom dead point
下中天／[天體]下中天　lower transit, lower culmination
下阻岩床／下阻岩床　positive confining bed
下作用车钩／下作用式車鉤　bottom operation coupler
下作用水阀／下作用水閥　under lever faucet
夏季季候风／夏季季候風　summer monsoon
夏季区带／夏期區[域]　summer zone
夏季用润滑油／夏季用潤滑油　summer oil
夏季载重线／夏期載重線　summer load line
夏利玛尔花园／夏利瑪爾花園　Shalamar bagh in Kashmir
夏令时／夏令時　summer time
夏热冬冷地区／夏熱冬冷地區　hot summer and cold winter zone
夏热冬暖地区／夏熱冬暖地區　hot summer and warm winter zone
夏至点／夏至[點]　summer solstice
先锋阶段／先鋒期　pioneer stage
先锋剧场／實驗劇場　experimental theater
先锋群落／先驅群落　pioneer community
先锋树种／先鋒樹種　pioneer tree species
先锋植物／先驅植物　pioneer plant
先锋种／先驅種　pioneer species
先拱后墙法／先拱後牆法　arched roof in advance of wall tunneling method, arch first lining method, flying arch method
先进的长途运输系统／先進長途運輸系統　advanced rural transportation system, ARTS
先进的城市[公共]运输系统／先進公共運輸系統　advanced public transportation system, APTS
先进的驾驶员信息系统／電子公路監理網　advanced driver information system, ADIS
先进的交通管理系统／先進交通管理系統　advanced traffic management system, ATMS
先进的汽车控制系统／先進車輛控制系統　advanced vehicle control system
[先进]柔性防热材料／[先進]柔性熱防護材料　advanced flexible thermal protection material
[先进]柔性绝热材料／[先進]柔性熱絕緣材料　advanced flexible insulation material
先期固结压力／先期固結壓力　preconsolidation pressure
先墙后拱法／先牆後拱法　wall in advance of arched roof tunneling method, side wall first lining method
先张法／先張法，先拉法　pretensioning method
先张法预应力混凝土结构／先張法預應力混凝土結構　pretensioned prestressed concrete structure
先张法预应力梁／先張法預應力梁　pretensioned prestressed concrete girder
先知楼／先知樓　house of the prophet
先钻／預鑽　subdrilling

先钻后扩法/先鑽後擴法　reaming after boring method
纤蛇纹石/蛇紋石板　chrysotile
纤维/纖維　fiber
纤维板/纖維板　fiberboard
纤维缠绕成形/繞線成形　filament winding moulding
纤维混凝土/纖維[增強]混凝土　fiber concrete
纤维混凝土路面/纖維混凝土鋪面　fiber concrete pavement
纤维浸润性/纖維潤濕性　fiber wetness
纤维拉伸强度/纖維抗拉強度　tensile strength of fiber
纤维绳/纖維[繩]索,纖維纜線　fiber rope
纤维水泥板/纖維水泥平板　fiber cement flat sheet
纤维素纤维/纖維素纖維　cellulose fiber
纤维索/纖維[繩]索,纖維纜線　fiber rope
纤维育苗器/纖維育苗器　wood fiber plant grower
纤维预处理/纖維預處理　pretreatment of fiber
纤维增强复合材料/纖維強化複合材　fiber reinforced composite
纤维增强硅酸钙板/纖維增強矽酸鈣板　fiber reinforced calcium silicate sheet
纤维增强塑料筋/纖維增強塑膠筋　fiber reinforced plastic rod
[纤维]织物/織物,蒙布　fabric
纤维质淤泥/纖維質淤泥　fiberous peat
鲜活货物/鮮活貨物　fresh and living goods, fresh and live freight
闲置包/閒置包　idle package
闲置船/停航　lay up
闲置土地/閒置土地　idle land
弦杆/[桁]弦,弦材　chord, chord member
弦宽/弦長　chord length
咸潮/鹹潮　salt tide
咸淡水交接面/淡鹽水界面　fresh salt water interface
咸水/鹽水　saline water
咸水入侵/鹽水入侵　saline water intrusion
涎流冰/涎流冰　salivary flow ice
衔接轮/側輥軸　side roller
舷边动力滚柱/舷側動力滾子　side power roller
舷边角钢/舷緣板角鐵　stringer angle
舷侧/舷側　broadside
舷侧板/側邊板　side plate
舷侧阀/舷側閥　ship side valve
舷侧肋骨/舷側縱材　side longitudinal
舷侧竖桁/側深橫肋　side transverse
舷侧拖网船/舷側拖網船,側拖網漁船　beam trawler
舷侧外板/船側外板列　side plating
舷侧纵桁/側加強肋,側縱材　side stringer
舷窗/舷[側圓]窗,客艙窗戶　side light, side scuttle, cabin window
舷窗[内]盖/舷窗内蓋,内窗蓋　deadlight
舷灯/舷燈　sidelight
舷灯遮板/舷燈遮光板　screen of sidelight
舷顶列板/舷側厚板列　sheer strake
舷弧/舷弧　sheer
舷角/相對方位　relative bearing
舷门/舷門,舷側艙口　side port
舷门灯/梯口燈　gangway light
舷门跳板/舷門跳板　side ramp
舷内/船内　inboard
舷旁排出口/舷外排出口　overboard discharge outlet
舷墙/舷牆　bulwark
舷墙门/梯口通道　gangway port
舷墙排水口/舷牆排水口　bulwark freeing port
舷墙梯/舷牆梯　bulwark ladder
舷墙系索器/舷牆繫索器　bulwark gripper
舷伸甲板/張出甲板,舷外平臺　sponson deck
舷梯/舷梯　gangway ladder, accommodation ladder
舷梯绞车/舷梯絞車,舷梯絞機　accommodation ladder winch
舷梯强度试验/舷梯安全限試驗　proof test for accommodation ladder
舷外吊杆/舷外吊桿　outboard boom
舷外挂机/舷外機　outboard engine
舷外甲板/張出甲板,舷外平臺　sponson deck
舷外跨距/伸出[舷外]距離　outreach, boom outreach
舷外排出阀/舷外排洩閥,舷側排洩閥　overboard discharge valve
舷外排水孔/舷外排水孔　overboard scupper
舷外作业/舷外作業　outboard work
显路径编程/顯路徑程式設計　explicit path programming
显燃期/顯燃期　sensible combustion period
显热/顯熱,可感熱　sensible heat
显热蓄热/顯熱加熱再生　sensible heat regeneration
显色性/演色性　color rendering
显色指数/顯色指數,顯色指標,現色性指數　color rendering index
显示方法/顯示法　display method
显示方式/顯示方式　display mode
显示符号/顯示符號　display symbol
显示距离/顯示距離　range of a signal
LED显示屏/LED顯示屏　LED screen

显示屏亮度/顯示屏亮度　display screen luminance
CRT 显示器/陰極射線管顯示器　cathode ray tube display, CRT display
显示式[测量]仪器/顯示式[量測]儀器　displaying measuring instrument
显示图像/顯示影像　display image
显示仪器/顯示儀表　display instrument
显示元素/顯示元件　display element
显微镜检查/顯微鏡試驗　microscopic test
显微镜室/顯微鏡室　microscope room
显微裂纹/微觀裂紋　microscopic crack
显微摄影/顯微攝影　photomicrograph
显微组织/微結構　microstructure
显性性状/優勢遺傳性質　dominate character
险恶地/障礙地區　foul ground
险情检查/險情檢查　examination of dangerous situation
险升坡/陡昇坡　steep ascent
险性事故/大事故　bad accident, dangerous accident
县公路/縣道　county highway, county road
县级医院/縣立醫院　county hospital
县市公路/縣市公路　prefectural highway
县域城镇体系/縣域城鎮體系　county seat town and township system of county
县域村镇体系规划/縣域村鎮體系規劃　town and village system planning for a county
县域规划/區域規劃,地區計劃　county regional planning
现场拌和/工地配料,工地配合　job mix
现场拌和试验/現場拌和試驗　field mixing test
现场测量/現場量測　on-site measurement
现场调度/現場調度,就地調度　on-site dispatching
[现场]工程签证单/[現場]工程簽證單　project verification form
现场焊接/現場焊接,工地焊接　field welding
现场纪录/現場記錄　record on spot
现场检测方法/現場檢驗方法　in situ check and test method
现场剪切触探仪/原位剪力試驗計　iskymeter
现场剪切试验/原位置剪切試驗　in situ shear test
现场鉴别/野外鑒別法　field identification
现场浇制桩/場鑄樁　cast-in-place pile
现场校正/現場矯直　straightened up in place
现场勘测/現場調查　site investigation
现场勘探/基址探測　site exploration
现场考察/現場稽查　site inspection
现场渗透试验/現場滲水試驗　field seepage test
现场十字板试验/現場十字片試驗　field vane test
现场试验/現場試驗,現場測試　field test
现场通信/現場通信　on-scene communication
现场通信管制/現場通信管制　control of on-scene communication
现场土壤剪切仪/原位剪力試驗計　iskymeter
现场修理/現場修理　on-site repair
现场压实试验/碾壓試驗　field compaction test
现场指挥/現場指揮　on-scene commander, OSC
现场总线/現場總經　fieldbus
现场总线控制系统/現場匯流排控制系統　fieldbus control system
现代建筑运动/現代化運動　modern movement
现代派建筑教育/現代派建築教育　modernist architecture education
现代侵蚀/近期侵蝕　recent erosion
现代文保技术/現代文保技術　modern conservation technique of heritage
现代育种技术/現代育種技術　smart breeding
现代主义城市规划/現代主義都市規劃　modernist urban planning
现代主义建筑/現代主義建築,現代派建築　modernism in architecture
现代自由式插花/現代自由式插花　modern freestyle flower arrangement
现浇混凝土/場鑄混凝土　cast-in-place concrete
现浇混凝土结构/場鑄混凝土結構　cast-in-situ concrete structure
现浇混凝土桩/場鑄混凝土樁　in situ concrete pile
现金流量表/現金流程表,現金來源去向表　cash flow statement
现有船/現成船,現存船舶　existing ship
现有服务指数/現有服務指數　present service index, PSI
现有公路/既有公路　existing highway
现在车/現在車　car on hand
现状图/現狀圖,形勢圖,態勢圖　existing situation map, status chart
限定空间/限航空域　restricted space
限定要素/限定要素　determinant element
限额赔偿/有限賠償　limited compensation
限额设计/限額設計　design on prescribed cost
限航区/限航區　restricted area
限建区/限建區　construction limited area, construction restricted area
限界/限界　gauge, clearance
限界改善/限界改善　clearance improvement
限界架/限界框　clearance limit frame
限界检测车/限界測定車　clearance car, clearance

inspection car
限界检查／限界檢查　checking of clearance, clearance check measurement
限界检查器／限界檢查器　clearance treadle
限界门／限界門　warning portal
限界图／限界圖，限界輪廓　clearance diagram
限界线／邊際線　margin line
限量危险品／限量危險品　dangerous goods in limited quantity
限流电抗器／限流電抗器　inductive reactor, current limiting reactor
限流起动器／限流起動器　current limiting starter
限期拆除／限期拆除　dismantle within limited time
限燃层／限燃層　restrictor
限时人工解锁／限時人工解鎖　manual time release
限速／限制速度　limiting speed
限速标志／限速標誌，速限標誌　stated speed sign, speed-limiting sign
限速器／限速器　speed-limiting governor
限位开关／極限開關，限制開關　limit switch
限压阀／限制閥，極限閥　limiting valve
限用操作员证书／限用值機員證書　restricted operator certificate, ROC
限于吃水船／吃水受限船　vessel constrained by her draught
限于吃水船号灯／吃水限制號燈　deep draught vessel light
限运货物／限運貨物　restricted goods
限制／限制，約束　restriction, restraint
限制标志／限制標誌　restrictive sign
限制电压／極限電壓　measured limiting voltage
限制动压／限制動力壓力　limit dynamic pressure
限制公路／限制公路，自由大道　limited way
限制建设区／限制建設區　development-restricted zone
限制降落区标志／限制降落區域標誌　restricted landing area mark
限制马赫数／最佳馬赫數　optimum Mach number
限制坡度／限制坡度　ruling grade, limiting grade
限制器／限制器　limiter
限制牵引力／限界牽引力，限界曳引力　limiting tractive force, limiting tractive power
限制区[域]／限[制]區　restricted area, limiting zone
限制速度／限制速率　limited speed, speed restriction
限制特性／限制特性　limited characteristic
限制纬度／限制緯度　limiting latitude
限制性三体问题／狹義三體問題　restricted three-body problem

限制因子／限制因子　limiting factor
限制用户／限制用戶　limited subscriber
限制轴重／限制軸重　axle load limited
限重标志／重量限制標誌　weight limit sign
线／線　thread, string
PE线／保護導體　protective conductor
PEN线／PEN線，保護接地中性導體　protective earthing and neutral conductor
线材／線材　wire rod
线侧平式站房／線側平式站房　level parallel station building
线侧上式站房／線側上式站房　high level station building
线侧式站房／線側式站房，通過式站房　parallel station building
线侧下式站房／線側下式站房　low-lying station building
线岔／架空交叉　overhead crossing
线传热系数／線性傳熱係數　linear heat transfer coefficient
线读出／線內讀出　line readout
线端平式站房／線端平式站房　level terminal station building
线段／段，節　section
线对／線對　pair
线间距[离]／相鄰線路　distance between centers of tracks, midway between tracks
线脚／緣材，線板　molding
线控制／線控制　line control, linked control
线框表示法／線[圖]框表示法　wire frame representation
线框模型／線框模型　wire frame model
线路／鐵路路線，永存性公路或鐵路　track, permanent way
线路标志／線路標誌　road way sign, permanent way sign
线路测量／路線測量，路線勘查　route survey
线路大修／線路大修，軌道更新作業　major repair of track, track renewal, track overhauling
线路点／線路點　field location
线路电压降／線路電壓降　line drop
线路放大器／線上放大器　line amplifier
线路封锁／軌道封鎖　track blockade, closure of track
线路复测／線路複測　repetition survey of existing railway, resurvey of existing railway
线路机具／線路機具　permanent way tool
线路机械／線路機械　permanent way machine

线路接触器/線路接觸器　line contactor
线路利用率/線路效率　line efficiency
线路滤波器/線路濾波器　line filter
线路爬行/線路爬行　track creeping
线路平面图/線路平面圖,軌道布置圖　track plan, line plan
线路平剖面图/軌道表示盤　track chart
线路清理机械/鐵路路線整理機　permanent way clearing machine
线路区段/軌道區段　track section
线路全长/軌道全長　total track length
线路所/閉塞信號控制站　block post
线路踏勘/路線勘測　route reconnaissance
线路维修/鐵路維修　maintenance of track
线路维修规则/線路維修規則　rules of maintenance of way
线路有效长/軌道有效長　effective track length
线路杂音/線路雜訊,線路噪聲　line noise
线路占用表示/線路占用表示　track occupancy indication
线路遮断表示器/線路遮斷表示器　track obstruction indicator
线路中断/線路中斷　line interruption
线路中心线/軌道中[心]線　central line of track
线路中修/軌道中修　intermediate repair of track, track intermediate repair
线路纵断面/線路縱斷面　track profile
线路纵断面图/線路縱斷面圖　track profile, line profile
线铝合金/線鋁合金　wire aluminum alloy
线膨胀/線膨脹　linear expansion
线圈高度/線圈高度　coil height
线群/線群　group of lines
线群出站信号机/線群出站信號機　group starting signal
线烧蚀率/線燒蝕率　linear ablative rate
线束/線束,路線群,軌道群　track group, group of tracks
线束减速器/線束減速器　group retarder
线弹性结构/線型彈性結構　linear elastic structure
线条试验/線條試驗　thread test
线头脱落/線頭脫落　wire lead drop out
线位移/線性變位　linear displacement
线向校正/線向校正　rectification of alignment
线向调和/線向調和　harmony of alignment
线形衬板/面板,裙板　lining board
线形设计/線向設計,定線設計　alignment design
线形协调/線形協調　alignment coordination

线形要素/線形要素　alignment element
线型航站楼/線型航站樓,前列式航站樓　linear terminal
线性/線性　linearity
线性插值法/線性交集法　linear intersection method
线性灯/線性燈器,線光　linear light, linear modulator
线性规划/線性規劃　linear programming
线性化理论/線性化理論　linearized theory
线性膨胀/線膨脹　linear expansion
线性扫描/線性掃描　linear scanning
线性扫描率/線性掃描速率　linear sweep rate
线性弹性断裂力学/線彈性破裂力學　linear elastic fracture mechanics
线性调频/線性調頻　linear FM
线性调频脉冲/線性調頻脈衝　chirp
线性通道/線性河槽　linear channel
线性效率系数/線性效率係數　coefficient of linear effect
线性蓄水库/線性蓄水庫　linear reservoir
线性预应力/線性預力　linear prestress
线性原理/線性原理　principle of linearity
线性运动/線性運動　linear motion
线压力/線壓力　linear pressure
线障脉冲测试器/脈衝回波線障測試儀　pulse echo fault locator
线阵[列]探测器/線性陣列偵檢器　linear array detector
线支承/線支承　line bearing
乡/鄉,鎮區　township
乡村/鄉村　country, village, rural area
乡村道路/鄉村道路,郊區道路,市外道路　rural road
乡村复兴/鄉村復興　rural revival
乡村规划/鄉村規劃,農村規劃　rural planning, country planning
乡村规划编制成果/鄉村規劃成果,農村規劃成果　products of rural planning
乡村建设规划许可证/鄉村建設規劃許可證　permit for rural construction plan, building permit for construction in township and village
乡村景观/田園景觀　rural landscape
乡村旅游/鄉村旅遊　rural tourism
乡村社区/村莊社區,村落社區　village community
乡村生活方式/鄉村生活方式,鄉村生活風格　rural life style
乡村生活模式/鄉村生活模式　country life pattern
乡村衰退/鄉村衰變　rural decay

乡村转型/農村轉型　rural transformation
乡公路/鄉公路　township highway
乡规划/鄉[鎮]規劃　township planning
乡郊地区/鄉村區　rural area
乡里制度/鄉裡制度　village neighborhood system
乡趣园/鄉趣園　rustic garden
乡土建筑/本土建築　vernacular architecture
乡土建筑遗产/鄉土建築遺產　built vernacular heritage
乡土景观/鄉土地景　vernacular landscape
乡土树种/鄉土樹種　indigenous tree species, native tree species
乡贤祠/鄉賢祠　memorial hall for distinguished local
乡域规划/鄉鎮區規劃　township area planning
乡镇/農業市鎮　rural town
乡镇卫生院/鄉村醫院　rural hospital
相参应答机/同調應答機　coherent transponder
相错式接头/錯接式接頭　alternate joint, staggered joint
相对 GPS/相對全球定位系統　relative GPS
相对标高/相對高度　relative elevation
相对测量/相對量測　relative measurement
相对沉降量/相對沈陷量　relative settlement
相对定位/相對定位　relative positioning
相对方位/相對方位　relative bearing
相对风速/相對風速　relative speed of wind
相对辐射定标/相對輻射校正　relative radiometric calibration
相对刚度/相對勁度　relative stiffness
相对高程/相對高度　relative elevation
相对高度/相對高度,相對波高　relative height
相对光谱灵敏度/相對光譜靈敏度　relative spectral sensitivity
相对光谱响应/相對光譜響應　relative spectral response
相对含水量/相對含水量　relative water content
相对航高/相對航高　relative flying height
相对计程仪/相對計程儀　relative log
相对加速度/相對加速度　relative acceleration
相对孔径/相對孔徑,相對口徑　relative aperture
相对密实度/相對密實度　relative density, relative compactness
相对密实度试验/相對密實度試驗　relative density test
相对免赔额/起賠限額　franchise
相对摩擦系数/相對摩擦係數　relative friction coefficient
相对频率/相對頻率　relative frequency

相对日照时数/相對日照期間　relative sunshine duration
相对深度/相對深度　relative depth
相对生长速率/相對生長率　relative growth rate, RGR
相对生长系数/相對生長係數　relative growth coefficient
相对湿度/相對濕度　relative humidity
相对式接头/對接[式]接頭　opposite joint, butt joint
相对速度/相對速度,相對速[率]　relative speed, relative velocity
相对速率/相對速率　relative speed
相对位移/相對變位　relative displacement
相对误差/相對誤差　relative error
相对效率/相對效率　relative efficiency
相对旋转劲度/相對旋轉勁度　relative rotational stiffness
相对旋转效率/相對轉動效率　relative rotative efficiency
相对运动雷达/相對運動雷達　relative motion radar, RM radar
相对[运动]显示/相對運動顯示　relative motion display
相干/相干,同調,相參　coherent
相干函数/相干函數　coherence function
相干回波/同調回波　coherent echo
相干接收/相干接收,同調接收　coherent receiving
相干接收机/相干接收器,同調接收器　coherent receiver
相干雷达/同調雷達　coherent radar
相干散射/相干散射,同調散射　coherent scattering
相干调制/相干調製　coherrent modulation
相干载波/同調載波　coherent carrier
相干噪声/相參雜波　coherent noise
相关尺寸标准/自動尺度更換　associative dimensioning
相关方程/相關方程式　correlate equations
相关接收机/相關接收機　correlation receiver
相关色温/相關色溫　correlated color temperature
相关系数/相關係數　coefficient of correlation, correlation coefficient
相关因素/相關因數　correlation factor
相关指数/相關指數　correlation index
相互接近/互相接近　approaching one another
相互作用/相輔作用　coaction
相容性/相容性　compatibility
相容质量矩阵/相容質量矩陣　compatible mass

matrix
相似/相似，類比　analogy
相似参数/相似參數　similarity parameter
相似理论/相似性理論　similarity theory
相似律/相似定律　similarity law
相似系数/相似係數　coefficient of similarity
相似性指数/相似度指數　index of similarity
相似[性]准则/相似性判據　similarity criterion
相应水位/對應水位　corresponding water level
香炉/香爐　cernser burner, incense burner
厢房/厢房　wing room
厢式挂车/厢式掛車　van trailer
厢式货车/箱式載重車　van truck
箱/箱　case
箱底承载能力/箱底負載能力　floor loading capability
箱格导柱/[貨櫃]導槽　cell guide
箱涵/箱涵　box culvert
箱间段/銜接槽　inter-tank section
箱梁型护栏/箱形梁護柵　box girder fence
箱门封条/箱門密封墊　door seal gasket
箱内作业叉车/箱内作業叉車　inside container operation fork lift
箱式变电站/箱式變電站，箱形變電站　box-type substation
箱式托盘/箱形托貨板　box pallet
箱式验潮仪/箱式驗潮儀　box gage
箱形舱盖/箱形艙蓋　pontoon hatch cover, pontoon cover
箱形拱桥/箱型拱橋　box arch bridge
箱形机架/箱形機架　box frame
箱形基础/箱形基礎　box foundation
箱形框架结构/箱框構造　box frame construction
箱[形]梁/箱形[大]梁　box girder
箱[形]梁桥/箱形梁橋　box girder bridge
箱形内龙骨/方形内龍骨　box keelson
箱形桥台/箱形橋臺　box type abutment
箱形中桁材/箱形中線縱梁　duct center girder
箱形桩/箱型鋼樁，對焊方鋼樁　box pile
箱序号/貨櫃序號　container serial number
箱主代号/櫃主碼　container owner code
箱装货/箱裝貨　cased cargo
镶板/鑲板　panel board
镶合浇筑/鑲合澆鑄　match casting
镶辑复照图/攝影索引圖　index of photography
镶木地板/鑲嵌地板，拼花地板　parquetry
镶木细工/拼木　wood mosaic
镶嵌玻璃/鑲嵌玻璃，馬賽克玻璃　mosaic glass,

decorated glass
镶嵌花坛/鑲嵌花壇　mosaic bed
镶嵌性/鑲嵌性　mosaic
镶嵌阵列/鑲嵌陣列　mosaic array
镶刃刀头/插式鑽頭　insert bit
镶套/襯套　bushing
镶隅/鑲隅　inset corner stone
详查型侦察卫星/詳查型偵察衛星　close look reconnaissance satellite
详图/詳圖，細節　detail
详细符号/詳細符號　detailed symbol
详细规划/詳細規劃，細部規劃　detailed planning, detail planning
详细设计/細部設計　detail design
响度/響度　loudness
响度级/響度級，響度水準　loudness level
响墩信号/爆響號誌　torpedo, detonating signal
响应/回應　response
响应控制/回應控制　response control
响应量子效率/響應量子效率　responsive quantum efficiency, RQE
响应率/響應度　responsibility
响应谱/回應譜　response spectrum
响应时间指数/反應時間指數　response time index, RTI
响应速度/響應速度，反應速度　speed of response
响应特性/響應特性　response characteristic
响应滞后/反應落後　response lag
向岸风/向岸風，向濱風　onshore wind
向岸流/向岸流　onshore current
向东航程/東橫距　easting
向后/向後　aback, astern
向量多边形/向量多邊形　vector polygon
向量分析/向量分析　vector analysis
向流性/向流性　rheotaxis
向前/向前，前方，正车　ahead
向前倒缆/向前斜出各纜　forward-leading springs
向上风/居上風，頂風　in the wind
向上拉/向上緊　bowse up
向上式凿岩机/頂鑽　stoper
向上通风/向上通氣　upward ventilation
向台指示器/向臺指示器　to indicator
向位换算/方向換算　conversion of directions
向西航行/往西航　westing
向下拉/向下緊　bowse down
向下弹射/向下彈射　downward ejection
向斜/向斜　syncline
向心式涡轮/向心式渦輪機　centripetal turbine

向心预应力/同心預力 concentrical prestress
项目管理/項目管理,專案管理 project management
项目后评价/項目後評價 post project evaluation
项目建议书/項目建議書,專案申請報告 project proposal, proposed task of project
项目经理/專案經理 project manager
项目评估/計劃評估 project appraisal
项目质量管理/工程品質管理 project quality management
项目资本金/項目資本金 equity
项目资源管理/項目資源管理 project resources management
巷/巷道,公定航道 lane, alley
巷号/巷號 lane letter
巷宽/巷寬 lane width
巷设定/巷設定 lane set
巷识别/巷識別,航道識別 lane identification, LI
巷识别计/巷識別計 lane identification meter
相变[材料]储热装置/相變[材料]儲熱裝置 phase change material device
相地/相地,工址調查 site investigation, site study planning
CCD相机/CCD攝影機 charge-coupled device camera, CCD camera
相机检定主距/鏡箱焦距 calibrated focal length of camera
相控调压/相位控制 phase control
相控阵测量雷达/相控陣測量雷達 phased array instrumentation radar
相控阵雷达/相列雷達 phased array radar
相控阵天线/相控陣天線,相位陣列天線 phased array antenna
相面解法/相面解法 phase plane solution
相敏轨道电路/檢相軌道電路 phase detecting track circuit
相片传真机/照片傳真設備 photographic facsimile apparatus
相片镶嵌图/像片鑲嵌圖 photo-mosaic
相石/相石 stone selection
相速度/相位速度 phase velocity
相位/相[位] phase
相位编码/相位編碼 phase coding
相位差/相[位]差,偏距,偏位 offset, phase difference
相位传递函数/相傳遞函數 phase transfer function, PTF
相位抖动测量仪/相位抖動測量儀 phase jitter tester
相位分离/相位分離 phase separation
相位共振/相共振 phase resonance
相位检波器/相位偵檢器 phase detector
相位历程/相位歷史 phase history
相位日变化/相位日變 diurnal phase change
相位扫描/相位掃描 phase scanning
相位调制/相位調變,調相 phase modulation
相位突然异常/相位突然異常 sudden phase anomaly, SPA
相位滞后/相延 phase lag
相线/相[位]線 phase line
相序/相序 phase sequence
相移键控/相移鍵控 phase shift keying, PSK
象皮石/象皮石 xiangpi stone
象棋/西洋棋 chess
象限角/象限角,方位角 quadrantal angle, quadrantal bearing
象限自差/象限自差 quadrantal deviation
象形文字阶梯/象形文字階梯 hieroglyphic stairway
象形文字阶梯广场/象形文字階梯廣場 hieroglyphic stairway plaza
像变形/影像畸變 distortion of image
像差/像差 aberration
像差渐晕/像差漸暈 aberration vignetting
像点/像點 image point
像幅/像面幅度 frame of image, format
像畸变/影像畸變 distortion of image
像面照度/像面照度 illuminance of image plane
像片地平线/主水平線 horizon trace
像片方位元素/元素的定向 orientation element
像片框标/像片框標 fiducial mark of the photograph
像片索引图/像片索引圖,航線覆蓋圖 photo index
像片镶嵌图/像片鑲嵌圖,相片鑲嵌圖 photo mosaic
像片遥测/像片遥測 photographic extension
像散/像散現象,散光 astigmatism
像素/像素,圖素 pixel, picture element
像素中心距/像素間距 pixel pitch
像移/影像運動 image motion
像移补偿/影像運動補償[作用] image motion compensation, IMC
像移补偿畸变/影像運動補償[作用]畸變差 image motion compensation distortion
像移补偿精度/影像運動補償精度 accuracy of image motion compensation
像移补偿装置/影像運動補償裝置 image motion compensation device
像元/像素 pixel
像元分辨率/像素解析度 pixel resolution

像元复位偏压/像素復位偏壓　pixel reset bias
像元复位时钟/像素重定時鐘　pixel reset clock
像元配准/像素註冊,像素登記　pixel registration
像主点/像主點　principal point
橡胶挡泥板/橡膠護舷　rubber fender
橡胶地板/橡膠鋪面板　rubber flooring
橡胶垫/橡皮墊　rubber mat, rubber pad
橡胶垫板/橡膠墊板　rubber tie plate
橡胶堆/橡膠堆　rubber-metal pad
橡胶改性沥青/膠粉改性瀝青　rubber modified asphalt
橡胶缓冲器/橡膠緩衝器　rubber draft gear
橡胶接缝/橡膠墊　rubber joint
橡胶沥青/橡膠化瀝青,橡皮化瀝青　rubberized asphalt
橡胶沥青装置/橡膠瀝青工場　rubber asphalt unit
橡胶摩擦式缓冲器/橡皮摩擦緩衝器　rubber friction draft gear
橡胶乳液黏结剂/水泥橡膠液　rubber latex cement
橡胶水泥/橡膠水泥　rubber cement
橡胶弹簧/橡皮彈簧　rubber spring
橡胶弹性导柱式轴箱定位装置/橡膠彈性導柱式軸箱定位裝置　rubber elastic guide post type journal box positioning device
橡胶支座/橡膠軸承　rubber bearing
橡胶轴承/橡膠軸承　rubber bearing
橡皮成形/橡皮墊成形　rubber pad forming
橡皮带/橡皮帶　rubber belt
橡皮膏液压成形/橡皮膏液壓成形　rubber cell hydroforming
橡皮拉深/橡皮墊拉製　rubber pad drawing
橡皮艇/橡皮艇　rubber boat
肖氏硬度/反跳硬度　scleroscope hardness
肖氏硬度试验/蕭式硬度試驗　Shore hardness test
削平木枕/枕木之修削　tie adzing
消冰/除冰　deicing
消冰剂污染/防凍劑汙染,防冰劑汙染　deicing agent pollution
消波设施/消波設施　attenuating shock wave equipment
消侧音器/消側音電路裝置　anti-sidetone device
消除应力热处理/消力熱處理　stress relief heat treatment
消磁按钮开关/消磁按鈕開關　degauss push button switch
消磁场/消磁場　degaussing range
消磁船/消磁船　degaussing vessel, degaussing ship
消毒/消毒　disinfection

消毒池/消毒池,氯接觸槽　disinfecting pool, chlorine contact chamber
消毒剂/消毒劑　disinfectant
消毒室/消毒室　sterilizing room
消防泵/消防泵,滅火泵,救火泵　fire pump
消防部署/消防部署　firefighting station
消防车/消防車　fire engine
消防车库/消防機器房　fire engine room
消防船/消防船,救火船,消防艇　fire boat, firefighting ship
消防电梯/緊急專用電梯　fire lift, emergency elevator
消防规范/防火規則　fire protecting rules
消防给水/消防給水　fire supply
消防给水系统/消防給水系統　fire water supply system, fire water system
消防局/消防隊　fire department, fire authority
消防控制室/消防控制室,火警控制室　fire control room, fire protection control room
消防控制站/火警控制站　fire control station
消防控制中心/消防控制中心　fire protection control room
消防联动控制器/消防聯動控制器　integrated fire controller
消防联动控制系统/聯合消防系統　integrated fire control system
消防炮/消防炮　fire monitor
消防器材/消防設備,滅火設備　fire fighting apparatus and materials
消防软管/水龍帶　fire hose
消防设施/消防設備　fire fighting equipment
消防栓/消防栓,水龍頭　hydrant, fire plug
消防栓箱/消防栓箱　fire-hydrant cabinet
消防水泵间/消防水罐室　fire water tank room
消防水压力/消防水壓　fire pressure
消防水源/消防水池　fire protection water source
消防系统/消防系統,滅火系統　fire extinguishing system, firefighting system
消防需水率/消防用水量　fire demand rate
消防巡逻制度/火警巡邏系統　fire patrol system
消防演习/消防演習　fire fighting drill
消防应急广播/消防應急廣播　fire public address
消防用水/消防用水　water for fire fighting
消防用水量/消防需水量　fire demand
消防员装备/消防員裝具　fireman outfit
消防站/消防站,火警布署站　fire station
消防专用水/消防用水　water for fire fighting
消防总管/主消防水管,救火主水管　fire main

消光/消光,熄滅　extinction
消光系数/消光係數　extinction coefficient, extinction index
消耗式冷剂冷藏集装箱/冷藏貨櫃,冷凍貨櫃　refrigeration container
消火栓/消防栓,水龍頭　hydrant, fire plug
消火栓水量测试/消防水量試驗　hydrant flow test
消火栓系统/消火栓系統　hydrant system
消极空间/負形空間　negative space
消力槛/消力檻,擋板門檻　baffle sill
消灭曲线/衰減曲線　curve of extinction
消能减震/耗能減震　energy dissipation and earthquake response reduction
消能支撑/消能支撐　energy dissipation brace
消能装置/消能裝置　energy killer
消泡剂/消泡劑　defoaming agent
消球差透镜/消球差透鏡　aspherical lens
消融/消冰,冰融　ablation
消色差透镜/消色差透鏡　achromatic lens
消色体/消色體　achromatic body
消声/抑噪　noise suppression
消声衬/抑噪襯　noise suppression gasket, noise suppression liner
消声结构/消聲結構　noise elimination structure
消声量/消聲量　sound deadening capacity
消声喷管/抑噪噴嘴　noise suppression nozzle
消声器/消音器,噪音抑制器,静噪器　silencer, noise silencer, muffler
消声器插入损失/消音器介入損耗　insertion loss of silencer
消声室/無回音室,無響室　anechoic chamber, anechoic room, free-field room
消声弯头/消聲彎頭　bend muffler
消石灰/消石灰,熟石灰　slaked lime, hydrated lime
消絮凝剂/擴散劑　deflocculation agent
消旋体/消旋體　despinner
消漩装置/消漩裝置　vortex suppression devices
消压状态/消壓狀態　state of decompression
消音器/消音器　silencer
消杂光/消去雜散光　eliminate stray light
硝化/硝化作用　nitrification
硝酸酯增塑聚醚推进剂/硝酸酯增塑聚醚推進劑　nitrate ester plasticized polyether propellant, NEPP propellant
销钉板/板榫　plate dowel
销钉拼接板/榫續接　pin splice
销接/榫接　pin connection
销连接/銷釘接合　doweled joint
销栓作用/銷栓作用　dowel action
小半径曲线黏降/小半徑曲線黏降　reduction of adhesion on minimal radius
小半涨潮/小半漲潮　quarter flood
小雹/小雹　small hail
小爆破/小爆破　light shot
小便收集/尿液收集　urine collection
小不对称弹头/小不對稱彈頭　nose with small asymmetry
小不对称弹头试验/小不對稱彈頭試驗　small asymmetric nose testing
小潮/小潮　neap tide
小潮差/小潮差　neap tide range
小潮升/小潮昇　neap rise, NR
小城市/小城市,小都市　small city
小导管预注浆/小導管注漿,微管預灌漿　pre-grouting with small duct, pre-grouting with micropipe
小岛/小島　isle
小方格铺砌/簡易鋪面　random paving
小幅液体晃动力学/小幅液體晃動力學　small-amplitude-slosh liquid dynamics
小改正/小修正　small correction
小管出流器/小管出流器　mini tube emitter
小规模更新/小規模更新　small-scale regeneration
小孩票/兒童票　child ticket
小河/小河,小灣　creek
小河弯/次級蜿蜒　submeander
小横梁/橫梁,交叉拉桿,軌枕　crosstie
小环比对/小環驗證　minor loop validation
小环境/人造環境,微環境　microenvironment
小尖塔/小尖塔,尖柱,尖端　pinnacle
小件寄存处/行李間　luggage room, luggage storage
小街/小街　local street
小径/[小]徑　alley, path
小距/低螺距　low pitch
小客车[交通量]单位/小客車單位　passenger car unit, PCU
小浪/微浪　smooth sea
小流量加注/小流量[率]裝填　low flow rate filling
小流量加注控制/小流量裝填控制　slow filling control
小卖部/速食櫃,小吃店　snack counter, buffet
小锚/小錨,艇錨,小移船錨　kedge anchor
小木作/小木作　smaller non-structural carpentry, xiao muzuo
小瀑布/小瀑布　cascade
小气候/小氣候,微氣候　microclimate

小桥/小橋 small bridge, short span bridge, minor bridge
小青砖/小青磚 small brick
小区公园/鄰里公園 neighborhood park
小区路/小區路 community road
小区试验/小區試驗 plot experiment
小区游园/社區公園,小庭院 community garden, small garden
小群落/小群落 microcommunity, microcoenose
小扰动方程/小擾動方程式 small perturbation equation
小扰动位势方程/小擾動位势方程式 small perturbation potential equation
小生境/小生境,小棲息地 microhabitat
小石子混凝土/小石子混凝土 micro-aggregate concrete
小时变化系数/每時變化係數 hourly variation coefficient
150小时长期试车/150小時持久試車 150 h endurance test
小时高峰系数/小時高峰係數 maximum factor of hourly consumption
小时降雨率/雨率 rainfall rate
小时率/小時率 hour rate
小式/小式 xiaoshi-style
小水线面双体船/小水線面雙體船 small water plane area twin hull, SWATH, small water plane twin hull ship
小套公寓/簡易公寓 efficiency apartment
小艇/小艇 cutter, small craft
小艇结/鬆套結 slippery hitch
小湾/小灣,小河 creek
小卫星/小衛星 small satellite, mini satellite
小行星/小行星,小遊星 minor planet, asteroid
小型车运价/小型車運價 rate for small vehicle
小型翻地犁/翻地犁 uncovering plough
小型客车/小型客車,小公共汽車 small-sized bus, mini-bus
小型客车票价/小型客車票價 ticket price of mini-bus
小型临时工程/小型臨時工程項目 small-scale temporary project
小型三轮汽车/馬達三輪車 motor pedicab
小型线路机械/小型線路機械 light permanent way machine
小型液压捣固机/輕型液壓砸道機,剗道機 light hydraulic tamping machine
小型枕底清筛机/小型枕底清篩機 small ballast undercutting cleaner
小熊β/小熊β,北極二,帝 Kochab
小修/小修 minor overhaul
小循环运行/小循環運行 partial circulation operation
小烟管/煙管 smoke tube
小游园/小遊園 petty street garden
小运转机车/小運轉機車 locomotive for district transfer, transfer locomotive train
小站电气集中联锁/小站繼電器聯鎖 relay interlocking for small station
小直径隧道/微型隧道 micro-tunnel
小直径隧道掘进机/微型掘進 micro-tunneller
笑气/笑氣,一氧化二氮 laughing gas, nitrous oxide
效果图/效果圖,精描圖,寫實圖 rendering
楔/楔,尖劈 wedge
楔缝式锚杆/狹縫楔型錨桿 slit wedge type rock bolt
楔固/楔挖法 wedging
楔块拱/分塊拱 voussoir arch
楔式切割/楔形炸法 wedge cut
楔形缝/楔形縫 keyed joint
楔形绿地/楔形綠地,楔形綠化地帶 green wedge, green land of wedge
楔形锚具/楔式錨碇 wedge anchorage
楔形内接/楔狀內接 wedge inscribing
楔形掏槽/楔形炸法 wedge cut
楔形柱/錐形柱 tapered column
楔状绿地/楔狀綠地 wedge-shaped green space
歇山/歇山 hip-and-gable roof, xieshan
协定航线/航路 shipping route
协方差分析/共變[異]數分析 analysis of covariance
协会/機構 institution
协调避碰操纵/協調避碰操縱 coordinated collision avoidance maneuver
协调侧滑法/協調側滑法 coordinated sideslip method
协调加载/協調負載 coordinated loading
协调精确度/協調準確度 coordination accuracy
协调空间/協調空間 coordination space
协调控制/連鎖控制 coordinated control
协调路线/協調線路 coordination route
协调扭转/相容扭轉 compatibility torsion
协调世界时/協調世界時 coordinated universal time, universal time coordinated, UTC
协调条件/適合條件 condition of compatibility
协调转弯/協調轉彎 coordinate turn
协同干扰/合作式干擾技術 cooperative jamming

协同规划/協同計劃　collaborative planning
协同进化/共[同]演化　coevolution
协同作用/協同作用,協力作用　synergism
协议/協定　protocol, agreement
协议规范/協定規格　protocol specification
协议书/協議,協定　agreement
协议书表格/協議書表格　form of agreement
协作横移线搜寻/協調橫移線搜索　coordinated creep line search
胁迫/逆壓,逆境　stress
斜舱壁/斜艙壁　sloping bulkhead
斜槽口/斜口　skew notch
斜撑/斜支木　raking strut
斜撑式满布木拱架/斜撐式滿布木拱架　full span wooden inclined strut centering
斜撑桅杆式架梁起重机/斜撐桅桿式架梁起重機　cross stay derrick girder erecting machine
斜程能见度/斜視能見度　slant visibility
斜搭接/斜搭接　scarf joint
斜垫圈/斜墊圈　beveled washer
斜洞门/斜洞門　skew tunnel portal, skew portal
斜度/坡度,比降　gradient pitch
斜对称/歪對稱　skew symmetry
斜对称载荷/對角載荷　diagonally symmetrical loading force
斜杆/斜構件,斜材,木橫撐　diagonal member, branch bar strut
斜钢筋/斜鋼筋　diagonal bar
斜格梁桥/斜格梁橋　skew grillage girder bridge
斜沟/斜溝　oblique gutter
斜管沉淀池/斜管沈澱池　tube settler
斜轨枕垫钣/斜軌枕墊鈑　inclined tie plate
斜夯/坡面夯實　slope tamping
斜桁/[縱帆]斜桁　gaff
斜环标/斜環樺　skewed-ring dowel
斜激波/斜震波　oblique shock wave
斜脊/斜脊,屋頂角　hip
斜交叉/斜式交叉　skew intersection
斜交涵洞/斜涵洞　skew culvert
斜交角/斜[交]角,複斜角　skew angle
斜交桥/斜[式]橋　skew bridge, skewed bridge
斜角连接/斜接頭　splayed joint
斜接/斜對接合　oblique butt joint
斜接近/斜曝光　oblique exposure
斜接近段长度/斜接近段長度　oblique exposure length
斜接近段的等效距离/斜曝光等效間距　equivalent distance of the oblique exposure

斜接头/嵌接頭　scarfed joint
斜井/斜井,斜坑　inclined shaft
斜距/斜距離　slope distance
斜距分辨率/斜距解析度　slant range resolution
斜拉破坏/對角拉力破壞　diagonal tension failure
斜拉桥/斜拉橋,斜張橋　cable stayed bridge
斜拉索结构/斜拉索結構,懸索跨越結構　cable stayed structure
斜拉-悬索组合体系桥/混合索支承梁橋體系　hybrid cable supported bridge system
斜缆/斜拉索　stay cable, inclined cable
斜肋骨/斜肋骨　cant frame
斜肋楼板/斜交格子板　diagrid floor
斜链形悬挂/傾斜鏈線　inclined catenary, srew catenary
斜梁/斜梁　cant beam, sloped beam
斜列式停车/斜列式停車　diagonal parking
斜裂缝/斜裂縫　diagonal crack
斜路缘/斜面緣石　sloped curb
斜面升船机/斜面昇船機　incline ship lift
斜坡跑道/斜坡跑道　slope of the runway
斜坡烧蚀试验/斜坡法燒蝕試驗　ramp method of ablation test
斜坡式防波堤/斜坡式防波堤,拋石防波堤　sloping breakwater, mound breakwater, mound-type breakwater
斜坡式码头/斜坡式碼頭　sloping wharf
斜剖线/斜剖面線　diagonal line, diagonal
斜嵌接/斜嵌接合　oblique scarf joint
斜切/斜切　beveling
斜切轨条/斜切軌條　step rail
斜切喷管/斜切噴管　oblique cut nozzle, nozzle with scarfed exit plane
斜全榫/斜全榫　beveled housing
斜筛/斜篩機　inclined screen
斜双凹界面/斜雙凹介面　double skew notch
斜索/拉索　stay cable
斜索面斜拉桥/斜索面斜拉橋　cable stayed bridge with inclined cable plane
斜调/傾斜調整　slope regulation
斜投影/斜軸投影　oblique projection
斜腿刚构桥/斜腿剛架橋　slant legged rigid frame bridge
斜腿刚架桥/斜腿剛架橋,斜撐梁橋　strutted beam bridge, rigid frame bridge with inclined leg, slant legged rigid frame bridge
斜纹/斜紋　oblique to grain
斜压破坏/對角壓力破壞　diagonal compression

failure
斜翼飞机/斜翼機　oblique wing airplane
斜支承/斜支承　inclined support
斜支距/斜支距　oblique offset
斜支木/斜支木　raking strut
斜置技术/斜置技術　skewed sensor technology
斜置式内燃机/斜置引擎　diagonal engine, inclined engine
斜桩/斜樁　batter pile, raking pile, spur pile
谐波/諧波　harmonic
谐波电流百分比测定/諧波電流百分比測定　measurement of percentage of harmonic current
谐波发射/諧波發射　harmonic emission
谐波分量/諧波分量,諧波成分　harmonic component
谐波分析/諧波分析　harmonic analysis
谐波干扰/諧波干涉　harmonic interference
谐波含量/諧波含量　harmonic content
谐波源/諧波源　harmonic source
谐波振动/諧波振動　harmonic vibration
谐摇/同步　synchronous rolling, synchronism
谐振/諧振,共振　resonance
谐振单元/諧振元件　resonant element
携带电话机/便攜電話機　portable telephone set
写实色彩/寫實色彩　treat color
泄放旋塞阀/排洩旋塞　drain cock
泄洪沉积池/洪池　detention pool
泄洪道/洩洪道　floodway
泄洪量/溢流量　overflow discharge
泄洪区/溢洪區　field of spillway
泄滑下水/洩滑下水　evacuation-slide launching
泄降率/比洩降　specific drawdown
泄降时间/洩降時間　time of drawdown
泄流排水管/輔助下水道　relief sewer
泄漏/洩漏,漏出,滲漏　leakage, leak, breakthrough
泄漏电流/漏電流　leakage current
泄漏率/滲漏率　leakage rate
泄漏探测器/檢漏器　leak finder
泄水道/沖沙口　scour outlet
泄水洞/排水洞　drain cavern, drain tunnel
泄水沟/排水溝　drain ditch, drainage ditch
泄水管/出水管　effluent pipe, outlet conduit
泄水孔/洩水孔,排濕孔　weep hole, drainage opening
泄水量/退水[量]　escapage
泄压/洩壓　depressurization
泄压阀/洩壓閥,保險閥　relief valve
泄压口/洩壓口　pressure relief opening

泄油池/洩油池　oil leakage sump
泻溜/瀉溜　earth-debris flow
卸车数/卸車數　number of car unloading
卸荷阀/卸載閥　unloading valve
卸荷腔/平衡腔　unloading cavity
卸货/卸貨　discharging, unloading, unship
卸货港/卸貨港　port of discharge
卸货区/卸貨區　unloading zone
卸架砂筒/卸架砂筒　sand cylinder for centering unloading
卸扣/卸扣　shackle
卸载/卸載,卸貨　load shedding, unloading
屑末探测器/切屑檢測器　chip detector
蟹耙式清岩机/蟹耙式清岩機　rake-up ballast remover
蟹爪式装岩机/蟹爪式裝岩機　crab rock loader
蟹爪式装载机/連續裝載機　gathering loader
心电图室/心電圖室　electrocardiogram room, ECG room
心肺功能检查/心肺功能檢驗　cardiovascular and pulmonary function test
心轨/鼻[尖]軌,岔心尖軌　point rail, nose rail
心环/繩眼襯環　thimble
心理精神检查/心理精神檢查　psycho-psychiatric examination
心理需要/心理需要　psychological need
心理学选拔/心理學選拔　psychological selection
心理训练/心理訓練　psychological training
心理应激/心理壓力　psychological stress
心理咨询室/心理諮詢室　psychological consultation room, psychological counseling room
心理作用/心理影響,心理衝擊　psychological impact
心盘面自由高/心盤面自由高　free height of center plate wearing surface from rail top
心盘载荷/中心板負載　load on center plate
心盘座/心盤座　center filler
心式牵引变压器/心式牽引變壓器　core-type traction transformer
心土搅糊/基層土搗固　subsoil puddling
心土黏闭/基層土搗固　subsoil puddling
心土镇压/基層土壓實　subsoil compacting
心形[方向]特性图/心形極圖解　cardioid polar diagram
心宿二(天蝎 α)/心宿二,大火(天蝎 α)　Antares
心血管功能检查/心血管功能檢查　cardiovascular function examination
芯/[模]芯　core
芯[包层表面]不圆度/鐵芯非圓性　non-circularity

of core cladding
芯［包层表面］同心度／芯［包層表面］同心度　core cladding concentricity
芯级一级落区／芯級一級落區　core and first stage impact area
芯径／核心直径　core diameter
芯柱／核心柱　core column
辛氏法则／辛普生法則　Simpson rules
锌／鋅　zinc
锌基合金／鋅基合金　zinc-base alloy
锌银蓄电池／鋅銀蓄電池　zinc-silver battery
新奥法／新奥［工］法，新奥地利隧洞施工法　new Austrian tunneling method, NATM
新版图／新版海圖　new edition chart
新拌混凝土／未凝混凝土　fresh concrete
新陈代谢／新陳代謝　metabolism
新陈代谢派／新陳代謝派　metabolism
新城／新市鎮　new town
新城市主义／新都市主義　new urbanism
新城运动／新市鎮運動　new town movement
新风／新風　fresh air
新风机房／新風機房　fresh air room
新风机组／新風機組　fresh air handling unit
新风冷负荷／新風冷負荷　cooling load from outdoor air, cooling load for ventilation
新风量／新風量　fresh air requirement
新风系统／新風換氣系統　fresh air ventilation system
新古典主义／［西方］古典復興　neo-classicism, classical revival
新技术群／新技術群　neo-technic complex
新建／新建築物　construction of new building
新建区／新區　newly built district
新建铁路／新建鐵路　newly built railway
新浇混凝土／未凝混凝土　fresh concrete
新杰森条款／紐哲遜條款　New Jason clause
新理性主义／新理性主義　new rationalism
新能源／新能源　new energy
新农村／新村　new village
新区／新區　newly built district
新区开发／新區發展　new district development
新区域主义／新區域主義　new regionalism
新社区／新社區　new community
新生地／新生地　reclaimed land
新生交通／新生交通　generted traffic
新市镇／新市鎮　new town
新市镇发展计划／新市鎮發展計劃　new town development plan

新特有种／新特有種，新固有種　neo-endemic species
新危险物标志／新危險物標誌　new danger mark
新鲜空气量／新鮮空氣量　quantity of fresh air
新现代／新現代　new modern
新兴城镇／新市鎮　new town
新兴工业城市／新工業市　new industrial city
新型城镇化／新型都市化　new type of urbanization
新艺术运动／新藝術運動　art nouveau
新月／新月，朔　new moon
新月拱／新月拱　crescent arch
新泽西护栏／紐澤西［混凝土］護欄　New Jersey safety barrier
新植代／新生代植物　cenophyte
薪炭林／薪炭材　firewood forest, fuelwood forest
信标／信標，示標，指［向］標　beacon
信标捕获时间／信標獲取時間　beacon acquisition time
信标登记／示標登記　beacon register
信标电文／示標信文　beacon message
信标定位概率／示標定位概率　beacon location probability
信标发射天线／示標發射天線　beacon transmit antenna
信标检测概率／示標檢測概率　beacon detection probability
信标识别／示標識別　beacon identification
信标识别数据／示標識別數據　beacon identification data
信标台／信標發射臺　beacon station
信标信号／示標號誌　beacon signal
信串比／訊號對串音比　signal to crosstalk ratio
信道／信道　channel
信道编码／通道編碼　channel encoding
信道存储／頻道存儲　channel storage
信道空闲信号／通道空閒信號　channel free signal
信道模型／頻道模型　channel model
信道容量／通道容量　channel capacity
信道申请／頻道申請　channel request
信风／信風　trade wind
信号／信號，訊號　signal
信号变压器／信號變壓器　signal transformer
信号标志／信號標誌　signal mark
信号表示／信號指示　signal indication
信号场地／信號區　signal area
信号处理机／信號處理機　signal processor
信号大修／信號大修　signal overhaul repair, signal major repair
信号弹／信號彈　signal shell

信号[灯]/信號燈,號誌柱,交通號誌　signal light, signal lamp, traffic signal
信号点/信號點　signal location
信号电路/信號回路　signal circuit
信号电源室/信號電力室　signal power room
信号发生器/信號發生器　signal generator
信号阀/[應急]信號閥　signal valve
信号分解器/訊號分解器　signal resolver
信号复示器/信號複示器,信號中繼器　signal repeater
信号故障/信號故障　signal fault
信号关闭/信號關閉　signal at stop
信号关闭表示/信號關閉表示　stop signal indication
信号机点灯电路/信號點燈電路　signal lighting circuit
信号机点灯电源/信號機點燈電源　signal lighting power source
信号机后方/號誌[機]外方　in rear of a signal
信号机前方/號誌[機]内方　in advance of a signal
信号集中修/信號集中維護　signal centralized maintenance
信号继电器/信號繼電器　signal relay
信号检修/信號檢修　signal inspection, signal check-out maintenance
信号开放/信號開放　signal at clear
信号开放表示/信號開放表示　cleared signal indication
信号控制/信號控制　signal control
信号控制电路/信號控制電路　signal control circuit
信号控制交叉口/燈號控制交叉口　signalized crossing, signalized intersection
信号控制器/號誌控制器　signal controller
信号铃流发生器/信號音與鈴流發生器　tone and ringing generator
信号楼/信號塔　signal tower
信号面/號誌面　signal face
信号桥/信號橋　signal bridge
信号设备/信號設備　signaling appliance
信号绳/信號繩　signal line
信号调节器/信號調節器　signal conditioner
信号停止开关/號誌行止開關　signal shutdown switch
信号托架/信號托架　signal bracket
信号桅/信號桅　signal mast
信号维修/信號維修　signal maintenance
信号握柄/號誌閘柄　signal lever
信号无效标/信號無效標　signal out of order sign
信号系统/號誌系統　signal system

信号显示/信號顯示　signal aspect and indication
信号选别器/信號選別器　signal slot
信号烟雾/煙[霧信]號　smoke signal
信号音/音響訊號,音頻訊號　sound signal
信号整治/信號整治　signal renovation
信号指示器/號誌指示　signal indicator
信号质量检测/信號品質檢測　signal quality detection
信号中修/信號中修　signal intermediate repair
信号周期/信號週期　signal cycle
信令电流/信號電流　signaling current
信令电路/信令電路　signaling circuit
信令分组/信號分組　signaling packet
信文标志/信文標誌　message marker
信文范围/信文欄　message field
信文筛选因素/信文篩檢因素　message filtering factor
信文转换时间/信文轉換時間　message transfer time
信息/資訊,消息,訊息　information
信息安全/資訊安全　information safety, information security
信息处理/資訊處理　information processing
信息处理机/資訊處理機　information processing machine
信息处理用房/資訊處理室　information processing room
信息点/資訊點　telecommunication outlet, TO
信息发送台/資訊發送臺　information sending station
信息反馈重发纠错/自動重發糾錯　error correction by information feed back repetition
信息格式/資訊格式　information format
信息化应用系统/資訊技術應用系統　information technology application system, ITAS
信息交换/資訊交換　information exchange
信息接收台/資訊接收臺　information receiving station
信息可视化/資訊視覺化　information visualization
信息流/資訊流　information flow
信息设施系统/資訊科技系統基礎建設　information technology system infrastructure, ITSI
信息速率/資訊率　information rate
信息网络系统/資訊網路系統　information network system
信息源择优/最佳訊息源選擇　optimal information source selection
信用卡电话/信用卡電話　credit card call

信用证/信用狀　letter of credit
信噪比/信噪比,訊噪比　signal-noise ratio, signal to noise ratio
兴波阻力/興波阻力,成波阻力　wave making resistance
兴波阻尼/興波阻尼　wave making damping
兴奋剂检测室/興奮劑檢查室　doping control room
星表/星表　star catalog
星捕获/星獲得　star acquisition
星捕获概率/星獲得機率　probability of star acquisition
星-地[测控]校飞试验/星-地[測控]校飛試驗　dynamic matching TT and C test between satellite and station
星-地静态[测控]匹配试验/星-地静態[測控]匹配試驗　static matching TT and C test between satellite and station
星跟踪/星體追蹤　star track
星光制导/天文導引　celestial guidance
星号/星號　star number
星基导航系统/衛星基導航系統　satellite-based navigational system
星基多普勒轨道和无线电定位组合系统/都卜勒衛星測軌和無線電定位系統　Doppler orbitography and radiopositioning integrated system by satellite, DORIS
星际航行/星際航行　interplanetary and interstellar navigation
星际探测器/[行]星際航天器　interplanetary spacecraft
星-箭电磁兼容性试验/星-箭電磁相容性試驗　launcher-satellite EMC test
星箭分离/星箭分離　satellite rocket separation
星-箭分离试验/星-箭分離試驗　satellite-launcher separation test
星-箭匹配/衛星發射載具匹配　satellite and launch vehicle matching
星空模拟器/星空模擬機　sky simulator
星历/天文曆　ephemeris
星历计算/星曆計算　ephemeris calculation
星历数据/衛星運行數據表,衛星軌道數據,天文曆數據　ephemeris data
星敏感器/恆星傳感器　star sensor, stellar sensitometer
星球仪/示星球　star globe
星-三角启动/星-三角起動　star-delta starting
星扫描器/星掃描儀　star scanner
星上电源控制设备/衛星電源控制裝置　satellite power control device
星识别/星識別　star recognition
星搜索/星搜尋　star search
星体跟踪器/星體追蹤儀　star tracker, stellar tracker
星图/天象圖　sky diagram
星图仪/星圖儀　star mapper
星位角/星位角　parallactic angle
星下点/星下點　sub-satellite point
星下点参数/衛星星下點參數　sub-satellite point parameters
星下点轨迹/衛星星下點軌跡　sub-satellite track
星形拱/星形拱頂　stellar vault
星形链/星形鏈　star chain
星形柔性桨毂/星形柔性螺旋槳毂　starflex hub
星形-三角形接法/星形三角連接　star-delta connection
星形投影/星形投影　star projection
星形网[络]/星形網路　star network
星形药柱/星狀藥柱　star grain
星形发动机/星形發動機,星形引擎　radial engine
星宿一(长蛇α)/星宿一(長蛇α)　Alphard
星载数据收集分系统/衛星[基]資料收集子系統　satellite base data collection subsystem
星载致冷器/星載致冷器　space borne refrigerator
星罩半罩翻转吊具/半整流罩翻轉吊索　half-fairing turning sling
星罩工作梯/整流罩工作梯　fairing working ladder
星座/星座　constellation
行包保管/行李儲藏服務　luggage storage service
行包标签/行李標籤　luggage label
行包承运/行李承運　acceptance of luggage consignment
行包地道/行李地道　luggage tunnel
行包丢失/行李丢失　loss of luggage
行包货位/行李貨位　luggage lot
行包交付/行李交付　luggage delivery
行包赔偿率/行李補償率　luggage compensation rate
行包坡道/行李坡道　luggage ramp
行包事故/鐵路行李包裹運輸　luggage and parcel traffic accident
行包收集间/行李收集間　temporary luggage room
行包受理/行李受理　luggage acceptance
行包损坏/行李損失　damage of luggage
行包提取处/行李寄存處　luggage claim room, luggage out counter
行包托运/行李托運　luggage consignment
行包邮政地道/行李郵政地道　tunnel for luggage

行 557

and postbag
行包运价/行李運價　luggage transport rate
行包正运率/行李正運率　luggages transport regularity rate
行波场/進行波前進波場　progressive wave field
行波管/進行波管,前進波管　progressive wave tube, traveling wave tube, TWT
行波[声]试验/進行波試驗,前進波試驗　progressive wave test
行车闭塞法/行車閉塞法　train block system
行车道/車行道　traveled way
行车激振/行車激振　vibration excited by moving truck
行车记录设备/行車記錄設備　train movement recording equipment
行车津贴/行車津貼　operation subsidy
行车路单/貨運提單　waybill
行车路线/車行道　traveled way
行车碾压/行車碾壓　traffic bound, free bound
行车凭证/行車憑證　running token
行车视距/行車視距　driving sight distance
行车信号[机]/行車信號機　train signal
行车指挥自动化/交通管理自動化　automation of traffic control
行车中断/行車中斷　traffic interruption
行程/動程　throw
行程编码/掃描長度編碼[法]　run length encoding
行程车速/回送速度　travel speed, journey speed
行程缸径比/衝程口徑比　stroke-bore ratio
行程利用率/行程利用率　operation mileage rate
行程时间/旅程時間,旅行時間　travel time, journey time
行程时间比/行程-時間比　travel time ratio
行道树/行道樹,街頭樹,街道樹　avenue tree, street tree, roadside tree
行动规划/實施計劃　action plan
行动式索斗挖掘机/履式拖斗挖土機　walking dragline
行宫/行宮　imperial retreat
行进盲道/行進盲道　go-ahead blind sidewalk
行近流速/漸近流速,行近速度,來流速度　approach velocity
行李/行李　luggage, baggage
行李包裹承运/行李包裹承運　acceptance of luggages and parcels
行李包裹交付/行李包裹交付　dilivery of luggages and parcels
行李包裹托运/行李包裹托運　consigning of luggages and parcels
行李舱/行李艙,行李間　luggage room, baggage compartment, luggage compartment
行李车/行李車　baggage car, luggage van
行李处理系统/行李處理系統　baggage handling system, BHS
行李房/行李房,行李間　luggage room, luggage office, baggage office
行李架/行李架　luggage rack, baggage rack
行李票/行李票　luggage ticket, baggage ticket
行李室/行李房　luggage compartment, baggage room
行李损坏赔款限额/行李損失責任限制　limit of liability for loss of or damage to luggage
行李提取厅/行李認領大堂　baggage reclaim hall
行人安全岛/行人穿越島　pedestrian island
行人安全设施/行人安全裝置　pedestrian safety device
行人按钮信号控制机/行人按鈕號誌控制器　pedestrian push button signal controller
行人避车处/庇護人孔,避車洞　refuge manhole
行人管制/人行道交通管理　pedestrian control
行人过街标志/行人過街標誌　pedestrian crossing sign
行人过街信号灯/行人過街號誌燈　pedestrian crossing signal lamp
行人横穿设施/行人橫穿設施　pedestrian crossing device
行人护栏/行人柵欄　pedestrian barrier
行人检测器/行人偵測器,行人感知器　pedestrian detector
行人交通/行人交通　pedestrian traffic
行人信号/行人專用號誌　pedestrian signal
行人信号相/行人時相　pedestrian phase
行人信号相位/行人號誌時相　pedestrian signal phase
行人引发控制器/行人觸動控制器　pedestrian actuated controller
行驶时间/行駛時間　running time
行驶速度/行駛速度,行車速率　running speed, travel speed
行驶性能试验/行駛性能試驗　travel performance test
行驶延误/運行延誤,運行延滯　operational delay
行驶阻力测定/行駛電阻量測　moving resistance measurement
行为背景/行爲背景　context of the behavior
行为测量/行爲測量　behavioral measure

行为场景/行爲場所　behavior setting
行为地图/行爲地圖　behavior map
行为环境/行爲環境　behavioral environment
行为空间/行爲空間　behavioral space
行为心理学/行爲主義心理學　behavioristic psychology
行星/行星　planet
行星辐射收支/行星輻射收支　planetary radiation budget
行星轨道/行星軌道　planetary orbit
行星际磁场/行星際磁場　interplanetary magnetic field
行星考察机器人/行星探測機器人　planetary exploration robot
行星视运动/行星視運動　planet apparent motion
行星型齿轮转动机构/太陽行星齒輪　sun and planet gear
行星演化指数/行星演化指數　planetary evolution index
行游比/行游比　ratio of transportation and tourism time
行政办公楼/行政大樓,市政大樓　administration building
行政办公区/行政辦公室　administrative office zone
行政办公用地/行政辦公用地　administrative office land use, land for administration
行政村/行政村　administrative village
行政监督/制度監督　institutional supervision
行政楼层/行政辦公樓層　executive floor
行政强制执行/行政強制執行　mandatory administrative execution
行政区/行政區　administrative region, administrative district
行政审批一体化平台/行政審批一體化平臺　administrative approval integration platform
行政套房/行政套房　executive suite
行政中心/行政中心　administrative center
形变模量/變形模數　modulus of deformation
形变热处理/形變熱處理　thermomechanical treatment, TMT
形变压力/形變壓力,單位變形力　deformation pressure
形变阻力/形變曳力,形變抵抗　deformation drag
U形玻璃/U形玻璃,槽形玻璃　U-shape glass
Z形[操纵]试验/Z形[操縱]試驗,蛇航[操縱]試驗　zigzag test
U形铲/U形鏟　U-blade
形成层/形成層　cambium

L形传动/L形傳動　L-drive
V形传动/V形驅動　V-drive
Z形传动/Z形傳動,Z形驅動　Z transmission, Z drive
U形存水弯/U形存水彎　running trap
T形刚构桥/T形剛構橋　T-shaped rigid frame bridge
T形刚架桥/T形鋼構橋　T-shaped rigid frame bridge
L形钢/角鋼　L-bar, L-section
T形钢/T形材　T-section, T-steel
U形管/U形管　U-pipe
形函数/形狀函數　shape function
K形桁架/K式桁架　K-truss
W形护栏/W形護欄　W-type guardrail
D形环/D形環,拉繫環　D-ring
A形机架/A形托架　A-frame
T形交叉/丁字交叉　T-intersection
Y形交叉/Y形交叉　Y-intersection
T形接头/T形接頭,三通管接　T-joint
X形结点/X形接頭　X-joint
Y形结点/Y形接頭　Y-joint
T形截面/T形斷面　T-section
L形块码头/L形塊碼頭　L-block type wharf
T形立体交叉/丁字立體交叉　T-grade separation
Y形立体交叉/Y形立體交叉　Y-grade separation
V形链/V形鏈　V-mode chain
T形梁/T形梁　T-shaped beam
U形梁/U形梁　U-shaped beam
T形梁桥/T[形]梁橋　T-beam bridge
U形剖面/U形剖面　U-section
V形起重柱/V形吊桿柱　V-type derrick post
V形桥墩/V形墩　V-shaped pier
Y形[桥]墩/Y形橋墩　Y-shaped pier
T形桥台/T形橋臺　T-abutment
U形桥台/U形橋臺　U-abutment, U-shaped abutment
S形曲线/S曲線,反向曲線　S-curve
ω形燃烧室/環形燃燒室　annular combustor, toroidal combustion chamber
形式主义者/形式主義者　formist
Z形试验/Z形試驗,蛇航試驗　standard maneuvering test
A形索塔/A架索塔　A-framed tower
T形天线/T形天線　T-aerial, T-antenna
Z形推进/Z形推進　Z-peller propulsion
U形推土机/U形推土機　U-dozer
T形尾翼/T形尾[翼]　T-tail

V形尾翼/V形尾翼　V-tail
形象规划/形象規劃　image plan
形心/形心　centroid, centroid of area
U形压力计/U形管流體壓力計　U-tube manometer
H形柱/H形柱　H-column
形状函数/形狀函數　shape function
形状记忆合金/形狀記憶合金　shape memory alloy
形状稳性力臂/形狀穩度力臂　lever of form stability
形状稳性力臂曲线/[穩度]交叉曲線　cross curves of stability
形状系数/形狀係數　form coefficient
形状阻力/形狀抵抗　form resistance
形阻/形狀阻力　form drag
H型柴油机/H型柴油機　H-type diesel engine
V型柴油机/V型柴油機　V-type diesel engine
B型超声波室/B型超音[檢查]室,B超室　B-mode ultrasound room
型吃水/型吃水量,模吃水　molded draft
S型辐板/S型輻板　S-type wheel plate, S-plate
型钢/型鋼　section steel, shaped steel
型钢混凝土/鋼骨鋼筋混凝土　steel reinforced concrete
型钢混凝土梁/鋼骨鋼筋混凝土梁　girder with rolled steel section encased in concrete
型辊成形/型輥成形　contour roll forming
型号合格审定基础/型別檢定基礎　type certification basis
型号合格审定试飞/驗證試飛,驗證飛行試驗　type certification flight test
型号合格证/機型證書　type certificate
型号认可证书/型號認可證書　validation of type certificate
型号审定专用条件/型別檢定證專用條件　type certification special condition
型宽/型寬　molded breadth
MP型链/多脈搏型鏈　multi-pulse mode chain, MP mode chain
JM12型锚具/JM12型錨具　JM12 anchorage
型煤/煤磚　moulded coal
型面喷管/特型噴管　contoured nozzle
型排水量/型排水量,模排水量　molded displacement
型排水体积/型排水體積　molded volume
型深/型深,[船]模深　molded depth, molded depth of vessel
型式/型,式　type
型式试验/型式試驗,典型試驗　type test
A型显示/A型顯示　A-scope

型线/型線,模線　molded lines
型线放样/放樣　laying down, laying off of hull lines
型线光顺/線型整順　lines fairing
型线图/線型[圖]　lines, lines plan
型砧/型鐵砧,花砧　swage block
型值/船線坐標　offsets
型值表/船線坐標表　offset table, table of offsets
性别结构/性別結構　gender structure
性能标准/性能標準　performance standard
TEMPEST性能测量/TEMPEST性能量測　TEMPEST performance measurement
性能测试/性能試驗　performance testing
性能管理系统/性能管理系統,飛行管理系統　performance management system
性能监视器/性能監測器　performance monitor
性能降级/性能降低,性能劣化　degradation of performance
性能校飞/性能飛行校準　performance calibration flight
性能试验/性能試驗,性能測驗　performance test
性能验证测试/性能審認試驗　performance verification test
性信息素/性費洛蒙,性傳訊素　sex pheromone
汹涛阻力/洶濤阻力,狂浪阻力　rough water resistance, rough sea resistance
胸径/胸[高直]徑　diameter at breast height
胸墙/胸牆　crown wall
雄性不育/雄性不育,雄性不稔　male sterility
休眠期/休眠的　dormant
休憩公园/休憩公園　recreation park
休息区/休息區　rest area
休息区标志/休息區標誌　rest area sign
休息室/休息室,門廳　lounge, foyer
休息娱乐区/遊憩區　recreation area
休闲/休閒　leisure
休闲车/娛樂車輛,大型旅行車　recreational vehicles, RV
休养城市/休閒城市　resort city
休渔期/休漁期　fishing season off
休止角/止傾角,靜止角　angle of repose
修补/修補　patching
修补接头效率/修補接頭效率　repair joint efficiency
修补木枕/修補木枕　tie repairing
修车库/修車庫　motor repair shop, car repair pit, freight car temporary repairing shed
修车台位长度/修車臺位長度　length of repair position
修车线/修車線　repair track in station, repair siding

修船坞/修船塢　repairing dock
修道院园林/修道院園林　estate of priory
修复/修整,再處理　reconditioning
修复工程/修復工作　rehabilitation work
修复性维修/修復性維修　corrective maintenance
修剪/修剪　clip, trim
修剪车/修剪車　pruning vehicle
修建设计/構造設計　construction design
修建性详细规划/修建性細部規劃,配置計劃,基地計劃　detailed construction planning, site planning
修理/修理,檢修　repair
修理尺寸/修理尺寸　repair size
修理船/修理艦　repair ship
修理单/修理單　repair list
修理港/修理港　repair port
修理站/修理站　service station
修配/修配　fit-up
修缮/復舊,恢復,保存　restoration, preservation
修整器/修整器　shaping equipment
修正功率/已校功率　corrected power
修正惯性系数/修正慣性參數　modified inertia parameter
修正回路/修正回路　corrective loop
修正牛顿公式/修正牛頓方程式　modified Newtonian equation
修正图/訂正圖　revised drawing
修正因子/修正因子　correction factor
修正值/修正　correction
修正总概算/修正總概算　amended sum of approximate estimate, revised general estimate
修枝剪/修枝剪　pruning shear
锈/銹　rust
锈钢板/銹鋼板　stain steel
嗅味阈值/嗅覺閾值,嗅覺低限　odor threshold
溴化锂吸收式制冷装置/溴化鋰水吸收冷凍裝置　lithium bromide water absorption refrigerating plant
须弥座/須彌座　Sumeru pedestal, Xumizuo
虚电路/虛擬電路　virtual circuit
虚功/虛功　virtual work
虚功互等定理/虛功互換原理　reciprocal virtual work theorem
虚功原理/虛功原理　principle of virtual work
虚呼叫/虛擬呼叫,虛擬通話　virtual call
虚交点/虛交點　imaginary intersection point
虚警/誤警,假警報　false alarm
虚警率/誤警率　false alarm rate
虚空间/錯覺空間　illusory space
虚力/虛力　virtual force

虚拟城市/虛擬都市　virtual city
虚拟摩擦角/假摩擦角　virtual angle of friction
虚拟施工/虛擬建設　virtual construction
虚拟现实/虛擬現實,虛擬實境　virtual reality, VR
虚拟终端/虛擬終端機　virtual terminal
虚坡/虛坡度,假想坡度　virtual grade
虚声源法/虛聲源法　image sound source method
虚位移/虛變位　virtual displacement
虚位移原理/虛變位原理　principle of virtual displacement
虚线/虛線　hidden line
虚指令/錯誤指令,僞指令,誤發指令　false command
虚指令概率/僞指令概率　false command probability
虚轴/虛軸　dummy axis
需水峰/高峰需水量　peak demand
需水量/需水量　water demand, water requirement
需氧法/好氣法　aerobic process
需氧菌/需氣性菌　aerobe
需氧塘/好氣池　aerobic pond
需氧污泥消化/需氣汙泥消化　aerobic sludge digestion
需氧细菌/需氣性細菌　aerobic bacteria
需要停车次数/停車需求　parking demand
需用功率/需求功率　power required
需用推力/需求推力　thrust required
徐变/蠕變,潛變　creep
徐变试验/潛變試驗　creep test
徐变系数/潛變係數　creep coefficient
许可舱长/[艙區]許可長度　permissible length, permissible length of compartment
许用应力/容許應力　permissible stress, allowable stress
序列视景/序列視景　serial vision
畜牧场/牧場,動物農場　animal farm, livestock farm
续灌/續灌　continuous irrigation
续航发动机/續航發動機　sustained motor
续航力/續航[能]力　cruising ability, endurance, cruising radius
续航时间/航時,續航力　endurance
絮凝/絮凝,絮狀沈澱　flocculation
絮凝池/混凝池,絮凝櫃　flocculation basin, flocculating tank
絮凝剂/絮凝劑　flocculant, flocculation agent
蓄冰机房/蓄冰機房　room for ice storage
蓄电池/蓄電池[組],電瓶　accumulator battery, storage battery, accumulator

蓄电池充电系统试验/蓄電池充電系統試驗 checks of battery charging-arrangement
蓄电池电路/蓄電池電路 battery circuit
蓄电池供电/蓄電池供電 storage battery power supply
蓄电池机车/蓄電池機車 battery locomotive
蓄电池起重机/蓄電池起重機 battery crane
蓄电池室/[蓄]電池室 battery room
蓄电池箱/蓄電池箱 storage battery box, accumulator box
蓄洪/洪水吸收,攔洪 flood absorption
蓄冷水池/蓄冷水池 thermal storage tank
蓄能制动/儲能制動 energy-storing brake
蓄排放设施/蓄排放設施 detention and controlled drainage equipment
蓄热器/蓄熱器,再生器,熱交換器 regenerator, heat accumulator, heat storage
蓄热式加热器/蓄積[式]加熱器 storage-type heater
蓄热式热交换器/回熱式熱交換器,再生熱交換器,交流換熱器 regenerative heat exchanger
蓄热系数/蓄熱係數 coefficient of heat accumulation
蓄水池式发电厂/堰蓄式發電廠 pondage type power plant
蓄水库容/潴蓄容量 conservation storage
蓄水曲线/潴蓄曲線 storage curve
蓄水周期/潴蓄週期 storage cycle
蓄压器/蓄壓器,儲壓器,積儲器 accumulator, hydraulic capacitor
蓄滞洪区/分滯洪區 flood detention basin
宣港/港口申報 declaration of port
宣石/宣石 Xuan stone
宣载/載重噸申報 declaration of dead weight tonnage of cargo
轩辕十四(狮子α)/軒轅十四(獅子α) Regulus
悬/懸,吊 hang
悬板桥/應力帶橋 stressed ribbon bridge
悬臂/懸臂 cantilever arm
悬臂板/懸臂板,懸挑梁板,挑板 cantilever slab
悬臂灌注法/懸臂工法 cast-in-place cantilever construction, free cantilever segmental concreting with suspended formwork
悬臂架设法/懸臂架設法 cantilever erection
悬臂浇注/懸臂澆鑄 free cantilever casting
悬臂梁/懸臂梁 cantilever beam
悬臂梁桥/懸臂梁橋 cantilever beam bridge, cantilever girder bridge
悬臂拼装法/懸臂拼裝法 cantilever erection method, cantilevered assembling construction, free cantilever erection with segments of precast concrete
悬臂式挡土墙/懸臂式擋土牆 cantilever retaining wall
悬臂式交通标志/懸臂交通標誌 cantilever traffic sign
悬臂式棚洞/懸臂式棚洞 cantilever shed tunnel, cantilever shed gallery
悬臂式铺轨机/懸臂式鋪軌機 rail laying machine with cantilever
悬臂式铺轨排机/懸臂式鋪軌排機 track panel laying machine with cantilever
悬臂自升式钻井平台/懸臂自昇式鑽油平臺 cantilever jack-up drilling platform, cantilever jack-up drilling unit
悬带桥/懸帶橋,吊帶橋 suspended ribbon bridge
悬吊滑轮/懸吊滑輪 suspension pulley
悬吊式顶棚/懸吊天花板 suspended ceiling
悬浮导向分别控制/懸浮導向分別控制 separate control lift and guidance
悬浮导向兼用/懸浮導向兼用 combined lift and guidance
悬浮固体/浮游物 suspended solids
悬浮力/懸浮力 lift force
悬浮炉/粉煤鍋爐 pulverized-coal fired boiler
悬浮泥沙/浮游土 suspended sediment
悬浮燃料/漿體燃料 slurry fuel
悬浮生长生物法/懸浮性微生物生長法 suspended-growth biological process
悬浮系统/懸吊系統 suspension system
悬浮系统动力学/懸浮系統動力學 dynamics of suspension system
悬浮组件/懸浮模塊 suspension module
悬高杆长比/懸高桿長比 suspension height boom length ratio
悬挂舵/懸舵,吊舵 hanging rudder, spade rudder, under hung rudder
悬挂结构/懸掛結構 suspension structure
悬挂膜结构/吊式膜結構 suspended membrane structure
悬挂式脚手架/懸式腳手架 suspended scaffolding
悬挂投放装置/懸掛投放裝置 suspension and release equipment
悬挂系统/懸吊系統 suspension system
悬降区标志/懸降區域標誌 winching area mark
悬接接头/懸接式接頭 suspended joint
悬距/氣隙 clearance, air gap
悬空脚手架/懸空腳手架 hanging stage, hanging scaffold

悬跨/懸跨　suspended span
悬拉桥/索橋　cable-suspension bridge
悬篮/懸籃　hanging basket
悬链锚腿系泊/懸垂法錨泊　catenary anchor leg mooring, CALM
悬球/懸球　ball suspension
悬山/懸山　overhanging gable roof, xuanshan
悬伸型艉/懸伸艉　counter stern
悬式座架/懸式座架　suspension mounting
悬索/懸索　mounted overhead, suspended cable
悬索结构/懸索結構　cable suspended structure
悬索桥/吊橋　suspension bridge
悬索铁路/懸吊軌道　hanging railway
悬停/懸停,懸浮,懸空　hovering
悬停飞行/懸空飛行　hovering flight
悬停回转/懸空迴轉　turning in hover
悬停升限/懸空昇限　hovering ceiling
悬停效率/懸空效率　hovering efficiency
悬停指示器/懸空指示器　hovering indicator
悬线/懸線,吊索　suspending wire
悬移质/懸浮物質　suspended load
悬移质取样器/浮土採樣器　suspended load sampler
旋臂机试验/旋轉臂試驗　whirling arm testing
旋臂起重机/旋轉吊車　rotary crane
旋臂试验/[船模]強制迴旋試驗　rotating arm test
旋臂水池/旋臂水槽　rotating arm basin
旋回圈/旋迴圈,迴轉圈,迴旋圈　turning circle
旋回性/迴轉能力　turning ability
旋回性指数/迴旋指數　turning indices
旋回直径/旋迴直徑　final diameter
旋回周期/迴旋週期　turning period
旋剪法/旋剪法　gyratory-shear method
旋进性/迴轉偏移　gyroscopic precession
旋流风口/旋流風口　twist outlet, swirl diffuser
旋流加力燃烧室/渦流後燃器　swirl afterburner
旋流曝气/旋流曝氣　spiral-flow aeration
旋流器/旋流器,迴旋式噴嘴　swirler
旋流燃烧/旋流燃燒　swirl-flow combustion
旋流式空气扩散/旋流式空氣擴散　spiral-airflow diffusion
旋片快门/轉盤快門　rotating disc shutter
旋桥/轉橋　turn bridge
旋入管接头/外螺紋活管套節　male union
旋塞/旋塞　cock
旋刷刮板清扫车/旋轉式掃路機　rotary broom slat sweeper
旋水域/迴旋水區,旋迴水區　turning circle
旋梯/旋梯　spiral stage

旋网/旋網　round haul net
旋涡/旋渦,渦流,渦旋　vortex, swirl
旋涡泵/旋流泵　helical flow pump, regenerative pump
旋涡破碎/渦流崩解　vortex breakdown
旋涡式雾化器/旋渦式霧化器　swirl type atomizer
旋涡阻尼/旋渦阻尼　eddy-making damping
旋翼/旋翼,轉子　rotor
旋翼反扭矩/反扭矩尾槳　antitorque of rotor
旋翼风车制动/旋翼風車制動　rotor windmill braking
旋翼机/旋翼飛機　autogyro
旋翼桨毂/旋翼轂　rotor hub
旋翼桨盘载荷/旋翼槳盤負載　rotor disk loading
旋翼桨叶/轉子葉片　rotor blade
旋翼拉力/旋翼推力　rotor thrust
旋翼前进比/旋翼前進比　rotor advance ratio
旋翼入流比/旋翼內流比　rotor inflow ratio
旋翼刹车系统/旋翼刹車系統　rotor brake system
旋翼实度/旋翼實度　rotor solidity
旋翼塔实验/旋翼塔試驗　rotor tower test
旋翼尾流/旋翼尾流　rotor wake
旋翼涡环/旋翼渦流環　rotor vortex ring
旋翼中心间距/旋翼中心間距　distance between rotor centers
旋翼轴前倾角/旋翼軸前傾角　forward tilting angle of rotor shaft
旋翼锥度/旋翼錐度　rotor coning
旋圆双半结/繞轉加雙半套結　round turn and two half-hitches
旋振/旋式顫振　whirl mode flutter
旋轴剪草机/旋軸剪草機　spindle mower
旋转/旋轉　slewing
旋转变流机/旋轉式換流機　rotary convertor
旋转餐厅/旋轉餐廳　revolving restaurant
旋转冲唤钻机/旋轉打擊鑽　rotary percussion drill
旋转冲量/旋轉衝量　rotation impulse
旋转锄/旋轉鋤　rotary hoe
旋转磁场/旋轉磁場　rotating field, rotational magnetic field, rotating magnetic field
旋转弹试验/旋轉彈試驗　rotating rocket testing
旋转刀具圆周速度测定/旋轉刀具圓週速度測定　rotary tool circular velocity measurement
旋转动导数/旋轉動力導數　rotary dynamic derivative
旋转法施工/旋轉法施工　erection by swing method
旋转格式/旋轉格式　Jameson scheme
旋转号盘电话机/旋轉號盤電話機　rotary dial

telephone set
旋转环形天线／旋轉環形天線　rotary loop antenna
旋转计量器／迴轉計量器　rotation recorder
旋转角速度／迴轉速率　turning rate
旋转壳／旋轉殼　revolutionary shell, rotational shell
旋转门／旋轉門　swing gate, revolving door
旋转面壳／迴轉面殼　shell of revolution
旋转盘雾化粉末／旋轉圓盤霧化粉末　rotating disk atomized powder
旋转剖面／旋轉斷面　revolved section
旋转起重机／旋轉起重機,旋轉吊車　swing crane, slewing crane
旋转伞／旋轉傘　rotating parachute
旋转筛／迴轉式篩　rotary screen
旋转失速／旋轉失速　rotating stall
旋转式拨号盘／旋轉撥號盤　rotary dial
旋转式除雪机／旋轉鏟雪車　rotary snow plough
旋转式分配器／旋轉式灑布機　rotary distributor
旋转式通风机／旋輪鼓風機　rotary blower
旋转式凿岩机／旋轉式鑿岩機　rotary jack hammer
旋转式钻机／旋轉式鑽機,旋挖鑽機　swiveling drill, swiveling drill machine, rotary drill machine
旋转视窗／旋轉視窗　clear view screen
旋转挺杆起重机／全迴轉起重機　swing-jib crane
旋转头磁记录器／螺旋形掃描記錄器　helical scan recorder
旋转腕臂／旋轉腕臂　hinged cantilever
旋转心脏形方向图／旋轉心形線方向圖　rotating cardioid pattern
旋转压碎机／旋轉軋碎機　rotary crusher
旋转运动／旋轉運動,迴轉運動　rotary motion, rotational motion
旋转轴／旋轉軸　axis of revolution
旋转钻进／轉式鑽探　rotary drilling
旋子彩画／旋子彩畫　tangent circle pattern
漩水／渦流,旋渦,漩渦　eddy
选拔综合评定／選拔綜合評估　selection integrated evaluation
选港货／卸地待定货　optional cargo
选呼／選擇呼號　selective call
选件／選件　option
选控信号／選控信號　selectivity signal
选矿厂／選礦廠　concentrator, mineral processing plant
选路／選線,路徑選擇　route selection
选路制信号／選線信號　route signaling
选煤厂／選煤廠,洗煤廠　coal preparation plant
选频电平表／選頻電平表　selective level meter

选线／選線,路徑選擇　route selection
选卸货／卸地待定货　optional cargo
选择／選擇　selecting
选择船位／假定船位　assumed position
选择港／待擇港　optional port
选择呼叫／選擇呼叫　selective calling
选择呼叫号码／選擇呼叫號碼　selective calling number
选择经度／經度採用值　assumed longitude
选择可用性／選擇可用性　selective availability, SA
选择利用性／選擇可用性　selective availability, SA
选择前向纠错／選擇前向偵錯　selective forward error correction
选择前向纠错方式／選擇前向偵錯模式　selective error correcting mode
选择纬度／緯度採用值　assumed latitude
选择性／選擇性　selectivity
选择性保护／選擇性保護　selectivity protection
选择性腐蚀／選擇腐蝕　selective corrosion
选择性广播发射台／選擇性廣播發射臺　selective broadcast sending station, SBSS
选择性广播接收台／選擇性廣播接收臺　selective broadcast receiving station, SBRS
选择与决策模型／選擇與決策模型　decision and choice modelling, DCM
选择育种／選擇性繁殖　selection breeding
选址／選位　siting
选址勘察／地盤測量　siting investigation, siting survey
选址意见书／選址意見書　written proposal on the choice of location, permission notes for location, permission note for location
选种室／選種室　seed selection room
眩光／眩光　glare
旋风分离器／旋風分離器　cyclone separator
旋风燃烧／旋風燃燒　cyclone combustion
旋风式除尘器／旋風除塵器,旋風吸塵器,離心除塵器　cyclone dust collector
旋风筒式空气滤清器／旋風式空氣過濾器　cyclone type air filter
旋压／旋壓　spinning, metal spinning
旋压成形／旋壓成形　spin shaping, spin forming
渲染／渲染　render
削弱磁场／削弱磁場　weakened field
靴梁／靴梁　boot beam plate
穴灌／穴灌　bunch irrigation
穴施／穴施　hole fertilizer
穴蚀／穴蝕現象,穴塌　cavitation

学生出游/郊遊,學校組織的旅行　school trip
学生活动中心/學生活動中心　students activity center
学生票/學生票　student ticket
学生宿舍/學生宿舍,學員宿舍　students dormitory
学童过街标志/學童過街標誌　children crossing sign
学徒/學徒,實習生　apprentice
学徒制建筑教育/學徒制建築教育　apprenticeship of architectural education
学习控制/學習控制　learning control
学校标志/學校標誌　school sign
学校园/學校園　school garden
学院派建筑教育/學院派建築教育　classical architecture education
雪暴/雪暴　blizzard
雪崩/雪崩,冰崩　dehris, avalanche, snow slip
雪崩防治/雪崩保護　snow slide protection
[雪的]水当量/雪水等量　water equivalent of snow
雪地/雪地　snowfield
雪盖/雪罩　snow mantle
雪盖冰/雪蓋冰　snow-covered ice
雪害/雪害　snow hazard, snow blockade
雪害地段路基/雪害地段路基　subgrade in snow damage zone, subgrade in snow disaster zone
雪荷载/雪荷載　snow load
雪茄吧/雪茄吧　cigar bar
雪犁/排雪犁　snow plough
雪犁车/掃雪車　snow plough car
雪粒/雪粒　snow grain
雪橇运动/雪橇運動　sled movement
雪蕈/雪蕈　snow mushroom
雪原/雪地　snowfield
雪质/雪質　quality of snow
血库/血庫　blood bank
血液透析室/血液透析室　hemodialysis room
血中酒精浓度/血中酒精濃度　blood-alcohol concentration
熏舱/熏艙消毒,煙熏法,熏蒸法　fumigation
熏蒸室/熏蒸室　fumigation room
旬间装车计划/旬裝車計劃　ten day car loading plan
寻的导弹反干扰/自動歸向飛彈抗干擾　homing missile ECCM
寻的制导/歸向導引,追蹤導引　homing guidance
寻位/定位　locating, position fix, positioning
寻位信号/定位信號　locating signal
寻位与归航信号/定位與導向信號　locating and homing signals
巡道工/軌道檢查員　track walker, track patrolling man
巡道工无线电通信/軌道檢查員無線電通訊　radio communication for track walker
巡航/巡航,巡弋　cruise
巡航编队与部署/巡航編隊與序列　cruising formation and disposition
巡航工况管理/巡航操作形式管理　cruising operating mode management
巡航机组/巡航機組　cruising engine unit
巡航速度/巡航速率,巡航船速　cruising speed
巡航涡轮机/巡航渦輪機　cruising turbine
巡回监测器/圓轉偵測器　circular monitor
巡回养护/巡迴養護　patrol maintenance
巡逻船/巡邏艇　patrol boat
巡逻艇信号/巡邏艇信號　patrol boat signal
巡视检查/巡視檢查　walkaround inspection
巡洋舰/巡洋艦　cruiser
巡洋舰[型]艉/巡洋艦型艉　cruiser stern
询问脉冲/訊問脈衝　interrogation pulse
询问模式/詢問模式　interrogation mode
循环/循環,週　cycle
循环泵/循環泵,環流泵　circulating pump
循环比/回流比　recirculation ratio
循环床锅炉/循環液化床鍋爐　circulating fluidized bed boiler
循环代偿障碍/循環代償失調　circulatory decompensation
循环挡板/循環隔板　circulating baffle plate
循环调度法/循環調度法　cyclic dispatching method
循环柜/循環櫃　circulating tank
循环滑油舱/循環[潤]滑油櫃　circulating lubrication oil tank
循环滑油柜/循環[潤]滑油櫃　circulating lubrication oil tank
循环给水系统/再循環水系統　recirculation water system
循环检查制/循環檢查制　cyclic scanning system
循环检验/連續檢驗　continuous survey
循环交路/循環交路　loop routing
循环经济园区/循環經濟園區　circular economy park
循环冷却水系统/循環冷卻水系統　recirculating cooling water system
循环冷却系统/循環冷卻系統　circulation cooling system
循环流化床锅炉/循環液化床鍋爐　circulating fluidized bed boiler
循环码/循環碼　cyclic code

循环码副帧同步/循環碼副幀同步　cyclic code subframe synchronization
循环冗余检验/循環冗餘檢測　cyclic redundancy check, CRC
循环润滑/環流潤滑　circulating lubrication
循环时间/循環時間,週期時間　cycle time
循环寿命/循環壽命,週期壽命　cycle life
循环水倍率/循環水率　circulating water ratio
循环水槽/環流水槽,回流水槽　circulating water tank, circulating water channel, circulating tank
循环水量/循環流　circulating flow
循环直达列车/循環直達列車　shuttled block train
循环周期/循環週期　circulating period
循环作业量测定/循環作業量測定　determination of operating cycle production quantity
循证设计/循證設計　evidence-based design
训练池/訓練池　training pool
训练船/訓練船　training vessel, training ship
训练飞行/訓練飛行　training flight
训练馆/練習館　practice hall
训练手册/訓練手冊　training manual, training handbook
训练塔/訓練塔　training tower
训练综合评定/訓練綜合評估　training comprehensive evaluation
迅速减压/快速減壓　rapid decompression
驯化/馴化,馴養　domestication

Y

压板/平臺板　holding plate, platen
压比/壓力比　pressure ratio
压槽/壓槽　rolling groove
压差变换器/壓差指示器　differential pressure conditioner
压差传感器/壓差傳感器　differential pressure transducer
压差液面计/壓差液位指示器　differential pressure liquid level indicator
压差阻力/壓力阻抗　pressure drag
压电机构/壓電裝置　piezoelectric device
压电式传感器/壓電式感測器　piezoelectric transducer
压电式加速度计/壓電式加速度計　piezoelectric accelerometer
压电式天平/壓電式平衡儀　piezoelectric type balance
压电效应/壓電效應　piezoelectric effect
压电引信/壓電引信　piezoelectric fuze
压顶/頂石,封頂　coping, capping
压顶板/横支材　capping piece
压舵/壓舵,整流舵　counter rudder
压杆/壓桿,受壓鋼筋　turn the control wheel, compression bar
压感侦车器/壓觸式車輛感知器　pressure-sensitive vehicle detector
压钩坡/壓鉤坡　coupler compression grade, coupler compressing grade
压焊/壓焊,壓接　pressure welding
压痕/壓痕　indentation
压花玻璃/壓花玻璃　patterned glass
压花地坪/壓花地坪　embossed floor
压浆/壓漿　mud jacking
压浆泵/壓漿泵　mudjack
压紧板/押板　keep plate
压紧装置/捏縮裝置　pinch device
压坑式推力室/壓坑式推力室　indented thrust chamber
压块/壓料塊　pressing block
压溃荷载/崩壞載重　collapse load
压扩/壓縮擴展　companding

压扩律/壓擴律　companding law
压拉双作用预应力/壓拉雙作用預應力　prestressing with subsequent compression and tension
压力比表/壓力比表　pressure ratio gage
压力表/壓力計　pressure gage
压力舱/加壓艙室　pressurized module
压力传感器/壓力傳感器,壓力轉換器,壓力感應器　pressure transducer, pressure sensor, pressure transmitter
压力法/壓力法　pressure method
压力分布/壓力分布　pressure distribution
压力分布试验/壓力分布試驗　pressure distribution test
压力风缸/壓力箱　pressure reservoir
压力缸/壓力圓筒　pressure cylinder
压力管/壓力管　pressure pipe, pressure tube
压力管道水压试验/壓力管道水壓強度　water pressure test for pressure pipeline
压力盒/壓力盒,壓力計,壓力盤　pressure cell
压力级/壓力級　pressure stage
压力计/壓力計　pressure gage
压力继电器/壓力繼電器　pressure relay
压力加油/壓力加油　pressure refueling
压力空隙比曲线/壓力孔隙比曲線　pressure-void ratio curve
压力控制阀/壓力控制閥　pressure control valve
压力控制分系统/壓力控制子系統　pressure control subsystem
压力流/湧泉流　artesian flow
压力流雨水排水系统/壓力流雨水排水系統,虹吸式屋面雨水排水系統　full pressure storm water system
压力平衡阀/壓力平衡閥　pressure balance valve
压力气化煤气/加壓煤氣　pressurized gas
压力区/壓力區　pressure zone
压力容器/壓力容器,壓力槽　pressure vessel
压力升高比/昇壓速度　pressure step-up ratio, rate of pressure rise
压力式波高计/壓力式波高計　pressure type wavemeter
压力式涵洞/壓力[式]涵洞　outlet submerged

culvert, pressure culvert
压力试验/壓力試驗 pressure test
压力室/壓力室 pressure chamber
压力输水管/壓力輸水道 pressure aqueduct
压力水柜/壓力水櫃 water pressure tank
压力探测仪/壓力測深器 pressure sounder
压力通风/强制通風 forced draught
压力图/壓力表 pressure chart
压力系数/壓力係數 pressure coefficient
压力线/壓力線 pressure line
压力响应因子/壓力反應因子 pressure response factor
压力引信/壓力引信 pressure fuze
压力折减系数/壓力折減係數 operating pressure derating coefficient for various operating temperature
压力真空切断阀/壓力真空斷路器 pressure and vacuum breaker
压力中心/壓力中心 pressure center, center of pressure
压力-重力式滑油系统/重力進給潤滑系統 gravity forced-feed oiling system
压力注油防腐法/壓力注油防腐法 pressure creosoting
压力铸造/壓鑄,模鑄 die casting, pressure die casting
压路机/壓路機,壓路滾軸 roller, road roller
压滤/壓濾 filter pressing
压滤机/壓濾機 filter press
压铆/壓鉚接 press riveting
压铆机/擠壓鉚釘器 squeeze riveter
压铆系数/壓縮鉚接係數 coefficient of squeezed riveting
压密注浆/擠壓灌漿工法 compaction grouting
压敏漆/壓力感測塗料 pressure sensitive paint
压气机/壓縮機,壓縮器 compressor
压气机喘振试验/壓縮機顫動試驗 compressor surging test
压气机耗功/壓縮機功率輸入 power input to compressor
压气机机匣/壓縮機箱 compressor casing
压气机基元级/壓縮機元素級 compressor element stage
压气机流道/壓縮機流徑 compressor passage, compressor flow path
压气机特性/壓縮機特性 compressor characteristics
压气机叶轮/壓氣機葉輪 blower impeller
压气机增压比/壓縮機壓力比 compressor pressure ratio
压气机转子/壓縮機轉子 compressor rotor
压气浇置设备/壓氣澆置設備 pneumatic placing equipment
压气排水打捞/壓縮空氣排水浮昇 raising by dewatering with compressed air
压气式防波堤/壓氣防波堤 pneumatic breakwater
压气涡轮/壓縮汽輪機 compressor turbine
压汽式蒸馏装置/蒸汽壓縮蒸餾裝置 vapor compression distillation plant
压强/壓力[強度] pressure
压强计/壓力計,壓力表,測壓計 manometer
压强温度敏感系数/壓力溫度靈敏度 temperature sensitivity of pressure
压强系数/壓力係數 pressure coefficient
压强总冲/總壓力衝量 total pressure impulse
压曲/壓曲,屈曲 buckling
压曲临界荷载/彎折載重 crippling load
压曲系数/屈曲係數 buckling coefficient
压屈系数/屈曲係數 buckling coefficient
压燃式发动机/壓燃式引擎 self-ignition engine
压入式通风/壓入式通風 blowing system of ventilation
压入桩/頂入樁 jacked pile
压射冲头/柱塞,活塞 plunger, injection piston
压实/壓實,夯實 compaction
压实标准/壓實標準 compacting criteria
压实度/壓實[程]度 degree of compaction
压实度试验/壓實試驗 compactness test
压实度自动检测装置/壓實度自動檢測裝置 automatic compactometer
压实厚度/壓實厚度 compaction depth
压实机械试验/壓實機械試驗 compaction machine test
压实宽度测定/壓實寬度測定 compacting width measurement
压实能量/壓實能量 compaction energy
压实设备/夯實設備,夯實用具 compaction equipment, compacting equipment
压实深度测定/壓實深度測定 compacting depth measurement
压实水/壓縮水 water of compaction
压实速度测定/壓實速度測定 rolling speed measurement
压实系数/密實係數,壓實因數,夯實因數 compacting factor, compacting coefficient, compaction factor
压实性/夯實性 compactibility

压实因数试验/夯實因數試驗 compacting factor test
压式水阀/壓縮龍頭 compression faucet
压水试验/壓水試驗,地層滲透試驗 water head test, packer test
压送式拌和机/壓送式拌和機 canif-mixer
压碎值/壓碎值 crushing value
压碎值试验/壓碎值試驗 crushing value test
压缩/壓縮 compression
压缩比/壓縮比 compression ratio
压缩波/壓縮波 compression wave
压缩多变指数/壓縮多方指數 polytropic index of compression
压缩[固结]试验/壓縮[固結]試驗 compression consolidation test, compression test
压缩过程/壓縮過程 compression process
压缩环/壓縮脹圈 compression ring
压缩混凝土桩/壓縮混凝土樁 pressure concrete pile
压缩机/壓縮機,壓縮器 compressor
压缩机油/壓縮機油 compressor oil
压缩空气病/壓縮空氣病 compressed air sickness
压缩空气打桩机/壓縮空氣打樁機 compressed air pile driver
压缩空气机车/壓縮空氣機車 compressed air locomotive
压缩空气起动系统/壓縮空氣起動系統 compression air starting system
压缩空气设备全面的气密性试验/壓縮空氣設備全面的氣密性試驗 test for over-all air-tightness of compressed air equipment
压缩空气站/壓縮空氣站 compressed air station
压缩空气振动器/壓氣振動器 compressed air vibrator
压缩力/壓[縮]力 compressive force
压缩模量/壓縮模量 constrained modulus
压缩欺骗干扰/壓縮欺騙式干擾 compression deception jamming
压缩气体/壓縮氣體 compressed gas
压缩气体反作用控制系统/壓縮氣體反作用控制系統 pressurized-gas reaction control system
压缩始点温度/壓縮初溫 compression beginning temperature
压缩始点压力/壓縮始點壓力 compression beginning pressure
压缩式冷水机组/壓縮式水冷卻器 compression-type water chiller
压缩试验/壓縮試驗,耐壓試驗,抗壓試驗 compression test

压缩室容积/壓縮室容積 compression chamber volume
压缩天然气/壓縮天然氣 compressed natural gas
压缩天然气加气站/壓縮天然氣加氣站,壓縮天然氣燃料供應站 compressed natural gas fueling station, CNG fueling station
压缩图/壓縮圖 compression diagram
压缩系数/壓縮係數 coefficient of compressibility
压缩行程/壓縮衝程 compression stroke
压缩性/[可]壓縮性 compressibility
压缩性修正量/壓縮修正 compressibility correction
压缩压力/壓縮壓力 compression pressure
压缩压力计/壓縮計 compression gage
压缩载荷/壓縮載重 compressive load
压缩终点温度/壓縮終端溫差 compression terminal temperature
压缩终点压力/壓縮終點壓力 compression terminal pressure
压条/壓條 layering, planting by layer
压条繁殖/堆壓法 mound layering
压[弯]梁机/彎樑器 beam bender
压向下风/乘風而駛,乘風而馳 drive
压心系数/壓心係數 center of pressure coefficient
压型钢板/壓型鋼板,異型鋼板 profiled steel sheet
压檐木/橫支材 capping piece
压油机/機力注油器 mechanical lubricator
压载/壓載,壓艙 ballast, ballasting
压载泵/壓載[水]泵,壓艙[水]泵 ballast pump
压载舱漆/壓載艙漆 ballast tank paint
压载水/壓載水,壓艙水 ballast water
压载[水]舱/壓載艙 ballast tank, ballast water tank
压载水系统/壓艙水系統 ballast system, ballasting system
压载水总管/壓載管路 ballast line, ballast main line
压载状态/壓載船況 ballast condition
压桩机/壓樁機 pile press machine
压阻加速度计/壓[電電]阻加速度計 piezoresistor accelerometer, piezoresistive accelerometer
压阻力/壓阻力 pressure resistance
押运/護航 escorting
垭口/埡[口],隘[口],坳[口] pass
鸭式布局/前翼構型 canard configuration
鸭式飞机/前翼型飛機 canard airplane
芽变/芽變,芽條變異 bud sport, bud mutation
芽变选种/芽變選種 selection of bud sport
芽插/芽插 bud cutting
芽接/芽接 bud grafting
崖/[懸]崖 cliff

崖锥/崖錐 talus cone
衙署/衙署 government office, yashu
哑点/零點,無效點,消盡點 null point
哑控/静音 muting
哑罗经/啞羅經 dumb card compass, pelorus
雅典宪章/雅典憲章 Charter of Athens
亚表土层测探法/地下測定 subsurface sounding
亚单元/次級單位 subunit
亚钢管/亞鋼管 semisteel pipe
亚高山带/亞高山帶 subalpine zone
亚克力板/壓克力 acrylic
亚区/次[區]域 subregion
亚山地带/山麓地帶 submontane zone
亚声速风洞/次音速風洞 subsonic wind tunnel
亚声速后缘/次音速後緣 subsonic trailing edge
亚声速流/次音速流 subsonic flow
亚声速前缘/次音速前緣 subsonic leading edge
亚述建筑/亞述建築 Assyrian architecture
亚音速/次音速 subsonic velocity
亚种/亞種 subspecies
亚种群/亞族群 subpopulation
氩弧焊/氩弧焊接,氩[氣電弧]焊 argon-arc welding
咽喉道岔/咽喉道岔 throat point
咽喉区长度/喉道長度 throat length
咽喉信号机/咽喉信號機 signal in throat section
烟/煙 fume
烟草厂/卷煙廠 tobacco factory
烟尘初始排放浓度/煙塵初始排放濃度 smoke density at end of boiler unit
烟尘排放浓度/煙密度 smoke density
烟尘污染/爐煙塵汙染 smoke dust pollution
烟囱/煙囪 chimney, stack
烟囱标记/煙囪標記 funnel mark
烟囱漆/煙囪漆 funnel paint
烟道/煙道 flue, gas pass
烟斗形通风筒/煙斗形通風筒 cowl head ventilator
烟度/煙度 limit of smoke
烟度排放标准/煙排放標準 smoke emission standard
烟风洞/煙風洞 smoke wind tunnel
烟管/煙管 smoke tube
烟害/煙害 smoke pollution, fume pollution, injury from smoke
烟灰沉积物/煙灰沈積物 soot deposit
烟灰着火/煙灰著火 soot fire
烟火信号/煙火信號 pyrotechnic signal
烟迹式烟度计/濾紙測煙計 Bosch filter paper smoke meter
烟盔/防煙盔 smoke helmet
烟粒/油煙,煙灰 soot
烟流法/煙流法 smoke flow method
烟幕/煙幕 smokescreen
烟浓度/煙幕濃度 smoke concentration
烟气/煙[霧] smoke
烟气分析/煙道氣分析,氣體分析 flue gas analysis, gas analysis
烟气露点/煙[道]氣露點 flue gas dew point
烟气排放连续监测/連續性煙道排氣監測 continuous emission monitoring
烟气排放在线监测/連續性煙道排氣監測 continuous emission monitoring
烟气脱氮/煙氣脫氮,煙氣脫硝 flue gas denitrification, NOx removal from flue gas
烟气脱硝技术/煙氣脫硝,煙氣脫氮 flue gas denitrification, NOx removal from flue gas
烟雾/煙[霧] smoke
烟箱/煙箱 smokebox
烟箱大门/煙箱前端 smokebox front
烟箱管板/煙箱管板 smokebox tube sheet
烟箱小门/煙箱門 smokebox door
烟叶烘房/煙葉烘房,烤煙房 tobacco oast house
淹灌/淹灌 flood irrigation
淹没/泛濫,淹水 submergence
淹没丁坝/淹沒丁壩 submerged spur dike
淹没陆地/淹水地 submerged land
淹没面积/氾濫區,泛濫面積 flooded area, inundated area
淹水地区/淹水區 inundated district
延长杆/伸長桿 extension rod
延迟/延遲,延時 delay
延迟爆破/延遲爆破 delay blasting
延迟电气雷管/延遲電雷管 delay electric blasting cap
延迟交货/延遲交貨 delay in delivery
延迟开航/延遲發航 delay of ship
延迟裂纹/延遲龜裂 delayed cracking, delayed crack
延迟时间/時間延遲,時滯,滯留時間 time lag, detention period
延迟性修正量/延遲補正 lag correction
延度/延度,延性 ductility
延度试验/延性試驗 ductility test
延发雷管/延遲引發雷管 delay-action detonator
延期/延期 extension of time, extension of time for completion
延期回扣制/延期回扣制度 deferred rebate system
延期违约偿金/違約罰金 liquidated damages

延伸报警/延伸警報　extension alarm
延伸海事声明/海事後續報告,補充海事報告　extended protest
延伸喷管/加長噴嘴　extendible nozzle
延伸线/延長線,標線　extension line
延伸轴/延伸軸　extension shaft
延绳钓/延繩釣,長繩釣　long line
延时电路/延時電路　time delay circuit
延时机构/延遲機構　delay mechanism
延时样本/延時樣本　time-extension sample
延时遥测/延時遥測　delayed telemetry
延时引爆/延遲引爆　delayed exploding
延时指令/延遲指令　delayed command
延寿/壽命延長　lifetime extension
延误/延誤　delay
延误时间/延遲時間　delay time
延性/延性,延度　ductility
延性材料/延性材料　ductile material
延性破坏/延性破壞　ductile failure
延续进路/延續進路　successive route
延滞费/延滯費,滯船費　demurrage
I$_a$严格自然保护区/I$_a$嚴格自然保護區　I$_a$-strict nature reserve
严寒地区/大寒帶　severe cold zone
严酷度/嚴重性　severity
严密性试验/氣密試驗　airtightness test, gastightness test
严重故障/嚴重故障　major failure
严重破坏/嚴重破壞　severe damage
岩爆/岩爆,炸石　rock burst
岩崩/墜石　fall rock
岩层/岩層　rock stratum
岩洞类/岩洞類　caves type
岩堆/崖錐,落石堆　talus
岩堆地段路基/岩堆地段路基　subgrade in rock deposit zone, subgrade in talus zone, subgrade in scree zone
岩缝泉/岩縫泉　joint spring
岩缝填充物/岩縫添加料　joint filling material
岩浆岩/岩漿岩　magmatic rock
岩块填料/岩塊填料　rock block filler, rock filler
岩棉/岩綿　rock wool
岩溶水文学/石灰岩區水文學　karst hydrology
岩生花卉/岩生花卉　rock flower
岩生植物/岩生植物　lithophyte, rock plant
岩石/岩[石]　rock
岩石层/岩界,岩圈　lithosphere
岩石单轴饱和抗压强度/岩石飽和單軸抗壓強度　uniaxial saturated compressive strength of rock
岩石[分布]图/岩石地質圖　solid map
岩石基础/岩石基礎　rock foundation
岩石坚硬程度/岩石堅硬度　hardness degree of rock
岩石路基/岩石地基　rock subgrade
岩石圈/岩圈,岩界　lithosphere
岩石隧道/岩石隧道　tunnel in rock, rock tunnel
岩石学/岩石學　petrography
岩石压力/岩石壓力　rock pressure
岩石应力量测/岩體應力測量　rock stress measurement
岩石园/岩石園,岩石庭院,假山花園　rock garden
岩体基本质量/岩體基本品質　rock mass basic quality
岩体力学/岩石力學　rock mechanics
岩体完整程度/岩體完整度　rock mass completeness
岩土工程分级/地工分級　categorization of geotechnical project
岩土工程勘察/土質調查　soil survey, geotechnical investigation
岩土工程学/大地工程　geotechnical engineering
岩土力学/地工技術　geotechnique
岩土特性指标试验/土質特性指標試驗　geotechnical index property test
岩相/岩相　lithofacies, rock facies
岩屑堆积/岩錐堆積土　talus deposit
岩屑锥/崖錐　talus cone
岩心/岩心,石心　core
岩心采取率/岩心採取率　percentage of coring
岩心取样/岩心樣本　core sample
岩心取样器/岩心取樣器　core sampler
岩心提断器/岩心採取器　core catcher
岩心钻机/岩心鑽探機　core boring machine
岩柱/礁柱　rock pillar
岩锥堆积土/岩錐堆積土　talus deposit
沿岸标/沿岸標誌　alongshore mark
沿岸冰带/冰總　ice fringe
沿岸测量/沿岸測量　coastwise survey
沿岸地形/沿岸地形　coastal feature
沿岸航行/沿岸航行　coastal navigation, coastal trip
沿岸警告/沿海警告　coastal warning
沿岸流/沿岸流　littoral current, coastal current
沿岸漂流物/沿岸漂流物　littoral transport
沿岸漂沙/海岸漂砂　beach drift
沿岸沙洲/沿岸砂洲　longshore bar
沿岸通航带/沿岸通航區　inshore traffic zone
沿岸图/沿岸海圖,沿海海圖　coastal chart
沿[海]岸沉积/沿岸沈積物　littoral deposit

沿海船/沿海船,沿岸航行船　coasting service vessel, coaster vessel, coaster
沿海地区/海岸區,沿岸區　coastal area
沿海防护林/海岸保安林　coast protection forest
沿海航行/近岸航行　coastwise navigation, coastal trip
沿海航运/沿海航運,沿海貿易　cabotage
沿海航运权/沿海航運權　right cabotage
沿海路线/沿海航路　coastal route
沿海平原/沿海平原　coastal plain
沿路载货区/路緣載貨區　curb loading zone
沿溪线/谷線　valley line
沿线走行公里/沿線走行公里　running kilometer on the road
研究工作室/研究工作室　research studio
研究机/研究用飛機　research aircraft
研究型城市设计/研究型都市設計　research oriented urban design
研究性试飞/研究試飛　research flight test
研究性试验/研究性試驗　research test, investigation test
研究中心/研究中心　research center
研磨/研磨,研光　lapping
研制试验/發展測試　development test
盐厂/［製］鹽廠　salt works
盐度/鹽度,含鹽量　brine density, salinity
盐度计/鹽度計,鹽分計　salinometer
盐分法/鹽液法　salt-solution method
盐分平衡/鹽分均衡　salt balance
盐分污染/鹽分汙染　saline contamination
盐分指标/鹽分指數　salt index
盐害/鹽害,鹽分失調　salt stress, salt injury
盐碱化/鹼土化　salinization
盐碱土/鹽鹼土　saline-alkali soil
盐劈［作用］/鹽水楔　salt wedge
盐侵蚀/鹽蝕　salt corrosion
盐泉/鹽水泉　saline spring
盐生群落/鹽水群集　salt community
盐生植物/鹽土植物　halophyte
盐蚀模拟试验/鹽霧模擬試驗　salt-fog simulated test
盐水泵/鹽水泵,鹵水泵　brine pump
盐水腐蚀/鹽水腐蝕　salt water corrosion
盐水浓度法/鹽液法　salt-solution method
盐水入侵/鹽水侵害　salt water encroachment
盐水体系/鹽水管系統　salt water system
盐土/鹽土,白鹼土　solonchak
盐稳定土［壤］/鹽穩定土壤　salt stabilized soil

盐雾试验/鹽霧試驗　salt spray test
盐楔［作用］/鹽水楔　salt wedge
盐液测流法/鹽分法　saline method
盐胀/鹽脹　salt heaving
盐渍化岩石/鹽漬化岩石　saline rock
盐渍土地区路基/鹽漬土地區路基　subgrade in salty soil zone, subgrade in saline soil region
颜料/顏料　pigment
颜色适应性/顏色適應性　color adaptability
檐/檐　eave, yan
檐板/簷板　curtain plate
檐壁/檐壁　frieze
檐部/額枋簷飾　entablature
檐椽/檐椽　eave rafter, yanchuan
檐口/飛檐,屋檐　cornice, eaves
檐幕/檐幕　transverse curtain
檐柱/檐柱　eave column
衍射/繞射　diffraction
衍射光栅/繞射光柵　diffraction grating
衍射系数/繞射係數　diffraction coefficient
掩蔽/掩蔽,掩罩　masking
掩蔽锚地/安全錨地　protected anchorage
眼板/眼板　eye plate, pad eye
眼点/視點　eyepoint
眼高/眼高　height of eye
眼高差/眼高差　dip
眼高差改正/眼高差修正　dip correction
眼环/環板　ring plate
眼环［插］接/眼索接琵琶頭　eye splice
眼镜式开挖法/眼鏡型開挖隧道法　spectacle type tunnelling method
偃［偏垂］角/偃角　hade
演播室/播音室,播像室　studio
演示飞行/示範飛行,飛行表演　demonstration flight
演替/演替,消長　succession
演习区/演習區　exercise area, practice area
演员活门/舞臺暗坑門　flaps
厌氧法/厭氧法　anaerobic process
厌氧塘/厭氧塘　anaerobic pond
厌氧细菌/厭氧菌　anaerobic bacteria
厌氧消化/厭氧消化　anaerobic digestion
厌氧性废水处理/廢汙厭氧處理　anaerobic waste treatment
宴会厅/宴會廳　banquet hall, ballroom
宴会厅前厅/客廳,前室　anteroom
验槽/施工驗槽　examination of foundation pit excavated
验潮器/檢潮器,潮位計　tide gage

验潮仪/驗潮儀　tidal meter
验潮站/檢潮所　tide gage station
验船师/驗船師,檢驗師　surveyor
验道/驗道,路口查驗　road inspection
验货/買方檢查貨物,到貨驗收　inspection of goods
验收/驗收,接受,認可　acceptance, acceptance after inspection
验收记录/檢驗記錄　inspection record
验收试飞/驗收試飛　acceptance flight test
验收试验/驗收試驗,允收測試,接收測試　acceptance test
验收证书/驗收證明書　acceptance certificate
验算荷载/驗算荷載　check load, checking load
验线/驗線　inspection of property line
验证/驗證,檢定　verification
验证板/見證板　witness plate
验证机/驗證[發動]機　demonstration engine
验证性试验/驗證性試驗　proving test
燕尾槽/鳩尾槽　dovetail groove
燕尾榫/鳩尾榫　dovetail tenon
扬尘货/揚塵貨,粉狀貨　dusty cargo, dusty goods
扬弹机/彈藥昇降機　ammunition hoist
扬帆结/上桅揚帆結　topsail halyard bend
扬弃爆破/揚棄爆破　abandoned blasting, abandonment blasting
扬声电话机/揚聲電話機　loudspeaking telephone set
扬声调度单机/揚聲調度單機　dispatching loudspeaker set
扬声器/揚聲器,擴音器　loudspeaker
扬声器通信/揚聲器通信　loudspeaker signaling
扬水灌溉/抽水灌溉　lift irrigation
扬水站/揚水站　relift station
羊角/繫索扣　cleat
羊角碾/羊腳輥　taper-foot roller
羊足压路机/羊腳滾壓機　sheep-foot roller
阳[电]极/陽極　anode
阳光控制镀膜玻璃/陽光控制鍍膜玻璃　solar control coated glass
阳极保护/陽極防蝕,電鍍保護　anodic protection, sacrificial protection
阳极防腐/陽極防蝕　anodic protection
阳极[氧]化/陽極處理　anodizing
阳离子交换/陽離子置換量　cation exchange capacity
阳离子乳化沥青/陽離子乳化瀝青　cationic emulsified bitumen
阳畦/陽畦　local solar shed
阳伞效应/傘狀效應　umbrella effect
阳生植物/陽生植物　sun plant

阳台/陽臺　balcony
阳台绿化/陽臺綠化　balcony greening
阳性地被植物/陽性地被植物　positive ground cover plant
阳性植物/陽性植物　heliophyte, positive plant
杨氏模量/楊氏模數　Young modulus
洋葱头穹顶/洋蔥形圓頂　onion dome
洋风式/西式　foreign style
洋流/洋流　ocean current
洋流图/洋流[分布]圖　ocean current chart
洋区/洋區　ocean regions
洋区码/洋區碼　ocean region code
仰拱/仰拱　invert, inverted arch
仰焊位置/仰焊,仰姿　overhead position, overhead position of welding
仰极/仰極　elevated pole
仰极高度/仰極高度　polar altitude
仰角/仰角,高程　elevation
仰角单元/仰角引導單元　elevation unit
仰角误差/仰角誤差　elevation error
仰坡/前坡　front slope, overlaying slope
仰视景观/仰視景觀　upward landscape
养地作物/養地作物,益土作物　crop of improving soil fertility
养分/養分　nutrient
养分三要素/養分三要素　three essential nutrients
养分循环/營養循環,元素循環　nutrient cycle
养蜂室/養蜂場　bee house
养护薄膜/養護薄膜　curing membrane
养护池/養護槽　curing tank
养护对策/養護對策　maintenance counterproposal
养护费用/養護費,維修成本,保養成本　maintenance cost
养护工程/保養計劃　maintenance project
养护管理/維護管理　maintenance management
养护里程/養護里程　maintenance mileage
养护室/養護室　curing room, curing chamber
养护质量/維護品質　maintenance quality
养鸡场/家禽飼養場　poultry yard
养老院/老人養護中心,老人安養院　nursing home for senior
养路表报/養路表報　maintenance-of-way report and form, track work form
养路道班/養路班,養路工作人員　maintenance gang
养路电话/線路養護電話　track maintenance telephone
养路段/養路段,修護組　maintenance section, maintenance office

养路费/公路養路費　highway maintenance fee
养路工/養路道班工　trackman, machine operator, track mechanics
养路工区/養路工區,線路養護區　track maintenance section, permanent way gang
养路工长/線路領工員　track foreman
养路管理电脑系统/養路管理電腦系統　computer aided track maintenance and management system
养路领工区/養路領工區　track subdivision, track maintenance subdivision
养路领工员/養路領工員　track master, track supervisor
养路总段/養路組　maintenance division
养马场/養馬場　horse ranch
养禽场/家禽飼養所　poultry farm
养鱼场/養魚場　fish farm
氧饱和/飽和氧量　oxygen saturation
氧垂曲线/氧垂曲線　oxygen sag curve
氧分压/氧分壓　oxygen partial pressure
氧分压控制/氧分壓控制　oxygen partial pressure control
氧分压强/氧分壓　oxygen partial pressure
氧复合/氧複合　oxygen recombination
氧过多症/氧過剩　oxygen excess
氧化安定性/氧化穩定性　oxidation stability
氧化处理/氧化處理　oxidation treatment
氧化废水/氧化汙水　oxidized wastewater
氧化沟/氧化溝　oxidation ditch
氧化剂/氧化劑,氧化物質　oxidizing substance, oxidizer
氧化剂光电传感器/氧化劑光電感測器　oxidizer photoelectric sensor
氧化剂过滤器/氧化劑過濾器　oxidizer filter
氧化剂加注口/氧化劑加注導管　oxidizer filler
氧化剂加注口支架/氧化劑加注口支架　oxidizer filling port support mount
氧化剂加注连接器/氧化劑加載連接器　oxidizer loading connector
氧化剂加注软管/氧化劑加載軟管　oxidizer loading flexible hose
氧化剂加注系统/氧化劑加注系統　oxidizer loading system
氧化剂流量/氧化劑流率　oxidizer flow rate
氧化剂箱/氧化劑箱　oxidizer tank
氧化剂溢出连接器/氧化劑溢流連接器　oxidizer overflow connector
氧化剂溢出软管/氧化劑溢流軟管　oxidizer overflow flexible hose

氧化剂运输车/氧化劑搬運車　oxidizer transporter
氧化剂增压系统/氧化劑加壓系統　oxidizer pressurizing system
氧化沥青/氧化瀝青　oxidized asphalt
氧化率/氧化率　oxidation rate
氧化钛/氧化鈦　titanium oxide
氧化塘/氧化池　oxidation pond
氧化污泥/氧化汙泥　oxidized sludge
氧化焰/氧化焰　oxidizing flame
氧矛切割/氧吹管切割　oxygen lance cutting
氧气电弧切割/氧氣電弧截割　oxy-arc cutting
氧气呼吸器/氧氣呼吸器　oxygen breathing apparatus
氧气面罩/氧氣面罩　oxygen mask
氧气排放塔/氧氣排氣塔　gas oxygen exhaust tower
氧气示流器/氧氣流量指示器　oxygen flow indicator
氧气调节器/氧氣調節器　oxygen regulator
氧气系统/氧氣系統　oxygen system
氧气压力比/氧氣壓力比　oxygen pressure ratio
氧气余压/氧氣餘壓　oxygen overpressure
氧气余压表/氧氣餘壓表　oxygen overpressure indicator
氧气站/氧氣站　oxygen station
氧摄取率/攝氧速率　oxygen uptake rate
氧乙炔焊/氧乙炔焊接,氧乙炔熔接　oxy-acetylene welding
氧乙炔焰/氧乙炔焰　oxy-acetylene flame
氧债/氧債　oxygen debt
氧张力/氧氣分壓　oxygen tension
样板/樣板,型板,模板　template
样板房/樣板住宅　model house
样板工程/樣板工程　sample project
样本/樣本,樣品,試樣　sample
样本量/樣本數　sample size
样带/樣帶　belt transect
样带法/直線接觸種類鑒定記載法　line transect
样地/樣地,樣區　sample plot
样地记录[表]/群落匯總表　samples to record
样方/樣方　quadrat
样机试验/原型測試,原型試驗　prototype test
样品/樣品,試樣,樣本　sample
样品供给泵/樣品供給泵　sample feed pump
样条/條材　batten
样箱/模型打樣　mock-up
腰横缆/舯橫纜　waist breast
腰线/腰線　waist line
邀请招标/邀請招標　invitation tender, selective tendering, selective bidding

窑内干燥/爐乾　kiln drying, oven-dried
窑烧砖/磚窯　brick kiln
摇鞍/搖擺桿　swing rocker
摇摆火箭发动机/懸掛式火箭發動機　gimbaled rocket engine
摇摆漂移率/顫動漂移率　wobbling drift rate
摇摆软管/搖擺軟管　flexible hose assembly, gimbal bellows
摇摆筛/搖[動]篩　swinging screen
摇摆试验/橫搖試驗　rolling experiment, rolling test
摇摆误差/搖擺誤差　rolling error
摇臂式起落架/搖臂式起落架　levered suspension landing gear
摇杆/主桿　main rod
摇头振动/偏搖　yawing vibration, hunting vibration
摇枕挡/搖枕縱向擋　bolster guide
摇枕挡间隙/搖枕擋間隙　bogie bolster play
摇枕吊/承梁吊桿　bolster hanger, swing hanger
摇枕吊轴/擺動吊掛,索式懸吊　swing hanger cross beam
摇枕弹簧/承梁彈簧　bolster spring
摇轴支座/[橋架]搖軸支座,[桁架]伸縮支座　rocker bearing
摇桩/搖樁　vibrant pile
遥操作技术/遙操作　teleoperation
遥操作系统/遠程作業系統　remote operating system
遥测/遙測[術],電測　telemetry, remote measurement, remote metering
遥测标准/遙測標準　telemetry standards
遥测参数/遙傳參數　telemetry parameter, telemetered parameter, telemetered measurement
遥测大纲/遙測程式　telemetry program
遥测地面站/遙測地面站　telemetry earth station
遥测分系统/遙測子系統　telemetry subsystem
遥测供电控制系统/遙測供電控制系統　power supply control system for telemetering system
遥测和指令系统/遙測命令系統　telemetry and command system
遥测缓变参数/遙測緩變參數　slow variation telemetry parameter
遥测计算机字/遙測計算機字　telemetry computer word
遥测监视网/遙測監視網　telemetry and monitor network
遥测检测系统/遙測檢測系統　telemetry checkout system
遥测[接收]站/遙測接收站　telemetry receive station
遥测连续参数/連續遙測參數　continuous telemetry parameter
遥测脉冲参数/脈波遙測參數　pulse telemetry parameter
遥测前端/遙測前端　telemetry front end
遥测容量/遙測容量　telemetry capacity
遥测实施方案/遙測實施方案　telemetry implement plan
遥测试验[导]弹/遙測飛彈　telemetry missile, instrumented missile
遥测数据处理/遙測資料處理　telemetry data processing, telemetry data reduction
遥测速变参数/遙測速變參數　fast variation telemetry parameter
遥测外测数据时间零点对齐/遙測追蹤資料調零　telemetry and tracking data time zero alignment
遥测误差/遙測誤差　telemetry errors
遥测系统/遙測系統　telemetry system
遥测信号中断/遙測訊號消失　telemetering signal blackout
遥测信息/遙測資訊　telemetry information
遥测[信息]仿真/遙測模擬　telemetry information simulation
遥测引信/遙測引信　telemetry fuze
遥测站/遙測臺站　telemetry station
PC遥测站/個人電腦遙測臺站　personal computer telemetry station
遥测指令参数/遙測指令參數　event telemetry parameter
遥测字符/遙測符號　telemetry symbol
遥感/遙[感探]測　remote sensing
遥感地面接收站/遙測地面接收站　ground station of remote sensing
遥感分系统/遙測分系統　remote sensing subsystem
遥感技术/遙感技術　remote sensing technique
遥感平台/遙感平臺　platform for remote sensing
遥感器/遙感器,遙測器　remote sensor
遥感数据处理中心/遙測資料處理中心　data processing center of remote sensing
遥感图像/遙測圖像　remote sensing picture
遥感卫星/遙感衛星　remote sensing satellite
遥感相机/遙測相機　remote sensing camera
遥感影像/遙感探測影像　remote sensing image
遥控/遙控,遠方指揮,遙[遠命]令　telecontrol, telecommand, remote control
遥控飞行器/遙控載具　remotely piloted vehicle
遥控分控台/遙控副控臺　telecommand sub-console
遥控分系统/遙控子系統　telecommand subsystem

遥控混凝土喷射机/遥控喷射　robot spray
遥控机器人/遠程機器人　telerobot
遥控机械手/遥控操動器　teleoperator
遥控区段/遥控區段　remotely controlled section
遥控扫雷航海勤务/遥控掃雷航海勤務　remote control mine-sweeping navigation service
遥控设备/遥控設備　telecommand equipment
遥控水雷/遥控水雷　remote-controlled mine
遥控调焦/遥控調焦　remote focusing
遥控系统/指揮與管制系統,命令與控制系統　command and control system
遥控异常报警/遥控異常警報　remote control abnormal alarm
遥控站/遥控站　command and control station, telecommand station
遥控指令/遥控指令　telecommand
遥控终端/遥控終端　telecommand terminal
遥控主控台/遥控主控制臺　telecommand master console
遥控转发/遥控轉發　telecontrol repeat
遥控装定/遠程設置　remote setting
遥调/遥調　remote regulation
遥现技术/遥現　telepresence
遥信/遥控監視　remote surveillance
遥信区段/遥信區段　remote surveillance section
遥医学/遠距醫療　telemedicine
咬边/過熔低陷　undercut
咬缸/咬缸,[氣]缸膠著　cylinder sticking, piston seizure
咬口缝/端折咬合,卷邊接縫　lock seam
咬黏/黏著　seizure
咬入角/碎石機顎角　angle of nip
药房/藥房,藥局　pharmacy
药壶爆破/藥壺爆破　pot hole blasting
药剂泵/複式泵　compound pump
药剂科/藥劑科,藥劑部　pharmacy department
药库/藥庫　medicine store
药品检验所/藥品檢驗所　drug control department
药芯焊丝/含焊劑芯焊線,複合焊線　flux-combined wire, flux-cored wire
药用植物/藥用植物　medicinal plant, pharmaceutical plant
药用植物园/芳草園　herb garden
药柱燃烧速率/藥柱燃燒率　grain burning rate
药柱肉厚/藥柱厚度　grain web thickness
药柱通气面积/藥柱通氣面積　grain port area
要车计划表/要車計劃表　car planned requisition list
钥匙路签/鑰匙路簽　staff with a key

椰糠/椰糠　coir dust
冶金缺陷/冶金缺陷　metallurgical defect
冶炼车间/冶煉車間　smelting shop
野餐区/野餐區　picnic place
野花组合/野生花卉　wild flowers mix
野鸟喂食器/野鳥餵食器　bird feeder
野趣园/野趣園　wild plants botanical garden
野奢旅游/野奢旅遊　wild luxury travel
野生动物/野生動物　wildlife
野生动物保护区/野生動物保護區　wild animal refuge area
野生苗/野生植物　wilding
野生植物园/野生植物園　wild plants garden
野生种/野生種　wild species
野生种质资源/野生遺傳資源　wild genetic resources
野外持水量/田間持水量　field water retaining capacity
野外渗透系数/野外滲透係數　field coefficient of permeability
野外游憩用地/景觀遊憩用地　landscape restoration land
野营区/野營區　camp site
业务办公区/業務辦公區　business-office zone
业务代码/業務代碼　service code
业务公电/業務通知　service advice
业务衡准数/服勤基準數,管運標準數　criterion of service numeral
业务通信系统/業務通信系統,業務通訊系統　service communication system
业务信号/業務信號　service signal
业主/業主,所有權人　employer, owner, property owner
业主大会/業主大會　owner assembly
业主委员会/業主委員會　owner committee
叶背/葉背　back of blade
叶插/葉插　leaf cutting
叶端/葉端　blade end
叶端损失系数/葉端損失係數　root and tip loss factor
叶根/葉根　blade root
叶根空化/葉根空化　root cavitation
叶厚比/葉厚比　blade thickness ratio
叶尖漏泄损失/葉梢漏洩損失　tip-leakage loss
叶浆搅拌式沥青乳化机/葉槳攪拌式瀝青乳化機　paddle bitumen emulsifying machine
叶轮/葉輪　impeller, blade wheel
叶轮式粉碎机/衝擊式碎石機　impeller breaker
叶面参考线/葉片參考線　blade reference line

叶面积比/葉面積比　leaf area ratio, LAR
叶面积指数/葉面積指數　leaf area index, LAI
叶面空化/螺槳葉正面空化　face cavitation
叶面喷肥/葉面施肥　foliar fertilization
叶面施肥/葉面施肥　foliage fertilization
叶面吸收/葉面吸收　foliar absorption
叶盘耦合振动/葉盤耦合振動　blade-disc coupling vibration
叶盘转子结构/槳盤轉子構形　blisk rotor configuration
叶片/葉片　blade, vane
叶片泵/轉葉泵　rotary vane pump, vane pump
叶片颤振/葉片顫振　blade flutter
[叶片]出口角/葉片出流角,輪葉出口角　blade outlet angle
叶片动频/葉片動頻　blade natural frequency under rotation
叶片高度/葉片高　blade height
叶片进口角/輪葉入口角,葉片入流角　blade inlet angle
叶片造型/葉片造型　blade profiling
叶片噪声/葉片噪音　blade noise
叶片阻尼凸台/葉片阻尼凸臺　part-span shroud of blade
叶频/葉頻　blade frequency
叶切面/葉片剖面　blade section
叶栅稠度/葉柵固性　cascade solidity
叶栅风洞/串聯葉片風洞　cascade wind tunnel
叶梢/葉尖　blade tip
叶梢空化/葉尖空化　tip cavitation
叶饰/葉理　foliation
叶素/葉片元素　blade element
叶形桁架/月牙形桁架　lenticular truss
叶型/葉型,翼剖面,葉片輪廓[剖面]　profile, blade profile
叶元体/葉片元素　blade element
叶元体理论/葉片元素理論　blade element theory
页岩/頁岩　shale
页岩沥青/頁岩瀝青,頁岩焦油　shale tar
曳纲/曳綱,曳繩,拖索　warp
曳纲滑轮/曳綱滑輪　warp block
曳光管/閃焰　flare
曳开桥/曳開橋　draw bridge
曳绳钓/曳繩鈎　troll line
曳绳钓起线机/曳繩鈎起繩機　trolling gurdy
曳绳钓渔船/曳繩鈎漁船　troller, trolling boat
曳网/地曳網　drag net
夜航命令簿/夜航命令簿　night order book
夜间飞行/夜航　night flight
夜间人口/夜間人口　night population, nighttime population
夜间施工噪声/夜間建築施工雜訊　night construction noise
夜间效应/夜間效應　night effect
夜间信号/夜間信號,夜標　night signal
夜景照明/夜景照明　nightscape lighting
夜视六分仪/夜視六分儀　night vision sextant
夜总会/夜總會　night club
液舱/液艙　liquid tank
液舱鉴定/液艙櫃檢查　inspection of tank
液氮加注补加车/液氮裝載補加車　liquid nitrogen loading and topping vehicle
液氮加注测控系统/液氮加注量測與控制系統　liquid nitrogen loading measuring and control system
液氮加注系统/液氮加注系統　liquid nitrogen loading system
液氮加注液路系统/液氮加注液路系統　liquid nitrogen loading liquid line system
液氮调试/液氮測驗　liquid nitrogen test
液氮系统/液氮系統　liquid nitrogen system
液氮用气系统/液氮分配系統　liquid nitrogen distribution system
液肥混合调配器/液肥混合調配器　liquid fertilizer mixer-proportioner
液浮摆式加速度计/液浮擺式加速度計,液浮擺式加速度儀　liquid floated pendulous accelerometer
液浮喷管/液承噴嘴　liquid bearing nozzle
液浮陀螺加速度计/液浮擺式積分陀螺加速度儀　floated PIGA
液浮陀螺仪/液浮陀螺儀,液體羅經,液浮迴轉儀　fluid compass, floated gyro, liquid floated gyroscope
液-固耦合动力学/液-固耦合動力學　fluid-structure interaction dynamics
液罐挂车/貯槽拖車　tank trailer
液罐货车/油槽[卡]車　tank truck
液化/液化[作用]　liquefaction
液化等级/液化等級　liquefaction category
液化可燃性气体/液化可燃氣　liquefied flammable gas
液化气船/液化氣體船　liquefied gas carrier
液化气体/液化氣體　liquefied gas
液化石油气/液化石油氣　liquefied petroleum gas, LPG
液化石油气舱/液化石油氣艙　liquefied petroleum

gas tank
液化石油气厂/液化石油氣儲配站 liquefied petroleum gas plant, LPG plant
液化石油气储存/液化石油氣儲存 LPG storage
液化石油气储配站/液化石油氣儲配站,液化石油氣氣化站 LPG vaporizing station, LPG distribution station
液化石油气船/液化石油氣船 liquefied petroleum gas carrier, LPG carrier
液化石油气供应/液化石油氣供應 LPG supply, distribution of LPG
液化石油气混气站/液化石油氣混氣站 liquefied petroleum gas-air mixing station
液化石油气气化站/液化石油氣氣化站 liquefied petroleum gas vaporizing station
液化石油气运输/液化石油氣運輸 LPG transportation
液化天然气/液化天然氣 liquefied chemical gas, liquefied natural gas, LNG
液化天然气舱/液化天然氣艙 liquefied natural gas tank
液化天然气储配站/壓縮天然氣儲配站 LNG stored and distribution station
液化天然气船/液化天然氣船 liquefied natural gas carrier, LNG carrier
液化指数/液化指數 liquefaction index
液化作用破坏/液化性破壞 liquefaction failure
液货/液狀貨 liquid cargo, fluid cargo
液货泵/液貨泵 liquid pump
液货船/液貨船 tanker, liquid cargo ship
液货船管系/液貨船管路系統 tanker piping system
液货阀/貨油閥 cargo oil valve
液晶法/液晶法 liquid crystal method
液晶显示屏/液晶顯示器 liquid crystal display, LCD
液控单向阀/液控止回閥 hydraulic control non-return valve
液冷服/液冷服 liquid-cooled suit, liquid cooling garment
液冷头盔/液冷頭盔 liquid-cooled helmet
液力变扭器/液壓扭矩變換器 hydraulic torque converter
液力传动/液壓傳動 hydraulic transmission
液力传动内燃机车/液壓傳動機車 diesel-hydraulic locomotive
液力传动系统/液力傳動系統 hydraulic transmission system
液力传动箱/液壓傳動機構,液力變速箱 hydraulic transmission gear box
液力换向传动箱/液力換向傳動箱 hydrodynamic reverser
液力机械传动/流體機械傳動 hydromechanical drive
液力耦合器/液壓耦合器 hydraulic coupler
液力气动式缓冲器/液壓氣動式緩衝器 hydropneumatic draft gear
液力循环元件/液壓機構 hydraulic unit
液力制动操纵阀/液力制動操作閥 hydrodynamic brake operating valve
液力制动阀/液力制動閥 hydrodynamic brake valve
液力制动器/液壓軔,液壓刹車,液力刹車 hydraulic brake
液密/液密 resistant to liquid, liquid-tight
液面负荷/表面載重 surface load
液面高度指示牌/液面高度指示牌 liquid level indicating plate, telltale
液面计/浮標觀測 float gauging
液氢氮配气台/液氫氮配氣臺 liquid hydrogen nitrogen gas distribution board
液氢加泄配气台/液氫進-出配氣臺 liquid hydrogen fill-drain gas distribution board
液氢加泄自动脱落连接器/液氫進-出自動脫落連接器 liquid hydrogen fill-drain auto-disconnect coupler
液氢加泄自动脱落连接器支架/液氫進-出自動脫落連接器支架 liquid hydrogen fill-drain auto-disconnect coupler support mount
液氢加注测控系统/液氫加載量測與控制系統 liquid hydrogen loading measuring and control system
液氢加注活门测试工作梯/液氫加載閥閥[門]工作梯 liquid hydrogen loading valve checking ladder
液氢加注监测系统/液氫加載監測系統 liquid hydrogen loading monitoring system
液氢加注控制机/液氫加載控制器 liquid hydrogen loading controller
液氢加注控制台/液氫加載控制臺 liquid hydrogen loading test-control desk
液氢加注连接器接头/液氫加載連接器接頭 liquid hydrogen loading connector fitting
液氢加注微机站/液氫加載微電腦站 liquid hydrogen loading microcomputer station
液氢加注系统/液氫加注系統 liquid hydrogen loading system
液氢加注液路系统/液氫加載液路系統 liquid hydrogen loading liquid line system

液氢铁路加注运输车/液氫鐵路裝載車　liquid hydrogen railway loading vehicle
液氢箱/液態氫槽　liquid hydrogen tank
液塑限联合测定仪/液塑限聯合測定儀　liquid plastic combine tester
液态/液態　liquid state
液态模锻/液態金屬鍛造　liquid metal forging, melted metal squeezing
液体比重/液體比重　specific gravity of liquid, specific weight of liquid
液体比重测定/液體比重測定　hydrometry
液体动力润滑/流體動力潤滑　hydrodynamic lubrication
液体晃动力学/液體晃動力學　liquid sloshing dynamics
液体晃动试验/液體晃動試驗　liquid sloshing test
液体晃动载荷/液體晃動載荷　liquid sloshing load
液体回路/流體回路　fluid loop
液体火箭推进剂/液體火箭推進劑　liquid rocket propellant
液体货物/液貨　liquid cargo
液体静力润滑/流體靜力潤滑　hydrostatic lubrication
液体静力水准仪/流體靜力水準器　hydrostatic leveling instrument
液体沥青/液態瀝青，膠狀瀝青　liquid asphalt
液体罗经/濕羅經　liquid compass
液体起动系统/液體啟動系統　liquid start system
液体润滑/液體潤滑　liquid lubrication
液体散货/液體散貨　liquid bulk cargo
液体推进剂/液體推進劑　liquid propellant
液体[推进剂]火箭发动机/液體[推進劑]火箭發動機　liquid propellant rocket engine
液体物质/液體物質　liquid substance
液体压载/液體壓艙物　liquid ballast
液体阻尼器/液體阻尼器　liquid damping vessel
Ⅰ液位/Ⅰ液位　1st liquid level
Ⅱ液位/Ⅱ液位　2nd liquid level
Ⅲ液位/Ⅲ液位　3rd liquid level
液位计/液位計　level gage
液涡轮/液渦輪　liquid turbine
液限/液限　liquid limit, LL
液限试验/液限試驗　liquid limit test
液相色谱仪/液體色譜儀　liquid chromatograph
液性限度/液性限度　liquid limit
液性指数/液性指數　liquidity index
液压泵/液力泵　hydraulic pump
液压比例自控系统/自動液壓比例系統　automatic hydraulic proportioning system
液压变矩器/液壓變矩器　hydraulic moment converter, hydraulic moment variator
液压变速[传动]装置/液力變速驅動裝置　hydraulic variable speed driver
液压舱盖/液壓艙口蓋　hydraulic hatch cover
液压操纵阀/液力操縱閥　hydraulic operated valve
液压操纵货油阀/液力操作液貨閥　hydraulic operated cargo valve
液压成形/液壓成形　hydraulic forming
液压传动/液壓傳動，液力傳動，液壓驅動　hydraulic transmission drive, hydraulic transmission, hydrostatic drive
液压传动泵/水動式抽水機　hydraulically driven pump
液压传动装置/液力傳動機構　hydraulic transmission gear
液压锤/液壓錘，液力錘　hydraulic hammer
液压打桩机/水壓式打樁機　hydraulic pile driver
液压捣固机/液壓搗固機，液壓砸道機，剳道機　hydraulic tamping machine
液压舵机/液壓操舵裝置　hydraulic steering engine, hydraulic actuator
液压发送器/液壓傳動器　hydraulic transmitter
液压防碰设备/油壓式防舷材　hydraulic fender
液压放大器/液壓放大器　hydraulic amplifier
液压附件集成/液壓附件整合　hydraulic accessory integration
液压复合舵机/集成液壓操舵裝置　integrated hydraulic actuator
液压缸/液壓缸　hydro cylinder
液压缓冲护栏/液壓緩衝護欄　hydraulic cushion guardrail
液压缓冲器/液力緩衝器　hydraulic buffer
液压换向阀/液力方向控制閥　hydraulic directional control valve
液压机/液壓機　hydraulic machine, hydraulic press
液压减速[传动]装置/液壓減速裝置　hydraulic reduction gear
液压减振器/液壓減振器　hydraulic damper
液压接头/液壓接頭　hydraulic joint
液压静力触探仪/液壓靜力觸探儀　hydraulic static cone penetrometer
液压卷扬机/水力噴射器　hydraulic ejector
液压控制/液壓操縱　hydraulic control
液压控制阀/液壓控制閥　hydraulic control valve
液压块/水壓臺　hydraulic block
液压拉延/液壓拉製　hydro-drawing, hydraulic

drawing
液压离合器/液壓離合器　hydraulic clutch, hydraulically controlled clutch, hydraulic friction clutch
液压联轴器/液壓聯結器　hydraulic coupling, oil injection coupling
液压密封/液壓密封　hydraulic seal
液压起货机/液壓起貨機　hydraulic cargo winch
液压气动式铆钉枪/壓氣釘鉚機　hydro-pneumatic riveter
液压刹车系统/液壓刹車系統　hydraulic brake system
液压上支撑/液壓上支撐　hydraulic top bracing
液压升降机/液壓昇降機,液力昇降機　hydraulic elevator
液压式缓冲器/液壓式緩衝器　hydraulic draft gear
液压式排气阀传动机构/液力致動排氣閥機構　hydraulically actuated exhaust valve mechanism
液压式调速器/液壓調速器,液力調速器　hydraulic governor
液压式张拉千斤顶/液壓拉伸千斤頂　hydraulic tensioning jack
液压式振动台/液壓振動產生器　hydraulic vibration generator
液压试验/液壓試驗　hydraulic pressure test
液压伺服阀/液力伺服閥　hydraulic servo valve
液压伺服马达/液力伺服馬達　hydraulic servomotor
液压松土器/油壓式分裂器　hydraulic ripper
液[压]锁/液壓鎖　hydraulic lock
液压锁闭装置/液力鎖閉設施　hydraulic blocking device
液压挖掘机/液壓挖掘機　hydraulic excavator
液压稳定器/液壓穩定器　hydraulic pressure stabilizer
液压系统/液壓系統　hydraulic system
液压-橡皮囊成形/液壓-橡膠隔膜成形　rubber-diaphragm hydraulic forming
液压蓄能器/液壓儲蓄器　hydraulic accumulator
液压压拔套管机/液壓壓拔套管機　hydraulic casing extractor
液压岩石破碎机/液壓岩石破碎機　hydraulic rock breaker
液压遥控传动装置/液壓遙控裝置　hydraulic telemotor
液压油柜/液壓油櫃　hydraulic oil tank
液压油滤/液壓油濾　hydraulic filter
液压[油]马达/液壓馬達　fluid motor, hydraulic motor
液压油箱/液壓油箱　hydraulic tank
液压余度控制/液壓縮減控制　hydraulic redundancy control
液压元件试验/液壓元件試驗　hydraulic element test
液压原动机/水力原動機　hydraulic prime mover
液压圆锥破碎机/油壓錐形碎石機　hydro-cone crusher
液压凿岩机/液壓鑿岩機　hydraulic jack hammer
液压执行机构/液力致動機構　hydraulic actuating gear
液压制动器/液壓軔,液壓刹車,液力刹車　hydraulic brake
液压致动机构/液壓致動裝置　hydraulic actuating unit
液压助力器/液壓增壓器,液力增壓器　hydraulic booster
液压桩头破碎器/液壓樁頭破碎器　hydraulic pile head splitter
液压自动找平装置/液壓自動平層裝置　hydraulic automatic leveling device
液氧/液[態]氧　liquid oxygen
液氧泵/液氧泵　liquid oxygen pump
液氧氮配气台/液氧氮分配系統　liquid oxygen nitrogen distribution board
液氧地面用气系统/液氧地面供氣系統　liquid oxygen ground gas distribution system
液氧固定贮罐/液氧儲存槽　liquid oxygen storage tank
液氧过冷器/液氧過冷器　liquid oxygen supercooler
液氧加泄配气台/液氧進-出氣分配系統　liquid oxygen fill-drain gas distribution board
液氧加泄自动脱落连接器/液氧進-出自動脫落連接器　liquid oxygen fill-drain auto-disconnect connector
液氧加泄自动脱落连接器支架/液氧進-出自動脫落連接器支架　liquid oxygen fill-drain auto-disconnect connector support mount
液氧加注补加车/液氧裝載補加車　liquid oxygen loading and topping truck
液氧加注测控系统/液氧加注量測與控制系統　liquid oxygen loading measuring and control system
液氧加注场地控制台/液氧加注場地控制臺　on-site liquid oxygen loading console
液氧加注控制机/液氧加注控制器　liquid oxygen loading controller
液氧加注控制台/液氧加注控制臺　liquid oxygen loading test-control desk

液氧加注连接器接头/液氧加載連接器接頭　liquid oxygen loading connector fitting
液氧加注系统/液氧加注系統　liquid oxygen loading system
液氧加注液路系统/液氧加注液路系統　liquid oxygen loading liquid line system
液氧煤油火箭发动机/液氧煤油火箭發動機　liquid oxygen-kerosene rocket engine
液氧箱/液態氧槽　liquid oxygen tank
液氧液氢火箭发动机/氫氧火箭發動機　liquid oxygen-liquid hydrogen rocket engine
液氧转换器/液態氧轉化器　liquid oxygen converter
一般冲刷/一般冲刷　general scour
一般符号/基本符號　general symbol, basic symbol
一般工业固体废物/一般工業固體廢物　general industrial solid waste
一般公路/普通公路　ordinary highway, mixed traffic highway
一般故障/輕微故障　minor failure
一般路基/一般路基　general subgrade, ordinary subgrade
一般漫射照明/一般擴散照明　general diffused lighting
一般闪光/一般閃光　ordinary flash
一般摄动/普通攝動　general perturbation
一般事故/一般事故　ordinary accident
一般条件/一般條件　general condition
一般通信/一般通信　general communication
[一般]显色指数/通用演色指數　general color rendering index
一般行包/一般行李　normal luggage
一般性检查/一般檢驗　general inspection
一般照明/一般照明　general lighting
一般镇/一般鎮　common town
一次拌成稳定土搅拌机/一次成型穩定土攪拌機　single pass soil stabilizer, single pass stabilized soil road mixer
一次泵冷水系统/冷激水系統　chilled water system
一次参数/一次參數　primary parameter
一次场/一次場　primary field
一次电池/一次電池[組],原電池[組]　primary battery
一次电池供电/一次電池供電　primary cell power supply
一次风/一次空氣,主空氣,初級空氣　primary air
一次惯性力/一次慣性力　the first order inertia force
一次回风/一次回風　primary return air
一次货物作业平均停留时间/一次貨物作業平均停留時間　average detention time of local car for loading or unloading
一次空气/一次空氣,主空氣,初級空氣　primary air
一次力矩补偿器/一次力矩補償器　the first order moment compensator
一次磨耗车轮/一次磨耗車輪　one-wear wheel
一次能源/初級能源　primary energy
一次配电系统/一次配電系統　primary distribution system
一次碰撞/初級碰撞　primary collision
一次屏蔽水系统/一次遮罩水系統　primary shield water system
一次屏障/主防壁　primary barrier
一次群/一次群　primary group
一次水/一次水　primary water
一次污染/一次汙染　primary pollution
一次污染物/初始汙染物,原生汙染物　primary pollutant
一次性返回器/一次性返回器　expendable recoverable capsule
一次性使用运载器/一次性使用運載火箭,消耗性發射載具　expendable launch vehicle
一次指令/一次指令　once command
一等三角测量/一等三角測量　first order triangulation
一等三角点/一等三角點　first order triangulation station
一等水准/一等水準[測量]　first order level, first order leveling
一等作图仪/一级作圖儀　first order plotting instrument
一点多址微波通信系统/點對多點微波系統　point-to-multipoint microwave system
一点锚/一字力錨　riding one-point anchors
一点透视/一點透視　one-point perspective
一二年生花卉/一二年生植物　annual and biennial plant
一股流/一股流　primary air
一挂/一掛　a hoist
一贯[测量]单位制/一致[測量]單位制　coherent system of unit of measurement
一贯导出测量单位/一致導出測量單位　coherent derived unit of measurement
一回路/一次回路　primary loop
一级半火箭/一级半火箭　one and a half stage rocket
一级保护区/一級保護區　the first class preservation district

一级泵/初始泵,主泵　primary pump
一级标准太阳电池/一級標準太陽電池　primary standard solar cell
一级处理/初級處理,初步處理　primary treatment
一级公路/一級公路　first-class highway
一级强化处理/強化一級處理　enhanced primary treatment
一级水手/一等水手　able-bodied seaman, AB
一级无线电电子证书/第一級無線電電子員證書　first-class radio electronic certificate
一级注册建筑师/一級註冊建築師　grade 1 registered architect
一阶段设计/一階段設計　one-step design, one-phase design
一阶矩/一次力矩　first moment
一年生花卉/一年生花卉　annuals
一年生植物/一年生植物　annual plant
[一批]货物/貨物　consignment
一切险/一切險,全險　all risks
一日游/一日遊　day tour
一送多受/一送多受　single feeding and multiple receiving track circuit
一体从板座/一體從板座　rear draft check casting
一体构架转向架/剛架轉向架　rigid frame truck
一天航程/一日行程　day run
一维定常管流/一維定常管流　one-dimensional steady channel flow
一维碰撞/一維衝撞　one dimension collision
一位侧/一位側　left side of car
一位端/一位端　B end of car
一系悬挂/單級懸掛　single stage suspension
一氧化碳监测仪/一氧化碳檢測器　carbon monoxide detector
一氧化碳允许浓度/一氧化碳容許濃度　carbon monoxide allowable concentration
一致性/符合性　conformity
一致性测试/符合測試　conformance testing
一字锚泊/一字雙錨泊　moor
一字双锚泊/雙錨繫泊　mooring to two anchors
一字形桥台/一字形橋臺,直線橋臺　head wall abutment, straight abutment
伊红次甲基蓝琼脂/曙紅亞甲藍培養劑　eosin-methylene-blue agar, EMB
伊丽莎白·莫伊尼汉的天堂/伊麗莎白·莫伊尼漢的天堂　Elizabeth Moynihan Paradise
伊利石/伊利石　illite
伊索拉·贝拉庄园/伊索拉·貝拉莊園　Villa Isola Bella

衣冠冢/衣冠冢　cenotaph
衣帽间/衣帽間　cloakroom
医疗/醫療　medical care
医疗车/診療車　hospital car
医疗电文/醫療信文　medical messages
医疗花园/醫療花園　healing gardens
医疗技术部/醫療技術部　medical technology department
医疗救护工程/醫療救護工程　medical aid engineering
医疗设备厂/醫療用品廠　medical appliance manufactory
医疗设备科/醫學工程科　medical engineering section
医疗卫生建筑/醫療大樓　medical building
医疗卫生用地/醫療衛生用地　medical and sanitary land use, land for health care
医疗援助/醫療協助　medical assistance
医疗运输/醫療運送　medical transport
医疗站/醫療救護站　medical station
医疗指导/醫療指導　medical advice
医务室/醫務室,診療所　medical premises, clinic
医学选拔/醫學選拔　medical selection
医用电梯/醫院用梯　hospital elevator
医用氧舱/醫用高壓氧艙　medical hyperbaric oxygen chamber, medical hyperbaric chamber pressurized with medical oxygen
医用氧气加压舱/醫用高壓氧艙　medical hyperbaric oxygen chamber, medical hyperbaric chamber pressurized with medical oxygen
医用中心供氧系统/醫用中心供氧系統　centralized oxygen-supply system
医用中心吸引系统/醫用中心吸引系統　centralized vacuum-supply system
医院/醫院　hospital
医院船/醫院船　hospital ship
医院街/醫院街　hospital street
医院污水/醫院汙水　hospital sewage
仪表板/控制臺,電子儀器座　console
仪表电路/儀器電路　instrument circuit
仪表飞行/儀器飛行,儀器飛航　instrument flight
仪表飞行规则/儀器飛航規則　instrument flight rules, IFR
仪表飞行规则的直线进近/儀表飛行直線進場　straight-in approach-IFR
仪表校正/儀器校正　instrument correction
仪表进近程序/儀器進場程式　instrument approach procedure, IAP

仪表精度/儀器準確度　instrument accuracy
仪表灵敏度/儀表靈敏度　instrument sensitivity
仪表跑道/儀器飛行跑道　instrument runway
仪表气象条件/儀器飛行氣象條件　instrument meteorological condition, IMC
仪表引航技术/盲目導航技術　blind pilotage techniques
仪表与照明分系统/儀表與照明分系統　instrumentation and illumination subsystem
仪表准确度/儀器準確度　instrument accuracy
仪表着陆系统/儀器降落系統　instrument landing system, ILS
仪表着陆系统关键区/儀錶著陸系統警戒區　instrument landing system critical area
仪表着陆系统基准高/ILS 參考空層高度　ILS reference datum height, ILS RDH
仪表着陆系统敏感区/ILS 敏感區　ILS sensitive area
仪器舱/儀器艙　instrument compartment, instrument module
仪器常数/儀器常數　instrument constant
仪器高/儀器高　instrument height
仪器高测法/儀器高測法　height of instrument method
仪器检查/儀器檢查　inspect by instrument
仪器仪表/儀表和儀器,儀器和裝置　instrument and apparatus
仪器仪表厂/儀表廠　instrument and meter factory
仪式广场/儀式廣場　ceremonial plaza
宜居城市/宜居都市　livable city
宜人试验/人員檢定試驗　man-rating test
移泊/移位　shifting
移测装置/移動量測裝置　movable measuring device
移车台/移車臺,遷車臺　traveling platform
移船锚/小移船錨,小錨,艉錨　kedge anchor
移点器/移點器,定心器,求新器　plumbing fork
移动/衝程　travel
移动备用方式/移動備用系統　movable reservation system
移动标志/移動標誌　portable sign
移动单元/行動單元　mobile unit
移动地球站/行動地球臺,行動衛星電臺　mobile earth station
移动地球站信息信道/行動地球臺資訊頻道　MES message channel
移动地球站状态/行動地球臺狀態　mobile earth station status
移动电台/移動電臺,機動電臺　mobile station
移动风域/移動風域　moving fetch
移动杠杆/移動槓桿　truck live lever
移动罐柜/可攜式櫃　portable tank
移动轨条/移動軌條　movable rail
移动绞机/移動絞機　shift winch
移动模架/移動模架　form traveler
移动配料机/移動灑水機　traveling distributor
移动牵引变电所/可動牽引變電站　movable traction substation
移动牵引变压器/可動牽引變壓器　movable traction transformer
移动式吊车/可動式吊車　mobile hoist
移动式辅燃气轮机/移動式輔燃氣[渦]輪機　mobile auxiliary gas turbine
移动式机器人/移動式機器人　mobile robot, locomotive robot
移动式洁净小室/清潔臺　clean booth
移动式沥青混合料搅拌设备/移動式瀝青攪拌站　mobile asphalt mixing plant
移动式沥青混合设备/移動式瀝青拌和機　portable asphalt plant
移动式联合碎石机组/移動式碎石廠　mobile crushing plant
移动式门架/活動式橋門臺架　traveling gantry
移动式模型/移動式模型　traveling form
移动式泡沫灭火系统/移動式泡沫滅火系統　mobile foam extinguishing system
移动式平台/移動式平臺　mobile platform, mobile unit
移动式破碎设备/移動式軋碎機　portable crushing plant
移动式起重机/移動式吊車,吊運車　traveler, portable crane
移动式稳定土厂拌设备/行動式穩定土廠拌站　mobile stabilized soil mixing plant
移动式压缩机/移動式空氣壓縮機　portable compressor
移动式装卸机械/移動式裝卸機械　mobile handling machinery
移动式钻井平台/移動式鑽探平臺,可動式鑽油臺　mobile drilling platform, mobile drilling unit
移动通信/移動通信,行動通信　mobile communication
移动通信基站/移動通信基站　cell site, mobile telecommunication base station
移动通信基站机房/移動通信基站房　mobile communication base station room
移动通信卫星/移動通訊衛星　mobile

communication satellite
移动微波通信/移動微波通信,移動微波通訊 mobile microwave communication
移动信号/移動信號 movable signal
移动性/機動性,可動性 mobility
移动业务/行動業務 mobile service
移动重量式减摇装置/多重式穩定器 moving-weight stabilizer
移交车/移交車 loaded cars to be delivered at junction stations
移交证书/接管證書 taking over certificate
移民/移民 immigration
移频电报/移頻電報 frequency shift telegraphy
移频轨道电路/移頻軌道電路 frequency shift modulated track circuit
移频自动闭塞/移頻自動閉塞 automatic block with audio frequency shift modulated track circuit
移位寄存器/移位暫存器 shift register
移线船位/移線定位,航進定位 running fix, RF
移相器组件/相移器組件 phase shifter package
移行装吊车/移行裝吊車 creeper crane
移栽/移植 transplant
移载法/移重法 shifting weight method
遗产地/遺產地 heritage site
遗产管理规划/遺產管理計劃 heritage management planning
遗产监测/遺產監測 heritage monitoring
遗产评估/遺產評估 assessment of heritage
遗产完整性/遺產完整性 integrity of heritage
遗产再利用/遺產再利用 heritage utilization, reuse
遗产真实性/遺產真實性 authenticity of heritage
遗传/遺傳 heredity
遗传变异/遺傳變異 genetic variation
遗传力/遺傳力,可遺傳性 heritability
遗传性状/遺傳性狀 genetic charactor
颐和园/頤和園 Yi-He Yuan Imperial Garden, Summer Palace
疑存/疑有 existence doubtful, ED
疑位/可疑位置 position doubtful, PD
乙级分隔/B級區 B class division
乙炔发生器/乙炔發生器 acetylene generator
乙炔站/乙炔站 acetylene station
乙烯基地坪涂料/乙烯基地坪塗料 ethylene base floor coating
已定位报警/經定位之警報 located alert
已修正结果/修正結果 corrected result
已装船提单/[已]裝船載貨證券 on board bill of lading, shipped bill of lading

以太网/乙太網路 Ethernet
椅/椅 chair
艺术插花/藝術插花 artistic flower arrangement
艺术地坪/藝術地坪 art paving
艺术价值/藝術價值 artistic value
艺术与工艺运动/藝術與工藝運動 arts and crafts movement
刈幅/刈幅 swath
议标/協議招標 negotiated tendering, negotiated bidding
异步/異步,非同步 asynchronous
异步传输/非同步傳輸 asynchronous transmission
异步电动机/異步電動機,非同步電動機 asynchronous motor
异步辅助电动机/異步輔助電動機,非同步輔助電動機 asynchronous auxiliary motor
异步通信/異步通信 asynchronous communication
异步陀螺电机/異步陀螺電機,非同步陀螺電機 asynchronous gyro motor
异侧下锚/異側下錨 different-side anchor
异常/異常 anomaly
异常潮位/異常潮位 anomalous tide level
异常潮汐/非常潮 abnormal tide
异常处理/異常處置 exception handling
异常磁区/磁異常區 magnetic anomaly
异常磨损/異常磨損 abnormal wear
异常喷射/異常噴射 abnormal injection
异常喷油/異常噴射 abnormal injection
异常侵蚀/異常侵蝕 abnormal erosion
异程式系统/異程式系統 direct return system
异频单工无线电通信/異頻單工無線電通訊 different-frequency simplex radio communication
异响/異響 abnormal noise
异向凝结[作用]/周動混凝 perikinetic coagulation
异形钢丝/麻面鋼線 deformed wire
异形轨/中轉軌條 compromise rail
异形轨条/異形軌條 transition rail
异形接头/異形接頭,異軌接頭 compromise joint, transition joint
异形接头夹板/異形魚尾板 compromise joint bar
异形柱结构/異形柱結構 special shaped column structure
异养菌总数/總異營菌 total heterotrophic bacteria count
异养生物/異養生物,他營生物 heterotroph, heterotrophic organism
异源多倍体/異源多倍體 allopolyploid
异源校准/異源校準 different source calibration

异质结太阳电池/異質結太陽電池,異接面太陽電池 heterojunction solar cell
抑制/抑制 suppression
抑制的毒性/抑制性毒性 inhibitory toxicity
抑制偏摆试验/止擺試驗 yaw checking test
抑制栽培/抑制栽培 retarding culture
抑制载波发射/遏止載波發射 suppressed carrier emission
邑/[都]邑 yi, city
译码/譯碼 decoding
译码器/譯碼機,解碼器 decoder
易爆货/易爆炸貨 explosive cargo
易爆危险品旗/危險品裝卸旗 powder flag
易铲污泥/易鏟汙泥,可鏟汙泥 workable sludge, spadable sludge
易腐货[物]/易腐貨[物],易腐品,易壞貨物 perishable goods, perishable freight, perishable cargo
易流态化物质/易液化物質 material which may liquefy
易燃/易燃,可燃 flammable
易燃固体/易燃固體 flammable solid
易燃货物/易燃貨物 inflammable freight, inflammable cargo
易燃限度/易燃限度 inflammable limit
易燃液体/易燃液體,可燃液體 flammable liquid
易溶色粉/易溶色粉 washable distemper
易溶性岩石/易溶性岩石 strongly soluble rock
易熔合金/易熔合金 fusible alloy
易熔塞/[可]熔塞 fusible plug
易碎货[物]/易碎貨[物] fragile goods
易行车/易行車 easy rolling car
易行线/易行線 easy running track
易自燃固体/易自燃固體 flammable solid liable to spontaneous combustion
驿道/郵路,驛程,投遞路線 post road
驿站/驛站 post house, yizhan
疫点/疫點 epidemic site
疫区/疫區 epidemic area
逸出/逸出 escape
逸流/逸流,洩漏,漏洩 leakage
意大利船级社/義大利驗船協會 Registro Italiano, RI
意大利式园林/意大利式園林 Italian style garden
意大利文物建筑保护学派/義大利文物建築保護學派 Italian school of built heritage conservation
意境/意境 artistic conception, poetic imagery
意外紧急制动/意外緊急制動 undesirable emergency braking, UEB
意外事件分析/意外事故分析 contingency analysis
意象地图/心智圖 mental map
溢出/溢出,漫溢 spilling, spill
溢洪道/溢洪道,溢流式溢水道 flood spillway, overflow spillway
溢洪桥/溢流壩頂橋 spillway bridge
溢呼/溢呼,全忙呼叫 overflow call
溢浆孔/溢漿孔 grout vent
溢流段长度/溢流段長度 crest length of overflow section
溢流段[断面]/溢流斷面 overflow section
溢流阀/溢流閥 overflow valve
溢流管/溢流管,溢水管 overflow pipe
溢流量/溢流量 overflow discharge
溢流率/溢流率 overflow rate
溢流水深/溢流深 overflow depth
溢流[下水]道/輔助下水道 relief sewer
溢流堰顶/溢流頂 crest of overflow
溢散光/溢散光 spill light, spray light
溢卸/溢卸 over-landed, over-delivery
溢油柜/溢流櫃 overflow tank
翼刀/翼刀,翼面擋流板 wing fence
翼轨/翼軌,側翼軌道 wing rail
翼尖/翼尖 wing tip
翼尖外挂/翼尖運載 wing tip carriage
翼尖涡/翼尖渦 wing tip vortex
翼肋/翼肋 wing rib
翼梁/翼梁 wing spar
翼轮式曝气器/翼輪式曝氣器 paddle-wheel aerator
翼墙/[側]翼牆 wing wall, wing masonry
翼墙式洞门/翼牆式隧道洞門 wing wall tunnel portal
翼梢涡/翼尖渦旋 wing tip vortex
翼梢小翼/小翼,翼翹 winglet
翼身融合/翼身融合 blended wing-body configuration
翼弦/翼弦 wing chord
翼形/翼切形 airfoil, airfoil profile
翼形厚度/剖面厚度 profile thickness
翼形中弧线/翼[切]形中線 airfoil mean camber line, profile mean line
翼缘/翼緣,凸緣 flange
翼缘板/翼板 flange plate
翼缘卷曲/翼板卷曲 flange curling
翼载荷/機翼負載 wing loading
翼展/翼展 span, wing span
翼柱形药柱/翼柱形藥柱 finocyl grain

因果链/因果鏈　chains of causation
阴/陰　covered
阴极保护/陰極防蝕[法]　cathodic protection
阴极射线管显示屏/陰極射線管顯示器　cathode ray tube display, CRT display
阴离子乳化沥青/陰離子乳化瀝青　anionic emulsified bitumen
阴影/陰影　shading
阴影法/暗影法　shadowgraph technique
阴影分析/陰影分析　shadowing analysis
阴影功率下降/陰影功率下降　degradation from shadowing power
阴影面积/窳陋區　area blighted
阴影屏蔽/陰影遮罩　shadow shield
阴影扇形/扇形陰影　shadow sector
阴影图/陰影圖　shadow diagram
阴影仪/陰影顯像　shadowgraph system
荫棚/蔭棚　shade-frame
荫生植物/耐陰植物,遮陰植物　shade plant
荫性地被植物/陰性地被植物　negative ground cover plant
荫性植物/嗜陰植物,陰地植物,耐陰植物　sciophyte, shade-tolerant plant
音控防鸣电路/音控防鳴器　voice-operated anti-singing circuit
音控门限电平/聲控繼電器電路　threshold level of voice-operated circuit
音量/音量　volume
音量表/音量計,風量計　volume meter
音频/音頻,聲頻　acoustic frequency, audio frequency
音频频率响应/音頻錄放幅頻響應　audio frequency response
音频通信电路/音訊通信電路　audio communication circuit
音频线/音頻線　audio cable
音频信号分配器/音頻信號分配器　audio signal distributor
音频选叫/聲頻選擇呼叫　VF selective calling
音频终端装置/音頻終端裝置,聲頻終端裝置　audio frequency terminating set
音频转接段/音頻段　audio frequency section
音频组合选呼/音頻組合選擇呼號　selective call with audio frequency coding
音色/音色,音品　timbre
音速/音速　sonic speed
音箱/揚聲器,喇叭　speaker
音响告警装置/音響預警裝置　aural alerting device
音响航标/音響訊號,音頻訊號　sound signal
音响环境仿真/聲響環境模擬　audio environment simulation
音响控制室/傳音控制室　acoustical control room
音响榴弹/音響信號彈　sound signal shell
音响信号器具/音響信號器具　sound signal instrument
音选调度电话分机/音選調度電話分機　dispatching telephone subset with VF selective calling
音选调度电话汇接分配器/音選調度電話匯接分配器　tandem distributor for dispatching telephone with VF selective calling, tandem distributor
音选调度电话滤波器/音選調度電話濾波器　bridging filter for dispatching telephone with VF selective calling
音选调度电话总机/音選調度電話主機　dispatching telephone control board with VF selective calling
音选双向增音机/雙向增音器,雙向轉發器　two-way repeater for VF selective calling, two-way repeater
音选同线电话分机/音選同線電話分機　party-line telephone subset with VF selective calling
音选同线电话分配器/音選同線電話分配器　party-line telephone distributor for VF selective calling
音选同线电话总机/音選同線電話總機　party-line telephone control board with VF selective calling
音乐教室/音樂室　music room
音乐厅/音樂廳,演奏廳　concert hall
音质/聲[學]的　acoustic
音质设计/音質設計　acoustical design
银行/銀行　bank
银行分理处/銀行分行　bank branch
银河/銀河　Milky Way
银河系/銀河系　Milky Way, galaxy
银河宇宙线/銀河宇宙射線　galactic cosmic ray
引爆控制系统/引爆控制系統　fuzing control system
引爆系统/發火系統　fuzing system, armament
引爆指令/起爆指令　initiation command
引潮力/引潮力,生潮力,起潮力　tide generating force, tide producing force
引出线/指線　leader line
引船驳岸/引船駁岸　ship-directional quay
引船绞盘/卷索絞盤　warping capstan
引导/導向　designation
引导参数计算/指示參數計算　designating parameter calculation
引导范围/指示範圍　designation range
引导滑车/導滑車　leading block

引导雷达/指示雷達　designation radar
引导伞/導傘　pilot parachute
引导数据/指示資料　designating data
引导系统/指示系統　designating system
引导信号/誘導號誌　calling-on signal
引导性风洞/引導性風洞　pilot wind tunnel
引道/引道,進路　approach
引道坡度/銜接坡度,漸近坡度　approach grade
引道区/進近區　approach zone
引堤/引堤　backward displacement of levee
引发自检/激發自我測試　initiated self-test
引风机/引風機,抽風機　induced draft fan
引航/地標航行　piloting
引航班/導航組　piloting team
引航船/引水船　pilot vessel
引航费/引水費　pilotage
引航锚地/引水錨地　pilot anchorage
引航信号/引領信號　homing signal
引航学/引水術　pilotage
引航员/引水[人]　pilot
引航员软梯/引水[人]梯　pilot ladder
引航员升降装置/引水員昇降機　pilot hoist
引航站/引水站　pilot station
引进桁架/引進桁架　pilot truss
引进架设法/引進架設法　launching erection
引进螺帽/引進螺帽　pilot nut
引缆/傳遞索　messenger
引缆回收索/回收索　messenger return line
引力辅助控制/引力輔助控制　gravity aided control
G_z 引起的意识丧失/G_z 引起的意識喪失　G_z induced loss of consciousness
引气混凝土/加氣混凝土　air entraining concrete
引气剂/輸氣劑　air entraining admixture, air entraining agent
引气减水剂/引氣減水劑　air entraining and water reducing admixture
引前相供电臂/引前相供電臂　leading phase feeding section
引桥/引[道栈]橋　approach, approach bridge, approach spans
引桥式码头/引[道栈]橋式碼頭　pier with approach trestle, pier with approach bridge
引入管/供應管　service pipe, inlet pipe
引入架/引入架　lead-in rack
引入试验架/引入測試架　lead-in test rack
引入线/上坡軌道　lead track
引射喷管/引射器噴嘴　ejector nozzle
引射器/引射器,引射泵,彈射器　ejector, injector

引射式燃烧器/噴射式燃燒器　injection burner
引射式预混燃烧器/引射式預混燃燒器　atmospheric burner, natural draft burner
引伸计/伸展計　extensometer
引水坝/引水壩　intake dam
引水航路/引水航路　pilot fairway
引水率/分水比　diversion ratio
引水锚地/引水錨地　pilot anchorage
引水渠道/引水路　headrace channel
引水隧洞/導流隧洞,引水路　diversion tunnel, headrace
引水信号/引水信號　pilot signal
引水堰/引水堰　intake weir
引水站/引水站　pilot station
引下线/引下線　down-conductor system
引信/引信,信管　fuze
引信安全性试验/引信安全性試驗　fuze safety test
引信半实物仿真/引信半硬體模擬　hardware in loop fuze simulation
引信冲击试验/引信衝擊試驗　fuze shock test
引信单元测试/引信單位測試　fuze unit test
引信电磁全尺寸动态仿真/引信電磁全尺寸動態模擬　fuze electromagnetic full-scale dynamic simulation
引信电磁缩比动态仿真/引信電磁縮比動態模擬　fuze electromagnetic scaled dynamic simulation
引信电源/引信電源供應器　fuze power supply
引信跌落试验/引信拋投試驗　fuze drop test
引信定向天线/引信定向天線　directional antenna of fuze
引信动态仿真/引信動態模擬　fuze dynamic simulation
引信反应区/引信反應區　fuze reaction zone
引信仿真/引信模擬　fuze simulation
引信分辨力/引信解析能力　resolution capability of fuze
引信辅天线/引信輔天線　auxiliary fuze antenna
引信挂飞试验/引信繫留試驗　fuze captive carrying test
引信火箭橇试验/引信火箭滑道試驗　rocket sled test for fuze
引信静态仿真/引信靜態模擬　fuze static simulation
引信抗干扰性/引信反干擾　fuze counter-jamming
引信雷达方程/引信雷達測距方程　fuze radar range equation
引信例行试验/引信例行測試　fuze routine test
引信灵敏度/引信靈敏度　fuze sensitivity
引信灵敏度测试/引信靈敏度試驗　fuze sensitivity

test
引信盲区/引信死區 fuze dead zone
引信启动/引信啟動 fuze actuation
引信启动半径/引信啟動半徑 fuze actuation radius
引信启动概率/引信啟動機率 probability of fuze actuation
引信启动规律/引信啟動定律 actuation law of fuze
引信启动角/引信啟動角,引信致動角 fuze actuation angle
引信启动角散布/引信啟動角散布 dispersion of fuze actuation angle
引信启动距离/引信致動距離 fuze actuation distance
引信启动区/引信啟動區,引信致動區 fuze actuation zone
引信敲击试验/引信打擊試驗 fuze strike test
引信全向天线/引信全向性天線 omnidirectional antenna of fuze
引信绕飞试验/引信繞飛試驗 flyover test for fuze
引信柔性滑轨试验/引信火箭繩索滑道試驗 rope-sled test for fuze
引信数学仿真/引信數學模擬 fuze mathematical simulation
引信水声仿真/引信水聲模擬 fuze hydro-acoustic simulation
引信瞬发度/引信瞬時性 fuze instantaneity
引信瞬发度试验/引信瞬時性試驗 fuze instantaneity test
引信天线/引信天線 fuze antenna
引信天线波瓣倾角/引信天線方向圖傾角 inclination angle of fuze antenna pattern
引信天线方向图/引信天線方向圖 fuze antenna pattern
引信物理仿真/引信物理模擬 fuze physical simulation
引信延迟时间/引信遲延時間 fuze delay time
引信延时性能试验/引信延時性能試驗 fuze time-delay characteristic test
引信与战斗部配合/引信與彈頭配合 fuze-warhead matching
引信与战斗部配合效率/引信與彈頭配合效率 fuze-warhead matching efficiency
引信振动试验/引信振動試驗 fuze vibration test
引信执行电路/引信起動電路 fuze firing circuit
引信主天线/引信主天線 main fuze antenna
引信装定/引信裝定 fuze setting
引信准动态仿真/引信準動態模擬 fuze quasi-dynamic simulation

引信作用距离/引信作用距離 fuze function range
引战配合光学仿真/引信與彈頭配合光學模擬 optical simulation of fuze-warhead matching
引战配合计算机图形仿真/引信與彈頭配合電腦圖形處理模擬 computer graphic simulation of fuze-warhead matching
引战配合数学仿真/引信與彈頭配合數學模擬 mathematical simulation of fuze-warhead matching
引战协调性/引戰配合 fuze-warhead matching capability, fuze-warhead coordination
引种/引種 introduction
引种驯化/引種馴化 introduction and acclimatization
引种植物/引進植物,外來植物 introduced plant
饮料厂/飲料廠 beverage factory
饮食广场/美食廣場 food plaza
饮水泵/飲用水泵 drinking water pump
饮水舱/飲用水艙 drinking water tank
饮水喷头/飲水噴頭 drinking fountain
饮水器/飲水器 water drinker
饮水泉/飲水泉 water springs
饮水箱/飲用水箱 potable water tank
饮用水/飲用水,可飲水 potable water
饮用水标准/飲用水標準 drinking water standards
饮用水臭氧消毒器/飲用水臭氧消毒器 drinking water ozone disinfector
饮用水矿化器/飲用水礦化器 mineralizing equipment of drinking
饮用水系统/飲用水系統 drinking water system
饮用杂用双水系统/二元供水系統 dual water supply systems
隐蔽/隱蔽 concealment
隐蔽港/隱蔽港 hidden harbor
隐蔽工程/隱蔽工程,隱蔽工事 concealed work, hidden project, hidden construction work
隐蔽工程检查/隱蔽工程檢查 hidden project inspection
隐蔽工程验收/隱蔽工程驗收 inspection and approval of concealed work, hidden work acceptance
隐化池/隱化池 imhoff tank
隐患性故障/隱患性故障 hidden fault
隐头喷泉/隱頭噴泉 secret fountain
隐线/虛線 hidden line
隐形/隱形 stealth
隐形材料/隱形材料,隱身材料 stealth material
隐形技术/隱形技術,隱身技術 stealth technique, stealth technology
隐性性状/隱性性狀 recessive charactor
印度洋区/印度洋區域 Indian Ocean Region, IOR

印染厂/印染廠　printing and dyeing plant
印刷厂/印刷機　printing press
印制电路板插座/印刷電路板插座　printed circuit board socket
饮马槽广场/飲馬槽廣場　Plaza del Bebedero los Caballos
应付票据/付款單　bills payable
应付日期/到期日　due date
20英尺集装箱/20呎貨櫃相當數量　twenty equivalent unit, TEU
英德石/英德石　Yingde stone
英国式园林/英國式園林　English style garden
英国文物建筑保护学派/英國文物建築保護學派　British school of built heritage conservation
膺架浇筑法/膺架澆鑄法　cast-on scaffolding method
鹰架式架设法/鷹架式架設法　erection with scaffolding method
迎风格式/上風格式　up-wind scheme
迎风换抢/迎風槕餞　tacking
迎角/衝角,攻角　angle of attack
迎角指示器/攻角指示器　angle of attack indicator
迎客厅/迎客大廳　arrival hall
迎面碰撞/正面碰撞,正面衝撞,對撞　head on collision
荧光/熒光[性]　fluorescence
荧光灯/螢光燈,日光燈　fluorescent lamp
荧光检漏/螢光檢漏　fluorescence leak detection
荧光屏/熒光屏　fluoroscope, fluorescent screen
荧光渗透探伤/螢光滲透探傷　fluorescent penetrant flaw detection
荧光微丝法/螢光微絲法　fluorescence microtuft method
盈亏平衡分析/損益平衡分析　break-even analysis
营救浮环/營救浮環　buoyant rescue quoit
营救器电台/營救器電臺　survival station
营救训练/救難訓練　rescue training
营养厨房/營養廚房　dietary kitchen
营养繁殖/營養繁殖　vegetative propagation
营养科/營養科　nutriology department
营养缺乏/營養缺乏　nutrition deficiency
营养失调/營養失調　nutritional disorder
营养土/營養土　nutrition soil
营养物质/營養物質　nutrition substance
营养液/培養液　culture solution
营养诊断/營養診斷　nutrition diagnosis
营业厅/營業廳　business hall
营业外支出/營業外支出,非營業性支出　non-operating outlay

营业线路公里/營運里程　operating kilometer
营业性运输/營業性運輸　for hire transport
营业站/營業站　operating station
营运标志/營運標誌　operation sign
营运吃水/航務吃水　operating draft
营运范围/營運範圍　operation area
营运方式/營運方式　operation manner
营运里程/營運里程,運營里程　operation mileage
营运汽车/營業車輛　for hire vehicle
营运收入/營業收入　operation revenue
营运速度/營運速度,運轉速率　operation speed, operational speed
营运线路/營運線路　operation route
营运线路图/營運線路圖　operational route map
营运证/營運證　operation certificate
营运支出/營運支出　operation expenditure
营造法式/營造法式　Treatise on Architectural Methods, Yingzao Fashi
营造法原/營造法原　Source of Architectural Methods, Yingzao Fayuan
影壁/影壁,照壁　screen spirit wall
影视外景基地/影視旅遊基地　movie and television base
影响半径/影響半徑　radius of influence
影响表/影響表　influence table
影响电流/影響電流　influencing current
影响范围分析/影響圈分析　sphere of influence analysis
影响量/影響量　influence quantity
影响面/影響面　influence surface
影响面积/影響圈,影響範圍　influence area
影响圈/影響圈　influence circle
影响线/影響線　influence line
影像地图/攝影[地]圖　photographic map
[影像]再现/再現,重顯　reconstruction
影印件/影印件　photostat printing
应变/應變　strain
应变部署表/部署表　muster list, station bill
应变动测/應變動測　deformation dynamic inspection
应变计/應變計,應變儀　strain gage, strainmeter
应变率/應變率　strain rate
应变率向量/應變率向量　strain rate vector
应变能/應變能　strain energy
应变能密度/應變能密度　strain energy density
应变偏[张]量/偏差應變張量　deviatoric tensor of strain
应变强度/[單位]應變　strain intensity
应变强化/應變硬化　strain hardening

应变软化/應變軟化　strain softening
应变时效/應變時效,應變老化　strain ageing
应变式天平/應變規式平衡儀　strain gage balance
应变势能/應變勢能　potential energy of strain
应变速度/應變速度　strain velocity
应变向量/應變向量　strain vector
应变巡检箱/應變巡檢箱　strain scanning unit
应变仪/應變儀,應變計　strain gage, strain indicator
应变仪传感器/應變計測感器　strain gage transducer
应变硬化/應變硬化　strain hardening
应答编码/應答編碼　encoding the response
应答跟踪/訊問追蹤　interrogating tracking
应答机/詢答機,轉頻器,識別器　transponder
应答信号/收到信號,確認信號　acknowledge signal
应舵时间/迴轉回應延遲　delay of turning response
应急避难设施/應急設備,緊急設備　emergency shelter facilities
应急舱口/逃生艙口　escape hatch
应急操舵装置/應急操舵裝置,應急舵機　emergency steering gear
应急操纵/應急操縱　emergency maneuvering
应急撤离/緊急撤離　emergency evacuation
应急撤离设备/緊急疏散裝置　emergency evacuated equipment
应急出口/緊急出口,太平門　emergency exit
应急处理/緊急處置　emergency handling
应急处理程序/緊急處理程式　emergency processing program
应急灯/應急燈　emergency light
应急电池/應急電池　emergency cell
应急电话/緊急電話　emergency telephone
应急电话标志/緊急電話標誌　emergency telephone sign
应急电缆/應急電纜,緊急電纜　emergency cable
应急电气设备/應急電力設備　emergency electric equipment
应急电源/緊急電源[供應]　emergency power supply, electric source for safety service
应急电站/應急電站,應急動力站　emergency electrical power plant, emergency power station
应急动力装置/緊急動力單元　emergency power unit
应急舵/應急舵　jury rudder
应急发电柴油机/應急柴油發電機　emergency generator diesel engine
应急发电机/應急發電機　emergency generator
应急返回/應急返回　emergency return

应急返回着陆区/應急返回降落區　landing zone of emergency return
应急辅助鼓风机/應急鼓風機　emergency blower, emergency standby blower
应急供电/應急電力供應　emergency electrical power supply
应急供氧阀/應急供氧閥　emergency oxygen supply valve
应急供氧系统/應急供氧系統　emergency oxygen supply system
应急关闭系统/應急自動關閉裝置　emergency automatic shutdown device, emergency shutdown system
应急管理系统/緊急管理系統　emergency management system
应急航行机组/應急航行機組　take-home engine unit
应急回收程序/應急回收程式　emergency recovery sequence
应急救生站/應急救生站　emergency rescue station
应急救生着陆区/緊急救援降落區　landing zone of emergency rescue
应急救灾无线电通信/應急救災無線電通信　radio communication for emergency purpose
应急空气压缩机/應急用空氣壓縮機　emergency air compressor
应急离机系统/緊急逃生系統　emergency escape system
应急罗经/應急羅經　emergency compass
应急模式/應急模式　contingency mode
应急配电板/應急配電板　emergency switchboard
应急起动/應急起動　emergency starting
应急刹车系统/應急刹車系統　emergency brake system
应急设施/緊急響應設施　emergency response facility
应急食品/應急食物　contingency food
应急疏水试验/應急洩水試驗　emergency draining test
应急说明/應急說明　emergency instruction
应急速闭阀/應急速閉閥　quick-closing emergency valve
应急天线/應急天線　emergency antenna
应急停车/緊急停車　emergency stop
应急停车带/緊急停車地帶　emergency parking strip
应急停车装置/緊急關閉設施　emergency shutdown device
应急卫星通信/應急衛星通訊　emergency satellite

communication
应急下降/緊急下降　emergency descent
应急消防泵/應急消防泵,應急救火泵　emergency fire pump
应急训练/應急訓練　emergency training
应急氧源/應急氧氣瓶　emergency oxygen tank
应急业务/應急業務　emergency service
应急照明/應急照明,應急燈　emergency lighting
应急照明系统/應急照明系統　emergency lighting system
应急状态/應急工作狀態　emergency rating
应急着陆/緊急著陸,緊急落地　emergency landing
应急着陆区/緊急著陸區　emergency landing zone
应急准备/應急準備　emergency preparedness
应力/應力　stress
应力标示图/應力標示圖　stress profile
应力波方程法/應力波方程式法　stress wave equation method
应力次数曲线/應力計數曲線　stress-number curve
应力幅/應力幅度　stress amplitude
应力腐蚀/應力腐蝕　stress corrosion
应力腐蚀断裂/應力腐蝕龜裂　stress corrosion cracking
应力腐蚀裂纹/應力腐蝕龜裂　stress corrosion cracking
应力恢复法/應力恢復法　stress recovery method
应力极限/應力極限範圍　limiting range of stress
应力集中/應力[之]集中　stress concentration, concentration of stress
应力集中系数/應力集中因數　factor of stress concentration
应力集中因数/應力集中因數　factor of stress concentration
应力计/應力計　stress meter
应力解除法/應力消除法　stress relief method
应力控制张拉/應力控制張拉　prestressing under stress control
应力路径/應力線路　stress path
应力蒙皮结构/承[應]力蒙皮結構　stressed-skin construction
应力疲劳/應力疲勞　stress fatigue
应力偏[张]量/偏差應力張量　deviatoric tensor of stress
应力强度/應力強度,單位應力　stress intensity
应力强度因子/應力強度因子　stress intensity factor
应力强度因子阈值/應力強度因子閾值　threshold of stress intensity factor
应力区/應力區,主壓力區　stress block

应力释放/去應力　destressing
应力松弛/應力鬆弛　stress relaxation
应力椭圆/主應力橢圓　ellipse of stress
应力往复线图/應力反復線圖　stress-endurance diagram
应力吸收薄膜/應力吸收薄膜　stress absorbing membrane
应力严重系数法/應力嚴重係數法　stress severity factor method
应力-应变曲线/應力-應變曲線　stress-strain curve
应力圆/應力圓　stress circle
应用空气动力学/應用空氣動力學　applied aerodynamics
应用软件/應用軟體　application software
应用生态学/應用生態學　applied ecology
应用卫星/應用衛星　applied satellite
应用液/使用溶液　working solution
硬表层/地殼,外殼　crust
硬搓[绳]/硬搓索法　hard lay
硬错误/硬體錯誤　hard error
硬地面/硬面　hardstand
硬点/硬點　hard spot
硬度/硬度　hardness
硬度计/硬度計　hardometer
硬度试验/硬度試驗　hardness test
硬度数/硬度數　hardness number
硬横跨/門形桿架,門式框架　portal structure
硬化混凝土/硬化混凝土　hardened concrete
硬化时间/硬化時間　curing time
硬件/硬體　hardware
硬聚氯乙烯管/UPVC 管線　unplasticized polyvinyl chloride pipe
硬壳式结构/硬殼式[結構],單殼式　monocoque structure, monocoque
硬盔/硬盔　rigid helmet
硬沥青/瀝青　pitch
硬练砂浆强度试验/硬練砂漿強度試驗　early dry mortar strength test
硬路肩/路肩,隔離墩　hard shoulder
硬铝合金/硬鋁,杜拉鋁　duralumin
硬木材/硬木材　hardwood
硬黏土/硬黏土,韌黏土　firm clay, stiff clay
硬盘/硬磐　hardpan
硬判决/硬式判斷,硬式決定　hard decision
硬钎焊/硬焊,銅焊　brazing
硬山/硬山　flush gable roof
硬式传动机构/硬式傳動機構　push-pull rod system
硬式航天服/硬質太空衣　hard space suit

硬卧车/硬臥車　semi-cushioned berth sleeping car, semi-cushioned couchette
硬性洗涤剂/硬清潔劑　hard detergent
硬岩/硬岩,堅石　hard rock, hard stone
硬叶林/硬葉[樹]林,常綠林　sclerophyllous forest, durisilvae
硬质合金/硬質合金　hard alloy, cemented carbide
硬质聚氨酯泡沫塑料/硬質聚氨酯泡沫塑膠　rigid polyurethane foams
硬质裂纹黏土/硬裂黏土　stiff-fissured clay
硬质塑料/剛性塑膠　rigid plastic
硬质纤维板/硬質纖維板　stiff fiberboard
硬质岩石/硬岩　hard rock
硬质阳极[氧]化/硬質陽極處理　hard anodizing
硬砖/過燒磚　clinker brick
硬着陆/硬著陸,重落地　hard landing
硬座车/硬座車　semi-cushioned seat coach
哟-哟装置/哟-哟裝置　yo-yo device
拥包/隆起　upheaval, swelling
拥挤度/擁塞度　degree of congestion
拥挤人群管理培训/群眾管理訓練　crowd management training
壅塞/阻塞,阻氣,阻流　choking
壅水/壅水,回水　back water
壅水高度/壅水高度　back water height, height of backwater
永磁式力矩器/永磁式扭矩產生器　permanent magnet torquer
永磁陀螺电机/永磁陀螺電機　permanent magnet gyro motor
永磁悬浮系统/永久磁鐵懸承系統　permanent magnet suspension system, PMSS
永磁直流力矩电机/永磁[性]直流轉矩電動機　permanent magnet DC torque motor
永定柱/永定柱　yongdingzhu
永久变形/永久變形　permanent deformation
永久衬砌/永久式襯砌　permanent lining
永久船磁/永久船磁　ship permanent magnetism
永久磁铁/永久磁鐵　permanent magnet
永久冻土下位水/永冰淹水,永冰下水　subpermafrost water
永久荷载/永久荷載,永久負載　permanent load, permanent action
永久建筑/永久性建物　permanent building
永久校正/永久校正　permanent adjustment
永久链路/永久鏈路　permanent link
永久式模板/永久性内襯　permanent shuttering
永久水平缆线/永久水平纜線　fixed horizontal cable

永久线路[中线]桩/永久標誌　permanent monument
永久效应/永久效應　permanent effect
永[久性]冻土/永凍土　permafrost
永久性建筑/永久建築　permanent building
永久性桥/永久性橋梁　permanent bridge
永久性损伤/永久損害　permanent damage
永久性修理/徹底檢查　permanent repair
永久虚[拟]电路/永久虛擬線路,固定虛擬電路　permanent virtual circuit
永久压载/固定壓艙物　permanent ballast
永久应变/永久應變　permanent strain
永久硬度/永久硬度　perpetual hardness, permanent hardness
永久作用/永久作用　permanent action
泳道/比賽泳道　racing lane
涌潮/湧潮,怒潮　tidal bore, sea bore
涌级/湧級　swell scale, scale of swell
涌浪/湧浪,長浪　swell, surge
涌浪补偿器/湧浪補償器,波浪補償器　swell compensator
涌浪高度/湧高　swell height
涌泉灌/湧泉灌　bubbler irrigation
涌水/湧水　gushing water
涌水头/湧水頭　bubbler
用材林/用材林　timber forest
用地边界/用地邊界　land use boundary
用地标高/地面高程　ground elevation, land elevation
用地分类/土地利用分類,土地利用型　land use classification
用地红线/用地紅線　boundary line of land, property line of land
用地兼容性/用地相容性,土地利用相容性　land use compatibility
用地面积/用地面積　site area, size of the land
用地平衡/用地平衡,土地使用平衡　land use balance
用电负荷/電力負載　electrical load
用电负荷指标/電機線電負載指標　electrical load index
用户等效距离误差/用戶等效距離誤差　user equivalent range error, UERE
用户电报/用户電報　telex subscriber telegraph
用户电报电话/用户電報電話　telex telephony, TEXTEL
用户电报书信业务/電報交換書信業務　telex letter service
用户电报业务/電報交換業務　telex service

用户码/用戶碼　subscriber number
用户热力站/用戶熱力站　consumer thermal substation
用户试验/用戶使用測試　user test
用户水表/用戶水表　service meter
用户引入线/用戶引入線　subscriber lead-in
用户主机/用戶主機站　subscriber main station
用户坐标系/用戶坐標系統　user coordinate system, UCS
用气定额/煤氣消耗量定額,煤氣耗用量定額　gas consumption quota
用气量/煤氣耗用量　gas consumption
用水定额/用水定額,用水配額　water consumption norm, water consumption quota
用水量/用水量,水消耗量,水能耗　water supply volume, water consumption
用水量标准/供水量標準　water demand standard
用途分区/用途地帶　use zoning
用益物权/用益物權　usufruct
佣金/佣金　commission
优化/優化,最佳化,最適化　optimization
优化操纵/最適操作條件,最適操作狀況　optimum handling, optimum operation
优化设计/最適設計　optimal design
优势度/優勢度　dominance
优势度指数/優勢度指數　dominace index
优势频率/優勢頻率　dominant frequency
优势树种/優勢樹種　dominant tree species
优势种/優勢種　dominant species
优先标志/優先標誌　priority sign
优先公路/優先公路　preferential highway
优先街道/優先街道　preferential street
优先权/優先權　right of priority
优先时差/優先時差　priority phase offset
优先通行车道/優先車道　priority lane
优选元器件清单/優選零件清單　preferred parts list
优质工程/優質工程　high grade project
优质杂排水/優質雜排水　high grade gray water
邮船/郵船　mail ship
邮电通信建筑/電信建築　telecommunication building
邮件舱/郵件艙,郵件室　mail room
邮件处理中心/郵件處理中心　mail processing center, postal center
邮件及行李间/郵件及行李間　mail and baggage room
邮件转运站/郵件轉運站　post transfer station
邮局/郵局,郵政中心　post office

邮旗/郵旗　mail flage
邮箱业务/郵箱業務　mailbox service
邮政车/郵車　postal car, mail van
邮政间/郵政間　post office compartment
邮政设施/郵政設施　mail facility, post facility
油包/油包　oil box
油泵定时标记/泵定時記號　pump timing mark
油舱涂料/油艙塗料　oil tank coating
油尺/燃油油桿　fuel dipstick
油船/油輪,運油船　oil carrier, oil tanker
油船锚地/油輪錨地　oil tanker anchorage
油导筒式轴箱定位装置/油導筒式軸箱定位裝置　oil guide cylinder type journal box positioning device
油底壳/油池,油槽,滴油盤　oil sump, oil pan
油动机/伺服馬達　servomotor
油断路器/油斷路器　oil circuit-breaker
油分离器/油分離器　oil separator, oil extractor
油分计/油含量計　oil content meter
油分瞬时排放率/油分瞬間排洩率　instantaneous rate of discharge of oil content
油封/油封　oil sealing
油封期/拆封前儲存壽命　storage life before unpack
油港/油港　oil harbor
油管/油管　oil pipe
油环/止油圈,油封　oil ring
油回火钢丝/油回火鋼線　oil-tempered wire
油迹/油跡　traces of oil
油结胶/油黏結　caking of oil
油浸式牵引变压器/油浸式牽引變壓器　oil-immersed type traction transformer
油井水泥/油井專用水泥　oil-well cement
油井钻工/挖井工　well sinker
油锯/鏈鋸　chain saw
油卷/油卷　lubricating roll
油类/油類　oil
油类沉积物/油[類]殘留物　oily residues
油冷/油冷　oil cooling
油量测量系统/油量量測系統　fuel quantity measurement system
油流法/油流法　oil flow technique
油滤/滑油濾　oil filter
油轮清洁海洋指南/油輪海洋清潔指南　clean seas guide for oil tankers
油码头/油碼頭,油終端站　oil terminal, oil wharf
油毛毡/油毛氈　bituminous felt
油密/油密　resistant to oil, oil-tight
油密舱壁/油密艙壁　oil-tight bulkhead
油泥/油泥　sludge

油泥焚化炉/油泥焚化爐　sludge incinerator
油泥柜/油泥[艙]櫃,汙油[泥]櫃　sludge tank
油破布/含油破布　oily rags
油漆/[油]漆,塗料　coating, paint
油漆间/油漆間,油漆庫　paint store, paint room
油漆饰面车间/塗裝工場　painting shop
油漆稀释剂/油漆稀釋劑,松節油精　turpentine substitute
油气比/油氣比　fuel-air ratio
油气分离器/油氣分離器,除氣器,分油器　oil-air separator, deaerator, oil separator
油气化炉/油氣化爐　oil gasifier
油-气悬挂拖车/油-氣鉤狀拖車　oil-gas hooked trailer
油气炸弹/油氣彈　fuel-air bomb
油燃烧器/燃油器　oil burning unit
油润滑/油潤滑　oil lubricating
油、散、矿船/礦砂散裝貨與油兼用船　ore-bulk-oil carrier, OBO
油砂/油砂層　oil sand
油石比/油石比　bitumen aggregate ratio
油水分离器/油水分離器　oil-water separator
油水分离设备/油水分離設備,油水分離裝置　oil-water separating equipment
油水界面/油水分界面　oil-water interface
油水界面探测仪/油水分界面探測儀,油水介面計　oil-water interface detector
油位表/油位表　fuel level gage
油污染/油汙　oil pollution
油污水/[含]油汙水　oily water
油污水处理船/油汙水處理船　oily water disposal boat
油污损害/油汙損害　damage from oil pollution
油雾浓度探测器/油霧偵測器　oil mist detector
油线室/軸箱包裝室　journal box packing room
油箱/[燃]油箱,油櫃,油艙　oil tank, fuel tank
油箱增压/油箱增壓　tank pressurization
油箱姿态误差/油箱姿態誤差　tank attitude error
油性混合物/含油混合物　oily mixture
油压动力室/油壓動力室　hydraulic pressure engine room
油压继电器/油壓繼電器　oil pressure relay
油压千斤顶张拉/液壓千斤頂預力　hydraulic jack prestressing
油压式护舷材/油壓式護舷材　oil pressure fender
油压试验/驗油,油驗　oil test
油压压差控制器/油壓差控制器　oil pressure differential controller

油浴式空气滤清器/油浴空氣過濾器　oil bath air filter
油渣泵/汙油泵　sludge pump
油毡/油氈　linoleum
油毡防水层/防水層瀝青氈,油毛氈　water proof asphalt felt
油枕/油枕　treated wooden tie
油制气/油[煤]氣　oil gas
鱿鱼钓机/魷[魚]釣機,釣魷魚機　squid angling machine
鱿鱼钓渔船/魷[魚]釣船　squid angling boat
游步道/遊步道　path
游步甲板/散步甲板　promenade deck
游车/遊車　idle car
游船码头/碼頭區　terminal
游动火箭发动机/微調火箭發動機　vernier rocket engine, vernier rocket motor
游客/觀光客　tourist
游客服务中心/遊客服務中心　tourist reception center
游客规模/遊客規模　tourist scale
游客量/旅遊容量　tourist capacity
游客增长率/觀光客增長率,觀光客生長率　growth rate of tourists
游客中心/遊客中心　tourist center
游览车/遊覽車　park sightseeing bus
游览船/遊覽船,觀光船　excursion boat, excursion vessel
游览解说系统/遊覽解說系統　tour interpretation system
游览路线/遊覽路線,遊覽線路　touring route
游览区/遊覽區,觀光區　excursion area, open-to-public area, esthetic area
游乐园/娛樂公園,露天遊樂場　amusement park
游离二氧化碳/自由二氧化碳　free carbon dioxide
游离氯/單體氯　free chlorine
游离碳含量/游離碳含量,自由碳含量　free carbon content
游离碳含量试验/游離碳含量試驗,自由碳含量試驗　free carbon content test
游离性余氯/自由有效餘氯　free residual chlorine
游憩/遊憩　recreation
游憩草坪/遊憩草坪　recreational lawn
游憩功能/休閒娛樂功能　recreational function
游憩机会谱/遊憩機會譜　recreation opportunity spectrum
游憩意向综合体/綜合旅遊區　recreation image complex

游人调查/遊人調查　visitors investigation
游人分析/遊人分析　garden visitors analysis
游人管理/遊人管理　visitors management
游人规则/遊人規則　visitors regulation
游人容[纳]量/遊人容納量　visitors capacity
游人统计/遊人統計　visitors statistics
游人中心/遊人中心　visitors center
游丝/遊絲　hair wire
游艇/遊艇　pleasure craft, pleasure yacht, yacht
游艇停泊区/遊艇停泊區　yacht landing area
游戏厅/遊戲室,球藝室　game room
游线/旅遊線路　tour track
游移河槽/暫用水道　shifted channel
游泳池/游泳池　swimming pool
游泳池池水净化设备机房/游泳池水處理室　water treatment room for swimming pool
[游泳池]混合流式循环/複合循環　pool water combined circulation
[游泳池]给水排水工程/給排水工程　water supply and drainage engineering of swimming pool
[游泳池]逆流式循环/反循環　pool water reverse circulation
[游泳池]顺流式循环/層流式循環　pool water down-flow circulation
[游泳池]循环净化给水系统/循環淨化給水系統　circulation treating water supply system of swimming pool
[游泳池]直流净化给水系统/直流淨化給水系統　once through treated water supply system of swimming pool
[游泳池]直流式给水系统/單流水系統　once through water supply system of swimming pool
游泳馆/室内游泳池　natatorium, aquatic center
游泳设施/游泳設施　swimming facility
游泳运动/游泳　swimming
有酬载荷/酬載,有效載荷,有效負載　payload
有挡锚链/日字鏈　stud chain
有毒货/毒性貨　poisonous cargo
有毒物质/有毒物質　poisonous substance
有舵雪橇滑道/有舵雪橇滑道　bobsleigh
有缝线路/有接頭軌道　jointed track
有盖漏斗车/有蓋漏斗車　covered hopper car
有杆锚/有桿錨,普通錨　stock anchor
有功负荷/動力負載　power load, power loading
有功功率/有效功率,瓩功率,有效電力　active power, kW power
有功功率自动分配装置/有效功率自動分配裝置　automatic distributor of active power

有箍车轮/輪箍式車輪　tired wheel, tyred wheel
有轨电车/有軌電車道　tram, trolley
有轨运输/軌道交通　track transportation
有害地段/有害地段　harmful district
有害干扰/有害干擾　harmful interference
有害货/有害貨物　noxious cargo, harmful cargo
有害生物监测/有害生物監測　pest inspection
有害生物综合治理/有害生物綜合管理　integrated pest management, IPM
有害水/有害水　harmful water
有害物质/有害物質　harmful substance, HS
有害物质报告/有害物質報告　harmful substance report
有害液体物质/有毒液體物質　noxious liquid substance
有机多功能透波材料/有機多功能透電磁波材料　organic multifunctional electromagnetic wave transparent material
有机发光二极管显示屏/有機發光二極體顯示器　organic light emitting diode display, OLED display
有机肥料/有機肥料　organic fertilizer
有机废弃物肥料/有機廢棄物肥料　organic waste fertilizer
有机负荷/有機負荷　organic loading
有机覆盖物/有機覆蓋物　organic mulch
有机高分子材料/有機高分子化材料　organic high polymer materials
有机更新/有機更新　organic renewal
有机功能材料/有機機能材料　organic functional material
有机过氧化物/有機過氧化物　organic peroxide
有机建筑/有機建築　organic architecture
有机结合料/有機黏結劑　organic binder
有机聚合物/有機聚合物　organic polymer
有机疏散/有機疏散　organic decentralization
有机酸/有機酸　organic acid
有机物含量试验/有機物質含量試驗　organic matter content test
有机物质降解作用/有機物分解　organic matter degradation
有机纤维增强塑料/有機纖維強化塑膠　organic fiber reinforced plastic
有机性疏散/有機性疏散　organic decentralization
有机营养/植物有機營養　organic nutrition
有机杂质/有機雜質　organic impurity
有机载体锅炉/有機載體鍋爐　organic fluid boiler
有机质含量/有機物質含量　organic matter content
有机[质]土/有機[質]土　organic soil

有机主义者/有機主義者　organist
有极继电器/極化繼電器,極化電驛　polarized relay
有菌手术室/有菌手術室　general operation room
有利地段/有利地段　favorable area to earthquake resistance, favorable area
有林地/林地　forest land
有路面公路/鋪砌公路　paved highway
有黏结预应力混凝土结构/有黏結預應力混凝土結構　bonded prestressed concrete structure
有缺陷框架/不完整架構　imperfect frame
有人增音机/有人增訊站,有人中繼站　attended repeater
有色金属/非鐵金屬　non-ferrous metal
有色金属冶炼厂/有色金屬冶煉廠　non-ferrous metal plant, non-ferrous metal refinery
有色金属制品厂/有色金屬製品廠　non-ferrous metal products factory
有调中转车/有調中轉車　transit car with resorting
有调中转车停留时间/有調中轉車停留時間　detention time of car in transit with resorting
有限变形/有限變形　shake clown
有限差分法/有限差分法,有限差數法,定差法　finite difference method
有限点火/有限點火　finite burn
有限幅波/有限振幅波　finite amplitude wave
有限基本解法/有限基本解法　method of finite fundamental solution
有限竞争性招标/有限競爭性招標　invitation tender
有限使用期产品/有限使用壽命產品　limited operating life item
有限寿命产品/有限壽命產品　limited life item
有限条法/有限帶板法　finite strip method
有限位移理论/有限位移理論　finite displacement theory
有限翼展机翼/有限翼展機翼　finite span wing
有限预应力/有限預應力　limited prestressing
有限预应力混凝土/有限預力混凝土　limited prestressing concrete
有限元法/有限元[素]法　finite element method
有限元分析/有限元素分析　finite element analysis
有限元计算/有限元素計算　finite element calculation
有限元网络/有限元網格　mesh of finite element
有限振幅波/有限振幅波　finite amplitude wave
有限贮存期产品/有限庫存壽命產品　limited shelf life item
有线电视机房/有線電視工作間　cable TV plant room

有线广播电视机房/有線廣播電視機房　cable broadcast and TV room
有线及卫星电视系统/電纜電視系統　cable television and satellite television system
有线校零/有線校零　cable zero calibration
有线遥测/有線遙測　wire telemetry
有效半径/有效半徑　effective radius
有效表土层/有效表土層　effective topsoil layer
有效波/指示波　significant wave
有效波法/指示波法　significant wave method
有效波高/有義波高,指示浪高,顯著波高　significant wave height
有效波倾角/有效波斜度　effective wave slope
有效波周期/有義波週期,指示波浪週期　significant wave period
有效尺寸/有效尺寸　effect size
有效的/有效的,有用的　useful
有效反射面积/有效反射區　effective reflection area
有效辐射功率/有效輻射功率　effective radiated power
有效覆盖压力/有效超載壓力　effective overburden pressure
有效干舷/有效乾舷　effective freeboard
有效感觉噪声水平/有效感知噪音位準　effective perceived noise level, EPNL
有效刚度/有效勁度　effective stiffness
有效高度/有效高度,實際高度　virtual height, effective height
有效[工作]深度/可用水深　available depth
有效功率/有效功率　effective power
有效供油行程/有效供油衝程　effective delivery stroke
有效积温/有效日照量,積效日照量　effective accumulative insolation, effective accumulative temperature, total effective temperature
有效截[面]面积/有效橫斷面積,淨斷面積　net sectional area, effective cross-sectional area
有效孔隙率/有效孔隙率　effective porosity
有效宽度/有效寬度　effective width
有效粒度/有效粒徑　effective size of grain
有效粒径/有效徑　effective diameter
有效磷/有效磷　available phosphorus
有效绿灯时间/有效綠燈時間　effective green time
有效面积/有效面積　effective area
有效碾压深度/有效碾壓深度　effective rolling depth
有效区域/有效面積　effective area
有效全向辐射功率/有效等方向性輻射電力　effective isotropically radiated power

有效燃油消耗率/有效燃油消耗率　effective specific fuel consumption
有效热效率/有效熱效率　effective thermal efficiency, effective brane thermal efficiency, useful thermal efficiency
有效日照/有效日照　effective sunshine
有效容积/有效容積　effective volume
有效融雪[量]/有效融雪　effective snow melt
有效杀伤半径/有效殺傷半徑　effective kill radius
有效烧蚀热/有效燒蝕熱　effective ablation heat
有效射程/有效射程　effective range
有效声号/有效聲號　effective sound signal
有效速度/有效流速　effective velocity
有效土层/有效土層　effective soil layer
有效推力/有效推力　effective thrust
有效温度/有效溫度　effective temperature, ET
有效吸收/有效吸收量　effective absorption
有效稀释度/有效稀釋率　available dilution
有效效率/有效效率　effective efficiency
有效压缩比/有效壓縮比　effective compression ratio
有效意识时间/有效意識時間　time of useful consciousness
有效翼缘宽度/翼緣有效寬度　effective width of flange
有效应力/有效應力　effective stress
有效应力参数/有效應力參數　effective stress parameter
有效预应力/有效預力,最終預力　effective prestress, final prestress
有效载荷舱/有效載荷艙　payload module
有效载荷分离/有效載荷分離　payload separation
有效载荷试验场/有效載荷試驗場　payload range
有效载荷整流罩/酬載護罩　payload fairing
有效载荷转运/酬載轉移　payload transfer
有效载荷准备间/有效載荷準備間　payload preparation room
有效站台长度/有效月臺長度　effective length of platform
有效张力/有效拉力　effective tension
有形损耗/有形損耗　tangible wear
有旋流/旋流　rotational flow
有压隧洞/有壓隧洞　pressurized tunnel
有眼环的短索/末端附眼環短索　lizard
有氧运动/有氧運動　aerobic exercise
有氧运动室/韻律教室　aerobics classroom
有益干扰/有利干擾　beneficial interference
有意搁浅/故意擱淺　voluntary stranding
有翼导弹气动特性/有翼導彈氣動特性　aerodynamic characteristics of winged missile
有用的/有用的,有效的　useful
有源降压装置/有源降壓裝置　active degrade voltage apparatus
有源卫星/運作中衛星　active satellite
有源噪声[振动]控制/主動式噪音控制　active noise vibration control
有载自动调节/有載自動調節　autoregulation on load
有证标准物质/有證參考物質,有證參考材料　certified reference material
有中梁底架/有中梁底架　underframe with center sill
有阻尼自由振动/受阻自由振動　damped free vibration
有坐标格网海图/有格海圖　gridded chart
右侧浮标/右舷通過浮標　starboard hand buoy
右车道/右側車道　right lane
右焊法/反向焊接　backhand welding
右开道岔/右開道岔　right hand turnout
右开式/右開式　right hand model
右满舵/右滿舵　hard starboard
右舷/右舷　starboard, starboard side
右舷发动机/右舷引擎　starboard engine
右[向]捻/右搓索　right lay
右旋/右旋,右轉　right hand turning, right-handed turning
右旋柴油机/右轉柴油機　right hand rotation diesel engine
右旋钢索/右旋纜索　right hand lay
右旋螺旋杆/右旋螺桿　right hand screw
右旋螺旋桨/右旋螺槳　right-handed propeller
右转发动机/右轉動力機　right hand engine
右转弯/右轉　right turn
右转[弯]车道/右轉車道　right turn lane
右转弯导向线/右轉車道導引線　right turn guide line
右转弯匝道/右轉匝道　right turn ramp
[幼儿]隔离室/隔離室　isolation room
幼儿活动室/幼兒活動室　kindergarten activity room
幼儿寝室/幼兒室　kindergarten dormitory
幼儿音体活动室/幼兒音體活動室　kindergarten musical and multi-activity room
幼儿园/幼兒園,幼稚園,託兒所　nursery, kindergarten
幼年河/幼年河　young river
幼鱼栖息场/幼魚棲息場　fish nursery ground
囿/囿　hunting park, you

诱变育种/誘變育種　mutation breeding
诱导比/誘導比　induction ratio
诱导标志/誘導標誌　induction sign
诱导环境/誘導環境　induced environment
诱导器/誘導器　induction unit
诱导式空气调节系统/誘導式空調系統　induction air conditioning system
诱导阻力/誘導阻力　induced drag
诱鸟区/誘鳥區　bird sanctuary area
诱杀/撲滅　luring insect pest
诱杀性植物/誘殺的植物　trap plant
诱增交通量/誘發交通量,衍生交通量　induced traffic volume
釉面砖/釉面磚　glazed tile
迂回进路/迂回路由,備用路由,可選用的路由　detour route, alternative route
迂回线/迂回線　roundabout line
迂回运输/迂回式運輸,繞行運輸　roundabout transport, roundabout traffic, circuitous traffic
迂回中继/迂回長途中繼法　alternative trunking
淤灌/放淤法　colmatage
淤积/淤積,淤塞　silting, siltation, silting up
淤积池/沈泥池　silt basin
淤积黏土/淤積黏土　warved clay
淤锚/錨埋入　anchor embedded
淤泥/淤泥,泥漿,汙泥　mud, silt, sludge
淤塞/淤塞　silting up
余度舵机/多餘驅動器　redundancy actuator
余度供电/冗餘電力供應　redundant electrical power supply
余度管理/冗餘管理　redundancy management
余度技术/冗餘技術　redundancy technology
余度结构/冗餘結構　redundancy architecture
余高/焊縫凸量　reinforcement
余割平方波束天线/餘割平方波束天線　cosecant-squared beam antenna
余氯/餘氯　residual chlorine
余面/餘面　lap
余能/輔能　complementary energy
余气系数/過量空氣係數　excess air coefficient
余热锅炉/廢熱鍋爐　waste heat boiler, heat recovery boiler, exhaust heat boiler
余速损失/餘速損失　leaving velocity loss
余暇生活空间/餘暇生活空間　leisure time living space
余氧系数/餘氧係數　excess oxidizer coefficient
余药分数/餘藥分數　sliver fraction
余振自谱分析/殘餘振動自我頻譜分析　residual vibration auto-spectrum analysis
余震/餘震　after shock
鱼舱/魚艙　fish hold
鱼粉加工船/捕魚加工船　fish meat factory ship
鱼腹梁/魚腹梁　fish-belly sill
鱼腹式桁架/月牙形桁架　lenticular truss
鱼雷快艇/魚雷[快]艇　torpedo motor boat, torpedo boat
鱼类洄游/魚群洄遊　fishing mass migration
鱼群/魚群　fish school
鱼群密度/魚群密度　concentration of fish
鱼群探测器/魚群探測器,魚群探尋器　fish finder
鱼群指示标/魚群指示浮標　fish group indicating buoy
鱼肉分选机/魚肉採取機　meat separator
鱼尾板/護緣板　shin
鱼尾螺栓/魚尾螺栓　belt fishtail, fishtail bolt
鱼形桁架/月牙形桁架　lenticular truss
娱乐康体用地/娛樂康體用地　land for recreation facility
娱乐性景观环境用水/娛樂性景觀環境用水　water for recreational environment use
娱乐演出区/娛樂演出區　entertaining performance place
娱乐中心/娛樂中心　entertainment center, amusement center, recreation center
渔场/漁場　fishing ground
渔场图/漁場圖　fishing chart
渔船/漁船　fishing boat, fishing ship, fishing vessel
渔港/漁港　fishing harbor
渔港规章/漁港規則　regulations of fishery harbor
渔港监督艇/漁港監督艇　fishing port supervision boat
渔监/漁業監督　fishing supervision
渔礁/漁礁　fish reef
渔具/漁具　fishing tackle, fishing gear
渔捞限制/漁撈限制　fishing restriction
渔捞作业/漁撈作業　fishing operation
渔区/漁區　fishing area, fishing zone
渔汛/漁期　fishing season, catching season
渔业灯/捕魚燈　fishing light
渔业调查船/漁業研究船　fishery research boat, fishery research ship, fishery research vessel
渔业法规/漁業法規　fishery rules and regulations
渔业公司/漁業公司　fisheries company
渔业加工船/漁業加工船,漁[獲]加工船　fisheries factory ship, fishery factory ship, fish factory ship
渔业权/漁業權　fishing right

渔业实习船/漁業訓練船　fisheries training boat, fishery training vessel
渔业协定/漁業協定　fishery agreement
渔业巡逻船/漁業巡邏船　fishery patrol boat
渔业指导船/漁業指導船　fishery guidance ship, fishery guidance boat
渔栅/漁栅　fishing stake
渔政/漁業行政　fishery administration
渔政船/漁政船　fishery administration vessel
隅点/象限點　intercardinal point
逾期交付/延期交貨　delayed delivery
逾期提货/逾期提貨　delayed pick up
瑜伽/瑜伽　yoga
宇宙速度/宇宙速度　cosmic velocity
宇宙线/宇宙射線　cosmic ray
宇宙线爆发/宇宙線爆炸　cosmic ray burst
宇宙线强度/宇宙線強度　cosmic ray intensity
羽流/卷流,煙流　plume
羽流试验/煙流試驗　plume testing
羽毛球场/羽球場　badminton court
羽毛球运动/羽球　badminton
羽蛇神金字塔/羽蛇神金字塔　The Pyramid of Kukulkan
羽焰/裙焰　exhaust plume
雨层云/雨層雲　nimbo stratus
雨岛效应/雨島效應　rain island effect
雨滴/雨滴　rain drop
雨洪管理设计/景觀暴雨管理　drainage design and storm water management
雨花石/雨花石　Yuhua stone
雨回波衰减补偿技术/雨回聲衰減補償技術　rain echo attenuation compensation technique, REACT
雨季施工/雨季施工　raining season construction, rainy season construction
雨量/雨量　rainfall
雨量-持续时间-面积分析/雨量延時面積分析　depth-duration-area analysis
雨量分配系数/雨量分配係數　rainfall distribution coefficient
雨量计/雨量計,雨量器　rain gage, pluviometer
雨量记录器/雨量計　rain recorder
雨量逆增/雨量逆轉　inversion of rainfall
雨量器/降雨計　pluviometer
雨量强度频率/雨量強度頻率　intensity frequency of rainfall
雨量强度曲线/雨量強度曲線　intensity curve of rainfall
雨量损失/雨量損失　storm loss

雨林/雨林　rain forest, hygrodrymium
雨淋灭火系统/滅火系統　deluge system
雨篷/天篷,遮篷　canopy
雨蚀/雨水浸蝕　rain erosion
雨水/雨水,天水　meteoric water
雨水泵房/雨水泵室　rainwater pump room
雨水泵站/雨水泵站,滯洪抽水站　stormwater pumping station
雨水池/雨水池　stormwater tank
雨水冲刷/雨水沖刷　rainwash
雨水储存设施/雨水儲存裝置　rainwater storage equipment
雨水观察井/集水井　catch basin
雨水管/降水口,流水口　down spout, drain spout
雨水管道/雨水管,雨水溝,暴雨下水道　storm sewer
雨水花园/雨水花園　rain garden
雨水集蓄水池给水系统/集蓄水池給水系統　rain-well water supply system
雨水口/雨水口,排水孔　inlet, scupper, storm water inlet
雨水利用/雨水利用　use of rainwater
雨水利用系统/雨水利用系統　rain utilization system
雨水流量/雨水流量　discharge of storm sewage
雨水排除规划/雨水排除規劃　storm drainage planning
雨水排水系统/雨水排水系統,暴雨排水系統　rain system, stormwater system
雨水侵蚀/雨水浸蝕　rain erosion
雨水渠/雨水管　stormwater sewer
雨水渗透/雨水浸透　rain penetration
雨水收集给水系统/雨水收集給水系統　rain collection and water supply system
雨水收集系统/雨水收集利用系統　rainwater collection system
雨水下水道溢出/雨水溢流下水道　stormwater overflow sewer
雨水源河/雨水源河　rain-fed stream
雨天/雨日　rainy day
雨天流量/雨天水量　wet weather flow
雨天事故/雨天交通事故,雨天交通意外　wet traffic accident
雨雪干扰抑制/抗雨雪干擾　anti-clutter rain
语言传输指数/語音傳輸指數　speech transmission index, STI
语言干扰级/語言干擾位準　speech interference level
语言教室/語言教室　language classroom

语义学/語意學　semantic
语音告警/語音警報　phonic warning
语音-数据群呼/語音-數據群呼　voice-data group call
语音通信系统/語音通信系統　voice communication system
郁闭度/鬱閉度,葉層密度,林冠密度　crown density, shade density, canopy density
郁闭林冠/鬱閉冠層,鬱閉樹冠　closed canopy
育成鸡舍/育成雞舍　mature bird housing
育雏鸡舍/育雛器,孵卵器　brooder
育种/育種,繁殖　breeding
浴间坐台/浴間座　in-tub seat
浴室/浴室　bathroom
预办闭塞/預辦閉塞　preworking a block
预拌砂浆/預拌砂漿　ready-mixed mortar
预包装火箭发动机/預包裝火箭發動機　prepackaged rocket engine
预报波向/預報波向　forecasted wave direction
预曝光/預暴露　pre-exposure
预备舵工/預備舵手　lee helmsman
预备费/預備費　contingency
预备航次/預備航程　preliminary voyage
预备航天员/太空人候選者　astronaut candidate
预备间/特別房艙　state room
预备林/預備林,保留林　reserve forest
预测不满意百分率/預計不滿率　predicted percentage dissatisfied, PPD
预测导引律/預測導引律　predicted guidance law
预测平均热感觉/預測平均投票數　predictive mean vote, PMV
预测危险区/預測危險區　predicted area of danger, PAD
预处理/預處理　pretreatment
预触发器/預觸發器　pre-trigger
预防接种证书/預防接種證書　vaccination certificate
预防维修制/預防性保養系統　preventive maintenance system
预防[性]维护/預防維護,預防維修,預防保養　preventive maintenance
预防性修理/預防性修理　preventive repair
预放电/預放電　preliminary discharge
预付运费/預付運費,預支運費　advanced freight
预告/預告　preliminary notice
预告标/預告標　warning sign for approaching a station
预告信号/來臨信號　approaching signal
预告信号机/遠距號誌[機]　distant signal

预拱度/預拱量,預拱值　camber, precamber
预计到达时间/預計到達時間　estimated time of arrival, ETA
预计开航时间/預計離開時間　estimated time of departure, ETD
预计值/預計值,預報值　predicted value
预[加]应力/預力　prestressing
预加应力阶段/預力階段　prestressing stage
预检分诊室/預檢分診室　screening track, fast track
预借提单/預借載貨證券　advanced bill of lading
预浸料/預浸布　prepreg
预警机/預警機　early warning airplane
预警时间/告警時間　pre-warning time
预警卫星/早期警報衛星,早期預警衛星　early warning satellite
预可行性研究/初步可行性研究,可行性前期研究　pre-feasibility study
预冷/預冷　pre-cooling
预冷器/預冷器　pre-cooler
预冷系统/預冷系統　chilldown system
预裂爆破/預裂爆破　presplit blasting
预留变形量/預留變形量　deformation allowance
预留沉落量/預留沈落量　reserve settlement, settlement allowance
预留第二线/預留第二線　reserved second line
预留活载发展系数/預留活荷載增加因數　preserved live load increasing factor
预留金/預備金　reserve
预留孔/預留孔穴　preformed hole
预留强度/預留強度　reserved strength
预留用地/保留地　reservation area, reserved land
预滤池/初步過濾,粗濾　preliminary filter, prefilter
预埋件/預埋件　embedded parts
预膜/預膜　prefilming
预膜剂/預膜劑　prefilming agent
预扭导流片/預扭導流片　prerotating vane
预排进路/預排進路　presetting of a route
预曝气/預曝氣　preaeration
预切槽/預切槽　precutting trough
预燃[燃烧]室/預燃室　precombustion chamber, prechamber
预燃室喷嘴/預燃室噴嘴　precombustion chamber nozzle
预燃室式燃烧室/預燃室　precombustion chamber, prechamber
预热/預熱　preheating, preheat
预热锅炉/預熱鍋爐　preheating boiler
预热器/預熱器　preheater

预热送风/熱風　hot blast
预试/預試法　pretesting
预算成本/預算成本,計劃成本　budgeted cost
预算定额/預算定額　budget rating, rating norm for budget
预填骨料灌浆混凝土/預填骨料灌漿混凝土　colcrete
预通气/預曝氣　preaeration
预弯法/預彎法　preflex method
预弯法预应力/預彎法預應力　prestressing without tendon by pre-bending
预弯梁桥/預彎梁橋　preflex girder bridge
预温固定法/預溫固定法　refastening-down
预吸氧/預吸氧　preoxygenation
预舾装/預舾裝　pre-outfitting
预洗/預洗　prewash
预先浸湿/預濕法　prewetting
预先润湿/預濕法　prewetting
预先装定/預置　presetting
预压/預加荷載　preloading
预压法/預壓密工法　preloading method
预压固结荷载/預壓重量　preconsolidation load
预压压实/預載夯實　preloading compaction
预验收/工程預驗收　engineering pre-acceptance
预氧化/預氧化　preoxidized
预应力/預[應]力　prestress
预应力传递/預力傳遞　transfer prestress
预应力传递长度/預應力傳遞長度　transmission length of prestress
预应力度/預力度　degree of prestressing
预应力反拱/預力反拱　prestressing camber
预应力钢/預力鋼　prestressing steel
预应力钢结构/預應力鋼結構　prestressed steel structure
预应力钢筋腱外形/鋼腱縱斷面　tendon profile
预应力钢筋张拉机/預應力鋼筋張力機　prestressed steel bar tensioning machine
预应力混凝土/預應力混凝土　prestressed concrete
预应力混凝土结构/預[應]力混凝土結構　prestressed concrete structure
预应力混凝土路面/預力混凝土路面　prestressed concrete pavement
预应力混凝土桥/預力混凝土橋　prestressed concrete bridge
预应力混凝土轨枕/預力混凝土軌枕　prestressed concrete sleeper
预应力混凝土桩/預力混凝土樁　prestressed concrete pile

预应力阶段/預力階段　prestressing stage
预应力筋/[鋼]腱　tendon
预应力筋孔道/鋼腱道　tendon duct
预应力壳/預力薄殼　prestressed shell
预应力锚杆/預應力岩石錨桿　prestressed rock bolt
预应力千斤顶/預應力千斤頂　prestressing jack
预应力损失/預[應]力損失　loss of prestress
预应力台座/預加應力臺　prestressing bed
预应力体系/預力系統　prestressing system
预张拉/先拉力　pretension
预制/預製　prefabrication
预制场/預製場　prefabrication yard, casting yard
预制钢壳钻孔基础/預製鋼殼鑽孔基礎　prefabricated steel shell bored foundation
预制混凝土/預鑄混凝土　precast concrete
预制混凝土构件/混凝土預製構件　precast concrete unit, precast concrete member
预制混凝土路面/預鑄混凝土路面　precast concrete pavement
预制件挂车/預製拖車　prefab trailer
预制建筑/預鑄房屋　prefabricated building
预制灭火系统/預製滅火系統　pre-engineered extinguishing system
预制桩/預鑄樁　precast pile
预钻插桩法/預鑽插樁法　socketing pile in prebored hole
预作用自动喷水灭火系统/預作用噴水滅火系統,預動式　preaction sprinkler system
阈限系数/界限係數　threshold factor
阈限值/低限值　threshold limit value
阈[值]/閾值　threshold
阈值星等/閾值星等　magnitude of threshold
遇水膨胀橡胶/遇水膨脹橡膠　hydrophilic expansion rubber
遇水易燃固体/遇濕易燃固體　flammable solid when wet
遇险/遇險,遇難　distress
遇险报告/遇難信文　distress message
遇险报警/遇險警報　distress alerting
DSC遇险报警/數位選擇呼叫遇險警報　DSC distress alerts
遇险报警转发/遇險報中繼　distress alert relay
遇险船员/遇險船員　distressed seaman
遇险电传呼叫/遇險電傳呼叫　distress telex call
遇险电话呼叫/遇險電話呼叫　distress telephone call
遇险和安全通信/遇險與安全通信　distress and safety communications
遇险呼叫/遇難呼叫,求救呼叫　distress call

遇险呼叫程序/遇險呼叫程式　distress call procedure
遇险呼叫格式/遇險呼叫格式　distress call format
遇险火光信号/遇難照明彈　distress flare
遇险阶段/遇險階段　distress phase
遇险求救程序/遇險程式　distress procedures
遇险收妥承认/遇險收到確認　distress acknowledgement
遇险通信/遇險通信　distress communication
遇险通信业务/遇險業務　distress traffic
遇险信道/遇險頻道　distress channel
遇险信号/遇險信號,遇難信號　distress signal
遇险优先等级/遇險優先順序　distress priority
遇险优先呼叫/遇險優先呼叫　distress priority call
遇险优先申请信息/優先請求遇險信文　distres priority request message
遇险者/遇險人員　person in distress
御街/禦街　Yu Jie, royal street
愈合组织/愈合組織　healing organization
愈伤组织/愈傷組織,新生組織　callus
渊潭/淵潭　deep pool and pond
元胞自动机/細胞自動機,格狀自動機　cellular automate, cellular automaton
元件/元件　element
元件破损事故/元件破損事故　element breakdown accident
元件烧毁事故/元件燒毀事故　element burnout accident
元素宇宙丰度/元素宇宙豐度　cosmic abundance of elements
园凳/園凳　garden bench
园建工程师/園林建設工程師　construction engineer of landscape architecture
园景/園林景觀　garden scenery
园景树/園景樹,獨賞樹　specimen tree
园廊/遊廊,走廊　veranda, gallery, colonnade
园篱/園籬　garden fence, garden hedge
园林/園林　garden and park
园林保留地/園林保留地　reserve garden
园林匾额楹联/園林區額楹聯　inscribed tablet in garden
园林布局/園林布局　garden layout
园林城市/園林城　landscape garden city
园林道路设计/園林道路設計　garden road design, garden path design
园林灯具/園林燈具　garden nightscape lighting
园林地貌创作/園林地貌創作　topographical design
园林地形改造/園林地形改造　topographical reform
园林动物/園林動物　landscape animal
园林分区/園林分區　garden zoning
园林分区规划/園林分區規劃　garden block planning
园林工程/園林工程　garden engineering, landscape engineering
园林工具/園林工具　garden instrument, garden implement
园林管理/園林管理　garden management
园林管理规划/園林管理規劃　management plan
园林规划/園林規劃　garden planning, landscaping planning, landscape planning
园林规划说明书/園林規劃說明書　garden planning direction
园林规划图/園林規劃圖　garden planning map
园林机具设备/園林機具設備　gardening machine
园林机械/園林機械　garden machine
园林给水/景觀給水　landscape water supply
园林给水系统/景觀供水系統　landscape water supply system
园林技术管理/園林技術管理　garden technical management
园林建筑/園林建築[物]　garden building
园林建筑学/園林建築學　garden architecture
园林空间/園林空間　garden space
园林理水/園林理水　water system layout in garden
园林露天剧场/園林露天劇場　open garden theater
园林露天舞池/園林露天舞池　open garden dance space
园林绿地/園林綠地　landscape green area
园林绿地灌溉/綠化灌溉　landscape irrigation
园林绿地灌溉系统/園林綠地灌溉系統　irrgation system for landscape
园林美学/園林美學　garden aesthetics
园林苗圃/園林苗圃　garden nursery
园林排水/園林排水　landscape drainage
园林区划/園林區劃　garden area division
园林色彩艺术/園林色彩藝術　art of garden color
园林设备/園林設備　garden equipment
园林设计/園林設計,庭園設計,景觀設計　garden design, landscape design
园林设计师/園林設計師　landscape architect, garden designer
园林生态规划/造園生態規劃　landscape architecture ecological planning
园林生态环境/造園生態區　landscape architecture ecotope

园林生态系统/造園生態系 landscape architecture ecosystem
园林施工/園林施工 garden layout, garden construction
园林史/園林[歷]史 landscape history, garden history
园林水电工程师/園林建設總公司高級工程師 hydroelectric engineer of landscape architecture
园林水景/園林水景 water scene of garden
园林微生物/園林微生物 landscape microbe
园林系统/公園系統 park system
[园林]项目部/項目團隊,專案團隊 project department, project team
[园林]项目计划/專案計劃 project plan
[园林]项目团队/專案團隊,項目團隊 project department, project team
[园林]项目周期/景觀項目週期 project cycle
园林小品/園林小品 small garden ornament
园林小气候/園林小氣候 landscape microclimate
园林形式/園林形式 garden style
园林学史/園林學史 history of garden architecture
园林夜景照明/園林夜景照明 gardener nightscape lighting
园林艺术/園林藝術 garden art
园林艺术布局/園林藝術布局 artistic layout of garden
园林意境/園林意境 poetic imagery of garden
园林楹联/園林楹聯 couplet written on scroll, couplet on pillar
园林植物/園藝植物,景觀植物,園藝花木 landscape plant, garden plant
园林植物群落/景觀植物群落 landscape phytobiocoenose
园林总体规划/園林總體規劃 garden master planning
园林座椅/庭園椅子 garden chair
园路布局/道路設計 road layout
园路工程/園路工程 garden paving engineering
园路结构设计/園路結構設計 road structural design
园路设计/園路設計 garden path design
园路台阶/園路臺階 garden road step
园路线形设计/公路線形設計 road alignment design
园貌维修/園貌維修 garden feature maintenance
园内交通管理/園内交通管理 park traffic control
园桥/園橋 garden bridge
园台/園臺 platform
园亭/涼亭,蔭亭 garden pavilion, pavilion

园土/園土 garden soil
园外交通管理/園外交通管理 traffic control out of park entrance
园椅/園椅,庭園椅子 garden chair, garden seat
园艺/園藝 horticulture
园艺疗法/園藝療法 horticultural therapy
园艺治疗/園藝療法 horticultural therapy
园址测量图/園址測量圖 garden site survey map
园桌/園桌 garden table
原材料加工工厂/原料加工廠 raw material processing plant
原地/原位,就地 in situ
原动机自动起动装置/原動機自動起動器 prime mover automatic starter
原废水/原廢水 raw wastewater
原件收付/原件收付 original piece receipt and delivery
原料加工车间/原料加工車間 raw material handling plant
原料库/原料[儲存]庫 raw material storage
原木/原木 log
原球茎/蘭菌共生體 protocorm
原生矿物/原礦石 primary mineral
原生水/原生水 primitive water
原生土/原位土壤 soil in situ, in-situ soil
原生污染物/原生汙染物,初始汙染物 primary pollutant
原生演替/初級演替,初級消長 primary succession
原生植被/本地植物 secondary vegetation, native vegetation
原生种/初始種 initial species
原始固结/原始壓密 virgin consolidation
原始环境系统/原始環境系統 wilderness environment system
原始孔隙度/原孔隙度 original porosity
原始林/原始林 virgin forest
原始数据/原始資料,初級資料 original data, raw data
原始完整性/原始完整性 original integrality
原水/生水,未經淨化水 raw water
原条/原條 timber stripe
原位/原位,就地 in situ
原位测量/原位量測 in situ measurement
原位测试/原位試驗,現地實驗 in situ test
原位强度/原位強度 in situ strength
原位维修/原位維修 on site maintenance
原位直剪试验/原位直剪試驗 in situ direct shear test

原污泥/原汙泥　raw sludge
原污水/原汙水　raw sewage
原物归安/原物歸安　anastylosis of heritage
原型飞行试验/原型飛行試驗　protoflight test
原型机试飞/原型試飛　prototype flight test
原油/原油　crude oil
原油船/原油輪　crude oil tanker, crude oil carrier
原油洗舱/原油洗艙　crude oil washing, COW
原油洗舱系统/原油洗艙系統　crude oil washing system, crude oil cleaning system
原住民/原住民　existing resident
原状/原狀　undisturbed
原状土/原狀土　parent soil
原状土样/原狀土樣,原狀標本　undisturbed sample, undisturbed soil sample
原子级加工/原子等級加工　atomic scale machining
原子能/核能　nuclear energy
原子频标/原子頻標　atom frequency standard
原子氢焊/氫原子焊　atomic-hydrogen welding, atomic-hydrogen arc welding
原子时/原子時　atomic time, AT
原子氧/原子氧　atom oxygen
原子氧流量模式/原子氧流量模式　atomic oxygen fluence model
原子氧试验/原子氧試驗　atomic oxygen test
圆舭艇型/圓舭型船體　round-bilge hull
圆材结/木材[套]結　timber hitch
圆点曲线终点/圓曲線終點　end of circular curve
圆顶环/圓頂環　dome ring
圆锭/圓錠　round lozenge
圆度/圓度　circularity, roundness
圆端形桥墩/圓端形橋墩　round-ended pier
圆概率误差/圓形概差　circular error probable, CEP
圆钢/圓鋼　round steel
圆拱顶/圓拱頂　dome proper
圆规/小圓規　bow compass
圆弧法/圓弧法　circular arc method
圆环效应/管壁效應　annular effect
圆缓点/圓緩點　point of curve to spiral
圆极化/圓極化　circular polarization
圆角多边形风洞/多邊形風洞　polygon wind tunnel
圆角区/內圓角區　fillet area
圆截面风洞/圓筒風洞　circular wind tunnel
圆明园/圓明園　Yuanming Yuan Imperial Garden
圆木/圓木,圓形木材　log
圆木桥/圓木橋　log bridge
圆木桩/圓木樁　log peg
圆盘给料机/盤式進料器,盤飼機　disk feeder

圆频率/圓[週]頻率　circular frequency
圆曲线/圓[弧]曲線　circular curve
圆曲线终点/圓曲線終點　end of circular curve
圆扫描/圓形掃描　circular scan
圆石路面/圓石路面　cobble stone pavement
[圆]筒仓/[圓]筒倉　silo
圆筒喷灌器/圓筒噴灌器　rotor sprinkler
圆筒形浮标/筒形浮標　cylindrical buoy
圆筒形壳/圓筒形殼　circular cylindrical shell
圆头钉/圓頭釘　round headed nail
圆头铆钉/圓頭鉚釘　round-head rivet, snaphead rivet
圆形编队/圓形編隊　circular formation
圆形端头/鉚釘頭　button head
圆形基础/圓形基礎　circular foundation
圆形桥墩/圓形橋墩　circular pier
圆形筒壳/圓筒形殼　circular cylindrical shell
圆形尾/圓形艉　round stern
圆-圆系统/圓-圓系統　ρ-ρ system
圆直点/切線點,相切點,曲線終點　point of tangent, PT
圆周波数/圓週波數　radian wave number
圆柱/圓柱體　circular column
圆柱测径规/柱形塞規　cylindrical plug, cylindrical gage
圆柱度/圓柱度　cylindricity
圆柱滚子轴承/[圓柱]滾子軸承　roller bearing, cylindrical roller bearing
圆柱壳/圓筒薄殼　cylindrical shell
圆柱体号型/圓筒形號標　cylinder shape
圆柱体抗压强度/圓柱抗壓強度　cylindrical compressive strength
圆柱体压力试验/圓柱體壓力試驗　cylindrical compression test
圆柱投影/圓筒投影法　cylindrical projection
圆柱形镉镍蓄电池/圓柱狀鎳鎘蓄電池　cylindrical cadmium-nickel battery
圆柱坐标机器人/筒狀機器人　cylindrical robot
圆锥/圓錐物　cones
圆锥贯入度仪/圓錐貫入器　cone penetrometer
圆锥滚子轴承/滾錐軸承　taper roller bearing, tapered roller bearing
圆锥号型/圓錐形號標　conical shape
圆锥离合器/錐形離合器　cone clutch
圆锥破碎机/錐式碎石機　cone crusher
圆锥扫描/錐形掃描　conical scanning
圆锥扫描地球敏感器/錐形掃描地球感測器　conical scanning earth sensor, conical scanning horizon

sensor
圆锥扫描跟踪/圓錐形掃描追蹤　conical scanning tracking
圆锥扫描雷达/圓錐形掃描雷達　conical scanning radar
圆锥式碎石机/錐式碎石機　cone crusher
圆锥投影/圓錐投影法　conical projection
圆锥误差/角錐誤差　coning error
缘石标记/緣石標線　curb marking
缘石坡道/緣石坡道，路緣坡道　curb ramp
缘藻类/緣藻類　greenalgae
源/［流］源　source
源包/資料封包　source packet
源点地址/源位址　source address
源流/源流　source flow
源流强度/源流強度　strength of source flow
源区电磁脉冲/源地電磁脈波　source-region electromagnetic pulse
源头削减/源削減　source reduction
远场/遠場　far field
远场区/遠場區　far field area
远程待爆/遠程備炸　long distance arming
远程待爆时间/遠程備炸時間　long distance arming time
远程发令/遠程命令　remote commanding
远程监督分区/遠程監督分區　relayed surveillanced subsection
远程监控/遠程監督及控制　remote monitor and control
远程扫描/長距程掃描　long-range scanning
远程网路/遠程網路　relayed surveillanced network
远程巡航速度/遠端巡航速度　long-range cruising speed
远程终端/遠端［終端機］　remote terminal
远地点/遠地點　apogee
远地点发动机/遠地點發動機　apogee engine
远地点火箭发动机/遠地點踢進器　apogee kick rocket engine, apogee kick rocket motor
远地点注入/遠地點注入　apogee injection
远动工区/遠動工區　work district for telemechanical system
远端串音/遠端串音，遠端串話　far-end crosstalk
远端串音衰减/遠端串音衰減　far-end crosstalk attenuation
远供系统/遠供系統　remote power feeding system
远海测量/遠洋測量　pelagic survey
远红外/遠紅外　far infrared
远机位/遠端停機位　remote aircraft stand

远焦的/遠焦的，非焦性的　afocal
远景/遠景　distant view
远景规划/長期規劃　long-term planning
远距离测量/長途量測　long distance measurement
远距离控制/遙控　remote control
远距离水位指示计/遠隔水位指示器　remote water level indicator
远距用户/遠距用戶　distant subscriber
远控［消防］炮灭火系统/遠控［消防］炮滅火系統　remote-controlled fire monitor extinguishing system
远离/遠離　away from
远破波/碎波　broken wave
远破波高/碎波浪高　breaking wave height
远破波力/碎波浪力　breaking wave force
远日点/遠日點　aphelion
远心柔顺装置/遙軸順應性裝置　remote center compliance device, RCC device
远星点/遠星點　apastron
远洋船/遠洋船［舶］　ocean going vessel, ocean going ship, ocean trader
远洋码头/遠洋碼頭　oceanic wharf
远洋提单/海運載貨證券　ocean bill of lading
远洋渔业/遠洋漁業　distant fishery
远缘杂交育种/遠緣雜交育種　distant hybridization breeding
远缘杂种/遠緣雜種　distant hybrid
远月点/遠月點　apocynthion
远震/遠震　far earthquake
苑/苑　imperial park, yuan
约定参照标尺/約定參考標度　conventional reference scale
约定层次/契約層次　indenture level
约定最大持续功率/約定最大連續輸出功率　contract maximum continuous rating, contract MCR
约克-安特卫普规则/約克-安特衛普規則　York-Antwerp Rules
约束/約束，拘束　constraint
约束单元/限制單元　constraint element
约束混凝土/約束混凝土　confined concrete
约束结构/束縛結構　restrained structure
约束力矩/拘束力矩　restraining moment
约束砌体/約束砌體　confined masonry
约束运行/約束運行　constrained operation
月潮/太陰潮　lunar tide
月潮间隙/月中天潮汐間歇　lunitidal interval
月池/月池　new moon pool
月出/月出　moon rise

月洞门/月洞門,月亮門 moon gate
月度货物运输计划/月度貨物運輸計劃 monthly freight traffic plan
月高峰系数/月高峰係數 maximum uneven factor of monthly consumption
月检/月檢,每月檢查 monthly inspection
月龄/月齡 moon age
月没/月没 moon set
月平均日交通量/月平均日交通量 monthly average daily traffic volume, MADT volume
月球/月球 moon
月球地质/月球地質 geology of Moon
月球视运动/月視運動 moon apparent motion
月球探测工程系统/月球探測工程系統 lunar exploration engineering system
月球探测器/月球太空船 lunar spacecraft
月球探测卫星/月球探測衛星 lunar exploration satellite
月食/月食 lunar eclipse
月坛/月壇 Temple of Moon, Yue Tan
月相/月相 lunar phases
月牙板/月牙板 reverse link, quadrant link
月牙板滑块/月牙板滑塊 reverse link block, die block
乐池/樂池,樂團席 orchestra pit
阅读灯/閱讀燈 reading lamp
阅览室/閱覽室 reading room
跃层/躍層 spring layer
跃层住宅/躍層公寓 duplex apartment
跃升/攢昇 zoom
跃水现象/躍水現象 porpoising
跃移[作用]/跳躍,躍動 saltation
越冬室/越冬室 wintering bee house
越级/過覆 overstep
越岭隧道/越嶺隧道,穿山隧道,山嶺隧道 over mountain line tunnel, summit tunnel
越岭线/越嶺線 ridge crossing line
越岭选线/越嶺選線 location of mountain line, location of line in mountain region, location over mountain
越区干扰/超越干擾 overshooting interference
越区供电/越區供電 over-zone feeding
越区灌溉/越丘灌溉 plot-to-plot irrigation
越行站/越行站 overtaking station
越秀木/越秀木 Yuexiu wood
越野车/越野車 cross-country vehicle
越野滑雪/越野滑雪 cross-country skiing
越站乘车/越站乘車 overtaking the station

越障限制重量/障礙限制重量 obstacle limiting weight
云底高度/雲底高 cloud base height
云顶高度/雲頂高度 cloud top height
云高/雲高 cloud height
云量/雲量 cloud amount
云母/雲母 mica
云幂/雲幕 cloud ceiling
云幂灯/雲幕燈,艙頂燈 ceiling light, ceiling projector
云幂高度/雲幕高 ceiling height
云幂气球/雲幕氣球 ceiling balloon
云幂仪/雲幕計 ceilometer
云图[册]/雲圖冊 cloud atlas
云纹法/雲紋法 moire method
云状/雲狀 cloud form
云状空化/雲狀空化 cloud cavitation
匀砂/匀砂 sand brooming
匀熵流/均熵流 homoentropic flow
匀质列车/匀質列車 even mass train
允许间隙/容許間隙 permissible clearance
允许磨损/容許磨損 permissible wear
允许逃逸/容許逃脱 permit escape
允许预推信号/容許預推信號 permissive prehumping signal
允许轴载荷/允許軸載荷 allowable load on journals of same axle
允许自毁/允許自毀 self-destruction permissible
允许阻塞度/容許阻塞度 permitted blockage percentage
陨石/隕石 meteorite
运兵船/運兵船 troopship
运畜船/牲口船 cattle ship, cattle carrier
运达期限/運達期限 time limit of shipment arrival
运动病/動量症 motion sickness
运动波/[運]動波 kinematic wave
运动补偿设备/運動補償設備 motion compensation equipment
运动草坪/運動草坪 sports lawn
运动场/運動場,體育場 stadium, arena, athletic field
运动场草坪/運動場草坪 sports turf
运动地面/運動地面 sport floor
运动定律/運動律 law of motion
运动仿真器/運動模擬器 motion simulator
运动功能减退/運動減退,動作減退 hypokinesia
运动基[训练]仿真器/運動基訓練模擬機 motion base training simulator, MBTS

运动俱乐部/運動俱樂部　sports club
运动空间/運動空間　motion space
运动模拟/動力模擬　kinematic simulation
运动耐力/運動耐力　exercise tolerance
运动黏度/運動黏度,動力黏度,動黏[滯]性　kinematic viscosity, kinematical viscosity
运动伞/運動傘　sport parachute
运动设施/運動設施,體育設施　athletic facility, sports facility
运动稳定性/運動穩定性　kinematic stability
运动学/運動學　kinematics
运动学相似性/運動相似性　kinematic similarity
运动员更衣室/運動員更衣室　locker room
运动员席/運動員席　sportsman seat
运动中心/運動中心　center of motion
运动周期/運動週期　period of motion
运费/運費　freight
运费保险/運費保險　freight insurance
运费吨/運費噸,載貨容積噸,貨物噸　freight ton
运费付讫/運費付訖　carriage paid
运费率/[貨物]運費率　freight rate
运费清单/運費清單　freight manifest
运费未收/運費由收貨人支付　carriage forward
运河操纵/運河中操縱　maneuvering in canal
运河灯/運河燈　canal light
运河吨位/運河噸位　canal tonnage
运河航标/運河助航標　navigation aids on canal
运货飞船/運貨太空船　cargo spacecraft
运价/運價,費率　tariff, rate
运价本/價目表,費率規章,收費制　tariff
运价比差/運價比差　rate ratio
运价加成/運價加成　rate addition
运价减成/運價減成　rate reduction
运粮船/糧食船　victualler
运量/運輸量　volume
运量波动系数/貨物運輸量波動係數　freight volume fluctuation coefficient
运量预测/運[輸]量預測　transport volume forecast, traffic volume forecast
运煤船/運煤船　collier, coal carrier
运苗车/運苗車　vehicle for tree transportation
运木船/運木船,木材運輸船　log carrier, timber carrier
运泥船/運泥船　sludge boat
运输安全管理/運輸安全管理　safety management of traffic
运输安全监察/運輸安全監督　safety supervision of traffic
运输安全检查/運輸安全檢查　safety inspection of traffic
运输安全控制系统/運輸安全控制系統　safety control system of traffic
运输安全评估/運輸安全評估　safety evaluation of traffic
运输安全系统工程/鐵路運輸安全系統工程　safety system engineering of traffic
运输包装/運輸包裝[件]　packing for transport, transport package
运输标志/運輸標誌　transport mark
运输成本/運輸成本　traffic cost
运输成本计划/運輸成本計劃　traffic cost plan
运输船/運輸船,運輸艦　transport ship
运输方案/運輸方案　traffic program
运输服务业/運輸服務業　transport service industry
运输工程学/運輸工程　transportation engineering
运输工作技术计划/運輸工作技術計劃　plan of technical indices for freight traffic
运输工作日常计划/運輸工作日常計劃　day-to-day traffic working plan
运输管理费/運輸管理費　transport administration fee
运输规划/運輸規劃　transportation planning
运输合同/運送契約　contract of carriage
运输和起吊载荷/運輸和起吊載荷　transport and hoisting load
运输环境/運輸環境　transportation environment
运输机/運輸機　transport airplane
运输计划/運輸計劃圖　transportation plan
运输搅拌混凝土/車拌混凝土　transit-mixed concrete
运输结构/交通結構　transport structure
运输经济学/運輸經濟學　transportation economics
运输类飞机/運輸類飛機　airplane in transportation category
运输类旋翼机/運輸類別旋翼機　rotorcraft in transportation category
运输里程/運輸里程　carriage mileage
运输量/輸送量　transportation volume
运输路线/運輸路線　transit route
运输能力/運輸容量　transport capacity
运输起竖发射车/運輸-起竖-發射車　transporter-erector-launcher, TEL
运输设施/運輸設施　transportation facility
运输市场/運輸市場　transport market
运输市场管理/運輸市場管理　transport market control

运输试验/運送測試　transportation test
运输收入/交通規費　traffic revenue
运输收入率/交通規費率　rate of traffic revenue
运输弹性系数/運輸彈性係數　transport elasticity coefficient
运输体系/運輸系統　transport system
运输条件/運輸情況　traffic condition
运输网/運輸網　transportation network
运输系数/輸送係數　transport coefficient
运输系统计划/運輸系統計劃　transportation system plan
运输限制/運輸限制　traffic limitation, traffic restriction
运输责任期/運輸責任期　transport liability period
运输支出/運輸支出　traffic expenditure
运输重量测定/裝船重量測定　shipping weight measurement
运输走廊/運輸走廊　transportation corridor
运土机械/土工機械,移土工設施　earth-moving machine, earth-moving plant
运土列车/運土列車　earth-moving train
运行/運算,操作　operate
运行安全/作業安全　operation security
[运行]轨道/軌道　running orbit
运行过渡工况/運轉情況工況　transitional running condition
运行检查/運行檢查　running inspection
运行剖面/運行剖面圖　operation profile
运行时间/運轉時間　running time
运行速度/運行速度,運行速率　operating speed
运行调节/運行調節　operation regulation
运行图描绘仪/運行圖描繪儀　train diagram plotter
运行图天窗/運行圖天窗　sky-light in the train diagram, gap in the train diagram
运行图周期/運行圖週期　period in the train diagram
运行阻力/運轉阻力,行駛阻力　running resistance
运行阻力试验/運轉阻力試驗,行駛阻力試驗　test for running resistance
运营成本/作業成本　operation cost
运营吨公里/運營噸公里　freight tonne kilometer
运营期/運轉期　operating period
运营铁路/運營鐵路　railway in operation, operating railway
运营通风/運轉通風　operation ventilation
运营系统模拟/運營系統模擬　simulation of operation system
运用车/運用車　serviceable car, car for traffic use, cars open to traffic
运用车保有量/運用車保有量　number of serviceable car held
运用车工作量/運用車工作量　serviceable car operation capacity
运用机车/運用機車　locomotive in operation
运用机车台数/運用機車臺數　number of locomotive in service
运用考验/運用試驗,運作試驗,實用試驗　service test
运用试验/運行試驗　service test, operation test
运载火箭/發射載具　carrier rocket, launch vehicle
运载火箭轨道理论/運載火箭軌道理論　theory of launch vehicle trajectory
运载火箭气动特性/運載火箭氣動特性　aerodynamic characteristics of launch vehicle
运载火箭遥测/發射載具遙測　launch vehicle telemetry
运载火箭运动理论/運載火箭運動理論　theory of launch vehicle motion
运载火箭转运/發射載具轉移　launch vehicle transfer
运载火箭装配测试厂房/發射載具裝配測試廠房　launch vehicle assembly and test building
运载可靠度/運載可靠度　carrying reliability
运载器垂直运输/運載器垂直運輸　vertical state transportation of launch vehicle
运载体/載具　vehicle
运载体坐标系/載具坐標系　vehicle coordinate system
运转变扭器/運行扭矩變速器　running torque converter
运转车长/運轉車長　train guard
运转曲线/運行線圖　run curve
运转试验/運轉試驗　running trial, running test
运转室/運轉室　operation office for train receiving departure, traffic operation office
晕船药/暈船藥　anti-seasickness medicine
韵律教室/韻律教室　aerobics classroom

Z

匝道/匝道,斜坡　ramp
匝道标线/匝道標線　ramp marking
匝道集成系统控制/匝道集成系統控制　ramp integrated system control
匝道交通调节/匝道儀控　ramp metering
匝道连接处/匝道連接處　ramp junction
匝道桥/坡橋,引橋　ramp bridge
匝道通行能力/匝道通行能力　ramp capacity
杂草植物/宅旁植物　ruderal plant
杂光/雜散光　stray light
杂光系数/雜散光係數　coefficient of stray light
杂合体/雜合子,異型合子　heterozygote
杂货/雜貨　general cargo
杂货船/雜貨船　general cargo ship
杂货码头/雜貨碼頭　general cargo wharf
杂技场/競技場,馬戲場　circus
杂交育种/雜交育種　cross breeding
杂交元/雜交元　hybrid element
杂类危险物质/雜項危險物質　miscellaneous dangerous substance
杂乱回波/混雜回波　clutter echo
杂木林/雜木林,雜樹林　spinney
杂排水/中水　gray water
杂散电流腐蚀/迷走電流腐蝕,漏洩電流腐蝕　stray-current corrosion
杂散发射/混附發射　spurious emission
杂砂岩/硬砂岩　greywacke
杂填土/雜填土　miscellaneous fill
杂物吊杆/吊柱,吊架　davit
杂音测试器/聲電位差計　psophometer
杂音抑制器/噪音抑制器　noise suppressor
杂音抑制线圈/雜訊抑制線圈　noise suppression coil
杂种优势/雜種優勢　heterosis
灾害调查/損害調查　damage survey
灾害性地质/災害地質　disaster geology
灾难性故障/毀滅性故障　catastrophic fault
栽培变种/栽培品種　cultivated variety
栽培类型/栽培型　cultivated form
栽培植被/栽培植被　cultivated vegetation
栽植机/栽植機,種植機　planting machine
再拌和/重拌　remixing
再补充/再移植,補植　restocking
再城市化/再都市化　reurbanization
再充风/再充風　recharging
再次制订计划/再計劃　replanning
再分杆/中間對角線,細分成員　intermediate diagonal, subdivided member
再固结/再壓密　reconsolidation
再混合/重拌　remixing
再集中[化]/再集中　recentralization
再利用/再[利]用　reuse
再平衡/再平衡　rebalance
再热/再熱　reheat
再热器/再熱器,重熱器,復熱器　reheater
再热式汽轮机/再熱式蒸汽渦輪機　reheat steam turbine
再热系数/再熱因數,重熱因數　reheat factor
再入/重返　reentry
再入等离子鞘/再入等離子體外殼　reentry plasma sheath
再入点/再入點,重入點　reentry point
再入段/再進入階段　reentry phase
再入[段]测量/再進入階段量測　reentry phase measurement
再入方式/再入方式　reentry mode
再入防热/再入熱防護　reentry thermal protection
再入飞行器/重返載具　reentry vehicle
再入飞行器升阻比/再入飛行器昇阻比　lift-drag ratio of reentry vehicle
再入飞行器稳定裕度/再入飛行器穩定裕度　stabilization margin of reentry vehicle
再入飞行器压心/再入飛行器壓心　aerodynamic pressure center of reentry vehicle
再入飞行器质心/再入飛行器質心　mass center of reentry vehicle
再入高度/重返高度　reentry altitude
再入轨道/重返軌跡　reentry trajectory
再入黑障区/再入黑障區域　reentry blackout zone
再入环境/再入環境　reentry environment
再入加热/再入加熱　reentry heating
再入角/再入角　reentry angle
再入控制/再入[大氣層]控制　reentry control

再入气动总加热量/再入氣動總加熱量　total amount of reentry aerodynamic heating
再入气体动力学/再入氣體動力學　reentry gas dynamics
再入速度/重返[大氣層]速度　reentry velocity
再入遥测/再入遥測　reentry telemetry
再入载荷/再入負載　reentry load
再入最大热流密度/再入最大熱流密度　maximum density of reentry heat flow rate
再生/再生　regeneration
再生冷却/再生冷卻　regenerative cooling
再生沥青混合料/再生瀝青混合料　reclaimed asphalt mixture
再生式空气预热器/再生式空氣預熱器,迴轉式空氣預熱器　rotary air heater
再生式热交换器/再生[式]熱交換器　regenerative heat exchanger, heat regenerative exchanger
再生式生命保障系统/再生式維生系統　regenerative life support system
再生水/再生水,淨化水　reclaimed water, renovated water
再生水泵站/再生水抽水站　reclaimed water pumping station
再生水厂/再生水廠　water reclamation plant, water recycling plant
再生水利用规划/中水利用規劃　reclaimed water utilization planning
再生水利用系统/再生水利用系統　reclaimed water utilization system
再生水平/再生水準　regeneration level
再生系统/再生系統　regeneration system
再生橡胶/再製橡膠　reclaimed rubber
再生效率/再生效率　regeneration efficiency
再生原水/再生水　regenerated water
再生噪声/再生雜訊噪音　regenerated noise
再生纸种植器/再生紙種植器　reclaimed paper container
再生制动/[電力]再生制動,再生剎車　regenerative braking, regenerative brake
再生中继/再生中繼　regeneration and repetition
再适应/再適應　readaptation
再调节水库/重調整水庫　reregulating reservoir
再吸收/再吸收　resorption
再循环/再循環,回流　recycle, recirculation
再循环阀/再循環閥　recirculation valve
再压缩/再壓縮　recompression
再引入/再引入　reintroduction
再用轨/代用軌　second hand rail, relaying rail
再造林/跡地造林　reafforestation, reforestation
再振铃/再振鈴　re-ringing
在轨爆炸/在軌爆炸　explosion on orbit
在轨测试/軌道上測試　in-orbit test
在轨管理/在軌管理　in-orbit management
在轨破裂/在軌破裂　rupture on orbit
在航/航行中　underway
在上风/居上風,頂風　in the wind
在线测量/線上量測　on-line measurement
在线测试/連線測試　on-line test
在线修/線上維護　on-line maintenance
在用汽车/在用車　vehicle in use
在职培训/在職訓練　in service training
在子午线上航行/經線航法　meridian sailing
载波/載波　carrier wave
载波电报终端机/載波電報終端機　carrier telegraph terminal
载波电话增音机/載波電話中繼器　carrier telephone repeater
载波电话终端机/載波電話終端機　carrier telephone terminal
载波调度电话中继器/載波調度電話中繼器　carrier adaptor for dispatching telephone
载波功率/載波功率　carrier power
载波频率/載波頻率　carrier frequency
载波通信/載波通信　carrier communication
载波同步/載波同步　carrier synchronization
载波遥接话路/載波遥接話路　carrier channel connected to telephone line
载波用户/載波用戶　carrier subscriber
载驳船/駁船搬運船,子母船,浮貨櫃船　lighter aboard ship, LASH, barge carrier
载车渡船/汽車輪渡　auto ferry
载弹量/裝彈量　store-carrying capacity
载供系统/載波供應系統　carrier supply system
载荷比例阀/載荷比例閥　load proportional valve
载荷传感阀/負載感測器　load sensor valve
载荷等级数/負重等級,負載分類號碼　load classification number, LCN
载荷历程/載荷歷程　load history
载荷谱/負載波譜　loading spectrum
载荷情况/負載情況　load condition
载荷曲线/負荷曲線,載重曲線　load curve
载荷任务训练/酬載任務訓練　payload mission training
载荷设计/負載設計　load design
载荷专家/酬載專家　payload specialist, PS
载货舱位/貨艙空間　cargo space

载货甲板/載貨甲板　cargo deck
载货量/載貨量　cargo deadweight
载货汽车/卡車　motor truck
载货清单/載貨單,艙單　manifest
载货容积/貨艙空間　cargo space
载机/空中載體　aerial carrier
载机运动补偿/飛機運動補償　aircraft motion compensation
载客量利用率/載客量利用率　bus capacity utilization rate
载冷剂/冷卻劑　cooling medium, coolant
载冷剂泵/冷卻劑泵　coolant pump
载流承力索/電流輸送懸鏈線　current-carrying catenary
载漏/載漏,載波漏失　carrier leak
载频/載波頻率　carrier frequency
载频放大器/載波放大器　carrier amplifier
载频同步/載頻同步,載波頻率同步　carrier frequency synchronization
载频周期匹配/週波匹配　radio cycle match
载人飞船发射/載人太空船發射　manned spacecraft launch
载人飞船工程/載人宇宙飛船工程　manned spacecraft engineering
[载人]飞船加注间/載人太空船加注間　manned spacecraft loading room
载人飞船系统/載人宇宙飛船系統　manned spacecraft system
载人飞船遥测/載人飛船遥測　manned spacecraft telemetry
[载人]飞船装配测试厂房/載人太空船裝配測試廠房　manned spacecraft assembly and test building
载人航天/載人太空飛行　manned space flight
载人航天发射场/載人太空飛行發射場　launch site for manned space flight
载人航天工程系统/載人航太工程系統　manned space engineering system
载人航天技术/載人太空科技　manned space technology
载人航天器/載人太空船　manned spacecraft
载人航天器回收/載人太空船回收　manned spacecraft recovery
载人离心机/人體離心機　human centrifuge
载人潜水器/有人潛水器　manned submersible
载人振动实验设备/載人振動器　manned vibrator
载损鉴定/貨損檢查　inspection on hatch and cargo
载运能力/載運能力　transport competency
载运违禁品/載運違禁品　carriage of contraband

载噪比/載波雜訊比,載波雜音比　carrier-to-noise ratio
载重/裝載量,超重量　loading capacity
S载重/S載重　S loading
载重吨位/載重噸位　loaded tonnage
载重量/載重[量]　deadweight
载重量标尺/載重標尺　deadweight scale
载重量利用率/載重量利用率　truck loading capacity utilization rate
载重汽车/載重車　loaded car
载重[水]线/載重[水]線　load water line
载重线标志/載重線標誌,船舶載重線　load line mark, plimsoll line mark
载重线检验/載重線檢驗　load line survey
载重线勘划/載重線勘劃　load line assignment
载重线区域/載重線區域　load line area
载重线圆圈/載重線圈　load line disc
载重线证书/載重線證書　load line certificate
载重与平衡/載重平衡　weight and balance
载装手册/裝載手册　loading manual
暂冲式风洞/間歇風洞　intermittent wind tunnel
暂存库/待驗倉庫,暫時庫容,暫時貯存　temporary storage
暂估价/暫定金額　provisional sum
暂列金额/暫定金額　provisional sum
暂时硬度/暫態硬度　temporary hardness
暂停/暫停,臨時停車　standing
暂押室/臨時拘留室　temporary detention room
暂住人口/暫住人口　temporary resident population
錾平锤/鏨面錘,琢面錘　chipping hammer
遭遇段/交會軌道段　encounter phase of trajectory
遭遇周期/遭遇週期　period of encounter
凿边/鑽鏨,打除　chiselling
凿缝/鑽鏨,打除　chiselling
凿井吊泵/沈泵　sinking pump
凿井装岩机/直井出碴機　shaft mucker
凿削/鏨平　chipping
凿岩机/鏨岩機,鑽岩機　rock drill, jack hammer, air hammer drill
凿岩机推进器/鑽穿速　drill feed
凿岩钎/鑽鋼　drill steel
凿岩台车/鏨岩臺車,鑽孔臺車　rock drilling jumbo, drilling jumbo
凿岩钻车/鏨岩鑽車　drill wagon for jack hammer
凿子/鏨子　cold set
早爆/過早起爆　premature blast
早后期声能比/早後期聲能比　early-to-late arriving sound energy ratio

早凝/早凝　premature stiffening
早期反射声/早期反射　early reflection
早期故障率/早期故障率　infant mortality
早期基督教建筑/早期基督教堂式建築　early Christian architecture
早期强度/早期強度　early strength
早期失效期/早期失效期　incipient failure period
早期衰变时间/早期衰減時間　early decay time, EDT
早期现代主义/早期現代主義　early modernism
早期抑制快速响应喷头/早期滅火快速反應灑水噴頭　early suppression fast response sprinkler
早强硅酸盐水泥/早強水泥　high-early-strength portland cement
早强混凝土/早強混凝土　early strength concrete
早强减水剂/早強減水劑　hardening accelerating and water reducing admixture
早燃/先期點火　pre-ignition
早炸/早爆炸　early burst
藻海/藻海　sargasso sea
藻胶酸钠/藻鈉凝集補助劑　sodium alginate
藻井/藻井　domed coffered ceiling, zaojing
皂化/皂化　saponification
造/造　way of construction, zao
造币厂/鑄幣廠　mint factory
造船厂/造船廠　ship yard, shipyard
造船台/造船碼頭　building berth
造床流量/造河流量　formative discharge
造价分析/造價分析　cost analysis
造价工程师/成本工程師　cost engineer
造景/造景　landscaping
造景类用水/造景類用水　water for waterscape use
造林/造林　afforestation
造桥机/造橋機　bridge fabrication machine
造型/模製,造模翻砂,成型　molding
造型地貌/造型地貌　imaginative geomorphologic figuration
造型工艺/模具化過程,成模過程　moulding process
造型机/造模機,塑造機　molding machine
造型修剪/修剪,樹木整型,剪枝　topiary, pruning
造园学/造園學,造園術,造園法　garden making, landscape gardening
造纸厂/造紙廠　paper mill
噪度/噪度,噪音量　perceived noisiness
噪声/噪音,雜訊　noise
噪声等级/噪音度　noise level
噪声等效曝光量/雜訊等效曝光[量]　noise equivalent exposure, NEE

噪声等效反射比差/雜訊等效反射比差　noise equivalent reflectance difference, NERD
噪声等效功率/雜訊等效功率,等效雜訊功率　noise equivalent power, NEP
噪声等效温差/雜訊等效溫度差　noise equivalent temperature difference, NETD
噪声等值线/噪音等值線　noise isoline
噪声发生器/雜波產生器　noise generator
噪声烦劳度/噪音吵鬧度　noise annoyance
噪声干扰/噪音干擾　noise jamming
噪声合格证/噪音許可證　noise certificate
噪声缓解/消音　noise abatement
噪声检定值/噪音額定數　noise rating number, NRN
噪声降低/噪音防治　abatement noise
噪声角/雜訊角　noise angle
噪声控制/噪音控制,噪音管制　noise control
噪声雷达引信/雜訊雷達引信　noise radar fuze
噪声敏感度/雜訊靈敏度　noise sensitivity
噪声敏感建筑物/噪音敏感建築物　noise sensitive building
噪声频谱/雜訊譜　noise spectrum
噪声评价/噪音準則　noise criterion
噪声评价曲线/噪音判據曲線　noise criterion curve, NC-curve
噪声容限/雜訊容限　noise margin
噪声试验/噪音試驗　noise level test
噪声衰减/噪音衰減,雜訊衰減　noise attenuation
噪声污染/噪音汙染　noise pollution
噪声污染级/噪音汙染位準　noise pollution level
噪声系数/噪音因數　noise factor
噪声抑制/噪音抑制,雜訊減低　noise attenuation
责任故障/責任故障　chargeable fault
责任级/責任層級　level of responsibility
责任事故/責任事故　responsible accident
责任限制/責任限制　limitation of liability
增大截面加固法/增大截面加固法　structure member strengthening with reinforced concrete
增幅速率选择电路/增幅速率選擇電路　envelope growth selection circuit
增幅选择/增幅選擇　envelope growth selection
增量调制/差量調變,二階調變　delta modulation
增面燃烧/增面燃燒　progressive burning
增黏剂/增黏劑,膠黏劑　viscosity index improver, tackifier
增强电热式肼单组元推进系统/增強電熱式肼單組元推進系統　augmented electrothermal monopropellant hydrazine system

增强群呼接收机/強化群呼接收機 enhanced group calling receiver, EGC receiver
增强群呼系统/強化群呼系統 enhanced group call system
增强群呼业务码/強化群呼業務碼 enhanced group call service code
增强群呼译码器/強化群呼解碼器 EGC decoder
增强塑料/強化塑膠,補強塑膠 reinforced plastic
增强相/強化相 reinforcing phase
增升装置/增昇裝置 high lift device
"增速"按钮/"增速"按鈕 push button "up"
增塑剂/塑化劑 plasticizer
增稳系统/穩定增強系統 stability augmentation system
增效作用/增效作用 synergism
增压/增壓,加壓 supercharge, pressurization, supercharging
增压泵/增壓泵 booster pump, boost pump
[增]压比/增壓比,壓力比 pressure ratio, supercharging ratio
增压柴油机/增壓式柴油機 supercharged diesel engine
增压度/渦輪增壓度 degree of turbocharging, degree of supercharging
增压发动机/增壓發動機,增壓引擎 supercharged engine
[增压]后冷器/補助冷卻器 aftercooler
增压级/增壓級 booster stage
增压气源/加壓氣來源 pressurization air source
增压器出口温度/增壓器排放溫度 discharge temperature of super charger
增压器喘振/渦輪增壓器波振 turbocharger surge
增压器机油滤清器/渦輪增壓器機油濾清器 oil precision filter for turbocharger
增压器配机试验/渦輪增壓器配對試驗 turbocharger matching test
增压器涡轮特性/增壓器渦輪特性 turbocharger turbine characteristics
[增压器]压气机/增壓器,吹風機,鼓風機 blower
增压涡轮泵/增壓渦輪泵 boost turbopump, booster turbopump
增压系统辅助鼓风机/渦輪增壓器輔助鼓風機 turbocharging auxiliary blower
增压系统应急鼓风机/渦輪增壓器應急鼓風機 turbocharging emergency blower
增压压力/增壓[壓]力 boost pressure, supercharging pressure
增压预冷/加壓預冷 pre-cooling by pressurization
增压中冷/增壓中間冷卻 charge inter-cooling
增压座舱/壓力艙 pressurized cabin
增益/增益 gain
增长管理/成長管理 growth management
增长极理论/成長極理論 growth pole theory
增长交通量/增長交通量 increment of traffic volume
增长率法/生長速率法 growth rate method
增值税/增值稅 incremental tax
憎水性/疏水性 hydrophobicity
憎水性集料/疏水集料 hydrophobic aggregate
扎绳头/紮頭,繩頭紮束 whipping
渣粒球性/渣粒球性 sediment sphericity
渣油/殘存油 residual oil
渣油路面/渣油路面 residue oil pavement
渣滓/渣滓,沈澱 sediment
轧钢厂/輥軋廠 rolling mill
轧辊/輥子,滾子 roller
轧制/[輥]軋 rolling
轧制边/滾邊 rolled edge
闸板阀/閘門,門閥 gate valve
闸板转换阀/閘門變換閥 gate change-over valve
闸阀/閘閥,拉式閘門 gate valve, draw gate
闸门/閘門,拉門 draw gate
闸门板/閘門板 gate sheet
闸门槽/閘門槽,拉門溝 gate groove
闸门立柱/閘門立柱 meeting post
闸[门]桥/閘門橋 water gate bridge
闸片/制動墊,軔襯,刹車襯 brake lining, brake pad
闸式潜水器/閘式潛水器 lock-in lock-out submersible
闸瓦/閘瓦,刹車片 brake shoe
闸瓦背/閘瓦背 brake shoe back
闸瓦插销/閘瓦插銷 brake shoe key
闸瓦间隙自动调节器/自動鬆緊調整器 automatic slack adjuster
闸瓦试验台/軔塊慣性臺架 brake shoe inertia dynamometer
闸瓦托/軔座,刹車座 brake head
闸瓦压力/閘瓦壓力,制動塊壓力 brake shoe pressure
闸压成形/折板機成形 press-brake forming
闸引水工程/閘門引水工程 gate diversion work
栅顶/梁格狀頂 grid, gridiron
栅格翼/網狀彈翼 lattice fin
栅式进水口/格柵式進水口,算式進水口 grated inlet
栅线调查/栅線調查 screen line count

炸弹舱/炸彈艙　bomb bay
炸弹口径/炸彈口徑　bomb caliber
炸毁线/破壞線　destruction line
炸毁指令/破壞命令　destruct command
炸药/炸藥,爆炸品　explosive
摘车修/摘車修　car detached repair
摘挂调车/摘掛調車　detaching and attaching of car
摘挂列车/摘掛列車　pick-up and drop train
摘机状态/拿起話筒　off-hook
摘蕾/除芽　flower bud picking
摘心/摘心　pick the top young sprout
宅基地/農村宅基地,自用住宅　homestead, rural housing land
宅间绿地/宅間綠地,住宅區補充綠地　residential supplementary green space, green space between houses or apartments
宅间小路/宅間小路　residential lane
宅园/宅園　home garden
窄带干扰/窄頻干擾　narrow band interference
窄带随机振动/窄帶隨機振動　narrow band random vibration
窄带直接印字/狹頻帶直接印字　narrow band direct print
窄带直接印字电报/狹頻帶直接電報　narrow band direct-printing telegraphy
窄带直接印字电报设备/狹頻帶直接印字電報設備　narrow band direct-printing telegraph equipment, NBDP telegraph equipment
窄轨/窄軌　narrow gage
窄轨铁路/窄軌鐵路　narrow gage railway
窄桥标志/窄橋標誌　narrow bridge sign
沾污/沾染　contamination
毡房/氈包,圓頂帳蓬　yurt
斩波调压/截波控制　chopper control
展成法/演生　generating
[展馆]参观走廊/參觀走廊　visitor gallery
展开立面图/展開立面圖　developed elevation drawing
展开面积/展開面積　developed area
展[览]馆/展覽館,陳列館,展示館　exhibition hall
展览室/展覽室,展示室　exhibition room
展览温室/展覽溫室　public conservatory
展廊/展覽會場,特展區　exhibition gallery
[展品]摄影室/攝影室　photographic studio
[展品]修复室/文物修復工作室　conservation laboratory
展平机构/變平機構　flatten mechanism
展期检验/延期檢驗　extension survey
展厅/展示館,陳列館,展覽館　exhibition hall
展弦比/展弦比,寬高比　aspect ratio
展线/展線,延伸線　route development, extension of line, line development
展线系数/延伸係數　coefficient of extension line, coefficient of developed line
占地面积/占地面積　site area
占线表示/占線表示　occupancy indication
占用带宽/占用頻帶寬　occupied bandwidth
栈道/棧道　boardwalk, trestle on a cliff
栈桥/棧橋,突堤,排架橋　trestle, jetty, trestle bridge
栈桥式码头/棧橋式碼頭,突堤碼頭　jetty, trestle type wharf
战斗部/彈頭　warhead
战斗部动态杀伤区/戰鬥部動態殺傷區　dynamic killing zone of warhead
战斗船/戰艦　fighting boat
战斗弹遥测/作戰飛彈遙測　operational missile telemetry
战斗[导]弹/作戰飛彈　operational missile
战斗工况管理/戰鬥操作方式管理　combat operating mode management
战斗航海勤务/戰鬥航海勤務　combating navigation service
战斗转弯/急爬昇轉彎　chandelle
战列舰/戰[鬥]艦　battle ship
战略规划/戰略規劃,策略[性]規劃　strategic planning
战略通信卫星/戰略通訊衛星　strategic communication satellite
战术空中导航系统/戰術導航判讀系統　tactical air navigation system, TACAN system
战术通信卫星/戰術通訊衛星　tactical communication satellite
战争条款/戰時險條款　war risk clause
站场/站場　station yard
站场感应通信/站場感應通信　station-yard inductive communication
站场监视电视/站場監視電視　station-yard monitor TV
站场客运建筑/站場客運設備　passenger service facilities
站场排水/站場排水　station-yard drainage
站场通信/站場通信　station-yard communication
站场无线电通信/站場無線電通訊　station-yard radio communication
站场无线电中继转发台/站場無線電中繼臺,站場無

線電中繼站　station-yard radio relay set
站场型网路/站場型網路　geographical circuitry
站到站/貨櫃站到站　container freight station to container freight station, CFS to CFS
站点服务半径/站點服務半徑　station service radius
站调楼/指揮調度臺　yard controller tower
站房平台/站房平臺　platform for station building
站间联系电路/站間聯繫電路　liaison circuit between stations
站间行车电话/站間行車電話　interstation train operation telephone
站界/站界，車站限界　station limit
站界标/站界標　station limit sign
站内道口联系电路/站內道口聯繫電路　liaison circuit with highway crossings within the station
站内作业/站內轉運　yard work
站坪长度/站位長度　length of station site
站坪坡度/站坪坡度　grade of station site
站前广场/車站廣場　station square, station place
站台/月臺　platform
站台票/月臺票　platform ticket
站台屏蔽门/月臺門　platform screen door
站线/站線，車場軌道，站內軌道　siding, station track, yard track
站线有效长/站線有效長度　effective length of station track
站修/站修　repair track maintenance
张紧器/張力器　tensioner
张开型裂纹/張開型裂紋　opening mode of crack
张拉程序/施拉程式　stressing sequence, tensioning procedure
张拉结构/張力結構　tension structure, tensile structure
张拉控制应力/張拉控制應力，預力控制應力　control stress for prestressing, jacking control stress
张拉膜/張力膜　tensile membrane
张拉膜结构/張力膜結構　tensile membrane structure
张拉千斤顶/張拉千斤頂　tensioning jack, drawing jack
张拉试验/拔樁試驗　pulling test
张力场/張力場　tension field
张力场梁/張力場梁　tension field beam
张力传感器/張力轉換器　tension transducer
张力杆/張力桿　tensioning bar
张力控制器/張力控制器　tension control assembly
张力轮/拉緊帶輪　straining pulley, tension pulley

张力腿平台/張力腳式鑽油臺　tension leg platform, TLP
张力增量/張力增量　tension increment
张量场/張量場　tensor field
张量分析/張量分析　tensor analysis
张索加油装置/張索加油裝置　span wire fuel rig
张弦结构/串結構　string structure
章动/章動　nutation
章动敏感器/章動感測器　nutation sensor
章动频率/章動頻率　nutation frequency
章动阻尼器/章動阻尼器　nutation damper
樟子松/歐洲赤松　pinus sylvestris
涨潮/漲潮　flood tide, rising tide
涨潮标志/洪水位，高潮位標誌，泛水標誌　flood mark
涨潮持续时间/漲潮[持續]期　duration of flood, duration of flood tide
涨潮顶点/最高潮　high tide
涨潮力/漲潮力　tidal flood strength
涨潮历时/漲潮期　duration of rise
涨潮流/漲潮流　flood current, flood stream, tidal flood current
涨落周期/漲落週期　cycle of fluctuation
涨圈式密封/漲圈型密封環　piston ring type seal
丈杆/測桿　measuring rod
丈量/量測，測定　measure
丈量吨位/丈量噸位，量計噸位　measurement tonnage
丈人一(天鴿 α)/丈人一(天鴿 α)　Phact
账务机构/賬務機構　accounting authority
账务机构识别码/賬務機構識別碼　accounting authority identification code, AAIC
胀壳式锚杆/擴孔錨碇型　expansion type rock bolt
胀形/膨脹　bulging
障碍物/障礙物，阻塞　obstacle, clogging
障碍物灯/航空障礙燈　obstacle light
障碍物探测/障礙物探測　obstruction sounding
障碍物限界面/障礙物限界面　obstruction restriction surface
障碍物限制面/障礙物限制面　obstacle restrictive surface
障碍照明/障礙照明　obstacle lighting
障景/障景　obstructive scenery
障景种植/障景種植　screen planting
招标/招標　call for tenders, call for bids, invitation for bid
招标活动行政监督/招標活動行政監督　administrative supervision of tender

招标控制价/招標控制價　regulated maximum bidding price
招待所/招待所　hostel
招投标程序/投標手續　tender procedure, bid procedure
招引注意信号/引起注意信號　signal to attract attention
着发机构/擊發裝置　percussing device
着火/著火,燃燒　ignition
着火点/著火點,[引]燃點　ignition point, ignition temperature, fire point
爪板/棘齒板　claw plate
爪形冲击锤/爪形衝擊錘　cross chipper hammer
找顶/找頂　top cleaning
找平层/找平層　leveling layer
找小坑/找小坑　spot surfacing
沼气/[汙水]沼氣　biogas, sewage gas
沼气池/沼氣池　biogas digester
沼气电站/沼氣電站　methane power station
沼气发电/沼氣發電　methane electricity generation
沼生植物/池沼植物　helophyte
沼泽/沼澤　swamp
沼泽群落/沼澤群落　limnodium
沼泽土/沼澤土　bog soil
沼泽淤泥/沼澤淤泥　boglime lake marl
沼泽园/沼澤園　bog and marsh garden
沼泽植被/沼澤性植被　mire vegetation
沼泽植物/沼澤植物　marsh plant
兆欧表/高阻表,邁格表　megger
照壁/照壁,影壁　screen spirit wall
照查锁闭/檢核鎖定裝置　check locking
照度计/照度計　illuminance meter
照度均匀度/照度均匀度　uniformity ratio of illuminance
照距/光照距,光強度視程　luminous range
照明/照明　lighting, illumination
照明灯/照明燈　illuminating lamp
照明灯具/燈具　lamp and lantern
照明电路/照明電路　lighting circuit
照明功率密度/照明功率密度　lighting power density, LPD
照明光源/照明光源,採光光源　lighting source
照明过渡/照明過渡　lighting transition
照明过渡段/照明過渡區段　lighting transition section
照明节电率/節能率　energy saving ratio
照明配电箱/照明配電箱,照明配電盤　lighting distribution box, lighting power distribution panel
照明设备/照明設備　lighting facility
照明适应段/照明適應段　lighting adaptation section
照明稳压器/照明穩壓器　illumination voltage stabilizer
照明装置/照明設備　illumination equipment
照射/照射,暴露,曝光　exposure
照射途径/曝露途徑　exposure pathway
[照相]干板/照相底版　photographic dry plate
照相馆/照相館　photo studio
照相枪/照相槍　gun camera
照相望远镜/照相望遠鏡,攝影望遠鏡　photographic telescope
照准尺/視準尺　sight rule
罩壳/蓋,套　cover
罩面/覆蓋　overlay
遮蔽/遮蔽　masking, sheltering
遮蔽光弧/遮光弧　obscured sector
遮蔽甲板/遮蔽甲板　shelter deck
遮蔽甲板船/遮蔽甲板船　sheltered deck vessel
遮蔽角/遮光角,遮罩角　shielding angle
遮断比/遮斷比　cut-off
遮断信号/遮斷信號　obstruction signal
遮断信号按钮/遮斷信號按鈕　obstruction signal button
遮断预告信号机/遮斷預告號誌機　approach obstruction signal
遮光片/遮光片　antiglare screen, antidazzling screen
遮光罩/遮光物　shade
遮拦比/遮攔比　ratio of obstruction
遮阳/遮陽,物鏡遮光罩　sunshade
遮阳板/遮陽板,擋板　sun-shield, visor
遮阳金属百叶帘/遮陽金屬百葉簾　metal venetian blind for shading
遮阳篷/天遮,天篷[遮]　awning
[遮阳]天篷帘/遮陽天篷簾　sky-light blind
遮阳系数/遮陽係數　shading coefficient
遮障/隔板,隔屏　screen
折/收,卷　furl
折板/折板,多稜薄殼　folded plate, folded slab
折边肘板/卷邊腋板,凸緣腋板　flanged bracket
折尺/折尺　folding scale
折点/折點　breakpoint
折点氯化/折點氯消毒　breakpoint chlorination
折叠家具/折疊式家具　folding furniture
折叠门/折[疊]門　folding door
折叠频率/卷折頻率　foldover frequency
折叠式舱口盖/折疊[式]艙口蓋　folding hatch

折叠式舱盖/折式艙蓋 folding hatchcover
折叠式减摇鳍装置/折鳍穩定器 folding fin stabilizer
折叠式太阳电池阵/折疊式太陽電池陣 fold-out type solar array
折叠式箱型货盘/折疊式箱形托貨板 folding box pallet
折叠推拉窗/推拉折頁窗 sliding folding window
折叠座椅/折椅 folding seat
折断/折斷 break off
折反式光学系统/折反式光學系統 refractive and reflective optical system
折光差/折光差 refraction
折光系数/折射係數 refraction coefficient
折合水准/折算水準 reduced level
折减弹性模量/抗減彈性模數 reduced elastic modulus
折角塞门/角旋塞 angle cock
折角型船艇/硬稜船體 hard chine hull
折射/折射 refraction
折射角/折射角 angle of refraction
折射率分布/折射率剖面圖 refractive-index profile
折射式光学系统/折射光學系統 refractive optical system
折射图/折射圖 refraction diagram
折射系数/折射因數 refraction factor
折算热负荷/折算熱輸入 reduced heat input
折贴角/折貼角 crimped angle
折线法/多邊形法 polygon method
折线形屋架/弓形屋架 segmental roof truss
折线张拉/彎曲鋼腱 deflected tendon
折中主义/折衷主義 eclecticism
辙叉/轍叉,岔心,交叉 frog, crossing
辙叉跟长/轍叉跟長度 heel length of frog
辙叉跟端/岔心踵端 heel end of frog, frog heel
辙叉跟宽/岔心踵端開程 heel spread of frog
辙叉号数/岔心號數 frog number
辙叉角/轍叉角,岔心角,岔道角 frog angle, crossing angle
辙叉心轨尖端/岔心實際交點 actual point of frog
辙叉心轨理论尖端/轍叉理論交叉點,岔心理論交點 theoretical point of frog
辙叉咽喉/叉喉,轉轍喉,翼軌彎曲點 throat of frog
辙叉有害空间/轍叉有害空間 gap in the frog, open throat, unguarded flange-way
辙叉趾长/轍叉趾長 toe length of frog
辙叉趾端/岔心趾端 toe end of frog, frog toe

辙叉趾宽/趾端開口距 toe spread of frog
锗砷化镓太阳电池/鍺砷化鎵太陽電池 Ge-gallium arsenide solar cell
褶皱/褶皺,褶曲 fold
针对性维修/條件性維護 conditional maintenance
针阀/針閥 needle valve
针灸科/針灸科 department of acupuncture and moxibustion
针孔/針孔,銷孔 pinhole
针入度/針入度 penetration, penetration degree
针入度试验/穿入試驗,穿插試驗 penetration test
针入度指数/穿入度指數 penetration index
针叶林/針葉林 needle-leaved forest, coniferous forest
针叶乔木群落/針葉喬木林 conisilvae
针叶树/針葉樹,松柏類 conifer
针织厂/針織廠 knitting mill
针状星云/針狀星雲 acicular nebula
侦察船/偵查艦 scout, scout ship
侦察分系统/偵察子系統 reconnaissance subsystem
侦察机/偵察機 reconnaissance airplane
侦察卫星/偵察衛星 reconnaissance satellite
侦察相机/偵察攝影機 space-born reconnaissance camera
珍善本书库/善本書庫 rare book stack
珍珠岩/珍珠岩 perlite
帧/[資訊]框 frame
帧传输/幀傳遞 frame transfer
帧读出/幀讀出 frame readout
帧格式/框格式 frame format
帧频/框頻,圖框頻率 frame frequency
帧首定界符/訊框起始定界符 frame start delimiter
帧速率/幀率,框速率 frame rate
帧同步/幀同步,框同步 frame synchronization
帧同步码/幀同步碼,框同步碼 frame sync pattern
帧抓取器/框接收器 frame grabber
真北/真北 true north
真北方向角/真北方向角 true north bearing
真出没/真出没 true rise and set
真地平/真地平線,真水平線 true horizon
真地平圈/天球水平線圈 celestial horizon
真方位/真方位 true bearing, TB
真风/真風 true wind
真缝/真縫 true joint
真高度/真高度 true altitude
真航向/真航向 true course, TC, true heading
真近点角/真近點角,真近點距 true anomaly
真空/真空 vacuum

真空安全阀/真空減壓閥　pressure vacuum relief valve
真空泵/真空泵　evacuation pump, vacuum pump
真空泵抽气速率/真空泵體積流率,泵抽速　volume flow rate of a vacuum pump
真空泵极限压力/真空泵極限壓強　vacuum ultimate pressure of a pump
真空比冲/真空比衝　vacuum specific impulse
真空[变相]锅炉/真空[變相]鍋爐　vacuum boiler
真空玻璃/真空玻璃　vacuum glass
真空插管浇注/真空管鑄造　vacuum tube casting
真空沉积涂层/真空沈積塗層　vacuum deposited coating
真空充电与放电试验/真空充電與放電試驗　vacuum charging and discharging test
真空充气/真空充氣　vacuum gas filling
真空充油/真空充油　vacuum oil filling
真空抽气系统/真空抽氣系統　vacuum pumping system
真空除气/真空除氣　vacuum degassing, vacuum deaeration
真空除氧/真空脫氣機　vacuum deaerate
真空淬火/真空淬火　vacuum quenching, vacuum hardening
真空电子束焊/真空電子束焊接　vacuum electron beam welding
真空度/真空度　vacuum, degree of vacuum
真空镀[膜]/真空沈積　vacuum deposition
真空断路器/真空斷路器　vacuum circuit-breaker
真空多层绝热/真空多層絕緣　vacuum multi-layer insulation
真空阀门/真空閥　vacuum valve
真空放电/真空放電　vacuum discharge
真空封接/真空密封　vacuum seal
真空干摩擦/真空乾摩擦　vacuum dry friction
真空干燥/真空乾燥　vacuum seasoning
真空灌胶/真空灌膠　vacuum glue pouring
真空光学试验台/真空光學試驗臺　vacuum optical test bench
真空烘烤/真空加熱除氣　vacuum bakeout
真空混凝土/真空混凝土　vacuum concrete
真空检漏/真空偵漏,真空檢漏　vacuum leak detection
真空检漏系统/真空偵漏系統　vacuum leak detecting system
真空浇注/真空鑄造　vacuum casting
真空金属软管/真空金屬軟管　vacuum metal flexible pipe
真空金属硬管/真空金屬硬管　vacuum metal hard pipe
真空浸渍/真空浸漬　vacuum impregnation
真空冷焊/真空冷焊　vacuum cold welding
真空冷焊试验/真空冷焊試驗　vacuum cold welding test
真空冷凝器/真空冷凝器　vacuum condenser
真空流导/真空流導　vacuum conductance
真空排水/真空系統排水　vacuum drain
真空破坏器/真空破除器　vacuum breaker
真空钎焊/真空硬焊　vacuum brazing
真空热处理/真空熱處理　vacuum heat treatment
真空热环境/熱真空環境　thermal vacuum environment
真空升华/真空昇華　vacuum sublimation
真空试验/真空試驗　vacuum test
真空室/真空室,真空艙　vacuum chamber
真空速/真空速　true airspeed
真空推力/真空推力　vacuum thrust
真空脱水工艺/真空脫水技術　vacuum dewatering technique
真空吸尘清扫车/[真空]吸塵器　vacuum sweeper
真空吸尘装置/真空吸塵裝置,真空淨化設備　vacuum cleaning installation, vacuum cleaner, cleaning vacuum plant
真空吸水机械/真空吸水機械　vacuum water sucker
真空系统/真空系統　vacuum system
真空压力表/真空壓力器　vacuum manometer
真空硬钎焊/真空硬焊　vacuum brazing
真空预压/真空預壓　vacuum preloading
真空蒸发/真空蒸發　vacuum evaporation
真空蒸馏/真空蒸餾　vacuum distillation
真空制动/真空靭,真空刹車　vacuum brake
真空制动装置/真空制動裝置　vacuum brake equipment
真空主断路器/真空線路斷路器　line vacuum circuit-breaker
真空作业混凝土/真空法混凝土　vacuum processed concrete
真密度/真密度　true density
真内摩擦角/真内[部]摩擦角　true angle of internal friction
真石漆/真石漆　sand textured building coating based on synthetic resin emulsion
真实断面图/足尺斷面　true section
真实刚度/真實勁度　true stiffness
真实高度/真實高度　true height
真实孔径侧视雷达/真實孔徑側視雷達　real

aperture side-looking radar
真实孔径长度/真實孔徑長度　length of real aperture
真实孔径分辨率/真實孔徑解析度　resolution of real aperture
真实孔径雷达/真實孔徑雷達　real aperture radar
真实气体/真實氣體　real gas
真实气体效应/真實氣體效應　real gas effect
真实速度/真速　true velocity
真实天线/真實天線　real antenna
真实性/真實性,本真　authenticity
真实应力/真應力　true stress
真太阳/真太陽　true sun
真太阳日/真太陽日　true solar day
真误差/真誤差　true error
真型试验/足尺试验　full-scale test
真运动雷达/真運動雷達　true motion radar, TM radar
真[运动]显示/真運動顯示　true motion display
真蒸汽压力/真蒸汽壓力　true vapour pressure
砧木/砧木　rootstock
诊断参数/診斷參數　diagnostic parameter
诊断方法/診斷方法　diagnostic method
诊断工艺/診斷技術　diagnostic technology
诊断规范/診斷規範　diagnostic norm
诊断周期/診斷週期　interval between diagnosis
诊断专家系统/診斷專家系統　diagnostic expert system
诊室/診察室　consulting room
枕间夯实机/軌枕夯實機　crib consolidating machine
枕梁/車體承梁　body bolster
枕木塞/道釘孔塞,軌枕栓　tie plug
枕形壁灯/枕形壁燈　pillow shaped wall lamp
阵发性客流/間歇性客運交通　intermittent passenger traffic
阵风/陣風,疾風　gust
阵风风洞/陣風風洞　gust wind tunnel
阵风缓和/陣風衰減　gust alleviation
阵风速率/陣風速率　gust speed
阵风响应/陣風反應　gust response
阵风性/風陣性,風陣係数　gustiness
阵风因子/陣風因子　gust wind factor
阵风载荷/陣風負載　gust load
阵风载荷减缓/陣風負載衰減　gust load alleviation
阵列探测器/偵檢器陣列　detector array
阵列天线/陣列天線　array antenna
阵雨/陣雨,驟雨　shower
振摆误差/擺矩振動誤差　vibropendulous error

振冲/振衝　vibroflotation
振冲法/面振法　vibroflotation method
振冲器/振動衝擊器　vibrating impacter
振荡极限/回擺極限　oscillation limit
振荡器/振盪器　oscillator
振荡燃烧/振盪燃燒　oscillating combustion
振荡压路机/振盪壓路機　oscillatory roller
振荡中心/擺動中心　center of oscillation
振捣棒/内部震動機　poker vibrator
振捣混凝土/震實混凝土　vibrated concrete
振动/振動　vibration
振动沉拔桩机/振動沈拔樁機,振動打拔樁機　vibration pile driver extractor, vibro-driver extractor
振动沉拔桩架/振動打拔樁架　vibratory pile driving and extracting frame
振动沉桩/振動打椿　vibration piling
振动冲击夯/振動衝擊夯,振動搗緊機　vibratory tamper, vibratory rammer
振动传递率/振動傳遞率　vibration transmissibility
振动打桩机/振動打樁機　vibrating pile driver, vibratory driver, vibro pile driver
振动环境/振動環境　vibration environment
振动[火]箭/振動[火]箭　vibration test rocket
振动给料机/振動給料機　vibrating feeder
振动加速度/振動加速度　vibration acceleration
振动监测仪/振動監視器　vibration monitor
振动料仓/儲料斗　surge bin
振动烈度/振動烈度　vibration severity
振动流法/振流法　vibrating-flow method
振动轮激振力测定/振動輪激振力測定　vibration drum exciting force measurement
振动轮频率测定/振動輪頻率測定　drum vibration frequency measurement
振动轮振幅测定/振動輪振幅測定　drum vibration amplitude measurement
振动模态/振動模[態]　mode of vibration
振动模态频率/振動模態頻率　vibration modal frequency
振动能/振動能　vibrational energy
振动辗压机/振動壓實機　vibration compactor, vibration roller
振动碾/振動滾壓機　vibrating roller
振动漂移率/振動漂移率　vibration drift rate
振动平板夯/振動板壓實機,振動壓密法　vibratory plate compactor
振动筛/振動篩　vibrating screen
振动式输送机/搖振帶式輸送機　shaking conveyor
振动试验/振動試驗　vibration test

振动台/振動臺,搖振臺　vibration table, shaking table
振动推土机/振動推土機　vibrating dozer
振动弦式变换器/振動線轉換器　vibrating wire converter
振动响应/振動響應　vibration response
振动压路机/振動式滾壓機,震實機　vibratory roller
振动压密/振動壓密法　vibro densification
振动压实/振動壓實,振動夯實　vibrating compaction
振动压实机/震板夯實機　vibrating plate compactor
振动严酷度/振動烈度　vibration severity
振动抑制/減震　vibration suppression
振动允许界限/振動容許限度　allowable limits of vibration
振动噪声/振動噪音　vibration noise
振动中心/擺動中心　center of oscillation
振动桩锤/震動打樁機　vibratory pile hammer
振抖/顫動　fluttering
振幅/振幅　amplitude, amplitude of vibration
振幅共振/共振幅　amplitude of resonance
振幅频谱/振幅譜　amplitude spectrum
振梁加速度计/振梁加速度計,振動電波加速計　vibrating beam accelerometer
振铃/振鈴　ringing
振铃器/發信設備　signaling equipment
振铃信号振荡器/振鈴信號振盪器　ringing signal oscillator
振弦加速度计/振盪帶加速器　vibrating string accelerometer
振型/振型,振動模式,振動模態　vibration mode, vibration shape, mode of vibration
振型分解法/振型疊加法　modal analysis method
振型密度/振型密度　mode shape density
振型能量/振型能量　mode shape energy
振型斜率/振型斜率　mode shape slope
震动沉桩法/震動沈樁法　pile vibro-sinking method
震陷/震陷　earthquake subsidence
震源/震源　earthquake focus, hypocenter
震灾/震災,地震災害　earthquake damage, seismic hazard
震中/震中　earthquake epicenter, epicenter
震中距/震央距離　distance from epicenter
镇/集鎮,市鎮　town
镇规划/市鎮規劃,城鎮規劃　town planning
镇浪油/鎮浪油　wave quelling oil
镇流器/鎮流電阻器,鎮定物　ballast resistor, ballast
镇域/鎮域　administrative region of town
镇域规划/鎮域規劃　town administrative area planning
镇域镇村体系/鎮域鎮村體系　town and village system of town
争议/争端　dispute
征地/土地徵收　compulsory land acquisition, expropriation
征地范围/土地徵收區片　land expropriation area
征地面积/土地徵收面積　land acquisition area
蒸发沉积/蒸發沈積,汽化沈積　evaporating deposition
蒸发池/蒸發塘　evaporation pond
蒸发防冰/蒸發防冰　evaporative anti-icing
蒸发管/蒸發器　vaporizer
蒸发管束/蒸發管排　evaporator tube bank
蒸发计/蒸發計　atmidometer
蒸发冷却/蒸發冷卻　evaporative cooling
蒸发量/蒸發[容量],蒸發率　evaporation capacity, evaporative capacity
蒸发率/蒸發率　rate of evaporation
蒸发皿系数/蒸皿係數　pan coefficient
蒸发能力/蒸發勢　evaporation power
蒸发盘管/蒸發盤管　evaporating coil
蒸发器/蒸發器　evaporator
蒸发潜热/蒸發潛熱　latent heat of vaporization
蒸发污染物/蒸發汙染物　evaporative pollutant
蒸发压力调节阀/背壓調整器　evaporator pressure regulator, back pressure regulator
蒸发压缩制冷/蒸汽壓縮冷凍　vapor compression refrigeration
蒸馏法/蒸餾法　distillation method
蒸馏器/蒸餾器　distiller
蒸馏试验/蒸餾試驗　distillation test
蒸馏水柜/蒸餾水櫃　distilling tank, distilled water tank
蒸馏水室/蒸餾水室　distilled water room
蒸馏温度/蒸餾溫度　distillation temperature
蒸馏装置/蒸餾設備　distillation plant
蒸汽/蒸汽　steam
蒸汽采暖装置/蒸汽採暖裝置　steam heating equipment
蒸汽船/輪船　steam ship
蒸汽打桩机/蒸汽打樁機　steam pile driver, steam pile hammer
蒸汽动力发电厂/蒸汽發電廠　steam power plant, steam power station
蒸汽动力装置/蒸汽動力裝置　steam power plant
蒸汽舵机/蒸汽舵機　steam steering engine
蒸汽供暖/蒸汽供暖,蒸汽加熱　steam heating

蒸汽供暖系统/暖汽系統　steam heating system
蒸汽锅炉/蒸汽鍋爐　steam boiler
蒸汽机车/蒸汽機車　steam locomotive
蒸汽机车连杆/蒸汽機車連桿　steam locomotive side rod
蒸汽机车热工特性/蒸汽機車熱工特性　thermo-characteristic of steam locomotive
蒸汽机车洗修/蒸汽機車洗修　steam locomotive boiler washout repair
蒸汽机船/汽船,輪船　steamer, steam ship, SS
蒸汽机动力装置/蒸汽機動力設備　steam engine power plant
蒸汽机-废汽汽轮机联合装置/蒸汽機與排汽渦輪機複合機　combined steam engine and exhaust turbine installation
蒸汽截止阀/停汽閥　steam stop valve
蒸汽警笛/汽笛　steam whistle
蒸汽扩散/蒸汽擴散　vapor diffusion
蒸汽滤器/濾汽器　steam strainer
蒸汽灭火系统/蒸汽窒火系統　steam smothering system, steam fire extinguishing system
蒸汽喷射油气抽除装置/噴汽清除[有害]氣體系統　steam ejector gas-freeing system
蒸汽喷射制冷/蒸汽噴射冷凍　steam jet refrigeration
蒸汽屏法/蒸汽屏法　vapor screen technique
蒸汽屏显示/蒸汽屏顯示　vapor-screen method of flow visualization
蒸汽起货机/蒸汽吊貨絞機　steam cargo winch
蒸汽起重机/蒸汽吊車　steam crane
蒸汽热网/蒸汽熱網　steam heat supply network
蒸汽渗透系数/蒸汽滲透性係數　coefficient of vapor permeability
蒸汽渗透阻/蒸汽擴散阻力　vapor resistivity
蒸汽式沥青熔化装置/蒸汽式瀝青熔化裝置　asphalt steam pipe melter
蒸汽室/汽櫃　steam chest
蒸汽疏水阀/蒸汽袪水器,汽阱　steam trap
蒸汽塔/蒸汽塔　turret
蒸汽透平/蒸汽渦輪[機],汽輪機　steam turbine
蒸汽雾化油燃烧器/蒸汽霧化燃油器　steam atomizing oil burner
蒸汽熏舱管系/蒸汽窒火管路系統　tank steaming-out piping system
蒸汽循环冷却系统/蒸汽冷卻循環系統　vapor cycle cooling system
蒸汽压力/汽壓力　vapor pressure
蒸汽养护/蒸汽養護　steam curing

蒸汽养生/蒸汽養護　steam curing
蒸汽浴室/蒸汽浴室　steam bathroom
蒸汽直接作用泵/直聯蒸汽泵　direct acting steam pump
蒸汽制冷压缩机/氣體壓縮冷卻機　vapor refrigeration compressor
蒸-燃联合动力装置/組合蒸汽燃氣渦輪機動力設備　combined steam and gas turbine power plant
蒸散势/蒸發散勢　potential evapotranspiration
蒸腾计/葉蒸計　phytometer
蒸腾抑制剂/蒸騰抑制劑　transpiration retardan
蒸压砖/蒸壓磚　autoclaved brick
蒸养混凝土/蒸汽養護混凝土　steam cured concrete
蒸养砖/蒸養磚　steam cured brick
整备品重量/整備品重量　servicing weight
整备线/整備線　servicing siding
整备线配置系数/整備線分配因數　allocation factor of service track
整车分卸/整車分卸　car load freight unloaded at two or more stations
整车货[物]/整車貨物　car load freight, full truck load, FTL
整车货物运输/整車貨物運輸　truck load transport
整车运价/整車運價　truck load rate
整定值/標置值　setting value
整锻曲轴/實心曲柄軸　solid crankshaft
整剪绿篱/整剪綠籬　clipped hedge
整块码头岸壁/整塊碼頭岸壁　monolithic wharf
整块模板/整塊模板　monolithic form
整理道床/道碴整理　ballast trimming
整理水池/整理水池　unravel water tank
整流变压器/整流器[用]變壓器　rectifier transformer
整流舵/整流舵,壓舵　counter rudder
整流方式/整流方式　mode of rectification
整流继电器/整流器繼電器　rectifier relay
整流器/整流器　rectifier
整流器供电/整流器供電　rectifier power supply
整流误差/校正誤差　rectification error
整流叶片/整流葉片,静子葉片　straightening vane, stator vane
整流罩/整流罩,整流片　fairing
整流罩半罩铁轮支架车/半整流鐵輪支架車　half-fairing iron wheel carriage
整流罩半罩运输车/半整流罩拖車　half-fairing trailer
整流罩舵/整流舵,球形舵　counter rudder, bulb rudder, bulb-type rudder

整流罩分离试验/整流罩分離試驗　fairing separation test
整流罩公路运输车/整流罩拖車　fairing trailer
整流罩扣罩间/整流罩扣罩間　fairing install room
整流罩落区/酬載護罩碰撞區域　impact area of payload fairing
整流罩铁路运输车/整流罩鐵路運輸車　fairing rail transporter
整流罩-有效载荷公路运输车/整流罩酬載拖車　fairing-payload trailer
整流罩装配型架/整流罩裝配架　fairing assembling frame
整片路面/薄層鋪面　sheet pavement
整平/整修軌面　smoothing iron
整平层/水平面基層,水準層　leveling course
整容室/整容室　face-lifting chamber
整体壁板/整體壁板　integral panel
整体车轮/整體車輪　solid wheel, monobloc wheel
整体承载结构/整體承載結構　monocoque structure, integral loadcarrying structure
整体城市设计/都市設計規劃　integrated urban design
整体道床/整體道床,整體混凝土底座　solid bed, integrated ballast bed, monolithic concrete bed
整体二极管太阳电池/整體二極體太陽電池　integral diode solar cell
整体盖片/整體圍帶[罩蓋]　integral cover
整体规划/綜合規劃,廣博規劃　comprehensive planning
整体规划图/綜合規劃圖　comprehensive plan
整体活塞/整體活塞　one-piece piston
整体剪切破坏/全剪破壞　general shear failure
整体结构/整體結構　integral structure
整体列车/固定編組列車　integral train
整体式衬砌/整體式襯砌　integral lining
整体式浮船坞/整體式浮船塢　single unit floating dock
整体式码头/巨塊式碼頭　monolithic type wharf
整体稳定性/整體穩定性　overall stability
整体[性]保护/整體保護　integrated conservation, holistic conservation
整体油箱/整體油箱　integral fuel tank
整体运输/整體運輸　integral transportation
整箱货/整櫃貨,整櫃裝載,全貨櫃之貨物　full container load, FCL
整星二级故障/衛星二級故障　second-class failure of satellite
整星三级故障/衛星三級故障　third-class failure of satellite
整星一级故障/衛星一級故障　first-class failure of satellite
整形/整形　shaping, trimming
整形草坪/整形草坪　formal lawn
整形花坛/整形花壇　formal flower bed
整形修理/整形修理　form correction repair
整形种植/整形種植　architectural planting
整形树/整形樹　topiary tree
整正轨缝/整正軌縫　dispersal of rail gaps, adjusting joint gaps up to standard
整正曲线/曲線整正,曲線校正　curve adjusting, curve lining
整正水平/整正水準　adjusting of cross level
整治/整治,復健　regularization, rehabilitation
整治冻害轨道/整治凍害軌道　treatment of frost heaving track
整治水位/調節水位　regulated water stage
正铲[挖掘机]/正鏟挖掘機　front shovel, face shovel
正铲挖泥船/戽斗挖泥船　bucket dredger, dipper dredger
正常低水位/正常低水位　normal low water level, NLWL
正常动作继电器/正常動作繼電器　normal acting relay
正常断层/常態斷層　normal fault
正常返回/正常返回　normal return
正常负载黏土/正常負載黏土　normally loaded clay
正常高水位/正常高水位　normal high water level, NHWL
正常工作条件/正常操作條件　normal operating condition
正常固结/正常壓密的　normally consolidated
正常固结土/正常壓密土壤　normally consolidated soil
正常海滩/正常海灘　normal beach
正常环境/正常環境　normal environment
正常回收程序/正常回收程式　normal recovery sequence
正常类飞机/普通類飛機　airplane in normal category
正常类旋翼机/普通類旋翼機　rotorcraft in normal category
正常路缘/直面路緣　normal curb
正常密黏土/正常壓密黏土　normally consolidated clay
正常模式/巡航模式,巡弋模式　cruise mode

正常磨损/正常磨損,正常磨耗 normal wear
正常排水量/正常排水量 normal displacement
正常起动程序/正常起動程式 normal starting sequence
正常侵蚀/自然銷蝕 normal erosion
正常使用功率/常用[定額]出力 normal service rating
正常使用极限状态/使用極限狀態 serviceability limit state
正常式布局/正常構型 normal configuration
正常输出/可靠出量 firm output
正常损耗/正常損耗 normal loss
正常通气性/正常通風 normal aeration
正常退水曲线/正常退水曲線 normal recession curve
正常位移/正常位移 normal displacement
正常蓄水位/正常高水位 normal high water level, NHWL
正常运行/正常運轉 normal operation
正常照明/正常照明 normal lighting
正常状态/正常狀況 normal condition
正常[状态]仿真/正常狀態模擬 normal state simulation
正常姿态/標準姿態 normal attitude
正车/正車,向前,前方 ahead
正车操纵阀/正車操縱閥 ahead maneuvring valve
正车汽轮机/正車蒸汽渦輪機 ahead steam turbine
正车燃气轮机/正車燃氣渦輪機 ahead gas turbine
正点/準時,按預定計劃,按時間表 on schedule
正定位/正定位 pull-off mode
正洞门/正洞門 orthonormal tunnel portal, straight tunnel portal, orthonormal portal
正舵/正舵 amidships
正反馈/正反饋 positive feedback
正反转双风扇/正反轉雙風扇 counterrotating fan
正浮/正浮,縱平浮,直柱 zero trim, floating on even keel, upright
正浮位置/正浮位置 upright position
正割弹性模量/正割彈性模數 secant modulus of elasticity
正庚烷不溶物/正庚烷不溶物 n-heptane insoluble
正横/正横 abeam
正横接近法/正横接近法 abeam approaching method
正横距离/正横距離 distance abeam
正后方/正後方 dead astern
正火/正常化 normalizing
正激波/正震波 normal shock wave

正极/正極 positive electrode
正极柱/正端子,陽端子 positive terminal
正己烷当量/正己烷當量 hexane equivalent
正脊/正脊 principal ridge
正加速度/正加速度 positive acceleration
正检[星]/正檢[星] flight and engineering model, FEM
正交叉/十字交叉 right-angled intersection
正交的/正交的 orthogonal
正交反力/正向反力,法向反力 normal reaction
正交[各向]异性/異面異彈性 orthotropy
正交极化/正交極化 cross polarization
正交桥/正交橋 right bridge
正交性检查/正交性檢查 orthogonality check
正交性判据/正交性判據 orthogonality criterion
正交异性板/正交異[向]性板 orthotropic slab, orthotropic plate
正交异性钢桥面/正交異向性鋼床板橋 orthotropic steel bridge deck
正接/正極性 straight polarity
正螺旋试验/渦旋試驗 direct spiral test
正面角焊缝/正面填角焊道,填角焊接 front fillet weld, fillet weld in normal shear, fillet welding
正面开口式水涡轮/正面開口式水渦輪 frontal type water turbine
正前方/正前方 dead ahead
正桥/主橋 main bridge
正时灯/點火正時燈 timing light
正时图/正時圖 timing diagram
正式测量图/正式測量圖,官方測量圖 ordinance survey map
正式试验/正式試驗,驗收試驗 official test
正台阶法/正臺階法 positive benching tunnelling method
正态分布/正態分布 normal distribution
正投影/正投影 front screen projection
正投影法/正射投影 orthographic projection
正弯矩/下垂力矩 sagging moment
正文/正文 text
正文结束信号/電文結束信號 end-of-text signal
正文开始信号/電文信號開始 start-of-text signal
正吻/正吻 ridge ornament
正弦表面波/正弦表面波 sinusoidal surface wave
正弦波/正弦波 sine wave, sinusoidal wave
正弦定频试验/正弦暫停試驗 sine dwell test
正弦扫描试验/正弦掃掠試驗 sine sweep test
正弦调谐/正弦調諧 sine tuning
正弦振动试验/正弦振動試驗 sine vibration test

正线/幹線,主線　main line
正响应区/正響應區　positive response zone
正向传播/正向傳播　forward propagation
正向加速度/正加速度　positive acceleration
正向信道/正向通道　forward channel
正循环钻机/循環鑽土機　circulation drill
正循环钻孔法/正循環鑽孔法　circulation boring method
正样[星]/飛行模型　flight model, FM
正应变/線性應變　linear strain
正则模态/正模　normal mode
正蒸汽分配/正蒸汽分配　positive steam distribution
正轴投影/正軸投影　normal projection
正装/正裝　right-handed machine
正自流水头/正湧泉水頭,正湧泉高差　positive artesian head
证券交易所/證券交易所　stock exchange
证人室/證人室　witness room
政策规划/政策性計劃　policy plan
政委/政工官　political officer
政务电报/公務電報　government telegram
之字路线车站/之字線車站　switch-back station
之字形线/鋸齒線　zigzag line
支撑/支撐　mast, shoring, bracing
支撑材/支撐材　bar timbering
支撑杆/抗壓構材　strut and tie
支撑式桥台/支撐式橋臺　supported type abutment
支撑体系/支撐系統　bracing system
支撑系统/支撐系統　bracing system
支撑应力/承載應力　bearing stress
支承/支承,懸吊　suspension
支承板/支承墊板　bearing plate
支承刚度/支承勁度　support stiffness
支承连杆/支承鉸桿　support link
支承面/平面支承　surface bearing
支承强度/承載強度　bearing strength
支承式伸缩装置/支柱式伸縮裝置　support type expansion installation
支承托架/支撐托架　frame support bracket
支承液体/支持液體　supporting liquid
支承桩/支[承]樁　bearing pile
支持级/助理級　support level
支持绝缘子/支持絕緣子　supporting insulator
支持器/支撐物　supporter
支持绳索/吊索　holding rope
支挡结构/支護結構　retaining structure
支挡桩/竪樁　soldier pile
支导线/不閉合導線,自由導線　free traverse

支点/支點　pivot point
支电话所/支電話局　minor telephone office
支付/給付　payment
支杆式应变天平/支桿應變規式平衡儀　strain gage balance with sting
支搁板挡土墙/支架式擋土牆　shelf retaining wall
支拱板条/[檁]矢木　lagging
支架/支架,支柱　support
支架干扰修正/支架干擾修正[量]　support interference correction
支架项圈/支架頂圈　heading collar
支流/支流　side stream, tributary, branch river
支路/岔道　local road, collector road, branch road
支配机车/支配機車　disposal locomotive
支配性故障/主導故障　dominant fault
支渠/支渠　branch canal, lateral canal
支索/牽索,拉條　stay
支线/支線,支路　branch, branch line
支线传送装置/支線輸送裝置　branch line conveyer
支线公路/公路支線　branch highway, feeder highway
支线卷扬机/支線卷揚機　branch line winder
支线客机/支線運輸機　feeder liner
支线运输/輔助運務　feeder service
支援滑行道/支援滑行道　support taxiway
支摘窗/支摘窗　removable window
支柱/支柱　pillar, post
支柱侧面限界/支柱側面限界　mast gage
支柱式起落架/套筒式起落架　telescopic landing gear
支座/支座,支承,支架　bearing, support
支座反力/支承反力　support reaction
支座摩阻力/摩擦軸承　friction of bearing
芝加哥建筑学派/芝加哥建築學派　Chicago school of architecture
芝加哥千禧公园/芝加哥千禧公園　Chicago Millennium Park
芝加哥学派/芝加哥學派　Chicago school
枝插/枝插,莖插　stem cutting
枝接/枝接,接木　stem grafting
枝下高/枝下高　clear bole height
枝状管网/分支網路　branching network, branched network
织女一(天琴α)/織女一(天琴α)　Vega
知识表达技术/知識表達技術　knowledge presentation technique
知识库/知識庫　knowledge base
执行调度/執行調度　operation dispatching

执行机构/執行機構　routine organization
执行角/執行角　execution angle
执行器/執行器,致動器　actuator
执行指令/執行命令　execute command
执业范围/執業範圍　scope of professional activities
直插用户/直插用戶　direct plug-in subscriber
直尺/直尺　straightedge
直达干扰/直達干擾　leakage
直达港/直達港　direct port
直达货/直達貨　direct cargo
直达客运/直達客運　non-stop bus service, express bus service
直达声/直達音　direct sound
直达提单/直達載貨證券　direct bill of lading
直达运输/聯運運輸,直達交通　non-stop transportation, non-stop fast freight
直道/筆直的道路　straight road
直动泵/直接出力泵　direct acting pump
直辐板/直輪板　straight wheel plate
直管/直管　straight pipe
直管形荧光灯/直管熒光燈,雙端螢光燈　straight tubular fluorescent lamp
直轨器/直軌器　rail straightening tool, rail straightener
直航船/直航船舶　stand-on vessel
直缓点/緩和曲線起點　point of tangent to spiral, TS
直击雷/直擊雷　direct lightning flash
直交式排水系统/直交式排水系統　perpendicular system
直交停车/直交停車　perpendicular parking
直角拐肘/直角曲柄　right angle crank
直角航线程序/直角航線程式　racetrack procedure
直角交叉/垂直交叉,十字形交叉　rectangular crossing, square crossing
直角截止阀/直角停止閥,直角關閉閥　angle shut-off valve
直角坐标法/直角坐標法　rectangular coordinate method
直角坐标机器人/矩形機器人　rectangular robot
直接测量法/直接量測法　direct method of measurement
直接潮/直接潮,順潮　direct tide, fair tide
直接传动/直接傳動　direct transmission
直接费/直接成本　direct cost
直接刚度/直接勁度　direct stiffness
直接刚度法/直接勁度法　direct stiffness method
直接供电方式/直接供電方式　direct feeding system

直接过滤/直接過濾　direct filtration
直接荷载/直接載重　direct load
直接缓解/直接釋放,串聯釋放,一次電流釋放　direct release
直接换装/直接換裝　direct transshipment
直接记录/直接記錄　direct recording
直接加热/直接加熱　direct heating
直接剪切试验/直接剪切試驗　direct shear test
直接剪切仪/直接剪力[試驗]儀　direct shear apparatus
直接金属掩模/直接金屬掩模　direct metal mask
直接进入阀/直接進風閥　direct admission valve
直接进入法返回/直接進入法返回　direct reentry return mode
[直接]径流/直接徑流　direct runoff
直接距离测量/直接距離測量　direct distance surveying
直接力控制/直接加力控制　direct force control
直接连接/直接連接　lug connection, direct connection
直接喷射燃烧室/直接噴射燃燒室　direct injection combustion chamber
直接启动/直接起動,全[電]壓起動　direct-on-line starting
直接驱动/直接驅動　direct drive, gearless drive
直接日辐射/直接日射　direct solar radiation
直接视野/直接視野　direct field of vision
直接数控/直接數值控制　direct numerical control, DNC
直接数字控制系统/直接數位控制系統　direct digital control system, DDC system
直接效益/直接利潤,直接利潤　direct benefit
直接印字电报/直接印字電報　direct-printing telegraphy
直接原因/直接原因　immediate cause
直接照明/直接照明　direct lighting
直接蒸发式空气冷却器/直接蒸發空氣冷卻器　direct evaporating air cooler
直接装注油管/直接注入管路　direct loading pipe line, direct filling line
直结轨道/直結軌道　track fastened directly to steel girder
直径系数/直徑因數　Taylor advance coefficient, Taylor diameter constant, diameter factor
直立/直柱,正浮　upright
直立斗式输送机/直立斗式輸送機　vertical bucket conveyor
直立护木/直立護木　vertical fender

直 625

直立式防波堤/直立[式防波]堤　vertical breakwater
直立式路缘石/直立缘石　vertical curb
直立式码头/垂直面碼頭　vertical face wharf
直立式炭化炉/竪罐蒸餾爐　vertical retort
直立[型]艏/直立型艏　straight stem, vertical bow
直链形悬挂/折線懸鏈　polygonal catenary
直列式柴油机/直列式柴油機,直列型柴油機　straight type diesel engine, in-line type diesel engine
直列式传爆系列/直達線導火藥　direct line explosive train
直列式发动机/直列型動力機　straight type engine
直列式内燃机/直列引擎,單排引擎　in line engine
直棂窗/直欞窗　grill window, zhilingchuang
直流传动/直流[電]驅動　direct current drive, DC drive
直流电动发电机/電動發電機　dynamotor
直流电动机/直流馬達　direct current motor, DC motor
直流[电弧]焊/直流電弧焊接　direct-current arc welding
直流电弧焊机/直流電弧焊接器　direct current arc welder, DC arc welder
直流电力机车/直流電力機車　DC electric locomotive
直流电力牵引制/直流電傳動　DC electric traction system
直流电力推进装置/直流電力推進裝置　DC electric propulsion plant
直流电流互感器/直流比流器　DC current transformer
直流电桥/直流電橋　direct current bridge
直流电源屏/直流電源屏　DC power supply panel
直流电站/直流電站　DC power station
直流发电机/直流發電機　direct current generator
直流辅助电动机/直流輔助馬達或電動機　DC auxiliary motor
直流辅助发电机/直流輔助發電機　DC auxiliary generator
直流高速断路器/直流高速斷路器　DC high speed circuit-breaker
直流供电制/直流電源系統　DC power supply system
直流轨道电路/直流軌道電路　DC track circuit
直流锅炉/直流鍋爐,單流鍋爐　once through boiler, mono-tube boiler
直流过滤/線性篩選　in-line filtration
直流继电器/直流繼電器　DC relay
直流接触器/直流接觸器　DC contactor
直流控制发电机/直流控制發電機　DC control generator
直流冷却水系统/直流冷却水系統　once-through cooling water system
直流励磁机/直流勵磁機　DC exciter
直流喷嘴/直流噴嘴　orifice element
直流起动发电机/直流起動發電機　DC starting generator, dynastarter
直流牵引变电所/直流牽引變電站　DC traction substation
直流牵引电动机/直流牽引電動機　DC traction motor
直流燃烧/順流式燃燒　straight-flow combustion
直流燃烧室/順流燃燒室　through flow combustor
直流扫力/單[向]流驅氣　uniflow scavenging
直流扫气/單[向]流驅氣　uniflow scavenging
直流式锅炉/直通式鍋爐　straight-through boiler
直流水系统/直流水系統　once-through water system
直流斩波器/直流截波器　DC chopper
直流制/直流系統　DC system
直流主发电机/[直流]主發電機　DC main generator
直馏矿物油/純礦油　straight mineral oil
直馏沥青/直餾瀝青　straight-run bitumen
直馏沥青胶泥/直煉瀝青膠　straight-run asphalt cement
直埋电缆/地下電纜,埋設電纜　buried cable
直埋敷设/直埋敷設　integral pipetrench, directly buried installation
直爬梯/貓梯,屋頂用梯子　catladder, vertical ladder
直桥/直橋　straight bridge
直燃式溴化锂吸收式制冷机/直燃式溴化鋰吸收式製冷機　direct-fired lithium-bromide absorption-type refrigerating machine
直射辐射/直接輻射　direct radiation
直射喷嘴/直射式噴嘴　plain orifice atomizer
直射日光/直射日光　sunlight
[直升]导管浇筑混凝土法/特密管灌鑄混凝土　tremie concreting
直升飞机起降场/直昇機坪　helicopter pad
直升机/直昇機　helicopter
直升机场/直昇機場　heliport
直升机地面共振/直昇機地面共振　helicopter ground resonance
直升机功率传递系数/直昇機功率傳遞係數　helicopter power utilization coefficient
直升机功率载荷/直昇機動力負載　helicopter power loading

直升机回避区/直昇機禁止飛行區域　helicopter forbidden region
直升机甲板/直昇機甲板　helicopter deck
直升机救生套/直昇機救生環索　helicopter rescue strop
直升机起落装置/直昇機起落架　helicopter landing gear
直升机前飞升限/直昇機實用昇限　helicopter service ceiling
直升机援助/直昇機援助　assistant by helicopter
直升机着舰装置/直昇機著艦裝置　helicopter deck-landing devices
直升机着水装置/直昇機浮筒式起落架　helicopter floatation gear
直升机作业/直昇機作業　helicopter operation
直式桥台/直橋臺　stub abutment
直梯/直立梯　vertical ladder
直通场/直通場　through yard
直通交路/直通交路　through routing
直通截止阀/直通截止閥　through shut-off valve
直通客流/直通客流　through passenger flow
直通空气制动装置/直通空氣制動閥裝置　straight air brake equipment
直通列车/直通列車　transit train
直通旅客列车/直通客運列車　through passenger train
直通式货运站/直通式貨運站　through-type freight station
直通型运行/直通式運行　straight-through operation
直通制动管/直通制動管　direct air brake pipe
直线/直線　straight line
直线电动机/直線電動機,線性電動機,線性馬達　linear motor
直线法/直線法　method of line
直线钢腱/直線鋼腱　straight tendon
直线加速器成像室/直線加速器室　linear accelerator room
直线尖轨/直線尖軌　straight switch
直线进近着陆/直接落地　straight-in landing
直线掏槽/平眼抽心孔式　burn cut
直线同步电动机/線性同步電[動]機　linear synchronous motor
直线涡流/直線渦流　rectilinear vortex
直线行驶性能试验/直線性能試驗　straight line running test
直线形码头/直線形碼頭　straight line type wharf
直线异步电动机/直線異步電動機　linear asynchronous motor

直线运动/直線運動　rectilinear motion
直泻槽/直瀉槽　vertical chute
直卸式拌和机/不傾式拌和機　non-tilting mixer
直行车道/直行車道　direct-through lane
直行纹理/直紋　straight grain
直压式采暖装置/直壓式採暖裝置　direct pressure steam heating equipment
直压式暖汽调整阀/直壓式暖汽調整閥　car pressure regulater
直叶片/直葉片　straight blade
直饮水/直飲水　fine drinking water
直饮水原水/直飲水原水　raw water of fine drinking water
直圆点/曲線起點　point of curve, PC
K 值/K 值　K value
pH 值/pH 值,酸鹼值　pH value
值班/當值　on shift
值班调度/值班調度　routine dispatching
值班供暖/值班採暖　standby heating
值班室/值勤室　duty room
值机大厅/值機大廳,旅客登記大堂　check-in hall
K 值试验/K 值試驗　test for K value of complete car
职业病危害防护设施/職業病危害防護設施　facility for occupational hazard
职业接触限值/職業性暴露限度　occupational exposure limit
职业结构/職業結構　occupation structure
职住平衡/就業-居住平衡　job-housing balance
植被/植被,植物覆蓋　vegetation, vegetative cover
植被垂直[地]带/高程植被帶　altitudinal vegetation zone, vertical vegetation zone
植被[地]带/植被帶,植物帶　vegetation zone
植被地带性/植被格局　zonation of vegetation
植被分类/植生分類　vegetation classification
植被覆盖率/植被覆蓋率　vegetation coverage
植被格局/植被水準[地]帶　vegetation pattern
植被固坡/植被固坡　planting protect slope
植被区划/植被區劃　vegetation regionalization
植被水平[地]带/水平植被帶　horizontal vegetation zone
植被型/植被型,植生型　vegetation form, vegetation type
植被制图/植被製圖　vegetation mapping
植草/植草　grass planting
植草浅沟/灘槽,潮溝　swale
植篱/樹籬　hedge
植苗工/鋪草工　sodding work

植生袋/植生袋　soil sack, vegetation bag
植树箱/植樹箱　planting box
植物保护/植物保護　plant protection
植物保健绿地/植物保健綠地　plant health garden
植物病虫防治/植物病蟲防治　disease and insect control
植物地理学/植物地理學　plant geography, phytogeography
植物分布学/植物分布學　phytochorology, plant chorology
植物覆盖/植物覆蓋　plant mulching
植物个体生态学/植物個體生態學　plant autoecology
植物工厂/植物工廠　plant factory
植物固沙/植物固砂　sand consolidation by planting
植物耗水强度/植物耗水率　water consumption rate of plant
植物基因工程育种/植物分子育種　plant molecular breeding
植物监测/植物監測　plant monitoring
植物检疫法/植物檢疫法　plant quarantine method
植物景观/植物景觀　plant landscape, flora landscape
植物垃圾/植物垃圾　botanic waste
植物垃圾处理/植物廢物處理　botanic waste treatment
植物酪脂胶/植物酪脂膠　vegetable protein glue
植物历史学/植物歷史學　plant history
植物量/植物量　phytomass
植物配植/植物配植　plant arrangement, planting arrangement
植物配置/[園林]植物配置　plant disposition, planting arrangement
植物气候学/植物氣候學　plant climatology
植物区系/植物區系　flora
植物区系地理学/植物區系地理學　floristic geography
植物区系学/植物區系學　florology, floristics
植物区系组成/植物區系組成　floral composition, floristic composition
植物圈/植物圈　phytosphere, vegetation circle
植物群落/植物群落　phytocoenosis, phytocoenosium, phytocommunity
植物群落季相/植物群落季相　seasonal aspect stages of plant community
植物群落结构/植物群落結構　plant community structure
植物群落生态学/植物群落生態學　plant synecology
植物群落学/植物群落學　phytocoenology, phytocoenostics
植物生态地理学/植物生態地理學　plant ecological geography
植物生态配置/植物生態配置　plant ecological arrangement
植物生态系统/植物生態系統　plant ecosystem
植物生态学/植物生態學　plant ecology
植物生物学/植物生物學　plant biology
植物生长阻滞含水量/植物生長阻滯含水量　water content of inhibiting plant growth
植物纤维绳/天然纖維索　natural fiber rope
植物形态学/植物形態學　plant morphology
植物修复/植物修復,植物復育法　phytoremediation
植物学/植物學　botany, plant science
植物养护管理/植物養護管理　plant maintenance and management
植物营养/植物營養　plant nutrition
植物园/植物園　botanical garden
植物造型/整形觀賞樹木　topiary
植物展览温室/植物溫室　plants greenhouse
植物整形修剪/植物修剪　plant trimming and pruning
植物志/植物誌,植物區系　flora
植物滞尘/植物滯塵　dust-retention of plant
植物种群生态学/植物族群生態學　plant population ecology
植物专类园/專類園　specific categorized plant garden
止冲流速/不沖刷速度　non-scouring velocity
止荡锚/止擺錨　yaw checking anchor
止回阀/止回閥,單向閥,逆止閥　check valve, back pressure valve, flap trap
止裂/止裂　crack arrest
止轮器/止輪鐵鞋　wheel skid
止水/止水　water stop
止水带/止水帶,水封　water stop, water stop tie
止水胶垫/止水橡膠帶　rubber water stop
止水栓/止水栓　kerb stop, kerb cock
止水铜片/止水銅片　water stopping copper
止推环/推力環　thrust ring
止推块/支承塊　thrust block
止推轴承盖/推力軸承蓋　thrust bearing cap
止推轴瓦/推力軸承殼　thrust bearing shell
止推座/支承塊　thrust block
止脱结/止脱結,止脱繩　mousing
止移板/防動板　shifting board
止转块/剎車塊板　scotch block

纸草花式柱/紙莎草形柱　papyrus column
纸带发报机/卷帶發送器　tape transmitter
纸浆车/紙漿車　pulp car
纸面石膏板/石膏板　gypsum plasterboard
纸上定线/紙上定線　paper location, paper location of line
纸上封锁/紙上封鎖　paper blockade
纸上封锁区/紙上封鎖區　paper blockade zone
纸鸢/鳶,風箏　kite
纸制品/紙製品　paper products
指北针/指北針　north arrow
指标差/指標誤差　index error
指标改正量/指標改正　index correction
指标镜/[六分仪]器鏡　index-mirror
指导船长/駐埠船長　port captain
指导司机/指導司機　driver instructor
指导性施工组织设计/指導性施工組織設計　design for guiding construction organization, guiding design for construction scheme
指点信标/標誌信號　marker beacon
指定配合比/指定配合　specified mix
指定仲裁员/指定仲裁人　appointed arbitrator
指挥电话/指令電話　command telephone
指挥电话总机/指揮電話控制板　command telephone control board
指挥调度设备/指令調度設備　command dispatching equipment
指挥调度体制/指令調度體系　command dispatching hierarchy
指挥调度通信系统/指令調度通訊系統　command dispatching and communication system
指挥调度系统/指令調度系統　command dispatching system
指挥工程/指揮工程　command engineering
指挥舰/指揮艦　commanding ship
指挥控制中心/指揮管制中心　command and control center
指挥控制中心计算机/指控中心電腦　command and control center computer
指挥区/命令區　command area
指挥室围壳/[潛艇]指揮室　sail
指挥塔台/指揮塔　direct tower, command tower
指挥通信/命令通信　command communication
指接/指形接合　finger joint
指令编码/命令編碼　command encoding
指令长度/指令長度　length of command code
指令重发/指令重傳　command retransmission
指令代码/指令碼,命令碼　command code

指令电路/指令電路　command circuit
指令舵角/指令舵角　ordered rudder angle
指令发射机/指令發射機　command transmitter
指令格式/命令格式　command format
指令和数据获取/指令和數據攫取　command and data acquisition
指令和数据获取站/指令和數據攫取站　command and data acquisition station
指令接收机/命令接收機,指令接收器　command receiver
指令解调器/命令解調器　command demodulator
指令连发/指令連續傳輸　command continual transmission
指令容量/指令容量　command capacity
指令信息/命令資訊　command information
指令译码器/指令譯碼器　instruction decoder
指令引信/指令引信　command fuze
指令长/指揮官　commander
指令执行机构/指令執行單元　command execution unit
指令制导/指令導引　command guidance
指令终端/命令終端　command terminal
指路标志/[方向]指示標誌　guide sign, direction sign
指南/指南　guide book
指配频带/指配頻帶　assigned frequency band
指配频率/指配頻率　assigned frequency
指示标志/指示標誌　mandatory sign, instructive mark, indication sign
指示灯/指向[標誌]燈　direction sign luminaire, indicator lamp, pilot lamp
指示浮筒/位置浮標　position buoy
指示功/指示功　indicated work
指示功率/指示功率,指示馬力　indicated horse power, IHP, indicated power
指示空速/指示空速　indicated airspeed
指示马力/指示馬力　indicated horse power
指示器/指示器　indicator
指示牵引力/指示牽引力　indicated tractive effort
指示群落/指標群落　indicator community
指示[燃]油消耗率/指示[馬力]燃油消耗率　indicated specific fuel oil consumption, indicated specific fuel consumption, ISFC
指示热效率/指示熱效率　indicated thermal efficiency
指示提单/指示載貨證券　order bill of lading
指示压力系数/指示壓力係數,表壓[力]係數　coefficient of indicated pressure

指示值/指標數　indicated number
指示植物/指標植物　indicator plant
指示种/指標[物]種　ecological indication species
指数分布/指數分布　exponential distribution
指向精度/指向準確度　pointing accuracy
指向力/指向力　directive force
指向力矩/尋子午線力矩　meridian-seeking torque, meridian-seeking moment
指向系数/方向指數　direction index
指向线/指向線　arrow marking
趾板/趾板　toe slab
制材/製材　sawing lumber
制材表/製材表　shop bill
制茶厂/製茶廠　tea factory
制荡板/制水板　swash plate
制荡舱壁/制水艙壁　swash bulkhead
制导/導引,導航　guidance
制导关机/導引關機　guidance cutoff
制导误差/導引誤差　guidance error
制导系统/導引系統　guidance system
制导系统测试/導引系統測試　guidance system test
制导引信/導引引信　guidance fuze
制导炸弹/導向炸彈　guided bomb
制动/制動,刹车　braking, retrogradation
制动安定性/制動安定性　service stability
制动倍率/槓桿比率　leverage ratio
制动比压/制動比壓　brake pressurize
制动波速/制動傳播率　braking propagation rate
制动不衰竭性/制動不衰竭性　inexhaustibility
制动舱/制動艙　retro module
制动岔道/制動岔道　catch points
制动撑架/制動撑架　braking bracing
制动初速/制動初速　initial speed at brake application
制动电抗器/制動電抗器　braking reactor
制动电路/制動電路　braking circuit
制动电阻柜/制動電阻櫃　braking resistor cubicle
制动电阻器/制動電阻器　braking resistor
制动电阻元件/制動電阻器柵　braking resistor grid
制动墩/制動墩　braking pier, abutment pier
制动反应时间/制動反應時間　brake reaction time
制动方式/制動方式　brake mode
制动缸/韌缸,刹车缸　brake cylinder
制动缸后杠杆/制動缸後槓桿　auxiliary lever
制动缸活塞行程/活塞行程　piston travel
制动缸前杠杆/韌缸槓桿　cylinder lever
[制动缸压力]保持阀/單向閥,止回閥　retaining valve

制动杠杆传动效率/制動槓桿傳動效率　brake rigging efficiency
制动鼓车床/刹车鼓車床　brake drum lathe
制动管减压量/制動管減壓量　brake pipe pressure reduction
制动管路/制動管路　brake piping
制动火箭/後推火箭　retro-rocket
制动火箭发动机/制動火箭發動機　retro-rocket motor
制动机/刹車閘　brake
制动检修所/制動檢修所　brake inspection point
制动角/制動角　retro-angle
制动接触器/制動接觸器　braking contactor
制动距离/停止距離　brake distance, stopping distance
制动块/刹車塊板　scotch block
制动拉杆/制動拉桿　lever connection
制动力/制動力,刹车力　braking force, braking effort
制动力矩/制動扭矩　brake torque, braking torque
制动梁/韌梁,刹車梁　brake beam
制动梁槽钢/制動梁槽鋼　brake beam compression channel
制动梁弓形杆/制動梁弓形桿　brake beam tension rod
制动梁拉杆/制動拉桿,韌拉桿　brake beam pull rod
制动梁下拉杆/制動梁下拉桿　brake beam bottom rod
制动梁支柱/制動梁支柱　brake beam strut
制动灵敏度/靈敏度　sensitivity
制动率/制動率　braking ratio
制动能高/制動能高　velocity hump crest of retarder
制动盘/刹車碟　brake disc
制动平均有效压力/制動平均有效壓力　brake mean effective pressure
制动软管/軟管　hose
制动软管连接器/軟管接頭,軟管接合　brake hose coupling
制动时间/制動時間　braking time
制动试验台/刹車試驗器　brake tester
制动室/制動室　brake repair room
制动衰竭性/提淨性　exhaustibility
制动速度/制動速度　retro-speed
制动索/制索器　rope stopper
[制动]踏板力计/腳制動踏板壓力計　foot brake pedal pressure gage
制动蹄磨床/刹車蹄磨床　brake shoe grinder
制动铁鞋/韌塊,刹車塊,刹車蹄片　brake shoe,

skate
制动位/制動位置,减速器位置,缓行器位置 retarder location
制动稳定性/不靈敏度 insensitivity
制动系统/制動系統,韌系统,刹车系统 brake system
制动效率/制動效率,刹車效能 brake efficiency
制动性能试验/制動性能試驗 braking ability test
制动延迟距离/反應制動距離 brake lag distance
制动员室/制動員室 brakeman cabin
制动支管/韌支管,刹车支管 brake branch pipe
制动支管三通/支管T形接頭 branch pipe tee
制动主管/刹车管,韌管 brake pipe
[制动]柱塞/韌管,刹车管 spool, brake pipe
制动转矩/制動扭矩 brake torque, braking torque
制动装置/制動裝置 brake equipment, brake gear
制动[装置]试验/制動馬力試驗,刹車試驗 brake test
制舵器/制舵器 rudder stopper
制际串音/系统間串音 inter-system crosstalk
制剂室/制劑室 drug manufacturing room
制冷/冷却,冷藏,冷凍 refrigeration
制冷吨/冷凍噸 refrigerating ton
制冷机房/製冷站,冷凍機房 refrigeration station, refrigeration plant room
制冷剂/冷凍劑,冷媒 refrigeration agent, refrigerant
制冷剂泵/冷媒泵 refrigerating medium pump
制冷剂计量装置/冷凍劑計算裝置 refrigerant metering device
制冷加温装置/製冷加溫裝置 refrigeration and heating equipment
制冷量/冷凍能量 refrigerating capacity
制冷系数/冷凍性能係數 coefficient of refrigerating performance
制冷系统/冷凍系統 refrigeration system
制冷循环/冷凍循環 refrigeration cycle
制粒机/製粒機 pelletizer
制链器/錨鏈扣 chain stopper
制链爪/止鏈爪,拉線爪,吊鏈鉤 devil claw
制流板/制水板 swash plate
制索结/絆索套結 stopper hitch
制索器/制鏈器,停止器 stopper
制糖厂/糖廠 sugar refining plant, sugar mill
制图/製圖 drafting
制图法/圖解力學 graphics
制图机/製圖儀 drafting machine
制图学/圖解力學 graphics

制外[测量]单位/[量測]制外單位 off-system unit of measurement
制压箱/減壓水槽 break-pressure tank
[制]盐场/[製]鹽廠 salt works
制氧机/製氧機 oxygenator factory
制氧机厂/製氧機廠 oxygenator factory
制药厂/製藥廠 pharmaceutical factory
制约停车/禁止暫停 restricted stopping
制止危及海上航行安全非法行为公约/制止危及海上航行安全非法行爲公約 Convention for the Suppression of Unlawful Acts against the Safety of Maritime Navigation
质点/質點 material point, mass point, particle
质控填土/工程回填材料 engineered fill
质扩散/質量擴散 mass diffusion
质量/①質量,②品質 ①mass, ②quality
质量保修制度/品質保修制度 rule on quality repair guarantee
质量保证/品質保證 quality assurance
质量保证大纲/品質保證計劃 quality assurance program
质量保证模式/品質保證模式 quality assurance mode
质量保证体系/品質保證體系 quality assurance system
质量不平衡力矩/質量不平衡扭矩 mass unbalance torque
质量策划/品質規劃 quality planning
质量成本/[相關]品質成本 cost of quality, quality-related costs
质量定律/質量律 mass law
质量反馈/品質回饋 quality feedback
质量方针/品質政策 quality policy
质量分析/品質分析 quality analysis
质量改进/品質改進 quality improvement
质量工程师/品質工程師 quality engineer
质量功能展开/品質功能展開 quality function deploy, QFD
质量管理/品質管理,品質管制 quality management, quality control
质量惯性矩/質量慣性矩 mass moment of inertia
质量环/品質環 quality loop
质量集中系统/質量集中系統 concentrated mass system
质量计划/品質計劃 quality plan
质量记录跟踪卡/品質記錄追蹤卡 quality record tracing card
质量监督/品質監督,品質監視 quality surveillance,

quality superintendence
质量矩阵/質量矩陣　mass matrix
质量控制/品質控制,品質管制　quality control
质量控制试验/品質管制試驗　quality control test
质量排出式控制/質量排出式控制　mass expulsion control
质量排出装置/質量擠壓裝置　mass expulsive device
质量平衡/質量平衡　mass balance
质量评价/品質評價　quality assessment
质量认证/品質認證　quality certification
质量烧蚀率/質量燒蝕率　mass ablative rate
质量审核/品質稽核　quality audit
质量审核员/品質稽核員　quality auditor
质量事故/品質事故　quality accident
质量手册/品質手冊　quality manual
质量守恒定律/質量守恆律　law of conservation mass
质量损失/品質損失　quality loss
质量体系/品質體系　quality system
质量问题归零/品質問題歸零　turning quality problem to zero
质量性状/品質性狀　qualitative charactor
质量要求/品質要求　requirements for quality
质量与可靠性/品質與可靠度　quality and reliability, Q and R
质量与可靠性信息系统/品質與可靠度資訊系統　Q and R information system, Q and R data system
质量责任制/品質責任制　quality responsibility system
质量指标/品質指數　quality index
质量中心/質量中心,累積中心　mass center
质量中心轴/質量中心軸　axis of mass center
质谱计非相干散射模式/質譜儀不相干散射模式　mass spectrometer incoherent scatter mode
质谱仪/質譜儀　mass spectrometer
质调节/恆流量控制　constant flow control
质心/質[量中]心,累積中心　center of mass, mass center
质心测定/質心測定　center of mass determination
质心跟踪/重心追蹤　centroid tracking
质心位置测定/質心位置測定　mass center test
质心位置偏差/質心偏差　deviation of mass center
质询条款/解釋條款　interpellation clause
治疗室/治療室　therapy room
致命故障/嚴重失效　critical failure
致命性故障/致命故障,關鍵性故障　critical fault
秩序感/秩序感,條理性　sense of order
窒息法/窒息法　smothering method

蛭石/蛭[蒙特]石　vermiculite
智慧城市/智慧都市　smart city, sapiential city
智慧城市规划/智慧都市規劃　smart city planning
智慧景区/智慧[風]景區　smart scenic area, wisdom scenic spot
智慧旅游/智慧旅遊　smart tourism
智慧社区/智慧社區　intelligent community
智慧生态城市/智慧生態都市　smart-ecological city
智能避碰系统/智慧型避碰系統　intelligent collision avoidance system
智能材料/智能材料,敏感材料　intelligent material
智能车路系统/智慧型車輛公路系統　intelligent vehicle highway system, IVHS
智能传感器/智慧轉換器　intelligent transducer
智能灯控系统/智能燈光控制系統　intelligent light control system
智能低压断路器/智能低壓斷路器　intelligent low-voltage circuit-breaker
智能电网/智慧電網　smart power grid
智能定时开关/智能定時開關　intelligent time switch
智能化集成系统/智慧型整合系統　intelligent integration system, IIS
智能建筑/智慧型大樓　intelligent building
智能交通系统/智慧型[交通]運輸系統　intelligent transportation system, ITS
智能决策支持系统/智慧決策支援系統　intelligent decision support system
智能控制系统/智慧控制系統　intelligent control system
智能蒙皮/智慧皮層　smart skins
滞尘能力/滯塵能力　dust-retention ability
滞尘效应/滯塵效應　dust-retention effect
滞尘植物/滯塵植物　dust holding plant
滞航/頂風緩航　heave to
滞洪沉积池/滯洪沈積池　retention pool
滞后角/滯後角　lag angle
滞后[现象]/滯後[現象],遲滯[現象]　hysteresis
滞后相供电臂/滯後相供電臂　lagging phase feeding section
滞后响应区/滯後響應區　hysteresis response zone
滞回曲线/滯回曲線,滯後曲線　hysteresis curve, hysteresis loop
滞回性能/滯回性能　hysteretic behavior, restoring force behavior
滞留费/船舶滯留費,碇泊費,入港稅　groundage
滞留时间/滯留時間,停留時間　residence time, retention time

滞留用地/滞留用地　stranded site
滞流河川/緩流河川　sluggish stream
滞流系数/滞流係數,減速係數　coefficient of retardation, retardance coefficient
滞期/延滯期　demurrage
滞燃期/延燃期間,延遲期間　delay period, combustion lagging period, combusting delay period
滞水水库/保水水庫　retention reservoir
滞弹性/滯彈性　anelasticity
滞止/停滯　stagnation
滞止蒸汽参数/停滯蒸汽參變數　stagnation steam parameter
置换/更換,替換[件]　replacement
置石/置石　stone arrangement, stone layout
置信度/可信度,信任度　confidence factor, confidence level
中波、短波广播发射台/中、短波廣播發射臺　medium wave and short wave transmitting station, MW and SW transmitting station
中波、短波收音台/中、短波接收臺,中、短波接收站　medium wave and short wave receiving station, MW and SW receiving station
中餐厅/中餐廳　Chinese restaurant
中舱/中心艙　center tank
中层/堆積　pile up
中层拖网/中層拖網　mid-water trawl
中长隧道/中長隧道　medium tunnel
中承式桥/半穿式橋　half through bridge
中垂/舯垂[現象]　sagging
中单翼/中置翼　midwing
中档/緩衝軌條　intermediate rail
中等城市/中等都市,中型都市　medium-sized city
中等交通/中量交通　medium traffic
中等破坏/中等破壞　moderate damage
中等职业学校/職業中學,職業技術學校　vocational middle school
中点电压/中點電壓　mid-point voltage
中点圆破坏/中點圓破壞　mid-point circle failure
中殿/[教堂的]中殿,中央廣場　nave
中断服务程序/中斷服務常規　interrupt service routine
中断管理程序/中斷管理程式　interruption management program
中断系统/中斷系統　interrupt system
中断限/中斷限度,中止限度　abort limit
中断性交通流/中斷的交通流　interrupted traffic flow
中分纬度/中間緯度　middle latitude

中分纬度改正量/中緯修正量　correction of middle latitude
中分纬度算法/中緯航法　middle latitude sailing
中腐水性生物/中腐水性生物　mesosaprobien
中高层住宅/中高層住宅　medium high house
中高频无线电设备/中高頻無線電裝置　MF-HF radio installation
中耕/中耕　row, intertillage
中拱/舯拱　hogging
中拱弯矩/拱勢力矩　hogging moment
中和/中和　neutralization
中和变压器/中和變壓器,中性變壓器　neutralizing transformer
中和轨温/中性溫度　neutral temperature
中和面/中性面　neutral plane
中桁材/中線縱梁,內龍骨　center girder, keelson
中横剖面/舯[橫]剖面　midship section
中横剖面系数/舯剖面係數　midship section coefficient
中红外/中紅外線　middle infrared
中弧线/拱線　camber line
中华巴洛克/巴羅克風格　Chinese Baroque style
中-活载/中-活載　China railway standard live loading, CRS-live loading
中机型船/舯機艙船　amidships engined ship
中级路面/中級路面　intermediate class pavement
中级压紧配合/中級壓緊配合　medium force fit
中继泵/增壓泵,加力泵　booster pump
中继泵站/加壓站　booster pump station
中继传输方式/中繼傳輸波式,繼電器傳輸波式　relay transmission mode
中继电路/中繼電路　trunk circuit
中继光学系统/中繼光學系統　relay optical system
中继器/中繼器　repeaters
中继线/中繼線,幹線　trunk
中继信号机/中繼信號機　transition signal
中继用户/中繼用戶　trunk subscriber
中继站/中繼站,轉播站,轉發站　repeater station
中间仓库/中間倉庫　interim store
中间层/中間層　intermediate layer
中间车道/中間車道,中央車道　center lane, middle lane
中间齿轮箱/中間減速器　intermediate gear box
中间处理/中級處理　intermediate treatment
中间带/中間帶　median
中间带排水/中間帶排水　median drainage
中间电缆盒/中間電纜盒　intermediate cable terminal box

中间港/中途港　intermediate port
中间工艺检验/中間工藝檢驗　intermediate inspection at the technological process
中间轨道法/中間軌道方法　intermediate orbit method
中间缓冲装置/中間緩衝器　intermediate buffer
中间继电器/中間斷電器,輔助繼電器,輔助替續器　auxiliary relay, intermediate relay
中间壳体/中間殼體　intermediate casing
中间肋骨/中間肋骨　intermediate frame
中间冷却器/中間冷却器　intercooler
中间配线架/中間接線板　intermediate distributing frame
中间坡/中等坡度　intermediate grade
中间漆/中間塗層　intermediate coat
中间牵引装置/中間牽引機構　intermediate draw gear
中间燃料油/中間燃油　intermediate fuel oil
中间色表/中間色表　intermediate color appearance
中间设备/中間設備　intermediate equipment
中间试验/中間試驗　intermediate test
中间试验车间/中間試驗車間　pilot testing plant
中间视觉/中間視覺　mesopic vision
中间室/中間室,中間箱　middle chamber
中间体/管托架　pipe bracket
中间线路滤波器/中間線路濾波器　intermediate line filter
中间验收/中間驗收　intermediate acceptance
中间站/中間站　intermediate station
中间站公务电话/中間站公務電話　interstation telephone
中间站台/中間月臺　intermediate platform
中间轴/中間軸　intermediate shaft
中间轴承/中間軸承　plummer block, intermediate shaft bearing, intermediate bearing
中间柱/中間柱　single suspension mast
中间状态/中間態　intermediate rating
中介轴/延伸軸　extension shaft
中空玻璃/中空玻璃　sealed insulating glass
中空飞行/中空飛行　mid airway flight
中空假山/中空假山　frame hill
中跨/中跨　mid span
中浪/和浪　moderate sea
中冷器/中間冷却器　intercooler
中梁/中梁　center sill
中梁悬臂部/倒懸　overhang, cantilever portion of center sill
中裂乳化沥青/中裂乳化瀝青　medium breaking emulsified bitumen
中磷闸瓦/中磷閘瓦　medium phosphor cast iron brake shoe
中锚/中錨,流錨　stream anchor
中内龙骨/中線內龍骨　center-line keelson, center keelson
中能见度/能見度中等　visibility moderate
中凝液体沥青/中凝液態瀝青　medium curing liquid asphalt
中频带磁记录器/中頻磁帶記錄器　intermediate-frequency tape recorder
中频燃烧不稳定性/中頻燃燒不穩定　intermediate-frequency combustion instability
中频通信/中頻通信　MF communication
中频无线电设备/中頻無線電裝置　MF radio installation
中期检验/中期檢驗　intermediate survey
中期天气预报/中期預報　medium-range forecast
中强钢丝/中強度鋼絲　medium strength steel wire
中桥/中橋　major bridge, middle span bridge, medium bridge
中曲面/中曲面　middle surface
中热硅酸盐水泥/中熱卜特蘭水泥　moderate heat Portland cement
中砂/中砂　medium sand
中生代/中生代　mesozoic era
中生树种/中生樹種　mesophilous tree species
中生植物/中生植物,適潤植物　mesophyte
中湿类型/中濕類型　median dampness type
中世纪建筑/中古時代建築　medieval architecture
中试/前導研究　pilot studies
中试厂/中間[試驗]工廠　pilot plant
中枢重调/中樞重調　central readjustment
中数耐受极限/中數可忍限值,中數忍限　median tolerance limit
中水/中水,回收水,再生水　reclaimed water, non potable reclaimed water
中水处理站/中水站,再生水處理站　reclaimed water station
中水分食品/中濕[性]食品　intermediate moisture food
中水设施/中水設施　equipments and facilities of reclaimed water
中水位桥/中水位橋　medium water level bridge
中水系统/中水系統,再生水系統　water reclaim system
中水原水/再生水原水　raw water of reclaimed water

中水装置/廢水回收設備　wastewater reclamation facilities, intermediate water facilities
中速柴油机/中速柴油機　medium speed diesel engine
中碳钢/中碳鋼　medium carbon steel
中天/中天　transit, meridian passage, culmination
中天顶距/[過]子午圈天頂距　meridian zenith distance
中天高度/中天高度　meridian altitude
中天观测/中天高度觀測　meridian observation
中庭/中庭,天井　patio, atrium
中途返回/中途返回　midway return operation
中途港/中途港　intermediate port
中途加压站/接力水泵場　relay pumping station
中途转换/中途轉換　throwing of switch under car, gear shifting in car driving
中位车速/中速　median speed
中位水道/中位水道　intermediate water channel
中温植物/溫帶生物　mesotherm
中文译码机/中文譯碼機　Chinese character code translation equipment
中线/中心線　center line
中线标记/中心標線　center line marking
中线测量/中[心]線測量　center line survey
中线面/中線面　center plane, center line plane
中线桩/中心樁　center line stake
中小学校建筑/學校建築　school building
中心城区/中心城區　central city area
中心城区规划/中心都市規劃　central city planning
中心城市/中心城市,中心都市　central city
中心冲头/中心衝孔　center-punching
中心村/中心村　central village, key village
中心岛/中央島,分向島　center island, central island
中心岛标线/中央島標線,分向島標線　center island marking
中心地理论/中地理論　central place theory
中心地区/中心地區　central area
中心点/支點　pivot point
中心电话所/中央電話局　central telephone office
中心电台/中心站　center station
中心光点/中心光點　pipper
中心广场/中心廣場　central plaza
中心交通区/主要交通區　central traffic district
中心搅拌厂/集中式拌和廠　central mixing plant
中心控制/中心控制,集中控制,集控　centralized control
中心控制器/中央控制器　central controller
中心扩大显示/中心擴大顯示　center-expand display
中心绿岛/中心綠島　center green island
中心锚结/中心錨結　mid-point anchor
中心锚结线夹/中心錨結線夾　mid-point anchor clamp
中心面/中心面　centroidal surface
中心排油阀/中心出油閥　central oil outlet valve
中心偏移/偏心　off-centering
中心区/中心區　center area
中心商务区/中心商業區　central business district, CBD
中心式舞台/中心式舞臺,圓形舞臺　arena stage
中心受压柱/中心受壓柱　centrally compressed column
中心投影/中心投影法　center projection, central projection
中心系泊定位钻井船/中心繫泊定位鑽探船　turret moored drilling ship, center moored drilling ship
中心线/中心線　center line
中心[消毒]供应部/中心消毒供應室　central sterilized supply department, CSSD
中心销/中心銷　center pin, king pin, pivot pin
中心镇/中心鎮　central town, key town
中心柱/中心柱　center mast
中行车/中行車　middle rolling car
中型客车/中型客車　medium bus
中型清筛机/中型清篩機　medium ballast undercutting cleaner
中性导体/中性導體　neutral conductor
中性点/中性點　neutral point
中性浮力仿真器/中性浮力模擬機　neutral buoyancy simulator
中性浮力试验/中性浮力試驗　neutral buoyancy test
中性流/中線電流　neutral current
中性滤光片/全波長濾光器　neutral filter
中性色/中性色,無彩色　neutral color
中性土/中性土　neutral soil
中性土植物/中性土植物　neutrophilous soil plant
中性温度/中性溫度　neutral temperature
中性线/中性線　neutral line
中性焰/中性火焰　neutral flame
中性植物/日照中性植物　day neutral plant
中性轴/中性軸,中和軸,中立軸　neutral axis
中修/中繼維修　intermediate maintenance
中压透平/中壓渦輪機　intermediate pressure turbine
中央操纵机构/中央操縱機構　central control mechanism
中央处理单元/中央處理單元　central processor unit
中央处理器/中央處理機　central processing unit,

CPU
中央大学建筑系/中央大學建築系　Department of Architecture in Central University
中央带/中央帶　center strip, median strip
中央导洞法/中央導洞法, 中央導坑法　central pilot tunneling method
中央导坑/中央導坑, 中設導坑　central heading, center drift
中央电池/［共電制］中央電池組　central battery
中央分割岛/車道分隔島　divisional island
中央分隔带/中央分隔帶　median separator, central separator, medial divider
中央分隔带护栏/路中護欄　median barrier
中央分隔带开口/中央分向島開口　median opening
中央分隔岛/路中間島　medial island
中央浮标/航道中流浮標　mid-channel buoy
中央隔离带/路中央行車帶　median strip
中央公园/中央公園　central park
中央缓冲器/中央緩衝器　central draft gear
中央活力区/中心活力區　central activity zone
中央计量站/中央測量站　central measuring station
中央空调器/中央空調　central air conditioner
中央空调系统/中央空調系統, 中央空氣調節系統　central air conditioning system
中央冷却系统/中央冷卻系統　central cooling system
中央领导枝/中央領導枝　central leadership branch
中央商务区/中心商業區　central business district
中央商务住宅/中央商務住宅　central serviced apartment
中央商业区/中心商業區, 中央商圈　central commercial area, central business district
中央实验室/中央實驗室　central laboratory
中央楔块/中心楔塊　center wedge
中央行政区/中央行政區　central government administration district
中药厂/中藥廠　traditional Chinese medicine factory
中药店/傳統中藥店　traditional Chinese medicine store
中英混合式园林/中英混合式園林　Anglo-Chinese style garden
中涌/中湧　moderate swell
中游/中游　middle reach
中站面/中站面　midstation plane
中植代/中生植物, 適潤植物　mesophyte
中制导/中途導引　midcourse guidance
中转仓库/通棧, 貨物棚　transit shed
中转车平均停留时间/中轉車平均停留時間　average detention time of car in transit
中转劳务包干费/中轉勞務包乾費　transshipment service package charge
中桩高程测量/中樁高程測量　center stake leveling
中桩填挖高度/中樁填挖高度　height of cut and fill at center stake
中子功率表/中子功率表　neutron power meter
中纵剖面/中心縱剖面　longitudinal section in center place
终点地址/目的地位址　destination address
终点电压/終止電壓　final voltage
终点站/終點站, 終端站　terminal station, terminus
终点站设施/終站設施　terminal facility
终端/終端［機］, 終端臺, 終端設備　terminal
终端电缆盒/電纜終端盒　cable terminal box
终端伏尔/終端多向導航臺　terminal VOR, TVOR
终端杆/終端桿　terminal pole
终端管制区/終端管制區域　terminal control area
终端盒/接線盒　terminal box
终端式站房/終端式站房　terminal station building
终端效应/端基效應　terminal effect
终端站/終端站　terminal station
终航向/終結航向　final course
终结信号/終止信號　finishing signal
终末沉降速度/臨界沈降速度　terminal settling velocity
终凝/終凝　final setting
终凝时间/終凝時間, 最終凝結時間　age of hardening, final setting time
终期置换/最終置換　final replacement
终碛/終［冰］碛, 端［冰］碛　terminal moraine
终夜灯/終夜燈　whole night lamp
终止合同/合約終止, 契約終止　termination of contract
钟表机构/時鐘機構　clock mechanism
钟表时间引信/時鐘定時引信　clock time fuze
钟锤拉索/拉鈴把手　bell pull
钟浮标/鐘浮標　bell buoy
钟鼓楼/鐘鼓樓　bell and drum tower
钟乳拱/鍾乳石拱頂　stalactite vault
钟乳石/鐘乳石, 石鐘乳　stalactite
舯/舯　midship
舯拱/舯拱　hogging
舯剖面惯性矩/舯剖面慣性矩　moment of inertia of midship section
舯剖面积/舯剖面積　area of midship section
舯剖面模数/舯剖面模數　modulus of midship section

舯剖面系数/舯剖面係數　midship section coefficient
舯突出部/舯膨出部　bulge
种/［物］種　species
种间竞争/種間競爭　interspecific competition
种内竞争/種內競爭　intraspecific competition
种群/種群,族群　population
种群变化/族群變化　population change
种群波动/族群變動　population fluctuation
种群大小/族群大小　population size
种群调查/族群普查　census
种群动态/族群動態　dynamic of population, population dynamics
种群分析/族群分析　population analysis
种群结构/族群結構　population structure
种群密度/族群密度　population density
种群灭绝/族群絕滅　population extinction
种群生态学/族群生態學　population ecology
种条/種條　breeding branches
种质创新/種質創新　germplasm enhancement
种质库/種質資源庫,品種資源庫,基因庫　germplasm bank
种质资源/種質資源　germplasm resources
种子/種子　seed
种子催芽/種子發芽　seed germination
种子加工与储藏/種子加工與儲藏　seed processing and storage
种子检验/種子檢驗　seed testing
种子库/種子庫　seed storage
种子液肥喷洒机/種子液肥噴灑機　hydro seeder
踵板/踵部底板　heel slab
中标/中標　award of contract
中标通知书/中標通知書,簽訂合同通知書　notification of award
仲裁/仲裁,公斷　arbitration
仲裁裁决/仲裁判斷　arbitration award
仲裁条款/仲裁條款　arbitration clause
仲裁庭/仲裁法庭　arbitration tribunal
仲裁委员会/仲裁委員會　board of arbitration
仲裁员/仲裁人　arbitrator
种植成活率/種植成活率　ratio of living tree, planting survival rate
种植大样图/種植大樣圖　detail planting design
种植地面/種植地面　planting floor
种植地区/種植地區　vegetation block
种植工程/種植工程　planting engineering
种植基质/種植基質　planting medium
种植模块/種植模塊　planting module
种植容器/種植容器　combined container, planting container
种植设计/種植設計,綠化設計,植樹計劃　planting design
种植土/果園土　planting soil
种植屋面/種植屋頂　green roof
种植箱/移植箱,苗木箱　plant box
重车行程/重車行程　loaded mileage
重车重心/重車重心　center of gravity for loaded car
重车重心高/重車重心高　center of gravity height of loaded car
重锤夯实法/重錘夯實法　heavy tamping method
重大改装/重大改裝　major conversion
重大件运输船/重大件貨運輸船　heavy and lengthy cargo carrier
重大建设项目/重大建設項目　major projects construction
重大事故/重大事故　grave accident
重大问题/重大問題　significant problem
重大问题报告/重大問題報告　significant problem report
重点货物/重點貨物　priority goods
重点污染物/重點汙染物　priority pollutant
重点物资运输计划/重點物資運輸計劃　priority materials transport plan
重点照明/補強照明　accent lighting
重点镇/重點鎮　major town
重吊杆/重吊桿　heavy derrick, jumbo boom
重吊起货机/重貨起重機　heavy lift derrick cargo winch
重工业/重工業　heavy industry
重工业区/重工業區　heavy industrial district
重骨料/重骨料　heavy aggregate
重交通/高運量　heavy traffic
重金属/重金屬　heavy metal
重力波/重力波　gravity wave
重力场/重力場　gravitational field
重力调车/重力調車　gravity shunting
重力拱坝/重力式拱壩　gravity arch dam
重力柜/重力櫃　gravity tank
重力焊/重力式［電弧］焊接　gravity welding
重力给水法/重力給水　gravity water supply
重力继电器/重力繼電器　gravitation type relay
重力加油/重力加油,自流式加油　gravity refuelling
重力校正/重力［誤差］改正　correction for gravity, gravity correction
重力勘探/重力式探查　gravitational prospecting
重力流雨水排水系统/重力流雨水排水系統　gravity storm water system

重力滤池/重力濾池　gravity filter
重力模型/重力模型,引力模式　gravity model
重力侵蚀/重力沖蝕　gravity erosion
重力生理学/重力生理學　gravitational physiology
重力式挡土墙/重力式擋土牆　gravity retaining wall
重力式吊艇架/重力[小艇]吊架　gravity type boat davit, gravity-type davit, gravity davit
重力式斗式提升机/重力式斗昇機　gravity bucket elevator
重力式防碰设备/重力式護木　gravity fender
重力式供给系统/重力供給系統　gravity feed system
重力式护[舷]木/重力式防舷材　suspended fender
重力式码头/重力式碼頭　gravity wharf
重力式锚碇/重力式錨碇　gravity anchor
重力式平台/重力式鑽油臺　gravity platform
重力式[桥]墩/重力式橋墩　gravity pier
重力式桥台/重力式橋臺　gravity abutment
重力式屋面雨水排水系统/重力式屋面雨水排水系統　gravity pressure roof storm water system
重力式下水/重力下水　gravity launching
重力式箱码头/重力沈箱碼頭　gravity caisson wharf
重力势能/重力位能　gravitational potential energy
重力输水管/重力輸水管　gravity aqueduct
重力水/重力水　gravity water
重力损失/重力損失　gravity losses
重力梯度捕获/重力姿態獲取　gravity gradient acquisition
重力梯度杆/重力梯度桿　gravity gradient boom
重力梯度力矩/重力梯度力矩　gravity gradient torque
重力梯度稳定/重力梯度穩定　gravity gradient stabilization
重力梯度姿态控制系统/重力梯度姿態控制系統　gravity gradient attitude control system
重力系泊塔/重力繫泊塔　gravity mooring tower
重力系统/重力系統　gravitational system
重力悬水/重力懸水　gravity suspended water
重力异常图/重力異常圖　gravity anomaly chart
重力油柜/重力油櫃　gravity oil tank
重量/重量　weight
重量百分比/重量百分比　percentage by weight
重量代换系统/重量代換系統　weight replacing system
重量吨/重量噸　weight ton
重量货/過秤貨　deadweight cargo
重量鉴定/重量檢定　inspection of weight
重量曲线/重量曲線　weight curve

重量稳性力臂/重量穩度力臂　lever of weight stability
重黏土/重黏土　heavy clay soil
重丘区/重丘區　hilling terrain
重水/重水　heavy water
重稳距/定傾[中心]高度　metacentric height
重箱里程/重箱里程　loaded container mileage
重心/重心　center of gravity
重心垂向坐标/垂向重心　vertical center of gravity
重心高度/重心高　height of center of gravity
重心横向坐标/横向重心　transverse center of gravity
重心后限/重心後限　afterward limit of center of gravity
重心距中距离/縱向重心與舯距離　longitudinal distance from amidships to the center of gravity
重心前限/重心前限　forward limit of center of gravity
重心纵向坐标/縱向重心　longitudinal center of gravity
重型钢轨/重轨　heavy rail
重型轨道/重型軌道　heavy track
重型轨道车/重型軌道車　heavy rail motor car, heavy motor trolley
重型击实试验/重型擊實試驗　modified compaction test
重型平板挂车/重載拖車　heavy haul trailer
重型钻岩机/重型鑽岩機　heavy drifter
重要负载/重要負載　important load
重要构件/主構件　primary member
重要件/重要零件　important part
重要天气/顯著天氣　significant weather
重要细节/重要細節,關鍵細節　critical detail
重油/重油　heavy oil
重载列车/重載列車　heavy haul train
重载铁路/重載鐵路　heavy haul railway
重症监护室/加護病房,加護病室　intensive care unit, ICU
重质混凝土/重質混凝土　heavy weight concrete
重质货物/重質貨物　heavy freight
重质燃料油/重燃油　heavy fuel oil
舟/船,小艇　boat
舟桥/浮桥　pontoon bridge, floating bridge, bateau bridge
周边地面/周邊地面　perimeter region
周边灌浆/周邊灌漿　rim grout
周边接缝/周邊接縫　perimetrical joint
周边炮眼/周界炮孔,修切炮孔　trimmer, trim hole,

rim hole
周边式/周邊式　perimetric layout, perimetric pattern
周边张力/環張力　ring tension
周计时/以週計時　time of week, TOW
周交通量变化图/每週交通量型　weekly traffic pattern
周界/周圍　perimeter
周界防范/周界防範　perimeter precaution
周界交通量调查/周界交通調查　cordon count
周年光行差/週年光行差　annual aberration
周年日/週年日　anniversary date
周期/週期　period
周期变距操纵杆/迴旋桿　cyclic-pitch stick
周期测量系统/定期測量系統　period measurement system
周期长/循環長度　cycle length
周期风/週期風　periodic wind
周期回升/週期性復原　cyclic recovery
周期流/週期流　periodic current
周期性/週期性　periodicity, periodism
周期性变化/週期性變化　cyclic variation
周期性传热/週期性傳熱　periodic heat transfer
周期性干扰力矩/週期性擾動扭矩　periodic disturbing torque
周期性耗竭/週期性涸竭　cyclic depletion
周期性检查/定期檢查,定期檢驗　periodical inspection
周期性力矩/週期性力矩　cyclic torque
周期性闪光/週期性閃光　cyclic flashing
周期性污染/週期性汙染　periodic pollution
周期振动/週期振動　periodic vibration
周日视运动/每日視運動　diurnal apparent motion
周围焊接/環焊　boxing
周围环境/周圍環境　ambient environment
周炸引信/週炸引信　ambient fuze
周转/週轉　turnover
周转轨/週轉軌　inventory stock rail
周转库/週轉庫　revolution storage
洲际导弹/洲際彈道飛彈　intercontinental missile
轴/軸　axis
X 轴/X 軸線　X-axis
Y 轴/Y 軸線　Y-axis
Z 轴/Z 軸線　Z-axis
轴测图/軸測圖,立體正投影圖　axonometric drawing
轴测图线性尺寸/軸測圖線性尺寸　axonometric drawing linear dimension

轴承/軸承,方位　bearing
轴承端盖/軸承端蓋　roller bearing end cap
轴承刮削/軸承刮削　scraping of bearing
轴承合金/軸承合金　antifrictional metal, bearing metal
轴承和功率传输组件/軸承和功率傳輸組件　bearing and power transfer assembly, BAPTA
轴承间隙/軸承間隙　bearing clearance
轴承力/軸承力　bearing force
轴承圈/軸承圈　collar bearing
轴承支架/橋承　bearing bridge
轴带发电机/軸驅動發電機　shaft-driven generator
轴端轴承/軸端軸承　axle end bearing
轴对称流/軸對稱流　axisymmetrical flow
X 轴分量/X 軸分量　X-component
轴功率/軸功率　shaft power
轴毂/軸轂,螺[槳]轂　propeller boss, shaft bossing
轴颈/軸頸　journal
轴颈后肩/軸頸後肩　journal back fillet
轴颈中心距/軸頸中心距離　distance between journal centers
轴距/輪基距　wheelbase
轴力图/軸力圖　axial force diagram
轴列式/車軸配置　axle arrangement
轴领/軸頸環　end collar, axle collar
轴流风扇/軸流扇　axial-flow fan
轴流式汽轮机/軸流[蒸汽]渦輪機　axial flow steam turbine
轴流式通风/軸流式風扇通風　ventilation by axial flow fan
轴流式通风机/軸流式風扇　axial fan
轴流式涡轮机/軸流式渦輪[機]　axial flow turbine
轴流式压气机/軸流[式]壓縮機　axial flow compressor
轴流[水]泵/軸流泵　axial flow pump
轴流通风机/軸流通風機,軸流鼓風機　axial flow blower
轴流压气机/軸流式壓縮機　axial flow compressor
轴马力/軸馬力　shaft horse power
轴身/軸體　axle body
轴隧/軸道　shaft tunnel
轴隧艇室/軸道凹部　tunnel recess
轴套/軸套,軸襯　shaft liner
轴头销/軸頭銷　gudgeon pin
轴瓦/徑向滑動軸承　plain journal bearing
轴瓦垫/軸瓦墊　journal bearing wedge
轴温/軸溫　journal temperature
轴系/軸系　shafting

轴系传动装置/軸系傳動裝置　transmission gear of shafting
轴系校中/軸線校中,軸線校準,軸系校準　shafting alignment, shaft alignment, centering for shafting
轴系接地装置/軸接地裝置　shafting-grounding device
轴系扭转振动/軸系扭轉振動　torsional vibration of shafting
轴系误差修正/軸系誤差修正　correction of axis system error
轴系效率/軸系效率　shafting efficiency, transmission efficiency of shafting
轴系找中/軸系對準,對中　centering of shafting
轴系振动/軸系振動　shafting vibration
轴系制动器/軸系制動器,軸遊轉防止裝置　shaft-locking device, shafting brake
轴系纵向振动/軸系縱向振動　longitudinal vibration of shafting, axial vibration of shafting
轴线/軸線　axis, axial line
轴线上叶厚/軸線上葉厚　blade thickness on axial line
轴箱/軸箱　journal box, axle box
轴箱承台/軸承臺,軸承托架,托架軸承　side frame pedestal bearing boss
轴箱挡/軸箱導架　axle box guide
轴箱导框/側框架托架　side frame pedestal
轴箱导框间隙/軸箱導框間隙　axle box play
轴箱盖/軸箱蓋　journal box lid
轴箱后盖/軸箱裏蓋　journal box rear cover
轴箱前盖/軸箱前蓋[板]　journal box front cover
轴箱弹簧/軸箱彈簧　journal box spring
轴箱弹簧支柱/軸箱彈簧支柱　journal box spring guide post
轴箱体/軸箱體　journal box body
轴箱托板/軸架拉條　pedestal brace
轴箱轴承/軸箱軸承　axle box bearing
轴向超载/軸向負荷係數　axial load factor
轴向减振器/縱向振動阻尼器　longitudinal vibration damper
轴向静压梯度/軸向靜壓梯度　static pressure gradient along tunnel axis
轴[向]力/軸向力,法向力,正交力　axial force, normal force
轴向力平衡装置/軸向推力平衡裝置　axial thrust balancing device
轴向推力/軸向推力　axial thrust
轴向位移保护装置/軸向位移保護設施　axial displacement protective device, axial displacement limiting device
轴向压力/軸壓力　axial pressure
轴向振动/軸向振動　axial vibration
轴向柱塞式液压马达/軸向活塞式液力馬達　axial-piston hydraulic motor
轴心轨迹/軸心軌跡　orbit of shaft center
轴心抗拉强度/軸向抗拉強度　axial tensile strength
轴心抗压强度/軸心抗壓強度　axial compressive strength
轴压比/軸壓比　axial compression ratio
轴压试验/軸壓縮試驗　axial compression test
轴载/軸重　axle load
轴载荷/軸載荷　load on axle journal
轴制动器/軸制動器,軸靭　shaft brake
轴中央部/軸心　axle center
轴重/軸[載]重,軸負荷　axle load, axle weight
轴重检测器/軸重偵測器　axle weight detector
轴重仪/軸重儀,軸重計　axle load meter
轴重转移/軸負載轉移　axle load transfer
轴重转移补偿装置/軸重轉移補償裝置　axle load transfer compensation device
轴装盘形制动/軸裝盤形制動　axle-mounted disc brake
肘板/肘板,腋板　knee plate, knee, bracket
肘杆机构/肘節機構　toggle mechanism
肘销/關節銷　knuckle pin
昼光/晝光,日光　daylight
昼间飞行/白晝飛行　day flight
昼间信号/晝間信號　day signal
昼夜等效[连续 A]声级/晝夜等效持續 A 加權聲壓位準　day-night equivalent continuous A-weighted sound pressure level
昼夜节律/晝夜間律,生理時鐘　circadian rhythm
昼夜通用信号/晝夜通用信號　day and night signal
皱曲纹/皺度　rugosity
皱纹套管/皺紋套管　spirally wound sheath
皱折/起皺,蒙皮挫曲　wrinkle
珠宝店/珠寶店　jewelry shop
珠宝饰品厂/珠寶飾品廠　jewelry work
珠承喷管/珠承噴嘴　bead support nozzle
株高/株高　plant height
诸元计算/合成資料計數　synthesized data count
猪舍/豬舍　pig barn
竹地板/竹地板　bamboo floor
竹家具/竹家具　bamboo furniture
竹胶合板/竹夾板　bamboo plywood
竹类/竹[材]　bamboo
竹林/竹林　bamboo forest

竹排/竹筏　bamboo raft
竹栓/竹栓　bamboo bolt
竹亭/竹亭　bamboo pavilion
竹筒排水管/竹管　bamboo drain
逐级/逐步　step-by-step
逐渐沉陷/逐進性沈落　progressive settlement
逐跨施工法/逐跨工法　span-by-span construction
逐区灌溉/越丘灌溉　plot-to-plot irrigation
逐时冷负荷综合最大值/逐時冷負荷綜合最大值　maximum sum of hourly cooling load
主按键开关组/主鍵開關組　main button switch group, main key switch set
主被动引信/主被動引信　active-passive fuze
主标志/主標誌　main mark
主标准/原級標準　primary standard
主波束效率/主光束效率　main beam efficiency
主操舵装置/主操舵裝置　main steering gear
主槽/主通道　main channel
主柴油机/主柴油機　main diesel engine
主潮/主潮　principle tide
主车钟/主車鐘　main engine telegraph
主成分分析/主成分分析　principal component analysis, PCA
主尺度/主要尺寸　principal dimensions
主尺度比/尺度比　dimension ratio
主船体/主船殼　main hull
主串通路/主串通路　disturbing channel
主导产业/主導產業　leading industry
主导风向/恆風向　prevailing wind direction
主灯/主燈　main light
主灯丝断丝报警/主燈絲斷絲報警　alarm for burnout of a main filament
主等高线/主等高線　principal contour
主地下水面/主要地下水面　main water-table
主电动机/主馬達　main motor
主电路/主電路,幹線　power circuit, main circuit
主电路短路保护系统试验/主電路短路保護系統試驗　test on short-circuit protection system of main circuit
主电路过载保护系统试验/主電路過載保護系統試驗　test on overload protection system of main circuit
主电路库用插座/主電路庫用插座　main circuit socket for shed supply
主电路库用转换开关/主電路庫用轉換開關　main circuit transfer switch for shed supply
主电源/主電源　main electric power source, main source of electrical power, primary electrical power source
主动安全性/主動式安全　active safety
主动齿轮/主動齒輪,驅動機構　driving gear
主动段/主動段　powered-flight phase
主动段测控/加速階段追蹤、遥測和指令站　TT and C of boost phase
主动段救生/主動段救生　power flight phase escape
主动舵/主動舵　active rudder
主动隔振/主動隔離　active vibration isolation
主动红外探测器/主動紅外相關器　active infrared correlation device
主动间隙控制/主動間隙控制　active clearance control
主动控制隔振装置/主動振動隔離裝置　active vibration isolating device
主动控制技术/主動控制技術　active control technology
主动轮对/主傳動輪組　main driving wheel set
主动式热控制/主動熱控制　active thermal control
主动式引信/主動式引信　active fuze
主动适应性/主動調適　active accommodation
主动水舱式减摇装置/主動減搖水艙穩定器　stabilizing system with active anti-rolling tanks
主动土压力/主動土壓力　active earth pressure
主动微波遥感/有源微波遥感　active microwave remote sensing
主动章动控制/主動章動控制　active nutation control
主动姿态控制/主動姿態控制　active attitude control
主动姿态稳定/主動姿態穩定　active attitude stabilization
主断路器/線路斷路器　line circuit-breaker
主舵杆/主舵桿　rudder main stock
主发电柴油机/主柴油發電機　main generator diesel engine
主发电机/主發電機　main generator
主发电机组/主發電機組　main generating set
主发动机/主[火箭]發動機,續航發動機　sustainer motor, sustainer, main engine
主阀/主閥,總閥　main valve
主飞行操纵系统/基本飛行控制系統　primary flight control system
主飞行显示器/主要飛行顯示器　primary flight display
主辅结合线网/主輔結合線網　network of transport arteries and branch lines
主干/主幹　in the middle of the trunk
主干道/幹道　trunk road

主干电缆/主電纜,主幹纜線,幹線纜線　main cable
主干路/幹道,幹線道路　arterial road
主钢缆/承載索　jackstay
主钩/主鉤　main hook
主钩起重量/主鉤起重量　main hook load
主固结/主壓密　primary consolidation
主观混响时间/主觀混響時間　subjective reverberation time
主管机关/主管機關,主管官署　administration
主惯性矩/主慣性矩　principal moment of inertia
主惯性轴/慣性主軸線　principal axis of inertia
主光学系统/主光學系統　primary optical system
主轨/主軌　main rail
主锅炉/主鍋爐　main boiler
主航道/主航道　main channel
主河槽/主河槽,洪水河床　main river channel, major bed
主荷载/主載重　primary load
主滑行道/主滑行道　main runway
主机/主機,主控機車　main engine, leading locomotive
主机房/電腦房　primary computer room
主机工况监测器/主機狀況偵測器　main engine condition monitor
主机故障应急处理/主機故障應急操縱　main engine fault emergency maneuver
主机航程/主機航程　distance by engine RPH
主机航速/引擎轉速,機速　engine speed
主机基座/主機座,主機臺　main engine bed, main engine foundation
主机校中/主機校中　determination for main engine location
主机遥控屏/主機遙控屏　main engine remote control panel
主机转速表/主機轉速表　main engine revolution speedometer
主极铁心/主極鐵心　mainpole core
主极线圈/主極線圈　mainpole coil
主给水系统/主給水系統　main feed system
主甲板/主甲板　main deck
主减速器/主變速箱　main gearbox
主降机场/主降機場　regular aerodrome
主叫/呼叫　calling
主叫控制复原方式/主叫控制復原方式　calling subscriber release
主叫用户/主叫用戶,主叫方　calling party
主接线/主[接線]系統　primary system
主景/主景　main feature

主景植物/主景植物　accent plant
主空气瓶/主空氣瓶　main air bottle
主控线路/主控線路　master control circuit
主控项目/主控項目　dominant item
主控站/主控[制]站　master control station, primary station
主控制机/主控制器　master controller
主跨/主跨　main span
主拉杆/主繫桿　main tie
主肋骨/主肋骨　main frame
主冷凝器循环泵/主冷凝器循環泵　main condenser circulating pump
主冷却剂系统/主冷卻劑系統　main coolant system
主力/主力　principal load
主连杆/主連桿　main connecting rod
主梁腹板/梁腹板　girder web
主梁荷载/梁載重　girder load
主梁中心距/主梁中心間隔　center-to-center distance of main girder
主令电器/主控開關,總開關　master switch
主令控制器/主控制器　master controller
主流/主流,幹流　main stream
主路/主道,幹線　main road
主轮距/輪軌距　wheel track
主罗经/主羅經　master compass
主螺栓/大螺栓　king bolt
主跑道/主跑道　primary runway
主配电板/主配電盤　main switchboard
主平行线/主平行線　principal parallel line
主起动阀/主起動閥　main starting valve
主起落架/主起落架　main gear
主汽阀/主停止閥　main stop valve
主汽轮机/主汽輪機,主蒸汽渦輪機　main steam turbine
主汽轮机组/主蒸汽渦輪機組　main steam turbine set
主桥/主橋　main bridge
主曲拐销/主曲柄銷　main crank pin
主曲率/主曲率　principal curvature
主群/主群　master group
主燃气轮机/主燃氣渦輪機　main gas turbine
主燃气轮机组/主燃氣渦輪機組　main gas turbine set
主燃区/主燃燒區　primary combustion zone
主伞/主傘　main parachute
主商业中心/主商業中心　main commercial center
主竖区/主要垂直區域　main vertical zone
主台/主臺　master station, main stage

主台信号/主臺信號 master signal
主台座/主托架 master pedestal
主弹性联轴节/主彈性聯軸節 main elastic coupling
主题标识符/主題標識符 subject indicator character
主题表示类型/主題顯示之形式 subject indication type
主题公园/主題樂園 theme park
主题形象/主題形象 theme image
主体功能区/主體功能區 development priority zone
主体功能区规划/主體功能區規劃 development priority zone planning
主体建筑/主體建築 main building
主体建筑控制线/主體建築控制線 main building control line
主体结构工程/骨架工程 skeleton work
主体群落/主群落 main community
主通气立管/主通氣立管 main vent stack
主推进机舱/主推進機器 main propelling machinery room
主推进装置/主推進裝置 main propulsion unit
主拖缆/主拖纜 main towing line
主陀螺/子午迴轉儀 meridian gyro
主弯矩/主力矩 primary moment
主席台/司令臺 rostrum, platform
主线/主線 principal line
主线圈/主線圈 main coil
主线收费站/主線收費站 mainline toll station
主信号/主號誌 main signal
主循环泵/主循環泵 main circulating pump
主压载水舱/主壓載艙 main ballast tank
主要编组站/主要編組站 main marshalling station
主要道路/主要道路 main road, major road
主要港/重要港埠 major port
主要公路/主要公路 major highway
主要构件/主構件 primary member
主要河川/主要河川 trunk river
主要路线/幹線[路] main route
主要入口/主要入口 main entrance
主要要素/主要特徵，主要項目 principal particulars
主要园路/主要園路 main garden road
主要原因/主要原因 major cause
主应变/主應變 principal strain
主应变轴/應變主軸 principal strain axis
主应力/主應力 primary stress, principal stress
主用发信机/主發射機 main transmitter
主用收信机/主接收機 main receiver
主用天线/主天線 main antenna
主站/主臺,主測站 master station, primary station

主振器/主控振盪器 master oscillator
主震/主震 main shock
主蒸汽管/蒸汽管 steam pipe
主整流柜隔离开关/主整流櫃隔離開關 isolating switch for main silicon rectifier cubicle
主枝/主枝 main branch
主轴/主軸 main axis, principal axis, main shaft
主轴承/主軸承 main bearing
主轴承盖/主軸承蓋 main bearing cap
主轴承螺母/主軸承[壓緊]螺母 main bearing nut
主轴承螺栓/主軸承柱螺栓 main bearing stud
主轴承镗床/主軸承鑽孔機 main bearing boring machine
主轴承座/主軸承座 main bearing seat, main bearing housing
主轴颈/曲柄軸頸 crankshaft journal, crank journal, main journal
主轴瓦/主軸承殼 main bearing shell
主轴线测设/主軸線設定 setting out of main axis
主轴箱/軸承 headstock
主转子/主轉子 main rotor
主桩/主樁 key pile
主着陆场/主登陸位置 major landing site
助[导]航设备/助航設施 navigation aid
助航标志/導航設備 navigation aid
助航灯光/助航燈光 navigational lighting aid
助滤剂/助濾劑 filtering aid
助凝剂/助凝劑 coagulant aid
助艏缆/前艏纜 forward bow spring
助推发动机/助推發動機 booster engine, booster motor
助推级翻转吊具/助推翻轉吊索 booster turning sling
助推级公路运输车/助推拖車 booster trailer
助推级七管连接器工作梯/助推七管連接器工作梯 booster seven pipe connector working ladder
助推级水平测试工作梯/助推水平測試工作梯 booster horizontal checking ladder
助推级水平吊具/助推水平吊索 booster horizontal sling
助推级铁路运输车/助推鐵路運輸車 booster rail transporter
助推级铁轮支架车/助推鐵輪運輸臺車 booster iron wheel carriage
助推器/助推器 booster
助推器配气台/助推器配氣臺 gas distribution board of booster
助艉缆/艉向後倒纜 forward back spring leading

aft, head aft spring
住舱/住艙　living quarter
住房按揭贷款/住房抵押貸款　house mortgage loan
住房补贴/住宅補貼　housing subsidy
住房调查/住宅調查　housing survey
住房法规/住宅法　housing code
住房公积金/住房公積金　housing accumulation fund
住房管理/住宅行政　housing administration
住房建设规划/住宅施工規劃　housing construction planning
住房建设计划/住宅建設計劃　housing development plan
住房金融/住宅信贷　housing finance
住房体制改革/住宅政策改革　housing policy reform
住房问题/住宅問題　housing problem
住房协会/住宅協會　housing association
住房需求/住宅需求　housing demand
住房政策/住宅政策　housing policy
住房租赁市场/住房租賃市場　house leasing market
住户大小/户量　household size
住户规模/户量　household size
住区/住區,居民點　settlement
住院部/住院部　inpatient department
住宅/住宅,屋子,起站　dwelling house, home
住宅标准/居住標準　dwelling standard
住宅布局/住宅布局　housing layout
住宅布置/住宅布置　residential layout
住宅单元/居住房屋,居住建築物　residential building unit
住宅地下排水管/家庭地下排水　house subdrain
住宅废水/家庭廢水　house wastewater
住宅建设规划/住宅建設計劃　housing development plan
住宅建筑方案/住宅方案　housing scheme
住宅建筑[面积]净密度/住屋面積淨密度　net floor area density of residential building
住宅建筑面积毛密度/住屋面積毛密度　gross floor area density of residential building
住宅建筑套密度/住屋單位密度　residential building unit density
住宅类型/住房類型　housing type
住宅密度/居住密度　residential density
住宅平均层数/住宅平均層數　average stories of house
住宅情况/居住水準　dwelling condition
住宅区/住宅區　residential district
住宅区道路/私人産業道路　estate road
住宅市镇/住宅市鎮,眠憩市鎮　bed town, residential town
住宅性能评定/住宅性能評定　housing performance assessment
住宅专项维修资金/住宅維修資金,住宅維修基金　residential special maintenance fund
住宅专用地区/住宅專用區　exclusive residential district
住宅组群/集團住宅　group house
住宅组团/住宅組團,住宅建築群　housing group, housing cluster
贮备电池/蓄電池　reserve battery
贮存可靠度/儲存可靠度　storage reliability
贮存期/貯藏時間　storage life
贮存试验/儲存試驗　storage test
贮存寿命加速试验/貯藏時間加速試驗　storage life accelerated test
贮存载荷/儲存負載　storage load
贮罐/儲存槽,儲藏箱　storage tank
贮木场/貯木池　timber basin
贮囊渗透速率/貯囊滲透速率　bladder specific penetration mass
贮箱排空效率/貯箱排空效率　propellant tank expulsion efficiency
贮箱气检/貯箱氣檢　gas leak inspection of tank
贮箱容积效率/貯箱容積效率　propellant tank volumetric efficiency
贮液池/蓄水池　reservoir
贮液桶/受液器　liquid receiver
注册/註冊,登記　register, registration
注册城市规划师/註冊規劃師　registered urban planner
注册城市规划师执业资格/註冊城市規劃師執業資格　registered urban planner qualification
注册港/註冊港,船籍港　port of registry
注册监督/註冊監督　register supervision
注册建筑师/註冊建築師　registered architect
注册建筑师继续教育/關於註冊建築師繼續教育問題　continuing education for registered architect
注册建筑师继续教育证书/註冊建築師繼續教育證書　certificate of continuing education for registered architect
注册建筑师执业资格考试/註冊建築師執業資格考試　examination for registered architect
注防腐油/注防腐油　creosoting
注记装置/註記裝置　annotation equipment
注浆/灌漿　grouting
注浆泵/灌漿泵,水泥漿泵　grouting pump, injection pump

注浆机/灌漿機,洋灰攪拌機,水泥攪拌機 grouting machine, grouter
注浆型锚杆/灌漿岩石錨桿 grouted rock bolt
注入管/注入管 filling pipe, filling piping, filling line
注入站/注入站,注入臺 injection station
注砂筒/注砂筒 sand volume apparatus
注射成形/射出成形 injection moulding
注射施肥/注射式施肥 injection fertilization
注射室/注射室 injection room
注水井/注水井 injection well
注水口/注水口,上水口 filling pipe end
注水器/注射器 injector
注水式船坞/注水式船塢 flooding dock
注水试验/揚水試驗 pumping test, water injection test
注销登记/撤銷登記 registration of withdrawal
注意标志/注意標誌 notice mark
注意信号/注意號誌 caution signal
驻波/駐波,定波 stationary wave, standing wave, clapotis
驻场设计/現場設計 on site service
驻车场停车周转率/停車使用率 parking turnover rate
驻车容量/停車容量 parking capacity
驻地监理工程师/駐地監理工程師 resident supervising engineer
驻点/止流點,停滯點 stagnation point
驻点温度/停滯温度 stagnation temperature
驻留时间/照射目標時間 dwell time
驻室/駐室 plenum chamber
柱/柱 column
柱板式挡土墙/板樁式擋土牆 pile plank retaining wall
柱比法/喻柱法,類比拉法 column analogy
柱插/柱插,鑽座 stake pocket
柱础/柱礎,柱座 column base
柱灯/柱[頭]燈 pillar lamp
柱墩式栈桥/柱支式橋墩 column supported pier
柱架式钻/柱架式鑽 mounting colume drill
柱间距/柱間 intercolumniation
柱间支撑/柱間支撑 column bracing
柱脚/柱礎,柱座 column base
柱距/柱距 column spacing, truss interval
柱孔[旋]钻/螺旋手鑽 post-hole auger
柱帽/柱帽,柱頭 capital
柱塞/柱塞,活塞 plunger, injection piston
柱塞泵/柱塞泵,唧子泵 plunger pump, ram pump

柱塞偶件/柱塞偶合件 plunger matching parts
柱塞套/柱塞套筒 plunger sleeve
柱塞套筒组件/柱塞與套筒組件 plunger and sleeve assembly
柱身/柱身 shaft
柱式/柱式,式樣 order
柱式洞门/柱式洞門 post-tunnel portal
柱式举升机/柱式昇降機 post lift
柱式轮廓标/柱式輪廓標 post delineator
柱式[桥]墩/柱式橋墩 column pier, shaft pier
柱式钻架/柱支鑽架 column drill
柱头/柱頭,柱帽 capital
柱头灯/柱頭燈 chapiter lamp, column headlight
柱头枋/柱頭枋 column-top joist, zhutoufang
柱头铺作/柱頭鋪作 column-top bracket set, zhutou puzuo
柱网/柱網 column grid, column network
柱稳半潜式钻井平台/柱穩定型鑽油船 column stabilized semisub drilling rig, column stabilized semi-submersible drilling unit
柱心力矩/核力矩 core moment
柱形浮标/柱形浮標 pillar buoy
柱形音频LED控制器/柱形音頻LED控制器 cylindrical audio LED controller
柱状施工法/柱狀施工法 column method of execution
柱状桅/柱狀桅 pole mast
柱座/柱座 stylobate
柱座标志/柱座標誌 stanchion sign
蛀干害虫/蛀幹害蟲 trunk pest
铸钢/鑄鋼 cast steel
铸钢车轮/鑄鋼輪 cast steel wheel
铸工车间/鑄工場 casting shop, foundry shop
铸件/鑄件 cast, casting
铸件清理车间/清理場 casting cleaning, fettling shop
铸件线收缩率/收縮[量] shrinkage, cissing
铸石/鑄石 cast stone
铸铁/鑄鐵 cast iron
铸铁管/鑄鐵管 cast iron pipe, CIP
铸铁管片/鑄鐵砌塊 cast-iron segment
铸铁铺面/鐵板鋪面 iron paving
铸铁闸瓦/鑄鐵閘瓦 cast iron brake shoe
铸型/鑄模 mold
铸压成型/壓鑄成型 die casting moulding
铸造/鑄造 foundry, casting, founding
铸造车间/鑄工場 casting shop, foundry shop
铸造高温合金/鑄造高溫合金 cast superalloy

铸造合金/鑄造合金　casting alloy, foundry alloy
铸造机座/鑄造機座　cast frame
铸造铝合金/鑄造鋁合金　cast aluminium alloy
铸造镁合金/鑄造用鎂合金　cast magnesium alloy
铸造钛合金/鑄造用鈦合金　cast titanium alloy
筑岛沉井/築島沈井　sinking open caisson on built island
筑路/築路　road construction
筑路机械/築路機械　road machinery
筑路机械大修/築路機械大修　major repair of road machine
筑路机械全过程管理/築路機械全過程管理　all-life period management of road construction machine
筑路机械小修/築路機械現場修理　current repair of road construction machine
筑路机械中修/築路機械中修　medium repair of road construction machine
筑路焦油/路用柏油　road tar
抓铲挖掘机/蛤殼形挖掘機　clam-shell excavator
抓斗/抓斗　grab, grapple
抓斗式起重机/蚌殼式吊挖機　clam-shell grabbing crane
抓斗挖泥船/抓斗[式]挖泥船,抓式挖泥機　grapple dredger, grab dredger
抓斗稳索/抓索　grab line, grab stabilizer line
抓岩机/抓石斗　rock grab
专机飞行/專機飛行　state flight
专家控制系统/專家控制系統　expert control system
专科大学/[專科]大學,學院　institute, college
专科医院/專科醫院　specialized hospital
专类公园/專類公園　theme park, specific garden
专类花境/專類花境　theme border
专类花园/專類花園　specified flower garden
专卖店/特許商店　speciality shop, exclusive agency, franchised store
专门性博物馆/專業博物館　specialized museum
专门性美术馆/專業美術館　specialized art museum
专门性图书馆/專業圖書館　specialized library
专设安全系统/專設安全系統　engineering safety system
专属经济区/專屬經濟區　exclusive economic zone
专属渔区/專屬漁業區　exclusive fishery zone
专题展厅/專業展區　specialized exhibition hall
专题制图仪/主題繪圖儀　thematic mapper, TM
专向/專向　special way
专项城市设计/專項都市設計　special urban design
专项规划/專項規劃　subject planning
专项旅游/專項旅遊　specific tour

专业负责人/專業負責人　professional leader
专业技术训练/專業技術訓練　professional technique training
专业救助/專業救助業務　specialized salvage service
专业性货运站/專業性貨運站　specialized freight station
专用标志/特殊標誌　special mark
专用泊位/專用船席,專用碼頭　appropriated berth
专用测试设备/專用測試設施　special test facility
专用车道/專用車道　accommodation lane
专用车行路/專用車行路　special dealers road
专用道路/專用道路　private road
专用灯/整補作業燈　task light
专用电话网/專用電話網路　private telephone network
专用电路/私用電路　private circuit
专用符号/特別符號　special symbol
专用工艺装备/專用工藝裝備　special tooling
专用公路/專用公路　accommodation highway
专用供水/專用給水,私用給水　private water supply
专用航道/專用航道　special purpose channel
专用货车/專用貨物列車　special purpose freight car
专用基金/特種基金,專款　special fund
专用集装箱/專用集裝箱,專用貨櫃　specific purpose container
专用教室/特殊教室　special classroom
专用龙头/專用水栓　private tap
专用绿地/專用綠地　specified green space
专用汽车/專用汽車　special purpose vehicle
专用清洁压载泵/清潔壓艙水泵　clean ballast pump
专用清洁压载水舱/清潔壓艙水專用艙　dedicated clean ballast tank
专用实验室/特殊制程實驗室　special lab
专用数据网/專用數據網路　private data network
专用铁道/工業鐵路　industrial railway
专用铁路/專用鐵路,專用鐵道　special purpose railway, exclusive railway
专用停车场/專用停車場　special parking lot, tied car park
专用通气立管/專用通氣立管　specific vent stack
专用通信网/專用通信網　private communication network
专用外部设备/專用周邊設備　special peripheral equipment
专用卫星通信网/專屬衛星通信網路　dedicated satellite communication network
专用下水道/私人下水道　private sewer
专用线/專用[支]線　private siding, special line,

private line
专用消防口/專用消防口 fire-firing access
专用压载舱保护位置/隔離壓艙水艙保護位置 protective location of segregated tank ballast
专用压载水/隔離壓艙水 segregated ballast
专用压载[水]舱/隔離壓載水艙 segregated ballast tank, SBT
专用压载系统/隔離壓載系統 segregated ballast system
专有名称权/專有名稱權 proper name right
专运列车无线电通信/特別列車無線電通訊 radio communication for special train
砖/磚 brick
砖红壤/磚紅壤 latosol
砖混结构/磚混結構 masonry-concrete structure
砖块路面/磚鋪路面 brick pavement
砖木结构/磚木結構 masonry-timber structure
砖铺路面/磚鋪路面 brick pavement
砖砌体/磚砌體 brick masonry
砖砌体结构/磚石結構 brick masonry structure
砖桥/磚橋 brick bridge
砖作/磚工 brick work
转包/轉讓合同 assignment of contract
转变长度/缓和長度 transition length
转变点/轉點 change point
转变滑行道/繞轉滑行道 turnaround taxiway
转场/運渡 ferry
转车机/迴轉裝置,盤車裝置 turning gear
转出式吊艇架/旋臂吊架 radial davit
转船货/轉船貨 transshipment cargo
转船力矩/船舶迴轉力矩 moment of turning ship
转船提单/轉口載貨證券 transshipment bill of lading
转船条款/轉船條款 transshipment clause
转点/轉[向]點 turning point, TP, turning station
转垛/轉垛 stacking area adjustment
转舵阶段/轉舵階段 maneuvering period
转舵时间/轉舵時間 time of rudder movement
转发无线电话遇险信号/轉發遇險通報 mayday relay
转发信标/轉發信標 responder beacon
转化处理/轉化處理 conversion treatment
转环/轉環 swivel
转换/轉換 translation
转换层/轉換層 transfer story
转换阀/變換閥 change-over valve
转换机构/變換機構 change-over mechanism
转换开关/換向開關,換路開關 change-over switch, transfer switching equipment
转换塞门/切換旋塞 cut-out cock
转换时间,轉換時間,轉移時間,傳遞時間 transfer time
转换锁闭器/轉換鎖閉器 switch-and-lock mechanism
转换效率/轉換效率 conversion efficiency
转换柱/轉換柱 transition mast
转换字符/轉換字元 hand-over-word, HOW
转极时间/轉極時間 pole-changing time
转极值/轉極值 pole-changing value
转接盒/互連裝置 interconnecting device
转矩/轉矩,扭矩 torque
转矩系数/轉矩係數 torque coefficient
转矩仪/轉矩計 torque meter
转口港/轉口港 port of transshipment
转口货/轉口貨,過路貨,接運貨 transit cargo
转口提单/接運載貨證券 transit bill of lading
转捩/換裝,過渡 transition
转[内]电/轉電 switch to internal power
转体架桥法/轉體架橋法 bridge erection by swinging method
转体施工法/轉體架橋法,施工擺動 construction by swing
转弯半径/轉彎半徑,迴旋半徑 turning radius
转弯侧滑仪/轉彎傾斜儀 turn and bank indicator
转弯车道/轉向車道 turning lane
转弯曲度/轉彎曲度 turning curvature
转弯驶出/出口轉向 exit turn
转弯速率/轉彎速率 turning speed
转弯线/轉彎線 turning guide marking
转弯阳角/轉捩點角 angle at turning point
转向/轉向,轉動 turning, altering course
转向点/轉向點 turning point
转向点浮标/轉向點浮標 turning buoy
转向杆/曲桿 deflecting bar
转向工况管理/迴轉操作形式管理 turning operating mode management
转向架/轉向架 truck, bogie
转向架侧架/轉向架側框架 truck side frame
转向架独立供电/轉向架獨立供電 bogie individual power supply
转向架对角线/轉向架構架對角線,車架對角線 truck frame diagonal
转向架构架/轉向架構架,車架 truck frame
转向架基础制动/轉向架基礎刹車裝置 truck brake

rigging
转向架承式牵引电动机/轉向架承式牽引電動機　bogie mounted traction motor
转向架扭曲刚度/轉向架扭曲剛度　truck rigidity against distorsion
转向架式车/轉向架車　bogie car
转向架摇枕/轉向架承梁　truck bolster
转向架制动组件/轉向架制動組件　truck-mounted brake assembly
转向架中心/轉向架樞心　bogie pivot center
转向架中心距离/轉向架樞軸節距　distance between bogie pivot centers, bogie pivot pitch
转向架组全轴距/組合式轉向架全軸距　wheelbase of combination truck
转向角/偏轉角,撓曲角　deflection angle
转向喷管/變向噴嘴,向量噴嘴　vectoring nozzle
转向上风/轉向上風　bear down
转向设备/轉向設備　turning facilities
转向下风/轉向下風　bear up
转向线/Y形線　turn-around wye, Y-track
转向性能试验/轉向試驗　turning test
转向旋翼航空器/傾轉旋翼飛機　tilt rotor aircraft
转向摇臂/搖臂　pitman arm
转移轨道/轉移軌道　transfer orbit
转移轨道三轴稳定/轉移軌道三軸穩定　transfer orbit three-axis stabilization
转移轨道自旋稳定/轉移軌道自旋穩定　transfer orbit spin stabilization
转移交通量/分流交通量　diverted traffic volume
转移条件/轉移狀況　transfer condition
转移位置线/轉移位置線　position line transferred
转移站/轉運站,換乘站　transfer station
转印法/複印法　transfer process
转运/轉運,轉移　transfer
转载间/轉載間　transit hall
转载平台/轉換平臺　transfer platform
转辙机/轉轍器　switch machine
转辙机安装装置/轉轍機安裝裝置　switch machine installation
转辙角/轍叉角,岔心角　switch angle
转辙器号数/轉轍器號數　switch number
转辙器座/轉轍器座　switch stand
转辙锁闭器/插桿鎖　plunger lock
转辙装置/轉轍鎖定　switch and lock movement
转注/轉注　transit-fueling
转租/轉租　subletting, subchartering
转臂式轴箱定位装置/轉臂式軸箱定位裝置　rocker type journal box positioning device

转动/迴轉　turn
转动车钩煤车/旋轉式運煤車　rotary dumping coal car
转动导缆孔/萬向導纜孔　universal chock
转动刚度/旋轉勁度　rotational stiffness
转动关节/旋轉接合器　rotary joint
转动惯量/慣性矩　moment of inertia
转动配合/轉動配合　running fit
转动喷管/可轉動噴管,可轉動噴管　rotatable nozzle
转动式车钩/旋轉式聯結器,旋轉式耦合器　rotary dump coupler
转动套环/覆環　shroud ring
转动座椅/旋轉座　rotating seat
转斗式提升机/轉斗式提昇機　rotary bucket elevator
转角/旋轉角　angle of rotation
转角挠度方程/撓度方程　slope deflection equation
转角铺作/轉角鋪作　corner column-top bracket set
P-V转角示功图/失相圖　out-of-phase diagram
转流/潮流旋轉　turn of tidal current
转轮式换热器/迴轉式熱交換器　rotary heat exchanger, heat wheel
转盘/轉盤,轉臺　turntable
转盘式钻机/轉盤鑽機　rotary table rig
转盘钻井/轉式鑽探　rotary drilling
转鳍机构/傾轉鰭機構　fin-tilting gear
转式流速计/迴轉式流速計　rotary meter
转艏性/航向改變性　course changing quality
转数计数器/轉數計　revolution counter
转速变换器/變速器　speed changer
转速表/轉速表,轉速計　tachometer
转速表传动装置/轉速計傳動裝置　transmission gear of tachometer
转速波动率/速率變動率,速率波動係數　coefficient of speed fluctuation, rate of speed fluctuation
转速法/轉速法　engine-speed method
转速继电器/轉速繼電器　tachometric relay
转速禁区/速限區　barred-speed range
转速控制/轉動速率控制　rotation velocity control
转速控制量/自旋速率控制量　spin rate control quantity
转速同步器/轉速諧調器　speed synchronizer
转速悬挂/轉速懸掛　speed hang-up
转塔式系泊系统/轉塔式繫泊系統　turret mooring system
转台/[旋]轉臺　turntable, revolving stage
转筒[鼓]洗涤器/鼓型清洗機　drum washer
转筒筛/旋轉篩　revolving screen

转筒式混合器/桶形拌和機　barrel mixer
转叶式转舵机构/轉葉式操舵裝置　rotary vane steering gear
转轴/轉軸　shaft
转柱舵/轉柱舵　rotating cylinder rudder
转子/轉子,旋翼　rotor
转子动量矩/轉子角動量　rotor angular momentum
转子临界转速/臨界轉子速率　critical rotor speed
转子平衡/轉子平衡　rotor balancing
转子式除雪机/旋轉式除雪機　rotary snow remover
转子式翻车机/轉式卸土車　rotary car dumper
转子式沥青乳化机/旋轉式瀝青乳化機　rotary bitumen emulsifying machine
转子式汽笛/汽笛,號笛　air whistle, air horn
转子式碎石机/轉子式碎石機　rotator crusher
转子式稳定土搅拌机/旋轉穩定土拌和機　rotary soil stabilizer, rotary stabilized soil road mixer
转子相对位移/轉子相對位移　relative rotor displacement
转子叶片/轉子葉片　rotor blade
庄园/莊園　manor, villa garden
桩/樁　pile
桩标/樁標　spar buoy, pile beacon
桩承台/樁鑽油臺　pile platform
桩垫木/樁墊　dolly
桩钉/樁釘　peg nail
桩定坡面点/定坡橛　slope staking
[桩]动测法/[樁]動測法　dynamic measurement of pile
桩箍/樁頭箍　pile hoop
桩贯入试验/樁貫入試驗　pile penetration test
桩横向荷载试验/樁橫向荷載試驗　lateral loading test of pile
桩基础/樁基[礎]　pile foundation
桩基系泊塔/樁基繫泊塔　piled mooring tower
桩基 c 值法/樁基 c 值法　subsoil reaction modulus c method for laterally loaded pile
桩基 m 值法/樁基 m 值法　subsoil reaction modulus m method for laterally loaded pile
桩校法/樁校法　peg adjustment method
桩景树/主樁樹　king pile tree
桩帽/樁帽　driving cap, driving helmet, pile helmet
桩墙移动/樁牆移動　sheeting movement
桩群/樁群　pile group, pile cluster
桩入土长度/樁入土長度　embeded length of pile
桩式桥/樁橋　pile bridge
桩[式桥]墩/樁橋墩　pile pier
桩式消防栓/柱式消防栓　pillar hydrant

桩头/樁頭　pile head
桩腿/樁腿　spud leg
桩完整性试验/樁完整性試驗　pile integrity test
桩靴/樁鞋　drive shoe
桩轴向荷载试验/樁軸向荷載試驗　axial loading test of pile
装裱室/裝裱室　mounting room
装裱修整室/裝裱修整室　mounting and trimming room
装舱检查/滿載吃水檢查　loading survey
装拆式钢桥/裝拆式鋼橋　fabricated and detachable steel bridge
装车机/帶式裝載機　train loader
装车数/裝車數　number of car loadings
装车调整/裝車調整　adjustment of car loading
装船通知单/下貨單　shipping note
装船要素/裝船要素　shipment element
装定角度/安裝角　setting angle
装管规则/裝管規則　plumbing regulation
装货泊位/裝貨船席　loading berth
装货单/裝貨通知單　shipping order
装货港/裝貨港　port of loading, port of shipment
装货口/裝貨口　hatch
装货落空损失费/裝貨落空損失費　compensation for failure of loading
装货码头/裝載場　loading terminal
装货清单/裝貨清單　loading list, cargo list
装货网络/裝貨網路　loading network
装货准单/載貨單　shipping bill
装料站/裝載場　loading terminal
装配/裝配,組裝　assembly
装配标记/裝配記號　assembly mark
装配车间/裝配車間　assembling shop
装配符号/裝配記號　assembly mark
装配附件/裝配件　mounting fittings
装配螺栓/固定螺栓　fitting-up bolt
装配式衬砌/裝配式襯砌,預製襯砌　precast lining, prefabricated lining
装配式混凝土结构/裝配式混凝土結構　prefabricated concrete structure
装配式建筑/預組房屋,預製房屋　prefabricated building
装配式结构/組裝結構　assembled structure
装配式墙板/裝配式外牆板　concrete exterior wall panel
装配式桥/裝配式橋　fabricated bridge
装配式水泥混凝土路面/裝配式混凝土路面,裝配式混凝土護面　fabricated concrete pavement

装配图/装配示意圖　assembly diagram
装配型架/裝配型架　assembly jig
装配型架垂直停放平台/裝配垂直支架　assembling frame vertical stand
装配型架铁轮支架车/整流罩鐵輪臺車　assembling frame iron wheel carriage
装配应力/裝接應力　assembly stress
装配整体式混凝土结构/裝配整體式混凝土結構　assembled monolithic concrete structure
装燃料/裝載燃料　bunkering
装哨浮标/鳴笛浮標　whistling buoy
装饰[混凝土]砌块/裝飾用[混凝土]砌塊　decorative concrete block
装饰井盖/裝飾面　decorative cover
装饰色彩/裝飾顏料　ornament color
装饰性种植/觀賞木栽培　ornamental planting
装饰艺术派/裝飾派藝術,藝術裝飾　art deco
装饰植物/裝飾植物　decorative plant
装土机/積土機　earth loader
装箱/裝櫃　stuffing
装箱单/裝箱單　packing list
[装卸]搬运/搬運,輸送　handling
装卸场/裝卸場,裝卸停機坪　loading and unloading yard, loading apron
装卸吊具工作梯/裝卸吊具工作梯　handing hoisting device working ladder
装卸定额/裝卸定額　handling quota
装卸吨/裝卸噸　stevedore ton
装卸方式/裝卸方式　handling mode
装卸费率/裝卸費率　rate of handling charge
装卸工/裝卸工,碼頭裝卸工人　stevedore
装卸工班定额/裝卸工班定額　handling shift quota
装卸工班效率/裝卸工班效率　handling shift efficiency
装卸工人/裝卸工　stevedore
装卸工人生产率/裝卸工人生產率　handling worker productivity
装卸工时产量/裝卸工時產量　handling hourly output
装卸工时定额/裝卸工時定額　handling hourly quota
装卸工序/裝卸工序　handling procedure
装卸工艺/裝卸工藝　handling technology
装卸工艺流程/裝卸工藝流程　handling technological process
装卸工艺设计/裝卸工藝設計　handling technology design
装卸工作成本/裝卸工作成本　handling operation cost
装卸工作单/裝卸工作單　handling sheet
装卸工作停歇时间/裝卸工作停歇時間　handling intermittence time
装卸换算吨/裝卸換算噸　converted tons of handling
装卸货驳/裝卸貨物駁船　stevedoring barge
装卸货场/裝卸貨場,貨區　loading and unloading area, loading and unloading yard
装卸货天数/許可裝卸日數　laydays
装卸机械/裝卸機械　handling machinery
装卸机械化方案/裝卸機械化方案　handling mechanization scheme
装卸机械化系统/裝卸機械化系統　handling mechanization system
装卸机械计时包用费/裝卸機械計時包用費　chartered handling equipment time-based charge
装卸机械利用率/裝卸機械利用率　utilization ratio of machine handling
装卸机械生产率/裝卸機械生產率　handling machinery productivity
装卸机械完好率/裝卸機械完好率　percentage of machine handling in good condition
装卸机械效率指标/裝卸機械效率指標　handling machinery efficiency index
装卸机械走行费/裝卸機械走行費　travel expense of handling equipment
装卸机械作业量/裝卸機械作業量　handling volume by machine
装卸检修所/裝卸檢修所　inspection and service point for car before loading or after unloading
装卸距离/裝卸距離　handling distance
装卸能力/裝卸能力　handling capacity
装卸期限/約定裝卸時間　laytime
装卸事故/裝卸事故　loading and unloading accident
装卸线/裝卸線　loading and unloading track
装卸效率/裝卸效率　handling efficiency
装卸站台/裝載平臺　loading and unloading platform, loading and unloading dock
装卸长/領班,工頭　foreman
装卸直接费用/裝卸直接費用　handling direct cost
装卸质量标准/裝卸品質標準　handling quality standard
装卸质量合格率/裝卸品質合格率　loading and unloading quality conformity rate
装卸自然吨/裝卸自然噸　actual ton of handling
装卸作业机械化/裝卸作業機械化　handling mechanization
装卸作业量/裝卸作業量　handling volume
装卸作业线/裝卸作業線　handling operation line

装卸作业指标／裝卸工作指數 index of handling operation
装卸作业自动化／裝卸作業自動化 handling automation
装卸作业组织／裝卸作業組織 handling organization
装岩机／裝岩機 rock loader
装药／裝藥 charge
装油港站／裝油終端站 oil-loading terminal
装有电报或电话通信的系泊浮筒／裝有電報或電話通信之繫泊浮筒 mooring buoy with telephonic or telegraphic communications
装缘植物／裝緣植物 edging plant
装载／裝載,裝貨 loading, lade
装载铲／積土機鏟 loading shovel
装载吃水／負載吃水,載重吃水 load draught
装载和污底工况管理／裝載與汙底作業形式管理 load and fouling hull operating mode management
装载机／裝載機 loader
装载检查／滿載吃水檢查 loading survey
装载检验／裝卸檢查 stowage survey
装载挖掘机／裝載挖掘機 loader excavator
装载系数／裝載係數,負荷係數 loading coefficient, coefficient of load
装载限界／裝載[高寬]限界 loading clearance limit, loading gage
装载仪／負荷指示器 load indicator
装载重量／總車重 laden weight
壮年河／成熟河川 mature river
状况监测维护／狀態監視維修 status monitoring maintenance
状态参数／狀態參數 state parameter
状态方程／狀態方程式 equation of state
状态非线性分析／狀態非線性分析 nonlinear stability analysis
状态监控／狀態監控 condition monitoring
状态检修／狀態檢修 repair based on condition of component
状态修／狀態修 repair according to condition
状态询问／狀況詢問 status enquiry
状态转移图／狀態變遷圖 state transition diagram
撞锤张力器／撞錘張力機 ram tensioner
撞击／撞擊,衝擊 impact, shock bump
撞击动力学／碰撞動力學 impact dynamics
撞击范围／衝撞範圍 impingement area
撞击声／衝擊音 impact sound
撞击声改善量／衝擊音改良 impact sound improvement
撞击声隔声频谱修正量／衝擊音頻譜修正量 spectrum adaptation term for impact sound
撞击声压级／衝擊聲壓位準 impact sound pressure level
撞击式喷注器／衝擊注射器 impinger injector
撞击中心／撞心 center of percussion
撞人事故／撞人事故 pedestrian accident
追悼室／悼念廳,靈堂 mourning hall
追肥／追肥料 fertilizer, topdressing
追钩／追鉤 catch up
追光室／追光室 spot-light room
追过／追越 out-foot, overtaking
追行角灯／追行角燈 light angle of approach
追越船／超越船,追趕船 overtaking vessel
追越声号／追越信號 overtaking sound signal
追踪／追蹤 homing
追踪攻击／追擊戰鬥 pursuit attack
追踪列车间隔时间／追蹤列車間隔時間 time interval between trains spaced by automatic block signal
追踪运行图／追蹤運行圖 train diagram for automatic block signal
锥度规／斜度計,推拔規 taper gage
锥壳／錐形殼 conical shell
锥锚／錨錐 anchorage cone
锥式破碎机／錐式碎石機 cone crusher
锥体护坡／錐體護坡 quadrant revetment, truncated cone banking
锥效应／錐形效應 coning effect
锥形／錐形,楔形 taper
锥形变薄旋压／管形剪力旋壓 cone spinning, tube shear spinning
锥形导槽／錐形導槽 conic guide
锥形反转出料混凝土搅拌机／錐形反轉出料混凝土攪拌機 tapered reverse tilting concrete mixer
锥形浮标／圓錐形浮標 conical buoy
锥形护坡／截錐護坡 truncated cone banking
锥形交通路标／交通錐 traffic cone
锥形搅拌机／錐形拌和機 conical mixer
锥形块石／錐形塊石 telford stone
锥形流／錐形流 conical flow
锥形流法／錐形流法 conical flow method
锥形锚具／錐形錨具,錐形錨座 cone anchorage, conical wedge anchorage
锥形扭转／錐形彎度 conical camber
锥形喷管／錐形噴嘴 conical nozzle
锥形倾翻出料混凝土搅拌机／錐形出料混凝土攪拌機 tapered tilting concrete mixer
锥形梢／錐形梢 coned dowel

锥形掏槽/方尖拔心　pyramid cut
锥形物/圓錐物　cones
锥柱形药柱/錐柱形藥柱　conocyl grain
锥状砾堆/錐狀礫堆　conical accumulation
坠落试验/墜落試驗　drop test
坠铊/平衡載重,配重,平衡錘　balance weight
坠铊补偿器/平衡錘張緊裝置　balance weight tensioner
缀板/撐板,條板　stay plate, tie plate, batten plate
缀材/格構支撐　lattice strut
缀花草坪/綴花草坪　compose flowers lawn, decorated flower lawn
缀条/綴條,繫桿　lacing bar
准备/準備　readiness
准备工作/準備工作　preparatory work
准备计划/準備計劃　preparatory plan
准备进路/準備進路　preparation of the route
准备就绪通知书/準備完成通知書　notice of readiness
准备开动/準備開航,備便放鬆　clear for running
准备开航/準備開航,備便放鬆　clear for running
准备完好率/準備率　readiness rate
准成像导引头/準像歸航器　quasi-image homing head
准分子激光光刻/準分子光刻法　excimer lithography
准峰值检波器/準峰檢波器　quasi-peak detector
准工业区域/準工業區　semi-industrial district
准轨铁路/標準軌距鐵道　standard-gage railway
准平稳/準滯留　quasi-stationary
准平稳风/準平穩風　quasi-steady-state wind
准确度/準確度　accuracy
准确度等级/準確度等級　accuracy class
准实时落点计算/近即時落點計算　near-real-time impact calculation
C准则/C準則　C criterion
D准则/D準則　D criterion
准正交各向异性板法/準正交各向異切塊法　quasi orthotropic slab method
准正弦波/準正弦　quasi-sinusoid
准直/校正,瞄準　collimation
准直透镜/光學準直透鏡　collimating lens
桌/桌　table
桌球房/撞球室　billiard room, billiard parlor
卓越周期/卓越週期,顯著週期　predominant period
浊点/濁點,雲點　cloud point
浊度/[渾]濁度　turbidity, turbidimeter
着舰系统/航艦著陸系統　carrier landing system

着陆/著陸,降落　landing
着陆场/登陸位置　landing site
着陆冲击/降落撞擊　landing shock, landing impact
着陆冲击耐力/降落衝擊耐力　landing impact tolerance
着陆灯/落地燈　landing light
着陆点/著陸點　landing point
着陆点精度/著陸點精度　landing point accuracy
着陆点散布范围/著陸點散布面　dispersion area of landing point
着陆点实时预报/著陸點即時預報　landing point real-time prediction
着陆段/著陸階段　landing phase
着陆分系统/著陸子系統　landing subsystem
着陆辅助设备/著陸救護設施　landing aids
着陆滑跑距离/落地滾行距離　distance of landing run
着陆缓冲分系统/著陸緩衝子系統　impact attenuation subsystem
着陆缓冲火箭/著陸緩衝火箭　landing impact attenuation rocket
着陆进场/著陸進場　landing approach
着陆距离/著陸距離　landing distance
着陆能量/著陸能量　landing energy
着陆散布度/著陸散布度　landing discursiveness
着陆速度/落地速率　landing speed
着陆跳跃/著陸彈跳　landing bounce
着陆限制重量/著陸限制重量　landing limiting weight
着陆预报/降落預報　landing forecast
着陆撞击/著陸撞擊,降落衝擊　landing impact
着色玻璃/著色玻璃　colored glass, tined glass
着色磨石子/著色磨石子　terrazzo-mix
着色渗透检测/染色滲透試驗　dye penetrant flaw testing
着色水泥/著色水泥　colored Portland cement
姿态/姿態　attitude
姿态保持/姿態保持　attitude hold, attitude keeping
姿态捕获/姿態獲取　attitude acquisition
姿态参数/姿態參數　attitude parameter
姿态测定系统/姿態測定系統　attitude determination system, ADS
姿态测量/姿態量測　attitude measurement
姿态测量精度/姿態量測精度　attitude measurement accuracy
姿态测量系统/姿態量測系統　attitude measurement system
姿态动力学/姿態動力學　attitude dynamics

姿态估计/姿態估計　attitude estimation
姿态航向基准系统/姿態航向角參考系統　attitude heading reference system
GPS姿态和轨道确定系统/全球定位系統姿態與軌道測定系統　GPS attitude and orbit determination system
姿态机动/姿態機動　attitude maneuver
姿态几何/姿態幾何　attitude geometry
姿态角/姿態角,仰角　attitude angle
姿态角传感器/姿態角換能器　attitude angle transducer
姿态角速度/姿態變化率　attitude angular velocity, attitude rate
姿态控制/姿態控制　attitude control
姿态控制分系统/姿態控制分系統　attitude control subsystem
姿态控制规律/姿態控制律　attitude control law
姿态控制火箭发动机/姿態控制火箭發動機　attitude control rocket engine, attitude control rocket motor
姿态控制精度/姿態控制精度　attitude control accuracy
姿态控制量/姿態控制量　attitude control quantity
姿态控制模式/姿態控制模式　attitude control mode
姿态控制系统/姿態控制系統　attitude control system
姿态控制系统带宽/姿態控制系統帶寬　bandwidth of attitude control system
姿态控制训练器/姿態控制訓練機　attitude control trainer
姿态敏感器/姿態感測器　attitude sensor
姿态漂移/姿態漂移　attitude drift
姿态确定/姿態測定　attitude determination
GPS姿态确定/全球定位系統姿態測定　GPS attitude determination
姿态确定精度/姿態測定精度　attitude determination accuracy
姿态扰动/姿態擾動　attitude disturbance
姿态失稳/姿態不穩定　attitude instability
姿态稳定/姿態穩定　attitude stabilization
姿态稳定度/姿態穩定性　attitude stability
姿态误差/姿態誤差　attitude error
姿态误差校正/姿態誤差校正　attitude error rectification
姿态预估/姿態預測　attitude prediction
姿态运动/姿態運動　attitude motion
姿态再次捕获/姿態重新取得　attitude reacquisition
姿态指引指示器/姿態指引器　attitude director indicator
资本成本/資本成本,資本費用　capital cost
资本金净利润率/資本回收[率]　return on equity, ROE
资产负债率/資產負債比率　asset liability ratio
资费表/價目表,費率規章,收費制　tariff
资格考试/資格考試　qualification examination
资格考试合格证书/資格考試合格證書　competency certificate of qualifying examination
资金来源/資金來源　financial source
资源禀赋/資源稟賦　resource endowment
资源舱/資源艙　resource module
资源管理保护区/資源管理保護區　protected areas with sustainable use of natural resources
资源容量/資源容量　resource capacity
资源型区位/資源型區位　resource oriented location
子车/子車　car without axle generator
子城/子城　zi cheng, auxiliary town
子程序/副程式　sub-program, subroutine
子代/子代,雜交後代　filial generation
子级/子級　substage
子结构/子結構　substructure
子母炸弹/子母炸彈　dispenser bomb
子母战斗部/子母彈頭　cluster warhead
子母钟/子母鐘　primary-secondary clocks
子圈/子午線下半部　lower branch of meridian
子午角/子午線角　meridian angle
子午圈/子午圈　meridian circle
子午圈曲率半径/子午線曲率半徑　meridian radius of curvature
子午卫星系统/子午衛星系統　transit
子午线/子午線,經線　meridian
子午线测量/子午線測定　meridian determination
子午仪/子午儀,中星儀　meridian instrument
子午仪系统/子午儀系統　Transit system
子帧/子構架　minor frame
子阵/子陣列　subarray
紫光太阳电池/紫光太陽電池　violet solar cell
紫禁城/紫禁城　Forbidden City
紫外臭氧光谱仪/紫外光臭氧光譜儀　ultraviolet ozone spectrometer, UOS
紫外光/紫外光　ultraviolet light
紫外扫描仪/紫外線掃描器　ultraviolet scanner
紫外试验/紫外線試驗　ultraviolet test
紫外太阳光谱仪/紫外太陽光譜儀　ultraviolet solar spectrometer, USS
紫外遥感/紫外遙測　ultraviolet remote sensing
自办站/自有站　self-owned terminal

自备电源/自備電源　power source provided by the owner, self-contained power
自备式导航/自備助航　self-contained navigation
自闭电路/自閉電路　self-stick circuit
自闭式安全门/自閉式安全門　automatic self-closing safety door
自变量/自變數　argument
自补偿静校[准]/自補償靜態校準　self-compensation static calibration
自测/自測　self-testing
自差/自差　deviation
自差表/自差表　deviation table
自差补偿装置/自差補償設施　deviation compensation device
自差分GPS/自差分全球定位系統　self-differential GPS, SDGPS
自差校正场/迴旋場所　swinging ground
自差曲线/自差曲線　deviation curve
自差式无线电引信/自差式無線電引信　autodyne radio fuze
自差系数/自差係數　coefficient of deviation
自带行李/隨身行李　cabin luggage
自导向径向转向架/自導向徑向轉向架　self-steering radial truck
自动摆动槽/自動旋轉斜槽　automatic swing chute
自动报警/自動警報器　auto alarm
自动曝光控制装置/自動曝露控制裝置　automatic exposure control device
自动闭塞/自動閉塞系統　automatic block system
自动闭塞联系电路/自動閉塞聯繫電路　liaison circuit with automatic blocks
自动避碰系统/自動避碰系統　automatic collision avoidance system
自动并联运行/自動并聯運轉　automatic parallel operation
自动拨号双向电话/自動撥號雙向電話　automatic dial-up two-way telephony
自动补加/自動補加　auto-topping
自动操纵作业/自動操作　automatic operation
自动操作/自動操作　automatic operation
自动测量仪/自動測量儀　automatic measuring instrument
自动测试模块/自動測試模組　automatic test module
自动测试设备/自動測試裝備　automatic test equipment, ATE
自动测向仪/自動[無線電]測向儀,自動定向器　automatic direction finder, ADF, automatic radio direction finder
自动抄车号/自動抄車號　automatic car identification
自动车辆定位/自動車輛定位　automatic vehicle location, AVL
自动称重/自動稱量　automatic weighing
自动充气调节伞/AIM伞　automatic inflation modulation parachute, AIM parachute
自动除渣分杂机/自動除渣澄清器　automatic dislodging clarifier
自动吹灰器/自動吹灰器　automatic soot blower
自动导航仪/自動導航儀　automatic navigator
自动导向系统/自動導向系統　automated guideway system
自动点灯/自動調光　automatic lighting
自动点火/自動點火　automatic ignition
自动电话机/自動電話機　automatic telephone set
自动电连接器/電自動偶合器　electric automatic coupler
自动电平调节系统/自動電平調節系統　automatic level regulating system
自动电压调节器/自動電壓調整器　automatic voltage regulator, AVR
自动扶梯/昇降[階]梯,自動[鏈]梯,活動樓梯　escalator, moving staircase
自动扶梯隧道/階梯式自動電梯隧道　escalator tunnel
自动扶正部分封闭救生艇/自行扶正部分圍蔽救生艇　self-right partially enclosed lifeboat
自动负荷控制/自動負載控制　automatic load control, ALC
自动高度调整装置/自動平層裝置　automatic leveling device
自动跟踪/自動追蹤　automatic tracking
自动过渡控制/自動過渡控制　automatic transition control
自动焊/自動焊接　automatic welding
自动航海通告系统/自動航船布告系統　automatic notice to mariners system, ANMS
自动呼叫/自動呼叫　automatic call, automatic calling
自动化编组站/自動化編組站　automatic marshalling station
自动化测试/自動測試　automatic test, automated testing
自动化驼峰/自動駝峰　automatic hump
自动化驼峰系统/自動化駝峰系統　automatic hump yard system
自动画线装置/自動道路標線　autoset road marking

自动缓解/自動緩解　false release by itself
自动机动攻击系统/自動操縱攻擊系統　automatic maneuvering attack system, AMAS
自动机械天平/自動機械天平　automatic mechanobalance
自动激活锌银电池/自動啟動鋅銀蓄電池　automatically activated zinc-silver battery
自动加载/自動加載　autoloading
自动驾驶仪/自動駕駛儀　autopilot
自动检错重发设备/自動錯誤請求設備　automatic retransmission on request equipment, ARQ equipment
自动减速/自動減速　automatic slow down
自动搅拌机/自動計量器　automatic batcher
自动校平装置/自動準平裝置　autolevelling assembly
自动解列/自動解除并聯　automatic parallel off
自动纠错/自動改錯　automatic error correction
自动聚焦机构/自動調焦裝置　autofocus mechanism
[自动]开闭器/轉轍電路控制器,開關電路控制器　switch circuit controller
自动空气断路器/自動空氣斷路器　automatic air circuit breaker
自动空气制动装置/自動氣閘裝置　automatic air brake equipment
自动控制/自動控制　automatic control
自动栏木/自動欄木　automatic operated barrier
自动雷达标绘仪/雷達自動測繪設備　automatic radar plotting aids, ARPA
自动力矩检定/自動力矩檢定　autostress rating
自动沥青拌和厂/自動瀝青拌和廠　automatic bituminous mixing plant
自动门/自動門　automatic door
自动瞄准/自動瞄準[跟蹤]　automatic aiming
自动模式/自動模式　automatic mode
自动目标数据交接系统/自動瞄準資訊交互系統　automatic target handoff system, ATHS
自动拍发器/自動鍵發設施　automatic keying device
自动排气活门/自動排氣閥　automatic exhaust valve
自动配料厂/自動配料廠　automatic batching plant
自动配平系统/自動調整系統　automatic trim system
自动喷灌控制器/自動灑水系統　automatic sprinkler system
自动喷水、报警和探测系统/自動噴水器與火警警報及滅火系統　automatic sprinkler, fire alarm and fire detection system
自动喷水灭火机/自動噴水滅火器　automatic water spraying fire extinguisher
自动喷水灭火系统/自動噴水滅火系統　automatic sprinkler system
自动喷水-泡沫联用系统/自動噴水-泡沫聯用系統　automatic combined sprinkler-foam system
自动喷调装置/自動噴調裝置　injection timer
自动膨胀阀/自動膨脹閥　automatic expansion valve
自动频率控制/自動頻率控制　automatic frequency control
自动平舱煤船/自動均載煤船　self-trimming collier
自动起动空气压缩机/自動起動空氣壓縮機　auto-starting air compressor
自动气割/自動氣焰截割　automatic gas cutting
自动清洗滤器/自動清洗過濾器　auto-clean strainer
自动请求重发方式/自動複傳申請　automatic repetition request mode
自动人行道/自動人行道　moving pavement
自动洒水探火系统/自動探火噴水系統　automatic sprinkler fire detection system
自动撒砂/自動撒沙　automatic sanding
自动扫描/自動掃描　auto scanning
自动刹车系统/自動刹車系統　autobrake system
自动式主起动阀/自動起動空氣關斷閥　automatic starting air shut-off valve
自动售货式食堂/自助餐廳,自動販賣機　automat
自动售检票/自動收票款裝置,自動收費　automatic fare collection, AFC
自动疏水/自動排洩裝置　automatic drainage
自动送进系统/自動傳送系統　automatic feed system
自动探火喷水系统/自動探火噴水系統　automatic sprinkler fire detection system
自动调光采光/自動調光採光　automatic dimming daylighting
自动调焦装置/自動聚焦裝置　automatic focusing device
自动调节机能/自動調節機能　homeostasis
自动调谐/自動調諧　automatic tuning
自动调压/電壓自動調節　automatic voltage regulation
自动调整片系统/自動調整片系統　automatic tab system
自动调整楔铁装置/自動補償器,自動校正器　automatic compensator
自动停车/自動停車,列車自動停車　auto-stop, automatic train stop
自动停车装置/自動停車裝置,列車自動停車裝置　automatic shut-down device, automatic train stop

equipment

自动通过按钮电路/自動通過按鈕電路 automatic pass-through button circuit

自动同步装置/自動同步設施 automatic synchronizing device

自动弯沉仪/自動撓度計 autodeflectometer

自动系泊绞车/自動繫泊絞車 automatic mooring winch

自动显示仪表/自動顯示儀 automatic display instrument

自动限时解锁/自動限時解鎖器,自動限時釋放[器] automatic time release

自动消防炮灭火系统/自動消防炮滅火系統 automatic fire monitor extinguishing system

自动信号/自動號誌 automatic signal

自动悬停控制/自動停懸飛行控制 automatic hovering control

自动旋转洒水喷头/自動旋轉灑水噴頭 automatic rotating sprinkler

自动巡路平地机/自動推土機 autopatrol

自动延绳机/自動延繩機 autolongline machine

自动验潮仪/自動測潮計 automatic tide gage

自动业务/自動業務 automatic service

自动液压大型捣固车/自動液壓大型搗固機 auto-leveling-lifting-lining-tamping machine

自动应答/自動應答,自動回應 automatic answering

自动用户电报试验/自動電傳試驗 automatic telex test

自动油门系统/自動油門系統 autothrottle system

自动增益控制/自動增益控制 automatic gain control

自动找平装置/自動平層裝置 automatic leveling device

自动止回阀/自動止回閥 automatic non-return valve

自动制动阀/自動剎車閥 automatic brake valve

自动终端情报服务/自動化航站資訊服務 automatic terminal information service, ATIS

自动转接/自動轉接 automatic switching over

自动着陆/自動著陸 automatic landing

自动着陆系统/自動著陸系統 autolanding system

自读水准尺/自讀標尺 self-reading staff

自发性景观/自發性景觀 spontaneous landscape

自放电/自放電 self-discharge

自放电率/自放電率 self-discharge rate

自封铆接/自封鉚接 self-sealed riveting

自复式按键开关/自我復位按鈕開關 self-reset push-key switch

自复式按钮/自複式按鈕 non-stick button

自感振动/自激振動 self-excited vibration

自功率谱/自功率頻譜 auto-power spectrum

自供空气救生艇/自供空氣系統救生艇 lifeboat with self-contained air support system

自航船/自航船,機動船,動力船 self-propelled ship, power-driven vessel

自航发射/[鱼雷]自滑發射 swim-out, swim-out discharge

自航链斗挖泥船/自航聯斗式挖泥船 self-propelled bucket dredger

自航试验/自行推動試驗 self-propulsion test

自航挖泥船/自航式挖泥船 self-propelling dredger, self-propelled dredger

自航吸式挖泥船/自航吸式挖泥船 self-propelling suction dredger

自航因子/自推因子 self-propulsion factor

自耗系数/衰減係數 decay coefficient

自环检测/自環路測試 self-loop test

自毁/自毀 self-destruction

自毁机构/自毀機構 self-destructor

自毁时间/自毀時間 self-destruction time

自毁指令/自毀指令 self-destruction command

自毁装置/自毀裝置 self-destruction device

自击式喷嘴/自擊式噴嘴 like-impinging injector element

自激/自激,自勵 self-excitation

自激振动/自激振動 self-excited vibration

自给空气支持系统/自供空氣支援系統 self-contained air support system

自记式转速表/記錄轉速計 recording tachometer

自记水位计/自記水尺 recording water gage

自驾车营地/自駕車營地 self-driving tours camp

自驾游/自駕遊 self-driving tour

自检功能/自核功能 self-checking function

自检指令/自檢指令,自檢命令 self-checking command

自建房/自建住宅 self-help housing

自交不亲和/自交不親和性 self-incompatibility

自交系/自交系 inbred line

自校准/自我修正 self-correction

自解期/自解期 auto-oxidation phase, period of endogenous respiration

自净时间/自淨時間 clean-down capability

自净梯度/自動洗淨坡度 self-cleansing gradient

自净作用/自淨作用 self-purification

自净[作用]常数/自淨常數 self-purification constant

自控器/自控器 automatic controller
自来水/自來水 tap water
[自来]水厂/[自來]水廠,給水廠 water supply and treatment plant, water supply and purification plant
自理行包/手提行李 hand luggage
自理装卸/自理裝卸 self-handling
自力式流量控制阀/直接流量控制閥 self-operated flow control valve
自力式调节阀/自行式調整器 self-operated regulator, self-acting control valve
自励/自勵,自激 self-excitation
自励交流发电机/自激交流發電機 self-excited AC generator
自亮浮灯/[救生圈]自燃燈,自燃信號燈 self-igniting buoy light, self-igniting light
自流/自然流量 natural flow
自流井出水率/湧泉率 artesian capacity
自流平地面/自流平地面 self-leveling floor
自流式循环水系统/自然式循環水系統 scoop circulating water system
自流式溢流堰/非束縮堰 free weir
自流水排泄/湧泉流量 artesian discharge
自流水总管道/重力輸水管道 gravity main
自流压力/湧泉壓力 artesian pressure
自流预冷/自流預冷 pre-cooling by auto-flow
自落式混凝土搅拌设备/重力式混凝土拌和廠 gravity concrete mixing plant
自落式稳定土搅拌设备/重力式穩定土廠拌站 gravity stabilized soil mixing plant
自锚式吊桥/自錨式吊橋,自錨式懸索橋 self-anchored suspension bridge
自锚式悬索桥/自錨式懸索橋,自錨式吊橋 self-anchored suspension bridge
自密实混凝土/自密實混凝土 self-compacting concrete
自耦变压启动/自耦變壓器起動 auto-transformer starting
自耦变压器/自耦變壓器,單卷變壓器 autotransformer, AT
自耦变压器供电方式/自耦變壓器供電方式 autotransformer feeding system
自耦变压器供电线/自耦變壓器供電線 AT-feeder
自耦变压器起动/自耦變壓器起動 auto-transformer starting
自耦变压器所/自耦變壓器所 auto-transformer post, ATP
自耦牵引变压器/自耦牽引變壓器 traction autotransformer

自抛光防污涂料/自拋光防汙漆,自磨型防汙漆 self-polishing copolymer antifouling paint
自喷井/自噴井,自流井 flowing well, artesian well
自起动装置/自動起動器 automatic starter, automatic starting device
自清洗粗滤器/自清洗濾器,自淨過濾器 self-cleaning strainer
自清洗分油机/自清洗分離器 self-cleaning separator
自清洗式滤器/自清洗濾器,自淨過濾器 self-cleaning strainer
自然保存/自然保育 natural preservation
自然保护/自然保育 natural conservation
自然保护区/自然保育區,天然保育區 nature reserve area, nature protection area, nature conservation area
自然保留地/自然保留區 nature reserve area
自然保育/自然保育 conservation of nature, nature conservation
自然层流翼型/自然層流翼形剖面 natural laminar flow aerofoil profile
自然沉淀/自然沈澱,單純沈澱 plain sedimentation
自然村/自然村 natural village
自然地貌/自然地貌 natural feature
自然电位测量/自然電位能測量 self-potential survey
自然电位法/自然電位法 spontaneous potential method
自然对流/自然對流 natural convection
自然防治/自然控制 natural control
自然肥力/自然肥力 natural fertility
自然服务/自然服務 nature service
自然更新/天然更新 natural regeneration
自然行诉/自然源轄地,自然管轄地 natural forum
自然环境/自然環境 natural environment
自然缓解/自然緩解 unintended release, undesired release
自然纪念物/自然紀念物 natural monument or feature
自然减速/標稱速降 nominal speed loss
自然接地体/自然接地極 natural grounding electrode
自然景观/自然景觀,天然景觀 natural landscape
自然景观保护区/自然保護區 natural reserve
自然控制/自然控制 natural control
自然老化/自然老化,自然時效 natural aging
自然疗法/自然療藥 nature remedies
自然流道/自然流道 natural escape
自然磨损/自然耗損 ordinary wear and tear

自然排水/自然排水　natural drainage
自然区/自然區域　natural region
自然生态系统/自然生態系　natural ecosystem
自然声景/自然聲景　nature soundscape
自然时效［处理］/自然時效,自然老化　natural aging
自然式道路系统/自然式道路系統　informal road system
自然式花篱/自然式花籬　natural flowering hedge
自然式渗排水道/灘槽,潮溝　swale
自然式园林/自然式園林　natural garden style, natural style garden
自然式种植/自然式種植　nature planting
自然调节/自然調節　natural regulation
自然通风/自然通風　natural draught, natural draft, natural ventilation
自然通风装置/自然通風裝置　natural ventilation equipment
自然土壤/底土,堅硬土層,未動土　natural soil
自然系统/自然生態系　natural ecosystem
自然选择/自然淘汰,天擇　natural selection
自然循环/自然循環　natural circulation
自然循环锅炉/自然循環鍋爐　natural circulation boiler
自然演替/自然演替　natural succession
自然养护/自然發酵　natural curing
自然遗产/自然遺產　natural heritage
自然与文化遗产保护/自然與文化遺產保護　conservation of natural and cultural heritage
自然灾害/自然災害,天災　natural catastrophe
自然增长率/自然增加率　rate of natural increase
自然振动/自然振動　natural vibration
自然植被/天然植被,天然植生　natural vegetation
自然制动/自然制動　unintended braking, undesired braking
自然资源/自然資源,天然資源　natural resources
自燃点/自燃點　spontaneous combustion point
自燃推进剂/自燃推進劑　hypergolic propellant
自燃推进剂火箭发动机/自燃推進劑火箭發動機　hypergolic propellant rocket engine
自燃烟雾信号/自動煙號　self-activating smoke signal
自溶/自解　autolysis
自润滑材料/自潤滑材料　self-lubricating material
自扫舱装置/自行收艙裝置　self stripping unit
自身标识/自船識別碼　self-identification
自［身］起动系统/自啟動系統　self-start system
自升式模板/爬模法　self-climbing formwork
自升式钻井平台/昇降式鑽油臺　jack-up rigs, jack-up drilling unit
自生应力/自生應力　selfstress
自生增压系统/自生加壓系統　autogenous pressurization system
自适应壁/自我調整壁　adaptive wall
自适应操舵仪/適應自動操舵儀　adaptive autopilot
自适应机翼/適應性機翼　adaptive wing
自适应控制/自適［應］控制　adaptive control
自适应弹射座椅/自我調整彈射椅　adaptive ejection seat
自适应天线阵/適應式陣列天線　adaptive array antenna
自适应网格技术/適應網格技術　adaptive grid technique
自适应望远镜/自適應望遠鏡　adaptive telescope
自适应信号控制系统/自適應交通控制系統　adaptive traffic signal control system
自适应延时/自適應遲延　adaptive delay
自适应遥测/自適應遙測術　adaptive telemetry
自适应引信/自適應引信　adaptive fuze
自适应自动驾驶仪/適應自動駕駛儀　adaptive autopilot
自锁阀/自鎖閥　latching valve
自调节/自［動］調節　self-regulation
自通风式电动机/自通風電動機　self-ventilated motor
自卫干扰/自衛干擾　self-screening jamming
自卫距离/自遮罩距離　self-screening range
自我就业/自我雇用,自營作業　self-employment
自我心理调节/自我心理調節　psychological self-regulation
自吸［式］离心泵/自注離心泵,自引離心泵　self-priming centrifugal pump
自吸式水泵/自吸泵,自引泵　self-prime pump
自响信号浮标/自動發聲浮標　automatic sound buoy
自卸车/自動卸車　dumping car
自卸挂车/傾卸拖車　dump trailer
自卸货车/自卸卡車,翻斗車　dump truck
自卸汽车/自卸汽車　dumping truck
自行车/自行車　bicycle
自行车车道/自行車道,腳踏車道　bike lane
自行车功量计/自行車測功器,腳踏車測功器　bicycle ergometer
自行车馆/自由車場　velodrome
自行车交通/自行車交通　bicycle transport
自行车交通规划/自行車交通規劃　bicycle traffic planning
自行车交通设施/自行車設施　bicycle facility

自行车路/自行車道　cycle path
自行车旅游/自行車旅遊　bicycle tour
自行车棚/自行車棚　bicycle shed
自行车赛场/自由車場　velodrome
自行车式起落架/自行車式起落架　bicycle landing gear
自行车停车场/自行車停放處　bicycle parking lot
自行车停放规划/自行車停放規劃　bicycle parking planning
自行车停放规则/自行車停放規則　bicycle parking rule
自行车运动/自行車運動　cycling
自行车专用道/自行車徑　bicycle track
自行式铲运机/刮運機,拖拉機式鏟運機　motor scraper, tractor scraper
自行式沥青混凝土摊铺机/自走式瀝青鋪路機　self-propelled asphalt paver
自行式平地机/自行式平土機,自動平土機　motor grader, wheel grader
自行式桥梁检测架/自行式橋梁檢測架　self-propelled bridge inspection cradle
自修/自行檢修　self repair
自修复系统/自修復系統　self-repairing system
自修正风洞/自校正風洞　self-correcting wind tunnel
自旋扫描地球敏感器/自旋掃描地球感測器　spin scanning earth sensor, spin scanning horizon sensor
自旋速率敏感器/自旋速率感測器　spinning rate sensor
自旋体/槳鼻罩　spinner
自旋稳定/自旋穩定　spin stabilization
自旋轴/螺旋軸,旋轉軸　spin axis
自选市场/超級市場,超市　supermarket
自循环通气/自循環通氣　self-circulation venting
自养生物/自養生物　autotroph
自应力混凝土/自應力混凝土　self-stressing concrete
自应力硫铝酸盐水泥/自應力硫鋁酸鹽水泥　self-stressing sulphoaluminate cement
自应力水泥/自應力水泥　self-stressing cement
自用车辆/自用車輛　private vehicle
自由场/自由聲場,自由音場　free sound field
自由场室/自由音場室　free-field room
自由车轮/獨立車輪　independent wheel
自由车速/自由速率　free speed
自由导线/自由導線,不閉合導線　free traverse
自由度/自由度　degree of freedom, DOF
自由锻/平模鍛造　open die forging, flat die forging
自由飞风洞/自由飛行風洞　free flight wind tunnel
自由飞模型/自由飛行模型　free flight model
自由[飞行]段测量/自由飛行段量測　free flight phase measurement
自由飞行机器人/自由飛行機器人　free flying robot
自由分子流/自由分子流　free molecular flow
自由港市/自由港市　free port town
自由桁架/自由桁架　free truss
自由活塞空气压缩机/自由活塞壓縮機　free piston compressor, free piston air compressor
自由活塞燃气轮机/自由活塞燃氣渦輪機　free piston gas turbine
自由降落下水/自由降落下水　free-fall launching
自由交通流/無阻車流　free traffic flow
自由流/自由流　free stream
自由流车速/自由車流速率　free flow speed
自由流线/自由流線　free streamline
自由落体/自由落體　free falling body
自由落体试验/自由落體試驗　free-fall testing
自由贸易区/自由貿易區　free trade zone
自由内接/自由內接　free inscribing
自由膨胀率/自由膨脹率　free swelling rate
自由气球/自由氣球　free balloon
自由区/自由區　free district
自由射流/自由噴射流,自由噴束　free jet
自由式道路系统/自由式道路系統　free style road system
自由陀螺仪/自由陀螺,自由迴轉儀　free gyroscope, free gyro
自由弯曲试验/自由彎曲試驗　free bend test
自由涡/自由渦[旋]　free vortex
自由涡轮/自由渦輪　free turbine
自由涡面/自由渦面　free vortex surface
自由液面效应/自由液面效應　free surface effect
自由液面修正/自由液面修正　free surface correction
自由溢流[口]/自由放流口　free outfall
自由溢流堰顶/自落式溢洪道　free overfall spillway
自由引水/自由引水　optional pilotage
自由振动/自由振動　free vibration
自由振动法/自由振動法　free oscillation method
自由装填式药柱/獨立式藥柱　free standing grain
自由自航船模试验/自航船模[運動]試驗　free-running model test
自由-自由状态/自由-自由狀態　free-free state
自有港/私有港　private port
自愈/自愈性　autogenous healing
自粘防水卷材/自粘型膠粘帶　self-adhesive waterproof sheet, self-adhesive asphalt membrane

自振频率/自振頻率　natural frequency of vibration
自振周期/自振週期,固有振動週期　natural period of vibration
自整角机/同步器　synchro
自整位式轴承/自動對正軸承　self-aligning bearing
自制/自束　self-restraint
自重/自重,空重,皮重　tare weight, light weight, own weight
自重系数/自重係數　ratio of light weight to loading capacity
自重修正/支承修正　tare correction
自主导航/自主導航　autonomous navigation
自主对准/自動校準　self-alignment
自主式导航设备/自備助航設備　self-contained navigational aids
自主式机器人/自律機器人　autonomous robot
自主式敏感器/獨立式感測器　autonomous sensor
自主卫星/自主衛星　autonomous satellite
自主位置保持/自主位置保持　autonomous station keeping
自主姿态确定/自律姿態測定　autonomous attitude determination
自助餐厅/自助餐廳　cafeteria
自助还书处/自助還書處　self-service department
自助旅社/自助旅社　youth hostel
自助旅游/自助旅遊　self-help travel
自助银行/自助銀行　self-service bank
自转下滑/自動旋轉下滑　autorotative glide
自转下降/自動旋轉著陸　autorotative descent
自装式刮运机/自裝式刮運機,四輪刮運機　four-wheel scraper
自准区仿真/自準區模擬　self-accurate area simulation
字/字　word
字长/字長　word length
T字灯/T字燈　Tee light
字符/字元　character
字符检验/字元核對　character check
字节/數元組　byte
8字结/8字結　figure-of-eight knot, figure-eight knot
字母电报/字母電報　alphabetical telegraph
字母拼读法/字母拼音　letter pronunciation
字母旗/字母旗　alphabetical flag
宗祠/家廟　ancestral hall, family shrine
宗教建筑/宗教建築　religious architecture
宗教设施用地/宗教設施用地　land for religion facility

综合布线电缆单元/綜合布線電纜裝置　cable unit of generic cabling system
综合布线工作区/綜合布線工作區　generic cabling system work area
综合布线集合点链路/綜合布線系統鏈結合并點　consolidation point link of generic cabling system
综合布线进线间/綜合布線進氣室　generic cabling inlet chamber
综合布线缆线/綜合布線系統主纜　generic cabling system cable
综合布线链路/綜合布線系統鏈結　generic cabling system link
综合布线系统/綜合布線系統　generic cabling system
综合部分负荷性能系数/整合性能係數　integrated part load value, IPLV
综合测试/整合測試　integrated test, integrated checkout
综合产品小组/整合性產品小組　integrated product team, IPT
综合大学/大學　university
综合单价/綜合單價　comprehensive unit price
综合单位水文图/合成單位歷線　synthetic unit hydrograph
综合导航/組合導航,整合航海　integrated navigation
综合电缆/複合電纜　composite cable
综合电信营业厅/綜合電信營業廳　general telecommunication business hall
综合调查船/綜合調查船　comprehensive research ship, comprehensive research vessel
综合动态显示器/綜合動態顯示器　synthetic dynamic display
综合法测图/綜合法測圖　panimatric photo
综合防灾避险/綜合防災　comprehensive disaster prevention
综合防灾能力/都市綜合防減災能力　capacity of urban comprehensive disaster prevention
综合飞行-推力控制/綜合飛行控制系統　integrated flight-propulsion control
综合概算/綜合概算　comprehensive approximate estimate
综合公园/綜合公園　comprehensive park
综合管道/組合管道　composite duct
综合管沟/綜合管溝　integral pipe trench
综合管廊/綜合管廊,綜合敷管廊道　comprehensive pipe gallery
综合光缆/複合光纜　combined optical fiber cable
综合规划图/綜合計劃　comprehensive plan

综合规划总图/總體規劃圖　comprehensive master plan
综合航空电子系统/集成航空電子系統　integrated avionics system
综合后勤保障/綜合後勤支援　integrated logistic support
综合化电子战系统/整合式電子戰系統　integrated EW system, INEWS
综合环境可靠性试验/組合環境可靠度試驗　combined environment reliability test
综合环境试验/組合環境試驗　combined environment test
综合火力飞行控制系统/綜合火力控制系統　integrated fire-flight control system, IFFCS
综合架/綜合架　composite rack
综合交通管理/綜合交通管理　comprehensive traffic management
综合校飞/整合飛行校準　integrated calibration flight
综合开发/綜合開發　comprehensive development
综合抗震能力/綜合抗震能力　comprehensive seismic capability
综合利用坝/多目標壩　multipurpose dam
综合楼/綜合建築,建築綜合體　multi-functional building, building complex
综合屏蔽系数/綜合遮罩因數　combination shielding factor
综合启动器/綜合起動器　composite starter
综合区/綜合區　mixed-use area, comprehensive area, mixed-use district
综合试验/綜合實驗　integrated experiment, complex experiment
综合温度/日光大氣溫度　solar-air temperature
综合稳定基层/綜合穩定土底基層　comprehensive stabilized base
综合效率/綜合效率　combined efficiency
综合性办公楼/綜合性辦公樓　multi-use office building, office building complex
综合性博物馆/綜合博物館　comprehensive museum
综合性货运站/綜合貨物站　general freight station, general goods station
综合性美术馆/綜合性美術館　general art museum
综合训练/綜合訓練　integrated training
综合演练/綜合演練　integrated rehearsal
综合养护车/複合養護車　combined maintenance truck
综合业务数字网/整合服務數位網路,整體服務數位網路　integrated service digital network
综合医院/綜合醫院　general hospital
综合运输/綜合運輸　comprehensive transport, multimode transport, intermode transport
综合运输系统/綜合運輸體系　comprehensive transportation system
综合遮阳/綜合遮陽　comprehensive sunshade
综合折旧率/複合折舊率,合成折舊率　composite depreciation rate
综合诊断/綜合診斷　general inspection and diagnosis
综合柱状图/綜合柱狀剖面圖　composite columnar section
综控设备室/設備控制室　control equipment room
棕地/棕地,棕色地帶　brown land
棕地更新/棕色地帶再生　brown field regeneration
棕榈叶式柱/棕櫚葉式柱　palm column
棕壤/棕土　brown forest soil, brown soil
总包合同/總價契約　lump-sum contract
总变化系数/總變化係數　overall peaking variation factor
总布置图/總[布置]圖　general arrangement, general plan
总长/全長　length overall, LOA
总车吨位日/總車噸位日　total vehicle ton day
总车客位日/總車客位日　total vehicle seat day
总车日/總車日　total vehicle days
总成本/總成本　total cost
总成大修/總成大修　unit major repair
总成互换修理法/總成互換修理法　unit exchange repair method
总成小修/總成小修　unit current repair
总成修理/總成修理　unit repair
总承包服务费/總承包服務費　general contracting service charge of construction
总承包合同/總契約　general contract
总尺寸/總尺寸　overall
总冲[量]/總衝量　total impulse
总出站信号机/通行信號　advance starting signal
总初级生产量/總基礎生產量　gross primary production
总大肠菌类/總大腸菌類　total coliform
总单位重量/統體單位重　gross unit weight
总氮量/總氮量　total nitrogen
总等电位连接/主等電位聯結　main equipotential bonding, MEB
总电离剂量/總電離劑量　total ionizing dose
总段/船體結構,船[體分]段　blocks
总段建造法/[船體]分段建造法　block method of

hull construction
总段舾装／船段舾裝　block outfitting
总吨位／總噸位　gross tonnage, GT
总风缸／總風缸　main air reservoir
总辐射／總體輻射　global radiation
总辐照度／總輻射度,太陽輻照度　global irradiance, solar global irradiance
总付运费／[總額]包載運貨　lumpsum freight
总负载裕量／總過載裕度　overall load margin
总概算／總估計　sum of approximate estimate, total estimate, summary estimate
总功率分配单元／總功率分配單元　bus power distribution unit
总固体／總固體[量]　total solid
总含盐量／總溶鹽量　total dissolved salt
总焓探针／總焓探針　total enthalpy probe
总合同／總契約　general contract
总剂量／總劑量　total dose
总价包干／包乾價格　all-in price
总价合同／總價合同,一攬子合同　lump sum contract
总检查／總檢查　general inspection
总碱值／總鹼值　total base number, TBN
总建筑面积／總樓地板面積　total floor area
总建筑师／總建築師　chief architect
总截面／總斷面　gross section
总径流[量]／總徑流　total runoff
总距／集體螺距　collective pitch
总距操纵杆／集體桿　collective pitch stick
总控制室／總控制室,主控制室　master control room
总脉冲次数／總脈衝次數　total pulses
总能量控制／總和能量控制　total energy control
总排水管／汙水總管　main sewer
总排[水]量／總排水量　total displacement
总配线架／總配線架,主配線架　main frame, main distribution frame
总平面规划／總平面規劃,建設場地規劃,總平面設計　site planning
总平面图／總平面圖,地盤圖,地基圖　master plan, site plan, general plan
总日辐射／總日射,全天日射　global solar radiation
总容积／總容積,總體積　total volume, gross volume
总容量／總容量　aggregate capacity, gross capacity
总溶解固体／總溶解固體　total disolved solid
总生育率／總生育率　total fertility
总声压级／總聲壓位準　overall sound pressure level
总视差／總視差　total parallax
总速率／總速率　overall speed

总酸值／總酸值　total acid number, TAN
总体布置图／總圖,總計劃　general plan
总体城市设计／總體都市設計　comprehensive urban design
总体规划／總計劃,總圖　general plan
总体规划编制成果／整體規劃成果　comprehensive planning outcome
总体结构系统／總體結構系統　general structural system
总体模态／總體模態　global mode
总体破坏／總體破壞　total failure
总体设计要求／設計要求項目　general design requirement
总体失稳／總體挫曲　general buckling
总统套房／總統套間　presidential suite
总投资／總投資　total investment
总投资收益率／投資報酬[率]　return on investment, ROI
总图／總平面圖,地基圖,一般圖　master plan, general chart, site plan
总图设计／總圖設計　site layout
总位移／總偏離　excursion
总温[度]／總溫度　total temperature
VXI总线测试／VXI匯流排測試　VXI bus test
总线网[络]／匯流排網路　bus network
总效率／總效率　total efficiency, overall efficiency
总谐波失真／總諧波失真　total harmonic distortion
总修正角／總修正角　total correcting angle
总需氧量／最終需氧量　ultimate oxygen demand
总悬浮颗粒物／總懸浮微粒量　total suspended particulate, TSP
总悬浮微粒／總懸浮顆粒物　total suspended particle
总压／總壓力　total pressure
总压控制／總壓控制　total pressure control
总压强／總壓力　total pressure
总压头／總落差　total head
总压下量／總縮減量　total reduction
总扬程／全揚程,總抽高差　total pump head
总应力／總應力　total stress
总硬度／總硬度　total hardness
总用泵／通用泵,常用泵　general service pump
总有机卤化物／總有機鹵素　total organic halogen
总有机碳量／總有機碳　total organic carbon, TOC
总预算／預算總額　total budget
总云量／總雲量　total cloud amount
[总]载重量／載重量　dead weight, DW
总振动／總體振動　global vibration
总重／總重　gross weight

总重吨公里/總重噸公里　gross ton-kilometer
总昼光照度/全晝光照度　global illuminance
总装配/總裝[配]　general assembly
总装式锅炉/組合鍋爐　packaged boiler
总装直属件/總裝直屬件　final assembly parts
总纵强度/縱向強度　longitudinal strength
总纵强度试验/縱向強度試驗　longitudinal strength test
总纵弯曲/縱[向]彎曲　longitudinal bending
总纵弯曲正应力/縱向彎應力　longitudinal bending stress, normal stress due to longitudinal bending moment
总阻力/總阻力　total resistance
纵波/縱波　longitudinal wave
纵舱壁/縱[向]艙壁　longitudinal bulkhead
纵荡/縱移,激變　surging
纵电动势/縱電動勢　longitudinal electro-motive force
纵断面/縱斷面　section, profile
纵断面测量/縱斷面測量　profile survey, profile surveying
纵断面分析仪/縱剖面分析儀　longitudinal profile analyzer
纵断面设计/縱斷面設計　profile design
纵断水平测量/縱斷水準測量　longitudinal levelling
纵队/縱隊　column formation
纵帆/縱帆　fore-and-aft sail, fore and after sail
纵缝/縱向節理　longitudinal joint
纵谷/縱向谷　longitudinal valley
纵骨/縱材　longitudinal
纵骨架/縱肋系統　longitudinal framing system, longitudinal frame system
纵过道/縱過道　longitudinal aisle
纵桁/縱桁　longitudinal girder
纵横奇偶检验/縱橫奇偶校驗　vertical horizontal parity
纵横制电话交换机/縱橫制電話交換機　crossbar telephone switching system
纵筋/縱向鋼筋,縱向支材　longitudinal bar
纵距/前進距離,進距　advance
纵梁/縱向梁,縱材　stringer, longitudinal beam
纵列式区段站/縱列式編組站　longitudinal type district station
纵列式停车/平行停車　parallel parking
纵裂/縱裂　ware crack
纵面线形/縱面定線,垂直定線　vertical alignment
纵坡折减/縱坡折減　grade compensation
纵剖面图/縱剖面圖　longitudinal section plan

纵剖线/縱剖面線　buttock line, buttocks
纵侵角/俯仰角　trim angle
纵倾/俯仰　trim
纵倾角/俯仰角,配平角　trimming angle, trim angle
纵倾力距/俯仰力矩　pitching moment, trimming moment
纵倾平衡泵/俯仰水泵　trimming pump
纵伸挂车/可調軸距拖車　adjustable wheelbase trailer
纵深防护/縱深防護　longitudinal-depth protection
纵深防护体系/縱深防護系統　longitudinal-depth protection system
纵稳心/縱定傾中心　longitudinal metacenter
纵稳心半径/縱定傾半徑　longitudinal metacentric radius
纵稳心高度/縱定傾中心在基線以上高度　longitudinal metacentric height above baseline
纵稳性/縱[向]穩度　longitudinal stability
纵稳性高度/縱定傾[中心]高,縱重穩距　longitudinal metacentric height, longitudinal stability height
纵稳性力臂/縱穩度力臂　longitudinal stability lever
纵线标记/縱線標誌　longitudinal marking
纵向补给装置/艉向補給裝置　astern replenishing rig
纵向操纵/縱向控制　longitudinal control
纵向缠绕/縱向纏繞　longitudinal winding
纵向冲击/縱向衝擊　longitudinal impact
纵向冲距/縱向衝距,正[慣性]滑行距離　head reach
纵向重叠率/縱向重疊率　longitudinal overlap
纵向磁棒/縱向磁棒　fore-and-aft magnet
纵向定线/縱向定線　longitudinal alignment
纵向扼流线圈/縱向扼流圈　longitudinal choke coil
纵向发展/立體發展　vertical development
纵向钢筋/縱向鋼筋　longitudinal reinforcement
纵向滑道/縱向滑道　end slipway
纵向间隔/縱向隔離　longitudinal separation
纵向力/縱向力　longitudinal force
纵向连续带光源/縱向連續帶光源　longitudinal continuous band illuminant
纵向裂缝/縱向裂痕,縱向破裂　longitudinal crack
纵向耦合振动/縱向耦合振動　coupled longitudinal vibration
纵向排水/縱向排水　longitudinal drainage
纵向平台/縱向月臺　longitudinal platform
纵[向]强度/縱向強度　longitudinal strength
纵向强化/縱向強化　longitudinal strengthening
纵向强力构件/縱向強度構件　longitudinal strength

member
纵向弹性模量/縱向彈性模數　modulus of longitudinal elasticity
纵向通风/縱向通風,縱流式通風　longitudinal ventilation
纵向拖拉法/縱向拖拉法,縱向拖拉安裝　erection by longitudinal pulling method, erection by longitudinal pulling
纵向弯曲试验/縱向彎折試驗　longitudinal bend test
纵向下水/艉向下水　end launching
纵向运动/縱向運動　longitudinal motion
纵向枕木/縱向軌枕　longitudinal sleeper, longitudinal tie
纵向振动/縱向振動　longitudinal vibration
纵向止移板/縱防動板　longitudinal shifting board
纵斜/後傾　rake
纵摇/縱搖,縱向[俯仰]運動　pitching, pitch motion
纵摇变形角/俯仰變形角　pitch deformation angle
纵摇角/縱搖角,俯仰角　pitch angle
纵摇周期/縱搖週期　period of pitching, pitching period
纵摇阻尼控制器/縱搖阻尼控制　pitch damping control
纵重稳距/縱定傾中心高　longitudinal metacentric height
纵轴/縱軸　longitudinal axis
走板/布線板　running board
走道板/走道板　walkway plate
走合/跑合,試車,試運轉　running in
走合期驾驶/走合期駕駛　driving in running in period
走合维护/跑合維護　running in maintenance
走廊/走廊,廊道,通道　corridor
走廊回风/走廊回風　air return through corridor
走廊交通管理计划/走廊交通管理計劃　corridor traffic management program
走马廊/迴廊　cloister, loggia
走锚/拖錨　dragging anchor
走石/走石　moving stone
走私/走私　smuggling
走线架/走線架　chute, chamfer
走向断层/規律斷層　strike fault
走行部灯/走行部燈　bogie lamp
走行装置/操作機構,傳動機構,運轉機構　running gear
租船费/租傭費　charterage
租船合同/租傭契約　charter party
租船提单/傭船載貨證券　charter party bill of lading
租船运费/傭船運費　charter freight
租地/租地　rented land
租金支付/租金支付　payment of hire
租赁价值/租值　rental value
租期/租期　period of hire
租税价/租值　rental value
租用电路/租用電路　leased circuit
足尺布局/全尺寸布局　full-scale layout, prototypic layout
足尺模型试验/足尺試驗　full-scale test
足尺试验/足尺寸試驗,全尺寸試驗,實尺寸試驗　full-scale test
足球场/足球場　football field, football stadium
足球场草坪/足球場草坪　soccer turf
足球运动/足球運動　soccer
足浴馆/足浴館　pediluvium studio
ISO9000族/ISO9000族　ISO9000 family
阻车器/停车装置　stop device
阻挡式护栏/阻擋式護欄　block-out safety fence
阻断/阻塞,封鎖　blockade
阻垢剂/阻垢劑　scale inhibitor
阻火包/阻火包　fireproof bag
阻火器/防焰網,避火器,消焰器　flame trap, flame arrester
阻抗电桥/阻抗電橋　impedance bridge
阻抗复合消声器/阻抗式消聲器　impedance compound muffler
阻抗轨隙连接器/電阻抗結接　impedance bond
[阻抗]匹配变压器/阻抗匹配變壓器　impedance matching transformer
阻抗匹配层/阻抗匹配層　impedance matching layer
阻抗匹配法/阻抗匹配法　impedance match method
阻力/阻力,拖曳力　drag force, drag, resistance
阻力发散/阻力發散　drag divergence
阻力公式/阻力公式,曳力公式　drag equation
阻力加速度/負加速度　drag acceleration
阻力平衡/阻力平衡　hydraulic resistance balance
阻力伞/阻力傘　drag parachute
阻力试验/阻力試驗　resistance test
阻力损失/阻力損失　drag loss
阻力系数/阻力係數　resistance coefficient, drag coefficient
阻力效应/阻力效應,拖曳效應　drag effect
阻尼/阻尼,減幅　damping
阻尼比/阻尼比　damping ratio
阻尼材料/阻尼材料　damping material
阻尼常数/阻尼常數　damping constant
阻尼导数/阻尼導數　damping derivative

阻尼结构/阻尼結構　damping structure
阻尼矩阵/阻尼矩陣　damping matrix
阻尼力/阻尼力　damping force
阻尼器/阻尼器,阻尼板　damper
阻尼系数/阻尼係數,阻尼因數　damping factor
阻尼液/阻尼流體　damping fluid
阻尼因数/阻尼因數,阻尼係數　damping factor
阻尼振动/阻尼振動,衰減振動　damped vibration
阻尼重物/鎮偏重物　damping weight
阻汽器/蒸汽袪水器,汽阱　steam trap
阻燃/耐燃物　flame resistant
阻燃材料/難燃材料　flame resistant material
阻燃电缆/耐燃性電纜　flame retardant cable
阻燃剂/阻燃劑　fire retardancy
阻燃性/耐火性,抗焰性,防延燃性　flame resistance, flame retardancy
阻塞/阻塞,阻流,擁塞　blockage, choking, congestion
阻塞比/阻塞比　blockage ratio
阻塞度/阻塞度　blockage percentage
阻塞干扰/阻塞干擾　block interference
阻塞工程/阻塞工程　block work
阻塞力/阻塞力　blocked force
阻塞密度/堵塞密度　jam density
阻塞试验/阻塞試驗　blockage test
阻塞物/阻塞　clogging
阻塞效应/阻塞效應　blockage effect
阻塞修正/阻塞修正　blockage correction
阻水面积/阻水面積　current obstruction area
阻水墙/隔牆,膜壁　diaphragm wall
阻索器/停止器,制鏈器　stopper
阻锈剂/阻蝕劑,抑蝕劑,腐蝕抑制劑　corrosion inhibitor
组重复周期/組重複週期　group repetition interval, GRI
组分/組分　constituent
组分试验/組分試驗　constituent test
组合/組匣,單元塊　unit-block
组合报警/群警報　group alarm
组合测量/組合測量　measurement in a closed series
组合衬砌/組合襯砌　composite lining
组合传动机车/組合傳動機車　coupled axle drive locomotive
组合窗/混合窗　combination window
组合大梁/組合梁　built-up girder
组合导航/組合導航,整合航海　integrated navigation
组合导航系统/組合導航系統　integrated navigation system

组合灯/組合燈　combination lamp, grouped lamp
组合电源/飛機整體驅動發電機　integrated drive generator, IDG
组合端子/組合端子　terminal of a unit block
组合断层/複雜斷層　compound fault
组合发动机/組合發動機　combined engine, hybrid engine
组合分配系统/組合分配系統　combined distribution system
组合钢模板/聯體鋼範本　combined steel formwork
组合柜/組合櫃,組匣櫃　modular block rack
组合活塞/複合活塞　composite piston
组合继电器/組合繼電器　combination relay
组合家具/組合式家具,積木式家具　combination furniture
组合架/組合架　unit-block assembly rack
组合接触器/組合接觸器　grouping contactor
组合结构/組合結構　composite structure
组合井/複管井　compound well
组合肋板/空架[底]肋板　bracket floor
组合梁/組合梁,合成梁　composite beam, built-up beam
组合梁桥/組合梁橋　composite beam bridge, composite girder bridge
组合梁式斜拉桥/組合橋面板斜張橋　composite deck cable stayed bridge
组合列车/組合列車　combined train
组合楼盖/組合樓蓋　composite floor system
组合模式/組合模式　integrated mode
组合起动屏/群起動盤　group starter panel
组合驱动/聯軸驅動　coupled axle drive
INS-GPS组合式导航系统/集成式INS-GPS導航系統　integrated INS-GPS navigation system
组合式电气集中联锁/組合式繼電聯鎖裝置　unit-block type relay interlocking
组合式高度表/組合高度表　combined altimeter
组合式锅炉/複合鍋爐　composite boiler
组合式空气调节机组/組合式空氣調節機組,組合式空氣處理機　modular air handling unit
组合式桥台/組合式橋臺　composite abutment
组合[式]曲轴/組合曲柄軸　built-up crankshaft
组合式信号机构/組合式信號機構　modular signal mechanism
组合式压路机/組合式壓路機　combination roller
组合式柱式/混合柱式　composite order
组合式转向架/組合式轉向架　combination truck
组合式纵向通风/合成縱流式通風　composite longitudinal ventilation

组合损失/組合損失 assembling loss
组合体/組合體 composite unit
组合体系拱桥/綜合體系拱橋 combined system arch bridge
组合网架/組合空間桁架 composite space truss
组合线法/組合線法 procedure assembly line
组合悬索吊架法/組合懸索吊架法 compound catenary system
组合压气机/組合壓縮機 combined compressor
组合应力/組合應力,合成應力 combined stress
组合与测试/整合及測試 integration and test
组合站/結合站 combined station
组合制导/整合導引 integrated guidance
组合柱/合成柱 composite column
组合砖砌体/組合磚砌體 composite brick masonry
组呼/群呼 group calling
组货服务费/組貨服務費 freight sales charge
组件实际效率/模組實際效率 practical module efficiency
组件试验/組合測試 assembly test, test of assembly
组件效率/模組效率 module efficiency
组培快繁/組培快繁 tissue culture and rapid propagation
组培育苗/組培育苗 micropropagation
组批/組批 combined lots
组拼式架桥机/裝配式架橋機 assembly girder-erecting machine
组团路/組團路 group road
组团绿地/組團綠地 sub-community green space, group green space
组团住宅/集團住宅 group house
组匣/組匣 modular block
组匣端子/組匣端子 terminals of a modular block
组匣式电气集中联锁/組匣式繼電聯鎖裝置 modular type relay interlocking
组织/組織 structure
组织培养/組織培養 tissue culture
组植/組植 group planting
组装图/裝配圖 assembly drawing
祖母结/假平結 granny knot
钻爆法/鑽爆法,鑽炸法 drilling and blasting method
钻孔/鑽孔 hole drilling
钻孔测量/鑽孔測量 borehole surveying
钻孔垂[直]度检测/鑽孔垂直度檢測 bored hole verticality measurement
钻孔灌注桩/板樁結構物灌注樁 cast-in-place pile
钻孔机/衝孔機 punching machine
钻孔扩端法/鑽孔擴端法 boring-and-underreaming method
钻孔冷却/鏇孔冷卻 bore-colded
钻孔泥浆试验/鑽孔泥漿試驗 boring slurry test
钻孔潜望镜/鑽孔潛望鏡 borehole periscope
钻孔照相机/鑽孔照相機 borehole camera
钻孔直径检测/鑽孔直徑檢測 bored hole diameter measurement
钻孔柱状图/鑽孔柱狀圖 boring log
钻孔桩/鑽掘[式基]樁 bored pile
钻入桩脚/鑽樁 drilled pile
钻探/鑽探 boring prospecting, boring, drilling
钻探船/鑽探船,鑽油船,鑽井船 drilling ship, drilling vessel
钻探设备/鑽探設備 drilling rig
钻芯法混凝土检测仪/鑽芯法混凝土檢測儀 concrete core drilling testing apparatus
钻芯取样检验/取芯鑽探檢驗 core drilling inspection
钻削/鑽鑿 drilling
钻岩船/鑽岩船 rock drill boat
钻岩机/鑿岩機 rock driller
钻蛀性害虫/穿孔性昆蟲 boring insect
钻斗/鑽孔葉片 drilling bucket
钻杆/鑽桿 boring rod, drill rod, drilling rod
钻井/鑽井 drilling well
钻井驳/鑽油駁 drilling barge
钻井船/鑽油船 drilling vessel, drilling ship
钻井供应船/鑽油臺補給船 drilling tender
钻井平台/鑽油[平]臺 drilling unit, drilling rig, drilling platform
钻井设备/鑽孔裝置 boring rig
钻石钻头/鑽石鑽頭 diamond bit
钻头提取器/鑽頭取出器 drill extractor
最长稳态工作时间/最長穩態工作時間 maximum steady-state burn time
最大安全速度/最大安全速率 maximum safe speed
最大包络曲线/最大包絡曲線 maximum envelope curve
最大波高/最大浪高 maximum wave height
最大测量深度/最大測量深度 maximum measuring depth
最大常用减压/最大常用減壓 full service reduction
最大常用制动/最大行車制動 full service braking
最大超高率/最大超高率 maximum superelevation rate
最大吃水/最大吃水 maximum draft
最大持水量/最大容水量 maximum water holding

capacity
最大持续电压/最大連續電壓　maximum continuous voltage
最大持续工作电压/最大連續工作電壓　maximum continuous operating voltage
最大持续功率/［額定］最大連續出力　maximum continuous rating, MCR
最大持续交流电压/最大連續交流電壓　maximum continuous alternating current voltage
最大持续直流电压/最大連續直流電壓　maximum continuous direct current voltage
最大冲击［响应］谱/最大衝擊［響應］譜　maximum shock response spectrum
最大磁场/最大磁場　maximum field
最大动压载荷/最大動壓負載　maximum dynamic pressure load
最大舵角/滿舵角　hard-over angle
最大反作用力矩/最大反作用扭矩　maximum reaction torque
最大服务交通量/最大服務流量　maximum service volume
最大服务流率/最大服務流率　maximum service flow rate
最大俯角/最大俯角　maximum downward tilt angle
最大复原力臂角/最大扶正力臂角　angle of maximum righting lever
最大复原力矩/最大扶正力矩　maximum righting moment
最大干密度/最大乾密度　maximum dry density
最大高度/最大高度　maximum height
最大工作范围/最大工作範圍，最大作用距離　maximum operating range
最大功耗/最大功率消耗［量］　maximum power consumption
最大功率/最大功率，最大動力　maximum power
最大功率点/最大動力點　maximum power point
最大航程速度/最大航程速度　speed for maximum range
最大荷载/最大載重　maximum load
最大横剖面/最大横剖面　maximum section
最大横剖面系数/最大横剖面係數　maximum transverse section coefficient
最大滑行重量/最大滑行重量　maximum taxi weight
最大活载剪力/最大活載剪力　maximum live shear
最大角加速度/最大角加速度　maximum angular acceleration
最大角速度/最大角速率　maximum angular rate

最大抗拉应力/極限張應力　ultimate tensile stress
最大可能洪水/最大可能洪水　maximum possible flood, maximum probable precipitation
最大可能雨量/最大可能雨量　maximum probable rainfall
最大可用增益/最大可用增益，最大可達增益　maximum available gain
最大空间/最大空間　maximum space
最大宽［度］/最大寬度，全寬　maximum breadth, extreme breadth
最大力矩/最大扭矩　maximum torque
最大连续状态/連續最大出力　maximum continuous rating
最大流量/尖峰流量　peak rate of flow
最大平飞速度/最大平飛速率　maximum level speed
最大坡度/最大坡度　maximum grade
最大起飞重量/最大起飛重量　maximum takeoff weight, maximum take-off weight
最大起升高度/最大提昇高度　maximum height of lift
最大起重量/最大起重量　maximum lifting capacity
最大倾斜位置/最大傾斜位置　maximum inclining position
最大燃油量限制螺钉/最大燃油量限制螺釘　maximum fuel limit screw
最大热负荷/最大熱負載　maximum heating load
最大容许稳定运行功率/容許最大穩定運轉功率　maximum permissible stable operation power
最大容许压力/最大容許壓力　maximum allowable pressure, maximum permissible pressure
最大升力系数/最大昇力係數　maximum lift coefficient
最大声压级/最大聲壓位準　maximum sound pressure level
最大湿密度/最大濕密度，最大濕比重　maximum wet density
最大时用水量/最大時用水量，最高時用水量　maximum hourly water consumption
最大使用限制速度/最大操作速度　maximum operation limit speed
最大输出功率/最大輸出功率　maximum output power
最大输出力矩/最大輸出扭矩　maximum output torque
最大水平视角/最大水平視角　maximum horizontal visual angle
最大瞬时流量/最高瞬間流量　maximum instantaneous discharge

最大摊铺生产率测定/最大攤鋪生產率測定 maximum paving capacity measurement
最大停机坪重量/最大停機坪重量 maximum ramp weight
最大推力/最大推力 maximum thrust
最大外移位置/最大外移位置 maximum outward position
最大弯矩/最大彎矩 maximum bending moment
最大稳性力臂/最大穩度力臂 maximum stability lever
最大稳性力臂角/最大穩度力臂角 angle of maximum stability lever
最大误差/最大誤差 maximum error
最大限制信号/最大限制信號 most restrictive signal
最大压强/最大壓強 maximum pressure
最大叶宽/最大葉寬 maximum blade width, maximum width of blade
最大叶宽比/最大葉寬比 maximum blade width ratio
最大允许车重/許可總車重 maximum permissible weight
最大允许误差/最大容許誤差 maximum permissible error
最大允许信号/最大允許信號 most favorable signal
最大允许烟雾传输时间/最大允許煙霧傳輸時間 maximum smoke transport time
最大运用功率/最大平均輸出功率 maximum service output power
最大轴原理/最大軸原理 maximum axis principle
最大轴重/最大軸上允許載荷 maximum allowable axle load
最大主应力/最大主應力 major principle stress
最大状态/最大額定值 maximum rating
最大着陆重量/最大落地重量 maximum landing weight
最大纵坡/最大縱坡度 maximum longitudinal gradient
最低安全高度/最低安全高度 minimum safe flight altitude, minimum safety altitude
最低安全配员/船員最低安全配額 minimum safe manning
最低保证强度/最低保證強度 guaranteed minimum strength
最低潮/最低潮,最低水 dead tide, lowest low water, LLW
最低吹风时间/最低吹風時間 minimum duration of wind
最低发光强度/最低照明強度 minimum luminous intensity
最低发射条件/最低發射條件 lowest launching condition
最低工作稳定转速试验/最低穩定轉速試驗 minimum steady speed test
最低可接受值/最低可接受值 minimum acceptable value
最低空载稳定转速/最低空載轉速 minimum idling stabilized speed
最低空载转速试验/最低空轉速試驗,最低空載速度試驗 minimum no-load speed test
最低起动压力/最低起動壓力 minimum starting pressure
最低扇区高度/最低防區高度,最小搜索區高度 minimum sector altitude, MSA
最低水位/最低水位 lowest water level, LWL
最低速率/最低速率 compulsory minimum speed
最低稳定行驶速度测定/最低穩定行駛速度測定 minimum steady travelling speed measurement
最低稳定转速/最低穩定轉速 minimum stable engine speed
最低下降高度/最低下降高度 minimum descent altitude, MDA, minimum steady height
最低下降水位/最低下降水位 bottom surge water level
最低限速标志/最低限速標誌 minimum stated speed sign
最低有效位/最低有效位元 least significant bit
最低运费/起碼運費 minimum freight
最低运费吨/起碼運費噸 minimum freight ton
最低运费提单/起碼運費載貨證券 minimum freight bill of lading
最低运转时间/最短操作時間 minimum operating time
最短绿灯时段/最短綠燈時段 minimum green period
最短时间/最短時間 minimum period
最短停车视距/最短不超車視距 minimum non-passing sight distance
最概率船位/最可能船位 most probable position, MPP
最高爆发压力/最高爆發壓力,尖峰壓力 maximum explosive pressure, peak pressure, maximum firing pressure
最高爆发压力表/最高爆發壓力表 maximum explosion pressure gage
最高波/最高波 highest wave

最高潮/最高水位　highest high water, HHW
最高空载转速/最大無負載速度　maximum no-load speed
最高燃烧温度/最大燃燒溫度　maximum combustion temperature
最高燃烧压力/最高燃燒壓力　maximum combustion pressure
最高日供水量/最高日供水量,最大日供水量　maximum daily water supply
最高日用水量/最大日用水量　maximum daily water consumption
最高水位/最高水位　highest water level, HWL
最高速度/最高速[率],飛速[率],強速　flank speed, maximum speed
最高行驶速度测定/最高行駛速度測定　maximum travelling speed measurement
最高预示环境/最高預測環境　maximum predicted environment
最高转速/最高速[率]　maximum speed
最后不合法航次/最後違法航程　illegitimate last voyage
最后的/最後的,極限的　ultimate
最后合法航次/最後合法航程　legitimate last voyage
最后机会原则/最後機會原則　last opportunity rule
最后文件/葳事檔　final act
最坏情况分析/最壞情況分析　worst condition analysis
最佳城市规模/最優都市規模　optimal city size
最佳弹道估计/彈道最佳估計　best estimation of trajectory
最佳发射条件/最佳發射條件　optimal launching condition
最佳负荷分配/最佳負載分配　optimum load sharing
最佳负载/最佳負載　optimum load
最佳工作电流/峰值電流　optimum operating current
最佳工作电压/最佳運轉電壓　optimum operating voltage
最佳含水量/最佳含水量,最適宜含水量　optimum water content, optimum moisture content, best moisture content
最佳含水量曲线/最佳含水量曲線　optimum
最佳航迹定线/最佳船舶航路　optimum track ship routing
最佳航速/最佳航速　optimum speed
最佳航线/最佳航路　optimum route
最佳航线拟定/最佳航線擬定　optimum routing
最佳混响时间/最佳混響時間　optimum reverberation time
最佳级配/最佳級配　optimum gradation
最佳决策/最佳決定　optimum decision
最佳密度/最適密度　optimum density, best density
最佳配合/最佳配合　optimized matching
最佳匹配点/最佳匹配點,最佳吻合點　optimum matching point
最佳启动点/最佳啟動點　optimum actuation point
最佳启动规律/最佳啟動定律　optimized actuation law
最佳启动时刻/最佳啟動時刻　optimum actuation moment
最佳速度/最佳速率　optimum speed
最佳性能/最佳性能　optimum performance
最佳帧同步码/最佳幀同步碼　optimal frame sync pattern
最接近时间/最接近之時刻　time of closet approach, TCPA
最近会遇点/最接近點　closest point of approach, CPA
最近会遇距离/最接近點距離　distance to closest point of approach, DCPA
最近会遇时间/最接近點時間　time to closest point of approach, TCPA
最近距离/最小距離　minimum distance
最近陆地/最近陸地　nearest land
最近视距/最近視線距離　minimum sight distance
最轻设计/最小設計重量　minimum weight design
最上升水位/最上昇水位　top surge, top surge water level
最少水泥含量/最少水泥含量　minimum cement content
最深分舱载重线/最深艙區劃分載重線　deepest subdivision loadline
最适需水量/最適需水量　optimum water requirement
最小包涵曲线/最小包涵曲線　minimum envelope curve
最小测量深度/最小測量深度　minimum measuring depth
最小车[头]间距/最小車頭間距　minimum headway
最小冲量极限环/最小衝量極限環　minimum impulse limit cycle
最小传热阻/最小熱阻　minimum thermal resistance
最小磁场/最小磁場　minimum field
最小电脉冲宽度/最小電脈寬　minimum electrical pulse width, MEPW
最小二乘法/最小二乘法　least square method
最小功原理/最小功定理　theorem of least work

最小加力状态/最小加力额定值 minimum augmentation rating
最小间距/最小間距 minimum spacing
最小接收场强/最小接收場強度 minimum receiving field strength
最小可分辨温差/最小可解析温差 minimum resolvable temperature difference, MRTD
最小可探测温差/最小可檢测温差 minimum detectable temperature difference, MDTD
最小可用接收电平/最小可用接收電平 minimum available receiving level
最小配筋率/最小鋼筋比 minimum steel ratio
最小平飞速度/最小平飛速率 minimum level speed
最小坡段长度/最小坡長 minimum length of grade section
最小倾覆力矩/最小翻覆力矩 minimum capsizing moment
最小曲线半径/最小曲線半徑 minimum radius of curve
最小日照间距/最小日照間距 minimum sunshine spacing
最小势能原理/最小勢能原理 principle of minimum potential energy
最小填土高度/最小填土高度 minimum height of fill
最小填筑高度/最小填築高度 minimum fill height of subgrade, minimum height of fill
最小新风量/最小新風量 minimum fresh air requirement
最小余能原理/最小餘能原理 principle of minimum complementary energy
最小主应力/最小主應力 minor principal stress
最小纵坡/最小縱坡度 minimum longitudinal gradient
最优观测几何条件/最優觀測幾何條件 optimal station geometry
最优控制/最佳控制 optimal control
最有效位/最高有效位元 most significant bit
最远视距/最遠視線距離 longest sight distance
最终报告/最終報告 final report
最终处置/最終處置 ultimate disposal
最终需氧量/最終需氧量 ultimate oxygen demand
作坊/作坊,車間,工場 workshop
左侧浮标/左舷通過浮標 port hand buoy
左焊法/[右手]左向焊法,前進焊法 forehand welding
左开道岔/左開道岔 left hand turnout
左开式/左開式 left hand model

左邻舰/左側船艦 next ship on the left
左满舵/左滿舵 hard port
左舷/左舷 port side
左舷发动机/左舷引擎 port engine
左舷浮标/左舷通過浮標 port hand buoy
左向旋转/左向旋轉,逆時針旋餞 left hand rotation
左旋/左旋,左轉 left hand turning
左旋柴油机/左旋柴油機 left hand rotation diesel engine
左旋圆极化/左旋圓形極化 left hand circular polarization
左翼舰/左翼船艦 left flank ship
左右错位交叉口/左右錯列交叉 right left staggered junction
左右对称/左右對稱 bilateral symmetry
左右舵停船/循環操舵停船法 rudder circling stop
左右通航标/分道航行標 separate channel mark
左指法则/左指法則 left thumb rule
左转/左轉 left turn
左转机组/左轉機組 left hand revolving engine unit
左转扭绞/左搓索 left hand lay
左转[弯]车道/左轉車道 left turn lane
左转弯导向线/左轉車道導引線 left turn guide line
左转弯匝道/左轉變匝道 left turn ramp
作/作 type of work, zuo
作物需水量/作物需水量 water requirement of crops
作业编程/任務程式設計 task programming
作业标志/作業標誌 working signal
作业程序/任務程式 task program
作业废弃物/操作所生廢棄物 operational wastes
作业控制中心/作業控制中心 operations control center
作业面/作業[平]面,工作平面 working plane
[作业]跳板/跳板 plank stage
作业性能试验/作業性能試驗 operating performance test
作业循环时间测定/操作週期測定 determination of operating cycle
作用/作用 action
作用标准值/作用標準值 characteristic value of action
作用部/作用部 service portion
作用阀/作用閥 application valve
作用范围/作用範圍 range of action
作用分项系数/作用分項係數 partial safety factor for action, action subcoefficient
作用距离/作用距離 ranging coverage, range of

action
作用力/作用力　active force
作用面积/灑水噴頭作用面積　area of sprinkler operation
作用频遇值/作用頻遇值　frequent value of action
作用区/接觸區　zone of contact
作用设计值/作用設計值　design value of action
作用效应/作用效應　effect of action, action effect
作用效应基本组合/作用效應基本組合　fundamental combination for action effects
作用效应偶然组合/作用效應偶然組合　accidental combination for action effects
作用效应系数/作用效應係數　coefficient of action effect
作用效应组合/作用效應組合　combination for action effects
作用准永久值/作用准永久值　quasi permanent value of action
作用组合/作用組合　combination of actions
作用组合值/作用組合值　combination value of actions
作用组合值系数/作用組合值係數　coefficient for combination value of actions
作战能力/戰鬥性能　combat capability
作战情报中心室/戰情中心　combat information center, CIC
坐板升降结/工作吊板套結　bosuns chair hitch
坐标/坐標　coordinate
坐标变换矩阵/坐標變換矩陣　transformation matrix of coordinates
坐标变换器/坐標變換器, 坐標轉換裝置　coordinate conversion device, coordinate transformation device
坐标测量仪/坐標儀表　coordinate instrumentation
坐标法/坐標法　coordinate method
坐标方位角/坐標方位角　plane-coordinate azimuth
坐标图形/坐標圖形　coordinate graphics
坐标系/坐標系統　coordinate system
坐标转换/坐標變換　coordinate transformation
坐凳栏杆/坐凳欄杆　seat rail
坐底式钻井平台/坐底式鑽油平臺　submersible drilling platform, submersible drilling unit
坐式便器/坐式便器　western toilet, seat-type water closet
坐坞强度/坐塢強度　docking strength
座板/底座　seat
座舱/座艙　cabin
座舱安全活门/座艙安全閥　cabin safety valve
座舱大气风速/座艙大氣風速　wind rate of cabin
座舱风扇/座艙風扇　cabin fan
座舱盖/座艙罩　canopy
座舱高度/座艙高度　cabin altitude
座舱高度压差表/座艙高度壓差表　cabin altitude and pressure difference gage
座舱供气/座艙供氣　cabin air supply
座舱露点/座艙露點　cabin dew point
座舱热交换器/座艙熱交換器　cabin heat exchanger
座舱压力调节器/座艙壓力調節器, 座艙壓力調整器　cabin pressure regulator
座舱压力制度/座艙壓力[調節]表　cabin pressure schedule
座舱仪表系统/座艙儀表系統　cabin instrument system
座舱应急卸压活门/座艙緊急放卸閥　cabin emergency dump valve
座舱增压/座艙加壓　cabin pressurization
座环/整流環　stay ring
座宽/座寬度　seat width
座式继电器/擱板式繼電器　shelf-type relay
座席电路/座席電路　operator circuit
[座席]横排曲率/[座席]橫排曲率　curvature of stall

附 录

国际单位制

1. 国际单位制（Le Système International d'Unités）及其国际简称 SI 是在 1960 年第 11 届国际计量大会上通过的。国际单位制单位由基本单位、导出单位（包括辅助单位在内的具有专门名称的导出单位和组合形式的导出单位，组合形式的导出单位本附录不予收录）及其倍数单位构成。

2. 圆括号中的名称，是它前面的名称的同义词。

3. 无方括号的量的名称与单位名称均为全称。方括号中的字，在不致引起混淆、误解的情况下，可以省略。去掉方括号中的字即为其名称的简称。

表1 基本单位

量的名称	单位名称	单位符号
大陆名/台湾名	大陆名/台湾名	
长度/長度	米/公尺	m
质量/質量	千克(公斤)/公斤	kg
时间/時間	秒/秒	s
电流/電流	安[培]/安培	A
热力学温度/熱力學溫度	开[尔文]/克耳文	K
物质的量/物[質]量	摩[尔]/莫耳	mol
发光强度/發光強度	坎[德拉]/燭光	cd

表2 包括辅助单位在内的具有专门名称的导出单位

量的名称	导出单位		
	单位名称	单位符号	换算关系
大陆名/台湾名	大陆名/台湾名		
[平面]角/[平面]角	弧度/弧度,弳度	rad	$1\ rad = 1\ m/m = 1$
立体角/立體角	球面度/立弳	sr	$1\ sr = 1\ m^2/m^2 = 1$
频率/頻率	赫[兹]/赫	Hz	$1\ Hz = 1\ s^{-1}$
力/力	牛[顿]/牛頓	N	$1\ N = 1\ kg \cdot m/s^2$
压力,压强,应力/壓力,壓強,應力	帕[斯卡]/帕斯卡	Pa	$1\ Pa = 1\ N/m^2$
能[量],功,热量/能[量],功,熱[量]	焦[耳]/焦耳	J	$1\ J = 1\ N \cdot m$
功率,辐[射能]通量/功率,輻射能通量	瓦[特]/瓦特	W	$1\ W = 1\ J/s$
电荷[量]/電荷量	库[仑]/庫侖	C	$1\ C = 1\ A \cdot s$
电压,电动势,电位,(电势)/電壓,電動勢,電位,(電勢)	伏[特]/伏特	V	$1\ V = 1\ W/A$
电容/電容	法[拉]/法拉	F	$1\ F = 1\ C/V$
电阻/電阻	欧[姆]/歐姆	Ω	$1\ \Omega = 1\ V/A$
电导/電導	西[门子]/西門	S	$1\ S = 1\ \Omega^{-1}$

(续表)

量的名称	导出单位		
	单位名称	单位符号	换算关系
大陆名/台湾名	大陆名/台湾名		
磁通[量]/磁通量	韦[伯]/韋伯	Wb	1 Wb=1 V·s
磁通[量]密度,磁感应强度/磁通[量]密度,磁感應強度	特[斯拉]/特士拉	T	1 T=1 Wb/m²
电感/電感	亨[利]/亨利	H	1 H=1 Wb/A
摄氏温度/攝氏温度	摄氏度/攝[氏温]度	℃	1 ℃=1 K
光通量/光通量	流[明]/流明	lm	1 lm=1 cd·sr
[光]照度/照度	勒[克斯]/勒克斯	lx	1 lx=1 lm/m²

表3 由于人类健康安全防护需要而确定的具有专门名称的导出单位

量的名称	导出单位		
	单位名称	单位符号	换算关系
大陆名/台湾名	大陆名/台湾名		
[放射性]活度/放射活性	贝可[勒尔]/贝克	Bq	1 Bq=1 s⁻¹
吸收剂量/吸收劑量 比授[予]能/比授能 比释动能/比釋動能	戈[瑞]/戈雷	Gy	1 Gy=1 J/kg
剂量当量/等價劑量,當量劑量	希[沃特]/西弗	Sv	1 Sv=1 J/kg

表4 国际单位制词头

因数	词头名称	词头符号
	大陆名/台湾名	
10^{24}	尧[它]/佑	Y
10^{21}	泽[它]/皆	Z
10^{18}	艾[可萨]/艾	E
10^{15}	拍[它]/拍	P
10^{12}	太[拉]/太,兆	T
10^{9}	吉[咖]/吉,十亿	G
10^{6}	兆/百萬	M
10^{3}	千/千	k
10^{2}	百/百	h
10^{1}	十/十	da
10^{-1}	分/分	d
10^{-2}	厘/厘	c

(续表)

因数	词头名称	词头符号
	大陆名/台湾名	
10^{-3}	毫/毫	m
10^{-6}	微/微	μ
10^{-9}	纳[诺]/奈	n
10^{-12}	皮[可]/披,微微	p
10^{-15}	飞[母托]/飛,毫微微	f
10^{-18}	阿[托]/阿,微微微	a
10^{-21}	仄[普托]/介	z
10^{-24}	幺[科托]/攸	y

注:词头与基本单位、导出单位共同组成一个新单位,即构成倍数单位。词头只用于构成倍数单位,不单独使用。

表5 可与国际单位制单位并用的计量单位

量的名称	单位名称	单位符号	换算关系
大陆名/台湾名	大陆名/台湾名		
时间/時間	分/分	min	1 min=60 s
	[小]时/[小]時	h	1 h=60 min=3 600 s
	日,(天)/日,天	d	1 d=24 h=86 400 s
[平面]角/[平面]角	度/度	°	1°=(π/180) rad
	[角]分/[角]分	′	1′=(1/60)°=(π/10 800) rad
	[角]秒/[角]秒	″	1″=(1/60)′=(π/648 000) rad
体积/體積	升/公升	L,(l)	1 L=1 dm³=10⁻³ m³
质量/質量	吨/公噸	t	1 t=10³ kg
	原子质量单位/原子質量單位	u	1 u≈1.660 540×10⁻²⁷ kg
旋转速度/轉速	转每分/每分鐘轉速	r/min	1 r/min=(1/60) s⁻¹
长度/長度	海里/海里,浬	n mile	1 n mile=1 852 m(只用于航行)
速度/速度	节/節	kn	1 kn=1 n mile/h=(1 852/3 600) m/s(只用于航行)
能/能	电子伏/電子伏[特]	eV	1 eV≈1.602 177×10⁻¹⁹ J
级差/位準差	分贝/分貝	dB	
线密度/線密度	特[克斯]/德士	tex	1 tex=10⁻⁶ kg/m
面积/面積	公顷/公頃	hm²	1 hm²=10⁴ m²

注:1. 平面角单位度、分、秒的符号,在组合单位中采用(°)、(′)、(″)的形式。例如,不用°/s,而用(°)/s。

2. 升的符号中,小写字母l为备用符号。

3. 公顷的国际通用符号为ha。

希腊字母表

大写	小写	名 称	大写	小写	名 称
A	α	阿尔法	N	ν	纽
B	β	贝塔	Ξ	ξ	克西
Γ	γ	伽马	O	ο	奥米克戎
Δ	δ	德尔塔	Π	π	派
E	ε	艾普西隆	P	ρ	柔
Z	ζ	泽塔	Σ	σ	西格马
H	η	伊塔	T	τ	陶
Θ	θ	西塔	Υ	υ	宇普西隆
I	ι	约(yāo)塔	Φ	φ	斐
K	κ	卡帕	X	χ	希
Λ	λ	拉姆达	Ψ	ψ	普西
M	μ	谬	Ω	ω	奥米伽

地质年代表

宙 Eon	代 Era	纪 Period	世 Epoch	生物发展阶段 Development of Organisms	距今时间(百万年) Time(Ma BP)
显生宙(PH) Phanerozoic	新生代(Kz) Cenozoic	第四纪(Q) Quaternary	全新世(Q_h) Holocene	现代人类出现。	0.0117
			更新世(Q_p) Pleistocene	生物绝大部分与现在类似。智人出现。	2.58
		新近纪(N) Neogene	上新世(N_2) Pliocene	生物面貌与现在接近,哺乳类形体变大。直立人出现。	5.333
			中新世(N_1) Miocene	类人猿出现。	23.03
		古近纪(E) Paleogene	渐新世(E_3) Oligocene	哺乳类迅速发展,被子植物繁盛。	33.9
			始新世(E_2) Eocene		56.0
			古新世(E_1) Paleocene		66.0
	中生代(Mz) Mesozoic	白垩纪(K) Cretaceous		被子植物出现,末期恐龙等大批生物绝灭。	~145.0
		侏罗纪(J) Jurassic		鸟类出现,爬行类及苏铁等裸子植物繁盛。	201.3±0.2
		三叠纪(T) Triassic		哺乳类出现。	251.902±0.024
	古生代(Pz) Paleozoic	二叠纪(P) Permian		无脊椎动物和裸子植物发展。	298.9±0.15
		石炭纪(C) Carboniferous		爬行类出现,蕨类植物繁盛。	358.9±0.4
		泥盆纪(D) Devonian		昆虫、原始鱼类、蕨类和原始裸子植物出现。	419.2±3.2
		志留纪(S) Silurian		原始鱼类、原始陆生植物出现。	443.4±1.5
		奥陶纪(O) Ordovician		无颌类脊椎动物出现,海生藻类发育。	485.4±1.9
		寒武纪(∈) Cambrian		小壳动物出现,藻类、三叶虫开始繁盛。	541.0±1.0
前寒武纪 Precambrian	元古宙(PT) Proterozoic			藻类、细菌繁盛,软体无脊椎动物出现。	2500
	太古宙(AR) Archean				4000
	冥古宙 Hadean				~4600

注:本表各地质时代的距今时间按国际地层委员会 2018 年 8 月资料。其中未经全球地质年龄测定的标准方法确定的用近似值表示(数字前加"~")。

元素周期表